THE K&W GUIDE TO COLLEGES

FOR STUDENTS WITH LEARNING DIFFERENCES

13TH EDITION

It's hard to believe that so many years have gone by since Marybeth and I were talking in her office at the high school. I had come in to see what she had in her files and approached her with questions. We discovered that we had a mutual desire to understand what college options were available for students with learning differences.

Our children have grown. My children, with learning differences and Attention Deficit Disorder, have moved forward and found success in their lives as adults. But each time we update our edition of the ***K&W Guide***, I remember my concerns about how to figure out where would be the best college environment. I wondered if there would be the right type of support for their specific learning challenges. Both Marybeth and I were working with students who had a diagnosis, she as the college counselor at our local high school, myself as a psychotherapist in private practice.

Colleges have come a long way since the day we tried to interest a publisher in our book and were told, "There is no audience for this type of resource book." Students are more informed about their learning issues and parents are more educated about how to understand their children's learning style. Colleges have so many different types and levels of support that it's become more important than ever to be able to distinguish what is and isn't necessary for the college student.

This book was created to help students feel confident about what they can expect from a college and for parents and professionals to be able to understand if the college is truly a "good match." It's very difficult for any parent to see their student as they are today and not for whom they hope they will be one day. It's very important that when looking for a college and a college support program that the parent takes a step back, looks at the child in front of them and recognizes what they need in the immediate, not years from the time they enter college.

It's much easier today, many editions later, for Marybeth and I to feel confident and comfortable approaching colleges and requesting detailed information. At one time there were only a select few. Today students have a large group from which to pick. But pick carefully. Look at courses required to enter and courses required to graduate. Keep in mind that getting in is the first hurdle, staying in is the true challenge.

We are so appreciative of Random House and The Princeton Review for their continued confidence and support in guaranteeing that we as authors of the ***K&W Guide*** are given the opportunity to write our book to serve a very deserving population of amazing learners.

The ***K&W Guide*** is created by us with a great deal of passion and hope, that families will feel they have an excellent resource to provide guidance and that their students will feel confident that there is a dream to dream.

Marybeth Kravets and Imy Wax

Co-authors of the ***K&W Guide***.

PrincetonReview.com

THE K&W GUIDE TO COLLEGES

FOR STUDENTS WITH LEARNING DIFFERENCES

13TH EDITION

MARYBETH KRAVETS, MA

AND IMY F. WAX, MS

Penguin
Random
House

The Princeton Review
24 Prime Parkway, Suite 201
Natick, MA 01760
E-mail: editorialsupport@review.com

 Published in the United States by Random House LLC., New York, and simultaneously in Canada by Random House of Canada Limited, Toronto.

A Penguin Random House Company.

ISBN: 978-1-101-92038-1
ISSN: 1934-4775

Printed in the United States of America on partially recycled paper.

9 8 7 6 5 4 3 2

13th Edition

Editorial

Robert Franek, VP Test Prep Books, Publisher
David Soto, Director of Content Development
Kristen O'Toole, Editorial Director
Stephen Koch, Student Survey Manager
Pia Aliperti, Editor

Random House Publishing Team

Tom Russell, VP, Publisher
Alison Stoltzfus, Publishing Director
Ellen L. Reed, Production Manager
Jake Eldred, Associate, Managing Editor
Suzanne Lee, Designer

Dedication

This book is a labor of love. It is written to help individuals throughout the world who have been identified as having Learning Differences or Attention Deficit Hyperactivity Disorder and who are seeking the right match and fit for life after high school. Just as importantly, the ***K&W Guide*** is for those students who have never been officially identified as having a learning difference. It is an educational tool for all of the families, professionals, and friends who know someone who has a learning difference or other learning issues who have hopes and dreams.

Acknowledgments

To the families of Marybeth Kravets and Imy F. Wax for their patience and support in this endeavor: Wendy, Steve, Allison, Connor, Isabel, Cooper, Mark, Sara, David, Robbie, Bennett, Cathy (in loving memory), Dan, Andrea, BJ, Matthew, Leia, Maisey, Blue, Howard, Lisa, Bill, Niaya, Ellis, Gary, Tamar, Jordan, Eli, Debrah, Judy, Greg, Jamie, Joey, Benji, Goldie, and Sadie.

To all of the colleges who provide services and programs to promote the educational endeavors and dreams of students with learning differences or attention deficit hyperactivity disorder. We would like to thank all of the contributors in the ***K&W Guide*** who share their thoughts and experiences with learning differences and attention deficit/hyperactivity disorder. Our appreciation to Dr. Miriam Pike, Head of School for Wolcott School, Chicago, Illinois and Stephanie Gordon, Transition Coordinator and Learning Disability Specialist, Deerfield High School, Deerfield, Illinois, for their professional assistance, Wendy Perlin, Jamie Goodman, Sara Hermanoff and Carol Sharp for their support in researching information and to Karen Rodgers Photography for the authors' pictures on the back cover of the book. karenrodgersphot@sbcglobal.net

CONTENTS

FOREWORD

I did not yet have college-bound kids, but I did have children who struggled academically—and I sensed that I might one day need them. I thought I might come away with a few tips, a recommendation or two and call it a day.

Instead of being mere speakers, what I found were magicians of sorts, unlocking a world of possibilities in higher education that I never thought possible. There was help out there—lots of it—for parents like me, who knew the value of a college degree, but had children who didn't fit in any of the prescribed boxes (academic whiz, athletic superstar, musical prodigy). In fact, more often than not, it was me who stayed up late writing those English papers and finishing the science project. How could they possibly get admitted anywhere if I was still going through their lockers and backpacks, searching for missing assignments with the intensity of a bloodhound?

But here were Kravets and Wax, proffering the then-groundbreaking idea that with the proper supports in place, students who learn differently could not only survive college, but could thrive.

Fast forward 20 years. As a reporter for the Chicago Tribune, not only have I relied on this team as expert sources in numerous stories, but I turned to them when seeking help for friends and relatives, always finding their counsel to be invaluable. It's true that the world is a different place than it was back when I first caught their "act" in that high school gym. Today, people have a greater understanding of learning differences, the role of medication and accommodations, such as untimed tests and note-takers.

Still, while the workplace offers all kinds of environments—from solitary telecommuting to the chaos of a restaurant kitchen—academia can be resistant to change, where giant lecture halls and "chalk and talk" still prevail. That's what makes this guide such an essential resource. The authors draw from hundreds of campus visits; they know the people who are in the offices, the ones who are genuinely committed to support services and ones who are just going through the motions.

But don't expect the institution to do all the heavy lifting. The best tutoring center in the world is useless if the student does not seek help. So, drawing from conversations with Kravets and Wax—along with my own lived experiences and years of reporting on college admissions—here are my three best tips to make the transition go smoother.

1. **Be your own best advocate.** Finance 101 is full? Chemistry has you confounded? Don't just glumly accept the situation and slink back to your dorm room. More often than not, educators choose this path because they genuinely want to help students succeed, so find the right people and courteously explain your plight. It is the rare professor who won't go the extra mile to assist a student who is truly motivated (and not just during finals week). This applies for when you are in emotional trouble, as well. Depression, eating disorders, drug abuse are all too common maladies on campuses today. Be alert to symptoms before they turn into a crisis. Knowing how and when to ask for assistance is a sign of strength, not weakness—and a skill that will serve you well across your lifetime.
2. **Say "yes".** The ultimate goal of any university is to turn out graduates, but also well-rounded individuals and good citizens. So engage in campus life by joining at least one club, activity or intramural sport. Being open to new experiences is one way to discover your passion and boost your knowledge base (I learned more about interviewing by working on my college newspaper than from my journalism classes).

Moreover, you will increase your chances of making friends and feel more connected to the community by saying "let's" rather than "let's not." College is one of the last places where you can take risks—be an athlete, an actor, an activist—with few consequences. So be open to the dazzling array of opportunities that will come your way. A semester abroad may require a leap of faith—but can also yield unimagined growth and adventures. When you're walking across the stage at commencement, it's too late.

3. Grade point average is not destiny. Daniel Goleman coined the term and wrote the book "Emotional Intelligence" and here's where you can hit it out of the park. In any company, the best salesperson is typically not the smartest, but the one who is the most persistent and can endure a soul-sucking amount of rejection. Remember that when you are trying to slog your way through some tedious text.

While it may look like your classmates have sailed through high school, no one is insulated from challenges forever. Believe it or not, you are already ahead of the game because you have learned to navigate those icy patches. You've developed some compensatory characteristics—such as empathy, resilience and collaboration—while many of your peers have yet to strengthen those muscles. Sadly, this is even more true today, when "helicopter parents" routinely intervene on behalf of their child with teachers, coaches and even potential employers, determined to remove every obstacle in their youngster's way.

As you start on this new journey, the odds are good that you have already learned one of life's most important lessons: The key to success is not about avoiding all conflicts—but having the information and tools to cope with those setbacks.

Bonnie Miller Rubin
Journalist and author

Thoughts From . . .

Thoughts from . . .
Kinko's Founder Paul Orfalea

It's no secret that I hate the words "disabled" and "disability," particularly when applied to those of us who struggle in school just because we don't fit society's narrow, industrial model of assembly line education. My dyslexia and ADHD have been labeled as "learning disabilities," despite the fact that I learn very well, as do you. If I have to be labeled, I want to be labeled accurately.

I hate the word, but I always ask my coworkers to come to me with solutions, not problems, so it's only fair that instead of complaining about the word "disabled," I should offer some alternatives.

The prefix "dis" means "not," so disabled means "not abled." That sucks, not least because it's wrong. People like me, with dyslexia and ADHD, are not without abilities. So I looked up some other Latin and Greek prefixes that could go in front of the word "abled" to better describe us.

Here are some possible replacements for the word "disabled," in alphabetical order:

Auto-abled = self-abled. For anyone who has come as far as you, such that you now need a book like this to explore your college options, "auto-abled" must have the ring of truth. I'm sure it seems like you've had to fight many battles on your own and figure everything out by yourself. But that's not quite true, is it? Family, friends, and community play an important role in helping us recognize and develop our abilities, so I don't think auto-abled will do it.

Bene-abled = well-abled. True, but not very specific. In fact, this could be the word some people would invent to describe everyone they don't label as "disabled," so let's just forget I ever mentioned it.

Dyna-abled = able to be abled. This has possibilities, but really, it describes almost everyone. If we're going to be labeled, we want a label we can wear proudly as members of an exclusive club.

Frater-abled = brother-abled. This also has potential, since those of us currently labeled "disabled" often rely on others for assistance. But then again, so does everyone—at least if they are honest.

Hetero-abled = mixed-abled. This one is too likely to cause snickering among the immature, which would certainly include me. Besides, once again, the term would include just about everybody.

Ideo-abled = enabled by ideas. I like this, because I've always been obsessed with the power of ideas, and there's no doubt in my mind that creativity is one of the great undervalued abilities of so-called learning-disabled people. Your ideas can work 24/7/365 and bring you wealth, opportunity, and influence. Let's add this to the short list of new words to describe how awesome we really are.

Idios-abled = one's own ability. Suggests uniqueness, and that's a powerful idea too. I've often said that education will take its great leap forward when every student is recognized as a unique individual, meaning we all have learning differences. Viewed this way, it is the educational system that is disabled, since it lacks the wherewithal to serve its constituency of unique human beings who display an infinite diversity of learning styles.

Poly-abled = many abilities. Absolutely true, but absolutely true for everyone and therefore serves no useful purpose. Hmmm. A label that serves no useful purpose. We'll come back to that thought later.

Subter-abled = secret abilities. That's sure how it feels. All through my childhood, my parents knew I could do more than the so-called experts believed. I wasn't sure, but they stuck with me and their belief became my belief. If students with dyslexia and ADHD were labeled "subter-abled," would teachers and administrators be motivated to seek out and nurture hidden abilities?

Trans-abled = across-abled. Considering the barriers we sometimes have to cross, this one makes some sense too.

So now we have invented ten new words to describe people with learning differences, and the really amusing thing is that the only word under consideration that does not describe people with dyslexia, ADHD, and other learning differences is "disabled." It's an outright lie, and one we need to expose and eliminate from the language.

We need a new word to replace a bad idea, but I don't think a single word will do the trick. As your own success proves, you are not someone with a learning disability. You are you. Your name is the only label that can accurately describe your ambition, your experience, your talent, your willpower, your curiosity, and your character. Be yourself.

Education has always required both mastering the educational material and mastering available resources. This book is a resource of resources—a marvelous tool for a group as diverse as us. Use this book to find a college that best fits YOU, and offers resources aligned with your motivation, interests and needs.

By helping you find a good fit, this book can play an important role in freeing you to be yourself while getting the most from an educational system that was not originally designed for you or me, but is now trying hard to adapt to our needs. It took a long time, but the world is starting to understand that every student is a unique individual, and every student has learning differences. The ***K&W Guide*** empowers us to make the most of our abilities. And until we can get a new word, at least we can build partnerships with those who respect us for what we can do.

Kinko's Founder Paul Orfalea is a serial entrepreneur and philanthropist, and the author of ***Copy This! Lessons from a Hyperactive Dyslexic who Turned a Bright Idea Into One of America's Best Companies.***

Thoughts from . . .
The Head of a High School

Success Prep for Students with Learning Differences: The Wolcott Way

Word blindness, minimal brain dysfunction, hyperactivity, dyslexia, specific learning disability, attention deficit disorder, attention deficit hyperactivity disorder, learning disorder, learning differences, learning and attention issues; these are all terms that have been used to describe bright people who learn differently yet struggle to achieve their potential in typical learning environments.

Since 1877 when German neurologist Adolf Kussamaul described word blindness, and 1904, when Fidgety Phil was published in the British journal Lancet, people have been searching for explanations of the deficiencies of groups of people who did not learn or behave in ways they were expected. This deficit based approach has resulted in a body of research, knowledge and practices that have helped to advance our understanding and support for these groups.

In alignment with this approach, students with learning and attentional differences need to demonstrate how deficient and disabled they are to be eligible to access learning. Educational programs are designed to remediate their deficits and often the goals are to make students function similarly to their typical developing peers. Federally regulated documents, IEPs and 504 Plans, are required to access basic accommodations to do things such as complete tests in school. Even with IEP or 504 accommodations, high school students with learning differences need to be approved by ACT and SAT to receive accommodations on college testing.

However, the deficit model has largely ignored the qualities in the same groups of people that are associated with success. While many young adults struggle to succeed, many highly successful adults have publicly identified their learning and attentional differences. The Yale Center for Dyslexia and Creativity, Understood, and CHADD - The National Resource on ADHD among other organizations, list numerous highly successful adults with learning and attention differences.

What if schools considered a strength based approach to the same groups of people?

The Frostig Center and the National Center for Learning Disabilities have explored characteristics of adults with learning and attentional differences associated with success. The Frostig Center's (1999) longitudinal studies identified the Success Attributes of self-awareness, proactivity, perseverance, goal-setting, support systems, and emotional coping strategies. More recently, The National Center for Learning Disabilities Student Voices A Study of Young Adults with Learning and Attentional Issues (2015) identified three common factors associated with thriving after high school; supportive home life, strong sense of self confidence and strong connections to friends and community.

Based upon these lines of research, alternate terms such as creative problem solvers, resilient, persistent, innovative, resourceful, self-confident, connected, self-advocates, successful, and thriving may be used to describe the same people with learning differences.

What if high schools valued students with learning differences for both their challenges and strengths?

At Wolcott School, an independent college preparatory high school for students with learning differences, students benefit from a balanced approach to secondary education. Students experience a rigorous high school education in an environment where how students learn is as important as what they learn. Students thrive as they develop their areas of strengths and challenges in academics, interests and thinking dispositions. Learning emphasizes high level thinking skills while the workload is manageable, allowing participation in leadership, athletics, clubs and activities.

In order to be prepared for college success, high school students with learning differences need to experience a balanced approach to learning, supported by educators and families who value their strengths and talents.

Miriam Pike, PhD
Head of School
Wolcott School, Chicago
wolcottschool.org

Raskind, M. H., Goldberg, R. J., Higgins, E. L., & Herman, K. L. (1999). Patterns of change and predictors of success in individuals with learning disabilities: Results from a twenty-year longitudinal study. *Learning Disabilities Research and Practice*, 14 (1), 35-49. - See more at: http://frostig.org/our-research/frostig-published-articles/#sthash.xCcKEUNb.dpuf

http://www.ncld.org/wp-content/uploads/2015/08/Student-Voices-Executive-Summary.pdf

http://dyslexia.yale.edu/successfuldyslexics.html

https://www.understood.org/en

http://www.chadd.org/Advocacy/ADHD-Champions.aspx

Thoughts from . . .

A High School Counselor

Marybeth Kravets and Imy Wax are the premier experts in the country on how colleges serve students with learning differences and related issues. This book is a must-have for any counselor or therapist who wants to help such students. It is up-to-date, easy to use, and unbiased. I recommend it enthusiastically.

Jon Reider
Director of College Counseling
San Francisco University High School

Thoughts from . . .

A University Vice President

The K&W Guide to College Programs & Services for Students with Learning Differences is an incredible resource for students and families embarking on the college search process. In my 20 plus years of professional experience at the University of Arizona, I have read hundreds of resources and guides, and assisted thousands of students in finding their best college fit. I am always so impressed with the initiative and determination of students on the quest for the perfect college experience. It can be a daunting process, but resources like this make all the difference. I believe this resource will help you find your place.

Marybeth Kravets has been a long time friend and supporter of the University of Arizona (UA). It has been her dedication to support for all students, especially those with learning challenges, that helped shape my focus on and belief in a comprehensive admission review process. Marybeth also helped us create our very first High School and Independent Counselor Advisory Board for the UA. Not only did she help us create it, she served on it for two years. The Board provided invaluable insight into our work at the University and allowed us to better recruit and enroll the new class each year.

In this newest edition, Ms. Kravets and Ms. Wax provide the most current and comprehensive information on college support programs and services. This Guide has been meticulously researched and will benefit parents and students throughout the entire college application process – all while keeping the right "fit" and best environment for learning as the most important factors. Enjoy!

Kasey Urquidez, Ed.D.
Vice President, Enrollment Management & Student Affairs Advancement,
and Dean, Undergraduate Admissions, University of Arizona

Thoughts from . . .

A College Support Program Assistant Director

The K&W Guide to Colleges for Students With Learning Differences is an outstanding resource. During my career as Assistant Director, Admissions & Recruitment, for the Strategic Alternative Learning Techniques (SALT) Center at the University of Arizona, families have consistently referenced this valuable resource. Such unwavering use makes it the definitive research tool for parents and students who are looking for post-secondary academic support programs and services.

Over the years, I have had the pleasure of working with Marybeth Kravets, who is an empathetic and compassionate crusader; helping students who learn differently fulfill their educational dreams. Ms. Kravets and co-author, Imy Wax, have created an unrivaled source that helps in the selection of the best possible opportunity for success in college. The guide's well-organized format highlights each college's enrollment size, admission requirements and academic support options.

In addition to finding a compatible college and support program, trends show that students who have a basic self-understanding of their condition and have developed or improved personal learning strategies, struggle less intensely in college. My colleagues and I have found that students who demonstrate this degree of self-awareness and self-determination benefit most from comprehensive support services, such as those offered by the SALT Center. These students also tend to be positive, motivated, have initiative and set realistic goals that play to their academic strengths. Consequently, they are better able to capitalize on the benefits of academic support programs and services, which will contribute to their goal of achieving success in college and life.

In this new edition, Ms. Kravets and Ms. Wax provide the most current and comprehensive information on college support programs and services. This essential guide is meticulously researched and will benefit parents and students who are looking for the right combination of college and academic support. Best wishes for your college search.

David Cillo, M.Ed.,
Assistant Director, Admissions & Recruitment,
The University of Arizona SALT Center

THOUGHTS FROM . . .
A COLLEGE SUPPORT PROGRAM ASSISTANT DIRECTOR

Success: What Does It Look Like?

I have been working in the field of education for about 35 years. I love working with students and with educators. My passion is to support students on their path to success. It's very simple to make that statement, but what does it mean? What is success?

The online dictionary defines success as "the favorable outcome of something attempted." That definition leaves a great deal of room for individual interpretation. Success looks differently depending on what is attempted. For a 4-year-old, learning to tie his or her shoes is a success. To the middle school student, making the team or the cheering squad is a success. In high school it may be having a date for the prom. However, the parents may have another point of view. Success to them is seeing their son or daughter graduate from high school.

High school has been completed with a favorable outcome. Success!! So, what is next...a job, vocational training, college, etc.? Decisions must be made. The goal is to accomplish a favorable outcome in whatever is attempted.

If the decision is to continue your education, making the right choice, and finding the right fit is extremely important. Check out the facts of the school. *The K&W College Guides to Colleges for Students with Learning Differences* is a great place to start. The information you will find in this guide is accurate and specific. Does the school offer the program of study that you are interested in? Is it the right size for you? Do you prefer the city or a more rural area? Do you qualify for additional academic support or accommodations? If so, does the school offer the support that you need? Visit the campus. Talk to admissions, the director of the support program, and someone in the program of study that you are interested in. In many school these appointments can be made through the admissions office along with a tour of the campus.

Remember as you are choosing a school, your goal is to be successful. Ask yourself if the choice you are making will give you the best chance of a favorable outcome. Once you have made that decision, use your campus resources. Talk to your instructors, advocate for yourself, work with your advisors, and establish a trusting and respectful relationship with your advisors. If you qualify for additional academic support or accommodations get connected with those resources right away.

The resource people on campus want the same thing for you that you want—a favorable outcome. Do your homework, research, visit the campus, and determine the best fit for you, the place where you can experience success!

At the University of Denver, we have two programs that provide support to students with learning differences. The Disability Services Office is the office you will find on every campus, however services will vary. On our campus this office determines the accommodations a student qualifies for and helps the student implement their accommodation. I am director of the Learning Effectiveness Program (LEP). The LEP is a fee for service program. Services provided through LEP include weekly academic counseling, organizational/time management assistance, and subject specific tutoring by tutors trained to work with students with learning differences. We have a staff of eighteen, which includes a director, associate director, enrollment coordinator, organizational/time management specialists, tutoring coordinator, and academic counselors. Our staff serves as a resource to the campus community, talking to professors, leading workshops, etc. We use Universal Design for Learning (UDL) techniques in our program and provide training in UDL principles across campus and in the community. The Universal Design for Learning is a set of principles for curriculum development that give all students equal opportunities to learn. UDL provides a flexible approach to learning that is customized and adjusted for individual needs.

As far back as second grade when I used to help students in my class that couldn't get their work done, I have been interested in how people learn and why learning comes more easily to some than to others. When I had the opportunity to receive training to become a Learning Disabilities Specialist specifically for college students, I jumped at the chance. I loved every minute of the training and amazingly a position for a Learning Disabilities Specialist at a community college became available. I moved from my position as a Testing Specialist to a Learning Disabilities Specialist at another college. The time that I was in that role was a time of great growth for me. I thought I was in my dream job, but little did I know that my real dream job was in Denver, Colorado. I have been director of LEP for four years and I love it! Lives are changed through our program. We work with students on an individual basis meeting them where they are and traveling beside them, guiding them through the college experience. Our desire is to equip students with the skills they need to be successful. The Four Cornerstones of LEP Student Development are: self-awareness, self-determination, self-advocacy, and accountability. When students graduate, we want them to take these cornerstones with them as they pursue their dreams and in turn make a life changing impact on the lives of others.

Over the past six years LEP has grown in size and services. We have hired additional counselors with expertise in a wider range of learning differences and have added new tutoring/testing rooms. We are excited to be able to reach out and provide services to more students.

My wildest dream is to see a learning center available to all students on every college campus, free of charge where all students can receive academic counseling, organizational/time management assistance, and subject specific tutoring. What college student could not at some time benefit from such support? Success starts with a vision. I am going for a favorable outcome!

Jimmie Smith,
Director, Learning Effectiveness Program,
University of Denver

Thoughts from . . .
Diercetor of ASD College Support Program

Because the challenges for individuals with Autism Spectrum Disorder (ASD) face are so unique and individualized, in order for college students with ASD to have the best chance at success, they need a defined on-campus support program that is designed specifically to offer support with the many issues that they will likely deal with. This program must be separate from the Office of Disability Support Services, where all students can receive academic and testing accommodations, which is most often not enough support for this population.

In 2007, when I started the Bridges to Adelphi Program (BAP) at Adelphi University in Garden City, NY, there were very few college support programs available for students with ASD. There was little research available, and from what I could tell from most of the college administrators that I spoke with, there was something between denial that there were students with (what was then known as) Asperger Syndrome on their campuses, and no best practices or resources to consult. That program that I started in 2007 with 3 students who were referred to me from the Office of Disability Support Services, now offers comprehensive, individualized, academic, social, and vocational support services to over 100 current Adelphi undergraduate and graduate students from all over the United States, the Caribbean, and China, who have self-disclosed with what is now diagnosed as ASD.

With the continuing rise in prevalence of ASD, now at 1 in 45 (Center for Disease Control, 2015), a greater awareness of the condition, increased research, and improved and earlier interventions and strategies for individuals with ASD have set the stage for increasing numbers of individuals with ASD to enroll in institutions of higher education. However, while these students may have the cognitive ability to successfully process college level academics, they may also experience significant challenges with communication, executive functioning, sensory issues, understanding social interactions, and managing their anxieties and emotions(Nagler & Shore, 2013).

The Bridges to Adelphi Program, which is fee-based, is based on social learning theory (Bandura, 1977) and cognitive behavioral principles (Beck, Rush, Shaw, & Emery, 1979) as theoretical foundations. A unique feature of BAP is that the staff consists almost exclusively of Adelphi graduate students who are studying psychology, social work, education, or communication disorders. Each student who enrolls in BAP is assigned at least two staff members to work with them a minimum of four times per week on academic issues. These meetings focus on executive functioning strategies to help the student remain aware of, and plan for, upcoming assignments, exams and meetings; and assignment completion, exam preparation, and research. In their meetings, staff is very interested in assessing how students think, learn, and work, so that we can design their supports to meet each student's individual strength and needs.

BAP also offers a variety of socialization opportunities, which are overseen by the staff. Two evenings a week, "Open Group" meetings are offered. These groups are driven by student interests. Students are also offered weekly "Men's" and "Women's" groups. These groups are more focused on subjects that college students need to talk about; and offer rich discussions on relationships, dating, romance, and associated topics. As well, twice a month students are offered group events, both on and off campus. These events include trips to a bowling alley or pool hall, Dave & Busters, or a local restaurant. BAP students are also offered the opportunity to meet weekly with a Peer Mentor, a volunteer undergraduate student who is asked to encourage BAP student's to attend campus activities or join campus clubs.

However, the most important social opportunity for students may occur in the BAP office, which is open Mondays through Fridays from 8am-8pm, and on Saturdays from 9am-4pm. Students are encouraged to hang around and socialize with each other in a safe and predictable environment. They often order food in together, play video games; talk about their classes; and over the years many friendships have been made.

Our research show outstanding outcomes. In 2014–15, BAP retained 95 percent of the students enrolled in the program. And the average GPA for the past four semesters has consistently been approximately 3.30. But these are not the only goals of BAP. We are also focused on developing independent and successful adults who, when they graduate, will find meaningful employment in their areas of study, at competitive wages.

To address these goals, we have developed a vocational program that offers BAP students complete vocational testing batteries, individual and group vocational meetings, assistance with resume writing and job interview skills, and help finding both on and off campus internships. BAP has also entered in partnerships with outside agencies that have programs that help adults with ASD find jobs and provide training for the employers, and on the job support for the employees.

This (very) brief outline of the services that the Bridges to Adelphi offers can serve as a guideline to parents of students with ASD. It is strongly advised that you go to each school that you and your child are considering. Take a campus tour when classes are in session to make certain that your child can feel comfortable there. Meet with an admissions officer. Meet with the Office of Disability Support Services to learn the criteria and documentation needed to receive services. And most importantly meet with the people that run the ASD support program on the campus. One last suggestion. Start early; don't wait for senior year to begin preparing for the transition from high school to college.

Mitch Nagler MA, LMHC, Director, Bridges to Adelphi Program
Assistant Director, Student Counseling Center
p – 516.877.3665
e – mnagler@adelphi.edu

Thoughts from . . .

Matthew Cohen, Esq., Attorney, Chicago Illinois

Obtaining Accommodations for College Students with Disabilities

Many children with disabilities have the potential to be highly successful in post-secondary school and beyond, particularly if provided the appropriate accommodations that they need to function within the school environment. Whether trade school, junior college, Liberal Arts College or major university, educational institutions are required to provide reasonable accommodations to students that are able to document the presence of a disability and the need for accommodation. However, the procedures for obtaining accommodations are very different in relation to getting into and participating in higher education than they are in elementary and high school. In the public school system, the responsibility lies with the school district to identify children suspected of having disabilities, to evaluate them (with parent consent), and to develop and implement individualized educational programs (IEPs) or Section 504 plans designed to meet their unique needs. Unfortunately, the law governing special education, the Individuals with Disabilities Education Act (IDEA) does not apply to higher education.

Further, while Section 504 applies to many colleges and universities, the rules for how it applies are different than within public elementary and high schools. Eligibility under the IDEA or Section 504 in public school does NOT automatically ensure that a student will be eligible for accommodations in college or, if eligible, will automatically qualify for the same services or accommodations. In order to maximize the likelihood that the student will receive appropriate accommodations in college, planning by the parents, the student, and the school district must begin well before the child applies for college. Some of these steps will be briefly highlighted below.

The Right to Accommodations

Two different federal laws govern the right to accommodations in relation to higher education. The first is the Americans with Disabilities Act of 1990 (the ADA), which has two different sections that are relevant to higher education. Title II of the ADA regulates local and state governmental entities, which includes community colleges, state colleges and universities. Title III of the ADA regulates what are called places of public accommodation. All private colleges and universities are places of public accommodation. However, those colleges that are religiously controlled are exempt from the coverage of the ADA.

In addition to regulating the provision of "reasonable accommodations" within colleges and universities, the ADA also provides the right to reasonable accommodations from agencies that administer the tests that are used for college and graduate admissions and for licensing upon graduation. Thus, the ACT, SAT, MCAT, LSAT and the like are all operated by organizations that are required to comply with the requirements of the ADA.

The second law, which governs the right to reasonable accommodations in higher education, is Section 504 of the Rehabilitation Act of 1973. Section 504 provides very similar protections as the ADA, but has two significant differences. First, in order for Section 504 to be applicable, the organization must be a recipient of federal financial assistance. Second, as there is no exception under Section 504 for colleges that are religiously controlled, those religiously controlled colleges that do accept federal funds must adhere to the Section 504 disability regulations even though the ADA does not apply. While most colleges and universities do receive federal financial assistance, and are therefore governed by Section 504, not all do. Thus, the non-discrimination laws apply to all colleges and universities except those that are religiously controlled and do not take federal financial assistance.

What Needs to Happen during High School?

First, all students in special education should have a transition plan in place starting at the age of 16 (or earlier, based on state law or individual need). This plan should include the student's input about their long-term goals; assessment of the student's continuing needs, and the development and implementation of a plan to facilitate the student's accomplishment of realistic post-secondary goals. Notably, the first step in the transition planning process is to conduct a transition assessment, including age appropriate assessment of the student's functioning and needs in relation to training, education, employment and independent living skills. 34 CFR 300.320(b). This plan must include the course of study necessary to reach the student's measurable post-secondary goals. This plan, when done right, can often provide important support for the student to prepare them for college, before they even get there. Notably, the transition plan can address not only academic and vocational goals, but also life skills, organizational or executive functioning needs, social deficits and a variety of other issues that may impact a student's ability to function successfully in college even if they meet the college's admissions criteria.

Second, the student needs to identify what colleges may be appropriate, given the student's disability (ies). The K&W Guide and consultation with college counselors can be invaluable in helping to determine whether particular colleges or even types of colleges are realistic for the student, with or without the provision of accommodations. If the student is going to take the SAT and/or ACT, the school and the family must take the necessary steps , typically with involvement from the high school's college counselors, to secure accommodations on those tests as well. For those students who do badly on such tests, it is worth investigating schools that place less emphasis on those tests or don't require them at all, a trend that has been gathering momentum recently.(www.fairtest.org)

Third, before a student receiving special education graduates, the school district is now required to complete a document called a Summary of Performance. According to the IDEA, when a student's special education eligibility is terminated due to graduation or aging out of school, the school must provide a summary of the child's "academic achievement, functional performance and recommendations on how to assist the child in meeting their post-secondary goals." 34 CFR 300.305. (e)(3). This document can be of enormous value both in documenting the nature of the child's disability and in providing support for the provision of particular accommodations. As the Summary of Performance statement is a relatively new requirement of the special education system and not all schools are fully familiar with it, parents should be sure that this is provided before the student graduates.

Who is Entitled to Accommodations Under the Disability Rights Laws?

Under both the ADA and Section 504, a person is entitled to reasonable accommodations if they meet a number of criteria. First, the person must have a physical or mental impairment that substantially limits a major life activity. There are a variety of different major life activities, but some of the most important, for purposes of accommodations in college, are learning, reading, concentrating, thinking and communicating. Second, the person must meet the general qualifications for participation in the program or activity that they are applying for, either with or without accommodations. Third, they must establish that they: a) have a physical or mental impairment, b) need specific accommodations and c) that these accommodations are "reasonable."

It is important to note that the burden is on the student to identify themselves as having a disability, provide documentation supporting this, and request accommodations. Unlike in elementary and high school, the burden is on the student to tell the college they have a disability and seek accommodations, not on the college to figure it out for themselves. The student is not obligated to disclose the disability, either in the application process or after admission, but they are not entitled to accommodations unless they make the disclosure and document the need for assistance. This is generally done by communication with the college or university's Disability Services Office.

The Americans with Disabilities Act Amendments of 2008, substantially expanded the grounds for a person to be determined to have a disability and eligible for accommodations, by overturning a number of court cases that had dramatically restricted the eligibility criteria. These cases held, among other things, that if mitigating measures, such as medication, neutralized the effect of the person's disability on their life functioning, they would no longer be deemed to be a person with a disability under the ADA. The ADA Amendments reversed those cases and expanded the ADA eligibility criteria as follows:

The ADA Amendments define a person as being a person with a disability if they have:

(A) a physical or mental impairment that substantially limits one or more major life activities of such individual;
(B) a record of such an impairment, or
(C) being regarded as having such impairment as described in paragraph (3).

The Amendments defined "Major life activities" as including but not being limited to, caring for oneself, performing manual tasks, seeing, bending, speaking, breathing, learning, reading, concentrating, thinking, communicating and working.

They also defined A major life activity to include the operation of a major bodily function, including but not limited to, functions of the immune system, normal cell growth, digestive, bowel, bladder, neurological, brain, respiratory, circulatory, endocrine and reproductive functions.....

An impairment that substantially limits one major life activity need not limit other major life activities in order to be considered a disability.

Further, an impairment that is episodic or in remission is a disability if it would substantially limit a major life activity when active.

One of the most important changes made by the 1998 amendments was the elimination of the use of mitigating measures as a basis for concluding that a person did not have a protected disability. This means that individuals that rely on special equipment, supports or accommodations that allow them to function at a level that is not regarded as impaired are still eligible as people with disabilities despite the use of these mitigating measures. Put another way, if a mitigating measure masks the impact of the disability to such an extent that the disability no longer appears impairing, but would be without the mitigating measure, the person still must be recognized as a person with a disability. Examples of mitigating measures provided in the law include:

(I) medication, medical supplies, equipment, or appliances, low-vision devices (which do not include ordinary eyeglasses or contact lenses), prosthetics including limbs and devices, hearing aids and cochlear implants or other implantable hearing devices, mobility devices, or oxygen therapy equipment and supplies
(II) use of assistive technology;
(III) reasonable accommodations or auxiliary aids or services; or
(IV) learned behavioral or adaptive neurological modifications.

These new standards reinstate the original and far broader reach of the ADA (and by parallel interpretation, Section 504). However, these criteria are very different than those used under the IDEA for children in special education Again, however, unlike the public schools, where the responsibility lies with the school to identify, evaluate and plan a program for children suspected of having a disability, the ADA and Section 504 give the responsibility for establishing the presence of a disability to the student seeking the accommodation. In other words, if the student wants reasonable accommodations, they must come forward, identify that they have a disability, document the disability and the need for accommodation and specifically request the provision of such accommodations. In fact, under these laws, the colleges may not ask questions about disability in the application/admissions process and the student need not disclose the existence of a disability at that stage.

Students seeking information about how a particular college will respond to the student's disability and whether it will have appropriate services to meet the student's needs can and should contact the school's Office of Disability Services (different colleges use different names). The Disability Services staff will be able to share information about the types of services that are provided, the types of students that are effectively served by the college or university, and help the student to determine when and what information to share (pre or post-application) in securing accommodations.

Although this is less often an issue, it should also be pointed out that under both laws, students are protected from discrimination if they have a history of disability or are perceived to have a disability. Thus, a school could not discriminate against an individual who is HIV Positive but has no symptoms, simply because of their HIV-Positive status. This would be discrimination based on the student being regarded as having a disability, even though they were not at that time actually disabled.

The Need for Documentation

Because the burden rests with the student to document that they actually have a disability, it is important that the student carefully document the existence of the impairment. This requires several different kinds of documentation. First, the colleges and universities are interested in the student's history in relation to their disability. Clinical reports which provide the diagnosis and which track the progression of the disorder are useful in establishing that the disability has been present on a long-standing basis. Second, schools are interested in current evaluations, typically at least within the past three years if not more current. Often, evaluations can be obtained from the school districts during this period, which may provide the necessary information. However, under some circumstances, the student may need to obtain outside clinical evaluations. This may be necessary for several reasons. First, if the student does not have a current school district evaluation, the outside evaluation may be the only option for obtaining current diagnostic material. Second, and particularly for students who are high functioning or even gifted, or who have more subtle disabilities, more sophisticated private testing may provide data that offers support for the presence of a disability that is not present in the public school's testing.

In addition to clinical material, the colleges and universities are very interested in whether the student has been receiving special education and/or Section 504 services. Colleges tend to be more receptive to the provision of accommodations when the student has a history of having received special education or Section 504 accommodations for a long period of time. Colleges tend to be more skeptical of the student's entitlement to accommodations if the student went through most or all of school without assistance and only became eligible for services late in high school. Unfortunately, there is a sense that some students deliberately seek eligibility around the junior year of high school for the primary purpose of obtaining accommodations on the SAT and ACT and for purposes of accommodations in college. While this may sometimes happen, there are also many students whose disability does not become a major problem or become obvious until the rigors of high school expose the problems that the student had previously been able to cope with successfully. Nonetheless, providing documentation of a prior history of accommodations is very useful in establishing both general eligibility for accommodations and justifying the need for the particular accommodations being requested. The graduate exam administrators (for the MCAT, LSAT, etc.) also look closely at whether there is a history of accommodation in high school and college, so these processes have a domino effect as the student progresses through college.

While students with late-diagnosed disabilities are not excluded from being considered for accommodations, either for college board testing, or once admitted, there is no question that those students are viewed with greater scrutiny and may need even more documentation to establish that they have areal impairment and require accommodations. Notably, recent research has suggested that the criteria for diagnosing AD/HD may be modified to allow for diagnosis based on symptoms that manifest themselves in adolescence, rather than in childhood, because of growing information that suggests that not all students with AD/HD meet criteria in elementary school. This may make it easier for some late-diagnosed students to make the case for eligibility.

Obtaining Accommodations After Admission

As indicated, the college may not ask questions that directly or indirectly seek to identify whether a student has a disability during the application process. However, some students may choose to share information about their disability during the application process or even use the disability as material in application essays for sharing ways that they have coped with adversity or otherwise. Whether and what to share in the application process is a difficult decision, which typically should be made with the benefit of consultation from parents, college counselors and even the disabilities services staff at the college the student is interested in attending.

Once the student has been admitted, however, if the student wants accommodations, they must contact the Office of Disability Services, present their documentation of disability and formally request accommodations. A wide variety of accommodations are available, from preferential seating to extra time for assignments or tests, to use of a note-taker, to use of a tape recorder or word processor for completion of assignments. The nature of potential accommodations is extensive, in that there is no specified list. Instead, accommodations are developed to respond to the needs of the particular individual. On the other hand, just because a student seeks a particular accommodation, or even received that accommodation previously in public school, does not mean that the college or university is obligated to provide it.

In particular, unlike special education, the college or university is not obligated to provide individual tutoring or 1-1 aides. If they elect to do so, as some do, they may charge extra for those services. The colleges must make their own judgment as to whether a request for a particular accommodation is "unduly burdensome," rather than reasonable. That determination will be based on a variety of factors, including but not limited to the quality of the student's documentation supporting the need for the accommodation, whether the student has a history of receiving the accommodation, the size of the college and its ability to provide the accommodation, and whether the college feels the accommodation simply goes beyond what is reasonable for the student to be accommodated.

In addition, the college has the right to refuse requested accommodations if the college believes and can establish that the proposed accommodation will "fundamentally alter" the basic mission, organization or mode of operation of the school. This comes up most often in circumstances when the student is requesting a total waiver of a particular requirement for graduation, such as exemption from math or foreign language requirements. Under some circumstances, alternatives to these requirements can be agreed upon which will work for the student and satisfy the college, but this is not always the case.

What To Do if the Accommodation is Denied or is not Being provided?

Unlike public school, where the school district is charged with the responsibility for insuring compliance with the IEP or 504 plan, there is less direct responsibility for enforcement placed on the college or university. At the outset, colleges handle the process of alerting faculty of the accommodation plan in a variety of ways. In some, the Office of Disability Services takes initial responsibility for notifying the faculty, while in others the burden is put on the student to bring the accommodations plan to the attention of the faculty member. Once the plan has been presented, the staff person is supposed to carry the plan out, but implementation often varies with the personality, understanding, and sensitivity of the individual staff member. Where there is a problem with compliance, the student generally is well advised to follow a series of steps:

1) Try to work it out directly with the faculty member
2) Seek the help of the Office of Disability Services staff
3) Seek to work things out with higher ups in the particular department or Dean's Office
4) Determine what the school's internal grievance procedure is. Typically, colleges have two sets of grievance procedures, a general grievance procedure relating to any problem involving a student, and a specific grievances procedure for handling disability related complaints. In consultation with the Office of Disability Services staff, parents, and perhaps private counsel, the student may opt to use the disability grievance procedure, the general grievance procedure or both. In either event, the student should be aware that there are typically specific timelines and documentation requirements contained in the grievance procedures.

5) If these efforts are unsuccessful, or if the problem is sufficiently severe to warrant more serious action, the student may file complaints with the US Department of Education, Office for Civil Rights or the US Department of Justice, for violation of Section 504 or the ADA respectively.

Obviously, these are last resort measures and students are best off resolving matters informally and amicably within the school structure wherever possible.

When seeking to obtain reasonable accommodations, documentation is critical. As indicated above, the ADAA of 2008 provides more expansive standards for demonstrating that the individual has a disability that substantially limits major life functions. Even given this important expansion of the scope of these laws, parents and students should be thorough in gathering as much information about the student's difficulties, both historically and currently, as possible. School records, clinical data, anecdotal information and evidence of the actual impact of the impairment are all critical to receiving recognition as a person with a disability and obtaining the desired accommodations. If a student is late diagnosed, it is even more important to seek information showing the historical presence of the disability (unless it is based on a recent medical condition or accident). This can include information about extra tutorial or therapeutic help the student received outside of school, informal accommodations that were provided by the teachers, staff or parents, anecdotal or report card information documenting that the student was having difficulties early on, even though they were not identified as related to a disability, and statements by the student and parents describing the ways that the disability adversely affected the student's functioning, even if they were able to progress academically or were not formally diagnosed. Once the accommodations have been secured, the student must develop and judiciously implement self-advocacy skills to insure that the accommodations are provided as intended and as needed. When in doubt, students should seek assistance from their Office of Disability Services, or if necessary, from outside agencies such as OCR,(www.ed.gov./about/offices/list/ocr and www.hhs.gov.ocr) or from knowledgeable lawyers. Students and parents can obtain more information about disability rights in higher education and the process of securing accommodations at two excellent websites: www.heath.gwu.edu and www.ahead.org.

Matt Cohen has represented children and adults with disabilities in regard to public and higher education for approximately 30 years. He regularly writes on disability law topics and lectures regularly on these subjects throughout the United States. His law firm, based in Chicago, has represented children, college students and adults throughout the United States.

Matt Cohen, Esq.
Matthew Cohen & Associates, Chicago IL
866-787-9270
www.mattcohenandassociates.com
disablethelabels@blogspots.com

Thoughts from . . .
a Parent

Neither my husband nor I have a background in education or learning differences. With regard to each of our four children and their elementary school education, we followed the path taken by most parents—we found a nearby school that matched our family's priorities and philosophies, enrolled, and stepped aside. We assumed that by sending our kids to a small, nurturing elementary school, the learning piece would take care of itself. We never anticipated how wrong we could be!

Over the years, we learned that our kids—each of them bright and motivated—were not what were called neuro-typical learners. Given their individual learning profiles, they each required extra support. There were struggles with de-coding, executive function, attention, the list seemed to grow as the word-load increased. Fortunately, their elementary school was able, for the most part, able to offer the support they needed.

When it came time for high school, our goal was to find an environment where our kids would not only be successful, but also be prepared to succeed beyond high school. In our research, we discovered that our city did not have a school where the teachers understood that 'how' they teach is as important as 'what' they teach; where the critical school/life balance was valued and efforts were made to help students achieve that healthy balance; where students' strengths were leveraged for academics as well as for a robust array of extra-curricular activities, from sports to theater, composting to robotics. As our children approached high school, it became clear to us that we needed to assemble a critical mass and found a high school established on these principles.

As parents, we have transformed from educational spectators to active participants. In the process, we have seen that for so many students, the right school can make all the difference both in students' day-to-day learning and in how they frame their dreams for the future.

It was with this acquired understanding about the nuanced differences between schools, and a clear picture of our eldest daughter's learning strengths and areas for growth that we embarked on the college application process for the first time. Much to our pleasure, we learned that her drive, focus, and self-awareness made the application process infinitely easier than it could have been. What helped most is that she began the process with specific questions in mind—what supports did she need in order to succeed in college and which colleges could provide those supports?

The K & W Guide to Colleges for Students with Learning Differences was critical to helping us frame the questions and begin to gather answers. The Guide is encyclopedic in the amount of information it offers about programs across the country. By skimming The Guide, we gained a fuller sense of the range of supports that colleges offer. Studying The Guide more deeply allowed us to develop a clearer understanding of how individual colleges differ. Certainly, when it came time to visit campuses, we felt very prepared.

Our daughter worked extremely hard to be successful in high school and to develop the self-awareness and self-advocacy skills necessary to succeed in college. We have found that success often comes down not to knowing the answers, but to knowing what questions to ask. I think The Guide is a ground-breaking resource for students with learning differences and a vital tool for helping them identify the important questions as they navigate the college application process.

Jennifer Levine and Jeff Aeder are the founders of Wolcott School,
Chicago Illinois

Thoughts from . . .
A Student

As a senior in high school, I have a good understanding of my learning strengths and challenges. I am a strong self-advocate and am very organized. However, I know math will always be a struggle, and that I benefit from using the audio version of reading assignments. I went into my college search knowing that I would do better in a college with a more structured learning support program, one that can help me stay organized, efficient, and focused on the assignments and teacher expectations.

Personally, I am much more comfortable entering a new situation if I know what to expect. I like to do a lot of research before starting something new. For me, The K & W Guide was a great place to start. As soon as I began creating a list of schools that I was interested in, I studied The Guide. It helped me understand what services the different colleges offered and how schools differed in the ways they supported students with learning differences.

I am one of those kids who took lots of notes during college tours. It was the best way for me to remember what I liked and did not like, and note what distinguished one school from another. I liked that *The Guide* gave me ideas about what to ask students, professors, admissions officers, and those who provided learning support.

For me, the college application process was difficult—lots of details, essays, timelines, etc. But, it was also manageable. I felt there were many colleges that fit my learning profile and personal interests. Fast forward a few months to the receipt of acceptance letters—I was pleased to have eight colleges to choose from that matched my priorities. I think my college application process was very positive because we put so much thought into identifying schools that were the right fit. With all of the research that I have done, I feel like I am going off to college having eliminated a whole set of uncertainties about what support different schools can and cannot offer. Given the number of surprises ahead, I am happy to have eliminated a whole category already!

Mollie Aeder
High School Senior
Wolcott School Class of 2016

General Guidelines for Documentation of a Learning Disability

1. A comprehensive psycho-educational or neuropsychological evaluation that provides a diagnosis of a learning disability must be submitted. The report should indicate the current status and impact of he learning disability in an academic setting. If another diagnosis is applicable (e.g., ADHD, mood disorder), it should be stated.
2. The evaluation must be conducted by a professional who is certified/licensed in the area of learning disabilities, such as a clinical or educational psychologist, school psychologist, and neuropsychologist or learning disabilities specialist. The evaluator's name, title, and professional credentials and affiliation should be provided.
3. The evaluation must be based on a comprehensive assessment battery:
   - **Aptitude**: Average broad cognitive functioning must be demonstrated on an individually administered intelligence test, preferably administered during high school or beyond, such as the WAIS, WISC, Woodcock-Johnson Cognitive Battery, and Kaufman Adolescent and Adult Intelligence Test. Subtest scaled scores/subtest scores should be listed.
   - **Academic Achievement**: A comprehensive academic achievement battery, such as the WJ and WIAT should document achievement deficits relative to potential. The battery should include current levels of academic functioning in relevant areas, such as reading, oral and written language, and mathematics. Standard scores and percentiles for administered subtests should be stated. Specific achievement tests can also be included, such as the Nelson-Denny Reading Test and Test of Written Language (TOWL), as well as informal measures (e.g., informal reading inventories and writing samples).
   - **Information Processing**: Specific areas of information processing (e.g., short- and long-term memory, auditory and visual perception/processing, executive functioning) should be assessed.
   - **Social-Emotional Assessment**: To rule out a primary emotional basis for learning difficulties and provide information needed to establish appropriate services, a social-emotional assessment, using formal assessment instruments and/or clinical interview, should be conducted.
   - **Clinical Summary**: A diagnostic summary should present a diagnosis of a specific learning disability; provide impressions of the testing situation; interpret the testing data; and indicate how patterns in the student's cognitive ability, achievement, and information processing reflect the presence of a learning disability. Recommendations should be provided for specific accommodations based on disability-related deficits. For students just graduating high school, an evaluation reflecting current levels of academic skills should have been administered while in high school; for students who have been out of school for a number of years, documentation will be considered on a case-by-case basis. Additional documents that do not constitute sufficient documentation, but that may be submitted in addition to a psychological, psycho-educational or neuropsychological evaluation include an individualized education plan (IEP), a 504 plan, and/or an educational assessment.

General Guidelines for Documentation of Attention Deficit/Hyperactivity Disorder (ADHD)

Students requesting accommodations and services on the basis of an Attention Deficit/Hyperactivity Disorder (AD/HD) are required to submit documentation that establishes a disability and supports the need for the accommodations recommended and requested.

1. A *qualified* professional must conduct the evaluation. Professionals who conduct the assessment, make the diagnosis of ADHD, detail symptoms, provide relevant history, determine functional limitations, and provide recommendations for accommodation must be qualified professionals defined as licensed mental health professionals. Primary care or general practice physicians are not considered qualified to complete an AD/HD evaluation.
2. Documentation must be current (typically within three years. The provision of accommodations is based upon an assessment of the current impact of the student's disability on learning in the college setting.
3. Documentation *must* be comprehensive. Requirements for any diagnostic report are:

- A medical or clinical diagnosis of AD/HD based on DSM criteria
- Assessment/testing profile and interpretation of the assessment instruments used that supports the diagnosis. Acceptable measures include objective measures of attention and discrimination or valid and reliable observer or self-report. Acceptable measures are
    - Conner's Continuous Performance Task (CPT)
    - Test of Variables of Attention (TOVA)
    - Behavioral Assessment System for Children
    - Conner's Adult AD/HD Rating Scale (CAARS)
    - CAARS-L; the long version of the self-report form
    - CARRS-O; the observer form
    - Brown Attention Deficit Disorder Scale
- A clear description of the functional limitations in the educational setting, specifying the major life activities that are affected to a substantial degree because of the disability
- Relevant history, including developmental, family, medical, psychosocial, pharmacological, educational and employment. AD/HD is by definition first exhibited in childhood. Therefore, the assessment should include historical information establishing symptoms of AD/HD throughout childhood, adolescence and into adulthood.
- A description of the specific symptoms manifesting themselves at the present time that may affect the student's academic performance
- Medications the student is currently taking, as well as a description of any limitations that may persist even with medication
- Co-existing conditions, including medical and learning disabilities that should be considered in determining reasonable accommodations

General Guidelines for Documentation of Asperger's Disorder and Other Pervasive Developmental Disorders

1. Documentation of Diagnosis:

   Documentation of an evaluation completed by a qualified professional and resulting in a diagnosis of Asperger's or other Pervasive Developmental Disorder should be provided. A qualified professional may include a psychiatrist, developmental pediatrician, clinical psychologist, neuropsychologist, or licensed mental health professional that has comprehensive training and direct experience working with Asperger's and other Pervasive Developmental Disorders.

   The evaluation report should contain a summary of a comprehensive diagnostic interview identifying the presenting problem, a developmental history, medical history, academic performance, relevant family history and relevant social/emotional/behavioral factors. It should also contain the credentials of the diagnosing professional.

2. Documentation of a Current Evaluation:

   The provision of accommodations in a college setting is based upon an assessment of the current impact a student's disability has on learning. An evaluation should provide a detailed description of the student's current functioning in the following areas:

   - Executive functioning
   - Pragmatic language
   - Social behavior patterns
   - Restricted, repetitive and/or stereotyped patterns of behavior, interests or activities
   - Sensory needs or concerns
   - Motor planning

   Supporting evidence should include results of aptitude and achievement testing, standardized testing of language skills, standardized scales of symptoms related to Asperger's or other Pervasive Developmental Disorders, as well as clinical observations.

   The evaluation should describe the current impact that the student's limitations resulting from the disorder have on learning and functioning within a college setting. Medical information relating to the student's diagnosis should include the impact of prescribed medication on the student's ability to meet the demands of the postsecondary educational environment. Additionally, an evaluation should include recommendations for accommodations and a rationale for the accommodations based on specific features/symptoms of the student's diagnosis. Relevant information regarding current treatment and prognosis should be provided.

3. Historical Documentation:

   Because Asperger's Disorder and other Pervasive Developmental Disorders are often manifested during childhood (though not always diagnosed), historical information regarding the student's academic performance, communication characteristics, and social patterns in elementary, secondary and postsecondary education should be provided. This information can be found in documents such as IEPs, Section 504 Plans, speech therapy evaluations, occupational therapy evaluations, social-emotional assessments, psychological/neuropsychological reports, and/or psychiatric evaluations.

THE JOURNEY

Edward M. Hallowell, M.D. and David Keevil, Psy.D., The Hallowell Center[1]:

Going to college is a rite of passage. The time for college finally arrives, and with considerable fanfare our children go: they go away from home, friends, and family, and go toward a "grown up" life of freedom and independence.

As this time arrives, parents and children often have powerful and competing urges on both sides: to hold on tight and never let go, or to sever all connections and begin anew. Of course many parents tend toward the former urge, while their adolescents yearn for the latter.

When you're a parent, so many instincts protest against letting go. The world is often a cruel and dangerous place, and you are all too aware of your child's newness—their youth and fragility. When you're young, it's blissful to dream of a new life that is entirely yours. And so much in our world supports that dream: songs, sitcoms, the exalted fables of popular culture.

If your child has ADHD or LD, you may feel even more acutely the urge to hold tight. Your child may be impulsive; he or she may seem emotionally unprepared for the challenges ahead, and may have only a vague understanding of the sometimes tedious and always disciplined work required at college. You may be particularly aware of all the effort "behind the scenes" that went into getting your child even this far—the homework assistance, the teachers meetings, the evaluations and treatments, and the countless hours of "extra help" along the way.

Your child with ADHD or LD may yearn particularly for the independence of college life. He or she may be awfully tired of feeling dependent on all the help you and others have offered. College may feel like a chance to "throw off the yoke" and finally succeed on one's own, free of dependence.

This tension, between the urge to hold on and the urge to let go, is very real for all of us who are parents, and it is very real for our children. I suppose the good and bad news is that this tension is life-long: we never really outgrow these competing urges. They just take on different shapes and sizes as we all continue to grow and mature.

What I want to tell you here—something I'm sure you already understand—is that the way to resolve this conflict is not to choose one side or the other—not to hold on even tighter, or pull away so hard that you are impossible to hold—but to mix them together, to balance them. In order to do this, you need to stay connected.

What do I mean by "stay connected"? I mean three things. First, hold on to what you have. Second, stay flexible. And third, grow new connections. Let me tell you a little more about each of these ideas.

Hold on to what you have.

Maybe it looks as if I'm saying that you shouldn't let go. Actually, some letting go will be essential, for both parent and child. Parents will probably unpack the car, move things into their child's room, get a last hug, and drive away. Students will spend their first night in a college dorm, go to their first campus party, register for classes, and set their own study schedule. But in the midst of all this necessary letting go, remember to hold on to what's important from the past as well.

What is important from the past? Every new college student will have his or her own list, but I hope most lists will include these headlines:

- Your parents love you, and will continue to love you no matter what;
- You have a home to return to, where you are welcome;
- You have friends who care about you;
- You have specific strengths and abilities you carry with you;
- You have learned many essential skills for coping with your ADHD or LD, and college is a tremendous opportunity to learn and use many more.

Here's an idea for parents: as your child with ADHD or LD prepares for college, devote some time to making a detailed, truthful, loving, and relentlessly supportive list of what your child will "carry" to college, and offer it to your child as a gift. And here's an idea for new college students with ADHD or LD: make your own list of what you will carry with you, as a personal, intimate reminder of what is strong and sustaining in your life.

Each list is a testament to the connections that will endure and sustain.

Stay Flexible

In nature, the best connections—the strongest and most sustaining—are flexible. Think of how a tree sways in the wind, allowing it to stay connected both to the ground and to the air, through its branches and leaves. Connections that are rigid tend to snap and crack apart under strain. Flexibility allows us to grow and flourish.

What does this mean for parents, and for their child with ADHD or LD? It means not to attach too rigidly to any one thing—to any one expectation, to any one vision of the future, to any one marker of "success." Think "trial and error"; think "a different drummer"; think "two steps forward, one and a half steps back."

One of the exciting and dismaying things about people with ADHD is that we do not always follow the pack. We may act impulsively, or "forget" to act at all. We may make associative connections between seven different ideas, but drop the one that's on next Monday's test. These and many other behaviors can lead to difficulty and risk. And they can lead to creativity and discovery.

Parents: if your child goes off to college and marches through in four years with a high grade point average, then good for your child! But this may well not happen. And if you tie your happiness to such expectations—if your expectations are too rigid—then you may well be disappointed, or unhappy, or angry, or dismissive. As a result, the connection between you and your child, and between your child and his or her positive self-understanding, may snap and crack apart. And that's not a good thing for anyone. Keep the connections flexible, pliant, and resilient. Cut each other slack, practice forgiveness, and keep your sense of humor.

And expect surprises. Life is always a dress rehearsal, and people flub their lines and miss their cues all the time. People with ADHD or LD may play a love scene when we expected tragedy, or start tap-dancing during the soliloquy. There's nothing to be gained by throwing them off the stage. Rather, find out how your script might be re-written, and how they can accustom themselves to the action around them. Stay flexible!

Grow New Connections

Many adolescents with ADHD or LD who head off to college have already received a great deal of help over the years. They may be sick of help! But if they avoid help at college they will be missing one of the most important lessons college has to teach: how to find and use help. Think of preparing for college as preparing to find and use help: from teachers, from tutors, from other students, from administrators, from friends and family.

Finding and using help is not the same thing as offering excuses, or getting others to do your work. It is the same thing as growing new connections. College is a community of learners. The vast majority of human beings learn best in community—we learn from others and with others. A student who has something to prove by "going it alone" is mistaking a lack of connections for maturity.

One of the wonderful things about this K & W Guide is that it helps students and their parents plan the best ways to find and use help. With this Guide you can map out new, essential connections: with colleges and universities who understand your needs; with appropriate support services on campus; with departments and faculty members who will understand, challenge and respect you. Use this guide to start planning now, and to further develop your ability to find and use help. Ask yourself: what kind of help might I need? How will I recognize when I need it? How will I go about finding it? How will I ask, and who will I ask? The answers you discover will change and grow as you change and grow. Remember, stay connected, and stay flexible!

In Closing

Bon voyage! You have an exciting trip ahead of you, climbing to the top of your own particular mountain. If you have ADHD or LD the path may be particularly challenging, and the air particularly thin at times. But you will get there. The people who love and respect you will not stand on the summit with you—that is yours alone. But I hope and trust they will help you along the paths you choose (and the paths that choose you), by remaining connected with you, assisting you in ways you find helpful, and sharing with you the wonder and excitement of your discoveries.

4 The Hallowell Center, Sudbury, MA, is dedicated to promoting cognitive and emotional well being in children and adults. www.DrHallowell.com

GETTING READY

The purpose of *The K&W Guide* is to help students with learning differences such as Specific Learning Disabilities (LD), Attention Deficit Hyperactivity Disorder (ADHD) or Asperger Syndrome Disorder (ASD) acquire the basic knowledge necessary to begin the college exploration process and get ready to make appropriate college selections.

To get ready students need to:

- Understand their strengths and weaknesses.
- Be able to articulate the nature of their learning disabilities.
- Understand the compensatory skills developed to accommodate the learning differences.
- Describe the services they received in high school.
- Identify short-term and long-term goals.
- Select appropriate college choices to match individual needs.

GUIDELINES FOR THE SEARCH AND SELECTION PROCESS

Self-Assessment

- What is the student's disability?
- When was the disability diagnosed?
- What is the student's level of performance in high school?
- Is the student enrolled in college-prep courses, modified courses, or individualized, special-education courses?
- What are the student's individual strengths and weaknesses?
- Is it easier for the student to learn from a lecture, reading the material, or having the material read to her?
- Does the student perform better on written assignments or oral presentations?
- Which subjects are easier, and which are more difficult?
- What are the student's favorite and least favorite courses and why?
- What are the student's short-term and long-term goals?
- Are these goals realistic?
- Is the student striving to improve in academic areas?
- What accommodations are being provided?
- Is the student actively utilizing resource assistance and learning compensatory strategies?
- What does the student plan to study in college?
- What skills and competencies are required for the career goals being pursued?
- When were the last diagnostic tests given?
- What level of services/accommodations is needed in college? Structured programs, comprehensive services, or basic services?

Articulation

- Does the student understand the disability?
- Can the student describe the disability?
- Does the student comprehend how the disability impacts learning?
- Can the student explain the nature of the disability?
- Can the student explain the accommodations being utilized as well as any curriculum modifications received?
- Can the student explain necessary accommodations to teachers?

Academic Assessment

Does the student have difficulty with written language?

- using appropriate words
- organizing thoughts
- writing lengthy compositions
- using correct punctuation and sentence structure
- expressing thoughts clearly

Does the student have trouble with verbal expression?

- retrieving appropriate words
- understanding what others are saying
- using words in the correct context
- carrying on conversations

Does the student have a problem with hand-eye coordination?

- finding certain information on a page
- performing tasks that require fine motor coordination

Does the student get frustrated reading?

- decoding unfamiliar words
- understanding reading assignments
- completing reading assignments within a time frame

Does the student often misspell words?

- mix up the sequence of letters
- become confused when spelling irregular words

Does the student experience difficulty performing mathematics?

- multiplication table and fractions
- sequencing of steps of various mathematical questions

Does the student have difficulty concentrating?

- fidgets or squirms
- distracted by noises
- difficulty following instructions
- difficulty finishing assignments

What are the student's study habits?

- attentive in class for an extended period of time
- easily distracted
- needs extra time to respond to questions
- note-taking skills
- memory
- time management
- time orientation
- organization

How is the student's handwriting ability?

- assignments are difficult to read
- appropriate capitalization used

- stays within the lines when writing
- leaves enough space between words

Exploration and Timelines

FRESHMAN YEAR

- Maintain an academic mindset
- Develop a four-year academic plan
- Meet with guidance counselor
- Know that grades are cumulative- stay focused
- Become familiar with college resources and websites
- Understand basic factors considered in college admission
- Understand your learning differences
- Zone in on learning time management skills, assertiveness training, stress management and exam preparation strategies
- Consider developing a digital portfolio
- Identify personal academic goals and benchmarks
- Read, read, and read. This is the best way to increase your vocabulary as you begin an early preparation for taking standardized tests.
- Become an active listener
- Become skilled at moving knowledge from short term memory to long term memory
- Become a skilled note taker
- Learn how to use assistive technology
- Set goals
- Register for sophomore year—take college prep core courses

SOPHOMORE YEAR

- Explore options.
- Consider taking the ACT Aspire (if available)- request appropriate testing accommodations
- Meet with counselor and case manager.
- Review testing and documentation.
- Review course registration for junior year
- Students considering four year colleges/universities should be enrolled in as many mainstreamed, college preparatory courses as possible.
- Use college web sites to explore for information.
- Register online as a prospective student
- Contact the service providers on the college campus.
- Work on developing good self-advocacy skills
- Understand learning style and strengths and challenges
- Understand the disability

JUNIOR YEAR

- Consider taking the PSAT—request appropriate testing accommodations
- Review achievement level.
- Review course registration for senior year
- Students considering four-year colleges/universities should be enrolled in as many mainstreamed, college preparatory courses as possible.
- Use college web sites to explore for information

- Review the level of services in high school.
- Identify the level of services needed in college.
- Be able to articulate the disability.
- Be comfortable asking for support and accommodations.
- Participate in the IEP process and be actively involved in the IEP meeting.
- Be involved in writing your Summary of Performance (SOP)
- Visit colleges.
- Register for the ACT/SAT, standardized or non-standardized.
- Request necessary updated psycho-educational testing. (Including the most current version of The Wechsler Adult Intelligence Scale)

SENIOR YEAR

- Submit general applications.
- Submit special applications (if required).
- Schedule interviews (if appropriate).
- Write a personal statement and self-disclose the disability.
- Answer essay questions (if required).
- Be involved in writing your Summary of Performance (SOP)
- Release current psycho-educational testing if required for a Support Program; otherwise release after determining what college the student will attend
- Release documentation of other health-related disabilities once it has been determined what college the student will attend.
- Be sure that the documentation includes a description of the disability and recommended accommodations.
- Be sure to get copies of the entire special education file including testing assessments and IEP summaries to have in your personal files after graduation.
- Students under the age of eighteen must have their parents' signature to release documentation to each of the colleges.

Campus Visits

- The student should call to make an arrangement for a visit.
- Visit while classes are in session.
- Meet with admissions and special support service providers.
- Take a guided tour.
- Attend a class.
- Eat a meal on campus.
- Drive around the boundaries of the campus.
- Take pictures, take notes, and talk to students on campus.
- Take parents or family members along (but not in the interview).
- Get available information on disability services
- E-mail or write thank-you notes.

Interviews

To prepare for interviews, students should know:

- Strengths and weaknesses
- The accommodations needed
- How to describe learning differences

If an interview is required prior to an admission decision:

- View the interview as an opportunity.
- Prepare a list of questions.
- Know that interviews, if required, are either required of all applicants or required for a special program or special admission practice.

Questions the Director of Support Services may ask:

- When was the learning difference first diagnosed?
- What type of assistance has the student been receiving in high school?
- What kind of accommodations will the student need in college?
- Can the student describe the learning difficulties?
- Can the student articulate strengths and weaknesses?
- How has the learning difference affected the student's learning?
- What high school courses were easy (or more difficult)?
- Is the student comfortable self-identifying the learning difference?
- Can the student self-advocate?
- What does the student plan to choose as a major?
- Is the student motivated?

Questions students and/or parents may ask:

- What are the admission requirements?
- Is there any flexibility in admission policy? Course substitutions? GPA?
- What is the application procedure?
- Is a special application required?
- What auxiliary testing is required?
- Are there extra charges or fees for the special programs or services?
- Are there remedial or developmental courses?
- What is the procedure for requesting course waivers or substitutions?
- Who is the contact person for learning differences?
- What are the academic qualifications of the individual who provides services to students with learning differences?
- What services and accommodations are available: Testing accommodations? Note takers? Books on tape? Skills classes? Support groups? Priority registration? Professional tutors? Peer tutors? Advising? Computer-aided technology? Scribes? Proctors? Oral tests? Use of computers and spell-checker in class? Use of calculators in class? Distraction-free environment for tests? Learning differences specialists? Advocacy with professors? Faculty in-services?
- How long has the program been in existence?
- How many students are receiving services?
- How long can students access services?
- What is the success rate of students receiving services?

For a successful interview:

- Develop a list of questions.
- Know the accommodations needed.
- Provide new information.
- Practice interviewing.

- Be able to describe strengths and weaknesses.
- Talk about extracurricular activities.
- Take notes.
- Get the business card of the interviewer.
- Try to relax.
- Have fun!

Letters of Recommendation

- Obtain descriptive letters from counselors, teachers, and case managers.
- Have recommenders address learning style, degree of motivation, level of achievement, abilities, attitudes, self-discipline, determination, creativity, mastery of subject matter, academic risks, and growth.
- Have a teacher describe the challenge in a difficult course.
- Advise recommenders when letters are due.

We have just highlighted some of the areas of importance. Now it is time to begin to use the information in this guide that describes the various programs and services at various colleges and universities in the United States.

College Interview Preparation Form For Students With Learning Differences

NAME: ______________________________ DATE: ______________

ADDRESS: ______________________________

PHONE: ______________________________

Description of Learning Difference:

____

____

When Diagnosed:

____

____

Special Help Received:

Tutoring ______________________________

LD Resource ______________________________

Remedial Reading ______________________________

Study Skills ______________________________

Other ______________________________

Which were helpful and why?

____

____

____

____

Current high school:

____

Describe this school:

____

____

____

GPA ____________________

SAT ____________________

ACT ____________________

Comment on your abilities in the following areas and describe them:

____

____

Memory:

____

Attention:

____

Time management:

____

Time orientation:

____

Describe strategies you have used to compensate for your Learning Difference:

____

Why were these strategies successful/unsuccessful for you?

____

____

____

When was your last diagnostic testing?

What is taking these kinds of tests like for you?

Describe your skills in the following areas. If your learning difference interferes in any of these areas, describe strategies you have used to compensate:

Reading

Writing

Spelling

Math

Test-taking

Note-taking

What is your favorite subject? Least favorite?

How would your favorite teacher describe you?

____

____

____

How would your least favorite teacher describe you?

____

____

____

What do you see as your own personal strengths?

____

____

What are your weaknesses?

____

____

What kinds of activities are you involved in?

____

____

____

What do you hope to get out of college?

____

____

What level of learning support do you need in college?

____

____

Which of the following services will be appropriate for you?

Extended Time Tests ________

Distraction Reduced
Environment for Tests ________

Taped Texts ________

LD Specialist ________

ADHD Coach ________

ASD Specialist ________

Skills Courses in Time
Management/Test Taking/
Organization/Note taking ________

Tutors ________

Note takers ________

Counseling ________

Reduced Course Load ________

Study Skills ________

Support Group ________

What are your career interests?

____

____

____

How to Use This Guide

The K&W Guide to Colleges for Students with Learning Differences includes information on colleges and universities that offer services to students with learning differences such as specific learning disabilities, Attention Deficit Hyperactivity Disorder or Asperger Syndrome Disorder.

Learning Disability (LD): A learning disability is a neurological condition that interferes with an individual's ability to store, process, or produce information.

Attention Deficit Hyperactive Disorder (ADHD): ADHD individuals generally have problems paying attention or concentrating. They can't seem to follow directions and are easily bored or frustrated with tasks. They also tend to move constantly and are impulsive, not stopping to think before they act. These behaviors are generally common in children. But they occur more often than usual and are more severe in a child with ADHD.

Autism Spectrum Disorder (ASD): are a group of developmental disabilities that can cause significant social, communication and behavioral challenges.

No two colleges are identical in the programs or services they provide, but there are some similarities. For the purpose of this guide, the services and programs at the various colleges have been grouped into three categories.

Structured Programs (SP)

Colleges with Structured Programs offer the most comprehensive services for students with learning disabilities. The director and/or staff are certified in learning disabilities or related areas. The director is actively involved in the admission decision and, often, the criteria for admission may be more flexible than general admission requirements. Services are highly structured and students are involved in developing plans to meet their particular learning styles and needs. Often students in Structured Programs sign a contract agreeing to actively participate in the program. There is usually an additional fee for the enhanced services. Students who have participated in a Structured Program or Structured Services in high school such as the Learning Disabilities Resource Program, individualized or modified coursework, tutorial assistance, academic monitoring, note-takers, test accommodations, or skill classes might benefit from exploring colleges with Structured Programs or Coordinated Services.

Coordinated Services (CS)

Coordinated Services differ from Structured Programs in that the services are not as comprehensive. These services are provided by at least one certified learning disability specialist. The staff is knowledgeable and trained to provide assistance to students to develop strategies for their individual needs. The director of the program or services may be involved in the admission decision, be in a position to offer recommendations to the admissions office on the potential success of the applicant, or to assist the students with an appeal if denied admission to the college. Receiving these services generally requires specific documentation of the learning disability—students are encouraged to self-identify prior to entry. Students voluntarily request accommodations or services in the Coordinated Services category, and there may be specific skills courses or remedial classes available or required for students with learning disabilities who are admitted probationally or conditionally. High school students who may have enrolled in some modified or remedial courses, utilized test accommodations, or required tutorial assistance, but who typically requested services only as needed, might benefit from exploring colleges with Coordinated Services or Services.

Services (S)

Services are the least comprehensive of the three categories. Colleges offering Services generally are complying with the federal mandate requiring reasonable accommodations to all students with appropriate and current documentation. These colleges routinely require documentation of the disability in order for the students with LD/ADHD to receive accommodations. Staff and faculty actively support the students by providing basic services to meet the needs of the students. Services are requested on a voluntarily basis, and there may be some limitations as to what is reasonable and the degree of services available. Sometimes, just the small size of the student body allows for the necessary personal attention to help students with learning disabilities succeed in college. High school students who require minimum accommodations, but who would find comfort in knowing that services are available, knowing who the contact person is, and knowing that this person is sensitive to students with learning disabilities, might benefit from exploring colleges providing Services or Coordinated Services.

Categories used to Describe the Programs and Services at Colleges and Universities

The categories on the following pages describe the topics of information used in this guide. Each college in the book is covered on two pages, beginning with pertinent information describing the learning disability program or services. This is followed by special admission procedures, specific information about services offered, and concludes with general college information. Please note the statement preceding the section on services and accommodations which states "Services and Accommodations are determined individually for each student based on current and appropriate documentation." Some categories are answered with: N/A (not applicable) because not all colleges were able to fit into every category included in this guide; NR (not reported) because some colleges were unable to provide the information we requested; and Y/N (Yes/No) because the answer is dependent on individual situations. The authors have made a conscientious effort to provide the most current information possible. However, names, costs, dates, policies, and other information are always subject to change, and colleges of particular interest or importance to the reader should be contacted directly for verification of the data.

Nota Bene: The score ranges published in this edition are from the old SAT, administered prior to March 2016. For the most up-to-date information on SAT score concordance, college and university admission policies, and the new SAT, please visit PrincetonReview.com.

School Profiles

Auburn University at Montgomery

P.O. Box 244023 Montgomery, AL 36124-4023
Phone: 334-244-3615 • Fax: 334-244-3795
E-mail: admissions@aum.edu • Web: www.aum.edu
Support: S • Institution: Public

Programs or Services for Students with Learning Differences

By providing opportunities for enhancing educational, technological, vocational and self-advocacy skills, the Center for Disability Services helps individuals with disabilities to become more self-reliant, self-motivated, and more successful citizens of the community.

Admission Information for Students with Learning Differences

College entrance test required: Yes
Interview required: Not Applicable
Essay required: Not Applicable
Additional Application Required for LD/ADHD/ASD: Yes
What documentation required for LD: Psychoeducational based on DSM-V standards, to include IQ and achievement and behavioral checklist scores.
With general application: No
To receive services after enrolling: Yes
What documentation required for ADHD: Neuropsychological and/or psychoeducational evaluation based on DSM-V standards.
With general application: No
To receive services after enrolling: Yes
What documentation required for ASD: Psychoeducational based on DSM-V standards, to include IQ and achievement standard test scores.
With general application: No
To receive services after enrolling: Yes
LD/ADHD/ASD documentation submitted to: Center for Disability Services
ASD Specific Program: NR
Special Ed. HS course work accepted: Yes
Specific course requirements of all applicants: Yes
Separate application required for program services: True
Total # of students receiving LD/ADHD/ASD services: 8
Acceptance into program means acceptance into college: No

Admissions

Minimum 18 ACT or 860 SAT score (taken before March 2016) or 940 SAT (taken March 2016 or after) and 2.3 GPA. If applying as a Bridge student, a minimum 17 ACT or 820 SAT score (taken before March 2016) or 900 SAT (taken March 2016 or after) and 2.3 GPA is required. Even if a student does not fully meet all the requirements for admission to Auburn Montgomery, the student still may find a home through the Bridge Program. This program is designed for students who meet specific academic criteria in order to enroll in courses designed to prepare them for full admission. The Bridge program provides qualified students with extra academic support for one semester prior to gaining full admission to AUM. During the Bridge semester, students will be enrolled in courses designed specifically for "bridging the gap" to a continued and successful college career. Bridge courses consist of a University Success course, as well as a Math and/or English course. Throughout the semester, faculty and staff on the Bridge team will assist students by implementing skill-building exercises for success in college. The Bridge program is designed to help familiarize students with our campus resources, while showing students how to thrive at AUM.

Additional Information

The Bridge program is one semester, and can begin Fall, Spring or Summer semester.Students who are successful in English, math and College Success, earning a "C" or higher in each course, will be moved to full admissions status. If a student does not earn a "C" in each course during Bridge, they must enroll elsewhere and earn 24 credit hours from an accredited institution to re-apply to AUM. The Center for Disability Services provides accommodations. Students with disabilities are encouraged to provide reasonable notification to instructors for exam accommodations. If CDS proctors the exam, it is the student's responsibility to contact CDS at least five days prior to an exam. Other Accommodations and Services include: Test accommodations including extended time frames, Proctored exams, Priority registration, Note-taking assistance, Tutor referral, Computer training, and Referral to outside sources.

General Support Services Information

Contact Information
Name of program or department: Center for Disability Services
Telephone: 334-244-3754
Fax: 334-244-3907
Website: www.aum.edu/cds

Accommodations or Services for Students with Learning Differences

Accommodations are decided upon an individual basis after a thorough review of appropriate, current documentation. The accommodations requests must be supported through the documentation provided and must be logically linked to the current impact of the condition on academic functioning.

Allowed in exams
Calculator: Yes
Dictionary: Yes
Computer: Yes
Spellchecker: Yes
Extended test time: Yes
Scribes: Yes
Proctors: Yes
Oral exams: Yes
Note-takers: Yes
Support services for students with LD: Yes
Support services for students with ADHD: Yes
Support services for students with ASD: Yes
Distraction-reduced environment: Yes
Tape recording in class: Yes
Electronic texts: Yes
Kurzweil reader: NR
Audio books: Yes
Other assistive technology: Yes
Priority registration: Yes
Added costs of services: No
LD specialists: No
ADHD coaching: Yes
ASD specialists: Yes
Professional tutors: No
Peer tutors: Not Applicable
Max. hours/wk. for services: NR
How professors are notified of student approved accommodations: By student

General Admissions Information

Office of Admissions: 334-244-3615

Entrance Requirements

Academic units recommended: 3 English, 3 math, 2 science, 2 science labs, 2 foreign language, 2 social studies, 2 history, 2 academic electives. High school diploma is required and GED is accepted. SAT or ACT required. If ACT, ACT with writing accepted. TOEFL required of all international applicants: minimum paper TOEFL 500 or minimum internet TOEFL 61.

Application deadline: 8/15
Notification: NR
Average GPA: 3.3
ACT Composite middle 50% range: 19-23
SAT Math middle 50% range: 470-540
SAT Critical Reading middle 50% range: 450-520
SAT Writing middle 50% range: NR-NR
Graduate top 10% of class: 16
Graduated top 25% of class: 40
Graduated top 50% of class: 76

COLLEGE GRADUATION REQUIREMENTS

Course waivers allowed: No
In what course: Math (as a course substitution, no waiver)
Course substitutions allowed: Yes
In what course: Math

Additional Information

Environment: This public school was founded in 1967. It has a 500-acre campus.

Student Body
Undergrad enrollment: 4,257
% Women: 64
% Men: 36
% Out-of-state: 5.2

Cost information
In-state tuition: $8,700
Out-of-state tuition: $19,560
Room & board: $5,520

Housing Information
University Housing: Yes
Percent living on campus: 19.8

Greek System
Fraternity: Yes
Sorority: Yes
Athletics: NAIA

Jacksonville State University

700 Pelham Road North, Jacksonville, AL 36265
Phone: 256-782-5268 • Fax: 256-782-5953
E-mail: info@jsu.edu • Web: www.jsu.edu
Support: CS • Institution: Public

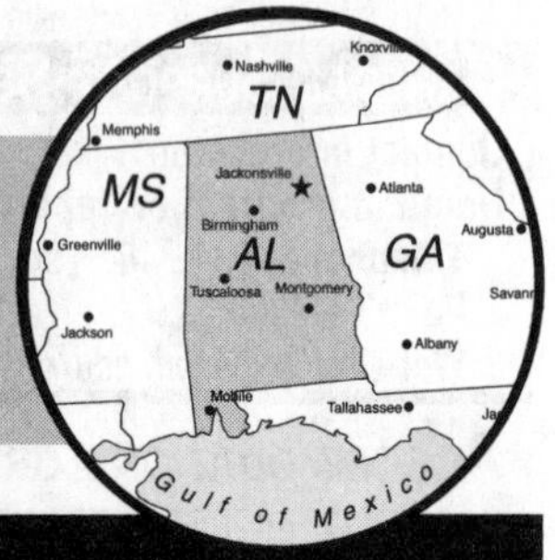

Programs or Services for Students with Learning Differences

Disability Support Services(DSS) offers services for students with learning differences including specific learning disabilities, ADHD, and Autism Spectrum Disorder. Once students have been admitted to the institution, DSS assists the student with reasonable accommodations and supportive services. Accommodations are based on medical and psychological records, history of past use of accommodations, and communication with the student about needed services and accommodations. Suggested documentation for a student with a learning difference includes most recent psycho educational testing, current achievement tests, high school academic records including Individualized Education Plans (IEPs) or 504 Plans. DSS staff will work with each student to develop an Individualized Postsecondary plan (IPP). Copies of the IPP can be obtained each semester for the student to present to their instructors.

Admission Information for Students with Learning Differences

College entrance tests required: Yes
Interview required: No
Essay required: No
Additional application required for LD/ADHD/ASD: NR
What documentation required for LD: Psycho ed evaluation to include: relevant historical info, instructional interventions, related services, age diagnosed, objective data (aptitude, achievement, info processing), test scores (standard, percentile and grade equivalents) and describe functional limitations.
With general application: No
To receive services after enrolling: Yes
What documentation required for ADHD: Diagnosis based on DSM-V; history of behaviors impairing functioning in academic setting; diagnostic interview; history of symptoms; evidence of ongoing behaviors.
With general application: No
To receive services after enrolling: Yes
What documentation required for ASD: Diagnosis based on DSM-V; history of behaviors impairing functioning in academic setting; diagnostic interview; history of symptoms; evidence of ongoing behaviors.
With general application: No
To receive services after enrolling: Yes
LD/ADHD/ASD documentation submitted to: Disability Support Services
ASD Specific Program: NR
Special Ed. HS course work accepted: Yes
Specific course requirements for all applicants: Yes
Separate application required: Request for Services (Applying to DSS) can be completed online or printable version available
Total # of students receiving LD/ADHD/ASD services: 150
Acceptance into program means acceptance into college: Students must be admitted and enrolled in the university first and then request services.

Admissions

Unconditional Admission-ACT composite 20 or above, SAT combined Critical Reading and Math 950 or above. Conditional Admission- ACT composite 17-19, SAT Combined Critical Reading and Math 830-940. Applicants must also provide evidence of High School Graduation with an acceptable diploma. GED is acceptable in lieu of high school graduation. Freshman applicants must submit an official high school transcript showing course work through the junior year at the time of application and submit a final high school transcript after graduation showing date of graduation and type of diploma. TOEFL required of all international applicants minimum paper TOEFL 500, minimum Internet based TOEFL 61.

Additional Information

JSU offers a support group for students with ASD. The group meets weekly during the fall and spring semesters. ADHD coaching is also available. The Center for Autism Studies (CAS) provides an avenue for research and education in Autism Spectrum Disorders, including early identification, intervention, behavior management, differentiation of instruction, and family dynamics. CAS represents a way to contribute to the state and national information on ASD and build an infrastructure of research and support for individuals with ASD.

General Support Services Information

Contact Information
Name of program or department: Disability Support Services
Telephone: 256-782-8380
Fax: 256-782-8383

Accommodations or Services For Students With Learning Differences

Accommodations are decided upon an individual basis after meeting with a student and reviewing relevant documentation.

Allowed in exams
Calculator: Yes
Dictionary: Yes
Computer: Yes
Spellchecker: Yes
Extended test time: Yes
Scribes: Yes
Proctors: Yes
Oral exams: Yes
Note-takers: Yes
Services for students with LD: Yes
Services for students with ADHD: Yes
Services for students with ASD: Yes
Distraction-reduced environment: Yes
Tape recording in class: Yes
Audio books: NR
Electronic texts: Yes
Kurzweil Reader: No
Other assistive technology: Yes
Priority registration: Yes
Added costs for services: No
LD specialists: Yes
ADHD coaching: Yes
ASD specialists: Yes
Professional tutors: No
Peer tutors: 40, ACE Program
Max. hours/wk. for services: Weekdays and evenings
How professors are notified of LD/ADHD: Copy of IPP is provided to student to disclose to professors.

General Admissions Information

Office of Admissions: NR

Entrance Requirements

TOEFL required of all international applicants.

Application deadline: NR
Notification: NR
Average GPA: 2.99
ACT Composite middle 50% range: 17-23
SAT Math middle 50% range: 400-530
SAT Critical Reading middle 50% range: 420-530
SAT Writing middle 50% range: NR-NR
Graduated top 10% of class: NR
Graduated top 25% of class: NR
Graduated top 50% of class: NR

COLLEGE GRADUATION REQUIREMENTS

Course waivers allowed: Yes
In what course: Handled on a case by case basis
Course substitutions allowed: Yes
In what course: Handled on a case by case basis

Additional Information

Environment: NR

Student Body
Undergrad enrollment: 7,138
% Women: 58
% Men: 42
% Out-of-state: 12

Cost information
In-state tuition: $4,040
Out-of-state tuition: $8,080
Room & board: $3,312
Housing Information
University Housing: Yes
Percent living on campus: 15

Greek System
Fraternity: Yes
Sorority: Yes
Athletics: Division I

The U. of Alabama in Huntsville

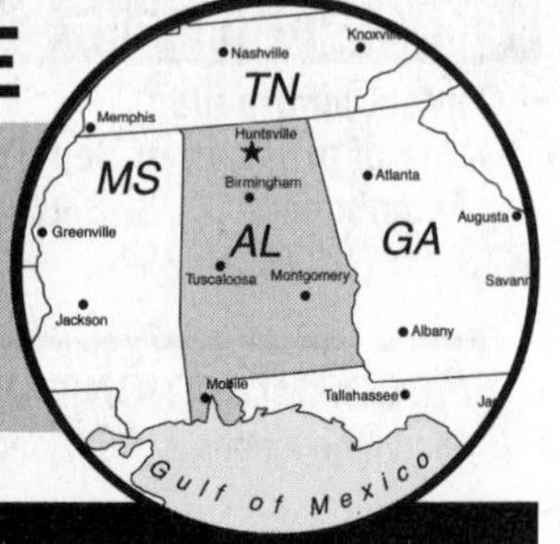

301 Sparkman Drive, Huntsville, AL 35899
Phone: 256-824-6070 • Fax: 256-824-6073
E-mail: admitme@uah.edu • Web: www.uah.edu
Support: S • Institution type: 4-year public

Programs or Services for Students with Learning Differences

The Office of Student Development Services offers a variety of services and accommodations to assist students with disabilities in eliminating barriers they encounter in pursuing higher education. The office's main objective is to provide access to academic, social, cultural, recreational, and housing opportunities at the university. A student is considered registered with Disability Support Services (DSS) when they have completed all application paperwork, their intake/registration paperwork has been approved, and they have had an interview with a 504 Coordinator. The services offered through this office encourage students to achieve and maintain autonomy.

Admission Information for Students with Learning Differences

College entrance tests required: Yes
Interview required: No
Essay required: No
Additional application required for LD/ADHD/ASD: NR
What documentation required for LD: Psycho ed evaluation to include: relevant historical info, instructional interventions, related services, age diagnosed, objective data (aptitude, achievement, info processing), test scores (standard, percentile and grade equivalents) and describe functional limitations.
With general application: No
To receive services after enrolling: Yes
What documentation required for ADHD: Diagnosis based on DSM-V; history of behaviors impairing functioning in academic setting; diagnostic interview; history of symptoms; evidence of ongoing behaviors.
With general application: No
To receive services after enrolling: Yes
What documentation required for ASD: Diagnosis based on DSM-V; history of behaviors impairing functioning in academic setting; diagnostic interview; history of symptoms; evidence of ongoing behaviors.
With general application: No
To receive services after enrolling: Yes
LD/ADHD/ASD documentation submitted to: Disability Support Services
ASD Specific Program: NR
Special Ed. HS course work accepted: Yes
Specific course requirements for all applicants: Yes
Separate application required: Yes
Total # of students receiving LD/ADHD/ASD services: 150
Acceptance into program means acceptance into college: Students must be admitted and enrolled in the university first and then request services.

Admissions

Admission is based on grades and test scores. Additionally, applicants should have 4 years of English, 3 years of social studies, 3 years of math, 2 years of science, and a total of 20 Carnegie units. Deficiencies must be removed within one year.

ACT	SAT	GPA
17 or below	700 or below	3.25
18	740	3.00
19	790	2.75
20–21	860	2.50
22	920	2.25
23	970	2.00
24 or above	1010 or above	1.15

There is no special LD admission process. If a student becomes subject to academic suspension, the suspension is for a minimum of one term, and the student must petition the Admissions Committee for approval to reenroll.

Additional Information

Students should forward their documentation to Disability Support Services. Disability Support Services provides the mandated services, including testing accommodations, reduced distraction environments for tests, readers, proctors, scribes, note-takers, and specialized adaptive computers, Institution organized Peer Assisted Study Sessions (PASS), covering math, chemistry classes along with many others are available to all students. In addition the Student Success Center provides centralized access to academic coaching, tutorial services, and the writing center to all students on campus. All students have access to skills classes in time management, test-taking strategies, and study skills. Services and accommodations are available for undergraduate and graduate students.

General Support Services Information

Contact Information
Name of program or department: Student Development Services
Telephone: 256-824-6203
Fax: 256-824-6672

Accommodations or Services For Students With Learning Differences

Accommodations are decided upon an individual basis after a thorough review of appropriate, current documentation. The accommodations requested must be supported through the documentation provided and must be logically linked to the current impact of the condition on academic functioning.

Allowed in exams
Calculator: Yes
Dictionary: Yes
Computer: Yes
Spellchecker: Yes
Extended test time: Yes
Scribes: Yes
Proctors: Yes
Oral exams: Yes
Note-takers: Yes
Services for students with LD: Yes
Services for students with ADHD: Yes
Services for students with ASD: Yes
Distraction-reduced environment: Yes
Tape recording in class: Yes
Audio books: NR
Electronic texts: Yes
Kurzweil Reader: Yes
Other assistive technology: Yes
Priority registration: Yes
Added costs for services: No
LD specialists: No
ADHD coaching: NR
ASD specialists: NR
Professional tutors: NR
Peer tutors: NR
Max. hours/wk. for services: Unlimited
How professors are notified of LD/ADHD: By both student and director

General Admissions Information

Office of Admissions: 256-824-2773

Entrance Requirements

Academic units required: 4 English, 3 math, 3 science, 4 social studies, 6 academic electives. **Academic units recommended:** 4 English, 4 math, 4 science, 2 science labs, 2 foreign language, 4 social studies, 6 academic electives. High school diploma is required and GED is accepted. SAT or ACT required. If ACT, ACT with writing accepted. TOEFL required of all international applicants: minimum paper TOEFL 500 or minimum internet TOEFL 62.

Application deadline: 8/20
Notification: NR
Average GPA: 3.64
ACT Composite middle 50% range: 23-29
SAT Math middle 50% range: 510-650
SAT Critical Reading middle 50% range: 510-640
SAT Writing middle 50% range: NR-NR
Graduated top 10% of class: 28
Graduated top 25% of class: 50
Graduated top 50% of class: 83

COLLEGE GRADUATION REQUIREMENTS

Course waivers allowed: Yes
In what course: Individual case-by-case decisions
Course substitutions allowed: Yes
In what course: Individual case-by-case decisions

Additional Information

Environment: This public school was founded in 1950. It has a 400-acre campus.

Student Body
Undergrad enrollment: 6,013
% Women: 43
% Men: 57
% Out-of-state: 10

Cost information
In-state tuition: $9,192
Out-of Tuition: $21,506
Room & board: $8,433

Housing Information
University Housing: Yes
Percent living on campus: 20

Greek System
Fraternity: Yes
Sorority: Yes
Athletics: Division II

The U. of Alabama at Tuscaloosa

Box 870132, Tuscaloosa, AL 35487-0132
Phone: 205-348-5666 • Fax: 205-348-9046
E-mail: admissions@ua.edu • Web: www.ua.edu
Support: S • Institution: 4-year public

Programs or Services for Students with Learning Differences

Documented physical or mental condition that substantially limits one or more major life activities may be eligible for services and accommodations. Those seeking services for LD and/or ADHD must provide documentation including a narrative report of a psychoeducational or neuropsychological evaluation; a summary of areas of testing; actual test scores; overall summary and diagnosis; and recommendations and suggested strategies for student, professors, and academic advisors. The Office of Disability Services may request further testing. Complete documentation requirements can be found at www.ods.ua.edu.

Admission Information for Students with Learning Differences

College entrance test required: Yes
Interview required: No
Essay required: Not Applicable
Additional Application Required for LD/ADHD/ASD: NR
What documentation required for LD: Students requesting accommodations on the basis of attention deficit-hyperactivity disorder (ADHD) must provide documentation by a physician.
With general application: No
To receive services after enrolling: Yes
What documentation required for ADHD: Students requesting accommodations on the basis of an Autism Spectrum Disorder (ASD) must provide documentation by a professional who has undergone comprehensive training and has relevant experience in differential diagnosis.
With general application: No
To receive services after enrolling: Yes
What documentation required for ASD: Students requesting accommodation on the basis of a specific learning disability must provide documentation from a professional who has under
With general application: No
To receive services after enrolling: Yes
LD/ADHD/ASD documentation submitted to: Office of Disability Services
ASD Specific Program: UA-ACTS
Special Ed. HS course work accepted: NR
Specific course requirements of all applicants: NR
Separate application required for program services: Yes
Total # of students receiving LD/ADHD/ASD services: NR
Acceptance into program means acceptance into college: No

Admissions

All students must meet regular entrance requirements. Decisions about the potential for academic success at UA are based on performance on the ACT and/or SAT, GPA, and courses. EX: A student with a 21 ACT or 1000 SAT [critical reading and math scores only] along with a GPA of 3.0 should be successful at the University. ACT with Writing or SAT with Writing required. 4 yrs. English, 4 years Social Sciences, 3 yrs. Math, 3 yrs. Natural Sciences, 1 unit of foreign language, and 4 units of academic courses (recommend courses in fine arts or computer literacy, with additional courses in mathematics, natural sciences, and foreign language.) Students who exceed the minimum number of units in math, natural sciences, or foreign language will be given additional consideration. An interview with the Office of Disability Services is recommended.

Additional Information

Accommodations are tailored to individual needs according to diagnostic testing. Accommodations may include: early registration; testing modifications; academic aids such as taping lectures, use of calculators, dictionaries, spell checkers, note takers, and materials in alternative formats. UA-ACTS program provides individualized services to help studetns develop appropriate skills for self-advocacy, daily living, and social interaction that will contribute to their success as an independent adult.

General Support Services Information

Contact Information
Name of program or department: Office of Disability Services
Telephone: 205-348-4285
Fax: 205-348-0804
Website: www/pds/ia/edi

Accommodations or Services For Students With Learning Differences

Accommodations are decided upon an individual basis after a thorough review of appropriate, current documentation. The accommodations requests must be supported through the documentation provided and must be logically linked to the current impact of the condition on academic functioning.

Allowed in exams
Calculator: Yes
Dictionary: Yes
Computer: Yes
Spellchecker: Yes
Extended test time: Yes
Scribes: Yes
Proctors: Yes
Oral exams: Yes
Note-takers: Yes
Support services for students with LD: Yes
Support services for students with ADHD: Yes
Support services for students with ASD: Yes
Distraction-reduced environment: Yes
Tape recording in class: Yes
Electronic texts: Yes
Kurzweil reader: NR
Audio books: Yes
Other assistive technology: Yes
Priority registration: Yes
Added costs of services: No
LD specialists: No
ADHD coaching: Yes
ASD specialists: Yes
Professional tutors: No
Peer tutors: Not Applicable
Max. hours/wk. for services: NR
How professors are notified of student approved accommodations: By student

General Admissions Information

Office of Admissions: 205-348-5666

Entrance Requirements

Academic units required: 4 English, 3 math, 3 science, 2 science labs, 1 foreign language, 4 social studies, 5 academic electives. **Academic units recommended:** 4 English, 3 math, 3 science, 2 science labs, 2 foreign language, 4 social studies, 5 academic electives. High school diploma is required and GED is accepted. SAT or ACT required. If ACT, ACT with writing accepted. TOEFL required of all international applicants: minimum paper TOEFL 550 or minimum internet TOEFL 79.

Application deadline: NR
Notification:NR
Average GPA: 3.66
ACT Composite middle 50% range: 22-31
SAT Math middle 50% range: 490-610
SAT Critical Reading middle 50% range: 490-600
SAT Writing middle 50% range: 480-600
Graduate top 10% of class: 37
Graduated top 25% of class: 57
Graduated top 50% of class: 82

COLLEGE GRADUATION REQUIREMENTS

Course waivers allowed: No
In what course: NR
Course substitutions allowed: Yes
In what course: Substitutions are sometimes granted, but no courses are waived. Courses cannot be substituted if doing so would substantially alter the nature of the program or if the course is required as part of the student's major.

Additional Information

Environment: This public school was founded in 1831. It has a 1000-acre campus.

Student Body
Undergrad enrollment: 31,958
% Women: 55
% Men: 45
% Out-of-state: 53.7

Cost information
In-state tuition: $10,170
Out-of-state tuition: $25,950
Room & board: $9,030

Housing Information
University Housing: Yes
Percent living on campus: 26.4

Greek System
Fraternity: Yes
Sorority: Yes
Athletics: Division I

UNIVERSITY OF ALASKA—ANCHORAGE

3211 Providence Drive, Anchorage, AK 99508-8046
Phone: 907-786-1480 • Fax: 907-786-4888
E-mail: enroll@uaa.alaska.edu • Web: www.uaa.alaska.edu
Support: S • Institution type: 4-year public

AK
Anchorage
Gulf of Alaska

PROGRAMS OR SERVICES FOR STUDENTS WITH LEARNING DIFFERENCES

The University of Alaska—Anchorage provides equal opportunities for students who have disabilities. Academic support services are available to students with learning disabilities. Staff trained to work with students with disabilities coordinate these services. To allow time for service coordination, students are encouraged to contact the Disability Support Services (DSS) office several weeks before the beginning of each semester. Ongoing communication with the staff throughout the semester is encouraged.

ADMISSION INFORMATION FOR STUDENTS WITH LEARNING DIFFERENCES

College entrance tests required: Yes
Interview required: No
Essay required: No
Additional application required for LD/ADHD/ASD: NR
What documentation required for LD: Psycho ed evaluation to include: relevant historical info, instructional interventions, related services, age diagnosed, objective data (aptitude, achievement, info processing), test scores (standard, percentile and grade equivalents) and describe functional limitations.
With general application: No
To receive services after enrolling: Yes
What documentation required for ADHD: Diagnosis based on DSM-V; history of behaviors impairing functioning in academic setting; diagnostic interview; history of symptoms; evidence of ongoing behaviors.
With general application: No
To receive services after enrolling: Yes
What documentation required for ASD: Psycho ed evaluation
With general application: NR
To receive services after enrolling: Yes
LD/ADHD/ASD documentation submitted to: Disability Support Services
ASD Specific Program: NR
Special Ed. HS course work accepted: Yes
Specific course requirements for all applicants: NR
Separate application required: No
Total # of students receiving LD/ADHD/ASD services: 90 plus
Acceptance into program means acceptance into college: The University of Alaska—Anchorage has open enrollment; students are accepted to the university and then may request services.

ADMISSIONS

All students must meet the same admission requirements. The university has an open enrollment policy. However, admission to specific programs of study may have specific course work or testing criteria that all students will have to meet. While formal admission is encouraged, the university has an open enrollment policy that allows students to register for courses in which they have the adequate background. Open enrollment does not guarantee subsequent formal admission to certificate or degree programs. Individuals with learning disabilities are admitted via the standard admissions procedures that apply to all students submitting applications for formal admission. Students with documentation of a learning disability are eligible to receive support services once they are enrolled in the university. LD students who self-disclose during the admission process are referred to DSS for information about services and accommodations.

ADDITIONAL INFORMATION

Classes are available for all students in the areas of vocabulary building and study skills. There is no separate tutoring for students with learning disabilities. Tutorial help is available for all students in the reading and writing labs and the Learning Resource Center. With appropriate documentation, students with LD or ADHD may have access to accommodations such as testing modifications, distraction-free testing environments, scribes, proctors, note-takers, calculators, dictionaries, and computers in exams, and access to assistive technology. Services and accommodations are available for undergraduate and graduate students. The Academic Coach Center helps students develop academic skills. It is offered in individual sessions with a peer coach.

General Support Services Information

Contact Information
Name of program or department: Disability Support Services
Telephone: 907-786-4530
Fax: 907-786-4531

Accommodations or Services For Students With Learning Differences

Accommodations are decided upon an individual basis after a thorough review of appropriate, current documentation. The accommodations requested must be supported through the documentation provided and must be logically linked to the current impact of the condition on academic functioning.

Allowed in exams
Calculator: Yes
Dictionary: Yes
Computer: Yes
Spellchecker: Yes
Extended test time: Yes
Scribes: Yes
Proctors: Yes
Oral exams: Yes
Note-takers: Yes
Services for students with LD: Yes
Services for students with ADHD: Yes
Services for students with ASD: Yes
Distraction-reduced environment: Yes
Tape recording in class: Yes
Audio books: NR
Electronic texts: Yes
Kurzweil Reader: Yes
Other assistive technology: Yes
Priority registration: Yes
Added costs for services: No
LD specialists: No
ADHD coaching: NR
ASD specialists: NR
Professional tutors: No
Peer tutors: Yes
Max. hours/wk. for services: Unlimited
How professors are notified of LD/ADHD: By student initiated letters sent through Disability Support

General Admissions Information

Office of Admissions: 907-786-1480

Entrance Requirements

High school diploma is required and GED is accepted. SAT or ACT required. TOEFL required of all international applicants: minimum paper TOEFL 450.

Application deadline: 7/1
Notification: NR
Average GPA: NR
ACT Composite middle 50% range: NR-NR
SAT Math middle 50% range: 440-570
SAT Critical Reading middle 50% range: 430-580
SAT Writing middle 50% range: NR-NR
Graduated top 10% of class: 13
Graduated top 25% of class: 32
Graduated top 50% of class: 62

COLLEGE GRADUATION REQUIREMENTS

Course waivers allowed: Yes
In what course: Individual case-by-case decisions
Course substitutions allowed: Yes
In what course: Individual case-by-case decisions

Additional Information

Environment: This public school was founded in 1954. It has a 384-acre campus.

Student Body
Undergrad enrollment: 17,129
% Women: 58
% Men: 42
% Out-of-state: 9.6
Cost information
In-state tuition: $4,950
Out-of-state tuition: $17,400
Room & board: $9,827
Housing Information
University Housing: Yes
Percent living on campus: NR
Greek System
Fraternity: NR
Sorority: NR
Athletics: Division II

UNIVERSITY OF ALASKA—FAIRBANKS

PO Box 757480, Fairbanks, AK 99775-7480
Phone: 907-474-7500 • Fax: 907-474-5379
E-mail: admissions@uaf.edu • Web: www.uaf.edu
Support: S • Institution type: 4-year public

PROGRAMS OR SERVICES FOR STUDENTS WITH LEARNING DIFFERENCES

The University of Alaska is committed to providing equal opportunity to students with disabilities. Disability Services at The University of Alaska—Fairbanks provides assistance to students with documented disabilities. The purpose of Disability Services (DS) is to provide equal access to higher education for students with disabilities. Campus services include the Academic Advising Center, which is responsible for advising incoming freshmen and students with undeclared majors. It provides explanations of programs and their requirements and assists students with choosing majors, selecting electives, and choosing classes consistent with their academic and career goals. Student Support Services provides academic and personal support, including developmental classes and tutoring for students who are economically disadvantaged, do not have a parent who graduated from college, or have a documented disability. Disabled Students of UAF is an organization that provides peer support groups for UAF students experiencing disabilities. The Student Development and Learning Center provides tutoring, individual instruction in basic skills and counseling, career-planning services, and assessment testing. Disability Services welcomes inquiries and seeks to make the college experience a success for students with disabilities.

ADMISSION INFORMATION FOR STUDENTS WITH LEARNING DIFFERENCES

College entrance tests required: Yes
Interview required: No
Essay required: No
Additional application required for LD/ADHD/ASD: NR
What documentation required for LD: Psycho ed evaluation to include: relevant historical info, instructional interventions, related services, age diagnosed, objective data (aptitude, achievement, info processing), test scores (standard, percentile and grade equivalents) and describe functional limitations.
With general application: No
To receive services after enrolling: Yes
What documentation required for ADHD: Diagnosis based on DSM-V; history of behaviors impairing functioning in academic setting; diagnostic interview; history of symptoms; evidence of ongoing behaviors.
With general application: No
To receive services after enrolling: Yes
What documentation required for ASD: Psycho ed evaluation
With general application: NR
To receive services after enrolling: Yes
LD/ADHD/ASD documentation submitted to: Disability Services
ASD Specific Program: NR
Special Ed. HS course work accepted: Yes
Specific course requirements for all applicants: Yes
Separate application required: No
Total # of students receiving LD/ADHD/ASD services: 30–40
Acceptance into program means acceptance into college: Students must be admitted and enrolled in the university first and then request services.

ADMISSIONS

To enter as a freshman for a baccalaureate degree there are two options: 1) high school diplomas, 2.5 in core courses and GPA 3.0 and no cut-off on ACT/SAT; 2) high school diploma, 2.5 in core courses, a minimum 2.5 GPA and ACT 18 or SAT 1290. Core curriculum 4 years English, 3 years math, 3 years social sciences, and 3 years natural or physical sciences. Foreign languages are recommended. Students can be provisionally accepted if they make up course deficiencies with a C or better in each of the developmental or university courses and complete nine credits of general degree requirements with a C or better.

ADDITIONAL INFORMATION

Services include individual counseling to determine necessary accommodations; arrangements for special services such as readers, scribes, and note-takers; advocacy with faculty and staff; assistance to faculty and staff in determining appropriate accommodations; help in determining specific needs for students with learning disabilities; and referral to campus and community agencies for additional services. Basic study-skills classes are offered for all students and may be taken for credit. Services and accommodations are provided for any student registered for at least 1 credit.

General Support Services Information

Contact Information
Name of program or department: Disability Services
Telephone: 907-474-5655
Fax: 907-474-5688

Accommodations or Services For Students With Learning Differences

Accommodations are decided upon an individual basis after a thorough review of appropriate, current documentation. The accommodations requested must be supported through the documentation provided and must be logically linked to the current impact of the condition on academic functioning.

Allowed in exams
Calculator: No
Dictionary: Yes
Computer: Yes
Spellchecker: Yes
Extended test time: Yes
Scribes: Yes
Proctors: Yes
Oral exams: Yes
Note-takers: Yes
Services for students with LD: Yes
Services for students with ADHD: Yes
Services for students with ASD: Yes
Distraction-reduced environment: Yes
Tape recording in class: Yes
Audio books: NR
Electronic texts: Yes
Kurzweil Reader: Yes
Other assistive technology: Yes
Priority registration: No
Added costs for services: No
LD specialists: No
ADHD coaching: NR
ASD specialists: NR
Professional tutors: No
Peer tutors: No
Max. hours/wk. for services: N/A
How professors are notified of LD/ADHD: By student

General Admissions Information

Office of Admissions: 907-474-7500

Entrance Requirements

Academic units required: 4 English, 3 math, 3 science, 1 science labs, 3 social studies, **Academic units recommended:** 2 foreign language. High school diploma is required and GED is not accepted. SAT or ACT required. If ACT, ACT with writing recommended. TOEFL required of all international applicants: minimum internet TOEFL 79.

Application deadline: 6/15
Notification: Rolling starting 1/1
Average GPA: 3.27
ACT Composite middle 50% range: 18-26
SAT Math middle 50% range: 480-610
SAT Critical Reading middle 50% range: 480-610
SAT Writing middle 50% range: 450-570
Graduated top 10% of class: 18
Graduated top 25% of class: 38
Graduated top 50% of class: 69

COLLEGE GRADUATION REQUIREMENTS

Course waivers allowed: No
In what course: N/A
Course substitutions allowed: Yes
In what course: Depends on documentation

Additional Information

Environment: This public school was founded in 1917. It has a 2,250-acre campus.

Student Body
Undergrad enrollment: 7,610
% Women: 58
% Men: 42
% Out-of-state: 14

Cost information
In-state tuition: $6,360
Out-of-state tuition: $21,030
Room & board: $8,380
Housing Information
University Housing: Yes

Percent living on campus: 30
Greek System
Fraternity: NR
Sorority: NR
Athletics: Division II

Arizona State University

PO Box 870112, Tempe, AZ 85287-0112
Phone: 480-965-7788 • Fax: 480-965-3610
E-mail: ugradinq@asu.edu • Web: www.asu.edu
Support: CS • Institution type: 4-year public

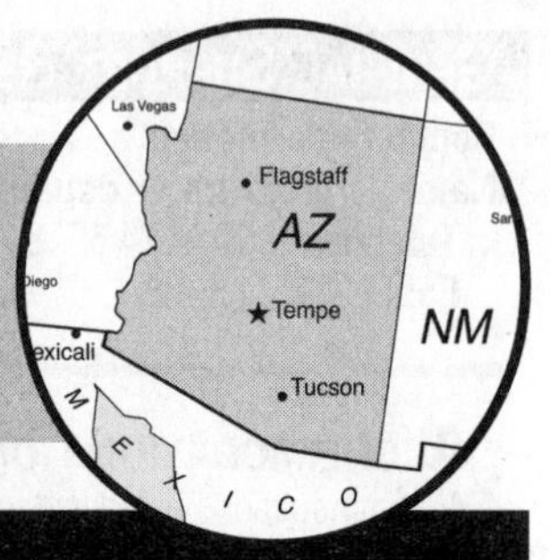

Programs or Services for Students with Learning Differences

The Arizona State University (ASU) Disability Resource Centers (DRC) on each ASU campus facilitate access to educational, social, and career opportunities for qualified ASU students with disabilities, including but not limited to students with learning disabilities and attention deficit hyperactivity disorder. Qualified DRC professional staff on each ASU campus are recommending and implementing reasonable and effective disability accommodations, resources, services, and auxiliary aids upon student request to facilitate student access. DRC services and accommodations are recommended individually for each student. DRC students are provided with self-advocacy training and academic resources and referrals, e.g., Student Success Centers, Writing Centers, Career Services, Enrollment Services, Student Financial Assistance, academic advising referrals, TRiO Student Support Services (for qualified applicants), etc., and encouraged to seek out methods for attaining the highest possible goals and achievement. All DRC services and accommodations are recommended and provided on an individual basis upon request as appropriate for qualified/eligible students. DRC is an access facilitator assisting qualified students in becoming academically and socially independent. DRC professional staff provides and facilitates a wide range of academic support services and accommodations for qualified students in addition to faculty and staff education and training. The centers also provide ASU pre-entry consultation regarding disability accommodations eligibility upon request.

Admission Information for Students with Learning Differences

College entrance test required: Yes
Interview required: NR
Essay required: Not Applicable
Additional Application Required for LD/ADHD/ASD: Not Applicable
What documentation required for LD: Psycho ed evaluation
With general application: Not Applicable
To receive services after enrolling: Not Applicable
What documentation required for ADHD: The DRC will accept diagnoses of an Autism Spectrum Disorder that is based on comprehensive, age-appropriate, psychoeducational evaluations that demonstrate current functional limitations of the disability.
With general application: Not Applicable
To receive services after enrolling: Not Applicable
What documentation required for ASD: Psycho ed evaluation
With general application: Not Applicable
To receive services after enrolling: Not Applicable
LD/ADHD/ASD documentation submitted to: Disability Resource Center
ASD Specific Program: NR
Special Ed. HS course work accepted: Not Applicable
Specific course requirements of all applicants: Yes
Separate application required for program services: Yes
Total # of students receiving LD/ADHD/ASD services: 167
Acceptance into program means acceptance into college: Not Applicable

Admissions

Students with LD submit the ASU application, self-disclose and submit documentation. Courses required: 4 English, 4 math, 3 science, 2 social science, 2 foreign language and 1 fine arts. Applicants must meet at least one of the following: Top 25 percent or 3.0 GPA or 22 ACT (24 ACT non-resident) or SAT 1040 (1110 non-resident). All applicants not meeting these standards are evaluated through an Individual Review process. To appeal a denial write a letter "Why ASU", describe ability for success, send 3 recommendations demonstrating motivation and perseverance, and gradual upward trend in courses and grades. Admissions and disability support personnel review appeals. If applicants are denied after an appeal students may become a non-degree-seeking applicant. Transcripts not required. Non-degree candidates may live in residential housing at ASU and attend local community college. After 24 credits and 2.0, GPA students may apply for regular admission at ASU.

Additional Information

Academic support accommodations include consultation, individualized program recommendations, registration information and advisement referrals, academic tutoring, Computer Tech Center, learning strategies instruction, library research assistance, supplemental readers, mastery of Alternative Learning Techniques Lab, note-taking, testing accommodations, and diagnostic testing referrals. DSR will accept current diagnosis of ADHD based on appropriate diagnostic information that includes a clinical history, instruments used for the diagnosis, narrative, DSM diagnosis, and recommendations for accommodations.

General Support Services Information

Contact Information
Name of program or department: Disability Resource Center
Telephone: (480)727-1368
Fax: (480) 727-5459
Website: NR

Accommodations or Services For Students With Learning Differences

Accommodations are decided upon an individual basis after a thorough review of appropriate, current documentation. The accommodations requests must be supported through the documentation provided and must be logically linked to the current impact of the condition on academic functioning.

Allowed in exams
Calculator: Yes
Dictionary: Yes
Computer: Yes
Spellchecker: Yes
Extended test time: Yes
Scribes: Yes
Proctors: Yes
Oral exams: Yes
Note-takers: Yes
Support services for students with LD: Yes
Support services for students with ADHD: Yes
Support services for students with ASD: Yes
Distraction-reduced environment: Yes
Tape recording in class: Yes
Electronic texts: Yes
Kurzweil reader: NR
Audio books: Yes
Other assistive technology: Yes
Priority registration: Yes
Added costs of services: No
LD specialists: Yes
ADHD coaching: Yes
ASD specialists: Yes
Professional tutors: No
Peer tutors: Yes
Max. hours/wk. for services: NR
How professors are notified of student approved accommodations: NR

General Admissions Information

Office of Admissions: 480-965-7788

Entrance Requirements

Academic units required: 4 English, 4 math, 3 science, 3 science labs, 2 foreign language, 1 social studies, 1 history, and 1 units from above areas or other academic areas. High school diploma is required and GED is accepted. SAT or ACT recommended. If ACT, ACT with writing accepted. TOEFL required of all international applicants: minimum paper TOEFL 500 or minimum internet TOEFL 61.

Application deadline: NR
Notification: Rolling starting 9/1
Average GPA: 3.49
ACT Composite middle 50% range: 23-28
SAT Math middle 50% range: 520-640
SAT Critical Reading middle 50% range: 510-630
SAT Writing middle 50% range: NR-NR
Graduate top 10% of class: 29
Graduated top 25% of class: 60
Graduated top 50% of class: 89

COLLEGE GRADUATION REQUIREMENTS

Course waivers allowed: No
In what course: Math, Foreign Language
Course substitutions allowed: Yes
In what course: Math, Foreign Language

Additional Information

Environment: This public school was founded in 1885. It has a 1963.73-acre campus.

Student Body
Undergrad enrollment: 41,828
% Women: 43
% Men: 57
% Out-of-state: 25

Cost information
In-state tuition: $9,484
Out-of-state tuition: $24,784
Room & board: $11,061

Housing Information
University Housing: Yes
Percent living on campus: 22

Greek System
Fraternity: Yes
Sorority: Yes
Athletics: Division I

NORTHERN ARIZONA UNIVERSITY

PO Box 5633, Flagstaff, AZ 86011-5633
Phone: 928-523-5511 • Fax: 928-523-0226
E-mail: undergraduate.admissions@nau.edu • Web: www.nau.edu
Support: S • Institution type: 4-year public

PROGRAMS OR SERVICES FOR STUDENTS WITH LEARNING DIFFERENCES

Disability Resources promotes educational opportunities for students with disabilities at Northern Arizona University. DSS assists students in their persistence to graduate by providing resources, services, and auxiliary aids so that they may realize their life goals. The goal of Disability Resources is to assist students in achieving their academic goals while at the same time creating an environment conducive to learning and building students' self-esteem. The belief is that by receiving supportive assistance, the student will become an independent learner and self-advocate.

ADMISSION INFORMATION FOR STUDENTS WITH LEARNING DIFFERENCES

College entrance tests required: Yes
Interview required: No
Essay required: No
Additional application required for LD/ADHD/ASD: NR
What documentation required for LD: Psycho ed evaluation to include: relevant historical info, instructional interventions, related services, age diagnosed, objective data (aptitude, achievement, info processing), test scores (standard, percentile and grade equivalents) and describe functional limitations.
With general application: No
To receive services after enrolling: Yes
What documentation required for ADHD: Diagnosis based on DSM-V; history of behaviors impairing functioning in academic setting; diagnostic interview; history of symptoms; evidence of ongoing behaviors.
With general application: No
To receive services after enrolling: Yes
What documentation required for ASD: Psycho ed evaluation
With general application: NR
To receive services after enrolling: Yes
LD/ADHD/ASD documentation submitted to: Disability Resources
ASD Specific Program: NR
Special Ed. HS course work accepted: Yes
Specific course requirements for all applicants: Yes
Separate application required: No
Total # of students receiving LD/ADHD/ASD services: 117
Acceptance into program means acceptance into college: Students must be admitted and enrolled in the university first and then request services.

ADMISSIONS

There are no special admissions criteria for students with learning disabilities. General admission requirements for unconditional admission include: 4 years of English, 4 years of math; 2 years of social science with 1 year being American history; 2–3 years of science lab with additional requirements; 1 year of fine arts; and 2 years of a foreign language. (Students may be admitted conditionally with course deficiencies, but not in both math and science). In-state residents should have a 2.5 GPA, be in the top 50 percent of their high school class (a 3.0 GPA or being in the upper 25 percent of their graduating class is required for non-residents), or earn an SAT combined score of 930 (1010 for non-residents) or an ACT score of 22 (24 for non-residents). Conditional admissions is possible with a 2.5–2.99 GPA or being in the top 50 percent of their graduating class and strong ACT/SAT scores. Exceptional admission may be offered to 10 percent of the new freshmen applicants or transfer applicants. The Writing section of the ACT is not required.

ADDITIONAL INFORMATION

Skills classes are available in note-taking, study techniques, reading, memory and learning, overcoming math anxiety, speed reading, time management, test-taking strategies. The university offers the following courses: How to Make Math Easy, How to Get Started Writing, How to Edit Writing, and How to Prepare for Final Exams. All services and accommodations are available for undergraduate and graduate students.

General Support Services Information

Contact Information
Name of program or department: Disability Resources
Telephone: 928-523-8773
Fax: 928-523-8747
E-mail: DR@nau.edu

Accommodations or Services For Students With Learning Differences

Accommodations are decided upon an individual basis after a thorough review of appropriate, current documentation. The accommodations requested must be supported through the documentation provided and must be logically linked to the current impact of the condition on academic functioning.

Allowed in exams
Calculator: Yes
Dictionary: Yes
Computer: Yes
Spellchecker: Yes
Extended test time: Yes
Scribes: Yes
Proctors: Yes
Oral exams: Yes
Note-takers: Yes
Services for students with LD: Yes
Services for students with ADHD: Yes
Services for students with ASD: Yes
Distraction-reduced environment: Yes
Tape recording in class: Yes
Audio books: NR
Electronic texts: Yes
Kurzweil Reader: Yes
Other assistive technology: Yes
Priority registration: Yes
Added costs for services: No
LD specialists: No
ADHD coaching: NR
ASD specialists: NR
Professional tutors: No
Peer tutors: 100
Max. hours/wk. for services: Unlimited
How professors are notified of LD/ADHD: By student

General Admissions Information

Office of Admissions: 928-523-5511

Entrance Requirements

Academic units required: 4 English, 4 math, 3 science, 3 science labs, 2 foreign language, 1 social studies, 1 history, and 1 units from above areas or other academic areas. High school diploma is required and GED is accepted. SAT or ACT required for some. If ACT, ACT with writing accepted. TOEFL required of all international applicants: minimum paper TOEFL 525 or minimum internet TOEFL 70.

Application deadline: NR
Notification: NR
Average GPA: 3.52
ACT Composite middle 50% range: 20-25
SAT Math middle 50% range: 460-570
SAT Critical Reading middle 50% range: 460-580
SAT Writing middle 50% range: 450-560
Graduated top 10% of class: 22
Graduated top 25% of class: 53
Graduated top 50% of class: 85

COLLEGE GRADUATION REQUIREMENTS

Course waivers allowed: No
Course substitutions allowed: Yes
In what course: There is a math substitution (not waiver) program for individuals with a math learning disability. It only applies to the liberal studies math requirement.

Additional Information

Environment: This public school was founded in 1899. It has a 740-acre campus.

Student Body
Undergrad enrollment: 33,000
% Women: 59
% Men: 41
% Out-of-state: 29

Cost information
Room & board: NR
Housing Information
University Housing: Yes
Percent living on campus: 29

Greek System
Fraternity: Yes
Sorority: Yes
Athletics: Division I

University of Arizona

PO Box 210040, Tucson, AZ 85721-0040
Phone: 520-621-3237 • Fax: 520-621-9799
E-mail: appinfo@arizona.edu • Web: www.arizona.edu
Support: SP • Institution type: 4-year public

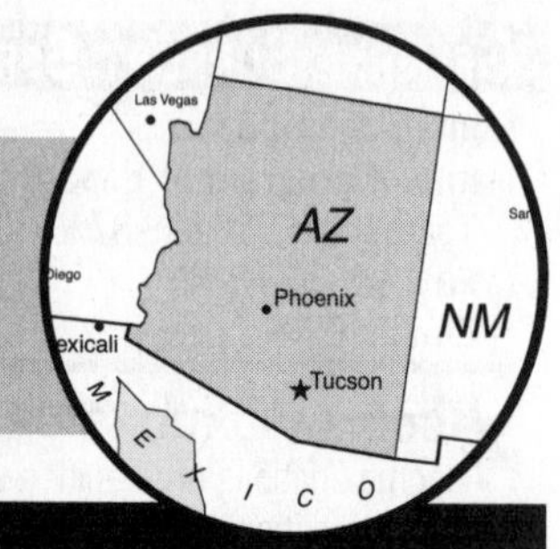

Programs or Services for Students with Learning Differences

The SALT Center (Strategic Alternative Learning Techniques) is a fee-based academic support program that provides a comprehensive range of enhanced services to University of Arizona students who have learning and/or attention challenges. The SALT Center's innovative approach is recognized nationwide as one of the most successful for empowering students in the university setting. The range of services in the SALT Center facilitates student learning, self-advocacy, and independence. Students take ownership of their education through working with a Strategic Learning Specialist to create an Individualized Learning Plan; engaging in strategies for time management, organization, reading and writing; utilizing tutoring by peer tutors who are internationally certified by the College Reading and Learning Association; and accessing assistive technology in the SALT Center's technology lab.

Admission Information for Students with Learning Differences

College entrance tests required: Yes
Interview required: No
Essay required: Yes
Additional application required for LD/ADHD/ASD: NR
What documentation required for LD: Psycho ed evaluation to include: relevant historical info, instructional interventions, related services, age diagnosed, objective data (aptitude, achievement, info processing), test scores (standard, percentile and grade equivalents) and describe functional limitations.
With general application: Yes if requested as part of Structured Program application
To receive services after enrolling: Yes
What documentation required for ADHD: Diagnosis based on DSM-V; history of behaviors impairing functioning in academic setting; diagnostic interview; history of symptoms; evidence of ongoing behaviors.
With general application: Yes if requested as part of Structured Program application
To receive services after enrolling: Yes
What documentation required for ASD: Psycho ed evaluation
With general application: NR
To receive services after enrolling: Yes
LD/ADHD/ASD documentation submitted to: NR
ASD Specific Program: NR
Special Ed. HS course work accepted: NR
Specific course requirements of all applicants: NR
Separate application required: NR
Total # of students receiving LD/ADHD/ASD services: NR
Acceptance into program means acceptance into college: NR

Admissions

Students must submit a general application to the University and a SALT application. Students may check the box on the general application indicating they are interested in SALT. Students are admitted to the University and then reviewed by SALT. General admission criteria include: 4 English, 4 math, 3 science, 2 social studies, 2 foreign language, 1 fine art. Deficiencies can be made up in English with ACT sub score of 21, Math ACT sub score 24 and science ACT sub score 20. Most applicants are admissible with required courses and either 24 ACT (22 ACT resident) or SAT 1110) SAT 1040 resident) or top ¼ of the class. SALT application should be submitted early in the process. All SALT applicants should answer 3 essay questions: 1) Why are you applying to SALT and how do you plan to use the services; 2) Describe a difficult situation you have encountered in your life, and tell how you handled the situation; 3) Tell about your strengths, skills and talents. Students can submit documentation of a disability to Admissions and to SALT or answer SALT question #4 which asks for a description of academic challenges and the support services used to manage those challenges.

Additional Information

The SALT program provides comprehensive services for four years. The fee for the lower division is $5,600 per year (includes tutoring) and for upper division the fee is $2,600 plus $21 per hour for tutoring. Life and ADHD coaching is $1350 for three months. The SALT program includes: 1) Tutoring that models learning strategies specific to the subject matter; most UA courses are supported; schedule tutors online through TutorTrac™; meet with tutors individually; attend a group review session for courses; 2) Strategic Learning Specialist is a point person for SALT and campus resources; designs Individualized Learning Plan; teaches strategies to help improve academics; monitors academic progress; and 3) Educational Technology to print, study and research; draft essays using dictation software; listen to course readings; brainstorm and organize thoughts using the latest learning apps. Life and ADHD Coaching is designed for students who benefit from the support, structure and accountability coaches provide in this partnership.

General Support Services Information

Contact Information
Name of program or department: SALT Center (Strategic Alternative Learning Techniques)
Telephone: 520-621-8493
Fax: 520-626-3260

Accommodations or Services For Students With Learning Differences

Accommodations are decided upon an individual basis after a thorough review of appropriate, current documentation. The accommodations requested must be supported through the documentation provided and must be logically linked to the current impact of the condition on academic functioning.

Allowed in exams
Calculator: Yes
Dictionary: Yes
Computer: Yes
Spellchecker: Yes
Extended test time: Yes
Scribes: Yes
Proctors: Yes
Oral exams: Yes
Note-takers: Yes
Services for students with LD: Yes
Services for students with ADHD: Yes
Services for students with ASD: Yes
Distraction-reduced environment: Yes
Tape recording in class: Yes
Audio books: Yes
Electronic texts: Yes
Kurzweil Reader: Yes
Other assistive technology: Yes
Priority registration: Yes
Added costs for services: $2,800 per semester
LD specialists: Yes
ADHD coaching: Yes
ASD specialists: No
Professional tutors: Yes
Peer tutors: Yes
Max. hours/wk. for services: Yes
How professors are notified of LD/ADHD: Student and SALT

General Admissions Information

Office of Admissions: 520-621-3237

Entrance Requirements

Academic units required: 4 English, 4 math, 3 science, 3 science labs, 2 foreign language, 2 social studies, 1 visual/performing arts. **Academic units recommended:** 4 English, 4 math, 3 science, 3 science labs, 2 foreign language, 2 social studies, 1 visual/performing arts. High school diploma is required and GED is accepted. SAT or ACT recommended. If ACT, ACT with writing accepted. TOEFL required of all international applicants: minimum internet TOEFL 70.

Application deadline: 5/1
Notification: NR
Average GPA: 3.38
ACT Composite middle 50% range: 21-27
SAT Math middle 50% range: 480-620
SAT Critical Reading middle 50% range: 480-600
SAT Writing middle 50% range: 470-590
Graduated top 10% of class: 28
Graduated top 25% of class: 54
Graduated top 50% of class: 84

COLLEGE GRADUATION REQUIREMENTS

Course waivers allowed: No
Course substitutions allowed: Yes
In what course: Course substitutions are typically in math or second language; approval must come from college/major department.

Additional Information

Environment: This public school was founded in 1885. It has a 378-acre campus located in the center of Tuscon.

Student Body
Undergrad enrollment: 33,732
% Women: 51
% Men: 49
% Out-of-state: 31

Cost information
In-state tuition: $11,400
Out-of Tuition: $32,600
Room & board: $9,840

Housing Information
University Housing: Yes
Percent living on campus: 19.9

Greek System
Fraternity: Yes
Sorority: Yes
Athletics: Division I

Arkansas State University

PO Box 1570 State University, AR 72467
Phone: 870-972-3024 • Fax: 870-972-3406
E-mail: admissions@astate.edu • Web: www.astate.edu
Support: S • Institution: Public

Programs or Services for Students with Learning Differences

To provide students with disabilities access to resources that will enable them to manage daily activities in the university setting.

Admission Information for Students with Learning Differences

College entrance test required: Yes
Interview required: No
Essay required: Not Applicable
Additional Application Required for LD/ADHD/ASD: Yes
What documentation required for LD: Documentation of disability from a professional
With general application: No
To receive services after enrolling: Yes
What documentation required for ADHD: Documentation of disability from a professional
With general application: No
To receive services after enrolling: Yes
What documentation required for ASD: Documentation of disability from a professional
With general application: No
To receive services after enrolling: Yes
LD/ADHD/ASD documentation submitted to: Disability Services
ASD Specific Program: NR
Special Ed. HS course work accepted: Not Applicable
Specific course requirements of all applicants: NR
Separate application required for program services: True
Total # of students receiving LD/ADHD/ASD services: 555
Acceptance into program means acceptance into college: No

Admissions

Same for all students.

Additional Information

Contact the Office of Disability Services.

General Support Services Information

Contact Information
Name of program or department: Disability Services
Telephone: 870-972-3964
Fax: 870-972-3351
Website: www.astate.edu/a/disability

Accommodations or Services for Students with Learning Differences

Accommodations are decided upon an individual basis after a thorough review of appropriate, current documentation. The accommodations requests must be supported through the documentation provided and must be logically linked to the current impact of the condition on academic functioning.

Allowed in exams
Calculator: Yes
Dictionary: Yes
Computer: Yes
Spellchecker: Yes
Extended test time: Yes
Scribes: Yes
Proctors: Yes
Oral exams: Yes
Note-takers: Yes
Support services for students with LD: Yes
Support services for students with ADHD: Yes
Support services for students with ASD: Yes
Distraction-reduced environment: Yes
Tape recording in class: Yes
Electronic texts: Yes
Kurzweil reader: NR
Audio books: Yes
Other assistive technology: Yes
Priority registration: Yes
Added costs of services: No
LD specialists: Yes
ADHD coaching: Yes
ASD specialists: Yes
Professional tutors: No
Peer tutors: Not Applicable
Max. hours/wk. for services: NR
How professors are notified of student approved accommodations: By both student and director

General Admissions Information

Office of Admissions: 870-972-3024

Entrance Requirements

Academic units required: 4 English, 4 math, 3 science, 3 science labs, 1 social studies, 2 history. **Academic units recommended:** 2 foreign language. High school diploma is required and GED is accepted. SAT or ACT required. If ACT, ACT with writing accepted. TOEFL required of all international applicants: minimum paper TOEFL 500 or minimum internet TOEFL 61.

Application deadline: 8/24
Notification:NR
Average GPA: 3.51
ACT Composite middle 50% range: 21-26
SAT Math middle 50% range: 470-540
SAT Critical Reading middle 50% range: 400-540
SAT Writing middle 50% range: 420-480
Graduate top 10% of class: 27
Graduated top 25% of class: 49
Graduated top 50% of class: 74

COLLEGE GRADUATION REQUIREMENTS

Course waivers allowed: Yes
In what course: Accommodations for physical education requirement.
Course substitutions allowed: Yes
In what course: College Algebra and Foreign Language.

Additional Information

Environment: This public school was founded in 1909. It has a 941-acre campus.

Student Body
Undergrad enrollment: 9,592
% Women: 57
% Men: 43
% Out-of-state: 10.7

Cost information
In-state tuition: $6,000
Out-of-state tuition: $12,000
Room & board: $8,140

Housing Information
University Housing: Yes
Percent living on campus: 30.2

Greek System
Fraternity: Yes
Sorority: Yes
Athletics: Division I

U. of Arkansas—Fayetteville

232 Silas Hunt Hall, Fayetteville, AR 72701
Phone: 479-575-5346 • Fax: 479-575-7515
E-mail: uofa@uark.edu • Web: www.uark.edu
Support: S • Institution type: 4-year public

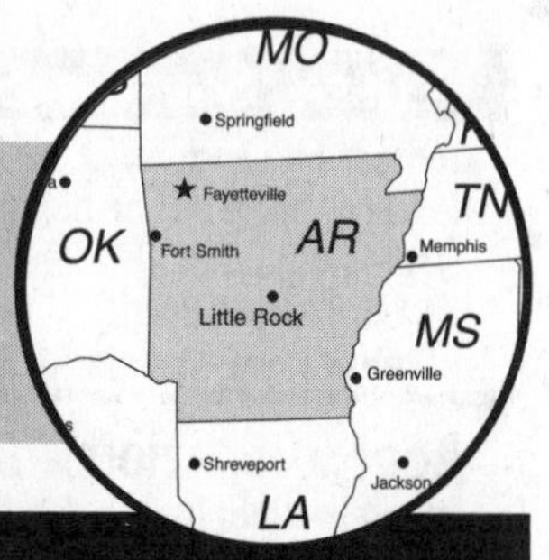

Programs or Services for Students with Learning Differences

The Center for Educational Access (CEA) is the office responsible for facilitating campus access and accommodations for students with disabilities. The philosophy of the CEA is to provide an environment in which students are encouraged to develop independence, the ability to self-advocate, and knowledge of resources that will enable them to take advantage of opportunities available in the modern world. The Enhanced Learning Center offers tutoring services to all University of Arkansas students free of charge. Supplemental Instruction (SI) is an academic enrichment program that increases student performance and retention. SI offers enrolled students regularly scheduled, out-of-class review sessions in historically difficult courses. Sessions are led by experienced students who excel in the difficult subject matter. SI is free to all UA students.

Admission Information for Students with Learning Differences

College entrance tests required: Yes
Interview required: No
Essay required: No
Additional application required for LD/ADHD/ASD: NR
What documentation required for LD: Psycho ed evaluation to include: relevant historical info, instructional interventions, related services, age diagnosed, objective data (aptitude, achievement, info processing), test scores (standard, percentile and grade equivalents) and describe functional limitations.
With general application: No
To receive services after enrolling: Yes
What documentation required for ADHD: Diagnosis based on DSM-V; history of behaviors impairing functioning in academic setting; diagnostic interview; history of symptoms; evidence of ongoing behaviors.
With general application: No
To receive services after enrolling: Yes
What documentation required for ASD: Psycho ed evaluation
With general application: NR
To receive services after enrolling: Yes
LD/ADHD/ASD documentation submitted to: Center for Educational Access
ASD Specific Program: NR
Special Ed. HS course work accepted: NR
Specific course requirements of all applicants: Yes
Separate application required: No
Total # of students receiving LD/ADHD/ASD services: NR
Acceptance into program means acceptance into college: Students must be admitted and enrolled prior to requesting services.

Admissions

Guaranteed general admission to the University of Arkansas requires a minimum GPA of 3.0 and an ACT score of 20 (or SAT of 930). Students who do not meet qualifications may be admitted on the basis of individual review of their application portfolios. Course requirements include: 4 years of English, 4 years of math, 3 years of social studies, 3 years of science, and 2 electives to be chosen from English, foreign languages, oral communication, mathematics, computer science, natural sciences, and social studies.

Additional Information

The University of Arkansas is committed to ensuring student success through a powerful convergence of programs and services. While at the university, we help students meet their challenges confidently. SSS has a friendly, resourceful, and helpful staff committed to helping students succeed.

Learning Disability Program/Services

Contact Information
Name of program or department: Center for Educational Access
Telephone: 479-575-3104
Fax: 479-575-7445

Accommodations or Services For Students With Learning Differences

Accommodations are decided upon an individual basis after a thorough review of appropriate, current documentation. The accommodations requested must be supported through the documentation provided and must be logically linked to the current impact of the condition on academic functioning.

Allowed in exams
Calculator: Yes
Dictionary: Yes
Computer: Yes
Spellchecker: Yes
Extended test time: Yes
Scribes: Yes
Proctors: Yes
Oral exams: No
Note-takers: Yes
Services for students with LD: Yes
Services for students with ADHD: Yes
Services for students with ASD: Yes
Distraction-reduced environment: Yes
Tape recording in class: Yes
Audio books: NR
Electronic texts: Yes
Kurzweil Reader: Yes
Other assistive technology: Yes
Priority registration: Yes
Added costs for services: No
LD specialists: No
ADHD coaching: NR
ASD specialists: NR
Professional tutors: No
Peer tutors: Yes
Max. hours/wk. for services: N/A
How professors are notified of LD/ADHD: Student

General Admissions Information

Office of Admission: 479-575-5346

Entrance Requirements

Academic units required: 4 English, 4 math, 3 science (2 science labs), 3 social studies, 2 academic electives. **Academic units recommended:** 2 foreign language. High school diploma is required, and GED is accepted. ACT with or without Writing component accepted. TOEFL required of all international applicants: minimum paper TOEFL 550, minimum computer TOEFL 213.

Application deadline: 8/15
Average GPA: 3.56
ACT Composite middle 50% range: 23–28
SAT Math middle 50% range: 520–630
SAT Critical Reading middle 50% range: 500–610
SAT Writing middle 50% range: NR
Graduated top 10% of class: 31%
Graduated top 25% of class: 58%
Graduated top 50% of class: 87%

COLLEGE GRADUATION REQUIREMENTS

Course waivers allowed: N/A
Course substitutions allowed: N/A

Additional Information

Environment: Urban area about 200 miles northwest of Little Rock.

Student Body
Undergrad enrollment: 19,027
% % Women: 49%
% % Men: 51%
% Out-of-state: 33%

Cost Information
In-state tuition: $7,175
Out-of Tuition: $17,600
Room & board: $8,200

Housing Information
University housing: Yes
% Living on campus: 33%

Greek System
Fraternity: Yes
Sorority: Yes
Athletics: Division I

UNIVERSITY OF THE OZARKS

415 N College Avenue, Clarksville, AR 72830
Phone: 479-979-1227 • Fax: 479-979-1417
E-mail: admiss@ozarks.edu • Web: www.ozarks.edu
Support: SP • Institution: Private

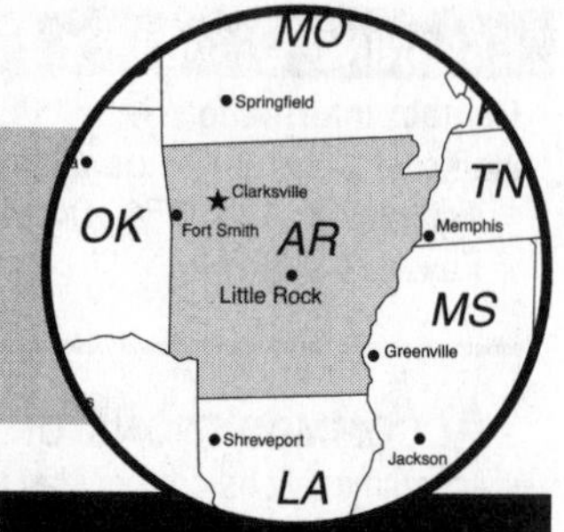

PROGRAMS OR SERVICES FOR STUDENTS WITH LEARNING DIFFERENCES

The Jones Learning Center believes that students with specific learning disabilities and AD/HD are entitled to services that best insure that they have access to information and ideas taught on campus and to alternative ways to show that they have learned that information. The Learning Center emphasizes an interactive learning environment. Instruction is individualized and personalized. Enhanced services include individualized programming; assistive technology; centralized accessibility; and a supportive atmosphere with a 4:1 student-to-staff ratio, which provides students even greater opportunity to realize their true academic potential. Ideas, instructional materials, and activities are presented on a variety of different levels commensurate with the educational needs of the individual student. This program is very comprehensive in every area. At the beginning of each semester the course load and needs of the student are assessed to determine what services will be needed.

ADMISSION INFORMATION FOR STUDENTS WITH LEARNING DIFFERENCES

College entrance test required: Yes
Interview required: No
Essay required: Recommended
Additional Application Required for LD/ADHD/ASD: NR
What documentation required for LD: Medical evaluation. Psychoeducational assessment is recommended.
With general application: Yes
To receive services after enrolling: Yes
What documentation required for ADHD: Psychoeducational assessment
With general application: Yes
To receive services after enrolling: Yes
What documentation required for ASD: Psychoeducational assessment that includes the most current WAIS, a comprehensive individually administered achievement measure, and processing assessment as well as behavioral information.
With general application: Yes
To receive services after enrolling: Yes
LD/ADHD/ASD documentation submitted to: Student Success Center
ASD Specific Program: Living and Learning Community
Special Ed. HS course work accepted: Yes
Specific course requirements of all applicants: Yes
Separate application required for program services: Yes
Total # of students receiving LD/ADHD/ASD services: NR
Acceptance into program means acceptance into college: Yes

ADMISSIONS

Students complete a special application. Applicants must be 18 or older; complete high school or obtain a GED; demonstrate average or above-average I.Q.; have a learning disability or Attention Deficit Disorder as a primary disability; provide diagnostic information from previous evaluations; complete the admissions packet and visit campus. If the psychoeducational evaluation is not current, applicants may choose to update the documentation during a two-day campus visit. This evaluation is offered for an additional fee. Applicants with some areas of concern for the admissions committee may be admitted on a one-year trial basis. This conditional admission is only available to students applying to the Jones Learning Center. There are no specific high school courses and no minimum ACT/SAT score value or grade point average required for admission.

ADDITIONAL INFORMATION

Students are assigned to a program coordinator who meets daily with the student and assists in the individualized planning of the students' program of study, acts as an advocate, and monitors the students' progress. Students receive help in understanding their learning styles, utilizing their strengths, circumventing deficits and building skills, and becoming independent learners and self-advocates. Skills classes are offered in study skills/writing (for credit), and math (for credit). Enhanced services include testing accommodations; one-to-one administration of a test with a reader and staff to take dictation, if needed; assistive technology available throughout the building; peer tutoring; and note-takers. Developmental services include opportunities to improve basic skills in writing and math. Students with ADD and/or LD may receive services from the Learning Center. The Living and Learning Community is a new program at University of the Ozarks for high-functioning students with Autism Spectrum Disorder (ASD). The Living and Learning Community's goal is to support the growing number of students on the autism spectrum that are now attending college.

General Support Services Information

Contact Information
Name of program or department: Student Success Center
Telephone: 479-979-1300
Fax: 479-979-
Website: www.ozarks.edu

Accommodations or Services For Students With Learning Differences

Accommodations are decided upon an individual basis after a thorough review of appropriate, current documentation. The accommodations requests must be supported through the documentation provided and must be logically linked to the current impact of the condition on academic functioning.

Allowed in exams
Calculator: Yes
Dictionary: Yes
Computer: Yes
Spellchecker: Yes
Extended test time: Yes
Scribes: Yes
Proctors: Yes
Oral exams: Yes
Note-takers: Yes
Support services for students with LD: Yes
Support services for students with ADHD: Yes
Support services for students with ASD: Yes
Distraction-reduced environment: Yes
Tape recording in class: Yes
Electronic texts: Yes
Kurzweil reader: NR
Audio books: Yes
Other assistive technology: Yes
Priority registration: Yes
Added costs of services: Yes
LD specialists: Yes **ADHD coaching:** Yes
ASD specialists: Yes
Professional tutors: Yes
Peer tutors: Yes
Max. hours/wk. for services: NR
How professors are notified of student approved accommodations: By both student and director

General Admissions Information

Office of Admissions: 479-979-1227

Entrance Requirements

Academic units recommended: 4 English, 4 math, 3 science, 2 science labs, 2 foreign language, 1 social studies, 2 history. High school diploma is required and GED is accepted. SAT or ACT required. If ACT, ACT with writing accepted. TOEFL required of all international applicants: minimum paper TOEFL 500.

Application deadline: NR
Notification: NR
Average GPA: 3.31
ACT Composite middle 50% range: 19-25
SAT Math middle 50% range: 443-560
SAT Critical Reading middle 50% range: 450-570
SAT Writing middle 50% range: NR-NR
Graduate top 10% of class: 18
Graduated top 25% of class: 44
Graduated top 50% of class: 76

COLLEGE GRADUATION REQUIREMENTS

Course waivers allowed: No
In what course: NR
Course substitutions allowed: Yes
In what course: Course substitutions are not needed for foreign language because alternatives are given for all students. The same will be available in the 16-17 school year for math.

Additional Information

Environment: This private school, affiliated with the Presbyterian Church, was founded in 1834. It has a 56-acre campus.

Student Body
Undergrad enrollment: 630
% Women: 55
% Men: 45
% Out-of-state: 29

Cost information
Tuition: $21,450
Room & board: $6,500

Housing Information
University Housing: Yes
Percent living on campus: 65

Greek System
Fraternity: No
Sorority: No
Athletics: Division III

CALIFORNIA POLYTECHNIC STATE UNIVERSITY—SAN LUIS OBISPO

Admissions Office, San Luis Obispo, CA 93407-0031
Phone: 805-756-2311 • Fax: 805-756-5400
E-mail: admissions@calpoly.edu • Web: www.calpoly.edu
Support: CS • Institution: Public

PROGRAMS OR SERVICES FOR STUDENTS WITH LEARNING DIFFERENCES

The goal of the program is to assist students with learning disabilities using their learning strengths. The Disability Resource Center (DRC) assists students with disabilities in achieving access to higher education, promotes personal and educational success, and increases the awareness and responsiveness of the campus community. DRC is actively involved with students and faculty and provides a newsletter and open house to keep the university population aware of who it is and what it does. Incoming students are encouraged to meet with college advisors, in conjunction with DRC staff, to receive assistance in the planning of class schedules. This allows for the selection of appropriate classes to fit particular needs and personal goals. It is the responsibility of each student seeking accommodations and services to provide a written, comprehensive psychological and/or medical evaluation verifying the diagnosis. The Cal Poly Student Learning Outcomes model promotes student personal growth and the development of self-advocacy for full inclusion of qualified students with verified disabilities. The promotion of student self-reliance and responsibility are necessary adjuncts to educational development. For learning disabilities the assessments must be done by a licensed educational psychologist, psychologist, neurologist, or LD specialist. The diagnosis of ADHD must be done by a licensed educational psychologist, psychologist, psychiatrist, neurologist, or physician.

ADMISSION INFORMATION FOR STUDENTS WITH LEARNING DIFFERENCES

College entrance test required: Yes
Interview required: No
Essay required: No
What documentation required for LD: Psycho ed evaluation
With general application: No
To receive services after enrolling: Yes
What documentation required for ADHD: Psycho ed evaluation
With general application: No
To receive services after enrolling: Yes
With general application: No
To receive services after enrolling: Yes
What documentation required for ASD: Psycho ed evaluation
With general application: NR
To receive services after enrolling: Yes
LD/ADHD/ASD documentation submitted to: Support program/services
ASD Specific Program: NR
Special Ed. HS course work accepted: No
Specific course requirements of all applicants: No
Separate application required for program services: N/A
Total # of students receiving LD/ADHD/ASD services: NR
Acceptance into program means acceptance into college: NR

ADMISSIONS

Students with LD must meet the same admission criteria as all applicants, and should submit a general admission application to the Admissions Office. General requirements include: 4 years English, 3 years math, 1 year U.S. history or government, 1 year lab science, 2 years foreign language, 1 year fine arts, and 3 years electives. On a case-by-case basis, foreign language substitutions may be allowed. All documentation should be sent directly to the Disability Resource Center, and students who self-disclose will receive information. Admission decisions are made by the Admissions Office.

ADDITIONAL INFORMATION

Incoming students are strongly urged to contact the DRC if disability related assistance is required. Academic accommodations are designed to meet a student's disability-related needs without fundamentally altering the nature of the instructional program, and are not intended to provide remediation. Supportive services may include: alternative format materials, assistive listening devices, notetaking, taped textbooks, test accommodations, tutorial services and writing assistance. DRC may recommend the services of the Academic Skills Center of Student Academic Services and enrollment in English and math classes offering additional support. There is also a peer mentoring program, Partners for Success, and a career mentoring program available to all students. Students requesting accommodations, which include using a computer, dictionary or spellchecker during an exam, will need the professor's permission. The university cannot provide psychoeducational assessment services. Services and accommodations are available to undergraduate and graduate students.

General Support Services Information

Contact Information
Name of program or department: Disability Resource Center (DRC)
Telephone: 805-756-1395
Fax: 805-756-5451

Accommodations or Services For Students With Learning Differences

Accommodations are decided upon an individual basis after a thorough review of appropriate, current documentation. The accommodations requests must be supported through the documentation provided and must be logically linked to the current impact of the condition on academic functioning.

Allowed in exams
Calculator: Yes
Dictionary: Yes
Computer: Yes
Spellchecker: Yes
Extended test time: Yes
Scribes: Yes
Proctors: Yes
Oral exams: Yes
Note-takers: Yes
Services for students with LD: Yes
Services for students with ADHD: Yes
Services for students with ASD: Yes
Distraction-reduced environment: Yes
Tape recording in class: Yes
Kurzweil reader: Yes
Audio books from learning ally: Yes
Other assistive technology: Yes
Priority registration: Yes
Added costs of services: No
LD specialists: Yes
ADHD coaching: NR
ASD specialists: NR
Professional tutors: NR
Peer tutors: No
Max. hours/wk. for services: 0
How professors are notified of student approved accommodations: Student

General Admissions Information

Office of Admissions: 805-756-2311

Entrance Requirements

Academic units required: 4 English, 3 math, 2 science, 2 science labs, 2 foreign language, 1 social studies, 1 history, 1 academic electives, 1 visual/performing arts. **Academic units recommended:** 4 science, 2 science labs, 4 foreign language, 1 social studies, 1 history, 1 academic electives, 2 visual/performing arts. High school diploma is required and GED is accepted. SAT or ACT required. If ACT, ACT with writing accepted. TOEFL required of all international applicants: minimum paper TOEFL 550 or minimum internet TOEFL 80.

Application deadline: 11/30
Notification: 4/1
Average GPA: 3.92
ACT Composite middle 50% range: 26-31
SAT Math middle 50% range: 580-690
SAT Critical Reading middle 50% range: 550-650
SAT Writing middle 50% range: NR-NR
Graduated top 10% of class: 49
Graduated top 25% of class: 84
Graduated top 50% of class: 98

COLLEGE GRADUATION REQUIREMENTS

Course waivers allowed: No
Course substitutions allowed: Yes
In what course: On a case-by-case basis, individuals may be granted course substitutions (not waivers) in quantitative reasoning (in very limited non-math related majors) by the VP of Academic Affairs and foreign language substitutions with department approval.

Additional Information

Environment: This public school was founded in 1901. It has a 9678-acre campus.

Student Body
Undergrad enrollment: 20,049
% Women: 47
% Men: 53
% Out-of-state: 14

Cost information
In-state tuition: $5,472
Room & board: $12,009

Housing Information
University Housing: Yes
Percent living on campus: 36

Greek System
Fraternity: Yes
Sorority: Yes
Athletics: Division I

California State Polytechnic University—Pomona

3801 West Temple Avenue, Pomona, CA 91768
Phone: 909-869-3210 • Fax: 909-869-4529
E-mail: admissions@csupomona.edu • Web: www.cpp.edu/
Support: CS • Institution: Public

Programs or Services for Students with Learning Differences

The Disability Resource Center (DRC) Vision Statement: The Disability Resource Center's unwavering dedication to the promotion of equal access and opportunity for students with disabilities will be realized by our commitment to facilitating graduation and developing community leaders and contributors. http://www.dsa.csupomona.edu/drc/

Admission Information for Students with Learning Differences

College entrance test required: Yes
Interview required: No
Essay required: No
Additional Application Required for LD/ADHD/ASD: NR
What documentation required for LD: Report with scores for aptitude and achievement testing. Visit Documentation Standards at: www.cpp.edu/~drc/
With general application: No
To receive services after enrolling: Yes
What documentation required for ADHD: Diagnostic information and historical data should be summarized in a report. Visit Documentation Standards at: www.cpp.edu/~drc/
With general application: No
To receive services after enrolling: Yes
What documentation required for ASD: Psycho ed evaluation
With general application: No
To receive services after enrolling: Yes
LD/ADHD/ASD documentation submitted to: Disability Resource Center
ASD Specific Program: NR
Special Ed. HS course work accepted: NR
Specific course requirements of all applicants: NR
Separate application required for program services: NR
Total # of students receiving LD/ADHD/ASD services: 155
Acceptance into program means acceptance into college: NR

Admissions

Students must meet the university's regular entrance requirements, including C or better in the subject requirements of 4 years of English, 3 years of math, 1 year of U.S. history, 2 years of science lab, 2 years of a foreign language, 1 year of visual or performing arts, and 3 years of academic electives and a qualifiable eligibility index based on high school GPA and scores on either ACT or SAT. Special admits are very limited. Applicants with LD are encouraged to complete college-prep courses. However, if students are unable to fulfill a specific course requirement because of a learning disability, alternative college-prep courses may be substituted. Substitutions may be granted in foreign language, science lab, and math. Substitutions may be authorized on an individual basis after review and recommendation by applicant's guidance counselor in consultation with the Director of DSS. Course substitutions could limit access to some majors. Students are encouraged to self-disclose a learning disability if it would help to explain lower grades. Students who self-disclose are reviewed by DSS, which provides a recommendation to admissions.

Additional Information

Support services include counseling, advocacy services, registration, note-takers, readers, tutors, testing accommodations, and specialized equipment. Skills classes are not offered through DSS, but are available in other departments in the areas of reading skills, test preparation, test-taking strategies, and study skills. Services and accommodations are available to undergraduate and graduate students. Cal Poly offers a summer program for any high school student.

General Support Services Information

Contact Information
Name of program or department: Disability Resource Center
Telephone: 909-869-3333
Fax: 909-869-3271
Website: www.cpp.edu/~drc/accommodations-and-services

Accommodations or Services For Students With Learning Differences

Accommodations are decided upon an individual basis after a thorough review of appropriate, current documentation. The accommodations requests must be supported through the documentation provided and must be logically linked to the current impact of the condition on academic functioning.

Allowed in exams
Calculator: Yes
Dictionary: Yes
Computer: Yes
Spellchecker: Yes
Extended test time: Yes
Scribes: Yes
Proctors: Yes
Oral exams: Yes
Note-takers: Yes
Support services for students with LD: Yes
Support services for students with ADHD: Yes
Support services for students with ASD: Yes
Distraction-reduced environment: Yes
Tape recording in class: Yes
Electronic texts: Yes
Kurzweil reader: NR
Audio books: NR
Other assistive technology: Yes
Priority registration: Yes
Added costs of services: No
LD specialists: Yes
ADHD coaching: No
ASD specialists: No
Professional tutors: No
Peer tutors: No
Max. hours/wk. for services: NR
How professors are notified of student approved accommodations: By both student and director

General Admissions Information

Office of Admissions: 909-869-3210

Entrance Requirements

Academic units required: 4 English, 3 math, 2 science, 2 science labs, 2 foreign language, 1 social studies, 1 history, 1 academic electives, 1 visual/performing arts. **Academic units recommended:** 4 math. High school diploma is required and GED is accepted. SAT or ACT required. If ACT, ACT with writing accepted. TOEFL required of all international applicants: minimum paper TOEFL 525.

Application deadline: 11/30
Notification: Rolling starting 10/2
Average GPA: 3.49
ACT Composite middle 50% range: 20-27
SAT Math middle 50% range: 470-610
SAT Critical Reading middle 50% range: 450-570
SAT Writing middle 50% range: NR-NR
Graduate top 10% of class: NR
Graduated top 25% of class: NR
Graduated top 50% of class: NR

COLLEGE GRADUATION REQUIREMENTS

Course waivers allowed: No
In what course: NR
Course substitutions allowed: Yes
In what course: It depends on the student and the disability. However, there have been course substitutions for Math.

Additional Information

Environment: This public school was founded in 1938. It has a 1437-acre campus.

Student Body
Undergrad enrollment: 22,157
% Women: 44
% Men: 56
% Out-of-state: 1

Cost information
In-state tuition: $5,472
Out-of-state tuition: $16,632
Room & board: $15,238

Housing Information
University Housing: Yes
Percent living on campus: 10

Greek System
Fraternity: Yes
Sorority: Yes
Athletics: Division II

California State U.—Fullerton

PO Box 6900, Fullerton, CA 92834-6900
Phone: 657-278-7788 • Fax: 657-278-7699
E-mail: admissions@fullerton.edu • Web: www.fullerton.edu
Support: CS • Institution: Public

Programs or Services for Students with Learning Differences

The Student Support Services Program is a wide network of support services that help ensure academic and personal success in college. The program is designed to increase retention and graduation rates for underrepresented students. Students are encouraged to fulfill their academic and career potential by participating in an exceptional support environment. Each participant is teamed with an academic counselor for one-on-one mentoring and advisement. The emphasis is on providing students with personal attention and access to support services that include academic advisement; tutoring (referrals for individual and group tutoring including review sessions in select courses and development of study group); co-curricular events; peer mentoring for first-time freshmen; workshops and study-skills courses in reading, writing, math and other subjects, as well as time management; counseling; and an introduction to campus resources.

Admission Information for Students with Learning Differences

College entrance test required: Yes
Interview required: No
Essay required: No
Additional Application Required for LD/ADHD/ASD: NR
What documentation required for LD: Psycho ed evaluation to include: relevant historical info, instructional interventions, related services, age diagnosed, objective data (aptitude, achievement, info processing), test scores (standard percentile and grade equivalents) and describe functional limitations.
With general application: No
To receive services after enrolling: Yes
What documentation required for ADHD: Diagnosis based on DSM-V; history of behaviors impairing functioning in academic setting; diagnostic interview; history of symptoms; evidence of ongoing behaviors.
With general application: No
To receive services after enrolling: Yes
What documentation required for ASD: Psycho ed evaluation
With general application: NR
To receive services after enrolling: Yes
LD/ADHD/ASD documentation submitted to: Disabled Student Services
ASD Specific Program: NR
Special Ed. HS course work accepted: No
Specific course requirements of all applicants: Yes
Separate application required for program services: No
Total # of students receiving LD/ADHD/ASD services: NR
Acceptance into program means acceptance into college: Students must be accepted and enrolled prior to requesting services.

Admissions

Students are admitted on an eligibility index based on high school GPA in college-prep courses and scores on ACT or SAT. Lower GPA requires higher scores on the test. Other factors such as impaction and residency status are also considered. The foreign language requirement may be waived in rare cases when supported by the testing data supporting a relevant learning disability. ACT or SAT Reasoning Test required. All applicants must have 2 social science, 4 English, 3 math, 2 science (science with a lab, 1 biological and 1 physical), and 2 foreign language. The GPA is calculated based on the college-prep courses completed in grades 10, 11, and if available, 12. Students must have at least a C in these courses. Grades of D or less cannot be validated by a higher second semester grade in any of the following disciplines: social science/history, English, laboratory science, visual/performing arts, and electives. Students must have C or higher in all semesters of English, other lab sciences than chemistry, social sciences/history, and visual/performing arts to have the course counted toward the required preparatory units. Applicants within the local area will be required to meet the minimum eligibility requirement of 2900 based on GPA and SAT result or a 694 based on GPA and ACT result. Students outside of the local area should not anticipate receiving an admissions decision until late January or February.

Additional Information

The Intensive Learning Experience (ILE) program is designed to monitor the progress of any students fulfilling remedial compliance requirements and help students make successful progress in fulfilling the graduation requirements. ILE staff helps students on class planning, study skills, transfer work, campus resources, time management, and campus organizations. If not exempt from the English Placement Test (EPT) and Entry Level Mathematics (ELM), freshman must pass the EPT and/or ELM to move into the GE-level mathematics and English courses. If students do not pass they must take a developmental English and/or math course to fulfill the remedial compliance requirements. ILE provides students with an accommodation letter for professors each semester.

General Support Services Information

Contact Information
Name of program or department: Disabled Student Services
Telephone: 657-278-3112
Fax: (657) 278-2408
Website: www.fullerton.edu/dss/about_dss

Accommodations or Services For Students With Learning Differences

Accommodations are decided upon an individual basis after a thorough review of appropriate, current documentation. The accommodations requests must be supported through the documentation provided and must be logically linked to the current impact of the condition on academic functioning.

Allowed in exams
Calculator: Yes
Dictionary: Yes
Computer: Yes
Spellchecker: Yes
Extended test time: Yes
Scribes: Yes
Proctors: Yes
Oral exams: Yes
Note-takers: Yes
Support services for students with LD: NR
Support services for students with ADHD: NR
Support services for students with ASD: NR
Distraction-reduced environment: Yes
Tape recording in class: Yes
Electronic texts: Yes
Kurzweil reader: Yes
Audio books: NR
Other assistive technology: Yes
Priority registration: Yes
Added costs of services: No
LD specialists: Yes
ADHD coaching: NR
ASD specialists: NR
Professional tutors: No
Peer tutors: No
Max. hours/wk. for services: NR
How professors are notified of student approved accommodations: By student

General Admissions Information

Office of Admissions: 657-278-7788

Entrance Requirements

Academic units required: 4 English, 3 math, 2 science, 2 science labs, 2 foreign language, 1 social studies, 1 history, 1 academic electives, 1 visual/performing arts. **Academic units recommended:** 4 English, 3 math, 2 science, 2 science labs, 3 foreign language, 1 social studies, 1 history, 1 academic electives, 1 visual/performing arts. High school diploma is required and GED is accepted. SAT or ACT required. TOEFL required of all international applicants: minimum paper TOEFL 500 or minimum internet TOEFL 61.

Application deadline: 11/30
Notification: NR
Average GPA: 3.57
ACT Composite middle 50% range: 19-24
SAT Math middle 50% range: 470-570
SAT Critical Reading middle 50% range: 460-560
SAT Writing middle 50% range: NR-NR
Graduate top 10% of class: 24
Graduated top 25% of class: 66
Graduated top 50% of class: 96

COLLEGE GRADUATION REQUIREMENTS

Course waivers allowed: NR
Course substitutions allowed: NR

Additional Information

Environment: This public school was founded in 1957. It has a 225-acre campus.

Student Body
Undergrad enrollment: 33,144
% Women: 55
% Men: 45
% Out-of-state: 1

Cost information
In-state tuition: $5,472
Out-of-state tuition: $16,632
Room & board: $13,510

Housing Information
University Housing: Yes
Percent living on campus: 2

Greek System
Fraternity: Yes
Sorority: Yes
Athletics: Division II

California State U.—Long Beach

1250 Bellflower Boulevard, Long Beach, CA 90840
Phone: 562-985-5471 • Fax: 562-985-4973
E-mail: eslb@csulb.edu • Web: www.csulb.edu
Support: CS • Institution: Public

Programs or Services for Students with Learning Differences

The mission of the Disabled Student Services is to assist students with disabilities as they secure their university degrees at California State University, Long Beach. The Disabled Student Services Support Services and Advising Program provides accommodations for students with disabilities. Students who need accommodations must provide adequate medical verification of their disability and contact the office to receive services.

Admission Information for Students with Learning Differences

College entrance test required: Yes
Interview required: No
Essay required: 5
Additional application required for LD/ADHD/ASD: NR
What documentation required for LD: Acceptable documentation should consist of a psycho-educational report and/or other professional verification. Documentation should be dated within the last 3 years from time of application. Note: Individual Educational Plans (IEP's) are not generally an acceptable form of verification for the California State University (CSU) system.
With general application: No
To receive services after enrolling: Yes
What documentation required for ADHD: A psycho-educational report and/or other professional verification from an appropriately licensed professional with a DSM-5 diagnosis and/or medical verification.
With general application: No
To receive services after enrolling: Yes
What documentation required for ASD: www.csulb.edu/autism
With general application: No
To receive services after enrolling: Yes
LD/ADHD/ASD documentation submitted to: Both support services and admissions
ASD Specific Program: NR
Special Ed. HS course work accepted: N/A
Specific course requirements of all applicants: Yes
Separate application required for program services: No
Total # of students receiving LD/ADHD/ASD services: NR
Acceptance into program means acceptance into college: NR

Admissions

Special Admission Information: The Special Admission process is a means by which applicants, who may not meet the California State University Long Beach (CSULB) admission requirements due to a disability, but who are "otherwise qualified," may request special consideration for admission. The DSS Special Admissions Committee facilitates this process by consulting with Enrollment Services while providing additional information about each applicant's special circumstances. It is the committee's function to evaluate disability documentation using guidelines established by the California State University (CSU) system. All applicants are reviewed on a case-by-case basis. All final special admission decisions are made by Enrollment Services. A student wishing to be considered for special admission must first apply through the CSULB admission process. Applicants who are "otherwise qualified" based on a review of their documentation will be forwarded to Enrollment Services for Special Admissions consideration. Enrollment Services will then weigh the committee's recommendations as they relate to the total CSULB applicant pool for that term. If Enrollment Services agrees that a Special Admissions applicant is "otherwise qualified" and all competitive admission standards have been met, both the applicant and Disabled Student Services will be notified regarding Enrollment. Some applicants may be "conditionally" admitted via an enrollment exception. Enrollment Services will require these candidates to remediate their academic deficiency either prior to or subsequent to enrollment to CSULB. (e.g., students who qualify for Special Admissions whose math deficiency is waived for admission purposes will be required to complete a mathematics course substitution in the area of critical thinking to fulfill their missing General Education Breadth requirement during their first semester of attendance at CSULB).

Additional Information

The Stephen Benson Program for Students with Learning Disabilities (SBP) was created to serve the needs of CSULB students who have a diagnosed learning disability. The program was established in 1980 and continues to be one of the most recognized post-secondary LD programs in the state. Typically, the SBP serves approximately 500 students with learning disabilities each semester. A learning disability can interfere with a student's ability to assimilate or process information in several ways. The purpose of the SBP is to provide students, with documented learning disabilities, a support system to assist them in attaining their academic goals.

General Support Services Information

Contact Information
Name of program or department: CSULB—Disabled Student Services
Telephone: 562-985-5401
Fax: 562-985-4529

Accommodations or Services For Students With Learning Differences

Accommodations are decided upon an individual basis after a thorough review of appropriate, current documentation. The accommodations requests must be supported through the documentation provided and must be logically linked to the current impact of the condition on academic functioning.

Allowed in exams
Calculator: Yes
Dictionary: Yes
Computer: Yes
Spellchecker: Yes
Extended test time: Yes
Scribes: Yes
Proctors: Yes
Oral exams: Yes
Note-takers: Yes
Services for students with LD: Yes
Services for students with ADHD: Yes
Services for students with ASD: Yes
Distraction-reduced environment: Yes
Tape recording in class: Yes
Kurzweil reader: Yes
Audio books from learning ally: Yes
Other assistive technology: Yes
Priority registration: Yes
Added costs of services: No
LD specialists: Yes
ADHD coaching: NR
ASD specialists: NR
Professional tutors: NR
Peer tutors: Yes
Max. hours/wk. for services: NR
How professors are notified of student approved accommodations: Student

General Admissions Information

Office of Admissions: 562-985-5471

Entrance Requirements

Academic units required: 4 English, 3 math, 2 science, 2 science labs, 2 foreign language, 1 social studies, 1 history, 1 academic electives, and 1 units from above areas or other academic areas. High school diploma is required and GED is accepted. SAT or ACT required. If ACT, ACT with writing accepted. TOEFL required of all international applicants: minimum paper TOEFL 525.

Application deadline: 11/30
Notification: Rolling starting 12/1
Average GPA: 3.52
ACT Composite middle 50% range: 20-25
SAT Math middle 50% range: 480-600
SAT Critical Reading middle 50% range: 460-570
SAT Writing middle 50% range: NR-NR
Graduated top 10% of class: NR
Graduated top 25% of class: NR
Graduated top 50% of class: NR

COLLEGE GRADUATION REQUIREMENTS

Course waivers allowed: No
Course substitutions allowed: Yes
In what course: 1. Math 2. Other General Education courses as needed; on a case-by-case basis by way of an appeal through Academic Affairs.

Additional Information

Environment: This public school was founded in 1949. It has a 322-acre campus.

Student Body
Undergrad enrollment: 31,523
% Women: 56
% Men: 44
% Out-of-state: 1

Cost information
In-state tuition: $5,472
Out-of Tuition: $11,160
Room & board: $11,880

Housing Information
University Housing: Yes
Percent living on campus: 9

Greek System
Fraternity: Yes
Sorority: Yes
Athletics: Division I

California State U.—Northridge

Admissions and Records, CSU Northridge, Northridge, CA 91330-8207
Phone: 818-677-3700 • Fax: 818-677-3766
E-mail: admissions.records@csun.edu • Web: www.csun.edu
Support: CS • Institution: Public

Programs or Services for Students with Learning Differences

Disability Resources and Educational Services (DRES) recognizes that students with disabilities can be quite successful in the university setting if appropriate educational support services are offered to them. In an effort to assist students with disabilities in reaching their full potential, the program offers a comprehensive and well-coordinated system of educational support services that allow students to be judged on the basis of their ability rather than disability. In order to accommodate different needs DRES has developed an individualized learning plan called "journey to success". Students must register with DRES to be eligible.

Admission Information for Students with Learning Differences

College entrance test required: Yes
Interview required: Yes
Essay required: NR
Additional Application Required for LD/ADHD/ASD: NR
What documentation required for LD: Must contain a specific diagnosis, indicating whether the disability is temporary or permanent, and a concise description of the functional limitations imposed by the disability. Copies of the assessment containing the results of a diagnostic interview, an assessment of aptitude, academic achievement, and information processing as well as a diagnosis with functional limitations are recommended.
With general application: No
To receive services after enrolling: Yes
What documentation required for ADHD: Neuropsychological assessment signed by physician, other licensed health care professional, or rehabilitation counselor. The report should contain a specific diagnosis, indicating whether the disability is temporary or permanent, and a concise description of the functional limitations.
With general application: No
To receive services after enrolling: yes
What documentation required for ASD: Psycho ed evaluation
With general application: No
To receive services after enrolling: Yes
LD/ADHD/ASD documentation submitted to: Disability Resources and Educational Services
ASD Specific Program: NR
Special Ed. HS course work accepted: yes
Specific course requirements of all applicants: Yes
Separate application required for program services: No
Total # of students receiving LD/ADHD/ASD services: NR
Acceptance into program means acceptance into college: NR

Admissions

There is no special admission process. However, if a student applies to the university and is rejected, they may appeal the descision. Students must get a C or better in: 4 years English, 3 years math, 1 year U.S. history, 1 year science, 2 years foreign language, 1 year visual/performing arts, and 3 years of electives. An eligibility index combining GPA and ACT or SAT is used.

Additional Information

During the Transition years students can expect staff to assist them in: managing workloads, developing compensatory strategies for life-long learning, learning self-advocacy skills, and learning how to access services. In the Foundation years students can expect staff to continue with a mentor relationship, map out career strategies, encourage the student to join co-curricular activities that contribute to personal and social growth and continuing relationship-building with faculty. Assistance in developing appropriate learning strategies is provided on an individual basis.

General Support Services Information

Contact Information
Name of program or department: Disability Resources and Educational Services
Telephone: 818-677-2684
Fax: 818-677-4932
Website: www.csun.edu/dres/student-services

Accommodations or Services For Students With Learning Differences

Accommodations are decided upon an individual basis after a thorough review of appropriate, current documentation. The accommodations requests must be supported through the documentation provided and must be logically linked to the current impact of the condition on academic functioning.

Allowed in exams
Calculator: Yes
Dictionary: Yes
Computer: Yes
Spellchecker: Yes
Extended test time: Yes
Scribes: Yes
Proctors: Yes
Oral exams: Yes
Note-takers: Yes
Support services for students with LD: Yes
Support services for students with ADHD: Yes
Support services for students with ASD: NR
Distraction-reduced environment: Yes
Tape recording in class: Yes
Electronic texts: NR
Kurzweil reader: Yes
Audio books: Yes
Other assistive technology: Yes
Priority registration: Yes
Added costs of services: No
LD specialists: Yes
ADHD coaching: NR
ASD specialists: NR
Professional tutors: No
Peer tutors: Yes
Max. hours/wk. for services: 2
How professors are notified of student approved accommodations: Student

General Admissions Information

Office of Admissions: 818-677-3700

Entrance Requirements

Academic units required: 4 English, 3 math, 1 science, 2 science labs, 2 foreign language, 2 history, 1 academic electives, and 1 units from above areas or other academic areas. High school diploma is required and GED is accepted.High school diploma is required and GED is not accepted. SAT or ACT required. TOEFL required of all international applicants: minimum paper TOEFL 500.

Application deadline: NR
Notification: Rolling starting 11/30
Average GPA: NR
ACT Composite middle 50% range: NR-NR
SAT Math middle 50% range: NR-NR
SAT Critical Reading middle 50% range: NR-NR
SAT Writing middle 50% range: NR-NR
Graduate top 10% of class: NR
Graduated top 25% of class: NR
Graduated top 50% of class: NR

COLLEGE GRADUATION REQUIREMENTS

Course waivers allowed: NR
Course substitutions allowed: NR

Additional Information

Environment: This public school was founded in 1956. It has a 350-acre campus.

Student Body
Undergrad enrollment: 36,917
% Women: 54
% Men: 46
% Out-of-state: 1

Cost information
In-state tuition: $6,564
Out-of-state tuition: $11,028
Room & board: $9,962

Housing Information
University Housing: Yes
Percent living on campus: 8

Greek System
Fraternity: Yes
Sorority: Yes

Athletics: Division I

CAL. STATE U.—SAN BERNARDINO

5500 University Parkway, San Bernardino, CA 92407-2397
Phone: 909-537-5188 • Fax: 909-537-7034
E-mail: moreinfo@mail.csusb.edu • Web: www.csusb.edu
Support: CS • Institution: Public

PROGRAMS OR SERVICES FOR STUDENTS WITH LEARNING DIFFERENCES

The Learning Disability Program is dedicated to assuring each student an opportunity to experience equity in education. Each student must complete an assessment, and then the staff helps to develop compensatory methods for handling assignments and classroom projects. Careful attention is paid to helping the student acquire learning skills and formulating and implementing specific strategies for note-taking and management of written materials. Recommendations are designed for each student as a result of a psychometric assessment, personal interview, and academic requirements. The emphasis of the plan is to assist the students with a learning disability in finding techniques to deal with it in college and in the job market.

ADMISSION INFORMATION FOR STUDENTS WITH LEARNING DIFFERENCES

College entrance tests required: Yes
Interview required: Yes
Essay required: No
Additional application required for LD/ADHD/ASD: NR
What documentation required for LD: Psycho ed evaluation to include: relevant historical info, instructional interventions, related services, age diagnosed, objective data (aptitude, achievement, info processing), test scores (standard, percentile and grade equivalents) and describe functional limitations.
With general application: No
To receive services after enrolling: Yes
What documentation required for ADHD: Diagnosis based on DSM-V; history of behaviors impairing functioning in academic setting; diagnostic interview; history of symptoms; evidence of ongoing behaviors.
With general application: No
To receive services after enrolling: Yes
What documentation required for ASD: Psycho ed evaluation
With general application: NR
To receive services after enrolling: Yes
LD/ADHD/ASD documentation submitted to: Services for Students with Disabilities
ASD Specific Program: NR
Special Ed. HS course work accepted: No
Specific course requirements of all applicants: Yes
Separate application required: Yes
Total # of students receiving LD/ADHD/ASD services: 140–156
Acceptance into program means acceptance into college: Students must be admitted and enrolled in the university first and then request services.

ADMISSIONS

The eligibility index requirements for out-of-state, non-resident students are higher than for California residents. For non-resident students, a GPA of 3.61 or higher qualifies with any test score. A 2.45 is the minimum regular admission GPA. The average GPA for admissions is a 3.23. The average ACT is 18 and a mid 50% range of 16-20. The average SAT is 950 (Math and Critical Reading) and the mid 50% range of 790-990. Special admission may be requested through the Learning Disability Program if the student has a deficiency in course entrance requirements. The Director of the LD Program provides recommendations on the admissibility of those students who do not meet regular admissions requirements. Occasionally, the special admit will consider students who do not meet the required GPA or test scores. These requirements can be substituted, and the student can make up the deficiency on campus once enrolled.

ADDITIONAL INFORMATION

Services and accommodations for students with appropriate documentation could include the following: the use of calculators, dictionaries, computers, or spellchecker during exams; extended time on tests; distraction-free testing environments; oral exams; note-takers; proctors; scribes; tape recorders in class; books on tape; assisting technology; and priority registration. Specific services include assessment counseling and testing accommodations. Students on academic probation have two quarters to raise their GPA to a 2.0. The LD Program provides continual academic support.

General Support Services Information

Contact Information
Name of program or department: Services to Students with Disabilities
Telephone: 909-537-5238
Fax: 909-537-7090

Accommodations or Services For Students With Learning Differences

Accommodations are decided upon an individual basis after a thorough review of appropriate, current documentation. The accommodations requested must be supported through the documentation provided and must be logically linked to the current impact of the condition on academic functioning.

Allowed in exams
Calculator: Yes
Dictionary: No
Computer: Yes
Spellchecker: Yes
Extended test time: Yes
Scribes: Yes
Proctors: Yes
Oral exams: Yes
Note-takers: Yes
Services for students with LD: Yes
Services for students with ADHD: Yes
Services for students with ASD: Yes
Distraction-reduced environment: Yes
Tape recording in class: Yes
Audio books: NR
Electronic texts: Yes
Kurzweil Reader: Yes
Other assistive technology: Yes
Priority registration: Yes
Added costs for services: No
ADHD coaching: NR
ASD specialists: NR
LD specialists: Yes
Professional tutors: No
Peer tutors: No
Max. hours/wk. for services: N/A
How professors are notified of LD/ADHD: By student

General Admissions Information

Office of Admissions: 909-537-5188

Entrance Requirements

Academic units required: 4 English, 3 math, 2 science, 2 science labs, 2 foreign language, 1 social studies, 1 history, 1 academic electives, 1 visual/performing arts. High school diploma is required and GED is accepted. SAT or ACT recommended. If ACT, ACT with writing accepted. TOEFL required of all international applicants: minimum paper TOEFL 500 or minimum internet TOEFL 61.

Application deadline: NR
Notification: NR
Average GPA: 3.21
ACT Composite middle 50% range: 16-20
SAT Math middle 50% range: 400-500
SAT Critical Reading middle 50% range: 400-490
SAT Writing middle 50% range: 390-480
Graduated top 10% of class: NR
Graduated top 25% of class: NR
Graduated top 50% of class: NR

COLLEGE GRADUATION REQUIREMENTS

Course waivers allowed: No
Course substitutions allowed: Yes
In what course: General education, math

Additional Information

Environment: This public school was founded in 1965. It has a 430-acre campus.

Student Body
Undergrad enrollment: 17,721
% Women: 60
% Men: 40
% Out-of-state: 0.4

Cost information
Out-of Tuition: $11,160
Room & board: $9,372

Housing Information
University Housing: Yes
Percent living on campus: 7.8

Greek System
Fraternity: Yes
Sorority: Yes
Athletics: Division II

College of the Siskiyous

800 College Avenue, Weed, CA 96094
Phone: 530-938-5555 • Fax: 530-938-5367
E-mail: registration@siskiyous.edu • Web: www.siskiyous.edu
Support: CS • Institution type: 2-year public

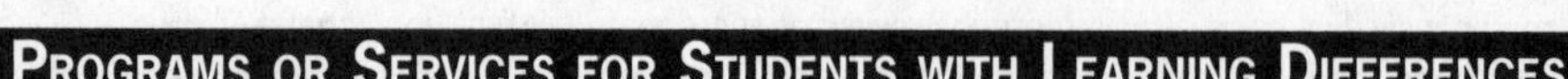

Programs or Services for Students with Learning Differences

The Disabled Student Programs and Services Office (DSP&S) is dedicated to meeting the needs of students with disabilities. The goal of DSP&S is to assist students to overcome barriers to allow access to the college's regular programs and activities. Support services are provided for students with a wide variety of disabilities. Any student who has a documented disability and demonstrates a need for a service that is directly related to the educational limitation is eligible for support services.

Admission Information for Students with Learning Differences

College entrance tests required: Yes
Interview required: No
Essay required: No
Additional application required for LD/ADHD/ASD: NR
What documentation required for LD: Psycho ed evaluation to include: relevant historical info, instructional interventions, related services, age diagnosed, objective data (aptitude, achievement, info processing), test scores (standard, percentile and grade equivalents) and describe functional limitations.
With general application: No
To receive services after enrolling: Yes
What documentation required for ADHD: Diagnosis based on DSM-V; history of behaviors impairing functioning in academic setting; diagnostic interview; history of symptoms; evidence of ongoing behaviors.
With general application: No
To receive services after enrolling: Yes
What documentation required for ASD: Psycho ed evaluation
With general application: NR
To receive services after enrolling: Yes
LD/ADHD/ASD documentation submitted to: Disabled Student Programs and Services
ASD Specific Program: NR
Special Ed. HS course work accepted: No
Specific course requirements of all applicants: No
Separate application required: Yes
Total # of students receiving LD/ADHD/ASD services: 50
Acceptance into program means acceptance into college: Students must be admitted and enrolled in the college first and then request services.

Admissions

Students with LD/ADHD who self-disclose during the admission process may receive advice from DSP&S during the admission process. Basically, this advice would provide descriptions of appropriate courses the students may take and the services and accommodations they may be eligible to receive. There are not any minimum admission requirements for a specific class rank, GPA, or ACT/SAT score. Applicants must have a high school diploma or equivalent certification.

Additional Information

There is an LD specialist available in the Disabled Students Programs and Services Office. There are support services available for students who have a documented disability and demonstrate a need for a service that is directly related to their educational limitations. They may include academic advising, registration assistance, an LD assessment, tutoring, readers, note-takers, testing accommodations, and adaptive educational equipment. The COS High Tech Center is designed to provide computer access and technology to students with disabilities to educate and prepare them for academic success and today's work force. In addition, all students have access to skills classes in areas such as time management, organization, study strategies, and test-taking strategies.

Groups served: Acquired Brain Impairment (ABI); A verified deficit in brain functioning which results in a total or partial loss of cognitive, communicative, motor, psycho-social, and/or sensory perceptual abilities; Communicatively Challenged; An impairment in the processes of speech, language, or hearing; Developmentally Delayed Learners; A student exhibiting below-average intellectual functioning and potential for measurable achievement; Learning Challenged Students with at least average intelligence who exhibit one or more deficits in processing; Physically Challenged; Students with visual, mobility, or orthopedic impairment; Psychologically Challenged; A persistent psychological or psychiatric disorder, emotional or mental disorder; Other Challenges (This category includes all other verifiable disabilities and health-related limitations that adversely affect education performance but do not fall into any of the other categories.) **Other challenges include:** conditions having limited strength, vitality, or alertness due to chronic or acute health problems. Examples are: attention deficit disorders (ADD); epilepsy; heart conditions; HIV/AIDS; cancer. This disability group can be verified by a licensed physician

General Support Services Information

Contact Information
Name of program or department: Disabled Student Programs and Services
Telephone: 530-938-5297
Email: dsps@siskiyous.edu

Accommodations or Services For Students With Learning Differences

Accommodations are decided upon an individual basis after a thorough review of appropriate, current documentation. The accommodations requested must be supported through the documentation provided and must be logically linked to the current impact of the condition on academic functioning.

Allowed in exams
Calculator: No
Dictionary: No
Computer: Yes
Spellchecker: No
Extended test time: Yes
Scribes: Yes
Proctors: Yes
Oral exams: Yes
Note-takers: Yes
Services for students with LD: Yes
Services for students with ADHD: Yes
Services for students with ASD: Yes
Distraction-reduced environment: Yes
Tape recording in class: Yes
Audio books: NR
Electronic texts: Yes
Kurzweil Reader: Yes
Other assistive technology: Yes
Priority registration: No
Added costs for services: No
LD specialists: Yes
ADHD coaching: NR
ASD specialists: NR
Professional tutors: No
Peer tutors: Yes
Max. hours/wk. for services: Unlimited
How professors are notified of LD/ADHD: By student

General Admissions Information

Office of Admissions: 530-938-5555

Entrance Requirements

There are no specific requirements for courses, GPA, class rank, or test scores. TOEFL required of all internationalapplicants: minimum paper TOEFL 470, minimum computer TOEFL 150.

Application deadline: None
Notification: Rolling
Average GPA: NR
ACT Composite middle 50% range: NR-NR
SAT Math middle 50% range: NR-NR
SAT Critical Reading middle 50% range: NR-NR
SAT Writing middle 50% range: NR-NR
Graduated top 10% of class: NR
Graduated top 25% of class: NR
Graduated top 50% of class: NR

COLLEGE GRADUATION REQUIREMENTS

Course waivers allowed: No
Course substitutions allowed: Yes
In what course: Students can petition for a substitute course.

Additional Information

Environment: NR

Student Body
Undergrad enrollment: 4,587
% Women: 53
% Men: 44
% Out-of-state: 27

Cost information
In-state tuition: $1,154
Out-of-state tuition: $6,194
Room & board: $4,770

Housing Information
University Housing: Yes
Percent living on campus: NR

Greek System
Fraternity: No
Sorority: No
Athletics: NJCAA

Loyola Marymount University

1 LMU Drive, Los Angeles, CA 90045-8350
Phone: 310-338-2750 • Fax: 310-338-2797
E-mail: admissions@lmu.edu • Web: www.lmu.edu
Support: S • Institution: Private

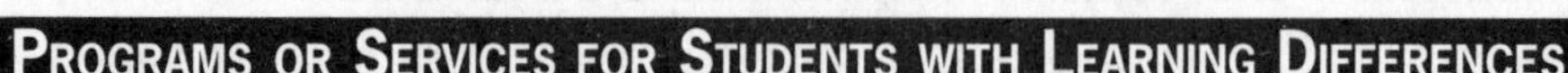

Programs or Services for Students with Learning Differences

The Office of Disability Support Services (DSS) provides specialized assistance and resources that enable students with physical, perceptual, emotional, and learning disabilities to achieve maximum independence while they pursue their educational goals. Assisted by staff specialists from all areas of the university, the DSS Office works to eliminate physical and attitudinal barriers. To be eligible for services, students must provide documentation of the disability from a licensed professional. At the Learning Resource Center students can receive tutoring in over 250 LMU classes, attend workshops, and access assistance in writing, reading, and math with LRC specialists.

Admission Information for Students with Learning Differences

College entrance test required: Yes
Interview required: No
Essay required: No
Additional application required for LD/ADHD/ASD: NR
What documentation required for LD: Most current psychoeducational evaluation, transcripts, accommodations in high school, SAT/ACT scores/accommodations, IEP or 504 if attended public school, medical documents if on medication
With general application: No
To receive services after enrolling: Yes
What documentation required for ADHD: psychoeducational evaluation, transcripts, accommodations in high school, SAT/ACT scores/accommodations, IEP/504 if attended public high school
With general application: No
To receive services after enrolling: Yes
What documentation required for ASD: Psycho ed evaluation
With general application: No
To receive services after enrolling: Yes
LD/ADHD/ASD documentation submitted to: Support program/services
ASD Specific Program: NR
Special Ed. HS course work accepted: No
Specific course requirements of all applicants: No
Separate application required for program services: Yes
Total # of students receiving LD/ADHD/ASD services: 80
Acceptance into program means acceptance into college: NR

Admissions

There is no special admissions process for students with disabilities. The admission decision will be based upon the student's grade point average, SAT/ACT scores, strength of curriculum, the application essay, letters of recommendation, and extracurricular activities. Enrolled students have an average GPA of 3.75. Students are encouraged to have completed 4 years English, 3 years social sciences, 3 years foreign language, 3 years math (4 years for engineering and science), and 1 year elective.

Additional Information

There is an Academic Resource Center where all students can find specialists and tutors. There is course-specific tutoring, study skills programs (which include learning time management, overcoming test anxiety, conquering math word problems, mastering the textbook, preparing for exams, and studying efficiently), and other academic support programs with full-time professional staff members prepared to assist with writing, reading, math, ESL, and Disability Support Services. Assistive technology includes: equipment that enlarges print, Kurzweil 3000, Jaws and Dragon Dictate. Specific accommodations for LD students with appropriate documentation could include: priority registration, notetakers, readers, transcribers, alternate testing conditions, taped books, and advocacy.

General Support Services Information

Contact Information
Name of program or department: Office of Disability Support Services (DSS)
Telephone: 310-338-4216
Fax: 310-338-5344

Accommodations or Services For Students With Learning Differences

Accommodations are decided upon an individual basis after a thorough review of appropriate, current documentation. The accommodations requests must be supported through the documentation provided and must be logically linked to the current impact of the condition on academic functioning.

Allowed in exams
Calculator: Yes
Dictionary: Yes
Computer: Yes
Spellchecker: Yes
Extended test time: Yes
Scribes: Yes
Proctors: Yes
Oral exams: Yes
Note-takers: Yes
Services for students with LD: Yes
Services for students with ADHD: Yes
Services for students with ASD: Yes
Distraction-reduced environment: Yes
Tape recording in class: Yes
Audio books from learning ally: Yes
Electronic texts: NR
Kurzweil Reader: Yes
Other assistive technology: Yes
Priority registration: Yes
Added costs for services: No
LD specialists: Yes
ADHD coaching: NR
ASD specialists: NR
Professional tutors: NR
Peer tutors: Yes
Max. hours/wk. for services: 1 ea. subj.
How professors are notified of student approved accommodations: Student

General Admissions Information

Office of Admissions: 310-338-2750

Entrance Requirements

Academic units recommended: 4 English, 3 math, 2 science, 2 science labs, 3 foreign language, 3 social studies, 1 academic electives. High school diploma is required and GED is accepted. SAT or ACT required. If ACT, ACT with writing accepted. TOEFL required of all international applicants: minimum paper TOEFL 550 or minimum internet TOEFL 80.

Application deadline: 1/15
Notification: Rolling starting 11/1
Average GPA: 3.75
ACT Composite middle 50% range: 25-30
SAT Math middle 50% range: 560-660
SAT Critical Reading middle 50% range: 550-640
SAT Writing middle 50% range: 550-650
Graduated top 10% of class: 44
Graduated top 25% of class: 76
Graduated top 50% of class: 93

COLLEGE GRADUATION REQUIREMENTS

Course waivers allowed: No
Course substitutions allowed: No

Additional Information

Environment: This private school, affiliated with the Roman Catholic Church, was founded in 1911. It has a 128-acre campus.

Student Body
Undergrad enrollment: 6,259
% Women: 56
% Men: 44
% Out-of-state: 24

Cost information
Tuition: $41,876
Room & board: $14,470

Housing Information
University Housing: Yes
Percent living on campus: 51

Greek System
Fraternity: Yes
Sorority: Yes
Athletics: Division I

Menlo College

1000 El Camino Real, Atherton, CA 94027
Phone: 650-543-3753 • Fax: 650-543-4103
E-mail: admissions@menlo.edu • Web: www.menlo.edu
Support: CS • Institution: Private

Programs or Services for Students with Learning Differences

The Menlo College Academic Success Center (ASC) welcomes all students including those with learning, psychological, and attention challenges. In its new configuration with the Bowman Library, now the Learning Community Commons, services have broadened to include library staff and resources. Students who present proper documentation of a disability may qualify for accommodations. All students are welcome to utilize the services of the Academic Success Center.

Admission Information for Students with Learning Differences

College entrance test required: Yes
Interview required: No
Essay required: Not Applicable
Additional Application Required for LD/ADHD/ASD: NR
What documentation required for LD: Psychoeducational testing or IEP from high school
With general application: No
To receive services after enrolling: Yes
What documentation required for ADHD: Psychoeducational testing or psychiatrist or physician's report
With general application: No
To receive services after enrolling: Yes
What documentation required for ASD: Psychoeducational testing or IEP from high school
With general application: No
To receive services after enrolling: Yes
LD/ADHD/ASD documentation submitted to: ASC
ASD Specific Program: NR
Special Ed. HS course work accepted: Not Applicable
Specific course requirements of all applicants: NR
Separate application required for program services: NR
Total # of students receiving LD/ADHD/ASD services: 41
Acceptance into program means acceptance into college: No

Admissions

Students are admitted to Menlo College on their own merits, without regard to disability. If students choose to self-disclose their learning challenges, they are encouraged to meet with the Academic Success Center in advance of their arrival to arrange for early set-up of accommodations. Menlo values the individual strengths and diversity that students bring to Menlo, so we choose not to follow a specific formula when making our admission decisions. Each applicant is reviewed individually, and the acceptance decisions are based on many factors including the strength of your course curriculum, the school you attend(ed), and your grades and test scores. In addition, we consider your extracurricular activities, community involvement, employment, and leadership roles. Menlo College is most interested in the quality of students' activities, rather than the quantity. Essay required regarding either 1) Academic strengths or weaknesses, or 2) Reasons for seeking college education, or 3) Learning experiences you hope to have, or 4) Why Menlo Counselor teacher recommendation, ACT/SAT.

Additional Information

The Academic Success Center provides a 'one-stop' center for information and resources that are key to academic and career success. The services include: advising, advocacy, assistive technology, note takers, books on tape, tutoring lab and writing center, testing and tutoring, documentation analysis and faculty liaison for Students with Disabilities. The Academic Success Center will help students improve test performance, obtain or update their Degree Check Sheet(s), understand why they may attend class regularly, but feel like they're missing important points or having trouble completing tests in the allotted time, feel like they don't have enough time to get everything done, not sure how to take notes, need a tutor or study group, or want information on meeting with your academic advisor.

General Support Services Information

Contact Information
Name of program or department: ASC
Telephone: 650-543-3845
Fax: 650-543-4120
Website: www.menlo.edu/academics/resources

Accommodations or Services for Students with Learning Differences

Accommodations are decided upon an individual basis after a thorough review of appropriate, current documentation. The accommodations requests must be supported through the documentation provided and must be logically linked to the current impact of the condition on academic functioning.

Allowed in exams
Calculator: Yes
Dictionary: Yes
Computer: Yes
Spellchecker: Yes
Extended test time: Yes
Scribes: Yes
Proctors: Yes
Oral exams: Yes
Note-takers: Yes
Support services for students with LD: Yes
Support services for students with ADHD: Yes
Support services for students with ASD: Yes
Distraction-reduced environment: Yes
Tape recording in class: Yes
Electronic texts: Yes
Kurzweil reader: NR
Audio books: Yes
Other assistive technology: Yes
Priority registration: No
Added costs of services: No
LD specialists: Yes
ADHD coaching: No
ASD specialists: NR
Professional tutors: Yes
Peer tutors: NR
Max. hours/wk. for services: NR
How professors are notified of student approved accommodations: By both student and director

General Admissions Information

Office of Admissions: 650-543-3753

Entrance Requirements

Academic units recommended: 4 English, 3 math, 3 science, 2 foreign language, 3 social studies. High school diploma is required and GED is accepted. SAT or ACT required. If ACT, ACT with writing accepted. TOEFL required of all international applicants: minimum paper TOEFL 500 or minimum internet TOEFL 61.

Application deadline: 4/1
Notification: NR
Average GPA: 3.3
ACT Composite middle 50% range: 19-25
SAT Math middle 50% range: 470-563
SAT Critical Reading middle 50% range: 450-533
SAT Writing middle 50% range: 450-525
Graduate top 10% of class: NR
Graduated top 25% of class: NR
Graduated top 50% of class: NR

COLLEGE GRADUATION REQUIREMENTS

Course waivers allowed: Yes
In what course: Foreign language and math
Course substitutions allowed: Yes
In what course: Foreign language and math

Additional Information

Environment: This private school was founded in 1927. It has a 45-acre campus.

Student Body
Undergrad enrollment: 768
% Women: 45
% Men: 55
% Out-of-state: 19

Cost information
Tuition: $39,250
Room & board: $13,150

Housing Information
University Housing: Yes
Percent living on campus: 60

Greek System
Fraternity: No
Sorority: No
Athletics: NAIA

OCCIDENTAL COLLEGE

1600 Campus Road, Los Angeles, CA 90041-3314
Phone: 323-259-2700 • Fax: 323-341-4875
E-mail: admission@oxy.edu • Web: www.oxy.edu
Support: S • Institution: Private

PROGRAMS OR SERVICES FOR STUDENTS WITH LEARNING DIFFERENCES

The dean's office coordinates academic support services for all students, including those with disabilities, who want to enhance their academic success. Students who have a documented disability requiring academic accommodation and who wish to apply for academic accommodation in addition to the general academic support services need to make an appointment with the dean's office as far in advance of the semester of enrollment as possible. The purpose of this meeting is to acquaint the student with the available resources, determine the accommodations required by the student, and complete appropriate forms requesting services. If relevant documentation has not been previously submitted to the dean's office, students should bring it to this meeting. The documentation should support assessments completed within the past 3 years. Accommodations for students with documented disabilities are determined by individual student needs.

ADMISSION INFORMATION FOR STUDENTS WITH LEARNING DIFFERENCES

College entrance test required: Yes
Interview required: No
Essay required: Not Applicable
Additional Application Required for LD/ADHD/ASD: Yes
What documentation required for LD: Psycho-educational evaluation/assessment
With general application: No
To receive services after enrolling: Yes
What documentation required for ADHD: Psycho-educational evaluation/assessment
With general application: No
To receive services after enrolling: Yes
What documentation required for ASD: Psycho-educational evaluation/assessment
With general application: No
To receive services after enrolling: Yes
LD/ADHD/ASD documentation submitted to: Disability Services
ASD Specific Program: NR
Special Ed. HS course work accepted: Not Applicable
Specific course requirements of all applicants: Yes
Separate application required for program services: Yes
Total # of students receiving LD/ADHD/ASD services: 320
Acceptance into program means acceptance into college: No

ADMISSIONS

Same as for all students

ADDITIONAL INFORMATION

The most typically successful student at Occidental College is a self-advocate who understands and can explain his or her academic needs, when appropriate, to professors and others providing academic assistance. The student seeks assistance related to the disability, as needed, from the CAE coordinator. If concerns or questions arise, the student contacts the coordinator of the CAE to resolve or clarify. If extended time for exams, note-taking, alternative formats to text, or other academic accommodations are needed, the student carries out his or her responsibilities for receiving these accommodations, including timely scheduling of exam proctoring appointments, communicating with professors, seeking out student note-takers, and notifying the CAE of assigned readings. Alternative courses to the foreign language requirement are offered on a case-by case basis and with presentation of psychoeducational documentation that specifically justifies the need in the area of foreign language. In such cases, the student will make arrangements through the coordinator of Academic Support Services. Occidental College does not provide daily support and consultation for learning disabled students. Students are encouraged to find fellow students as note-takers, and the college will make available two-ply paper for use by volunteer note-takers and will honor volunteer note-takers with bookstore gift certificates. Students enrolled at Occidental College who have not been previously diagnosed and who have reason to suspect they may have a learning disability or ADHD are encouraged to meet with the coordinator of Academic Support Services to determine appropriate action. Occidental College does not administer diagnostic assessments, but will assist students in making arrangements to be tested by a qualified professional. The cost of the evaluation is the responsibility of the student.

General Support Services Information

Contact Information
Name of program or department: Disability Services
Telephone: (323) 259-2969
Fax: (323) 341-4927
Website: www.oxy.edu/disability-services

Accommodations or Services For Students With Learning Differences

Accommodations are decided upon an individual basis after a thorough review of appropriate, current documentation. The accommodations requests must be supported through the documentation provided and must be logically linked to the current impact of the condition on academic functioning.

Allowed in exams
Calculator: Yes
Dictionary: Yes
Computer: Yes
Spellchecker: Yes
Extended test time: Yes
Scribes: Yes
Proctors: Yes
Oral exams: Yes
Note-takers: Yes
Support services for students with LD: Yes
Support services for students with ADHD: Yes
Support services for students with ASD: Yes
Distraction-reduced environment: Yes
Tape recording in class: Yes
Electronic texts: Yes
Kurzweil reader: NR
Audio books: Yes
Other assistive technology: Yes
Priority registration: Yes
Added costs of services: No
LD specialists: Yes
ADHD coaching: Yes
ASD specialists: No
Professional tutors: No
Peer tutors: Yes
Max. hours/wk. for services: NR
How professors are notified of student approved accommodations: By student

General Admissions Information

Office of Admissions: 323-259-2700

Entrance Requirements

Academic units recommended: 4 English, 3 math, 3 science, 3 foreign language, 2 social studies, 3 history. High school diploma is required and GED is accepted. SAT or ACT required. If ACT, ACT with writing recommended. TOEFL required of all international applicants: minimum paper TOEFL 600.

Application deadline: 1/15
Notification: 3/25
Average GPA: 3.64
ACT Composite middle 50% range: 28-31
SAT Math middle 50% range: 600-690
SAT Critical Reading middle 50% range: 600-690
SAT Writing middle 50% range: 605-690
Graduate top 10% of class: 55
Graduated top 25% of class: 90
Graduated top 50% of class: 99

COLLEGE GRADUATION REQUIREMENTS

Course waivers allowed: No
In what course: No waiver, but can substitute Foreign Language, Math
Course substitutions allowed: Yes
In what course: Math, Foreign Languages

Additional Information

Environment: This private school was founded in 1887. It has a 120-acre campus.

Student Body
Undergrad enrollment: 2,112
% Women: 57
% Men: 43
% Out-of-state: 52

Cost information
Tuition: $48,690
Room & board: $13,946

Housing Information
University Housing: Yes
Percent living on campus: 82

Greek System
Fraternity: Yes
Sorority: Yes
Athletics: Division III

Reedley College

995 North Reed Avenue, Reedley, CA 93654
Phone: 559-638-3641 • Fax: 559-638-5040
E-mail: emerzian@scccd.org • Web: www.reedleycollege.com
Support: CS • Institution type: 2-year public

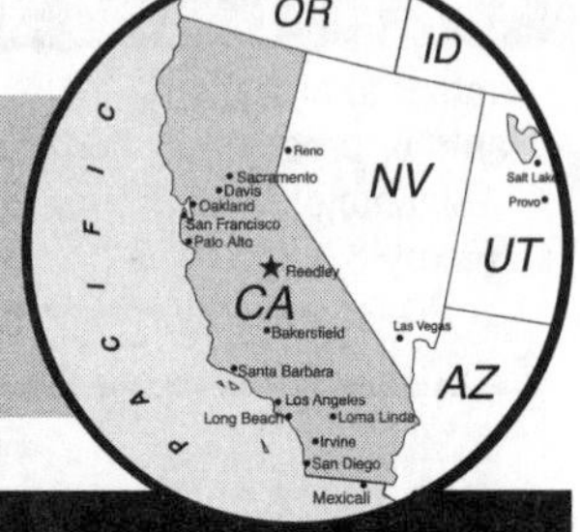

Programs or Services for Students with Learning Differences

The Disabled Student Program and Services (DSP&S) focuses on abilities, not disabilities. DSP&S offers services to students with learning disabilities beyond those provided by conventional programs at the college and enables students to pursue their individual educational, vocational, and personal goals successfully. The Learning Disabilities Program assesses the needs and skill levels of each student, tailoring a specific educational course of study designed to bring out the best in an individual at a college level. The instructional program in reading, writing, math, and other academics prepares students to function in the classroom, in their vocation, and throughout life. The LD Program provides special instruction and attention for students with specific educational needs not available in mainstream classes.

Admission Information for Students with Learning Differences

College entrance tests required: No
Interview required: Yes
Essay required: No
Additional application required for LD/ADHD/ASD: NR
What documentation required for LD: Psycho ed evaluation to include: relevant historical info, instructional interventions, related services, age diagnosed, objective data (aptitude, achievement, info processing), test scores (standard, percentile and grade equivalents) and describe functional limitations.
With general application: No
To receive services after enrolling: Yes
What documentation required for ADHD: Diagnosis based on DSM-V; history of behaviors impairing functioning in academic setting; diagnostic interview; history of symptoms; evidence of ongoing behaviors.
With general application: No
To receive services after enrolling: Yes
What documentation required for ASD: Psycho ed evaluation
With general application: NR
To receive services after enrolling: Yes
LD/ADHD/ASD documentation submitted to: Disabled Student Program and Services
ASD Specific Program: NR
Special Ed. HS course work accepted: Yes
Specific course requirements of all applicants: No
Separate application required: No
Total # of students receiving LD/ADHD/ASD services: 125
Acceptance into program means acceptance into college: Students must be admitted and enrolled in the university first and then request services.

Admissions

Reedley is an open-door admission college. Students present a high school diploma, certificate of high school completion equivalent, or LD/special education test results. There is no minimum GPA or required courses required for admission. ACT/SAT tests are not required for admission. There is a separate application to access services for students with learning disabilities. This application, however, is submitted after admission.

Additional Information

The LD Program services includes 3 main service components of testing, accommodations and instruction: LD assessments, learning strategies instruction from an LD specialist, small class sessions, adaptive instruction, matriculation and integration with mainstream classes, individualized student contact, and specialized educational counseling. In addition, students can access the following accommodations if they provide appropriate documentation: the use of calculators, dictionaries, computers, or spellchecker in exams; extended time on tests; scribes; proctors; oral exams; note-takers; tape recorder in class; books on tape; assistive technology; and priority registration. American Sign Language may be substituted for foreign language, and students are responsible for providing information about their disability to their professors. Transition to College Services provides outreach and support to local high school seniors on an IEP/504 plan. The program is designed to connect high school students with disabilities with services through DSP&S prior to graduating high school. Services may include: online college application assistance, college placement testing, academic advising, completing the DSP&S intake. For more information, contact: Jackie Smith, Transition to College Counselor/Coordinator, Voice: (559) 638-0332, TTY: (559) 638-0356.

General Support Services Information

Contact Information
Name of program or department: Disabled Students Program and Services (DSP&S)
Telephone: 559-638-0332
Fax: 559-638-0382

Accommodations or Services For Students With Learning Differences

Accommodations are decided upon an individual basis after a thorough review of appropriate, current documentation. The accommodations requested must be supported through the documentation provided and must be logically linked to the current impact of the condition on academic functioning.

Allowed in exams
Calculator: Yes
Dictionary: Yes
Computer: Yes
Spellchecker: Yes
Extended test time: Yes
Scribes: Yes
Proctors: Yes
Oral exams: Yes
Note-takers: Yes
Services for students with LD: Yes
Services for students with ADHD: Yes
Services for students with ASD: Yes
Distraction-reduced environment: Yes
Tape recording in class: Yes
Audio books: NR
Electronic texts: Yes
Kurzweil Reader: Yes
Other assistive technology: Yes
Priority registration: Yes
Added costs for services: No
LD specialists: Yes
ADHD coaching: NR
ASD specialists: NR
Professional tutors: No
Peer tutors: Yes
Max. hours/wk. for services: Unlimited
How professors are notified of LD/ADHD: By student

General Admissions Information

Office of Admissions: NR

Entrance Requirements

Application deadline: None
Notification: Rolling
Average GPA: NR
ACT Composite middle 50% range: NR-NR
SAT Math middle 50% range: NR-NR
SAT Critical Reading middle 50% range: NR-NR
SAT Writing middle 50% range: NR-NR
Graduated top 10% of class: NR
Graduated top 25% of class: NR
Graduated top 50% of class: NR

COLLEGE GRADUATION REQUIREMENTS

Additional Information

Environment: The college is located 30 miles southeast of Fresno.

Student Body
Undergrad enrollment: 7,718
% Women: 56
% Men: 44
% Out-of-state: NR

Cost information
Out-of-state tuition: $3,977.00
Room & board: NR

Housing Information
University Housing: Yes
Percent living on campus: NR

Greek System
Fraternity: No
Sorority: No
Athletics: NJCAA

San Diego State University

5500 Campanile Dr, San Diego, CA 92182-7455
Phone: 619-594-6336
Web: www.sdsu.edu
Support: CS • Institution: Public

Programs or Services for Students with Learning Differences

The Learning Disability Program at San Diego State is part of Student Disability Services. The LD Program is designed to provide assessment, accommodations, and advocacy. Students must provide documentation prior to receiving services. Students with learning disabilities may be assessed using nationally standardized batteries. The university believes that students with learning disabilities can be successful at San Diego State and will provide the appropriate services to foster their success.

Admission Information for Students with Learning Differences

College entrance test required: Yes
Interview required: Not Applicable
Essay required: Not Applicable
Additional Application Required for LD/ADHD/ASD: Yes
What documentation required for LD: Documentation is evaluated on a case-by-case basis. Typically successful documentation includes a recent psycho-educational evaluation, history of accommodations and evidence of functional limitations.
With general application: No
To receive services after enrolling: Yes
What documentation required for ADHD: Evaluation from appropriately trained licensed professional documenting diagnosis.
With general application: No
To receive services after enrolling: Yes
What documentation required for ASD: Documentation is evaluated on a case-by-case basis. Typically successful documentation includes a recent psycho-educational evaluation, history of accommodations and evidence of functional limitations.
With general application: No
To receive services after enrolling: Yes
LD/ADHD/ASD documentation submitted to: Student Disability Services
ASD Specific Program: NR
Special Ed. HS course work accepted: Not Applicable
Specific course requirements of all applicants: Yes
Separate application required for program services: Yes
Total # of students receiving LD/ADHD/ASD services: NR
Acceptance into program means acceptance into college: No

Admissions

Students with disabilities must meet the university's admissions criteria. Under exceptional circumstances, students who are denied admission may appeal the decision. If the circumstances involve disability, contact Student Disability Services. Applicants must have 4 years English, 3 years math, 2 years social science, 2 years lab science, 2 years foreign language, 1 year visual or performing arts (in same course), and 1 year academic elective. Students are evaluated based on identified major and are ranked against other applicants in same major.

Additional Information

Students are encouraged to get volunteer note-takers from among other students enrolled in the class. Limited tutoring is available based on documented functional limitations related to subject matter. Tutoring, when authorized, is available at no charge. Students with learning disabilities may request permission to tape a lecture. Students will also need permission from the professor to use a calculator, dictionary, computer, or spellchecker in exams. High Tech Center is an assistive technology center available to students with disabilities. Services and accommodations are available for undergraduates and graduate students.

General Support Services Information

Contact Information
Name of program or department: Student Disability Services
Telephone: 619-564-6473
Fax: 619-594-4315
Website: http://newscenter.sdsu.edu/student_affairs/sds/

Accommodations or Services For Students With Learning Differences

Accommodations are decided upon an individual basis after a thorough review of appropriate, current documentation. The accommodations requests must be supported through the documentation provided and must be logically linked to the current impact of the condition on academic functioning.

Allowed in exams
Calculator: Yes
Dictionary: Yes
Computer: Yes
Spellchecker: Yes
Extended test time: Yes
Scribes: Yes
Proctors: Yes
Oral exams: Yes
Note-takers: Yes
Support services for students with LD: Yes
Support services for students with ADHD: Yes
Support services for students with ASD: Yes
Distraction-reduced environment: Yes
Tape recording in class: Yes
Electronic texts: Yes
Kurzweil reader: NR
Audio books: Yes
Other assistive technology: Yes
Priority registration: Yes
Added costs of services: No
LD specialists: Yes
ADHD coaching: No
ASD specialists: Yes
Professional tutors: Yes
Peer tutors: Yes
Max. hours/wk. for services: NR
How professors are notified of student approved accommodations: By student

General Admissions Information

Office of Admissions: 619-594-6336

Entrance Requirements

Academic units required: 4 English, 3 math, 2 science, 2 science labs, 2 foreign language, 1 social studies, 1 history, 1 academic electives, 1 visual/performing arts. **Academic units recommended:** 4 math. High school diploma is required and GED is accepted. SAT or ACT required. If ACT, ACT with writing accepted. TOEFL required of all international applicants: minimum paper TOEFL 550 or minimum internet TOEFL 80.

Application deadline: 11/30
Notification: NR
Average GPA: 3.69
ACT Composite middle 50% range: 22-28
SAT Math middle 50% range: 510-630
SAT Critical Reading middle 50% range: 500-600
SAT Writing middle 50% range: 490-590
Graduate top 10% of class: 33
Graduated top 25% of class: 73
Graduated top 50% of class: 96

COLLEGE GRADUATION REQUIREMENTS

Course waivers allowed: No
Course substitutions allowed: Yes
In what course: Mathematics; Foreign Language

Additional Information

Environment: This public school was founded in 1897. It has a 300-acre campus.

Student Body
Undergrad enrollment: 29,234
% Women: 54
% Men: 46
% Out-of-state: 8

Cost information
In-state tuition: $5,472
Out-of-state tuition: $16,632
Room & board: $15,826

Housing Information
University Housing: Yes
Percent living on campus: 15

Greek System
Fraternity: Yes
Sorority: Yes
Athletics: Division I

San Francisco State University

1600 Holloway Avenue, San Francisco, CA 93132
Phone: 415-338-6486 • Fax: 415-338-3880
E-mail: ugadmit@sfsu.edu • Web: www.sfsu.edu
Support: CS • Institution: Public

Programs or Services for Students with Learning Differences

The Disability Program and Resource Center (DPRC) is available to promote and provide equal access to the classroom and campus-related activities. A full range of support services is provided so that students may define and achieve personal autonomy at SFSU. The staff is sensitive to the diversity of disabilities, including those only recently recognized as disabilities requiring reasonable accommodations. Confidential support services are available. All students registered with DPRC are eligible for disability management advising. This consists of helping students access services from DPRC; manage DPRC services and school in general; problem-solve conflicts/concerns that are disability-related with individuals, programs, and services on campus; and understand "reasonable accommodation" under the law. Generally, the campus community is sensitive, but if an oversight occurs, students do have protection under Section 504 and the ADA. Students are encouraged to contact DPRC for guidance in pursuing a grievance. Resolution of a violation can often be achieved informally without completing the formal grievance procedure.

Admission Information for Students with Learning Differences

College entrance test required: Yes
Interview required: Yes
Essay required: Yes
Additional Application Required for LD/ADHD/ASD: NR
What documentation required for LD: Psycho ed evaluation to include: relevant historical info, instructional interventions, realted services, age diagnosed, objective data (aptitude, achievement, info processing), test scores (standard, percentile and grade equivalents) and describe functional limitations.
With general application: Gen App ADHD
To receive services after enrolling: Yes
What documentation required for ADHD: Diagnosis based on DSM-V; history of behaviors impairing functioning in academic setting; diagnostic interview; history of symptoms; evidence of ongoing behaviors.
With general application: No
To receive services after enrolling: Yes
What documentation required for ASD: Diagnosis based on DSM-V; history of behaviors impairing functioning in academic setting; diagnostic interview; history of symptom; evidence of ongoing behaviors; psycho ed evaluation.
With general application: Yes
To receive services after enrolling: Yes
LD/ADHD/ASD documentation submitted to: Disability Programs and Resource Center
ASD Specific Program: NR
Special Ed. HS course work accepted: Yes
Specific course requirements of all applicants: Yes
Separate application required for program services: Yes
Total # of students receiving LD/ADHD/ASD services: 571
Acceptance into program means acceptance into college: Students must be admitted and enrolled before requesting services.

Admissions

Students with LD apply to the university through the regular application process. If the student is not eligible for regular admission for a disability-related reason, DPRC can provide special admissions assistance. To obtain special admissions assistance, students need to register with the DPRC office, provide verification of the disability, and notify the Admissions Office that the DPRC has the appropriate verification. When these steps have been taken, the Admissions Office will consult with the DPRC before making a decision. The admissions contact person can request substitutions of high school courses in math, foreign language, and science. Students with LD who are judged unable to fulfill specific requirements may take course substitutions. Substitutions are authorized on an individual basis after review and recommendation by the high school or community college counselor. Students taking substitutions must have 15 units of college-prep study. High school case managers may write summaries and provide a clinical judgment. The DPRC wants information about achievement deficits and may require the student to attend an admissions interview.

Additional Information

The DPRC offers a drop-in center with available tutorial services. The DPRC can also arrange for test accommodations and note-takers and will advocate for the student. The staff is very involved and offers comprehensive services through a team approach. There are no developmental courses offered at the university. However, there are skills classes. Students with documented LD may request assistance in locating tutors. Other services may include registration assistance, campus orientation, note-takers, readers, test-taking assistance, tutoring, disability-related counseling, and referral information. Go to the DPRC website for information on how to register with the department at http://www.sfsu.edu/~dprc/registering.html

General Support Services Information

Contact Information
Name of program or department: Disability Programs and Resource Center
Telephone: 415-338-2472
Fax: 415-338-1041
Website: http://access.sfsu.edu/content/staff

Accommodations or Services For Students With Learning Differences

Accommodations are decided upon an individual basis after a thorough review of appropriate, current documentation. The accommodations requests must be supported through the documentation provided and must be logically linked to the current impact of the condition on academic functioning.

Allowed in exams
Calculator: Yes
Dictionary: Yes
Computer: Yes
Spellchecker: Yes
Extended test time: Yes
Scribes: Ues
Proctors: Yes
Oral exams: No
Note-takers: Yes
Support services for students with LD: Yes
Support services for students with ADHD: Yes
Support services for students with ASD: Yes
Distraction-reduced environment: Yes
Tape recording in class: Ues
Electronic texts: NR
Kurzweil reader: Yes
Audio books: NR
Other assistive technology: Yes
Priority registration: Yes
Added costs of services: Yes
LD specialists: Yes
ADHD coaching: No
ASD specialists: No
Professional tutors: Yes
Peer tutors: Yes
Max. hours/wk. for services: NR
How professors are notified of student approved accommodations: By student

General Admissions Information

Office of Admissions: 415-338-6486

Entrance Requirements

Academic units required: 4 English, 3 math, 2 science, 2 science labs, 2 foreign language, 1 social studies, 1 history, 1 academic electives, 1 visual/performing arts. **Academic units recommended:** 4 English, 4 math, 2 science, 2 science labs, 2 foreign language, 1 social studies, 1 history, 1 academic electives, 1 visual/performing arts. High school diploma is required and GED is accepted. SAT or ACT required. If ACT, ACT with writing accepted. TOEFL required of all international applicants: minimum paper TOEFL 500 or minimum internet TOEFL 61.

Application deadline: 11/30
Notification: Rolling starting 10/1
Average GPA: 3.23
ACT Composite middle 50% range: 18-24
SAT Math middle 50% range: 430-550
SAT Critical Reading middle 50% range: 430-540
SAT Writing middle 50% range: NR-NR
Graduate top 10% of class: NR
Graduated top 25% of class: NR
Graduated top 50% of class: NR

COLLEGE GRADUATION REQUIREMENTS

Course waivers allowed: Yes
Course substitutions allowed: Yes

Additional Information

Environment: This public school was founded in 1899. It has a 142-acre campus.

Student Body
Undergrad enrollment: 26,906
% Women: 56
% Men: 44
% Out-of-state: 1
Cost information
In-state tuition: $5,472
Out-of-state tuition: $16,632
Room & board: $12,234
Housing Information
University Housing: Yes
Percent living on campus: 11.4
Greek System
Fraternity: Yes
Sorority: Yes
Athletics: Division II

San Jose State University

One Washington Square, ADMIN 110, San Jose, CA 95192-0168
Phone: 408-924-6000 • Fax: 408-924-2050
E-mail: aec-info@sjsu.edu • Web: www.sjsu.edu
Support: CS • Institution: Public

Programs or Services for Students with Learning Differences

San Jose State University is a major, comprehensive public university located in the center of San Jose and in the heart of Silicon Valley. SJSU is the oldest state university in California. Its distinctive character has been forged by its long history, by its location, and by its vision—a blend of the old and the new, of the traditional and the innovative. Among its most prized traditions is an uncompromising commitment to offer access to higher education to all persons who meet the criteria for admission, yielding a stimulating mix of age groups, cultures, and economic backgrounds for teaching, learning, and research. SJSU takes pride in and is firmly committed to teaching and learning, with a faculty that is active in scholarship, research, technological innovation, community service, and the arts.

Admission Information for Students with Learning Differences

College entrance test required: Yes
Interview required: No; However students are required to schedule and appointment with a Disability Coordinator.
Essay required: No
Additional application required for LD/ADHD/ASD: NR
What documentation required for LD: WJ and WAIS. DRC will accept the WIAT test results—standard scores are required for all assessments. AEC will accept historical documentation for consideration of services and accommodations.
With general application: No
To receive services after enrolling: Yes
What documentation required for ADHD: Documentation from a licensed professional trained/specializing in AD/HD and licensed to use the DSM IV/V criteria for AD/HD diagnosis
With general application: No
To receive services after enrolling: Yes
What documentation required for ASD: Differential diagnosis of autism—the following professionals would generally be considered qualified to evaluate and diagnose autism spectrum disorders provided they have comprehensive training in the Spectrum Disorders and direct experience with an adolescent or adult autism population: clinical psychologists, neuropsychologists, psychiatrists, and other relevantly trained medical doctors. It is in the student's best interest to provide recent and appropriate documentation; however the AEC will accept historical documentation for consideration of services and accommodations.
With general application: No
To receive services after enrolling: Yes
LD/ADHD/ASD documentation submitted to: Support program/services
ASD Specific Program: NR
Special Ed. HS course work accepted: N/A
Specific course requirements of all applicants: Yes
Separate application required for program services: No
Total # of students receiving LD/ADHD/ASD services: 725
Acceptance into program means acceptance into college: Students must be admitted and enrolled before requesting services.

Admissions

Pre-Admission Counseling—the following are services provided to prospective students: Application Workshops are conducted at local high school and community colleges by an SJSU representative to help you understand how CSUmentor and additional online resources can assist you. Pre-admission counseling is offered in the Student Services Center for prospective students. Pre-admission counseling is an important step in preparing for college as an undergraduate student. An Admission Counselor will review the following information: CSU & EOP application process, the online application process, pre-admissions undergraduate advising, admission requirements for first time freshmen and transfer students, A-G subject requirements, testing, and GPA requirements for first time freshmen, the Four Basic Skill requirements for transfer students.

Additional Information

The Accessible Education Center (AEC) strives to provide an array of academically related services for students with learning disabilities. Accommodations for curriculum requirements are determined on a case-by-case basis and provided specifically for coursework in which learning disability impacts curriculum requirements. Students can be self identified or referred to the AEC. All students are encouraged to meet with professional staff well in advance of the start of classes to discuss their academic needs and to set up appropriate services. An Educational Assistant is employed by the Accessible Education Center (AEC_ to work on a one-to-one basis with a student registered with the AEC, whose disability impairment(s) prevents the student from meeting curriculum requirements. Eligibility for an Educational Assistant is determined by the AEC's Director or Counselors and is determined on a case-by-case basis. Students must meet with the AEC Director or a Coordinator each semester the service is needed.

General Support Services Information

Contact Information
Name of program or department: Accessible Education Center (AEC) formerly The Disability Resource Center
Telephone: 408-924-6000
Fax: 408-924-5999

Accommodations or Services For Students With Learning Differences

Accommodations are decided upon an individual basis after a thorough review of appropriate, current documentation. The accommodations requests must be supported through the documentation provided and must be logically linked to the current impact of the condition on academic functioning.

Allowed in exams
Calculator: Yes
Dictionary: Yes
Computer: Yes
Spellchecker: Yes
Extended test time: Yes
Scribes: Yes
Proctors: Yes
Oral exams: Yes
Note-takers: Yes
Services for students with LD: Yes
Services for students with ADHD: Yes
Services for students with ASD: Yes
Distraction-reduced environment: Yes
Tape recording in class: Yes
Audio books: NR
Electronic texts: NR
Kurzweil Reader: Yes
Other assistive technology: Yes
Priority registration: Yes
Added costs of services: No
LD specialists: Yes
ADHD coaching: NR
ASD specialists: NR
Professional tutors: NR
Peer tutors: NR
How professors are notified of student approved accommodations: Student

General Admissions Information

Office of Admissions: 408-283-7500

Entrance Requirements

Academic units required: 4 English, 3 math, 2 science, 2 science labs, 2 foreign language, 1 social studies, 1 history, 1 academic electives, 1 visual/performing arts. High school diploma is required and GED is accepted. SAT or ACT required. If ACT, ACT with writing accepted. TOEFL required of all international applicants: minimum paper TOEFL 550 or minimum internet TOEFL 80.

Application deadline: 11/30
Notification: Rolling starting 2/22
Average GPA: 3.4
ACT Composite middle 50% range: 20-26
SAT Math middle 50% range: 470-610
SAT Critical Reading middle 50% range: 450-570
SAT Writing middle 50% range: 450-560
Graduated top 10% of class: NR
Graduated top 25% of class: NR
Graduated top 50% of class: NR

COLLEGE GRADUATION REQUIREMENTS

Course waivers allowed: No
Course substitutions allowed: Yes
In what course: General education quantitative reasoning substitutions made on case-by-case basis, must be disability related

Additional Information

Environment: This public school was founded in 1857. It has a 154-acre campus.

Student Body
Undergrad enrollment: 26,822
% Women: 48
% Men: 52
% Out-of-state: 1.02

Cost information
In-state tuition: $5,472
Out-of Tuition: $14,400
Room & board: $14,217

Housing Information
University Housing: Yes
Percent living on campus: 13

Greek System
Fraternity: Yes
Sorority: Yes
Athletics: Division I

Santa Clara University

500 El Camino Real, Santa Clara, CA 95053
Phone: 408-554-4700 • Fax: 408-554-5255
E-mail: Admission@scu.edu • Web: www.scu.edu
Support: CS • Institution: Private

Programs or Services for Students with Learning Differences

The primary mission of Disabilities Resources is to enhance academic progress, promote social involvement, and build bridges connecting the various services of the university for all students. This goal is met by providing: academic intervention programs, opportunities to increase students' personal understanding of their disability, role models, and community outreach. Disabilities Resources is a resource area within the Drahmann Center that helps to ensure equal access to all academic and programmatic activities for students with disabilities. This goal is met through the provision of Academic Support Services, contact with other university offices, educational programming on disability issues for the university, and, most importantly, assistance in teaching students effective self-advocacy skills under the student development model. Students must submit proper documentation to obtain services through the Office of Disability Resources. The documentation needs to have been completed within the past 3 years to be valid and must include a diagnostic statement, the date of the disability's onset, if appropriate; what procedures and measures (formal and informal) were used to assess the condition: what functional limitations there are and how they will affect academics; if appropriate, all psychometric testing results (standard scores or percentile scores); and, if appropriate, what the examiners' recommendations are for specific academic accommodations for a documented disability of ADHD, a narrative listing in history of ADD/ADHD/ASD, must be completed by a certified medical professional addressing treatment plan.

Admission Information for Students with Learning Differences

College entrance test required: Yes
Interview required: No
Essay required: 4
Additional Application Required for LD/ADHD/ASD: NR
What documentation required for LD: Psycho ed evaluation within past 3 years
With general application: No
To receive services after enrolling: Yes
What documentation required for ADHD: Documentation must be done by professional
With general application: No
To receive services after enrolling: Yes
What documentation required for ASD: Documentation by a qualified professional
With general application: No
To receive services after enrolling: Yes
LD/ADHD/ASD documentation submitted to: Disabilities Resources
ASD Specific Program: NR
Special Ed. HS course work accepted: No
Specific course requirements of all applicants: No
Separate application required for program services: Yes
Total # of students receiving LD/ADHD/ASD services: 116
Acceptance into program means acceptance into college: NR

Admissions

Students should meet the minimum high school course requirements: History and Social Science: 3 years English: 4 years, Mathematics: 3 years required; 4 years recommended Laboratory Science: 2 years required; 3 years recommended, Language Other Than English: 2 years required; 3 years recommended; 4 years preferred, Visual and Performing Arts: 1 year recommended. Applicants select one of the academic schools/colleges: the College of Arts and Sciences, the Leavey School of Business, or the School of Engineering. While the selectivity between schools and programs does not vary greatly, academic readiness for the program of interest will be gauged based on a student's expressed interest.

Additional Information

The disabilities resources staff meets individually with students. Some of the academic accommodations provided by DSR include notetaking, library assistance, and test accommodations. Other support services include priority registration; tutoring or academic counseling: and workshops on legal issues and self-advocacy. The DR is in the process of purchasing computer-aided technology to assist the students. Graduate students with learning disabilities are offered the same services and accommodations as those provided for undergraduate students. Students can be better served if the professional documentation they submit specifically identifies the accommodations needed for the student to be successful in college. This should include the student's strengths and weaknesses and any required modifications. All lower division students have access to peer tutoring, drop-in-math lab, and a drop-in-writing center. Some accommodations would need to be approved by the professor.

General Support Services Information

Contact Information
Name of program or department: Disabilities Resources
Telephone: 408-554-4109
Fax: NR
Website: www.scu.edu/disabilities/

Accommodations or Services For Students With Learning Differences

Accommodations are decided upon an individual basis after a thorough review of appropriate, current documentation. The accommodations requests must be supported through the documentation provided and must be logically linked to the current impact of the condition on academic functioning.

Allowed in exams
Calculator: Yes
Dictionary: Yes
Computer: Yes
Spellchecker: Yes
Extended test time: Yes
Scribes: Yes
Proctors: Yes
Oral exams: No
Note-takers: Yes
Support services for students with LD: Yes
Support services for students with ADHD: Yes
Support services for students with ASD: NR
Distraction-reduced environment: Yes
Tape recording in class: Yes
Electronic texts: NR
Kurzweil reader: Yes
Audio books: Yes
Other assistive technology: Yes
Priority registration: Yes
Added costs of services: No
LD specialists: Yes
ADHD coaching: NR
ASD specialists: NR
Professional tutors: No
Peer tutors: Yes
Max. hours/wk. for services: NR
How professors are notified of student approved accommodations: Both student and director

General Admissions Information

Office of Admissions: 408-554-4700

Entrance Requirements

Academic units required: 4 English, 3 math, 2 science, 2 science labs, 2 foreign language, 3 social studies, 1 academic electives. **Academic units recommended:** 4 English, 4 math, 3 science labs, 3 social studies, 1 academic electives, 1 visual/performing arts. High school diploma is required and GED is not accepted. SAT or ACT required. If ACT, ACT with writing accepted. TOEFL required of all international applicants: minimum paper TOEFL 575 or minimum internet TOEFL 90.

Application deadline: 1/7
Notification: NR
Average GPA: 3.67
ACT Composite middle 50% range: 27-32
SAT Math middle 50% range: 620-710
SAT Critical Reading middle 50% range: 590-690
SAT Writing middle 50% range: NR-NR
Graduate top 10% of class: 50
Graduated top 25% of class: 83
Graduated top 50% of class: 98

COLLEGE GRADUATION REQUIREMENTS

Course waivers allowed: NR
Course substitutions allowed: NR

Additional Information

Environment: This private school, affiliated with the Roman Catholic Church, was founded in 1851. It has a 106-acre campus.

Student Body
Undergrad enrollment: 5,385
% Women: 49
% Men: 51
% Out-of-state: 27
Cost information
Room & board: $13,965
Housing Information
University Housing: Yes
Percent living on campus: 52
Greek System
Fraternity: No
Sorority: No
Athletics: Division I

Santa Monica College

1900 Pico Boulevard, Santa Monica, CA 90405
Phone: 310-434-4000 • Fax: 310-434-3645
E-mail: admission@smc.edu • Web: www.smc.edu
Support: CS • Institution type: 2-year public

Programs or Services for Students with Learning Differences

The college is dedicated to helping students with LD achieve their goals by assisting them in becoming independent, college students. These goals are met by screening, testing, and certifying learning disabilities; developing individual plans and recommending appropriate academic accommodations to provide academic equity; and teaching compensatory learning strategies and fostering self-awareness of learning strengths and weaknesses. Students must be evaluated to determine eligibility for the program. This evaluation is achieved in an 8-week assessment workshop where students discover their learning strengths and weaknesses through a series of tasks. Academic and thinking skills are assessed. Test results will be compared to guidelines provided by the State of California, to determine whether a student qualifies for ongoing support services student with LD. The LD specialist interprets test results and makes individual recommendations on how to improve learning and study strategies.

Admission Information for Students with Learning Differences

College entrance tests required: No
Interview required: No
Essay required: No
Additional application required for LD/ADHD/ASD: NR
What documentation required for LD: Psycho ed evaluation to include: relevant historical info, instructional interventions, related services, age diagnosed, objective data (aptitude, achievement, info processing), test scores (standard, percentile and grade equivalents) and describe functional limitations.
With general application: No
To receive services after enrolling: Yes
What documentation required for ADHD: Diagnosis based on DSM-V; history of behaviors impairing functioning in academic setting; diagnostic interview; history of symptoms; evidence of ongoing behaviors.
With general application: No
To receive services after enrolling: Yes
What documentation required for ASD: Psycho ed evaluation
With general application: NR
To receive services after enrolling: Yes
LD/ADHD/ASD documentation submitted to: Center for Students with Disabilities
ASD Specific Program: NR
Special Ed. HS course work accepted: Yes
Specific course requirements for all applicants: No
Separate application required: Yes
Acceptance into program means acceptance into college: Students must be admitted and enrolled in the university first and then request services.

Admissions

Students may enroll at Santa Monica College if they have graduated from high school, are 18 or 16 years and submit a Student Score Report for passing the California High School Proficiency examination. Assessment tests are required to enroll in English or math courses unless the student meets the exemption criteria. Orientations can be completed in person or online. After the orientation, the student will be able to proceed with enrollment.

Additional Information

After the assessment process, an Individual Educational Plan is developed with recommendations for needed skills training and appropriate accommodations. Following is a list of accommodations and services that the student may be eligible for as indicated in his/her educational plan: Test Proctoring; Priority Registration when appropriate; Volunteer Note takers; Alternate Media; Study Strategies Classes; Tutoring; High Tech Training Center; Academic Advisement (DSPS Counselor). Learning Disabilities Study Strategy Classes: Counseling 51: Test taking/Memory Strategies; Counseling 52: Textbook/Memory Strategies; Counseling 54: Organizational Strategies; Counseling 56: Written Language Strategies; Counseling 57: Listening, Note taking and Memory; Counseling 58: Math Strategies; Counseling 59: Textbook Strategies Using Technology Services at High Tech Training Center. *Teach courses in industry-standard applications integrated with assistive technology and ergonomics to students with disabilities enrolled in SMC academic courses.

General Support Services Information

Contact Information
Name of program or department: Learning Disability Program/Center for Students with Disabilities
Telephone: 310-434-4265
Fax: 310-434-4272

Accommodations or Services For Students With Learning Differences

Accommodations are decided upon an individual basis after a thorough review of appropriate, current documentation. The accommodations requested must be supported through the documentation provided and must be logically linked to the current impact of the condition on academic functioning.

Allowed in exams
Calculator: Yes
Dictionary: Yes
Computer: Yes
Spellchecker: Yes
Extended test time: Yes
Scribes: No
Proctors: Yes
Oral exams: Yes
Note-takers: Yes
Services for students with LD: Yes
Services for students with ADHD: Yes
Services for students with ASD: Yes
Distraction-reduced environment: Yes
Tape recording in class: Yes
Audio books: NR
Electronic texts: Yes
Kurzweil Reader: Yes
Other assistive technology: Yes
Priority registration: Yes
Added costs for services: No
LD specialists: Yes
ADHD coaching: NR
ASD specialists: NR
Professional tutors: No
Peer tutors: Yes
Max. hours/wk. for services: N/A
How professors are notified of LD/ADHD: By student

General Admissions Information

Office of Admissions: NR

Entrance Requirements

Application deadline: NR
Notification: NR
Average GPA: NR
ACT Composite middle 50% range: NR-NR
SAT Math middle 50% range: NR-NR
SAT Critical Reading middle 50% range: NR-NR
SAT Writing middle 50% range: NR-NR
Graduated top 10% of class: NR
Graduated top 25% of class: NR
Graduated top 50% of class: NR

COLLEGE GRADUATION REQUIREMENTS

Course waivers allowed: Yes
In what course: Math proficiency exam
Course substitutions allowed: Yes
In what course: Math proficiency exam

Additional Information

Environment: NR

Student Body
Undergrad enrollment: 30,619
% Women: 53
% Men: 47
% Out-of-state: NR

Cost information
In-state Tuition: $1,600
Out-of-state Tuition: $9,000
Room & board: N/A

Housing Information
University Housing: Yes
Percent living on campus: N/A

Greek System
Fraternity: No
Sorority: No
Athletics: NJCAA

Santa Rosa Junior College

Santa Rosa Campus: 1501 Mendocino Avenue, Santa Rosa, CA 95401
Phone: 707-527-4685 • Fax: 707-527-4798
Petaluma Campus: 680 Sonoma Mtn. Parkway, Petaluma, CA 94954
Phone: 707-527-4685 • Fax: 707-527-4798
E-mail: admininfo@santarosa.edu • Web: www.santarosa.edu
Support: CS • Institution type: 2-year public

Programs or Services for Students with Learning Differences

The Disability Resources Department provides students with disabilities equal access to a community college education by providing academic accommodations, support services, and advocacy services. Santa Rosa Junior College is a state supported community college that accepts all students who apply for and meet the state eligibility criteria for general admission to the college. In order to receive disability services, valid documentation that verifies a learning disability must be submitted. Learning disabilities testing must have been completed by a licensed, qualified professional using appropriate standardized testing. Santa Rosa Junior College creates a campus climate in which diverse learning styles and equal access for students with disabilities can be realized.

Admission Information for Students with Learning Differences

College entrance tests required: No
Interview required: No
Essay required: No
Additional application required for LD/ADHD/ASD: NR
What documentation required for LD: Psycho ed evaluation to include: relevant historical info, instructional interventions, related services, age diagnosed, objective data (aptitude, achievement, info processing), test scores (standard, percentile and grade equivalents) and describe functional limitations.
With general application: No
To receive services after enrolling: Yes
What documentation required for ADHD: Diagnosis based on DSM-V; history of behaviors impairing functioning in academic setting; diagnostic interview; history of symptoms; evidence of ongoing behaviors.
With general application: No
To receive services after enrolling: Yes
What documentation required for ASD: Psycho ed evaluation
With general application: NR
To receive services after enrolling: Yes
LD/ADHD/ASD documentation submitted to: Disability Resources
ASD Specific Program: NR
Special Ed. HS course work accepted: Yes
Specific course requirements of all applicants: No
Separate application required: No
Total # of students receiving LD/ADHD/ASD services: 500
Acceptance into program means acceptance into college: Students must be admitted and enrolled in the college first and then request services.

Admissions

Admission to Santa Rosa is open to students with a high school diploma or a GED, or are 18 years of age or older. Students with learning disabilities must meet state eligibility requirements verifying a learning disability to qualify for services. Students must demonstrate: average to above-average intellectual ability, adequate measured achievement in at least one academic area or employment setting, a severe processing deficit in one or more areas, and a severe discrepancy between aptitude and achievement in one or more academic areas. All students must demonstrate appropriate behavior and an ability to benefit from the instructional program.

Additional Information

The College Skills Program offers limited specialized classes. Support services include limited assessment for learning disabilities, advising, assistive technology, alternate media, and liaison. Services are also provided to students with medical verification of other disabilities, such as blind/low-vision, deaf/hearing impaired, physical disabilities, psychological disabilities, chronic health impaired, etc.

General Support Services Information

Contact Information
Name of program or department: Disability Resources Department
Santa Rosa Campus: Telephone: 707-527-4278
Fax: 707-524-1768
Petaluma Campus:Telephone: 707-778-2492
Fax: 707-778-2497

Accommodations or Services For Students With Learning Differences

Accommodations are decided upon an individual basis after a thorough review of appropriate, current documentation. The accommodations requested must be supported through the documentation provided.

Allowed in exams
Calculator: Yes
Dictionary: Yes
Computer: Yes
Spellchecker: Yes
Extended test time: Yes
Scribes: Yes
Proctors: Yes
Oral exams: Yes
Note-takers: Yes
Services for students with LD: Yes
Services for students with ADHD: Yes
Services for students with ASD: Yes
Distraction-reduced environment: Yes
Tape recording in class: Yes
Audio books: NR
Electronic texts: Yes
Kurzweil Reader: NR
Other assistive technology: NR
Priority registration: Yes
Added costs for services: No
LD specialists: Yes
ADHD coaching: NR
ASD specialists: NR
Professional tutors: NR
Peer tutors: NR
Max. hours/wk. for services: NR
How professors are notified of LD/ADHD: By student

General Admissions Information

Office of Admissions: NR

Entrance Requirements

Application deadline: NR
Notification: NR
Average GPA: NR
ACT Composite middle 50% range: NR-NR
SAT Math middle 50% range: NR-NR
SAT Critical Reading middle 50% range: NR-NR
SAT Writing middle 50% range: NR-NR
Graduated top 10% of class: NR
Graduated top 25% of class: NR
Graduated top 50% of class: NR

COLLEGE GRADUATION REQUIREMENTS

Course waivers allowed: Yes
In what course: Student must attempt math course/s before a waiver is granted.
Course substitutions allowed: No

Additional Information

Environment: NR

Student Body
Undergrad enrollment: NR
% Women: NR
% Men: NR
% Out-of-state: NR

Cost information
Room & board: NR

Housing Information
University Housing: No
Percent living on campus: NR

Greek System
Fraternity: No
Sorority: No
Athletics: NR

Sierra College

5000 Rocklin Road, Rocklin, CA 95677
Phone: 916-789-0553 • Fax: 916-789-2967
E-mail: gmodder@sierracollege.edu • Web: www.sierracollege.edu
Support: CS • Institution type: 2-year public

Programs or Services for Students with Learning Differences

The goals of the Learning Opportunity Center are to assist students with learning disabilities in reaching their academic/vocational goals, help the students strengthen and develop their perceptual skills, and provide the support needed to maximize student success. Sierra College subscribes to the psychometric-evaluation model established by the California Community College System. This six-step process includes intake screening, measured achievement, ability level, processing deficit, aptitude-achievement discrepancy, and eligibility recommendation. Students are evaluated individually through the Learning Disabilities Orientation course. This is a mainstreamed program with no special classes, but it does provide support and accommodations for students with learning disabilities.

Admission Information for Students with Learning Differences

College entrance tests required: No
Interview required: No
Essay required: No
Additional application required for LD/ADHD/ASD: NR
What documentation required for LD: Psycho ed evaluation to include: relevant historical info, instructional interventions, related services, age diagnosed, objective data (aptitude, achievement, info processing), test scores (standard, percentile and grade equivalents) and describe functional limitations.
With general application: No
To receive services after enrolling: Yes
What documentation required for ADHD: Diagnosis based on DSM-V; history of behaviors impairing functioning in academic setting; diagnostic interview; history of symptoms; evidence of ongoing behaviors.
With general application: No
To receive services after enrolling: Yes
What documentation required for ASD: Psycho ed evaluation
With general application: NR
To receive services after enrolling: Yes
LD/ADHD/ASD documentation submitted to: Disabled Student Program and Services
ASD Specific Program: NR
Special Ed. HS course work accepted: Yes
Specific course requirements for all applicants: NR
Separate application required: No
Total # of students receiving LD/ADHD/ASD services: 350
Acceptance into program means acceptance into college: Students must be admitted and enrolled in the university first and then request services.

Admissions

Sierra College has an open admissions policy for those students who meet the regular entrance requirements. ACT/SAT are not required, and there are no cutoffs for GPA, class rank, or test scores. Additionally, no specific courses are required for admission. Any student who holds a high school diploma or GED is admitted. Services are provided to all enrolled students with appropriate documentation.

Additional Information

To receive services and accommodations, students must meet the eligibility requirements set forth by the state of California for students with learning disabilities. Skills courses are available in reading, math, writing, study strategies, English as a second language, and spelling. These skills classes are offered for college credit. In addition, students can get assistance in test-taking techniques, priority registration, and peer tutoring. Other services include assessment and evaluation of learning disabilities, individual education plans, identification of students' learning styles and modalities, perceptual training programs, test-taking facilitation, compensatory learning strategies/techniques, computer-assisted instruction, and classroom accommodations. They screen for ADD/ADHD and Visual Perception. They offer classes to improve perceptual skills.

General Support Services Information

Contact Information
Name of program or department: Learning Opportunities Center/Disabled Student Programs and Services (DSP&S)
Telephone: 916-789-2939

Accommodations or Services For Students With Learning Differences

Accommodations are decided upon an individual basis after a thorough review of appropriate, current documentation. The accommodations requested must be supported through the documentation provided and must be logically linked to the current impact of the condition on academic functioning.

Allowed in exams
Calculator: Yes
Dictionary: Yes
Computer: Yes
Spellchecker: Yes
Extended test time: Yes
Scribes: No
Proctors: Yes
Oral exams: Yes
Note-takers: Yes
Services for students with LD: Yes
Services for students with ADHD: Yes
Services for students with ASD: Yes
Distraction-reduced environment: Yes
Tape recording in class: Yes
Audio books: NR
Electronic texts: Yes
Kurzweil Reader: No
Other assistive technology: Yes
Priority registration: Yes
Added costs for services: No
LD specialists: Yes
ADHD coaching: NR
ASD specialists: NR
Professional tutors: No
Peer tutors: Approximately 100
Max. hours/wk. for services: Unlimited
How professors are notified of LD/ADHD: By student

General Admissions Information

Office of Admissions: NR

Entrance Requirements

Application deadline: NR
Notification: NR
Average GPA: NR
ACT Composite middle 50% range: NR-NR
SAT Math middle 50% range: NR-NR
SAT Critical Reading middle 50% range: NR-NR
SAT Writing middle 50% range: NR-NR
Graduated top 10% of class: NR
Graduated top 25% of class: NR
Graduated top 50% of class: NR

COLLEGE GRADUATION REQUIREMENTS

Course waivers allowed: Yes
In what course: Waivers are provided on an individual basis.
Course substitutions allowed: Yes
In what course: Substitutions are provided on an individual basis.

Additional Information

Environment: The campus is located in the foothills of the Sierra Nevada Mountains, approximately twenty minutes from Sacramento and 105 miles east of San Francisco.

Student Body
Undergrad enrollment: 34,900
% Women: 52
% Men: 48
% Out-of-state: NR

Cost information
Room & board: $3,700/semester

Housing Information
University Housing: Yes
Percent living on campus: NR

Greek System
Fraternity: No
Sorority: No
Athletics: NJCAA

Sonoma State University

1801 East Cotati Avenue, Rohnert Park, CA 94928
Phone: 707-664-2778 • Fax: 707-664-2060
E-mail: student.outreach@sonoma.edu • Web: www.sonoma.edu
Support: S • Institution: Public

Programs or Services for Students with Learning Differences

Disability Services for Students ensures that people with disabilities receive equal access to higher education. We work to protect and promote the civil rights of students with disabilities. We challenge and support students to develop self-determination and independence as people with disabilities. In reaching its determinations about appropriate accommodations, DSS considers factors such as the documentation from professionals specializing in the area of the student's diagnosed disability, the student's functional limitations, and the student's input and accommodation history in regard to particular needs and limitations. DSS works with the student and relevant faculty and staff through an interactive process designed to achieve an accommodation that meets the needs of all parties.

Admission Information for Students with Learning Differences

College entrance test required: Yes
Interview required: No
Essay required: No
Additional application required for LD/ADHD/ASD: NR
What documentation required for LD: http://www.sonoma.edu/dss/media/print/ld_guidelines.pdf
With general application: No
To receive services after enrolling: Yes
What documentation required for ADHD: http://www.sonoma.edu/dss/media/print/certification_adhd.pdf
With general application: No
To receive services after enrolling: Yes
What documentation required for ASD: Psycho ed evaluation
With general application: NR
To receive services after enrolling: Yes
LD/ADHD/ASD documentation submitted to: Disability Support Services
ASD Specific Program: NR
Special Ed. HS course work accepted: No
Specific course requirements of all applicants: Yes
Separate application required for program services: 3
Total # of students receiving LD/ADHD/ASD services: NR
Acceptance into program means acceptance into college: NR

Admissions

Admission to Sonoma State University is competitive since we receive more applications than we can accommodate. Under special provisions approved by the California State University, Sonoma State University utilizes a combination of the undergraduate admissions requirements outlined in the Basic California State University Admissions Requirements. Supplementary admissions criteria for first-time freshmen include, but are not limited to, high school grade point averages, test scores (SAT I or ACT), and high school course preparation. In order to be considered for admission, you must file a complete undergraduate application at CSU Mentor. Sonoma State University is a selective admissions campus. Therefore it is important to apply during the designated applications periods. Wherever possible, we admit students on a rolling basis upon completion of an admissions file. So early application and prompt response to requests for application support documents will speed your admissions notification. Determination and Notification of Admission: After applications for admission have been received in the Office of Admissions and Records, they are processed and matched with required transcripts and test scores. Evaluation of the records is made to determine whether applicants meet the admissions requirements.

Additional Information

The Disability Services for Students office (DSS) welcomes Sonoma State University students who are interested in receiving accommodation services related to their disability. The Learning Center provides academic support services including tutorial services for students with learning differences(no fee). The Learning Skills Service Program provides individualized instruction, computer based learning, learning plans based on learning strengths and multiple intelligences, mentoring with PALs, study skills workshops, and small group tutoring. The Tutorial Center provides individual and small group learning assistance in a broad range of academic subjects.

General Support Services Information

Contact Information
Name of program or department: Disability Services for Students
Telephone: 707-664-2677
Fax: 707-664-3330

Accommodations or Services For Students With Learning Differences

Accommodations are decided upon an individual basis after a thorough review of appropriate, current documentation. The accommodations requests must be supported through the documentation provided and must be logically linked to the current impact of the condition on academic functioning.

Allowed in exams
Calculator: Yes
Dictionary: Yes
Computer: Yes
Spellchecker: Yes
Extended test time: Yes
Scribes: Yes
Proctors: Yes
Oral exams: Yes
Note-takers: Yes
Services for students with LD: Yes
Services for students with ADHD: Yes
Services for students with ASD: Yes
Distraction-reduced environment: Yes
Tape recording in class: Yes
Audio books from learning ally: Yes
Electronic texts: NR
Kurzweil Reader: Yes
Other assistive technology: Yes
Priority registration: Yes
Added costs of services: No
LD specialists: No
ADHD coaching: NR
ASD specialists: NR
Professional tutors: NR
Peer tutors: NR
How professors are notified of student approved accommodations: Student

General Admissions Information

Office of Admissions: 707-664-2778

Entrance Requirements

Academic units required: 4 English, 3 math, 2 science, 1 science labs, 2 foreign language, 2 history, 1 academic electives, 1 visual/performing arts, and 1 units from above areas or other academic areas. High school diploma is required and GED is accepted. SAT or ACT required. If ACT, ACT with writing accepted. TOEFL required of all international applicants: minimum paper TOEFL 500 or minimum internet TOEFL 61.

Application deadline: 11/30
Notification: Rolling starting 11/1
Average GPA: 3.21
ACT Composite middle 50% range: 19-24
SAT Math middle 50% range: 440-550
SAT Critical Reading middle 50% range: 440-550
SAT Writing middle 50% range: 440-540
Graduated top 10% of class: NR
Graduated top 25% of class: NR
Graduated top 50% of class: NR

COLLEGE GRADUATION REQUIREMENTS

Course waivers allowed: No
Course substitutions allowed: Yes
In What Courses: Case by case basis

Additional Information

Environment: This public school was founded in 1960. It has a 269-acre campus.

Student Body
Undergrad enrollment: 8,615
% Women: 62
% Men: 38
% Out-of-state: NR

Cost information
Out-of Tuition: $16,632
Room & board: $11,799

Housing Information
University Housing: Yes
Percent living on campus: 22

Greek System
Fraternity: Yes
Sorority: Yes
Athletics: Division II

STANFORD UNIVERSITY

Undergraduate Admission, Stanford, CA 94305-6106
Phone: 650-723-2091 • Fax: 650-725-2846
E-mail: admission@stanford.edu • Web: www.stanford.edu
Support: CS • Institution: Private

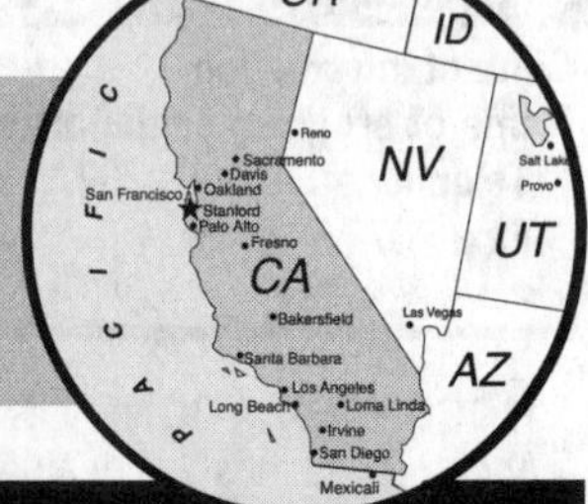

PROGRAMS OR SERVICES FOR STUDENTS WITH LEARNING DIFFERENCES

The Office of Accessible Education (OAE) provides services and resources to students with disabilities. Students who may be eligible for services have a variety of disabilities, including mobility impairments, chronic illness, sensory disabilities, learning disabilities, and psychological disabilities. The center's goal is to enable students with disabilities to participate fully in the educational experience at Stanford while meeting the academic standards maintained by the University. The Schwab Learning Center, affiliated with the OAE, offers enhanced services specifically for students with learning disabilities and attention deficit hyperactivity disorder. The center was established in 2002 by an endowment from Charles and Helen Schwab. Services may include screening assessments for learning disabilities, individual learning strategy sessions, individual tutoring in various academic disciplines, workshops for faculty and teaching staff, as well as community outreach programs. The funding support provided by Mr. and Mrs. Schwab allows Stanford University to offer services and resources above and beyond what is required by federal and state disability laws.

ADMISSION INFORMATION FOR STUDENTS WITH LEARNING DIFFERENCES

College entrance test required: Yes
Interview required: No
Essay required: Not Applicable
Additional Application Required for LD/ADHD/ASD: NR
What documentation required for LD: Documentation from students with Attention-Deficit Hyperactivity/ Disorder (ADHD) attending Stanford University must demonstrate the current functional impact of the disability on one or more major life activities (e.g., concentrating, learning, thinking,
With general application: No
To receive services after enrolling: Yes
What documentation required for ADHD: Psycho ed evaluation
With general application: No
To receive services after enrolling: Yes
What documentation required for ASD: Documentation from students with a Learning Disability attending Stanford University must demonstrate the current functional impact of the disability on one or more major life activities (e.g., reading, learning, concentrating, thinking, working etc.) and
With general application: No
To receive services after enrolling: Yes
LD/ADHD/ASD documentation submitted to: Office of Accessible Education
ASD Specific Program: NR
Special Ed. HS course work accepted: NR
Specific course requirements of all applicants: Yes
Separate application required for program services: NR
Total # of students receiving LD/ADHD/ASD services: NR
Acceptance into program means acceptance into college: No

ADMISSIONS

Stanford seeks to enroll students with excellent academic records who show evidence of their personal achievement outside the classroom and who have used the resources available to them to their fullest potential. The policy on the admissions of students iwth learning disabilities makes clear there is now separate academic program. Students should take a strong college-preparatory curriculum, including honors and Advanced Placement courses.

ADDITIONAL INFORMATION

Students seeking services or accommodations for specific learning disabilities or attention deficit hyperactivity disorder must submit psychoeducational evaluations that are recent enough to reflect current levels of functioning. There are no skill courses offered. Tutoring is available through the SLC and on campus through the Center for Teaching and Learning. A peer support group is available. Other accommodations can include note-taking services, typist/scribe services, course materials in alternate format, letters to professors for course/exam accommodations, and exam room accommodation. Services and accommodations are offered to undergraduate and graduate students.

General Support Services Information

Contact Information
Name of program or department: Office of Accessible Education
Telephone: 650-723-1066
Fax: NR
Website: NR

Accommodations or Services For Students With Learning Differences

Accommodations are decided upon an individual basis after a thorough review of appropriate, current documentation. The accommodations requests must be supported through the documentation provided and must be logically linked to the current impact of the condition on academic functioning.

Allowed in exams
Calculator: Yes
Dictionary: Yes
Computer: Yes
Spellchecker: Yes
Extended test time: Yes
Scribes: Yes
Proctors: No
Oral exams: No
Note-takers: Yes
Support services for students with LD: Yes
Support services for students with ADHD: Yes
Support services for students with ASD: Yes
Distraction-reduced environment: Yes
Tape recording in class: Yes
Electronic texts: Yes
Kurzweil reader: NR
Audio books: Yes
Other assistive technology: Yes
Priority registration: No
Added costs of services: No
LD specialists: Yes
ADHD coaching: NR
ASD specialists: Yes
Professional tutors: Yes
Peer tutors: Yes
Max. hours/wk. for services: 10
How professors are notified of student approved accommodations: By student

General Admissions Information

Office of Admissions: 650-723-2091

Entrance Requirements

Academic units recommended: 4 English, 4 math, 3 science, 3 science labs, 3 foreign language, 3 social studies, 3 history. High school diploma is required and GED is accepted. SAT or ACT required. If ACT, ACT with writing required.

Application deadline: 1/3
Notification: 4/1
Average GPA: 3.95
ACT Composite middle 50% range: 31-35
SAT Math middle 50% range: 700-800
SAT Critical Reading middle 50% range: 690-780
SAT Writing middle 50% range: 690-780
Graduate top 10% of class: 96
Graduated top 25% of class: 99
Graduated top 50% of class: 100

COLLEGE GRADUATION REQUIREMENTS

Course waivers allowed: No
Course substitutions allowed: Yes

Additional Information

Environment: This private school was founded in 1885. It has a 8180-acre campus.

Student Body
Undergrad enrollment: 6,999
% Women: 48
% Men: 52
% Out-of-state: 61

Cost information
Tuition: $45,729
Room & board: $14,107

Housing Information
University Housing: Yes
Percent living on campus: 93

Greek System
Fraternity: Yes
Sorority: Yes
Athletics: Division I

U. of California—Berkeley

110 Sproul Hall, Berkeley, CA 94720-5800
Phone: 510-642-3175 • Fax: 510-642-7333
E-mail: 510-642-3175 • Web: www.berkeley.edu
Support: CS • Institution: Public

Programs or Services for Students with Learning Differences

The Disabled Student Program (DSP) seeks to ensure that students with disabilities have equal access to educational opportunities and student life at UC—Berkeley. DSP works to sustain a supportive environment that provides appropriate and necessary disability-related accommodations, enables students to demonstrate their knowledge and skills, facilitates students' success in academic pursuits, and promotes independence. DSP's services assist students as they develop their skills and the qualities needed to meet their educational, personal, and professional goals. DSP also works to support the efforts of the campus community to ensure full participation of students with disabilities in every aspect of university life. DSP is a recipient of a TRIO Student Support Services Grant. Funds are used to provide a variety of services for students, helping them to achieve academic success, complete graduation requirements and plan successful post-graduation educations or careers. For services, DSP must have verification of the disability on file. Students with LD must submit a psychoeducational evaluation completed by a qualified professional. Students with ADHD must submit a letter from a qualified professional who has an expertise in diagnosing ADHD in adults.

Admission Information for Students with Learning Differences

College entrance tests required: Yes
Interview required: No
Essay required: Yes
Additional application required for LD/ADHD/ASD: NR
What documentation required for LD: Psycho ed evaluation to include: relevant historical info, instructional interventions, related services, age diagnosed, objective data (aptitude, achievement, info processing), test scores (standard, percentile and grade equivalents) and describe functional limitations.
With general application: No
To receive services after enrolling: Yes
What documentation required for ADHD: Diagnosis based on DSM-V; history of behaviors impairing functioning in academic setting; diagnostic interview; history of symptoms; evidence of ongoing behaviors.
With general application: No
To receive services after enrolling: Yes
What documentation required for ASD: Psycho ed evaluation
With general application: NR
To receive services after enrolling: Yes
LD/ADHD/ASD documentation submitted to: Disabled Student Program
ASD Specific Program: NR
Special Ed. HS course work accepted: No
Specific course requirements of all applicants: Yes
Separate application required: No
Total # of students receiving LD/ADHD/ASD services: 242
Acceptance into program means acceptance into college: Students must be admitted and enrolled in the university first and then request services.

Admissions

An LD and admission specialist are available to meet applicants with LD interested in UC Berkeley. Specialists will review the transcript and give advice on how to proceed with the application. DSP works closely with admissions. There are two tiers for admission: Tier I is an automatic admission; Tier II applicants may need other criteria to be admitted. The impact of a disability could be a factor in an admission for a Tier II applicant. When an applicant self-discloses a disability, DSP requests documentation, and a statement about the impact of the disability. DSP uses this information to answer questions about the applicant from the Admissions Office. In general, applicants have 4 English, 2 social science, 3 math (4 years recommended), 2 science (3 recommended), 2 foreign language (3 years recommended), 1 visual/performing arts, and 1 year academic elective from previous areas.

Additional Information

DSP provides academic accommodations; consulting with instructors about accommodations; academic strategies and study skills; academic advising, adaptive technology, support groups, and a course "Facilitating Success" for students with LD/ADHD that centers on understanding learning differences, maximizing strengths, academic planning, research, writing, exam preparation, and using university resources; priority registration; specialists to help in problem-solving strategies and solutions to difficult problems; informational workshops on topics like understanding disabilities and individual learning styles; reading, writing, and research efficiency; memory strategies, self-advocacy; computer applications that facilitate learning; and career or graduate school planning.

General Support Services Information

Contact Information
Name of program or department: Disabled Students' Program
Telephone: 510-642-0518
Fax: 510-643-9686

Accommodations or Services For Students With Learning Differences

Accommodations are decided upon an individual basis after a thorough review of appropriate, current documentation. The accommodations requested must be supported through the documentation provided and must be logically linked to the current impact of the condition on academic functioning.

Allowed in exams
Calculator: Yes
Dictionary: NR
Computer: NR
Spellchecker: Yes
Extended test time: Yes
Scribes: Yes
Proctors: Yes
Oral exams: No
Note-takers: Yes
Services for students with LD: Yes
Services for students with ADHD: Yes
Services for students with ASD: Yes
Distraction-reduced environment: Yes
Tape recording in class: Yes
Audio books: NR
Electronic texts: Yes
Kurzweil Reader: Yes
Other assistive technology: Yes
Priority registration: Yes
Added costs for services: No
LD specialists: Yes
ADHD coaching: NR
ASD specialists: NR
Professional tutors: No
Peer tutors: Some individual tutoring is available through the TRIO grant.
Max. hours/wk. for services: NR
How professors are notified of LD/ADHD: By student

General Admissions Information

Office of Admissions:

Entrance Requirements

Academic units required: 4 English, 3 math, 2 science, 2 science labs, 2 foreign language, 2 history, 1 academic electives, 1 visual/performing arts. **Academic units recommended:** 4 English, 4 math, 3 science, 3 science labs, 3 foreign language, 2 history, 1 academic electives, 1 visual/performing arts. High school diploma is required and GED is accepted. SAT or ACT required. If ACT, ACT with writing required. TOEFL required of all international applicants: minimum paper TOEFL 550 or minimum internet TOEFL 80.

Application deadline: 11/30
Notification: NR
Average GPA: 3.85
ACT Composite middle 50% range: 28-33
SAT Math middle 50% range: 630-760
SAT Critical Reading middle 50% range: 600-730
SAT Writing middle 50% range: 610-740
Graduated top 10% of class: 98
Graduated top 25% of class: 100
Graduated top 50% of class: 100

COLLEGE GRADUATION REQUIREMENTS

Course waivers allowed: Yes
In what course: Math waivers are considered on a case-by-case basis.
Course substitutions allowed: Yes
In what course: Foreign language requirement can be substituted with cultural courses on a case-by-case basis.

Additional Information

Environment: This public school was founded in 1868. It has a 1,232-acre campus.

Student Body
Undergrad enrollment: 27,126
% Women: 52
% Men: 48
% Out-of-state: 15

Cost information
In-state tuition: $0
Out-of Tuition: $35,928
Room & board: $15,422

Housing Information
University Housing: Yes
Percent living on campus: 26

Greek System
Fraternity: Yes
Sorority: Yes
Athletics: Division I

U. of California—Los Angeles

1147 Murphy Hall, Los Angeles, CA 90095-1436
Phone: 310-825-3101 • Fax: 310-206-1206
E-mail: ugadm@saonet.ucla.edu • Web: www.ucla.edu
Support: CS • Institution: Public

Programs or Services for Students with Learning Differences

UCLA complies with state, federal, and university guidelines that mandate full access for students with disabilities, including learning disabilities. UCLA complies with the requirement to provide reasonable accommodations for documented students to allow them to participate in their academic program to the greatest extent possible. Students with other documented types of learning disabilities, including attention deficit hyperactive disorder and traumatic brain injury, are also served by the LD program. The UCLA LD program is coordinated by a full-time learning disabilities specialist and offers a full range of accommodations and services. Services are individually designed and include counseling, special test arrangements, note-taker services, readers, priority enrollment, adaptive technology, and individual tutoring. An active support group provides opportunities for students to discuss mutual concerns and enhance learning strategies. Workshops and speakers address skill development and topics of interest. In the Peer Mentor Program, continuing students with learning disabilities serve as resources to entering students.

Admission Information for Students with Learning Differences

College entrance tests required: Yes
Interview required: No
Essay required: Yes
Additional application required for LD/ADHD/ASD: NR
What documentation required for LD: Psycho ed evaluation to include: relevant historical info, instructional interventions, related services, age diagnosed, objective data (aptitude, achievement, info processing), test scores (standard, percentile and grade equivalents) and describe functional limitations.
With general application: No
To receive services after enrolling: Yes
What documentation required for ADHD: Diagnosis based on DSM-V; history of behaviors impairing functioning in academic setting; diagnostic interview; history of symptoms; evidence of ongoing behaviors.
With general application: No
To receive services after enrolling: Yes
What documentation required for ASD: Psycho ed evaluation
With general application: NR
To receive services after enrolling: Yes
LD/ADHD/ASD documentation submitted to: Office for Students with Disabilities
ASD Specific Program: NR
Special Ed. HS course work accepted: No
Specific course requirements of all applicants: Yes
Separate application required: No
Total # of students receiving LD/ADHD/ASD services: 225–300
Acceptance into program means acceptance into college: Students must be admitted and enrolled in the university first and then request services.

Admissions

There are no special admissions criteria for students with learning disabilities. In an academic review, the university will assess and balance a variety of academic factors to determine the overall scholastic strength of each applicant. UCLA does not use a formula. The comprehensive review includes the remainder of the freshman applicants after the academic review. While commitment to intellectual development and academic progress continues to be of primary importance, the personal statement also forms an integral part of this review. All applicants are required to submit the SAT or ACT. To be competitive, students usually score in the high 20s on the ACT or high 1100s on the SAT. Required courses are 4 years English, 2 years history/social science, 3 years math, 2 years foreign language, 2 years science lab (3 years recommended), and 2 years electives.

Additional Information

The LD Program includes tutors for individual classes, peer mentors, support group meetings, learning skills workshops, advocacy, referrals to campus resources, priority enrollment, orientation program, LD screening, and disability management counseling by four LD specialists including disability awareness, learning, and time management strategies, self-advocacy skills, and interpretation of evaluation reports. Accommodations could include alternatives in printed materials: (taped textbooks, computerized voice synthesizer, and Learning Ally); test-taking procedures (extended time, proctor to assist with reading and writing, distraction-free test area, computer for essay exams, or spellchecker); note-taking (note-takers or taped lectures); writing essays and papers (word processors with voice synthesizers or composition tutors); reduced course load; extended time to complete a program.

General Support Services Information

Contact Information
Name of program or department: Office for Students with Disabilities
Telephone: 310-825-1501
Fax: 310-825-9656

Accommodations or Services For Students With Learning Differences

Accommodations are decided upon an individual basis after a thorough review of appropriate, current documentation. The accommodations requested must be supported through the documentation provided and must be logically linked to the current impact of the condition on academic functioning.

Allowed in exams
Calculator: Yes
Dictionary: Yes
Computer: Yes
Spellchecker: Yes
Extended test time: Yes
Scribes: Yes
Proctors: Yes
Oral exams: No
Note-takers: Yes
Services for students with LD: Yes
Services for students with ADHD: Yes
Services for students with ASD: Yes
Distraction-reduced environment: Yes
Tape recording in class: Yes
Audio books: NR
Electronic texts: Yes
Kurzweil Reader: Yes
Other assistive technology: Yes
Priority registration: Yes
Added costs for services: No
LD specialists: Yes
ADHD coaching: NR
ASD specialists: NR
Professional tutors: No
Peer tutors: Yes
Max. hours/wk. for services: Unlimited
How professors are notified of LD/ADHD: By both student and director

General Admissions Information

Office of Admissions: 310-825-3101

Entrance Requirements

Academic units required: 4 English, 3 math, 2 science, 2 science labs, 2 foreign language, 2 history, 1 academic electives, 1 visual/performing arts. **Academic units recommended:** 4 English, 4 math, 3 science, 3 science labs, 3 foreign language, 2 history, 1 academic electives, 1 visual/performing arts. High school diploma is required and GED is accepted. SAT or ACT required. If ACT, ACT with writing required. TOEFL required of all international applicants: minimum paper TOEFL 550 or minimum internet TOEFL 83.

Application deadline: 11/30
Notification: Rolling starting 3/31
Average GPA: 4.33
ACT Composite middle 50% range: 25-33
SAT Math middle 50% range: 600-750
SAT Critical Reading middle 50% range: 570-700
SAT Writing middle 50% range: 580-720
Graduated top 10% of class: 97
Graduated top 25% of class: 100
Graduated top 50% of class: 100

COLLEGE GRADUATION REQUIREMENTS

Course waivers allowed: No
Course substitutions allowed: Yes
In what course: Foreign language and math as appropriate based on documentation, history, and recommendation.

Additional Information

Environment: This public school was founded in 1919. It has a 419-acre campus.

Student Body
Undergrad enrollment: 29,585
% Women: 56
% Men: 44
% Out-of-state: 11

Cost information
In-state tuition: $0
Out-of Tuition: $35,928
Room & board: $13,452

Housing Information
University Housing: Yes
Percent living on campus: NR

Greek System
Fraternity: Yes
Sorority: Yes
Athletics: Division I

U. of California—San Diego

9500 Gilman Drive, La Jolla, CA 92093-0021
Phone: 858-534-4831 • Fax: 858-534-5723
E-mail: admissionsinfo@ucsd.edu • Web: www.ucsd.edu
Support: CS • Institution: Public

Programs or Services for Students with Learning Differences

The primary objective of the Office for Students with Disabilities (OSD) is to integrate mainstream students with learning disabilities into campus programs, services, and activities. Academic accommodations are designed to meet disability related needs without fundamentally altering the program; and may include part-time enrollment, exception to minimum academic progress requirements, substitution of course work required for graduation, and alternative test formats. This program is not intended to provide remediation. Students seeking accommodations must provide a comprehensive written evaluation that meets the following requirements: Assessments, including test scores and sub-test scores, must be provided. Testing must be current, valid, reliable, and appropriate for college age students. A narrative report needs to discuss the student's educational, medical and family histories and any presenting concerns related to learning disabilities. If co-occurring conditions exist, they need to be discussed within the context of a DSM IV diagnosis on all 5 axes. A discussion of the student's current and functional limitations needs to occur.

Admission Information for Students with Learning Differences

College entrance test required: Yes
Interview required: No
Essay required: Yes
Additional Application Required for LD/ADHD/ASD: NR
What documentation required for LD: Psycho ed evaluation to include: relevant historical info, instructional interventions, related services, age diagnosed, objective data (aptitude, achievement, and info processing), test scores (standard, percentile and grade equivalents) and describe functional limitations.
With general application: No
To receive services after enrolling: Yes
What documentation required for ADHD: Diagnosis based on DSM-V; history of behaviors impairing functioning in academci setting; diagnostic interview; history of symptoms; evidence of ongoing behaviors.
With general application: No
To receive services after enrolling: Yes
What documentation required for ASD: Psycho ed evaluation
With general application: NR
To receive services after enrolling: Yes
LD/ADHD/ASD documentation submitted to: Office for Students with Disabilities
ASD Specific Program: NR
Special Ed. HS course work accepted: NR
Specific course requirements of all applicants: Yes
Separate application required for program services: Yes
Total # of students receiving LD/ADHD/ASD services: 100
Acceptance into program means acceptance into college: Student must be admitted and enrolled in the university first and then reviewed for LD services.

Admissions

There is no special admissions process for students with learning disabilities. All applicants must meet the same admission criteria. Students must satisfy subject, GPA, and examination requirements. 15 units of high school courses must be completed to fulfill the subject requirements. At least 7 of those 15 units must be taken in the last 2 years of high school and a grade of "C" or greater must be earned: History (2 years), English (4 years), Math (3 years, although 4 years are recommended), Lab science (2 years, although 3 years are recommended), Language other than English (2 years although 3 years are recommended), Visual and Performing Arts (1 year), College Prep Electives (1 year). Students need to earn a minimum GPA based on "a-g" courses taken in the 10th and 11th grades. California residents with a 3.0 GPA or above satisfy the minimum scholarship requirement if they achieve a correlating score on the SAT/ACT tests listed in the UC Admissions Index; Non-California residents must have a 3.4 GPA or higher in "a-g" courses and achieve a correlating score in the UC Admissions Index. The UC Admissions Index may be found at: http://www.universityofcalifornia.edu/admissions/freshman/california-residents/admissions-index/index.html

Additional Information

Depending upon the current functional limitations imposed by the diagnosed disability, accommodations may include the following: extended test time, note-taking, permission to tape record lectures, priority registration, calculators, etc.

General Support Services Information

Contact Information
Name of program or department: Office for Students with Disabilities
Telephone: 858.534.4382
Fax: 858.534.4650
Website: NR

Accommodations or Services for Students With Learning Differences

Accommodations are decided upon an individual basis after a thorough review of appropriate, current documentation. The accommodations requests must be supported through the documentation provided and must be logically linked to the current impact of the condition on academic functioning.

Allowed in exams
Calculator: Yes
Dictionary: Yes
Computer: Yes
Spellchecker: Yes
Extended test time: Yes
Scribes: Yes
Proctors: Yes
Oral exams: Yes
Note-takers: Yes
Support services for students with LD: NR
Support services for students with ADHD: Yes
Support services for students with ASD: NR
Distraction-reduced environment: Yes
Tape recording in class: Yes
Electronic texts: Yes
Kurzweil reader: Yes
Audio books: NR
Other assistive technology: Yes
Priority registration: Yes
Added costs of services: No
LD specialists: Yes
ADHD coaching: NR
ASD specialists: NR
Professional tutors: No
Peer tutors: Yes
Max. hours/wk. for services: Unlimited
How professors are notified of student approved accommodations: By students

General Admissions Information

Office of Admissions: 858-534-4831

Entrance Requirements

Academic units required: 4 English, 3 math, 2 science, 2 science labs, 2 foreign language, 2 history, 1 visual/performing arts. **Academic units recommended:** 4 English, 4 math, 3 science, 3 science labs, 3 foreign language, 2 history, 1 academic electives, 1 visual/performing arts. High school diploma is required and GED is accepted. SAT or ACT required. If ACT, ACT with writing required. TOEFL required of all international applicants: minimum paper TOEFL 550.

Application deadline: 11/30
Notification: Rolling starting 3/15
Average GPA: 4
ACT Composite middle 50% range: 27-32
SAT Math middle 50% range: 630-770
SAT Critical Reading middle 50% range: 580-680
SAT Writing middle 50% range: 590-700
Graduate top 10% of class: 100
Graduated top 25% of class: 100
Graduated top 50% of class: 100

COLLEGE GRADUATION REQUIREMENTS

Course waivers allowed: NR
Course substitutions allowed: NR

Additional Information

Environment: This public school was founded in 1960. It has a 1,976-acre campus.

Student Body
Undergrad enrollment: 26,590
% Women: 48
% Men: 52
% Out-of-state: 6

Cost information
In-state tuition: $0
Out-of-state tuition: $36,334
Room & board: $12,254

Housing Information
University Housing: Yes
Percent living on campus: 43

Greek System
Fraternity: Yes
Sorority: Yes
Athletics: Division II

U. of California—Santa Barbara

Office of Admissions, Santa Barbara, CA 93106-2014
Phone: 805-893-2881 • Fax: 805-893-2676
E-mail: admissions@sa.ucsb.edu • Web: www.ucsb.edu
Support: CS • Institution: Public

Programs or Services for Students with Learning Differences

The Disabled Student Program (DSP) is a department within the Division of Student Affairs that works to increase the retention and graduation ratio of students with temporary and permanent disabilities, assure equal access to all educational and academic programs, and foster student independence. The university is strongly committed to maintaining an environment that guarantees students with disabilities full access to educational programs and activities. The DSP office serves as a campus liaison regarding issues and regulations related to students with disabilities. DSP provides reasonable accommodations to students with disabilities; specific accommodations are determined on an individual basis. Admitted students should upload documentation to the DSP online system following the completion of an online application. The online system can be accessed at http://dsp.sa.ucsb.edu. Students enter the program via the DSP portal using their NetID and password following admission to the university. When students are set to a status of 'Ready for Meeting' they should schedule an appointment with a disabilities specialist. Accommodations and academically related services are not designed to provide remediation, but to accommodate a disorder that impairs the student's ability to acquire, process, or communicate information. Each accommodation will be made available to the extent that it does not compromise the academic integrity of the student's academic program.

Admission Information for Students with Learning Differences

College entrance test required: Yes
Interview required: No
Essay required: Yes
Additional Application Required for LD/ADHD/ASD: NR
What documentation required for LD: Psycho ed evaluation
With general application: No
To receive services after enrolling: Yes
What documentation required for ADHD: Psycho ed evaluation
With general application: No
To receive services after enrolling: Yes
What documentation required for ASD: Psycho ed evaluation
With general application: No
To receive services after enrolling: Yes
LD/ADHD/ASD documentation submitted to: The Disabled Students Program
ASD Specific Program: NR
Special Ed. HS course work accepted: No
Specific course requirements of all applicants: Yes
Separate application required for program services: Yes
Total # of students receiving LD/ADHD/ASD services: 499
Acceptance into program means acceptance into college: Students must be admitted and enrolled at university before requesting services.

Admissions

All students must meet the university requirements for admissions. Students may self-disclose their disability in their personal statement. Each essay is reviewed by three readers who assign a score to the application. The university seeks high achieving students who have made the most of their circumstances and are involved in a variety of activities. For California students applying as freshman must have a minimum 3.0 weighted GPA in 10th and 11th grade classes and be enrolled in college prep classes. The average weighted GPA for freshman admitted is 4.15. For out of state freshman the minimum required GPA is 3.43. The SAT or ACT with writing is required. For transfer students 60 semester or 90 quarter transferable units are required. Once a student is admitted to the university, they may apply to the Disabled Students Program.

Additional Information

Students with disabilities submit an on-line application for academic accommodations using the DSP website http://dsp.sa.ucsb.edu Documentation of incoming students for the fall quarter is reviewed by the Documentation Review Committee beginning the third week of June each year. Students receive an email regarding their DSP status. Students are invited to a fall DSP orientation program and meet with their disabilities specialist. Non-remedial drop in, group and individualized tutoring, as well as study skills workshops, are offered through the campus tutoring center, Campus Learning Assistance Services (CLAS) for all university students.

General Support Services Information

Contact Information
Name of program or department: The Disabled Students Program
Telephone: 805-893-2182
Fax: 805-893-7127
Website: http://dsp.sa.ucsb.edu/home

Accommodations or Services For Students With Learning Differences

Accommodations are decided upon an individual basis after a thorough review of appropriate, current documentation. The accommodations requests must be supported through the documentation provided and must be logically linked to the current impact of the condition on academic functioning.

Allowed in exams
Calculator: NR
Dictionary: NR
Computer: NR
Spellchecker: NR
Extended test time: Yes
Scribes: NR
Proctors: NR
Oral exams: NR
Note-takers: Yes
Support services for students with LD: NR
Support services for students with ADHD: NR
Support services for students with ASD: NR
Distraction-reduced environment: NR
Tape recording in class: NR
Electronic texts: NR
Kurzweil reader: NR
Audio books: NR
Other assistive technology: NR
Priority registration: NR
Added costs of services: NR
LD specialists: NR
ADHD coaching: NR
ASD specialists: NR
Professional tutors: No
Peer tutors: NR
Max. hours/wk. for services: NR
How professors are notified of student approved accommodations: NR

General Admissions Information

Office of Admissions: 805-893-2881

Entrance Requirements

Academic units required: 4 English, 3 math, 2 science labs, 2 foreign language, 2 history, 1 academic electives, 1 visual/performing arts. **Academic units recommended:** 4 math, 3 science labs, 3 foreign language. High school diploma is required and GED is accepted. SAT or ACT required. If ACT, ACT with writing required. TOEFL required of all international applicants: minimum paper TOEFL 550 or minimum internet TOEFL 80.

Application deadline: 11/30
Notification: 3/1
Average GPA: 4.02
ACT Composite middle 50% range: 24-30
SAT Math middle 50% range: 580-700
SAT Critical Reading middle 50% range: 550-670
SAT Writing middle 50% range: 560-680
Graduate top 10% of class: 100
Graduated top 25% of class: 100
Graduated top 50% of class: 100

COLLEGE GRADUATION REQUIREMENTS

Course waivers allowed: NR
Course substitutions allowed: NR

Additional Information

Environment: This public school was founded in 1909. It has a 989-acre campus.

Student Body
Undergrad enrollment: 20,607
% Women: 53
% Men: 47
% Out-of-state: 5

Cost information
In-state tuition: $0
Out-of-state tuition: $36,948
Room & board: $14,192

Housing Information
University Housing: Yes
Percent living on campus: 39

Greek System
Fraternity: Yes
Sorority: Yes
Athletics: Division I

UNIVERSITY OF SAN FRANCISCO

2130 Fulton Street, San Francisco, CA 94117
Phone: 415-422-6563 • Fax: 415-422-2217
E-mail: admission@usfca.edu • Web: www.usfca.edu
Support: CS • Institution: Private

PROGRAMS OR SERVICES FOR STUDENTS WITH LEARNING DIFFERENCES

The mission of Student Disability Services, (SDS) is to help USF students with disabilities serve as fully contributing and actively participating members of the University community while acquiring and developing the knowledge, skills, values, and sensitivity to become women and men for others. Toward that end, SDS promotes a fully integrated University experience for students with disabilities by ensuring that students have equal access to all areas of student life and receive appropriate educational support and services to foster their academic and personal success.

ADMISSION INFORMATION FOR STUDENTS WITH LEARNING DIFFERENCES

College entrance test required: Yes
Interview required: No
Essay required: Not Applicable
Additional Application Required for LD/ADHD/ASD: Yes
What documentation required for LD: Comprehensive Documentation Documentation should be comprehensive and must include the following: Evidence of Early Impairment Relevant historical information is essential since ADHD is by definition, first exhibited in childhood and manifests itself in m
With general application: No
To receive services after enrolling: Yes
What documentation required for ADHD: Psycho ed evaluation
With general application: No
To receive services after enrolling: Yes
What documentation required for ASD: Documentation The following guidelines are provided in the interest of assuring that documentation is appropriate to verify eligibility and to support requests for reasonable accommodations, academic adjustments, and/or auxiliary aids. The learning specia
With general application: No
To receive services after enrolling: Yes
LD/ADHD/ASD documentation submitted to: Student Disability Services
ASD Specific Program: No
Special Ed. HS course work accepted: Not Applicable
Specific course requirements of all applicants: NR
Separate application required for program services: Yes
Total # of students receiving LD/ADHD/ASD services: 197
Acceptance into program means acceptance into college: No

ADMISSIONS

Same as General Admissions

ADDITIONAL INFORMATION

Services include trained tutors, instruction in study skills and coping strategies, academic advising, maintaining regular contact with the LD coordinator, diagnostic testing, individual or small group instruction for educational building, and helping students improve their understanding of their learning disability. Assistive technology includes Kurzweil, Dragon Naturally Speaking, and so on. Extended time for course examinations may be a reasonable accommodation for students with specific types of disabilities. SDS reviews the documentation submitted by the student as part of the intake process and indicates extended time on a letter of accommodation when appropriate. Students with attention deficit hyperactivity disorder request services through SDS. A comprehensive neuropsychological or psychoeducational assessment report by a qualified professional clearly stating the presence of this disorder is required. The University of San Francisco's Learning and Writing Center aims to help all students to connect with one another and with professional staff members to achieve their academic best. Services in the Learning Center include tutors, academic workshops, and opportunities for study group information, and computer and other learning resources. The Writing Center provides professional writing assistance. For a complete and comprehensive listing of documentation guidelines and how to access services, please visit the website: www.usfca.edu/acadserv/academic/services/sds.

General Support Services Information

Contact Information
Name of program or department: Student Disability Services
Telephone: 4154222613
Fax: 4154225906
Website: NR

Accommodations or Services For Students With Learning Differences

Accommodations are decided upon an individual basis after a thorough review of appropriate, current documentation. The accommodations requests must be supported through the documentation provided and must be logically linked to the current impact of the condition on academic functioning.

Allowed in exams
Calculator: Yes
Dictionary: Yes
Computer: Yes
Spellchecker: Yes
Extended test time: Yes
Scribes: Yes
Proctors: Yes
Oral exams: Yes
Note-takers: Yes
Support services for students with LD: Yes
Support services for students with ADHD: Yes
Support services for students with ASD: Yes
Distraction-reduced environment: Yes
Tape recording in class: Yes
Electronic texts: Yes
Kurzweil reader: NR
Audio books: Yes
Other assistive technology: Yes
Priority registration: Yes
Added costs of services: No
LD specialists: Yes
ADHD coaching: Yes
ASD specialists: Yes
Professional tutors: No
Peer tutors: Yes
Max. hours/wk. for services: NR
How professors are notified of student approved accommodations: By both student and director

General Admissions Information

Office of Admissions: 415-422-6563

Entrance Requirements

Academic units required: 4 English, 3 math, 2 science, 2 foreign language, 3 social studies, 6 academic electives, and 2 units from above areas or other academic areas. High school diploma is required and GED is accepted. SAT or ACT required. If ACT, ACT with writing required. TOEFL required of all international applicants: minimum internet TOEFL 79.

Application deadline: 1/15
Notification: NR
Average GPA: 3.63
ACT Composite middle 50% range: 24-28
SAT Math middle 50% range: 540-640
SAT Critical Reading middle 50% range: 530-620
SAT Writing middle 50% range: 520-620
Graduate top 10% of class: 25
Graduated top 25% of class: 67
Graduated top 50% of class: 94

COLLEGE GRADUATION REQUIREMENTS

Course waivers allowed: No
Course substitutions allowed: Yes
In what course: This is all done on a case-by-case basis.

Additional Information

Environment: This private school, affiliated with the Roman Catholic Church, affiliated with the Jesuit Church, was founded in 1855. It has a 55-acre campus.

Student Body
Undergrad enrollment: 6,782
% Women: 62
% Men: 38
% Out-of-state: 20

Cost information
Tuition: $44,040
Room & board: $13,990

Housing Information
University Housing: Yes
Percent living on campus: 32

Greek System
Fraternity: Yes
Sorority: Yes
Athletics: Division I

UNIVERSITY OF SOUTHERN CALIFORNIA

Office of Admission/John Hubbard Hall, Los Angeles, CA 90089-0911
Phone: 213-740-1111 • Fax: 213-821-0200
E-mail: admitusc@usc.edu • Web: www.usc.edu
Support: CS • Institution: Private

PROGRAMS OR SERVICES FOR STUDENTS WITH LEARNING DIFFERENCES

Disability Services and Programs is responsible for delivery of services to students with learning disabilities. It offers a comprehensive support program in the areas of educational therapy, content area tutoring, study skills instruction, special exam administration, liaison with textbook-taping services, advocacy, and network referral system. The learning specialists, graduate assistants, and learning assistants are available to students for academic therapy. A computer lab is available for computer-assisted learning and for word processing when working with a staff person. After admission, students with LD are counseled by advisors who dialogue with the learning specialist and who are sensitive to special needs. Educational counseling is done by the learning specialist. Off-campus referrals are made to students desiring comprehensive diagnostic testing. The support structure for students with documented learning disabilities is one that is totally individualized; there is no special program per se. Support is given at the request of the student. The learning disabilities specialist and/or grad assistants at USC are prepared to act as advocates when appropriate for any student experiencing academic problems that are related to the learning disability. USC aims to assure close, personal attention to its students even though it is a large campus.

ADMISSION INFORMATION FOR STUDENTS WITH LEARNING DIFFERENCES

College entrance test required: Yes
Interview required: No
Essay required: Yes
Additional Application Required for LD/ADHD/ASD: NR
What documentation required for LD: Psycho Ed evaluation toinclude: relevant historical info, instructional interventions, related services, age diagnosed, objective data (aptitude, achievement, info processing), test scores (standard, percentile and grade equivalents) and describe functional limitations.
With general application: No
To receive services after enrolling: Yes
What documentation required for ADHD: Diagnosis basedon DSM; history of behaviors impairing functioning inacademic setting; diagnostic interview; history of symptoms; evidence of ongoing behaviors.
With general application: NR
To receive services after enrolling: Yes
What documentation required for ASD: Psycho ed evaluation
With general application: NR
To receive services after enrolling: Yes
LD/ADHD/ASD documentation submitted to: Disability Services and Programs
ASD Specific Program: NR
Special Ed. HS course work accepted: Yes
Specific course requirements of all applicants: Yes
Separate application required for program services: NR
Total # of students receiving LD/ADHD/ASD services: 350
Acceptance into program means acceptance into college: Students must be admitted and enrolled in the university first and then request services.

ADMISSIONS

There are no special admissions for students with learning disabilities. Course requirements include 4 years of English, 3 years of math, 2 years of natural science, 2 years of social studies, 2 years of a foreign language, and 4 year-long electives. (The foreign language requirement is not waived in the admission process). It is helpful for comparison purposes to have both timed and untimed SAT or ACT test results. Transfer students are admitted on the basis of their college course work as well as the high school record. It is the student's responsibility to provide recent educational evaluations for documentation as part of the admissions application process. Testing must be current within 3 years, or 5 years for transfer or returning students.

ADDITIONAL INFORMATION

The services provided are modifications that are determined to be appropriate for students with LD. During the first 3 weeks of each semester, students are seen on a walk-in basis by the staff in the LD Support Services. Students requesting assistance must have a planning appointment with an LD specialist or grad assistant; provide a copy of the current class schedule; and be sure that eligibility has been determined by documenting specific learning disabilities. Learning assistance most often involves one-on-one attention for academic planning, scheduling, organization, and methods of compensation. Students may have standing appointments with learning assistants and subject tutors. After one "no-show" or three canceled appointments, standing appointments will be canceled. Course accommodations could include taping of lectures, note-taking, extended time for tests, use of word processor, proofreader, limiting scheduling of consecutive exams, and advocacy. Other services include support groups, counseling, and coaching.

General Support Services Information

Contact Information
Name of program or department: Disability Services and Programs
Telephone: 213-740-0776
Fax: 213-740-8216
Website: https://kortschakcenter.usc.edu/

Accommodations or Services For Students With Learning Differences

Accommodations are decided upon an individual basis after a thorough review of appropriate, current documentation. The accommodations requests must be supported through the documentation provided and must be logically linked to the current impact of the condition on academic functioning.

Allowed in exams
Calculator: Not Applicable
Dictionary: Not Applicable
Computer: Yes
Spellchecker: Not Applicable
Extended test time: Yes
Scribes: Yes
Proctors: Yes
Oral exams: Not Applicable
Note-takers: Yes
Support services for students with LD: Yes
Support services for students with ADHD: Yes
Support services for students with ASD: Not Applicable
Distraction-reduced environment: Not Applicable
Tape recording in class: Yes
Electronic texts: Not Applicable
Kurzweil reader: NR
Audio books: No
Other assistive technology: Yes
Priority registration: NR
Added costs of services: NR
LD specialists: NR
ADHD coaching: NR
ASD specialists: NR
Professional tutors: No
Peer tutors: NR
Max. hours/wk. for services: NR
How professors are notified of student approved accommodations: NR

General Admissions Information

Office of Admissions: 213-740-1111

Entrance Requirements

Academic units required: 4 English, 3 math, 2 science, 2 science labs, 2 foreign language, 2 social studies, 3 academic electives. **Academic units recommended:** 4 English, 4 math, 3 science, 3 science labs, 3 foreign language, 3 social studies, 3 academic electives. High school diploma is required and GED is not accepted. SAT or ACT required. If ACT, ACT with writing accepted. TOEFL required of all international applicants.

Application deadline: 1/15
Notification: 4/1
Average GPA: 3.73
ACT Composite middle 50% range: 30-33
SAT Math middle 50% range: 650-770
SAT Critical Reading middle 50% range: 620-730
SAT Writing middle 50% range: 650-750
Graduate top 10% of class: 88
Graduated top 25% of class: 97
Graduated top 50% of class: 100

COLLEGE GRADUATION REQUIREMENTS

Course waivers allowed: NR
In what course: NR
Course substitutions allowed: NR
In what course: NR

Additional Information

Environment: This private school was founded in 1880. It has a 155-acre campus.

Student Body
Undergrad enrollment: 18,810
% Women: 51
% Men: 49
% Out-of-state: 32

Cost information
Tuition: $49,464
Room & board: $13,855

Housing Information
University Housing: Yes
Percent living on campus: 30

Greek System
Fraternity: Yes
Sorority: Yes
Athletics: Division I

University of the Pacific

3601 Pacific Avenue, Stockton, CA 95211
Phone: 209-946-2211 • Fax: 209-946-2413
E-mail: admissions@pacific.edu • Web: www.pacific.edu
Support: S • Institution: Private

Programs or Services for Students with Learning Differences

There is no special program for students with learning disabilities, but the university does have a Learning Disabilities Support Program. This program offers assistance through tutoring, study skills classes, support groups, and testing accommodations. Documentation for LD must include psychoeducational evaluations from a professional. The documentation for ADHD must be from a medical doctor. Documentation should be sent to the Director of the Office of Services for Students with Disabilities. Students register for services after admission by contacting the Office of Services for Students with Disabilities. Student confidentiality is protected. The ultimate goal is for the student to earn a degree that is unmodified and unflagged. Faculty and staff are dedicated to providing students with learning disabilities all reasonable accommodations so that they may enjoy academic success. The LD Support Program helps keep University of the Pacific in compliance with the Americans with Disabilities Act and Section 504 of the Rehabilitation Act. Compliance is accomplished without compromising University of the Pacific standards, placing undue financial or administrative burden on the university, fundamentally altering the nature of programs, or extending unreasonable accommodations.

Admission Information for Students with Learning Differences

College entrance test required: NR
Interview required: No
Essay required: Recommended
Additional Application Required for LD/ADHD/ASD: NR
What documentation required for LD: Psycho ed evaluation
With general application: No
To receive services after enrolling: Yes
What documentation required for ADHD: Psycho ed evaluation
With general application: No
To receive services after enrolling: Yes
What documentation required for ASD: Psycho ed evaluation
With general application: NR
To receive services after enrolling: Yes
LD/ADHD/ASD documentation submitted to: Services for Students with Disabilities
ASD Specific Program: No
Special Ed. HS course work accepted: No
Specific course requirements of all applicants: Yes
Separate application required for program services: NR
Total # of students receiving LD/ADHD/ASD services: NR
Acceptance into program means acceptance into college: NR

Admissions

UOP welcomes students with learning disabilities. Although there is no special admission procedure, students are given special consideration. There is no minimum ACT/SAT requirement. There are two alternative methods for admissions: (1) probationary admissions for the marginal student—C/D average with no special requirements, but the university advisor is notified of status; no required test score; and no quota regarding the number of students admitted; and (2) special admissions—students who begin college courses in the summer prior to freshman year and receive at least a C average in two courses and one study skills class (can take those courses at any local community college).

Additional Information

All admitted students are eligible for LD services with the appropriate assessment documentation. Academic Support Services offers services to improve learning opportunities for students with LD and are provided within reasonable limits. These services could include diagnostic assessment, accommodations for academic needs, electronic books and alternate formatting, readers, tutorials for academic courses, and referrals to appropriate resources. Skills courses for credit are available in reading, study skills, writing, and math. Services and accommodations are available for undergraduate and graduate students.

General Support Services Information

Contact Information
Name of program or department: Services for Students with Disabilities
Telephone: 209.946.3221
Fax: 209.946.2278
Website: www.pacific.edu/disabilities

Accommodations or Services For Students With Learning Differences

Accommodations are decided upon an individual basis after a thorough review of appropriate, current documentation. The accommodations requests must be supported through the documentation provided and must be logically linked to the current impact of the condition on academic functioning.

Allowed in exams
Calculator: Yes
Dictionary: Yes
Computer: Yes
Spellchecker: Yes
Extended test time: Yes
Scribes: Yes
Proctors: Yes
Oral exams: Yes
Note-takers: Yes
Support services for students with LD: Yes
Support services for students with ADHD: Yes
Support services for students with ASD: Yes
Distraction-reduced environment: Yes
Tape recording in class: Yes
Electronic texts: Yes
Kurzweil reader: NR
Audio books: Yes
Other assistive technology: Yes
Priority registration: Yes
Added costs of services: No
LD specialists: No
ADHD coaching: Yes
ASD specialists: Yes
Professional tutors: No
Peer tutors: NR
Max. hours/wk. for services: NR
How professors are notified of student approved accommodations: By director

General Admissions Information

Office of Admissions: 209-946-2211

Entrance Requirements

Academic units recommended: 4 English, 2 foreign language, 2 social studies, 1 history, 1 academic electives, 1 visual/performing arts. High school diploma is required and GED is accepted. SAT or ACT required. If ACT, ACT with writing accepted. TOEFL required of all international applicants: minimum paper TOEFL 475 or minimum internet TOEFL 52.

Application deadline: 1/15
Notification: Rolling starting 1/11
Average GPA: 3.45
ACT Composite middle 50% range: 22-29
SAT Math middle 50% range: 520-660
SAT Critical Reading middle 50% range: 490-620
SAT Writing middle 50% range: 490-630
Graduate top 10% of class: 33
Graduated top 25% of class: 66
Graduated top 50% of class: 90

COLLEGE GRADUATION REQUIREMENTS

Course waivers allowed: No
In what course: NR
Course substitutions allowed: Yes
In what course: math fundamental skills and foreign language.

Additional Information

Environment: This private school was founded in 1851. It has a 175-acre campus.

Student Body
Undergrad enrollment: 3,735
% Women: 52
% Men: 48
% Out-of-state: 7

Cost information
Tuition: $42,414
Room & board: $12,858

Housing Information
University Housing: Yes
Percent living on campus: 46

Greek System
Fraternity: Yes
Sorority: Yes
Athletics: Division I

Whittier College

13406 Philadelphia Street, Whittier, CA 90608
Phone: 562-907-4238 • Fax: 562-907-4870
E-mail: admission@whittier.edu • Web: www.whittier.edu
Support: S • Institution: Private

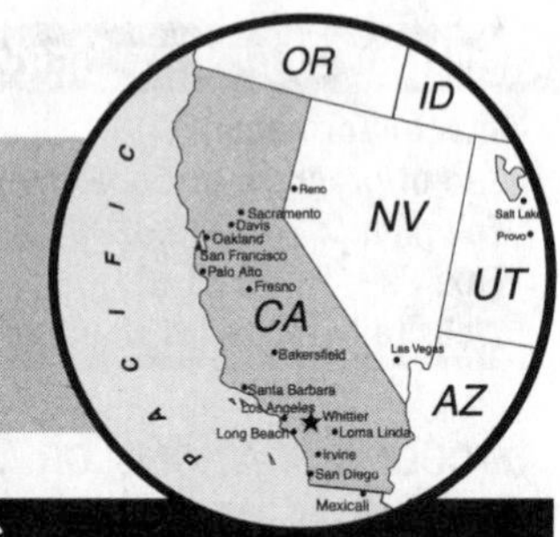

Programs or Services for Students with Learning Differences

The director of The Office of Disability Services provides assistance to students with documented disabilities. Accommodation requests are made through the director's office. Students with disabilities must make their needs known to the director of Disability Services to receive accommodations. To arrange for services, students must self-disclose the disability and make an individual appointment to discuss their accommodation requests with the director. Learning Support Services offers additional services: peer tutoring, workshops on study skills, and basic English and math skills assistance. These services are provided at no cost.

Admission Information for Students with Learning Differences

College entrance tests required: Yes
Interview required: No
Essay required: No
Additional application required for LD/ADHD/ASD: NR
What documentation required for LD: Psycho ed evaluation to include: relevant historical info, instructional interventions, related services, age diagnosed, objective data (aptitude, achievement, info processing), test scores (standard, percentile and grade equivalents) and describe functional limitations.
With general application: No
To receive services after enrolling: Yes
What documentation required for ADHD: Diagnosis based on DSM-V; history of behaviors impairing functioning in academic setting; diagnostic interview; history of symptoms; evidence of ongoing behaviors.
With general application: No
To receive services after enrolling: Yes
What documentation required for ASD: Psycho ed evaluation
With general application: No
To receive services after enrolling: Yes
LD/ADHD/ASD documentation submitted to: Disability Services
ASD Specific Program: NR
Special Ed. HS course work accepted: NR
Specific course requirements of all applicants: Yes
Separate application required: No
Total # of students receiving LD/ADHD/ASD services: 22
Acceptance into program means acceptance into college: Student must be admitted and enrolled in the university first and then reviewed for LD services.

Admissions

There is no special admissions process for students with disabilities. All applicants are expected to meet the same admission criteria. Students must submit the ACT or SAT Reasoning and have a minimum of a 2.0 GPA; the recommended courses include 4 years of English, 3–4 years of math, 2–3 years of a foreign language, 2–3 years of social studies, and 2–3 years of science labs.

Additional Information

The use of calculators, dictionaries, computers, or spellcheckers in exams would be considered on a case-by-case basis, depending on appropriate documentation and student needs. Students with appropriate documentation will have access to note-takers, readers, extended exam times, alternative exam locations, proctors, scribes, oral exams, books on tape, and priority registration. All students have access to a Math Lab, a Writing Center, a Learning Lab, and academic counseling.

The Office of Disability Services also assists students with Self Advocacy Academic Support and Counseling Supportive Education Services Case Management Services (SES) helps students learn to cope with symptoms that can affect their college experience. Such symptoms can include problems with concentration, learning difficulties, test anxiety, trouble with organization, and understanding individual strengths and weaknesses.

General Support Services Information

Contact Information
Name of program or department: Disability Services
Telephone: 562-907-4840
Fax: 562-907-4827

Accommodations or Services For Students With Learning Differences

Accommodations are decided upon an individual basis after a thorough review of appropriate, current documentation. The accommodations requested must be supported through the documentation provided and must be logically linked to the current impact of the condition on academic functioning.

Allowed in exams
Calculator: Yes
Dictionary: Yes
Computer: Yes
Spellchecker: Yes
Extended test time: Yes
Scribes: Yes
Proctors: Yes
Oral exams: No
Note-takers: Yes
Services for students with LD: Yes
Services for students with ADHD: Yes
Services for students with ASD: Yes
Distraction-reduced environment: Yes
Tape recording in class: Yes
Audio books: NR
Electronic texts: Yes
Kurzweil Reader: Yes
Other assistive technology: Yes
Priority registration: Yes
Added costs for services: No
LD specialists: No
ADHD coaching: NR
ASD specialists: NR
Professional tutors: No
Peer tutors: 15–30
Max. hours/wk. for services: Unlimited
How professors are notified of LD/ADHD: By both student and director

General Admissions Information

Office of Admissions: 562-907-4238

Entrance Requirements

Academic units required: 3 English, 2 math, 1 science, 1 science labs, 2 foreign language, 1 social studies. **Academic units recommended:** 4 English, 3 math, 2 science, 3 foreign language, 2 social studies. High school diploma is required and GED is accepted. SAT or ACT required. If ACT, ACT with writing required. TOEFL required of all international applicants: minimum paper TOEFL 550.

Application deadline: NR
Notification: Rolling starting 12/30
Average GPA: 3.52
ACT Composite middle 50% range: 20-26
SAT Math middle 50% range: 470-590
SAT Critical Reading middle 50% range: 463-580
SAT Writing middle 50% range: 450-560
Graduated top 10% of class: 25
Graduated top 25% of class: 1
Graduated top 50% of class: 93

COLLEGE GRADUATION REQUIREMENTS

Course waivers allowed: Yes
In what course: Foreign language, math
Course substitutions allowed: Yes
In what course: Foreign language as an admissions requirement

Additional Information

Environment: This private school was founded in 1887. It has a 75-acre campus.

Student Body
Undergrad enrollment: 1,650
% Women: 56
% Men: 44
% Out-of-state: 16
Cost information
Room & board: NR
Housing Information
University Housing: Yes
Percent living on campus: 50
Greek System
Fraternity: Yes
Sorority: Yes
Athletics: Division III

COLORADO STATE U.—PUEBLO

LARC, Suite 169, 2200 Bonforte Blvd, Pueblo, CO 81001
Phone: 719-549-2462 • Fax: 719-549-2419
E-mail: info@colostate-pueblo.edu • Web: www.csupueblo.edu
Support: S • Institution: Public

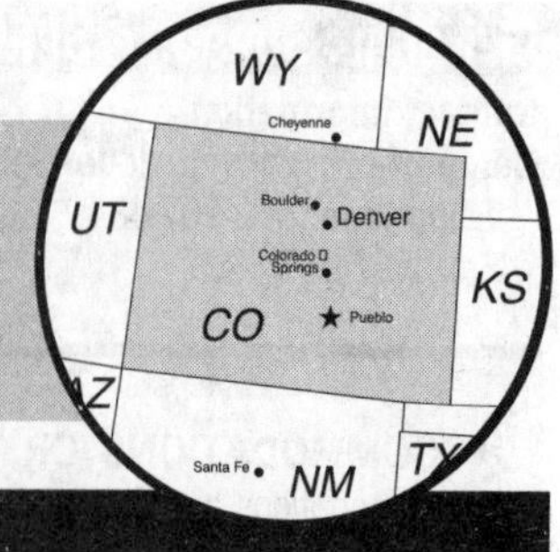

PROGRAMS OR SERVICES FOR STUDENTS WITH LEARNING DIFFERENCES

The Mission of the Disability Resource Office at Colorado State University—Pueblo is to ensure provision of reasonable academic accommodations and support, designed to enhance academic effectiveness and promote independence in students with documented disabilities.

ADMISSION INFORMATION FOR STUDENTS WITH LEARNING DIFFERENCES

College entrance tests required: Yes
Interview required: No
Essay required: No
Additional application required for LD/ADHD/ASD: NR
What documentation required for LD: Psycho ed evaluation to include: relevant historical info, instructional interventions, related services, age diagnosed, objective data (aptitude, achievement, info processing), test scores (standard, percentile and grade equivalents) and describe functional limitations.
With general application: No
To receive services after enrolling: No
What documentation required for ADHD: Diagnosis based on DSM-V; history of behaviors impairing functioning in academic setting; diagnostic interview; history of symptoms; evidence of ongoing behaviors.
With general application: No
To receive services after enrolling: Yes
What documentation required for ASD: Diagnosis based on DSM-V; history of behaviors impairing functioning in academic setting; list of current medications.
With general application: No
To receive services after enrolling: No
LD/ADHD/ASD documentation submitted to: Disability Resource Office
ASD Specific Program: NR
Special Ed. HS course work accepted: NR
Specific course requirements for all applicants: NR
Total # of students receiving LD/ADHD/ASD services: NR
Acceptance into program means acceptance into college: No

ADMISSIONS

Colorado State University—Pueblo's admission process is designed to promote diversity within the student population and to assure equal access to qualified applicants. The final admission decision is based on the applicant's potential for attaining a degree at the university. All first-time freshmen must submit their high school transcripts with GPA and ACT/SAT scores along with CSU—Pueblo's application. Applicants who do not meet admission standards are encouraged to submit personal statements explaining their circumstances and to show academic progress throughout high school.

ADDITIONAL INFORMATION

Skills classes are offered in note-taking strategies, study skills, and textbook-reading strategies. The request for the use of a dictionary, computer, or spellchecker during exams will depend on the student's documented needs and permission from the professor. Students with specific needs are encouraged to provide documentation that specifically identifies the disability and the accommodations needed. Tutoring is available through Student and Academic Services. The Academic Improvement Program helps students who are on GPA alerts or academic probation develop an Academic Improvement Plan to promote success. The writing room offers one-on-one writing assistance. The staff of Student Academic Services is committed to assisting all students in their academic lives. Students registered with the Disability Resource & Support Center at Colorado State University-Pueblo are provided with access to the University's self service Assistive Technology Lab. The lab has the following assistive technology software programs available for students to utilize: JAWS; Zoom Text; Dragon Naturally Speaking; Kurzweil 1000; Kurzweil 3000.

General Support Services Information

Contact Information
Name of program or department: Disability Resource Office
Telephone: 719-549-2648
Fax: 719-549-2195

Accommodations or Services For Students With Learning Differences

Accommodations are decided upon an individual basis after a thorough review of appropriate, current documentation. The accommodations requested must be supported through the documentation provided.

Allowed in exams
Calculator: Yes
Dictionary: Yes
Computer: Yes
Spellchecker: Yes
Extended test time: Yes
Scribes: Yes
Proctors: Yes
Oral exams: Yes
Note-takers: Yes
Services for students with LD: Yes
Services for students with ADHD: No
Services for students with ASD: No
Distraction-reduced environment: Yes
Tape recording in class: Yes
Audio books from learning ally: No
Electronic texts: Yes
Kurzweil Reader: Yes
Other assistive technology: Yes
Priority registration: No
Added costs for services: No
LD specialists: No
ADHD coaching: No
ASD specialists: No
Professional tutors: No
Peer tutors: No
Max. hours/wk. for services: As needed
How professors are notified of LD/ADHD: By student

General Admissions Information

Office of Admissions: 719-549-2461

Entrance Requirements

Academic units required: 4 English, 3 math, 3 science, 2 science labs, 2 foreign language, 2 social studies, 1 history, **Academic units recommended:** 4 English, 3 math, 3 science, 2 science labs, 2 foreign language, 2 social studies, 1 history. High school diploma is required and GED is accepted. SAT or ACT required. If ACT, ACT with writing accepted. TOEFL required of all international applicants: minimum paper TOEFL 500.

Application deadline: 8/1
Notification: Rolling starting 8/1
Average GPA: 3.1
ACT Composite middle 50% range: 18-22
SAT Math middle 50% range: 420-550
SAT Critical Reading middle 50% range: 420-530
SAT Writing middle 50% range: NR-NR
Graduated top 10% of class: 2
Graduated top 25% of class: 8
Graduated top 50% of class: 36

COLLEGE GRADUATION REQUIREMENTS

Course waivers allowed: No
Course substitutions allowed: Yes
In what course: NR

Additional Information

Environment: This public school was founded in 1933. It has a 275-acre campus.

Student Body
Undergrad enrollment: 4,798
% Women: 58
% Men: 42
% Out-of-state: 7

Cost information
Out-of Tuition: $13,543
Room & board: $6,300

Housing Information
University Housing: Yes
Percent living on campus: NR

Greek System
Fraternity: Yes
Sorority: Yes
Athletics: Division II

Regis University

3333 Regis Boulevard, Denver, CO 80221-1099
Phone: 303-458-4900 • Fax: 303-964-5534
E-mail: regisadm@regis.edu • Web: www.regis.edu
Support: CS • Institution: Private

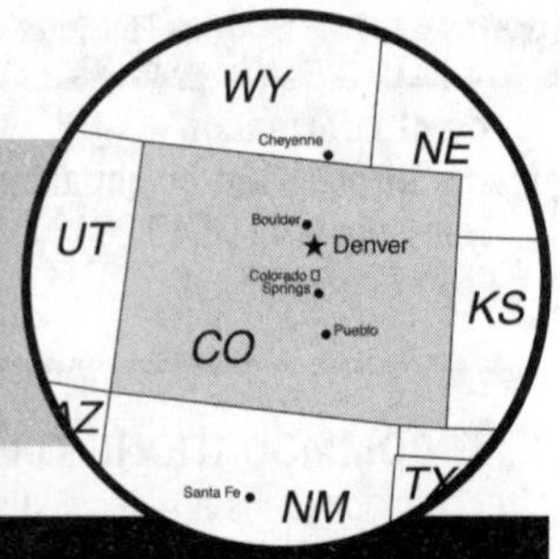

Programs or Services for Students with Learning Differences

The Commitment Program, created in 1976, provides learning support courses, peer mentoring, study groups, and priority advising and registration for approximately 50 freshmen who are provisionally admitted to the university. Commitment students may not participate in varsity sports or off-campus employment during their freshman year, and are obliged to make regular use of academic support provided by the Program. Two Commitment study rooms are available all day every day, and weekly Forum meetings offer career counseling, study skills, time management, and other first-year enrichment services. LS courses (including critical reading and writing, and math and science learning strategies) apply toward elective credit. The director of the program works closely with the Office of Disability Services to support students in need of specific accommodations. In keeping with the Jesuit mission of "educating men and women in the service others," Commitment students work throughout the academic year in a variety of Father Woody Service Projects.

Admission Information for Students with Learning Differences

College entrance tests required: Yes
Interview required: No
Essay required: No
Additional application required for LD/ADHD/ASD: NR
What documentation required for LD: Psycho ed evaluation to include: relevant historical info, instructional interventions, related services, age diagnosed, objective data (aptitude, achievement, info processing), test scores (standard, percentile and grade equivalents) and describe functional limitations.
With general application: No
To receive services after enrolling: Yes
What documentation required for ADHD: Diagnosis based on DSM-V; history of behaviors impairing functioning in academic setting; diagnostic interview; history of symptoms; evidence of ongoing behaviors.
With general application: No
To receive services after enrolling: Yes
What documentation required for ASD: Evaluations must be conducted by a qualified impartial professional. Eval to include: letterhead, diagnosis based on DSM-V criteria, history, comprehensive testing, comprehensive standardized IQ test (including cognitive/achievement scores), communication assessment, ADOS, ADI-R, GARS, GADS, AAA, impact of current medication to meet the demands of post-secondary environment, current functional limitations.
With general application: NR
To receive services after enrolling: Yes
LD/ADHD/ASD documentation submitted to: Disability Services
ASD Specific Program: NR
Special Ed. HS course work accepted: NR
Specific course requirements for all applicants: NR
Separate application required: No
Total # of students receiving LD/ADHD/ASD services: 1–150
Acceptance into program means acceptance into college: Students are reviewed by Freshman Commitment and a recommendation is provided to the Admissions Committee for a final decision.

Admissions

There is no special admission for students with LD. Interview not required. Minimum GPA 2.56, SAT of 930, or ACT of 20 and 15 academic units. Students may be considered with 17 ACT or 810 SAT and 2.3 GPA. Students need to show sufficient evidence of motivation and ability to succeed in college, even though they may not have the required GPA or test scores. Recommendations and extracurricular activities will be considered. Students admitted on probation typically have stronger test scores and lower GPAs and are admitted on one semester probation. They need a 2.0 GPA to return the second semester. Other students may be admitted into the Freshman Commitment Program. These students usually have lower test scores and a C-plus average. Probationary admission is for two semesters.

Additional Information

Disability Services provides self-advocacy training; test-taking and learning strategies assistance; academic monitoring; note-takers; readers; scribes; extended testing time; and course substitutions. Students in the Commitment Program remain for one year and, with successful completion, are officially admitted to the college. They must pass all required commitment courses with a C or better, not fall below a 2.0 GPA in non-Commitment courses, and agree not to participate in varsity sports or other activities that interfere with class attendance while in the program. There are learning support courses, study groups, and tutorials. Tutors available and all students must pass 3 hours of math. There is a math learning support course or a remedial math class available prior to taking the regular college algebra class.

General Support Services Information

Contact Information
Name of program or department: Student Disability Services
Telephone: 303-458-4951
Fax: 303-964-6595
E-mail: disability@regis.edu

Accommodations or Services For Students With Learning Differences

Accommodations are decided upon an individual basis after a thorough review of appropriate, current documentation. The accommodations requested must be supported through the documentation provided and must be logically linked to the current impact of the condition on academic functioning.

Allowed in exams
Calculator: Yes
Dictionary: Yes
Computer: Yes
Spellchecker: Yes
Extended test time: Yes
Scribes: Yes
Proctors: Yes
Oral exams: Yes
Note-takers: Yes
Services for students with LD: Yes
Services for students with ADHD: Yes
Services for students with ASD: Yes
Distraction-reduced environment: Yes
Tape recording in class: Yes
Audio books: NR
Electronic texts: Yes
Kurzweil Reader: Yes
Other assistive technology: Yes
Priority registration: No
Added costs for services: No
LD specialists: No
ADHD coaching: NR
ASD specialists: NR
Professional tutors: No
Peer tutors: Varies
Max. hours/wk. for services: Unlimited
How professors are notified of LD/ADHD: By student

General Admissions Information

Office of Admissions: 303-458-4900

Entrance Requirements

Academic units recommended: 4 English, 3 math, 2 science, 1 science labs, 2 foreign language, 2 social studies, 1 academic electives. High school diploma is required and GED is accepted. SAT or ACT required. If ACT, ACT with writing accepted. TOEFL required of all international applicants: minimum paper TOEFL 550 or minimum internet TOEFL 82.

Application deadline: 8/1
Notification: Rolling starting 9/15
Average GPA: 3.52
ACT Composite middle 50% range: 21-27
SAT Math middle 50% range: 470-590
SAT Critical Reading middle 50% range: 480-580
SAT Writing middle 50% range: 480-570
Graduated top 10% of class: 21
Graduated top 25% of class: 50
Graduated top 50% of class: 79

COLLEGE GRADUATION REQUIREMENTS

Course waivers allowed: Yes
In what course: All students must take 3 hours of math. Foreign culture courses are substituted for foreign language if the documentation verifies a disability.
Course substitutions allowed: Yes
In what course: All students must take 3 hours of math. Foreign culture courses are substituted for foreign language if the documentation verifies a disability.

Additional Information

Environment: This private school, affiliated with the Roman Catholic Church, was founded in 1877. It has a 90-acre campus.

Student Body
Undergrad enrollment: 4,499
% Women: 61
% Men: 39
% Out-of-state: 37

Cost information
Tuition: $33,110
Room & board: $10,040

Housing Information
University Housing: Yes
Percent living on campus: NR

Greek System
Fraternity: No
Sorority: No
Athletics: Division II

U. of Colorado—Boulder

552 UCB, Boulder, CO 80309-0552
Phone: 303-492-6301 • Fax: 303-735-2501
Web: www.colorado.edu/
Support: CS • Institution: Public

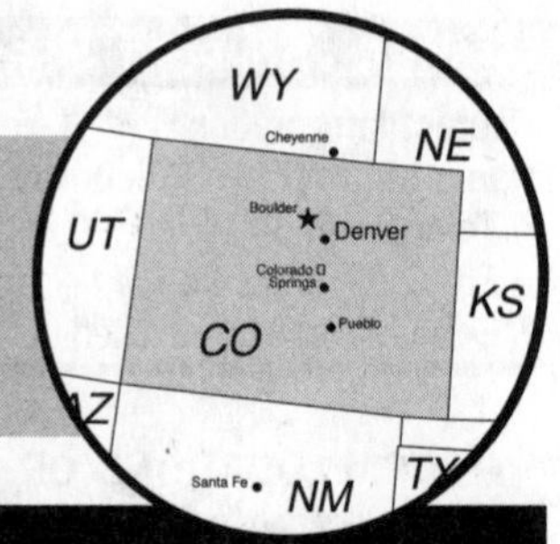

Programs or Services for Students with Learning Differences

Mission Disability Services ensures that students with disabilities receive reasonable accommodations and services to participate fully in the academic environment. Vision: We envision a fully accessible, integrated, and universally designed campus community. Students with disabilities are one of the many groups that make up our campus community and a diverse community broadens our understanding and appreciation for the contributions of each individual. Philosophy: Disability Services provides leadership and guidance regarding accommodations and universal access, which requires a collaborative relationship among all members of the university community. Core Values: Human variation is natural and vital in the development of dynamic communities; building and using an academic success toolkit (i.e., self-advocacy skills, resources, various study strategies) is essential for all students; responsibility for meaningful and universal access belongs to all; a diverse and stimulating university community is a shared responsibility; disability is diversity; universal design is essential for achieving inclusion and social participation of all.

Admission Information for Students with Learning Differences

College entrance test required: Yes
Interview required: No
Essay required: Not Applicable
Additional Application Required for LD/ADHD/ASD: Yes
What documentation required for LD: Psycho-educational evaluation
With general application: No
To receive services after enrolling: Yes
What documentation required for ADHD: Psycho ed evaluation
With general application: No
To receive services after enrolling: Yes
What documentation required for ASD: Psycho-educational evaluation
With general application: No
To receive services after enrolling: Yes
LD/ADHD/ASD documentation submitted to: Disability Services
ASD Specific Program: NR
Special Ed. HS course work accepted: No
Specific course requirements of all applicants: Yes
Separate application required for program services: No
Total # of students receiving LD/ADHD/ASD services: NR
Acceptance into program means acceptance into college: NR

Admissions

There is not a special admission process for students with disabilities. All students are considered under the same competitive admissions criteria. All application information should be submitted to admissions, but documentation should be submitted directly to Disability Services. Mid 50 percent GPA for Arts and Science is 3.2.-3.85, ACT 23-28 class rank 59%-89%. Guaranteed admission to Arts and Science is top 10 percent or 3.8 GPA or 3.5 GPA and 1150 SAT or 25 ACT or 3.25 GPA and 1260 SAT or 28 ACT. Mid 50 percent for College of Engineering is 3.7-4.0 GPA, 27-32 CT, rank 80%-97%. Guaranteed admission to College of Engineering is top 5 percent or 3.8 HPA or 1280 SAT (Critical Reading 610 and Math 670)) or 29 English and 30 Math on ACT.

Additional Information

Services provided through Disability Services include an opportunity to meet with a disability specialist to identify appropriate accommodations, campus resources, advocacy, and short-term academics strategies. The Disability Specialist provides individualized support to students with all kinds of disabilities. This support can take many forms including informal academic advising, advocacy, and letters to professors designating reasonable accommodation, if appropriate. Disability Specialists assist students in developing strategies for time management, organization, study skills, test preparation, and transition to and beyond life at the university.

General Support Services Information

Contact Information
Name of program or department: Disability Services
Telephone: 303-492-8671
Fax: 303-492-5601
Website: NR

Accommodations or Services For Students With Learning Differences

Accommodations are decided upon an individual basis after a thorough review of appropriate, current documentation. The accommodations requests must be supported through the documentation provided and must be logically linked to the current impact of the condition on academic functioning.

Allowed in exams
Calculator: NR
Dictionary: NR
Computer: NR
Spellchecker: NR
Extended test time: Yes
Scribes: NR
Proctors: Yes
Oral exams: NR
Note-takers: Yes
Support services for students with LD: Yes
Support services for students with ADHD: Yes
Support services for students with ASD: NR
Distraction-reduced environment: Yes
Tape recording in class: NR
Electronic texts: Yes
Kurzweil reader: NR
Audio books: NR
Other assistive technology: Yes
Priority registration: No
Added costs of services: NR
LD specialists: Yes
ADHD coaching: NR
ASD specialists: NR
Professional tutors: No
Peer tutors: NR
Max. hours/wk. for services: NR
How professors are notified of student approved accommodations: By student

GENERL ADMISSIONS INFORMATION

Office of Admissions: 303-492-6301

Entrance Requirements

Academic units required: 4 English, 4 math, 3 science, 2 science labs, 3 foreign language, 3 social studies, 1 history, and 1 units from above areas or other academic areas. High school diploma is required and GED is accepted. SAT or ACT required. If ACT, ACT with writing accepted.

Application deadline: 1/15
Notification: 4/1
Average GPA: 3.62
ACT Composite middle 50% range: 24-30
SAT Math middle 50% range: 540-660
SAT Critical Reading middle 50% range: 530-640
SAT Writing middle 50% range: NR-NR
Graduate top 10% of class: 28
Graduated top 25% of class: 57
Graduated top 50% of class: 89

COLLEGE GRADUATION REQUIREMENTS

Course waivers allowed: No
In what course: NR
Course substitutions allowed: No
In what course: NR

Additional Information

Environment: This public school was founded in 1876. It has a 600-acre campus.

Student Body
Undergrad enrollment: 27,010
% Women: 45
% Men: 55
% Out-of-state: 40

Cost information
In-state tuition: $9,312
Out-of-state tuition: $31,410
Room & board: $13,194

Housing Information
University Housing: Yes
Percent living on campus: 29

Greek System
Fraternity: Yes
Sorority: Yes
Athletics: Division I

University of Colorado—Colorado Springs

1420 Austin Bluffs Parkway, Colorado Springs, CO 80918
Phone: 719-255-3084
E-mail: go@uccs.edu • Web: www.uccs.edu
Support: CS • Institution: Public

WY
NE
UT
KS
CO
AZ
NM
TX
Cheyenne
Boulder
Denver
Colorado Springs
Pueblo
Santa Fe

Programs or Services for Students with Learning Differences

University of Colorado—Colorado Springs is committed to providing equal educational opportunity for all students who meet the academic admission requirements. The purpose of Disability Services is to provide comprehensive support to meet the individual needs of students with disabilities. Students are expected to utilize the resources of Disability Services to the degree they determine necessary.

Admission Information for Students with Learning Differences

College entrance tests required: Yes
Interview required: No
Essay required: No
Additional application required for LD/ADHD/ASD: NR
What documentation required for LD: Psycho ed evaluation to include: relevant historical info, instructional interventions, related services, age diagnosed, objective data (aptitude, achievement, info processing), test scores (standard, percentile and grade equivalents) and describe functional limitations.
With general application: No
To receive services after enrolling: Yes
What documentation required for ADHD: Diagnosis based on DSM-V; history of behaviors impairing functioning in academic setting; diagnostic interview; history of symptoms; evidence of ongoing behaviors.
With general application: No
To receive services after enrolling: Yes
What documentation required for ASD: Psycho ed evaluation
With general application: NR
To receive services after enrolling: Yes
LD/ADHD/ASD documentation submitted to: Disability Services
ASD Specific Program: NR
Special Ed. HS course work accepted: No
Specific course requirements of all applicants: Yes
Separate application required: No
Total # of students receiving LD/ADHD/ASD services: 40
Acceptance into program means acceptance into college: Student must be admitted and enrolled in the university first and then reviewed for LD services.

Admissions

An applicant's learning disability is not considered in an admission decision. All applicants are required to meet the Minimum Academic Preparation Standards (MAPS), including 4 years of English, 3 years of math (4 years for engineering and business), 3 years of natural science, 2 years of social science, 2 years of a foreign language, and 1 year of an elective; fine and performing arts are encouraged. Courses taken before 9th grade are accepted as long as the documentation provided shows that the courses were completed. American Sign Language is a qualified substitute for a foreign language. Successfully completing 2 years of a foreign language will satisfy the foreign language requirement regardless of whether the courses were taken before the 9th grade. Students with deficiencies may be admitted to the university provided they meet the other admission standards of test scores, rank in class, and GPA (minimum of 2.8), provided they make up any deficiencies in the MAPS prior to graduation.

Additional Information

Students with learning disabilities receive information in their acceptance letter about contacting Disability Services if they wish to request accommodations or services. Students must request services and submit appropriate documentation. Students must meet with Disability Services to discuss support services and/or accommodations that are appropriate. Strategy development is offered in study skills, reading, test performance, stress reduction, time management, and writing skills. Disability Services offers the use of volunteers who use carbonless paper provided by the support services. Services and accommodations are available for undergraduate and graduate students with learning disabilities. Tutors are available for all university students in labs; tutors are also provided for students with disabilities.

General Support Services Information

Contact Information
Name of program or department: Disability Services
Telephone: 719-262-3354
Fax: 719-262-3195

Accommodations or Services For Students With Learning Differences

Accommodations are decided upon an individual basis after a thorough review of appropriate, current documentation. The accommodations requested must be supported through the documentation provided and must be logically linked to the current impact of the condition on academic functioning.

Allowed in exams
Calculator: NR
Dictionary: Yes
Computer: Yes
Spellchecker: Yes
Extended test time: Yes
Scribes: Yes
Proctors: Yes
Oral exams: Yes
Note-takers: No
Services for students with LD: Yes
Services for students with ADHD: Yes
Services for students with ASD: Yes
Distraction-reduced environment: Yes
Tape recording in class: Yes
Audio books: NR
Electronic texts: Yes
Kurzweil Reader: Yes
Other assistive technology: Yes
Priority registration: No
Added costs for services: No
LD specialists: Yes
ADHD coaching: NR
ASD specialists: NR
Professional tutors: No
Peer tutors: No
Max. hours/wk. for services: N/A
How professors are notified of LD/ADHD: By student

General Admissions Information

Office of Admissions: 719-255-3084

Entrance Requirements

Academic units required: 4 English, 4 math, 3 science, 2 science labs, 1 foreign language, 3 social studies, 1 history, 2 academic electives, **Academic units recommended:** 4 English, 4 math, 3 science, 2 science labs, 1 foreign language, 3 social studies, 1 history, 2 academic electives. High school diploma is required and GED is accepted. SAT or ACT required. If ACT, ACT with writing accepted. TOEFL required of all international applicants: minimum paper TOEFL 550.

Application deadline: NR
Notification: NR
Average GPA: 3.31
ACT Composite middle 50% range: 21-25
SAT Math middle 50% range: 472-600
SAT Critical Reading middle 50% range: 470-590
SAT Writing middle 50% range: 450-560
Graduated top 10% of class: 13
Graduated top 25% of class: 36
Graduated top 50% of class: 70

COLLEGE GRADUATION REQUIREMENTS

Course waivers allowed: No
In what course: N/A
Course substitutions allowed: Yes
In what course: American Sign Language is accepted as a foreign language.

Additional Information

Environment: This public school was founded in 1965. It has a 504-acre campus.

Student Body
Undergrad enrollment: 9,051
% Women: 53
% Men: 47
% Out-of-state: 11

Cost information
Room & board: NR
Housing Information
University Housing: Yes
Percent living on campus: 13

Greek System
Fraternity: NR
Sorority: Yes
Athletics: Division II

University of Denver

Office of Admission, Denver, CO 80208
Phone: 303-871-2036 • Fax: 303-871-3301
E-mail: admission@du.edu • Web: www.du.edu
Support: SP • Institution: Private

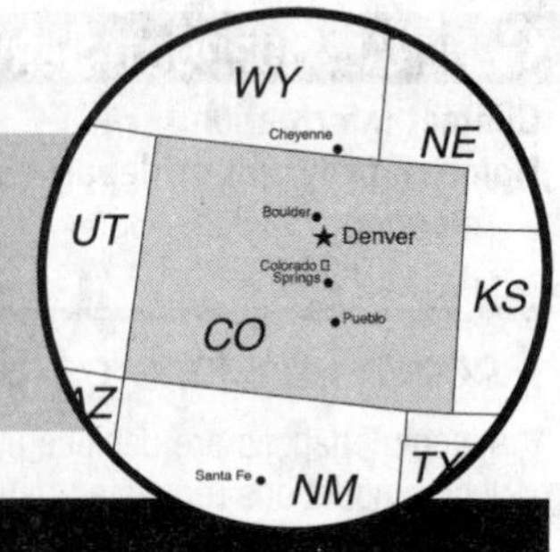

Programs or Services for Students with Learning Differences

The Learning Effectiveness Program (LEP) is a comprehensive program structured to provide students with individualized support. LEP counselors work one-on-one with students to determine their learning strengths and to develop skills that will allow them to be successful university students. LEP helps students understand their learning difference and how it impacts their collegiate experience; develop organizational and learning strategies based on their strengths; identify, implement and effectively use University resources; emphasize continual development of self-advocacy skills; find balance between social and academic activities; discover confidence, inherent motivation, and self-awareness; and develop educational goals consistent with their life's passion and objectives. THE LEP serves approximately 230 students each year. There is a fee for students enrolled in the LEP. The Disability Services program is a separate program that provides accommodations at no cost to any student who has a documented disability or medical issue as required by the Americans with Disabilities Act and Section 504 of the Rehabilitation Act. DSP accommodations may include but are not limited to: extended time on tests, alternate-format text, and note-taking services.

Admission Information for Students with Learning Differences

College entrance test required: Yes
Interview required: No
Additional application required for LD/ADHD/ASD: NR
What documentation required for LD: We require a full psychoeducational evaluation within the last three years. Ideally, we are looking for an aptitude test and an achievement test, though we are not strictly tied to a discrepancy model for diagnosis. If you have questions regarding appropriate testing, please contact the program.
With general application: No
To receive services after enrolling: Yes
What documentation required for ADHD: Full evaluation documenting the diagnosis of ADHD, impact this has on student and recommended accommodations
With general application: No
To receive services after enrolling: Yes
What documentation required for ASD: Same as above
With general application: No
To receive services after enrolling: Yes
LD/ADHD/ASD documentation submitted to: Support program/services
ASD Specific Program: NR
Special Ed. HS course work accepted: No
Specific course requirements of all applicants: Yes
Separate application required for program services: Yes
Total # of students receiving LD/ADHD/ASD services: NR
Acceptance into program means acceptance into college: NR

Admissions

Admission to the university is distinct from enrollment in the LEP. All potential DU candidates must submit a general admissions application, essay, recommendations, activity sheet, high school transcript, and ACT/SAT scores. Students applying to LEP must be accepted by DU and make separate application to the LEP, as well as provide documentation of LD/ADHD through recent diagnostic tests. Strengths, weaknesses, maturity level, ability to handle frustration, and feelings about limitations should also be included in documentation sent to the LEP. A campus visit and interview with LEP is recommended after submission of all documentation and testing. Interviews should be scheduled as far in advance as possible. DU looks for students who have challenged themselves academically and recommend 4 years English, 3-4 years math, 3-4 years social studies, 3-4 years science and 3-4 foreign languages. The middle 50% GPA ranges from 3.51-4.0 The ACT or SAT is required and Denver will "super score" either the ACT or SAT to determine the highest composite score on either test. Extra-curricular activities are important as are the teacher/counselor recommendations.

Additional Information

LEP services are only available to students who are enrolled in the LEP program. The LEP is a fee-for-service program that provides services beyond the mandated accommodations provided under Section 504. There is an additional fee per year for this program. The director is an LD specialist and the staff is composed of professionals in a variety of academic disciplines and have been trained to work with students with learning differences. Professional tutoring is also available to students enrolled in this program. Students who feel that they need only basic accommodations and do not wish to participate in the comprehensive program should contact Disability Services Program at 303-871-2372 to make those arrangements. Learning disability assessments are available on campus through the Counseling Center.

General Support Services Information

Contact Information
Name of program or department: Disability Services Program
Telephone: 303-871-2372
Fax: 303-871-3939

Accommodations or Services for Students with Learning Differences

Accommodations are decided upon an individual basis after a thorough review of appropriate, current documentation. The accommodations requests must be supported through the documentation provided and must be logically linked to the current impact of the condition on academic functioning.

Allowed in exams
Calculator: Yes
Dictionary: No
Computer: Yes
Spellchecker: No
Extended test time: Yes
Scribes: Yes
Proctors: Yes
Oral exams: Yes
Note-takers: Yes
Services for students with LD: Yes
Services for students with ADHD: Yes
Services for students with ASD: Yes
Distraction-reduced environment: Yes
Tape recording in class: Yes
Kurzweil reader: Yes
Audio books from learning ally: Yes
Other assistive technology: Yes
Priority registration: Yes
Added costs of services: Yes
LD specialists: Yes
ADHD coaching: NR
ASD specialists: NR
Professional tutors: Yes
Peer tutors: No
How professors are notified of student approved accommodations: Student

General Admissions Information

Office of Admissions: 303-871-2036

Entrance Requirements

Academic units recommended: 4 English, 2 science labs. High school diploma is required and GED is accepted. SAT or ACT required. If ACT, ACT with writing accepted. TOEFL required of all international applicants: minimum paper TOEFL 550 or minimum internet TOEFL 80.

Application deadline: 1/15
Notification: 3/15
Average GPA: 3.68
ACT Composite middle 50% range: 25-30
SAT Math middle 50% range: 560-660
SAT Critical Reading middle 50% range: 550-640
SAT Writing middle 50% range: 510-620
Graduated top 10% of class: 42
Graduated top 25% of class: 74
Graduated top 50% of class: 95

COLLEGE GRADUATION REQUIREMENTS

Course waivers allowed: No
Course substitutions allowed: Yes
In what course: In the area of foreign language, students may qualify to take substitution courses which still expose them to new cultures and identities, but do not have the intensive grammar component.

Additional Information

Environment: This private school was founded in 1864. It has a 125-acre campus.

Student Body
Undergrad enrollment: 5,643
% Women: 54
% Men: 46
% Out-of-state: 57

Cost information
Tuition: $43,164
Room & board: $11,498

Housing Information
University Housing: Yes
Percent living on campus: 47

Greek System
Fraternity: Yes
Sorority: Yes
Athletics: Division I

UNIVERSITY OF NORTHERN COLORADO

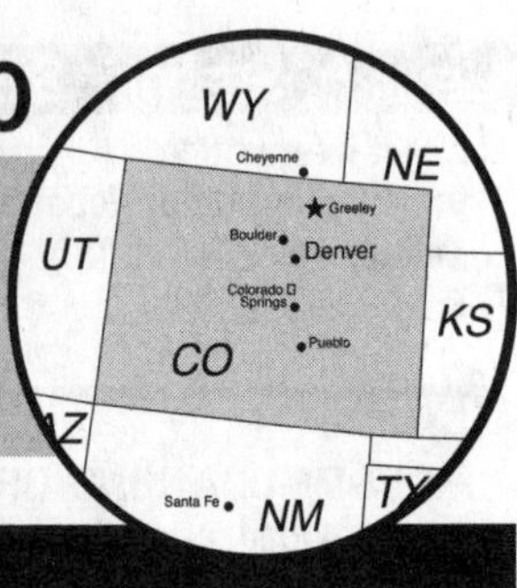

UNC Admissions Office, Greeley, CO 80639
Phone: 970-351-2881 • Fax: 970-351-2984
E-mail: admissions@unco.edu • Web: www.unco.edu
Support: S • Institution: Public

PROGRAMS OR SERVICES FOR STUDENTS WITH LEARNING DIFFERENCES

Although the university does not offer a formal LD program, individual assistance is provided whenever possible. The Disability Support Services (DSS) provides access, accommodations, and advocacy for UNC students who have documented disabilities. Academic needs are determined by the documentation and a student interview. Students with disabilities have an equal opportunity to pursue their educational goals. DSS provides test accommodations, adaptive hardware and software, learning strategies, organizational skills, and a reader program. Students requesting accommodations at UNC must provide test instruments from a certified professional that measures general intellect, aptitude, and more specific information processing tests; academic and vocational measures of achievement; and a clinical interview, which is the primary measure of previous educational and psychological functioning. Suggestions of reasonable accommodations that may be appropriate at the postsecondary level are encouraged. These recommendations should be supported by the diagnosis. Students with ADHD must provide a medical or clinical diagnosis from a developmental pediatrician, neurologist, and psychiatrist, licensed clinical or educational psychologist, family physician, or a combination of such professionals.

ADMISSION INFORMATION FOR STUDENTS WITH LEARNING DIFFERENCES

College entrance test required: Yes
Interview required: Yes
Essay required: No
Additional Application Required for LD/ADHD/ASD: NR
What documentation required for LD: Psycho ed evaluation toinclude: relevant historical info, instructional interventions, related services, age diagnosed, objective data (aptitude,achievement, info processing), test scores (standard, percentileand grade equivalents) and describe functional limitations.
With general application: No
To receive services after enrolling: Yes
What documentation required for ADHD: Diagnosis basedon DSM-V; history of behaviors impairing functioning inacademic setting; diagnostic interview; history of symptoms;evidence of ongoing behaviors.
With general application: No
To receive services after enrolling: Yes
What documentation required for ASD: Psycho ed evaluation
With general application: NR
To receive services after enrolling: Yes
LD/ADHD/ASD documentation submitted to: Disability Support Services (DSS)
ASD Specific Program: NR
Special Ed. HS course work accepted: Yes
Specific course requirements of all applicants: Yes
Separate application required for program services: No
Total # of students receiving LD/ADHD/ASD services: 100
Acceptance into program means acceptance into college: Students must be admitted and enrolled in the university first and then request services.

ADMISSIONS

There is no special admission process for students with learning disabilities. All students with disabilities are admitted to UNC under the standard admission requirements of the university. The university uses class rank, GPA, and test scores to determine a selection index. UNC requires 3 years of math, and the classes must be college-prep. Pre-Algebra does not count. UNC recommends 4 years of English, 3 years of history/social sciences, and 3 years of natural science. When UNC evaluates a transcript for admissions, they only look at the math. The UNC has a special window for admitting students who do not meet UNC's freshman admission requirements but want to earn full admission into a degree program. Students wishing to participate in this program need to call the Admissions Office. Each applicant is judged on an individual basis. Students do not need to be LD to apply for this DSS program but must have a documented disability. To assist in determining eligibility for the program, current medical/clinical information is necessary. To receive services, students must request accommodations upon arrival at UNC. Students enrolled in the Challenge Program must take 12 hours of college credit and earn a GPA of 2.0 after one or two semesters to remain at UNC.

ADDITIONAL INFORMATION

Services for individuals with LD/ADHD includes learning strategies, organizational skills, and advocacy skills; reader program; test accommodations; assistance in arranging for note-takers; and assistive technology, including voice synthesizers, screen readers, screen enlargers, scanners, voice-recognition computer systems, large monitors, and word processing with spellchecker. Workshops are offered in student skills, organizational skills, study strategies, and time management. These workshops are electives and are not for credit. Services and accommodations are available for undergraduate and graduate students.

General Support Services Information

Contact Information
Name of program or department: Disability Support Services (DSS)
Telephone: 970-351-2289
Fax: 970-351-4166
Website: NR

Accommodations or Services For Students With Learning Differences

Accommodations are decided upon an individual basis after a thorough review of appropriate, current documentation. The accommodations requests must be supported through the documentation provided and must be logically linked to the current impact of the condition on academic functioning.

Allowed in exams
Calculator: Yes
Dictionary: Yes
Computer: Yes
Spellchecker: Yes
Extended test time: Yes
Scribes: Yes
Proctors: Yes
Oral exams: Yes
Note-takers: Yes
Support services for students with LD: NR
Support services for students with ADHD: NR
Support services for students with ASD: NR
Distraction-reduced environment: Yes
Tape recording in class: Yes
Electronic texts: Yes
Kurzweil reader: NR
Audio books: NR
Other assistive technology: Yes
Priority registration: Yes
Added costs of services: No
LD specialists: No
ADHD coaching: NR
ASD specialists: NR
Professional tutors: No
Peer tutors: Yes
Max. hours/wk. for services: NR
How professors are notified of student approved accommodations: By student

General Admissions Information

Office of Admissions: 970-351-2881

Entrance Requirements

Academic units recommended: 4 English, 4 math, 3 science, 2 science labs, 1 foreign language, 2 social studies, 1 history, 2 academic electives. High school diploma is required and GED is accepted. SAT or ACT recommended. If ACT, ACT with writing accepted. TOEFL required of all international applicants.

Application deadline: 8/1
Notification: Rolling starting 9/1
Average GPA: 3.23
ACT Composite middle 50% range: 19-25
SAT Math middle 50% range: 450-580
SAT Critical Reading middle 50% range: 460-580
SAT Writing middle 50% range: NR-NR
Graduate top 10% of class: 13
Graduated top 25% of class: 35
Graduated top 50% of class: 74

COLLEGE GRADUATION REQUIREMENTS

Course waivers allowed: NR
Course substitutions allowed: NR

Additional Information

Environment: This public school was founded in 1890. It has a 243-acre campus.

Student Body
Undergrad enrollment: 9,394
% Women: 63
% Men: 37
% Out-of-state: 13.8

Cost information
In-state tuition: $6,372
Out-of-state tuition: $17,958
Room & board: $10,360

Housing Information
University Housing: Yes
Percent living on campus: 35.8

Greek System
Fraternity: Yes
Sorority: Yes
Athletics: Division I

Western State Colorado University

600 N. Adams, Gunnison, CO 81231
Phone: 970-943-2119 • Fax: 970-943-2363
E-mail: admissions@western.edu • Web: www.western.edu
Support: S • Institution: Public

WY
Cheyenne
NE
Boulder
UT
Colorado Springs
Gunnison
Pueblo
KS
CO
AZ
Santa Fe
NM
TX

Programs or Services for Students with Learning Differences

Disability Services, located in Western's Academic Resource Center, coordinates support services for all qualified students with disabilities. We offer a variety of resources and accommodations to assist students as they pursue their academic and career goals. While providing a supportive environment, we encourage students to develop independence and take responsibility for their academic experiences. Personal consultation and workshops are available to help students improve learning, problem-solving, and self-advocacy skills.

Admission Information for Students with Learning Differences

College entrance tests required: Yes
Interview required: No
Essay required: No
Additional application required for LD/ADHD/ASD: NR
What documentation required for LD: Psycho ed evaluation to include: relevant historical info, instructional interventions, related services, age diagnosed, objective data (aptitude, achievement, info processing), test scores (standard, percentile and grade equivalents) and describe functional limitations.
With general application: No
To receive services after enrolling: Yes
What documentation required for ADHD: Diagnosis based on DSM-V; history of behaviors impairing functioning in academic setting; diagnostic interview; history of symptoms; evidence of ongoing behaviors.
With general application: No
To receive services after enrolling: Yes
What documentation required for ASD: Psycho ed evaluation
With general application: NR
To receive services after enrolling: Yes
LD/ADHD/ASD documentation submitted to: Disability Services
ASD Specific Program: NR
Special Ed. HS course work accepted: Yes
Specific course requirements of all applicants: Yes
Separate application required: No
Total # of students receiving LD/ADHD/ASD services: NR
Acceptance into program means acceptance into college: Students must be admitted and enrolled prior to requesting services.

Admissions

Admission to Western depends on academic performance and background, standardized test scores, and personal attributes. In addition to general admissions requirements, Western State recommends a personal essay and recommendations from teachers, counselors, or others who know the student's academic ability. The college tries to admit those students who have demonstrated their ability to succeed. Normally, students are admitted if they meet the following criteria: graduate from an accredited high school; have a cumulative GPA of 2.5 or better (on a 4.0 scale of college-prep courses) and/or rank in the upper two-thirds of the student's graduating class; and score 20 or higher on the ACT or 950 on the SAT. Western recommends 4 years of English, 3 years of mathematics to include algebra II, 2 years of natural science, and 2 years of social science. Modern language and computer science units are also important.

Additional Information

Students who choose to register for Learning Disability Program/Services typically do so soon after acceptance to Western. All accepted students will receive information regarding the Academic Resource Center, including Disability Services and the registration link (www.western.edu/dsinfo). Once registered, all students will go through an intake session with Disability Services staff to review policies, procedures, resources, and accommodations. Some of the services used by students include, but are not limited to, test accommodations, taped textbooks, readers, scribes, note-takers, and assistance with academic advising and course registration. Individual learning skills assistance is availalble through appointments and workshops, our staff works with students to help them develop effective learning skills and study strategies in areas such as reading, memory, test taking, note-taking, organization, and time management. We encourage students who wish to enhance motivation, develop an understanding of individual learning styles, and improve academic performance to use the Academic Resource Center's resources.

General Support Services Information

Contact Information
Name of program or department: Disability Services
Telephone: 970.943.7056
Fax: 970.943.3409

Accommodations or Services For Students With Learning Differences

Accommodations are decided upon an individual basis after a thorough review of appropriate, current documentation. The accommodations requested must be supported through the documentation provided and must be logically linked to the current impact of the condition on academic functioning.

Allowed in exams
Calculator: Yes
Dictionary: No
Computer: Yes
Spellchecker: Yes
Extended test time: Yes
Scribes: Yes
Proctors: Yes
Oral exams: Yes
Note-takers: Yes
Services for students with LD: Yes
Services for students with ADHD: Yes
Services for students with ASD: Yes
Distraction-reduced environment: Yes
Tape recording in class: Yes
Audio books: NR
Electronic texts: Yes
Kurzweil Reader: Yes
Other assistive technology: Yes
Priority registration: Yes
Added costs for services: No
LD specialists: No
ADHD coaching: NR
ASD specialists: NR
Professional tutors: No
Peer tutors: NR
Max. hours/wk. for services: NR
How professors are notified of LD/ADHD: By student

General Admissions Information

Office of Admissions: (970) 943-2119

Entrance Requirements

Academic units required: 4 English, 4 math, 3 science, 2 science labs, 1 foreign language, 3 social studies, 1 history, 2 academic electives, **Academic units recommended:** 2 foreign language. High school diploma is required and GED is accepted. SAT or ACT required. If ACT, ACT with writing accepted. TOEFL required of all international applicants: minimum paper TOEFL 550.

Application deadline: 8/1
Notification: Rolling starting 11/1
Average GPA: 2.87
ACT Composite middle 50% range: 17-23
SAT Math middle 50% range: 450-560
SAT Critical Reading middle 50% range: 460-580
SAT Writing middle 50% range: NR-NR
Graduated top 10% of class: NR
Graduated top 25% of class: NR
Graduated top 50% of class: NR

COLLEGE GRADUATION REQUIREMENTS

Course waivers allowed: No
Course substitutions allowed: Yes
In what course: Math substitutions may be approved for students with documented math learning disabilies, when appropriate.

Additional Information

Environment: This public school was founded in 1911. It has a 228-acre campus.

Student Body
Undergrad enrollment: 2,419
% Women: 43
% Men: 57
% Out-of-state: 28

Cost information
Room & board: NR

Housing Information
University Housing: Yes
Percent living on campus: 45

Greek System
Fraternity: NR
Sorority: NR
Athletics: Division II

Fairfield University

1073 North Benson Road, Fairfield, CT 06824-5171
Phone: 203-254-4100 • Fax: 203-254-4199
E-mail: admis@fairfield.edu • Web: www.fairfield.edu
Support: CS • Institution: Private

Programs or Services for Students with Learning Differences

The university provides services for students with disabilities through Student Support Services. There is no learning disability program, only services that are available for all students with disabilities. These services are designed to provide equal access to the learning environment. Students are supported while being encouraged to be self-advocates. Students with learning disabilities must provide documentation from an appropriate testing agent. Students with ADHD must have documentation from appropriate professionals who can provide behavior rating scales, ruling out other disabilities, and showing the onset of the ADHD between ages 7–12. All documentation should be submitted to Student Support Services.

Admission Information for Students with Learning Differences

College entrance test required: No
Interview required: No
Essay required: NR
Additional Application Required for LD/ADHD/ASD: No
What documentation required for LD: Psycho ed evaluation
With general application: No
To receive services after enrolling: Yes
What documentation required for ADHD: Psycho ed evaluation
With general application: No
To receive services after enrolling: Yes
What documentation required for ASD: Psycho ed evaluation
With general application: No
To receive services after enrolling: Yes
LD/ADHD/ASD documentation submitted to: Disability Support Services
ASD Specific Program: No
Special Ed. HS course work accepted: NR
Specific course requirements of all applicants: NR
Separate application required for program services: NR
Total # of students receiving LD/ADHD/ASD services: NR
Acceptance into program means acceptance into college: NR

Admissions

There is no special admissions process for students with learning disabilities. Admission criteria include ranking in top 40 percent of graduating class or better; maintaining a B average; scoring 25 ACT, although submitting ACT/SAT is optional; counselor recommendations; and college-prep courses including 4 years of English, 3–4 years of math, 2–4 years of a foreign language, 1–3 years of science lab, and 2–3 years of history. Courses taken in the Special Education Department may be acceptable. The mid 50 percent SAT Reasoning Test scores are 1720–1930, and ACT scores are 26–29. Once students have been admitted and have enrolled, they may initiate contact for services.

Additional Information

Skills courses are offered in study skills, note-taking strategies, time management skills, and strategies for success. These skills courses are not for credit. Students are offered meetings with a professional who has a background in teaching students with disabilities. Letters are sent to professors on students' request. All students have access to content tutoring and a Writing Center. Services and accommodations are available for undergraduate and graduate students.

General Support Services Information

Contact Information

Name of program or department: Disability Support Services

Telephone: 203-254-4000 x: 2615

Fax: NR

Website: www.fairfield.edu/disabilitysupport

Accommodations or Services For Students With Learning Differences

Accommodations are decided upon an individual basis after a thorough review of appropriate, current documentation. The accommodations requests must be supported through the documentation provided and must be logically linked to the current impact of the condition on academic functioning.

Allowed in exams
Calculator: Yes
Dictionary: Yes
Computer: Yes
Spellchecker: Yes
Extended test time: Yes
Scribes: Yes
Proctors: Yes
Oral exams: Yes
Note-takers: Yes
Support services for students with LD: Yes
Support services for students with ADHD: Yes
Support services for students with ASD: Yes
Distraction-reduced environment: Yes
Tape recording in class: Yes
Electronic texts: Yes
Kurzweil reader: NR
Audio books: Yes
Other assistive technology: Yes
Priority registration: Yes
Added costs of services: No
LD specialists: No
ADHD coaching: No
ASD specialists: No
Professional tutors: No
Peer tutors: Yes
Max. hours/wk. for services: 4
How professors are notified of student approved accommodations: By student

General Admissions Information

Office of Admissions: 203-254-4100

Entrance Requirements

Academic units required: 4 English, 3 math, 3 science, 2 science labs, 2 foreign language, 2 social studies, 2 history, **Academic units recommended:** 4 English, 4 math, 4 science, 4 foreign language, 2 social studies, 2 history. High school diploma is required and GED is not accepted. SAT or ACT considered if submitted. If ACT, ACT with writing accepted. TOEFL required of all international applicants: minimum paper TOEFL 550 or minimum internet TOEFL 80.

Application deadline: 1/15
Notification: 4/1
Average GPA: 3.41
ACT Composite middle 50% range: 25-29
SAT Math middle 50% range: 560-640
SAT Critical Reading middle 50% range: 540-630
SAT Writing middle 50% range: 550-640
Graduate top 10% of class: 31
Graduated top 25% of class: 69
Graduated top 50% of class: 97

COLLEGE GRADUATION REQUIREMENTS

Course waivers allowed: Yes

In what course: foreign language

Course substitutions allowed: Not Applicable

In what course: NR

Additional Information

Environment: This private school, affiliated with the Roman Catholic-Jesuit Church, was founded in 1942. It has a 200-acre campus.

Student Body
Undergrad enrollment: 3,970
% Women: 60
% Men: 40
% Out-of-state: 72
Cost information
Tuition: $44,250
Room & board: $13,520
Housing Information
University Housing: Yes
Percent living on campus: 75
Greek System
Fraternity: NR
Sorority: NR
Athletics: Division I

MITCHELL COLLEGE

437 Pequot Avenue, New London, CT 06320
Phone: 860-701-5011 • Fax: 860-444-1209
E-mail: admissions@mitchell.edu • Web: www.mitchell.edu/
Support: SP • Institution: Private

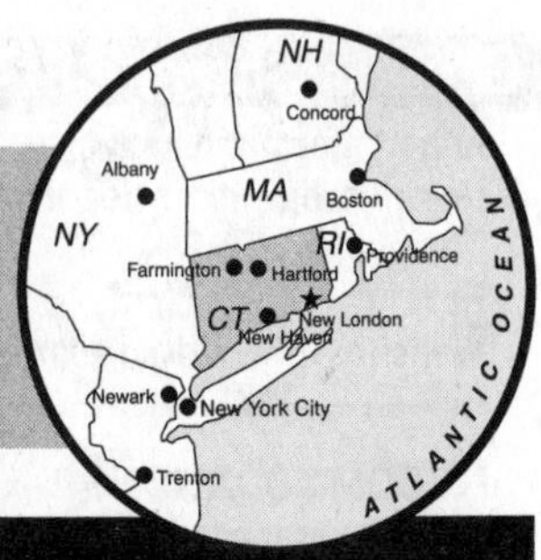

PROGRAMS OR SERVICES FOR STUDENTS WITH LEARNING DIFFERENCES

Mitchell College is dedicated to providing a student-centered, supportive learning environment that addresses the educational needs of all students, including those with disabilities. The Duques Academic Success Center offers academic and other supports through five functions—the Tutoring Center offers professional tutoring to all students; the Career Center helps students investigate and pursue career options; the Academic Advising Center offers professional academic advising: Disability Student Services (DSS) determines eligibility for services and arranges accommodations; and the Bentsen Learning Resource Center (LRC) for students with documented learning disabilities and ADHD. The LRC offers three levels of academic support. Students participating at Level 1 work with a LRC Specialist 3 times a week. An individualized program of support is developed based on a student's learning strengths, challenges, and goals. Close individual attention, frequent contact, and structured follow up are the main components of the fee-based program. Level 2 is an enhanced support program offering less-involved and less-directed assistance on an individual and/or small group basis, with up to 2 scheduled appointments a week. Level 3 is appropriate for students who can apply a variety of learning strategies across the curriculum, but who may still benefit from limited support and one weekly meeting with a learning specialist.

ADMISSION INFORMATION FOR STUDENTS WITH LEARNING DIFFERENCES

College entrance tests required: No
Interview required: Yes
Essay required: Yes
Additional application required for LD/ADHD/ASD: NR
What documentation required for LD: Psycho ed evaluation to include: relevant historical info, instructional interventions, related services, age diagnosed, objective data (aptitude, achievement, info processing), test scores (standard, percentile and grade equivalents) and describe functional limitations.
With general application: Yes if requested as part of Structured Program application
To receive services after enrolling: Yes
What documentation required for ADHD: Diagnosis based on DSM-V; history of behaviors impairing functioning in academic setting; diagnostic interview; history of symptoms; evidence of ongoing behaviors.
With general application: Yes if requested as part of Structured Program application
To receive services after enrolling: Yes
What documentation required for ASD: Psycho ed evaluation
With general application: NR
To receive services after enrolling: Yes
LD/ADHD/ASD documentation submitted to: DSS
ASD Specific Program: NR
Special Ed. HS course work accepted: NR
Specific course requirements for all applicants: No
Separate application required: Submittal of documentation currently constitutes application for eligibility determination.
Total # of students receiving LD/ADHD/ASD services: 300

ADMISSIONS

Students must first apply and be accepted into Mitchell College. Application requirements are listed on www.mitchell.edu and include the application itself, transcripts, at least one recommendation, a written personal statement, as well as an interview. Standardized tests are currently optional. A high school diploma or GED is required for admission. Applicants are evaluated holistically and admitted based on their potential. Generally, students who complete a college preparatory curriculum with a GPA of 2.0 or higher are admitted. Approximately 95 percent of those who are admitted receive financial aid, which can be applied to supplemental fees for services offered by the LRC. Students who are interested in participating in the LRC program need to complete a Request for Services Application. In addition, students need to submit documentation of a learning disability and or AD/HD to Disability Student Services.

ADDITIONAL INFORMATION

Mitchell College also has the "Thames Academy," a post-grad (PG) or pre-college transitional experience. It is a year of academic preparation that students take between the end of their high school education and the start of their college studies. Unlike traditional post-grad programs at prep schools, Thames Academy at Mitchell College provides college-level courses for credit. Located on Mitchell College Campus, the Academy provides a structured residential program within a collegiate environment and co-curricular interaction with two- and four-year students. Tuition for the 2016-2017 Thames Academy school year is $50,865.

General Support Services Information

Contact Information
Name of program or department: Bentsen Learning Resource Center
Telephone: 860-701-5145
Fax: 860-701-5090

Accommodations or Services For Students With Learning Differences

Accommodations are decided upon an individual basis after a thorough review of appropriate, current documentation. The accommodations requested must be supported through the documentation provided and must be logically linked to the current impact of the condition on academic functioning.

Allowed in exams
Calculator: Yes
Dictionary: Yes
Computer: Yes
Spellchecker: Yes
Extended test time: Yes
Scribes: Yes
Proctors: Yes
Oral exams: Yes
Note-takers: Yes
Services for students with LD: Yes
Services for students with ADHD: Yes
Services for students with ASD: Yes
Distraction-reduced environment: Yes
Tape recording in class: Yes
Audio books: NR
Electronic texts: Yes
Kurzweil Reader: Yes
Other assistive technology: Yes
Priority registration: N/A
Added costs for services: Yes
LD specialists: Yes
ADHD coaching: NR
ASD specialists: NR
Professional tutors: 10–12
Peer tutors: No
Max. hours/wk. for services: 4
How professors are notified of LD/ADHD: By student

General Admissions Information

Office of Admissions: 860-701-5011

Entrance Requirements

Academic units recommended: 4 English, 3 math, 3 science, 2 social studies, 2 history, 2 academic electives. High school diploma is required and GED is accepted. SAT or ACT not used. TOEFL required of all international applicants: minimum paper TOEFL 500.

Application deadline: NR
Notification: Rolling starting 12/15
Average GPA: 2.68
ACT Composite middle 50% range: NR-NR
SAT Math middle 50% range: NR-NR
SAT Critical Reading middle 50% range: NR-NR
SAT Writing middle 50% range: NR-NR
Graduated top 10% of class: NR
Graduated top 25% of class: NR
Graduated top 50% of class: NR

COLLEGE GRADUATION REQUIREMENTS

Course waivers allowed: No
Course substitutions allowed: Yes
In what course: Varies based on the student's history with the subject area and the school policies and procedures.

Additional Information

Environment: This private school was founded in 1938. It has a 68-acre campus.

Student Body
Undergrad enrollment: 858
% Women: 47
% Men: 53
% Out-of-state: 42

Cost information
Tuition: $26,774
Room & board: $12,492
Housing Information
University Housing: Yes
Percent living on campus: 56

Greek System
Fraternity: No
Sorority: No
Athletics: Division III

SOUTHERN CONNECTICUT STATE U.

SCSU—Admissions House, 131 Farnham Ave., New Haven, CT 06515-1202
Phone: 203-392-5644 • Fax: 203-392-5727
E-mail: adminfo@scsu.ctstateu.edu • Web: www.southernct.edu
Support: CS • Institution type: 4-year public

PROGRAMS OR SERVICES FOR STUDENTS WITH LEARNING DIFFERENCES

The mission of the DRC is to ensure educational equity for students with disabilities. The DRC assists students in arranging for individualized accommodations and support services. The Center of Excellence on ASD is a resource on campus as well as to the surrounding community.

ADMISSION INFORMATION FOR STUDENTS WITH LEARNING DIFFERENCES

College entrance test required: Yes
Interview required: No
Essay required: No
Additional application required for LD/ADHD/ASD: NR
What documentation required for LD: There is a wide variety of tests we review, there's no single test in particular. We usually follow the current industry standard tests administered by psychologists. Please go to www.southernct.edu/DRC for more information on our Doc policy
With general application: No
To receive services after enrolling: Yes
What documentation required for ADHD: There is a wide variety of tests we review, there's no single test in particular. We usually follow the current industry standard tests administered by psychologists. Please go to www.southernct.edu/DRC for more information on our Doc policy
With general application: No
To receive services after enrolling: Yes
What documentation required for ASD: There is a wide variety of tests we review, there's no single test in particular. We usually follow the current industry standard tests administered by psychologists. Please go to www.southernct.edu/DRC for more information on our Doc policy.
With general application: No
To receive services after enrolling: Yes
LD/ADHD/ASD documentation submitted to: Support program/services
ASD Specific Program: NR
Special Ed. HS course work accepted: N/A
Specific course requirements of all applicants: No
Separate application required for program services: Yes
Total # of students receiving LD/ADHD/ASD services: 400
Acceptance into program means acceptance into college: NR

ADMISSIONS

There is no special admissions process for students with learning disabilities. All applicants must meet the same criteria. Course requirements include 4 years of English, 3 years of math, 2 years of science, 2 years of a foreign language, 2 years of social studies, and 2 years of history.

ADDITIONAL INFORMATION

Qualified students are invited to contact the DRC and schedule an in-take appointment to discuss their needs. The DRC also supports Outreach Unlimited, which is a student organization primarily made-up of students with disabilities. The DRC provides assistance with developing compensatory strategies such as time management, study skills, and identifying strengths and weaknesses. The DRC also helps with course selection, promotion of self determination in areas of self advocacy, goal setting, and career development. DRC Specialists offer weekly appointments of a first come first serve basis. Students can make an appointment at any point during the semester.

General Support Services Information

Name of program or department: Disability Resource Center (DRC)
Telephone: 203-392-6828
Fax: 203-392-6829

Accommodations or Services For Students With Learning Differences

Accommodations are decided upon an individual basis after a thorough review of appropriate, current documentation. The accommodations requests must be supported through the documentation provided and must be logically linked to the current impact of the condition on academic functioning.

Allowed in exams
Calculator: Yes
Dictionary: Yes
Computer: Yes
Spellchecker: Yes
Extended test time: Yes
Scribes: Yes
Proctors: Yes
Oral exams: Yes
Note-takers: Yes
Services for students with LD: Yes
Services for students with ADHD: Yes
Services for students with ASD: Yes
Distraction-reduced environment: Yes
Tape recording in class: Yes
Audio books from learning ally: Yes
Electronic texts: NR
Kurzweil Reader: Yes
Other assistive technology: Yes
Priority registration: Yes
Added costs of services: No
LD specialists: Yes
ADHD coaching: NR
ASD specialists: NR
Professional tutors: Yes
Peer tutors: No
Max. hours/wk. for services: NR
How professors are notified of student approved accommodations: Student

General Admissions Information

Office of Admissions: 203-392-5644

Entrance Requirements

Academic units required: 4 English, 3 math, 2 science, 1 science labs, 2 foreign language, 2 social studies, 2 history. **Academic units recommended:** 4 English, 4 math, 3 science, 4 foreign language, 3 social studies, 3 history. High school diploma is required and GED is accepted. SAT or ACT required. If ACT, ACT with writing required. TOEFL required of all international applicants: minimum paper TOEFL 525.

Application deadline: 4/1
Notification: Rolling starting 12/1
Average GPA: NR
ACT Composite middle 50% range: 17-22
SAT Math middle 50% range: 410-530
SAT Critical Reading middle 50% range: 420-520
SAT Writing middle 50% range: 420-530
Graduated top 10% of class: 5
Graduated top 25% of class: 21
Graduated top 50% of class: 60

COLLEGE GRADUATION REQUIREMENTS

Course waivers allowed: No
In what course: N/A
Course substitutions allowed: Yes
In what course: Foreign Language

Additional Information

Environment: This public school was founded in 1893. It has a 168-acre campus.

Student Body
Undergrad enrollment: 8,525
% Women: 60
% Men: 40
% Out-of-state: 4

Cost information
Out-of Tuition: $15,137
Room & board: $10,687
Housing Information
University Housing: Yes
Percent living on campus: 31

Greek System
Fraternity: Yes
Sorority: Yes
Athletics: Division II

University of Connecticut

2131 Hillside Road, Storrs, CT 06268-3088
Phone: 860-486-3137 • Fax: 860-486-1476
E-mail: beahusky@uconn.edu • Web: www.uconn.edu
Support: CS • Institution: Public

Programs or Services for Students with Learning Differences

All students enrolled at UConn are eligible to apply to the Center for Students with Disabilities. The CSD engages in an interactive and individualized process with each student in order to determine reasonable and appropriate accommodations. The goal of the Center is to ensure a comprehensively accessible University experience where individuals with disabilities have the same access to programs, opportunities and activities as all others. Students are elibile for accomodations such as extended time on exams, notetaking assistance, alternate media for printed materials, foreign language and math substitutions, and assistive and learning technologies. In addition to accomodations, the center also offers an enhanced fee-for-service program, referred to as Beyond Access, which provides students with an opportunity to work one-on-one with a trained strategy instructor to work on developing skills such as: time management and organization, study skills, stress management, self-advocacy, memory and concentration, social skills, career preparation, health and wellness, and reading and writing strategies.

Admission Information for Students with Learning Differences

College entrance test required: Yes
Interview required: No
Essay required: NR
Additional application required for LD/ADHD/ASD: NR
What documentation required for LD: Please refer to the CSD website at http://www.csd.uconn.edu/documentation_guidelines.html
With general application: No
To receive services after enrolling: Yes
What documentation required for ADHD: Please refer to the CSD website at http://www.csd.uconn.edu/documentation_guidelines.html
With general application: No
To receive services after enrolling: Yes
What documentation required for ASD: Please refer to the CSD website at http://www.csd.uconn.edu/documentation_guidelines.html
With general application: No
To receive services after enrolling: Yes
LD/ADHD/ASD documentation submitted to: Support program/services
ASD Specific Program: NR
Special Ed. HS course work accepted: N/A
Specific course requirements of all applicants: Yes
Separate application required for program services: Yes
Total # of students receiving LD/ADHD/ASD services: 270
Acceptance into program means acceptance into college: NR

Admissions

There is no separate application or application process for students with LD seeking accomodations and/or disability services through the CSD. Students must meet regular admissions requirements for admissions into UConn. Course requirements include 4 English, 3 math, 2 social studies, 2 foreign language, 2 science, and 3 electives. Once a student is admitted to UConn, he/she can request accommodations by contacting the Center for Students with Disabilities (CSD)—see www.csd.uconn.edu for specific information regarding requesting accommodations. Students are required to submit documentation to the CSD in order to be eligible for accommodations.

Additional Information

Students enrolled in Beyond Access work closely with a trained Strategy Instructor (SI) to design and customize their program based on their individual goals and learning profile. Students can chose to meet with their SI for three hours a week (Track I) or one hour per week (Track II) to work on developing skills such as: time management and organization, study skills, stress management, self-advocacy, memory and concentration, social skills, career preparation, health and wellness, and reading and writing strategies. As this program goes beyond the legislative mandates, in order to provide the necessary materiais and resources, participation in this program includes a rate of $3,400 per semester for Track I and $1,700, per semester for Track II. Goals of Beyond Access helps students identify strengths and challenges in both their academic and personal life; increase awareness of strategies, skills, and technologies for application in and out of the classroom; create a positive learning environment through active networking and communication amongst students, staff, faculty and parents and family members; and to help students build the self-determination needed to advocate for themselves on campus.

General Support Services Information

Contact Information
Name of program or department: Center for Students with Disabilities
Telephone: 860-486-2020
Fax: 860-486-5799

Accommodations or Services For Students With Learning Differences

Accommodations are decided upon an individual basis after a thorough review of appropriate, current documentation. The accommodations requests must be supported through the documentation provided and must be logically linked to the current impact of the condition on academic functioning.

Allowed in exams
Calculator: Yes
Dictionary: Yes
Computer: Yes
Spellchecker: Yes
Extended test time: Yes
Scribes: Yes
Proctors: Yes
Oral exams: Yes
Note-takers: Yes
Services for students with LD: Yes
Services for students with ADHD: Yes
Services for students with ASD: Yes
Distraction-reduced environment: Yes
Tape recording in class: Yes
Audio books from learning ally: Yes
Electronic texts: NR
Kurzweil Reader: Yes
Other assistive technology: Yes
Priority registration: Yes
Added costs of services: N/A
LD specialists: Yes
ADHD coaching: NR
ASD specialists: NR
Professional tutors: NR
Peer tutors: Yes
Max. hours/wk. for services: 1
How professors are notified of student approved accommodations: Both student and director

General Admissions Information

Office of Admissions: 860-486-3137

Entrance Requirements

Academic units required: 4 English, 3 math, 2 science, 2 science labs, 2 foreign language, 2 social studies, 3 academic electives. **Academic units recommended:** 3 foreign language. High school diploma is required and GED is accepted. SAT or ACT required. If ACT, ACT with writing required. TOEFL required of all international applicants: minimum paper TOEFL 550 or minimum internet TOEFL 79.

Application deadline: 1/15
Notification: Rolling starting 3/1
Average GPA: NR
ACT Composite middle 50% range: 26-30
SAT Math middle 50% range: 590-690
SAT Critical Reading middle 50% range: 560-660
SAT Writing middle 50% range: 550-660
Graduated top 10% of class: 50
Graduated top 25% of class: 85
Graduated top 50% of class: 98

COLLEGE GRADUATION REQUIREMENTS

Course waivers allowed: No
In what course: N/A
Course substitutions allowed: Yes
In what course: Based on documented evidence of significant impairment, some students qualify for course substitutions in foreign language or math courses.

Additional Information

Environment: This public school was founded in 1881. It has a 4,104-acre campus.

Student Body
Undergrad enrollment: 18,395
% Women: 50
% Men: 50
% Out-of-state: 22

Cost information
In-state tuition: $10,524
Out-of Tuition: $32,066
Room & board: $12,436

Housing Information
University Housing: Yes
Percent living on campus: 71

Greek System
Fraternity: Yes
Sorority: Yes
Athletics: Division I

UNIVERSITY OF HARTFORD

200 Bloomfield Avenue, West Hartford, CT 06117
Phone: 860-768-4296 • Fax: 860-768-4961
E-mail: admissions@mail.hartford.edu • Web: www.hartford.edu
Support: CS • Institution: Private

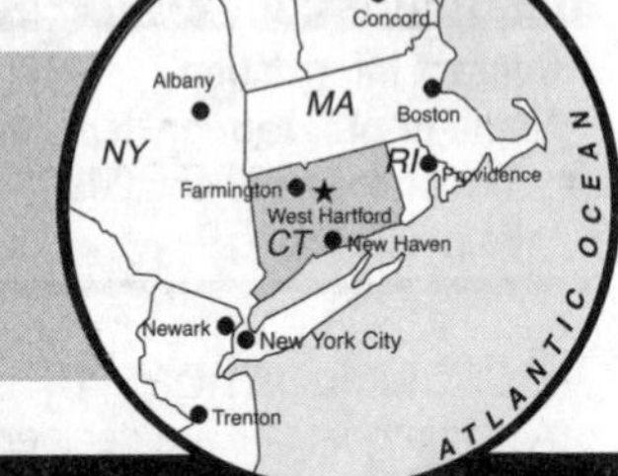

PROGRAMS OR SERVICES FOR STUDENTS WITH LEARNING DIFFERENCES

The Learning Plus program facilitates equal opportunity for academic achievement and is available to any student diagnosed with LD. Program objectives include help to: understand strengths and weaknesses; provide learning strategies; develop self-advocacy skills; connect with campus resources; develop decision-making skills; facilitate appropriate testing modifications; provide information to faculty and students regarding LD, classroom accommodations and testing modifications, and legal rights and responsibilities; and protect the confidentiality of student records. Learning Plus services include: Direct Strategies, in which students are assigned to an LP tutor and meet weekly for instruction in metacognitive skills such as information processing or organizational strategies; Check In, where students meet every other week with tutor for monitoring and organizational strategies; and Drop-In, for "as needed" assistance. Service determination depends on semester standing, GPA, and course curricula. Freshmen are assigned to Direct Strategies Instruction. Students with documentation are advised to contact the director of LP during the first week of classes. The director will discuss the disability, appropriate services, and classroom accommodations. Students are encouraged to discuss effective accommodations with professors. To receive services and accommodations from Learning Plus students should submit comprehensive documentation to the Director of Learning Plus, not admissions, after being accepted to the university.

ADMISSION INFORMATION FOR STUDENTS WITH LEARNING DIFFERENCES

College entrance test required: Yes
Interview required: No
Essay required: NR
Additional application required for LD/ADHD/ASD: NR
What documentation required for LD: WAIS and achievement testing.
With general application: No
To receive services after enrolling: Yes
What documentation required for ADHD: WAIS and achievement testing.
With general application: No
To receive services after enrolling: Yes
What documentation required for ASD: Psycho ed evaluation
With general application: No
To receive services after enrolling: Yes
LD/ADHD/ASD documentation submitted to: Learning Plus
ASD Specific Program: NR
Special Ed. HS course work accepted: Yes
Specific course requirements of all applicants: No
Separate application required for program services: No
Total # of students receiving LD/ADHD/ASD services: NR
Acceptance into program means acceptance into college: NR

ADMISSIONS

Students with learning disabilities do not apply to the Learning Plus Program, but do apply directly to one of the nine schools and colleges within the university. If admitted, students with learning disabilities may then elect to receive the support services offered. The Admissions Committee pays particular attention to the student's individual talents and aspirations, especially as they relate to programs available at the university. Some borderline applicants may be admitted as a summer admission. Course requirements include 4 years English, 3-3.5 years math, 2 years science, 2 years social studies, plus electives. Substitutions are allowed on rare occasions and depend on disability and major. Students may also apply to Hillyer College, which is a 2-year program with more flexible admission criteria. This is a developmental program, with flexible admission standards, offering many services. Hillyer provides students with the opportunity to be in a college atmosphere and, if successful, transfer into the 4-year program.

ADDITIONAL INFORMATION

Learning Plus is voluntary and students are required to seek assistance and to maintain contact. All modifications are determined on a case-by-case, course-by-course basis. The learning specialists are not content tutors. It is their goal to help students develop learning strategies and understand specific course material. Students are responsible for disclosing their LD to their professors. Skills classes are offered in study skills and math. Students can also receive one individual appointment weekly consisting of learning strategies from masters-level professionals. Instruction focuses on time management, organization strategies, reading, writing, mathematics, and course-specific study techniques. Some students with learning disabilities choose not to avail themselves of Learning Plus services. That is their privilege. The director of Learning Plus maintains confidential files of all documentation, should students request services at any time during their college career.

General Support Services Information

Contact Information
Name of program or department: DISABLED Students Services
Telephone: 860-768-5129
Fax: 860-768-4183

Accommodations or Services For Students With Learning Differences

Accommodations are decided upon an individual basis after a thorough review of appropriate, current documentation. The accommodations requests must be supported through the documentation provided and must be logically linked to the current impact of the condition on academic functioning.

Allowed in exams
Calculator: Yes
Dictionary: Yes
Computer: Yes
Spellchecker: Yes
Extended test time: Yes
Scribes: Yes
Proctors: Yes
Oral exams: Yes
Note-takers: Yes
Services for students with LD: Yes
Services for students with ADHD: Yes
Services for students with ASD: Yes
Distraction-reduced environment: Yes
Tape recording in class: Yes
Audio books from learning ally: No
Electronic texts: NR
Kurzweil Reader: Yes
Other assistive technology: Yes
Priority registration: Yes
Added costs of services: No
LD specialists: Yes
ADHD coaching: NR
ASD specialists: NR
Professional tutors: NR
Peer tutors: NR
How professors are notified of student approved accommodations: Both student and director

General Admissions Information

Office of Admissions: 860-768-4296

Entrance Requirements

Academic units required: 4 English, 2 math, 2 science, 2 social studies, 2 history, 4 academic electives. **Academic units recommended:** 3 math, 3 science, 2 foreign language. High school diploma is required and GED is accepted. SAT or ACT required. If ACT, ACT with writing accepted. TOEFL required of all international applicants: minimum paper TOEFL 550.

Application deadline: NR
Notification: Rolling starting 10/1
Average GPA: NR
ACT Composite middle 50% range: 20-25
SAT Math middle 50% range: 470-580
SAT Critical Reading middle 50% range: 470-580
SAT Writing middle 50% range: NR-NR
Graduated top 10% of class: NR
Graduated top 25% of class: NR
Graduated top 50% of class: NR

COLLEGE GRADUATION REQUIREMENTS

Course waivers allowed: Yes
In what course: N/A
Course substitutions allowed: Yes
In what course: Math and foreign language

Additional Information

Environment: This private school was founded in 1877. It has a 320-acre campus.

Student Body
Undergrad enrollment: 5,246
% Women: 51
% Men: 49
% Out-of-state: 51

Cost information
Tuition: $35,036
Room & board: $11,986

Housing Information
University Housing: Yes
Percent living on campus: 62

Greek System
Fraternity: NR
Sorority: NR
Athletics: Division I

University of New Haven

300 Boston Post Road, West Haven, CT 06516
Phone: 203-932-7319 • Fax: 203-931-6093
E-mail: admininfo@newhaven.edu • Web: www.newhaven.edu
Support: S • Institution: Private

Programs or Services for Students with Learning Differences

The primary responsibility of Campus Access Services (CAS) is to provide services and support that promote access to the university's educational programs and services for students with disabilities. Students must self-identify and submit documentation of a disability and the need for accommodations. Documentation should be submitted once the student is accepted to the university along with a signed DSR Intake form to request accommodations. Students must also follow the established policies and procedures for making arrangements for accommodations each semester. Staff members act as advocates, liaisons, planners, and troubleshooters. Staff is responsible for assuring access, but at the same time, they avoid creating an artificial atmosphere of dependence on services that cannot reasonably be expected after graduation. The Center for Learning Resources (CLR) offers free tutoring for all students, including students with disabilities. The Office of Academic Services offers academic assistance to all students. Academic skills counselors work one-on-one with students to strengthen their abilities and develop individualized study strategies, which focus on reading, note-taking, time management, learning/memory, and test-taking skills.

Admission Information for Students with Learning Differences

College entrance tests required: Yes
Interview required: No
Essay required: No
Additional application required for LD/ADHD/ASD: NR
What documentation required for LD: Psycho ed evaluation to include: relevant historical info, instructional interventions, related services, age diagnosed, objective data (aptitude, achievement, info processing), test scores (standard, percentile and grade equivalents) and describe functional limitations.
With general application: No
To receive services after enrolling: Yes
What documentation required for ADHD: Diagnosis based on DSM-V; history of behaviors impairing functioning in academic setting; diagnostic interview; history of symptoms; evidence of ongoing behaviors.
With general application: No
To receive services after enrolling: Yes
What documentation required for ASD: Psycho ed evaluation
With general application: NR
To receive services after enrolling: Yes
LD/ADHD/ASD documentation submitted to: Campus Access Services
ASD Specific Program: NR
Special Ed. HS course work accepted: Yes
Specific course requirements for all applicants: Yes
Separate application required: No
Total # of students receiving LD/ADHD/ASD services: NR
Acceptance into program means acceptance into college: Students must be admitted and enrolled in the university first and then request services.

Admissions

All applicants must meet the same admission requirements. SAT or ACT required. Students must submit a personal essay, and letter of recommendation. Foreign language is not required for admission. Students with learning disabilities may self-disclose if they feel that it would positively affect the admissions decision. Students admitted as a conditional admit are limited to four classes for the first semester.

Additional Information

CAS provides services that include the coordination of classroom accommodations, such as extended time for exams; use of a tape recorder, calculator, note-takers, and so on; access to readers, scribes, or books on tape; assistance during the course registration process; proctoring of tests when accommodations cannot be arranged for in the classroom; proctoring of English course post-tests and the Writing Proficiency Exam; and training in time management, organization, and test anxiety management. The office includes testing rooms and a mini computer lab with some adaptive software. The Center for Learning Resources has a Math Lab, Writing Lab, and Computer Lab. The CLR presents free workshops on preparing resumes and preparing for the Writing Proficiency Exam. The Office of Academic Services presents free workshops on improving study skills, such as getting organized, textbook and lecture note-taking techniques, and test preparation and strategies.

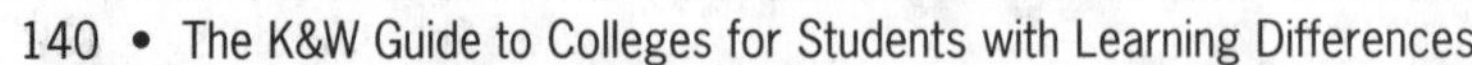

General Support Services Information

Contact Information
Name of program or department: Campus Access Services
Telephone: 203-932-7332
Fax: 203-931-6082

Accommodations or Services for Students With Learning Differences

Accommodations are decided upon an individual basis after a thorough review of appropriate, current documentation. The accommodations requested must be supported through the documentation provided and must be logically linked to the current impact of the condition on academic functioning.

Allowed in exams
Calculator: Yes
Dictionary: Yes
Computer: Yes
Spellchecker: Yes
Extended test time: Yes
Scribes: Yes
Proctors: Yes
Oral exams: No
Note-takers: Yes
Services for students with LD: Yes
Services for students with ADHD: Yes
Services for students with ASD: Yes
Distraction-reduced environment: Yes
Tape recording in class: Yes
Audio books: NR
Electronic texts: Yes
Kurzweil Reader: Yes
Other assistive technology: Yes
Priority registration: No
Added costs for services: No
LD specialists: No
ADHD coaching: NR
ASD specialists: NR
Professional tutors: No
Peer tutors: N/A
Max. hours/wk. for services: Unlimited
How professors are notified of LD/ADHD: By student

General Admissions Information

Office of Admissions: 203-932-7319

Entrance Requirements

Academic units recommended: 4 English, 3 math, 3 science, 2 science labs, 2 foreign language, 3 social studies. High school diploma is required and GED is accepted. SAT or ACT required. If ACT, ACT with writing accepted. TOEFL required of all international applicants: minimum internet TOEFL 80.

Application deadline: NR
Notification: Rolling starting 9/1
Average GPA: 3.4
ACT Composite middle 50% range: 21-26
SAT Math middle 50% range: 480-580
SAT Critical Reading middle 50% range: 480-580
SAT Writing middle 50% range: 470-570
Graduated top 10% of class: 16
Graduated top 25% of class: 40
Graduated top 50% of class: 78

COLLEGE GRADUATION REQUIREMENTS

Course waivers allowed: No
In what course: N/A
Course substitutions allowed: Yes
In what course: Courses that are not essential to the student's program of study

Additional Information

Environment: This private school was founded in 1920. It has a 78-acre campus.

Student Body
Undergrad enrollment: 5,002
% Women: 50
% Men: 50
% Out-of-state: 57

Cost information
Tuition: $35,000
Room & board: $9,200
Housing Information
University Housing: Yes
Percent living on campus: 53

Greek System
Fraternity: NR
Sorority: NR
Athletics: Division II

WESTERN CONNECTICUT STATE U.

Undergraduate Admissions Office, Danbury, CT 06810-6855
Phone: 203-837-9000 • Fax: 203-837-8338
E-mail: admissions@wcsu.edu • Web: www.wcsu.edu
Support: CS • Institution: Public

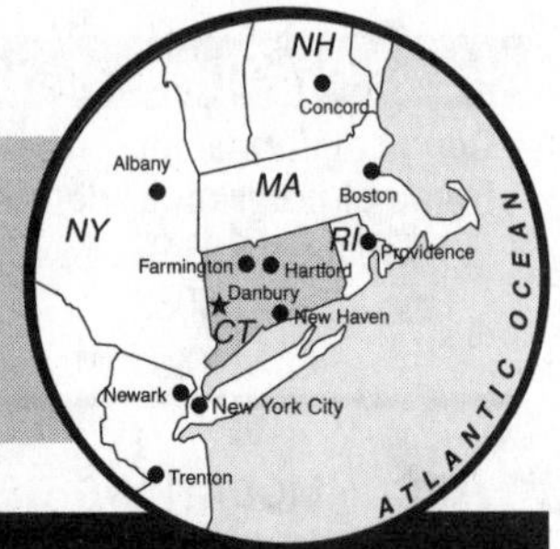

PROGRAMS OR SERVICES FOR STUDENTS WITH LEARNING DIFFERENCES

Two primary purposes of Students with Disabilities Services are to provide the educational development of disabled students and improve understanding and support in the campus environment. Students with learning disabilities will be assisted in receiving the services necessary to achieve their goals. Western Connecticut recognizes your right to reasonable accommodations and necessary services as a student qualified to be enrolled at this university. The Office of Disability Services directs and coordinates such services for students with disabilities that impact their educational experience. We provide advocacy, early registration, confidential counseling, empowerment counseling, complaint processing, accommodation planning, accommodation referrals, referrals to other university services, exam proctoring, accessibility, and other important services that are of value and consequence to students.

ADMISSION INFORMATION FOR STUDENTS WITH LEARNING DIFFERENCES

College entrance tests required: Yes
Interview required: No
Essay required: No
Additional application required for LD/ADHD/ASD: NR
What documentation required for LD: Psycho ed evaluation to include: relevant historical info, instructional interventions, related services, age diagnosed, objective data (aptitude, achievement, info processing), test scores (standard, percentile and grade equivalents) and describe functional limitations.
With general application: No
To receive services after enrolling: Yes
What documentation required for ADHD: Diagnosis based on DSM-V; history of behaviors impairing functioning in academic setting; diagnostic interview; history of symptoms; evidence of ongoing behaviors.
With general application: No
To receive services after enrolling: Yes
What documentation required for ASD: Psycho ed evaluation
With general application: NR
To receive services after enrolling: Yes
LD/ADHD/ASD documentation submitted to: Disability Services
ASD Specific Program: NR
Special Ed. HS course work accepted: Yes
Specific course requirements of all applicants: Yes
Separate application required: No
Total # of students receiving LD/ADHD/ASD services: NR
Acceptance into program means acceptance into college: Students must be admitted and enrolled in the university first and then request services.

ADMISSIONS

Students with learning disabilities submit the general application form. No alternative admission policies are offered. Students should have a 2.5 GPA (C-plus or better), with the average SAT of 894 (ACT may be substituted). Courses required include 4 years of English, 3 years of math, 2 years of science, 2 science labs, 2 years of a foreign language (3 years of a foreign language recommended), 1 year of social studies, 1 year of history, and 3 years of electives. Students are encouraged to self-disclose their disability on the application and submit documentation to be used after admission to determine services and accommodations.

ADDITIONAL INFORMATION

Services include priority registration, tutoring, testing accommodations, and advocacy and counseling. The university does not offer any skills classes. The university offers a special summer program for precollege freshmen with learning disabilities. Services and accommodations are available for undergraduate and graduate students.

General Support Services Information

Contact Information
Name of program or department: Disability Services
Telephone: 203-837-8946
Fax: 203-837-8848

Accommodations or Services For Students With Learning Differences

Accommodations are decided upon an individual basis after a thorough review of appropriate, current documentation. The accommodations requested must be supported through the documentation provided and must be logically linked to the current impact of the condition on academic functioning.

Allowed in exams
Calculator: Yes
Dictionary: No
Computer: Yes
Spellchecker: Yes
Extended test time: Yes
Scribes: Yes
Proctors: Yes
Oral exams: Yes
Note-takers: Yes
Services for students with LD: Yes
Services for students with ADHD: Yes
Services for students with ASD: Yes
Distraction-reduced environment: Yes
Tape recording in class: Yes
Audio books: NR
Electronic texts: Yes
Kurzweil Reader: No
Other assistive technology: Yes
Priority registration: Yes
Added costs for services: No
LD specialists: Yes
ADHD coaching: NR
ASD specialists: NR
Professional tutors: 1
Peer tutors: N/A
Max. hours/wk. for services: N/A
How professors are notified of LD/ADHD: By both student and director

General Admissions Information

Office of Admissions: 203-837-9000

Entrance Requirements

Academic units required: 4 English, 3 math, 2 science, 2 science labs, 2 foreign language, 1 social studies, 1 history. High school diploma is required and GED is accepted. SAT or ACT recommended. If ACT, ACT with writing accepted. TOEFL required of all international applicants: minimum paper TOEFL 550 or minimum internet TOEFL 79.

Application deadline: NR
Notification: Rolling starting 12/1
Average GPA: NR
ACT Composite middle 50% range: NR-NR
SAT Math middle 50% range: 450-540
SAT Critical Reading middle 50% range: 450-550
SAT Writing middle 50% range: 450-560
Graduated top 10% of class: 7
Graduated top 25% of class: 24
Graduated top 50% of class: 64

COLLEGE GRADUATION REQUIREMENTS

Course waivers allowed: Yes
In what course: As required depending on the student's disability
Course substitutions allowed: Yes
In what course: As required depending on the student's disability

Additional Information

Environment: This public school was founded in 1903. It has a 364-acre campus.

Student Body
Undergrad enrollment: 5,298
% Women: 53
% Men: 47
% Out-of-state: 6

Cost information
Room & board: NR

Housing Information
University Housing: Yes
Percent living on campus: 33

Greek System
Fraternity: Yes
Sorority: Yes
Athletics: Division III

University of Delaware

210 South College Avenue, Newark, DE 19716
Phone: 302-831-8123 • Fax: 302-831-6905
E-mail: admissions@udel.edu • Web: www.udel.edu
Support: CS • Institution: Public

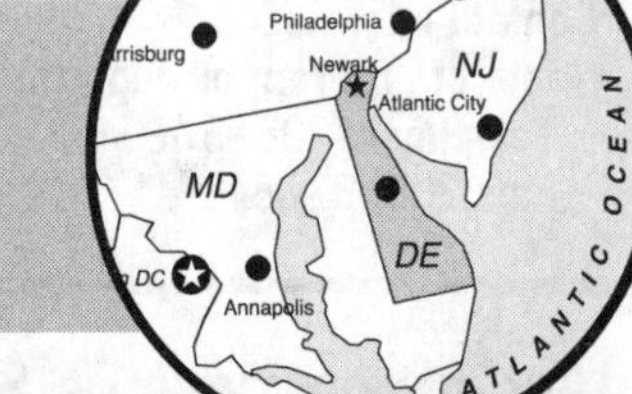

Programs or Services for Students with Learning Differences

Eligibility for reasonable accommodations is determined on a case-by-case basis upon receipt of appropriate documentation in order to determine that a disability exists and results in a functional limitation. Requested accommodations must be supported by the documentation and be logically linked to the current impact of the disability. Accommodations are provided in order to provide equal access to university course work, activities and programs. Accommodations may not interfere with or alter the essential skills of course curriculum.

Admission Information for Students with Learning Differences

College entrance tests required: Yes
Interview required: No
Essay required: Yes
Additional Application Required for LD/ADHD/ASD: NR
What documentation required for LD: Yes, after admission
With general application: No
To receive services after enrolling: Yes
What documentation required for ADHD: Yes, after admission
With general application: No
To receive services after enrolling: Yes
What documentation required for ASD: Psycho ed evaluation
With general application: NR
To receive services after enrolling: Yes
LD/ADHD/ASD documentation submitted to: Academic Success Services
ASD Specific Program: NR
Special Ed. HS course work accepted: NR
Specific course requirements of all applicants: Yes
Separate application required: NR
Total # of students receiving LD/ADHD/ASD services: NR
Acceptance into program means acceptance into college: Student must be admitted and enrolled in the university prior to requesting accommodation(s).

Admissions

Students must be otherwise qualified to admissions. Applicants are typically admitted to their first choice major if admitted to the university. Only list a second major if there is active interest. Courses required include 4 English, 3 math, 3 science, 4 social studies, 2 foreign language, and 2 electives. Foreign language taken prior to 9th grade is not counted. The university looks for academic rigor; grades in college prep classes, and highly recommends that applicants be enrolled in 5 academic core courses each semester. Essays are important and students must submit at least one recommendation from an academic source. Most students submit more recommendations. ACT with writing or SAT required and they will super score. Once admitted and committed to attending the university, students are encouraged to self-disclose their disability to the Office of Disability Support Services (DSS).

Additional Information

DSS reviews documentation and provides appropriate accommodations such as: assistive technology, note takers, notification to faculty, test accommodations, tutoring in conjunction with the Academic Enrichment Program in the Academic Enrichment Center. Support includes: individual and group tutoring, study skills workshops and classes and one-on-one academic assistance. The Summer Enrichment Program (SEP) is an academically intensive five-week residential program for incoming freshmen. Students can earn seven credits in math, English and a college transition course. Placement is determined by ACT/SAT. These students also participate in a variety of academic support meetings, cultural enrichment events, and personal, social and recreational activities. Participants are encouraged to participate in Office of Academic Enrichment activities throughout their freshman year and beyond.

General Support Services Information

Contact Information
Name of program or department: Disability Support Services (DSS)
Telephone: 302-831-4643
Fax: 302-831-3261

Accommodations or Services For Students With Learning Differences

Accommodations are decided upon an individual basis after a thorough review of appropriate, current documentation. The accommodations requested must be supported through the documentation provided and must be logically linked to the current impact of the condition on academic functioning. The following are possible accommodations.

Allowed in exams
Calculator: Yes
Dictionary: No
Computer: Yes
Spellchecker: Yes
Extended test time: Yes
Scribes: Yes
Proctors: Yes
Oral exams: No
Note-takers: Yes
Services for students with LD: Yes
Services for students with ADHD: Yes
Services for students with ASD: Yes
Distraction-reduced environment: Yes
Tape recording in class: Yes
Audio book: NR
Electronic texts: Yes
Kurzweil Reader: Yes
Other assistive technology: Yes
Priority registration: Yes
Added costs for services: No
LD specialists: Yes
ADHD coaching: NR
ASD specialists: NR
Professional tutors: No
Peer tutors: 150
Max. hours/wk. for services: N/A
How professors are notified of LD/ADHD: By both student and DSS

General Admissions Information

Office of Admissions: 302-831-8123

Entrance Requirements

Academic units required: 4 English, 3 math, 3 science, 2 science labs, 2 foreign language, 2 social studies, 2 history, 2 academic electives. **Academic units recommended:** 4 English, 4 math, 4 science, 3 science labs, 4 foreign language, 2 social studies, 2 history. High school diploma is required and GED is accepted. SAT or ACT required. If ACT, ACT with writing required. TOEFL required of all international applicants: minimum paper TOEFL 570 or minimum internet TOEFL 90.

Application deadline: 1/15
Notification: Rolling starting 11/1
Average GPA: 3.7
ACT Composite middle 50% range: 25-29
SAT Math middle 50% range: 560-660
SAT Critical Reading middle 50% range: 550-650
SAT Writing middle 50% range: 550-650
Graduated top 10% of class: 33
Graduated top 25% of class: 68
Graduated top 50% of class: 94

COLLEGE GRADUATION REQUIREMENTS

Course waivers allowed: No
Course substitutions allowed: Yes
In what course: Math and foreign language course substitution decisions are made on a case-by-case basis. Students are asked to attempt the class and work closely with a tutor before submitting a petition for a substitution.

Additional Information

Environment: This public school was founded in 1743. It has a 1000-acre campus.

Student Body
Undergrad enrollment: 17,575
% Women: 58
% Men: 42
% Out-of-state: 61

Cost information
In-state Tuition: $11,230
Out-of Tuition: $30,130
Room & board: $11,830

Housing Information
University Housing: Yes
Percent living on campus: 43

Greek System
Fraternity: Yes
Sorority: Yes
Athletics: Division I

American University

4400 Massachusetts Avenue, NW, Washington, DC 20016-8001
Phone: 202-885-6000 • Fax: 202-885-6014
E-mail: admissions@american.edu • Web: www.american.edu
Support: SP • Institution: Private

Programs or Services for Students with Learning Differences

The Academic Support Center (ASC) provides extensive support for students with documented learning disabilities and ADHD. Any student whose documentation meets university guidelines can access approved accommodations, work with a learning specialist, meet with the assistive technology specialist, use the Writing Lab, request peer tutors, and take advantage of group workshops. The Learning Services Program (LSP), within the ASC, is a mainstream freshman transition program offering additional support for students who apply to the program with learning disabilities that impact writing. There is a one-time fee for this program, and students must apply at the time they apply to the university. Disability services continue to be available until graduation.

Admission Information for Students with Learning Differences

College entrance test required: Test flexible
Interview required: No
Essay required: Required
Additional Application Required for LD/ADHD/ASD: Yes
What documentation required for LD: Psycho ed evaluation
With general application: No
To receive services after enrolling: Yes
What documentation required for ADHD: Psycho ed evaluation
With general application: No
To receive services after enrolling: Yes
What documentation required for ASD: For documentation details please visit: http://www.american.edu/ocl/asac/For-Students-Eligibility.cfm
With general application: No
To receive services after enrolling: Yes
LD/ADHD/ASD documentation submitted to: Academic Support and Access Center
ASD Specific Program: NR
Special Ed. HS course work accepted: NR
Specific course requirements of all applicants: NR
Separate application required for program services: Yes
Total # of students receiving LD/ADHD/ASD services: NR
Acceptance into program means acceptance into college: No

Admissions

Students with LD must be admitted to the university and then to the Learning Services Program. Students who wish to have program staff consult with the Admissions Office about their LD during the admissions process must submit a supplemental application to the Learning Services Program that requires documentation of the LD. Students should indicate interest in the program on their application. Special education courses taken in high school may be accepted if they meet the criteria for the Carnegie Units. The academic credentials of successful applicants with LD fall within the range of regular admissions criteria: the mean GPA is 2.9 for LD admits and 3.2 for regularly admitted students; ACT ranges from 24–29 for regular admits and 24–28 for LD admits or SAT 1110–1270 for regular admits and 1131 for LD admits. American Sign Language is an acceptable substitution for foreign language. The admission decision is made by a special Admissions Committee and is based on the high school record, recommendations, and all pertinent diagnostic reports.

Additional Information

All students work with an academic advisor in their school or college; students in the Learning Services Program have an advisor who consults on their learning disability. Students in the program meet weekly with a learning specialist for individual sessions that help them further develop college-level reading, writing, and study strategies—and with a writing tutor. Peer tutors assist with course content tutoring. Accommodations are based on diagnostic testing. Students are held to the same academic standards as all students but may meet these standards through nontraditional means.

General Support Services Information

Contact Information
Name of program or department: Academic Support and Access Center
Telephone: 202-885-3360
Fax: 202-885-1042
Website: http://www.american.edu/ocl/asac/index.cfm

Accommodations or Services for Students with Learning Differences

Accommodations are decided upon an individual basis after a thorough review of appropriate, current documentation. The accommodations requests must be supported through the documentation provided and must be logically linked to the current impact of the condition on academic functioning.

Allowed in exams
Calculator: Yes
Dictionary: Yes
Computer: Yes
Spellchecker: Yes
Extended test time: Yes
Scribes: Yes
Proctors: Yes
Oral exams: NR
Note-takers: Yes
Support services for students with LD: Yes
Support services for students with ADHD: Yes
Support services for students with ASD: Yes
Distraction-reduced environment: Yes
Tape recording in class: Yes
Electronic texts: Yes
Kurzweil reader: Yes
Audio books: NR
Other assistive technology: Yes
Priority registration: Yes
Added costs of services: Yes
LD specialists: Yes
ADHD coaching: NR
ASD specialists: NR
Professional tutors: No
Peer tutors: Yes
Max. hours/wk. for services: NR
How professors are notified of student approved accommodations: By student

General Admissions Information

Office of Admissions: 202-885-6000

Entrance Requirements

Academic units required: 4 English, 3 math, 3 science, 2 science labs, 2 foreign language, 2 social studies, 3 academic electives. **Academic units recommended:** 4 English, 4 math, 4 science, 3 foreign language, 4 social studies, 4 academic electives. High school diploma is required and GED is accepted. SAT or ACT considered if submitted. If ACT, ACT with writing required. TOEFL required of all international applicants: minimum paper TOEFL 550 or minimum internet TOEFL 80.

Application deadline: 1/15
Notification: 4/1
Average GPA: 3.66
ACT Composite middle 50% range: 26-30
SAT Math middle 50% range: 560-650
SAT Critical Reading middle 50% range: 590-690
SAT Writing middle 50% range: 570-670
Graduate top 10% of class: NR
Graduated top 25% of class: NR
Graduated top 50% of class: NR

COLLEGE GRADUATION REQUIREMENTS

Course waivers allowed: NR
Course substitutions allowed: NR

Additional Information

Environment: This private school, affiliated with the Methodist Church, was founded in 1893. It has a 84-acre campus.

Student Body
Undergrad enrollment: 7,909
% Women: 62
% Men: 38
% Out-of-state: 81

Cost information
Tuition: $44,046
Room & board: $14,526

Housing Information
University Housing: Yes
Percent living on campus: NR

Greek System
Fraternity: Yes
Sorority: Yes
Athletics: Division I

THE CATHOLIC U. OF AMERICA

620 Michigan Avenue, NE, Washington, DC 20064
Phone: 202-319-5305 • Fax: 202-319-6533
E-mail: cua-admissions@cua.edu • Web: www.cua.edu
Support: CS • Institution: Private

PROGRAMS OR SERVICES FOR STUDENTS WITH LEARNING DIFFERENCES

All prospective or current students with a diagnosed disability are encouraged to make contact with DSS in the early stages of their college planning or as soon as they identify a need for accommodations. DSS will send information about our services and documentation requirements to help the student prepare. DSS staff are also available to meet with the student at any time. DSS does not recommend that prospective students submit their documentation to Admissions. It is advisable to send documentation directly to DSS, after you have been admitted. Your eligibility for services/accommodations from DSS is a separate process and is done independently of the Office of Admissions. After documentation and the DSS Registration forms are reviewed, DSS will send an email notification to the student acknowledging receipt of the documentation and eligibility status. At any time during the Admissions process, students are welcome to meet with disability counselors to provide information about eligibility for academic support services and accommodations, appropriate documentation of disability, housing considerations, and transition issues.

ADMISSION INFORMATION FOR STUDENTS WITH LEARNING DIFFERENCES

College entrance test required: NR
Interview required: No
Essay required: Recommended
Additional Application Required for LD/ADHD/ASD: Yes
What documentation required for LD: DSS Registration Form as well as sufficient documentation related to their specific diagnosis. In the case of an ADHD/ADD diagnosis, a recent neuropsychological or psychoeducational evaluation is required
With general application: No
To receive services after enrolling: Yes
What documentation required for ADHD: DSS Registration Form as well as sufficient documentation related to their specific diagnosis. In the case of an Autism Spectrum Disorder, a recent neuropsychological or psychoeducational evaluation is required
With general application: No
To receive services after enrolling: Yes
What documentation required for ASD: DSS Registration Form as well as sufficient documentation related to their specific diagnosis. In the case of an LD diagnosis, a recent neuropsychological or psychoeducational evaluation is required
With general application: No
To receive services after enrolling: Yes
LD/ADHD/ASD documentation submitted to: Disability Support Services ; DSS
ASD Specific Program: NR
Special Ed. HS course work accepted: NR
Specific course requirements of all applicants: NR
Separate application required for program services: Yes
Total # of students receiving LD/ADHD/ASD services: 375
Acceptance into program means acceptance into college: No

ADMISSIONS

The Office of Undergraduate Admissions reviews each application on its own merits. Students with disabilities must meet the same standards as all other applicants. Documentation of your disability should not be sent with your application. Prospective students with disabilities are encouraged to write an additional personal statement. Once enrolled at the university, students with a learning disability that impairs the ability to acquire a foreign language may apply to substitute for the graduation language requirement. The decision to grant a substitution is based on an individual's learning history, documentation of a disability that impairs foreign language acquisition, and future educational goals. If a language substitution is granted two alternate courses are substituted. Students with a disability that impairs academic performance in the quantitative area may be eligible for a math substitution. This decision is based on learning history, documentation of a disability that impairs mathematical processing and future educational goals. Alternate courses are required if the substitution in math is approved. Math may not be substituted if required for graduation in the student's major.

ADDITIONAL INFORMATION

Once students have been admitted they should contact DSS and request an Intake Packet. DSS will review the application and documentation and determine accommodations and services. Students must complete a request form each semester to obtain an accommodation letter to give to professors. The Learning Specialist is available to meet one-on-one with students who are registered with DSS. The Learning Specialist helps students improve their learning. Services offered through DSS include time management skills, organizational skills, reading comprehension, study skills, test-taking skills, writing skills and stress management. Monthly emails are sent to students with learning strategy tips .

General Support Services Information

Contact Information
Name of program or department: Disability Support Services ; DSS
Telephone: 202-319-5211
Fax: 202-319-5126
Website: http://dss.cua.edu/Getting%20Started/smartstart.cfm

Accommodations or Services For Students With Learning Differences

Accommodations are decided upon an individual basis after a thorough review of appropriate, current documentation. The accommodations requests must be supported through the documentation provided and must be logically linked to the current impact of the condition on academic functioning.

Allowed in exams
Calculator: Yes
Dictionary: Yes
Computer: Yes
Spellchecker: Yes
Extended test time: Yes
Scribes: Yes
Proctors: Yes
Oral exams: Yes
Note-takers: Yes
Support services for students with LD: Yes
Support services for students with ADHD: Yes
Support services for students with ASD: Yes
Distraction-reduced environment: Yes
Tape recording in class: Yes
Electronic texts: Yes
Kurzweil reader: NR
Audio books: Yes
Other assistive technology: Yes
Priority registration: Yes
Added costs of services: Yes
LD specialists: Yes
ADHD coaching: Yes
ASD specialists: Yes
Professional tutors: No
Peer tutors: Yes
Max. hours/wk. for services: NR
How professors are notified of student approved accommodations: By student

General Admissions Information

Office of Admissions: 202-319-5305

Entrance Requirements

Academic units recommended: 4 English, 3 math, 3 science, 1 science labs, 3 foreign language, 4 social studies, and 1 units from above areas or other academic areas. High school diploma is required and GED is accepted. SAT or ACT considered if submitted. If ACT, ACT with writing accepted. TOEFL required of all international applicants: minimum paper TOEFL 550 or minimum internet TOEFL 80.

Application deadline: 1/15
Notification: Rolling starting 3/15
Average GPA: 3.38
ACT Composite middle 50% range: 22-28
SAT Math middle 50% range: 510-610
SAT Critical Reading middle 50% range: 510-620
SAT Writing middle 50% range: NR-NR
Graduate top 10% of class: NR
Graduated top 25% of class: NR
Graduated top 50% of class: NR

COLLEGE GRADUATION REQUIREMENTS

Course waivers allowed: No
In what course: Once a student has officially registered with DSS, they can apply for a Foreign Language or Math substitution. These are not exemptions and the university determines replacement courses the student will need to complete prior to graduation.
Course substitutions allowed: Yes
In what course: Math and Foreign Language

Additional Information

Environment: This private school, affiliated with the Roman Catholic Church, was founded in 1887. It has a 193-acre campus.

Student Body
Undergrad enrollment: 3,480
% Women: 53
% Men: 47
% Out-of-state: 97
Cost information
Tuition: $40,400
Room & board: $13,356
Housing Information
University Housing: Yes
Percent living on campus: 57
Greek System
Fraternity: Yes
Sorority: Yes
Athletics: Division III

The George Washington University

2121 Eye Street NW, Suite 201, Washington, DC 20052
Phone: 202-994-6040 • Fax: 202-994-0325
E-mail: gwadm@gwu.edu • Web: www.gwu.edu
Support: CS • Institution: Private

Programs or Services for Students with Learning Differences

Disability Support Services (DSS) provides support to learning disabled students so that they can participate fully in university life, derive the greatest benefit from their educational experiences, and achieve maximum personal success. Students must register to ensure that accommodations are appropriately communicated to university faculty, GW Housing, and Student Health. Students with LD/ADHD are served through DSS. The staff is committed to providing student-centered services that meet the individual needs of each student. The ultimate goal of DSS is to assist students with disabilities as they gain knowledge to recognize strengths, accommodate differences, and become strong self-advocates. Staff are available to discuss issues such as course load, learning strategies, academic accommodations, and petitions for course waivers or substitutions. DSS offers individual assistance in addressing needs not provided through routine services. Students with LD must provide documentation, including a comprehensive diagnostic interview, psychoeducational evaluation, and a treatment plan; test scores and an interpretation of overall intelligence, information processing, executive functioning, spatial ability, memory, motor ability, achievement skills, reading, writing, and math; and a specific diagnosis and description of the student's functional limitations in an educational setting.

Admission Information for Students with Learning Differences

College entrance tests required: Yes
Interview required: No
Essay required: N/A
Additional Application Required for LD/ADHD/ASD: NR
What documentation required for LD: Psycho ed evaluation to include: relevant historical info, instructional interventions, related services, age diagnosed, objective data (aptitude, achievement, info processing), test scores (standard, percentile and grade equivalents) and describe functional limitations.
With general application: No
To receive services after enrolling: Yes
What documentation required for ADHD: Diagnosis based on DSM-V; history of behaviors impairing functioning in academic setting; diagnostic interview; history of symptoms; evidence of ongoing behaviors.
With general application: No
With general application: NR
What documentation required for ASD: Psycho ed evaluation
With general application: NR
To receive services after enrolling: Yes
LD/ADHD/ASD documentation submitted to: Disability Support Services
ASD Specific Program: NR
Special Ed. HS course work accepted: No
Specific course requirements for all applicants: Yes
Separate application required: No
Total # of students receiving LD/ADHD/ASD services: 258
Acceptance into program means acceptance into college: Student must be admitted and enrolled in the university and then reviewed for services with Disability Support Services.

Admissions

GWU does not discriminate on the basis of disability in the recruitment and admission of students. There are no separate admissions procedures or criteria for disabled students. The minimal course requirements include 2 years of math (4 recommended), 4 years of English, 2 years of a foreign language (4 recommended), 2–3 years of social sciences (4 recommended), and 2–3 years of science (4 recommended). The score range for the ACT is 28-31 and for the SAT 1900–2100. The SAT Subject Tests are optional. Since there is no automatic referral from admissions or other campus offices, students are encouraged to contact DSS directly prior to or at the time of admission.

Additional Information

To be eligible, a student must provide to DSS documentation that substantiates the need for such services in compliance with Section 504 of the Rehabilitation Act and the Americans with Disabilities Act (ADA). Services provided without charge to students may include registration assistance, reading services, assistive technology, learning specialist services, note-taking assistance, test accommodations, and referrals. DSS does not provide content tutoring, although it is available on a fee basis from other campus resources.

GENERAL SUPPORT SERVICES INFORMATION

Contact Information
Name of program or department: Disability Support Services
Telephone: 202-994-8250
Fax: 202-994-7610

ACCOMMODATIONS OR SERVICES FOR STUDENTS WITH LEARNING DIFFERENCES

Accommodations are decided upon an individual basis after a thorough review of appropriate, current documentation. The accommodations requested must be supported through the documentation provided and must be logically linked to the current impact of the condition on academic functioning.

Allowed in exams
Calculator: Yes
Dictionary: Yes
Computer: Yes
Spellchecker: Yes
Extended test time: Yes
Scribes: Yes
Proctors: Yes
Oral exams: Yes
Note-takers: Yes
Services for students with LD: Yes
Services for students with ADHD: Yes
Services for students with ASD: Yes
Distraction-reduced environment: Yes
Tape recording in class: Yes
Audio book: NR
Electronic texts: Yes
Kurzweil Reader: Yes
Other assistive technology: Yes
Priority registration: Yes
Added costs for services: No
LD specialists: Yes
ADHD coaching: NR
ASD specialists: NR
Professional tutors: No
Peer tutors: No
Max. hours/wk. for services: NR
How professors are notified of LD/ADHD: By student

GENERAL ADMISSIONS INFORMATION

Office of Admissions: 202-994-6040

ENTRANCE REQUIREMENTS

Academic units required: 4 English, 2 math, 2 science, 1 science labs, 2 foreign language, 2 social studies. **Academic units recommended:** 4 English, 4 math, 4 science, 4 foreign language, 4 social studies. High school diploma is required and GED is not accepted. SAT or ACT required for some. If ACT, ACT with writing recommended. TOEFL required of all international applicants: minimum paper TOEFL 550.

Application deadline: 1/1
Notification: 4/1
Average GPA: NR
ACT Composite middle 50% range: 27-31
SAT Math middle 50% range: 600-700
SAT Critical Reading middle 50% range: 590-690
SAT Writing middle 50% range: 600-690
Graduated top 10% of class: 56
Graduated top 25% of class: 86
Graduated top 50% of class: 99

COLLEGE GRADUATION REQUIREMENTS

Course waivers allowed: No
Course substitutions allowed: Yes
In what course: Determination is made on a case-by-case basis, primarily in the areas of math and foreign language.

ADDITIONAL INFORMATION

Environment: This private school was founded in 1821. It has a 45-acre campus.

Student Body
Undergrad enrollment: 11,157
% Women: 56
% Men: 44
% Out-of-state: 97

Cost information
Tuition: $48,220
Room & board: $14,770

Housing Information
University Housing: Yes
Percent living on campus: 60

Greek System
Fraternity: Yes
Sorority: Yes

Athletics: Division I

Barry University

11300 North East Second Avenue, Miami Shores, FL 33161-6695
Phone: 305-899-3100 • Fax: 305-899-2971
E-mail: admissions@barry.edu • Web: www.barry.edu
Support: SP • Institution: Private

Programs or Services for Students with Learning Differences

Barry University offers a fee-for-service support program for students with LD. The Center for Advanced Learning (CAL) Program is a comprehensive, intensive, structured, and individualized approach to assisting students with LD throughout their college careers. It is designed to move students gradually toward increasing self-direction in academic, personal, and career activities. This program affirms Barry University's commitment to expand college opportunities to students with LD and provide the specialized services that can enhance college success. CAL program objectives: That all students have a right to fair and accessible education regardless of their challenges and learning differences; That with the right level of support, students can succeed; That individualized and specialized tutoring, mentoring, and advising services by compassionate, experienced professional staff; That CAL is dedicated to helping our students achieve their educational goals.

Admission Information for Students with Learning Differences

College entrance tests required: Yes
Interview required: Yes
Essay required: Yes
Additional Application Required for LD/ADHD/ASD: NR
What documentation required for LD: Pyschoeducational evaluation
With general application: Yes
To receive services after enrolling: Yes
What documentation required for ADHD: Pyschoeducational evaluation
With general application: Yes if requested as part of Structured Program application
To receive services after enrolling: Yes
What documentation required for ASD: Psycho ed evaluation
With general application: NR
To receive services after enrolling: Yes
To receive services after enrolling: Yes
LD/ADHD/ASD documentation submitted to: Director of CAL Program
ASD Specific Program: NR
Special Ed. HS course work accepted: Yes
Specific course requirements of all applicants: Yes
Separate application required: No
Total # of students receiving LD/ADHD/ASD services: 45
Acceptance into program means acceptance into college: Yes

Admissions

Students with learning disabilities/ADHD must meet the regular admission criteria for the university, which includes 2.0 GPA, ACT of 17 or above, or SAT of 800 or above, and 4 years of English, 3–4 years of math, 3 years of natural science, and 3–4 years of social science. There is a process of individual review by learning disability professionals for those students who have a diagnosed disability and who do not meet the general admission criteria. These students must provide appropriate and current LD/ADHD documentation and be interviewed by the Director of the CAL Program. Students admitted are expected to meet all requirements established for them and those of the specific university program in which they enroll.

Additional Information

The CAL Program includes a full range of professionally managed and intensive support services that includes the following: Review of diagnostic information allowing for development of a personalized educational plan; individual and small-group subject-area tutoring; instruction in learning and study strategies; academic advising; assistance in developing interpersonal skills; individual and small-group personal, academic, and career counseling; assistance in obtaining study aids and training in the use of assistive technology; computer access; special test administration services; and advocacy with faculty. Additionally, all students have access to a math lab, reading and writing centers, and selected educational seminars. All instructional staff hold advanced degrees in their area of specialization, no peer tutors are used.

General Support Services Information

Contact Information
Name of program or department: Office of Disability Services in Landon Building. CAL Program in Garner Building
Telephone: 305-899-3488
Fax: 305-899-3056

Accommodations or Services For Students With Learning Differences

Accommodations are decided upon an individual basis after a thorough review of appropriate, current documentation. The accommodations requested must be supported through the documentation provided and must be logically linked to the current impact of the condition on academic functioning.

Allowed in exams
Calculator: Yes
Dictionary: Yes
Computer: Yes
Spellchecker: Yes
Extended test time: Yes
Scribes: Yes
Proctors: Yes
Oral exams: Yes
Note-takers: Yes
Services for students with LD: Yes
Services for students with ADHD: Yes
Services for students with ASD: Yes
Distraction-reduced environment: Yes
Tape recording in class: Yes
Audio book: Yes
Electronic texts: Yes
Kurzweil Reader: Yes
Other assistive technology: Yes
Priority registration: No
Added costs for services: Yes
LD specialists: Yes
ADHD coaching: No
ASD specialists: No
Professional tutors: Yes
Peer tutors: No
Max. hours/wk. for services: Unlimited
How professors are notified of LD/ADHD: By both student and director

General Admissions Information

Office of Admissions: 305-899-3100

Entrance Requirements

Academic units recommended: 4 English, 3 math, 3 science, 3 social studies. High school diploma is required and GED is accepted. SAT or ACT required. If ACT, ACT with writing accepted. TOEFL required of all international applicants: minimum internet TOEFL 61.

Application deadline: NR
Notification: NR
Average GPA: 3.14
ACT Composite middle 50% range: 18-21
SAT Math middle 50% range: 420-520
SAT Critical Reading middle 50% range: 440-520
SAT Writing middle 50% range: NR-NR
Graduated top 10% of class: NR
Graduated top 25% of class: NR
Graduated top 50% of class: 100

COLLEGE GRADUATION REQUIREMENTS

Course waivers allowed: No
Course substitutions allowed: Must submit request and be approved by the specific department

Additional Information

Environment: This private school, affiliated with the Roman Catholic Church, was founded in 1940. It has a 122-acre campus.

Student Body
Undergrad enrollment: 4,619
% Women: 63
% Men: 37
% Out-of-state: 26
Cost information
Tuition: $28,160
Room & board: $9,300
Housing Information
University Housing: Yes
Percent living on campus: 35
Greek System
Fraternity: Yes
Sorority: Yes
Athletics: Division II

Beacon College

105 E. Main Street, Leesburg, FL 34748
Phone: 352-638-9731 • Fax: 352-787-0721
E-mail: admissions@beaconcollege.edu • Web: www.beaconcollege.edu
Support: SP • Institution: Private

Programs or Services for Students with Learning Differences

Beacon College was founded to award bachelor degrees to students with learning disabilities, ADHD and other learning differences. The College is committed to student success, offering academic and personal support services that help each student achieve his or her goals. The four-year graduation rate of 83.3% far surpasses the national average for students with learning disabilities, proving the effectiveness of the teaching model founded at the College. Every Beacon student leaves the College with stronger critical thinking skills and, due to a strong four-year Career Development program, professional skills designed to help each student understand his or her specific skill set and goals. Career Development courses, along with professional internships, help insure each student embarks on the appropriate career path after leaving Beacon. The fact that 83.3% of graduating students either obtain a job or continue in their education after leaving Beacon demonstrates the success of this program.

Admission Information for Students with Learning Differences

College entrance tests required: No
Interview required: No
Essay required: No
Additional Application Required for LD/ADHD/ASD: NR
What documentation required for LD: Psycho ed evaluation to include: relevant historical info, instructional interventions, related services, age diagnosed, objective data (aptitude, achievement, info processing), test scores (standard, percentile and grade equivalents) and describe functional limitations.
With general application: Yes if requested as part of Structured Program application
To receive services after enrolling: Yes
What documentation required for ADHD: Diagnosis based on DSM-V; history of behaviors impairing functioning in academic setting; diagnostic interview; history of symptoms; evidence of ongoing behaviors.
With general application: Yes if requested as part of Structured Program application
To receive services after enrolling: Yes
What documentation required for ASD: Psycho ed evaluation
With general application: NR
To receive services after enrolling: Yes
LD/ADHD/ASD documentation submitted to: Admissions
ASD Specific Program: NR
Special Ed. HS coursework accepted: Yes
Specific course requirements for all applicants: Standard High School Diploma
Separate application required for program services: No
Total % of students receiving LD/ADHD/ASD services: 100%
Acceptance into program means acceptance into college: NR

Admissions

In order to be considered for admissions to Beacon College, an applicant must submit: a completed application, non-refundable $50.00 application fee, and psychoeducational evaluation (completed within three years) that documents a learning disability, or AD/HD. The evaluation must include a complete WAIS with sub-test scores and assessments in reading and math. Official high school transcripts showing successful completion of a standard high school diploma or GED is also required. Beacon College does not place heavy emphasis on SAT/ACT scores. Interviews are preferred and provide a better understanding of the applicant.

Additional Information

Beacon College provides a comprehensive educational support services for students with learning disabilities or ADHD. Beacon serves a culturally diverse group of men and women from across the United States and internationally. Out-of-state students make up 65 percent of the student population at Beacon College. The average age of students ranges from 20–24 years of age, and 45 percent of students transfer to Beacon from another college or university. In order to meet the needs of our students, the average class size is approximately 12–15 students. The cornerstone of educational support services at Beacon College is our Academic Mentoring Program. In order to foster success, each student receives one-to-one academic mentoring services, which are designed to enhance academic performance and develop skills for life-long learning. The Field Placement Program allows students to complete supervised hours in the workplace to enhance their resumes and further their employment skills. The Cultural Studies Abroad Program gives students the opportunity to experience the life, history, culture, cuisine, architecture, music, and literature of exotic places. During the past ten years, students and professors have traveled to Italy, Greece, France, Spain, Australia, Russia, Sweden, Austria, England, and Ireland.

GENERAL SUPPORT SERVICES INFORMATION

Contact Information
Telephone: 855-220-5376
Fax: 352-787-0796

ACCOMMODATIONS OR SERVICES FOR STUDENTS WITH LEARNING DIFFERENCES

Accommodations are decided upon an individual basis after a thorough review of appropriate, current documentation. The accommodations requested must be supported through the documentation provided and must be logically linked to the current impact of the condition on academic functioning.

Allowed in exams
Calculator: Yes
Dictionary: Yes
Computer: Yes
Spellchecker: Yes
Extended test time: Yes
Scribes: Yes
Proctors: Yes
Oral exams: Yes
Note-takers: Yes
Services for students with LD: Yes
Services for students with ADHD: Yes
Services for students with ASD: Yes
Distraction-reduced environment: Yes
Tape recording in class: Yes
Audio book: NR
Electronic texts: Yes
Kurzweil Reader: Yes
Other assistive technology: Various voice-activated dictation software, WordQ, Inspiration, and computerized reading programs.
Priority registration: N/A
Added costs for services: No
LD specialists: Yes
ADHD coaching: NR
ASD specialists: NR
Professional tutors: Yes
Peer tutors: NR
Max. hours/wk. for services: Based on need.
How professors are notified of LD/ADHD: Both Student and Director

GENERAL ADMISSIONS INFORMATION

Office of Admissions: 352-638-9731

ENTRANCE REQUIREMENTS

Academic units required: 4 English, 1 math, 1 science, 1 social studies, 2 history, 3 academic electives. High school diploma is required and GED is accepted. SAT or ACT not used. If ACT, ACT with writing accepted. TOEFL required of all international applicants: minimum paper TOEFL 525.

Application deadline: 8/1
Notification: Rolling starting 9/1
Average GPA: 2.8
ACT Composite middle 50% range: NR-NR
SAT Math middle 50% range: NR-NR
SAT Critical Reading middle 50% range: NR-NR
SAT Writing middle 50% range: NR-NR
Graduated top 10% of class: NR
Graduated top 25% of class: NR
Graduated top 50% of class: NR

COLLEGE GRADUATION REQUIREMENTS

Course waivers allowed: Yes
In what course: Math
Course substitutions allowed: Yes
In what course: Math

ADDITIONAL INFORMATION

Environment: This private school was founded in 1989.

Student Body
Undergrad enrollment: 235
% Women: 38
% Men: 63
% Out-of-state: 80

Cost information
Tuition: $36,178
Room & board: $11,100

Housing Information
University Housing: Yes
Percent living on campus: 95

Greek System
Fraternity: Yes
Sorority: Yes
Athletics: NR

Florida A&M University

Suite G-9, Tallahassee, FL 32307-3200
Phone: 850-599-3796 • Fax: 850-599-3069
E-mail: ugrdadmissions@famu.edu • Web: www.famu.edu
Support: SP • Institution: Public

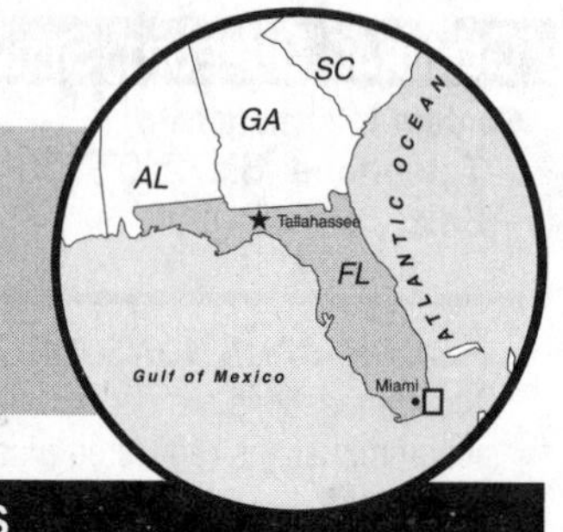

Programs or Services for Students with Learning Differences

The Center for Disability Access and Resources (CeDAR) at Florida A & M University provides comprehensive services and accommodations to FAMU students with disabilities. As an advocate for students with disabilities, the CeDAR collaborates with faculty, staff, and community partners to provide accommodations for the unique needs of students both in and out of the classroom. The mission is to provide enriching support programs, services, and reasonable accommodations. CeDAR hopes to foster a sense of empowerment in students with disabilities by educating them about their legal rights and responsibilities so that they can make informed choices, be critical thinkers, and self advocates. The goal is to ensure students with disabilities have access to the same programs, opportunities, and activities available to all FAMU students. The team works to celebrate and reward the unique backgrounds, viewpoints, skills, and talents of all CeDAR students.

Admission Information for Students with Learning Differences

College entrance test required: Yes
Interview required: No
Essay required: Required
Additional Application Required for LD/ADHD/ASD: Yes
What documentation required for LD: Certification of Attention-Deficit Disorder/Hyperactivity Disorder
With general application: NR
To receive services after enrolling: Yes
What documentation required for ADHD: Psychological Disability Verification Form
With general application: NR
To receive services after enrolling: Yes
What documentation required for ASD: High School IEP form, Psychological Disability Verification Form
With general application: NR
To receive services after enrolling: Yes
LD/ADHD/ASD documentation submitted to: Center for Disability Access and Resources
ASD Specific Program: NR
Special Ed. HS course work accepted: Not Applicable
Specific course requirements of all applicants: Yes
Separate application required for program services: FALSE
Total # of students receiving LD/ADHD/ASD services: NR
Acceptance into program means acceptance into college: NR

Admissions

CeDAR helps applicants who do not meet standard admission criteria to be admitted to FAMU under alternate criteria when appropriate based on the applicant's disability. Students are reviewed under alternate criteria. In implementing this procedure, the CeDAR shall not compromise academic or admission standards in any way. Students requesting an alternate review must request this review in writing and provide documentation certifying the existence of a disability; and verifying functional limitations imposed. These applicants are forwarded to CeDAR by admissions and a review confirms that the applicant's disability necessitates using alternate criteria. CeDAR will make a recommendation to admissions. Students may be required to attend the CeDAR College Study Skills Institute held during the summer prior to entrance before a recommendation to admit is completed. General admission includes GPA 2.55-2.99 (extra weight for AP/IB and Honors). FAMU uses the highest sub scores of ACT or SAT and does not use the ACT composite or SAT total score. Requires 4 English.

Additional Information

The CeDAR offers a six-week summer transition program (CSSI; required attendance for some incoming students with a disability who request special admissions consideration)to students who will be graduating or have graduated from high school. This program provides students a chance to focus on remediation of skill deficits, technology, and researching their area of disability. There are no fees for services provided. Enrollment in the CeDAR ART Program comes with a recommendation for PROVISIONAL admission to the university for the preceding SUMMER term. Enrollees are required to attend and successfully complete the College Study Skills Institute (CSSI) held during the summer before a final recommendation for continued enrollment will be offered. The CeDAR ART Program is a two year commitment to the institution as a stipulation for a student's continued enrollment at FAMU.

General Support Services Information

Contact Information
Name of program or department: Center for Disability Access and Resources
Telephone: (850) 599-3180
Fax: 850.561-2513
Website: http://www.famu.edu/index.cfm?cedar&SPECIALAdmissionsPROCESS

Accommodations or Services for Students with Learning Differences

Accommodations are decided upon an individual basis after a thorough review of appropriate, current documentation. The accommodations requests must be supported through the documentation provided and must be logically linked to the current impact of the condition on academic functioning.

Allowed in exams
Calculator: Yes
Dictionary: Yes
Computer: Yes
Spellchecker: Yes
Extended test time: Yes
Scribes: Yes
Proctors: Yes
Oral exams: Yes
Note-takers: Yes
Support services for students with LD: Yes
Support services for students with ADHD: Yes
Support services for students with ASD: Yes
Distraction-reduced environment: Yes
Tape recording in class: Yes
Electronic texts: Yes
Kurzweil reader: NR
Audio books: Yes
Other assistive technology: No
Priority registration: No
Added costs of services: NR
LD specialists: Yes
ADHD coaching: No
ASD specialists: Yes
Professional tutors: No
Peer tutors: NR
Max. hours/wk. for services: NR
How professors are notified of student approved accommodations: By student

General Admissions Information

Office of Admissions: 850-599-3796

Entrance Requirements

Academic units required: 4 English, 4 math, 3 science, 2 science labs, 2 foreign language, 3 social studies, 2 academic electives. High school diploma is required and GED is accepted. SAT or ACT required. If ACT, ACT with writing required. TOEFL required of all international applicants: minimum paper TOEFL 500 or minimum internet TOEFL 61.

Application deadline: 5/15
Notification: NR
Average GPA: 3.36
ACT Composite middle 50% range: 18-23
SAT Math middle 50% range: 420-530
SAT Critical Reading middle 50% range: 420-540
SAT Writing middle 50% range: 400-510
Graduate top 10% of class: 14
Graduated top 25% of class: 40
Graduated top 50% of class: 80

COLLEGE GRADUATION REQUIREMENTS

Course waivers allowed: Yes
In what course: Depending on the course and program of study
Course substitutions allowed: Yes
In what course: Depending on the course and program of study

Additional Information

Environment: This public school was founded in 1887. It has a 419-acre campus.

Student Body
Undergrad enrollment: 8,128
% Women: 63
% Men: 37
% Out-of-state: 14.7

Cost information
In-state Tuition: $5,645
Out-of-state Tuition: $17,585
Room & board: $10,100

Housing Information
University Housing: Yes
Percent living on campus: 28

Greek System
Fraternity: Yes
Sorority: Yes
Athletics: Division I

Florida Atlantic University

777 Glades Road, Boca Raton, FL 33431-0991
Phone: 561-297-3040 • Fax: 561-297-2758
E-mail: admissions@fau.edu • Web: www.fau.edu
Support: CS • Institution: Public

Programs or Services for Students with Learning Differences

Student Accessibility Services (SAS) provides Comprehensive academic support services include advocacy, academic accommodations, Assistive Technology equipment/software training, Assistive Technology Computer Lab, Learning Strategies training, and an active student organization. SAS has offices across three of FAU's campuses – Boca Raton, Davie, and Jupiter; however, accessibility services are available for students attending any of the six FAU campuses.

Admission Information for Students with Learning Differences

College entrance test required: Yes

Interview required: No
Essay required: No
Additional Application Required for LD/ADHD/ASD: NR
What documentation required for LD: The documentation must address of the student's functional limitations within the academic setting, as well as suggestions for accommodating the student: 1. Aptitude: WAIS and the Woodcock Johnson Test of Cognitive Ability 2. Achievement: Current levels of academic functioning in all aspects of reading, mathematics, and written language are required. 3. Information processing: Information processing should be addressed.
With general application: No
To receive services after enrolling: Yes
What documentation required for ADHD: The documentation must address of the student's functional limitations within the academic setting, as well as suggestions for accommodating the student: 1. Interview: Clinical interview with the diagnostician; 2. Assessment: A standardized assessment of attention (e.g., Continuous Performance Test. ADHD should be clearly diagnosed utilizing DSM codes.
With general application: No
To receive services after enrolling: Yes
What documentation required for ASD: Psycho ed evaluation
With general application: NR
To receive services after enrolling: Yes
LD/ADHD/ASD documentation submitted to: SAS
ASD Specific Program: NR
Special Ed. HS course work accepted: No
Specific course requirements of all applicants: Yes
Separate application required for program services: Yes
Total # of students receiving LD/ADHD/ASD services: 0
Acceptance into program means acceptance into college: NR

Admissions

There is no special application process for students with LD/ADHD/ASD. However, students with disabilities may be eligible to substitute for certain admission requirements. Students not meeting admission criteria may subsequently be admitted by a faculty admission committee if they possess the potential to succeed in university studies or will enhance the university. Supporting documentation explaining circumstances that adversely affected the student's past academic performances should be submitted. An admissions counselor will assist each applicant in submitting supporting materials to be presented to the committee by the Director of Admissions. In some cases, these students are reviewed by the SAS, which provides a recommendation to admissions. Students who self-disclose and are admitted are then reviewed for services. Typical courses required for admission include 4 years of English, 4 years of math (Algebra I and higher), 3 years of science, 2 years of a foreign language, 3 years of social studies, and 4 electives.

Additional Information

Student Accessibility Services (SAS) has a process for students with disabilities to apply for accommodations. The student needs to fill out the SAS Application for Support Services and submit a copy of his/her most recent documentation of disability. See this link http://www.fau.edu/sas/

General Support Services Information

Contact Information
Name of program or department: Office for Students with Disabilities (OSD)
Telephone: 561-297-3880
Fax: Same as above

Accommodations or Services For Students With Learning Differences

Accommodations are decided upon an individual basis after a thorough review of appropriate, current documentation. The accommodations requests must be supported through the documentation provided and must be logically linked to the current impact of the condition on academic functioning.

Allowed in exams
Calculator: Yes
Dictionary: Yes
Computer: Yes
Spellchecker: Yes
Extended test time: Yes
Scribes: Yes
Proctors: Yes
Oral exams: Yes
Note-takers: Yes
Services for students with LD: Yes
Services for students with ADHD: Yes
Services for students with ASD: Yes
Distraction-reduced environment: Yes
Tape recording in class: Yes
Audio book: Yes
Electronic texts: NR
Kurzweil reader: Yes
Other assistive technology: Yes
Priority registration: No
Added costs of services: No
LD specialists: Yes
ADHD coaching: NR
ASD specialists: NR
Professional tutors: NR
Peer tutors: Yes
Max. hours/wk. for services: NR
How professors are notified of student approved accommodations: Student

General Admissions Information

Office of Admissions: 561-297-3040

Entrance Requirements

Academic units required: 4 English, 4 math, 3 science, 2 science labs, 2 foreign language, 3 social studies, 3 academic electives. **Academic units recommended:** 4 English, 4 math, 3 science, 2 science labs, 2 foreign language, 3 social studies, 3 academic electives. High school diploma is required and GED is accepted. SAT or ACT required. If ACT, ACT with writing required. TOEFL required of all international applicants: minimum paper TOEFL 550 or minimum internet TOEFL 80.

Application deadline: 5/1
Notification: Rolling starting 10/1
Average GPA: 3.5
ACT Composite middle 50% range: 21-25
SAT Math middle 50% range: 490-580
SAT Critical Reading middle 50% range: 480-570
SAT Writing middle 50% range: 480-560
Graduated top 10% of class: 11
Graduated top 25% of class: 35
Graduated top 50% of class: 78

COLLEGE GRADUATION REQUIREMENTS

Course waivers allowed: Yes
Course substitutions allowed: Yes
In what course: Varies; it depends on the major requirements and the disability. Substitutions used rather than waivers.

Additional Information

Environment: This public school was founded in 1961. It has a 860-acre campus.

Student Body
Undergrad enrollment: 25,209
% Women: 56
% Men: 44
% Out-of-state: 5

Cost information
In-state Tuition: $5,986
Out-of Tuition: $21,543
Room & board: $11,353

Housing Information
University Housing: Yes
Percent living on campus: 6

Greek System
Fraternity: Yes
Sorority: Yes
Athletics: Division I

Florida State University

874 Traditions Way, 108 SSB, Tallahassee, FL 32306-2400
Phone: 850-644-6200 • Fax: 850-644-0197
E-mail: admissions@admin.fsu.edu • Web: www.fsu.edu
Support: CS • Institution: Public

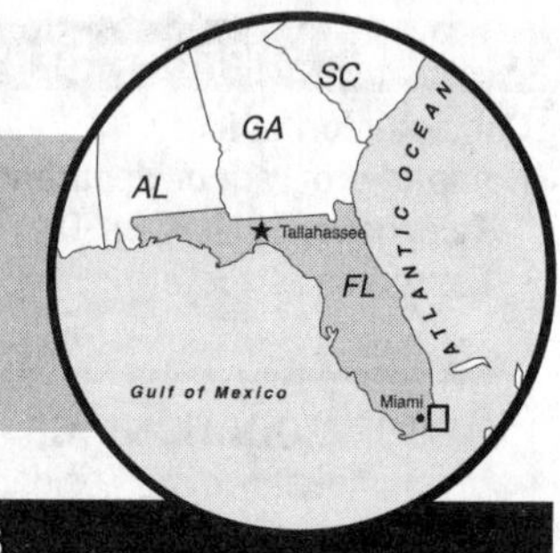

Programs or Services for Students with Learning Differences

The Student Disability Resource Center (SDRC) was established to serve as an advocate for Florida State students with disabilities and ensure that reasonable accommodations are provided. Florida State University is committed to providing a quality education to all qualified students and does not discriminate on the basis of race, creed, color, sex, religion, national origin, age, disability, genetic information, veterans' status, marital status, sexual orientation, gender identity, gender expression or any other legally protected group status. Providing services to more than 2,100 students, the Student Disability Resource Center is committed to ensuring the success of each Florida State University student. Through the provision of academic accommodations, testing support, assistive technologies, coaching and a space for students to feel part of the FSU community the SDRC creates an environment of success.

Admission Information for Students with Learning Differences

College entrance tests required: Yes
Interview required: No
Essay required: Yes
Additional Application Required for LD/ADHD/ASD: NR
What documentation required for LD: Psychoeducational assessment or supporting documentation with history of diagnosis and accommodations
With general application: No
To receive services after enrolling: Yes
What documentation required for ADHD: Psychoeducational assessment or supporting documentation with history of diagnosis and accommodations
With general application: No
To receive services after enrolling: Yes
What documentation required for ASD: Psychoeducational assessment or supporting documentation with history of diagnosis and accommodations
With general application: No
To receive services after enrolling: Yes
LD/ADHD/ASD documentation submitted to: Student Disability Resource Center
ASD Specific Program: NR
Special Ed. HS course work accepted: No
Specific course requirements of all applicants: Yes
Separate application required: No
Total # of students receiving LD/ADHD/ASD services: 700
Acceptance into program means acceptance into college: Students must be admitted and enrolled in the university first and then request services.

Admissions

Florida State University receives over 30,000 freshman applications each year. Because of the high number of applications the university receives, satisfying minimum requirements does not guarantee admission. The academic profile of the middle 50 percent of freshmen accepted in 2013 was: 3.9-4.7 weighted GPA; 26-30 ACT composite; 1730-1960 SAT total. In addition to the academic profile, a variety of other factors are also considered in the review process. These include the written essay, the rigor and quality of courses and curriculum, grade trends, class rank, strength of senior schedule in academic subjects, math level in the senior year, and number of years in a sequential foreign language. Applicants who bring other important attributes to the university community may also receive additional consideration. These applicants include students applying to the CARE Summer Bridge Program, visual and performing artists, and skilled athletes. Letters of recommendation are not required.

Additional Information

Students who choose to disclose their disability to receive accommodations must complete a Request for Services form provided by the SDRC. For an LD, documentation must be current (normed to the adult population) and provided by a qualified professional (Licensed psychologist.) Staff members assist students in exploring their needs and determining the necessary services and accommodations. Academic accommodations include alternate text formats, alternative testing location, extended time, reader and/or scribe, and inclass note-takers. Staff members meet individually with students with LD/ADHD. Services include teaching study skills, memory enhancement techniques, organizational skills, test-taking strategies, stress management techniques, ways to structure tutoring for best results, and skills for negotiating accommodations with instructors. Student Disability Union (SDU) act as a support group for students with disabilities.

General Support Services Information

Contact Information
Name of program or department: Student Disability Resource Center
Telephone: 850-644-9566
Fax: 850-645-1852

Accommodations or Services for Students with Learning Differences

Accommodations are decided upon an individual basis after a thorough review of appropriate, current documentation. The accommodations requested must be supported through the documentation provided and must be logically linked to the current impact of the condition on academic functioning.

Allowed in exams
Calculator: Yes
Dictionary: Yes
Computer: Yes
Spellchecker: Yes
Extended test time: Yes
Scribes: Yes
Proctors: Yes
Oral exams: No
Note-takers: Yes
Services for students with LD: Yes
Services for students with ADHD: Yes
Services for students with ASD: Yes
Distraction-reduced environment: Yes
Tape recording in class: Yes
Audio book: Yes
Electronic texts: Yes
Kurzweil Reader: No
Other assistive technology: Yes
Priority registration: Yes
Added costs for services: No
LD specialists: No
ADHD coaching: Yes
ASD specialists: No
Professional tutors: Yes
Peer tutors: Yes
Max. hours/wk. for services: N/A
How professors are notified of LD/ADHD: By student

General Admissions Information

Office of Admissions: 850-644-6200

Entrance Requirements

Academic units required: 4 English, 4 math, 3 science, 2 science labs, 2 foreign language, 1 social studies, 2 history, 3 academic electives. **Academic units recommended:** 4 English, 4 math, 4 science, 2 science labs, 4 foreign language, 2 social studies, 2 history, 3 academic electives. High school diploma is required and GED is accepted. SAT or ACT required. If ACT, ACT with writing required. TOEFL required of all international applicants: minimum paper TOEFL 550 or minimum internet TOEFL 80.

Application deadline: 1/15
Notification: NR
Average GPA: 3.91
ACT Composite middle 50% range: 25-29
SAT Math middle 50% range: 560-640
SAT Critical Reading middle 50% range: 560-640
SAT Writing middle 50% range: 560-640
Graduated top 10% of class: 38
Graduated top 25% of class: 75
Graduated top 50% of class: 97

COLLEGE GRADUATION REQUIREMENTS

Course waivers allowed: Yes
In what course: Foreign language, math.
Course substitutions allowed: Yes
In what course: Foreign language, math.

Additional Information

Environment: This public school was founded in 1851. It has a 452-acre campus.

Student Body
Undergrad enrollment: 32,948
% Women: 55
% Men: 45
% Out-of-state: 10

Cost information
In-state Tuition: $4,640
Out-of Tuition: $19,806
Room & board: $10,264

Housing Information
University Housing: Yes
Percent living on campus: 19.3

Greek System
Fraternity: Yes
Sorority: Yes
Athletics: Division I

Lynn University

3601 North Military Trail, Boca Raton, FL 33431-5598
Phone: 561-237-7900 • Fax: 561-237-7100
E-mail: admission@lynn.edu • Web: www.lynn.edu
Support: SP • Institution: Private

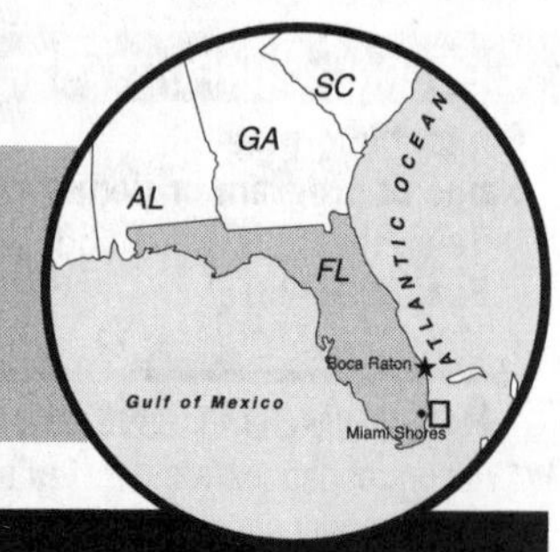

Programs or Services for Students with Learning Differences

The Comprehensive Support Program has experts in the field of learning pedagogy and nontraditional methodology providing extensive academic support for students with learning differences. This program includes group and individual tutoring, testing accommodations, an alternative testing environment, specialized classes, expert instructors who teach in a multimodality instruction and assessment format, workshops on anxiety and testing, progress updates, mid-term grades, and more. The coaching component of the program uses a diagnostic coaching model to addresses specific executive functioning issues such as organizational skills, procrastination, impulsivity, focus and attention, and study skills, etc.

Admission Information for Students with Learning Differences

College entrance tests required: Yes
Interview required: No
Essay required: NR
Additional Application Required for LD/ADHD/ASD: NR
What documentation required for LD: Psycho ed evaluation to include: relevant historical info, instructional interventions, related services, age diagnosed, objective data (aptitude, achievement, info processing), test scores (standard, percentile and grade equivalents) and describe functional limitations.
With general application: Yes if requested as part of Structured Program application
To receive services after enrolling: Yes
What documentation required for ADHD: Diagnosis based on DSM-V; history of behaviors impairing functioning in academic setting; diagnostic interview; history of symptoms; evidence of ongoing behaviors.
With general application: Yes if requested as part of Structured Program application
To receive services after enrolling: Yes
What documentation required for ASD: Psycho ed evaluation
With general application: NR
To receive services after enrolling: Yes
LD/ADHD/ASD documentation submitted to: Support Program/Services
ASD Specific Program: NR
Special Ed. HS course work accepted: Yes
Specific course requirements for all applicants: NR
Separate application required for program services: No
Total # of students receiving LD/ADHD/ASD services: 350
Acceptance into program means acceptance into college: Student must be admitted and enrolled in the university first and then offered services through IAL.

Admissions

Students should submit the general application to Lynn University. Admissions criteria are dependent on the level of services required. Students needing the least restrictive services should have taken college-prep high school courses. Some students may be admitted provisionally after submitting official information. Typically, these students have an ACT of 18 or lower or an SAT of 850 or lower and 2.5 GPA.

Additional Information

The IAL (Institute for Achievement and Learning) program features include: individual and group tutoring; study strategy sessions to enhance study and organizational skills; test anxiety sessions; faculty progress reports; extended time exams and alternative testing procedures; academic coaching and schedule planning; selected core courses offered through IAL trained faculty who teach students in a multimodality style in order to meet students' individual needs; communicative intervention with faculty and thematic instruction. The program uses a diagnostic coaching model to address behavioral issues such as organization skills, prioritizing of assignments and daily activities, strategies for procrastination, time management skills, coping with impulsivity, strategies to aid with focus and attention in and out of the classroom and study skills. There is an additional cost to participate in the IAL program program but program fees vary depending on the level of support required. There is an additional cost to participate in the IAL program program but program fees vary depending on the level of support required.

General Support Services Information

Contact Information
Name of program or department: Institute for Achievement and Learning
Telephone: 561-237-7064
Fax: 561-237-7873

Accommodations or Services For Students With Learning Differences

Accommodations are decided on an individual basis after a thorough review of appropriate, current documentation. Accommodations requested must be supported through the documentation provided and must be logically linked to the current impact of the condition on academic functioning.

Allowed in exams
Calculator: Yes
Dictionary: Yes
Computer: Yes
Spellchecker: Yes
Extended test time: Yes
Scribes: Yes
Proctors: Yes
Oral exams: Yes
Note-takers: No
Services for students with LD: Yes
Services for students with ADHD: Yes
Services for students with ASD: Yes
Distraction-reduced environment: Yes
Tape recording in class: Yes
Audio book: NR
Electronic texts: Yes
Kurzweil Reader: Yes
Other assistive technology: CCTV, Kurzweil Reader, Books on tape, Dragon Naturally Speak
Priority registration: Yes
Added costs for services: Yes
LD specialists: Yes
ADHD coaching: NR
ASD specialists: NR
Professional tutors: 46
Peer tutors: No
Max. hours/wk. for services: Unlimited
How professors are notified of LD/ADHD: Student

General Admissions Information

Office of Admissions: 561-237-7900

Entrance Requirements

Academic units recommended: 4 English, 4 math, 4 science, 2 social studies, 2 history. High school diploma is required and GED is accepted. SAT or ACT required for some. If ACT, ACT with writing accepted. TOEFL required of all international applicants: minimum paper TOEFL 525 or minimum internet TOEFL 71.

Application deadline: 8/1
Notification: Rolling starting 12/15
Average GPA: 3.07
ACT Composite middle 50% range: 19-24
SAT Math middle 50% range: 445-550
SAT Critical Reading middle 50% range: 450-540
SAT Writing middle 50% range: 430-540
Graduated top 10% of class: 10
Graduated top 25% of class: 25
Graduated top 50% of class: 57

COLLEGE GRADUATION REQUIREMENTS

Course waivers allowed: No
Course substitutions allowed: No

Additional Information

Environment: This private school was founded in 1962. It has a 123-acre campus.

Student Body
Undergrad enrollment: 2,003
% Women: 48
% Men: 52
% Out-of-state: 53

Cost information
Tuition: $32,800
Room & board: $11,640

Housing Information
University Housing: Yes
Percent living on campus: 46.4

Greek System
Fraternity: Yes
Sorority: Yes
Athletics: Division II

Stetson University

421 N. Woodland Blvd, DeLand, FL 32723
Phone: 386-822-7100 • Fax: 386-822-7112
E-mail: admissions@stetson.edu • Web: stetson.edu
Support: CS • Institution: Private

Programs or Services for Students with Learning Differences

The goal of Academic Success is to ensure equal access to the learning opportunities offered at Stetson University. This is accomplished through reasonable accommodations for the classroom, as well as, education for the campus community around principles of universal design and inclusion.

Admission Information for Students with Learning Differences

College entrance test required: No
Interview required: No
Essay required: Recommended
Additional Application Required for LD/ADHD/ASD: No
What documentation required for LD: Documentation from a professional in the field that provides a diagnosis, explanation of how diagnosis impacts the student, and recommendations for potential accommodations. This documentation can be in the form of a letter, Psychoeducational evaluation, IEP, 504 plan, etc.
With general application: No
To receive services after enrolling: No
What documentation required for ADHD: Documentation from a professional in the field that provides a diagnosis, explanation of how diagnosis impacts the student, and recommendations for potential accommodations. This documentation can be in the form of a letter, Psychoeducational evaluation, IEP, 504 plan, etc.
With general application: No
To receive services after enrolling: No
What documentation required for ASD: Documentation from a professional in the field that provides a diagnosis, explanation of how diagnosis impacts the student, and recommendations for potential accommodations. This documentation can be in the form of a letter, Psychoeducational evaluation, IEP, 504 plan, etc.
With general application: No
To receive services after enrolling: No
LD/ADHD/ASD documentation submitted to: Academic Success
ASD Specific Program: No
Special Ed. HS course work accepted: No
Specific course requirements of all applicants: Yes
Separate application required for program services: True
Total # of students receiving LD/ADHD/ASD services: 111
Acceptance into program means acceptance into college: No

Admissions

Average GPA is 3.8. ACT/SAT is optional. Courses required include: English 4 years, Mathematics 3 years, Science 3 years, Foreign Language 2 years, Social Studies 3 years.

Additional Information

There is a three step process to establish accommodations. First, students complete an Accommodations Profile on our website (www.stetson.edu/accessibility). This provides students with a chance to share their personal academic experience including strengths as a student, barriers encountered in the learning environment, and previous accommodations. Second, students provide supporting documentation. Guidelines for supporting documentation can also be found on our website. Finally, each student meets with a staff member to discuss and establish appropriate accommodations for their time at Stetson University. In addition to ensuring access for students, Academic Success also offers a number of resources focused on supporting a student's success. We offer tutoring in a number of courses across disciplines to help student's develop the content knowledge to be successful in their courses. We also offer success coaching to enhance overall academic skills including time management, note taking, active reading, test preparation, and test taking strategies. Any student interested in the social skills group can reach out to the Stetson University Counseling Center at counseling@stetson.edu.

General Support Services Information

Contact Information
Name of program or department: Academic Success
Telephone: 386-822-7345
Fax: 386-822-7322
Website: www.stetson.edu/accessibility

Accommodations or Services for Students with Learning Differences

Accommodations are decided upon an individual basis after a thorough review of appropriate, current documentation. The accommodations requests must be supported through the documentation provided and must be logically linked to the current impact of the condition on academic functioning.

Allowed in exams
Calculator: Yes
Dictionary: Yes
Computer: Yes
Spellchecker: Yes
Extended test time: Yes
Scribes: Yes
Proctors: Yes
Oral exams: Not Applicable
Note-takers: Yes
Support services for students with LD: Yes
Support services for students with ADHD: Yes
Support services for students with ASD: Yes
Distraction-reduced environment: Yes
Tape recording in class: Yes
Electronic texts: Yes
Kurzweil reader: NR
Audio books: Yes
Other assistive technology: Yes
Priority registration: Yes
Added costs of services: No
LD specialists: No
ADHD coaching: Yes
ASD specialists: No
Professional tutors: No
Peer tutors: Yes
Max. hours/wk. for services: NR
How professors are notified of student approved accommodations: By director

General Admissions Information

Office of Admissions: 386-822-7100

Entrance Requirements

Academic units required: 4 English, 3 math, 3 science, 2 foreign language, 2 social studies. High school diploma is required and GED is accepted. SAT or ACT required for some. If ACT, ACT with writing accepted. TOEFL required of all international applicants: minimum paper TOEFL 550 or minimum internet TOEFL 79.

Application deadline: NR
Notification: Rolling starting 9/1
Average GPA: 3.86
ACT Composite middle 50% range: 23.5-28
SAT Math middle 50% range: 520-620
SAT Critical Reading middle 50% range: 530-640
SAT Writing middle 50% range: 500-620
Graduate top 10% of class: 28
Graduated top 25% of class: 60
Graduated top 50% of class: 88

COLLEGE GRADUATION REQUIREMENTS

Course waivers allowed: No
In what course: NR
Course substitutions allowed: Yes
In what course: Foreign language

Additional Information

Environment: This private school was founded in 1883. It has a 175-acre campus.

Student Body
Undergrad enrollment: 3,084
Women: 57
Men: 43
Percent out-of-state: 32

Cost information
Tuition: $42,890
Room & board: $12,326

Housing Information
University Housing: Yes
Percent living on campus: 65

Greek System
Fraternity: Yes
Sorority: Yes
Athletics: Division I

UNIVERSITY OF CENTRAL FLORIDA

PO Box 160111, Orlando, FL 32816-0111
Phone: 407-823-3000 • Fax: 407-823-5625
E-mail: admission@ucf.edu • Web: www.ucf.edu
Support: CS • Institution: Public

PROGRAMS OR SERVICES FOR STUDENTS WITH LEARNING DIFFERENCES

The Office of Student Disability Services provides information and individualized services consistent with the student's documented disability. To be eligible for disability-related services, individuals must have a documented disability as defined by applicable federal and state laws. Individuals seeking services are required to provide recent documentation from an appropriate health care provider or professional. See www.sds.ucf.edu for specific documentation required.

ADMISSION INFORMATION FOR STUDENTS WITH LEARNING DIFFERENCES

College entrance test required: Yes
Interview required: Yes
Essay required: Yes
Additional Application Required for LD/ADHD/ASD: NR
What documentation required for LD: sycho Ed evaluation to include: relevant historical info, instructional interventions, related services, age diagnosed, objective data (aptitude,achievement, info processing), test scores (standard, percentile and grade equivalents) and describe functional limitations.
With general application: Yes
To receive services after enrolling: Yes
What documentation required for ADHD: Diagnosis based on DSM-V; history of behaviors impairing functioning in academic setting; diagnostic interview; history of symptoms;evidence of ongoing behaviors.
With general application: No
To receive services after enrolling: Yes
What documentation required for ASD: Students make an appointment with SDS Accessibility Consultant. Accommodations are based on student self-report and third party documentation (IEP, 504 Plan, evaluations, letter from treating professional provider, etc.)
With general application: No
To receive services after enrolling: Yes
LD/ADHD/ASD documentation submitted to: Student Accessibility Services
ASD Specific Program: NR
Special Ed. HS course work accepted: Yes
Specific course requirements of all applicants: Yes
Separate application required for program services: Yes
Total # of students receiving LD/ADHD/ASD services: NR
Acceptance into program means acceptance into college: NR

ADMISSIONS

Admission to the University of Central Florida requires graduation from an accredited high school with certain high school academic units, a cumulative high school GPA in those academic units, and SAT or ACT test scores. Course requirements include 4 years of English (at least 3 with substantial writing requirements); 3 years of mathematics (Algebra I and above); 3 years of natural science (at least 2 with labs); 3 years of social science; 2 sequential years of the same foreign language; 3 elective years (preferably from English, mathematics, natural science, social science, or foreign language areas). Students with disabilities who have not taken a foreign language in high school must submit, along with appropriate documentation, a letter from a school official verifying that not taking a foreign language was an accommodation for the disability. If a student needs special admission consideration based on a disability, the student should send the requested appropriate documentation to the Undergraduate Admissions Office. Satisfying minimum requirements does not guarantee admission to UCF since preference will be given to those students whose credentials indicate the greatest promise of academic success.

ADDITIONAL INFORMATION

The University Writing Center (UWC) provides free writing support to all undergraduates and graduates at the University of Central Florida. The Student Academic Resource Center (SARC) provides high-quality academic support programs, including tutoring and supplemental instruction, retention programs, academic advising programs, and various other academic programs and services. The Math Lab provides tutoring for students enrolled in mathematics courses.

General Support Services Information

Contact Information
Name of program or department: Student Accessibility Services
Telephone: 407-823-2371
Fax: 407-823-2372
Website: http://sas.sdes.ucf.edu/

Accommodations or Services For Students With Learning Differences

Accommodations are decided upon an individual basis after a thorough review of appropriate, current documentation. The accommodations requests must be supported through the documentation provided and must be logically linked to the current impact of the condition on academic functioning.

Allowed in exams
Calculator: Yes
Dictionary: Yes
Computer: Yes
Spellchecker: Yes
Extended test time: Yes
Scribes: Yes
Proctors: Yes
Oral exams: No
Note-takers: Yes
Support services for students with LD: Yes
Support services for students with ADHD: Yes
Support services for students with ASD: Yes
Distraction-reduced environment: Yes
Tape recording in class: Yes
Electronic texts: Yes
Kurzweil reader: NR
Audio books: Yes
Other assistive technology: NR
Priority registration: Yes
Added costs of services: No
LD specialists: No
ADHD coaching: Not Applicable
ASD specialists: No
Professional tutors: No
Peer tutors: Not Applicable
Max. hours/wk. for services: NR
How professors are notified of student approved accommodations: By director

General Admissions Information

Office of Admissions: 407-823-3000

Entrance Requirements

Academic units required: 4 English, 4 math, 3 science, 2 science labs, 2 foreign language, 3 social studies, 2 academic electives. High school diploma is required and GED is accepted. SAT or ACT required. If ACT, ACT with writing required. TOEFL required of all international applicants: minimum paper TOEFL 550 or minimum internet TOEFL 80.

Application deadline: 5/1
Notification: Rolling starting 9/15
Average GPA: 3.92
ACT Composite middle 50% range: 24-28
SAT Math middle 50% range: 540-640
SAT Critical Reading middle 50% range: 540-630
SAT Writing middle 50% range: 510-610
Graduate top 10% of class: 33
Graduated top 25% of class: 74
Graduated top 50% of class: 98

COLLEGE GRADUATION REQUIREMENTS

Course waivers allowed: No
In what course: NR
Course substitutions allowed: Yes
In what course: math, foreign language

Additional Information

Environment: This public school was founded in 1963. It has a 1415-acre campus.

Student Body
Undergrad enrollment: 54,513
% Women: 55
% Men: 45
% Out-of-state: 5.3

Cost information
In-state Tuition: $6,368
Out-of-state Tuition: $22,467
Room & board: $9,300

Housing Information
University Housing: Yes
Percent living on campus: 17

Greek System
Fraternity: Yes
Sorority: Yes
Athletics: Division I

UNIVERSITY OF FLORIDA

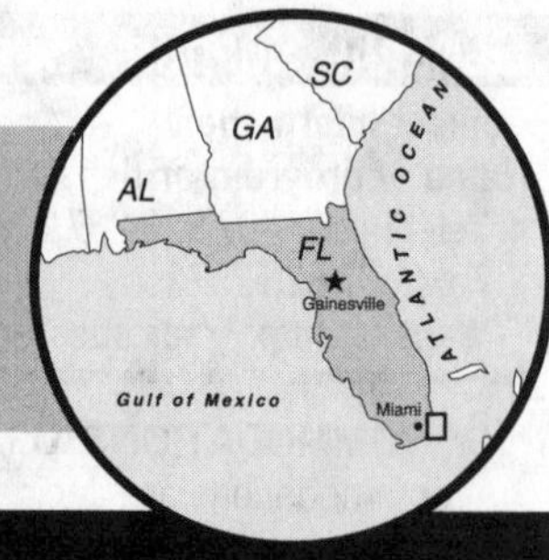

201 Criser Hall, Gainesville, FL 32611-4000
Phone: 352-392-1365 • Fax: 904-392-3987
E-mail: webrequests@registrar.ufl.edu • Web: www.ufl.edu
Support: CS • Institution: Public

PROGRAMS OR SERVICES FOR STUDENTS WITH LEARNING DIFFERENCES

The University of Florida offers a full range of support services designed to assist students with disabilities. Support services are individually tailored to each student's needs and those supports may be modified to meet the specific demands and requirements of individual courses. Advisement and support services are available to students on an as-needed basis.

ADMISSION INFORMATION FOR STUDENTS WITH LEARNING DIFFERENCES

College entrance test required: Yes
Interview required: No
Essay required: No
Additional Application Required for LD/ADHD/ASD: NR
What documentation required for LD: The University of Florida encourages a Psycho-Educational evaluation that meets the documentation guidelines outlined at https://www.dso.ufl.edu/drc/students/.
With general application: No
To receive services after enrolling: Yes
What documentation required for ADHD: The University of Florida encourages a psycho-educational evaluation that meets the documentation guidelines outlined at https://www.dso.ufl.edu/drc/students/.
With general application: No
To receive services after enrolling: Yes
What documentation required for ASD: The University of Florida encourages a Neuro-Psychological evaluation that meets the documentation guidelines outlinedat http://www.dso.ufl.edu/drc/students/.
With general application: No
To receive services after enrolling: Yes
LD/ADHD/ASD documentation submitted to: Admissions
ASD Specific Program: NR
Special Ed. HS course work accepted: N/A
Specific course: Yes
Separate application required for program services: No
Total # of students receiving LD/ADHD/ASD services: 350
Acceptance into program means acceptance into college: NR

ADMISSIONS

Applicants with learning disabilities apply to the university under the same guidelines as all other students. However, applicants with learning disabilities may request a 'disability consideration' review. Students should check the 'disability consideration' box on the general application to request 'disability consideration' review and submit disability documentation and a personal statement describing the impact of their learning disabilities on academic performance and/or standardized test scores, if applicable.

ADDITIONAL INFORMATION

The Dean of Students Office sponsors "Preview," a mandatory registration and orientation program. Disability Resource Center assistance can be provided regarding classroom accommodaitons, learning strategies, support groups, and foreign language and/or math course petitions. Services are available to focus on learning and success strategies.

General Support Services Information

Contact Information
Name of program or department: Disability Resource Center
Telephone: 352-392-8565 ext 200
Fax: 352-392-8570

Accommodations or Services For Students With Learning Differences

Accommodations are decided upon an individual basis after a thorough review of appropriate, current documentation. The accommodations requests must be supported through the documentation provided and must be logically linked to the current impact of the condition on academic functioning.

Allowed in exams
Calculator: Yes
Dictionary: Yes
Computer: Yes
Spellchecker: Yes
Extended test time: Yes
Scribes: Yes
Proctors: Yes
Oral exams: Yes
Note-takers: Yes
Services for students with LD: Yes
Services for students with ADHD: Yes
Services for students with ASD: Yes
Distraction-reduced environment: Yes
Tape recording in class: Yes
Audio book: Yes
Electronic texts: NR
Kurzweil Reader: Yes
Other assistive technology: Yes
Priority registration: Yes
Added costs of services: No
LD specialists: Yes
ADHD coaching: NR
ASD specialists: NR
Professional tutors: NR
Peer tutors: N/A
Max. hours/wk. for services: NR
How professors are notified of student approved accommodations: Student

General Admissions Information

Office of Admissions: 352-392-1365

Entrance Requirements

Academic units required: 4 English, 4 math, 3 science, 2 science labs, 2 foreign language, 3 social studies. High school diploma is required and GED is accepted. SAT or ACT required. If ACT, ACT with writing required.

Application deadline: 11/1
Notification: NR
Average GPA: NR
ACT Composite middle 50% range: 27-31
SAT Math middle 50% range: 590-680
SAT Critical Reading middle 50% range: 580-670
SAT Writing middle 50% range: 570-670
Graduated top 10% of class: 72
Graduated top 25% of class: 96
Graduated top 50% of class: 100

COLLEGE GRADUATION REQUIREMENTS

Course waivers allowed: No
Course substitutions allowed: Yes
In what course: Students may petition for foreign language and/or math course substitutions. The courses offered in substitution are decided on a by college and case-by-case basis.

Additional Information

Environment: This public school was founded in 1853. It has a 2000-acre campus.

Student Body
Undergrad enrollment: 35,043
% Women: 55
% Men: 45
% Out-of-state: 3.21

Cost information
In-state Tuition: $6,313
Out-of Tuition: $28,590
Room & board: $9,630

Housing Information
University Housing: Yes
Percent living on campus: 23.23

Greek System
Fraternity: Yes
Sorority: Yes
Athletics: Division I

Brenau University

500 Washington Street SE, Gainesville, GA 30501
Phone: 770-534-6162 • Fax: 770-538-4701
E-mail: admissions@brenau.edu • Web: www.brenau.edu
Support: SP • Institution: Private

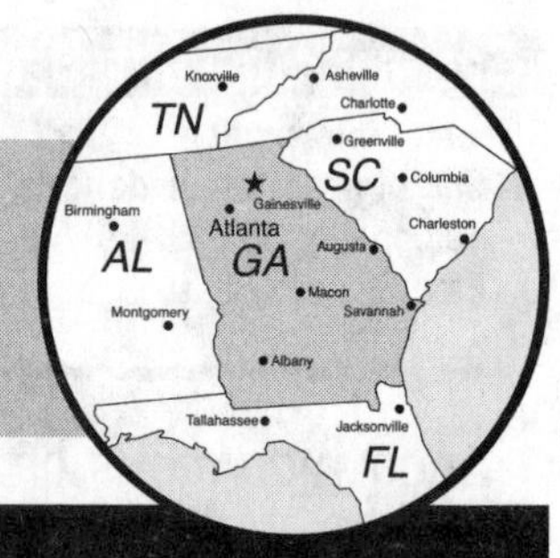

Programs or Services for Students with Learning Differences

The Brenau Learning Center is a program for students with a diagnosed learning disability or Attention Deficit Disorder. Students must also have average to above average academic aptitude with an adequate high school preparation for college studies. The program is designed to provide support services for students as they attend regular college courses. It also offers a more structured learning environment by offering tutoring by professional tutors and academic coaching for study strategies, organization, and time management. Students also receive additional support from the University First Year Experience that is provided to all students, and student-life services.

Admission Information for Students with Learning Differences

College entrance tests required: Yes
Interview required: No
Essay required: Yes
Additional Application Required for LD/ADHD/ASD: NR
What documentation required for LD: Current psychological report/transition plan from secondary school.
With general application: Yes
To receive services after enrolling: Yes
What documentation required for ADHD: Current psychological report/transition plan from secondary school.
With general application: Yes
To receive services after enrolling: Yes
What documentation required for ASD: Current psychological report/transition plan from secondary school.
With general application: Yes
To receive services after enrolling: Yes
LD/ADHD/ASD documentation submitted to: Admissions
ASD Specific Program: NR
Special Ed. HS course work accepted: No
Specific course requirements for all applicants: NR
Separate application required for program services: Yes
Total # of students receiving LD/ADHD/ASD services: 20
Acceptance into college means acceptance into program: Yes

Admissions

Freshmen applicants who have successfully completed a college prep high school curriculum at a regionally accredited high school with a minimum GPA of 2.5 and have composite SAT scores of at least 900 (ACT of 19) will ordinarily be granted admission. Evidence of satisfaction of these requirements shall only be in the form of an official, sealed transcript from authorized school personnel or an official, sealed G.E.D. certificate. Applicants who completed high school more than seven years prior to application are not required to submit SAT/ACT scores. SAT/ACT scores must be sent directly from the testing company or be included on official transcripts. All home-schooled students will be asked to come for an interview as well.

Additional Information

The Learning Center sponsors study skills and test-taking workshops each semester. It's also a resource for students with learning disabilities, such as attention deficit disorder. Learning Center students can register early and receive regular academic advising from the Director of the program. Study skills and computer skills courses are offered for credit. At all service levels students may take tests in an extended-time format where oral assistance is available. Learning Center students begin tutoring with professional tutors during the first week of the term and contract to regularly attend tutoring sessions throughout the semester. All LC students may receive one free hour of educational support per week in addition to scheduled tutoring. Students may be tutored in one to four academic classes per semester. LD services and accommodations are available for undergraduate and graduate students.

General Support Services Information

Contact Information
Name of program or department: Learning Center (LC)
Telephone: 770-534-6134
Fax: 770-297-5883

Accommodations or Services For Students With Learning Differences

Most students receive extended-time testing in the Learning Center facility. Time and a half is given for most "objective" selected response tests and double time for "essay" constructed-response exams. Students have the opportunity to have 2 hours of weekly scheduled tutoring by adults for each course selected. Most receive tutoring in English and core courses. One hour weekly with an academic specialist is also offered. These services are free. Students also receive instruction in study strategies such as reading textbooks and note-taking. The university has a strong First Year Experience course that supports all new students and strong student services. Students are also co-advised by the Director and major advisors.

Allowed in exams
Calculator: Yes
Dictionary: Yes
Computer: Yes
Spellchecker: Yes
Extended test time: Yes
Scribes: No
Proctors: Yes
Oral exams: No
Note-takers: Yes
Services for students with LD: Yes
Services for students with ADHD: Yes
Services for students with ASD: Yes
Distraction-reduced environment: Yes
Tape recording in class: Yes
Audio book: No
Electronic texts: Yes
Kurzweil Reader: Yes
Other assistive technology: Yes
Priority registration: Yes
Added costs for services: No
LD specialists: Yes
ADHD coaching: NR
ASD specialists: Yes
Professional tutors: Yes
Peer tutors: No
Max. hours/wk. for services: 9
How professors are notified of LD/ADHD: Both student and director

General Admissions Information

Office of Admissions: 770-534-6100

Entrance Requirements

Academic units required: 4 English, 4 math, 3 science, 2 foreign language, 3 social studies. High school diploma is required and GED is accepted. SAT or ACT required. If ACT, ACT with writing accepted. TOEFL required of all international applicants: minimum paper TOEFL 500 or minimum internet TOEFL 61.

Application deadline: NR
Notification: Rolling starting 8/1
Average GPA: NR
ACT Composite middle 50% range: NR-NR
SAT Math middle 50% range: 440-530
SAT Critical Reading middle 50% range: 450-550
SAT Writing middle 50% range: NR-NR
Graduated top 10% of class: NR
Graduated top 25% of class: NR
Graduated top 50% of class: NR

COLLEGE GRADUATION REQUIREMENTS

Course waivers allowed: No
Course substitutions allowed: No

Additional Information

Environment: This private school was founded in 1878. It has a 56-acre campus.

Student Body
Undergrad enrollment: 1,596
% Women: 90
% Men: 10
% Out-of-state: 5

Cost information
Tuition: $25,478
Room & board: $11,998

Housing Information
University Housing: Yes
Percent living on campus: 24

Greek System
Fraternity: No
Sorority: Yes
Athletics: NAIA

EMORY UNIVERSITY

Emory University, Boiseuillet Jones Center, Atlanta, GA 30322
Phone: 404-727-6036 • Fax: 404-727-4303
E-mail: admiss@emory.edu • Web: www.emory.edu
Support: CS • Institution: Private

PROGRAMS OR SERVICES FOR STUDENTS WITH LEARNING DIFFERENCES

Access, Disability Services and Resources is committed to advancing an accessible and "barrier-free" environment for its students, faculty, staff, patients, guests and visitors by ensuring that the principles of access, equity, inclusion and learning are applied and realized. As the administrative office responsible for: managing access needs, providing ADA accommodations, ensuring compliance with local, state and federal civil rights regulations pertaining to disability law, and serving as a critical resources for the enterprise, it is our role to embody Emory's commitment to its mission "in work and deed." Learning specialists are available to assist students in developing skills and strategies to define learning goals and individualized plans to reach a student's academic potential.

ADMISSION INFORMATION FOR STUDENTS WITH LEARNING DIFFERENCES

College entrance test required: Yes
Interview required: No
Essay required: No
Additional Application Required for LD/ADHD/ASD: NR
What documentation required for LD: Psycho ed evaluation
With general application: No
To receive services after enrolling: Yes
What documentation required for ADHD: Psycho ed evaluation
With general application: No
To receive services after enrolling: Yes
What documentation required for ASD: Psycho ed evaluation
With general application: No
To receive services after enrolling: Yes
LD/ADHD/ASD documentation submitted to: Support program/services
ASD Specific Program: NR
Special Ed. HS course work accepted: No
Specific course requirements of all applicants: No
Separate application required for program services: No
Total # of students receiving LD/ADHD/ASD services: NR
Acceptance into program means acceptance into college: NR

ADMISSIONS

Students with learning disabilities are required to submit everything requested by Admissions for all admissions. Teacher and/or counselor recommendations may be weighted more heavily in the admissions process. All applicants are evaluated individually and admitted based on potential for success. All first-year freshman applicants to Emory University are required to submit scores from either the SAT or the ACT. Emory University requires applicants to take the optional writing section of either the SAT or ACT. There is no preference given to one exam over the other. SAT and/or ACT scores are important but are not the deciding factors. Strong grades in rigorous courses may cause the committee to overlook below average standardized test scores, but high board scores will never make up for an applicant's weak course selection or grades.

Emory does not super score the ACT exam. For students who submit multiple ACT exam scores, the Admission Committee will review the overall score and sections scores for the ACT exam with the highest composite score. Emory requires the ACT with Writing test and does not review ACT exam scores when the writing test was not taken. The Admission Committee will super-score SAT exams taken for the same type of exam—but will not super-score across the old and the new formats.

ADDITIONAL INFORMATION

The needs of students with learning disabilities are met through academic accommodations and a variety of support services. Tutoring is offered by Emory College in most subjects on a one-on-one basis or in small groups. ADSR staff provides information for students about how to access specific accommodation needs once the student is accepted and begins his or her academic work. Information can be obtained about ADSR at www.ods.emory.edu.

General Support Services Information

Contact Information
Name of program or department: Access, Disability Services and Resources
Telephone: 404-727-9877
Fax: 404-727-1126

Accommodations or Services For Students With Learning Differences

Accommodations are decided upon an individual basis after a thorough review of appropriate, current documentation. The accommodations requests must be supported through the documentation provided and must be logically linked to the current impact of the condition on academic functioning.

Allowed in exams
Calculator: Yes
Dictionary: Yes
Computer: Yes
Spellchecker: Yes
Extended test time: Yes
Scribes: Yes
Proctors: Yes
Oral exams: Yes
Note-takers: Yes
Services for students with LD: Yes
Services for students with ADHD: Yes
Services for students with ASD: Yes
Distraction-reduced environment: Yes
Tape recording in class: Yes
Audio book: Yes
Electronic texts: NR
Kurzweil Reader: No
Other assistive technology: Yes
Priority registration: Yes
Added costs of services: No
LD specialists: No
ADHD coaching: NR
ASD specialists: NR
Professional tutors: NR
Peer tutors: Yes
Max. hours/wk. for services: 2
How professors are notified of student approved accommodations: Student

General Admissions Information

Office of Admissions: 404-727-6036

Entrance Requirements

Academic units recommended: 4 English, 4 math, 4 science, 2 science labs, 4 foreign language, 2 social studies, 2 history, 1 visual/performing arts. High school diploma is required and GED is not accepted. SAT or ACT required. If ACT, ACT with writing required. TOEFL required of all international applicants: minimum paper TOEFL 600.

Application deadline: 1/1
Notification: 4/1
Average GPA: 3.72
ACT Composite middle 50% range: 29-33
SAT Math middle 50% range: 650-770
SAT Critical Reading middle 50% range: 620-720
SAT Writing middle 50% range: 640-730
Graduated top 10% of class: 83
Graduated top 25% of class: 96
Graduated top 50% of class: 99

COLLEGE GRADUATION REQUIREMENTS

Course waivers allowed: No
Course substitutions allowed: No
In what course: Decisions made on a case-by-case basis

Additional Information

Environment: This private school, affiliated with the Methodist Church, was founded in 1836. It has a 56-acre campus.

Student Body
Undergrad enrollment: 6,867
% Women: 58
% Men: 42
% Out-of-state: 78

Cost information
Tuition: $45,700
Room & board: $13,130

Housing Information
University Housing: Yes
Percent living on campus: 64

Greek System
Fraternity: Yes
Sorority: Yes
Athletics: Division III

GEORGIA SOUTHERN UNIVERSITY

PO Box 8024, Statesboro, GA 30460
Phone: 912-478-5391 • Fax: 912-478-7240
E-mail: admissions@georgiasouthern.edu • Web: www.georgiasouthern.edu/
Support: CS • Institution: Public

PROGRAMS OR SERVICES FOR STUDENTS WITH LEARNING DIFFERENCES

Georgia Southern University wants all students to have a rewarding and pleasant college experience. The university offers a variety of services specifically tailored to afford students with learning disabilities an equal opportunity for success. These services are in addition to those provided to all students and to the access provided by campus facilities. Opportunities available through the Student Disability Resource Center, include special registration, which allows students to complete the course registration process without going through the standard procedure, and academic/personal assistance for students who are having difficulty with passing a class and need help with time management, note-taking skills, study strategies, and self-confidence. The university has a support group designed to help students with disabilities deal with personal and academic problems related to their disability.

ADMISSION INFORMATION FOR STUDENTS WITH LEARNING DIFFERENCES

College entrance test required: Yes
Interview required: No
Essay required: Not Applicable
Additional Application Required for LD/ADHD/ASD: NR
What documentation required for LD: Psycho ed evaluation
With general application: NR
To receive services after enrolling: Yes
What documentation required for ADHD: Psycho ed evaluation
With general application: NR
To receive services after enrolling: Yes
What documentation required for ASD: Psycho ed evaluation
With general application: NR
To receive services after enrolling: Yes
LD/ADHD/ASD documentation submitted to: Student Disability Resource Center
ASD Specific Program: No
Special Ed. HS course work accepted: No
Specific course requirements of all applicants: Yes
Separate application required for program services: Yes
Total # of students receiving LD/ADHD/ASD services: 121
Acceptance into program means acceptance into college: NR

ADMISSIONS

There is no special admission procedure for students with LD. All applicants must meet the same minimum requirements. Courses required include 4 English, 4 math, 3 science, 2 foreign language, and 3 social studies. The minimum SAT is 1010 or ACT 21. State minimum requirements for each portion of the SAT/ACT are 430 Critical reading, 400 Math/17 English, 17 Math. The minimum GPA is 2.0. Students not meeting the general admission requirements may be admitted through the Eagle Incentive Program (IEP). EIP is a summer program for students provisionally accepted for fall. Students who pass all summer courses and earn a "C" or better GPA. Students must have a minimum 920-1000 SAT or 20 ACT and meet state minimums for SAT Critical Reading and Math and ACT English and Math and complete the college prep curriculum required for general admission Students will be denied admission for fall if their EIP GPA is below a 2.0 or they fail one or more of the summer courses or they do not complete the required 8 summer credit hours.

ADDITIONAL INFORMATION

The Learning Support Program provides students admitted with inadequate skills in reading, composition, and/or math the opportunity to develop those skills to entry-level competency for regular freshman credit hours. If results of the placement tests reflect a need for assistance in developing academic skills of those who qualify for admission, students will be enrolled in a portion or in the entire Learning Support curriculum. Students may carry a maximum of 15 hours (including any Learning Support courses) except in their third semester when they are limited to 12 hours. Learning Support students are assigned an advisor in the Academic Success Center and must see this advisor for drop/add and registration (even if the student has declared a major). Students are not allowed to drop any required Learning Support classes. The only way a student can withdraw from a required Learning Support course is to withdraw from school.

General Support Services Information

Contact Information
Name of program or department: Student Disability Resource Center
Telephone: 912-478-1566
Fax: 912-478-1419
Website: NR

Accommodations or Services For Students With Learning Differences

Accommodations are decided upon an individual basis after a thorough review of appropriate, current documentation. The accommodations requests must be supported through the documentation provided and must be logically linked to the current impact of the condition on academic functioning.

Allowed in exams
Calculator: Yes
Dictionary: Yes
Computer: Yes
Spellchecker: Yes
Extended test time: Yes
Scribes: Yes
Proctors: Yes
Oral exams: Yes
Note-takers: Yes
Support services for students with LD: Yes
Support services for students with ADHD: Yes
Support services for students with ASD: Yes
Distraction-reduced environment: Yes
Tape recording in class: Yes
Electronic texts: Yes
Kurzweil reader: NR
Audio books: Yes
Other assistive technology: Yes
Priority registration: Yes
Added costs of services: No
LD specialists: Yes
ADHD coaching: Yes
ASD specialists: Yes
Professional tutors: No
Peer tutors: No
Max. hours/wk. for services: NR
How professors are notified of student approved accommodations: By student

General Admissions Information

Office of Admissions: 912-478-5391

Entrance Requirements

Academic units required: 4 English, 4 math, 4 science, 2 science labs, 2 foreign language, 3 social studies. High school diploma is required and GED is not accepted. SAT or ACT required. If ACT, ACT with writing required. TOEFL required of all international applicants: minimum paper TOEFL 523 or minimum internet TOEFL 69.

Application deadline: 5/1
Notification:NR
Average GPA: 3.29
ACT Composite middle 50% range: 21-25
SAT Math middle 50% range: 510-590
SAT Critical Reading middle 50% range: 520-590
SAT Writing middle 50% range: 480-570
Graduate top 10% of class: 17
Graduated top 25% of class: 49
Graduated top 50% of class: 76

COLLEGE GRADUATION REQUIREMENTS

Course waivers allowed: Yes
In what course: Foreign language and math
Course substitutions allowed: Yes
In what course: Foreign language and math

Additional Information

Environment: This public school was founded in 1906. It has a 700-acre campus.

Student Body
Undergrad enrollment: 17,963
% Women: 50
% Men: 50
% Out-of-state: 4

Cost information
In-state Tuition: $5,226
Out-of-state Tuition: $18,444
Room & board: $9,800

Housing Information
University Housing: Yes
Percent living on campus: 27

Greek System
Fraternity: Yes
Sorority: Yes
Athletics: Division I

Georgia State University

PO Box 4009, Atlanta, GA 30302-4009
Phone: 404-413-2500 • Fax: 404-413-2002
E-mail: admissions@gsu.edu • Web: www.gsu.edu
Support: CS • Institution: Public

Programs or Services for Students with Learning Differences

Georgia State University is committed to helping each student, including those students with disabilities; realize his or her full potential. This commitment is fulfilled through the provision of reasonable accommodations to ensure equitable access to its programs and services for all qualified students with disabilities. In general, the university will provide accommodations for students with disabilities on an individualized and flexible basis. It is the student's responsibility to seek available assistance and make his or her needs known. All students are encouraged to contact the Office of Disability Services and/or Student Support Services in the early stages of their college planning. The pre-admission services include information regarding admission requirements and academic support services. Students should register with both services before classes begin. This will assure that appropriate services are in place prior to the first day of classes. As a rule, the university does not waive academic requirements because of any disability. Therefore, the student should carefully evaluate degree requirements early in his or her studies. The only exception to this policy is if there is a documented learning disability that would hinder the learning of a foreign language, in which case a student may petition for a substitution in the foreign language requirement.

Admission Information for Students with Learning Differences

College entrance test required: Yes
Interview required: No
Essay required: No
Additional Application Required for LD/ADHD/ASD: NR
What documentation required for LD: Psycho ed evaluation toinclude: relevant historical info, instructional interventions, related services, age diagnosed, objective data (aptitude, achievement, info processing), test scores (standard, percentile and grade equivalents) and describe functional limitations.
With general application: No
To receive services after enrolling: Yes
What documentation required for ADHD: Diagnosis basedon DSM-V; history of behaviors impairing functioning in academic setting; diagnostic interview; history of symptoms; evidence of ongoing behaviors.
With general application: No
To receive services after enrolling: Yes
What documentation required for ASD: Psycho ed evaluation
With general application: NR
To receive services after enrolling: Yes
LD/ADHD/ASD documentation submitted to: Margaret A. Staton Office of Disabiltiy Services
ASD Specific Program: NR
Special Ed. HS course work accepted: NR
Specific course requirements of all applicants: NR
Separate application required for program services: NR
Total # of students receiving LD/ADHD/ASD services: 163
Acceptance into program means acceptance into college: Students must be admitted and enrolled in the university first and then request services.

Admissions

Students with LD must meet the same admission criteria as all other applicants. The university uses a predicted GPA of 2.1 for admission to a degree program or a GPA of 1.8 for admission to Learning Support Systems. This is determined by the ACT/SAT score and the high school GPA. The higher the GPA, the lower the ACT/SAT can be and vice versa. Course requirements include 4 years of English, 3 years of science, 3 years of math, 3 years of social science, and 2 years of a foreign language. (Substitutions are allowed for foreign language if the student has documentation that supports the substitution). Students may appeal an admission decision if they are denied and could be offered a probationary admission.

Additional Information

To receive LD services, students must submit documentation that evaluates intelligence; academic achievement in reading, math, and written language; auditory/phonological processing; language skills; visual-perceptual-spatial-constructural capabilities; attention; memory; executive function; motor skills; and social-emotional behavior. Student Support Services provides individual and group counseling, tutoring, advocacy, taped texts, advising, readers, learning lab, computer training, and referral for diagnosis of LD. The University Counseling Center provides study skills training; test-taking strategies; note-taking skills; textbook-reading skills; test anxiety and stress management, time management, and organizational techniques; thesis and dissertation writing; and personal counseling. Passport is a special section of the Personal and Academic Development Seminar Class offered through the Learning Support Program and is specifically designed for students with LD.

General Support Services Information

Contact Information
Name of program or department: Margaret A. Staton Office of Disabiltiy Services
Telephone: 404-413-1560
Fax: NR
Website: NR

Accommodations or Services For Students With Learning Differences

Accommodations are decided upon an individual basis after a thorough review of appropriate, current documentation. The accommodations requests must be supported through the documentation provided and must be logically linked to the current impact of the condition on academic functioning.

Allowed in exams
Calculator: Yes
Dictionary: Yes
Computer: Yes
Spellchecker: Yes
Extended test time: Yes
Scribes: No
Proctors: Yes
Oral exams: Yes
Note-takers: Yes
Support services for students with LD: Yes
Support services for students with ADHD: Yes
Support services for students with ASD: Yes
Distraction-reduced environment: Yes
Tape recording in class: Yes
Electronic texts: Yes
Kurzweil reader: No
Audio books: NR
Other assistive technology: Yes
Priority registration: Yes
Added costs of services: No
LD specialists: Yes
ADHD coaching: NR
ASD specialists: Yes
Professional tutors: No
Peer tutors: No
Max. hours/wk. for services: NR
How professors are notified of student approved accommodations: By student

General Admissions Information

Office of Admissions: 404-413-2500

Entrance Requirements

Academic units required: 4 English, 4 math, 4 science, 2 science labs, 2 foreign language, 3 social studies,
Academic units recommended: 4 English, 4 math, 4 science, 2 science labs, 2 foreign language, 3 social studies. High school diploma is required and GED is not accepted. SAT or ACT required. If ACT, ACT with writing accepted. TOEFL required of all international applicants: minimum paper TOEFL 550 or minimum internet TOEFL 79.

Application deadline: 3/1
Notification: 5/1
Average GPA: 3.4
ACT Composite middle 50% range: 20-25
SAT Math middle 50% range: 470-580
SAT Critical Reading middle 50% range: 480-580
SAT Writing middle 50% range: NR-NR
Graduate top 10% of class: 16
Graduated top 25% of class: 45
Graduated top 50% of class: 83

COLLEGE GRADUATION REQUIREMENTS

Course waivers allowed: NR
Course substitutions allowed: NR

Additional Information

Environment: This public school was founded in 1913. It has a 33-acre campus.

Student Body
Undergrad enrollment: 25,160
% Women: 59
% Men: 41
% Out-of-state: 4

Cost information
In-state Tuition: $8,112
Out-of-state Tuition: $26,322
Room & board: $13,342

Housing Information
University Housing: Yes
Percent living on campus: 18

Greek System
Fraternity: No
Sorority: No
Athletics: Division I

Reinhardt University

7300 Reinhardt Circle, Waleska, GA 30183
Phone: 770-720-5526 • Fax: 770-720-5899
E-mail: www.reinhardt.edu • Web: www.reinhardt.edu
Support: SP • Institution: Private

Programs or Services for Students with Learning Differences

The Academic Support Office (ASO) provides assistance to students with specific learning abilities or attention deficit disorders. Students are enrolled in regular college courses. The program focuses on compensatory skills and provides special services in academic advising, group tutoring, assistance in writing assignments, note-taking, testing accommodations, and coordination of assistive learning technologies. Reinhardt's ASO was established in 1982 to provide assistance to students with learning disabilities who meet regular college entrance requirements, have a diagnosed LD, and may or may not have received any LD services in the past due to ineligibility for high school services, or a recent diagnosis.

Admission Information for Students with Learning Differences

College entrance tests required: Yes
Interview required: Yes
Essay required: N/A
Additional Application Required for LD/ADHD/ASD: NR
What documentation required for LD: Psycho ed evaluation to include: relevant historical info, instructional interventions, related services, age diagnosed, objective data (aptitude, achievement, info processing), test scores (standard, percentile and grade equivalents) and describe functional limitations.
With general application: Yes if requested as part of Structured Program application
To receive services after enrolling: Yes
What documentation required for ADHD: Diagnosis based on DSM-V; history of behaviors impairing functioning in academic setting; diagnostic interview; history of symptoms; evidence of ongoing behaviors.
With general application: Yes if requested as part of Structured Program application
To receive services after enrolling: Yes
What documentation required for ASD: Psycho ed evaluation
With general application: NR
To receive services after enrolling: Yes
To receive services after enrolling: Yes
LD/ADHD/ASD documentation submitted to: Admissions
ASD Specific Program: NR
Special Ed. HS course work accepted: No
Specific course requirements for all applicants: Yes
Separate application required for program services: Yes
Total # of students receiving LD/ADHD/ASD services: 70
Acceptance into program means acceptance into college: Separate application required after student has enrolled

Admissions

Applicants with learning disabilities should request an ASO admission packet from Admissions; if they choose to self-disclose upon application, they should complete the regular application; note an interest in Academic Support; fill out the supplemental form from ASO; provide IEPs from as many years of high school, psychological evaluations documenting the disability, and three references addressing aptitude, motivation, ability to set realistic goals, interpersonal skills, and readiness for college; and submit SAT/ACT scores. Students applying to the ASO program may be asked to interview with the ASO faculty. Admission decisions are made by the Admission Office. Students choosing not to self-disclose upon application should request information from the ASO Director.

Additional Information

The ASO is staffed by three full-time faculty members. Additional tuition is required for students enrolled in ASO tutorials. A generous financial aid program is available to all qualified students. Academic Support Services include: faculty-led tutorials (for fee); academic advisement and counseling; accommodative services for students with documented LD/ADD such as individualized testing, note-takers, and the coordination of assistive technology. All students admitted and enrolled in the ASO Program attend a regular student orientation program plus have an interview and orientation with the faculty from the ASO Program.

General Support Services Information

Contact Information
Name of program or department: Academic Support Office (ASO)
Telephone: 770-720-5567
Fax: 770-720-5602
E-mail: AAA@reinhardt.edu

Accommodations or Services For Students With Learning Differences

Accommodations are decided upon an individual basis after a thorough review of appropriate, current documentation. The accommodations requested must be supported through the documentation provided and must be logically linked to the current impact of the condition on academic functioning.

Allowed in exams
Calculator: Yes
Dictionary: No
Computer: Yes
Spellchecker: Yes
Extended test time: Yes
Scribes: Yes
Proctors: Yes
Oral exams: Yes
Note-takers: Yes
Services for students with LD: Yes
Services for students with ADHD: Yes
Services for students with ASD: Yes
Distraction-reduced environment: Yes
Tape recording in class: Yes
Audio book: NR
Electronic texts: Yes
Kurzweil Reader: Yes
Other assistive technology: Yes
Priority registration: Yes
Added costs for services: Yes
LD specialists: Yes
ADHD coaching: NR
ASD specialists: NR
Professional tutors: 3
Peer tutors: No
Max. hours/wk. for services: Unlimited
How professors are notified of LD/ADHD: Both student and director

General Admissions Information

Office of Admissions: 770-720-5526

Entrance Requirements

Academic units required: 4 English, 4 math, 3 science, 3 social studies, **Academic units recommended:** 2 foreign language. High school diploma is required and GED is accepted. SAT or ACT required. If ACT, ACT with writing accepted. TOEFL required of all international applicants: minimum paper TOEFL 500.

Application deadline: NR
Notification: NR
Average GPA: 3.02
ACT Composite middle 50% range: 17-22
SAT Math middle 50% range: 430-530
SAT Critical Reading middle 50% range: 410-540
SAT Writing middle 50% range: NR-NR
Graduated top 10% of class: NR
Graduated top 25% of class: NR
Graduated top 50% of class: 63

COLLEGE GRADUATION REQUIREMENTS

Course waivers allowed: No
Course substitutions allowed: No

Additional Information

Environment: This private school, affiliated with the Methodist Church, was founded in 1883. It has a 600-acre campus.

Student Body
Undergrad enrollment: 1,035
% Women: 56
% Men: 44
% Out-of-state: 27

Cost information
Tuition: $19,946
Room & board: $7,568
Housing Information
University Housing: Yes
Percent living on campus: 43

Greek System
Fraternity: No
Sorority: No
Athletics: NAIA

UNIVERSITY OF GEORGIA

Terrell Hall, 210 South Jackson Street, Athens, GA 30602-1633
Phone: 706-542-8776 • Fax: 706-542-1466
E-mail: admproc@uga.edu • Web: www.uga.edu
Support: CS • Institution: Public

PROGRAMS OR SERVICES FOR STUDENTS WITH LEARNING DIFFERENCES

The Disability Resource Center (DRC) assists the university in fulfilling its commitment to educate and serve students with disabilities who qualify for admissions. The DRC coordinates and provides a variety of academic and support services to students, including students with learning disabilities (LD), attention deficit hyperactivity disorder (ADHD,and Asperger Syndrome (AS). Our mission is to promote equal educational opportunities and a welcoming environment for students with disabilities at the University of Georgia. The DRC staff are dedicated professionals with a wide variety of expertise in disability related issues. These encompass disability specific accommodations, universal design, program access, assistive technology, alternative text, architectural access, and disability law. Staff can hold regular meetings with students to discuss and monitor academic progress, assist students in understanding their disability, make referrals to other campus and community resources, and consult with faculty as needed. Documentation guidelines can be found on the DRC webpage http://drc.uga.edu/students/documentation-guidelines.

ADMISSION INFORMATION FOR STUDENTS WITH LEARNING DIFFERENCES

College entrance test required: Yes
Interview required: No
Essay required: Not Applicable
Additional Application Required for LD/ADHD/ASD: Yes
What documentation required for LD: Psycho ed evaluation
With general application: No
To receive services after enrolling: Yes
What documentation required for ADHD: Psycho ed evaluation
With general application: No
To receive services after enrolling: Yes
What documentation required for ASD: Psycho ed evaluation
With general application: No
To receive services after enrolling: Yes
LD/ADHD/ASD documentation submitted to: Disability Resource Center
ASD Specific Program: NR
Special Ed. HS course work accepted: No
Specific course requirements of all applicants: Yes
Separate application required for program services: Yes
Total # of students receiving LD/ADHD/ASD services: 374
Acceptance into program means acceptance into college: No

ADMISSIONS

There are no special admission criteria for students with disabilities. Students must meet the admissions criteria for the university. However, some students choose to write their admission essay related to their disability to help explain lower standardized scores or GPAs. Average GPA is 3.9.

ADDITIONAL INFORMATION

DRC staff refers students to campus resources as requested. The Academic Resource Center located in Milledge Hall provides a variety of academic assistance for all students on campus. ARC has a peer-based tutor program that includes drop-in labs for chemistry, math and physics, as well as appointment-based tutoring for over 60 courses and a Writing Center staffed with specialists who are experts in their field. Every fall academic success workshops on such issues as time management, stress management, and preparing for exams are offered.

General Support Services Information

Contact Information
Name of program or department: Disability Resource Center
Telephone: 706-542-8719
Fax: 706-542-7719
Website: drc.uga.edu

Accommodations or Services For Students With Learning Differences

Accommodations are decided upon an individual basis after a thorough review of appropriate, current documentation. The accommodations requests must be supported through the documentation provided and must be logically linked to the current impact of the condition on academic functioning.

Allowed in exams
Calculator: Yes
Dictionary: Yes
Computer: Yes
Spellchecker: Yes
Extended test time: Yes
Scribes: Yes
Proctors: Yes
Oral exams: Yes
Note-takers: Yes
Support services for students with LD: Yes
Support services for students with ADHD: Yes
Support services for students with ASD: Yes
Distraction-reduced environment: Yes
Tape recording in class: Yes
Electronic texts: Yes
Kurzweil reader: NR
Audio books: Yes
Other assistive technology: Yes
Priority registration: Yes
Added costs of services: No
LD specialists: Yes
ADHD coaching: No
ASD specialists: Yes
Professional tutors: No
Peer tutors: No
Max. hours/wk. for services: NR
How professors are notified of student approved accommodations: By student

General Admissions Information

Office of Admissions: 706-542-8776

Entrance Requirements

Academic units required: 4 English, 4 math, 4 science, 2 science labs, 2 foreign language, 3 social studies, **Academic units recommended:** 4 English, 4 math, 4 science, 2 science labs, 3 foreign language, 1 social studies, 2 history, 1 academic electives. High school diploma is required and GED is accepted. SAT or ACT required. If ACT, ACT with writing accepted. TOEFL required of all international applicants: minimum paper TOEFL 550 or minimum internet TOEFL 80.

Application deadline: 1/15
Notification: NR
Average GPA: 3.91
ACT Composite middle 50% range: 26-30
SAT Math middle 50% range: 580-670
SAT Critical Reading middle 50% range: 570-660
SAT Writing middle 50% range: 560-660
Graduate top 10% of class: 53
Graduated top 25% of class: 88
Graduated top 50% of class: 99

COLLEGE GRADUATION REQUIREMENTS

Course waivers allowed: No
Course substitutions allowed: Yes
In what course: Foreign Language; Math

Additional Information

Environment: This public school was founded in 1785. It has a 324-acre campus.

Student Body
Undergrad enrollment: 27,547
% Women: 57
% Men: 43
% Out-of-state: 8

Cost information
Out-of-state Tuition: $27,574
Room & board: $9,450

Housing Information
University Housing: Yes
Percent living on campus: 36

Greek System
Fraternity: Yes
Sorority: Yes
Athletics: Division I

DePaul University

1 East Jackson Boulevard, Chicago, IL 60604-2287
Phone: 312-362-8300 • Fax: 312-362-5749
E-mail: admission@depaul.edu • Web: www.depaul.edu
Support: CS • Institution: Private

Programs or Services for Students with Learning Differences

The Center for Students with Disabilities (CSD) is designed to service and support students with learning disabilities, attention deficit hyperactivity disorder, and all other disabilities. The immediate goals are to provide learning strategies based on students' strengths and weaknesses to assist students in the completion of course work. The ultimate goal is to impart academic and study skills that will enable the students to function independently in the academic environment and competitive job market. CSD provides intensive help on a one-on-one basis. It is designed to assist with regular college courses, improve learning deficits, and help the student learn compensatory skills. Students can choose to work with learning disability specialists with whom they can meet for up to 2 hours per week.

Admission Information for Students with Learning Differences

College entrance tests required: Yes
Interview required: Yes
Essay required: No
Additional Application Required for LD/ADHD/ASD: NR
What documentation required for LD: Psycho ed evaluation to include: relevant historical info, instructional interventions, related services, age diagnosed, objective data (aptitude, achievement, info processing), test scores (standard, percentile and grade equivalents) and describe functional limitations.
With general application: No
To receive services after enrolling: Yes
What documentation required for ADHD: Diagnosis based on DSM-V; history of behaviors impairing functioning in academic setting; diagnostic interview; history of symptoms; evidence of ongoing behaviors.
With general application: No
To receive services after enrolling: Yes
What documentation required for ASD: Psycho ed evaluation
With general application: NR
To receive services after enrolling: Yes
LD/ADHD/ASD documentation submitted to: Center for Students with Disabilities (CSD)
ASD Specific Program: NR
Special Ed. HS course work accepted: Yes
Specific course requirements of all applicants: Yes
Separate application required: Yes
Total # of students receiving LD/ADHD/ASD services: 350–400
Acceptance into program means acceptance into college: Students must be admitted and enrolled in the university first and then request services.

Admissions

There is no separate process for students with learning disabilities who wish to be considered for admission to the university. Students with learning disabilities must be first accepted to DePaul University before they can be accepted to the Center for Students with Disabilities (CSD). University admission requirements include a completed application, official high school transcripts, counselor recommendation, ACT/SAT score or responses to supplemental essay questions, and an application fee. DePaul is a test-optional for students applying for freshman admission. Students can choose to apply with or without ACT or SAT scores. For more information regarding requirements and the process please visit: http://www.depaul.edu/admission.

Additional Information

DePaul's Center for Students with Disabilities (CSD) coordinates DePaul University's provision of accommodations and other services to students pursuant to the Americans with Disabilities Act and Section 504 of the Rehabilitation Act of 1973. CSD provides support services for all enrolled students at DePaul; part-time and full-time, undergraduate and graduate, and across all Schools/Colleges within DePaul for all campuses. Recommendations for accommodations are determined by CSD staff after reviewing the documentation provided and an interview with the student. CSD follows the guidelines of the newly updated Americans with Disabilities Act (ADA) and related legislation to determine the most appropriate accommodations for the students. CSD provides appropriate accommodations and services for students related to the nature of their disability.

General Support Services Information

Contact Information
Name of program or department: Center for Students with Disabilities
Telephone: 773-325-1677
Fax: 773-325-3720

Accommodations or Services For Students With Learning Differences

Accommodations are decided upon an individual basis after a thorough review of appropriate, current documentation. The accommodations requested must be supported through the documentation aligned with ADA guidelines provided and must be logically linked to the current impact of the condition on academic functioning.

Allowed in exams
Calculator: Yes
Dictionary: Yes
Computer: Yes
Spellchecker: Yes
Extended test time: Yes
Scribes: Yes
Proctors: Yes
Oral exams: Yes
Note-takers: No
Services for students with LD: Yes
Services for students with ADHD: Yes
Services for students with ASD: Yes
Distraction-reduced environment: Yes
Tape recording in class: Yes
Audio book: NR
Electronic texts: Yes
Kurzweil Reader: Yes
Other assistive technology: Yes
Priority registration: Yes
Added costs for services: No
LD specialists: Yes
ADHD coaching: NR
ASD specialists: NR
Professional tutors: No
Peer tutors: No
Max. hours/wk. for services: 2
How professors are notified of LD/ADHD: By student

General Admissions Information

Office of Admissions: 312-362-8300

Entrance Requirements

Academic units required: 4 English, 3 math, 3 science, 2 science labs, and 2 units from above areas or other academic areas. **Academic units recommended:** 4 English, 3 math, 3 science, 2 science labs, 2 foreign language, and 2 units from above areas or other academic areas. High school diploma is required and GED is accepted. SAT or ACT recommended. If ACT, ACT with writing accepted. TOEFL required of all international applicants: minimum paper TOEFL 550 or minimum internet TOEFL 80.

Application deadline: 2/1
Notification: 3/15
Average GPA: 3.56
ACT Composite middle 50% range: 22-28
SAT Math middle 50% range: 490-610
SAT Critical Reading middle 50% range: 520-620
SAT Writing middle 50% range: NR-NR
Graduated top 10% of class: 20
Graduated top 25% of class: 54
Graduated top 50% of class: 87

COLLEGE GRADUATION REQUIREMENTS

Course waivers allowed: Yes
In what course: Foreign language (LD and ADHD)
Course substitutions allowed: Yes
In what course: Foreign language (LD and ADHD)

Additional Information

Environment: This private school, affiliated with the Roman Catholic Church, was founded in 1898. It has a 36-acre campus.

Student Body
Undergrad enrollment: 15,961
% Women: 34
% Men: 66
% Out-of-state: 23

Cost information
Tuition: $35,680
Room & board: $12,873

Housing Information
University Housing: Yes
Percent living on campus: 17

Greek System
Fraternity: Yes
Sorority: Yes
Athletics: Division I

Eastern Illinois University

600 Lincoln Avenue, Charleston, IL 61920
Phone: 217-581-2223 • Fax: 217-581-7060
E-mail: admissions@eiu.edu • Web: www.eiu.edu
Support: S • Institution: Public

Programs or Services for Students with Learning Differences

The Office of Disability Services provides support to students with LD/ADHD as appropriate with documentation. Eastern Illinois University's Students with Autism Transitional Education Program focuses on providing enhanced support in three main skill set areas. A solid foundation of Academic, Social , and Daily-living (ASD) skill sets is crucial for the success of post-secondary students.

Admission Information for Students with Learning Differences

College entrance test required: Yes
Interview required: Yes
Essay required: Not Applicable
Additional Application Required for LD/ADHD/ASD: No
What documentation required for LD: Psycho ed evaluation
With general application: NR
To receive services after enrolling: Yes
What documentation required for ADHD: Psycho ed evaluation
With general application: NR
To receive services after enrolling: Yes
What documentation required for ASD: Psycho ed evaluation
With general application: NR
To receive services after enrolling: Yes
LD/ADHD/ASD documentation submitted to: Student Disability Services
ASD Specific Program: STEP
Special Ed. HS course work accepted: Not Applicable
Specific course requirements of all applicants: Yes
Separate application required for program services: FALSE
Total # of students receiving LD/ADHD/ASD services: 150
Acceptance into program means acceptance into college: NR

Admissions

All applicants must meet the same admission criteria. Once admitted, students with LD or ADHD must provide appropriate documentation in order to access services and accommodations. The average GPA is 3.0 and average ACT 22.

Additional Information

STEP provides enhanced training at EIU on Academic, Social, and Daily-living skills (ASD) to allow students the opportunity to navigate their college experience successfully. In order to directly address these areas, the Transition Program provides opportunities for growth through: Individualized peer mentorships that work to develop ASD skill sets,
Personalized campus tours focused on the individual's schedule/routine each semester, Social skills groups that focus on utilizing interpersonal skills in the classroom and throughout the campus community, A positive educational work environment through regularly scheduled academic study tables, Social events tailored to interests of the participants of the program to enhance the opportunity for friendships, active involvement on campus , and vocational skill development, Physical fitness programs personalized to individual needs and abilities, Residential support through trained residence assistants,
Single-room option for an additional fee that supports the opportunity to decompress and regulate (based on availability), Early move-in date that allows for a calmer transition from the home to residence hall life, Regular daily-living skill trainings to ensure that students adequately adjust to adulthood, and Option for parental involvement to allow for optimum teamwork between the individual, campus supports, and the family. There is a fee of $2500 per semester.

General Support Services Information

Contact Information
Name of program or department: Student Disability Services
Telephone: 217-581-6583
Fax: NR
Website: http://www.eiu.edu/disablty/

Accommodations or Services For Students With Learning Differences

Accommodations are decided upon an individual basis after a thorough review of appropriate, current documentation. The accommodations requests must be supported through the documentation provided and must be logically linked to the current impact of the condition on academic functioning.

Allowed in exams
Calculator: Yes
Dictionary: Yes
Computer: Yes
Spellchecker: Yes
Extended test time: Yes
Scribes: No
Proctors: Yes
Oral exams: Yes
Note-takers: Yes
Support services for students with LD: Yes
Support services for students with ADHD: Yes
Support services for students with ASD: Yes
Distraction-reduced environment: Yes
Tape recording in class: Yes
Electronic texts: Yes
Kurzweil reader: NR
Audio books: Yes
Other assistive technology: Yes
Priority registration: Yes
Added costs of services: No
LD specialists: Yes
ADHD coaching: No
ASD specialists: NR
Professional tutors: No
Peer tutors: Yes
Max. hours/wk. for services: NR
How professors are notified of student approved accommodations: By student

General Admissions Information

Office of Admissions: 217-581-2223

Entrance Requirements

Academic units required: 4 English, 3 math, 3 science, 3 science labs, 3 social studies, 2 academic electives, **Academic units recommended:** 2 foreign language. High school diploma is required and GED is accepted. SAT or ACT required. If ACT, ACT with writing recommended. TOEFL required of all international applicants: minimum paper TOEFL 500 or minimum internet TOEFL 61.

Application deadline: 8/15
Notification: Rolling starting 8/1
Average GPA: 3.08
ACT Composite middle 50% range: 19-24
SAT Math middle 50% range: NR-NR
SAT Critical Reading middle 50% range: NR-NR
SAT Writing middle 50% range: NR-NR
Graduate top 10% of class: 9
Graduated top 25% of class: 31
Graduated top 50% of class: 69

COLLEGE GRADUATION REQUIREMENTS

Course waivers allowed: No
In what course: NR
Course substitutions allowed: No
In what course: NR

Additional Information

Environment: This public school was founded in 1895. It has a 320-acre campus.

Student Body
Undergrad enrollment: 7,202
% Women: 60
% Men: 40
% Out-of-state: 4

Cost information
In-state Tuition: $8,550
Out-of-state Tuition: $10,680
Room & board: $9,546
Housing Information
University Housing: Yes
Percent living on campus: 39

Greek System
Fraternity: Yes
Sorority: Yes
Athletics: Division I

Illinois State University

Office of Admissions, Normal, IL 61790-2200
Phone: 309-438-2181 • Fax: 309-438-3932
E-mail: admissions@illinoisstate.edu • Web: www.ilstu.edu
Support: CS • Institution: Public

Programs or Services for Students with Learning Differences

The mission of Disability Concerns is to ensure full and equal participation for persons with disabilities in the Illinois State University community through: Empowering individuals; Promoting equal access; Encouraging self-advocacy; Reducing attitudinal, physical, and communications barriers; Providing appropriate accommodations. The Disability Concerns program is designed to work with students who have learning disabilities towards the goal of becoming academically and socially successful while attending Illinois State University.

Admission Information for Students with Learning Differences

College entrance test required: Yes
Interview required: No
Essay required: Not Applicable
Additional Application Required for LD/ADHD/ASD: No
What documentation required for LD: Psycho ed evaluation
With general application: NR
To receive services after enrolling: No
What documentation required for ADHD: Psycho ed evaluation
With general application: NR
To receive services after enrolling: No
What documentation required for ASD: Psycho ed evaluation
With general application: NR
To receive services after enrolling: No
LD/ADHD/ASD documentation submitted to: Disability Concerns
ASD Specific Program: NR
Special Ed. HS course work accepted: Yes
Specific course requirements of all applicants: Yes
Separate application required for program services: FALSE
Total # of students receiving LD/ADHD/ASD services: 181
Acceptance into program means acceptance into college: NR

Admissions

Admissions criteria for students with learning disabilities are the same as for other students. Of freshman admitted fall 2013, one half earned composite ACT scores of 22 to 26, and the middle 50 percent had a high school grade point average between 3.15 and 3.83 on a 4.0 scale. High school courses required include: 4 years English, 3 years math (algebra, geometry, algebra II-trigonometry or higher), 2 years social science, 2 years natural science with laboratories, 2 years of one foreign language or 2 years of fine arts, and 2 years electives. Students with LD/ADHD who are denied admission may self-disclose and submit a letter of appeal. That appeal is then reviewed by the Office of Admissions. The appeal process is available to all students who are denied admission, but have special circumstances that need consideration.

Additional Information

The following are options for accommodations based on appropriate documentation and needs: note-takers, readers, e-text, scribes, computers, testing accommodations, conference with LD/ADHD specialist, and quiet study rooms. Skills courses are offered to all students in time management, test taking strategies, and study skills. Additionally, there is a writing center, math lab, and tutorial assistance for all students. One scholarship of $2,000.00 will be awarded. All applicants for the Disability Concerns Will To Succeed Scholarship must: Be a current client of Disability Concerns; be an undergraduate student enrolled in good standing at Illinois State University; possess a minimum of 2.5 GPA on a 4.0 GPA scale; candidate must meet the definition of a person with one of the following disabilities: Learning Disability; Attention Deficit/Hyperactivity Disorder; Medical Disability; Psychiatric Disability; Autism Spectrum Disorder; Communication Disorder.

General Support Services Information

Contact Information
Name of program or department: Disability Concerns
Telephone: 309-438-5853
Fax: 309-438-7713
Website: DisabilityConcerns.IllinoisState.edu

Accommodations or Services For Students With Learning Differences

Accommodations are decided upon an individual basis after a thorough review of appropriate, current documentation. The accommodations requests must be supported through the documentation provided and must be logically linked to the current impact of the condition on academic functioning.

Allowed in exams
Calculator: Yes
Dictionary: Yes
Computer: Yes
Spellchecker: Yes
Extended test time: Yes
Scribes: Yes
Proctors: Yes
Oral exams: Yes
Note-takers: Yes
Support services for students with LD: Yes
Support services for students with ADHD: Yes
Support services for students with ASD: Yes
Distraction-reduced environment: Yes
Tape recording in class: Yes
Electronic texts: Yes
Kurzweil reader: NR
Audio books: No
Other assistive technology: Yes
Priority registration: Yes
Added costs of services: No
LD specialists: Yes
ADHD coaching: No
ASD specialists: No
Professional tutors: No
Peer tutors: Not Applicable
Max. hours/wk. for services: NR
How professors are notified of student approved accommodations: By student

General Admissions Information

Office of Admissions: 309-438-2181

Entrance Requirements

Academic units required: 4 English, 3 math, 2 science, 2 science labs, 2 foreign language, 2 social studies, 2 academic electives. High school diploma is required and GED is accepted. SAT or ACT required. If ACT, ACT with writing accepted. TOEFL required of all international applicants: minimum paper TOEFL 550 or minimum internet TOEFL 79.

Application deadline: 4/1
Notification: Rolling starting 9/1
Average GPA: 3.32
ACT Composite middle 50% range: 21-26
SAT Math middle 50% range: NR-NR
SAT Critical Reading middle 50% range: NR-NR
SAT Writing middle 50% range: NR-NR
Graduate top 10% of class: NR
Graduated top 25% of class: NR
Graduated top 50% of class: NR

COLLEGE GRADUATION REQUIREMENTS

Course waivers allowed: No
In what course: NR
Course substitutions allowed: Yes
In what course: Determined on an individual basis.

Additional Information

Environment: This public school was founded in 1857. It has a 850-acre campus.

Student Body
Undergrad enrollment: 18,426
% Women: 55
% Men: 45
% Out-of-state: 2

Cost information
In-state Tuition: $13,168
Out-of-state Tuition: $20,984
Room & board: $9,850

Housing Information
University Housing: Yes
Percent living on campus: 32

Greek System
Fraternity: Yes
Sorority: Yes
Athletics: Division I

Lincoln College

300 Keokuk Street, Lincoln, IL 62656
Phone: 800-569-0556 • Fax: 217-732-7715
E-mail: admission@lincolncollege.com • Web: www.lincolncollege.edu
Support: CS • Institution: Private

Programs or Services for Students with Learning Differences

Lincoln College is committed to enhancing student achievement through a campus-wide approach to supportive services in combination with parental involvement. The college offers personal attention and a number of supportive services to assist students. All incoming first-year students are highly encouraged to take a one credit Frist Year Experience course to aid with their transition to college. All students have access to free tutoring in all subject areas through the Academic Success Center. Students can receive additional help as needed in the math lab, which is staffed by full-time math faculty 8 hours per week, and the writing lab. Students diagnosed with LD, AD/HD and other disabilities that negatively impact them in areas of time management, organization, or planning, can participate in the Academy of College Collaboration for Effective Student Success (ACCESS) Program which is a fee-based program that consists of a five-day intensive transition course before the fall semester begins, academic coaching sessions (at least two per week), academic advising, and ongoing communication between ACCESS coaches, parents, and instructors. The cost of the program is $2,250 per semester (in additional to regular tuition and fees) and students can enroll at any point during their academic career.

Admission Information for Students with Learning Differences

College entrance tests required: Yes
Interview required: Possibly, depends on ACT score, GPA, and high school curriculum
Essay required: Same as above
Additional Application Required for LD/ADHD/ASD: NR
What documentation required for LD: Psycho ed evaluation to include: relevant historical info, instructional interventions, related services, age diagnosed, objective data (aptitude, achievement, info processing), test scores (standard, percentile and grade equivalents) and describe functional limitations.
With general application: No
To receive services after enrolling: Yes
What documentation required for ADHD: Diagnosis based on DSM-V; history of behaviors impairing functioning in academic setting; diagnostic interview; history of symptoms; evidence of ongoing behaviors.
With general application: No
To receive services after enrolling: Yes
What documentation required for ASD: Psycho ed evaluation
With general application: NR
To receive services after enrolling: Yes
LD/ADHD/ASD documentation submitted to: Office of Disability Services
ASD Specific Program: NR
Special Ed. HS course work accepted: Yes
Specific course requirements of all applicants: NR
Separate application required: No
Total # of students receiving LD/ADHD/ASD services: NR
Acceptance into program means acceptance into college: Students are admitted and enrolled at the college and then reviewed for supportive services.

Admissions

Acceptance to Lincoln College is based on a student's high school record and standardized test scores. In select cases, a personal interview and letters of recommendation are required. Generally students with an ACT composite score of 16 and a cumulative GPA of a 2.00 or higher may be admitted without restriction. Those with an ACT composite score of 15 or lower may be admitted upon review by the Assistant Director of Admissions and if accepted are accepted on a conditional acceptance.

Additional Information

Lincoln College offers the Academic Development Seminar for students the week before fall semester starts. Students learn writing and speaking skills, effective library skills, and science lab orientation. They develop effective student technique; lab and field orientation; methods to evaluate social science graphs, charts, and maps; and concepts and values in the humanities. The Academic Writing Seminar is also offered one week in the summer to cover crucial college skills such as writing skill development, note-taking techniques, exam tips, speaking skills, writing to define and classify, college expectations, analytical thinking and writing, and writing to understand and evaluate.

General Support Services Information

Contact Information
Name of program or department: The Office for Disability Services; The ACCESS Program
Telephone: 800-569-0556
Fax: 217-735-4902

Accommodations or Services For Students With Learning Differences

Accommodations are decided upon an individual basis after a thorough review of appropriate, current documentation. The accommodations requested must be supported through the documentation provided and must be logically linked to the current impact of the condition on academic functioning.

Allowed in exams
Calculator: Yes
Dictionary: No
Computer: Yes
Spellchecker: Yes
Extended test time: Yes
Scribes: No
Proctors: Yes
Oral exams: Yes
Note-takers: No
Services for students with LD: Yes
Services for students with ADHD: Yes
Services for students with ASD: Yes
Distraction-reduced environment: Yes
Tape recording in class: Yes
Audio book: NR
Electronic texts: Yes
Kurzweil Reader: No
Other assistive technology: Yes
Priority registration: Yes
Added costs for services: Yes for ACCESS Program
LD specialists: Yes
ADHD coaching: NR
ASD specialists: NR
Professional tutors: 15
Peer tutors: No
Max. hours/wk. for services: Unlimited
How professors are notified of LD/ADHD: By student

General Admissions Information

Office of Admissions: (800) 569-0556

Entrance Requirements

TOEFL required of all international applicants.

Application deadline: NR
Notification: NR
Average GPA: NR
ACT Composite middle 50% range: NR-NR
SAT Math middle 50% range: NR-NR
SAT Critical Reading middle 50% range: NR-NR
SAT Writing middle 50% range: NR-NR
Graduated top 10% of class: NR
Graduated top 25% of class: NR
Graduated top 50% of class: NR

COLLEGE GRADUATION REQUIREMENTS

Course waivers allowed: Case-by-case basis
Course substitutions allowed: Case-by-case basis

Additional Information

Environment: NR

Student Body
Undergrad enrollment: NR
% Women: NR
% Men: NR
% Out-of-state: NR

Cost information
Tuition: $16,700
Room & board: $7,100

Housing Information
University Housing: Yes
Percent living on campus: NR

Greek System
Fraternity: NR
Sorority: NR
Athletics: Other

Loyola University—Chicago

820 North Michigan Avenue, Chicago, IL 60611
Phone: 312-915-6500 • Fax: 312-915-7216
E-mail: admission@luc.edu • Web: www.luc.edu/
Support: CS • Institution: Private

Programs or Services for Students with Learning Differences

SSWD serves students with disabilities by creating and fostering an accessible learning environment. We aim to empower students with diverse needs by enhancing their self-awareness, self-determination and self-advocacy. We promote awareness of the needs of students with disabilities and encourage the Loyola community to respect and care for each individual. Following in the steps of Loyola's Jesuit mission, SSWD is committed to serving all students no matter their gender, race, ethnicity, age, socio-economic status, sexual orientation, or disability. We work closely with campus partners, students, families, and the Chicago community to create a safe environment for students to succeed academically and personally.

Admission Information for Students with Learning Differences

College entrance test required: NR
Interview required: No
Essay required: Not Applicable
Additional Application Required for LD/ADHD/ASD: Yes
What documentation required for LD: Psycho ed evaluation
With general application: No
To receive services after enrolling: Yes
What documentation required for ADHD: Psycho ed evaluation
With general application: No
To receive services after enrolling: Yes
What documentation required for ASD: Psycho ed evaluation
With general application: No
To receive services after enrolling: Yes
LD/ADHD/ASD documentation submitted to: Services for Students with Disabilities
ASD Specific Program: No
Special Ed. HS course work accepted: Yes
Specific course requirements of all applicants: Yes
Separate application required for program services: Yes
Total # of students receiving LD/ADHD/ASD services: NR
Acceptance into program means acceptance into college: No
Total # of students receiving LD/ADHD/ASD services: NR
Acceptance into program means acceptance into college: Students must be admitted and enrolled prior to requesting services.

Admissions

There is no special admissions procedure for students with disabilities. All admission applications are handled on a case-by-case basis by the Admissions Office for the Undergraduate Admissions. The following units or courses are suggested for admission to Loyola University—Chicago: 4 years of English (required), 3–4 years of math, 3 years of social science, 2 or more years of a foreign language, and 3–4 years of natural or physical science. Each application is reviewed individually and thoroughly. The writing sample, counselor recommendations (up to 3 reommendations), student activities, grades (minimum 3.2 GPA), and standardized test scores are all considered to determine if Loyola will be a good academic match for the strengths and abilities of the applicant. Loyola does not require or use the new written sections on the SAT and ACT for admission or placement.

Additional Information

Students are encouraged to meet with a staff member in the Services for Students with Disabilities office early on to determine accommodations and services for the upcoming semester. Documentation should provide a clear description of the recommended accommodations, connect these to the impact of the condition, provide possible alternatives to the recommended accommodations, and include a statement regarding the level of need for accommodations.

General Support Services Information

Contact Information
Name of program or department: Services for Students with Disabilities
Telephone: 773508-3700
Fax: 773-508-3810
Website: www.luc.edu/sswd

Accommodations or Services For Students With Learning Differences

Accommodations are decided upon an individual basis after a thorough review of appropriate, current documentation. The accommodations requests must be supported through the documentation provided and must be logically linked to the current impact of the condition on academic functioning.

Allowed in exams
Calculator: Yes
Dictionary: Yes
Computer: Yes
Spellchecker: Yes
Extended test time: Yes
Scribes: Yes
Proctors: Yes
Oral exams: Yes
Note-takers: Yes
Support services for students with LD: Yes
Support services for students with ADHD: Yes
Support services for students with ASD: Yes
Distraction-reduced environment: Yes
Tape recording in class: Yes
Electronic texts: Yes
Kurzweil reader: NR
Audio books: Yes
Other assistive technology: Yes
Priority registration: Yes
Added costs of services: No
LD specialists: Yes
ADHD coaching: Yes
ASD specialists: No
Professional tutors: No
Peer tutors: Yes
Max. hours/wk. for services: NR
How professors are notified of student approved accommodations: By student

General Admissions Information

Office of Admissions: 312-915-6500

Entrance Requirements

Academic units required: 4 English, 3 math, 3 science, 2 foreign language, 2 social studies, 1 history. **Academic units recommended:** 4 English, 4 math, 3 science, 2 foreign language, 2 social studies, 2 history, 3 academic electives. High school diploma is required and GED is accepted. SAT or ACT required. If ACT, ACT with writing accepted. TOEFL required of all international applicants: minimum paper TOEFL 550 or minimum internet TOEFL 79.

Application deadline: NR
Notification: Rolling starting 10/15
Average GPA: 3.65
ACT Composite middle 50% range: 24-29
SAT Math middle 50% range: 518-630
SAT Critical Reading middle 50% range: 520-630
SAT Writing middle 50% range: 520-630
Graduate top 10% of class: 33
Graduated top 25% of class: 70
Graduated top 50% of class: 92

COLLEGE GRADUATION REQUIREMENTS

Course waivers allowed: No
In what course: They can receive substitutions (foreign language requirement substituted with foreign literature courses), but they cannot be exempted entirely
Course substitutions allowed: Yes
In what course: Foreign language is most common

Additional Information

Environment: This private school, affiliated with the Roman Catholic-Jesuit Church, was founded in 1870. It has a 105-acre campus.

Student Body
Undergrad enrollment: 11,079
% Women: 65
% Men: 35
% Out-of-state: 34.6

Cost information
Tuition: $40,052
Room & board: $13,770

Housing Information
University Housing: Yes
Percent living on campus: 41.3

Greek System
Fraternity: Yes
Sorority: Yes
Athletics: Division I

National Louis University

122 South Michigan Avenue, Chicago, IL 60603
Phone: 312-261-3550
E-mail: nlnuinfo@wheeling1.nl.edu • Web: www.nl.edu
Support: SP • Institution type: 4-year private

Programs or Services for Students with Learning Differences

The Learning & Library Center is designed to assist students with learning disabilities to pursue and complete a college education. It is a supportive program for students admitted by the university and enrolled in regular and developmental college courses. While the total services furnished in this program are provided by the university to all students who might experience difficulty with a regular college curriculum, emphasis is placed on individual program planning, tutoring, monitoring, arranged counseling, and special testing for the learning disabled. The center provides peer tutoring, contact with faculty, academic advising, and career and emotional counseling for students who make reasonable progress toward a degree in one of the college programs. Path to Academics, Community and Employment (P.A.C.E) is a three-year, post-secondary certificate program designed to meet the transitional needs for young adults with multiple intellectual, learning and developmental disabilities.

Admission Information for Students with Learning Differences

College entrance tests required: Yes
Interview required: No
Essay required: No
Additional Application Required for LD/ADHD/ASD: NR
What documentation required for LD: Psycho ed evaluation to include: relevant historical info, instructional interventions, related services, age diagnosed, objective data (aptitude, achievement, info processing), test scores (standard, percentile and grade equivalents) and describe functional limitations.
With general application: Yes if requested as part of Structured Program application
To receive services after enrolling: Yes
What documentation required for ADHD: Diagnosis based on DSM-V; history of behaviors impairing functioning in academic setting; diagnostic interview; history of symptoms; evidence of ongoing behaviors.
With general application: Yes if requested as part of Structured Program application
To receive services after enrolling: Yes
What documentation required for ASD: Psycho ed evaluation
With general application: NR
To receive services after enrolling: Yes
LD/ADHD/ASD documentation submitted to: Center for Academic Development
ASD Specific Program: NR
Special Ed. HS course work accepted: No
Specific course requirements of all applicants: NR
Separate application required: No
Total # of students receiving LD/ADHD/ASD services: 25
Acceptance into program means acceptance into college: Students must be admitted and enrolled in the university first and then request services.

Admissions

Students must meet regular admission requirements of a 2.0 GPA in college prep classes and be in top 50 percent of class. Minimum 19 ACT/750 SAT. Some may be admitted on a provisional basis as summer admits or as high-potential students. Criteria used in determining admissibility could include work experience, demonstrated leadership in community or extracurricular activities, motivation and attitude toward learning, and career objectives. In addition, an interview and letters of recommendation may be requested. Interested applicants should indicate interest and submit documentation to admission with permission to share with Learning Specialist. Applicants will meet with Learning Specialists for an informal assessment. Student documentation should highlight the ability to function at college level.

Additional Information

The Learning & Library Center is staffed by specialists. Services include: Summer Bridge Program, developmental reading, writing, and math courses; advising; individualized tutoring and monitoring; organizational skills training; and modification of course presentation and exams if appropriate. Path to Academics, Community and Employment (P.A.C.E) is a three-year, post-secondary certificate program designed to meet the transitional needs for young adults with multiple intellectual, learning and developmental disabilities.

General Support Services Information

Contact Information
Name of program or department: P.A.C.E. at NLU
Telephone: 312-261-37706
Email: paceprogram@nl.edu

Accommodations or Services For Students With Learning Differences

Accommodations are decided upon an individual basis after a thorough review of appropriate, current documentation. The accommodations requested must be supported through the documentation provided and must be logically linked to the current impact of the condition on academic functioning.

Allowed in exams
Calculator: Yes
Dictionary: Yes
Computer: Yes
Spellchecker: Yes
Extended test time: Yes
Scribes: Yes
Proctors: Yes
Oral exams: No
Note-takers: Yes

Services for students with LD: Yes
Services for students with ADHD: Yes
Services for students with ASD: Yes
Distraction-reduced environment: Yes
Tape recording in class: Yes
Audio book: NR
Electronic texts: No
Kurzweil Reader: No
Other assistive technology: Yes
Priority registration: Yes

Added costs for services: Yes for P.A.C.E. Program
LD specialists: Yes
ADHD coaching: NR
ASD specialists: NR
Professional tutors: 5
Peer tutors: 5
Max. hours/wk. for services: 2
How professors are notified of LD/ADHD: By both student and director

General Admissions Information

Office of Admission: 847-465-0575

Entrance Requirements

Academic units recommended: 4 English, 3 math, 2 science (1 science lab), 2 foreign language, 3 social studies. High school diploma is required, and GED is accepted.

Application deadline: NR
Notification: NR
Average GPA: 3.36
ACT Composite middle 50% range: NR-NR

Average SAT Math: 360
Average SAT Critical Reading: 410
Average SAT Writing: 320
Graduated top 10% of class: NR
Graduated top 25% of class: NR

Graduated top 50% of class: NR

COLLEGE GRADUATION REQUIREMENTS

Course waivers allowed: No
Course substitutions allowed: Yes
In what course: NR

Additional Information

Environment: There are 5 locations in the Chicago area.

Student Body
Undergrad enrollment: 1,700
% Women: 78
% Men: 22
% Out-of-state: 1

Cost information
Tuition: $12,000
Room & board: NR
Housing Information
University Housing: Yes
Percent living on campus: 5

Greek System
Fraternity: No
Sorority: No
Athletics: Division 1

NORTHERN ILLINOIS UNIVERSITY

Office of Admissions, DeKalb, IL 60115-2857
Phone: 815-753-0446 • Fax: 815-753-1783
E-mail: admissions@niu.edu • Web: www.niu.edu/admissions
Support: CS • Institution: 4-Year Public

PROGRAMS OR SERVICES FOR STUDENTS WITH LEARNING DIFFERENCES

NIU's Disability Resource Center does not have a "program" for students with learning disabilities, but provides accommodations, guidance, and advocacy to all students with disabilities.

ADMISSION INFORMATION FOR STUDENTS WITH LEARNING DIFFERENCES

College entrance test required: Yes
Interview required: Yes
Essay required: No
Additional Application Required for LD/ADHD/ASD: NR
What documentation required for LD: Letter from medical or counseling professional and/or I.E.P. from High School; and/or documentation from previous institution.
With general application: No
To receive services after enrolling: Yes
What documentation required for ADHD: Letter from medical or counseling professional and/or I.E.P. from High School; and/or documentation from previous institution.
With general application: No
To receive services after enrolling: No
What documentation required for ASD: Letter from medical or counseling professional and/or I.E.P. from High School; and/or documentation from previous institution.
With general application: No
To receive services after enrolling: No
LD/ADHD/ASD documentation submitted to: Disability Resource Center
ASD Specific Program: NR
Special Ed. HS course work accepted: No
Specific course requirements of all applicants: No
Separate application required for program services: NR
Total # of students receiving LD/ADHD/ASD services: 400
Acceptance into program means acceptance into college: No

ADMISSIONS

NIU's DRC does not have a program, therefore there is not a separate admissions process. All new students seeking access/accommodations participate in an initial interview then develop an Accommodation Plan. General admission requires 4 years English, 2 years math, 2 years science, and 2 years social studies. The Chance Program is only available to Illinois residents from targeted schools or who participate in certain academic preparatory programs.

ADDITIONAL INFORMATION

A student's Letter of Accommodation has a list of all approved accommodations, though some may require additional dialogue with faculty, i.e. providing support in situations that include clinical, field, or internship experiences. Accommodations are individualized for students and sometimes for specific courses. The guiding mission of the CHANCE Program is to identify, recruit, admit, and assist otherwise capable students whose pre-college education has not fully enabled them to take maximum advantage of their potential and the opportunities of higher education at NIU. CHANCE services include: individual and group academic, personal and career counseling, academic monitoring and follow-up throughout the student's undergraduate career, tutorial assistance for courses, academic skills-enhancement courses, introductory university transition skills-building course taught by a counselor and peer mentoring for freshmen and transfer students.

Support Services Information

Contact Information
Name of program or department: Disability Resource Center
Telephone: 815- 753-1303
Fax: 815-753-9570

Accommodations or Services For Students With Learning Differences

Accommodations are decided upon an individual basis after a thorough review of appropriate, current documentation. The accommodations requests must be supported through the documentation provided and must be logically linked to the current impact of the condition on academic functioning.

Allowed in exams
Calculator: Yes
Dictionary: Yes
Computer: Yes
Spellchecker: Yes
Extended test time: Yes
Scribes: Yes
Proctors: Yes
Oral exams: Yes
Note-takers: Yes
Support services for students with LD: No
Support services for students with ADHD: No
Support services for students with ASD: No
Distraction-reduced environment: Yes
Tape recording in class: Yes
Electronic texts: Yes
Kurzweil reader: Yes
Audio books: Yes
Other assistive technology: Yes
Priority registration: Yes
Added costs of services: No
LD specialists: No
ADHD coaching: Yes
ASD specialists: Yes
Professional tutors: No
Peer tutors: No
Max. hours/wk. for services: Unlimited
How professors are notified of student approved accommodations: By student

General Admissions Information

Office of Admissions: 815-753-0446

Entrance Requirements

Academic units required: 4 English, 2 math, 2 science, 1 science labs, 1 foreign language, 2 social studies, 1 history. **Academic units recommended:** 4 math, 4 science, 2 science labs, 2 foreign language, 3 social studies. High school diploma is required and GED is accepted. SAT or ACT required. TOEFL required of all international applicants: minimum paper TOEFL 525.

Application deadline: 8/1
Notification: NR
Average GPA: NR
ACT Composite middle 50% range: 19-25
SAT Math middle 50% range: NR-NR
SAT Critical Reading middle 50% range: NR-NR
SAT Writing middle 50% range: NR-NR
Graduate top 10% of class: 13
Graduated top 25% of class: 36
Graduated top 50% of class: 74

COLLEGE GRADUATION REQUIREMENTS

Course waivers allowed: NR
In what course: Course substitutions waiver rarely granted, depends on specific circumstance.
Course substitutions allowed: NR
In what course: NR

Additional Information

Environment: This public school was founded in 1895. It has a 546-acre campus.

Student Body
Undergrad enrollment: 15,027
% Women: 49
% Men: 51
% Out-of-state: 2.7

Cost information
In-state Tuition: $9,466
Out-of-state Tuition: $18,506
Room & board: $9,670

Housing Information
University Housing: Yes
Percent living on campus: 28

Greek System
Fraternity: Yes
Sorority: Yes
Athletics: Division I

Northwestern University

PO Box 3060, Evanston, IL 60204-3060
Phone: 847-491-7271 • Fax: NR
E-mail: ug-admission@northwestern.edu • Web: www.northwestern.edu
Support: CS • Institution: Private

Programs or Services for Students with Learning Differences

AccessibleNU is the campus resource that provides students with LD, ADHD and all other disabilities the tools, reasonable accommodations and support services needed to participate fully in the university Environment. A wide range of services are provided to students with disabilities enrolled in undergraduate, graduate, or professional schools, allowing them full access to programs and activities at Northwestern University. It is the responsibility of the student to provide documentation of disability, to inform the AccessibleNU office and to request accommodations and services if needed. A student who has a disability but has not registered with AccessibleNU is not entitled to services or accommodations.

Admission Information for Students with Learning Differences

College entrance tests required: Yes
Interview required: No
Essay required: Yes
Additional Application Required for LD/ADHD/ASD: NR
What documentation required for LD: Psycho ed evaluation to include: relevant historical info, instructional interventions, related services, age diagnosed, objective data (aptitude, achievement, info processing), test scores (standard, percentile and grade equivalents) and describe functional limitations.
With general application: No
To receive services after enrolling: Yes
What documentation required for ADHD: Diagnosis based on DSM-V; history of behaviors impairing functioning in academic setting; diagnostic interview; history of symptoms; evidence of ongoing behaviors.
With general application: No
To receive services after enrolling: Yes
What documentation required for ASD: Psycho ed evaluation
With general application: NR
To receive services after enrolling: Yes
LD/ADHD/ASD documentation submitted to: Services for Students with Disabilities
ASD Specific Program: NR
Special Ed. HS course work accepted: No
Specific course requirements of all applicants: NR
Separate application required: No
Total # of students receiving LD/ADHD/ASD services: 280
Acceptance into program means acceptance into college: Students must be admitted and enrolled in the university first and then request services.

Admissions

There is no special admissions procedure for students with learning disabilities or ADHD. All applicants must meet the general admission criteria. Most students have taken AP and honors courses in high school and been very successful in these competitive college-prep courses. ACT/SAT tests are required, and SAT Subject Tests are recommended. Foreign-language substitutions may be allowed and are decided on a case-by-case basis.

Additional Information

Some students who received disability-related services in high school may decide to try taking their Northwestern courses without any accommodations or services. AccessibleNU recommends that those students nonetheless provide documentation of their disability. In this way, the AccessibleNU office can easily serve the student if they later find that accommodations are needed. AccessibleNU maintains confidentiality of information, meaning that records contained in AccessibleNU files are housed only in the AccessibleNU office and are not part of the student's academic file. Support services may include testing accommodations, such as extended time and alternative test environment, note-taking services, materials in e-text and audio format, access to adaptive equipment and software, scribe, study strategy assistance, access to a computer to type exam responses, sign language interpreter, C-Print and assistance in activity relocation.

Support Services Information

Contact Information

Name of program or department: AccessibleNU, Alison May - Assistant Dean of Students & Director

Telephone: 847-467-5530

Fax: 847-467-5531

Email: accessiblenu@northwestern.edu

Accommodations or Services For Students With Learning Differences

Accommodations are decided upon an individual basis after a thorough review of appropriate, current documentation. The accommodations requested must be supported through the documentation provided and must be logically linked to the current impact of the condition on academic functioning.

Allowed in exams
Calculator: Yes
Dictionary: Yes
Computer: Yes
Spellchecker: Yes
Extended test time: Yes
Scribes: Yes
Proctors: Yes
Oral exams: Yes
Note-takers: Yes
Services for students with LD: Yes
Services for students with ADHD: Yes
Services for students with ASD: Yes
Distraction-reduced environment: Yes
Tape recording in class: Yes
Audio book: NR
Electronic texts: Yes
Kurzweil Reader: Yes
Other assistive technology: Yes
Priority registration: Yes
Added costs for services: No
LD specialists: Yes
ADHD coaching: NR
ASD specialists: NR
Professional tutors: No
Peer tutors: No
Max. hours/wk. for services: Usually 1 hour
How professors are notified of LD/ADHD: Student

General Admissions Information

Office of Admissions: 847-491-7271

Entrance Requirements

Academic units recommended: 4 English, 3 math, 2 science, 2 science labs, 2 foreign language, 2 social studies, 2 history, 1 academic electives. High school diploma or equivalent is not required. SAT or ACT required. If ACT, ACT with writing required. TOEFL required of all international applicants.

Application deadline: 1/1
Notification: 4/1
Average GPA: NR
ACT Composite middle 50% range: 31-34
SAT Math middle 50% range: 700-790
SAT Critical Reading middle 50% range: 690-770
SAT Writing middle 50% range: NR-NR
Graduated top 10% of class: 90
Graduated top 25% of class: 100
Graduated top 50% of class: 100

COLLEGE GRADUATION REQUIREMENTS

Course waivers allowed: No
Course substitutions allowed: Yes
In what course: On a case-by-case basis

Additional Information

Environment: This private school was founded in 1851. It has a 240-acre campus.

Student Body
Undergrad enrollment: 8,405
% Women: 51
% Men: 49
% Out-of-state: 67

Cost information
Tuition: $46,836
Room & board: $14,389

Housing Information
University Housing: Yes
Percent living on campus: 40

Greek System
Fraternity: Yes
Sorority: Yes
Athletics: Division I

Roosevelt University

430 South Michigan Avenue, Chicago, IL 60605
Phone: 312-341-2102 • Fax: 312-341-3523
E-mail: admission@roosevelt.edu • Web: www.roosevelt.edu/Home.aspx
Support: CS • Institution: Private

Programs or Services for Students with Learning Differences

The Learning and Support Services Program (LSSP) is designed to assist students with learning differences in their pursuit of a college education. Individualized tutoring is provided. A fee is included. Students with Learning Differences, not participating in the LSSP, often utilize Disability Services, under the same office as the LSSP.

Admission Information for Students with Learning Differences

College entrance test required: Yes
Interview required: Yes
Essay required: Yes
Additional Application Required for LD/ADHD/ASD: NR
What documentation required for LD: Psycho ed evaluation to include: relevant historical info, instructional interventions, related services, age diagnosed, objective data (aptitude, achievement, info processing), test scores (standard, percentile and grade equivalents) and describe functional limitations.
With general application: No
To receive services after enrolling: Yes
What documentation required for ADHD: Diagnosis based on DSM-V; history of behaviors impairing functioning in academic setting; diagnostic interview; history of symptoms; evidence of ongoing behaviors.
With general application: No
To receive services after enrolling: Yes
What documentation required for ASD: Diagnosis based on DSM-V; history of behaviors impairing functioning in academic setting; diagnostic interview; history of symptoms; evidence of ongoing behaviors.
With general application: No
To receive services after enrolling: Yes
LD/ADHD/ASD documentation submitted to: Academic Success Center
ASD Specific Program: NR
Special Ed. HS course work accepted: Yes
Specific course requirements of all applicants: Yes
Separate application required for program services: No
Total # of students receiving LD/ADHD/ASD services: 20–35
Acceptance into program means acceptance into college: Students must be admitted through the regular admissions process, and once enrolled, may request services.

Admissions

There is not a separate admissions process through the Academic Success Center. However, it is recommended that students write a letter to the ASC director to request services and state the purpose and reason for seeking help. After reviewing the letter, ASC staff holds an informal interview assessment with the student. Applicants send reports to the ASC with authorization for release of information. These reports should include the following: (1) most recent transcript and confidential records; (2) health and academic history; (3) test results and reports, including achievements, individual IQ, or other measurements of academic performance; and (4) the latest IEP. The ASC staff will evaluate the reports and a meeting will be held to determine eligibility into ASC.

Additional Information

The Learning and Support Services Program is available to students with learning disabilities, attention disorders, traumatic brain injury, and any other condition that presents learning disorders. Assistance is available in course selection, required course readings, assignments, and more. Depending on individual needs, tutoring assistance may include course-related training, time management, organizational skills, to name a few. Students are highly encouraged to utilize other appropriate resources, such as counseling, career development, campus life and tutoring center. Services and accommodations are available to undergraduate and graduate students.

General Support Services Information

Contact Information
Name of program or department: Academic Success Center
Telephone: 312-341-3810
Fax: 312-341-2471
Website: http://www.roosevelt.edu/StudentSuccess/AcademicSuccessCenter.aspx

Accommodations or Services For Students With Learning Differences

Accommodations are decided upon an individual basis after a thorough review of appropriate, current documentation. The accommodations requests must be supported through the documentation provided and must be logically linked to the current impact of the condition on academic functioning.

Allowed in exams
Calculator: Yes
Dictionary: Yes
Computer: Yes
Spellchecker: Yes
Extended test time: Yes
Scribes: Yes
Proctors: Yes
Oral exams: Not Applicable
Note-takers: Yes
Support services for students with LD: Yes
Support services for students with ADHD: Yes
Support services for students with ASD: Yes
Distraction-reduced environment: Yes
Tape recording in class: Yes
Electronic texts: Yes
Kurzweil reader: NR
Audio books: NR
Other assistive technology: Yes
Priority registration: NR
Added costs of services: No
LD specialists: NR
ADHD coaching: Yes
ASD specialists: NR
Professional tutors: No
Peer tutors: Yes
Max. hours/wk. for services: NR
How professors are notified of student approved accommodations: NR

General Admissions Information

Office of Admissions: 877-277-5978

Entrance Requirements

Academic units required: 4 English, 3 math, 2 science, 2 science labs, 2 social studies, **Academic units recommended:** 4 English, 4 math, 3 science, 3 science labs, 2 foreign language, 3 social studies, 2 history, 2 academic electives. High school diploma is required and GED is accepted. SAT or ACT required. If ACT, ACT with writing accepted. TOEFL required of all international applicants: minimum internet TOEFL 40.

Application deadline: NR
Notification: NR
Average GPA: 3.16
ACT Composite middle 50% range: 19-25
SAT Math middle 50% range: 470-610
SAT Critical Reading middle 50% range: 470-640
SAT Writing middle 50% range: 460-610
Graduate top 10% of class: 13
Graduated top 25% of class: 37
Graduated top 50% of class: 68

COLLEGE GRADUATION REQUIREMENTS

Course waivers allowed: Yes
In what course: Varies. Each request is considered individually and subject to department approval.
Course substitutions allowed: Yes
In what course: Varies, typically math.

Additional Information

Environment: This private school was founded in 1945. It has a 34-acre campus.

Student Body
Undergrad enrollment: 3,239
% Women: 64
% Men: 36
% Out-of-state: 15

Cost information
Tuition: $28,119
Room & board:NR

Housing Information
University Housing: Yes
Percent living on campus: 21

Greek System
Fraternity: No
Sorority: Yes
Athletics: NAIA

Shimer College

3424 S. State Street, Chicago, IL 60616
Phone: 312-235-3500 • Fax: 888-808-3133
E-mail: admission@shimer.edu • Web: www.shimer.edu/
Support: S • Institution: Private

Programs or Services for Students with Learning Differences

Shimer has no specific program for students with learning disabilities. Some students with relatively mild learning disabilities who have been unsuccessful in other settings have been successful at Shimer because of the unusual approach to education. Shimer offers an integrated curriculum where students read original sources and not textbooks. Students gather to discuss the books in small groups. Many students with learning disabilities who are motivated to seek the kind of education offered by Shimer have been successful. Students are responsible for seeking the supportive help they want. Class sizes vary from 8 to 12 students, and a great deal of individual attention is available to all students.

Admission Information for Students with Learning Differences

College entrance tests required: No
Interview required: Yes
Essay required: Yes
Additional Application Required for LD/ADHD/ASD: NR
What documentation required for LD: Psycho ed evaluation to include: relevant historical info, instructional interventions, related services, age diagnosed, objective data (aptitude, achievement, info processing), test scores (standard, percentile and grade equivalents) and describe functional limitations.
With general application: No
To receive services after enrolling: Yes
What documentation required for ADHD: Neuropsychological or psychoeducational assessment
With general application: No
To receive services after enrolling: Yes
What documentation required for ASD: Psycho ed evaluation
With general application: NR
To receive services after enrolling: Yes
LD/ADHD/ASD documentation submitted to: Dean of students
ASD Specific Program: NR
Special Ed. HS course work accepted: Yes
Specific course requirements of all applicants: NR
Separate application required: No
Total # of students receiving LD/ADHD/ASD services: NR
Acceptance into program means acceptance into college: Students must be admitted and enrolled in the university first and then request services.

Admissions

The goal of Shimer is to select students who will benefit from and contribute to its intellectual community. Each applicant is considered on an individual basis. Motivation, intellectual curiosity, and commitment to a rigorous and integrative educational program are important qualifications. Shimer will consider the application of any individual who has the potential to perform well. Admission standards are the same for all students. Once admitted, students with learning disabilities work with the Dean of Students office to document disability, request reasonable accommodation, and determine the level of support the college is able to provide. Students are required to have a personal interview, which can be conducted by telephone; write a personal essay; provide ACT/SAT scores (if available); and submit letters of recommendation to the Admission Office. There is no minimum GPA or specific high school courses required. ACT/SAT scores are considered in the admission decision, but they are not required. Writing samples and other personal contact will be used by the Admission Committee to make an evaluation. A campus visit is strongly encouraged. The essay portion of the application asks the applicant to provide an analysis of academic experience and offers the opportunity to demonstrate creative talent. These essays are major criteria in determining candidacy for admission. Shimer will accept a limited number of students on a threshold basis. These students often lack specific evidence of academic achievement, but they are able to convince the Admission Committee of their commitment and potential. These students receive additional mentoring and support from faculty. Continuation after one semester is dependent on academic achievement.

Additional Information

Classes, except in a rare instance, are never larger than 12 students. All courses are conducted through discussion, and all course reading is from original sources. Because of Shimer's faculty/student ratio, all students receive individualized attention from faculty, staff, and other students.

General Support Services Information

Contact Information
Name of program or department: Dean of the College
Telephone: 312-235-3518

Accommodations or Services For Students With Learning Differences

Accommodations are decided upon an individual basis after a thorough review of appropriate, current documentation. The accommodations requested must be supported through the documentation provided and must be logically linked to the current impact of the condition on academic functioning. Determination of accommodations may require an on-campus meeting.

Allowed in exams
Calculator: Yes
Dictionary: Yes
Computer: Yes
Spellchecker: Yes
Extended test time: Yes
Scribes: No
Proctors: No
Oral exams: Yes
Note-takers: No
Services for students with LD: Yes
Services for students with ADHD: Yes
Services for students with ASD: Yes
Distraction-reduced environment: Yes
Tape recording in class: Yes
Audio book: NR
Electronic texts: Yes
Kurzweil Reader: No
Other assistive technology: No
Priority registration: No
Added costs for services: No
LD specialists: No
ADHD coaching: NR
ASD specialists: NR
Professional tutors: Yes
Peer tutors: 1–3
Max. hours/wk. for services: Unlimited
How professors are notified of LD/ADHD: Dean of Students Office

General Admissions Information

Office of Admissions: 312-235-3555

Entrance Requirements

Academic units recommended: 4 English, 3 math, 3 science, 2 foreign language, 2 history, 1 visual/performing arts. High school diploma or equivalent is not required. SAT or ACT required for some. If ACT, ACT with writing accepted. TOEFL required of all international applicants: minimum paper TOEFL 625.

Application deadline: NR
Notification: Rolling starting 9/15
Average GPA: 2.99
ACT Composite middle 50% range: NR-NR
SAT Math middle 50% range: 500-640
SAT Critical Reading middle 50% range: 620-760
SAT Writing middle 50% range: 500-620
Graduated top 10% of class: NR
Graduated top 25% of class: NR
Graduated top 50% of class: NR

COLLEGE GRADUATION REQUIREMENTS

Course waivers allowed: No
Course substitutions allowed: No

Additional Information

Environment: This private school was founded in 1853. It has a 140-acre campus.

Student Body
Undergrad enrollment: 77
% Women: 47
% Men: 53
% Out-of-state: 50

Cost information
Tuition: $31,000
Room & board: $11,516

Housing Information
University Housing: Yes
Percent living on campus: 10

Greek System
Fraternity: No
Sorority: No
Athletics: Other

Southern Illinois U.—Carbondale

Undergraduate Admissions, Mailcode 4710, Carbondale, IL 62901
Phone: 618-536-4405
E-mail: admissions@siu.edu • Web: www.siu.edu
Support: SP • Institution: Public

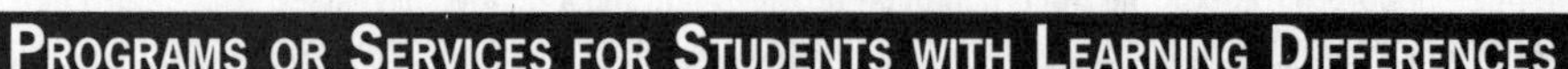

Programs or Services for Students with Learning Differences

Achieve provides comprehensive academic and social support for students with learning disabilities, adhd, and other learning differences, including students on the autism spectrum, at Southern Illinois University in Carbondale. We focus on providing intensive individualized support for students across a number of services and accommodations, integration of students into campus life, communication with all stakeholders to improve success, and guidance for students as they progress. Our mission is to anticipate and exceed the service needs of our students through the best practices of the field, and to teach and reinforce the skills students will need to be successful after they graduate.

Admission Information for Students with Learning Differences

College entrance test required: Yes
Interview required: Yes
Essay required: Required
Additional Application Required for LD/ADHD/ASD: NR
What documentation required for LD: Achieve requires as much comprehensive diagnostic and psychoeducational evaluations and records as can be provided. Achieve wants to see records across the lifespan, if possible. Measures of cognitive ability, academic ability, and social and emotional
With general application: Yes
To receive services after enrolling: Yes
What documentation required for ADHD: No specific diagnostic tool, rating scale, or professional statements are required, but clear and specific diagnostic materials which identify the disorder must be present.
With general application: Yes
To receive services after enrolling: Yes
What documentation required for ASD: Achieve requires as much comprehensive diagnostic and psychoeducational evaluations and records as can be provided. Achieve wants to see records across the lifespan, if possible. Measures of cognitive ability, academic ability, and social and emotional
With general application: Yes
To receive services after enrolling: Yes
LD/ADHD/ASD documentation submitted to: Disability Support Services
ASD Specific Program: The Achieve Program
Special Ed. HS course work accepted: NR
Specific course requirements of all applicants: Yes
Separate application required for program services: Yes
Total # of students receiving LD/ADHD/ASD services: 250
Acceptance into program means acceptance into college: Yes

Admissions

Application to the university and the Achieve Program are separate. Applicants must apply to both. Applicants to the Achieve Program are required to provide: Achieve Program application, $50.00 application fee, Professional Reference form, and documentation of disability. Visit the Achieve Program webpage (http://achieveprogram.siuc.edu/) for downloadable application materials. The Achieve program application can be submitted after completion of junior year of high school. For admission to the University please visit the admissions website: http://admissions.siu.edu/.

Additional Information

Achieve Program students are required to complete the same core curriculum requirements as all other students. The Achieve Program does teach its own sections of UCOL 101, a required course for all first semester freshmen. First year Achieve students are required to spend a minimum of five hours per week at the Achieve Program facilities either working independently, with a general tutor or course specific tutor. The student resource and math labs are staffed with peer tutors to assist with studying and preparing for exams, homework assignments, projects, and written work. Note-takers are assigned for some classes when instructor-provided course notes, PowerPoint presentations, and relevant information are unavailable. Students are encouraged to take their exams at the Achieve offices and may receive extended time as well as a reader or scribe if needed. Audio books are available for students with a demonstrated need, and the Achieve Program has a site license for Kurzweil software. Graduate assistants and staff work with students as case managers so that students have individualized attention and support. All staff is trained to assist students with organization and time management skill building. The Achieve Program has a private computer lab for Achieve students as well as wireless rooms.

General Support Services Information

Contact Information
Name of program or department: Disability Support Services
Telephone: (618) 453-5738
Fax: (618) 453-5700
Website: http://achieve.siu.edu/

Accommodations or Services For Students With Learning Differences

Accommodations are decided upon an individual basis after a thorough review of appropriate, current documentation. The accommodations requests must be supported through the documentation provided and must be logically linked to the current impact of the condition on academic functioning.

Allowed in exams
Calculator: Yes
Dictionary: Yes
Computer: Yes
Spellchecker: Yes
Extended test time: Yes
Scribes: Yes
Proctors: Yes
Oral exams: Yes
Note-takers: Yes
Support services for students with LD: Yes
Support services for students with ADHD: Yes
Support services for students with ASD: Yes
Distraction-reduced environment: Yes
Tape recording in class: Yes
Electronic texts: Yes
Kurzweil reader: NR
Audio books: Yes
Other assistive technology: Yes
Priority registration: Yes
Added costs of services: Yes
LD specialists: Yes
ADHD coaching: Yes
ASD specialists: Yes
Professional tutors: No
Peer tutors: Yes
Max. hours/wk. for services: NR
How professors are notified of student approved accommodations: By both student and director

General Admissions Information

Office of Admissions: 618-536-4405

Entrance Requirements

Academic units required: 4 English, 3 math, 3 science, 3 science labs, 3 social studies, 2 academic electives.
Academic units recommended: 4 English, 4 math, 3 science, 3 science labs, 3 social studies, 2 academic electives. High school diploma is required and GED is accepted. SAT or ACT required. If ACT, ACT with writing accepted. TOEFL required of all international applicants: minimum paper TOEFL 520 or minimum internet TOEFL 68.

Application deadline: 5/1
Notification: Rolling starting 9/1
Average GPA: 3.09
ACT Composite middle 50% range: 19-25
SAT Math middle 50% range: 470-600
SAT Critical Reading middle 50% range: 460-610
SAT Writing middle 50% range: NR-NR
Graduate top 10% of class: 10
Graduated top 25% of class: 32
Graduated top 50% of class: 61

COLLEGE GRADUATION REQUIREMENTS

Course waivers allowed: Yes
In what course: There is a process through which some waivers can be granted. The University offers many options for students to meet curriculum demands without a waiver.
Course substitutions allowed: Yes
In what course: The University offers many options for students to substitute courses to meet their graduation requirements.

Additional Information

Environment: This public school was founded in 1869. It has a 1136-acre campus.

Student Body
Undergrad enrollment: 13,031
% Women: 46
% Men: 54
% Out-of-state: 16

Cost information
In-state-tuition: $26,669
Out-of-state tution: $39,922
Room & board: $9,996

Housing Information
University Housing: Yes
Percent living on campus: 30

Greek System
Fraternity: Yes
Sorority: Yes
Athletics: Division I

Southern Illinois U.—Edwardsville

PO Box 1600, Edwardsville, IL 62026-1080
Phone: 618-650-3705 • Fax: 618-650-5013
E-mail: admissions@siue.edu • Web: www.siue.edu
Support: CS • Institution: Public

Programs or Services for Students with Learning Differences

SIUE's philosophy is to assist students in becoming as independent as possible, and every effort has been made to eliminate barriers to learning. SIUE offers a full range of resources to support students with disabilities and help them attain their educational goals. Students are encouraged to contact Disability Support Services (DSS) as soon as they decide to enroll at the university in order to plan academic accommodations. SIUE does not have special classes for students with learning disabilities; however, the university does offer academic development classes for students who need to develop their math, readying, and writing skills. New Horizons is an organization for students, faculty, and staff who are concerned with issues faced by students with disabilities on campus. New Horizons' activities include disability awareness events, fund-raising, guest speakers, and social activities.

Admission Information for Students with Learning Differences

College entrance test required: Yes
Interview required: No
Essay required: Not Applicable
Additional Application Required for LD/ADHD/ASD: Yes
What documentation required for LD: Specialist in the field must submit a completed outline of documentation to establish disability
With general application: No
To receive services after enrolling: Yes
What documentation required for ADHD: Psycho ed evaluation
With general application: No
To receive services after enrolling: Yes
What documentation required for ASD: Adult inteligence and achievement testing
With general application: No
To receive services after enrolling: Yes
LD/ADHD/ASD documentation submitted to: Disability Support Services
ASD Specific Program: Disability Support Services
Special Ed. HS course work accepted: No
Specific course requirements of all applicants: NR
Separate application required for program services: Yes
Total # of students receiving LD/ADHD/ASD services: NR
Acceptance into program means acceptance into college: No

Admissions

Students with learning disabilities are required to submit the same general application form as all other students. Students should submit documentation of their learning disability in order to receive services once enrolled. This documentation should be sent to DSS. Regular admissions criteria recommended: 4 years of English, 3 years of math, 3 years of science, 3 years of social science, 2 years of a foreign language or electives (students with deficiencies need to check with the Office of Admissions); grade point average of 2.5/4.0 and an ACT minimum of 18 (the average is 22.4) or SAT of 860-890. Students not meeting this criteria are encouraged to apply and may be subject to additional review; Students denied admission may appeal the decision.

Additional Information

The Learning Support Service is available to help students with disabilities improve their time management skills anddevelop effective study strategies. Current resources include advocacy, priority registration, books in alternate format,extended time testing (double time), assistance in writing/ready exams, and volunteer note takers. In addition, the DSSstaff members act as liaisons with faculty and staff regarding learning disabilities and accommodations needed bystudents. Services and accommodations are available for undergraduate and graduate students

General Support Services Information

Contact Information
Name of program or department: Disability Support Services
Telephone: 618-650-3726
Fax: 618-650-5691
Website: siue.edu/dss

Accommodations or Services For Students With Learning Differences

Accommodations are decided upon an individual basis after a thorough review of appropriate, current documentation. The accommodations requests must be supported through the documentation provided and must be logically linked to the current impact of the condition on academic functioning.

Allowed in exams
Calculator: Yes
Dictionary: No
Computer: Yes
Spellchecker: No
Extended test time: Yes
Scribes: Yes
Proctors: Yes
Oral exams: Yes
Note-takers: Yes
Support services for students with LD: Yes
Support services for students with ADHD: Yes
Support services for students with ASD: Yes
Distraction-reduced environment: Yes
Tape recording in class: Yes
Electronic texts: Yes
Kurzweil reader: NR
Audio books: Yes
Other assistive technology: Yes
Priority registration: Yes
Added costs of services: No
LD specialists: Yes
ADHD coaching: No
ASD specialists: No
Professional tutors: No
Peer tutors: No
Max. hours/wk. for services: NR
How professors are notified of student approved accommodations: By student

General Admissions Information

Office of Admissions: 618-650-3705

Entrance Requirements

Academic units required: 4 English, 3 math, 3 science, 3 science labs, 3 social studies, 2 academic electives. **Academic units recommended:** 2 foreign language. High school diploma is required and GED is accepted. SAT or ACT required. If ACT, ACT with writing accepted. TOEFL required of all international applicants: minimum paper TOEFL 550 or minimum internet TOEFL 79.

Application deadline: 5/1
Notification: Rolling starting 9/15
Average GPA: 3.37
ACT Composite middle 50% range: 20-26
SAT Math middle 50% range: 470-615
SAT Critical Reading middle 50% range: 430-558
SAT Writing middle 50% range: 440-570
Graduate top 10% of class: 17
Graduated top 25% of class: 43
Graduated top 50% of class: 73

COLLEGE GRADUATION REQUIREMENTS

Course waivers allowed: No
Course substitutions allowed: Yes
In what course: math, foreign language

Additional Information

Environment: This public school was founded in 1957. It has a 2660-acre campus.

Student Body
Undergrad enrollment: 11,781
% Women: 53
% Men: 47
% Out-of-state: NR

Cost information
In-state tuition: $7,296
Out-of-state Tuition: $20,498
Room & board: $9,211

Housing Information
University Housing: Yes
Percent living on campus: 30

Greek System
Fraternity: Yes
Sorority: Yes
Athletics: Division I

University of Illinois Springfield

One University Plaza Springfield, IL 62703-5407
Phone: 217-206-4847 • Fax: 217-206-6620
E-mail: admissions@uis.edu • Web: www.uis.edu
Support: S • Institution: Public

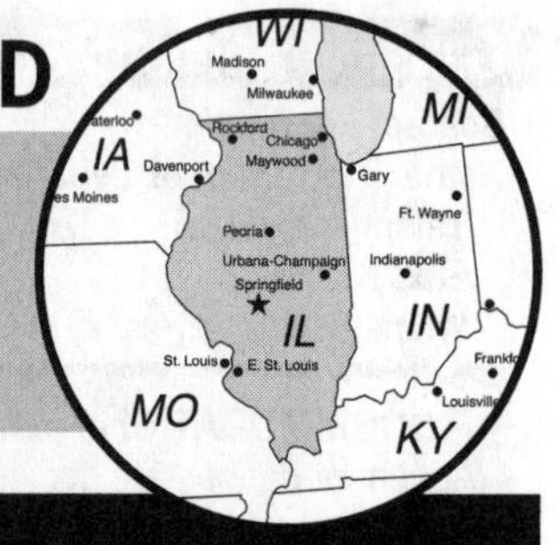

Programs or Services for Students with Learning Differences

To ensure students with disabilities receive the appropriate approved academic accommodations for their documented disability

Admission Information for Students with Learning Differences

College entrance test required: Yes
Interview required: No
Essay required: Not Applicable
Additional Application Required for LD/ADHD/ASD: No
What documentation required for LD: Diagnostic reports used to determine disability must be written within 3 years of the time of the request for academic accommodations. Include test scores that substantiate a significant impairment to learning/cognitive functioning and academic functioning. Describe present symptoms and functioning symptoms/ conditions regarding the diagnosis.
With general application: No
To receive services after enrolling: No
What documentation required for ADHD: Address current & 5-year old levels of functioning. Explain need for accommodations with summarized assessment procedures & results. Include evaluation results, if possible, revealing the significant impairment of daily life and academic functioning. Include history of functional limitations of major life activities - math/reading or written language, below average functioning measured by psychoeducational/neuropsychological, psychological evaluation.
With general application: No
To receive services after enrolling: No
What documentation required for ASD: Must include updated psycho educational testing. Testing must address the present impact of the student's disability on current academic functioning and should be completed within 5 years of the request for academic accommodations. Must clearly state a diagnosis of the specific learning disability.
With general application: No
To receive services after enrolling: No
LD/ADHD/ASD documentation submitted to: Disability Services
ASD Specific Program: No
Special Ed. HS course work accepted: Not Applicable
Specific course requirements of all applicants: Yes
Separate application required for program services: True
Total # of students receiving LD/ADHD/ASD services: 24
Acceptance into program means acceptance into college: No

Admissions

NR

Additional Information

NR

General Support Services Information

Contact Information
Name of program or department: Disability Services
Telephone: 217-206-6666
Fax: 217-206-7154
Website: http://www.uis.edu/disabilityservices/

Accommodations or Services for Students with Learning Differences

Accommodations are decided upon an individual basis after a thorough review of appropriate, current documentation. The accommodations requests must be supported through the documentation provided and must be logically linked to the current impact of the condition on academic functioning.

Allowed in exams
Calculator: Yes
Dictionary: Yes
Computer: Yes
Spellchecker: Yes
Extended test time: Yes
Scribes: Yes
Proctors: Yes
Oral exams: Yes
Note-takers: Yes
Support services for students with LD: Yes
Support services for students with ADHD: Yes
Support services for students with ASD: Yes
Distraction-reduced environment: Yes
Tape recording in class: Yes
Electronic texts: Yes
Kurzweil reader: NR
Audio books: Yes
Other assistive technology: Yes
Priority registration: Yes
Added costs of services: No
LD specialists: Yes
ADHD coaching: No
ASD specialists: Yes
Professional tutors: No
Peer tutors: Not Applicable
Max. hours/wk. for services: NR
How professors are notified of student approved accommodations: By student

General Admissions Information

Office of Admissions: 217-206-4847

Entrance Requirements

Academic units required: 4 English, 3 math, 3 science, 2 science labs, 2 foreign language, 3 social studies. High school diploma is required and GED is accepted. SAT or ACT required. If ACT, ACT with writing accepted. TOEFL required of all international applicants: minimum paper TOEFL 500 .

Application deadline: NR
Notification: Rolling starting 9/15
Average GPA: 3.42
ACT Composite middle 50% range: 20-26
SAT Math middle 50% range: 510-600
SAT Critical Reading middle 50% range: 430-530
SAT Writing middle 50% range: 428-600
Graduate top 10% of class: 19
Graduated top 25% of class: 46
Graduated top 50% of class: 75

COLLEGE GRADUATION REQUIREMENTS

Course waivers allowed: Yes
In what course: Math and foreign language. Depends upon individual circumstances
Course substitutions allowed: Yes
In what course: Math and foreign language. Depends upon individual circumstances

Additional Information

Environment: This public school was founded in 1969. It has a 746-acre campus.

Student Body
Undergrad enrollment: 2,937
% Women: 51
% Men: 49
% out-of-state: 13.4

Cost information
Room & board: NR

Housing Information
University Housing: Yes
Percent living on campus: 30.6

Greek System
Fraternity: No
Sorority: No
Athletics: Division II

U. of Illinois at Urbana-Champaign

901 West Illinois Street, Urbana, IL 61801-3028
Phone: 217-333-0302 • Fax: 217-244-4614
E-mail: http://admissions.illinois.edu/contact_u • Web: illinois.edu
Support: CS • Institution: Public

Programs or Services for Students with Learning Differences

The Division of Disability Resources and Educational Services (DRES) assists qualified students with disabilities in the pursuit of their higher education objectives. DRES assists students with disabilities in gaining access to and benefiting from all the related experiences that are an integral part of a University of Illinois education. Professional staff, including an LD specialist, two clinical psychologists, a career specialist, and an assistive information technology specialist, are available at DRES to assist students in the following areas: planning and implementing academic accommodations, developing compensatory strategies, coaching, for organization and time management, assistive information technology, test accommodations, counseling, and priority registration. Students who receive an offer of admission should submit their documentation to DRES. This documentation should include: diagnostic interviews (developmental, medical, family histories); WAIS, Woodcock-Johnson Tests of Cognitive Ability, Academic Achievement Battery, and a specific LD diagnosis by a qualified professional. ADHD documentation should include: evidence of early impairment, an extensive interview, developmental history, consideration of alternative causes, all appropriate neuropsych tests, extensive clinical summary, and specific DSM-IV diagnosis.

Admission Information for Students with Learning Differences

College entrance test required: NR
Interview required: Not Applicable
Essay required: Not Applicable
Additional Application Required for LD/ADHD/ASD: Yes
What documentation required for LD: Psycho ed evaluation
With general application: No
To receive services after enrolling: Yes
What documentation required for ADHD: Psycho ed evaluation
With general application: No
To receive services after enrolling: Yes
What documentation required for ASD: Psycho ed evaluation
With general application: No
To receive services after enrolling: Yes
LD/ADHD/ASD documentation submitted to: Disability Resources and Educational Services (DRES)
ASD Specific Program: NR
Special Ed. HS course work accepted: Not Applicable
Specific course requirements of all applicants: NR
Separate application required for program services: Yes
Total # of students receiving LD/ADHD/ASD services: 195
Acceptance into program means acceptance into college: No

Admissions

Applicants with LD/ADHD are expected to meet the same admission criteria as all other applicants. Applicants whose qualifications are slightly below a college's admission guidelines are encouraged to use the first essay on the application to provide additional information that could be useful in understanding the student's academic history. The university admits students to particular colleges on the basis of class rank, GPA, ACT/SAT scores, extracurricular activities, two application essays, achievements, and challenge of curriculum. Prospective students should contact the appropriate college for complete course requirements. Required courses include four years English, three to three and a half years math, two years foreign language, two years social science, two years lab science, and two courses from any of the five subject categories.

Additional Information

Accommodations are individually student-centered. The student is expected to declare and document all concurrent disabilities for which services are expected. The design and implementation of accommodations depend on the student's perspective of his/her functional limitations relative to the academic requirements of each course. Timely communication to the learning disability specialist of any situations that are projected to need accommodations during the semester is essential. Individual inquiries and early contacts prior to campus residency strengthen the process of accommodation. Students with LD/ADHD work with specialists to develop learning and compensatory strategies and access accommodation and services.

General Support Services Information

Contact Information
Name of program or department: Disability Resources and Educational Services (DRES)
Telephone: 217-333-1970
Fax: 217-244-0014
Website: www.disability.illinois.edu

Accommodations or Services For Students With Learning Differences

Accommodations are decided upon an individual basis after a thorough review of appropriate, current documentation. The accommodations requests must be supported through the documentation provided and must be logically linked to the current impact of the condition on academic functioning.

Allowed in exams
Calculator: Yes
Dictionary: Yes
Computer: Yes
Spellchecker: Yes
Extended test time: Yes
Scribes: Yes
Proctors: Yes
Oral exams: Yes
Note-takers: Yes
Support services for students with LD: Yes
Support services for students with ADHD: Yes
Support services for students with ASD: Yes
Distraction-reduced environment: Yes
Tape recording in class: Yes
Electronic texts: Yes
Kurzweil reader: NR
Audio books: Yes
Other assistive technology: Yes
Priority registration: Yes
Added costs of services: No
LD specialists: Yes
ADHD coaching: Yes
ASD specialists: Yes
Professional tutors: No
Peer tutors: NR
Max. hours/wk. for services: NR
How professors are notified of student approved accommodations: By student

General Admissions Information

Office of Admissions: 217-333-0302

Entrance Requirements

Academic units required: 4 English, 2 science labs, 2 foreign language, 2 social studies, 2 academic electives. **Academic units recommended:** 4 English, 4 math, 4 science labs, 4 foreign language, 4 social studies, 4 academic electives. High school diploma is required and GED is accepted. SAT or ACT required. If ACT, ACT with writing accepted. TOEFL required of all international applicants: minimum internet TOEFL 80.

Application deadline: 12/1
Notification: 2/13
Average GPA: NR
ACT Composite middle 50% range: 26-32
SAT Math middle 50% range: 700-790
SAT Critical Reading middle 50% range: 590-690
SAT Writing middle 50% range: 600-690
Graduate top 10% of class: 59
Graduated top 25% of class: 90
Graduated top 50% of class: 99

COLLEGE GRADUATION REQUIREMENTS

Course waivers allowed: No
Course substitutions allowed: Yes

Additional Information

Environment: This public school was founded in 1867. It has a 4724-acre campus.

Student Body
Undergrad enrollment: 32,959
% Women: 44
% Men: 56
% Out-of-state: 9

Cost information
In-state Tuition: $15,626
Out-of-state Tuition: $30,786
Room & board: $11,000

Housing Information
University Housing: Yes
Percent living on campus: 50

Greek System
Fraternity: Yes
Sorority: Yes
Athletics: Division I

UNIVERSITY OF ST. FRANCIS

500 Wilcox Street, Joliet, IL 60435
Phone: 815-740-2270 • Fax: 815-740-5078
E-mail: admissions@stfrancis.edu • Web: www.stfrancis.edu
Support: S • Institution: Private

PROGRAMS OR SERVICES FOR STUDENTS WITH LEARNING DIFFERENCES

The Office of Disability Services (ODS) is committed to ensuring equal access by fostering an accessible learning environment. We seek to empower students with disabilities through self-advocacy and developing independence to the fullest extent possible. The Academic Resource Center (ARC) offers a variety of opportunities and academic support services to help students to reach their potential and achieve their goals. Programs and services are available to enhance learning, improve skills and promote success in courses. In the center, students will find computers, study aids, study tables, comfortable spots for reading and friendly people to offer individualized help. Tutoring in a variety of subjects is available from students, faculty members or professional staff.

ADMISSION INFORMATION FOR STUDENTS WITH LEARNING DIFFERENCES

College entrance test required: Yes
Interview required: No
Essay required: Not Applicable
Additional Application Required for LD/ADHD/ASD: Yes
What documentation required for LD: If after the intake interview supplemental information is needed from an outside provider, recommended documentation is
With general application: No
To receive services after enrolling: Yes
What documentation required for ADHD: Psycho ed evaluation
With general application: No
To receive services after enrolling: Yes
What documentation required for ASD:
With general application: No
To receive services after enrolling: Yes
LD/ADHD/ASD documentation submitted to: Office of Disability Services
ASD Specific Program: NR
Special Ed. HS course work accepted: Yes
Specific course requirements of all applicants: Yes
Separate application required for program services: True
Total # of students receiving LD/ADHD/ASD services: 20
Acceptance into program means acceptance into college: No

ADMISSIONS

Freshmen Criteria 2.5 GPA/4.0 scale top 50% of class 20 ACT or 1390 SAT 4 yrs. English 3 yrs. math including Alg I, Geometry, Alg.II or higher 2 yrs. social studies 2 yrs. science including 1 with lab, 3 yrs fine arts, computers, or for. lang. 3 yrs. of electives Transfer Criteria 2.5 transfer GPA for most majors

ADDITIONAL INFORMATION

ARC offers students: New techniques for learning, exam preparation assistance, study aid, test preparation, workshops on time management, note-taking, learning styles, dosage calculations and memory techniques. ARC also provides supports in learning strategies such as reading, study habits, test taking, and test anxiety. Students may receive one-on-one assessment of learning strategies and coaching in study skills by making an appointment.

General Support Services Information

Contact Information
Name of program or department: Office of Disability Services
Telephone: 815-740-3204
Fax: 815-740-3726
Website: https://myusf.stfrancis.edu/portal/secure/content/15023

Accommodations or Services for Students with Learning Differences

Accommodations are decided upon an individual basis after a thorough review of appropriate, current documentation. The accommodations requests must be supported through the documentation provided and must be logically linked to the current impact of the condition on academic functioning.

Allowed in exams
Calculator: Yes
Dictionary: Yes
Computer: Yes
Spellchecker: Yes
Extended test time: Yes
Scribes: Yes
Proctors: Yes
Oral exams: Yes
Note-takers: Yes
Support services for students with LD: Yes
Support services for students with ADHD: Yes
Support services for students with ASD: Yes
Distraction-reduced environment: Yes
Tape recording in class: Yes
Electronic texts: Yes
Kurzweil reader: NR
Audio books: Yes
Other assistive technology: Yes
Priority registration: Yes
Added costs of services: No
LD specialists: No
ADHD coaching: No
ASD specialists: Yes
Professional tutors: Yes
Peer tutors: Yes
Max. hours/wk. for services: NR
How professors are notified of student approved accommodations: By student

General Admissions Information

Office of Admissions: 815-740-2270

Entrance Requirements

Academic units required: 4 English, 3 math, 2 science, 1 science labs, 2 social studies, 3 academic electives, and 3 units from above areas or other academic areas. High school diploma is required and GED is accepted. SAT or ACT required. If ACT, ACT with writing accepted. TOEFL required of all international applicants: minimum paper TOEFL 550 or minimum internet TOEFL 79.

Application deadline: 8/1
Notification: Rolling starting 9/1
Average GPA: 3.4
ACT Composite middle 50% range: 21-25
SAT Math middle 50% range: 470-630
SAT Critical Reading middle 50% range: 470-530
SAT Writing middle 50% range: 450-490
Graduate top 10% of class: 16
Graduated top 25% of class: 43
Graduated top 50% of class: 77

COLLEGE GRADUATION REQUIREMENTS

Course waivers allowed: Yes
In what course: Decided case by case and with approval of dean
Course substitutions allowed: Yes
In what course: Decided case by case and with approval of dean

Additional Information

Environment: This private school, affiliated with the Roman Catholic Church, was founded in 1920. It has a 22-acre campus.

Student Body
Undergrad enrollment: 1,323
% Women: 65
% Men: 35
% Out-of-state: 5

Cost information
Tuition: $29,630
Room & board: $9,084

Housing Information
University Housing: Yes
Percent living on campus: 26

Greek System
Fraternity: No
Sorority: Yes
Athletics: NAIA

Western Illinois University

1 University Circle, Macomb, IL 61455-1390
Phone: 309-298-3157 • Fax: 309-298-3111
E-mail: admissions@wiu.edu • Web: www.wiu.edu
Support: CS • Institution: Public

Programs or Services for Students with Learning Differences

Western Illinois University is committed to justice, equity, and diversity. Providing equal opportunities for students with disabilities is a campus-wide responsibility. Disability Resource Center is the office that coordinates academic accommodations for students with diagnosed disabilities who self-identify to the office. Remedial assisstance or a specialized curriculum is not available at WIU. Students requesting accommodations must provide current documentation verifying the specific disability.

Admission Information for Students with Learning Differences

College entrance test required: Yes
Interview required: No
Essay required: N/A
Additional Application Required for LD/ADHD/ASD: NR
What documentation required for LD/ADHD: While DRC staff does rely on third-party documentation, it is imperative that DRC staff speak with students regarding their experiences in the educational environment. When DRC reviews third-party information, they are looking for two key elements: The information is provided by an evaluator who is qualified to diagnose the condition, and documentation supports the requested accommodations.
With general application: Yes
To receive services after enrolling: Yes
What documentation required for ASD: Psycho ed evaluation
With general application: NR
To receive services after enrolling: Yes
LD/ADHD/ASD documentation submitted to: Disability Resource Center
ASD Specific Program: NR
Special Ed. HS course work accepted: N/A
Specific course requirements of all applicants: Yes
Separate application required for program services: NR
Total # of students receiving LD/ADHD/ASD services: NR
Acceptance into program means acceptance into college: Separate application required after student has enrolled.

Admissions

Students with learning disabilities must meet the same admission criteria as all applicants, which includes four years English, three years social studies, three years math, three years science, and two years electives. Applicants must also have a ACT 20/SAT 920 and a 2.5 GPA. Students not meeting these standards may be considered for alternative admission. The application should be supported by a letter of recommendation from the counselor and a letter of appeal from the student. The Academic Services Program provides an opportunity for admission to a limited number of students yearly who do not meet the regular WIU admissions. Students considered for alternative admissions must have an ACT of 16 and a high school cummulative GPA of 2.2. Students admitted in the Academic Services Program are chosen on the basis of demonstrated academic potential for success. Several criteria are considered including, but not limited to high school academic GPA, grade patterns, references, and student letter expressing interest in the program.

Additional Information

The purpose of the DRC exam service is to modify aspects of the testing environment in a manner that allows for accurate assessment of achievement. Exam accommodations include but are not limited to extended time, a reduced-distraction test environment, readers, scribes, and a computer for essay and short answer exams. While instructors may provide these accommodations to students if they wish, DRC offers an exam service for faculty who do not have the resources to provided necessary modifications within their respective departments. Students who plan to take exams using the DRC exam service, will meet with a DRC staff member to schedule exams. The university may allow course substitutions for students receiving DRC services, based on strong documentation of a weakness in a specific area. A student must write a letter of appeal to the Council on Admission, Graduation and Academic Standards (CAGAS). The student should send a copy of the appeal letter to Disability Resource Center. The letter of appeal should contain at least the following: The student's name, address, identification number, and major; the type of request; an explanation of the student's disability; the rationale for the request; a history of any previous attempts to complete courses that satisfy current requirements; and any history of similar requests granted by any college, university or high school. A letter from DRC should accompany the student's request verifying the disability, when they notified DRC of their disability, and an indication of how long the student has had the disability.

General Support Services Information

Contact Information
Name of program or department: Disability Resource Center
Telephone: 309-298-2512
Fax: 309-298-2361
Website: NR

Accommodations or Services For Students With Learning Differences

Accommodations are decided upon an individual basis after a thorough review of appropriate, current documentation. The accommodations requests must be supported through the documentation provided and must be logically linked to the current impact of the condition on academic functioning.

Allowed in exams
Calculator: Yes
Dictionary: Yes
Computer: Yes
Spellchecker: Yes
Extended test time: Yes
Scribes: Yes
Proctors: Yes
Oral exams: Yes
Note-takers: Yes
Support services for students with LD: Yes
Support services for students with ADHD: Yes
Support services for students with ASD: Yes
Distraction-reduced environment: Yes
Tape recording in class: Yes
Electronic texts: Yes
Kurzweil reader: NR
Audio books: No
Other assistive technology: NR
Priority registration: Yes
Added costs of services: No
LD specialists: Yes
ADHD coaching: No
ASD specialists: Not Applicable
Professional tutors: No
Peer tutors: Yes
Max. hours/wk. for services: NR
How professors are notified of student approved accommodations: By both student and director

General Admissions Information

Office of Admissions: 309-298-3157

Entrance Requirements

Academic units recommended: 4 English, 3 math, 3 science, 3 social studies, 2 academic electives. High school diploma is required and GED is accepted. SAT or ACT required. If ACT, ACT with writing accepted. TOEFL required of all international applicants: minimum paper TOEFL 550 or minimum internet TOEFL 79.

Application deadline: NR
Notification: 9/15
Average GPA: 3.2
ACT Composite middle 50% range: 18-23
SAT Math middle 50% range: NR-NR
SAT Critical Reading middle 50% range: NR-NR
SAT Writing middle 50% range: NR-NR
Graduate top 10% of class: 10
Graduated top 25% of class: 31
Graduated top 50% of class: 67

COLLEGE GRADUATION REQUIREMENTS

Course waivers allowed: NR
In what course: NR
Course substitutions allowed: Yes
In what course: NR

Additional Information

Environment: This public school was founded in 1899. It has a 1050-acre campus.

Student Body
Undergrad enrollment: 9,141
% Women: 50
% Men: 50
% Out-of-state: 11

Cost information
In-state tuition: $12,217
Out-of-state tuition: $16,533
Room & board: $9,580

Housing Information
University Housing: Yes
Percent living on campus: 44

Greek System
Fraternity: Yes
Sorority: Yes
Athletics: Division I

Wheaton College (IL)

501 College Avenue Wheaton, IL 60187
Phone: 630-752-5011 • Fax: 630-752-5285
E-mail: admissions@wheaton.edu • Web: www.wheaton.edu
Support: S • Institution: Private

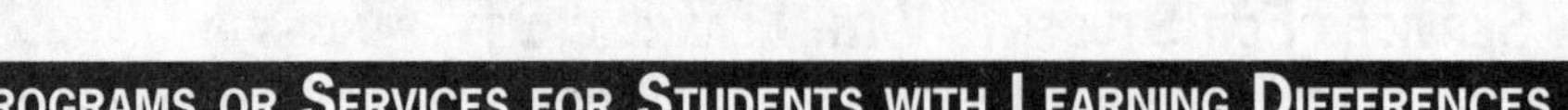

Programs or Services for Students with Learning Differences

The Academic and Disability Services Office exists to address the individual academic needs of students and cultivate a community-wide attitude of welcome and inclusiveness for students with disabilities. It strives to develop the God-given strengths of each student, and provides services both for students needing academic enrichment or assistance and for those dealing with learning, physical or mental health challenges.

Admission Information for Students with Learning Differences

College entrance test required: Yes
Interview required: No
Essay required: Not Applicable
Additional Application Required for LD/ADHD/ASD: Not Applicable
What documentation required for LD: Evaluation from a licensed psychologist or form completed by physician.
With general application: Not Applicable
To receive services after enrolling: Not Applicable
What documentation required for ADHD: A letter or evaluation from a physician, licensed psychologist or psychiatrist that includes diagnosis, impact/functional limitations, previous accommodations, specific recommendations.
With general application: Not Applicable
To receive services after enrolling: Not Applicable
What documentation required for ASD: Psychoeducational evaluation completed by a licensed psychologist or psychiatrist.
With general application: Not Applicable
To receive services after enrolling: Not Applicable
LD/ADHD/ASD documentation submitted to: Academic and Disability Services
ASD Specific Program: NR
Special Ed. HS course work accepted: Not Applicable
Specific course requirements of all applicants: NR
Separate application required for program services: False
Total # of students receiving LD/ADHD/ASD services:
Acceptance into program means acceptance into college: Not Applicable

Admissions

Applicants should have followed a challenging college preparatory curriculum. Advanced Placement and International Baccalaureate courses are encouraged if available. Applicants are expected to meet the unit requirements listed below: A minimum of 18 units should be earned in high school. Only courses taken in grades 9-12 are counted. An applicant should plan to complete at least 14 units by the end of his/her junior year. Of the 18 units, 15 must be earned in the academic areas of English, mathematics, science, social studies, and foreign language. Applicants are expected to have completed at least two years of one foreign language. Interviews are an optional part of the application process that allow the college to get to know applicants better. All applicants are required to complete the primary essay. Wheaton does superscore both the SAT and the ACT, using the highest critical reading and math scores from any sitting of the SAT test, and calculating the highest composite ACT score using sub scores from any sitting of the ACT test. A recommendation from one core academic teacher is required. A recommendation from a pastor, youth pastor, former pastor, Bible study leader, Christian school teacher, church official, or other mature Christian is required.

Additional Information

Through one-on-one counseling and academic workshops, students are offered the opportunity to improve existing skills, to develop new strategies, and to maximize their learning experience. A series of workshops are offered each year in the areas of time management, college reading and note-taking, college writing and research, exam preparation, procrastination and perfectionism. Individual meetings are available by appointment to offer accountability, coaching and accommodation advocacy. Academic counseling is available for all students. Accommodation approval and services for students with documented learning including assessment screening for potential learning challenges are available and can include: learning style assessment, academic coaching and accountability, and strategic learning improvement information.

General Support Services Information

Contact Information
Name of program or department: Academic and Disability Services
Telephone: 630-752-5674
Fax: 630-752-7226
Website: http://www.wheaton.edu/Student-Life/Student-Care/Academic-and-Disability-Services

Accommodations or Services for Students with Learning Differences

Accommodations are decided upon an individual basis after a thorough review of appropriate, current documentation. The accommodations requests must be supported through the documentation provided and must be logically linked to the current impact of the condition on academic functioning.

Allowed in exams
Calculator: No
Dictionary: No
Computer: Yes
Spellchecker: No
Extended test time: Yes
Scribes: Yes
Proctors: Yes
Oral exams: Yes
Note-takers: Yes
Support services for students with LD: Yes
Support services for students with ADHD: Yes
Support services for students with ASD: Yes
Distraction-reduced environment: Yes
Tape recording in class: Yes
Electronic texts: Yes
Kurzweil reader: NR
Audio books: Yes
Other assistive technology: Yes
Priority registration: No
Added costs of services: No
LD specialists: No
ADHD coaching: Yes
ASD specialists: Yes
Professional tutors: No
Peer tutors: Yes
Max. hours/wk. for services: NR
How professors are notified of student approved accommodations: By both student and director

General Admissions Information

Office of Admissions: 630-752-5011

Entrance Requirements

Academic units required: 4 English, 3 math, 3 science, 2 foreign language, 3 social studies, **Academic units recommended:** 4 English, 4 math, 4 science, 3 foreign language, 4 social studies, High school diploma is required and GED is accepted. SAT or ACT required. If ACT, ACT with writing accepted. TOEFL required of all international applicants: minimum paper TOEFL 587 or minimum internet TOEFL 95.

Application deadline: 1/10
Notification: 4/1
Average GPA: 3.68
ACT Composite middle 50% range: 27-32
SAT Math middle 50% range: 590-700
SAT Critical Reading middle 50% range: 600-710
SAT Writing middle 50% range: 600-700
Graduate top 10% of class: 52
Graduated top 25% of class: 75
Graduated top 50% of class: 93

COLLEGE GRADUATION REQUIREMENTS

Course waivers allowed: No
In what course: Foreign language substitution but no waivers
Course substitutions allowed: Yes
In what course: Foreign language, in rare cases public speaking

Additional Information

Environment: This private school was founded in 1860. It has a 80-acre campus.

Student Body
Undergrad enrollment: 2,432
% Women: 52
% Men: 48
% Out-of-state: 74

Cost information
Tuition: $32,950
Room & board: $9,200

Housing Information
University Housing: Yes
Percent living on campus: 90

Greek System
Fraternity: Yes
Sorority: Yes
Athletics: Division III

Anderson University

1100 East Fifth Street, Anderson, IN 46012-3495
Phone: 765-641-4080 • Fax: 765-641-4091
E-mail: info@anderson.edu • Web: www.anderson.edu
Support: SP • Institution: Private

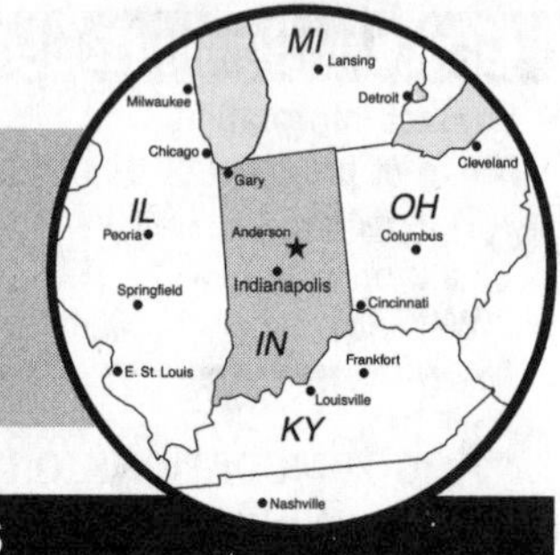

Programs or Services for Students with Learning Differences

It is the philosophy of Anderson University that those students who are qualified and have a sincere motivation to complete a college education should be given every opportunity to work toward that goal. Students with specific learning disabilities may be integrated into any of the many existing services at the Kissinger Learning Center or more individual programming may be designed. Students receive extensive personal contact through the program. The director of the program schedules time with each student to evaluate personal learning style in order to assist in planning for the most appropriate learning environment. One of the most successful programs is individual or small group tutorial assistance. Adjustment and emotional support is also provided. The college strives to provide the maximum amount of services necessary to assist students with learning disabilities in their academic endeavors, while being careful not to create an overdependency.

Admission Information for Students with Learning Differences

College entrance test required: Yes
Interview required: Yes
Essay required: Optional
Additional Application Required for LD/ADHD/ASD: NR
What documentation required for LD: If the student seeks accommodations, documentation of the disability and need for accommodations is required.
With general application: NR
To receive services after enrolling: Yes
What documentation required for ADHD: If the student seeks accommodations, documentation of the disability and need for accommodations is required.
With general application: NR
To receive services after enrolling: Yes
What documentation required for ASD: If the student seeks accommodations, documentation of the disability and need for accommodations is required.
With general application: NR
To receive services after enrolling: Yes
LD/ADHD/ASD documentation submitted to: Disability Services for Students
ASD Specific Program: NR
Special Ed. HS course work accepted: NR
Specific course requirements of all applicants: Yes
Separate application required for program services: No
Total # of students receiving LD/ADHD/ASD services: 34
Acceptance into program means acceptance into college: NR

Admissions

Students with specific learning disabilities who apply to Anderson do so through the regular admission channels. The university recommends that students have the following courses in their high school background: 4 years of English, 3 years of mathematics, 2 years of a foreign language, 3 years of science, and 3 years of social studies. Also considered in the evaluation of each application is the student's seriousness of purpose; personality and character; expressed willingness to live within the standards of the Anderson University community; and service to school, church, and community. Documentation of a specific learning disability must be included with the application. We encourage students to self-disclose because they may qualify for special consideration and be admitted through the LD program. Failure to disclose could result in nonacceptance based on standardized class scores, GPA, etc. Upon request for consideration for the program, prospective students are expected to make an on-campus visit, at which time a personal interview is arranged with the program director. All applicants are considered on an individual basis.

Additional Information

The Bridges Program at Anderson University offers a program to help students with specific learning disabilities and/or ADHD achieve their educational goals. The Bridges program provides these students an extra layer of support during the transition from high school to college.

During their first semester, students who are accepted into the Bridges program must take a two-credit-hour college survival skills/study skills course that is taught by a DSS staff member/members. Freshmen enrolled in the program are typically limited to a lighter course load during their first semester. Students are fully integrated into the university and follow the regular curriculum and requirements for graduation. Students who wish to apply to the Bridges program must notify the DSS director. Documentation of a specific learning disability and/or ADHD must be provided. Students applying for the program are required to have a personal interview with the program director.

General Support Services Information

Contact Information
Name of program or department: Disability Services for Students
Telephone: 765 6414223
Fax: NR
Website: www.anderson.edu/kissinger

Accommodations or Services For Students With Learning Differences

Accommodations are decided upon an individual basis after a thorough review of appropriate, current documentation. The accommodations requests must be supported through the documentation provided and must be logically linked to the current impact of the condition on academic functioning.

Allowed in exams
Calculator: NR
Dictionary: No
Computer: NR
Spellchecker: Yes
Extended test time: Yes
Scribes: Yes
Proctors: Yes
Oral exams: No
Note-takers: Yes
Support services for students with LD: NR
Support services for students with ADHD: Yes
Support services for students with ASD: No
Distraction-reduced environment: Yes
Tape recording in class: Yes
Electronic texts: Yes
Kurzweil reader: Yes
Audio books: No
Other assistive technology: Yes
Priority registration: No
Added costs of services: No
LD specialists: Yes
ADHD coaching: Yes
ASD specialists: No
Professional tutors: No
Peer tutors: Yes
Max. hours/wk. for services: Unlimited
How professors are notified of student approved accommodations: Both student and supervisor

General Admissions Information

Office of Admissions: 765-641-4080

Entrance Requirements

Academic units required: 4 English, 3 math, 3 science, 3 science labs, 2 foreign language, 1 social studies, 1 history. **Academic units recommended:** 4 English, 4 math, 4 science, 4 science labs, 3 foreign language, 2 social studies, 2 history, 5 academic electives, 1 computer science, 1 visual/performing arts. High school diploma is required and GED is not accepted. SAT or ACT required. If ACT, ACT with writing required. TOEFL required of all international applicants: minimum paper TOEFL 547 or minimum internet TOEFL 78.

Application deadline: 7/1
Notification: Rolling starting 9/1
Average GPA: 3.505
ACT Composite middle 50% range: 21-25
SAT Math middle 50% range: 470-570
SAT Critical Reading middle 50% range: 470-560
SAT Writing middle 50% range: NR-NR
Graduate top 10% of class: 24
Graduated top 25% of class: 53
Graduated top 50% of class: 86

COLLEGE GRADUATION REQUIREMENTS

Course waivers allowed: NR
Course substitutions allowed: NR
In what course: Case by case decision.

Additional Information

Environment: This private school, affiliated with the Church of God Church, was founded in 1917. It has a 100-acre campus.

Student Body
Undergrad enrollment: 1,907
% Women: 61
% Men: 39
% Out-of-state: 25

Cost information
Tuition: $27,520
Room & board: $9,380

Housing Information
University Housing: Yes
Percent living on campus: 77

Greek System
Fraternity: No
Sorority: No
Athletics: Division III

INDIANA UNIVERSITY

300 North Jordan Avenue, Bloomington, IN 47405-1106
Phone: 812-855-0661 • Fax: 812-855-5102
E-mail: iuadmit@indiana.edu • Web: www.iub.edu
Support: CS • Institution: Public

PROGRAMS OR SERVICES FOR STUDENTS WITH LEARNING DIFFERENCES

The goal of the Office of Disability Services for Students (DSS) is to provide services that enable students with disabilities to participate in, and benefit from all university programs and activities. There is no specific program for students with LD. However there is a Learning Disabilities Coordinator who provides supportive services necessary to help students pursue their academic objectives. The Briscoe Academic Support Center offers free assistance to all IU students, night and day. During the day, the center is used for study groups, meetings, and advising, and in the evenings it provides free tutoring, advising, and academic support to assist with course assignments and studying. No appointments are necessary. Students with LD must provide current and appropriate psychoeducational evaluations that address: aptitude; achievement; information processing; clear and specific evidence and identification of an LD; test scores/data must be included; evaluations must be done by a qualified professional; and current IEPs are helpful. Students with ADHD must provide documentation that includes: a clear statement of ADHD with a current diagnosis, including a description of supporting symptoms; current testing, preferably within 3 years; a summary of assessment procedures and evaluations used; a summary supporting diagnosis; medical history; suggestions of reasonable accommodations; and current IEP is helpful.

ADMISSION INFORMATION FOR STUDENTS WITH LEARNING DIFFERENCES

College entrance test required: Yes
Interview required: NR
Essay required: NR
Additional Application Required for LD/ADHD/ASD: NR
What documentation required for LD: https://studentaffairs.indiana.edu/disability-services-students/request-services/documenting-disability.shtml
With general application: NR
To receive services after enrolling: Yes
What documentation required for ADHD: https://studentaffairs.indiana.edu/disability-services-students/request-services/documenting-disability.shtml
With general application: NR
To receive services after enrolling: Yes
What documentation required for ASD: https://studentaffairs.indiana.edu/disability-services-students/request-services/documenting-disability.shtml
With general application: NR
To receive services after enrolling: Yes
LD/ADHD/ASD documentation submitted to: Disability Services for Students
ASD Specific Program: NR
Special Ed. HS course work accepted: NR
Specific course requirements of all applicants: NR
Separate application required for program services: NR
Total # of students receiving LD/ADHD/ASD services: NR
Acceptance into program means acceptance into college: NR

ADMISSIONS

There is no special admission process for students with learning disabilities. Each applicant is reviewed individually. IU is concerned with the strength of the college-prep program, including senior year, grade trends, and the student's class rank. Students falling below the minimum standards may receive serious consideration for admission if their grades have been steadily improving in a challenging college-prep program. 4 years English, 3 years math, 1 year science, 2 years social science, 2 years foreign language, plus additional courses in math, science, social science and/or foreign language to be competitive for admission. Indiana residents must complete Core 40 which includes a minimum of 28 semesters of college-prep courses. Nonresidents must complete a minimum of 32 semester college-prep classes. All students should be enrolled in at least 4 college-prep courses each semester. Students usually rank in the top one-third out-of-state and top half in-state. Students must take either the ACT with Writing or the SAT with Writing.

ADDITIONAL INFORMATION

Accommodations can be made to provide: test modifications, referrals to tutors, peer note-takers, books on tape, adaptive technology, and priority registration for students needing books on tape. Students must provide appropriate documentation and submit request for services. Students need to request a letter from DSS to give to their professors. No course requirements are waived automatically. Students who have difficulty with math or foreign language should discuss with DSS. The Student Academic Center offers workshops, courses for credit, and individualized academic assesments. No fees.

General Support Services Information

Contact Information
Name of program or department: Disability Services for Students
Telephone: (812) 855-7578
Fax: (812) 855-7650
Website: https://studentaffairs.indiana.edu/disability-services-students/index.shtml

Accommodations or Services For Students With Learning Differences

Accommodations are decided upon an individual basis after a thorough review of appropriate, current documentation. The accommodations requests must be supported through the documentation provided and must be logically linked to the current impact of the condition on academic functioning.

Allowed in exams
Calculator: NR
Dictionary: NR
Computer: NR
Spellchecker: NR
Extended test time: Yes
Scribes: Yes
Proctors: Yes
Oral exams: Yes
Note-takers: Yes
Support services for students with LD: Yes
Support services for students with ADHD: Yes
Support services for students with ASD: Yes
Distraction-reduced environment: Yes
Tape recording in class: Yes
Electronic texts: Yes
Kurzweil reader: NR
Audio books: NR
Other assistive technology: Yes
Priority registration: Yes
Added costs of services: NR
LD specialists: Yes
ADHD coaching: NR
ASD specialists: Yes
Professional tutors: No
Peer tutors: Yes
Max. hours/wk. for services: NR
How professors are notified of student approved accommodations: By student

General Admissions Information

Office of Admissions: 812-855-0661

Entrance Requirements

Academic units required: 4 English, 3 science, 2 science labs, 2 foreign language, 3 social studies. High school diploma is required and GED is accepted. SAT or ACT required. If ACT, ACT with writing required. TOEFL required of all international applicants: minimum paper TOEFL 550 or minimum internet TOEFL 79.

Application deadline: NR
Notification: NR
Average GPA: 3.64
ACT Composite middle 50% range: 24-30
SAT Math middle 50% range: 540-660
SAT Critical Reading middle 50% range: 520-630
SAT Writing middle 50% range: 510-620
Graduate top 10% of class: 34
Graduated top 25% of class: 68
Graduated top 50% of class: 95

COLLEGE GRADUATION REQUIREMENTS

Course waivers allowed: NR
Course substitutions allowed: NR

Additional Information

Environment: This public school was founded in 1820. It has a 1937-acre campus.

Student Body
Undergrad enrollment: 38,364
% Women: 51
% Men: 49
% Out-of-state: 32.59

Cost information
In-state Tuition: $9,087
Out-of-state Tuition: $32,945
Room & board: NR

Housing Information
University Housing: Yes
Percent living on campus: 35.15

Greek System
Fraternity: Yes
Sorority: Yes
Athletics: Division I

Manchester College

604 E. College Avenue N., Manchester, IN 46962
Phone: 260-982-5055 • Fax: 260-982-5239
E-mail: admitinfo@manchester.edu • Web: www.manchester.edu
Support: CS • Institution: Private

Programs or Services for Students with Learning Differences

Manchester College does not have a specific program for students with learning disabilities. The college is, however, very sensitive to all students. The key word at Manchester College is "success," which means graduating in 4 years. The college wants all students to be able to complete their degree in 4 years. The college does provide support services to students identified as disabled to allow them to be successful. The goal is to assist students in their individual needs.

Admission Information for Students with Learning Differences

College entrance tests required: Yes
Interview required: Yes
Essay required: No
Additional Application Required for LD/ADHD/ASD: NR
What documentation required for LD: Psycho ed evaluation to include: relevant historical info, instructional interventions, related services, age diagnosed, objective data (aptitude, achievement, info processing), test scores (standard, percentile and grade equivalents) and describe functional limitations.
With general application: No
To receive services after enrolling: Yes
What documentation required for ADHD: Diagnosis based on DSM-V; history of behaviors impairing functioning in academic setting; diagnostic interview; history of symptoms; evidence of ongoing behaviors.
With general application: No
What documenation required for ASD: Psycho ed evaluation
LD/ADHD/ASD documentation submitted to: Learning Support Services
ASD Specific Program: NR
Special Ed. HS course work accepted: Yes
Specific course requirements of all applicants: Yes
Separate application required: No
Total # of students receiving LD/ADHD/ASD services: 20–30
Acceptance into program means acceptance into college: Students must be admitted and enrolled in the university first and then request services.

Admissions

Students with learning disabilities submit the regular application form, and are required to meet the same admission criteria as all other applicants. Course requirements include 4 years of English, 2 years of math (3 years recommended), 2 years of science (3 years recommended), 2 years of science labs (3 years of science labs recommended), 2 years of a foreign language required, 2 years of social studies, 1 year of history (2 years recommended), and 1 year of an elective (2 years recommended). Average ACT is 22 or SAT Reasoning 990. Students are admitted to the college and use the support services as they choose. If special consideration for admission is requested, it is done individually, based on potential for graduation from the college. Manchester considers a wide range of information in making individual admission decisions. Students are encouraged to provide information beyond what is required on the application form if they believe it will strengthen their application or help the college to understand the students' performance or potential. Students who self-disclose the existence of a learning disability and are denied can ask to appeal the decision and have their application reviewed in a "different" way. The key question that will be asked is if the student can graduate in 4 years or, at the most, 5 years.

Additional Information

The Success Center provides tutoring for all students at the college. A course is offered presenting college level study skills with opportunities for students to apply these skills in their current course texts. Specific topics include time management, note-taking, vocabulary, text study techniques, test-taking, and memory strategies. Other topics include: college expectations, learning styles and assessments, self-management, and educational and career planning.

General Support Services Information

Contact Information
Name of program or department: Academic Success
Telephone: 260-982-5076
Fax: 260-982-5888

Accommodations or Services For Students With Learning Differences

Accommodations are decided upon an individual basis after a thorough review of appropriate, current documentation. The accommodations requested must be supported through the documentation provided and must be logically linked to the current impact of the condition on academic functioning.

Allowed in exams
Calculator: Yes
Dictionary: No
Computer: Yes
Spellchecker: Yes
Extended test time: Yes
Scribes: Yes
Proctors: Yes
Oral exams: Yes
Note-takers: Yes
Services for students with LD: Yes
Services for students with ADHD: Yes
Services for students with ASD: Yes
Distraction-reduced environment: Yes
Tape recording in class: Yes
Audio book: NR
Electronic texts: Yes
Kurzweil Reader: No
Other assistive technology: Yes
Priority registration: No
Added costs for services: No
LD specialists: Yes
ADHD coaching: NR
ASD specialists: NR
Professional tutors: No
Peer tutors: Yes
Max. hours/wk. for services: Unlimited
How professors are notified of LD/ADHD: By both student and director

General Admissions Information

Office of Admissions: 260-982-5055

Entrance Requirements

Academic units required: 4 English, 2 math, 2 science, 2 science labs, 1 social studies, 1 history, 2 academic electives. **Academic units recommended:** 4 English, 3 math, 3 science, 2 science labs, 2 foreign language, 2 social studies, 2 history, 2 academic electives, 1 computer science, 1 visual/performing arts. High school diploma is required and GED is accepted. SAT or ACT considered if submitted. If ACT, ACT with writing accepted. TOEFL required of all international applicants: minimum paper TOEFL 550 or minimum internet TOEFL 79.

Application deadline: NR
Notification: Rolling starting 9/1
Average GPA: 3.33
ACT Composite middle 50% range: 19-26
SAT Math middle 50% range: 440-550
SAT Critical Reading middle 50% range: 430-550
SAT Writing middle 50% range: 410-530
Graduated top 10% of class: 15
Graduated top 25% of class: 44
Graduated top 50% of class: 82

COLLEGE GRADUATION REQUIREMENTS

Course waivers allowed: No
Course substitutions allowed: No

Additional Information

Environment: This private school was founded in 1889. It has a 124-acre campus.

Student Body
Undergrad enrollment: 1,246
% Women: 52
% Men: 48
% Out-of-state: 12
Cost information
Tuition: $29,650
Room & board: $9,620
Housing Information
University Housing: Yes
Percent living on campus: 75
Greek System
Fraternity: No
Sorority: No
Athletics: Division III

University of Indianapolis

1400 East Hanna Avenue, Indianapolis, IN 46227-3697
Phone: 317-788-3216 • Fax: 317-788-3300
E-mail: admissions@uindy.edu • Web: www.uindy.edu
Support: SP • Institution: Private

Programs or Services for Students with Learning Differences

The University of Indianapolis offers a full support system for students with learning disabilities called BUILD (Baccalaureate for University of Indianapolis Learning Disabled). The goal of this program is to help students with learning disabilities reach their academic potential. All students with disabilities at the university have reasonable modifications available to them at no extra charge. The BUILD program offers accommodations significantly more in depth than just minimal requirements. Services are comprehensive, and the staff is knowledgeable about learning disabilities. The basic tenets of this collaboration include: Commitment to an understanding of one's strengths and difficulties, Honesty in academic endeavors, Dedication to one's own academic and personal growth, careful organization of time and information, personal accountability, persistence and hard work towards achieving goals, and utilization of all support offered at the University.

Admission Information for Students with Learning Differences

College entrance tests required: Yes
Interview required: Yes
Essay required: No
Additional Application Required for LD/ADHD/ASD: NR
What documentation required for LD: Psycho ed evaluation to include: relevant historical info, instructional interventions, related services, age diagnosed, objective data (aptitude, achievement, info processing), test scores (standard, percentile and grade equivalents) and describe functional limitations.
With general application: Yes if requested as part of Structured Program application
To receive services after enrolling: Yes
What documentation required for ADHD: Diagnosis based on DSM-V; history of behaviors impairing functioning in academic setting; diagnostic interview; history of symptoms; evidence of ongoing behaviors.
With general application: Yes if requested as part of Structured Program application
To receive services after enrolling: Yes
What documentation required for ASD: Psycho ed evaluation
With general application: NR
To receive services after enrolling: Yes
LD/ADHD/ASD documentation submitted to: BUILD
ASD Specific Program: NR
Special Ed. HS course work accepted: No
Specific course requirements of all applicants: Yes
Separate application required: Yes
Total # of students receiving LD/ADHD/ASD services: 80
Acceptance into program means acceptance into college: Students must be admitted by the university and then admitted to BUILD. If not accepted by admissions, a committee confers.

Admissions

Admission to the BUILD program occurs after a student has been accepted to the university. Students with LD must meet the university admissions requirements. However, consideration is given for individual strengths and weaknesses. The student must submit the following to the Office of Admissions: university application for admission, high school transcript, SAT or ACT scores. The student must submit the following to the BUILD Program: current documentation regarding I.Q. scores, reading and math proficiency level, primary learning style, and major learning difficulty. After BUILD reviews the information, interviews will be arranged for those applicants being considered for final selection into the BUILD Program. Acceptance into BUILD is determined by the program director.

Additional Information

All students and staff of the BUILD program are members of a unique educational community whose goal is to access each student's potential for success. Such a goal requires tremendous individual and cooperative effort on the part of each member of this community. The BUILD program supports self-advocacy. Students are expected to function independently as mature, responsible adults in fulfilling academic requirements and attaining their scholastic and personal goals. Students are expected to attend all class sessions and interact with professors. BUILD tutorial sessions are to support student academic endeavors. However, tutors will assist students, review class information, discern main concepts, set goals and recommend skills to reach goals. Students are expected to attend each tutorial session having already attempted homework and reading assignments. Tutors will be available to help explain unclear concepts; however, students are encouraged to meet frequently with professors.

General Support Services Information

Contact Information

Name of program or department: Baccalaureate for University of Indianapolis Learning Disabled (BUILD)
Telephone: 317-788-3536
Fax: 317-788-3585

Accommodations or Services For Students With Learning Differences

Accommodations are decided upon an individual basis after a thorough review of appropriate, current documentation. The accommodations requested must be supported through the documentation provided and must be logically linked to the current impact of the condition on academic functioning.

Allowed in exams
Calculator: Yes
Dictionary: Yes
Computer: Yes
Spellchecker: Yes
Extended test time: Yes
Scribes: Yes
Proctors: Yes
Oral exams: Yes
Note-takers: No
Services for students with LD: Yes
Services for students with ADHD: Yes
Services for students with ASD: Yes
Distraction-reduced environment: Yes
Tape recording in class: Yes
Audio book: NR
Electronic texts: No
Kurzweil Reader: Yes
Other assistive technology: Yes
Priority registration: No
Added costs for services: Yes
LD specialists: Yes
ADHD coaching: NR
ASD specialists: NR
Professional tutors: 25
Peer tutors: No
Max. hours/wk. for services: Unlimited
How professors are notified of LD/ADHD: By both student and director

General Admissions Information

Office of Admissions: 317-788-3216

Entrance Requirements

Academic units required: 4 English, 3 math, 2 science, 1 science labs, 2 foreign language, 2 social studies, 1 history, 3 academic electives, 1 computer science, 2 visual/performing arts. **Academic units recommended:** 4 English, 3 math, 3 science, 2 science labs, 3 foreign language, 2 social studies, 1 history, 3 academic electives, 1 computer science, 2 visual/performing arts. High school diploma is required and GED is accepted. SAT or ACT required. If ACT, ACT with writing accepted. TOEFL required of all international applicants: minimum paper TOEFL 500.

Application deadline: 8/20
Notification: Rolling starting 9/1
Average GPA: 3.42
ACT Composite middle 50% range: 19-25
SAT Math middle 50% range: 460-570
SAT Critical Reading middle 50% range: 450-560
SAT Writing middle 50% range: 440-550
Graduated top 10% of class: 27
Graduated top 25% of class: 56
Graduated top 50% of class: 88

COLLEGE GRADUATION REQUIREMENTS

Course waivers allowed: No
Course substitutions allowed: Yes
In what course: Modern language requirements

Additional Information

Environment: This private school, affiliated with the Methodist Church, was founded in 1902. It has a 65-acre campus.

Student Body
Undergrad enrollment: 4,205
% Women: 68
% Men: 32
% Out-of-state: 9
Cost information
Tuition: $23,590
Room & board: $9,090
Housing Information
University Housing: Yes
Percent living on campus: 35
Greek System
Fraternity: No
Sorority: No
Athletics: Division II

UNIVERSITY OF NOTRE DAME

220 Main Building, Notre Dame, IN 46556
Phone: 574-631-7505 • Fax: 574-631-8865
E-mail: admissions@nd.edu • Web: www.nd.edu
Support: S • Institution: Private

PROGRAMS OR SERVICES FOR STUDENTS WITH LEARNING DIFFERENCES

It is the mission of Disability Services to ensure that Notre Dame students with disabilities have access to the programs and facilities of the university. Disability Services is committed to forming partnerships with students to share the responsibility of meeting individual needs. At the University of Notre Dame, students with disabilities may use a variety of services intended to reduce the effects that a disability may have on their educational experience. Services do not lower course standards or alter essential degree requirements, but instead give students an equal opportunity to demonstrate their academic abilities. Students can initiate a request for services by registering with Disability Services and providing information that documents the disability. Individual assistance is provided in selecting the services that will provide access to the academic programs and facilities of the university.

ADMISSION INFORMATION FOR STUDENTS WITH LEARNING DIFFERENCES

College entrance test required: Yes
Interview required: No
Essay required: Yes
Additional Application Required for LD/ADHD/ASD: NR
What documentation required for LD: Psycho ed evaluation
With general application: No
To receive services after enrolling: Yes
What documentation required for ADHD: Psycho ed evaluation
With general application: No
To receive services after enrolling: Yes
What documentation required for ASD: Psycho ed evaluation
With general application: NR
To receive services after enrolling: Yes
LD/ADHD/ASD documentation submitted to: Disability Services
ASD Specific Program: NR
Special Ed. HS course work accepted: No
Specific course requirements of all applicants: No
Separate application required for program services: No
Total # of students receiving LD/ADHD/ASD services: 500
Acceptance into program means acceptance into college: NR

ADMISSIONS

Notre Dame will use the highest ACT composite score from a single testing date. The writing portion of the ACT is not required. Both the previous SAT and redesigned SAT are acceptable. The essay portion of the redesigned SAT is not required, and UND will superscore the SAT. The university will not superscore sub-scores from the current SAT with the redesigned SAT.Essays are the most enjoyable part of the application reading process that helps UND learn about important decisions you've made, adventures you've survived, lessons you've learned, family traditions you've experienced, challenges you've faced, embarrassing moments you've overcome. Interviews are not offered.

ADDITIONAL INFORMATION

Services for students with learning disabilities or Attention Deficit Disorder include taped textbooks, note-takers, exam modifications, assistance with developing time management skills and learning strategies, and screening and referral for diagnostic testing. Students may substitute American Sign Language for Foreign Language requirement. Tutors are available for all students from other resources. There is also a Writing Center for all students. Academic adjustments are modifications to how a student meets the academic requirements of a course or academic program. These modifications do not lower academic standards, but rather give a qualified student equal access to the educational opportunities of the University.

General Support Services Information

Contact Information
Name of program or department: Disability Services
Telephone: 574-631-7141
Fax: NR
Website: NR

Accommodations or Services For Students With Learning Differences

Accommodations are decided upon an individual basis after a thorough review of appropriate, current documentation. The accommodations requests must be supported through the documentation provided and must be logically linked to the current impact of the condition on academic functioning.

Allowed in exams
Calculator: NR
Dictionary: NR
Computer: Yes
Spellchecker: NR
Extended test time: Yes
Scribes: Yes
Proctors: Yes
Oral exams: Yes
Note-takers: Yes
Support services for students with LD: Yes
Support services for students with ADHD: Yes
Support services for students with ASD: Yes
Distraction-reduced environment: Yes
Tape recording in class: Yes
Electronic texts: NR
Kurzweil reader: Yes
Audio books: NR
Other assistive technology: NR
Priority registration: Yes
Added costs of services: NR
LD specialists: Yes
ADHD coaching: NR
ASD specialists: NR
Professional tutors: No
Peer tutors: Yes
Max. hours/wk. for services: NR
How professors are notified of student approved accommodations: Student

General Admissions Information

Office of Admissions: 574-631-7505

Entrance Requirements

Academic units required: 4 English, 3 math, 2 science, 2 science labs, 2 foreign language, 2 history, 3 academic electives. **Academic units recommended:** 4 English, 4 math, 4 science, 2 science labs, 4 foreign language, 4 history. High school diploma is required and GED is not accepted. SAT or ACT required. If ACT, ACT with writing accepted. TOEFL required of all international applicants: minimum paper TOEFL 560 or minimum internet TOEFL 100.

Application deadline: 1/1
Notification: 4/10
Average GPA: NR
ACT Composite middle 50% range: 32-34
SAT Math middle 50% range: 680-770
SAT Critical Reading middle 50% range: 670-760
SAT Writing middle 50% range: 650-750
Graduate top 10% of class: 91
Graduated top 25% of class: 98
Graduated top 50% of class: 100

COLLEGE GRADUATION REQUIREMENTS

Course waivers allowed: NR
Course substitutions allowed: NR

Additional Information

Environment: This private school, affiliated with the Roman Catholic Church, was founded in 1842. It has a 1250-acre campus.

Student Body
Undergrad enrollment: 8,462
% Women: 48
% Men: 52
% Out-of-state: 92
Cost information
Tuition: $47,422
Room & board: $13,846
Housing Information
University Housing: Yes
Percent living on campus: 79
Greek System
Fraternity: No
Sorority: No
Athletics: Division I

University of Saint Francis (IN)

2701 Spring Street, Fort Wayne, IN 46808
Phone: 260-399-8065 • Fax: 260-399-8161
E-mail: admis@sf.edu • Web: www.sf.edu
Support: CS • Institution type: 4-year private

Programs or Services for Students with Learning Differences

Student Academic Support Services (SASS) provides reasonable academic accommodations for students with diagnosed and documented disabilities. Students are self-advocates and develop skills to become independent learners. SASS provides accommodations to ensure students have access to the college environment. Students are encouraged to meet with the Director of SASS prior to the start of the semester to discuss accommodations available to provide the most opportunity for the student as the semester begins. SASS offers coordinated services to students with documentation but no formal program is available.

Admission Information for Students with Learning Differences

College entrance tests required: ACT or SAT
Interview required: No
Essay required: Not due to disability but may be for other admissions requirements
Additional Application Required for LD/ADHD/ASD: NR
What documentation required for LD: The most recent psychological evaluation and the most recent individual education plan.
With general application: NR
To receive services after enrolling: Yes
What documentation required for ADHD: Yes
With general application: NR
To receive services after enrolling: Psycho ed evaluation
What documentation required for ASD: Psycho ed evaluation
With general application: NR
To receive services after enrolling: Yes
LD/ADHD/ASD documentation submitted to: Academic Support Services
ASD Specific Program: NR
Special Ed. HS course work accepted: No
Specific course requirements of all applicants: Nothing based on disability
Separate application required: No
Total # of students receiving LD/ADHD/ASD services: Varies by semester
Acceptance into program means acceptance into college: Students must be admitted and enrolled in the university first and then request services. Coordinated services are offered; not a specific LD/ADHD program.

Admissions

High school students wishing to be directly admitted to USF must meet the criteria listed below. As a Franciscan institution, the college believes education should be available to everybody. There are a few things to keep in mind when applying: Applicants should have a 2.3 GPA on a 4.0 scale; earn a combined SAT score of 1000+ on the reading and math sections or earn an ACT composite score of 21+. As a Franciscan institution St Francis believes in getting to know an applicant as an individual and making their admissions decision carefully and thoughtfully. Students who may not meet all criteria are still evaluated for acceptance upon receipt of an essay.

Additional Information

Skills developing courses are offered based on need as determined standardized test scores. All university students are encouraged to access available tutoring; both peer and on-line tutoring are available. Disability accommodation are determined after documentation evaluation and student intake interview. Some regular accommodation include but are not limited to: distraction reduced testing environment, extended time, note-taking assistance, books in alternative formats, reading of exams, and others as determined on a case by case basis. Students are encouraged to meet with Assistant Director (or designee) weekly or as needed for assistance with organization, time management, and other study skills beneficial in college.

General Support Services Information

Contact Information
Name of program or department: Student Success and Academic Advising Center
Telephone: 260-339-8065
Fax: 260-339-8161

Accommodations or Services For Students With Learning Differences

Accommodations are decided upon an individual basis after a thorough review of appropriate, current documentation. The accommodations requested must be supported through the documentation provided and must be logically linked to the current impact of the condition on academic functioning.

Allowed in exams (When supported through documentation, determined on a case by case basis)
Calculator: Yes
Dictionary: Yes
Computer: Yes
Spellchecker: Yes
Extended test time: Yes
Scribes: Yes
Proctors: Yes
Oral exams: Yes
Note-takers: Yes
Services for students with LD: Yes
Services for students with ADHD: Yes
Services for students with ASD: Yes
Distraction-reduced environment: Yes
Tape recording in class: Yes, when student is present in class
Audio book: NR
Electronic texts: As available
Accommodations for students with ADHD: Yes, based on documentation
Kurzweil Reader: Yes
Other assistive technology: Yes
Priority registration: No
Added costs for services: No
LD specialists: No
ADHD coaching: NR
ASD specialists: NR
Professional tutors: Yes
Peer tutors: Yes
Max. hours/wk. for services: Predominantly during business hours but no limit per student per week.
How professors are notified of LD/ADHD: Confidential student summary latter delivered by student

General Admissions Information

Office of Admissions: 260-399-8000

Entrance Requirements

Academic units required: 4 English, 3 math, 2 science, 2 social studies, 1 history, 1 academic electives. **Academic units recommended:** 4 English, 4 math, 3 science, 3 social studies, 1 history, 4 academic electives, SAT or ACT required. If ACT, ACT with writing accepted. TOEFL required of all international applicants: minimum paper TOEFL 550 or minimum internet TOEFL 80.

Application deadline: NR
Notification: Rolling starting 8/1
Average GPA: 3.34
ACT Composite middle 50% range: 18-24
SAT Math middle 50% range: 430-540
SAT Critical Reading middle 50% range: 430-530
SAT Writing middle 50% range: 420-530
Graduated top 10% of class: 17
Graduated top 25% of class: 47
Graduated top 50% of class: 78

COLLEGE GRADUATION REQUIREMENTS

Course waivers allowed: Yes, in some courses
Course substitutions allowed: Yes, in some courses

Additional Information

Environment: The 70-acre campus is located west of Fort Wayne.

Student Body
Undergrad enrollment: 1,804
% Women: 71
% Men: 29
% Out-of-state: 9

Cost information
Tuition: $29,630
Room & board: $9,084

Housing Information
University Housing: Yes
Percent living on campus: 22

Greek System
Fraternity: NR
Sorority: NR
Athletics: NAIA

University of Southern Indiana

8600 University Boulevard, Evansville, IN 47712
Phone: 812-464-1765 • Fax: 812-465-7154
E-mail: enroll@usi.edu • Web: www.usi.edu
Support: S • Institution: Public

Programs or Services for Students with Learning Differences

Counseling Center staff provide resources to assist students with disabilities so they can participate in educational programming. This is accomplished by offering student support and advocacy, being available for student and faculty consultation, and providing specific accommodation resources. Students must have a professionally diagnosed disability to qualify for use disability resources.

Admission Information for Students with Learning Differences

College entrance test required: Yes
Interview required: Not Applicable
Essay required: Not Applicable
Additional Application Required for LD/ADHD/ASD: Not Applicable
What documentation required for LD: Psycho ed evaluation. Testing older than three ears may not be accepted.
With general application: Not Applicable
To receive services after enrolling: Not Applicable
What documentation required for ADHD: Psycho ed evaluation with complete diagnostic report or diagnostic narrative. Testing older than three years may not be accepted.
With general application: Not Applicable
To receive services after enrolling: Not Applicable
What documentation required for ASD: Psychological evaluation is preferred. Documentation from any qualified professional that meets requirements on website is accepted.
With general application: Not Applicable
To receive services after enrolling: Not Applicable
LD/ADHD/ASD documentation submitted to: Disability Resources
ASD Specific Program: NR
Special Ed. HS course work accepted: NR
Specific course requirements of all applicants: Yes
Separate application required for program services: Yes
Total # of students receiving LD/ADHD/ASD services: NR
Acceptance into program means acceptance into college: Not Applicable

Admissions

Admissions criteria are the same for all students; however, the admissions office will always work with students on an individual basis if needed. In general, students with a 3.6 GPA or higher are admitted with honors. Students with a 2.0–3.5 GPA are admitted in good standing, and students with a GPA below a 2.0 are accepted conditionally. The conditional admissions procedure is for new freshmen who earned below a 2.0 in English, math, science, and social studies. The following are required for those admitted conditionally: freshman seminar; 2.0 GPA; registration through the University Division rather than a specific major; enrollment in no more than 12 credit hours. ACT/SAT scores are used for placement purposes.

Additional Information

In order to use resources for a disability, professional documentation of a disability attached to the university's Verification of Disability form must be provided by the student. Skills classes are offered in basic grammar, algebra review, reading, and study skills. Credit is given for the hours, but the grades are Pass/No Pass. There are no paid note-takers, but special supplies and copy services are provided at no charge to allow the students to get copies of other students'notes. Other services include: assistance obtaining alternative format textbooks; test accommodations; and advocacy and counseling. Services and accommodations are available for undergraduate and graduate students.

General Support Services Information

Contact Information
Name of program or department: Disability Resources
Telephone: 812-464-1961
Fax: 812-464-1935
Website: http://www.usi.edu/disabilities

Accommodations or Services For Students With Learning Differences

Accommodations are decided upon an individual basis after a thorough review of appropriate, current documentation. The accommodations requests must be supported through the documentation provided and must be logically linked to the current impact of the condition on academic functioning.

Allowed in exams
Calculator: Yes
Dictionary: Yes
Computer: Yes
Spellchecker: Yes
Extended test time: Yes
Scribes: Yes
Proctors: Yes
Oral exams: Yes
Note-takers: Yes
Support services for students with LD: Yes
Support services for students with ADHD: Yes
Support services for students with ASD: Yes
Distraction-reduced environment: Yes
Tape recording in class: Yes
Electronic texts: Yes
Kurzweil reader: NR
Audio books: Yes
Other assistive technology: Yes
Priority registration: Yes
Added costs of services: No
LD specialists: NR
ADHD coaching: No
ASD specialists: Yes
Professional tutors: No
Peer tutors: Yes
Max. hours/wk. for services: NR
How professors are notified of student approved accommodations: By student

General Admissions Information

Office of Admissions: 812-464-1765

Entrance Requirements

Academic units recommended: 4 English, 4 math, 2 science, 2 foreign language, 2 social studies, 2 history, 2 academic electives. High school diploma is required and GED is accepted. SAT or ACT required. If ACT, ACT with writing recommended. TOEFL required of all international applicants: minimum paper TOEFL 525 or minimum internet TOEFL 71.

Application deadline: 8/15
Notification: NR
Average GPA: 3.27
ACT Composite middle 50% range: 19-24
SAT Math middle 50% range: 450-550
SAT Critical Reading middle 50% range: 440-550
SAT Writing middle 50% range: 420-525
Graduate top 10% of class: 12
Graduated top 25% of class: 33
Graduated top 50% of class: 71

COLLEGE GRADUATION REQUIREMENTS

Course waivers allowed: No
In what course: Substitutions are sometimes approved.
Course substitutions allowed: NR
In what course: Substitutions are only granted after committee review.

Additional Information

Environment: This public school was founded in 1965. It has a 330-acre campus.

Student Body
Undergrad enrollment: 8,130
% Women: 61
% Men: 39
% Out-of-state: 11

Cost information
In-state Tuition: $6,838
Out-of-state Tuition: $16,619
Room & board: $8,176

Housing Information
University Housing: Yes
Percent living on campus: 31

Greek System
Fraternity: Yes
Sorority: Yes
Athletics: Division II

Vincennes University

1002 North First Street, Vincennes, IN 47591
Phone: 800-742-9198 • Fax: 812-888-8888
E-mail: vuadmit@vinu.edu • Web: www.vinu.edu
Support: SP • Institution type: 4-year public

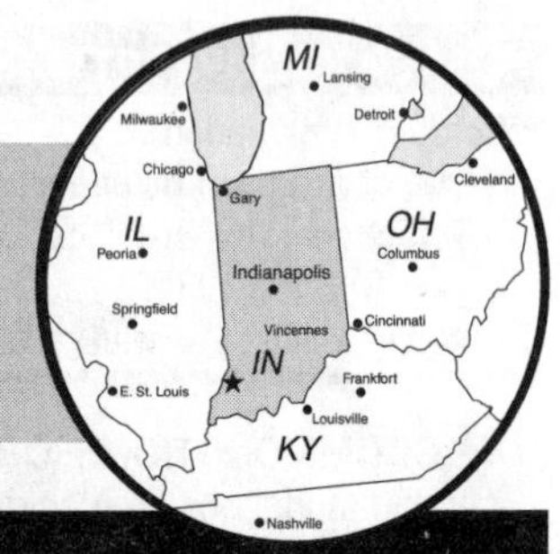

Programs or Services for Students with Learning Differences

Students Transition into Education Program (STEP) is a LD support program for students in the mainstream. Students' strengths are the emphasis; compensatory techniques rather than remediation are the thrust. STEP is designed to develop unique abilities, achieve academic potential, and develop a sense of self-worth and skills to function and learn independently. Students take four semesters in STEP I–IV: The course teaches requisite social, study, and self-awareness skills and serves as a support group. The curriculum is practical and emphasizes active thinking, independent learning, student accountability, and the acquisition of specific strategies proven to improve academic performance. STEP I addresses self-advocacy, compensatory techniques, coping, adaptation, stress, and socialization; II emphasizes socialization and metacognitive skills; III further develops social skills and solidifies study skills; IV emphasizes career planning, job-search, and social skills, and includes the STEP retreat. COPE Student Support Services (seperate from STEP) is a Trio Program requiring that the student meet one of three requirements: first generation college student, low income, or disabled.

Admission Information for Students with Learning Differences

College entrance tests required: No
Interview required: No
Essay required: No
Additional Application Required for LD/ADHD/ASD: NR
What documentation required for LD: Psycho ed evaluation to include: relevant historical info, instructional interventions, related services, age diagnosed, objective data (aptitude, achievement, info processing), test scores (standard, percentile and grade equivalents) and describe functional limitations.
With general application: Yes if requested as part of Structured Program application
To receive services after enrolling: Yes
What documentation required for ADHD: Diagnosis based on DSM-V; history of behaviors impairing functioning in academic setting; diagnostic interview; history of symptoms; evidence of ongoing behaviors.
With general application: Yes if requested as part of Structured Program application
To receive services after enrolling: Yes
What documentation required for ASD: Psycho ed evaluation
With general application: NR
To receive services after enrolling: Yes
LD/ADHD/ASD documentation submitted to: STEP
ASD Specific Program: NR
Special Ed. HS course work accepted: Yes
Specific course requirements of all applicants: NR
Separate application required: Yes
Total # of students receiving LD/ADHD/ASD services: 100–120
Acceptance into program means acceptance into college: Students must apply separately to the university and STEP or Cope. Students will be accepted to the university first and then to the STEP or Cope.

Admissions

Students with learning disabilities must submit the general application. SAT and ACT scores are not required for other majors, however they are used for placement in course levels appropriate to a student's academic preparation. If students have not taken the SAT or ACT, they will be required to take a placement test before they can register for classes. Students with learning disabilities must apply separately to STEP: Send the STEP application; psychological evaluation; and letters of recommendation from LD specialists, counselors, or teachers. The transcript is less important and recommendations more important. Admission is based on determination of student eligibility, available funding, and space remaining. Early application is important. Students applying to Cope should apply separately to the university prior to applying to STEP.

Additional Information

STEP benefits include an LD specialist for individualized tutoring/remediation, professional/peer tutoring, specialized remedial and/or support classes, weekly academic monitoring, special classes, reduced class load, auditing class before taking test modifications, papers rather than tests, and alternative ways to demonstrate competency. STEP does not exempt students from classes, class requirements, or provide taped books and note-takers. Cope provides individual counselor to assist with needs; tutoring; progress reports; academic advising; appropriate accommodations; academic support groups; and workshops on study skills, test anxiety, self-esteem, and interview skills. The Study Skills Center is open to all students.

General Support Services Information

Contact Information
Name of program or department: Students Transition into Education Program (STEP)
Telephone: 812-888-4212
Fax: 812-888-5531

Accommodations or Services For Students With Learning Differences

Accommodations are decided upon an individual basis after a thorough review of appropriate, current documentation. The accommodations requested must be supported through the documentation provided and must be logically linked to the current impact of the condition on academic functioning.

Allowed in exams
Calculator: Yes
Dictionary: Yes
Computer: Yes
Spellchecker: Yes
Extended test time: Yes
Scribes: Yes
Proctors: Yes
Oral exams: Yes
Note-takers: Yes
Services for students with LD: Yes
Services for students with ADHD: Yes
Services for students with ASD: Yes
Distraction-reduced environment: Yes
Tape recording in class: Yes
Audio book: NR
Electronic texts: Yes
Kurzweil Reader: Yes
Other assistive technology: Yes
Priority registration: Yes
Added costs for services: $425 per semester
LD specialists: Yes
ADHD coaching: NR
ASD specialists: NR
Professional tutors: 10–20
Peer tutors: 25–45
Max. hours/wk. for services: N/A
How professors are notified of LD/ADHD: By both student and director

General Admissions Information

Office of Admission: 800-742-9198

Entrance Requirements:
ACT/SAT not required for admission.

Application deadline: NR
Notification: NR
Average GPA: NR
ACT Composite middle 50% range: NR-NR
SAT Math middle 50% range: NR-NR
SAT Critical Reading middle 50% range: NR-NR
SAT Writing middle 50% range: NR-NR
Graduated top 10% of class: NR
Graduated top 25% of class: NR
Graduated top 50% of class: NR

COLLEGE GRADUATION REQUIREMENTS

Course waivers allowed: NR
Course substitutions allowed: NR

Additional Information

Environment: The school is located on 95 acres 45 minutes south of Terre Haute.

Student Body
Undergrad enrollment: 19,250
% Women: 45
% Men: 55
% Out-of-state: 36
Cost information
In-state tuition: $4,752
Out-of-state tuition: $11,812
Room & board: NR
Housing Information
University Housing: Yes
Percent living on campus: 44
Greek System
Fraternity: Yes
Sorority: Yes
Athletics: NJCAA

DRAKE UNIVERSITY

2507 University Avenue, Des Moines, IA 50311-4505
Phone: 515-271-3181 • Fax: 515-271-2831
E-mail: admission@drake.edu • Web: www.drake.edu
Support: S • Institution: Private

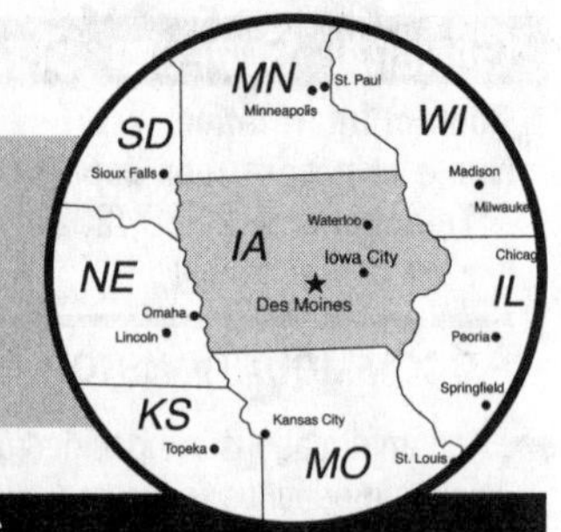

PROGRAMS OR SERVICES FOR STUDENTS WITH LEARNING DIFFERENCES

The Student Disability Services' purpose is to facilitate and enhance the opportunity for students with any type of disability to successfully complete their postsecondary education. The SDS is committed to enriching the academic experience of Drake students with disabilities through individualized assessment of accommodations and resource needs. To initiate a request for services, students should contact the SDS. An appointment will be made with a staff member to begin the registration process. Students are encouraged to meet with a SDS counselor each semester to identify accommodations that are needed. It is the students' responsibility to self-identify that they have a learning disability; to provide professional documentation of their disability; and to request the accommodations that they need. The SDS office maintains a collection of information on disabilities, and there are many sources on the instruction and evaluation of students with disabilities. SDS encourages faculty, staff, and students to contact the office if they are interested in this type of information.

ADMISSION INFORMATION FOR STUDENTS WITH LEARNING DIFFERENCES

College entrance test required: Yes
Interview required: No
Essay required: No
Additional Application Required for LD/ADHD/ASD: NR
What documentation required for LD: Psycho ed evaluation to include: relevant historical info, instructional interventions, related services, age diagnosed, objective data (aptitude, achievement, info processing), test scores (standard, percentile and grade equivalents) and describe functional limitations.
With general application: No
To receive services after enrolling: Yes
What documentation required for ADHD: Diagnosis based on DSM-V; history of behaviors impairing functioning in academic setting; diagnostic interview; history of symptoms; evidence of ongoing behaviors.
With general application: No
To receive services after enrolling: Yes
What documentation required for ASD: Psycho ed evaluation
With general application: NR
To receive services after enrolling: Yes
LD/ADHD/ASD documentation submitted to: Student Disability Services
ASD Specific Program: NR
Special Ed. HS course work accepted: Yes
Specific course requirements of all applicants: Yes
Separate application required for program services: No
Total # of students receiving LD/ADHD/ASD services: NR
Acceptance into program means acceptance into college: Student must be admitted and enrolled in the university first and then reviewed for LD services.

ADMISSIONS

There is no special admission process for students with learning disabilities. All applicants are expected to meet the same admission criteria, including 16 academic college-prep courses with a minimum of 4 years of English, 2 years of math, 2 years of science, 2 years of social studies, 1 year of history, and 2 years of a foreign language; 21 ACT or 970 SAT; and a minimum of a 2.0 GPA. Students must be admitted and enrolled in the university prior to seeking accommodations or services for a learning disability.

ADDITIONAL INFORMATION

The SDS can offer students appointments at the pre-admission and pre-enrollment stages; review of Drake's policies and procedures regarding students with disabilities; identification and coordination of classroom accommodations; assessment of service needs; note-takers, scribes, and readers; referral to appropriate campus resources; advocacy and liaison with the university community; and training on the use of assistive technology. Services provided by the SDS do not lower any course standards or change any requirements of a particular degree. The services are intended to allow equal access and provide an opportunity for students with disabilities to demonstrate their abilities.

General Support Services Information

Contact Information
Name of program or department: Student Disability Services
Telephone: 515-271-1835
Fax: NR

Accommodations or Services For Students With Learning Differences

Accommodations are decided upon an individual basis after a thorough review of appropriate, current documentation. The accommodations requests must be supported through the documentation provided and must be logically linked to the current impact of the condition on academic functioning.

Allowed in exams
Calculator: Yes
Dictionary: Yes
Computer: Yes
Spellchecker: Yes
Extended test time: Yes
Scribes: Yes
Proctors: Yes
Oral exams: Yes
Note-takers: Yes
Support services for students with LD: Yes
Support services for students with ADHD: Yes
Support services for students with ASD: Yes
Distraction-reduced environment: Yes
Tape recording in class: Yes
Electronic texts: Yes
Kurzweil reader: Yes
Audio books: NR
Other assistive technology: Yes
Priority registration: No
Added costs of services: No
LD specialists: No
ADHD coaching: NR
ASD specialists: NR
Professional tutors: No
Peer tutors: Yes
Max. hours/wk. for services: Unlimited
How professors are notified of student approved accommodations: By student

General Admissions Information

Office of Admissions: 515-271-3181

Entrance Requirements

Academic units recommended: 4 English, 3 math, 2 science, 1 science labs, 2 foreign language, 4 social studies. High school diploma is required and GED is accepted. SAT or ACT required. If ACT, ACT with writing accepted. TOEFL required of all international applicants: minimum paper TOEFL 530 or minimum internet TOEFL 71.

Application deadline: NR
Notification: Rolling starting 10/15
Average GPA: 3.71
ACT Composite middle 50% range: 24-30
SAT Math middle 50% range: 550-690
SAT Critical Reading middle 50% range: 520-670
SAT Writing middle 50% range: NR-NR
Graduate top 10% of class: 37
Graduated top 25% of class: 69
Graduated top 50% of class: 93

COLLEGE GRADUATION REQUIREMENTS

Course waivers allowed: NR
Course substitutions allowed: NR

Additional Information

Environment: This private school was founded in 1881. It has a 150-acre campus.

Student Body
Undergrad enrollment: 3,338
% Women: 56
% Men: 44
% Out-of-state: 69

Cost information
Tuition: $35,060
Room & board: $9,850

Housing Information
University Housing: Yes
Percent living on campus: 70

Greek System
Fraternity: Yes
Sorority: Yes
Athletics: Division I

Grand View University

1200 Grandview Avenue, Des Moines, IA 50316-1599
Phone: 515-263-2810 • Fax: 515-263-2974
E-mail: admissions@GrandView.edu • Web: www.admissions.grandview.edu
Support: CS • Institution: Private

Programs or Services for Students with Learning Differences

Accommodations are decided upon an individual basis after a thorough review of appropriate, current documentation. The accommodations requests must be supported through the documentation provided and must be logically linked to the current impact of the condition on academic functioning.

Admission Information for Students with Learning Differences

College entrance tests required: Yes
Interview required: No
Essay required: No
Additional Application Required for LD/ADHD/ASD: NR
What documentation required for LD: Verification of learning disabilities by licensed psychologist required.
With general application: NR
To receive services after enrolling: Yes
What documentation required for ADHD: Verification of learning disabilities by licensed psychologist required.
With general application: NR
To receive services after enrolling: Yes
What documentation required for ASD: Verification of learning disabilities by licensed psychologist required.
With general application: NR
To receive services after enrolling: Yes
Receive services after enrolling (ASD): Yes
LD/ADHD/ASD documentation submitted to: Academic Success
ASD Specific Program: NR
Special Ed. HS course work accepted: Yes
Specific course requirements of all applicants: No
Separate application required: No
Total # of students receiving LD/ADHD/ASD services: 15
Acceptance into program means acceptance into college: Students must be admitted and enrolled prior to requesting services.

Admissions

There is no special admissions process for students with LD and ADHD. There is a freshman academy for students who do not have sufficient preparation to undertake college work but show potential for success in college. Grand View has a personalized admission and enrollment policy. Consideration may be given to: class rank and test scores; quality of high school curriculum completed; co-curricular achievement; and maturity and seriousness of purpose as displayed through church, community, school, work, and family activities. Students planning to attend Grand View University are encouraged to pursue a college-preparatory course of study in high school. It is recommended that students complete: Four years of English, three years of math, three years of science, three years of social science and two years of foreign language. Admission to a particular program or major may be governed by different standards.

Additional Information

Academic Enrichment Center provides resources which complement classroom instruction enabling students to optimize their academic experience. Students can receive help with reading comprehension, study skills, organizational skills, developing a personal management plan, test-taking strategies, writing skills, personalized instruction in math, and peer tutoring. The Career Center provides services, resources, and educational opportunities by assisting students in developing, evaluating, initiating, and implementing personal career and life plans. Faculty members serve as academic advisors. Core courses can have substitutions options. Other services or accommodations offered for students with appropriate documentation include the use of calculators, computers, or spellcheckers; extended testing time; scribes; proctors; oral exams; note-takers; a distraction-free environment for taking tests; tape-recording of lectures; and services for students with ADHD.

GENERAL SUPPORT SERVICES INFORMATION

Contact Information
Name of program or department: Academic Enrichment Center
Telephone: 515-263-2971
Fax: 515-263-2824

ACCOMMODATIONS OR SERVICES FOR STUDENTS WITH LEARNING DIFFERENCES

Accomodations are granted on an individual basis after a thorough review of appropriate, current documentation. Students are encouraged to contact Joy Brandt at 515-263-2971 or jbrandt@grandview.edu to review policies and procedures, request accommodations, and to develop an accommodation plan.

Allowed in exams
Calculator: Yes
Dictionary: Yes
Computer: Yes
Spellchecker: Yes
Extended test time: Yes
Scribes: Yes
Proctors: Yes
Oral exams: Yes
Note-takers: Yes
Services for students with LD: Yes
Services for students with ADHD: Yes
Services for students with ASD: Yes
Distraction-reduced environment: Yes
Tape recording in class: Yes
Audio book: NR
Electronic texts: Yes
Kurzweil Reader: Yes
Other assistive technology: Yes
Priority registration: Yes
Added costs for services: No
LD specialists: Yes
ADHD coaching: NR
ASD specialists: NR
Professional tutors: NR
Peer tutors: Yes
Max. hours/wk. for services: Unlimited
How professors are notified of LD/ADHD: By student in collaboration with the director

GENERAL ADMISSIONS INFORMATION

Office of Admissions: 515-263-2810

ENTRANCE REQUIREMENTS

Academic units recommended: 4 English, 3 math, 3 science, 2 foreign language, 3 social studies. High school diploma is required and GED is accepted. SAT or ACT required. If ACT, ACT with writing recommended. TOEFL required of all international applicants: minimum paper TOEFL 550.

Application deadline: 8/15
Notification: Rolling starting 9/15
Average GPA: 3.2
ACT Composite middle 50% range: 19-23
SAT Math middle 50% range: 400-480
SAT Critical Reading middle 50% range: 380-450
SAT Writing middle 50% range: 360-440
Graduated top 10% of class: 15
Graduated top 25% of class: 33
Graduated top 50% of class: 64

COLLEGE GRADUATION REQUIREMENTS

Course waivers allowed: No
Course substitutions allowed: Yes
In what course: Substitutions/options vary and must qualify.

ADDITIONAL INFORMATION

Environment: This private school, affiliated with the Lutheran Church, was founded in 1896. It has a 35-acre campus.

Student Body
Undergrad enrollment: 2,096
% Women: 58
% Men: 42
% Out-of-state: 13

Cost information
Tuition: $24,800
Room & board: $8,690

Housing Information
University Housing: Yes
Percent living on campus: 37

Greek System
Fraternity: No
Sorority: No
Athletics: NAIA

Grinnell College

1103 Park Street, Grinnell, IA 50112-1690
Phone: 641-269-3600 • Fax: 641-269-4800
E-mail: askgrin@grinnell.edu • Web: www.grinnell.edu
Support: S • Institution: Private

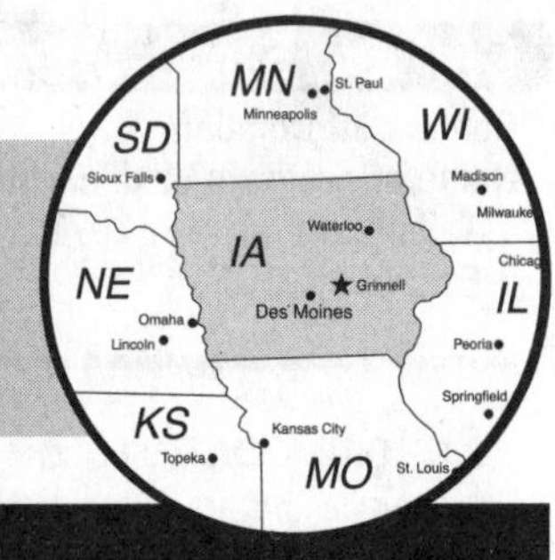

Programs or Services for Students with Learning Differences

Grinnell College is dedicated to educating young people whose achievements show a high level of intellectual capacity, initiative, and maturity. Every year, this highly qualified group of students includes people with learning disabilities. Grinnell is committed to providing academic adjustments and reasonable accommodations for students with disabilities who are otherwise qualified for admission. Many of Grinnell's characteristics make it a positive educational environment for all students: an open curriculum, small classes, easy access to professors, and openness to diversity. The Academic Advising Office coordinates services for students with LD, arranges for academic accommodations, acts as a liaison to the faculty, and offers personal, individual assistance. Once students are admitted and they accept the offer of admission, Grinnell likes to plan with them for any reasonable accommodation they will need in order to enjoy a successful experience. Students have the responsibility to make their needs known. The most important factors for college success are seeking help early and learning to be self-advocates. Students are encouraged to notify the Academic Advising Office about their needs before they arrive for the first semester. For planning purposes, sooner is always better.

Admission Information for Students with Learning Differences

College entrance test required: NR
Interview required: No
Essay required: Not Applicable
Additional Application Required for LD/ADHD/ASD: NR
What documentation required for LD: See documentation guidelines: https://www.grinnell.edu/about/offices-services/academic-advising/disability-services#documentation
With general application: Not Applicable
To receive services after enrolling: Yes
What documentation required for ADHD: See documentation guidelines: https://www.grinnell.edu/about/offices-services/academic-advising/disability-services#documentation
With general application: Not Applicable
To receive services after enrolling: Yes
What documentation required for ASD: See documentation guidelines: https://www.grinnell.edu/about/offices-services/academic-advising/disability-services#documentation
With general application: Not Applicable
To receive services after enrolling: Yes
LD/ADHD/ASD documentation submitted to: Disability Resources
ASD Specific Program: NR
Special Ed. HS course work accepted: NR
Specific course requirements of all applicants: NR
Separate application required for program services: Yes
Total # of students receiving LD/ADHD/ASD services: NR
Acceptance into program means acceptance into college: Not Applicable

Admissions

Admission to Grinnell is highly selective, and while there is no single factor that guarantees admission, it helps to have taken a challenging, balanced high school curriculum. The recommended secondary school program is: 4 years of English, 4 years of mathematics (at least through pre-calculus), 3 years of social studies, 3 years of lab science, and 3 years of a foreign language. First-year applicants may interview beginning in February of their junior years and until mid-December of their senior years. Interviews are not required for admission, and applicants may only interview once. ACT/SAT required.

Additional Information

Students need to meet with their faculty advisor and the Academic Advising Office to plan for their individual needs. The Academic Advising Office coordinates services for students and arranges for academic accommodations and assists students with LD to develop effective academic strategies. The Reading Lab helps students improve reading speed, vocabulary, and reading comprehension. The Science Learning Center and Math Lab provide instruction for students who want to strengthen their background in these areas. Individual tutoring and supplemental instruction is available in all subjects at no charge. Additional resources include referral for LD testing, reduced course loads, extended time for exams, personal counseling, an books in auditory (electronic) format. Skills classes for credit are offered in reading, writing, math and science.

General Support Services Information

Contact Information
Name of program or department: Disability Resources
Telephone: 6412693702
Fax: NR
Website: https://www.grinnell.edu/about/offices-services/accessibility-disability

Accommodations or Services For Students With Learning Differences

Accommodations are decided upon an individual basis after a thorough review of appropriate, current documentation. The accommodations requests must be supported through the documentation provided and must be logically linked to the current impact of the condition on academic functioning.

Allowed in exams
Calculator: Yes
Dictionary: Yes
Computer: Yes
Spellchecker: Yes
Extended test time: Yes
Scribes: Yes
Proctors: Yes
Oral exams: Yes
Note-takers: Yes
Support services for students with LD: Yes
Support services for students with ADHD: Yes
Support services for students with ASD: Yes
Distraction-reduced environment: Yes
Tape recording in class: Yes
Electronic texts: Yes
Kurzweil reader: NR
Audio books: Yes
Other assistive technology: Yes
Priority registration: Yes
Added costs of services: No
LD specialists: Yes
ADHD coaching: Yes
ASD specialists: Not Applicable
Professional tutors: No
Peer tutors: Yes
Max. hours/wk. for services: NR
How professors are notified of student approved accommodations: By both student and director

General Admissions Information

Office of Admissions: 641-269-3600

Entrance Requirements

Academic units recommended: 4 English, 4 math, 3 science, 3 science labs, 3 foreign language, 3 social studies, 3 history. High school diploma is required and GED is accepted. SAT or ACT required. If ACT, ACT with writing accepted. TOEFL required of all international applicants.

Application deadline: 1/15
Notification: Rolling starting 4/1
Average GPA: NR
ACT Composite middle 50% range: 30-33
SAT Math middle 50% range: 660-770
SAT Critical Reading middle 50% range: 640-740
SAT Writing middle 50% range: NR-NR
Graduate top 10% of class: 81
Graduated top 25% of class: 96
Graduated top 50% of class: 100

COLLEGE GRADUATION REQUIREMENTS

Course waivers allowed: No
Course substitutions allowed: No

Additional Information

Environment: This private school was founded in 1846. It has a 120-acre campus.

Student Body
Undergrad enrollment: 1,705
% Women: 55
% Men: 45
% Out-of-state: 88

Cost information
Tuition: $48,322
Room & board: $11,980

Housing Information
University Housing: Yes
Percent living on campus: 88

Greek System
Fraternity: No
Sorority: No
Athletics: Division III

Indian Hills Community College

623 Indian Hills Drive, Building 12, Ottumwa, IA 52501
Phone: 800-726-2585 • Fax: 641-683-5263
E-mail: disabilityservices@indianhills.edu • Web: www.indianhills.edu
Support: S • Institution type: 2-year Public

Programs or Services for Students with Learning Differences

Disability Services provides academic and physical accommodations and services for students with disabilities based on documented needs. Students with a documented learning disability or attention deficit hyperactivity disorder must provide current documentation which has been completed by a qualified professional such as a school counselor, physician, psychologist, or other health care professional. Statements must include: a description of the disability, a statement of how the disability prohibits one or more major life activities and is a barrier to the student's full participation in the program, and a description of the specific accommodations which might be provided. All requests for accommodations should be made as far in advance as possible. Students enrolling in credit programs are encouraged to make their requests for accommodations at the time they are applying for admission and preferably no later than 6 weeks prior to the beginning of each academic term. All student requests are dealt with in a confidential manner.

Admission Information for Students with Learning Differences

College entrance tests required: Compass
Interview required: No
Essay required: No
Additional Application Required for LD/ADHD/ASD: NR
What documentation required for LD: Psycho ed evaluation to include: relevant historical info, instructional interventions, related services, age diagnosed, objective data (aptitude, achievement, info processing), test scores (standard, percentile and grade equivalents) and describe functional limitations.
With general application: No
To receive services after enrolling: Yes
What documentation required for ADHD: Diagnosis based on DSM-V; history of behaviors impairing functioning in academic setting; diagnostic interview; history of symptoms; evidence of ongoing behaviors.
With general application: No
To receive services after enrolling: Yes
What documentation required for ASD: Psycho ed evaluation
With general application: NR
To receive services after enrolling: Yes
LD/ADHD/ASD documentation submitted to: Disability Services
ASD Specific Program: NR
Special Ed. HS course work accepted: Yes
Specific course requirements of all applicants: NR
Separate application required: No
Total # of students receiving LD/ADHD/ASD services: N/A
Acceptance into program means acceptance into college: Students must be admitted and enrolled in the college first and then request services.

Admissions

Indian Hills Community College is an "open-door" institution. All students must present a high school diploma or GED or must earn one while enrolled in order to receive a college degree. ACT/SAT tests are not required, and there are no specific high school courses required for admission.

Additional Information

Skill–Building courses are available through the Indian Hills Academic Success Center. These courses are designed to increase confidence and abilities in subjects where students may need some extra help. Courses are offered to help improve reading, writing, and math. The COMPASS test can help measure skill levels in reading, writing, and math, giving students the information they need when deciding whether they are ready for an advanced course or need to refresh knowledge by taking a Skill–Building course. The Professional Tutors in the Academic Success Center are equipped to help with math, writing, and reading courses. Assistance is available on a walk–in basis. Student Peer Tutors are available in most subjects for no charge, but this service is limited to the availability of tutors. While every effort is made to secure tutors, the Academic Success Center cannot guarantee that tutors can be arranged for every subject. Student peer tutoring sessions can be held during the day, evenings, or weekends, and may be individual or group sessions.

General Support Services Information

Contact Information
Name of program or department: Disability Services
Telephone: 641-683-5749
Fax: 641-683-5263

Accommodations or Services For Students With Learning Differences

Accommodations are decided upon an individual basis after a thorough review of appropriate, current documentation. The accommodations requested must be supported through the documentation provided and must be logically linked to the current impact of the condition on academic functioning. The following accommodations are determined on a case-by-case basis.

Allowed in exams
Calculator: Yes
Dictionary: Yes
Computer: Yes
Spellchecker: Yes
Extended test time: Yes
Scribes: Yes
Proctors: Yes
Oral exams: Yes
Note-takers: Yes
Services for students with LD: Yes
Services for students with ADHD: Yes
Services for students with ASD: Yes
Distraction-reduced environment: Yes
Tape recording in class: Yes
Audio book: NR
Electronic texts: Yes
Kurzweil Reader: Yes
Other assistive technology: Yes
Priority registration: No
Added costs for services: No
LD specialists: No
ADHD coaching: NR
ASD specialists: NR
Professional tutors: 9
Peer tutors: 20–30
Max. hours/wk. for services: Unlimited
How professors are notified of LD/ADHD: Disability Services shares accommodatiions

General Admissions Information

Office of Admission: 800-726-2585

Entrance Requirements

Academic units recommended: 4 English, 3 math, 3 science, 4 social studies, 2 foreign language. Some majors require specific math courses. Open admissions. High school diploma or GED equivalent accepted.

Application deadline: NR
Notification: NR
Average GPA: NR
ACT Composite middle 50% range: NR-NR
SAT Math middle 50% range: NR-NR
SAT Critical Reading middle 50% range: NR-NR
SAT Writing middle 50% range: NR-NR
Graduated top 10% of class: NR
Graduated top 25% of class: NR
Graduated top 50% of class: NR

COLLEGE GRADUATION REQUIREMENTS

Course waivers allowed: No
Course substitutions allowed: No

Additional Information

Environment: The college is located on 400 acres about 2 hours east of Iowa City or west of Des Moines.

Student Body
Undergrad enrollment: 8,065
% Women: 56
% Men: 44
% Out-of-state: 5

Cost information
In-state tuition: $4,800
Out-of-state tuition: $7,600
Room & board: $5,460

Housing Information
University Housing: NR
Percent living on campus: NR

Greek System
Fraternity: NR
Sorority: NR
Athletics: NR

Iowa State University

100 Enrollment Services Center, Ames, IA 50011-2011
Phone: 515-294-5836 • Fax: 515-294-2592
E-mail: admissions@iastate.edu • Web: www.iastate.edu
Support: CS • Institution: Public

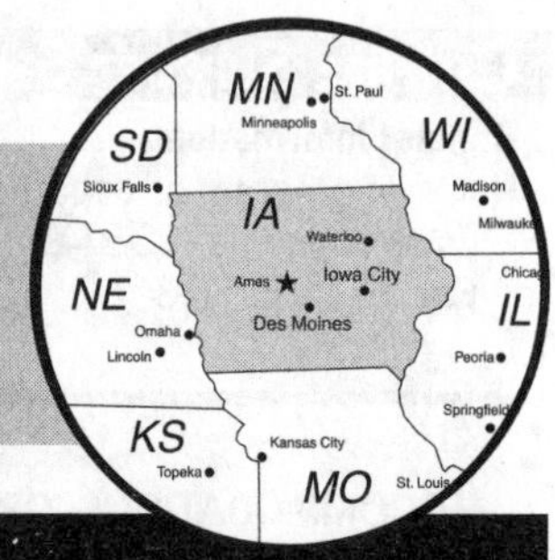

Programs or Services for Students with Learning Differences

ISU is committed to providing equal opportunities and facilitating the personal growth and development of all students. Staff from the Student Disability Resources Office assists students with issues relating to the documented disability. A thorough review of most current LD evaluation and documentation is completed to determine the possible accommodations needed. SDR staff also offers assistance in articulating needs to faculty and staff, and may serve as a liaison in student/staff negotiations. Documentation should include current diagnosis, functional limitations, and relevant information about the student and examiner's qualifications; behavioral observation of the way students present themselves, verbal and nonverbal communication, interpersonal skills and behavior during testing; a narrative describing developmental and educational history; a description of the effect of the disability on learning is required. Recommendations concerning possible accommodations is welcomed.

Admission Information for Students with Learning Differences

College entrance test required: Yes
Interview required: N/A
Essay required: No
Additional Application Required for LD/ADHD/ASD: NR
What documentation required for LD: Psych Ed evaluation
With general application: No
To receive services after enrolling: Yes
What documentation required for ADHD: Psych Ed evaluation
With general application: No
To receive services after enrolling: Yes
What documentation required for ASD: Psycho ed evaluation
With general application: NR
To receive services after enrolling: Yes
LD/ADHD/ASD documentation submitted to: Student Disability Resources
ASD Specific Program: NR
Special Ed. HS course work accepted: NR
Specific course requirements of all applicants: Yes
Separate application required for program services: NR
Total # of students receiving LD/ADHD/ASD services: NR
Acceptance into program means acceptance into college: NR

Admissions

Students with documented disabilities are held to Iowa State's regular freshman admission requirements (listed below). Those who feel their academic record does not accurately reflect their ability to succeed and, therefore, wish to be considered for admission on an individual basis are asked to submit additional documentation explaining their circumstances. This documentation should include: 1) A letter from the applicant requesting special consideration. This letter should identify the disability and include a description of how the disability impacts academic performance. 2) Information pertaining to accommodations and services used in high school or the most recent educational setting. 3) A recent typed report prepared by a qualified provider that contains a specific current diagnosis, treatment history, and existing functional impact as it relates to one's participation at Iowa State University. Please refer to www.dso.iastate.edu/dr/ for more details on documentation requirements. Freshman applicants are considered for admission based on their Regent Admission Index (RAI) score which is based on the following equation: RAI = (2 x ACT composite score) + (1 x percentile high school rank) + (20 x high school grade point average) + (5 x number of years of high school courses completed in the core subject areas) Students who achieve at least a 245 RAI and who meet the University's minimum high school course requirements will automatically qualify for admission. Students who achieve less than a 245 RAI will be considered for admission on an individual basis.

Additional Information

The Academic Learning Lab is a "learning-how-to-learn" center designed to help all students. Counselors work one-on-one to evaluate and identify problem study habits and devise strategies to improve them. The Learning Lab and Tutoring and Student Support Services are in one area called the Academic Success Center (ASC). ASC coordinates services including counseling, teaching reading, and study skills, and provides a list of tutors. The Writing Center is available to all students. The LD specialist provides information about readers, note-takers, and scribes. Peer Supplemental Instruction (SI) is an academic assistance program attached to very difficult courses. SI leaders attend classes and conduct biweekly sessions to help students learn and study the course material. Student Support Services is a federally funded program for students with LD and others qualified to receive academic support in the form of free tutoring and skill-building workshops.

General Support Services Information

Contact Information
Name of program or department: Student Disability Resources
Telephone: 5152947220
Fax: NR

Accommodations or Services For Students With Learning Differences

Accommodations are decided upon an individual basis after a thorough review of appropriate, current documentation. The accommodations requests must be supported through the documentation provided and must be logically linked to the current impact of the condition on academic functioning.

Allowed in exams
Calculator: Yes
Dictionary: Yes
Computer: Yes
Spellchecker: Yes
Extended test time: Yes
Scribes: Yes
Proctors: Yes
Oral exams: No
Note-takers: Yes
Support services for students with LD: Yes
Support services for students with ADHD: Yes
Support services for students with ASD: Yes
Distraction-reduced environment: Yes
Tape recording in class: Yes
Electronic texts: Yes
Kurzweil reader: Yes
Audio books: NR
Other assistive technology: Yes
Priority registration: Yes
Added costs of services: No
LD specialists: Yes
ADHD coaching: NR
ASD specialists: NR
Professional tutors: No
Peer tutors: NR
Max. hours/wk. for services: NR
How professors are notified of student approved accommodations: By student

General Admissions Information

Office of Admissions: 515-294-5836

Entrance Requirements

Academic units required: 4 English, 3 math, 3 science, 2 science labs, 2 foreign language, 2 social studies, **Academic units recommended:** 4 English, 4 math, 4 science, 3 science labs, 3 foreign language, 4 social studies. High school diploma is required and GED is accepted. SAT or ACT required. If ACT, ACT with writing accepted. TOEFL required of all international applicants: minimum paper TOEFL 530 or minimum internet TOEFL 71.

Application deadline: NR
Notification: NR
Average GPA: 3.5
ACT Composite middle 50% range: 22-28
SAT Math middle 50% range: 500-640
SAT Critical Reading middle 50% range: 460-620
SAT Writing middle 50% range: NR-NR
Graduate top 10% of class: 22
Graduated top 25% of class: 54
Graduated top 50% of class: 91

COLLEGE GRADUATION REQUIREMENTS

Course waivers allowed: NR
Course substitutions allowed: NR

Additional Information

Environment: This public school was founded in 1858. It has a 1794-acre campus.

Student Body
Undergrad enrollment: 30,034
% Women: 43
% Men: 57
% Out-of-state: 31

Cost information
In-state Tuition: $6,648
Out-of-state Tuition: $19,768
Room & board: $8,070

Housing Information
University Housing: Yes
Percent living on campus: 41

Greek System
Fraternity: Yes
Sorority: Yes
Athletics: Division I

Loras College

1450 Alta Vista, Dubuque, IA 52004-0178
Phone: 800-245-6727 • Fax: 563-588-7119
E-mail: admissions@loras.edu • Web: www.loras.edu
Support: SP • Institution: Private

Programs or Services for Students with Learning Differences

Loras College provides a supportive, comprehensive program for the motivated individual with a learning disability or AD/HD. Students can be successful in Loras' competitive environment if they have had adequate preparation, are willing to work with program staff, and take responsibility for their own learning. The Enhanced Program staff has three specialists to serve as guides and advocates, encouraging and supporting students to become independent learners. Students with LD or ADHD who are enrolled in college-preparatory courses in high school are the most appropriate candidates for the Loras program. Often high school students who previously were in support programs, but are not currently receiving services, are excellent candidates for the program if they have taken challenging classes.

Admission Information for Students with Learning Differences

College entrance test required: Yes
Interview required: Yes
Essay required: 5
Additional Application Required for LD/ADHD/ASD: NR
What documentation required for LD: Diagnostic evaluation, including IQ and achievement testing.
With general application: No
To receive services after enrolling: Yes
What documentation required for ADHD: Diagnostic evaluation, including IQ and achievement testing.
With general application: No
To receive services after enrolling: Yes
What documentation required for ASD: Diagnostic evaluation, including IQ and achievement testing.
With general application: No
To receive services after enrolling: Yes
LD/ADHD/ASD documentation submitted to: Support program/services
ASD Specific Program: Yes
Special Ed. HS course work accepted: Yes
Specific course requirements of all applicants: Yes
Separate application required for program services: Yes
Total # of students receiving LD services: 50-60
Acceptance into program means acceptance into college: Separate application required after students has enrolled.

Admissions

Students interested in the Enhanced Program should apply simultaneously to the College and the Enhanced Program. The Enhanced Program Application and current documentation should be submitted to the Lynch Learning Center. After the materials are reviewed, appropriate candidates will be invited for an official interview with an Lynch Learning Center staff member. All application materials for the Enhanced Program must be received by December 15, the priority application date. Students interested in the Enhanced Program are encouraged to apply early in their senior year to prevent delays in the process.

Additional Information

The Lynch Learning Center offers three levels of service for students with diagnosed disabilities. The Autism Specific Program is designed to help students with ASD thrive emotionally, academically and socially. Through the four-year program, students work directly with Lynch Learning Center staff members designated as Certified Autism Specialists. Students enrolled in the program will meet weekly with their Lynch Learning Center coach and attend weekly study table sessions and bi-monthly mentoring meetings. Students hone skills ranging from self-advocacy and organization to stress management and socialization in addition to specialized career prep including one-on-one résumé and cover letter counseling, job shadowing, and internship opportunities. To help acclimate students to campus, students have the opportunity to participate in a five-day summer transition program. The Enhanced Program is a comprehensive program designed to provide additional support for students with a primary disability of LD/ADHD, but students with other disabilities will be considered. The Enhanced Program includes a two-credit class, Learning Strategies, both semesters of the first-year; a weekly meeting with an Lynch Learning Center staff member; and peer tutors, as needed.

General Support Services Information

Contact Information
Name of program or department: Enhanced Program
Telephone: 563-588-7134
Fax: 563-588-7071

Accommodations or Services For Students With Learning Differences

Accommodations are decided upon an individual basis after a thorough review of appropriate, current documentation. The accommodations requests must be supported through the documentation provided and must be logically linked to the current impact of the condition on academic functioning.

Allowed in exams
Calculator: Yes
Dictionary: Yes
Computer: Yes
Spellchecker: Yes
Extended test time: Yes
Scribes: Yes
Proctors: Yes
Oral exams: Yes
Note-takers: Yes
Services for students with LD: Yes
Services for students with ADHD: Yes
Services for students with ASD: Yes
Distraction-reduced environment: Yes
Tape recording in class: Yes
Audio book: Yes
Electronic texts: NR
Kurzweil Reader: Yes
Other assistive technology: Yes
Priority registration: No
Added costs of services: Yes
LD specialists: Yes
ADHD coaching: NR
ASD specialists: Yes
Professional tutors: NR
Peer tutors: Yes
Max. hours/wk. for services: NR
How professors are notified of student approved accommodations: Student

General Admissions Information

Office of Admissions: 563-588-7236

Entrance Requirements

Academic units recommended: 4 English, 4 math, 3 science, 2 science labs, 3 social studies, 2 academic electives. High school diploma is required and GED is accepted. SAT or ACT required. If ACT, ACT with writing accepted. TOEFL required of all international applicants: minimum paper TOEFL 550 or minimum internet TOEFL 79.

Application deadline: NR
Notification: NR
Average GPA: 3.46
ACT Composite middle 50% range: 21-26
SAT Math middle 50% range: 460-570
SAT Critical Reading middle 50% range: 460-540
SAT Writing middle 50% range: NR-NR
Graduated top 10% of class: 22
Graduated top 25% of class: 46
Graduated top 50% of class: 77

COLLEGE GRADUATION REQUIREMENTS

Course waivers allowed: Yes
In what course: Waivers are possible for math after attempting math course work; no foreign language waivers are necessary because there is no foreign language requirement.
Course substitutions allowed: N/A

Additional Information

Environment: This private school, affiliated with the Roman Catholic Church, was founded in 1839. It has a 60-acre campus.

Student Body
Undergrad enrollment: 1,462
% Women: 48
% Men: 52
% Out-of-state: 62

Cost information
Tuition: $30,065
Room & board: $7,697

Housing Information
University Housing: Yes
Percent living on campus: 68

Greek System
Fraternity: Yes
Sorority: Yes
Athletics: Division III

MORNINGSIDE COLLEGE

1501 Morningside Avenue, Sioux City, IA 51106-1751
Phone: 712-274-5511 • Fax: 712-274-5101
E-mail: mscadm@morningside.edu • Web: www.morningside.edu
Support: CS • Institution: Private

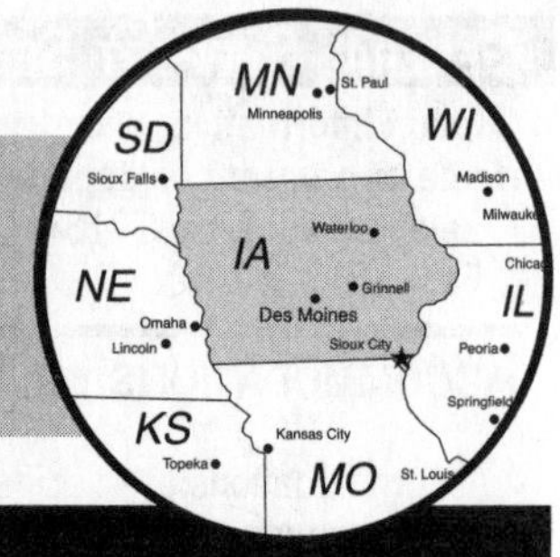

PROGRAMS OR SERVICES FOR STUDENTS WITH LEARNING DIFFERENCES

Students with learning disabilities can and do succeed in college. However, students with different learning styles may need assistance in order to be truly successful students. Morningside College will require supportive data to verify that a disability exists. These may include, but are not necessarily limited to, the following: high school records; specific plans recommended by qualified professionals and/or consultants; and satisfactory medical determination as required.

ADMISSION INFORMATION FOR STUDENTS WITH LEARNING DIFFERENCES

College entrance tests required: Yes
Interview required: Yes
Essay required: Yes
Additional Application Required for LD/ADHD/ASD: NR
What documentation required for LD: Psycho ed evaluation to include: relevant historical info, instructional interventions, related services, age diagnosed, objective data (aptitude, achievement, info processing), test scores (standard, percentile and grade equivalents) and describe functional limitations.
With general application: No
To receive services after enrolling: Yes
What documentation required for ADHD: Diagnosis based on DSM-V; history of behaviors impairing functioning in academic setting; diagnostic interview; history of symptoms; evidence of ongoing behaviors.
With general application: No
To receive services after enrolling: Yes
What documentation required for ASD: Psycho ed evaluation
With general application: NR
To receive services after enrolling: Yes
LD/ADHD/ASD documentation submitted to: Associate Dean for Academic Affairs
ASD Specific Program: NR
Special Ed. HS course work accepted: N/A
Specific course requirements of all applicants: NR
Separate application required: Yes
Total # of students receiving LD/ADHD/ASD services: 15–20
Acceptance into program means acceptance into college: Students must be admitted and enrolled prior to requesting services.

ADMISSIONS

Morningside's selective admissions program is based on the following criteria: class rank, college preparatory course work, GPA, ACT or SAT, essay participation recommended but not required, character, and personal abilities. Students with ACT of 20 or SAT of 1410, and either ranked in the top half of their class or have achieved a high school GPA of 2.5 meet the academic standards for admissions. First-year students who have been out of high school more than 5 years are not required to submit ACT or SAT test scores but are required to take math and/or English placement assessments. Students who have not completed high school may be admitted on the basis of a GED score.

ADDITIONAL INFORMATION

Reasonable accommodations for students might include the following: note-taking, copies of instructor's notes, tape-recording of class, reasonable equipment modification, preferential seating, books on tape, test-taking accommodations, word processor adaptations, and reader service. The Academic Support Center is open to all students. Academic Support Center staff helps students improve or strengthen their academics by providing free assistance in writing techniques. Writing specialists are available to help students with the basics as well as help proficient writers who want assistance for particular writing assignments or projects.. Staff and student tutors are available in the Academic Support Center for students who want help in areas such as accounting, biology, chemistry, economics, history, math, science, religion, and sociology. The Krone Advising Center houses a team of full-time, professional, first-year advisers.

General Support Services Information

Contact Information
Name of program or department: Academic Support Center
Telephone: 800-831-0806, ext. 5388
Fax: 712-274-5358

Accommodations or Services For Students With Learning Differences

Accommodations are decided upon an individual basis after a thorough review of appropriate, current documentation. The accommodations requested must be supported through the documentation provided and must be logically linked to the current impact of the condition on academic functioning.

Allowed in exams
Calculator: Yes
Dictionary: Yes
Computer: Yes
Spellchecker: Yes
Extended test time: Yes
Scribes: Yes
Proctors: Yes
Oral exams: Yes
Note-takers: Yes
Services for students with LD: Yes
Services for students with ADHD: Yes
Services for students with ASD: Yes
Distraction-reduced environment: Yes
Tape recording in class: Yes
Audio book: NR
Electronic texts: Yes
Kurzweil Reader: No
Other assistive technology: No
Priority registration: No
Added costs for services: No
LD specialists: No
ADHD coaching: NR
ASD specialists: NR
Professional tutors: 5–10
Peer tutors: 5–15
Max. hours/wk. for services: Unlimited
How professors are notified of LD/ADHD: Associate Dean

General Admissions Information

Office of Admissions: 712-274-5511

Entrance Requirements

Academic units recommended: 3 English, 2 math, 2 science, 3 social studies. High school diploma is required and GED is accepted. SAT or ACT required. If ACT, ACT with writing accepted. TOEFL required of all international applicants: minimum paper TOEFL 450.

Application deadline: NR
Notification: NR
Average GPA: 3.37
ACT Composite middle 50% range: 20-25
SAT Math middle 50% range: NR-NR
SAT Critical Reading middle 50% range: NR-NR
SAT Writing middle 50% range: NR-NR
Graduated top 10% of class: 15
Graduated top 25% of class: 42
Graduated top 50% of class: 78

COLLEGE GRADUATION REQUIREMENTS

Course waivers allowed: No
Course substitutions allowed: No

Additional Information

Environment: This private school, affiliated with the Methodist Church, was founded in 1894. It has a 68-acre campus.

Student Body
Undergrad enrollment: 1,214
% Women: 54
% Men: 46
% Out-of-state: 32

Cost information
Tuition: $27,620
Room & board: $9,010

Housing Information
University Housing: Yes
Percent living on campus: 64

Greek System
Fraternity: Yes
Sorority: Yes

Athletics: NAIA

Saint Ambrose University

518 West Locust Street, Davenport, IA 52803-2898
Phone: 563-333-6300 • Fax: 563-333-6297
E-mail: admit@sau.edu • Web: www.sau.edu
Support: CS • Institution: Private

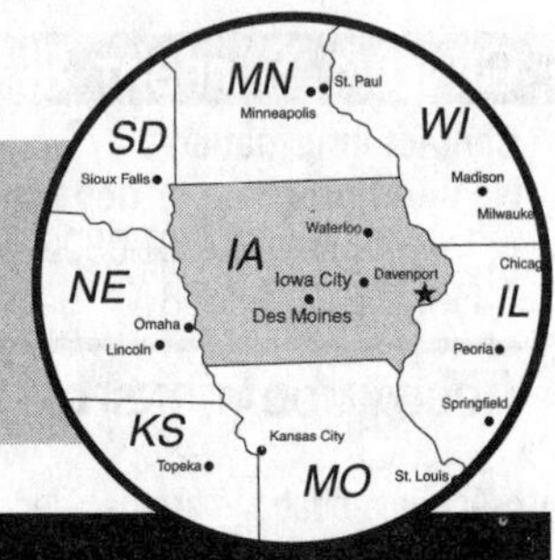

Programs or Services for Students with Learning Differences

Student Disability Services at St. Ambrose University has two primary goals. The first goal is to provide qualified students with disabilities services or reasonable accommodations intended to reduce the effects that a disability may have on their performance in a traditional academic setting. Services do not lower course standards or significantly alter degree requirements, but instead give students a better chance to demonstrate their academic abilities. The second goal of the office is to assist students with disabilities in developing learning strategies to compensate for their disability and to become independent learners. Any student can initiate a request for services by registering with Student Disability Services, and providing information that documents the disability.

Admission Information for Students with Learning Differences

College entrance test required: Yes
Interview required: No
Essay required: Not Applicable
Additional Application Required for LD/ADHD/ASD: Yes
What documentation required for LD: psycho ed evaluation
With general application: No
To receive services after enrolling: Yes
What documentation required for ADHD: documentation sufficient to confirm disability
With general application: No
To receive services after enrolling: Yes
What documentation required for ASD: documentation sufficient to confirm disability, suggest correct score from assessment that measure
With general application: No
To receive services after enrolling: Yes
LD/ADHD/ASD documentation submitted to: Student Disability Services
ASD Specific Program: NR
Special Ed. HS course work accepted: Yes
Specific course requirements of all applicants: NR
Separate application required for program services: Yes
Total # of students receiving LD/ADHD/ASD services: NR
Acceptance into program means acceptance into college: No

Admissions

Students meeting minimum admission requirements are not required to send additional information for admission purposes, but it is helpful in providing effective services. The general admission criteria include minimum ACT 20 or minimum 950 SAT; 2.5 GPA; with specific course requirements. Students who have completed junior year in high school may attend the Summer Transition Program to assess their ability for regular admission. Students who do not meet the criteria are encouraged to contact the Director for additional consideration.

Additional Information

Through Student Disability Services students may have access to the following services: academic advising; advocacy; alternate exam arrangements including extended time, large print, separate testing room, readers, scribes, or use of a computer; books in alternative format; assitive technology; equipment loans; LD specialist to provide one-to-one learning skills instruction; liaison with outside agencies; screening and referral for diagnosis of learning disabilities; and other accommodations to meet appropriate needs. A four-week Summer Transition Program is available for college-bound students with learning disabilities, Asperger's and/or ADHD who have completed their junior year in high school. Students do not have to be admitted to St. Ambrose to participate in this program, and completion of the program does not guarantee admission to St. Ambrose University. Students take either Intro to Psychology or Intro to Sociology, and engage in sessions where they receive instruction on study skills, note-taking, textbook reading, memorization strategies, and test preparation. Additional sessions are also required where students are engaged in informal discussion groups on topics such as rights and responsibilities of students with disabilities, selecting accommodations, understanding their disability, and self-advocacy. Learning disability specialists attend the psych class and assist students in applying learning skills to their course work.

General Support Services Information

Contact Information
Name of program or department: Student Disability Services
Telephone: 563-333-6275
Fax: NR
Website: NR

Accommodations or Services For Students With Learning Differences

Accommodations are decided upon an individual basis after a thorough review of appropriate, current documentation. The accommodations requests must be supported through the documentation provided and must be logically linked to the current impact of the condition on academic functioning.

Allowed in exams
Calculator: Yes
Dictionary: Yes
Computer: Yes
Spellchecker: Yes
Extended test time: Yes
Scribes: Yes
Proctors: Yes
Oral exams: Yes
Note-takers: Yes
Support services for students with LD: Yes
Support services for students with ADHD: Yes
Support services for students with ASD: Yes
Distraction-reduced environment: Yes
Tape recording in class: Yes
Electronic texts: Yes
Kurzweil reader: NR
Audio books: Yes
Other assistive technology: Yes
Priority registration: No
Added costs of services: No
LD specialists: Yes
ADHD coaching: Yes
ASD specialists: Not Applicable
Professional tutors: No
Peer tutors: Yes
Max. hours/wk. for services: 48
How professors are notified of student approved accommodations: By student

General Admissions Information

Office of Admissions: 563-333-6300

Entrance Requirements

Academic units recommended: 4 English, 3 math, 2 science, 2 science labs, 1 foreign language, 1 social studies, 1 history, 4 academic electives. High school diploma is required and GED is accepted. SAT or ACT required. If ACT, ACT with writing accepted. TOEFL required of all international applicants: minimum paper TOEFL 500.

Application deadline: NR
Notification: Rolling starting 10/1
Average GPA: 3.28
ACT Composite middle 50% range: 20-26
SAT Math middle 50% range: NR-NR
SAT Critical Reading middle 50% range: NR-NR
SAT Writing middle 50% range: NR-NR
Graduate top 10% of class: 21
Graduated top 25% of class: 44
Graduated top 50% of class: 74

COLLEGE GRADUATION REQUIREMENTS

Course waivers allowed: No
In what course: NR
Course substitutions allowed: Yes
In what course: Foreign Language

Additional Information

Environment: This private school, affiliated with the Roman Catholic Church, was founded in 1882. It has a 118-acre campus.

Student Body
Undergrad enrollment: 2,794
% Women: 58
% Men: 42
% Out-of-state: 57

Cost information
Tuition: $28,870
Room & board: $9,869
Housing Information
University Housing: Yes
Percent living on campus: 60

Greek System
Fraternity: No
Sorority: No
Athletics: NAIA

UNIVERSITY OF IOWA

107 Calvin Hall, Iowa City, IA 52242
Phone: 319-335-3847 • Fax: 319-333-1535
E-mail: admissions@uiowa.edu • Web: www.uiowa.edu
Support: CS • Institution: Public

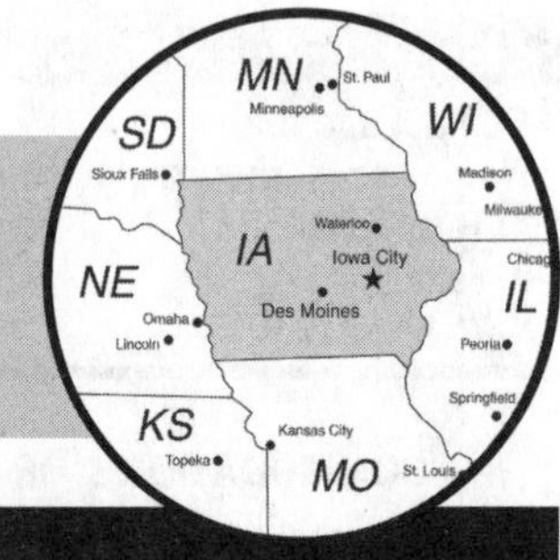

PROGRAMS OR SERVICES FOR STUDENTS WITH LEARNING DIFFERENCES

The mission of LD/ADHD Services in the University of Iowa's Student Disability Services (SDS) is to facilitate individualized academic accommodations for eligible students. Each student has an assigned staff adviser who assists the student in identifying appropriate course accommodations, communmincating classroom needs to faculty, accessing other related services and resources. Students with LD/ADHD who need disability servcies are encouraged to register with SDS as soon as possible. Students are encouraged to schedule an on-campus interview with the LD/ADHD coordinator to learn more about disability services for students with LD-ADHD and about the university.

ADMISSION INFORMATION FOR STUDENTS WITH LEARNING DIFFERENCES

College entrance test required: Yes
Interview required: No
Essay required: No
Additional Application Required for LD/ADHD/ASD: NR
What documentation required for LD: Psycho ed evaluation
With general application: No
To receive services after enrolling: Yes
What documentation required for ADHD: Psycho ed evaluation
With general application: No
To receive services after enrolling: Yes
What documentation required for ASD: Psycho ed evaluation
With general application: NR
To receive services after enrolling: Yes
LD/ADHD/ASD documentation submitted to: Student Disability Services
ASD Specific Program: NR
Special Ed. HS course work accepted: NR
Specific course requirements of all applicants: NR
Separate application required for program services: NR
Total # of students receiving LD/ADHD/ASD services: NR
Acceptance into program means acceptance into college: NR

ADMISSIONS

General admissions require 4 years English, 3 years math (2 yrs of algebra and 1 yr of geeometry), 3 years social studies, 3 years science, (including 1 yr from two of these-biology, chemistry, physics) and 2 years foreign language. Iowa residents must present a Regent Admission Index (RAI) score of 245 or above; residents of other states must present an RAI of 255 or above. RAI combines four factors: ACT or SAT, high school rank, high school cum grade-point average and the number of completed high school core courses. The College of Engineering requires successful completion of the High School Course Requirements, including demonstrated success (As or Bs) in math and science courses; and present ACT math and composite scores of 25 or above and present a Regent Admission Index score of 265 or higher. There is an "individual review" procedure for students who do not meet admission criteria due to a disability. Students must submit a admission application, transcript, and test scores; a letter disclosing the disability and requesting "individual review," describing how the disability affected academic performance and what accommodations and compensation strategies are used to strengthen performance in deficit areas; a description of resources used and a statement explaining why the student may not have completed high school requirements, if applicable; letters from 2 people, not related, who can attest to the applicant's ability to be successful; and a diagnostic report verifying the disability and providing information about both the process and findings of the diagnostic assessment. The report should contain specific recommendations concerning the eligible academic accommodations, including whether the student qualifies for foreign language or math substitutions, and be signed by a licensed professional with the license number.

ADDITIONAL INFORMATION

Students requesting disability-related services from Student Disability Services are required to provide satisfactory evidence of their eligibility for services. Services are determined on a case-by-case basis. They include priority registration for courses, assistance in communicating with faculty and administrators, facilitation of classroom accomodations, alternative examination services, text-to-audio services, counseling referrals, and tutoring referrals.

General Support Services Information

Contact Information
Name of program or department: Student Disability Services
Telephone: 319-335-1462
Fax: 319-335-3973
Website: https://sds.studentlife.uiowa.edu/

Accommodations or Services For Students With Learning Differences

Accommodations are decided upon an individual basis after a thorough review of appropriate, current documentation. The accommodations requests must be supported through the documentation provided and must be logically linked to the current impact of the condition on academic functioning.

Allowed in exams
Calculator: Yes
Dictionary: Yes
Computer: Yes
Spellchecker: Yes
Extended test time: Yes
Scribes: Yes
Proctors: Yes
Oral exams: No
Note-takers: Yes
Support services for students with LD: Yes
Support services for students with ADHD: Yes
Support services for students with ASD: Yes
Distraction-reduced environment: Yes
Tape recording in class: Yes
Electronic texts: Yes
Kurzweil reader: NR
Audio books: Yes
Other assistive technology: Yes
Priority registration: Yes
Added costs of services: Yes
LD specialists: Yes
ADHD coaching: No
ASD specialists: Yes
Professional tutors: No
Peer tutors: NR
Max. hours/wk. for services: NR
How professors are notified of student approved accommodations: By student

General Admissions Information

Office of Admissions: 319-335-3847

Entrance Requirements

Academic units required: 4 English, 3 math, 3 science, 2 foreign language, 3 social studies. **Academic units recommended:** 4 math, 4 foreign language. High school diploma is required and GED is accepted. SAT or ACT required. If ACT, ACT with writing recommended. TOEFL required of all international applicants: minimum paper TOEFL 530 or minimum internet TOEFL 80.

Application deadline: 4/1
Notification: Rolling starting 8/1
Average GPA: 3.66
ACT Composite middle 50% range: 23-28
SAT Math middle 50% range: 540-690
SAT Critical Reading middle 50% range: 460-630
SAT Writing middle 50% range: NR-NR
Graduate top 10% of class: NR
Graduated top 25% of class: NR
Graduated top 50% of class: NR

COLLEGE GRADUATION REQUIREMENTS

Course waivers allowed: No
Course substitutions allowed: Yes
In what course: World Language

Additional Information

Environment: This public school was founded in 1847. It has a 1900-acre campus.

Student Body
Undergrad enrollment: 23,357
% Women: 52
% Men: 48
% Out-of-state: 34

Cost information
In-state Tuition: $8,550
Out-of-state Tuition: $28,638
Room & board: $10,108

Housing Information
University Housing: Yes
Percent living on campus: 26

Greek System
Fraternity: Yes
Sorority: Yes
Athletics: Division I

University of Northern Iowa

1227 West 27th Street, Cedar Falls, IA 50614-0018
Phone: 319-273-2281 • Fax: 319-273-2885
E-mail: admissions@uni.edu • Web: www.uni.edu
Support: S • Institution: Public

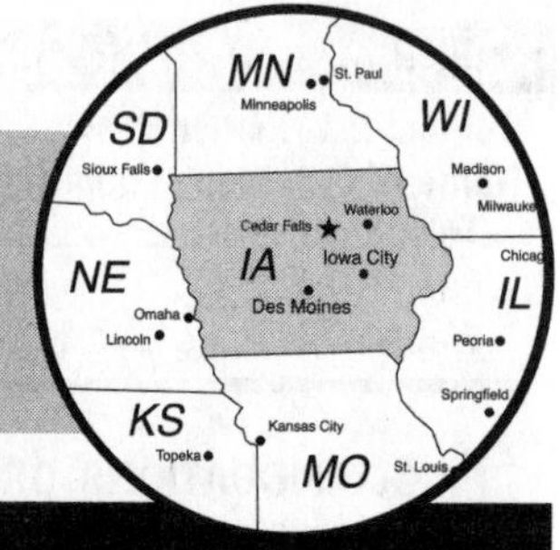

Programs or Services for Students with Learning Differences

Student Disability Services is dedicated to serving the special needs of students at the University of Northern Iowa. Student Disability Services works with students to ensure that all persons with disabilities have access to university activities, programs, and services. Specialized services are provided to enhance the overall academic, career, and personal development of each person with a physical, psychological, or learning disability. Services are available to currently enrolled students, who must apply for services, and provide appropriate documentation to support the accommodation request.

Admission Information for Students with Learning Differences

College entrance test required: Yes
Interview required: No
Essay required: Not Applicable
Additional Application Required for LD/ADHD/ASD: Yes
What documentation required for LD: Students are encouraged to submit a recent psychoeducational evaluation for documentation. If such documentation does not exist, they can submit a letter from their treating physician/psychologist or their most recent IEP/504 Plan.
With general application: No
To receive services after enrolling: Yes
What documentation required for ADHD: A letter from a mental health provider (i.e. psychologist, therapist, counselor), an IEP or 504 plan, or a psychoeducational evaluation.
With general application: No
To receive services after enrolling: Yes
What documentation required for ASD: Students are encouraged to submit a recent psychoeducational evaluation for documentation. If such documentation does not exist, they can submit their most recent IEP/504 Plan.
With general application: No
To receive services after enrolling: Yes
LD/ADHD/ASD documentation submitted to: Student Disability Services
ASD Specific Program: NR
Special Ed. HS course work accepted: No
Specific course requirements of all applicants: Yes
Separate application required for program services: Yes
Total # of students receiving LD/ADHD/ASD services: 119
Acceptance into program means acceptance into college: No

Admissions

There is no special admission process for students with learning disabilities. Students with disabilities are considered for admission on the same basis as all other applicants, and must meet the same academic standards. Students must have 4 years English, 3 years math, 3 years science, 3 years social studies, 2 years academic elective (can be foreign language). The university will accept college-preparatory courses taken through the special education department of the high school. Class rank and either the ACT or the SAT are considered.

Additional Information

Services available include individualized pre-enrollment interview and orientation to disability services; preferred registration; alternative testing arrangements; auxiliary aides. Academic services are available to all students at UNI who wish to receive additional academic support outside of the classroom. The Academic Learning Center provides students with a variety of supportive services that will enhance academic achievement and success. Students may access help in Writing Assistance in any of their classes. Students may schedule a single appointment to work on a specific assignment or a regular appointment to work on a variety of assignments. Assistance with math skills is also available in the Math Lab. Services include 1-to-1 and small group instruction; individual instruction and practice through a variety of self-instructional modes; and review lessons to support the development and practice of concepts/skills taught in math courses. Drop-in hours are available.

General Support Services Information

Contact Information
Name of program or department: Student Disability Services
Telephone: 319-273-2677
Fax: 319-273-7576
Website: www.uni.edu/sds

Accommodations or Services For Students With Learning Differences

Accommodations are decided upon an individual basis after a thorough review of appropriate, current documentation. The accommodations requests must be supported through the documentation provided and must be logically linked to the current impact of the condition on academic functioning.

Allowed in exams
Calculator: Yes
Dictionary: Yes
Computer: Yes
Spellchecker: Yes
Extended test time: Yes
Scribes: Yes
Proctors: Yes
Oral exams: Yes
Note-takers: Yes
Support services for students with LD: Yes
Support services for students with ADHD: Yes
Support services for students with ASD: Yes
Distraction-reduced environment: Yes
Tape recording in class: Yes
Electronic texts: Yes
Kurzweil reader: NR
Audio books: Yes
Other assistive technology: Yes
Priority registration: Yes
Added costs of services: No
LD specialists: No
ADHD coaching: Yes
ASD specialists: Not Applicable
Professional tutors: No
Peer tutors: Yes
Max. hours/wk. for services: 2
How professors are notified of student approved accommodations: By student

General Admissions Information

Office of Admissions: 319-273-2281

Entrance Requirements

Academic units required: 4 English, 3 math, 3 science, 3 social studies, 2 academic electives. **Academic units recommended:** 1 science labs, 2 foreign language. High school diploma is required and GED is accepted. SAT or ACT required. If ACT, ACT with writing accepted. TOEFL required of all international applicants: minimum paper TOEFL 550 or minimum internet TOEFL 79.

Application deadline: 8/15
Notification: NR
Average GPA: 3.5
ACT Composite middle 50% range: 20-25
SAT Math middle 50% range: NR-NR
SAT Critical Reading middle 50% range: NR-NR
SAT Writing middle 50% range: NR-NR
Graduate top 10% of class: 18
Graduated top 25% of class: 48
Graduated top 50% of class: 84

COLLEGE GRADUATION REQUIREMENTS

Course waivers allowed: No
In what course: NR
Course substitutions allowed: Yes
In what course: Depending on student need, UNI offers both foreign language and math course substitutions.

Additional Information

Environment: This public school was founded in 1876. It has a 910-acre campus.

Student Body
Undergrad enrollment: 10,169
% Women: 57
% Men: 43
% Out-of-state: 5.9

Cost information
In-state Tuition: $6,648
Out-of-state Tuition: $16,836
Room & board: $8,320

Housing Information
University Housing: Yes
Percent living on campus: 74

Greek System
Fraternity: Yes
Sorority: Yes
Athletics: Division I

WALDORF COLLEGE

106 South 6th Street, Forest City, IA 50436
Phone: 641-585-8112 • Fax: 641-585-8125
E-mail: admissions@waldorf.edu • Web: www.waldorf.edu
Support: SP • Institution: Private

PROGRAMS OR SERVICES FOR STUDENTS WITH LEARNING DIFFERENCES

The Learning Disabilities Program (LDP) fully integrates students with learning disabilities into mainstream courses. The program features a special orientation session, academic advising, tutoring, specialized services, and developmental courses. The LDP takes a holistic approach to address the social, emotional, and academic needs of the person with a learning disability. The LDP is learning strategies based. Students are accepted as individuals with the potential to succeed in college. The students have the opportunity to participate fully in college life and to experience academic success. Students benefit from a 12:1 student/instructor ratio; each student is provided a laptop computer to use while in attendance. To be eligible for the Waldorf LDP, students must meet the following criteria: have psychological and achievement test results, preferably no more than 2 years old; have been involved with intervention on some level during high school; and exhibit a positive attitude and potential for good college success when appropriate learning strategies and coping skills are used.

ADMISSION INFORMATION FOR STUDENTS WITH LEARNING DIFFERENCES

College entrance tests required: Yes
Interview required: Maybe
Essay required: NR
Additional Application Required for LD/ADHD/ASD: NR
What documentation required for LD: Psycho ed evaluation to include: relevant historical info, instructional interventions, related services, age diagnosed, objective data (aptitude, achievement, info processing), test scores (standard, percentile and grade equivalents) and describe functional limitations.
With general application: Yes if requested as part of Structured Program application
To receive services after enrolling: Yes
What documentation required for ADHD: Diagnosis based on DSM-V; history of behaviors impairing functioning in academic setting; diagnostic interview; history of symptoms; evidence of ongoing behaviors.
With general application: Yes if requested as part of Structured Program application
To receive services after enrolling: Yes
What documentation required for ASD: Psycho ed evaluation
With general application: Yes
To receive services after enrolling: Yes
LD/ADHD/ASD documentation submitted to: Learning Disability Program
ASD Specific Program: NR
Special Ed. HS course work accepted: Yes
Specific course requirements of all applicants: NR
Separate application required: NR
Total # of students receiving LD/ADHD/ASD services: 30
Acceptance into program means acceptance into college: Students are either admitted directly into the college and then must request LDP or are reviewed by Admissions and Academic Progress committee and a decision is made on acceptance.

ADMISSIONS

There is no special admissions process for students with learning disabilities. LDP students go through the regular admission procedures. General admission requirements include 4 years of English, 2 years of math and science; ACT 18 minimum; and a 2.56 GPA. There is a probationary admission for some students not meeting the regular criteria. These students will be asked to participate in a special interview, either by phone or in person, in order to be considered for LDP. The number of spaces in LDP is limited.

ADDITIONAL INFORMATION

Services in the LDP include the following: specialized academic advising regarding schedules and academic classes; priority time and scheduling with the learning specialist; counseling services available upon referral or request; special orientation for LDP students at the beginning of the academic year, tutor time above and beyond the regular services available to all students; academic coaches who work one-on-one with students; specialized materials and/or technology for LD students; priority registration for developmental and study skills classes; as-needed academic testing with a learning-style emphasis; instructor notification of learning disability; and academic progress monitoring that will be shared with the student, and parents if permission is given. There are skills classes for credit in study skills, math/pre-algebra, reading, and writing.

General Support Services Information

Contact Information
Name of program or department: Learning Disability Program
Telephone: 641-585-8207
Fax: 641-584-8194
Email: AACE@waldorf.edu

Accommodations or Services For Students With Learning Differences

Accommodations are decided upon an individual basis after a thorough review of appropriate, current documentation and meeting with the student. The accommodations requested must be supported through the documentation provided and must be logically linked to the current impact of the condition on academic functioning.

Allowed in exams
Calculator: Yes
Dictionary: Yes
Computer: Yes
Spellchecker: Yes
Extended test time: Yes
Scribes: Yes
Proctors: Yes
Oral exams: Yes
Note-takers: Yes
Services for students with LD: Yes
Services for students with ADHD: Yes
Services for students with ASD: Yes
Distraction-reduced environment: Yes
Tape recording in class: Yes
Audio book: NR
Electronic texts: Yes
Kurzweil Reader: Yes
Other assistive technology: Yes
Priority registration: Yes
Added costs for services: Yes
LD specialists: Yes
ADHD coaching: Yes
ASD specialists: Yes
Professional tutors: 8–10
Peer tutors: 25
Max. hours/wk. for services: Unlimited
How professors are notified of LD/ADHD: By director and student letters

General Admissions Information

Office of Admissions: NR

Entrance Requirements

SAT or ACT required. TOEFL required of all international applicants.

Application deadline: NR
Notification: Rolling starting 10/4
Average GPA: NR
ACT Composite middle 50% range: NR-NR
SAT Math middle 50% range: NR-NR
SAT Critical Reading middle 50% range: NR-NR
SAT Writing middle 50% range: NR-NR
Graduated top 10% of class: NR
Graduated top 25% of class: NR
Graduated top 50% of class: NR

COLLEGE GRADUATION REQUIREMENTS

Course waivers allowed: No
Course substitutions allowed: Yes
In what course: NR

Additional Information

Environment: NR

Student Body
Undergrad enrollment: 1,425
% Women: 37%
% Men: 63%
% Out-of-state: NR

Cost information
Tuition: $19,804
Room & board: $6,994
Housing Information
University Housing: Yes
Percent living on campus: 27

Greek System
Fraternity: No
Sorority: No
Athletics: NAIA

KANSAS STATE UNIVERSITY

119 Anderson Hall, Manhattan, KS 66506
Phone: 785-532-6250 • Fax: 785-532-6393
E-mail: k-state@k-state.edu • Web: www.k-state.edu
Support: CS • Institution: Public

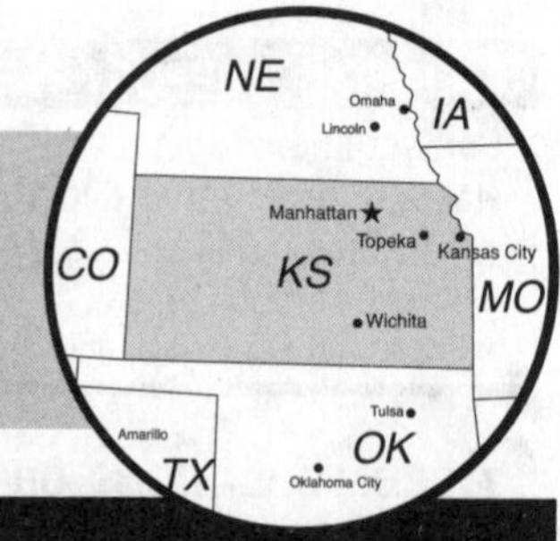

PROGRAMS OR SERVICES FOR STUDENTS WITH LEARNING DIFFERENCES

Kansas State provides a broad range of support services to students with learning disabilities through Disability Support Services (DSS), as well as through numerous other university departments. The goals of the program are to recommend and provide accommodations and assistance tailored to the students' needs. Faculty and staff are sensitive to the special needs of the students and will work with them in their pursuit of educational goals. DSS works with students to plan accommodations that best aid the students to overcome areas of difficulty. DSS does not modify or reduce the content of courses. Rather, DSS helps to set up ways for students to demonstrate academic knowledge without interference from the disability. To qualify for services students must provide DSS with documentation of a learning disability that includes: a complete record of all testing administered; a signed statement from a professional documenting LD; and information about strengths and weaknesses to help plan accommodations best suited to the student's needs. Many of the services provided take time to arrange. Consequently, students are encouraged to apply for services early in the process of planning for college.

ADMISSION INFORMATION FOR STUDENTS WITH LEARNING DIFFERENCES

College entrance test required: Yes
Interview required: Not Applicable
Essay required: Not Applicable
Additional Application Required for LD/ADHD/ASD: Yes
What documentation required for LD: Demonstrate current, functional limitations in the learning environment. Verification of history for receiving specific accommodations is strongly considered.
With general application: NR
To receive services after enrolling: Yes
What documentation required for ADHD: Demonstrate current, functional limitations in the learning environment. Verification of history for receiving specific accommodations is strongly considered.
With general application: NR
To receive services after enrolling: Yes
What documentation required for ASD: Demonstrate current, functional limitations in the learning environment. Verification of history for receiving specific accommodations is strongly considered.
With general application: NR
To receive services after enrolling: Yes
LD/ADHD/ASD documentation submitted to: Student Access Center
ASD Specific Program: NR
Special Ed. HS course work accepted: Not Applicable
Specific course requirements of all applicants: Yes
Separate application required for program services: Yes
Total # of students receiving LD/ADHD/ASD services: 400
Acceptance into program means acceptance into college: NR

ADMISSIONS

Kansas residents must complete the Kansas pre-college curriculum with at least a 2.0/4.0 GPA, AND achieve an ACT of 21, or above or a minimum SAT of 980, or rank in the top one-third of their graduating class, AND achieve a 2.0 GPA on all attempted college work. Non-Kansas residents must complete the Kansas pre-college curriculum with at least a 2.0/4.0 GPA AND Achieve an ACT composite of 21, or above or a minimum combined SAT of 980, or rank in the top one-third of their class, AND achieve a 2.0 GPA on all attempted college work. The Director of Disability Support Services may be asked to consult with admissions on individual applicants. Course requirements include 4 English, 3 math, 3 science, 3 social studies and 3 electives.

ADDITIONAL INFORMATION

To access support services students must provide DSS with verification of LD. Specific information about strengths and weaknesses help DSS plan accommodations best suited to students' needs. Students should contact DSS for services. Many services take time to arrange so early applications are encouraged. Students with LD may be eligible for services such as test-taking accommodations, readers, assistance in obtaining alternative text, note-takers. Tutoring is offered in some freshman/sophomore classes. All students may attend an orientation meeting prior to registration freshman year. Special courses are offered in Enhanced University Experience to learn note-taking, textbook-reading, and test-taking skills; math review for students experiencing difficulty with arithmetic computations; intermediate algebra; and college algebra. Services are available for undergrads and graduate students.

General Support Services Information

Contact Information
Name of program or department: Student Access Center
Telephone: 785-532-6441
Fax: 785-532-6457

Accommodations or Services For Students With Learning Differences

Accommodations are decided upon an individual basis after a thorough review of appropriate, current documentation. The accommodations requests must be supported through the documentation provided and must be logically linked to the current impact of the condition on academic functioning.

Allowed in exams
Calculator: Yes
Dictionary: Yes
Computer: Yes
Spellchecker: Yes
Extended test time: Yes
Scribes: Yes
Proctors: Yes
Oral exams: Yes
Note-takers: Yes
Support services for students with LD: Yes
Support services for students with ADHD: Yes
Support services for students with ASD: Yes
Distraction-reduced environment: Yes
Tape recording in class: Yes
Electronic texts: Yes
Kurzweil reader: NR
Audio books: Yes
Other assistive technology: Yes
Priority registration: Yes
Added costs of services: Not Applicable
LD specialists: Yes
ADHD coaching: Yes
ASD specialists: Yes
Professional tutors: No
Peer tutors: Not Applicable
Max. hours/wk. for services: 2
How professors are notified of student approved accommodations: By both student and director

General Admissions Information

Office of Admissions: 785-532-6250

Entrance Requirements

Academic units required: 4 English, 3 math, 3 science, 3 social studies, 3 academic electives. High school diploma is required and GED is accepted. SAT or ACT recommended. If ACT, ACT with writing accepted.

Application deadline: NR
Notification: NR
Average GPA: 3.49
ACT Composite middle 50% range: 22-28
SAT Math middle 50% range: 480-640
SAT Critical Reading middle 50% range: 470-600
SAT Writing middle 50% range: 440-580
Graduate top 10% of class: 22
Graduated top 25% of class: 47
Graduated top 50% of class: 75

COLLEGE GRADUATION REQUIREMENTS

Course waivers allowed: Yes
In what course: math, foreign language
Course substitutions allowed: Yes
In what course: math, foreign language

Additional Information

Environment: This public school was founded in 1863. It has a 668-acre campus.

Student Body
Undergrad enrollment: 19,859
% Women: 48
% Men: 52
% Out-of-state: 18

Cost information
In-state Tuition: $8,517
Out-of-state Tuition: $22,596
Room & board: $8,430

Housing Information
University Housing: Yes
Percent living on campus: 23

Greek System
Fraternity: No
Sorority: No
Athletics: Division I

PITTSBURG STATE UNIVERSITY

1701 South Broadway, Pittsburg, KS 66762
Phone: 620-235-4251 • Fax: 620-235-6003
E-mail: psuadmit@pittstate.edu • Web: www.pittstate.edu
Support: CS • Institution: Public

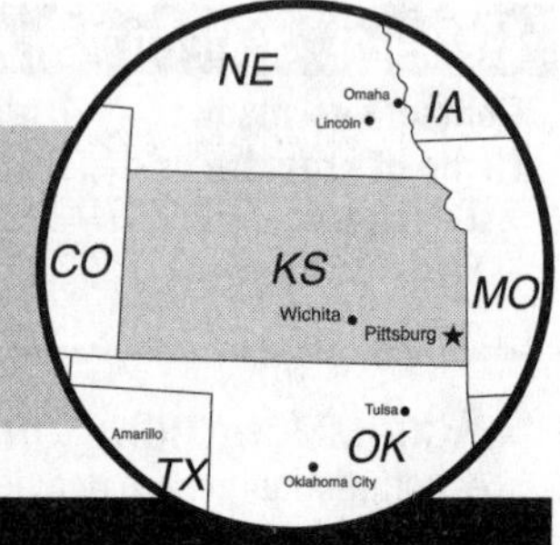

PROGRAMS OR SERVICES FOR STUDENTS WITH LEARNING DIFFERENCES

The Center for Student Accommodations at Pittsburg State University is committed to providing appropriate educational and related services to students with LD/ADHD and disabilities related to a mental illness. PSU works hard to help meet the needs of students with a disability. The specific type of assistance is determined on an individual basis. Previous records and an interview determine the type and degree of assistance appropriate for the student. The Center for Student Accommodations provides information, reasonable accommodations and direction to other campus resources for students with disabilities to ensure equal access at Pittsburg State University.

ADMISSION INFORMATION FOR STUDENTS WITH LEARNING DIFFERENCES

College entrance test required: NR
Interview required: Not Applicable
Essay required: Not Applicable
Additional Application Required for LD/ADHD/ASD: Yes
What documentation required for LD: Psycho ed evaluation
With general application: No
To receive services after enrolling: Yes
What documentation required for ADHD: Psycho ed evaluation
With general application: No
To receive services after enrolling: Yes
What documentation required for ASD: Psycho ed evaluation
With general application: No
To receive services after enrolling: Yes
LD/ADHD/ASD documentation submitted to: Center for Student Accommodations
ASD Specific Program: NR
Special Ed. HS course work accepted: Not Applicable
Specific course requirements of all applicants: Yes
Separate application required for program services: Yes
Total # of students receiving LD/ADHD/ASD services: NR
Acceptance into program means acceptance into college: No

ADMISSIONS

Complete the Kansas pre-college curriculum (or equivalent for non-residents) with at least a 2.0 GPA (2.5 for non-residents) on a 4.0 scale AND meet one of the following: ACT composite score of 21 or higher (980 SAT or higher); rank in the top 1/3 of high school graduating class; AND (if applicable) achieve at least a 2.0 GPA on any college credit taken in high school. There are provisions for a small number of exceptions to the qualified admission standards. If a student does not meet the requirements, the admission application will be reviewed individually and additional documents may be requested before an admission decision is made.

ADDITIONAL INFORMATION

Specific assistance is determined on an individual basis based on documentation and an interview. Services provided by the Center for Student Accommodations include: organization and time management skills and strategies, study skills strategies, testing modifications include extended time for tests, reading multiple choice and true-false tests verbatim, reading and defining words on a test (if the definition of that word does not give the student an unfair advantage in answering questions), providing scribes for short or long essay exams, provide recorders to record lectures and help obtain textbooks in a digital format. We will also monitor student's class attendance.

General Support Services Information

Contact Information
Name of program or department: Center for Student Accommodations
Telephone: 620-235-4309
Fax: 620-235-4190
Website: http://www.pittstate.edu/office/center-for-student-accommodations/

Accommodations or Services For Students With Learning Differences

Accommodations are decided upon an individual basis after a thorough review of appropriate, current documentation. The accommodations requests must be supported through the documentation provided and must be logically linked to the current impact of the condition on academic functioning.

Allowed in exams
Calculator: Yes
Dictionary: Yes
Computer: Yes
Spellchecker: Yes
Extended test time: Yes
Scribes: Yes
Proctors: Yes
Oral exams: Yes
Note-takers: Yes
Support services for students with LD: Yes
Support services for students with ADHD: Yes
Support services for students with ASD: Yes
Distraction-reduced environment: Yes
Tape recording in class: Yes
Electronic texts: Yes
Kurzweil reader: NR
Audio books: Yes
Other assistive technology: Yes
Priority registration: No
Added costs of services: No
LD specialists: Yes
ADHD coaching: Yes
ASD specialists: No
Professional tutors: No
Peer tutors: NR
Max. hours/wk. for services: NR
How professors are notified of student approved accommodations: By director

General Admissions Information

Office of Admissions: 620-235-4251

Entrance Requirements

Academic units recommended: 4 English, 4 math, 3 science, 3 social studies, 3 computer science. High school diploma is required and GED is accepted. If ACT, ACT with writing accepted. TOEFL required of all international applicants: minimum paper TOEFL 520 or minimum internet TOEFL 68.

Application deadline: NR
Notification: NR
Average GPA: 3.3
ACT Composite middle 50% range: 19-24
SAT Math middle 50% range: NR-NR
SAT Critical Reading middle 50% range: NR-NR
SAT Writing middle 50% range: NR-NR
Graduate top 10% of class: 13
Graduated top 25% of class: 35
Graduated top 50% of class: 67

COLLEGE GRADUATION REQUIREMENTS

Course waivers allowed: No
Course substitutions allowed: No

Additional Information

Environment: This public school was founded in 1903. It has a 443-acre campus.

Student Body
Undergrad enrollment: 6,270
% Women: 48
% Men: 52
% Out-of-state: 27

Cost information
In-state Tuition: $6,508
Out-of-state Tuition: $16,978
Room & board: $6,734

Housing Information
University Housing: Yes
Percent living on campus: 19

Greek System
Fraternity: Yes
Sorority: Yes
Athletics: Division II

University of Kansas

Office of Admissions, Lawrence, KS 66045-7576
Phone: 785-864-3911 • Fax: 785-864-5006
E-mail: adm@ku.edu • Web: www.ku.edu/
Support: CS • Institution: Public

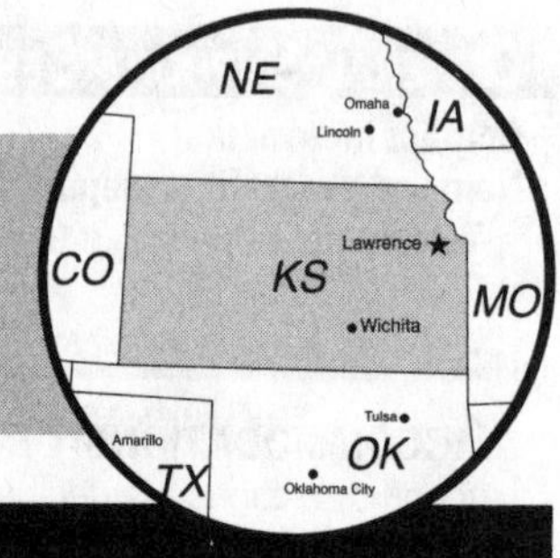

Programs or Services for Students with Learning Differences

The Academic Achievement and Access Center (AAAC) facilitates appropriate academic accommodations and auxiliary aids and services that are necessary to afford an individual with a disability an equal opportunity to participate in the University's programs and activities. Specifically, students must provide written documentation from a qualified professional on the nature and impact of the disability. The student and the AAAC will then engage in an interactive process to determine what, if any, accommodations are appropriate based on the student's disability and individual needs.

Admission Information for Students with Learning Differences

College entrance test required: Yes
Interview required: No
Essay required: NR
Additional Application Required for LD/ADHD/ASD: NR
What documentation required for LD: Psycho Ed evaulation to include: relevant historical info, instructional interventions, related services, age diagnosed, objective data (aptitude, achievement, info processing), test scores (standard, percentile and grade equivalents) and describe functional limitations.
With general application: No
To receive services after enrolling: Yes
What documentation required for ADHD: Diagnosis based on DSM-V; history of behaviors impairing functioning in academic setting; diagnostic interview; history of symptoms; evidence of ongoing behaviors.
With general application: No
To receive services after enrolling: Yes
What documentation required for ASD: Psycho ed evaluation
With general application: NR
To receive services after enrolling: Yes
LD/ADHD/ASD documentation submitted to: Academic Achievement and Access Center
ASD Specific Program: NR
Special Ed. HS course work accepted: Yes
Specific course requirements of all applicants: NR
Separate application required for program services: No
Total # of students receiving LD/ADHD/ASD services: 256
Acceptance into program means acceptance into college: Students must be admitted and enrolled in the university (denial can be appealed) and then request services.

Admissions

All applications are welcomed; assured admission is just one way to become a Jayhawk, and our individual review takes more into account. We encourage all students interested in the University of Kansas to complete an application, which will be reviewed individually by KU's admissions staff. Our review covers these factors: cumulative high school GPA, ACT or SAT scores, GPA in the core curriculum, and strength of courses. Students who don't meet the assured admissions requirements (below) will be asked to answer two to four short questions on the application, and responses will be included in the individual review. One way to guarantee a spot at KU is by meeting our assured admission criteria: 21+ ACT (1060+ SAT*) and 3.25+ GPA or 24+ ACT (1160+ SAT*) and 3.0+ GPA 2.0+ GPA (2.5+ for out-of-state students) in a college-prep curriculum.

Additional Information

Skill workshops are available in study skills, time management, stress management, and preparing for exams. Disability Resources also serves as an advocate or liaison for students. Tutoring services for students who meet qualifications are available through Supportive Educational Services at no cost. Tutoring Services offered through the Academic Achievement and Access Center are also available in most challenging entry level courses for a fee. Services and accommodations are available for undergraduate and graduate students.

GENERAL SUPPORT SERVICES INFORMATION

Contact Information
Name of program or department: Academic Achievement and Access Center
Telephone: 784-864-4064
Fax: 785-864-2817
Website: NR

ACCOMMODATIONS OR SERVICES FOR STUDENTS WITH LEARNING DIFFERENCES

Accommodations are decided upon an individual basis after a thorough review of appropriate, current documentation. The accommodations requests must be supported through the documentation provided and must be logically linked to the current impact of the condition on academic functioning.

Allowed in exams
Calculator: Yes
Dictionary: Yes
Computer: Yes
Spellchecker: Yes
Extended test time: Yes
Scribes: Yes
Proctors: Yes
Oral exams: Yes
Note-takers: Yes
Support services for students with LD: Yes
Support services for students with ADHD: Yes
Support services for students with ASD: Yes
Distraction-reduced environment: Yes
Tape recording in class: Yes
Electronic texts: Yes
Kurzweil reader: NR
Audio books: Yes
Other assistive technology: Yes
Priority registration: Yes
Added costs of services: No
LD specialists: Yes
ADHD coaching: NR
ASD specialists: Yes
Professional tutors: No
Peer tutors: NR
Max. hours/wk. for services: NR
How professors are notified of student approved accommodations: By student

GENERAL ADMISSIONS INFORMATION

Office of Admissions: 785-864-3911

ENTRANCE REQUIREMENTS

Academic units required: 4 English, 3 math, 3 science, 1 science labs, 3 social studies, 3 academic electives, **Academic units recommended:** 4 English, 4 math, 3 science, 3 social studies, 3 academic electives. High school diploma is required and GED is accepted. SAT or ACT required. If ACT, ACT with writing accepted. TOEFL required of all international applicants.

Application deadline: NR
Notification: Rolling starting 9/1
Average GPA: 3.5
ACT Composite middle 50% range: 22-28
SAT Math middle 50% range: NR-NR
SAT Critical Reading middle 50% range: NR-NR
SAT Writing middle 50% range: NR-NR
Graduate top 10% of class: 26
Graduated top 25% of class: 56
Graduated top 50% of class: 87

COLLEGE GRADUATION REQUIREMENTS

Course waivers allowed: No
Course substitutions allowed: Yes
In what course: college algebra only

ADDITIONAL INFORMATION

Environment: This public school was founded in 1866. It has a 1100-acre campus.

Student Body
Undergrad enrollment: 19,245
% Women: 50
% Men: 50
% Out-of-state: 27

Cost information
In-state Tuition: $10,802
Out-of-state Tuition: $26,640
Room & board: $10,076

Housing Information
University Housing: Yes
Percent living on campus: 25

Greek System
Fraternity: Yes
Sorority: Yes
Athletics: Division I

Bluegrass Community and Technical College

103 Oswald Building, Cooper Drive, Lexington, KY 40506
Phone: 859-246-6530 • Fax: 859-246-4678
E-mail: bl-dss@kctcs.edu • Web: www.bluegrass.kctcs.edu
Support: S • Institution type: 2-year Public

Programs or Services for Students with Learning Differences

Bluegrass Community and Technical College (BCTC) has made a firm commitment to providing high-quality postsecondary education to persons with disabilities. Disability Support Services staff seek to ensure equal access and full participation for persons with disabilities in postsecondary education, and empower students to obtain the life skills necessary for a fulfilling, productive lifestyle after leaving BCTC. Students can request services by visiting Disability Support Services (DSS). Full participation in the DSS program is encouraged from the initial admission contact throughout the student's academic career. Positive peer contacts as well as guidance from the DSS staff also play a major role in encouraging participation in the DSS program.

Admission Information for Students with Learning Differences

College entrance tests required: No
Interview required: No
Essay required: No
Additional Application Required for LD/ADHD/ASD: NR
What documentation required for LD: Psycho ed evaluation to include: relevant historical info, instructional interventions, related services, age diagnosed, objective data (aptitude, achievement, info processing), test scores (standard, percentile and grade equivalents) and describe functional limitations.
With general application: No
To receive services after enrolling: Yes
What documentation required for ADHD: Diagnosis based on DSM-V; history of behaviors impairing functioning in academic setting; diagnostic interview; history of symptoms; evidence of ongoing behaviors.
With general application: No
To receive services after enrolling: Yes
What documentation required for ASD: Psycho ed evaluation
With general application: NR
To receive services after enrolling: Yes
LD/ADHD/ASD documentation submitted to: Disability Support Services
ASD Specific Program: NR
Special Ed. HS course work accepted: Yes
Specific course requirements of all applicants: NR
Separate application required: No
Total # of students receiving LD/ADHD/ASD services: NR
Acceptance into program means acceptance into college: Students must be admitted and enrolled at LCC and then may request services.

Admissions

BCTC offers open-door admission to all applicants who meet the following requirements: proof of a high school diploma or the GED; ACT for placement not admission; 4 years of English, Algebra I and II, biology, chemistry or physics, U.S.history, and geometry. Any areas of deficiency can be made up at BCTC before enrolling in college courses; there is no required GPA or class rank. However, if a student scored below an 18 ACT in English, 20 Reading, or 21 Math, the student must take an assessment determined by the college. There is an articulation agreement between BCTC and the University of Kentucky.

Additional Information

DSS provides a full range of services, including academic advising, career counseling, supportive counseling, specialized computer software, recorded textbooks, note-takers, writers/scribes, tutors, and testing accommodation. The DSS coordinator serves as student liaison with college faculty, staff, and administrators; vocational rehabilitation counselors; and various other social service agencies. Tutoring services are available for students struggling in classes, not performing well on tests or having trouble writing papers. BCTC has a study skills specialist to assist with study strategies on an individual basis, in small group workshops, or in a classroom setting. he specialist administers a study skills assessment that helps identify areas of improvement in test preparation, test anxiety, note taking skills, textbook reading skills, memory techniques, math anxiety, time management and procrastination, concentration, and goal setting and motivation.

General Support Services Information

Contact Information
Name of program or department: Disability Support Services
Telephone: 859-246-6530
Fax: 859-246-4678

Accommodations or Services for Students with Learning Differences

Accommodations are decided upon an individual basis after a thorough review of appropriate, current documentation. The accommodations requested must be supported through the documentation provided and must be logically linked to the current impact of the condition on academic functioning.

Allowed in exams
Calculator: Yes
Dictionary: No
Computer: Yes
Spellchecker: Yes
Extended test time: Yes
Scribes: Yes
Proctors: Yes
Oral exams: Yes
Note-takers: Yes
Services for students with LD: Yes
Services for students with ADHD: Yes
Services for students with ASD: Yes
Distraction-reduced environment: Yes
Tape recording in class: Yes
Audio books: NR
Electronic texts: Yes
Kurzweil Reader: Yes
Other assistive technology: Yes
Priority registration: Yes
Added costs for services: No
LD specialists: No
ADHD coaching: NR
ASD specialists: NR
Professional tutors: No
Peer tutors: Yes
Max. hours/wk. for services: 2
How professors are notified of LD/ADHD: By director

General Admissions Information

Office of Admission: 859-246-6210

Entrance Requirements

Academic units recommended: 4 English, 3 math, 3 science, 3 U.S. history. Course deficiencies can be made up at BCTC. Open admissions. High school diploma or GED accepted. ACT is used for placement but not for admissions. GPA and class rank are not required.

Application deadline: NR
Notification: NR
Average GPA: NR
ACT Composite middle 50% range: NR-NR
SAT Math middle 50% range: NR-NR
SAT Critical Reading middle 50% range: NR-NR
SAT Writing middle 50% range: NR-NR
Graduated top 10% of class: NR
Graduated top 25% of class: NR
Graduated top 50% of class: NR

COLLEGE GRADUATION REQUIREMENTS

Course waivers allowed: No
Course substitutions allowed: Yes
In what course: Students may request subsitutions for courses with the approriate documentation.

Additional Information

Environment: The college is located on the campus of the University of Kentucky.

Student Body
Undergrad enrollment: NR
% Women: 58
% Men: 42
% Out-of-state: NR
Cost information
In-state Tuition: $147 per credit
Out-of-state Tuition: $515 per credit
Room & board: $6,975
Housing Information
University Housing: Yes
Percent living on campus: 1
Greek System
Fraternity: No
Sorority: No
Athletics: Intramural

Eastern Kentucky University

SSB CPO 54, Richmond, KY 40475
Phone: 859-622-2106 • Fax: 859-622-8024
E-mail: admissions@eku.edu • Web: www.eku.edu
Support: CS • Institution: Public

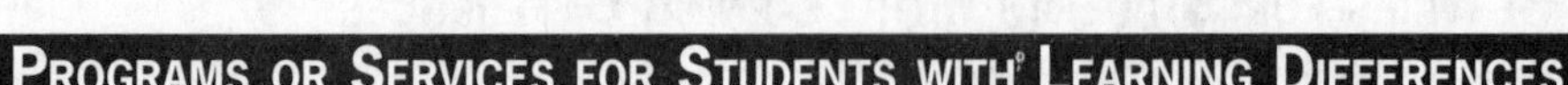

Programs or Services for Students with Learning Differences

The mission of Project SUCCESS is to respond effectively and efficiently to the individual educational needs of eligible university students with learning disabilities through a cost-effective, flexible program of peer tutors, academic coaching, focus groups, and assistive technology. Upon admittance Project SUCCESS develops an individualized program of services that serve to enhance the academic success of each student. The services a student utilizes will be determined in a conference between the student and the program director. At the core of our program is Academic Coaching and individualized tutoring services.

Admission Information for Students with Learning Differences

College entrance tests required: Yes
Interview required: Yes
Essay required: No
Additional Application Required for LD/ADHD/ASD: NR
What documentation required for LD: Psycho ed evaluation to include: relevant historical info, instructional interventions, related services, age diagnosed, objective data (aptitude, achievement, info processing), test scores (standard, percentile and grade equivalents) and describe functional limitations.
With general application: No
To receive services after enrolling: Yes
What documentation required for ADHD: Diagnosis based on DSM-V; history of behaviors impairing functioning in academic setting; diagnostic interview; history of symptoms; evidence of ongoing behaviors.
With general application: No
To receive services after enrolling: Yes
What documentation required for ASD: Psycho ed evaluation
With general application: NR
To receive services after enrolling: Yes
LD/ADHD/ASD documentation submitted to: OSID
ASD Specific Program: NR
Special Ed. HS course work accepted: Yes
Specific course requirements for all applicants: Yes
Separate application required for program services: Yes
Total # of students receiving LD/ADHD/ASD services: 250
Acceptance into program means acceptance into college: No

Admissions

Students who meet the following criteria will be granted full admission to the University: Have graduated from an accredited high school earning a minimum cumulative high school grade point average of 2.5 on a 4.0 scale; OR have submitted a minimum ACT composite score of 20 or SAT combined verbal/critical reading score of 950 or higher AND meet the Kentucky Pre-College Curriculum ANDhave submitted an official six-semester high school transcript, or a General Equivalency Diploma (GED), or documentation indicating completion of an EKU approved home-school or distance learning high school program.

Additional Information

Project SUCCESS services provided include academic coaching, one-on-one tutoring, note-taking services, e-texts, test accommodations, advocacy, weekly seminars. Skills classes are offered in study skills, reading skills, weekly workshops in transition, time management, learning and study strategies, test-taking skills, developmental math, developmental reading, and developmental writing. "Planning to Win" is a summer transitions program specifically designed for high school junior and graduating seniors with learning disabilities, attention deficit disorder and other cognitive disorders. The program is geared towards high school students who are planning to attend college in the fall as well as those who are only exploring post-secondary educational options at any college. Students attend three days of educational and inspiring workshops, fellowship with current college students and spend two nights in an EKU residence hall. The Planning to Win Program is focused on students; however parents and interested educators are also welcome.

General Support Services Information

Contact Information
Name of program or department: Office of Services for Individuals with Disabilities
Telephone: 859-622-2933
Fax: 859-622-6794

Accommodations or Services for Students with Learning Differences

Accommodations are decided upon an individual basis after a thorough review of appropriate, current documentation. The accommodations requested must be supported through the documentation provided and must be logically linked to the current impact of the condition on academic functioning.

Allowed in exams
Calculator: Yes
Dictionary: Yes
Computer: Yes
Spellchecker: Yes
Extended test time: Yes
Scribes: Yes
Proctors: Yes
Oral exams: Possibly
Note-takers: Yes
Services for students with LD: Yes
Services for students with ADHD: Yes
Services for students with ASD: Yes
Distraction-reduced environment: Yes
Tape recording in class: Yes
Audio books: NR
Electronic texts: Yes
Kurzweil Reader: No
Other assistive technology: Digital books (e-texts), assistive technology software including Zoomtext, Read and Write Gold, Inspiration, Window Eyes, JAWS
Priority registration: Yes
Added costs for services: Yes
LD specialists: Yes
ADHD coaching: NR
ASD specialists: NR
Professional tutors: No
Peer tutors: 35
Max. hours/wk. for services: 6
How professors are notified of LD/ADHD: Student

General Admissions Information

Office of Admissions: 859-622-2106

Entrance Requirements

Academic units required: 4 English, 3 math, 3 science, 1 science labs, 2 foreign language, 3 social studies, 7 academic electives, and 2 units from above areas or other academic areas. High school diploma is required and GED is accepted. SAT or ACT required. If ACT, ACT with writing accepted. TOEFL required of all international applicants: minimum paper TOEFL 500.

Application deadline: 8/1
Notification: Rolling starting 8/1
Average GPA: 3.22
ACT Composite middle 50% range: 19-24
SAT Math middle 50% range: NR-NR
SAT Critical Reading middle 50% range: NR-NR
SAT Writing middle 50% range: NR-NR
Graduated top 10% of class: 13
Graduated top 25% of class: 34
Graduated top 50% of class: 66

COLLEGE GRADUATION REQUIREMENTS

Course waivers allowed: Yes
In what course: Waivers and substitutions are determined on a case-by-case basis.
Course substitutions allowed: Yes
In what course: Waivers and substitutions are determined on a case-by-case basis.

Additional Information

Environment: This public school was founded in 1906. It has a 675-acre campus.

Student Body
Undergrad enrollment: 13,978
% Women: 56
% Men: 44
% Out-of-state: 13

Cost information
In-state Tuition: $7,920
Out-of-state Tuition: $17,640
Room & board: $8,188

Housing Information
University Housing: Yes
Percent living on campus: 25

Greek System
Fraternity: Yes
Sorority: Yes
Athletics: Division I

Thomas More College

333 Thomas More Parkway, Crestview Hill, KY 41017-3495
Phone: 859-344-3332 • Fax: 859-344-3444
E-mail: admissions@thomasmore.edu • Web: www.thomasmore.edu
Support: S • Institution: Private

Programs or Services for Students with Learning Differences

Thomas More College's Student Support Services program is committed to the individual academic, personal, cultural/social, and financial needs of the student. It is committed to promoting sensitivity and cultural awareness of the population served and to promoting varied on/off campus services and events that enhance the student's educational opportunities. A variety of support services are offered, including developmental courses, peer tutoring, and individual counseling. Students with deficits in speech/language, study skills, written expression, ongoing additional skills, perceptual skills, reading, speaking, math, fine motor, and ADHD with or without LD are admissible. Students may need 5 years to graduate. The college offers small classes, excellent faculty, and solid preparation for the future.

Admission Information for Students with Learning Differences

College entrance tests required: Yes
Interview required: No
Essay required: No
Additional Application Required for LD/ADHD/ASD: NR
What documentation required for LD: Psycho ed evaluation to include: relevant historical info, instructional interventions, related services, age diagnosed, objective data (aptitude, achievement, info processing), test scores (standard, percentile and grade equivalents) and describe functional limitations.
With general application: No
To receive services after enrolling: Yes
What documentation required for ADHD: Diagnosis based on DSM-V; history of behaviors impairing functioning in academic setting; diagnostic interview; history of symptoms; evidence of ongoing behaviors.
With general application: No
To receive services after enrolling: Yes
What documentation required for ASD: Psycho ed evaluation
With general application: NR
To receive services after enrolling: Yes
LD/ADHD/ASD documentation submitted to: Student Support Services
ASD Specific Program: NR
Special Ed. HS course work accepted: Yes
Specific course requirements of all applicants: Yes
Separate application required: No
Total # of students receiving LD/ADHD/ASD services: 10
Acceptance into program means acceptance into college: Students must be admitted and enrolled in the university first and then request services.

Admissions

First-year students must earn: 20 ACT composite score or 940 SAT combined Critical Reading + Mathematics score; 18 ACT English subscore or 450 SAT Critical Reading subscore; 2.5/4.0 GPA (80% or better/C+ average); with the following high school credits are required for entrance: English: 4 credits, Foreign Language: 2 credits; Social Science: 3 credits, Mathematics: 3 credits, Science: 3 credits, Arts Appreciation 1 credit and Computer Literacy 1 credit. Applicants lacking some of these units may be admitted at the discretion of the Admissions Committee. The college can waive ACT/SAT scores after considering the student's LD status.

Additional Information

The Office of Academic Student Support Services oversees four primary tasks: Assisting students with disabilities; Providing tutorial services in academic areas needed by the students; Student Success Workshops; and Peer Mentoring. Students with learning disabilities could be limited to 12–13 hours the first semester. Student progress will be monitored. Some students may be required to take developmental courses based on the college's assessment of reading, writing, and math skills. Skills classes are paired with world history, and there is college credit for skill classes in study skills, reading, and math. Some students are admitted on a conditional status and are given additional support through Student Support Services.

General Support Services Information

Contact Information
Name of program or department: Student Support Services
Telephone: 606-344-3521
Fax: 606-433-3638

Accommodations or Services for Students with Learning Differences

Accommodations are decided upon an individual basis after a thorough review of appropriate, current documentation. The accommodations requested must be supported through the documentation provided and must be logically linked to the current impact of the condition on academic functioning.

Allowed in exams
Calculator: Per accommodations
Dictionary: NR
Computer: Per accommodations
Spellchecker: No
Extended test time: Yes
Scribes: Yes
Proctors: Yes
Oral exams: Yes
Note-takers: Yes
Services for students with LD: Yes
Services for students with ADHD: Yes
Services for students with ASD: Yes
Distraction-reduced environment: Yes
Tape recording in class: Yes
Audio books: NR
Electronic texts: Yes
Kurzweil Reader: Yes
Other assistive technology: Per accommodations
Priority registration: No
Added costs for services: No
LD specialists: No
ADHD coaching: NR
ASD specialists: NR
Professional tutors: 2
Peer tutors: 40
Max. hours/wk. for services: Unlimited
How professors are notified of LD/ADHD: By student

General Admissions Information

Office of Admissions: 859-344-3332

Entrance Requirements

Academic units required: 4 English, 3 mathematics, 3 science, (1 science labs), 2 foreign language, 3 social studies. **Academic units recommended:** 2 Arts Appreciation and Computer Literacy. High school diploma is required and GED is accepted. SAT or ACT required. TOEFL required of all international applicants: minimum paper TOEFL 515.

Application deadline: 8/1
Notification: Rolling starting 3/15
Average GPA: 2.88
ACT Composite middle 50% range: 19-24
SAT Math middle 50% range: 460-600
SAT Critical Reading middle 50% range: 460-580
SAT Writing middle 50% range: NR-NR
Graduated top 10% of class: NR
Graduated top 25% of class: NR
Graduated top 50% of class: NR

COLLEGE GRADUATION REQUIREMENTS

Course waivers allowed: Yes
In what course: Foreign language and math
Course substitutions allowed: No

Additional Information

Environment: This private college has 100-acre suburban campus.

Student Body
Undergrad enrollment: 1,497
% Women: 51
% Men: 49
% Out-of-state: NR

Cost information
Tuition: $27,268
Room & board: $7,770
Housing Information
University Housing: Yes
Percent living on campus: 20

Greek System
Fraternity: Yes
Sorority: Yes
Athletics: Division III

UNIVERSITY OF KENTUCKY

100 Funkhouser Building, Lexington, KY 40506
Phone: 859-257-2000 • Fax: 859-257-3823
E-mail: admissions@uky.edu • Web: www.uky.edu
Support: CS • Institution: Public

PROGRAMS OR SERVICES FOR STUDENTS WITH LEARNING DIFFERENCES

The goal of the Disability Resource Center is to provide equal access to students with disabilities. We advocate for reasonable accommodations, removal of barriers, and acceptance of different learning methods. In partnership with students, faculty, and staff, our purpose is to achieve an accessible educational environment where students with disabilities have an equal opportunity to fully participate in all aspects of the university community.

ADMISSION INFORMATION FOR STUDENTS WITH LEARNING DIFFERENCES

College entrance test required: Yes
Interview required: No
Essay required: Not Applicable
Additional Application Required for LD/ADHD/ASD: Yes
What documentation required for LD: Psycho ed evaluation
With general application: Not Applicable
To receive services after enrolling: Yes
What documentation required for ADHD: Psycho ed evaluation
With general application: Not Applicable
To receive services after enrolling: Yes
What documentation required for ASD: Psycho ed evaluation
With general application: Not Applicable
To receive services after enrolling: Yes
LD/ADHD/ASD documentation submitted to: Disability Resource Center
ASD Specific Program: NR
Special Ed. HS course work accepted: No
Specific course requirements of all applicants: Yes
Separate application required for program services: No
Total # of students receiving LD/ADHD/ASD services: 448
Acceptance into program means acceptance into college: Not Applicable

ADMISSIONS

The University of Kentucky subscribes to a selective admission policy. The academic criteria are established by a faculty committee of the University Senate. The admission decision is based on factors, including cumulative high school grade pointaverage, completion of the precollege curriculum, ACT or SAT Reasoning score results, and special talents and abilities. High school minimum GPA is 2.0 to 2.49 with an average of 3.55. High school courses required: 4 English, 3 math, 3 science, 2 foreign language, 3 social studies, 5 academic electives, 1 health/physical education, and 1 visual/performing arts.

ADDITIONAL INFORMATION

The Academic Enhancement Program, referred to as The Study, helps students reach their academic goals. The Study includes academic study groups, tutoring, and learning skills workshops. Programs are purposefully designed to fosterinteractions that promote learning strategies and attitudes toward academic life that are characteristic of successful college students. The Writing Center offers free individual or group consultations for students, faculty, and staff. The Writing Center provides help for many kinds of writing: class assignments, creative writing, dissertations, scholarly monographs, grant applications, reports, articles, scholarship applications, and more. The Math Resource Center (Mathskeller) is specifically designed for students studying mathematics courses at the University of Kentucky, and tutors are free and available.

General Support Services Information

Contact Information
Name of program or department: Disability Resource Center
Telephone: (859) 257-2754
Fax: (859) 257-1980
Website: www.uky.edu/drc

Accommodations or Services For Students With Learning Differences

Accommodations are decided upon an individual basis after a thorough review of appropriate, current documentation. The accommodations requests must be supported through the documentation provided and must be logically linked to the current impact of the condition on academic functioning.

Allowed in exams
Calculator: No
Dictionary: No
Computer: Yes
Spellchecker: No
Extended test time: Yes
Scribes: Yes
Proctors: Yes
Oral exams: Yes
Note-takers: No
Support services for students with LD: Yes
Support services for students with ADHD: Yes
Support services for students with ASD: Yes
Distraction-reduced environment: Yes
Tape recording in class: Yes
Electronic texts: Yes
Kurzweil reader: NR
Audio books: Yes
Other assistive technology: Yes
Priority registration: Yes
Added costs of services: No
LD specialists: Yes
ADHD coaching: No
ASD specialists: Yes
Professional tutors: No
Peer tutors: Not Applicable
Max. hours/wk. for services: NR
How professors are notified of student approved accommodations: By student

General Admissions Information

Office of Admissions: 859-257-2000

Entrance Requirements

Academic units required: 4 English, 3 math, 3 science, 1 science labs, 2 foreign language, 3 social studies, 7 academic electives, 1 visual/performing arts, and 1 units from above areas or other academic areas. High school diploma is required and GED is accepted. SAT or ACT required. If ACT, ACT with writing accepted. TOEFL required of all international applicants: minimum paper TOEFL 527.

Application deadline: 2/15
Notification: 8/15
Average GPA: 3.6
ACT Composite middle 50% range: 22-28
SAT Math middle 50% range: 510-640
SAT Critical Reading middle 50% range: 490-620
SAT Writing middle 50% range: 480-610
Graduate top 10% of class: 30
Graduated top 25% of class: 57
Graduated top 50% of class: 85

COLLEGE GRADUATION REQUIREMENTS

Course waivers allowed: No
Course substitutions allowed: Yes
In what course: Possibly in math, statistics, foreign language, depending on the student's degree program and documentation of need.

Additional Information

Environment: This public school was founded in 1865. It has a 687-acre campus.

Student Body
Undergrad enrollment: 22,223
% Women: 52
% Men: 48
% Out-of-state: 28

Cost information
In-state Tuition: $10,936
Out-of-state Tuition: $24,268
Room & board: $10,192

Housing Information
University Housing: Yes
Percent living on campus: 28.8

Greek System
Fraternity: Yes
Sorority: Yes
Athletics: Division I

Western Kentucky University

Potter Hall 117, Bowling Green, KY 42101-1020
Phone: 270-745-2551 • Fax: 270-745-6133
E-mail: admission@wku.edu • Web: www.wku.edu
Support: CS • Institution: Public

Programs or Services for Students with Learning Differences

The purpose of SARC is to coordinate services and accommodations for students with documented disabilities. Our most common activities include reviewing disability documentation, meeting with students to determine appropriate accommodations, and partnering with other areas on campus to implement these accommodations. SARC strives to help students assume responsibility of their own educational experience. We assist students by providing access and opportunity in order for them to reach their full potential. The goal of the Student Accessibility Resource Center is to ensure that all students with disabilities are provided access to all facets of the Western Kentucky University experience; to facilitate and coordinate support services and programs that enable students with disabilities to maximize their educational potential; and to increase awareness among all members of the University so that students with disabilities are able to achieve academic success based on their abilities, not their disabilities.

Admission Information for Students with Learning Differences

College entrance tests required: Yes
Interview required: Yes
Essay required: N/A
Additional Application Required for LD/ADHD/ASD: NR
What documentation required for LD: Psycho ed evaluation to include: relevant historical info, instructional interventions, related services, age diagnosed, objective data (aptitude, achievement, info processing), test scores (standard, percentile and grade equivalents) and describe functional limitations.
With general application: No
To receive services after enrolling: Yes
What documentation required for ADHD: Diagnosis based on DSM-V; history of behaviors impairing functioning in academic setting; diagnostic interview; history of symptoms; evidence of ongoing behaviors.
With general application: No
To receive services after enrolling: Yes
What documentation required for ASD: Psycho ed evaluation
With general application: NR
To receive services after enrolling: Yes
LD/ADHD/ASD documentation submitted to: Support Program/Services
ASD Specific Program: NR
Special Ed. HS course work accepted: Yes
Specific course requirements for all applicants: Yes
Separate application required for program services: No
Total # of students receiving LD/ADHD/ASD services: 380
Acceptance into program means acceptance into college: No

Admissions

Students must meet one of the following requirements for admission:
ACT composite of 20 or greater, or SAT combined score of 1020 or greater (940 or greater combined score accepted for tests taken prior to March, 2016)*, or Unweighted high school GPA of 2.50 or higher, or achieve the required Composite Admission Index (CAI) score. Students admitted to WKU may be placed in an appropriate academic support program based on academic needs at the time of admission. Students will be notified regarding any academic placement by the appropriate office. ACT/SAT required but essay scores for the ACT and SAT are not evaluated for admission, scholarship, or placement purposes.

Additional Information

The program for students with LD offers students: adapted test administrations; textbooks in alternative format; short-term loan of special equipment; reading referral services; faculty liaison; peer tutoring; academic, personal, and career counseling; and assistance with the Reading and Learning Labs. Academic advisors assist students in course selection. The university combines intensive academic advisement with special seminars to provide support during the freshman year. The University Counseling Services Center provides assistance in personal, social, emotional, and intellectual development. Skills classes are offered in math, reading, vocabulary, study skills, and English through the Community College. College credit is given for these classes. Services and accommodations are available for undergraduate and graduate students. Students work directly with a counselor and meet twice weekly during the intital semester. Testing may be completed in the SDS facilities.

General Support Services Information

Contact Information
Name of program or department: Office for Student Disability Services
Telephone: 502-745-5004
Fax: 502-745-6289

Accommodations or Services for Students with Learning Differences

Accommodations are decided upon an individual basis after a thorough review of appropriate, current documentation. The accommodations requested must be supported through the documentation provided and must be logically linked to the current impact of the condition on academic functioning.

Allowed in exams
Calculator: Yes
Dictionary: N/A
Computer: Yes
Spellchecker: Yes
Extended test time: Yes
Scribes: Yes
Proctors: Yes
Oral exams: Yes
Note-takers: Yes
Services for students with LD: Yes
Services for students with ADHD: Yes
Services for students with ASD: Yes
Distraction-reduced environment: Yes
Tape recording in class: Yes
Audio books: NR
Electronic texts: Yes
Kurzweil Reader: No
Other assistive technology: Captioning
Priority registration: Yes
Added costs for services: No
LD specialists: Yes
ADHD coaching: NR
ASD specialists: NR
Professional tutors: 25
Peer tutors: 20
Max. hours/wk. for services: 20
How professors are notified of LD/ADHD: Both student and director

General Admissions Information

Office of Admissions: 270-745-2551

Entrance Requirements

Academic units required: 4 English, 3 math, 3 science, 1 science labs, 2 foreign language, 3 social studies, 1 history, 5 academic electives, and 1 units from above areas or other academic areas. High school diploma is required and GED is accepted. SAT or ACT required. If ACT, ACT with writing accepted. TOEFL required of all international applicants: minimum paper TOEFL 525 or minimum internet TOEFL 71.

Application deadline: 8/1
Notification: NR
Average GPA: 3.27
ACT Composite middle 50% range: 19-26
SAT Math middle 50% range: 440-570
SAT Critical Reading middle 50% range: 430-580
SAT Writing middle 50% range: NR-NR
Graduated top 10% of class: 22
Graduated top 25% of class: 44
Graduated top 50% of class: 74

COLLEGE GRADUATION REQUIREMENTS

Course waivers allowed: Yes
In what course: Courses that can be substituted are handled on a case-by-case basis.
Course substitutions allowed: Yes
In what course: NR

Additional Information

Environment: This public school was founded in 1906. It has a 235-acre campus.

Student Body
Undergrad enrollment: 17,310
% Women: 57
% Men: 43
% Out-of-state: 18

Cost information
In-state Tuition: $9,482
Out-of Tuition: $24,132
Room & board: $7,368

Housing Information
University Housing: Yes
Percent living on campus: 31

Greek System
Fraternity: Yes
Sorority: Yes
Athletics: Division I

LOUISIANA COLLEGE

1140 College Drive, Pineville, LA 71359-0560
Phone: 318-487-7259 • Fax: 318-487-7550
E-mail: admissions@lacollege.edu • Web: www.lacollege.edu
Support: SP • Institution: Private

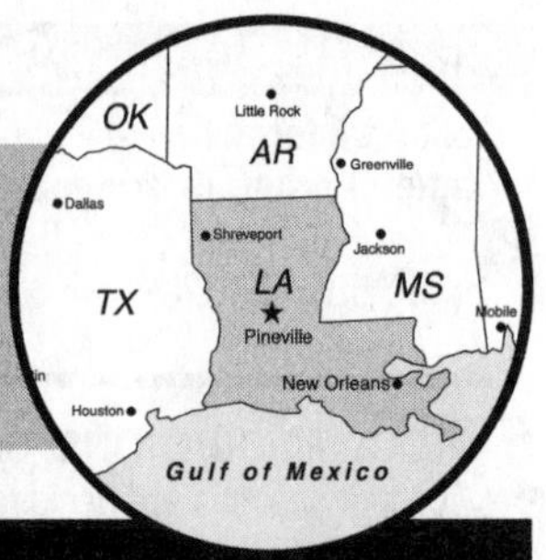

PROGRAMS OR SERVICES FOR STUDENTS WITH LEARNING DIFFERENCES

The goal of the Program to Assist Student Success (PASS) is to facilitate the academic success of students with disabilities and to serve as an advocate for the students. This highly individualized, limited enrollment program provides support services and personal attention to students who need special academic counseling, tutoring, or classroom assistance. Three levels of services are provided. Level I students are required to attend weekly individual counseling and tutoring sessions; the emphasis at this level is to provide individualized help to ensure the student's successful transition to college and to compensate for any identifiable disability. Level II students have, at a minimum, completed 24 hours of college credit at Louisiana College with at least a 2.5 GPA. Regularly scheduled individual counseling sessions continue to be provided; all other services continue to be available to the student as needed. Level III students have learned to compensate for their disability and are independently achieving college success; these students will have their progress monitored by the staff, and tutoring will continue to be available. Any student not maintaining a 2.5 GPA must remain in or return to Level I.

ADMISSION INFORMATION FOR STUDENTS WITH LEARNING DIFFERENCES

College entrance tests required: Yes
Interview required: Yes
Essay required: Yes
Additional Application Required for LD/ADHD/ASD: NR
What documentation required for LD: Psycho ed evaluation to include: relevant historical info, instructional interventions, related services, age diagnosed, objective data (aptitude, achievement, info processing), test scores (standard, percentile and grade equivalents) and describe functional limitations.
With general application: Yes if requested as part of Structured Program application
To receive services after enrolling: Yes
What documentation required for ADHD: Diagnosis based on DSM-V; history of behaviors impairing functioning in academic setting; diagnostic interview; history of symptoms; evidence of ongoing behaviors.
With general application: Yes if requested as part of Structured Program application
To receive services after enrolling: Yes
What documentation required for ASD: Psycho ed evaluation
With general application: NR
To receive services after enrolling: Yes
LD/ADHD/ASD documentation submitted to: Program to Assist Student Services
ASD Specific Program: NR
Special Ed. HS course work accepted: Yes
Specific course requirements of all applicants: NR
Separate application required: Yes
Total # of students receiving LD/ADHD/ASD services: 44
Acceptance into program means acceptance into college: Student must be admitted and enrolled in the university first and then request admission to PASS.

ADMISSIONS

All qualified applicants to PASS must submit the regular application, meet the general criteria for admission to Louisiana College, and have a diagnosed learning or physical disability. Successful applicants must have the intellectual potential (average to superior), the appropriate academic foundation (class standing and/or ACT/SAT scores), and the personal desire and motivation to succeed. The PASS director and staff make the final decision about admission to the program after reviewing the following: 20 or above on ACT or 930 or above on SAT; 4 years of English, 3 years of science, 3 years of social studies, and 3 years of math; 2.0 GPA; counselor's recommendation and other letters of reference; psychological or medical reports; and an essay outlining why the student feels he or she can succeed in college. At least one personal interview with student and parent(s) is required. Students are encouraged to apply early and there is an application evaluation fee of $25. Students may appeal to the Appeals Board if they are denied admission.

ADDITIONAL INFORMATION

Tutoring sessions are conducted in most subjects taken by Level I students. Additional tutorial help is available at the higher levels as needed. The PASS staff will carefully work with individual professors and the student's academic advisor to coordinate and accommodate the student's learning needs. Students admitted to PASS will remain in the program as long as they are at Louisiana College. Noncompliance with any component of the program may result in a student's dismissal from the program. Skills classes are offered in study techniques, test-taking strategies, and time management through orientation, and private tutoring from a PASS staff member. Incoming freshmen are encouraged to attend one summer session (5 weeks) to become familiar with the campus and college life. There is an additional fee for the PASS program that ranges from $450-$850 per semester, depending on the level of support provided.

General Support Services Information

Contact Information
Name of program or department: Program to Assist Student Success (PASS)
Telephone: 318-487-7629

Accommodations or Services for Students with Learning Differences

Accommodations are decided upon an individual basis after a thorough review of appropriate, current documentation. The accommodations requested must be supported through the documentation provided and must be logically linked to the current impact of the condition on academic functioning.

Allowed in exams
Calculator: Yes
Dictionary: Yes
Computer: Yes
Spellchecker: Yes
Extended test time: Yes
Scribes: Yes
Proctors: Yes
Oral exams: Yes
Note-takers: Yes
Services for students with LD: Yes
Services for students with ADHD: Yes
Services for students with ASD: Yes
Distraction-reduced environment: Yes
Tape recording in class: Yes
Audio books: NR
Electronic texts: Yes
Kurzweil Reader: Yes
Other assistive technology: Yes
Priority registration: No
Added costs for services: Yes
LD specialists: Yes
ADHD coaching: NR
ASD specialists: NR
Professional tutors: 3
Peer tutors: 50–60
Max. hours/wk. for services: 10
How professors are notified of LD/ADHD: By both student and director

General Admissions Information

Office of Admissions: 318-487-7259

Entrance Requirements

Academic units required: 4 English, 3 mathematics, 3 science, (2 science labs), 2 social studies, 1 history, 4 academic electives. **Academic units recommended:** 2 foreign language. High school diploma is required and GED is accepted. SAT or ACT required. TOEFL required of all international applicants: minimum paper TOEFL 550.

Application deadline: 8/15
Notification: Rolling starting 1/1
Average GPA: NR
ACT Composite middle 50% range: NR-NR
SAT Math middle 50% range: NR-NR
SAT Critical Reading middle 50% range: NR-NR
SAT Writing middle 50% range: NR-NR
Graduated top 10% of class: NR
Graduated top 25% of class: NR
Graduated top 50% of class: NR

COLLEGE GRADUATION REQUIREMENTS

Course waivers allowed: No
Course substitutions allowed: Yes
In what course: Appeals for substitutions must be made to special committee.

Additional Information

Environment: NR

Student Body
Undergrad enrollment: 1,256
% Women: 48
% Men: 52
% Out-of-state: 9

Cost information
Tuition: $10,560
Room & board: $5,086

Housing Information
University Housing: Yes
Percent living on campus: 56

Greek System
Fraternity: Yes
Sorority: Yes
Athletics: Division III

Louisiana State University

1146 Pleasant Hall, Baton Rouge, LA 70803
Phone: 225-578-1175 • Fax: 225-578-4433
E-mail: admissions@lsu.edu • Web: www.lsu.edu
Support: S • Institution: Public

Programs or Services for Students with Learning Differences

The purpose of Disability Services (DS) is to assist any student who finds his or her disability to be a barrier to achieving educational and/or personal goals. The office provides support services to students with learning disabilities. These services are provided to encourage students with LD/ADHD to achieve success in college. The consequences of a disability may include specialized requirements; therefore, the particular needs of each student are considered on an individual basis. DS dedicates its efforts to meeting both the needs of students with disabilities and the interests of faculty, staff, and the university as a whole. It is the practice of DS that issues concerning accommodations of students with disabilities in academic and other programs and activities be resolved between the student requesting the accommodation and the university employee representing the department within which the academic program or service is located. After intervention, if the student does not find the provision of an accommodation satisfactory, the student may file a formal grievance.

Admission Information for Students with Learning Differences

College entrance test required: Yes
Interview required: Not Applicable
Essay required: Not Applicable
Additional Application Required for LD/ADHD/ASD: Not Applicable
What documentation required for LD: Psycho ed evaluation
With general application: NA
To receive services after enrolling: Yes
What documentation required for ADHD: Full psychoeducational evaluation
With general application: Not Applicable
To receive services after enrolling: Not Applicable
What documentation required for ASD: Full psychoeducational evaluation
With general application: Not Applicable
To receive services after enrolling: Not Applicable
LD/ADHD/ASD documentation submitted to: Disability Services
ASD Specific Program: NR
Special Ed. HS course work accepted: Not Applicable
Specific course requirements of all applicants: NR
Separate application required for program services: Yes
Total # of students receiving LD/ADHD/ASD services: NR
Acceptance into program means acceptance into college: Not Applicable

Admissions

GPA: 3.0 academic GPA based on Required Core Units. An ACT composite score of 22, with at least 18 English subscore, 19 math subscore; or SAT scores of 1030 critical reading & math score, with at least 450 critical reading score and 460 math score. The writing section of the ACT/SAT is not required for admission. Students interested in Ogden Honors College consideration and top scholarships should complete the writing section. Students who are borderline to meeting admission requirements are still encouraged to apply. Other factors considered for admission may include choice of degree program, rank in class, credit in advanced placement or honors courses, rigor of the high school curriculum, and grade trends.

Additional Information

Specialized support services are based on individual disability-based needs. Services available include disability management counseling; adaptive equipment loan; note-takers; referral for tutoring; assistance with enrollment and registration; liaison assistance and referral to on-campus and off-campus resources; supplemental orientation to the campus; and advocacy on behalf of students with campus faculty, staff, and students. Learning Assistance Center is open to all students on campus. Computer labs, science tutoring, math lab, learning-skills assistance, supplemental instruction, and skills classes in time management, test-taking strategies, note-taking skills, reading skills, and study skills are available. The decision to provide accommodations and services is made by the SSD after reviewing documentation. Currently there are 175 students with LD and 300 students with ADHD receiving services and accommodations.

General Support Services Information

Contact Information
Name of program or department: Disability Services
Telephone: 225-578-5919
Fax: 225-578-4500
Website: NR

Accommodations or Services For Students With Learning Differences

Accommodations are decided upon an individual basis after a thorough review of appropriate, current documentation. The accommodations requests must be supported through the documentation provided and must be logically linked to the current impact of the condition on academic functioning.

Allowed in exams
Calculator: Yes
Dictionary: Yes
Computer: Yes
Spellchecker: Yes
Extended test time: Yes
Scribes: Yes
Proctors: Yes
Oral exams: Yes
Note-takers: Yes
Support services for students with LD: Yes
Support services for students with ADHD: Yes
Support services for students with ASD: Yes
Distraction-reduced environment: Yes
Tape recording in class: Yes
Electronic texts: Yes
Kurzweil reader: NR
Audio books: Yes
Other assistive technology: Yes
Priority registration: No
Added costs of services: Not Applicable
LD specialists: No
ADHD coaching: No
ASD specialists: Not Applicable
Professional tutors: No
Peer tutors: NR
Max. hours/wk. for services: NR
How professors are notified of student approved accommodations: By student

General Admissions Information

Office of Admissions: 225-578-1175

Entrance Requirements

Academic units required: 4 English, 4 math, 4 science, 2 foreign language, 3 social studies, 1 history, 1 visual/performing arts. High school diploma is required and GED is accepted. SAT or ACT required. If ACT, ACT with writing accepted. TOEFL required of all international applicants: minimum paper TOEFL 550 or minimum internet TOEFL 79.

Application deadline: 4/15
Notification: NR
Average GPA: 3.46
ACT Composite middle 50% range: 23-28
SAT Math middle 50% range: 510-630
SAT Critical Reading middle 50% range: 500-600
SAT Writing middle 50% range: NR-NR
Graduate top 10% of class: 25
Graduated top 25% of class: 54
Graduated top 50% of class: 82

COLLEGE GRADUATION REQUIREMENTS

Course waivers allowed: Yes
In what course: Foreign Languages
Course substitutions allowed: NR

Additional Information

Environment: This public school was founded in 1860. It has a 2000-acre campus.

Student Body
Undergrad enrollment: 25,572
% Women: 51
% Men: 49
% Out-of-state: 18

Cost information
In-state Tuition: $7,552
Out-of-state Tuition: $24,715
Room & board: $11,200

Housing Information
University Housing: Yes
Percent living on campus: 25

Greek System
Fraternity: Yes
Sorority: Yes
Athletics: Division I

Nicholls State University

PO Box 2050, Thibodaux, LA 70310
Phone: 985-448-4507 • Fax: 985-448-4929
E-mail: nicholls@nicholls.edu • Web: www.nicholls.edu
Support: S • Institution: Public

Programs or Services for Students with Learning Differences

The Louisiana Center for Dyslexia and Related Learning Disorders offers assistance to serious, capable students with learning disabilities at Nicholls State University who seek to earn an undergraduate degree. They believe that everyone has the right and the obligation to pursue the fulfillment of their learning potential. The center's programs are data driven, goal oriented, and committed to change. The center has close ties with leading scholars and researchers in dyslexia. The center is impressed with multisensory, linguistic, and direct instructional approaches, but to maintain its own integrity, it projects an orientation that is objective, open-minded, and directed toward the future. The goals of the center are focused on the need to increase the understanding of dyslexia and to upgrade and improve the accessibility and quality of the services that individuals with dyslexia depend upon to help them to become self-sufficient, well-adjusted, and contributing members of society.

Admission Information for Students with Learning Differences

College entrance tests required: Yes
Interview required: Yes
Essay required: NR
Additional Application Required for LD/ADHD/ASD: NR
What documentation required for LD: Psycho ed evaluation to include: relevant historical info, instructional interventions, related services, age diagnosed, objective data (aptitude, achievement, info processing), test scores (standard, percentile and grade equivalents) and describe functional limitations.
With general application: No
To receive services after enrolling: Yes
What documentation required for ADHD: Diagnosis based on DSM-V; history of behaviors impairing functioning in academic setting; diagnostic interview; history of symptoms; evidence of ongoing behaviors.
With general application: No
To receive services after enrolling: Yes
What documentation for ASD: Psycho ed evaluation
LD/ADHD/ASD documentation submitted to: LA Center for Dyslexia
ASD Specific Program: NR
Special Ed. HS course work accepted: Yes
Separate application required: Yes
Total # of students receiving LD/ADHD/ASD services: 0–150
Acceptance into program means acceptance into college: Student must be admitted and enrolled in the university first and then request to be reviewed for services.

Admissions

In-state applicants must meet all of the following: Completion of the Regents' Core 4 Curriculum (19 units) and minimum overall high school GPA of 2.0; at least a 21 ACT composite score OR a minimum overall high school GPA of 2.35/4.0; and have no need for a developmental English or math course. Out-of-state high schools, home school, or non-state approved high school graduates must meet one of the following: Same criteria as listed above; or have at least a 23 ACT composite score and have no need for a developmental English or math course; or meet the minimum core GPA on at least 17 units of the required HS Core 4 Curriculum, with at least a 21 ACT composite score and a minimum overall high school GPA of 2.35/4.0. Applications will be reviewed on an individual basis and an admissions decision will be made considering each applicant's potential for success and will include factors such as ACT score, special talents, and the University's commitment to a demographically diverse student population. Students who receive their GED or graduate from Non-Accredited Home School Programs who are under the age of 25 must submit ACT scores with a minimum 23 Composite score in order to be admitted and demonstrate no need for remedial coursework.

Additional Information

The Dyslexia Center provides a support system; equipment; remediation; academic planning; resources; and assistance. Accommodation forms with appropriate classroom and testing accommodations are given to professors. Typical accommodations may include but are not limited to extended time; use of an electronic dictionary; oral reader; or use of a computer. Students are enrolled in regular college classes. Other campus services for students with disabilities include the Office for Students with Disabilities; the Testing Center for special testing accommodations such as extended time or a quiet room; the Tutorial and Academic Enhancement Center for tutoring assistance; the university Counseling Center, which provides counseling directed at self-encouragement, self-esteem, assertiveness, stress management, and test anxiety; and the computer lab for assistance with written assignments. Assessment is available for a fee for students applying to the university.

General Support Services Information

Contact Information
Name of program or department: Office of Disability Services
Telephone: 985-448-4430

Accommodations or Services for Students with Learning Differences

Accommodations are decided upon an individual basis after a thorough review of appropriate, current documentation. The accommodations requested must be supported through the documentation provided and must be logically linked to the current impact of the condition on academic functioning.

Allowed in exams
Calculator: Yes
Dictionary: Yes
Computer: Yes
Spellchecker: Yes
Extended test time: Yes
Scribes: Yes
Proctors: Yes
Oral exams: Yes
Note-takers: Yes
Services for students with LD: Yes
Services for students with ADHD: Yes
Services for students with ASD: Yes
Distraction-reduced environment: Yes
Tape recording in class: Yes
Audio books: NR
Electronic texts: Yes
Kurzweil Reader: Yes
Other assistive technology: Yes
Priority registration: Yes
Added costs for services: No
LD specialists: No
ADHD coaching: NR
ASD specialists: NR
Professional tutors: No
Peer tutors: No
Max. hours/wk. for services: N/A
How professors are notified of LD/ADHD: By student

General Admissions Information

Office of Admissions: 985-448-4507

Entrance Requirements

Academic units required: 4 English, 3 math, 3 science, 2 foreign language, 1 social studies, 2 history, 2 academic electives. High school diploma is required and GED is accepted. SAT or ACT required. If ACT, ACT with writing accepted. TOEFL required of all international applicants: minimum paper TOEFL 500 or minimum internet TOEFL 61.

Application deadline: NR
Notification: Rolling starting 9/1
Average GPA: 2.86
Average ACT Composite: 21
SAT Math middle 50% range: NR-NR
SAT Critical Reading middle 50% range: NR-NR
SAT Writing middle 50% range: NR-NR
Graduated top 10% of class: 18
Graduated top 25% of class: 43
Graduated top 50% of class: 73

COLLEGE GRADUATION REQUIREMENTS

Course waivers allowed: No
Course substitutions allowed: No

Additional Information

Environment: This public school was founded in 1948. It has a 210-acre campus.

Student Body
Undergrad enrollment: 5,695
% Women: 61
% Men: 39
% Out-of-state: 4

Cost information
In-state Tuition: $7,378
Out-of-state Tuition: $18,310
Room & board: $9,290

Housing Information
University Housing: Yes
Percent living on campus: 20

Greek System
Fraternity: Yes
Sorority: Yes
Athletics: Division I

Tulane University

6823 St. Charles Avenue New Orleans, LA 70118
Phone: 504-865-5731 • Fax: 504-862-8715
E-mail: undergrad.admission@tulane.edu • Web: www.tulane.edu
Support: S • Institution: Private

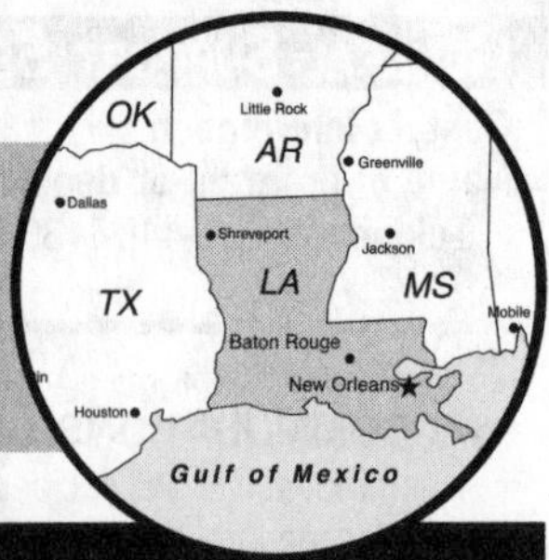

Programs or Services for Students with Learning Differences

The Goldman Office of Disability Services (ODS) is committed to providing equal access and a friendly environment for all who study and work at Tulane University. We offer accommodations and modifications of the academic or work environment to students and employees with psychological, medical/physical, and learning/developmental disabilities. Our staff members focus on leveling the playing field, and work directly with students, faculty and staff to accomplish this objective. When necessary, reasonable accommodations can be implemented to modify the academic environment to meet the needs of our students. Because no two students are alike, our staff members work collaboratively to develop an individualized plan which gives each student the same opportunity for success as their peers.

Admission Information for Students with Learning Differences

College entrance test required: NR
Interview required: No
Essay required: Not Applicable
Additional Application Required for LD/ADHD/ASD: No
What documentation required for LD: Although formal documentation is required for consideration of accommodations at Tulane University, the staff of the Goldman Office of Disability Services recognize that each individual experiences barriers to access differently.
With general application: NR
To receive services after enrolling: No
What documentation required for ADHD: Although formal documentation is required for consideration of accommodations at Tulane University, the staff of the Goldman Office of Disability Services recognize that each individual experiences barriers to access differently.
With general application: NR
To receive services after enrolling: No
What documentation required for ASD: Although formal documentation is required for consideration of accommodations at Tulane University, the staff of the Goldman Office of Disability Services recognize that each individual experiences barriers to access differently.
With general application: NR
To receive services after enrolling: No
LD/ADHD/ASD documentation submitted to: Goldman Office of Disability Services
ASD Specific Program: No
Special Ed. HS course work accepted: NR
Specific course requirements of all applicants: NR
Separate application required for program services: False
Total # of students receiving LD/ADHD/ASD services:
Acceptance into program means acceptance into college: NR

Admissions

SAT (pre-2016) composite 1950-2150 or ACT composite 30-33. Course requirements include 4 English, 3 math, 3 science, 3 social studies and 2 foreign language.

Additional Information

If a student is approved for testing accommodations, professors have the option of accommodating the student themselves or requesting that the student test in the Goldman Testing Center, proctored by ODS staff. Student Resources & Support Services (SRSS) was created to give students in need of support a single place to go for assistance. SRSS uses an individualized approach to help students connect to the resources that they may need on campus and in the New Orleans community. SRSS includes the Office of Case Management & Victim Support Services, Goldman Office of Disability Services, and the Office of Student Conduct. Case Management Services are designed to support students throughout their college career in order to best achieve their academic and co-curricular goals. Case Management helps the student identify the issues and appropriate resources and works collaboratively with the student to develop an action plan. Staff from Case Management also triage referrals and other reported information or concerns as it comes in, investigates and gathers additional information, prioritizes reports, and determines appropriate responses, sometimes in conjunction with Process of Care and/or the Behavioral Intervention Team. Case Managers are available to consult with students, faculty, staff, families, and community providers to determine the best approach to the student's current situation.

General Support Services Information

Contact Information
Name of program or department: Goldman Office of Disability Services
Telephone: 504-862-8433
Fax: 504-862-8435
Website: www.accessibility.tulane.edu

Accommodations or Services for Students with Learning Differences

Accommodations are decided upon an individual basis after a thorough review of appropriate, current documentation. The accommodations requests must be supported through the documentation provided and must be logically linked to the current impact of the condition on academic functioning.

Allowed in exams
Calculator: Yes
Dictionary: No
Computer: Yes
Spellchecker: No
Extended test time: Yes
Scribes: Yes
Proctors: Yes
Oral exams: Yes
Note-takers: Yes
Support services for students with LD: Yes
Support services for students with ADHD: Yes
Support services for students with ASD: Yes
Distraction-reduced environment: Yes
Tape recording in class: Yes
Electronic texts: Yes
Kurzweil reader: NR
Audio books: Yes
Other assistive technology: Yes
Priority registration: No
Added costs of services: No
LD specialists: No
ADHD coaching: No
ASD specialists: No
Professional tutors: No
Peer tutors: Yes
Max. hours/wk. for services: NR
How professors are notified of student approved accommodations: By student

General Admissions Information

Office of Admissions: 504-865-5731

Entrance Requirements

Academic units recommended: 4 English, 4 math, 4 science, 4 science labs, 3 foreign language, 3 social studies, 3 academic electives, High school diploma is required and GED is accepted. SAT or ACT required. If ACT, ACT with writing recommended. TOEFL required of all international applicants: minimum paper TOEFL 550 .

Application deadline: 1/15
Notification: 4/1
Average GPA: 3.506
ACT Composite middle 50% range: 29-32
SAT Math middle 50% range: 620-700
SAT Critical Reading middle 50% range: 620-710
SAT Writing middle 50% range: 640-720
Graduate top 10% of class: 55
Graduated top 25% of class: 85
Graduated top 50% of class: 96

COLLEGE GRADUATION REQUIREMENTS

Course waivers allowed: Yes
In what course: Foreign language
Course substitutions allowed: Yes
In what course: Foreign language

Additional Information

Environment: This private school was founded in 1834. It has a 110-acre campus.

Student Body
Undergrad enrollment: 8,339
% Women: 59
% Men: 41
% Out-of-state: 76

Cost information
Tuition:$45,758
Room & board: $13,758

Housing Information
University Housing: Yes
Percent living on campus: 45

Greek System
Fraternity: Yes
Sorority: Yes
Athletics: Division I

University of New Orleans

University of New Orleans Admissions, New Orleans, LA 70148
Phone: 504-280-6595 • Fax: 504-280-5522
E-mail: http://www.uno.edu/Admissions • Web: www.uno.edu
Support: S • Institution: Public

Programs or Services for Students with Learning Differences

The University of New Orleans is committed to providing all students with equal opportunities for academic and extracurricular success. The Office of Disability Services (ODS) coordinates all services and programs. In addition to serving its primary function as a liaison between the student and the university, the office provides a limited number of direct services to students with all kinds of permanent and temporary disabilities. Services begin when a student registered with the university contacts the ODS office, provides documentation of the disability, and requests assistance. ODS encourages student independence, program accessibility, and a psychologically supportive environment, so students may achieve their educational objectives. ODS also seeks to educate the campus community about disability issues.

Admission Information for Students with Learning Differences

College entrance tests required: Yes
Interview required: No
Essay required: No
Additional Application Required for LD/ADHD/ASD: NR
What documentation required for LD: Psycho ed evaluation to include: relevant historical info, instructional interventions, related services, age diagnosed, objective data (aptitude, achievement, info processing), test scores (standard, percentile and grade equivalents) and describe functional limitations.
With general application: No
To receive services after enrolling: Yes
What documentation required for ADHD: Diagnosis based on DSM-V; history of behaviors impairing functioning in academic setting; diagnostic interview; history of symptoms; evidence of ongoing behaviors.
With general application: No
To receive services after enrolling: Yes
What documentation required for ASD: Psycho ed evaluation
With general application: NR
To receive services after enrolling: Yes
LD/ADHD/ASD documentation submitted to: Office of Disability Services
ASD Specific Program: NR
Special Ed. HS course work accepted: Yes
Specific course requirements of all applicants: Yes
Separate application required: Yes
Acceptance into program means acceptance into college: Students must be admitted and enrolled in the university first and then request services.

Admissions

Students with LD should submit the general application form and are expected to meet the same admission standards as all other applicants. Students must complete an academic core curriculum 4 English, 4 math, 4 science, 4 social studies, 2 foreign language or 2 speech and 1 fine art. Other courses may be acceptable as substitutes for courses in the core curriculum. A minimum score at or above 19 Math (460 SAT); 18 English (450 SAT) is required to avoid remedial classes; plus one of the following: ACT composite score of 23 or greater (SAT 1060) or High School core GPA of 2.5 or greater. Students with less than 2.0 will not be admitted. Privateer Pathways Program: Applicants who do not meet the above test score requirements should refer to the Privateer Pathways Program, which include ACT English 16 and Math 17 or SAT English 410 or Math 400 or Compass English 61 (Writing) or Math 31 (Algebra).

Additional Information

Privateer Pathways is designed for students who, because of their ACT or SAT scores, need additional support in mathematics and/or English. Skills will be developed through the strategic delivery of academic support to students. The programs cover aspects such as time management, academic honesty, and financial aid. Bi-weekly Success Coaching is also available to first-year students. Each student will be individually evaluated for program eligibility based on high school transcripts and test scores. Participants will receive academic advising on courses required as part of the Pathways program.

General Support Services Information

Contact Information
Name of program or department: Office of Disability Services
Telephone: 504-280-6222
Fax: 504-280-3975

Accommodations or Services for Students with Learning Differences

Accommodations are decided upon an individual basis after a thorough review of appropriate, current documentation. The accommodations requested must be supported through the documentation provided and must be logically linked to the current impact of the condition on academic functioning.

Allowed in exams
Calculator: Yes
Dictionary: Yes
Computer: Yes
Spellchecker: Yes
Extended test time: Yes
Scribes: Yes
Proctors: Yes
Oral exams: Yes
Note-takers: Yes
Services for students with LD: Yes
Services for students with ADHD: Yes
Services for students with ASD: Yes
Distraction-reduced environment: Yes
Tape recording in class: Yes
Audio books: NR
Electronic texts: Yes
Kurzweil Reader: No
Other assistive technology: Yes
Priority registration: No
Added costs for services: No
LD specialists: No
ADHD coaching: NR
ASD specialists: NR
Professional tutors: No
Peer tutors: No
Max. hours/wk. for services: Referred to Learning Resource Center
How professors are notified of LD/ADHD: By both student and director

General Admissions Information

Office of Admissions: 504-280-6595

Entrance Requirements

Academic units required: 4 English, 4 math, 4 science, 2 foreign language, 4 social studies, 1 visual/performing arts. High school diploma is required and GED is accepted. SAT or ACT required. If ACT, ACT with writing accepted. TOEFL required of all international applicants: minimum paper TOEFL 550 or minimum internet TOEFL 213.

Application deadline: 7/25
Notification: NR
Average GPA: 3.25
ACT Composite middle 50% range: 21-25
SAT Math middle 50% range: 500-670
SAT Critical Reading middle 50% range: 500-630
SAT Writing middle 50% range: NR-NR
Graduated top 10% of class: 16
Graduated top 25% of class: 39
Graduated top 50% of class: 67

COLLEGE GRADUATION REQUIREMENTS

Course waivers allowed: No
Course substitutions allowed: Yes
In what course: Foreign language and math substitutions may be requested through individual colleges with appropriate documentation.

Additional Information

Environment: This public school was founded in 1956. It has a 195-acre campus.

Student Body
Undergrad enrollment: 7,152
% Women: 51
% Men: 49
% Out-of-state: 5

Cost information
In-state Tuition: $6,090
Out-of Tuition: $19,907
Room & board: $9,515

Housing Information
University Housing: Yes
Percent living on campus: 10

Greek System
Fraternity: Yes
Sorority: Yes
Athletics: Division I

Southern Maine Comm. College

2 Fort Road South, Portland, ME 04106
Phone: 207-741-5800 • Fax: 207-741-5760
E-mail: admissions@smccme.edu • Web: www.smccme.edu
Support: S • Institution: Public

Programs or Services for Students with Learning Differences

The Disability Services program is designed to offer academic support to students through various individualized services. Students can get professional faculty tutoring in their most difficult courses; learn about their specific learning style; improve concentration and memory; study more efficiently for tests; learn how to better manage their time; learn the basic skills that are the foundation of their specific technology; and use a computer toward processing, Internet research, and other computer applications.

Admission Information for Students with Learning Differences

College entrance tests required: Yes; SAT or Accuplacer
Interview required: No
Essay required: No
Additional Application Required for LD/ADHD/ASD: NR
What documentation required for LD: Psycho ed evaluation to include: relevant historical info, instructional interventions, related services, age diagnosed, objective data (aptitude, achievement, info processing), test scores (standard, percentile and grade equivalents) and describe functional limitations.
With general application: No
To receive services after enrolling: Yes
What documentation required for ADHD: Diagnosis based on DSM-V; history of behaviors impairing functioning in academic setting; diagnostic interview; history of symptoms; evidence of ongoing behaviors.
With general application: No
To receive services after enrolling: Yes
What documentation required for ASD: Psycho ed evaluation
With general application: NR
To receive services after enrolling: Yes
LD/ADHD/ASD documentation submitted to: Disability Services
ASD Specific Program: NR
Special Ed. HS course work accepted: Yes
Specific course requirements of all applicants: No
Separate application required: No
Total # of students receiving LD/ADHD/ASD services: 150
Acceptance into program means acceptance into college: Students must be admitted and enrolled in the university first and then request services.

Admissions

All students must meet the same admission criteria. There is no special admissions process for students with learning disabilities. All students have access to disability services, including those with a diagnosed learning disability. Some students are required to take the Accuplacer tests for placement into many courses. Students are exempt from the English portion with an SAT Critical Reading score of 450+ or ACT of 21. Students are exempt from Math portion of Accuplacer with SAT 490 Math or ACT 21.

Additional Information

The Learning Commons includes the Library, Writing Center and Tutoring Services . These services are available to all students. Students with diagnosed LD, as well as any student with academic needs, are provided with tutoring by faculty and students; access to resources in study skills in the form of personal advising/counseling, skill inventories, and study guides; and for LD, access to academic accommodations such as extended time on exams, testing in a quiet area, and note-takers or readers. Other services are learning assessments; faculty consulting; preparation of materials to assist students in all courses; study skills counseling; academic advising; counseling and support for students with learning disabilities; and access to multimedia self-teaching materials including computer-assisted instruction and videotapes.The college administers the Accuplacer test to any student who has not provided scores from the ACT or SAT.

General Support Services Information

Contact Information
Name of program or department: Counseling and Disability Services
Telephone: 207-741-5923

Accommodations or Services for Students with Learning Differences

Accommodations are decided upon an individual basis after a thorough review of appropriate, current documentation. The accommodations requested must be supported through the documentation provided and must be logically linked to the current impact of the condition on academic functioning.

Allowed in exams
Calculator: Yes
Dictionary: Yes
Computer: Yes
Spellchecker: Yes
Extended test time: Yes
Scribes: Yes
Proctors: Yes
Oral exams: Yes
Note-takers: Yes
Services for students with LD: Yes
Services for students with ADHD: Yes
Services for students with ASD: Yes
Distraction-reduced environment: Yes
Tape recording in class: Yes
Audio books: NR
Electronic texts: Yes
Kurzweil Reader: Yes
Other assistive technology: Yes
Priority registration: Yes
Added costs for services: No
LD specialists: No
ADHD coaching: NR
ASD specialists: NR
Professional tutors: 3
Peer tutors: 3
Max. hours/wk. for services: 3
How professors are notified of LD/ADHD: By both student and director

General Admissions Information

Office of Admission: 207-741-5800

Entrance Requirements

Academic units recommended: 4 English, 3 math, 1 lab science. High school diploma is required, and GED is accepted.

Application deadline: None
Notification: Rolling
Average GPA: NR
ACT Composite middle 50% range: NR-NR
SAT Math middle 50% range: NR-NR
SAT Critical Reading middle 50% range: NR-NR
SAT Writing middle 50% range: NR-NR
Graduated top 10% of class: NR
Graduated top 25% of class: NR
Graduated top 50% of class: NR

COLLEGE GRADUATION REQUIREMENTS

Course waivers allowed: Yes
In what course: Limited
Course substitutions allowed: Yes
In what course: Limited

Additional Information

Environment: The college, part of the Maine Community College System, is located on an 80-acre campus.

Student Body
Undergrad enrollment: 5,235
% Women: 51
% Men: 49
% Out-of-state: 0

Cost information
In-state Tuition: $2,760
Out-of-state Tuition: $5,520
Room & board: $8,788

Housing Information
University Housing: Yes
Percent living on campus: 8

Greek System
Fraternity: No
Sorority: No
Athletics: USCAA

University of New England

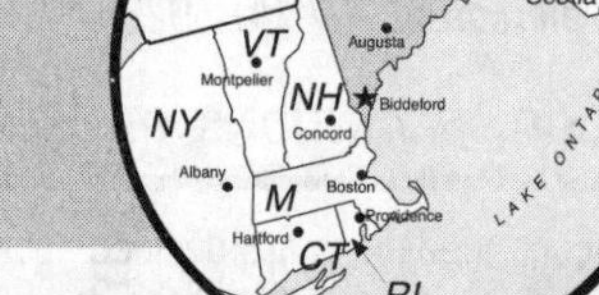

11 Hills Beach Road, Biddeford, ME 04005-9599
Phone: 207-602-2297 • Fax: 207-602-5900
E-mail: admissions@une.edu • Web: www.une.edu
Support: S • Institution: Private

Programs or Services for Students with Learning Differences

The University of New England's Disability Services exists to ensure that the university fulfills the part of its mission that seeks to promote respect for individual differences and to ensure that no one person who meets the academic and technical standards requisite for admission to, and the continued enrollment at, the university is denied benefits or subjected to discrimination at UNE solely by reason of the disability. Toward this end, and in conjunction with federal and state laws, the university both accepts and provides reasonable accommodations for qualified students. Students with learning disabilities or attention deficit disorder must provide current documentation that identifies the specific disability. All documentation should be submitted to Disability Services.

Admission Information for Students with Learning Differences

College entrance test required: NR **Interview required:** No
Essay required: Not Applicable
Additional Application Required for LD/ADHD/ASD: Not Applicable
What documentation required for LD: Psycho ed evaluation
With general application: No
To receive services after enrolling: Not Applicable
What documentation required for ADHD: Psycho ed evaluation
With general application: No
To receive services after enrolling: Not Applicable
What documentation required for ASD: Psycho ed evaluation
With general application: No
To receive services after enrolling: Not Applicable
LD/ADHD/ASD documentation submitted to: Disability Services
ASD Specific Program: NR
Special Ed. HS course work accepted: Not Applicable
Specific course requirements of all applicants: NR
Separate application required for program services: Yes
Total # of students receiving LD/ADHD/ASD services: NR
Acceptance into program means acceptance into college: No

Admissions

All applicants must meet the same admission criteria. There is no separate process for students with LD/ADHD. General admission criteria include 4 years English, 2–4 years math, 2–4 years social studies, 2–4 years science, and 2–4 years foreign language. It is recommended that students submit an essay and have an interview. Interviews are especially helpful for borderline applicants. After being admitted, students may submit documentation to Disability Services in order to request accommodations and services.

Additional Information

The Student Academic Success Center (SASC) provides a comprehensive array of academic support services including placement testing, courses, workshops, and tutoring. The mission of the Student Academic Success Center is to assist students to become independent learners so that they are able to meet the University's academic standards and attain their personal educational goals. In the Student Academic Success Center, professional staff members help students develop and maintain the skills they need to meed the challenges of undergraduate and graduate study. This is accomplished through individual consultations, workshops, and classroom presentations. The SASC Learning Specialist's time is spent working with students to assess progress and effectiveness in implementing practices designed to enable success. SASC provides a staff of peer, graduate, and professional tutors to support a wide selection of undergraduate courses.

General Support Services Information

Contact Information
Name of program or department: Disability Services
Telephone: 207-221-4418
Fax: 207-523-1919
Website: www.une.edu/studentlife/disability-services

Accommodations or Services For Students With Learning Differences

Accommodations are decided upon an individual basis after a thorough review of appropriate, current documentation. The accommodations requests must be supported through the documentation provided and must be logically linked to the current impact of the condition on academic functioning.

Allowed in exams
Calculator: Yes
Dictionary: Yes
Computer: Yes
Spellchecker: Yes
Extended test time: Yes
Scribes: Yes
Proctors: Yes
Oral exams: No
Note-takers: Yes
Support services for students with LD: Yes
Support services for students with ADHD: Yes
Support services for students with ASD: Yes
Distraction-reduced environment: Yes
Tape recording in class: Yes
Electronic texts: Yes
Kurzweil reader: NR
Audio books: Yes
Other assistive technology: Yes
Priority registration: Yes
Added costs of services: No
LD specialists: No
ADHD coaching: No
ASD specialists: No
Professional tutors: No
Peer tutors: NR
Max. hours/wk. for services: NR
How professors are notified of student approved accommodations: By student

General Admissions Information

Office of Admissions: 207-602-2297

Entrance Requirements

Academic units required: 4 English, 3 math, 3 science, 2 science labs, 2 social studies, 2 history, **Academic units recommended:** 4 math, 4 science, 3 science labs, 2 foreign language, 4 social studies, 4 history, 4 academic electives. High school diploma is required and GED is accepted. SAT or ACT required. If ACT, ACT with writing accepted. TOEFL required of all international applicants: minimum paper TOEFL 550.

Application deadline: NR
Notification: Rolling starting 12/15
Average GPA: 3.3
ACT Composite middle 50% range: NR-NR
SAT Math middle 50% range: 480-590
SAT Critical Reading middle 50% range: 480-580
SAT Writing middle 50% range: NR-NR
Graduate top 10% of class: NR
Graduated top 25% of class: NR
Graduated top 50% of class: NR

COLLEGE GRADUATION REQUIREMENTS

Course waivers allowed: No
Course substitutions allowed: No

Additional Information

Environment: This private school was founded in 1831. It has a 550-acre campus on the coast of Maine.

Student Body
Undergrad enrollment: 3,801
% Women: 73
% Men: 27
% Out-of-state: 68
Cost information
Tuition: $33,540
Room & board: $12,920
Housing Information
University Housing: Yes
Percent living on campus: 62
Greek System
Fraternity: No
Sorority: No
Athletics: Division III

Frostburg State University

FSU, 101 Braddock Road, Frostburg, MD 21532
Phone: 301-687-4201 • Fax: 301-687-7074
E-mail: fsuadmissions@frostburg.edu • Web: www.frostburg.edu
Support: S • Institution: Public

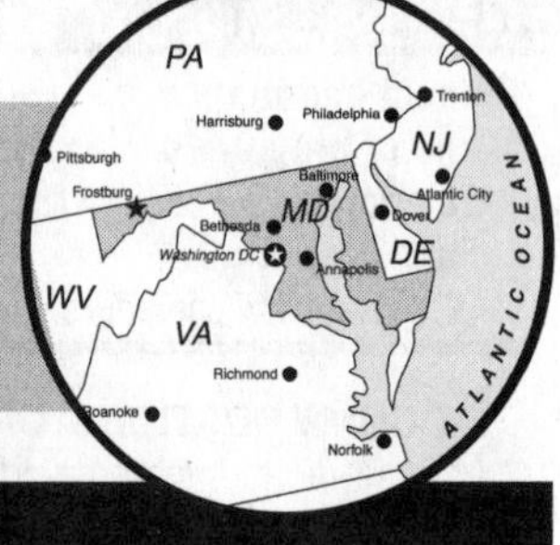

Programs or Services for Students with Learning Differences

Frostburg State University provides comprehensive support services for students with disabilities to assist them in achieving their potential. To be eligible for the services, admitted students must provide recent and appropriate documentation relating to their disability. Some of the services provided are extended time for testing, note takers, advocacy, electronic texts, priority registration, readers and scribes, and assistive technology. The goal of the program is to provide appropriate support services to enhance learning and to strive for student self-advocacy and understanding of and independence in their learning styles.

Admission Information for Students with Learning Differences

College entrance tests required: Yes
Interview required: No
Essay required: No
Additional Application Required for LD/ADHD/ASD: NR
What documentation required for LD: Psycho ed evaluation to include: relevant historical info, instructional interventions, related services, age diagnosed, objective data (aptitude, achievement, info processing), test scores (standard, percentile and grade equivalents) and describe functional limitations.
With general application: No
To receive services after enrolling: Yes
What documentation required for ADHD: Diagnosis based on DSM-V; history of behaviors impairing functioning in academic setting; diagnostic interview; history of symptoms; evidence of ongoing behaviors.
With general application: No
To receive services after enrolling: Yes
What documentation required for ASD: Statement of diagnosis from a qualified professional with recommendations for accomodations; statement of limitation and how the disability may affect the student; any assessment that were completed. ASD documentation not required with general application.
With general application: NR
To receive services after enrolling: Yes
LD/ADHD/ASD documentation submitted to: Disability Support Services
ASD Specific Program: NR
Special Ed. HS course work accepted: Yes
Specific course requirements of all applicants: Yes
Separate application required: No
Total # of students receiving LD/ADHD/ASD services: 250
Acceptance into program means acceptance into college: Students must be admitted and enrolled in the university first and then request services. There is an appeal procedure for students who are denied admission.

Admissions

There is no special admission procedure for students with learning disabilities. All students must complete the mainstream program in high school and meet all of the requirements for the university and the state. There is a Student Support Services/Disabled Student Services information form that must be completed by students to enroll in these programs. Admission to FSU is determined by the Admissions Office, which assesses an applicant's likelihood of success in a regular college program with support service assistance. Course requirements include 4 English, 3 math, 3 science, 2 science lab, 2 foreign language, and 3 social studies. If you have not taken the required courses, you may be admitted to the university with the understanding that courses in the deficient area(s) must be completed during the first year if you want to continue your studies. The average SAT Reasoning is 980 or ACT 21.

Additional Information

PASS is devoted to students' success in college. With PASS, FSU students can gain access to a variety of resources that will help them develop college skills and knowledge, strengthen their metacognitive process—including problem resolution and learning to learn skills—and other tools necessary for a college student's success. The following services are currently available to FSU students through PASS: Placement tests using the Nelson-Deny Reading Assessment, Developmental Math courses, Language Skills development, study skills and tutoring.

General Support Services Information

Contact Information
Name of program or department: Disability Support Services
Telephone: 301-687-4483
Fax: 301-687-4671

Accommodations or Services for Students with Learning Differences

Accommodations are decided upon an individual basis after a thorough review of appropriate, current documentation. The accommodations requested must be supported through the documentation provided and must be logically linked to the current impact of the condition on academic functioning.

Allowed in exams

Calculator: Yes
Dictionary: Yes
Computer: Yes
Spellchecker: Yes
Extended test time: Yes
Scribes: Yes
Proctors: Yes
Oral exams: Yes
Note-takers: Yes
Services for students with LD: Yes
Services for students with ADHD: Yes
Services for students with ASD: Yes
Distraction-reduced environment: Yes
Tape recording in class: Yes
Audio books: Not through the school but the student can get a student membership.
Electronic texts: Yes
Kurzweil Reader: Yes
Other assistive technology: Yes
Priority registration: Yes, when applicable
Added costs for services: No
LD specialists: No
ADHD coaching: We have someone that can work with students on time management, test taking skills, notetaking, etc.
ASD specialists: No
Professional tutors: 7
Peer tutors: Yes
Max. hours/wk. for services: Varies
How professors are notified of LD/ADHD: By student

General Admissions Information

Office of Admissions: 301-687-4201

Entrance Requirements

Academic units required: 4 English, 3 math, 3 science, 2 science labs, 2 foreign language, 3 history. High school diploma is required and GED is accepted. SAT or ACT required. If ACT, ACT with writing accepted. TOEFL required of all international applicants: minimum paper TOEFL 550.

Application deadline: NR
Notification: Rolling starting 11/1
Average GPA: 3.2
ACT Composite middle 50% range: 18-22
SAT Math middle 50% range: 440-540
SAT Critical Reading middle 50% range: 440-530
SAT Writing middle 50% range: 420-520
Graduated top 10% of class: 11
Graduated top 25% of class: 31
Graduated top 50% of class: 66

COLLEGE GRADUATION REQUIREMENTS

Course waivers allowed: No
Course substitutions allowed: Yes
In what course: Students may appeal for any course to be substituted. Appeals are determined on a case-by-case basis.

Additional Information

Environment: This public school was founded in 1898. It has a 260-acre campus in western Maryland.

Student Body
Undergrad enrollment: 4,631
% Women: 49
% Men: 51
% Out-of-state: 8

Cost information
In-state Tuition: $8,488
Out-of Tuition: $20,588
Room & board: $8,672

Housing Information
University Housing: Yes
Percent living on campus: 32

Greek System
Fraternity: Yes
Sorority: Yes
Athletics: Division III

McDaniel College

Two College Hill, Westminster, MD 21157
Phone: 410-857-2230 • Fax: 410-857-2757
E-mail: admissions@mcdaniel.edu • Web: www.mcdaniel.edu
Support: CS • Institution type: 4-year Private

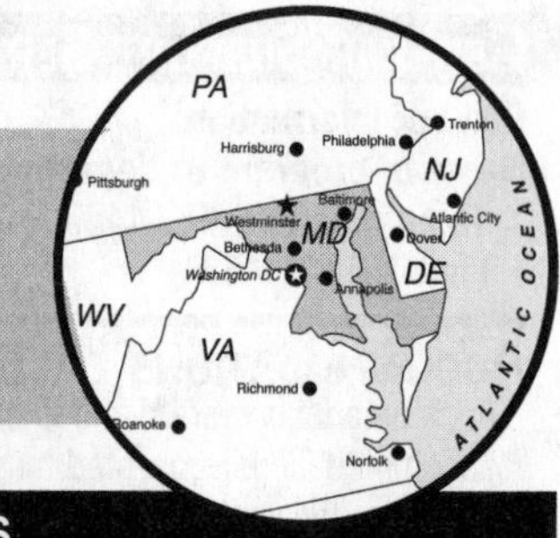

Programs or Services for Students with Learning Differences

Student Academic Support Services (SASS) ensures that all students with documented disabilities receive appropriate academic accommodations. The Mentorship Advantage Program (MAP) offers interactive workshops on topics such as socialization, organization, assistive technology, time management, resume writing and interviewing. The Providing Academic Support for Success (PASS) program offers students the opportunity to learn alongside their peers and supported by Graduate Assistants three evenings a week. The Academic Skills Program (ASP), a fee-based opportunity ($3,150 annual fee), provides students with weekly consultation with an Academic Counselor, academic skills tutoring with a SASS graduate assistant, use of supervised study/computer lab, learning style and priority registration.

Admission Information for Students with Learning Differences

College entrance tests required: Yes
Interview required: No
Essay required: Yes

Additional Application Required for LD/ADHD/ASD: NR
What documentation required for LD: Psycho ed evaluation to include: relevant historical info, instructional interventions, related services, age diagnosed, objective data (aptitude, achievement, info processing), test scores (standard, percentile and grade equivalents) and describe functional limitations.
With general application: No
To receive services after enrolling: Yes
What documentation required for ADHD: Diagnosis based on DSM-V; history of behaviors impairing functioning in academic setting; diagnostic interview; history of symptoms; evidence of ongoing behaviors.
With general application: No
To receive services after enrolling: Yes
What documentation required for ASD: Psycho ed evaluation
With general application: NR
To receive services after enrolling: Yes
LD/ADHD/ASD documentation submitted to: Academic Skills Center
ASD Specific Program: NR
Special Ed. HS course work accepted: No
Specific course requirements of all applicants: Yes
Separate application required: Yes
Total # of students receiving LD/ADHD/ASD services: 165
Acceptance into program means acceptance into college: Students must be admitted and enrolled in the university first and then request services.

Admissions

The admission process is the same for all applicants. General admission criteria include a minimum 2.75 GPA in core academic courses including 4 years English, 3 years math, 3 years science, 3 years social studies and 3 years of a foreign language (substitutions are allowed in foreign language if appropriate). Students with a 3.5 GPA do not have to submit an ACT or SAT. The average ACT is 21 and average SAT is 1000. Any documentation for LD or ADHD should be sent to ASC to be used after a student is admitted and enrolled.

Additional Information

McDaniel "Step Ahead" is an optional 5-day summer bridge opportunity offered for first-year students with disabilities. Intensive workshops, team-building activities and field trips are available for students to familiarize themselves with the resources, staff and peers who comprise and utilize McDaniel's SASS. Each participant is matched with a peer mentor. Some typical accommodations offered by the SASS include: note takers, alternative testing arrangements such as extra time, books on tape, computer with speech input, separate testing room, tape recorder, foreign language substitution and math substitution. Content tutors on campus are available and skills' tutoring with a Grad Assistant is also available on a limited basis. If there is sufficient support for a foreign language substitution, a recommendation is made to the provost of the college. If approved, cross-cultural studies courses may be suggested.

General Support Services Information

Contact Information
Name of program or department: Academic Skills Center
Telephone: 410-857-2504
Fax: 410-386-4617

Accommodations or Services for Students with Learning Differences

Accommodations are decided upon an individual basis after a thorough review of appropriate, current documentation. The accommodations requested must be supported through the documentation provided and must be logically linked to the current impact of the condition on academic functioning.

Allowed in exams
Calculator: Yes
Dictionary: Yes
Computer: Yes
Spellchecker: Yes
Extended test time: Yes
Scribes: Yes
Proctors: Yes
Oral exams: Yes
Note-takers: Yes
Services for students with LD: Yes
Services for students with ADHD: Yes
Services for students with ASD: Yes
Distraction-reduced environment: Yes
Tape recording in class: Yes
Audio books: NR
Electronic texts: Yes
Kurzweil Reader: Yes
Other assistive technology: Yes
Priority registration: Yes
Added costs for services: Yes
LD specialists: Yes
ADHD coaching: NR
ASD specialists: NR
Professional tutors: Yes
Peer tutors: 10
Max. hours/wk. for services: Unlimited
How professors are notified of LD/ADHD: By student

General Admissions Information

Office of Admissions: 410-857-2230

Entrance Requirements

Academic units required: 4 English, 3 math, 3 science, 3 science labs, 3 foreign language, 3 social studies, **Academic units recommended:** 4 English, 4 math, 4 science, 4 foreign language, 3 social studies, SAT or ACT required. If ACT, ACT with writing accepted. TOEFL required of all international applicants: minimum paper TOEFL 550 or minimum internet TOEFL 80.

Application deadline: NR
Notification: NR
Average GPA: 3.43
ACT Composite middle 50% range: 20-27
SAT Math middle 50% range: 480-590
SAT Critical Reading middle 50% range: 480-590
SAT Writing middle 50% range: NR-NR
Graduated top 10% of class: 26
Graduated top 25% of class: 51
Graduated top 50% of class: 82

COLLEGE GRADUATION REQUIREMENTS

Course waivers allowed: Yes
In what course: Foreign language
Course substitutions allowed: Yes
In what course: Foreign language

Additional Information

Environment: The college is located on 160 acres in a small town 30 miles northwest of Baltimore.

Student Body
Undergrad enrollment: 1,663
% Women: 54
% Men: 46
% Out-of-state: 34

Cost information
Tuition: $39,500
Room & board: $10,300

Housing Information
University Housing: Yes
Percent living on campus: 80

Greek System
Fraternity: Yes
Sorority: Yes
Athletics: Division III

SALISBURY UNIVERSITY

Admissions Office Salisbury, MD 21801
Phone: 410.543.6161 • Fax: 410.546.6016
E-mail: admissions@salisbury.edu • Web: www.salisbury.edu
Support: S • Institution: Public

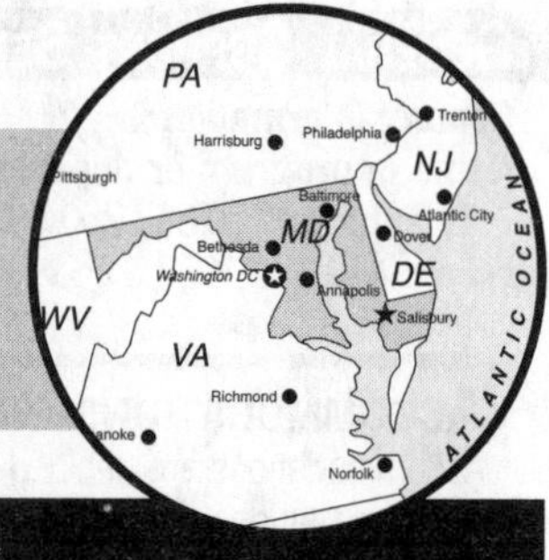

PROGRAMS OR SERVICES FOR STUDENTS WITH LEARNING DIFFERENCES

The OSDSS is committed to fostering accessible learning opportunities and environments for qualified students with disabilities. To support its mission, the OSDSS serves as a resource for students and instructors alike and values student self-empowerment, self-direction, and self-determination while believing that access to educational opportunities for students with disabilities should in no way compromise the intended learning outcomes of any educational opportunity or environment inside or outside of the classroom setting. The OSDSS aims to inform educate and support students with disabilities in ways in which allow them to achieve their educational, career, and life goals, on the basis of their personal skills, abilities, interests, and values. Equity in access, rights of privacy, and the integrity of academic programs, policies, and practices are emphasized by the OSDSS.

ADMISSION INFORMATION FOR STUDENTS WITH LEARNING DIFFERENCES

College entrance test required: No
Interview required: No
Essay required: Not Applicable
Additional Application Required for LD/ADHD/ASD: Yes
What documentation required for LD: Psycho-educational evaluation; psychiatrist or psychologist report; physician report.
With general application: No
To receive services after enrolling: Yes
What documentation required for ADHD: Psycho-educational Education
With general application: No
To receive services after enrolling: Yes
What documentation required for ASD: Psycho-educational Education
With general application: No
To receive services after enrolling: Yes
LD/ADHD/ASD documentation submitted to: Office of Student Disability Support Services
ASD Specific Program: NR
Special Ed. HS course work accepted: NR
Specific course requirements of all applicants: Yes
Separate application required for program services: True
Total # of students receiving LD/ADHD/ASD services:
Acceptance into program means acceptance into college: No

ADMISSIONS

Applicants must submit the completed application for admission, official high school transcripts, essay, and letter(s) of recommendation. Standardized SAT or ACT test scores are required for applicants with a weighted grade point average of 3.50 or less on a 4.0 scale. Applicants choosing to exclude standardized test scores should provide evidence of individual achievements and/or experiences which would not be evident from a review of the official high school transcripts. Leadership qualities, community service, artistic talent, athletic talent and diversity of background, including cultural, experiential and geographic, are additional factors used in the holistic review of each applicant.

ADDITIONAL INFORMATION

Once the OSDSS has evaluated the submitted disability documentation, confirmed that documentation meets the necessary criteria for receiving reasonable accommodations, and received the students' completed intake form, the student should contact the OSDSS in order to schedule an Intake Conference. At this meeting, the student and OSDSS staff member will discuss the students accommodation plans, strategies for a successful academic career, and campus resources and services, among other topics. All documentation submitted should contain a comprehensive written evaluation, prepared by a qualified professional, and should include a statement of diagnosis of a disability, a description of that disability and a description of the nature and severity of the students disability.

General Support Services Information

Contact Information
Name of program or department: Office of Student Disability Support Services
Telephone: 410-543-6070
Fax: 410-548-4052
Website: http://www.salisbury.edu/students/dss

Accommodations or Services for Students with Learning Differences

Accommodations are decided upon an individual basis after a thorough review of appropriate, current documentation. The accommodations requests must be supported through the documentation provided and must be logically linked to the current impact of the condition on academic functioning.

Allowed in exams
Calculator: Yes
Dictionary: Yes
Computer: Yes
Spellchecker: Yes
Extended test time: Yes
Scribes: Yes
Proctors: Yes
Oral exams: Yes
Note-takers: Yes
Support services for students with LD: Yes
Support services for students with ADHD: Yes
Support services for students with ASD: Yes
Distraction-reduced environment: Yes
Tape recording in class: Yes
Electronic texts: Yes
Kurzweil reader: NR
Audio books: Yes
Other assistive technology: Yes
Priority registration: Yes
Added costs of services: No
LD specialists: NR
ADHD coaching: Yes
ASD specialists: No
Professional tutors: No
Peer tutors: Yes
Max. hours/wk. for services: NR
How professors are notified of student approved accommodations: By student

General Admissions Information

Office of Admissions: 410.543.6161

Entrance Requirements

Academic units required: 4 English, 4 math, 3 science, 2 science labs, 2 foreign language, 3 social studies, **Academic units recommended:** 4 English, 4 math, 4 science, 3 science labs, 3 foreign language, 3 social studies, 3 academic electives, High school diploma is required and GED is accepted. SAT or ACT required for some. If ACT, ACT with writing accepted. TOEFL required of all international applicants: minimum paper TOEFL 79 or minimum internet TOEFL 550.

Application deadline: 1/15
Notification: 3/15
Average GPA: 3.69
ACT Composite middle 50% range: 21-26
SAT Math middle 50% range: 540-620
SAT Critical Reading middle 50% range: 540-620
SAT Writing middle 50% range: 530-605
Graduate top 10% of class: 20
Graduated top 25% of class: 54
Graduated top 50% of class: 89

COLLEGE GRADUATION REQUIREMENTS

Course waivers allowed: Yes
In what course: General Education courses, on a case-by-case basis.
Course substitutions allowed: Yes
In what course: Requests are evaluated on a case-by-case basis.

Additional Information

Environment: This public school was founded in 1925. It has a 155-acre campus 30 miles west of Ocean City, MD and 115 miles southeast of Baltimore, MD and Washington, D.C..

Student Body
Undergrad enrollment: 7,849
% Women: 57
% Men: 43
% Out-of-state: 13.5

Cost information
In-state tuition: $6,712
Out-of-state tuition: $15,058
Room & board: $11,010

Housing Information
University Housing: Yes
Percent living on campus: 42

Greek System
Fraternity: Yes
Sorority: Yes
Athletics: Division III

TOWSON UNIVERSITY

8000 York Road, Towson, MD 21252-0001
Phone: 410-704-2113 • Fax: 410-704-3030
E-mail: admissions@towson.edu • Web: www.towson.edu
Support: CS • Institution: Public

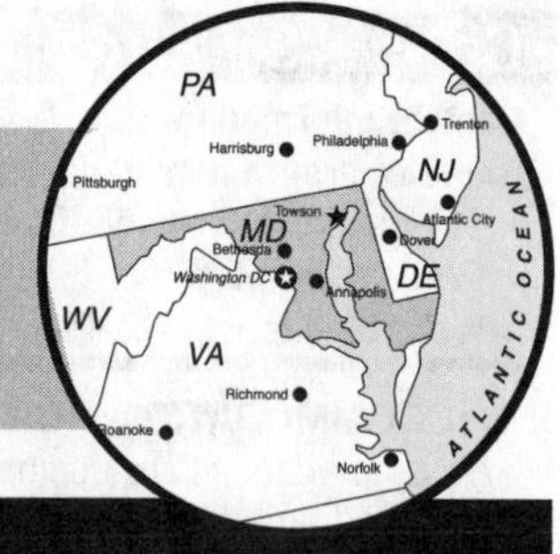

PROGRAMS OR SERVICES FOR STUDENTS WITH LEARNING DIFFERENCES

Towson University offers many services to students with disabilities, but it does not have a separate program for students with learning disabilities and/or attention deficit hyperactivity disorder. Eligibility for services is determined individually by the Disability Support Services (DSS) office based on documented need and personal interview. Students are encouraged to register with DSS as soon as possible after admission to the university to ensure timely provision of services. Once registered with Disability Support Services, students are issued a memo listing their accommodations that students are expected to present to professors. Towson University also offers all students tutorial services and a writing lab not affiliated with Disability Support Services.

ADMISSION INFORMATION FOR STUDENTS WITH LEARNING DIFFERENCES

College entrance test required: Yes
Interview required: No
Essay required: NR
Additional Application Required for LD/ADHD/ASD: Not Applicable
What documentation required for LD: Current psychiatrist or psychologist
With general application: Not Applicable
To receive services after enrolling: Not Applicable
What documentation required for ADHD: Psycho ed evaluation
With general application: Not Applicable
To receive services after enrolling: Not Applicable
What documentation required for ASD: Current psycho-educational evaluation
With general application: Not Applicable
To receive services after enrolling: Not Applicable
LD/ADHD/ASD documentation submitted to: Disability Support Services
ASD Specific Program: Hussman Center for Adults with Autism
Special Ed. HS course work accepted: Yes
Specific course requirements of all applicants: Yes
Separate application required for program services: Yes
Total # of students receiving LD/ADHD/ASD services: NR
Acceptance into program means acceptance into college: Not Applicable

ADMISSIONS

There is no question on the application that inquires about a learning disability. Students with learning disabilities who want to request services after they are admitted should provide documentation and information about their learning disability to the office of Disability Support Services only after they have been accepted to the university. The mid 50 percent SAT range for applicants (combined reading, math, and writing) is 1560-1770. Priority admission is granted to applicants with GPA of 3.0 and 4 years of English, 3 years of social science, 3 years of science lab, 3 years of math, and 2 years of a foreign language (waived with appropriate documentation). Courses taken in special education may be considered. Applicants with lower GPAs and test scores will be considered after their seventh semester grades on a space available basis, with priority given to those with the highest GPA.

ADDITIONAL INFORMATION

The Hussman Center for Adults with Autism brings together Towson University students and young adults on the autism spectrum to create a mutually rewarding learning environment. Social, educational and fitness programs support learning for adults with autism as they develop the tools needed to lead meaningful and engaged lives. The programs include fun social activities, art classes, comedy workshops, cooking classes, music, creative movement experiences as well as specialized training in language skills, personal fitness, and entry-level job skills. Many participants exhibit an increase in social interaction, wellness and community involvement after completing our programs. More than 300 Towson University students have been involved in service-learning experiences at the Hussman Center for Adults with Autism.

General Support Services Information

Contact Information
Name of program or department: Disability Support Services
Telephone: 410-704-2638
Fax: 410-704-4247

Accommodations or Services For Students With Learning Differences

Accommodations are decided upon an individual basis after a thorough review of appropriate, current documentation. The accommodations requests must be supported through the documentation provided and must be logically linked to the current impact of the condition on academic functioning.

Allowed in exams
Calculator: Yes
Dictionary: Yes
Computer: Yes
Spellchecker: Yes
Extended test time: Yes
Scribes: Yes
Proctors: Yes
Oral exams: Yes
Note-takers: Yes
Support services for students with LD: Yes
Support services for students with ADHD: Yes
Support services for students with ASD: Yes
Distraction-reduced environment: Yes
Tape recording in class: Yes
Electronic texts: Yes
Kurzweil reader: NR
Audio books: Yes
Other assistive technology: Yes
Priority registration: Yes
Added costs of services: No
LD specialists: Yes
ADHD coaching: No
ASD specialists: Yes
Professional tutors: No
Peer tutors: Yes
Max. hours/wk. for services: NR
How professors are notified of student approved accommodations: By student

General Admissions Information

Office of Admissions: 410-704-2113

Entrance Requirements

Academic units required: 4 English, 4 math, 3 science, 2 science labs, 2 foreign language, 3 social studies, 6 academic electives. High school diploma is required and GED is accepted. SAT or ACT required. If ACT, ACT with writing accepted. TOEFL required of all international applicants: minimum paper TOEFL 500 or minimum internet TOEFL 61.

Application deadline: 1/15
Notification: Rolling starting 11/6
Average GPA: 3.62
ACT Composite middle 50% range: 21-25
SAT Math middle 50% range: 500-590
SAT Critical Reading middle 50% range: 500-580
SAT Writing middle 50% range: 490-580
Graduate top 10% of class: 18
Graduated top 25% of class: 45
Graduated top 50% of class: 84

COLLEGE GRADUATION REQUIREMENTS

Course waivers allowed: No
Course substitutions allowed: Yes
In what course: Chiefly math. Foreign language is not required for most majors.

Additional Information

Environment: This public school was founded in 1866. It has a 328-acre campus.

Student Body
Undergrad enrollment: 19,049
% Women: 60
% Men: 40
% Out-of-state: 14

Cost information
In-state Tuition: $6,430
Out-of-state Tuition: $18,036
Room & board: $11,638

Housing Information
University Housing: Yes
Percent living on campus: 26

Greek System
Fraternity: Yes
Sorority: Yes
Athletics: Division I

U. OF MARYLAND—COLLEGE PARK

Mitchell Building College, Park, MD 20742-5235
Phone: 301-314-8385 • Fax: 301-314-9693
E-mail: um-admit@uga.umd.edu • Web: www.umd.edu
Support: CS • Institution: Public

PROGRAMS OR SERVICES FOR STUDENTS WITH LEARNING DIFFERENCES

The goal of the Disability Support Service is coordinate services which ensure individuvals with disabilities equal access to University programs. This goal is accomplished by: 1) providing and coordinating individually tailored direct services to students, faculty and staff, and campus visitors who have disabilities; 2) providing consultation to university staff regarding the Adaptive Technology needs of students and staff who have disabilities; 3) providing support and information to students and staff which promotes the development of advocacy and negotiation skills.

ADMISSION INFORMATION FOR STUDENTS WITH LEARNING DIFFERENCES

College entrance test required: Yes
Interview required: No
Essay required: Yes
Additional Application Required for LD/ADHD/ASD: NR
What documentation required for LD: Psycho-educational or neuropsychological evaluation (including Apititude and achievement testing). We will review IEP's for specificity and if specific enough, they may suffice as adequate documentation.
With general application: No
To receive services after enrolling: Yes
What documentation required for ADHD: Neuropsychological or Psycho-educational evaluation (including Apititude and achievement testing) or a comprehensive letter from a licensed counselor or psychologist, or a psychiatrist.
With general application: No
To receive services after enrolling: Yes
What documentation required for ASD: Psycho ed evaluation
With general application: No
To receive services after enrolling: Yes
LD/ADHD/ASD documentation submitted to: Support program/services
ASD Specific Program: NR
Special Ed. HS course work accepted: Yes
Specific course: Yes
Separate application required for program services: No
Total # of students receiving LD/ADHD/ASD services: 450

ADMISSIONS

Applicants must use the Coalition Application for Access and Affordability and Success to apply. Academic merit is assessed on the basis of each applicant's achievements and potential in a broad range of academic categories, as influenced by the opportunities and challenges faced by the applicant. These categories include: Educational Performance, Potential for College Success, Potential to Promote Beneficial Educational Outcomes and to Contribute to Campus and Community Life, Students' Persistence and Commitment to Educational Success. The review process considers more than 26 factors.

ADDITIONAL INFORMATION

Learning Assistance Service (LAS) is the academic support unit of the University Counseling Center. LAS exists to help students achieve their academic goals by providing a range of services. LAS also provides Academic Success Workshop series to help students become successful, active learners. Workshops focus on helping students manage their time and improve their approach to studying and learning at UM. LAS offers learning strategy courses to help develop college level learning strategies.

General Support Services Information

Contact Information
Name of program or department: Disability Support Service (DSS)
Telephone: 301-314-7682
Fax: 301-405-0813

Accommodations or Services for Students with Learning Differences

Accommodations are decided upon an individual basis after a thorough review of appropriate, current documentation. The accommodations requests must be supported through the documentation provided and must be logically linked to the current impact of the condition on academic functioning.

Allowed in exams
Calculator: Yes
Dictionary: Yes
Computer: Yes
Spellchecker: Yes
Extended test time: Yes
Scribes: Yes
Proctors: Yes
Oral exams: Yes
Note-takers: Yes
Services for students with LD: Yes
Services for students with ADHD: Yes
Services for students with ASD: Yes
Distraction-reduced environment: Yes
Tape recording in class: Yes
Audio books: Yes
Electronic texts: NR
Kurzweil Reader: Yes
Other assistive technology: Yes
Priority registration: Yes
Added costs of services: No
LD specialists: Yes
ADHD coaching: NR
ASD specialists: NR
Professional tutors: NR
Peer tutors: NR
Max. hours/wk. for services: NR
How professors are notified of student approved accommodations: Student

General Admissions Information

Office of Admissions: 301-314-8385

Entrance Requirements

Academic units required: 4 English, 4 math, 3 science, 2 science labs, 2 foreign language, 3 social studies, 3 history, **Academic units recommended:** 4 English, 4 math, 3 science, 2 science labs, 2 foreign language, 3 social studies, 3 history. High school diploma is required and GED is accepted. SAT or ACT required. If ACT, ACT with writing required. TOEFL required of all international applicants: minimum internet TOEFL 100.

Application deadline: 1/20
Notification: Rolling starting 4/1
Average GPA: 4.22
ACT Composite middle 50% range: NR-NR
SAT Math middle 50% range: 620-730
SAT Critical Reading middle 50% range: 590-690
SAT Writing middle 50% range: NR-NR
Graduated top 10% of class: NR
Graduated top 25% of class: NR
Graduated top 50% of class: NR

COLLEGE GRADUATION REQUIREMENTS

Course waivers allowed: No
Course substitutions allowed: Yes
In what course: Math, foreign language

Additional Information

Environment: A 1,382-acre campus in a small town setting near Washington, DC, and Baltimore.

Student Body
Undergrad enrollment: 27,443
% Women: 47
% Men: 53
% Out-of-state: 21

Cost information
In-state Tuition: $8,152
Out-of Tuition: $29,300
Room & board: $10,972

Housing Information
University Housing: Yes
Percent living on campus: 42

Greek System
Fraternity: Yes
Sorority: Yes
Athletics: Division I

American International College

1000 State Street, Springfield, MA 01109-3184
Phone: 413-205-3201 • Fax: 413-205-3051
E-mail: inquiry@aic.edu • Web: www.aic.edu
Support: SP • Institution: Private

Programs or Services for Students with Learning Differences

Supportive Learning Services (SLS) has been an integral part of the American International College campus since 1977. The staff recognizes that everyone learns differently and serves students as individuals with customized approaches and plans specific to their learning styles. AIC values their students' individual strengths above all things and truly believes they can achieve their dreams if given the right tools. This fee-based program provides the required tools, along with ongoing support and encouragement in the form of regular, individualized professional tutoring and academic coaching, group study sessions facilitated by professional educators, and skill-based workshops. SLS tutors work closely with college faculty and staff using a proactive advising model to support students. Assistance is available to each student in the program for the duration of his or her college career.

Admission Information for Students with Learning Differences

College entrance tests required: Yes
Interview required: Yes
Essay required: No
Additional Application Required for LD/ADHD/ASD: NR
What documentation required for LD: Psycho ed evaluation to include: relevant historical info, instructional interventions, related services, age diagnosed, objective data (aptitude, achievement, info processing), test scores (standard, percentile and grade equivalents) and describe functional limitations.
With general application: Yes if requested as part of Structured Program application
To receive services after enrolling: Yes
What documentation required for ADHD: Diagnosis based on DSM-V; history of behaviors impairing functioning in academic setting; diagnostic interview; history of symptoms; evidence of ongoing behaviors.
With general application: Yes if requested as part of Structured Program application
To receive services after enrolling: Yes
What documentation required for ASD: Psycho ed evaluation
With general application: NR
To receive services after enrolling: Yes
LD/ADHD/ASD documentation submitted to: Supportive Learning Services Program
ASD Specific Program: NR
Special Ed. HS course work accepted: No
Specific course requirements of all applicants: Yes
Separate application required: No
Total # of students receiving LD/ADHD/ASD services: 95
Acceptance into program means acceptance into college: Simultaneous admission decisions are made by the program and admissions.

Admissions

In addition to the standard AIC application, applicants to SLSP need to provide a recently administered Wechsler Adult Intelligence Scale, relevant diagnostic material, any supportive assistance they've received in the past and ACT or SAT scores. AIC evaluates high school coursework, grades and standardized test scores. However, they are equally interested in student activities, personal statement, and letters of recommendations. They understand that students are more than transcripts and test scores. A letter of recommendation is optional but is a good way for AIC to learn more about an applicant. Students can submit more than one, but the number of letters doesn't factor into their decision-making process. Personal statements are also optional, but they're a great way to tell the student's story first hand, and helps AIC learn about passions, interests, and goals. If a student is worried about GPA or test scores, or has had a personal experience that impacted academics, a personal statement can give the bigger picture. Interviews are optional. The admission decision is made simultaneously between admissions and SLSP.

Additional Information

Their expert staff reviews each student's documentation and gets to know them through a personal interview. Tutors then work creatively to find the best way to help them improve vital academic skills like: Goal setting, Organization and planning, Note taking, Time management, and Study skills, like volume reading and writing and Test taking. In addition to helping build academic skills, SLS staff can help students develop and practice self-advocacy skills and explore technologies that support academic success. Collegiate Disability Services (CDS), housed with SLS, ensures that all qualified students with disabilities receive accommodations & services that support an accessible, equitable, and inclusive learning and living environment at American International College. CDS staff works closely with Academics and Student Life to reduce or eliminate any disadvantages that may occur as a result of an individual's disability.

General Support Services Information

Contact Information
Name of program or department: Supportive Learning Services Program
Telephone: 413-205-3426
Fax: 413-205-3908

Telephone: 413-205-3426
Fax: 413-205-3908

Accommodations or Services for Students with Learning Differences

Accommodations are decided upon an individual basis after a thorough review of appropriate, current documentation. The accommodations requested must be supported through the documentation provided and must be logically linked to the current impact of the condition on academic functioning.

Allowed in exams
- **Calculator:** Yes
- **Dictionary:** No
- **Computer:** Yes
- **Spellchecker:** Yes

Extended test time: Yes
Scribes: Yes
Proctors: Yes
Oral exams: Yes
Note-takers: No
Services for students with LD: Yes
Services for students with ADHD: Yes
Services for students with ASD: Yes
Distraction-reduced environment: Yes
Tape recording in class: Yes
Audio books: NR
Electronic texts: Yes
Kurzweil Reader: Yes
Other assistive technology: Yes
Priority registration: Yes
Added costs for services: Yes
LD specialists: Yes
ADHD coaching: NR
ASD specialists: NR
Professional tutors: 9
Peer tutors: No
Max. hours/wk. for services: 5
How professors are notified of LD/ADHD: By both student and director

General Admissions Information

Office of Admissions: 413-205-3201

Entrance Requirements

Academic units recommended: 4 English, 3 math, 2 science, 2 science labs, 1 foreign language, 2 social studies, 4 academic electives. High school diploma is required and GED is accepted. SAT or ACT required. If ACT, ACT with writing accepted. TOEFL required of all international applicants: minimum paper TOEFL 550 or minimum internet TOEFL 80.

Application deadline: NR
Notification: Rolling starting 10/10
Average GPA: 2.8
ACT Composite middle 50% range: 16-23
SAT Math middle 50% range: 400-500
SAT Critical Reading middle 50% range: 390-480
SAT Writing middle 50% range: 380-480
Graduated top 10% of class: NR
Graduated top 25% of class: NR
Graduated top 50% of class: NR

COLLEGE GRADUATION REQUIREMENTS

Course waivers allowed: No
Course substitutions allowed: No

Additional Information

Environment: This private school has a 58-acre campus 75 miles from Boston and 30 miles north of Hartford.

Student Body
- **Undergrad enrollment:** 1,486
- **% Women:** 60
- **% Men:** 40
- **% Out-of-state:** 39

Cost information
- **Tuition:** $33,140
- **Room & board:** $6,430

Housing Information
- **University Housing:** Yes
- **Percent living on campus:** 50

Greek System
- **Fraternity:** No
- **Sorority:** No

Athletics: Division II

Boston College

140 Commonwealth Ave., Devlin Hall 208, Chestnut Hill, MA 02467-3809
Phone: 617-552-3100 • Fax: 617-552-0798
E-mail: ugadmis@bc.edu• Web: www.bc.edu
Support: CS • Institution type: 4-year private

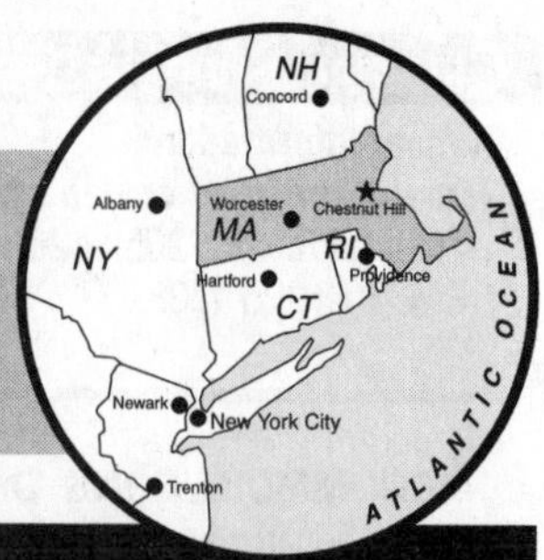

Programs or Services for Students with Learning Differences

There is no specific program at Boston College for students with LD. The Connors Family learning Center (CFLC) offers instructional support to faculty and graduate students, special services to students with LD and ADHD, and tutoring and skills workshops to all Boston College students. The CFLC provides academic support to more tha 450 BC students with LD. The CFLC aims to help students with LD to become independent learners who understand their abilities and disabilities and can act effectively as self-advocates. The CFLC also offers free tutoring to all students at BC. All tutors receive training and must be recommended or approved by the Chair of the Department for which the student will tutor. Students who are seeking support services are required to submit documentation to verify eligibility. Testing must be current, comprehensive, performed by a certified LD specialist or licensed psychologist, and there must be clear and specific evidence of a LD. Educational recommendations regarding the impact of the disability and accommodations recommended at the post secondary level must be included. Documentation for ADHD must include an in depth evaluation from the psychiatrist/psychologist/physician who made the diagnosis as well as specific educational recommendations.

Admission Information for Students with Learning Differences

College entrance test required: Yes
Interview required: Not Applicable
Essay required: Not Applicable
Additional Application Required for LD/ADHD/ASD: No
What documentation required for LD: Psycho ed evaluation within 4 years
With general application: NR
To receive services after enrolling: No
What documentation required for ADHD: Psycho ed evaluation
With general application: NR
To receive services after enrolling: No
What documentation required for ASD: Psycho ed evaluationi
With general application: NR
To receive services after enrolling: No
LD/ADHD/ASD documentation submitted to: The Connors Family Learning Center
ASD Specific Program: NR
Special Ed. HS course work accepted: Not Applicable
Specific course requirements of all applicants: Yes
Separate application required for program services: False
Total # of students receiving LD/ADHD/ASD services: NR
Acceptance into program means acceptance into college: NR

Admissions

Students must submit the application to one of the four undergraduate divisions: Morrissey College of Arts and Sciences,Carroll School of Management, Lynch School of Education or Connell School of Nursing. Students may submit the pre-2016 versions of the SAT and/or the redesigned SAT. The writing section is not required for new SAT or ACT. Boston College will superscore the redesigned SAT and ACT, but will not superscore sub-scores from the previous SAT with the redesigned SAT. SAT Subject Tests are optional. Boston College requires all applicants to submit the Boston College Writing Supplement.

Additional Information

Services offered by the Connors Family Learning Center include: individual consultations with a learning specialist; letters to faculty confirming and explaining the LD; reduced course load during the academic year combined with summer school; access to textbooks on CD; testing in a distraction free room; workshops on study skills and time management; and small group seminars on learning strategies.

General Support Services Information

Contact Information
Name of program or department: The Connors Family Learning Center
Telephone: 617-552-8093
Fax: NR
Website: http://www.bc.edu/connors

Accommodations or Services For Students With Learning Differences

Accommodations are decided upon an individual basis after a thorough review of appropriate, current documentation. The accommodations requests must be supported through the documentation provided and must be logically linked to the current impact of the condition on academic functioning.

Allowed in exams
Calculator: Yes
Dictionary: Yes
Computer: Yes
Spellchecker: Yes
Extended test time: Yes
Scribes: Yes
Proctors: Yes
Oral exams: Yes
Note-takers: Yes
Support services for students with LD: No
Support services for students with ADHD: Yes
Support services for students with ASD: No
Distraction-reduced environment: Yes
Tape recording in class: No
Electronic texts: No
Kurzweil reader: NR
Audio books: Yes
Other assistive technology: No
Priority registration: Yes
Added costs of services: No
LD specialists: Yes **ADHD coaching:** Yes
ASD specialists: No
Professional tutors: No
Peer tutors: Yes
Max. hours/wk. for services: 3
How professors are notified of student approved accommodations: By both student and director

General Admissions Information

Office of Admissions: 617-552-3100

Entrance Requirements

Academic units recommended: 4 English, 4 math, 4 science, 4 science labs, 4 foreign language, 4 social studies, 4 history. High school diploma is required and GED is accepted. SAT or ACT required. If ACT, ACT with writing accepted. TOEFL required of all international applicants: minimum paper TOEFL 600 or minimum internet TOEFL 100.

Application deadline: 1/1
Notification: 4/15
Average GPA: NR
ACT Composite middle 50% range: 30-33
SAT Math middle 50% range: 640-750
SAT Critical Reading middle 50% range: 620-720
SAT Writing middle 50% range: 640-730
Graduate top 10% of class: 79
Graduated top 25% of class: 95
Graduated top 50% of class: 99

COLLEGE GRADUATION REQUIREMENTS

Course waivers allowed: Yes
Course substitutions allowed: Yes
In what course: foreign language

Additional Information

Environment: This private school, affiliated with the Roman Catholic Church, was founded in 1863. It has a 386.1-acre campus.

Student Body
Undergrad enrollment: 9,192
% Women: 53
% Men: 47
% Out-of-state: 75

Cost information
Tuition: $48,540
Room & board: $13,496

Housing Information
University Housing: Yes
Percent living on campus: 84

Greek System
Fraternity: No
Sorority: No
Athletics: Division I

Boston University

233 Bay State Road, Boston, MA 02215
Phone: 617-353-2301 • Fax: 617-353-9695
E-mail: admissions@bu.edu • Web: www.bu.edu
Support: CS • Institution: Private

Programs or Services for Students with Learning Differences

Boston University recognizes that many students with a learning disability, attention deficit hyperactivity disorder, or psychiatry disability (including autism spectrum diagnoses) can succeed in a university if they are provided with support services and appropriate accommodations. The Office of Disability Services (ODS) is committed to assisting individuals with disabilities in achieving fulfillment and success in all aspects of university life. The primary objective of ODS is to foster academic excellence, personal responsibility, and leadership growth in students with disabilities through vigorous programming and the provision of reasonable accommodations. We further this commitment through the promotion of independence and self-advocacy in students with LD, ADHD, or other disabilities. The university does not waive program requirements or permit substitutions for required courses. Several degree programs have foreign language or mathematics requirements. The university considers these degree requirements essential to its programs.

Admission Information for Students with Learning Differences

College entrance tests required: Yes
Interview required: No
Essay required: No
Additional Application Required for LD/ADHD/ASD: NR
What documentation required for LD: Psycho ed evaluation to include: relevant historical info, instructional interventions, related services, age diagnosed, objective data (aptitude, achievement, info processing), test scores (standard, percentile and grade equivalents) and describe functional limitations.
With general application: No
To receive services after enrolling: Yes
What documentation required for ADHD: Diagnosis based on DSM-V; history of behaviors impairing functioning in academic setting; diagnostic interview; history of symptoms; evidence of ongoing behaviors.
With general application: No
To receive services after enrolling: Yes
What documentation required for ASD: Psycho ed evaluation
With general application: NR
To receive services after enrolling: Yes
LD/ADHD/ASD documentation submitted to: Office of Disability Services
ASD Specific Program: NR
Special Ed. HS course work accepted: No
Specific course requirements of all applicants: Yes
Separate application required: No
Total # of students receiving LD/ADHD/ASD services: 550
Acceptance into program means acceptance into college: Students must be admitted and enrolled in the university first and then request to be considered for services.

Admissions

The Office of Admissions makes all admissions decisions on an individual basis. BU expects that students with disabilities, including those with LD, will meet the same competitive admissions criteria as their peers without disabilities. Thus, there are no special admissions procedures for applicants with LD. ODS does not participate in any way in the application process or in admissions decisions. Admission is based on the strength of a student's secondary school record. For most programs at BU, the minimum requirements for consideration include 4 years of English, 3 years of mathematics (through pre calculus), 3 years of history and/or social science, 3 years of science (with laboratory components), and 2 years of a foreign language. Teacher and counselor recommendations and other personal qualifications as demonstrated by extracurricular activities are evaluated and weighed before admission decisions are made. The essay is considered a significant part of the application process. Activities in and out of school are important, and it is helpful if there is a match between the student's experiences or academic interests and the opportunities available at BU. Applicants must submit either the ACT or SAT with writing. The average ACT is 31 or SAT 1377 and the average GPA is an "A-".

Additional Information

The Office of Disability Services ("Disability Services") provides academic accommodations and services to students with learning and attentional disabilities. Disability Services arranges for academic accommodations for students with learning differences. Such accommodations may include the use of a note taker, course materials in alternative formats, reduced course load, or possibly examination-related accommodations such as extended time or a distraction-reduced environment. Students seeking accommodations must provide appropriate medical documentation of their disability so that Disability Services can determine the student's eligibility for accommodations; and if the student is eligible, determine appropriate academic accommodations.

General Support Services Information

Contact Information
Name of program or department: Office of Disability Services
Telephone: 617-353-3658
Fax: 617-353-9646

Accommodations or Services for Students with Learning Differences

Accommodations are decided upon an individual basis after a thorough review of appropriate, current documentation. The accommodations requested must be supported through the documentation provided and must be logically linked to the current impact of the condition on academic functioning.

Allowed in exams
Calculator: No
Dictionary: No
Computer: Yes
Spellchecker: Yes
Extended test time: Yes
Scribes: Yes
Proctors: Yes
Oral exams: Yes
Note-takers: Yes
Services for students with LD: Yes
Services for students with ADHD: Yes
Services for students with ASD: Yes
Distraction-reduced environment: Yes
Tape recording in class: Yes
Audio books: NR
Electronic texts: Yes
Kurzweil Reader: No
Other assistive technology: Yes
Priority registration: No
Added costs for services: Yes
LD specialists: Yes
ADHD coaching: NR
ASD specialists: NR
Professional tutors: None
Peer tutors: No
Max. hours/wk. for services: N/A
How professors are notified of LD/ADHD: By student

General Admissions Information

Office of Admissions: 617-353-2300

Entrance Requirements

Academic units required: 4 English, 3 math, 3 science, 3 science labs, 2 foreign language, 3 social studies, 3 history, **Academic units recommended:** 4 English, 4 math, 4 science, 4 science labs, 4 foreign language, 4 social studies, 4 history. High school diploma is required and GED is accepted. SAT or ACT required. If ACT, ACT with writing accepted. TOEFL required of all international applicants.

Application deadline: 1/3
Notification: 4/1
Average GPA: 3.61
ACT Composite middle 50% range: 27-31
SAT Math middle 50% range: 620-730
SAT Critical Reading middle 50% range: 580-680
SAT Writing middle 50% range: 600-690
Graduated top 10% of class: 58
Graduated top 25% of class: 89
Graduated top 50% of class: 99

COLLEGE GRADUATION REQUIREMENTS

Course waivers allowed: No
Course substitutions allowed: No

Additional Information

Environment: This private school was founded in 1839. It has a 132-acre campus.

Student Body
Undergrad enrollment: 17,932
% Women: 60
% Men: 40
% Out-of-state: 80

Cost information
Tuition: $47,422
Room & board: $14,520

Housing Information
University Housing: Yes
Percent living on campus: 75

Greek System
Fraternity: Yes
Sorority: Yes
Athletics: Division I

Clark University

950 Main Street, Worcester, MA 01610-1477
Phone: 508-793-7431 • Fax: 508-793-8821
E-mail: admissions@clarku.edu • Web: www.clarku.edu
Support: CS • Institution: Private

Programs or Services for Students with Learning Differences

Clark University is committed to providing equal access to otherwise qualified students with disabilities who are able to effectively function in a rigorous, campus-based, liberal-arts environment. Although Clark does not offer a specialized program, nor a learning center for students with disabilities, the University does provide a support service for qualified students who register with Student Accessibility Services. The director of Student Accessibility Services works with students to coordinate academic accommodations and services on campus. Student Accessibility Services is located in the Goddard Library, Room 430. This office is the point of contact for any student seeking accommodations.

Admission Information for Students with Learning Differences

College entrance test required: NR
Interview required: No
Essay required: Not Applicable
Additional Application Required for LD/ADHD/ASD: No
What documentation required for LD: Official documentation of disability from an appropriate licensed professional
With general application: No
To receive services after enrolling: No
What documentation required for ADHD: Official documentation of disability from an appropriate licensed professional
With general application: No
To receive services after enrolling: No
What documentation required for ASD: Typically students provide a Neuropsychological Evaluation, Psychoeducational Evaluation, or other learning evaluation
With general application: No
To receive services after enrolling: No
LD/ADHD/ASD documentation submitted to: Student Accessibility Services
ASD Specific Program: NR
Special Ed. HS course work accepted: NR
Specific course requirements of all applicants: NR
Separate application required for program services: FALSE
Total # of students receiving LD/ADHD/ASD services: NR
Acceptance into program means acceptance into college: No

Admissions

Special Services and the Office of Undergraduate Admissions work together in considering students for admission. Admission is based on ability rather than disability. Applicants must meet standard admissions requirements. An interview with Clark's Special Services Office is highly recommended. If a student requires any classroom accommodations or support services, a diagnostic assessment completed within the past 2 years must be submitted, documenting the learning disability. This documentation is needed to evaluate the applicant's needs and determine what services the university can provide. The university looks at a student's upward trend in high school, as well as the challenge of the curriculum and the number of mainstream courses the student has taken. Some special education courses in freshman year may be allowed if they have been followed by a college-prep curriculum during the rest of high school. The Director of Special Services makes a recommendation to the Admissions Office about the applicant, but the final decision rests with the Office of Admissions. The university values diversity in their applicants, but most students have taken 4 years of English, 3 years of mathematics, 3 years of science, 2 years of both a social science and a foreign language, and other credit electives, including the arts, recognized in the curriculum. The university feels that successful candidates for admission should have a strong senior-year course load (at least four, preferably five, solid academic courses).

Additional Information

An early orientation program 2 days prior to general orientation is designed to meet the needs of entering students with LD. This program is highly recommended as it provides intensive exposure to academic services on campus. Students take a reading comprehension and writing exam, and results are used to match students to the most appropriate academic program. Graduate students work with students on time management and organizational skills. Although note-takers are available, Special Services supplements this accommodation with the taping of lectures and highly recommends that students use a cassette recorder with a count. It is also recommended that freshmen students take only three courses in their first semester. All students must complete one math course in basic algebra prior to graduating. The overall GPA of freshmen receiving services from Special Services is a 2.7.

General Support Services Information

Contact Information
Name of program or department: Student Accessibility Services
Telephone: 508 798 4368
Fax: 508 421 3700

Accommodations or Services For Students With Learning Differences

Accommodations are decided upon an individual basis after a thorough review of appropriate, current documentation. The accommodations requests must be supported through the documentation provided and must be logically linked to the current impact of the condition on academic functioning.

Allowed in exams
Calculator: Yes
Dictionary: Yes
Computer: Yes
Spellchecker: Yes
Extended test time: Yes
Scribes: Yes
Proctors: Yes
Oral exams: Yes
Note-takers: Yes
Support services for students with LD: Yes
Support services for students with ADHD: Yes
Support services for students with ASD: Yes
Distraction-reduced environment: Yes
Tape recording in class: Yes
Electronic texts: Yes
Kurzweil reader: NR
Audio books: Yes
Other assistive technology: Yes
Priority registration: Not Applicable
Added costs of services: Not Applicable
LD specialists: Yes
ADHD coaching: Yes
ASD specialists: Yes
Professional tutors: No
Peer tutors: NR
Max. hours/wk. for services: NR
How professors are notified of student approved accommodations: By both student and director

General Admissions Information

Office of Admissions: 508-793-7431

Entrance Requirements

Academic units recommended: 4 English, 3 math, 3 science, 2 science labs, 2 foreign language, 2 social studies, 2 history. High school diploma is required and GED is accepted. SAT or ACT considered if submitted. If ACT, ACT with writing accepted. TOEFL required of all international applicants: minimum paper TOEFL 550.

Application deadline: 1/15
Notification: By both student and director
Average GPA: 3.66
ACT Composite middle 50% range: 26-30
SAT Math middle 50% range: 560-670
SAT Critical Reading middle 50% range: 560-670
SAT Writing middle 50% range: 560-670
Graduate top 10% of class: 44
Graduated top 25% of class: 77
Graduated top 50% of class: 99

COLLEGE GRADUATION REQUIREMENTS

Course waivers allowed: Not Applicable
In what course: All students must complete graduation requirements. These requirement are waived in only exceptional circumstances and all cases are considered on an individual basis based on documentation of disability.
Course substitutions allowed: Not Applicable
In what course: All students must complete graduation requirements. These requirement are waived in only exceptional circumstances and all cases are considered on an individual basis based on documentation of disability.

Additional Information

Environment: This private school was founded in 1887. It has a 50-acre campus.

Student Body
Undergrad enrollment: 2,397
% Women: 60
% Men: 40
% Out-of-state: 63

Cost information
Tuition: $42,800
Room & board: $8,450

Housing Information
University Housing: Yes
Percent living on campus: 70

Greek System
Fraternity: No
Sorority: No
Athletics: Division III

Curry College

1071 Blue Hill Avenue, Milton, MA 02186
Phone: 617-333-2210 • Fax: 617-333-2114
E-mail: curryadm@curry.edu • Web: www.curry.edu
Support: SP • Institution: Private

Programs or Services for Students with Learning Differences

The Program for Advancement of Learning (PAL) at Curry College is a comprehensive individualized program for students with specific learning disabilities and ADHD. Students in PAL participate fully in Curry College course work and extracurricular activities. The goal of PAL is to facilitate students' understanding of their individual learning styles and help them achieve independence as learners. Students' empowerment is developed via intensive study of their own strengths, needs, and learning styles. PAL is a place where students are honored for the strengths and talents they bring to the learning process and are given the chance to demonstrate their abilities. PAL students are leaders on campus. The PAL summer program is a 3-week course that is strongly recommended for new students to ease the transition to college and provide excellent preparation.

Admission Information for Students with Learning Differences

College entrance tests required: No
Interview required: No, but strongly recommended
Essay required: Yes
Additional Application Required for LD/ADHD/ASD: NR
What documentation required for LD: Psycho ed evaluation to include: relevant historical info, instructional interventions, related services, age diagnosed, objective data (aptitude, achievement, info processing), test scores (standard, percentile and grade equivalents) and describe functional limitations.
With general application: Yes if requested as part of Structured Program application
To receive services after enrolling: Yes
What documentation required for ADHD: Diagnosis based on DSM-V; history of behaviors impairing functioning in academic setting; diagnostic interview; history of symptoms; evidence of ongoing behaviors.
With general application: Yes if requested as part of Structured Program application
To receive services after enrolling: Yes
What documentation required for ASD: Psycho ed evaluation
With general application: NR
To receive services after enrolling: Yes
LD/ADHD/ASD documentation submitted to: Program for the Advancement of Learning (PAL)
ASD Specific Program: NR
Special Ed. HS course work accepted: Yes
Specific course requirements of all applicants: NR
Separate application required: Yes
Total # of students receiving LD/ADHD/ASD services: 275
Acceptance into program means acceptance into college: Yes

Admissions

Courses required for general admission include 4 English, 3 math, 2 science, 2 science lab, 1 social studies, 1 history, and 5 electives. For admission into the Program of the Advancement of Learning, applicants must submit a recent diagnostic evaluation describing a Specific Learning Disability and/or ADHD. Diagnostic evaluations must be less than three years old and contain the results of cognitive and achievement tests. In addition, an IEP or its equivalent is requested, if available. On-campus interviews are strongly recommended and may be required of some applicants. Space is limited for the program. Students applying to PAL are not required to submit SAT or ACT. Students may also respond to an "Optional" Supplement. Admission decisions are made jointly by PAL and the Office of Admissions.

Additional Information

PAL students must commit to the program for at least 1 year and have the option to continue with full or partial support beyond the first year. A 3-week 3-credit summer PAL summer session is strongly recommended. Students meet regularly with their own PAL instructor who is a learning specialist. The focus is on using the student's strengths to improve skills in areas such as listening, speaking, reading, writing, organization and time management, note-taking, and test-taking. Students also receive help with readings, papers, and assignments for classes as the basis for learning about their unique learning style. The specialist reviews diagnostic testing to help the student understand the profile of strengths and needs. Students earn three credits toward graduation for the first year. Skills classes, for credit, are offered through the Academic Enrichment Center in developmental reading, writing, and math. Another special offering is diagnostic testing, which available through the Educational Diagnostic Center at PAL at 617-333-2314.

General Support Services Information

Contact Information
Name of program or department: Program for Advancement of Learning (PAL)
Telephone: 617-333-2250
Fax: 617-333-2018

Accommodations or Services for Students with Learning Differences

Accommodations are decided upon an individual basis after a thorough review of appropriate, current documentation. The accommodations requested must be supported through the documentation provided and must be logically linked to the current impact of the condition on academic functioning.

Allowed in exams
Calculator: Yes
Dictionary: Yes
Computer: Yes
Spellchecker: Yes
Extended test time: Yes
Scribes: Yes
Proctors: Yes
Oral exams: NR
Note-takers: NR
Services for students with LD: Yes
Services for students with ADHD: Yes
Services for students with ASD: Yes
Distraction-reduced environment: Yes
Tape recording in class: Yes
Audio books: NR
Electronic texts: Yes
Kurzweil Reader: Yes
Other assistive technology: Yes
Priority registration: No
Added costs for services: Yes
LD specialists: Yes
ADHD coaching: NR
ASD specialists: NR
Professional tutors: Yes
Peer tutors: Yes
Max. hours/wk. for services: 2.5
How professors are notified of LD/ADHD: By student

General Admissions Information

Office of Admissions: 617-333-2210

Entrance Requirements

Academic units required: 4 English, 3 math, **Academic units recommended:** 2 science, 1 science labs, 2 foreign language, 2 social studies, 2 history. High school diploma is required and GED is accepted. SAT or ACT required for some. If ACT, ACT with writing accepted. TOEFL required of all international applicants: minimum paper TOEFL 500.

Application deadline: NR
Notification: Rolling starting 11/1
Average GPA: 2.8
ACT Composite middle 50% range: 18-21
SAT Math middle 50% range: 430-520
SAT Critical Reading middle 50% range: 420-520
SAT Writing middle 50% range: 420-520
Graduated top 10% of class: 5
Graduated top 25% of class: 18
Graduated top 50% of class: 53

COLLEGE GRADUATION REQUIREMENTS

Course waivers allowed: No
Course substitutions allowed: Yes
In what course: Varies

Additional Information

Environment: This private school was founded in 1879. It has a 137-acre campus.

Student Body
Undergrad enrollment: 2,900
% Women: 63
% Men: 37
% Out-of-state: 22
Cost information
Tuition: $34,730
Room & board: $13,900
Housing Information
University Housing: Yes
Percent living on campus: 52
Greek System
Fraternity: No
Sorority: No
Athletics: Division III

Dean College

Office of Admission, Franklin, MA 02038-1994
Phone: 508-541-1508 • Fax: 508-541-8726
E-mail: admission@dean.edu • Web: www.dean.edu
Support: SP • Institution: Private

Programs or Services for Students with Learning Differences

Students are able to enroll in the Arch Learning Community for one to four years depending on their individual needs. A step-down approach is utilized and provides greater services in the first two years as students are taught how to learn, followed by a measured decrease in services, to prepare students for graduation and their chosen career. The program offers learning support for students with diagnosed learning disabilities such as Attention Deficit Disorder, Asperger's Syndrome, ADHD, dyslexia, sensory processing, executive functioning disorder and nonverbal learning issues. The Arch program fee of $3,600 per semester will be assessed to students enrolling in the Learning Community. This fee is taken into consideration when calculating financial aid awards.

Admission Information for Students with Learning Differences

College entrance tests required: Yes
Interview required: No
Additional Application Required for LD/ADHD/ASD: NR
What documentation required for LD: Psycho ed evaluation to include: relevant historical info, instructional interventions, related services, age diagnosed, objective data (aptitude, achievement, info processing), test scores (standard, percentile and grade equivalents) and describe functional limitations.
With general application: Yes if requested as part of Structured Program application
To receive services after enrolling: Yes
What documentation required for ADHD: Diagnosis based on DSM-V; history of behaviors impairing functioning in academic setting; diagnostic interview; history of symptoms; evidence of ongoing behaviors.
With general application: Yes if requested as part of Structured Program application
To receive services after enrolling: Yes
What documentation required for ASD: Psycho ed evaluation
With general application: NR
To receive services after enrolling: Yes
LD/ADHD/ASD documentation submitted to: Support Program/Services
ASD Specific Program: NR
Special Ed. HS course work accepted: Yes
Specific course requirements for all applicants: NR
Separate application required for program services: Yes
Total # of students receiving LD/ADHD/ASD services: 100
Acceptance into program means acceptance into college: No

Admissions

There is no special admission process for students with learning disabilities. All students submit the same general application. Every application is carefully reviewed by admissions, and students are selected based on their academic performance in high school, recommendations, and personal accomplishments. There is no simple formula applied to an application. Dean strives to make the best match between what it offers as an institution and each student's skills, interests, and abilities. Students should have college-prep courses including four years English and three years math. Interviews are not required, but they are highly recommended, and students must submit a counselor's recommendation. SAT/ACT are required.

Additional Information

Accommodations may include, but are not limited to, electronic texts, access to computers, scribes and note-takers, and extended time for testing. The Learning Center provides free academic assistance and support services for all students through tutoring, workshops, and study groups. Professional and peer tutors are available to assist students in developing writing, math, and study skills, and to provide course-specific tutoring. Personalized Learning Services (PLS) offers tutorial support to students. Students may meet weekly with a learning, writing, or math academic coach one-to-one or in small groups. Learning and study strategies taught by specialist include test-taking; test preparation; note-taking skills; time management; academic organization; reading comprehension; research and writing skills; and self-awareness and advocacy. The fee for ARCH is $3,600 per semester.

General Support Services Information

Contact Information
Name of program or department: Disability Support Services
Telephone: 508-541-1768
Fax: 508-541-1829

Accommodations or Services for Students with Learning Differences

Accommodations are decided upon an individual basis after a thorough review of appropriate, current documentation. The accommodations requested must be supported through the documentation provided and must be logically linked to the current impact of the condition on academic functioning.

Allowed in exams
Calculator: Yes
Dictionary: No
Computer: Yes
Spellchecker: Yes
Extended test time: Yes
Scribes: Yes
Proctors: Yes
Oral exams: No
Note-takers: Yes
Services for students with LD: Yes
Services for students with ADHD: Yes
Services for students with ASD: Yes
Distraction-reduced environment: Yes
Tape recording in class: Yes
Audio books: NR
Electronic texts: No
Kurzweil Reader: Yes
Other assistive technology: Microsoft Speak, a word processing dictation program; Kurzweil reader
Priority registration: No
Added costs for services: Yes, $3,600 Arch (per semester)
LD specialists: Yes
ADHD coaching: NR
ASD specialists: NR
Professional tutors: 35
Peer tutors: 12–18
Max. hours/wk. for services: NR
How professors are notified of LD/ADHD: Student

General Admissions Information

Office of Admissions: 508-541-1508

Entrance Requirements

Academic units required: 3 English, 1 mathematics, 1 science, (1 science labs), 0 foreign language, 1 social studies, 1 history. **Academic units recommended:** 4 English, 2 mathematics, 2 science, (1 science labs), 1 foreign language, 2 social studies, 2 history, 1 academic elective. High school diploma is required and GED is accepted. SAT or ACT required. If ACT, ACT with Writing component accepted. TOEFL not required of all international applicants.

Application deadline: NR
Notification: Rolling starting 12/1
Average GPA: 2.2
ACT Composite middle 50% range: 15-20
SAT Math middle 50% range: 380-490
SAT Critical Reading middle 50% range: 390-490
SAT Writing middle 50% range: NR
Graduated top 10% of class: NR
Graduated top 25% of class: NR
Graduated top 50% of class: NR

COLLEGE GRADUATION REQUIREMENTS

Course waivers allowed: No
Course substitutions allowed: No

Additional Information

Environment: The campus is in a small town near both Boston, Massachusetts, and Providence, Rhode Island.

Student Body
Undergrad enrollment: 1,292
% Women: 52
% Men: 48
% Out-of-state: 53
Cost information
Tuition: $36,660
Room & board: $9,936
Housing Information
University Housing: Yes
Percent living on campus: 88
Greek System
Fraternity: No
Sorority: No
Athletics: NJCAA

Emerson College

120 Boylston Street, Boston, MA 02116-4624
Phone: 617-824-8600 • Fax: 617-824-8609
E-mail: admission@emerson.edu • Web: www.emerson.edu
Support: CS • Institution: Private

Programs or Services for Students with Learning Differences

Emerson College is committed to providing equal access to its academic programs and social activities for all qualified students with disabilities. While upholding this commitment, we maintain the high standards of achievement that are essential to the integrity of the college's programs and services. One of the primary goals of the DSO is to foster a welcoming and accessible environment for students across the campus. The school's philosophy is that students are independent and self-determined, and that students with disabilities—just like all students—have control over their lives at Emerson and they are ultimately responsible for making their own decisions. Emerson's Disability Services Office (DSO) offers academic accommodations and related services to qualified students with documented physical, medical, visual, hearing, learning, and psychological disabilities. Students with disabilities are not required to register with the DSO, but in order to receive accommodations they must self-identify to the DSO and request accommodations. Recommendations regarding accommodations for students with disabilities are determined on an individual basis. As part of the request process, students must provide recent documentation of their disabilities and have an interview with staff in the DSO. The documentation, prepared by a qualified professional, must substantiate the nature of the disability and its relationship to the requested accommodation.

Admission Information for Students with Learning Differences

College entrance tests required: Yes
Interview required: No
Essay required: Yes
Additional Application Required for LD/ADHD/ASD: NR
What documentation required for LD: Psycho ed evaluation
With general application: No
To receive services after enrolling: Yes
What documentation required for ADHD: Psycho ed evaluation
With general application: No
To receive services after enrolling: Yes
What documentation required for ASD: Psycho ed evaluation
With general application: No
To receive services after enrolling: Yes
LD/ADHD/ASD documentation submitted to: Disability Services Office
ASD Specific Program: NR
Special Ed. HS course work accepted: No
Specific course requirements for all applicants: NR
Separate application required for program services: No
Total # of students receiving LD/ADHD/ASD services: NR
Acceptance into program means acceptance into college: Student must be admitted and enrolled in the college to request services.

Admissions

Emerson College accepts the Common Application with a required Supplement. Admission is competitive. In choosing candidates for the entering class, we look for students who present academic promise in their secondary school record, recommendations, and writing competency, as well as personal qualities as seen in extracurricular activities, community involvement, and demonstrated leadership. There is no separate application for students with learning disabilities.

Additional Information

Emerson College offers academic support services, free of charge, to all undergraduate and graduate Emerson students. The College's Writing & Academic Resource Center (WARC) consists of three full-time professionals, graduate assistant writing tutors, and peer tutors. The professional staff provides academic counseling and support with study strategies and time management to individuals seeking academic support. Graduate writing tutors guide students in becoming more effective writers, and peer tutors assist students with course content. The center also offers grammar tutorials across the curriculum.

General Support Services Information

Contact Information
Name of program or department: Disability Services Office
Telephone: 617-824-8592
Fax: 617-824-8941

Accommodations or Services for Students with Learning Differences

Accommodations are decided on an individual basis after a review of current documentation and an interview conducted by a DSO staff member. The college reserves the right to determine the adequacy of the documentation and may request additional assessments and materials.

Allowed in exams
Calculator: Yes
Dictionary: Yes
Computer: Yes
Spellchecker: Yes
Extended test time: Yes
Scribes: Yes
Proctors: Yes
Oral exams: No
Note-takers: Yes
Services for students with LD: Yes
Services for students with ADHD: Yes
Services for students with ASD: No
Distraction-reduced environment: Yes
Tape recording in class: Yes
Audio books: No
Electronic texts: No
Kurzweil Reader: Yes
Other assistive technology: Print to Speech; JAWS; other adaptive software and hardware.
Priority registration: N/A
Added costs for services: No
LD specialists: Yes
ADHD coaching: No
ASD specialists: No
Professional tutors: No
Peer tutors: Yes
Max. hours/wk. for services: 4
How professors are notified of LD/ADHD: Student.

General Admissions Information

Office of Admissions: 617-824-8600

Entrance Requirements

Academic units required: 4 English, 3 math, 3 science, 3 foreign language, 3 social studies, **Academic units recommended:** 4 English, 3 math, 3 science, 3 foreign language, 3 social studies, 4 academic electives. High school diploma is required and GED is accepted. SAT or ACT required. If ACT, ACT with writing required. TOEFL required of all international applicants: minimum paper TOEFL 550 or minimum internet TOEFL 80.

Application deadline: 1/5
Notification: 4/1
Average GPA: 3.66
ACT Composite middle 50% range: 26-30
SAT Math middle 50% range: 560-650
SAT Critical Reading middle 50% range: 580-680
SAT Writing middle 50% range: 580-670
Graduated top 10% of class: 37
Graduated top 25% of class: 73
Graduated top 50% of class: 95

COLLEGE GRADUATION REQUIREMENTS

Course waivers allowed: Yes
In what course: Quantitative reasoning (math), world languages.
Course substitutions allowed: No
In what course: Students can choose to take American Sign Language to fulfill the World Language requirement.

Additional Information

Environment: This private school was founded in 1880. It has a 10-acre campus.

Student Body
Undergrad enrollment: 3,765
% Women: 61
% Men: 39
% Out-of-state: 76

Cost information
Tuition: $38,304
Room & board: $15,700
Housing Information
University Housing: Yes
Percent living on campus: 58

Greek System
Fraternity: Yes
Sorority: Yes
Athletics: Division III

Fitchburg State University

160 Pearl Street, Fitchburg, MA 01420-2697
Phone: 978-665-3144 • Fax: 978-665-4540
E-mail: admissions@fitchburgstate.edu • Web: www.fitchburgstate.edu
Support: S • Institution: Public

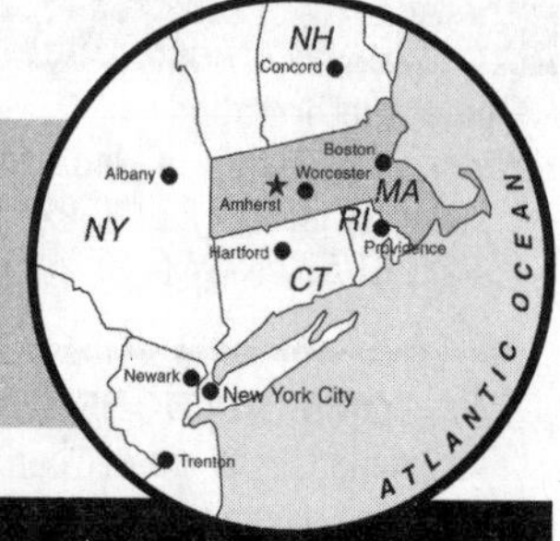

Programs or Services for Students with Learning Differences

The Disability Services Office provides support services and programs for students with disabilities. Disability Services empowers eligible students to succeed by striving to assure equal access and opportunity of curricular and extracurricular activities. Student autonomy is encouraged through the provision of reasonable accommodations, services, training in the use of assistive technology and self-advocacy. Disability Services will verify student eligibility for accommodations and for coordinating accommodations across campus. Students must request services themselves and must provide appropriate documentation to support the need for such services. Once students have obtained copies of their disability documentation from their high school or medical provider, to support the need for such services, they should meet with staff in the Disability Services office to register for services. Documentation must clearly state the diagnosis, describe the symptoms that impact the student's ability to function in the educational environment and provide specific recommendations for accommodations.

Admission Information for Students with Learning Differences

College entrance tests required: Yes
Interview required: No
Essay required: Yes
Additional Application Required for LD/ADHD/ASD: NR
What documentation required for LD: Psycho-Educational evaluation within the last 3 years and IEP if available.
With general application: Yes
To receive services after enrolling: Yes
What documentation required for ADHD: Diagnosis based on DSM-V; history of behaviors impairing functioning in academic setting; diagnostic interview; history of symptoms; evidence of ongoing behaviors.
With general application: No
To receive services after enrolling: Yes
What documentation required for ASD: Psych-Educational Evaluation within the last 3 years and IEP if available
With general application: No
To receive services after enrolling: Yes
LD/ADHD/ASD documentation submitted to: Disability Services Office
ASD Specific Program: NR
Special Ed. HS course work accepted: No
Specific course requirements of all applicants: Yes
Separate application required: Yes
Total # of students receiving LD/ADHD/ASD services: 280
Acceptance into program means acceptance into college: Students must be admitted and enrolled in the college prior to requesting services.

Admissions

Students requesting a waiver of ACT/SAT or foreign language requirement must submit the psycho-educational testing (within 3 years) with 504 Plan or IEP. Office of Admissions forwards testing to the Office of Disability Services for review who informs Admissions if a student meets the criteria for the waiver(s). If so applicants do not need to submit ACT/SAT or proof of completion of foreign language. (Must complete two additional college prep electives to substitute for the foreign language. General admission includes: 4 English, 3 math, 3 science (2 lab science), 2 social science, 2 foreign language, and 2 electives. GPA is based on all college-prep courses and weighs Honors and Advanced Placement courses. The university wants a weighted GPA of 3.0, however considers GPAs between 2.0-2.99 if students submit SAT/ACT scores meeting the sliding scale requirements. Applicants not meeting the sliding scale requirements will be considered on an individual basis for a limited number of admission exceptions. Applicants who meet the 3.0 GPA requirements do not have to use the sliding scale for admission, but still must submit competitive SAT/ACT scores if they are applying within 3 years of high school graduation.

Additional Information

The Office of Disability Services provides support services, programs and academic accommodations for students with documented disabilities. Some examples of academic accommodations include: testing accommodations, materials in an alternate format, adaptive software and computer equipment, assistive listening devices, sign language interpreters, reduced course load waiver (below 12 credits), academic skill building workshops, support with the development of leadership, self-advocacy and self-determination skills. To be eligible for academic accommodations, students must request services themselves and must provide appropriate documentation to support the need for such services. Requests for accommodations must be made in a timely manner and must be reasonable given the nature of the disability.

General Support Services Information

Contact Information
Name of program or department: Disability Services
Telephone: 978-665-4020
Fax: 978-665-4786

Accommodations or Services for Students with Learning Differences

To be eligible for academic accommodations, students must request services themselves and must provide appropriate documentation to support the need for such services. Requests for accommodations must be made in a timely manner and must be reasonable given the nature of the disability. All documentation received by the university is strictly confidential and is held in accordance with the Family Educational Rights and Privacy Act (FERPA)

Allowed in exams
Calculator: Yes
Dictionary: Yes
Computer: Yes
Spellchecker: Yes
Extended test time: Yes
Scribes: Yes
Proctors: Yes
Oral exams: Yes
Note-takers: Yes
Services for students with LD: Yes
Services for students with ADHD: Yes
Services for students with ASD: Yes
Distraction-reduced environment: Yes
Tape recording in class: Yes
Audio books: No
Electronic texts: Yes
Kurzweil Reader: Yes
Other assistive technology: Yes
Priority registration: No
Added costs for services: No
LD specialists: No
ADHD coaching: No
ASD specialists: No
Professional tutors: Yes
Peer tutors: Yes
Max. hours/wk. for services: Unspecified
How professors are notified of LD/ADHD: By student

General Admissions Information

Office of Admissions: 978-665-3144

Entrance Requirements

Academic units required: 4 English, 3 math, 3 science, 2 science labs, 2 foreign language, 1 social studies, 1 history, 2 academic electives. High school diploma is required and GED is accepted. SAT or ACT required. If ACT, ACT with writing accepted. TOEFL required of all international applicants: minimum paper TOEFL 550.

Application deadline: NR
Notification: Rolling starting 12/1
Average GPA: 3.1
ACT Composite middle 50% range: 19-23
SAT Math middle 50% range: 460-560
SAT Critical Reading middle 50% range: 450-560
SAT Writing middle 50% range: 450-540
Graduated top 10% of class: NR
Graduated top 25% of class: NR
Graduated top 50% of class: NR

COLLEGE GRADUATION REQUIREMENTS

Course waivers allowed: No
In what course: Varies
Course substitutions allowed: Yes

Additional Information

Environment: This public school was founded in 1894. It has a 78-acre campus.

Student Body
Undergrad enrollment: 4,172
% Women: 54
% Men: 46
% Out-of-state: 8

Cost information
In-state Tuition: $970
Out-of-state Tuition: $7,050
Room & board: $8,256

Housing Information
University Housing: Yes
Percent living on campus: 41

Greek System
Fraternity: Yes
Sorority: Yes
Athletics: Division III

MOUNT IDA COLLEGE

777 Dedham Street, Newton, MA 02459
Phone: 617-928-4553 • Fax: 617-928-4507
E-mail: admissions@mountida.edu • Web: www.mountida.edu
Support: SP • Institution: Private

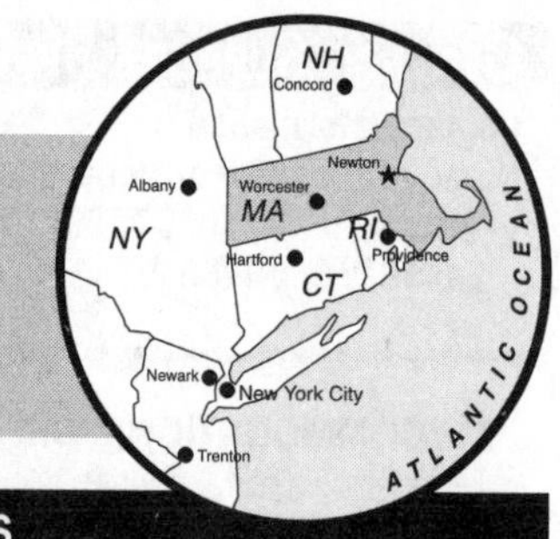

PROGRAMS OR SERVICES FOR STUDENTS WITH LEARNING DIFFERENCES

The Student Achievement Program (SAP) is a fee-for-service program that provides additional academic support for students with disabilities. The program focuses on developing and strengthening individual learning styles that create successful, independent learners. Students who join the SAP program have an assigned learning specialist who works with them one-on-one to build on strengths, identify strategies, and establish a clear pathway to success. Students can meet with their learning specialist one or two hours per week and focus on topics such as: time management and organization, study skills, stress management, self-advocacy, memory and concentration, social skills, career preparation, health and wellness, and reading and writing strategies. Academic workshops are offered throughout the semester as well. Fees range per semester from $2,200 to $6,600, depending on the number of sessions per week a student has with their learning specialist.

ADMISSION INFORMATION FOR STUDENTS WITH LEARNING DIFFERENCES

College entrance tests required: Yes
Interview required: No
Essay required: Yes
Additional Application Required for LD/ADHD/ASD: NR
What documentation required for LD: Psycho ed evaluation to include: relevant historical info, instructional interventions, related services, age diagnosed, objective data (aptitude, achievement, info processing), test scores (standard, percentile and grade equivalents) and describe functional limitations.
With general application: Yes if requested as part of Structured Program application
To receive services after enrolling: Yes
What documentation required for ADHD: Diagnosis based on DSM-V; history of behaviors impairing functioning in academic setting; diagnostic interview; history of symptoms; evidence of ongoing behaviors.
With general application: Yes if requested as part of Structured Program application
To receive services after enrolling: Yes
What documentation required for ASD: Psycho ed evaluation
With general application: NR
To receive services after enrolling: Yes
LD/ADHD/ASD documentation submitted to: Admissions
ASD Specific Program: NR
Special Ed. HS course work accepted: Yes
Specific course requirements of all applicants: Yes
Separate application required: Yes
Total # of students receiving LD/ADHD/ASD services: 150
Acceptance into program means acceptance into college: Students are admitted first to the college and then to the LOP.

ADMISSIONS

There is no special admissions process for students with learning disabilities. Open admissions is available. ACT/SAT are required for admission. An interview is strongly recommended. Students with disabilities should submit the WAIS–R, a test indicating appropriate reading grade level, and evaluative documentation of the learning disability. There is no formal application process to be enrolled in the SAP Program. Students interested in participating should complete a SAP enrollment form.

ADDITIONAL INFORMATION

The Student Achievement Program is open to any student who is interested in working with a Learning Specialist to meet his/her academic and personal goals. Please note: Students must first be admitted or be a current student in order to enroll. Once enrolled into the Student Achievement Program, students will meet regularly with their assigned professional learning specialist. During these sessions, students will gain important skills and strategies to help them make the most of their college experience. There is no formal application process to be enrolled in the program. Students interested in participating should complete the Student Achievement Program Enrollment form. Once the enrollment form is completed and returned, the student will be contacted and asked to complete the Service Agreement Form. Once the completed form is received, the student will receive a notification letter of enrollment in the program. The goals of the Student Achievement Program are to help students identify strengths and challenges in both their academic and personal life. Academic workshops help develop time management skills, reading and writing skills, and test-taking strategies.

General Support Services Information

Contact Information
Name of program or department: Learning Opportunities Program (LOP)
Telephone: 617-928-4648
Fax: 617-928-4648

Accommodations or Services for Students with Learning Differences

Accommodations are decided upon an individual basis after a thorough review of appropriate, current documentation. The accommodations requested must be supported through the documentation provided and must be logically linked to the current impact of the condition on academic functioning.

Allowed in exams
Calculator: Yes
Dictionary: Yes
Computer: No
Spellchecker: Yes
Extended test time: Yes
Scribes: No
Proctors: No
Oral exams: Yes
Note-takers: No
Services for students with LD: Yes
Services for students with ADHD: Yes
Services for students with ASD: Yes
Distraction-reduced environment: Yes
Tape recording in class: Yes
Audio books: NR
Electronic texts: Yes
Kurzweil Reader: Yes
Other assistive technology: Yes
Priority registration: No
Added costs for services: Yes
LD specialists: Yes
ADHD coaching: NR
ASD specialists: NR
Professional tutors: 7–10
Peer tutors: No
Max. hours/wk. for services: 2
How professors are notified of LD/ADHD: By student

General Admissions Information

Office of Admissions: 617-928-4553

Entrance Requirements

Academic units recommended: 4 English, 3 math, 3 science, 2 foreign language, 2 social studies. High school diploma is required and GED is accepted. SAT or ACT required. If ACT, ACT with writing recommended. TOEFL required of all international applicants: minimum paper TOEFL 525 or minimum internet TOEFL 70.

Application deadline: NR
Notification: NR
Average GPA: NR
ACT Composite middle 50% range: 15-20
SAT Math middle 50% range: 380-490
SAT Critical Reading middle 50% range: 390-490
SAT Writing middle 50% range: 400-500
Graduated top 10% of class: NR
Graduated top 25% of class: NR
Graduated top 50% of class: NR

COLLEGE GRADUATION REQUIREMENTS

Course waivers allowed: No
In what course: No foreign language requirement
Course substitutions allowed: Yes, under special conditions
In what course: Depends on the major and the learning style issues; not a usual accommodation

Additional Information

Environment: This private school was founded in 1899. It has a 72-acre campus.

Student Body
Undergrad enrollment: 1,460
% Women: 67
% Men: 33
% Out-of-state: 40
Cost information
Room & board: NR
Housing Information
University Housing: Yes
Percent living on campus: 64
Greek System
Fraternity: No
Sorority: No
Athletics: Division III

NORTHEASTERN UNIVERSITY

360 Huntington Avenue, Boston, MA 02115
Phone: 617-373-2200 • Fax: 617-373-8780
E-mail: admissions@neu.edu • Web: www.northeastern.edu
Support: SP • Institution: Private

PROGRAMS OR SERVICES FOR STUDENTS WITH LEARNING DIFFERENCES

For students with documented learning disabilities and/or ADHD, Northeastern offers both a comprehensive program and basic support services. The Learning Disabilities Program (LDP) is a comprehensive program for students with LD and/or ADHD. Students meet with a LD specialist for two regularly-scheduled one hour appointments each week. Content for meetings includes time management, organization, reading comprehension, expository writing, research and study skills, and self advocacy. The LDP is a fee-based service and requires an additional application and interview. The Disability Resource Center (DRC) offers accommodations to students with disabilities, including exam accommodations, notetaking services, and alternate format text. Students registered with the DRC may also meet with a LD specialist for support in using accommodations and for other disability-related needs. There is no charge for basic support services through the DRC.

ADMISSION INFORMATION FOR STUDENTS WITH LEARNING DIFFERENCES

College entrance test required: NR
Interview required: Yes
Essay required: Not Applicable
Additional Application Required for LD/ADHD/ASD: Yes
What documentation required for LD: Please see website for detailed information: www.northeastern.edu/drc
With general application: No
To receive services after enrolling: Yes
What documentation required for ADHD: Please see website for detailed information: www.northeastern.edu/drc
With general application: No
To receive services after enrolling: Yes
What documentation required for ASD: Please see website for detailed information: www.northeastern.edu/drc
With general application: No
To receive services after enrolling: Yes
LD/ADHD/ASD documentation submitted to: Disability Resource Center
ASD Specific Program: NR
Special Ed. HS course work accepted: Yes
Specific course requirements of all applicants: Yes
Separate application required for program services: Yes
Total # of students receiving LD/ADHD/ASD services: 223
Acceptance into program means acceptance into college: No

ADMISSIONS

There is no separate or different admissions process for students with learning disabilities or ADHD. However, students who are interested in the Learning Disabilities Program (LDP), must apply to the LDP as well as to the university. Students are encouraged to submit an application to the LDP immediately upon their decision to attend the university. The LDP also requires an interview for admission to the program. LDP application and additional information about the program are available at www.northeastern.edu/uhcs/idp. General admission requirements include: 4 years English, 3 years math, 3 years science, 3 years social studies, 3 years foreign language. The ACT or SAT are required.

ADDITIONAL INFORMATION

The LDP model is designed to support the academic development and achievement of students with learning disabilities and attention deficit disorders. LDP sessions can include targeted instruction and support in developing: Academic skills in reading, writing, executive functions, planning and managing time, and organizing materials. Students work on self regulated learning in obtaining goals, applying effective strategies, evaluating approaches and using resources. Academic mindsets involve maintaining motivation, persisting through challenges, and enhancing metacognition.

General Support Services Information

Contact Information
Name of program or department: Disability Resource Center
Telephone: 617.373.2676
Fax: 617.373.7500
Website: www.northeastern.edu/ldp

Accommodations or Services For Students With Learning Differences

Accommodations are decided upon an individual basis after a thorough review of appropriate, current documentation. The accommodations requests must be supported through the documentation provided and must be logically linked to the current impact of the condition on academic functioning.

Allowed in exams
Calculator: Yes
Dictionary: Yes
Computer: Yes
Spellchecker: Yes
Extended test time: Yes
Scribes: Yes
Proctors: Yes
Oral exams: Yes
Note-takers: Yes
Support services for students with LD: Yes
Support services for students with ADHD: Yes
Support services for students with ASD: Yes
Distraction-reduced environment: Yes
Tape recording in class: Yes
Electronic texts: Yes
Kurzweil reader: NR
Audio books: Yes
Other assistive technology: Yes
Priority registration: Not Applicable
Added costs of services: Yes
LD specialists: Yes
ADHD coaching: No
ASD specialists: Yes
Professional tutors: No
Peer tutors: NR
Max. hours/wk. for services: NR
How professors are notified of student approved accommodations: By student

General Admissions Information

Office of Admissions: 617-373-2200

Entrance Requirements

Academic units required: 4 English, 3 math, 3 science, 2 science labs, 2 foreign language, 3 social studies, 2 history, **Academic units recommended:** 4 math, 4 science. High school diploma is required and GED is accepted. SAT or ACT required. If ACT, ACT with writing accepted. TOEFL required of all international applicants: minimum internet TOEFL 92.

Application deadline: 1/1
Notification: 4/1
Average GPA: NR
ACT Composite middle 50% range: 31-34
SAT Math middle 50% range: 680-770
SAT Critical Reading middle 50% range: 660-740
SAT Writing middle 50% range: 640-730
Graduate top 10% of class: 70
Graduated top 25% of class: 94
Graduated top 50% of class: 99

COLLEGE GRADUATION REQUIREMENTS

Course waivers allowed: No
Course substitutions allowed: Yes
In what course: Foreign language course substitutions available for eligible students.

Additional Information

Environment: This private school was founded in 1898. It has a 73-acre campus.

Student Body
Undergrad enrollment: 17,990
% Women: 50
% Men: 50
% Out-of-state: 70

Cost information
Tuition: $32,300
Room & board: $13,000

Housing Information
University Housing: Yes
Percent living on campus: 48

Greek System
Fraternity: Yes
Sorority: Yes
Athletics: Division I

PINE MANOR COLLEGE

400 Heath Street, Chestnut Hill, MA 02467-2332
Phone: 617-731-7104 • Fax: 617-731-7102
E-mail: admission@pmc.edu • Web: www.pmc.edu
Support: CS • Institution: Private

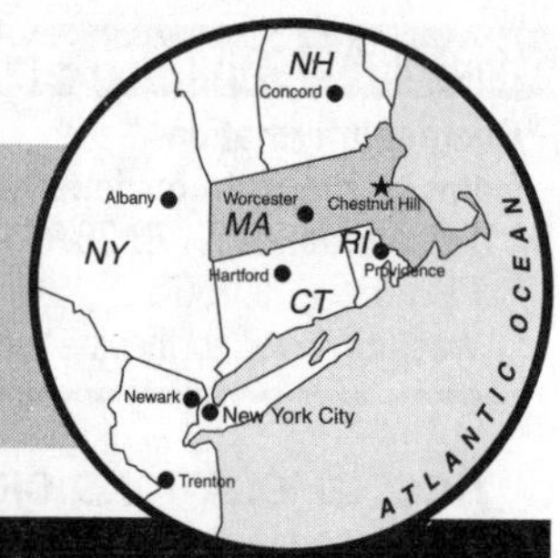

PROGRAMS OR SERVICES FOR STUDENTS WITH LEARNING DIFFERENCES

The Brown Learning Resource Center (LRC) is an expression of the College's strong commitment to the individual learning experience. The LRC supports and challenges students to realize their maximum academic potential in the way that best suits their individual learning styles. There are four full-time and three part-time professional tutors who provide tutoring that is individually tailored to the learning style and needs of the student. The tutoring is strategy-based and process-oriented. The LRC hopes that students with learning disabilities enter college with some compensatory techniques and study skills. The tutors furnish guidance and academic skills assistance to students whose learning disabilities create a gap between their true capacity and daily performance. The LRC serves the whole college population whether or not a student has a documented learning disability. There is no additional fee for this service.

ADMISSION INFORMATION FOR STUDENTS WITH LEARNING DIFFERENCES

College entrance test required: Yes
Interview required: No
Essay required: 5
Additional Application Required for LD/ADHD/ASD: NR
What documentation required for LD: We follow Association of Higher Ed and Disability (AHEAD) guidelines for disability documentation.
With general application: No
To receive services after enrolling: Yes
What documentation required for ADHD: We follow Association of Higher Ed and Disability (AHEAD) guidelines for disability documentation.
With general application: No
To receive services after enrolling: Yes
What documentation required for ASD: We follow Association of Higher Ed and Disability (AHEAD) guidelines for disability documentation.
With general application: No
To receive services after enrolling: Yes
LD/ADHD/ASD documentation submitted to: Both support services and admissions
ASD Specific Program: NR
Special Ed. HS course work accepted: Yes
Specific course: Yes
Separate application required for program services: No
Total # of students receiving LD/ADHD/ASD services: NR
Acceptance into program means acceptance into college: NR

ADMISSIONS

All applicants submit the same general application. Although not required, an interview is highly recommended. Courses required are 4 years English, 3 years math, 2 years science, 4 years social studies. Courses taken in special education are accepted. Admissions decisions are made by the Office of Admissions. However, the director of the LRC assists in interpreting testing and documentation and makes a recommendation to the Office of Admissions. Students are encouraged to self-disclose during the admission process. Once accepted, students should provide disability documentation to the LRC Director if they anticipate the need of academic accommodations. All students who submit disability documentation meet with the Director during Orientation to discuss accommodations.

ADDITIONAL INFORMATION

LRC tutors work with students on a regular, once or twice a week basis. Students also work closely with their academic advisors. LRC tutors offer diagnosis and remediation for students in academic difficulty; enrichment for successful students; and assistance to faculty and staff. In addition, the following accommodations have proved useful: reduced courseload each semester; additional time to complete exams, quizzes, or written assignments; a separate room for examinations; access to audio texts.

General Support Services Information

Contact Information
Name of program or department: Brown Learning Resource Center
Telephone: 617-731-7181
Fax: 617-731-7631

Accommodations or Services for Students with Learning Differences

Accommodations are decided upon an individual basis after a thorough review of appropriate, current documentation. The accommodations requests must be supported through the documentation provided and must be logically linked to the current impact of the condition on academic functioning.

Allowed in exams
Calculator: Yes
Dictionary: Yes
Computer: Yes
Spellchecker: Yes
Extended test time: Yes
Scribes: Yes
Proctors: Yes
Oral exams: Yes
Note-takers: Yes
Services for students with LD: Yes
Services for students with ADHD: Yes
Services for students with ASD: Yes
Distraction-reduced environment: Yes
Tape recording in class: Yes
Audio books: Yes
Electronic texts: NR
Kurzweil Reader: No
Other assistive technology: Yes
Priority registration: Yes
Added costs of services: No
LD specialists: Yes
ADHD coaching: NR
ASD specialists: NR
Professional tutors: NR
Peer tutors: Yes
Max. hours/wk. for services: 3
How professors are notified of student approved accommodations: Both student and director

General Admissions Information

Office of Admissions: 617-731-7104

Entrance Requirements

Academic units recommended: 4 English, 3 mathematics, 3 science, 2 foreign language, 2 social studies. High school diploma is required and GED is accepted. SAT or ACT required. If ACT, ACT with Writing component accepted. TOEFL required of all international applicants: minimum paper TOEFL 475.

Application deadline: NR
Notification: NR
Average GPA: NR
ACT Composite middle 50% range: NR-NR
SAT Math middle 50% range: NR-NR
SAT Critical Reading middle 50% range: NR-NR
SAT Writing middle 50% range: NR-NR
Graduated top 10% of class: NR
Graduated top 25% of class: NR
Graduated top 50% of class: NR

COLLEGE GRADUATION REQUIREMENTS

Course waivers allowed: Yes
Course substitutions allowed: N/A

Additional Information

Environment: Pine Manor is located on a 79-acre campus in Chestnut Hill, five miles west of Boston.

Student Body
Undergrad enrollment: 448
% Women: NR
% Men: NR
% Out-of-state: 36

Cost information
Tuition: $27,860
Room & board: $13,280

Housing Information
University Housing: Yes
Percent living on campus: 74

Greek System
Fraternity: No
Sorority: No
Athletics: Division III

SMITH COLLEGE

7 College Lane, Northampton, MA 01063
Phone: 413-585-2500 • Fax: 413-585-2527
E-mail: admission@smith.edu • Web: www.smith.edu
Support: S • Institution: Private

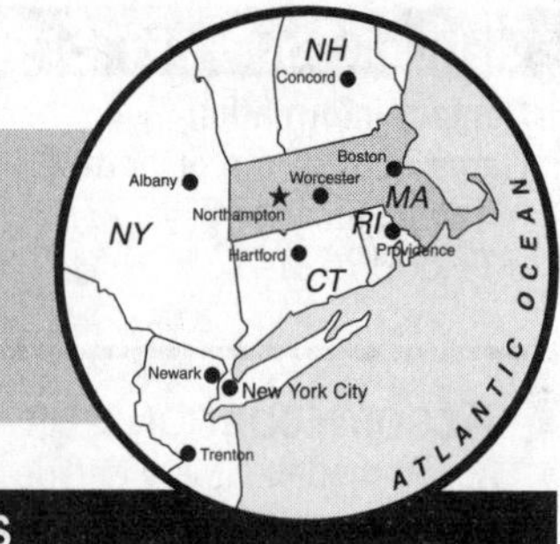

PROGRAMS OR SERVICES FOR STUDENTS WITH LEARNING DIFFERENCES

Smith College does not have a formal LD program. However, the college is both philosophically committed and legally required to enable students with documented disabilities to participate in college programs by providing reasonable accommodations for them. The Office of Disabilities Services (ODS) facilitates the provision of services and offers services aimed to eliminate barriers through modification of the program when necessary. A student may voluntarily register with ODS by completing a disability identification form and providing documentation of the disability, after which proper accommodations will be determined. Students with disabilities who need academic services are asked to make their needs known and file timely request forms for accommodations in course work each semester with ODS. Students are encouraged to tell professors about the accommodations needed. The college is responsible for providing that, within certain limits, students are not denied the opportunity to participate in college programs on the basis of a disability. The college will provide support services to students with appropriate evaluations and documentation. Students should contact the ODS for consultation and advice. Through the ODS office there are Peer Mentors.

ADMISSION INFORMATION FOR STUDENTS WITH LEARNING DIFFERENCES

College entrance tests required: Yes
Interview required: Yes
Essay required: Yes
Additional Application Required for LD/ADHD/ASD: NR
What documentation required for LD: Psycho ed evaluation to include: relevant historical info, instructional interventions, related services, age diagnosed, objective data (aptitude, achievement, info processing), test scores (standard, percentile and grade equivalents) and describe functional limitations.
With general application: No
To receive services after enrolling: Yes
What documentation required for ADHD: Diagnosis based on DSM-V; history of behaviors impairing functioning in academic setting; diagnostic interview; history of symptoms; evidence of ongoing behaviors.
With general application: No
To receive services after enrolling: Yes
What documentation required for ASD: Psycho ed evaluation
With general application: NR
To receive services after enrolling: Yes
LD/ADHD/ASD documentation submitted to: Office of Disability Services
ASD Specific Program: NR
Special Ed. HS course work accepted: No
Specific course requirements of all applicants: NR
Separate application required: Yes
Total % of students receiving LD/ADHD/ASD services: 20
Acceptance into program means acceptance into college: Students must be admitted to and enrolled in the university first and then request services.

ADMISSIONS

There is no special admissions procedure for students with learning disabilities. ACT/SAT are optional. Students may release scores at their discretion. Leniency may be granted in regard to a high school's waiving of foreign language requirements due to a learning disability. High school courses recommended are 4 years of English composition and literature, 3 years of a foreign language (or 2 years in each of 2 languages), 3 years of math, 2 years of science, and 2 years of history. Essays are required and help them understand how the student thinks, writes and what they are about. Recommendations are required. Interviews are highly recommended.

ADDITIONAL INFORMATION

The support services assist students to meet their requirements through modifications to programs when necessary. Courses are available in quantitative skills, study skills, and time management skills. The Special Needs Action Group for Support is a cross-disability, student-led group that meets regularly to provide support and peer mentoring and plan activities. Support services include readers, note-takers, scribes, assistive listening devices, typists, computing software and hardware, books on tape, writing counseling, peer tutoring, and time management/study skills training. If peer tutors are not available, other tutorial services may be sought.

General Support Services Information

Contact Information
Name of program or department: Office of Disability Services (ODS)
Telephone: 413-585-2071
Fax: 413-585-2206

Accommodations or Services for Students with Learning Differences

Accommodations are decided upon an individual basis after a thorough review of appropriate, current documentation. The accommodations requested must be supported through the documentation provided and must be logically linked to the current impact of the condition on academic functioning.

Allowed in exams
Calculator: Yes
Dictionary: No
Computer: Yes
Spellchecker: Yes
Extended test time: Yes
Scribes: Yes
Proctors: No
Oral exams: Yes
Note-takers: Yes
Services for students with LD: Yes
Services for students with ADHD: Yes
Services for students with ASD: Yes
Distraction-reduced environment: Yes
Tape recording in class: Yes
Audio books: NR
Electronic texts: Yes
Kurzweil Reader: Yes
Other assistive technology: Yes
Priority registration: Yes
Added costs for services: No
LD specialists: No
ADHD coaching: NR
ASD specialists: NR
Professional tutors: 2
Peer tutors: Yes
Max. hours/wk. for services: Unlimited
How professors are notified of LD/ADHD: By both student and director

General Admissions Information

Office of Admissions: 413-585-2500

Entrance Requirements
Academic units recommended: 4 English, 3 math, 3 science, 3 science labs, 3 foreign language, 2 history, 1 academic electives. High school diploma or equivalent is not required. SAT or ACT required for some. If ACT, ACT with writing accepted. TOEFL required of all international applicants: minimum paper TOEFL 600 or minimum internet TOEFL 90.

Application deadline: 1/15
Notification: NR
Average GPA: 3.94
ACT Composite middle 50% range: 28-32
SAT Math middle 50% range: 620-720
SAT Critical Reading middle 50% range: 620-740
SAT Writing middle 50% range: 630-720
Graduated top 10% of class: 64
Graduated top 25% of class: 90
Graduated top 50% of class: 100

COLLEGE GRADUATION REQUIREMENTS

Course waivers allowed: No
Course substitutions allowed: Yes
In what course: Foreign language

Additional Information

Environment: This private school was founded in 1871. It has a 147-acre campus.

Student Body
Undergrad enrollment: 2,478
% Women: 100
% Men: 00
% Out-of-state: 82

Cost information
Tuition: $47,620
Room & board: $16,010

Housing Information
University Housing: Yes
Percent living on campus: 95

Greek System
Fraternity: No
Sorority: No
Athletics: Division III

Springfield College

263 Alden Street, Springfield, MA 01109
Phone: 413-748-3136 • Fax: 413-748-3694
E-mail: admissions@spfldcol.edu • Web: www.springfieldcollege.edu
Support: CS • Institution type: 4-year private

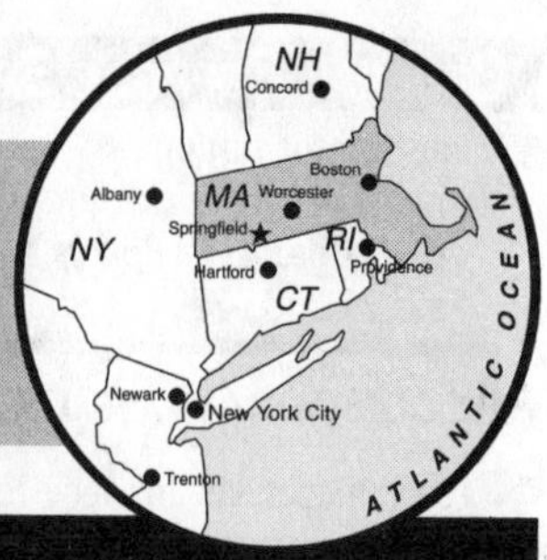

Programs or Services for Students with Learning Differences

Springfield College is committed to providing an equal educational opportunity and full participation in college activities for persons with disabilities. The Office of Learning Support Services provides services that ensure that students with disabilities are given an equal educational opportunity and the opportunity for full participation in all college programs and activities. In addition to supporting students with disabilities, Learning Support Services works with students who are having academic difficulty. Students can receive services by meeting with the director of Learning Support Services to verify eligibility for services, identify student needs, and determine appropriate services and accommodations. To receive services, students must provide documentation of their learning disabilities; the documentation must be current and comprehensive and contain specific evidence and identification of a learning disability. Documentation should not be older than 3 years.

Admission Information for Students with Learning Differences

College entrance tests required: Yes
Interview required: No
Essay required: Yes
Additional Application Required for LD/ADHD/ASD: NR
What documentation required for LD: Psycho ed evaluation to include: relevant historical info, instructional interventions, related services, age diagnosed, objective data (aptitude, achievement, info processing), test scores (standard, percentile and grade equivalents) and describe functional limitations.
With general application: No
To receive services after enrolling: Yes
What documentation required for ADHD: Diagnosis based on DSM-V; history of behaviors impairing functioning in academic setting; diagnostic interview; history of symptoms; evidence of ongoing behaviors.
With general application: No
To receive services after enrolling: Yes
What documentation required for ASD: Psycho ed evaluation
With general application: NR
To receive services after enrolling: Yes
LD/ADHD/ASD documentation submitted to: Office of Learning Support Services
ASD Specific Program: NR
Special Ed. HS course work accepted: No
Specific course requirements of all applicants: Yes
Separate application required: No
Total # of students receiving LD/ADHD/ASD services: 150–160
Acceptance into program means acceptance into college: Students must be admitted to and enrolled in the university first and then request services.

Admissions

There is no special admissions process for students with learning disabilities. All applicants must submit the same general application and meet the same admission criteria. There is no minimum GPA required, though the average GPA is a 3.0. Courses required include 4 years of English, 3 years of math, 2 years of history, and 2–3 years of science. Personal statements and interviews are required. Admissions decisions are made by the Office of Admissions.

Additional Information

Services provided through the Office of Learning Support Services include taped textbooks, taped lectures, readers, alternative testing, note-takers, tutors, computers with spell-check, reduced course loads, study skills and time management training, course accommodations, and assistance with course selection. Services and accommodations that may be appropriate for students with attention deficit hyperactivity disorder include testing accommodations, tape recording of lectures, assistance organizational skills, assistance with study skills, and access to adaptive technology. Services and accommodations that may be appropriate for students with learning disabilities include taped textbooks, readers, note-takers, tape recording of lectures, testing accommodations, reduced course load, assistance with study skills, assistance with organizational skills, and adaptive technology. Students experiencing academic difficulties may benefit from working one-on-one with an academic coach. Academic coaches help students put together a plan for success by focusing on each student's academic strengths and weaknesses. Academic coaches are available to help students address problems that impede academic progress, such as procrastination, time mismanagement, and related issues. Academic coaches develop plans to strengthen specific academic skills after an initial assessment. Tutoring is available for any Springfield College student who needs it. Faculty-approved tutors provide individual or small group sessions to students who are concerned about their academic performance.

General Support Services Information

Contact Information
Name of program or department: Learning Support Services
Telephone: 413-748-3431

Accommodations or Services for Students with Learning Differences

Accommodations are decided upon an individual basis after a thorough review of appropriate, current documentation. The accommodations requested must be supported through the documentation provided and must be logically linked to the current impact of the condition on academic functioning.

Allowed in exams
Calculator: Yes
Dictionary: Yes
Computer: Yes
Spellchecker: Yes
Extended test time: Yes
Scribes: Yes
Proctors: Yes
Oral exams: Yes
Note-takers: Yes
Services for students with LD: Yes
Services for students with ADHD: Yes
Services for students with ASD: Yes
Distraction-reduced environment: Yes
Tape recording in class: Yes
Audio books: NR
Electronic texts: Yes
Kurzweil Reader: Yes
Other assistive technology: Yes
Priority registration: No
Added costs for services: No
LD specialists: Yes
ADHD coaching: NR
ASD specialists: NR
Professional tutors: No
Peer tutors: No
Max. hours/wk. for services: Unlimited
How professors are notified of LD/ADHD: By both student and director

General Admissions Information

Office of Admission: 413-748-3136

Entrance Requirements

Academic units recommended: 4 English, 3 math, 3 science, 2 foreign language, 2 social studies, 4 academic electives. High school diploma is required, and GED is accepted. TOEFL required of all international applicants: minimum paper TOEFL 525.

Application deadline: NR
Notification: NR
Average GPA: NR
ACT Composite middle 50% range: NR-NR
SAT Math middle 50% range: NR-NR
SAT Critical Reading middle 50% range: NR-NR
SAT Writing middle 50% range: NR-NR
Graduated top 10% of class: NR
Graduated top 25% of class: NR
Graduated top 50% of class: NR

COLLEGE GRADUATION REQUIREMENTS

Course waivers allowed: Yes
In what course: Foreign language
Course substitutions allowed: Yes
In what course: Foreign language

Additional Information

Environment: The campus is in a suburban area about 30 minutes north of Hartford.

Student Body
Undergrad enrollment: 1,193
% Women: 73
% Men: 27
% Out-of-state: NR
Cost information
Tuition: $34,980
Room & board: $11,890
Housing Information
University Housing: Yes
Percent living on campus: NR
Greek System
Fraternity: No
Sorority: No
Athletics: NR

U. of Massachusetts—Amherst

University Admissions Center, Amherst, MA 01003-9291
Phone: 413-545-0222 • Fax: 413-545-4312
E-mail: mail@admissions.umass.edu • Web: www.umass.edu
Support: CS • Institution: Public

Programs or Services for Students with Learning Differences

Disabilities Services (DS) supports all students with documented disabilities. Students must register with DS and provide documentation to receive services. Students are assigned to work with a professional Consumer Manager to work on three objectives for the entire academic year: understanding and obtaining accommodations needed, identifying and utilizing resources, and identifying and implementing learning strategies. DS also provides Learning Specialists are trained in disability-related learning issues who apply unique, specific expertise and knowledge to student's academic needs. Learning Specialists' seek to match student's specific disabilities and skills to their specific learning requirements through the use of individualized learning techniques, study skills, reading techniques, organizational techniques and other active learning skills

Admission Information for Students with Learning Differences

College entrance test required: Yes
Interview required: No
Essay required: Not Applicable
Additional Application Required for LD/ADHD/ASD: Yes
What documentation required for LD: Psycho ed evaluation
With general application: No
To receive services after enrolling: Yes
What documentation required for ADHD: Psycho ed evaluation
With general application: No
To receive services after enrolling: Yes
What documentation required for ASD: Psycho ed evaluation
With general application: No
To receive services after enrolling: Yes
LD/ADHD/ASD documentation submitted to: Disability Services
ASD Specific Program: NR
Special Ed. HS course work accepted: Not Applicable
Specific course requirements of all applicants: NR
Separate application required for program services: Yes
Total # of students receiving LD/ADHD/ASD services: 484
Acceptance into program means acceptance into college: No

Admissions

Massachusetts residents with a learning disability who submit documentation of disability are eligible for exemption from the standardized test score requirement. Documentation includes a copy of either the Individualized Education Plan (IEP) or Section 504 plan OR a letter from the high school guidance counselor confirming that the student has a diagnosed learning disability.

High School Unit Requirements: Minimum subject matter requirements must be met (see chart below). The rigor of the curriculum is strongly considered. When assessing academic achievement, course grades as well as grade trends are important, including course selection and grades in relation to the desired major.

Additional Information

Students and Consumer Managers prepare accommodation forms for professors for accommodations such as: extended test time on exams and/or assignments, alternate test formats, and note taking. Learning Specialists assigned to students work on average, one hour per week (more meeting times may be needed). The Learning Specialist works with students to facilitate obstacles being experienced. Students with relevant documented LD can petition to substitute a foreign language requirement with cultural courses (called a foreign language modification). DS operates several programs such as: Access Program, Communication Access Program and Information Access Program.

General Support Services Information

Contact Information
Name of program or department: Disability Services
Telephone: (413) 545-0982
Fax: (413) 577-0122
Website: www.umass.edu/disability/index.html

Accommodations or Services For Students With Learning Differences

Accommodations are decided upon an individual basis after a thorough review of appropriate, current documentation. The accommodations requests must be supported through the documentation provided and must be logically linked to the current impact of the condition on academic functioning.

Allowed in exams
Calculator: Yes
Dictionary: Yes
Computer: Yes
Spellchecker: Yes
Extended test time: Yes
Scribes: Yes
Proctors: Yes
Oral exams: Yes
Note-takers: Yes
Support services for students with LD: Yes
Support services for students with ADHD: Yes
Support services for students with ASD: Yes
Distraction-reduced environment: Yes
Tape recording in class: Yes
Electronic texts: Yes
Kurzweil reader: NR
Audio books: Yes
Other assistive technology: Yes
Priority registration: Yes
Added costs of services: No
LD specialists: Yes
ADHD coaching: No
ASD specialists: Not Applicable
Professional tutors: No
Peer tutors: Not Applicable
Max. hours/wk. for services: NR
How professors are notified of student approved accommodations: By director

General Admissions Information

Office of Admissions: 413-545-0222

Entrance Requirements

Academic units required: 4 English, 3 math, 3 science, 2 science labs, 2 foreign language, 2 social studies, 2 academic electives. High school diploma is required and GED is accepted. SAT or ACT required. If ACT, ACT with writing recommended. TOEFL required of all international applicants: minimum internet TOEFL 80.

Application deadline: NR
Notification: NR
Average GPA: 3.83
ACT Composite middle 50% range: 25-30
SAT Math middle 50% range: 580-670
SAT Critical Reading middle 50% range: 550-640
SAT Writing middle 50% range: NR-NR
Graduate top 10% of class: 32
Graduated top 25% of class: 73
Graduated top 50% of class: 97

COLLEGE GRADUATION REQUIREMENTS

Course waivers allowed: No
Course substitutions allowed: Yes
In what course: Math, Analytical Reasoning, and Foreign Language

Additional Information

Environment: This public school was founded in 1863. It has a 1463-acre campus.

Student Body
Undergrad enrollment: 22,748
% Women: 49
% Men: 51
% Out-of-state: 20

Cost information
In-state Tuition: $13,790
Out-of-state Tuition: $30,123
Room & board: $12,028
Housing Information
University Housing: Yes
Percent living on campus: 58

Greek System
Fraternity: Yes
Sorority: Yes
Athletics: Division I

WHEATON COLLEGE (MA)

26 E Main Street, Norton, MA 02766
Phone: 508-286-8251 • Fax: 508-286-8271
E-mail: admission@wheatoncollege.edu • Web: wheatoncollege.edu
Support: S • Institution: Private

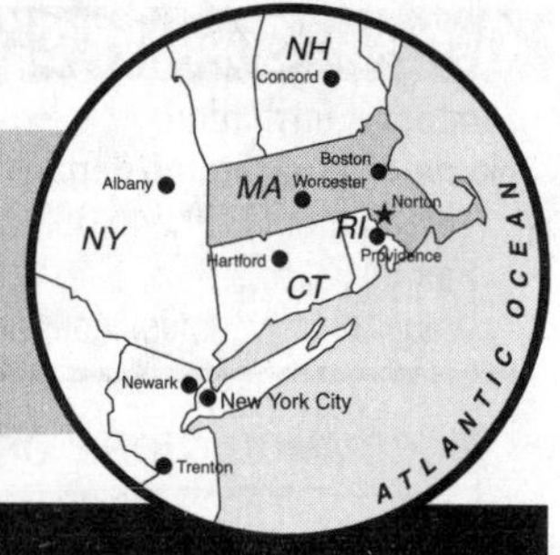

PROGRAMS OR SERVICES FOR STUDENTS WITH LEARNING DIFFERENCES

Wheaton College encourages life-long learning by assisting students to become self-advocates and independent learners. The college does not have a special program for students with LD. The Assistant Dean for College Skills serves as the 504/ADA coordinator. Students with LD can access services through the dean. The Academic Advising Center houses the Dean of Academic Advising who holds drop-in office hours and assists students with petitions to the Committee on Admissions and Academic Standing, Orientation, and Probation; general advising; and incomplete grade resolution. The advising staff can assist with pressing advising questions. Students also have access to tutors, peer advisors, and preceptors who offer assistance with study strategies. All students have access to these services.

ADMISSION INFORMATION FOR STUDENTS WITH LEARNING DIFFERENCES

College entrance test required: No
Interview required: No
Essay required: No
Additional Application Required for LD/ADHD/ASD: NR
What documentation required for LD: Psycho ed evaluation to include: relevant historical info, instructional interventions, related services, age diagnosed, objective data (aptitude, achievement, info processing), test scores (standard, percentile and grade equivalents) and describe functional limitations.
With general application: No
To receive services after enrolling: Yes
What documentation required for ADHD: Diagnosis based on DSM-V; history of behaviors impairing functioning in academic setting; diagnostic interview; history of symptoms; evidence of ongoing behaviors.
With general application: No
To receive services after enrolling: Yes
What documentation required for ASD: Psycho ed evaluation
With general application: NR
To receive services after enrolling: Yes
LD/ADHD/ASD documentation submitted to: Disability Services
ASD Specific Program: NR
Special Ed. HS course work accepted: Yes
Specific course requirements of all applicants: NR
Separate application required for program services: No
Total # of students receiving LD/ADHD/ASD services: 120
Acceptance into program means acceptance into college: Students must be admitted to and enrolled at the university before requesting services.

ADMISSIONS

All applicants must meet the same admission standards. Students with LD may choose to meet with the Assistant Dean for College Skills. Wheaton College does not require the ACT/SAT for admission. It is strongly suggested that students take 4 years of English, 3–4 years of math, 3–4 years of a foreign language, 2 years of social studies, and 3–4 years of science. Students are encouraged to take AP and honors courses and courses in visual/performing arts. Wheaton will accept courses taken in the special education department. Students with LD are encouraged to self-disclose and provide current documentation. All LD testing information should be sent to both admissions and support services.

ADDITIONAL INFORMATION

Services for students with LD can include classroom accommodations, college skills workshops, course tutoring program, general advising, and study strategy tutoring as well as strategy workshops. Reasonable accommodations are available for students with appropriate documentation. There is a summer program available for students who wish to participate. Proctors are not offered because Wheaton has an honor code for exams.

General Support Services Information

Contact Information
Name of program or department: Disability Services
Telephone: 5082868215
Fax: 5082865621
Website: NR

Accommodations or Services For Students With Learning Differences

Accommodations are decided upon an individual basis after a thorough review of appropriate, current documentation. The accommodations requests must be supported through the documentation provided and must be logically linked to the current impact of the condition on academic functioning.

Allowed in exams
Calculator: Yes
Dictionary: NR
Computer: Yes
Spellchecker: NR
Extended test time: Yes
Scribes: NR
Proctors: NR
Oral exams: NR
Note-takers: Yes
Support services for students with LD: Yes
Support services for students with ADHD: Yes
Support services for students with ASD: Yes
Distraction-reduced environment: Yes
Tape recording in class: Yes
Electronic texts: NR
Kurzweil reader: NR
Audio books: NR
Other assistive technology: Yes
Priority registration: No
Added costs of services: No
LD specialists: No
ADHD coaching: NR
ASD specialists: NR
Professional tutors: No
Peer tutors: NR
Max. hours/wk. for services: NR
How professors are notified of student approved accommodations: By both student and director

General Admissions Information

Office of Admissions: 508-286-8251

Entrance Requirements

Academic units required: 4 English, **Academic units recommended:** 4 math, 4 science, 4 foreign language, 4 social studies, 4 history. High school diploma is required and GED is accepted. SAT or ACT considered if submitted. If ACT, ACT with writing accepted. TOEFL required of all international applicants: minimum internet TOEFL 90.

Application deadline: 1/15
Notification: 4/1
Average GPA: 3.34
ACT Composite middle 50% range: 25-30
SAT Math middle 50% range: 550-665
SAT Critical Reading middle 50% range: 550-658
SAT Writing middle 50% range: 540-650
Graduate top 10% of class: 26
Graduated top 25% of class: 60
Graduated top 50% of class: 89

COLLEGE GRADUATION REQUIREMENTS

Course waivers allowed: No
In what course: Waivers are not permitted however students can petition for a foreign language substitution. There is not a waiver for the math requirement, however there are courses which integrate math concepts within a discipline. This is a viable option for students
Course substitutions allowed: NR

Additional Information

Environment: This private school was founded in 1834. It has a 400-acre campus.

Student Body
Undergrad enrollment: 1,598
% Women: 64
% Men: 36
% Out-of-state: 63

Cost information
Tuition: $47,390
Room & board: $12,165
Housing Information
University Housing: Yes
Percent living on campus: 95

Greek System
Fraternity: No
Sorority: No
Athletics: Division III

Wheelock College

200 The Riverway, Boston, MA 02215
Phone: 617-879-2206 • Fax: 617-879-2449
E-mail: undergrad@wheelock.edu • Web: www.wheelock.edu
Support: CS • Institution: Private

Programs or Services for Students with Learning Differences

The Disability Services Program at Wheelock College ensures that students with disabilities can participate in all facets of college life. They also provide and coordinate support services and programs that will enable students to maximize their educational potential. Students are encouraged to be independent individuals who know their strengths and develop compensatory skills for academic success. When working with students, the two major goals are to help with becoming independent and assisting in developing self-advocacy skills. Students with LD are encouraged to self-disclose to Disability Services. Students are required to provide documentation from a qualified professional. Disability Services will assist in identifying appropriate accommodations based on the documentation provided.

Admission Information for Students with Learning Differences

College entrance test required: Yes
Interview required: NR
Essay required: NR
Additional Application Required for LD/ADHD/ASD: NR
What documentation required for LD: Psycho ed evaluation to include: relevant historical info, instructional interventions, related services, age diagnosed, objective data (aptitude, achievement, info processing), test scores (standard, percentile and grade equivalents) and describe functional limitations.
With general application: No
To receive services after enrolling: Yes
What documentation required for ADHD: Diagnosis based on DSM-V; history of behaviors impairing functioning in academic setting; diagnostic interview; history of symptoms; evidence of ongoing behaviors.
With general application: NR
To receive services after enrolling: Yes
What documentation required for ASD: Psycho ed evaluation
With general application: NR
To receive services after enrolling: Yes
LD/ADHD/ASD documentation submitted to: Disability Services
ASD Specific Program: NR
Special Ed. HS course work accepted: Yes
Specific course requirements of all applicants: Yes
Separate application required for program services: NR
Total # of students receiving LD/ADHD/ASD services: 95
Acceptance into program means acceptance into college: Students must be admitted to and enrolled in the university prior to requesting services.

Admissions

There is no special admissions process for students with LD and ADHD. All applicants are expected to meet the general admission criteria. All students should have 4 years of English, 1 year of U.S. history and additional social studies, 3 years of college-prep math, and at least 1 year of science lab. Substitutions are not allowed for entrance requirements. Wheelock will accept courses in high school that were taken in the Special Education Department. Students should feel free to self-disclose their disabilities in the application process. Students must submit a copy of a graded paper written within the past year. It should be a minimum of 250 words and can be on any subject. Some examples are an English composition, a history thesis, a psychology report, or a literary critique.

Additional Information

With appropriate documentation, students may be eligible for the following services or accommodations: priority registration, letters informing the instructors of the disability and what reasonable accommodations the student will need, individual sessions with a learning specialist to help with time management, academic, and organizational skills support. The Writing Center is available for all students interested in assistance with writing skills, and peer tutors work one-on-one with the students. Students may request referrals for peer tutors, and study groups are available. In addition, workshops on the following topics are offered throughout the academic year: academic survival skills, reading skills, and evaluation of students' learning styles. Other academic support services include academic advising, and referrals for diagnostic testing.

General Support Services Information

Contact Information
Name of program or department: Disability Services
Telephone: 617 879 2030
Fax: 617 879 2163
Website: NR

Accommodations or Services For Students With Learning Differences

Accommodations are decided upon an individual basis after a thorough review of appropriate, current documentation. The accommodations requests must be supported through the documentation provided and must be logically linked to the current impact of the condition on academic functioning.

Allowed in exams
Calculator: No
Dictionary: No
Computer: No
Spellchecker: Yes
Extended test time: Yes
Scribes: Yes
Proctors: Yes
Oral exams: No
Note-takers: Yes
Support services for students with LD: Yes
Support services for students with ADHD: Yes
Support services for students with ASD: Yes
Distraction-reduced environment: Yes
Tape recording in class: Yes
Electronic texts: Yes
Kurzweil reader: Yes
Audio books: NR
Other assistive technology: Yes
Priority registration: Yes
Added costs of services: No
LD specialists: No
ADHD coaching: NR
ASD specialists: NR
Professional tutors: No
Peer tutors: Yes
Max. hours/wk. for services: NR
How professors are notified of student approved accommodations: By student

General Admissions Information

Office of Admissions: 617-879-2206

Entrance Requirements

Academic units required: 4 English, 3 math, 2 science, 1 science labs, 1 social studies, 2 history, 3 academic electives, **Academic units recommended:** 4 English, 3 math, 2 science, 1 science labs, 1 social studies, 2 history, 3 academic electives. High school diploma is required and GED is accepted. SAT or ACT required. If ACT, ACT with writing accepted. TOEFL required of all international applicants: minimum paper TOEFL 550 or minimum internet TOEFL 80.

Application deadline: 5/1
Notification: Rolling starting 1/20
Average GPA: 2.88
ACT Composite middle 50% range: 18-24
SAT Math middle 50% range: 400-520
SAT Critical Reading middle 50% range: 410-542
SAT Writing middle 50% range: 410-530
Graduate top 10% of class: 11
Graduated top 25% of class: 33
Graduated top 50% of class: 57

COLLEGE GRADUATION REQUIREMENTS

Course waivers allowed: NR
Course substitutions allowed: NR

Additional Information

Environment: This private school was founded in 1888. It has a 6-acre campus.

Student Body
Undergrad enrollment: 811
% Women: 84
% Men: 16
% Out-of-state: 39

Cost information
Tuition: $33,600
Room & board: $14,400
Housing Information
University Housing: Yes
Percent living on campus: 64

Greek System
Fraternity: No
Sorority: No
Athletics: Division III

ADRIAN COLLEGE

110 South Madison Street, Adrian, MI 49221
Phone: 517-265-5161 • Fax: 517-264-3331
E-mail: admissions@adrian.edu • Web: www.adrian.edu
Support: CS • Institution: Private

PROGRAMS OR SERVICES FOR STUDENTS WITH LEARNING DIFFERENCES

Adrian College has extensive academic support services for all students with disabilities. The more the students are mainstreamed in high school, the greater their chances of success at Adrian. There is no special or separate curriculum for students with learning disabilities.

ADMISSION INFORMATION FOR STUDENTS WITH LEARNING DIFFERENCES

College entrance tests required: Yes
Interview required: No
Essay required: N/A
Additional Application Required for LD/ADHD/ASD: NR
What documentation required for LD: Psycho ed evaluation to include: relevant historical info, instructional interventions, related services, age diagnosed, objective data (aptitude, achievement, info processing), test scores (standard, percentile and grade equivalents) and describe functional limitations.
With general application: No
To receive services after enrolling: Yes
What documentation required for ADHD: Diagnosis based on DSM-V; history of behaviors impairing functioning in academic setting; diagnostic interview; history of symptoms; evidence of ongoing behaviors.
With general application: No
To receive services after enrolling: Yes
What documentation required for ASD: Psycho ed evaluation
With general application: NR
To receive services after enrolling: Yes
LD/ADHD/ASD documentation submitted to: Support Program/Services
ASD Specific Program: NR
Special Ed. HS course work accepted: Yes
Specific course requirements for all applicants: NR
Separate application required for program services: Yes
Total # of students receiving LD/ADHD/ASD services: 37
Acceptance into program means acceptance into college: Separate application required after student has enrolled

ADMISSIONS

Students with learning disabilities must meet regular admission criteria. Students should demonstrate the ability to do college-level work through an acceptable GPA in college-preparatory classes (average 3.22) including four years English, three years math, social studies, science and language, ACT (average 19–24) or SAT. Furthermore, by their senior year in high school, students should, for the most part, be mainstreamed. Courses taken in special education will be considered for admission. The applications of students who self-disclose are reviewed by Academic Services staff, not to determine admissions, but to start a documentation file. There is a special admissions program designed for students who demonstrate academic potential. This Adrian College Enrichment Program (ACE) requires students to sign a contract and maintain a certain GPA each of the first two semesters.

ADDITIONAL INFORMATION

Academic Services Department offers a wide variety of services. Staff members help identify alternative study strategies and develop time management plans. Strategies for more effective reading, note-taking, and test-taking are also offered. The staff teaches a number of skills courses. Course adaptations help to make courses more understandable. Skills classes are available in reading, math, study skills and research paper writing, and students are granted credit toward their GPA. Tutorial assistance is available for all students. P.R.I.D.E. (Promoting the Rights of Individuals Everywhere) communicates information about the difficulties and accomplishments of people with disabilities.

General Support Services Information

Contact Information
Name of program or department: ACCESS, Academic Services
Telephone: 517-265-5161, ext. 4093
Fax: 517-264-3331

Accommodations or Services for Students with Learning Differences

Accommodations are decided upon an individual basis after a thorough review of appropriate, current documentation. The accommodations requested must be supported through the documentation provided and must be logically linked to the current impact of the condition on academic functioning.

Allowed in exams
Calculator: No
Dictionary: Yes
Computer: Yes
Spellchecker: Yes
Extended test time: Yes
Scribes: Yes
Proctors: Yes
Oral exams: Yes
Note-takers: Yes
Services for students with LD: Yes
Services for students with ADHD: Yes
Services for students with ASD: Yes
Distraction-reduced environment: Yes
Tape recording in class: Yes
Audio books: NR
Electronic texts: Yes
Kurzweil Reader: Yes, 1000 and 3000
Other assistive technology: Braille capabilities
Priority registration: No
Added costs for services: No
LD specialists: Yes
ADHD coaching: NR
ASD specialists: NR
Professional tutors: NR
Peer tutors: 100–110
Max. hours/wk. for services:
How professors are notified of LD/ADHD: Both student and director

General Admissions Information

Office of Admissions: 517-265-5161

Entrance Requirements

Academic units recommended: 4 English, 3 math, 2 science, 1 science labs, 2 foreign language, 1 social studies, 1 history, 2 academic electives. High school diploma is required and GED is accepted. SAT or ACT required. If ACT, ACT with writing accepted. TOEFL required of all international applicants: minimum paper TOEFL 500.

Application deadline: NR
Notification: Rolling starting 9/1
Average GPA: 3.3
ACT Composite middle 50% range: 20-25
SAT Math middle 50% range: 410-535
SAT Critical Reading middle 50% range: 430-515
SAT Writing middle 50% range: NR-NR
Graduated top 10% of class: 17
Graduated top 25% of class: 46
Graduated top 50% of class: 81

COLLEGE GRADUATION REQUIREMENTS

Course waivers allowed: No
Course substitutions allowed: No

Additional Information

Environment: This private school, affiliated with the Methodist Church, was founded in 1859. It has a 100-acre campus.

Student Body
Undergrad enrollment: 1,308
% Women: 47
% Men: 53
% Out-of-state: 24
Cost information
Tuition: $31,870
Room & board: $9,740
Housing Information
University Housing: Yes
Percent living on campus: 83
Greek System
Fraternity: Yes
Sorority: Yes
Athletics: Division III

CALVIN COLLEGE

3201 Burton Street SE, Grand Rapids, MI 49546
Phone: 616-526-6106 • Fax: 616-526-6777
E-mail: admissions@calvin.edu • Web: www.calvin.edu
Support: CS • Institution: Private

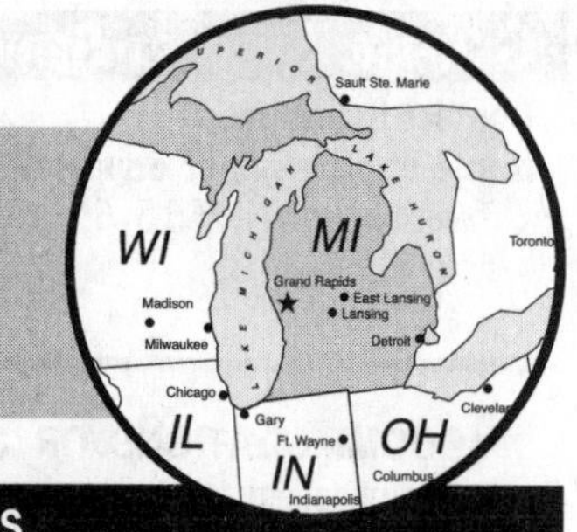

PROGRAMS OR SERVICES FOR STUDENTS WITH LEARNING DIFFERENCES

The mission of Student Academic Services is to ensure that otherwise qualified students are able to benefit from a distinctly Christian education based on liberal arts. The Coaching Program is for students with learning disabilities and/or ADHD and other students who specifically need help with time management and study skills. The coaches give suggestions and feedback as well as encouragement on how to manage academics with other areas of life. First-year students are encouraged to apply for the Coaching Program at the beginning of the fall semester. Once admitted, the student with a learning disability or ADHD may take advantage of all academic services. The student must understand, however, that academic standards at Calvin are rigorous. By taking advantage of appropriate services and by means of individual effort, it is assumed that academic progress will be made. The student and the disability coordinator maintain open communication with the appropriate faculty members to ensure academic integrity as well as reasonable expectations.

ADMISSION INFORMATION FOR STUDENTS WITH LEARNING DIFFERENCES

College entrance test required: Yes
Interview required: No
Essay required: Not Applicable
Additional Application Required for LD/ADHD/ASD: NR
What documentation required for LD: Please see our documentation requirements here: www.calvin.edu/academic/services/disability/documentation.html
With general application: NR
To receive services after enrolling: Yes
What documentation required for ADHD: Please see our documentation requirements here: www.calvin.edu/academic/services/disability/documentation.html
With general application: NR
To receive services after enrolling: Yes
What documentation required for ASD: Please see our documentation requirements here: www.calvin.edu/academic/services/disability/documentation.html
With general application: NR
To receive services after enrolling: Yes
LD/ADHD/ASD documentation submitted to: Disability Services
ASD Specific Program: NR
Special Ed. HS course work accepted: NR
Specific course requirements of all applicants: NR
Separate application required for program services: False
Total # of students receiving LD/ADHD/ASD services: NR
Acceptance into program means acceptance into college: NR

ADMISSIONS

There are no special admissions criteria for students with LD. Applicants are expected to have an ACT of 20 (19 English and 20 Math) or SAT of 940 (470 Critical Reading and 470 Math). The mid 50 percent for ACT is 23–25, and for SAT, it is 1090–1320. Courses required include: 3 English, 1 algebra, 1 geometry, and a minimum of 2 in any two of the following fields: social science, language, or natural science; one of the foreign language, math, social science, and natural science fields must include at least 3 years of study. The mid 50 percent GPA is 3.3–3.9. The Access Program provides an alternate entry track for first-time students who show promise of being successful at Calvin, but who cannot meet all of the admissions standards. The students are provided with placement testing in math and/or English, special advising, and enrollment in a college thinking and learning course during their first semester at Calvin. Depending on the outcome of the placement testing, additional developmental courses may be required as a condition of admission. The Access Program helps students develop new approaches, methods, and skills for learning by means of placement testing, academic advising, Academic Services Courses (ASC), and consultation with students' professors.

ADDITIONAL INFORMATION

The Office of Student Academic Services is a learning center is open to all students. SAS provides tutoring in most core and upper-level courses by trained upperclass students. Tutors meet with students each week to assist them in learning course content and in developing good approaches to learning. Classes are available in English, math, and study skills. These classes may be taken for college credit. The Coaching Program is an interactive relationship with another student who learns about the student's disability and learning style and then provides direction and strategies for the student.

General Support Services Information

Contact Information
Name of program or department: Disability Services
Telephone: 616.526.6155
Fax: 616.526.7066

Accommodations or Services For Students With Learning Differences

Accommodations are decided upon an individual basis after a thorough review of appropriate, current documentation. The accommodations requests must be supported through the documentation provided and must be logically linked to the current impact of the condition on academic functioning.

Allowed in exams
Calculator: Yes
Dictionary: Yes
Computer: Yes
Spellchecker: Yes
Extended test time: Yes
Scribes: Yes
Proctors: Yes
Oral exams: Yes
Note-takers: Yes
Support services for students with LD: Yes
Support services for students with ADHD: Yes
Support services for students with ASD: Yes
Distraction-reduced environment: Yes
Tape recording in class: Yes
Electronic texts: Yes
Kurzweil reader: NR
Audio books: Yes
Other assistive technology: Yes
Priority registration: Yes
Added costs of services: No
LD specialists: No
ADHD coaching: Yes
ASD specialists: NR
Professional tutors: No
Peer tutors: Yes
Max. hours/wk. for services: 1
How professors are notified of student approved accommodations: By student

General Admissions Information

Office of Admissions: 616-526-6106

Entrance Requirements

Academic units required: 3 English, 3 math, 2 science, 2 social studies, 3 academic electives, **Academic units recommended:** 4 English, 3 math, 2 science, 1 science labs, 2 foreign language, 3 social studies, 3 academic electives. High school diploma is required and GED is accepted. SAT or ACT required for some. If ACT, ACT with writing accepted. TOEFL required of all international applicants: minimum paper TOEFL 550 or minimum internet TOEFL 80.

Application deadline: 8/15
Notification: Rolling starting 11/1
Average GPA: 3.7
ACT Composite middle 50% range: 23-30
SAT Math middle 50% range: 530-670
SAT Critical Reading middle 50% range: 520-670
SAT Writing middle 50% range: NR-NR
Graduate top 10% of class: 28
Graduated top 25% of class: 56
Graduated top 50% of class: 82

COLLEGE GRADUATION REQUIREMENTS

Course waivers allowed: No
In what course: Students may be eligible for course substitutions.
Course substitutions allowed: Yes
In what course: Foreign Language

Additional Information

Environment: This private school, affiliated with the Christian Reformed Church, was founded in 1876. It has a 400-acre campus.

Student Body
Undergrad enrollment: 3,869
% Women: 55
% Men: 45
% Out-of-state: 44

Cost information
Tuition: $30,425
Room & board: $9,690

Housing Information
University Housing: Yes
Percent living on campus: 59

Greek System
Fraternity: No
Sorority: No
Athletics: Division III

Ferris State University

1201 South State Street, Big Rapids, MI 49307
Phone: 231-591-2100 • Fax: 231-591-3944
E-mail: admissions@ferris.edu • Web: www.ferris.edu
Support: CS • Institution: Public

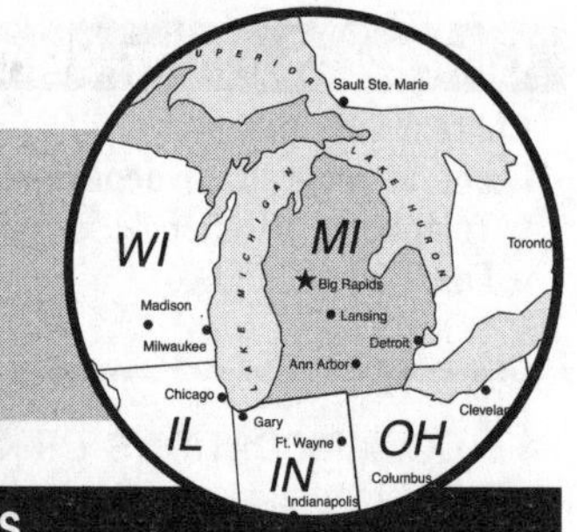

Programs or Services for Students with Learning Differences

Ferris State University is committed to a policy of equal opportunity for qualified students. The mission of Disabilities Services is to serve and advocate for students with disabilities, empowering them for self-reliance and independence. Ferris State does not have a program for students with learning disabilities, but does provide a variety of support services and accommodations for students with documented learning disabilities that interfere with the learning process. Ferris State does not, however, attempt to rehabilitate learning disabilities. To obtain support services, students need to meet with a counselor in the Educational Counseling and Disability Services. Students will complete a request for services application and a copy of the documentation of the disability. Documentation for LD/ADHD must be current and be submitted by a qualified professional. Professional development is offered to faculty and staff.

Admission Information for Students with Learning Differences

College entrance test required: Yes
Interview required: Yes
Essay required: Not Applicable
Additional Application Required for LD/ADHD/ASD: No
What documentation required for LD: Psycho ed evaluation
With general application: No
To receive services after enrolling: No
What documentation required for ADHD: Psycho ed evaluation
With general application: No
To receive services after enrolling: No
What documentation required for ASD: Psycho ed evaluation
With general application: No
To receive services after enrolling: No
LD/ADHD/ASD documentation submitted to: Educational Counseling & Disabilities Services
ASD Specific Program: NR
Special Ed. HS course work accepted: No
Specific course requirements of all applicants: Yes
Separate application required for program services: False
Total # of students receiving LD/ADHD/ASD services: 128
Acceptance into program means acceptance into college: No

Admissions

Students with learning disabilities must submit the general application form and should meet the same entrance criteria as all students. Qualified persons with disabilities may not be denied or subjected to discrimination in admission. There is no limit on the number of students admitted with disabilities. ACT scores are used for placement only and may not have an adverse effect on applicants with disabilities. No pre-admission inquiry regarding a possible disability can be made. Therefore, students with LD/ADHD are encouraged to self-disclose and provide information as to the extent of the disability. Sometimes a pre-admission interview is required if the GPA is questionable. In general, students should have a 2.0 GPA, but some programs require a higher GPA and specific courses. Diverse curricula offerings and a flexible admissions policy allow for the admission of most high school graduates and transfer students. Some programs are selective in nature and require the completion of specific courses and/or a minimum GPA.

Additional Information

Disability Services provides services and accommodations to students with LD or ADHD with appropriate documentation. These could include the Kurzweil Reading System; calculators for exams; Dragon Naturally Speaking extended testing times; electronic text; spellchecker for essay tests or exams; note-takers; word processing for essay tests; use of student supplied recording device in class; quiet areas for testing; educational counseling; and JAWS. The Academic Support Center offers tutoring for most courses. Flex tutoring is for in-depth clarification and review of subject material, and workshop tutoring is for short-term, walk-in assistance. The RSS is designed to help academically underprepared students succeed in college by offering assistance in reading, writing, and study skills. Students also have an opportunity to develop skills in goal setting, decision making, and time management. The Academic Support Center offers special instruction to assist students in improving their academic performance.

General Support Services Information

Contact Information
Name of program or department: Educational Counseling & Disabilities Services
Telephone: 231-591-3051
Fax: 231-591-3939
Website: www.ferris.edu/ecds

Accommodations or Services For Students With Learning Differences

Accommodations are decided upon an individual basis after a thorough review of appropriate, current documentation. The accommodations requests must be supported through the documentation provided and must be logically linked to the current impact of the condition on academic functioning.

Allowed in exams
Calculator: Yes
Dictionary: Yes
Computer: Yes
Spellchecker: Yes
Extended test time: Yes
Scribes: Yes
Proctors: No
Oral exams: Yes
Note-takers: Yes
Support services for students with LD: Yes
Support services for students with ADHD: Yes
Support services for students with ASD: Yes
Distraction-reduced environment: Yes
Tape recording in class: Yes
Electronic texts: Yes
Kurzweil reader: NR
Audio books: Yes
Other assistive technology: Yes
Priority registration: Yes
Added costs of services: NR
LD specialists: No
ADHD coaching: Yes
ASD specialists: NR
Professional tutors: No
Peer tutors: No
Max. hours/wk. for services: NR
How professors are notified of student approved accommodations: By both student and director

General Admissions Information

Office of Admissions: 231-591-2100

Entrance Requirements

Academic units recommended: 4 English, 4 math, 3 science, 2 foreign language, 3 social studies, 1 visual/performing arts, and 1 units from above areas or other academic areas. High school diploma is required and GED is accepted. SAT or ACT required. If ACT, ACT with writing accepted. TOEFL required of all international applicants: minimum paper TOEFL 500 or minimum internet TOEFL 61.

Application deadline: 8/1
Notification: NR
Average GPA: 3.24
ACT Composite middle 50% range: 19-24
SAT Math middle 50% range: NR-NR
SAT Critical Reading middle 50% range: NR-NR
SAT Writing middle 50% range: NR-NR
Graduate top 10% of class: NR
Graduated top 25% of class: NR
Graduated top 50% of class: NR

COLLEGE GRADUATION REQUIREMENTS

Course waivers allowed: No
Course substitutions allowed: No

Additional Information

Environment: This public school was founded in 1884. It has a 880-acre campus.

Student Body
Undergrad enrollment: 13,323
% Women: 52
% Men: 48
% Out-of-state: 6

Cost information
In-state Tuition: $10,970
Out-of-state Tuition: $17,562
Room & board: $9,434

Housing Information
University Housing: Yes
Percent living on campus: 26

Greek System
Fraternity: Yes
Sorority: Yes
Athletics: Division II

Finlandia University

601 Quincy Street, Hancock, MI 49930

Phone: 906-487-7274 • Fax: 906-487-7383

E-mail: admissions@finlandia.edu • Web: www.finlandia.edu

Support: SP • Institution: Private

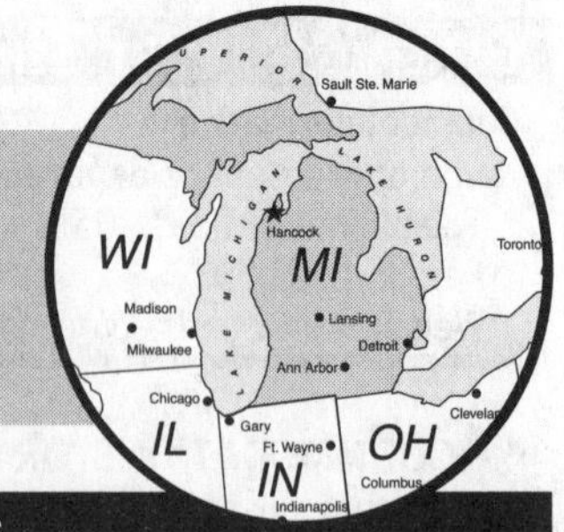

Programs or Services for Students with Learning Differences

Through Finlandia's Disability Student Services, students will receive individual counseling, tutoring, academic advising, and career counseling, but most importantly, students get an enormous amount of support and encouragement. Finlandia's DSS is designed for students needing personalized attention, additional support and reasonable accommodations. Careful academic planning is performed by the DSS Director to ensure that students carry a reasonable credit load that is sequential and well-balanced with attention to reading, written assignments, and other course requirements. The faculty is supportive, and written and verbal communication between the director and faculty is frequent. Student performance is monitored and there are weekly scheduled meetings. The director is the advisor and support person overseeing and coordinating each individual's program. Self-advocacy and compensatory skills are goals, rather than remediation.

Admission Information for Students with Learning Differences

College entrance tests required: No

Interview required: No

Additional Application Required for LD/ADHD/ASD: NR

What documentation required for LD: Psycho ed evaluation to include: relevant historical info, instructional interventions, related services, age diagnosed, objective data (aptitude, achievement, info processing), test scores (standard, percentile and grade equivalents) and describe functional limitations.

With general application: Yes if requested as part of Structured Program application

To receive services after enrolling: Yes

What documentation required for ADHD: Diagnosis based on DSM-V; history of behaviors impairing functioning in academic setting; diagnostic interview; history of symptoms; evidence of ongoing behaviors.

With general application: Yes if requested as part of Structured Program application

To receive services after enrolling: Yes

What documentation required for ASD: Psycho ed evaluation

With general application: NR

To receive services after enrolling: Yes

LD/ADHD/ASD documentation submitted to: Support Program/Services

ASD Specific Program: NR

Special Ed. HS course work accepted: Yes

Specific course requirements for all applicants: NR

Separate application required for program services: No

Total # of students receiving LD/ADHD/ASD services: 10–15

Acceptance into program means acceptance into college: No

Admissions

General admission requirements must be met by all applicants. In addition, students with learning disabilities should submit an evaluation, within the last three years, documenting the learning disability; an IEP; and a handwritten essay by the student describing the learning disability. Sometimes a telephone interview or visitation is requested to help determine eligibility for the program. An applicant must have the academic ability and background for work on a college level. Each applicant is evaluated individually by the DSS Director and the admissions staff.

Additional Information

The program director provides professors with a disability data sheet to request accommodations and also meets individually with faculty regarding student needs. Special services offered include alternative testing; individual counseling; career counseling; auxiliary aids and services; academic advising; computer-based instruction; support from the Teaching and Learning Center; and support from TRiO/Student Support Services. The director of the program will help them set up a plan for growth in areas that are challenging. Students will meet with their advisor once a week for as much or as little time as is needed.

General Support Services Information

Contact Information
Name of program or department: Disability Student Services
Telephone: 906-487-7276
Fax: 906-487-7535

Accommodations or Services for Students with Learning Differences

Accommodations are decided upon an individual basis after a thorough review of appropriate, current documentation. The accommodations requested must be supported through the documentation provided and must be logically linked to the current impact of the condition on academic functioning.

Allowed in exams
Calculator: Yes
Dictionary: Yes
Computer: Yes
Spellchecker: Yes
Extended test time: Yes
Scribes: Yes
Proctors: Yes
Oral exams: Yes
Note-takers: Yes
Services for students with LD: Yes
Services for students with ADHD: Yes
Services for students with ASD: Yes
Distraction-reduced environment: Yes
Tape recording in class: Yes
Audio books: NR
Electronic texts: Yes
Kurzweil Reader: Yes
Other assistive technology: No
Priority registration: No
Added costs for services: No
LD specialists: Yes
ADHD coaching: NR
ASD specialists: NR
Professional tutors: 7
Peer tutors: 5
Max. hours/wk. for services: Unlimited
How professors are notified of LD/ADHD: By both student and director

General Admissions Information

Office of Admissions: 906-487-7274

Entrance Requirements

High school diploma or GED accepted. Applicants must have the academic ability and background to work on a college level. ACT/SAT not required. TOEFL required of all international applicants, minimum paper TOEFL 400, minimum computer TOEFL 97.

Application deadline: NR
Notification: NR
Average GPA: NR
ACT Composite middle 50% range: NR-NR
SAT Math middle 50% range: NR-NR
SAT Critical Reading middle 50% range: NR-NR
SAT Writing middle 50% range: NR-NR
Graduated top 10% of class: NR
Graduated top 25% of class: NR
Graduated top 50% of class: NR

COLLEGE GRADUATION REQUIREMENTS

Course waivers allowed: No
Course substitutions allowed: Yes
In what course: Math

Additional Information

Environment: The school is located in a beautiful and rugged area of the Upper Peninsula of Michigan.

Student Body
Undergrad enrollment: 558
% Women: 61
% Men: 39
% Out-of-state: NR

Cost information
Tuition: $22,258
Room & board: $8,800

Housing Information
University Housing: Yes
Percent living on campus: NR

Greek System
Fraternity: No
Sorority: No
Athletics: NR

Grand Valley State University

1 Campus Drive, Allendale, MI 49401
Phone: 616-331-2025 • Fax: 616-331-2000
E-mail: admissions@gvsu.edu • Web: www.gvsu.edu
Support: S • Institution: Public

Programs or Services for Students with Learning Differences

The Office of Academic Support at Grand Valley State University provides academic support services and accommodations that enhance the learning environment for students with disabilities and helps educate the university community on disability issues. In addition to the regular services the university offers student skill assessment, academic and career advising, specialized tutoring, textbooks on tape, note-taking assistance, alternative test-taking assistance, peer mentoring, and counseling. OAS provides students with memoranda documenting their disability. The documentation will contain information on the nature of the disability and what academic accommodations the student may need.

Admission Information for Students with Learning Differences

College entrance test required: Yes
Interview required: No
Essay required: No
Additional Application Required for LD/ADHD/ASD: NR
What documentation required for LD: Psycho ed evaluation to include: relevant historical info, instructional interventions, related services, age diagnosed, objective data (aptitude, achievement, info processing), test scores (standard, percentile and grade equivalents) and describe functional limitations.
With general application: No
To receive services after enrolling: Yes
What documentation required for ADHD: Diagnosis based on DSM-V; history of behaviors impairing functioning in academic setting; diagnostic interview; history of symptoms; evidence of ongoing behaviors.
With general application: No
To receive services after enrolling: Yes
What documentation required for ASD: Psycho ed evaluation
With general application: NR
To receive services after enrolling: Yes
LD/ADHD/ASD documentation submitted to: Disability Support Resources
ASD Specific Program: NR
Special Ed. HS course work accepted: Yes
Specific course requirements of all applicants: Yes
Separate application required for program services: Yes
Total # of students receiving LD/ADHD/ASD services: 263
Acceptance into program means acceptance into college: Students must be admitted to and enrolled in the university prior to requesting services.

Admissions

Students are given the opportunity to provide documentation of their LD or ADHD. Information is reviewed by the Office of Academic Support and Admissions. Students interested in special accommodations need to submit both the regular admissions application and a separate application for the program. An evaluation report should include the summary of a comprehensive diagnostic interview. Standardized tests are required for admission. General admission requirements include 4 years of English, 3 years of math, 3 years of social science, and 2 years of science. The average ACT score is 23 or 1050–1080 SAT Reasoning and a 2.8 GPA.

Additional Information

Once admitted into the program students may request that an instructor progress report be sent to each of their professors. The purpose of this report is to inform students of their current academic standing in a class. Academic Support staff provide the following services: working with students to help them improve their academic weaknesses and increase their areas of strength; academic and career advising; specialized tutoring in addition to the general tutoring available for all students; seminars on reading textbooks, note-taking, time management, and test-taking strategies; tape recording of texts not available through RFBD; alternative test-taking; peer mentoring; and counseling. There is also the Organization for the Achievement of Disabled Students, which is a student organization whose goal is to advance the educational and career goals of students with disabilities.

General Support Services Information

Contact Information
Name of program or department: Academic Support (OAS)
Telephone: 616-331-2490
Fax: 616-331-3440

Accommodations or Services for Students with Learning Differences

Accommodations are decided upon an individual basis after a thorough review of appropriate, current documentation. The accommodations requested must be supported through the documentation provided and must be logically linked to the current impact of the condition on academic functioning.

Allowed in exams
Calculator: Yes
Dictionary: Yes
Computer: Yes
Spellchecker: Yes
Extended test time: Yes
Scribes: Yes
Proctors: Yes
Oral exams: Yes
Note-takers: Yes
Services for students with LD: Yes
Services for students with ADHD: Yes
Services for students with ASD: Yes
Distraction-reduced environment: Yes
Tape recording in class: Yes
Audio books: NR
Electronic texts: No
Kurzweil Reader: No
Other assistive technology: Yes
Priority registration: Yes
Added costs for services: No
LD specialists: No
ADHD coaching: NR
ASD specialists: NR
Professional tutors: No
Peer tutors: 140
Max. hours/wk. for services: 4
How professors are notified of LD/ADHD: By student

General Admissions Information

Office of Admissions: 616-331-2025

Entrance Requirements

Academic units required: 4 English, 3 math, 3 science, 2 science labs, 2 foreign language, 3 social studies. High school diploma is required and GED is accepted. SAT or ACT required. If ACT, ACT with writing recommended. TOEFL required of all international applicants: minimum paper TOEFL 550.

Application deadline: NR
Notification: NR
Average GPA: 3.53
ACT Composite middle 50% range: 21-26
SAT Math middle 50% range: NR-NR
SAT Critical Reading middle 50% range: NR-NR
SAT Writing middle 50% range: NR-NR
Graduate top 10% of class: 17
Graduated top 25% of class: 46
Graduated top 50% of class: 85

COLLEGE GRADUATION REQUIREMENTS

Course waivers allowed: NR
Course substitutions allowed: NR

Additional Information

Environment: This public school was founded in 1960. It has a 1275-acre campus.

Student Body
Undergrad enrollment: 21,971
% Women: 59
% Men: 41
% Out-of-state: 6

Cost information
Out-of-state Tuition: $16,344
Room & board: $8,360

Housing Information
University Housing: Yes
Percent living on campus: 28

Greek System
Fraternity: Yes
Sorority: Yes
Athletics: Division II

Michigan State University

250 Administration Building, East Lansing, MI 48824-1046
Phone: 517-355-8332 • Fax: 517-353-1647
E-mail: admis@msu.edu • Web: www.msu.edu
Support: CS • Institution: Public

Programs or Services for Students with Learning Differences

MSU is serious in its commitment to helping students no matter what the disability. The RCPD (Resource Center for Persons with Disabilities) mission is to be an advocate for the inclusion of students with disabilities into the total university experience. The RCPD responds to the needs of students by providing resources that equalize their chances for success and support their full participation in all university programs. Students must provide recent documentation and history in the form of a school report, psychologist's assessment, or certification by other recognized authority and must contain a clearly stated diagnosis. The Stern Tutoring and Alternative Techniques for Education (STATE) Program offers a structured environment, peer mentors, assistive technology, academic tutoring and instructional seminars on successful learning strategies to students with disabilities. The Building Opportunities for Networking and Discovery (BOND) program offers extensive opportunities for students with Autism Spectrum Disorders. Elements of the program include: Social learning experiences, facilitated support and skill building groups, individualized curriculum planning, outreach facilitation, integrative technology and civic engagement in the form of educational seminars and workshops to raise awareness and promote appreciation for diversity.

Admission Information for Students with Learning Differences

College entrance tests required: Yes
Interview required: No
Essay required: N/A
Additional Application Required for LD/ADHD/ASD: NR
What documentation required for LD: Psycho ed evaluation to include: relevant historical info, instructional interventions, related services, age diagnosed, objective data (aptitude, achievement, info processing), test scores (standard, percentile and grade equivalents) and describe functional limitations.
With general application: No
To receive services after enrolling: Yes
What documentation required for ADHD: Diagnosis based on DSM-V; history of behaviors impairing functioning in academic setting; diagnostic interview; history of symptoms; evidence of ongoing behaviors.
With general application: No
To receive services after enrolling: Yes
What documentation required for ASD: Psycho ed evaluation
With general application: NR
To receive services after enrolling: Yes
LD/ADHD/ASD documentation submitted to: RCPD
ASD Specific Program: NR
Special Ed. HS course work accepted: No
Specific course requirements for all applicants: Yes
Separate application required for program services: No
Total # of students receiving LD/ADHD/ASD services: 600
Acceptance into program means acceptance into college: Students must be admitted to and enrolled in the university first and then request services.

Admissions

Admission for students with learning disabilities to the university is based on the same criteria used for all other students. College Achievement Admissions Program (CAAP) is an alternative admissions procedure for students who have academic potential but who would be unable to realize that potential without special support services due to their economic, cultural, or educational background. Students with learning disabilities should send any documentation to RCPD.

Additional Information

Specialists are available by appointment in the RCPD to provide information to students. Accommodations include: E-text; study strategy tutoring; voice output computers; taping of lectures; extended time on tests; reader/scribe; quiet room for tests; scribes; advocacy assistance from specialists and letters to professors; support groups and consultation with service providers. Other resources on campus include: Learning Resource Center; Office of Supportive Services; MSU Counseling Center; and Academic Advising. The Learning Resource Center works with students with learning characteristics on an individual basis to help the student learn to utilize appropriate learning strategies and to mediate their learning environment. The Welcome Orientation Workshop (WOW) for incoming students with disabilities introduces students to the resources available at MSU.

General Support Services Information

Contact Information
Name of program or department: Resource Center for Persons with Disabilities
Telephone: 517-884-RCPD (7273)
Fax: 517-438-3191

Accommodations or Services for Students with Learning Differences

Accommodations are decided upon an individual basis after a thorough review of appropriate, current documentation. The accommodations requested must be supported through the documentation provided and must be logically linked to the current impact of the condition on academic functioning.

Allowed in exams
Calculator: Decision
Dictionary: No
Computer: Decision
Spellchecker: N/A
Extended test time: Yes
Scribes: Yes
Proctors: Yes
Oral exams: Yes
Note-takers: Yes
Services for students with LD: Yes
Services for students with ADHD: Yes
Services for students with ASD: Yes
Distraction-reduced environment: Yes
Tape recording in class: Yes
Audio books: NR
Electronic texts: Yes
Kurzweil Reader: Yes
Other assistive technology: Dragon Dictate, etc.
Priority registration: Yes
Added costs for services: No
LD specialists: Yes
ADHD coaching: NR
ASD specialists: NR
Professional tutors: 3
Peer tutors: 10
Max. hours/wk. for services: Unlimited
How professors are notified of LD/ADHD: Student

General Admissions Information

Office of Admissions: 517-355-8332

Entrance Requirements

Academic units required: 4 English, 3 math, 3 science, 1 science labs, 2 foreign language, 3 social studies, **Academic units recommended:** 4 math, 3 science, 1 science labs, 2 foreign language, 3 social studies. High school diploma is required and GED is accepted. SAT or ACT required. If ACT, ACT with writing required. TOEFL required of all international applicants: minimum paper TOEFL 550 or minimum internet TOEFL 79.

Application deadline: NR
Notification: Rolling starting 10/7
Average GPA: 3.68
ACT Composite middle 50% range: 23-28
SAT Math middle 50% range: 530-680
SAT Critical Reading middle 50% range: 450-580
SAT Writing middle 50% range: 460-580
Graduated top 10% of class: 31
Graduated top 25% of class: 67
Graduated top 50% of class: 95

COLLEGE GRADUATION REQUIREMENTS

Course waivers allowed: No
Course substitutions allowed: No
In what course: Individual consideration

Additional Information

Environment: This public school was founded in 1855. It has a 5200-acre campus.

Student Body
Undergrad enrollment: 39,143
% Women: 50
% Men: 50
% Out-of-state: 11.5

Cost information
In-state Tuition: $13,612
Out-of Tuition: $36,412
Room & board: $9,524

Housing Information
University Housing: Yes
Percent living on campus: 38.6

Greek System
Fraternity: Yes
Sorority: Yes
Athletics: Division I

Michigan Technological University

1400 Townsend Drive Houghton, MI 49931
Phone: 906-487-2335 • Fax: 906-487-2125
E-mail: mtu4u@mtu.edu • Web: www.mtu.edu
Support: CS • Institution: Public

Programs or Services for Students with Learning Differences

Disability Services will work with any student who would like to discuss academic success; one does not have to have a documented disability to talk to us. Our goal is to support the success of all students.

Admission Information for Students with Learning Differences

College entrance test required: Yes
Interview required: No
Essay required: Not Applicable
Additional Application Required for LD/ADHD/ASD: Not Applicable
What documentation required for LD: We prefer current documentation prepared by a specialist qualified to make the diagnosis, with suggestions for appropriate academic supports.
With general application: Not Applicable
To receive services after enrolling: Not Applicable
What documentation required for ADHD: We prefer current documentation prepared by a specialist qualified to make the diagnosis, with suggestions for appropriate academic supports.
With general application: Not Applicable
To receive services after enrolling: Not Applicable
What documentation required for ASD: We prefer current documentation prepared by a specialist qualified to make the diagnosis, with suggestions for appropriate academic supports.
With general application: Not Applicable
To receive services after enrolling: Not Applicable
LD/ADHD/ASD documentation submitted to: Student Disability Services
ASD Specific Program: NR
Special Ed. HS course work accepted: Not Applicable
Specific course requirements of all applicants: Yes
Separate application required for program services: True
Total # of students receiving LD/ADHD/ASD services: NR
Acceptance into program means acceptance into college: Not Applicable

Admissions

Admission for students with learning disabilities to the university is based on the same criteria used for all other students. College Achievement Admissions Program (CAAP) is an alternative admissions procedure for students who have academic potential but who would be unable to realize that potential without special support services due to their economic, cultural, or educational background. Admission is comptetitve and is based on academic performance in high school, strength and quality of curriculum, recent trends in academic performance, class rank, SAT/ACT, leadership, talents, conduct and diversity of experience. Middle 50% GPA is 3.4 -3.9 and ACT 24-28 or 1040-1210 (old SAT format).

Additional Information

Counseling Services offers support groups dependent on student interests and participation. Students run their own Autism Support group, The Spectrum Connection. Career Services works with Spectrum students on transitioning to careers. Accommodations include: Extended time for work done in class and on tests—students may be allowed 1.5 times the normally allotted time for tests; in some instances students will also be able to negotiate deadlines for other projects; a quiet or non-distractive environment for testing; consideration for spelling errors when spell-checking not available; a volunteer note-taker; instructor-provided course material; test reader and/or scribe; tape recording of lectures (with instructor permission); Kurzweil reader; and priority registration—students will be allowed to register early in the registration period, regardless of their class standing.

General Support Services Information

Contact Information
Name of program or department: Student Disability Services
Telephone: 906-487-2212
Fax: 906-487-3060
Website: https://www.mtu.edu/deanofstudents/students/disability/

Accommodations or Services for Students with Learning Differences

Accommodations are decided upon an individual basis after a thorough review of appropriate, current documentation. The accommodations requests must be supported through the documentation provided and must be logically linked to the current impact of the condition on academic functioning.

Allowed in exams
Calculator: Yes
Dictionary: Not Applicable
Computer: Yes
Spellchecker: Not Applicable
Extended test time: Yes
Scribes: Yes
Proctors: Yes
Oral exams: Not Applicable
Note-takers: Yes
Support services for students with LD: NR
Support services for students with ADHD: NR
Support services for students with ASD: Yes
Distraction-reduced environment: Yes
Tape recording in class: Yes
Electronic texts: Yes
Kurzweil reader: NR
Audio books: Yes
Other assistive technology: Yes
Priority registration: Yes
Added costs of services: No
LD specialists: Yes
ADHD coaching: Yes
ASD specialists: Not Applicable
Professional tutors: No
Peer tutors: Yes
Max. hours/wk. for services: NR
How professors are notified of student approved accommodations: By both student and director

General Admissions Information

Office of Admissions: 906-487-2335

Entrance Requirements

Academic units required: 3 English, 3 math, 2 science. **Academic units recommended:** 4 English, 4 math, 3 science, 2 foreign language, 3 social studies, 2 academic electives, 1 computer science, High school diploma is required and GED is accepted. SAT or ACT required. If ACT, ACT with writing accepted. TOEFL required of all international applicants: minimum paper TOEFL 550 or minimum internet TOEFL 79.

Application deadline: NR
Notification: Rolling starting 6/15
Average GPA: 3.66
ACT Composite middle 50% range: 24-29
SAT Math middle 50% range: 565-690
SAT Critical Reading middle 50% range: 545-665
SAT Writing middle 50% range: 505-625
Graduate top 10% of class: 28
Graduated top 25% of class: 62
Graduated top 50% of class: 92

COLLEGE GRADUATION REQUIREMENTS

Course waivers allowed: No
Course substitutions allowed: No

Additional Information

Environment: This public school was founded in 1885. It has a 925-acre campus.

Student Body
Undergrad enrollment: 5,721
% Women: 27
% Men: 73
% Out-of-state: 23

Cost information
In-state tuition: $13,986
Out-of-state tuition: $29,950
Room & board: $9,857

Housing Information
University Housing: Yes
Percent living on campus: 47

Greek System
Fraternity: Yes
Sorority: Yes
Athletics: Division II

NORTHERN MICHIGAN UNIVERSITY

1401 Presque Isle Avenue, Marquette, MI 49855
Phone: 906-227-2650 • Fax: 906-227-1747
E-mail: admiss@nmu.edu • Web: www.nmu.edu
Support: S • Institution: Public

PROGRAMS OR SERVICES FOR STUDENTS WITH LEARNING DIFFERENCES

Disability Services (DS) provides services and accommodations to all students with disabilities. The goal of DS is to meet the individual needs of students. Student Support Services is a multifaceted educational support project designed to assist students in completing their academic programs at NMU. The Student Support Services professional staff, peer tutors, mentors, and peer advisors provide program participants with individualized attention. Disability Services provides assistance and accommodations to students who have documented disabilities. Accommodation request are reviewed on an individual basis. Student are required to complete the Application for DS; provide appropriate documentation, which includes a diagnosis, symptoms of the disability, test scores and data that support the diagnosis, and recommendations regarding classroom accommodations; and schedule an appointment with the Disability Coordinator. Students with ADHD must provide appropriate documentation through a written report submitted by a medical doctor, psychiatrist, psychologist, counselor, or school psychologist to receive appropriate accommodations.

ADMISSION INFORMATION FOR STUDENTS WITH LEARNING DIFFERENCES

College entrance tests required: No
Interview required: No
Essay required: No
Additional Application Required for LD/ADHD/ASD: NR
What documentation required for LD: Psycho ed evaluation to include: relevant historical info, instructional interventions, related services, age diagnosed, objective data (aptitude, achievement, info processing), test scores (standard, percentile and grade equivalents) and describe functional limitations.
With general application: No
To receive services after enrolling: Yes
What documentation required for ADHD: Diagnosis based on DSM-V; history of behaviors impairing functioning in academic setting; diagnostic interview; history of symptoms; evidence of ongoing behaviors.
With general application: No
To receive services after enrolling: Yes
What documentation required for ASD: Psycho ed evaluation
With general application: NR
To receive services after enrolling: Yes
LD/ADHD/ASD documentation submitted to: Disability Services
ASD Specific Program: NR
Special Ed. HS course work accepted: Yes
Specific course requirements of all applicants: No
Separate application required: No
Total # of students receiving LD/ADHD/ASD services: 150
Acceptance into program means acceptance into college: Students must be admitted to and enrolled in the university first and then request services.

ADMISSIONS

There are no special admissions for students with learning disabilities. All students submit the same general application and are expected to have an ACT of 19 or higher and a high school GPA of at least 2.25. There are no specific high school courses required for admissions, though the university recommends 4 years English, 4 years math, 3 years history/social studies, 3 years science, 3 years foreign language, 2 years fine or performing arts, and 1 year computer instruction. Applicants not meeting all of the criteria will be fully considered by the Admission Review Committee. Applicants may be asked to take a pre-admission test or supply further information. A review of the applicant's academic background and potential for success may result in admission into the applicant's program of choice or admission on probation or into the College Transitions Program. Students will be asked to agree to certain conditions as part of their enrollment. Applicants denied admission may appeal to the Admissions Review Committee. Appeal letters should be submitted to the Director of Admissions.

ADDITIONAL INFORMATION

The coordinator of DS works one-on-one with students as needed, and will also meet with students who do not have specific documentation if they request assistance. Skill classes are offered in reading, writing, math, study skills, sociocultural development, and interpersonal growth. No course waivers are granted for graduation requirements from NMU. Substitutions, however, are granted when appropriate. Student Support Services provides each student with an individual program of educational support services, including academic advising; basic skill building in reading, math, and writing; counseling; career advisement; developmental skill building; mentoring; support groups and study groups; tutoring from paraprofessionals; specialized tutors; group tutoring or supplemental instruction; and workshops on personal development and study skills improvement.

General Support Services Information

Contact Information
Name of program or department: Disability Services
Telephone: 906-227-1700
Fax: 906-227-1714

Accommodations or Services for Students with Learning Differences

The process of determining whether a student is eligible for accommodations is a collaborative one. Students are encouraged to submit documentation which describes the current impact of their condition and its relevance to an academic setting.

Allowed in exams
Calculator: Yes
Dictionary: Yes
Computer: Yes
Spellchecker: Yes
Extended test time: Yes
Scribes: Yes
Proctors: Yes
Oral exams: Yes
Note-takers: Yes
Services for students with LD: Yes
Services for students with ADHD: Yes
Services for students with ASD: Yes
Distraction-reduced environment: Yes
Tape recording in class: Yes
Audio books: NR
Electronic texts: Yes
Kurzweil Reader: No
Other assistive technology: Yes
Priority registration: No
Added costs for services: No
LD specialists: No
ADHD coaching: NR
ASD specialists: NR
Professional tutors: No
Peer tutors: Yes
Max. hours/wk. for services: 2–4
How professors are notified of LD/ADHD: By student

General Admissions Information

Office of Admissions: 906-227-2650

Entrance Requirements

Academic units recommended: 4 English, 4 math, 4 science, 2 foreign language, 4 social studies. High school diploma is required and GED is accepted. SAT or ACT required. If ACT, ACT with writing accepted. TOEFL required of all international applicants: minimum paper TOEFL 500 or minimum internet TOEFL 61.

Application deadline: NR
Notification: NR
Average GPA: 3.13
ACT Composite middle 50% range: 19-24
SAT Math middle 50% range: NR-NR
SAT Critical Reading middle 50% range: NR-NR
SAT Writing middle 50% range: NR-NR
Graduated top 10% of class: NR
Graduated top 25% of class: NR
Graduated top 50% of class: NR

COLLEGE GRADUATION REQUIREMENTS

Course waivers allowed: No
Course substitutions allowed: Yes
In what course: Substitutions permitted to fulfill graduation requirements with appropriate documentation.

Additional Information

Environment: This public school was founded in 1899. It has a 350-acre campus.

Student Body
Undergrad enrollment: 8,451
% Women: 53
% Men: 47
% Out-of-state: 19.1

Cost information
In-state Tuition: $8,646
Out-of Tuition: $13,542
Room & board: $8,404

Housing Information
University Housing: Yes
Percent living on campus: 38

Greek System
Fraternity: Yes
Sorority: Yes
Athletics: Division II

UNIVERSITY OF MICHIGAN

515 E. Jefferson Street, Ann Arbor, MI 48109-1316
Phone: 734-764-7433 • Fax: 734-936-0740
Web: www.umich.edu
Support: CS • Institution: Public

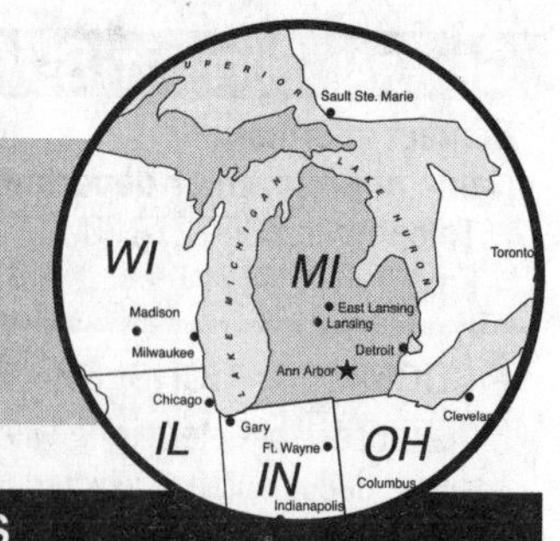

PROGRAMS OR SERVICES FOR STUDENTS WITH LEARNING DIFFERENCES

The philosophy of Services for Students with Disabilities (SSD) is based on the legal actions described in Section 504 of the Rehabilitation Act of 1973. SSD services are dependent on self-advocacy of the students and are "non-intrusive," giving the students the responsibility to seek out assistance. SSD offers selected student services that are not provided by other University of Michigan offices or outside organizations. SSD assists students in negotiating disability-related barriers to the pursuit of their education; strives to improve access to university programs, activities, and facilities; and promotes increased awareness of disability issues on campus. SSD encourages inquiries for information and will confidentially discuss concerns relating to a potential or recognized disability and, if requested, provide appropriate referrals for further assistance.

ADMISSION INFORMATION FOR STUDENTS WITH LEARNING DIFFERENCES

College entrance test required: Yes
Interview required: No
Essay required: Not Applicable
Additional Application Required for LD/ADHD/ASD: NR
What documentation required for LD: Psycho ed evaluation
With general application: No
To receive services after enrolling: Yes
What documentation required for ADHD: Psycho ed evaluation
With general application: No
To receive services after enrolling: Yes
What documentation required for ASD: Psycho ed evaluation
With general application: No
To receive services after enrolling: Yes
LD/ADHD/ASD documentation submitted to: Services for Students with Disabilities
ASD Specific Program: No
Special Ed. HS course work accepted: No
Specific course requirements of all applicants: Yes
Separate application required for program services: No
Total # of students receiving LD/ADHD/ASD services: 755
Acceptance into program means acceptance into college: Students must be admitted to and enrolled in the university prior to requesting services.

ADMISSIONS

Students with learning disabilities are expected to meet the same admission requirements as their peers. Courses required include: four years English, two years foreign language (four years recommended), three years math (four years recommended including algebra, trigonometry, and geometry), two years biological and physical sciences (three years recommended), three years history and the social sciences (two years history recommended, including one year of U.S. history), one year hands-on computer study is strongly recommended, as is one year in the fine or performing arts, or equivalent preparation. Score range for the ACT is 25–29 and SAT 1170–1340. There is no set minimum GPA as it is contingent on several other factors. For students with learning disabilities, the admissions office will accept letters of recommendation from LD specialists. When applying for admission to the University of Michigan, students with learning disabilities are encouraged to self-identify on the application form or by writing a cover letter.

ADDITIONAL INFORMATION

All accommodations are based on documented needs by the student. Services for students with learning disabilities include volunteer readers; volunteer tutors; referral for psychoeducational assessments; selected course book loans for taping; Franklin Spellers; free cassette tapes; APH 4-track recorders; advocacy and referral; advocacy letters to professors; limited scholarships; newsletters; volunteer note-takers; carbonized notepaper; free photocopying of class notes; free course notes service for some classes; many students eligible for assisted earlier registration; adaptive technology; and library reading rooms. SSD also provides appropriate services for students with "other health related disabilities" such as ADHD. There is a special summer program at the university for high school students with learning disabilities. Services and accommodations are available for undergraduates and graduates.

General Support Services Information

Contact Information
Name of program or department: Services for Students with Disabilities (SSD)
Telephone: 734-763-3000
Fax: 734-936-3947

Accommodations or Services for Students with Learning Differences

Accommodations are decided upon an individual basis after a thorough review of appropriate, current documentation. The accommodations requested must be supported through the documentation provided and must be logically linked to the current impact of the condition on academic functioning.

Allowed in exams
Calculator: Yes
Dictionary: Yes
Computer: Yes
Spellchecker: Yes
Extended test time: Yes
Scribes: Yes
Proctors: No
Oral exams: No
Note-takers: Yes
Services for students with LD: Yes
Services for students with ADHD: Yes
Services for students with ASD: Yes
Distraction-reduced environment: Yes
Tape recording in class: Yes
Electronic texts: No
Kurzweil Reader: Yes
Audio books: No
Other assistive technology: Yes
Priority registration: No
Added costs for services: No
LD specialists: Yes
ADHD coaching: No
ASD specialists: Yes
Professional tutors: Yes
Peer tutors: Yes
Max. hours/wk. for services: NR
How professors are notified of LD/ADHD: Student

General Admissions Information

Office of Admissions: 734-764-7433

Entrance Requirements

Academic units required: 4 English, 1 science labs. **Academic units recommended:** 4 English, 4 math, 4 science, 1 science labs, 4 foreign language, 4 social studies, 4 history, 1 computer science, 2 visual/performing arts. High school diploma is required and GED is accepted. SAT or ACT required. If ACT, ACT with writing required. TOEFL required of all international applicants: minimum paper TOEFL 600 or minimum internet TOEFL 100.

Application deadline: 2/1
Notification: Rolling starting 12/24
Average GPA: 3.83
ACT Composite middle 50% range: 29-33
SAT Math middle 50% range: 660-770
SAT Critical Reading middle 50% range: 630-730
SAT Writing middle 50% range: 640-730
Graduate top 10% of class: NR
Graduated top 25% of class: NR
Graduated top 50% of class: NR

COLLEGE GRADUATION REQUIREMENTS

Course waivers allowed: NR
Course substitutions allowed: NR

Additional Information

Environment: This public school was founded in 1817. It has a 3,177-acre campus.

Student Body
Undergrad enrollment: 28,312
% Women: 49
% Men: 51
% Out-of-state: 38

Cost information
In-state Tuition: $14,401
Out-of-state Tuition: $44,674
Room & board: $10,554

Housing Information
University Housing: Yes
Percent living on campus: 34

Greek System
Fraternity: Yes
Sorority: Yes
Athletics: Division I

Augsburg College

2211 Riverside Avenue, South Minneapolis, MN 55454
Phone: 612-330-1001 • Fax: 612-330-1590
E-mail: admissions@augsburg.edu • Web: www.augsburg.edu
Support: SP • Institution: Private

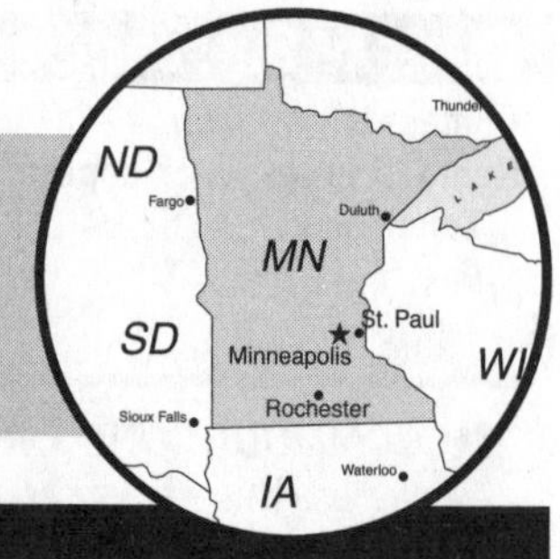

Programs or Services for Students with Learning Differences

CLASS illustrates its commitment to student success at Augsburg College by providing those academic services needed to accommodate individuals with learning, attentional, psychiatric or other cognitive-based disabilities, as well as students with physical disabilities and other health concerns including temporary disabilities. The foundation of CLASS, however, is deeply rooted in the promotion of student independence and the personal realization of one's full potential. Augsburg students who are eligible to receive CLASS services, once admitted, will work one-on-one with a CLASS Disability Specialist. The Specialist will work to provide academic guidance and service-related assistance whenever appropriate. No additional or supplemental fee is required for CLASS services.

Admission Information for Students with Learning Differences

College entrance tests required: Yes
Interview required: Yes
Essay required: N/A
Additional Application Required for LD/ADHD/ASD: NR
What documentation required for LD: Psycho ed evaluation to include: relevant historical info, instructional interventions, related services, age diagnosed, objective data (aptitude, achievement, info processing), test scores (standard, percentile and grade equivalents) and describe functional limitations.
With general application: Yes if requested as part of Structured Program application
To receive services after enrolling: Yes
What documentation required for ADHD: Diagnosis based on DSM-V; history of behaviors impairing functioning in academic setting; diagnostic interview; history of symptoms; evidence of ongoing behaviors.
With general application: Yes if requested as part of Structured Program application
To receive services after enrolling: Yes
What documentation required for ASD: Psycho ed evaluation
With general application: NR
To receive services after enrolling: Yes
LD/ADHD/ASD documentation submitted to: Support Program/Services
ASD Specific Program: NR
Special Ed. HS course work accepted: N/A
Specific course requirements for all applicants: Yes
Separate application required for program services: Yes
Total # of students receiving LD/ADHD/ASD services: 50–70
Acceptance into program means acceptance into college: Separate application required after student has enrolled.

Admissions

Students with disabilities are evaluated for admission to Augsburg College according to the same criteria and standards as other applicants. Once admitted to the college, students with disabilities complete the same General Education Core Curriculum and must meet the same essential course requirements (with or without reasonable academic accommodations) as students without disabilities. Students do not need to disclose their learning difference to Admissions, and it is not taken into consideration in admission decisions. Any documentation of a learning disability should be sent directly to CLASS and not included with the application to the college. Average GPA 3.2, average ACT 23, and average SAT 1125. Students who are admitted conditionally are required to access academic support through the Conditional Admit Program (CAP). Based on a student's entire application, the Admissions Committee will determine which of two CAP options will be required between Critical Thinking or a Caps Seminar.

Additional Information

To establish eligibility for services students must submit appropriate documentation for a cognitive-related disability that usually includes a current psychological, psycho-educational or neuro-psychological evaluation. In some cases, they may ask for a treating clinician to complete and return the Verification of Disability form as a supplement to other documentation. If a student has an Autism Spectrum Disorder they should fill out and return the PDD questionnaire in an effort to identify how the Pervasive Developmental Disorder diagnosis is currently and uniquely impacting the student. Students do not need to wait until they have been accepted to the college before determining their eligibility for CLASS services. They will review documentation for any prospective student who has applied for admission to Augsburg and will contact students about their eligibility once they have reviewed the documentation.

General Support Services Information

Contact Information
Name of program or department: Center for Learning and Adaptive Student Services (CLASS)
Telephone: 612-330-1053
Fax: 612-330-1137

Accommodations or Services for Students with Learning Differences

Accommodations are decided upon an individual basis after a thorough review of appropriate, current documentation. The accommodations requested must be supported through the documentation provided and must be logically linked to the current impact of the condition on academic functioning.

Allowed in exams
Calculator: Yes
Dictionary: Yes
Computer: Yes
Spellchecker: Yes
Extended test time: Yes
Scribes: Yes
Proctors: Yes
Oral exams: Yes
Note-takers: Yes
Services for students with LD: Yes
Services for students with ADHD: Yes
Services for students with ASD: Yes
Distraction-reduced environment: Yes
Tape recording in class: Yes
Audio books: NR
Electronic texts: No
Kurzweil Reader: Yes
Other assistive technology: Voice-recognition software
Priority registration: No
Added costs for services: No
LD specialists: Yes
ADHD coaching: NR
ASD specialists: NR
Professional tutors: 0
Peer tutors: 40–80
Max. hours/wk. for services: NR
How professors are notified of LD/ADHD: Student

General Admissions Information

Office of Admissions: 612-330-1001

Entrance Requirements

Academic units required: 4 English, 3 math, 3 science, 2 foreign language, 2 social studies. **Academic units recommended:** 4 social studies, 2 history. High school diploma is required and GED is accepted. SAT or ACT recommended. If ACT, ACT with writing accepted. TOEFL required of all international applicants: minimum paper TOEFL 550.

Application deadline: 8/15
Notification: Rolling starting 11/1
Average GPA: 3.27
ACT Composite middle 50% range: 19-25
SAT Math middle 50% range: 500-640
SAT Critical Reading middle 50% range: 510-640
SAT Writing middle 50% range: 480-600
Graduated top 10% of class: 11
Graduated top 25% of class: 37
Graduated top 50% of class: 69

COLLEGE GRADUATION REQUIREMENTS

Course waivers allowed: No
In what course: N/A
Course substitutions allowed: Yes
In what course: Foreign language

Additional Information

Environment: This private school, affiliated with the Lutheran Church, was founded in 1869. It has a 23-acre campus.

Student Body
Undergrad enrollment: 3,153
% Women: 55
% Men: 45
% Out-of-state: 13

Cost information
Tuition: $29,794
Room & board: $8,072

Housing Information
University Housing: Yes
Percent living on campus: 51

Greek System
Fraternity: No
Sorority: No
Athletics: Division III

MINNESOTA STATE U. MOORHEAD

Owens Hall, Moorhead, MN 56563
Phone: 218-477-2161 • Fax: 218-477-4374
E-mail: dragon@mnstate.edu • Web: www.mnstate.edu
Support: S • Institution: Public

PROGRAMS OR SERVICES FOR STUDENTS WITH LEARNING DIFFERENCES

The university is committed to ensuring that all students have equal access to programs and services. The Disability Resource Center (DRC) addresses the needs of students who have disabilities. The purpose of the DRC is to provide services and accommodations to students with documented disabilities, work closely with faculty and staff in an advisory capacity, assist in the development of reasonable accommodations for students, and provide equal access for otherwise qualified individuals with disabilities. A student with a documented learning disability may be eligible for services. DRC will assist in the development of reasonable accommodations for students with disabilities. To be eligible to receive services, students must provide appropriate documentation. This documentation should identify the nature and extent of the disability and provide information on the functional limitations as related to the academic environment. The documentation should provide recommended reasonable accommodations. Requests that would alter the academic standards are not granted. Students are responsible for monitoring their progress with faculty, requesting assistance, and meeting university standards.

ADMISSION INFORMATION FOR STUDENTS WITH LEARNING DIFFERENCES

College entrance tests required: Yes
Interview required: No
Essay required: No
Additional Application Required for LD/ADHD/ASD: NR
What documentation required for LD: Psycho ed evaluation to include: relevant historical info, instructional interventions, related services, age diagnosed, objective data (aptitude, achievement, info processing), test scores (standard, percentile and grade equivalents) and describe functional limitations.
With general application: No
To receive services after enrolling: Yes
What documentation required for ADHD: Diagnosis based on DSM-V; history of behaviors impairing functioning in academic setting; diagnostic interview; history of symptoms; evidence of ongoing behaviors.
With general application: No
To receive services after enrolling: Yes
What documentation required for ASD: Psycho ed evaluation
With general application: NR
To receive services after enrolling: Yes
LD/ADHD/ASD documentation submitted to: Director, Disability Services
ASD Specific Program: NR
Special Ed. HS course work accepted: Yes
Specific course requirements of all applicants: Yes
Separate application required: NR
Total # of students receiving LD/ADHD/ASD services: 25–50
Acceptance into program means acceptance into college: Students must be admitted to and enrolled in the university first and then request services.

ADMISSIONS

To be automatically admitted to Minnesota State University Moorhead, you must have graduated from high school or earned a GED and meet the following requirements: An ACT (preferred) composite score of 21 or SAT score of 1000 or above in Critical Reading and Math SAT admissions tests, or rank in the top 50% of your high school graduating class AND achieve a minimum score of 17 on the ACT or 830 on the SAT (Critical Reading and Math). If you are interested in MSU Moorhead and do not meet the above requirements, you are still encouraged to apply. Applications are reviewed based on such factors as strength of college preparation coursework, grade point average, academic progression, class rank, test scores, and probability of success. Additional information may be requested to help facilitate an admission decision. Visit msum.com for more information.

ADDITIONAL INFORMATION

Examples of general accommodations or services include the following: extended test times, reduced distraction testing environments, taped texts, note-taking, assistive technology, scribes, readers, tape-recording lectures, faculty liaisons, strategy development, priority registration, and individual support. Study skills courses are offered and students may earn credits for these courses. Services and accommodations are available for undergraduate and graduate students.

General Support Services Information

Contact Information
Name of program or department: Disability Services
Telephone: 218-477-4318
Fax: 218-477-2420

Accommodations or Services for Students with Learning Differences

Accommodations are decided upon an individual basis after a thorough review of appropriate, current documentation. The accommodations requested must be supported through the documentation provided and must be logically linked to the current impact of the condition on academic functioning.

Allowed in exams
Calculator: Yes
Dictionary: Yes
Computer: Yes
Spellchecker: Yes
Extended test time: Yes
Scribes: Yes
Proctors: Yes
Oral exams: Yes
Note-takers: Yes
Services for students with LD: Yes
Services for students with ADHD: Yes
Services for students with ASD: Yes
Distraction-reduced environment: Yes
Tape recording in class: Yes
Audio books: NR
Electronic texts: Yes
Kurzweil Reader: Yes
Other assistive technology: Yes
Priority registration: Yes
Added costs for services: No
LD specialists: No
ADHD coaching: NR
ASD specialists: NR
Professional tutors: No
Peer tutors: Yes
Max. hours/wk. for services: 1
How professors are notified of LD/ADHD: By both student and director

General Admissions Information

Office of Admissions: 218-477-2161

Entrance Requirements

Academic units required: 4 English, 3 math, 3 science, 1 science labs, 2 foreign language, 3 social studies, and 1 units from above areas or other academic areas. High school diploma is required and GED is accepted. SAT or ACT required. If ACT, ACT with writing accepted. TOEFL required of all international applicants: minimum paper TOEFL 500.

Application deadline: 6/15
Notification: NR
Average GPA: NR
ACT Composite middle 50% range: 20-25
SAT Math middle 50% range: 480-570
SAT Critical Reading middle 50% range: 445-520
SAT Writing middle 50% range: NR-NR
Graduated top 10% of class: 10
Graduated top 25% of class: 35
Graduated top 50% of class: 74

COLLEGE GRADUATION REQUIREMENTS

Course waivers allowed: Yes
In what course: Depends on the disability and requirements of the student's major
Course substitutions allowed: Yes
In what course: Depends on the disability and requirements of the student's major

Additional Information

Environment: This public school was founded in 1887. It has a 140-acre campus.

Student Body
Undergrad enrollment: 5,245
% Women: 60
% Men: 40
% Out-of-state: 33.1

Cost information
In-state Tuition: $6,898
Out-of Tuition: $13,796
Room & board: $7,398
Housing Information
University Housing: Yes
Percent living on campus: 24.78

Greek System
Fraternity: Yes
Sorority: Yes
Athletics: Division II

Saint Catherine University

2004 Randolph Avenue, Saint Paul, MN 55105
Phone: 651-690-8850 • Fax: 651-690-8868
E-mail: admissions@stkate.edu • Web: www.stkate.edu
Support: CS • Institution: Private

Programs or Services for Students with Learning Differences

St. Catherine University has two campuses where learning support is available. The Academic Success Center (Minneapolis Campus) provides a wide range of academic support. They offer individual and group tutoring, both online and in person with peer tutors and professional staff. The O'Neill Center for Academic Development (St. Paul campus) provides individual academic support through the Writing/Reading Center, the Math/Science Center, the Disability Resources Center and Student Mentors.

Admission Information for Students with Learning Differences

College entrance tests required: Yes, ACT or SAT
Interview required: No
Essay required: Yes
Additional Application Required for LD/ADHD/ASD: NR
What documentation required for LD: Psycho ed evaluation preferred along with educational history provided during meeting with an Access Consultant
With general application: No
To receive services after enrolling: Yes
What documentation required for ADHD: Diagnosis based on DSM-V; history of behaviors impairing functioning in academic setting; diagnostic interview; history of symptoms; evidence of ongoing behaviors.
With general application: No
To receive services after enrolling: Yes
What documentation required for ASD: Psycho ed evaluation
With general application: NR
To receive services after enrolling: Yes
LD/ADHD/ASD documentation submitted to: Resources for Disabilities
ASD Specific Program: NR
Special Ed. HS course work accepted: Yes
Specific course requirements of all applicants: NR
Separate application required: No
Total # of students receiving LD/ADHD/ASD services: 110
Acceptance into program means acceptance into college: Students must be admitted to and enrolled in the university first and then request services.

Admissions

There is no special admission procedure for students with learning disabilities, though the college tends to give special consideration if students self-disclose this information. Disclosure can help explain test scores, difficulties with certain course work, and so on. Saint Catherine University does not discriminate on the basis of disability in admission. A student may be accepted on a conditional basis, to a program which provides special advising, limited course lad and a course in strategies for success.

Additional Information

To access services, the student and Access Consultant discuss the anticipated demands of the courses for which the student is registered and develop accommodation letters. The letters identify the learning strategies and accommodations that will be used. For example, texts in alternative formats, testing accommodations, and note-takers are some of the more frequently offered accommodations. The specific nature of the disability is not addressed the student delivers the accommodation letters to her professors. Some students meet with Access Consultants on a weekly basis for time-management and study strategies. Within the O'Neill Center, a student may access assistance in writing, math and science courses.

General Support Services Information

Contact Information
Name of program or department: O'Neill Learning Center
Telephone: 651-590-6563
Fax: 651-690-6718

Accommodations or Services for Students with Learning Differences

Accommodations are decided upon an individual basis after a thorough review of appropriate, current documentation. The accommodations requested must be supported through the documentation provided and must be logically linked to the current impact of the condition on academic functioning.

Allowed in exams
Calculator: Yes
Dictionary: Yes
Computer: Yes
Spellchecker: Yes
Extended test time: Yes
Scribes: Yes
Proctors: Yes
Oral exams: Rarely
Note-takers: Yes
Services for students with LD: Yes
Services for students with ADHD: Yes
Services for students with ASD: Yes
Distraction-reduced environment: Yes
Tape recording in class: Yes
Audio books: NR
Electronic texts: Yes
Kurzweil Reader: Yes
Other assistive technology: Yes
Priority registration: Yes
Added costs for services: No
LD specialists: Yes
ADHD coaching: NR
ASD specialists: NR
Professional tutors: No
Peer tutors: 25–35 for Writing, Math, Science—available to all students, not just those with disabilities
Max. hours/wk. for services: Unlimited
How professors are notified of LD/ADHD: By both student and director

General Admissions Information

Office of Admissions: 651-690-8850

Entrance Requirements

Academic units recommended: 4 English, 3 math, 2 science, 4 foreign language, 2 social studies. High school diploma is required and GED is accepted. SAT or ACT required. If ACT, ACT with writing accepted. TOEFL required of all international applicants: minimum paper TOEFL 500.

Application deadline: NR
Notification: NR
Average GPA: 3.61
ACT Composite middle 50% range: 22-26
SAT Math middle 50% range: 490-560
SAT Critical Reading middle 50% range: 490-630
SAT Writing middle 50% range: NR-NR
Graduated top 10% of class: 23
Graduated top 25% of class: 52
Graduated top 50% of class: 87

COLLEGE GRADUATION REQUIREMENTS

Course waivers allowed: No
Course substitutions allowed: Yes
In what course: Math, foreign language

Additional Information

Environment: This private school, affiliated with the Roman Catholic Church, was founded in 1905. It has a 110-acre campus.

Student Body
Undergrad enrollment: 3,559
% Women: 97
% Men: 3
% Out-of-state: 11

Cost information
Tuition: $34,920
Room & board: $8,150

Housing Information
University Housing: Yes
Percent living on campus: 44

Greek System
Fraternity: No
Sorority: No
Athletics: Division III

St. Olaf College

1520 St. Olaf Avenue, Northfield, MN 55057
Phone: 507-786-3025 • Fax: 507-786-3832
E-mail: admissions@stolaf.edu • Web: wp.stolaf.edu
Support: S • Institution: Private

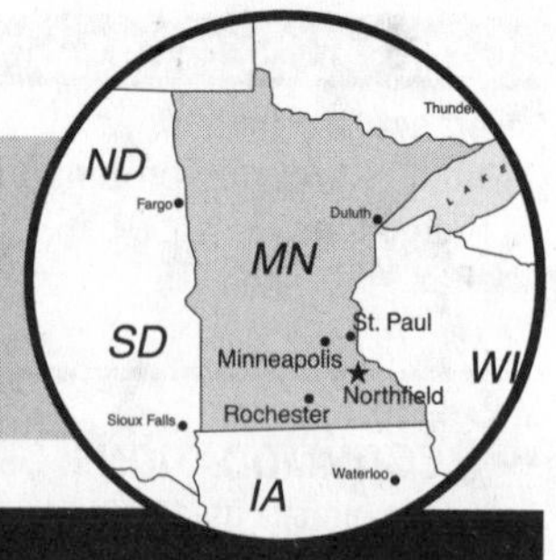

Programs or Services for Students with Learning Differences

The goal of the services at St. Olaf is to provide equal access to a St. Olaf education for all students with disabilities. The purpose is to create and maintain an environment in which students may achieve their fullest potential, limited to the least extent possible by individual disabilities. All faculty, staff, and students of the college are expected to adhere to this philosophy of equal access to educational opportunity and assume broad responsibility for its implementation. In order to receive services through Student Disability Services, students must provide a clear statement of diagnosed disability.

Admission Information for Students with Learning Differences

College entrance tests required: Yes
Interview required: N/A
Essay required: N/A
Additional Application Required for LD/ADHD/ASD: NR
What documentation required for LD: Clear statement of diagnosed disability with results from appropriate assessment instruments. Student Disability Services will work individually with students to determine whether documentation presented is sufficient.
With general application: NR
To receive services after enrolling: Yes
What documentation required for ADHD: Same documentation required for LD.
With general application: NR
To receive services after enrolling: Yes
What documentation required for ASD: Psycho ed evaluation
With general application: NR
To receive services after enrolling: Yes
LD/ADHD/ASD documentation submitted to: Support Program/Services
ASD Specific Program: NR
Special Ed. HS course work accepted: N/A
Specific course requirements for all applicants: Yes
Separate application required for program services: No
Total # of students receiving LD/ADHD/ASD services: 100
Acceptance into program means acceptance into college: N/A

Admissions

All applicants must meet the same competitive admission criteria. There is no separate application process for students with learning disabilities or attention deficit disorder. It's recommended that students have a strong academic curriculum. Once admitted, students with documented disabilities should have their current documentation sent to the Student Disability Services Office.

Additional Information

Any student who has a disability or who suspects they have a disability is welcome to make an appointment with an Access Specialist. Many students with ADHD, learning disabilities, mental health disabilities such as depression and anxiety, physical disabilities, chronic health conditions and ASD work with the Access Specialist. Examples of accommodations include (but not limited to) extend time on tests; distraction-free testing environment; use of a calculator, spellchecker or computer for exams; scribes; readers; note-takers; smart pens/recording devices; and alternate format texts. Also time management, organization, study skills, and coping strategies.

General Support Services Information

Contact Information
Name of program or department: Disability and Access Center (DAC)
Telephone: 507-786-3288
Fax: 507-786-3923

Accommodations or Services for Students with Learning Differences

Accommodations are decided upon an individual basis after a thorough review of appropriate, current documentation. The accommodations requested must be supported through the documentation provided and must be logically linked to the current impact of the condition on academic functioning.

Allowed in exams
Calculator: Yes
Dictionary: Yes
Computer: Yes
Spellchecker: Yes
Extended test time: Yes
Scribes: Yes
Proctors: N/A
Oral exams: Yes
Note-takers: Yes
Services for students with LD: Yes
Services for students with ADHD: Yes
Services for students with ASD: Yes
Distraction-reduced environment: Yes
Tape recording in class: Yes
Audio books: NR
Electronic texts: Yes
Kurzweil Reader: Yes
Other assistive technology: High Speed Scanner, Kurzweil license to go, Dragon Naturally Speaking, Inspiration, Pulse Smart Pen
Priority registration: Yes
Added costs for services: No
LD specialists: No
ADHD coaching: NR
ASD specialists: NR
Professional tutors: No
Peer tutors: 200–250
Max. hours/wk. for services: none
How professors are notified of LD/ADHD: Student

General Admissions Information

Office of Admissions: 507-786-3025

Entrance Requirements

Academic units recommended: 4 English, 4 math, 4 science, 2 science labs, 4 foreign language, 4 social studies. High school diploma is required and GED is accepted. SAT or ACT required. If ACT, ACT with writing accepted. TOEFL required of all international applicants: minimum internet TOEFL 90.

Application deadline: 1/15
Notification: 3/20
Average GPA: 3.59
ACT Composite middle 50% range: 26-31
SAT Math middle 50% range: 580-700
SAT Critical Reading middle 50% range: 560-710
SAT Writing middle 50% range: NR-NR
Graduated top 10% of class: 43
Graduated top 25% of class: 77
Graduated top 50% of class: 96

COLLEGE GRADUATION REQUIREMENTS

Course waivers allowed: No
Course substitutions allowed: Yes
In what course: Alternatives are rarely considered. A subcommittee must recommend substitutions and a faculty committee makes the decision. Most often a student is required to try a language with support from department, tutors, labs and study groups first.

Additional Information

Environment: This private school, affiliated with the Lutheran Church, was founded in 1874. It has a 300-acre campus.

Student Body
Undergrad enrollment: 3,046
% Women: 57
% Men: 43
% Out-of-state: 58

Cost information
Tuition: $44,180
Room & board: $10,080

Housing Information
University Housing: Yes
Percent living on campus: NR

Greek System
Fraternity: No
Sorority: No
Athletics: Division III

University of Minnesota, Morris

600 E 4th St, Morris, MN 56267
Phone: 320-589-6035 • Fax: 320-589-6051
E-mail: http://admissions.morris.umn.edu/contact • Web: www.morris.umn
Support: S • Institution: Public

Programs or Services for Students with Learning Differences

The Disability Resource Center is a catalyst for ensuring equal learning and working opportunities for students, faculty, staff and guests with disabilities by increasing the capacity of the University of Minnesota to eliminate physical, programmatic, policy, informational and attitudinal barriers. We promote barrier-free environments that facilitate equal opportunities for people with disabilities and that assist the University in meeting its obligations under federal and state statutes. We work to ensure access to University employment, courses, programs, facilities, services, and activities by providing or arranging reasonable accommodations, academic adjustments, auxiliary aids and services, training, consultation, and technical assistance.

Admission Information for Students with Learning Differences

College entrance test required: Yes
Interview required: No
Essay required: Not Applicable
Additional Application Required for LD/ADHD/ASD: Yes
What documentation required for LD: Psycho ed evaluation
With general application: No
To receive services after enrolling: Yes
What documentation required for ADHD: Psycho ed evaluation
With general application: No
To receive services after enrolling: Yes
What documentation required for ASD: Psycho ed evaluation
With general application: No
To receive services after enrolling: Yes
LD/ADHD/ASD documentation submitted to: Disability Resource Center
ASD Specific Program: LINK Peer Mentor Program
Special Ed. HS course work accepted: Yes
Specific course requirements of all applicants: Yes
Separate application required for program services: True
Total # of students receiving LD/ADHD/ASD services: 32
Acceptance into program means acceptance into college: No

Admissions

To apply, your high school transcript should include the following: 4 years of English; 4 years of math including one year each of elementary algebra, intermediate algebra, and geometry, 3 years of science with one year each of biological and physical science; 3 years of social studies, including United States history, and 2 years of a single second language. Primary review factors: Successful school performance, ACT/SAT, courses, and strength of the curriculum. Secondary review factors include: ACT/SAT writing test results, recommendations, interview, evidence of exceptional achievement, aptitude, or personal accomplishment not reflected in the academic record or standardized test scores, evidence of exceptional talent or ability in artistic, scholarly, leadership, or athletic performance, evidence that enrollment would enhance the cultural, gender, age, economic, racial, or geographic diversity of the student body, evidence of exceptional motivation, maturity, or responsibility, community involvement, work, or overcome barriers.

Additional Information

The mission of the Office of Academic Success is to ensure equal access to educational and academic supports, resources and information, and to promote excellence within the vision of lifelong professional and personal satisfaction in order to foster a University of Minnesota, Morris renewable, sustainable education, during the student's academic career. Structured, peer-led study sessions are available for select courses. Specially trained peer leaders facilitate regularly scheduled sessions that focus on both course content and effective study strategies. Mastering Skills for College Success is a 2-credit course offered each semester by Academic Assistance staff. This course aims to strengthen students' overall approach to learning in a college environment. Students develop individual learning plans tailored to their strengths.

General Support Services Information

Contact Information
Name of program or department: Disability Resource Center
Telephone: 320-589-6163
Fax: 320-589-6473
Website: NR

Accommodations or Services for Students with Learning Differences

Accommodations are decided upon an individual basis after a thorough review of appropriate, current documentation. The accommodations requests must be supported through the documentation provided and must be logically linked to the current impact of the condition on academic functioning.

Allowed in exams
Calculator: Yes
Dictionary: Yes
Computer: Yes
Spellchecker: Yes
Extended test time: Yes
Scribes: Yes
Proctors: Yes
Oral exams: Yes
Note-takers: Yes
Support services for students with LD: Yes
Support services for students with ADHD: Yes
Support services for students with ASD: Yes
Distraction-reduced environment: Yes
Tape recording in class: Yes
Electronic texts: Yes
Kurzweil reader: NR
Audio books: Yes
Other assistive technology: Yes
Priority registration: Yes
Added costs of services: No
LD specialists: No
ADHD coaching: Yes
ASD specialists: No
Professional tutors: No
Peer tutors: Yes
Max. hours/wk. for services: NR
How professors are notified of student approved accommodations: By both student and director

General Admissions Information

Office of Admissions: 320-589-6035

Entrance Requirements

Academic units required: 4 English, 4 math, 3 science, 2 foreign language, 3 social studies, High school diploma is required and GED is accepted. SAT or ACT required. If ACT, ACT with writing required. TOEFL required of all international applicants: minimum paper TOEFL 550 or minimum internet TOEFL 79.

Application deadline: 3/15
Notification: Rolling starting 9/15
Average GPA: 3.62
ACT Composite middle 50% range: 22-28
SAT Math middle 50% range: 510-640
SAT Critical Reading middle 50% range: 500-660
SAT Writing middle 50% range: 490-620
Graduate top 10% of class: 24
Graduated top 25% of class: 55
Graduated top 50% of class: 90

COLLEGE GRADUATION REQUIREMENTS

Course waivers allowed: Yes
In what course: Students may submit a petition for a waiver to be determined by a committee
Course substitutions allowed: Yes
In what course: Students may submit a petition for a substitution to be determined by a committee

Additional Information

Environment: This public school was founded in 1959. It has a 130-acre campus.

Student Body
Undergrad enrollment: 1,856
% Women: 54
% Men: 46
% Out-of-state: 13.2

Cost information
Tuition: $11,896
Room & board: $7,960
Housing Information
University Housing: Yes
Percent living on campus: 55.8

Greek System
Fraternity: No
Sorority: No
Athletics: Division III

Winona State University

175 Mark Street, Winona, MN 55987
Phone: 507-457-5100 • Fax: 507-457-5620
E-mail: admissions@winona.edu • Web: www.winona.edu
Support: S • Institution: Public

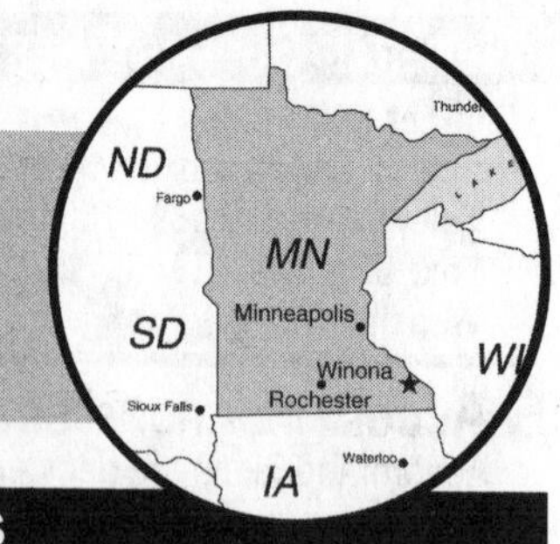

Programs or Services for Students with Learning Differences

"Helping Students Succeed" is the motto of WSU's Access Services. Many academic resources are offered free of charge to qualified students. Examples of academic accommodations include but are not limited to extended time on exams, low distraction test environments and alternate format textbooks. Winona State University values diversity in our community and is committed to ensuring equal access and opportunity to all qualified students. Access Services serves Winona State University students by providing academic accommodations for students who present qualifying documentation. As part of the Warrior Success Center the Access Services embodies the goal of student persistence to graduation. Winona State has the TRiO Student Support Service (SSS). TRIO is a community of support for first-generation, low-income, and students with documented disabilities designed to help students achieve their goals of graduation. SSS is dedicated to providing individualized academic and personal assistance to facilitate lifelong learning and development.

Admission Information for Students with Learning Differences

College entrance test required: Yes
Interview required: Not Applicable
Essay required: Not Applicable
Additional Application Required for LD/ADHD/ASD: Yes
What documentation required for LD: Psycho ed evaluation
With general application: No
To receive services after enrolling: Yes
What documentation required for ADHD: Psycho ed evaluation
With general application: No
To receive services after enrolling: Yes
What documentation required for ASD: Psycho ed evaluation
With general application: No
To receive services after enrolling: Yes
LD/ADHD/ASD documentation submitted to: Access Services for Students with Diabilities
ASD Specific Program: NR
Special Ed. HS course work accepted: Not Applicable
Specific course requirements of all applicants: Yes
Separate application required for program services: Yes
Total # of students receiving LD/ADHD/ASD services: NR
Acceptance into program means acceptance into college: No

Admissions

Winona State University Admissions requirements: ACT score of 21 or better with class rank in top 2/3 of high school class or Top 50 percent of graduating class with an ACT score of 18, 19, or 20. Course requirements include: 4 years English, 3 years math, 3 years science, 3 years social studies, 2 years foreign language (American Sign Language is accepted), and 1 additional year of an elective. The student's academic transcript will be reviewed to see that they have completed the Minnesota State University Preparation Requirements. Admissions decisions are processed in 15 to 20 days.

Additional Information

The mission of the Warrior Success Center (WSC) is to provide free and accessible services and resources for student success. WSC provides individualized advising to students and helps them identify majors and careers best suited to their unique interests, strengths and goals. WSC collaborates with a variety of programs and departments at WSU, as well as community partners. Services offered through Access Services includes advising, tutoring and supplemental instruction, study skills coaching, time management training, personal enrichment and skills development workshops, and leadership development.

General Support Services Information

Contact Information
Name of program or department: Access Services for Students with Diabilities
Telephone: 507-457-5878
Fax: 507-457-2957
Website: http://www.winona.edu/accessservices/

Accommodations or Services For Students With Learning Differences

Accommodations are decided upon an individual basis after a thorough review of appropriate, current documentation. The accommodations requests must be supported through the documentation provided and must be logically linked to the current impact of the condition on academic functioning.

Allowed in exams
Calculator: Yes
Dictionary: Yes
Computer: Yes
Spellchecker: Yes
Extended test time: Yes
Scribes: Yes
Proctors: Yes
Oral exams: Yes
Note-takers: Yes
Support services for students with LD: Yes
Support services for students with ADHD: Yes
Support services for students with ASD: Yes
Distraction-reduced environment: Yes
Tape recording in class: Yes
Electronic texts: Yes
Kurzweil reader: NR
Audio books: Yes
Other assistive technology: Yes
Priority registration: Yes
Added costs of services: No
LD specialists: No
ADHD coaching: No
ASD specialists: No
Professional tutors: Yes
Peer tutors: Yes
Max. hours/wk. for services: 1
How professors are notified of student approved accommodations: By both student and director

General Admissions Information

Office of Admissions: 507-457-5100

Entrance Requirements

Academic units required: 4 English, 3 math, 3 science, 3 science labs, 2 foreign language, 2 social studies, 1 history, 1 academic electives. High school diploma is required and GED is accepted. SAT or ACT required. If ACT, ACT with writing accepted. TOEFL required of all international applicants: minimum paper TOEFL 520 or minimum internet TOEFL 68.

Application deadline: 7/12
Notification: NR
Average GPA: 3.33
ACT Composite middle 50% range: 20-25
SAT Math middle 50% range: NR-NR
SAT Critical Reading middle 50% range: NR-NR
SAT Writing middle 50% range: NR-NR
Graduate top 10% of class: 9
Graduated top 25% of class: 30
Graduated top 50% of class: 69

COLLEGE GRADUATION REQUIREMENTS

Course waivers allowed: No
Course substitutions allowed: Yes
In what course: Substitution only available for courses that do not fundamentally alter the nature of the program or degree

Additional Information

Environment: This public school was founded in 1858. It has a 40-acre campus.

Student Body
Undergrad enrollment: 8,002
% Women: 61
% Men: 39
% Out-of-state: 30

Cost information
In-state Tuition: $7,103
Out-of-state Tuition: $12,800
Room & board: $8,120

Housing Information
University Housing: Yes
Percent living on campus: 30

Greek System
Fraternity: No
Sorority: No
Athletics: Division II

Evangel University

111 North Glenstone, Springfield, MO 65802
Phone: 417-865-2811 • Fax: 417-520-0545
E-mail: admissions@evangel.edu • Web: www.evangel.edu
Support: CS • Institution: Private

Programs or Services for Students with Learning Differences

The Academic Support Center supports the needs of all students at Evangel College. The center focuses on assisting students with improving academic skills so that they remain successful in college. The center offers study skills assistance, tutorial services, and individual college planning. Group and individual support counseling is also available. Classes covering study skills are offered for credit.

Admission Information for Students with Learning Differences

College entrance tests required: Yes
Interview required: No
Essay required: No
Additional Application Required for LD/ADHD/ASD: NR
What documentation required for LD: Psycho ed evaluation to include: relevant historical info, instructional interventions, related services, age diagnosed, objective data (aptitude, achievement, info processing), test scores (standard, percentile and grade equivalents) and describe functional limitations.
With general application: No
To receive services after enrolling: Yes
What documentation required for ADHD: Diagnosis based on DSM-V; history of behaviors impairing functioning in academic setting; diagnostic interview; history of symptoms; evidence of ongoing behaviors.
With general application: No
To receive services after enrolling: Yes
What documentation required for ASD: Psycho ed evaluation
With general application: NR
To receive services after enrolling: Yes
LD/ADHD/ASD documentation submitted to: Academic Support Center
ASD Specific Program: NR
Special Ed. HS course work accepted: Yes
Specific course requirements of all applicants: Yes
Separate application required: No
Total # of students receiving LD/ADHD/ASD services: 35
Acceptance into program means acceptance into college: Students must be admitted to and enrolled in the university first and then request services.

Admissions

There is no special application for students with learning disabilities. All students must meet the same admission criteria. Evangel College looks at the completed application. ACT test scores are required. Students should have at least a 2.0 GPA, a pastor's recommendation, and a high school recommendation. Course requirements include 3 years of English, 2 years of math, 2 years of social science, and 1 year of science. Students with documented LD can request a substitute for specific courses if their disability impacts their ability to learn that particular subject. Special admission to the SOAR Program is offered to students with ACT scores between 14–17. These students will be enrolled in study skills as well as other proficiency classes.

Additional Information

Some study skills classes are required for students who are admitted conditionally. The Academic Support Center offers tutoring, at no cost, in a variety of courses. The center offers resources in such topics as personal growth, goal setting, self-concept enrichment, stress management, memory and concentration, test-taking, underlining, note-taking, outlining, reading a textbook, research, writing term papers, time scheduling, reading efficiency, and vocabulary. Additional resources include the design and implementation of individualized programs with an instructor, personal professional counseling at no charge, career counseling with the Director of Career Development Services, reading labs for increased reading speed, and tutoring in other classes at no charge. SOAR is designed to assist selected provisionally admitted students during the first two semesters of college. SOAR courses focus on specific modules such as assessment and skills review in reading, math, and writing; study skills application; and career planning.

General Support Services Information

Contact Information
Name of program or department: Academic Development Center
Telephone: 417-865-2811
Fax: 417-865-9599

Accommodations or Services for Students with Learning Differences

Accommodations are decided upon an individual basis after a thorough review of appropriate, current documentation. The accommodations requested must be supported through the documentation provided and must be logically linked to the current impact of the condition on academic functioning.

Allowed in exams
Calculator: Yes
Dictionary: Yes
Computer: Yes
Spellchecker: Yes
Extended test time: Yes
Scribes: Yes
Proctors: Yes
Oral exams: Yes
Note-takers: Yes
Services for students with LD: Yes
Services for students with ADHD: Yes
Services for students with ASD: Yes
Distraction-reduced environment: Yes
Tape recording in class: Yes
Audio books: NR
Electronic texts: Yes
Kurzweil Reader: Yes
Other assistive technology: Yes
Priority registration: No
Added costs for services: No
LD specialists: Yes
ADHD coaching: NR
ASD specialists: NR
Professional tutors: 1
Peer tutors: 5
Max. hours/wk. for services: Unlimited
How professors are notified of LD/ADHD: By both student and director

General Admissions Information

Office of Admissions: 417-865-2811

Entrance Requirements

Academic units recommended: 3 English, 2 mathematics, 1 science, (1 science labs), 2 foreign language, 2 social studies, 3 academic electives. High school diploma is required and GED is accepted. SAT and SAT Subject Test or ACT required. TOEFL required of all international applicants: minimum paper TOEFL 490.

Application deadline: 8/15
Notification: Rolling starting 9/1
Average GPA: NR
ACT Composite middle 50% range: NR-NR
SAT Math middle 50% range: NR-NR
SAT Critical Reading middle 50% range: NR-NR
SAT Writing middle 50% range: NR-NR
Graduated top 10% of class: NR
Graduated top 25% of class: NR
Graduated top 50% of class: NR

COLLEGE GRADUATION REQUIREMENTS

Course waivers allowed: No
Course substitutions allowed: Yes
In what course: Math

Additional Information

Environment: The college is located on 80 acres in an urban area 225 miles west of St. Louis.

Student Body
Undergrad enrollment: 2,072
% Women: NR
% Men: NR
% Out-of-state: NR
Cost information
Tuition: $20,874
Room & board: $4,048
Housing Information
University Housing: Yes
Percent living on campus: 82
Greek System
Fraternity: No
Sorority: No
Athletics: Division II

Missouri State University

901 S. National, Springfield, MO 65897
Phone: 417-836-5517 • Fax: 417-836-6334
E-mail: info@missouristate.edu • Web: www.missouristate.edu
Support: SP • Institution: Public

Programs or Services for Students with Learning Differences

The Learning Diagnostic Clinic (LDC) is an academic support facility to assist students with learning disabilities. The staff includes psychologists and learning specialists. LDC provides two levels of academic support to 'qualified' individuals: One level of services includes those services that comprise basic accommodations guaranteed to the 'qualified' students with disabilities under the law; these services are offered at no cost. The next level is called 'Project Success,' an academic support program for college students with learning disabilities who desire more comprehensive services. This program provides academic and emotional support that will help to ease the transition to higher learning and the opportunity to function independently. If background and documentation do not support a diagnosis of LD, alternatives and suggestions are discussed with the student. If the student wishes to appeal a decision not to provide services, he/she is referred to the ADA/504 Compliance Officer.

Admission Information for Students with Learning Differences

College entrance test required: Yes
Interview required: No
Essay required:
Additional Application Required for LD/ADHD/ASD: NR
What documentation required for LD: Pyschoeducational Evaluation
With general application: No
To receive services after enrolling: Yes
What documentation required for ADHD: Letter from current physician.
With general application: No
To receive services after enrolling: Yes
What documentation required for ASD: Psycho ed evaluation
With general application: NR
To receive services after enrolling: Yes
With general application: No
To receive services after enrolling: Yes
LD/ADHD/ASD documentation submitted to: Support program/services
ASD Specific Program: NR
Special Ed. HS course work accepted: NR
Specific course requirements of all applicants: NR
Separate application required for program services: No
Total # of students receiving LD/ADHD/ASD services: 200
Acceptance into program means acceptance into college: NR

Admissions

Students must be admitted to the university to be eligible for the services, and students with learning disabilities must meet the same requirements for admission to the university as all other applicants. There is a special application to be completed as well as a required evaluation fee for students requesting special services. Eligibility for admissions is based on a sliding scale determined by ACT scores and class rank. Application procedures to Progress Success are: gain acceptance to by the university; self-identify and request application at LDC; submit application and requested information; and student is offered date for personal interview and testing or referred to other services; once interview and testing is completed the test data and information are evaluated by staff. The student is accepted or offered alternative suggestions.

Additional Information

Project Success is an academic support program for college students with a learning disability, ADHD, or other diagnosis who desire more comprehensive services than those covered under the Americans with Disabilities Act (ADA). Those enrolled in Project Success will be offered a wide variety of services tailored for students with learning disabilities. The student is assigned to a case manager who maintains contact, monitors progress, and assesses the effectiveness of accommodations. The fee for this level of accommodations is $1800 per semester for 2016-2017 school year.This is separate and above the basic services provided by the clinic. Basic services from LDC may include assistance in obtaining recorded textbooks, testing accommodations, and notetaking assistance; there is no fee for basic services.

General Support Services Information

Contact Information
Name of program or department: Learning Diagnostic Clinic (LDC)
Telephone: 417-836-4787
Fax: 417-836-5475

Accommodations or Services for Students with Learning Differences

Accommodations are decided upon an individual basis after a thorough review of appropriate, current documentation. The accommodations requests must be supported through the documentation provided and must be logically linked to the current impact of the condition on academic functioning.

Allowed in exams
Calculator: Yes
Dictionary: Yes
Computer: Yes
Spellchecker: Yes
Extended test time: Yes
Scribes: Yes
Proctors: Yes
Oral exams: Yes
Note-takers: Yes
Services for students with LD: Yes
Services for students with ADHD: Yes
Services for students with ASD: Yes
Distraction-reduced environment: Yes
Tape recording in class: Yes
Audio books: Yes
Electronic texts: NR
Kurzweil Reader: Yes
Other assistive technology: Yes
Priority registration: Yes
Added costs of services: No
LD specialists: Yes
ADHD coaching: NR
ASD specialists: NR
Professional tutors: NR
Peer tutors: NR
Max. hours/wk. for services: NR
How professors are notified of student approved accommodations: Both student and director

General Admissions Information

Office of Admissions: NR

Entrance Requirements

SAT or ACT required. If ACT, ACT with writing accepted. TOEFL required of all international applicants.

Application deadline: 7/20
Notification: NR
Average GPA: NR
ACT Composite middle 50% range: NR-NR
SAT Math middle 50% range: NR-NR
SAT Critical Reading middle 50% range: NR-NR
SAT Writing middle 50% range: NR-NR
Graduated top 10% of class: NR
Graduated top 25% of class: NR
Graduated top 50% of class: NR

COLLEGE GRADUATION REQUIREMENTS

Course waivers allowed: No
Course substitutions allowed: Yes
In what course: In special circumstances

Additional Information

Environment: The 200-acre rural campus is located 170 miles from Kansas City and 120 miles from St. Louis.

Student Body
Undergrad enrollment: 16,157
% Women: 56
% Men: 44
% Out-of-state: 7

Cost information
In-state Tuition: $4,920
Out-of-state Tuition: $9,840
Room & board: $5,294

Housing Information
University Housing: Yes
Percent living on campus: 24

Greek System
Fraternity: Yes
Sorority: Yes
Athletics: Division I

UNIVERSITY OF MISSOURI—COLUMBIA

230 Jesse Hall, Columbia, MO 65211
Phone: 573-882-7786 • Fax: 573-882-7887
E-mail: MU4U@missouri.edu • Web: www.missouri.edu
Support: CS • Institution: Public

PROGRAMS OR SERVICES FOR STUDENTS WITH LEARNING DIFFERENCES

Reasonable accommodations, auxiliary aids, and support services are provided by the Office of Disability Services (ODS) to ensure that any student with a disability will have equal access to the educational programs and activities at the university. MU does not have a stand-alone program oriented to students with specific learning disabilities; all students with disabilities are supported through ODS. Students with disabilities (including specific learning disabilities or ADD/ADHD) are required to adhere to the same academic standards as other students at the university. As in any higher education setting, students with disabilities have the responsibility to self-identify and are encouraged to request accommodations through ODS as early as possible. In most instances, students will be expected to provide documentation of disability; for learning disabilities this will likely be in the form of a diagnostic report, as well as documented evidence of having received accommodations previously. For entering freshmen, contacting ODS in advance of the start of their first semester is strongly encouraged.

ADMISSION INFORMATION FOR STUDENTS WITH LEARNING DIFFERENCES

College entrance tests required: Yes
Interview required: No
Essay required: No
Additional Application Required for LD/ADHD/ASD: NR
What documentation required for LD: Psycho ed evaluation to include: relevant historical info, instructional interventions, related services, age diagnosed, objective data (aptitude, achievement, info processing), test scores (standard, percentile and grade equivalents) and describe functional limitations.
With general application: No
To receive services after enrolling: Yes
What documentation required for ADHD: Diagnosis based on DSM-V; history of behaviors impairing functioning in academic setting; diagnostic interview; history of symptoms; evidence of ongoing behaviors.
With general application: No
To receive services after enrolling: Yes
What documentation required for ASD: Psycho ed evaluation
With general application: NR
To receive services after enrolling: Yes
LD/ADHD/ASD documentation submitted to: Office of Disability Services
ASD Specific Program: NR
Special Ed. HS course work accepted: Yes
Specific course requirements of all applicants: Yes
Separate application required: No
Total # of students receiving LD/ADHD/ASD services: 476
Acceptance into program means acceptance into college: Students must be admitted to and enrolled in the university first and then request services.

ADMISSIONS

There are no special admissions for students with learning disabilities. General admission is based on high school curriculum, ACT scores, and class rank. Applicants must have 4 years of English, 4 years of math, 3 years of social studies, 3 years of science, 2 years of a foreign language, and 1 unit of fine arts. Math, science, and foreign language requirements may be satisfied by completion of courses in middle school, junior high, or senior high. Any student with an ACT of 24 with the required courses is automatically admissible. Students with 23 ACT or 1050–1090 SAT need to rank within the top 52 percent of their graduating class. Students with 22 ACT or 1010–1040 SAT need to rank within the top 46 percent of their class. Students with 21 ACT or 970–1000 SAT need to rank within the top 31 percent of their class. Students with 19 ACT or 890–920 SAT need to rank within the top 22 percent of their class. Students with 18 ACT or 840–880 SAT need to rank within the top 14 percent of their class. Students with 17 ACT or 800–830 SAT need to rank within the top 6 percent of their class; ACT below 17 or SAT below 800 does not meet regular admission standards. Graduates of Missouri high schools who do not meet the standards for regular admission may be admitted on a conditional basis through a summer session program.

ADDITIONAL INFORMATION

Auxiliary aids and classroom accommodations include note-takers, lab assistants, readers, and assistive technology. Testing accommodations include time extensions, distraction-reduced environments, readers, scribes, or adaptive equipment. Coordinators can offer support and counseling in the areas of time management, study skills, learning styles, and other academic and social issues. Group support is also available. The Learning Center works cooperatively with ODS to provide individual tutoring free of charge. Other services include writing assistance, math assistance, test reviews, help with reading comprehension, and study skills training.

General Support Services Information

Contact Information
Name of program or department: Office of Disability Services (ODS)
Telephone: 573-882-4696
Fax: 573-884-5002

Accommodations or Services for Students with Learning Differences

Accommodations are decided on an individual basis after a thorough review of appropriate, current documentation, as well as an interview with an ODS Coordinator. The accommodations requested must be supported through the documentation provided and must be logically linked to the current impact of the condition on academic functioning.

Allowed in exams
Calculator: Yes
Dictionary: Yes
Computer: Yes
Spellchecker: Yes
Extended test time: Yes
Scribes: Yes
Proctors: Yes
Oral exams: Yes
Note-takers: Yes
Services for students with LD: Yes
Services for students with ADHD: Yes
Services for students with ASD: Yes
Distraction-reduced environment: Yes
Tape recording in class: Yes
Audio books: NR
Electronic texts: Yes
Kurzweil Reader: Yes
Other assistive technology: Yes
Priority registration: Yes
Added costs for services: No
LD specialists: Yes
ADHD coaching: Yes
ASD specialists: NR
Professional tutors: 7
Peer tutors: 120
Max. hours/wk. for services: Unlimited
How professors are notified of LD/ADHD: By student

General Admissions Information

Office of Admissions: 573-882-7786

Entrance Requirements

Academic units required: 4 English, 4 math, 3 science, 1 science labs, 2 foreign language, 3 social studies, and 1 units from above areas or other academic areas. High school diploma is required and GED is accepted. SAT or ACT required. If ACT, ACT with writing accepted. TOEFL required of all international applicants: minimum paper TOEFL 500 or minimum internet TOEFL 61.

Application deadline: NR
Notification: Rolling starting 9/1
Average GPA: NR
ACT Composite middle 50% range: 23-28
SAT Math middle 50% range: 530-660
SAT Critical Reading middle 50% range: 520-650
SAT Writing middle 50% range: NR-NR
Graduated top 10% of class: 27
Graduated top 25% of class: NR
Graduated top 50% of class: 87

COLLEGE GRADUATION REQUIREMENTS

Course waivers allowed: No
Course substitutions allowed: Yes
In what course: NR

Additional Information

Environment: This public school was founded in 1839. It has a 1372-acre campus.

Student Body
Undergrad enrollment: 27,654
% Women: 52
% Men: 48
% Out-of-state: 25

Cost information
In-state Tuition: $8,286
Out-of Tuition: $23,943
Room & board: $9,808

Housing Information
University Housing: Yes
Percent living on campus: 21

Greek System
Fraternity: Yes
Sorority: Yes
Athletics: Division I

University of Missouri—Kansas City

5100 Rockhill Road, Kansas City, mo 64114
Phone: 816-235-1111 • Fax: 816-235-5544
E-mail: admit@umkc.edu • Web: www.umkc.edu
Support: S • Institution: Public

Programs or Services for Students with Learning Differences

The Office of Services for Students with Disabilities's mission is to educate and support the student community. The provision of all reasonable accommodations and services is based upon assessment of the impact of the student's disabilities on his or her academic performance. Therefore, it is in the student's best interest to provide recent and appropriate documentation relevant to the student's learning environment.

Admission Information for Students with Learning Differences

College entrance test required: Yes
Interview required: Not Applicable
Essay required: Not Applicable
Additional Application Required for LD/ADHD/ASD: Not Applicable
What documentation required for LD: A letter from a qualified medical professional describing the condition and a description of its impact.
With general application: Not Applicable
To receive services after enrolling: Not Applicable
What documentation required for ADHD: A letter from a qualified medical professional describing the condition and a description of its impact.
With general application: Not Applicable
To receive services after enrolling: Not Applicable
What documentation required for ASD: We look for a wide range of testing that substantiate the diagnosis. Typically a WAIS and other work up.
With general application: Not Applicable
To receive services after enrolling: Not Applicable
LD/ADHD/ASD documentation submitted to: Office of Services for Students with Disabilities
ASD Specific Program: No
Special Ed. HS course work accepted: Not Applicable
Specific course requirements of all applicants: Yes
Separate application required for program services: True
Total # of students receiving LD/ADHD/ASD services: NR
Acceptance into program means acceptance into college: Not Applicable

Admissions

The admissions requirements are the same for all students.

Additional Information

All students with disabilities should enroll in classes as early as possible in the semester and let the Disability office know. This alerts them to the need to provide accommodations and allows them the time to make appropriate arrangements. Those students who are eligible to receive testing accommodations must meet with the professor early in the semester and discuss arrangements for testing. Contact the Office at 816-235-5696 and schedule an appointment. They will need documentation of your disability. There is also a Writing Center, and Math resource Center.

General Support Services Information

Contact Information
Name of program or department: Office of Services for Students with Disabilities
Telephone: 816-235-5696
Fax: 816-235-6363
Website: NR

Accommodations or Services for Students with Learning Differences

Accommodations are decided upon an individual basis after a thorough review of appropriate, current documentation. The accommodations requests must be supported through the documentation provided and must be logically linked to the current impact of the condition on academic functioning.

Allowed in exams
Calculator: Yes
Dictionary: Yes
Computer: Yes
Spellchecker: Yes
Extended test time: Yes
Scribes: Yes
Proctors: Yes
Oral exams: Yes
Note-takers: Yes
Support services for students with LD: Yes
Support services for students with ADHD: Yes
Support services for students with ASD: Yes
Distraction-reduced environment: Yes
Tape recording in class: Yes
Electronic texts: Yes
Kurzweil reader: NR
Audio books: Yes
Other assistive technology: Yes
Priority registration: Yes
Added costs of services: No
LD specialists: No
ADHD coaching: Yes
ASD specialists: NR
Professional tutors: No
Peer tutors: Not Applicable
Max. hours/wk. for services: NR
How professors are notified of student approved accommodations: By student

General Admissions Information

Office of Admissions: 816-235-1111

Entrance Requirements

Academic units required: 4 English, 4 math, 3 science, 1 science labs, 2 foreign language, 3 social studies, 1 visual/performing arts, High school diploma is required and GED is accepted. SAT or ACT required. If ACT, ACT with writing accepted. TOEFL required of all international applicants: minimum paper TOEFL 500 or minimum internet TOEFL 61.

Application deadline: NR
Notification: NR
Average GPA: 3.36
ACT Composite middle 50% range: 21-28
SAT Math middle 50% range: 520-710
SAT Critical Reading middle 50% range: 510-680
SAT Writing middle 50% range: NR-NR
Graduate top 10% of class: 32
Graduated top 25% of class: 57
Graduated top 50% of class: 82

COLLEGE GRADUATION REQUIREMENTS

Course waivers allowed: No
Course substitutions allowed: Yes
In what course: Math, foreign language

Additional Information

Environment: This private school was founded in 1929. It has a 191-acre campus.

Student Body
Undergrad enrollment: 11,253
% Women: 57
% Men: 43
% Out-of-state: 20

Cost information
In-state tuition: $8,103
Out-of-state tuition: $21,162
Room & board: $9,815

Housing Information
University Housing: Yes
Percent living on campus: 23

Greek System
Fraternity: Yes
Sorority: Yes
Athletics: Division I

Washington U. in St. Louis

Campus Box 1089, St. Louis, MO 63130-4899
Phone: 314-935-6000 • Fax: 314-935-4290
E-mail: admissions@wustl.edu • Web: wustl.edu
Support: CS • Institution: Private

Programs or Services for Students with Learning Differences

The Disability Resources (DR), a unit within Cornerstone: The Center for Advanced Learning at Washington University-St. Louis, recognizes that there are many types of disabilities that can hinder a student in achieving his or her true academic ability. It is the goal of DR to treat students with disabilities as individuals with specific needs and provide services responsive to those needs. DR provides a wide range of services and accommodations to help remove barriers posed by the students' disabilities. Students are encouraged to be their own advocates and have the major responsibility for securing services and accommodations. Reasonable accommodations will be made to assist students in meeting their individual needs. It is the goal of DR to incorporate students with disabilities into the mainstream of the university community. Any student who has a permanent or temporary psychological or physical disability is eligible for services. Students must self-identify and provide current documentation. The assistant director(s) of DR will work with the student to identify appropriate accommodations and services based on documentation and previous experiences. Most accommodations result from communication and agreements between the students and the classroom instructors.

Admission Information for Students with Learning Differences

College entrance test required: Yes
Interview required: NR
Essay required: NR
Additional Application Required for LD/ADHD/ASD: NR
What documentation required for LD: Please visit our "Documentation Guidelines" listed specifically for students with ADHD on the Disability Resources website at: cornerstone.wustl.edu/DisabilityResources/DocumentationGuidelines.aspx
With general application: NR
To receive services after enrolling: Yes
What documentation required for ADHD: Please visit our "Documentation Guidelines" listed specifically for students with ASD on the Disability Resources website at: cornerstone.wustl.edu/DisabilityResources/DocumentationGuidelines.aspx
With general application: NR
To receive services after enrolling: Yes
What documentation required for ASD: Please visit our "Documentation Guidelines" listed specifically for students with Learning Disabilities on the Disability Resources website at: cornerstone.wustl.edu/DisabilityResources/DocumentationGuidelines.aspx
With general application: NR
To receive services after enrolling: Yes
LD/ADHD/ASD documentation submitted to: Disability Resources
ASD Specific Program: NR
Special Ed. HS course work accepted: NR
Specific course requirements of all applicants: Yes
Separate application required for program services: NR
Total # of students receiving LD/ADHD/ASD services: 223
Acceptance into program means acceptance into college: NR

Admissions

Washington University gives full consideration to all applicants for admission. There is no special admissions process for students with learning disabilities. Students may choose to voluntarily identify themselves as learning disabled in the admissions process. If they chose to self-identify, details of the history and treatment of their disability, of how they have met different academic requirements in light of the disability, and the relationship between the disability and the students' academic record help the university to understand more fully the applicants' profiles. This information can be helpful in the application process to explain, for example, lower grades in certain subjects. Washington University is a competitive school and looks for students with rigorous academic preparation, including 4 years of English, 3-4 years of math, 3-4 years of science, and 3-4 years of social studies. Two years of a foreign language are preferred but not required.

Additional Information

Cornerstone: The Center for Advanced Learning provides support services to help the students to succeed academically. These include: essential study and test-taking skills, access to peer mentors, executive functioning, and time management and study techniques, etc. Common DR services and accommodations include, but are not limited to, readers or scribes, note-takers, assistance in obtaining accommodations for professional exams, referral for disability evaluation, audio taping class lectures, extra time to complete exams, alternative exam formats, and distraction-reduced exam sites. Services and accommodations are available for undergraduate and graduate students.

General Support Services Information

Contact Information
Name of program or department: Disability Resources
Telephone: 314-935-5970
Fax: 314-935-7559
Website: http://cornerstone.wustl.edu/DisabilityResources.aspx

Accommodations or Services for Students with Learning Differences

Accommodations are decided upon an individual basis after a thorough review of appropriate, current documentation. The accommodations requests must be supported through the documentation provided and must be logically linked to the current impact of the condition on academic functioning.

Allowed in exams
Calculator: Yes
Dictionary: Yes
Computer: Yes
Spellchecker: Yes
Extended test time: Yes
Scribes: Yes
Proctors: Yes
Oral exams: Yes
Note-takers: Yes
Support services for students with LD: Yes
Support services for students with ADHD: Yes
Support services for students with ASD: Yes
Distraction-reduced environment: Yes
Tape recording in class: Yes
Electronic texts: Yes
Kurzweil reader: NR
Audio books: No
Other assistive technology: Yes
Priority registration: NR
Added costs of services: No
LD specialists: Yes
ADHD coaching: Yes
ASD specialists: No
Professional tutors: No
Peer tutors: Yes
Max. hours/wk. for services: NR
How professors are notified of student approved accommodations: By student

General Admissions Information

Office of Admissions: 314-935-6000

Entrance Requirements

Academic units recommended: 4 English, 4 math, 4 science, 4 science labs, 2 foreign language, 4 social studies, 4 history. High school diploma is required and GED is accepted. SAT or ACT required. If ACT, ACT with writing accepted. TOEFL required of all international applicants.

Application deadline: 1/15
Notification: 4/1
Average GPA: NR
ACT Composite middle 50% range: 32-34
SAT Math middle 50% range: 710-790
SAT Critical Reading middle 50% range: 690-760
SAT Writing middle 50% range: 690-770
Graduate top 10% of class: 89
Graduated top 25% of class: 100
Graduated top 50% of class: 100

COLLEGE GRADUATION REQUIREMENTS

Course waivers allowed: NR
Course substitutions allowed: NR

Additional Information

Environment: This private school was founded in 1853. It has a 169-acre campus.

Student Body
Undergrad enrollment: 7,504
% Women: 53
% Men: 47
% Out-of-state: 93

Cost information
Tuition: $48,950
Room & board: $15,596

Housing Information
University Housing: Yes
Percent living on campus: 78

Greek System
Fraternity: Yes
Sorority: Yes
Athletics: Division III

Westminster College

Champ Auditorium, Westminster College, Fulton, MO 65251
Phone: 573-592-5251 • Fax: 573-592-5255
E-mail: admissions@westminster-mo.edu • Web: www.westminster-mo.edu/
Support: SP • Institution: Private

Programs or Services for Students with Learning Differences

Westminster College: The Learning Differences Program (LDP) provides the encouragement and support that students diagnosed with neurodevelopmental disorders need to be successful learners in the academic environment they share with regularly admitted students. Students selected for participation in the LDP represent about five percent of the total student population at Westminster. Long a part of Westminster's academic life, faculty, staff, and administrators readily accept and help accommodate students enrolled in the LDP. The LDP's services are tailored to meet the specific needs of students with professionally diagnosed neurodevelopmental disorders, including Attention Deficit/Hyperactivity Disorder, Dyscalculia, Dyslexia, Learning Disorder, and Disorder of Written Expression.

Admission Information for Students with Learning Differences

College entrance test required: Yes
Interview required: Yes
Essay required: NR
Additional Application Required for LD/ADHD/ASD: NR
What documentation required for LD: WAIS-R; (WISC III or IV) and written evaluation within 2 years; Woodcock-Johnson or WAIS
With general application: No
To receive services after enrolling: Yes
What documentation required for ADHD: Connors Parent/Teacher Rating Scale; various behavioral assessments
With general application: No
To receive services after enrolling: Yes
What documentation required for ASD: Psycho ed evaluation
With general application: NR
To receive services after enrolling: Yes
LD/ADHD/ASD documentation submitted to: Admissions
ASD Specific Program: NR
Special Ed. HS course work accepted: Yes
Specific course: Yes
Separate application required for program services: Yes
Total # of students receiving LD/ADHD/ASD services: NR
Acceptance into program means acceptance into college: NR

Admissions

There is a special application and admissions procedure for students with learning disabilities. Students submit a completed Westminster College application form and a separate application form for the LD program; results of an eye and hearing exam, WAIS, WJ, and achievement tests; SAT scores of 900-plus or ACT scores of 19-plus; two copies of their high school transcript; recent reports from school counselors, learning specialists, psychologists, or physicians who have diagnosed the disability; four recommendations from counselors or teachers familiar with their performance; and an evaluation from an educational specialist. An on-campus interview is required. Following the interview and a review of the file, the Professional Academic Staff confer and reach an admission decision usually within 1 week after the visit. Students are admitted directly into the college and then reviewed for LD services.

Additional Information

Students are mainstreamed and need a solid college-prep background in high school. There is a fee of $4,800 for the first year of the program and $2,800 each year thereafter. Students have access to unlimited tutoring. Learning resources include audio tapes of textbooks; self-instructional materials; special classes in study, reading, and listening skills; test-taking, time management, and English composition strategies; and word processors to assist in writing instruction. There is also the Academic Resource Center, which is a learning center that is open to all students.

General Support Services Information

Contact Information
Name of program or department: Learning Opportunity Center
Telephone: 573-592-5304
Fax: 573-592-5191

Accommodations or Services for Students with Learning Differences

Accommodations are decided upon an individual basis after a thorough review of appropriate, current documentation. The accommodations requests must be supported through the documentation provided and must be logically linked to the current impact of the condition on academic functioning.

Allowed in exams
Calculator: Yes
Dictionary: Yes
Computer: Yes
Spellchecker: Yes
Extended test time: Yes
Scribes: Yes
Proctors: Yes
Oral exams: Yes
Note-takers: Yes
Services for students with LD: Yes
Services for students with ADHD: Yes
Services for students with ASD: Yes
Distraction-reduced environment: Yes
Tape recording in class: Yes
Audio books: Yes
Electronic texts: NR
Kurzweil Reader: Yes
Other assistive technology: Yes
Priority registration: No
Added costs of services: Yes
LD specialists: Yes
ADHD coaching: NR
ASD specialists: NR
Professional tutors: NR
Peer tutors: Yes
Max. hours/wk. for services: NR
How professors are notified of student approved accommodations: Both student and director

General Admissions Information

Office of Admissions: 573-592-5251

Entrance Requirements

Academic units required: 4 English, 3 math, 2 science, 2 science labs, **Academic units recommended:** 2 foreign language, 2 social studies, 2 academic electives. High school diploma is required and GED is accepted. SAT or ACT required. If ACT, ACT with writing accepted. TOEFL required of all international applicants: minimum paper TOEFL 550.

Application deadline: NR
Notification: Rolling starting 10/1
Average GPA: 3.38
ACT Composite middle 50% range: 21-26
SAT Math middle 50% range: 530-615
SAT Critical Reading middle 50% range: 428-535
SAT Writing middle 50% range: 443-523
Graduated top 10% of class: 21
Graduated top 25% of class: 40
Graduated top 50% of class: 75

COLLEGE GRADUATION REQUIREMENTS

Course waivers allowed: No
Course substitutions allowed: Yes
In what course: Students can petition the academic dean for substitute courses in any area.

Additional Information

Environment: This private school, affiliated with the Presbyterian Church, was founded in 1851. It has a 86-acre campus.

Student Body
Undergrad enrollment: 953
% Women: 43
% Men: 57
% Out-of-state: 19
Cost information
Tuition: $23,200
Room & board: $9,480
Housing Information
University Housing: Yes
Percent living on campus: 85
Greek System
Fraternity: Yes
Sorority: Yes
Athletics: Division III

Montana State U.—Billings

1500 University Drive, Billings, MT 59101
Phone: 406-657-2158 • Fax: 406-657-2051
E-mail: cjohannes@msubillings.edu • Web: www.msubillings.edu
Support: S • Institution: Public

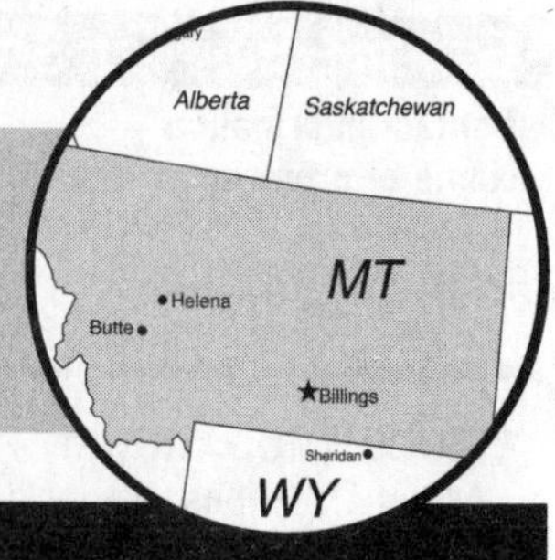

Programs or Services for Students with Learning Differences

The DSS mission statement is: Disability Support Services assists in creating an accessible university community where students with documented disabilities have an equal opportunity to fully participate in all aspects of the educational environment. We coordinate the provision of reasonable accommodations, advocate for an accessible and amenable learning environment, and promote self-determination for the students we serve.

Admission Information for Students with Learning Differences

College entrance tests required: Yes
Interview required: No
Essay required: No
Additional Application Required for LD/ADHD/ASD: NR
What documentation required for LD: Psycho ed evaluation to include: relevant historical info, instructional interventions, related services, age diagnosed, objective data (aptitude, achievement, info processing), test scores (standard, percentile and grade equivalents) and describe functional limitations.
With general application: No
To receive services after enrolling: Yes
What documentation required for ADHD: Diagnosis based on DSM-V; history of behaviors impairing functioning in academic setting; diagnostic interview; history of symptoms; evidence of ongoing behaviors.
With general application: No
To receive services after enrolling: Yes
What documentation is required for ASD: At whatever time the student is requesting service, counselor meets with the student to determine needs, no documentation required.
With general application: NR
To receive services after enrolling: Yes
LD/ADHD/ASD documentation submitted to: Disability Support Services
ASD Specific Program: NR
Special Ed. HS course work accepted: Yes
Specific course requirements of all applicants: Yes
Separate application required: No
Total # of students receiving LD/ADHD/ASD services: NR
Acceptance into program means acceptance into college: Students must be admitted to and enrolled in the university first and then request services.

Admissions

There is no special admission process for students with learning disabilities. All students must meet the same admission criteria. Freshmen applicants must meet one of the following conditions: ACT of 22 or SAT of 920, a 2.5 GPA; or rank in the top half of the class. Students must have 4 years of English, 3 years of math (students are encouraged to take math in their senior year), 3 years of social studies, 2 years of science lab (1 year must be earth science, biology, chemistry, or physics), and 2 years chosen from foreign language, computer science, visual/performing arts, and/or vocational education that meet the Office of Public Instruction guidelines. Students not meeting the college-preparatory requirements have four options: They can (1) apply for an exemption by writing a letter and addressing their special needs, talents, or other reasons; (2) enroll part-time in a summer session; (3) enroll as a part-time student with seven or fewer credits the first semester; or (4) attend a community college or other college and attempt at least 12 credits or make up any deficiency.

Additional Information

Students must request services, provide documentation specifying a learning disability or ADHD, make an appointment for an intake with DSS, meet with professors at the beginning of each semester, and work closely with DSS. DSS must keep documentation and intake on file, make a determination of accommodations, issue identification cards to qualified students, and serve as a resource and a support system. Services include course and testing accommodations, alternative testing, priority scheduling, technical assistance, liaison and referral services, taped textbooks, and career, academic, and counseling referrals. The use of a computer, calculator, dictionary, or spellchecker is at the discretion of the individual professor and based on the documented needs of the student. Services and accommodations are available for undergraduate and graduate students.

General Support Services Information

Contact Information
Name of program or department: Disability Support Services (DSS)
Telephone: 406-657-2283
Fax: 406-657-2187

Accommodations or Services for Students with Learning Differences

Accommodations are decided upon an individual basis after a thorough review of appropriate, current documentation. The accommodations requested must be supported through the documentation provided and must be logically linked to the current impact of the condition on academic functioning.

Allowed in exams
Calculator: Yes
Dictionary: No
Computer: Yes
Spellchecker: Yes
Extended test time: Yes
Scribes: Yes
Proctors: Yes
Oral exams: No
Note-takers: Yes
Services for students with LD: Yes
Services for students with ADHD: Yes
Services for students with ASD: Yes
Distraction-reduced environment: Yes
Tape recording in class: Yes
Audio books: Yes
Electronic texts: Yes
Kurzweil Reader: Yes
Other assistive technology: Yes
Priority registration: Yes
Added costs for services: No
LD specialists: No
ADHD coaching? No
ASD specialists on staff? No
Professional tutors: 1
Peer tutors: 10–20
Max. hours/wk. for services: Unlimited
How professors are notified of LD/ADHD: By student

General Admissions Information

Office of Admissions: 406-657-2158

Entrance Requirements

Academic units required: 4 English, 3 math, 2 science, 2 science labs, 3 social studies, and 2 units from above areas or other academic areas. High school diploma is required and GED is accepted. SAT or ACT required for some. If ACT, ACT with writing recommended. TOEFL required of all international applicants: minimum paper TOEFL 515 or minimum internet TOEFL 68.

Application deadline: NR
Notification: 9/1
Average GPA: NR
ACT Composite middle 50% range: 18-24
SAT Math middle 50% range: 440-560
SAT Critical Reading middle 50% range: 420-540
SAT Writing middle 50% range: NR-NR
Graduated top 10% of class: 8
Graduated top 25% of class: 31
Graduated top 50% of class: 63

COLLEGE GRADUATION REQUIREMENTS

Course waivers allowed: Yes
In what course: In foreign language and math under strict guidelines
Course substitutions allowed: Yes
In what course: In foreign language and math under strict guidelines

Additional Information

Environment: This public school was founded in 1927. It has a 92-acre campus.

Student Body
Undergrad enrollment: 4,034
% Women: 62
% Men: 38
% Out-of-state: 10

Cost information
In-state Tuition: $4,397
Out-of Tuition: $16,307
Room & board: $7,510

Housing Information
University Housing: Yes
Percent living on campus: 11

Greek System
Fraternity: Yes
Sorority: Yes
Athletics: Division II

MONTANA TECH OF THE U. OF MT

1300 West Park Street, Butte, MT 59701
Phone: 406-496-4256 • Fax: 406-496-4710
E-mail: enrollment@mtech.edu • Web: www.mtech.edu
Support: CS • Institution: Public

PROGRAMS OR SERVICES FOR STUDENTS WITH LEARNING DIFFERENCES

All persons with disabilities have the right to participate fully and equally in the programs and services of Montana Tech. Tech is committed to making the appropriate accommodations. Montana Tech's student life counselors are resources for students with disabilities. The counselors are a general resource for all students who may need assistance. Availability of services from Disability Services is subject to a student's eligibility for these and any other services. Students must provide appropriate and current documentation prior to requesting and receiving services or accommodations. All faculty and staff at the college are responsible for assuring access by providing reasonable accommodations. The Montana Tech Learning Center offers a variety of services to help students achieve their full academic potential. Tutors are available to help all students with course work in an assortment of subject areas. The Learning Center addresses the importance of developing basic college success skills.

ADMISSION INFORMATION FOR STUDENTS WITH LEARNING DIFFERENCES

College entrance tests required: Yes
Interview required: No
Essay required: No
Additional Application Required for LD/ADHD/ASD: NR
What documentation required for LD: Psycho ed evaluation to include: relevant historical info, instructional interventions, related services, age diagnosed, objective data (aptitude, achievement, info processing), test scores (standard, percentile and grade equivalents) and describe functional limitations.
With general application: No
To receive services after enrolling: Yes
What documentation required for ADHD: Diagnosis based on DSM-V; history of behaviors impairing functioning in academic setting; diagnostic interview; history of symptoms; evidence of ongoing behaviors.
With general application: No
To receive services after enrolling: Yes
What documentation required for ASD: Psycho ed evaluation
With general application: NR
To receive services after enrolling: Yes
LD/ADHD/ASD documentation submitted to: Disability Services
ASD Specific Program: NR
Special Ed. HS course work accepted: No
Specific course requirements of all applicants: Yes
Separate application required: No
Total # of students receiving LD/ADHD/ASD services: NR
Acceptance into program means acceptance into college: Students must be admitted to and enrolled in the university first and then request services.

ADMISSIONS

There is no special admission process for students with LD or ADHD. Applicants must have a 22 ACT or 1540 SAT Reasoning, or be in the upper 50 percent of their high school class, or have a 2.5 GPA. The GED is accepted. Students must have 14 academic high school credits, including 4 years of English, 2 years of science, 3 years of math, 3 years of social studies, and 2 years from other academic areas, including foreign language, computer science, visual/performing arts, and vocational education. Interviews are not required, and special education courses in high school are not accepted. Students who do not meet any of the general admission criteria may ask to be evaluated considering other factors. Students with LD/ADHD are encouraged to self-disclose in the admissions process.

ADDITIONAL INFORMATION

The following types of services are offered to students with disabilities: responses to requests for accommodation, assistance in working with faculty members, text accommodation in concert with instructors, access to assistive technology, note-taking, and career services. Documentation to receive services should be sent directly to Disability Services. Montana Tech offers compensatory classes for students with LD in both math and English. Services and accommodations are available for undergraduate and graduate students.

GENERAL SUPPORT SERVICES INFORMATION

Contact Information
Name of program or department: Disability Services
Telephone: 406-496-4129
Fax: 406-496-4757

ACCOMMODATIONS OR SERVICES FOR STUDENTS WITH LEARNING DIFFERENCES

Accommodations are decided upon an individual basis after a thorough review of appropriate, current documentation. The accommodations requested must be supported through the documentation provided and must be logically linked to the current impact of the condition on academic functioning.

Allowed in exams
Calculator: Yes
Dictionary: NR
Computer: Yes
Spellchecker: Yes
Extended test time: Yes
Scribes: Yes
Proctors: Yes
Oral exams: Yes
Note-takers: Yes
Services for students with LD: Yes
Services for students with ADHD: Yes
Services for students with ASD: Yes
Distraction-reduced environment: Yes
Tape recording in class: Yes
Audio books: NR
Electronic texts: Yes
Kurzweil Reader: Yes
Other assistive technology: Yes
Priority registration: Yes
Added costs for services: No
LD specialists: Yes
ADHD coaching: NR
ASD specialists: NR
Professional tutors: NR
Peer tutors: 0–12
Max. hours/wk. for services: Unlimited
How professors are notified of LD/ADHD: By both student and counselors

GENERAL ADMISSIONS INFORMATION

Office of Admissions: 406-496-4256

ENTRANCE REQUIREMENTS

Academic units required: 4 English, 3 math, 2 science, 2 science labs, 3 social studies, and 2 units from above areas or other academic areas. **Academic units recommended:** 4 math. High school diploma is required and GED is accepted. SAT or ACT required. If ACT, ACT with writing recommended. TOEFL required of all international applicants: minimum paper TOEFL 525 or minimum internet TOEFL 71.

Application deadline: NR
Notification: NR
Average GPA: 3.48
ACT Composite middle 50% range: 22-27
SAT Math middle 50% range: 540-630
SAT Critical Reading middle 50% range: 490-590
SAT Writing middle 50% range: 450-560
Graduated top 10% of class: 24
Graduated top 25% of class: 57
Graduated top 50% of class: 85

COLLEGE GRADUATION REQUIREMENTS

Course waivers allowed: No
Course substitutions allowed: No

ADDITIONAL INFORMATION

Environment: This public school was founded in 1893. It has a 113-acre campus.

Student Body
Undergrad enrollment: 2,751
% Women: 40
% Men: 60
% Out-of-state: 15

Cost information
In-state Tuition: $6,797
Out-of Tuition: $20,512
Room & board: $8,562

Housing Information
University Housing: Yes
Percent living on campus: 12

Greek System
Fraternity: No
Sorority: No
Athletics: NAIA

Rocky Mountain College

1511 Poly Drive, Billings, MT 59102-1796
Phone: 406-657-1026 • Fax: 406-657-1189
E-mail: admissions@rocky.edu • Web: www.rocky.edu
Support: CS • Institution: Private

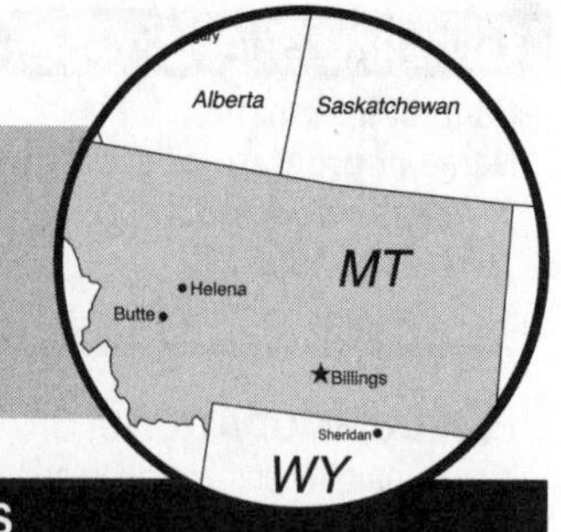

Programs or Services for Students with Learning Differences

Rocky Mountain College is committed to providing courses, programs, and services for students with disabilities. Services for Academic Success (SAS) provides a comprehensive support program for students with LD. To be eligible, participants must meet one of the primary criteria: come from a low-income family, be a first-generation college student, or have a physical or learning disability. Participants must also be U.S. citizens and have an academic need for the program. Students are responsible for identifying themselves, providing appropriate documentation, and requesting reasonable accommodations. The program tailors services to meet the needs of the individuals. SAS welcomes applications from students who are committed to learning and who are excited about meeting the challenges of college with the support provided by the SAS staff. The SAS program is supported by a grant from the U.S. Department of Education and funds from Rocky Mountain College. The small size of the college, together with the caring attitude of the faculty and an excellent support program, make Rocky a learning disability-friendly college.

Admission Information for Students with Learning Differences

College entrance tests required: Yes
Interview required: No
Essay required: No
Additional Application Required for LD/ADHD/ASD: NR
What documentation required for LD: Psycho ed evaluation to include: relevant historical info, instructional interventions, related services, age diagnosed, objective data (aptitude, achievement, info processing), test scores (standard, percentile and grade equivalents) and describe functional limitations.
With general application: No
To receive services after enrolling: Yes
What documentation required for ADHD: Diagnosis based on DSM-V; history of behaviors impairing functioning in academic setting; diagnostic interview; history of symptoms; evidence of ongoing behaviors.
With general application: No
To receive services after enrolling: Yes
What documentation required for ASD: Psycho ed evaluation
With general application: NR
To receive services after enrolling: Yes
LD/ADHD/ASD documentation submitted to: Services for Academic Success
ASD Specific Program: NR
Special Ed. HS course work accepted: No
Specific course requirements of all applicants: Yes
Separate application required: Yes
Total # of students receiving LD/ADHD/ASD services: 30–40
Acceptance into program means acceptance into college: Students must be admitted to and enrolled in the university first and then request services.

Admissions

There is no special admissions application for students with learning disabilities. All applicants must meet the same criteria, which include an ACT of 21 or SAT of 1000, a GPA of 2.5, and courses in English, math, science, and social studies. There is the opportunity to be considered for a conditional admission if scores or grades are below the cutoffs. To identify and provide necessary support services as soon as possible, students with disabilities are encouraged to complete a Services for Academic Success application when they are accepted. All documentation is confidential. Recommended courses for admissions include 4 years of English, 3 years of math, 3 years of social science, 2 years of science lab, and 2 years of a foreign language.

Additional Information

SAS provides a variety of services tailored to meet a student's individual needs. Services are free to participants and include developmental course work in reading, writing, and mathematics, study skills classes, tutoring in all subjects, academic, career, and personal counseling, graduate school counseling, accommodations for students with learning disabilities, alternative testing arrangements, taping of lectures or textbooks, cultural and academic enrichment opportunities, and advocacy. SAS staff meets with each student to talk about the supportive services the student needs and then develop a semester plan. Skills classes for college credit are offered in math, English, and studying techniques.

General Support Services Information

Contact Information
Name of program or department: Services for Academic Success (SAS)
Telephone: 406-657-1128
Fax: 406-259-9751

Accommodations or Services for Students with Learning Differences

Accommodations are decided upon an individual basis after a thorough review of appropriate, current documentation. The accommodations requested must be supported through the documentation provided and must be logically linked to the current impact of the condition on academic functioning.

Allowed in exams
Calculator: Yes
Dictionary: Yes
Computer: Yes
Spellchecker: Yes
Extended test time: Yes
Scribes: Yes
Proctors: Yes
Oral exams: Yes
Note-takers: Yes
Services for students with LD: Yes
Services for students with ADHD: Yes
Services for students with ASD: Yes
Distraction-reduced environment: Yes
Tape recording in class: Yes
Audio books: NR
Electronic texts: Yes
Kurzweil Reader: No
Other assistive technology: Yes
Priority registration: No
Added costs for services: No
LD specialists: Yes
ADHD coaching: NR
ASD specialists: NR
Professional tutors: 2
Peer tutors: 30
Max. hours/wk. for services: Unlimited
How professors are notified of LD/ADHD: By both student and director

General Admissions Information

Office of Admissions: 406-657-1026

Entrance Requirements

Academic units required: 4 English, 4 math, 3 science, 3 social studies, 2 history, 3 academic electives. High school diploma is required and GED is accepted. SAT or ACT required. If ACT, ACT with writing accepted. TOEFL required of all international applicants: minimum paper TOEFL 525.

Application deadline: NR
Notification: Rolling starting 9/1
Average GPA: 3.36
ACT Composite middle 50% range: 20-25
SAT Math middle 50% range: 450-550
SAT Critical Reading middle 50% range: 440-540
SAT Writing middle 50% range: 420-510
Graduated top 10% of class: 10
Graduated top 25% of class: 36
Graduated top 50% of class: 70

COLLEGE GRADUATION REQUIREMENTS

Course waivers allowed: No
Course substitutions allowed: Yes
In what course: NR

Additional Information

Environment: This private school was founded in 1878. It has a 60-acre campus.

Student Body
Undergrad enrollment: 1,007
% Women: 49
% Men: 51
% Out-of-state: 44
Cost information
Tuition: $22,442
Room & board: $7,160
Housing Information
University Housing: Yes
Percent living on campus: 49
Greek System
Fraternity: No
Sorority: No
Athletics: NAIA

UNIVERSITY OF MONTANA

Lommasson Center 103, Missoula, MT 59812
Phone: 406-243-6266 • Fax: 406-243-5711
E-mail: admiss@umontana.edu • Web: www.umontana.edu
Support: CS • Institution: Public

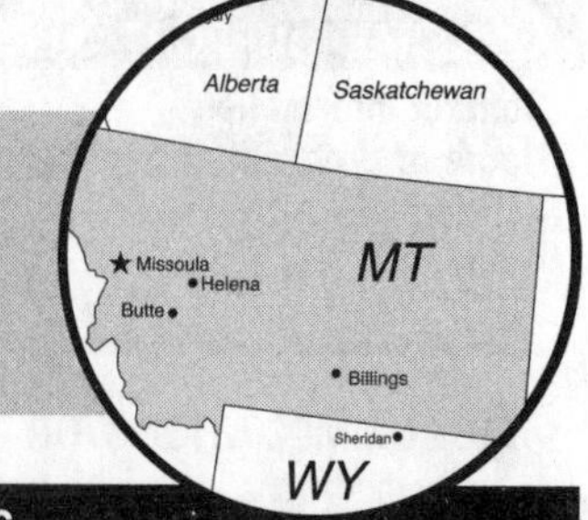

PROGRAMS OR SERVICES FOR STUDENTS WITH LEARNING DIFFERENCES

Disability Services for Students (DSS) ensures equal access to university students with disabilities. DSS is a stand-alone student affairs office at the university. It is staffed by more than ten full-time professionals. Students with learning disabilities have the same set of rights and responsibilities and the same set of services and reasonable program modifications, which are offered to other students with disabilities. Written documentation from a qualified diagnostician containing the diagnosis and functional limitations of the learning disability must be provided to DSS. However, the DSS office gives just as much weight to a student's self-report on how the disability impacts learning as the office does on a diagnostician's report. It should be noted that DSS does not operate in the same way that many special education programs in secondary schools do. At the university level, students have a right to access education, not a right to education. This means that DSS treats students as adults who either succeed or fail on their own merits. DSS assigns a coordinator to each student. The coordinator and the student collaborate to address barriers in the university program that may deny or limit full and equal program access. Students are encouraged to secure their rights through the student-coordinator relationship.

ADMISSION INFORMATION FOR STUDENTS WITH LEARNING DIFFERENCES

College entrance test required: NR
Interview required: No
Essay required: Not Applicable
Additional Application Required for LD/ADHD/ASD: Yes
What documentation required for LD: To register with Disability Services, medical records, psycho-educational testing, or school records are recommended as helpful documentation. We suggest that the documentation includes the following information: Credentials and contact information of the
With general application: No
To receive services after enrolling: Yes
What documentation required for ADHD: To register with Disability Services, medical records, psycho-educational testing, or school records are recommended as helpful documentation. We suggest that the documentation includes the following information: Credentials and contact information of the
With general application: No
To receive services after enrolling: Yes
What documentation required for ASD: To register with Disability Services, medical records, psycho-educational testing, or school records are recommended as helpful documentation. We suggest that the documentation includes the following information: Credentials and contact information of the
With general application: No
To receive services after enrolling: Yes
LD/ADHD/ASD documentation submitted to: Disability Services for Students
ASD Specific Program: NR
Special Ed. HS course work accepted: NR
Specific course requirements of all applicants: Yes
Separate application required for program services: Yes
Total # of students receiving LD/ADHD/ASD services: NR
Acceptance into program means acceptance into college: No

ADMISSIONS

Admissions criteria are the same for all applicants. However, consideration will be given to students who do not meet the general admissions criteria. General admission criteria include 22 on the ACT or 1540 on the SAT; ranking in the upper half of the class; and a 2.5 GPA, and successful completion of college prep program requirements. Disability Services will act as an advocate for students with learning disabilities during the admission process. Applicants not meeting admission criteria may request and receive a review of their eligibility by an Admissions Committee. Students should send documentation verifying the disability directly to the DSS office. The documentation should be written by a qualified professional and must include a diagnostic statement identifying the disability, a description of the diagnostic methodology, and the current functional limitations of the disability, the severity and longevity of the condition, and recommended modifications.

ADDITIONAL INFORMATION

Campus resources include academic and career advising, a study skill course, tutoring, math and writing centers, honors college, Student Fitness Center and outdoor programs, financial aid, housing, leadership development, diversity programs, health services including counseling, dental, and medical, and dietary and nutrition services.

General Support Services Information

Contact Information
Name of program or department: Disability Services for Students
Telephone: 406-243-2243
Fax: 406-243-5330
Website: www.umt.edu/disability

Accommodations or Services for Students With Learning Differences

Accommodations are decided upon an individual basis after a thorough review of appropriate, current documentation. The accommodations requests must be supported through the documentation provided and must be logically linked to the current impact of the condition on academic functioning.

Allowed in exams
Calculator: Yes
Dictionary: Yes
Computer: Yes
Spellchecker: Yes
Extended test time: Yes
Scribes: Yes
Proctors: Yes
Oral exams: No
Note-takers: Yes
Support services for students with LD: Yes
Support services for students with ADHD: Yes
Support services for students with ASD: Yes
Distraction-reduced environment: Yes
Tape recording in class: Yes
Electronic texts: Yes
Kurzweil reader: NR
Audio books: Yes
Other assistive technology: Yes
Priority registration: Yes
Added costs of services: No
LD specialists: Yes
ADHD coaching: Yes
ASD specialists: No
Professional tutors: No
Peer tutors: Not Applicable
Max. hours/wk. for services: NR
How professors are notified of student approved accommodations: By student

General Admissions Information

Office of Admissions: 243-6266

Entrance Requirements

Academic units required: 4 English, 3 math, 2 science, 2 science labs, 3 social studies, 2 history. **Academic units recommended:** 2 foreign language, 2 computer science, 2 visual/performing arts, and 2 units from above areas or other academic areas. High school diploma is required and GED is accepted. SAT or ACT required. If ACT, ACT with writing recommended. TOEFL required of all international applicants: minimum paper TOEFL 525 or minimum internet TOEFL 70.

Application deadline: NR
Notification: Rolling starting 9/15
Average GPA: 3.33
ACT Composite middle 50% range: 20-27
SAT Math middle 50% range: 490-600
SAT Critical Reading middle 50% range: 490-620
SAT Writing middle 50% range: 480-600
Graduate top 10% of class: 18
Graduated top 25% of class: 39
Graduated top 50% of class: 72

COLLEGE GRADUATION REQUIREMENTS

Course waivers allowed: No
In what course: Students can receive assistance with course substitution petition from Disability Services.
Course substitutions allowed: Yes

Additional Information

Environment: This public school was founded in 1893. It has a 220-acre campus.

Student Body
Undergrad enrollment: 10,778
% Women: 54
% Men: 46
% Out-of-state: 26

Cost information
In-state Tuition: $ 4,604
Out-of-state Tuition: $22,720
Room & board: $8,826

Housing Information
University Housing: Yes
Percent living on campus: NR

Greek System
Fraternity: Yes
Sorority: Yes
Athletics: Division I

University of Montana—Western

710 South Atlantic, Dillon, MT 59725
Phone: 406-683-7331 • Fax: 406-683-7493
E-mail: admissions@umwestern.edu • Web: www.umwestern.edu
Support: S • Institution: Public

Programs or Services for Students with Learning Differences

The U of Montana, Western strives to accommodate all students with special needs. These needs may be physical, social, and/or academic. Almost all services are free to the student. Both the Dean of Students and the Student Affairs Offices are in charge of making special accommodations available to students with learning disabilities. If an applicant has a documented learning disability and requests special accommodations for a class, he or she must contact the Associate Dean of Students so that arrangements can be made. The professor of the class, the Associate Dean, and the student will meet to set up an IEP for that class, and documentation will be kept on file in the Student Life Office.

Admission Information for Students with Learning Differences

College entrance tests required: Yes
Interview required: No
Essay required: No
Additional Application Required for LD/ADHD/ASD: NR
What documentation required for LD: Psycho ed evaluation to include: relevant historical info, instructional interventions, related services, age diagnosed, objective data (aptitude, achievement, info processing), test scores (standard, percentile and grade equivalents) and describe functional limitations.
With general application: No
To receive services after enrolling: Yes
What documentation required for ADHD: Diagnosis based on DSM-V; history of behaviors impairing functioning in academic setting; diagnostic interview; history of symptoms; evidence of ongoing behaviors.
With general application: No
To receive services after enrolling: Yes
What documentation required for ASD: Psycho ed evaluation
With general application: NR
To receive services after enrolling: Yes
LD/ADHD/ASD documentation submitted to: Disability Services
ASD Specific Program: NR
Special Ed. HS course work accepted: Yes
Specific course requirements of all applicants: Yes
Separate application required: No
Total # of students receiving LD/ADHD/ASD services: 21
Acceptance into program means acceptance into college: Students must be admitted to and enrolled in the university first and then request services.

Admissions

The college has no special requirements other than those outlined by the state Board of Regents: a valid high school diploma or GED. Criteria for general admission includes 4 years of English, 3 years of math, 3 years of science, 3 years of social studies, and 2 years from foreign language, computer science, visual/performing arts, or vocational education; a 2.5 GPA (minimum 2.0 for students with learning disabilities); a 20 ACT or 960 SAT; and ranking within the top 50 percent of the applicant's class. Students with documented learning disabilities may request waivers or substitutions in courses affected by the disability. Because Western Montana is a small university, each individual can set up an admissions plan. There is a 15 percent window of exemption for some students who do not meet admission requirements. These students can be admitted provisionally if they provide satisfactory evidence that they are prepared to pursue successfully the special courses required.

Additional Information

Students who present appropriate documentation may be eligible for some of the following services or accommodations: the use of calculators, dictionaries, computers, or spellcheckers during tests; extended time on tests; distraction-free environments for tests; proctors; scribes; oral exams; note-takers; tape recorders in class; books on tape; and priority registration. The Learning Center offers skill-building classes in reading, writing, and math. These classes do not count toward a student's GPA, but they do for athletic eligibility. Students whose ACT or entrance tests show that they would profit from such instruction will be placed in courses that will best meet their needs and ensure a successful college career. Free tutoring is available in most areas on a drop-in basis and/or at prescribed times. Services and accommodations are available for undergraduate and graduate students.

General Support Services Information

Contact Information
Name of program or department: Disability Services
Telephone: 406-683-7565
Fax: 406-683-7570

Accommodations or Services for Students with Learning Differences

Accommodations are decided upon an individual basis after a thorough review of appropriate, current documentation. The accommodations requested must be supported through the documentation provided and must be logically linked to the current impact of the condition on academic functioning.

Allowed in exams
Calculator: Yes
Dictionary: Yes
Computer: Yes
Spellchecker: Yes
Extended test time: Yes
Scribes: Yes
Proctors: Yes
Oral exams: Yes
Note-takers: Yes
Services for students with LD: Yes
Services for students with ADHD: Yes
Services for students with ASD: Yes
Distraction-reduced environment: Yes
Tape recording in class: Yes
Audio books: NR
Electronic texts: Yes
Kurzweil Reader: No
Other assistive technology: Yes
Priority registration: Yes
Added costs for services: No
LD specialists: No
ADHD coaching: NR
ASD specialists: NR
Professional tutors: 3
Peer tutors: 6
Max. hours/wk. for services: Unlimited
How professors are notified of LD/ADHD: By both student and director

General Admissions Information

Office of Admissions: 406-683-7331

Entrance Requirements

Academic units required: 4 English, 3 math, 2 science, 2 science labs, 3 social studies, 2 academic electives. High school diploma is required and GED is accepted. SAT or ACT required. If ACT, ACT with writing required. TOEFL required of all international applicants: minimum paper TOEFL 500.

Application deadline: NR
Notification: Rolling starting 9/1
Average GPA: 3.07
ACT Composite middle 50% range: 17-22
SAT Math middle 50% range: 390-530
SAT Critical Reading middle 50% range: 410-520
SAT Writing middle 50% range: NR-NR
Graduated top 10% of class: 4
Graduated top 25% of class: 21
Graduated top 50% of class: 49

COLLEGE GRADUATION REQUIREMENTS

Course waivers allowed: Yes
In what course: General education courses
Course substitutions allowed: Yes
In what course: General education courses

Additional Information

Environment: This public school was founded in 1893. It has a 34-acre campus.

Student Body
Undergrad enrollment: 1,469
% Women: 61
% Men: 39
% Out-of-state: 24

Cost information
In-state Tuition: $3,699
Out-of Tuition: $14,788
Room & board: $6,994

Housing Information
University Housing: Yes
Percent living on campus: 26

Greek System
Fraternity: Yes
Sorority: Yes
Athletics: NAIA

UNIVERSITY OF NEBRASKA—LINCOLN

1410 Q Street, Lincoln, NE 68588-0417
Phone: 402-472-2023 • Fax: 402-472-0670
E-mail: admissions@unl.edu • Web: www.unl.edu
Support: S • Institution: Public

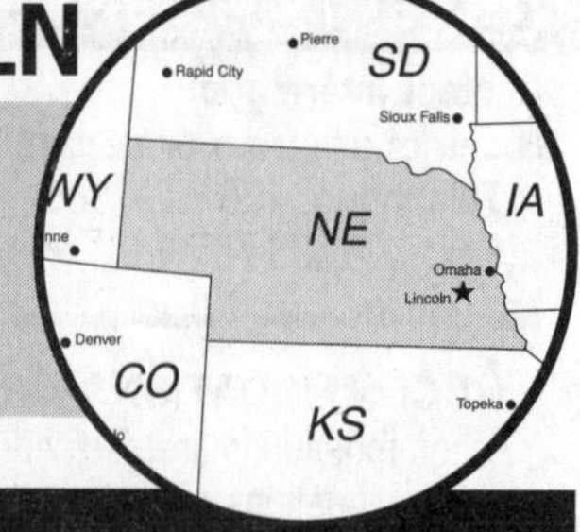

PROGRAMS OR SERVICES FOR STUDENTS WITH LEARNING DIFFERENCES

Services for Students with Disabilities (SSD) office provides special assistance to students with disabilities through individualized help and counseling. Because adjustment to college life and its academic demands is a new experience and there are special challenges confronting disabled students, SSD is committed to providing students with the support that will help them to reach their academic goals. SSD coordinates and delivers the services required to accommodate a disability. All accommodation requests are initiated at the SSD office with appropriate documentation.

ADMISSION INFORMATION FOR STUDENTS WITH LEARNING DIFFERENCES

College entrance test required: Yes
Interview required: No
Essay required: Not Applicable
Additional Application Required for LD/ADHD/ASD: Yes
What documentation required for LD: Psycho ed evaluation
With general application: No
To receive services after enrolling: Yes
What documentation required for ADHD: Psycho ed evaluation
With general application: No
To receive services after enrolling: Yes
What documentation required for ASD: Psycho ed evaluation
With general application: No
To receive services after enrolling: Yes
LD/ADHD/ASD documentation submitted to: Services for Students with Disabilities
ASD Specific Program: NR
Special Ed. HS course work accepted: No
Specific course requirements of all applicants: Yes
Separate application required for program services: No
Total # of students receiving LD/ADHD/ASD services: NR
Acceptance into program means acceptance into college: No

ADMISSIONS

All students applying for admission to UNL must meet the admission criteria. There is no special admission process for students with disabilities. The following is the current admission requirement: ACT composite score of 20 or higher, or an SAT total score (Critical Reading and Math only) of 950 or higher, or rank in the top half of graduating class along with meeting the following core requirements: 4 units of English (all units must include intensive reading & writing experiences), 4 units of math (algebra, algebra II & geometry are requred for student seeking admission, and one additional unit that builds on a knowledge of algebra), 3 units of social sciences (1 unit drawn from American and/or world history; 1 additional unit drawn from history, American government and/or geography; and a third unit drawn from any social science discipline), 3 units of natural sciences (At least 2 units selected from biology, chemistry, physics, and earth sciences. One of the above units must include laboratory instruction.), and 2 units of foreign language (both units must be in the same language). There is an appeal process for students with disabilities that are deferred admission.

ADDITIONAL INFORMATION

Accommodations are provided in an individualized manner for all students. Reasonable accommodations include: extended time on exams, a quiet distraction-reduced test environment, a reader, a scribe, an interpreter, Braille or large print exams, spelling assistance, the use of a computer or other adaptive equipment for exams, classroom notes, assistive notetaking device, transcriptionist in the classroom, and material in alternative formats which include Braille, and electronic texts. Other services provided include intercampus transportation coordination, priority registration, and assistance with advocacy.

General Support Services Information

Contact Information
Name of program or department: Services for Students with Disabilities
Telephone: 402-472-3787
Fax: 402-472-0080

Accommodations or Services For Students With Learning Differences

Accommodations are decided upon an individual basis after a thorough review of appropriate, current documentation. The accommodations requests must be supported through the documentation provided and must be logically linked to the current impact of the condition on academic functioning.

Allowed in exams
Calculator: Yes
Dictionary: Yes
Computer: Yes
Spellchecker: Yes
Extended test time: Yes
Scribes: Yes
Proctors: No
Oral exams: Yes
Note-takers: Yes
Support services for students with LD: Yes
Support services for students with ADHD: Yes
Support services for students with ASD: Yes
Distraction-reduced environment: Yes
Tape recording in class: Yes
Electronic texts: Yes
Kurzweil reader: NR
Audio books: Yes
Other assistive technology: Yes
Priority registration: Yes
Added costs of services: NR
LD specialists: No
ADHD coaching: No
ASD specialists: No
Professional tutors: No
Peer tutors: NR
Max. hours/wk. for services: NR
How professors are notified of student approved accommodations: By both student and director

General Admissions Information

Office of Admissions: 402-472-2023

Entrance Requirements

Academic units required: 4 English, 4 math, 3 science, 1 science labs, 2 foreign language, 2 social studies, 1 history. High school diploma is required and GED is accepted. SAT or ACT required. If ACT, ACT with writing accepted. Minimum internet TOEFL 70.

Application deadline: 5/1
Notification: Rolling starting 9/1
Average GPA: NR
ACT Composite middle 50% range: 22-28
SAT Math middle 50% range: 520-660
SAT Critical Reading middle 50% range: 500-640
SAT Writing middle 50% range: NR-NR
Graduate top 10% of class: 24
Graduated top 25% of class: 51
Graduated top 50% of class: 83

COLLEGE GRADUATION REQUIREMENTS

Course waivers allowed: No
Course substitutions allowed: Yes
In what course: Foreign Language

Additional Information

Environment: This public school was founded in 1869. It has a 617-acre campus.

Student Body
Undergrad enrollment: 19,979
% Women: 47
% Men: 53
% Out-of-state: 21

Cost information
Out-of-state Tuition: $20,760
Room & board: $9,961

Housing Information
University Housing: Yes
Percent living on campus: 43

Greek System
Fraternity: Yes
Sorority: Yes
Athletics: Division I

Wayne State College

1111 Main Street, Wayne, NE 68787
Phone: 402-375-7234 • Fax: 402-375-7204
E-mail: admit1@wsc.edu • Web: www.wsc.edu
Support: S • Institution: Public

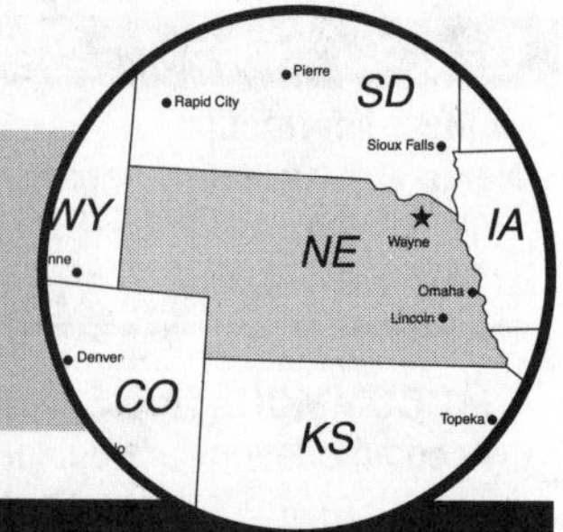

Programs or Services for Students with Learning Differences

At Wayne State College students with learning disabilities and ADHD are provided an individualized, cooperatively planned program of accommodations and services that are structured yet integrated within existing college services and programs. Accommodations are matched to the individual student's needs and are provided free of charge by the Counseling Center. In addition, WSC has a TRIO Student Support Services program known on campus as STRIDE. STRIDE (Students Taking Responsibility In Development and Education) is a program of student support services that includes individual attention, academic and personal support. STRIDE services help new students adjust more quickly and fully to college life. Students with disabilities are one of the populations eligible for STRIDE. STRIDE expects students to place a high priority on academic performance, invest the time and effort needed for college level learning, and take advantage of the services and programs available. Students with LD or ADD must complete a special application for STRIDE and submit written information, which verifies the disability diagnosis.

Admission Information for Students with Learning Differences

College entrance tests required: Yes
Interview required: No
Essay required: N/A
Additional Application Required for LD/ADHD/ASD: NR
What documentation required for LD: Psycho ed evaluation to include: relevant historical info, instructional interventions, related services, age diagnosed, objective data (aptitude, achievement, info processing), test scores (standard, percentile and grade equivalents) and describe functional limitations.
With general application: No
To receive services after enrolling: Yes
What documentation required for ADHD: Diagnosis based on DSM-V; history of behaviors impairing functioning in academic setting; diagnostic interview; history of symptoms; evidence of ongoing behaviors.
With general application: No
To receive services after enrolling: Yes
What documentation required for ASD: Psycho ed evaluation
With general application: NR
To receive services after enrolling: Yes
LD/ADHD/ASD documentation submitted to: Support Program/Services
ASD Specific Program: NR
Special Ed. HS course work accepted: Yes
Specific course requirements for all applicants: NR
Separate application required for program services: No
Total # of students receiving LD/ADHD/ASD services: 25
Acceptance into program means acceptance into college: Students must be admitted to and enrolled in the university first and then request services.

Admissions

Admission to Wayne State College is open to all high school graduates or students with a GED or equivalent. The college recommends that students take four years of English, three years of math, three years of social studies, and two years of science. Foreign language is not an entrance or graduation requirement. High school special education courses are accepted.

Additional Information

Through the STRIDE Program students have access to the following personal support services: a summer STRIDE pre-college experience, STRIDE peer mentor program, academic, and personal and career counseling; and academic support services including: academic advising and course selection guidance, a Succeeding in College course, one-on-one peer tutoring, writing skills, professional tutoring, individual study skills assistance in time management and organization, note-taking, study techniques and test taking strategies. The Counseling Center Office provides a cooperatively planned program of disability-related services and accommodations, which include: assistance in arranging accommodations, tape recorded textbooks and materials, and alternative exam arrangements.

General Support Services Information

Contact Information
Name of program or department: Counseling Center
Telephone: 402-375-7321
Fax: 402-375-7058

Accommodations or Services for Students with Learning Differences

Accommodations are decided upon an individual basis after a thorough review of appropriate, current documentation. The accommodations requested must be supported through the documentation provided and must be logically linked to the current impact of the condition on academic functioning.

Allowed in exams
Calculator: Yes
Dictionary: Yes
Computer: Yes
Spellchecker: Yes
Extended test time: Yes
Scribes: Yes
Proctors: Yes
Oral exams: Yes
Note-takers: Yes
Services for students with LD: Yes
Services for students with ADHD: Yes
Services for students with ASD: Yes
Distraction-reduced environment: Yes
Tape recording in class: Yes
Audio books: NR
Electronic texts: Yes
Kurzweil Reader: Yes
Other assistive technology: Kurzweil Program
Priority registration: Yes
Added costs for services: No
LD specialists: No
ADHD coaching: NR
ASD specialists: NR
Professional tutors: No
Peer tutors: 35
Max. hours/wk. for services: Unlimited
How professors are notified of LD/ADHD: Student

General Admissions Information

Office of Admissions: 402-375-7234

Entrance Requirements

Academic units recommended: 4 English, 3 math, 2 science, 2 foreign language, 3 social studies, 2 computer science, 2 visual/performing arts. High school diploma is required and GED is accepted. SAT or ACT recommended. If ACT, ACT with writing accepted. TOEFL required of all international applicants: minimum paper TOEFL 550.

Application deadline: NR
Notification: Rolling starting 9/15
Average GPA: 2.53
ACT Composite middle 50% range: 18-25
SAT Math middle 50% range: NR-NR
SAT Critical Reading middle 50% range: NR-NR
SAT Writing middle 50% range: NR-NR
Graduated top 10% of class: 9
Graduated top 25% of class: 29
Graduated top 50% of class: 59

COLLEGE GRADUATION REQUIREMENTS

Course waivers allowed: No
In what course: No foreign language requirement.
Course substitutions allowed: No
In what course: NR

Additional Information

Environment: This public school was founded in 1909. It has a 128-acre campus.

Student Body
Undergrad enrollment: 2,969
% Women: 57
% Men: 43
% Out-of-state: 13

Cost information
In-state Tuition: $347 per credit
Out-of-state Tuition: $795.20 per credit
Room & board: NR

Housing Information
University Housing: Yes
Percent living on campus: 46

Greek System
Fraternity: Yes
Sorority: Yes
Athletics: Division II

University of Nevada—Las Vegas

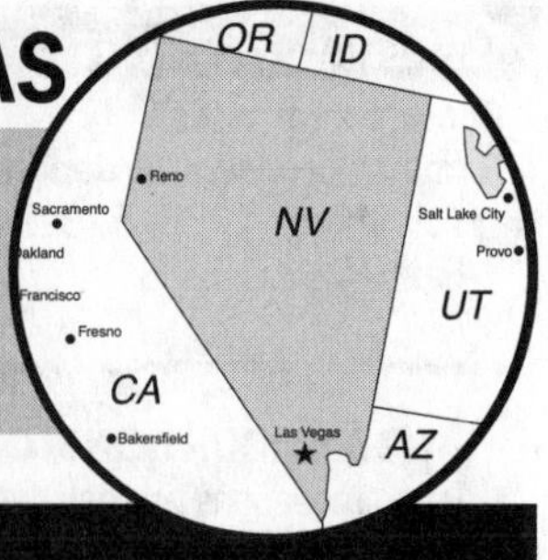

4505 Maryland Parkway, Las Vegas, NV 89154-1021
Phone: 702-774-8658 • Fax: 702-774-8008
E-mail: Undergraduate.Recruitment@ccmail.nevada.edu
Web: www.unlv.edu • Support: CS • Institution: Public

Programs or Services for Students with Learning Differences

The Disability Resource Center (DRC) provides academic accommodations for students with documented disabilities who are otherwise qualified for university programs. Compliance with Section 504 requires that reasonable academic accommodations be made for students with disabilities. These accommodations might include note-taking, testing accommodations, books on tape, readers, assistive technology, housing adjustments and dietary adjustments. To establish services, students will need to provide DRC with appropriate documentation of their disability. Appropriate accommodations will be determined after both a review of the reporting student's documentation of a disability as well as a discussion with that student to clarify his or her disability related needs.

Admission Information for Students with Learning Differences

College entrance tests required: No
Interview required: No
Essay required: N/A
Additional Application Required for LD/ADHD/ASD: NR
What documentation required for LD: Pyscho-educational evaluation (no more than three years old or done as an adult)
With general application: NR
To receive services after enrolling: Yes
What documentation required for ADHD: Same as above.
With general application: NR
To receive services after enrolling: Yes
What documentation required for ASD: Psycho ed evaluation
With general application: NR
To receive services after enrolling: Yes
LD/ADHD/ASD documentation submitted to: Support Program/Services
ASD Specific Program: NR
Special Ed. HS course work accepted: No
Specific course requirements for all applicants: Yes
Separate application required for program services: No
Total # of students receiving LD/ADHD/ASD services: 96 LD; 76 ADHD
Acceptance into program means acceptance into college: Any student attending classes at UNLV who has a documented disability may apply for accommodations through the Learning Enhancement Services.

Admissions

All applicants are expected to meet the same admission criteria. Freshmen applicants should have a weighted 3.0 grade point average (GPA) in the following high school academic courses: 4 years English, 3 years math, 3 years social science, and 3 years natural science with a total of 13 units. If a student has completed the 13 core high school courses but does not have a 3.0 GPA the student may fulfill any of the following admission requirements to be admissible to UNLV: Have a combined score from the SAT Critical Reading and Math sections of at least 1040, or an ACT composite score of at least 22, or a Nevada Advanced High School Diploma. If the applicant does not satisfy the minimum admission requirements the student may still be eligible for admission.

Additional Information

The Disability Resource Center offers help to all students on campus who have a diagnosed disability. Following their evaluation students meet with DRC specialists to develop a plan for services. Psychological services are available through the Counseling and Psychological Services Office. Assistance is provided year round to active students. Students remain active by requesting service each semester. Services are available to undergraduate, graduate, and continuing education students.

General Support Services Information

Contact Information
Name of program or department: Disability Resource Center (DRC)
Telephone: 702-895-0866
Fax: 702-895-0651

Accommodations or Services for Students with Learning Differences

Accommodations are decided upon an individual basis after a thorough review of appropriate, current documentation. The accommodations requested must be supported through the documentation provided and must be logically linked to the current impact of the condition on academic functioning.

Allowed in exams
Calculator: Yes
Dictionary: Yes
Computer: Yes
Spellchecker: Yes
Extended test time: Yes
Scribes: Yes
Proctors: Yes
Oral exams: Yes
Note-takers: Yes
Services for students with LD: Yes
Services for students with ADHD: Yes
Services for students with ASD: Yes
Distraction-reduced environment: Yes
Tape recording in class: Yes
Audio books: NR
Electronic texts: Yes
Kurzweil Reader: Yes
Other assistive technology: Yes
Priority registration: Yes
Added costs for services: No
LD specialists: Yes
ADHD coaching: NR
ASD specialists: NR
Professional tutors: No
Peer tutors: No
Max. hours/wk. for services: N/A
How professors are notified of LD/ADHD: Student

General Admissions Information

Office of Admissions: 702-774-8658

Entrance Requirements

Academic units required: 4 English, 3 math, 3 science, 2 science labs, 3 social studies. High school diploma is required and GED is accepted. SAT or ACT required. If ACT, ACT with writing accepted. TOEFL required of all international applicants: minimum paper TOEFL 500.

Application deadline: 7/1
Notification: 7/1
Average GPA: 3.28
ACT Composite middle 50% range: 18-25
SAT Math middle 50% range: 450-560
SAT Critical Reading middle 50% range: 440-560
SAT Writing middle 50% range: 420-530
Graduated top 10% of class: 23
Graduated top 25% of class: 52
Graduated top 50% of class: 82

COLLEGE GRADUATION REQUIREMENTS

Course waivers allowed: No
Course substitutions allowed: Yes
In what course: Foreign language is only required for English majors; substitutions are available. Math is required for graduation. All requests go to Academic Standards Committee after initial approval from the College Advisor, Chair of the Department, and Dean.

Additional Information

Environment: This public school was founded in 1957. It has a 337-acre campus.

Student Body
Undergrad enrollment: 23,801
% Women: 56
% Men: 44
% Out-of-state: 11.2

Cost information
In-state Tuition: $5,382
Out-of-state Tuition: $19,292
Room & board: NR

Housing Information
University Housing: Yes
Percent living on campus: 6.8

Greek System
Fraternity: Yes
Sorority: Yes
Athletics: Division I

COLBY-SAWYER COLLEGE

541Main Street, New London, NH 03257-7835
Phone: 603-526-3700 • Fax: 603-526-3452
E-mail: admissions@colbysawyer.edu • Web: www.colby-sawyer.edu
Support: CS • Institution: Private

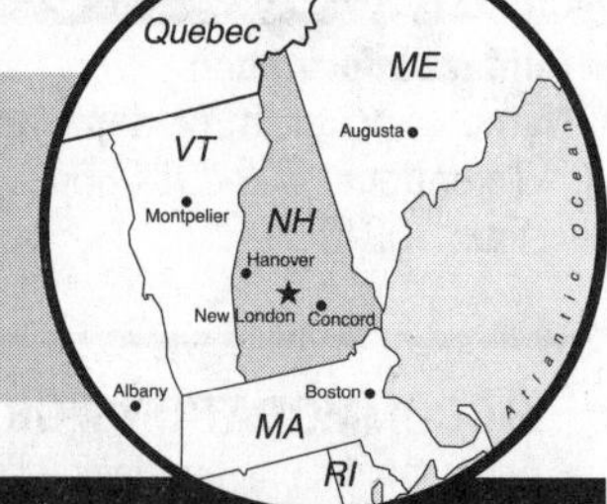

PROGRAMS OR SERVICES FOR STUDENTS WITH LEARNING DIFFERENCES

Students at Colby-Sawyer College are at the center of everything the college does, and the college excels at providing an individualized learning experience. Opportunities for faculty contact and academic support services are plentiful and initiated by the student. The curriculum at Colby-Sawyer College is writing intensive, requires critical reading and thinking skills and quantitative literacy abilities. Students are required to complete an internship related to their major. Colby-Sawyer College does not offer specialized programs for students with learning or any other disabilities. Through Access Resources (AR) Colby-Sawyer has Learning Specialists who provide services to students with documented disabilities. These specialists ensure that students have equal access to the curriculum..

ADMISSION INFORMATION FOR STUDENTS WITH LEARNING DIFFERENCES

College entrance tests required: Optional
Interview required: No
Essay required: Yes
Additional Application Required for LD/ADHD/ASD: NR
What documentation required for LD: Psychoeducational evaluation—aptitude and achievement results
With general application: No
To receive services after enrolling: Yes
What documentation required for ADHD: Diagnostic interview and substantiation and statement of diagnosis
With general application: No
To receive services after enrolling: Yes
What documentation required for ASD: Psycho ed evaluation
With general application: No
To receive services after enrolling: Yes
LD/ADHD/ASD documentation submitted to: Academic Development Center
ASD Specific Program: NR
Special Ed. HS course work accepted: Yes
Specific course requirements of all applicants: Yes
Separate application required: No
Total # of students receiving LD/ADHD/ASD services: 75
Acceptance into program means acceptance into college: Students must be admitted to and enrolled in the university first and then request services.

ADMISSIONS

There is no special admissions process for students with learning disabilities. Access Resources (AR) does not accept disability documentation prior to the student receiving an acceptance to the college and submitting an enrollment deposit. During the application process students do not disclose disability information, however, parents and students may schedule to meet with AR and bring documentation for review prior to acceptance. AR will inform students about what accommodations they can expect to receive and the documentation is returned to the student until enrolled in the college. To apply to the college students must submit one recommendation from either their counselor or a teacher. An essay is also required. Students must have 4 years English, 3 years math, 3 years science, and 3 years social studies. Foreign language is not required for admission. ACT or SAT submission is optional. The average GPA is 3.2.

ADDITIONAL INFORMATION

ADA Accommodations for students with documented disabilities are offered on an individualized basis. These include half-hour weekly meeting with a learning specialist for academic coaching, Live Scribe Echo Pens on loan, access to Kurzweil, and Dragon Naturally Speaking at the Academic Development Center and accommodations for testing. Professors are not required to modify curricular expectations (late submissions of work, modified assignments or exams, use of word banks-if not offered to entire class, etc.) Students need to have good self-advocacy and communication skills, the ability to analyze and synthesize information using college level material, the willingness to attend classes regularly. Well-established independent daily living skills, adequate time management skills supported by weekly meetings with a learning specialist, the willingness to seek tutoring support as needed.

General Support Services Information

Contact Information
Name of program or department: Academic Development Center
Telephone: 603-526-3711
Fax: 603-526-3115

Accommodations or Services for Students with Learning Differences

Accommodations are decided upon an individual basis after a thorough review of appropriate, current documentation. The accommodations requested must be supported through the documentation provided and must be logically linked to the current impact of the condition on academic functioning.

Allowed in exams
Calculator: Yes
Dictionary: Yes
Computer: Yes
Spellchecker: Yes
Extended test time: Yes
Scribes: Yes
Proctors: Yes
Oral exams: No
Note-takers: Yes
Services for students with LD: Yes **Services for students with ADHD:** Yes
Services for students with ASD: Yes
Distraction-reduced environment: Yes
Tape recording in class: Yes
Audio books: NR
Electronic texts: Yes
Kurzweil Reader: Yes
Other assistive technology: Yes
Priority registration: No
Added costs for services: No
LD specialists: Yes
ADHD coaching: Yes
ASD specialists: Yes
Professional tutors: 3–4
Peer tutors: 15–20
Max. hours/wk. for services: 1 hour per class per week plus 3 writing consultations per paper
How professors are notified of LD/ADHD: By student

General Admissions Information

Office of Admissions: 603-526-3700

Entrance Requirements

Academic units recommended: 4 English, 3 math, 3 science, 3 science labs, 2 foreign language, 3 social studies. High school diploma is required and GED is accepted. SAT or ACT required. If ACT, ACT with writing accepted. TOEFL required of all international applicants: minimum paper TOEFL 500.

Application deadline: 4/1
Notification: Rolling starting 1/1
Average GPA: 3
ACT Composite middle 50% range: 18-22
SAT Math middle 50% range: 440-530
SAT Critical Reading middle 50% range: 440-540
SAT Writing middle 50% range: NR-NR
Graduated top 10% of class: NR
Graduated top 25% of class: NR
Graduated top 50% of class: NR

COLLEGE GRADUATION REQUIREMENTS

Course waivers allowed: No
Course substitutions allowed: No

Additional Information

Environment: This private school was founded in 1837. It has a 200-acre campus.

Student Body
Undergrad enrollment: 948
% Women: 65
% Men: 35
% Out-of-state: 68
Cost information
Tuition: $29,620
Room & board: $10,340
Housing Information
University Housing: Yes
Percent living on campus: 90
Greek System
Fraternity: No
Sorority: No
Athletics: Division III

New England College

102 Bridge Street, Henniker, NH 03242
Phone: 603-428-2223 • Fax: 603-428-3155
E-mail: admission@nec.edu • Web: www.nec.edu
Support: CS • Institution: Private

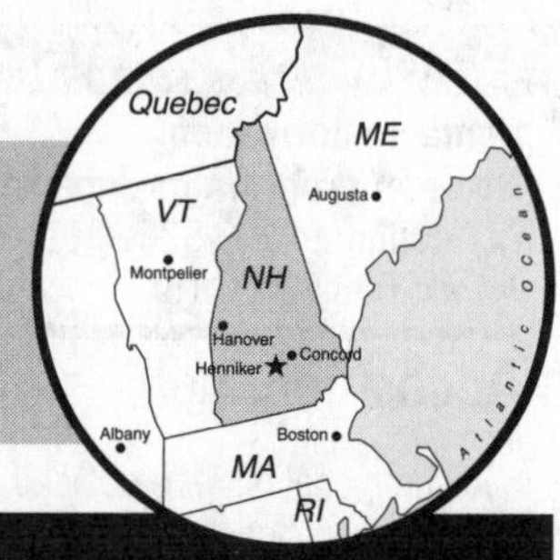

Programs or Services for Students with Learning Differences

Pathways Services provides services for all students in a welcoming and supportive environment. Students come to the center with a variety of academic needs. Some want help writing term papers. Some feel they read too slowly. Others are confused and anxious about their ability to perform as college students. Some students may have learning disabilities. The center provides individual or small group tutoring, academic counseling, and referral services. Tutoring is available in most subject areas. The center focuses primarily on helping students make a successful transition to New England College while supporting all students in their effort to become independent and successful learners. The support services meet the needs of students who do not require a formal, structured program, but who can find success when offered support and advocacy by a trained and experienced staff in conjunction with small classes and personal attention by faculty. Typically, these students have done well in mainstream programs in high school when given assistance. Students with learning disabilities are encouraged to visit NEC and Pathways Services to determine whether the support services will adequately meet their academic needs.

Admission Information for Students with Learning Differences

College entrance tests required: No
Interview required: As requested
Essay required: Required
Additional Application Required for LD/ADHD/ASD: NR
What documentation required for LD: Psycho ed evaluation to include: relevant historical info, instructional interventions, related services, age diagnosed, objective data (aptitude, achievement, info processing), test scores (standard, percentile and grade equivalents) and describe functional limitations.
With general application: No
To receive services after enrolling: Yes
What documentation required for ADHD: Diagnosis based on DSM-V; history of behaviors impairing functioning in academic setting; diagnostic interview; history of symptoms; evidence of ongoing behaviors.
With general application: No
To receive services after enrolling: Yes
What documentation required for ASD: Psycho ed evaluation
With general application: NR
To receive services after enrolling: Yes
LD/ADHD/ASD documentation submitted to: Disability Services
ASD Specific Program: NR
Special Ed. HS course work accepted: College prep courses
Specific course requirements of all applicants: Yes
Separate application required: No
Total % of students receiving LD/ADHD/ASD services: 20
Acceptance into program means acceptance into college: Students must be admitted to and enrolled in the university first and then request services. No special program.

Admissions

Students with learning disabilities submit the general New England College application. Students should have a 2.0 GPA. SAT/ACT results are optional. Course requirements include 4 years of English, 2 years of math, 2 years of science, and 2 years of social studies. Documentation of the learning disability should be submitted. An interview is recommended. Successful applicants have typically done well in mainstream programs in high school when given tutorial and study skills assistance.

Additional Information

Students may elect to use the Pathways Services with regular appointments or only occasionally in response to particular or difficult assignments. The center provides tutoring in content areas; computer facilities; study skills instruction; time management strategies; writing support in planning, editing, and proofreading; referrals to other college services; and one-on-one writing support for first-year students taking WR 101–102. Students are encouraged to use the word processors to generate writing assignments and to use the tutors to help plan and revise papers. The writing faculty works closely with the center to provide coordinated and supportive learning for all students. Professional tutors work with students individually and in small groups. These services are provided in a secure and accepting atmosphere. Currently, 20 percent of the student body has a diagnosed LD, and 10 percent have a diagnosed ADHD.

General Support Services Information

Contact Information
Name of program or department: Disability Services Office
Telephone: 603-428-2218
Fax: 603-428-2433

Accommodations or Services for Students with Learning Differences

Accommodations are decided upon an individual basis after a thorough review of appropriate, current documentation. The accommodations requested must be supported through the documentation provided and must be logically linked to the current impact of the condition on academic functioning.

Allowed in exams
Calculator: Yes
Dictionary: No
Computer: Yes
Spellchecker: Yes
Extended test time: Yes
Scribes: Yes
Proctors: Yes
Oral exams: Yes
Note-takers: Lecture notes
Services for students with LD: Yes
Services for students with ADHD: Yes
Services for students with ASD: Yes
Distraction-reduced environment: Yes
Tape recording in class: Yes
Audio books: NR
Electronic texts: Yes
Kurzweil Reader: No
Other assistive technology: No
Priority registration: No
Added costs for services: No
LD specialists: Yes
ADHD coaching: NR
ASD specialists: NR
Professional tutors: 7–10
Peer tutors: 5–7
Max. hours/wk. for services: 3
How professors are notified of LD/ADHD: Student provides professor with form.

General Admissions Information

Office of Admissions: 603-428-2223

Entrance Requirements

Academic units required: 4 English, 2 math, 2 science, 1 science labs, 2 social studies, **Academic units recommended:** 4 English, 3 math, 3 science, 2 science labs, 2 foreign language, 3 social studies. High school diploma is required and GED is accepted. SAT or ACT considered if submitted. TOEFL required of all international applicants: minimum paper TOEFL 550 or minimum internet TOEFL 13.

Application deadline: 9/1
Notification: Rolling starting 11/1
Average GPA: 3.14
Avg ACT Composite: 23 (20-27
SAT Avg Math: 534 (420-680)
SAT Avg Critical Reading: 507 (420-650
SAT Avg: 493 (430-620)
Graduated top 10% of class: 4
Graduated top 25% of class: 16
Graduated top 50% of class: 48

COLLEGE GRADUATION REQUIREMENTS

Course waivers allowed: No
Course substitutions allowed: No

Additional Information

Environment: This private school was founded in 1946. It has a 225-acre campus.

Student Body
Undergrad enrollment: 1,805
% Women: 59
% Men: 41
% Out-of-state: 83

Cost information
Tuition: $33,966
Room & board: $13,268

Housing Information
University Housing: Yes
Percent living on campus: 34

Greek System
Fraternity: Yes
Sorority: Yes
Athletics: Division III

Rivier University

420 South Main Street, Nashua, NH 03060
Phone: 603-897-8219 • Fax: 603-891-1799
E-mail: rivadmit@rivier.edu • Web: www.rivier.edu
Support: S • Institution: Private

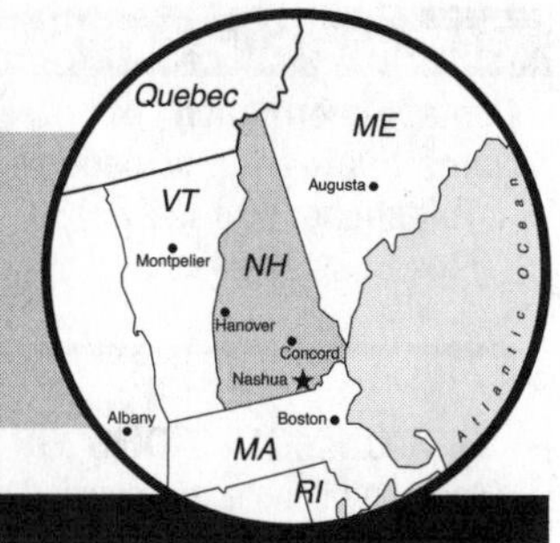

Programs or Services for Students with Learning Differences

Rivier University recognizes that learning styles differ from person to person. The college is committed to providing supports that allow all otherwise qualified individuals with disabilities an equal educational opportunity. Disability Services provides the opportunity for all individuals who meet academic requirements to be provided auxiliary services, facilitating their earning of a college education. To be eligible for support services, students are required to provide appropriate documentation of their disabilities to the coordinator of Disability Services. This documentation shall be provided from a professional in the field of psychoeducational testing or a physician and shall be current (completed within the past 3 to 5 years). This information will be confidential and is kept in the coordinator's office for the purpose of planning appropriate support services. To access services, students must contact the coordinator of Disability Services before the start of each semester to schedule an appointment and provide documentation; together the coordinator and the student will discuss and arrange for support services specifically related to the disability.

Admission Information for Students with Learning Differences

College entrance tests required: Yes **Interview required:** No
Essay required: Yes
Additional Application Required for LD/ADHD/ASD: NR
What documentation required for LD: Psycho ed evaluation to include: relevant historical info, instructional interventions, related services, age diagnosed, objective data (aptitude, achievement, info processing), test scores (standard, percentile and grade equivalents) and describe functional limitations.
With general application: No
To receive services after enrolling: Yes
What documentation required for ADHD: Diagnosis based on DSM-V; history of behaviors impairing functioning in academic setting; diagnostic interview; history of symptoms; evidence of ongoing behaviors.
With general application: No
To receive services after enrolling: Yes
What documentation required for ASD: Psycho ed evaluation
With general application: NR
To receive services after enrolling: Yes
LD/ADHD/ASD documentation submitted to: Disability Services
ASD Specific Program: NR
Special Ed. HS course work accepted: NR
Specific course requirements of all applicants: NR
Separate application required: No
Total # of students receiving LD/ADHD/ASD services: NR
Acceptance into program means acceptance into college: Students must be admitted to and enrolled in the university first and then request services.

Admissions

There is no special admissions process for students with LD. All applicants must meet the same criteria. Students should have a combined SAT of 820, a GPA in the top 80 percent of their graduating class, and take college-prep courses in high school. Courses required include 4 years of English, 2 years of a foreign language (though this may be substituted), 1 year of science, 3 years of math, 2 years of social science, and 4 years of academic electives. Applicants not meeting the general admission requirements may inquire about alternative admissions. The college offers a probational admit option that requires students to maintain a minimum 2.0 GPA their first semester.

Additional Information

Services available include academic, career, and personal counseling; preferential registration; classroom accommodations including tape recording of lectures, extended times for test completion, testing free from distractions, and note-takers; student advocacy; a writing center for individualized instruction in writing; and individualized accommodations as developed by the coordinator of Disability Services with the student. Services and accommodations are available for undergraduate and graduate students.

General Support Services Information

Contact Information
Name of program or department: Disability Services
Telephone: 603-897-8497
Fax: 603-897-8887

Accommodations or Services for Students with Learning Differences

Accommodations are decided upon an individual basis after a thorough review of appropriate, current documentation. The accommodations requested must be supported through the documentation provided and must be logically linked to the current impact of the condition on academic functioning.

Allowed in exams
Calculator: Yes/No
Dictionary: No
Computer: Yes
Spellchecker: Yes/No
Extended test time: Yes
Scribes: Yes
Proctors: Yes
Oral exams: Yes
Note-takers: Yes
Services for students with LD: Yes
Services for students with ADHD: Yes
Services for students with ASD: Yes
Distraction-reduced environment: Yes
Tape recording in class: Yes
Audio books: NR
Electronic texts: Yes
Kurzweil Reader: Yes
Other assistive technology: Yes
Priority registration: Yes
Added costs for services: No
LD specialists: No
ADHD coaching: NR
ASD specialists: NR
Professional tutors: No
Peer tutors: Yes
Max. hours/wk. for services: N/A
How professors are notified of LD/ADHD: By both student and director

General Admissions Information

Office of Admissions: 603-897-8219

Entrance Requirements

Academic units recommended: 4 English, 3 math, 1 science, 1 science labs, 2 foreign language, 2 social studies, 1 history, 3 academic electives. High school diploma is required and GED is accepted. SAT or ACT required. If ACT, ACT with writing recommended. TOEFL required of all international applicants: minimum paper TOEFL 500.

Application deadline: NR
Notification: Rolling starting 11/1
Average GPA: 3.08
ACT Composite middle 50% range: 17-21
SAT Math middle 50% range: 410-510
SAT Critical Reading middle 50% range: 410-510
SAT Writing middle 50% range: 420-520
Graduated top 10% of class: 6
Graduated top 25% of class: 27
Graduated top 50% of class: 71

COLLEGE GRADUATION REQUIREMENTS

Course waivers allowed: No
Course substitutions allowed: Yes
In what course: Each course subtitution is looked at individually.

Additional Information

Environment: This private school, affiliated with the Roman Catholic Church, was founded in 1933. It has a 68-acre campus.

Student Body
Undergrad enrollment: 1,437
% Women: 84
% Men: 16
% Out-of-state: 38

Cost information
Tuition: $25,410
Room & board: $9,798
Housing Information
University Housing: Yes
Percent living on campus: 43

Greek System
Fraternity: No
Sorority: No
Athletics: Division III

University of New Hampshire

UNH Office of Admissions, Durham, NH 03824
Phone: 603-862-1360 • Fax: 603-862-0077
E-mail: admissions@unh.edu • Web: www.unh.edu
Support: CS • Institution: Public

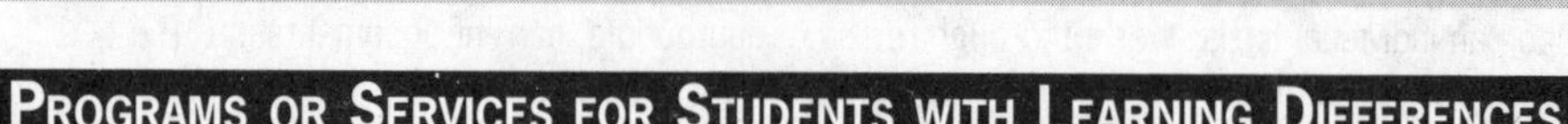

Programs or Services for Students with Learning Differences

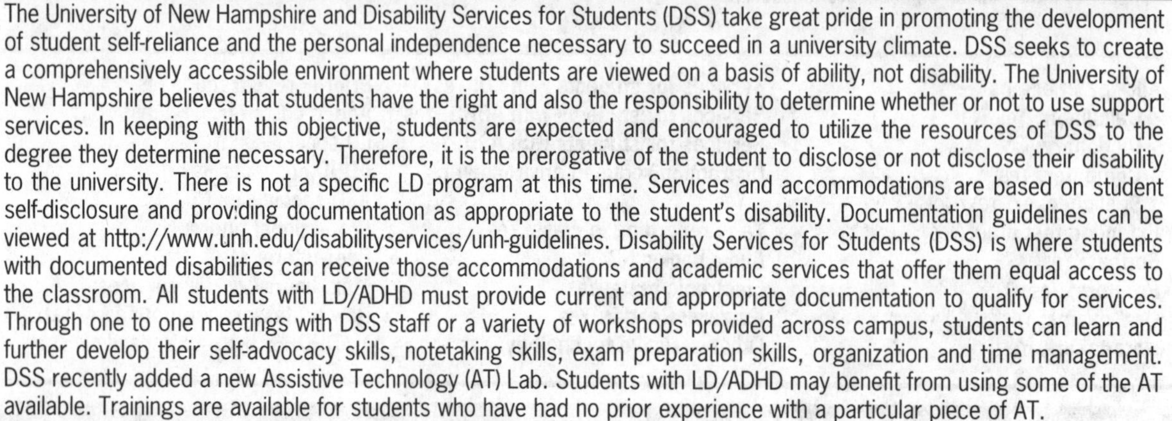

The University of New Hampshire and Disability Services for Students (DSS) take great pride in promoting the development of student self-reliance and the personal independence necessary to succeed in a university climate. DSS seeks to create a comprehensively accessible environment where students are viewed on a basis of ability, not disability. The University of New Hampshire believes that students have the right and also the responsibility to determine whether or not to use support services. In keeping with this objective, students are expected and encouraged to utilize the resources of DSS to the degree they determine necessary. Therefore, it is the prerogative of the student to disclose or not disclose their disability to the university. There is not a specific LD program at this time. Services and accommodations are based on student self-disclosure and providing documentation as appropriate to the student's disability. Documentation guidelines can be viewed at http://www.unh.edu/disabilityservices/unh-guidelines. Disability Services for Students (DSS) is where students with documented disabilities can receive those accommodations and academic services that offer them equal access to the classroom. All students with LD/ADHD must provide current and appropriate documentation to qualify for services. Through one to one meetings with DSS staff or a variety of workshops provided across campus, students can learn and further develop their self-advocacy skills, notetaking skills, exam preparation skills, organization and time management. DSS recently added a new Assistive Technology (AT) Lab. Students with LD/ADHD may benefit from using some of the AT available. Trainings are available for students who have had no prior experience with a particular piece of AT.

Admission Information for Students with Learning Differences

College entrance test required: Yes
Interview required: No
Essay required: Not Applicable
Additional Application Required for LD/ADHD/ASD: Yes
What documentation required for LD: A neuropsychological evaluation or other comprehensive tool to identify impact & needs.
With general application: No
To receive services after enrolling: Yes
What documentation required for ADHD: Best practices within the field
With general application: No
To receive services after enrolling: Yes
What documentation required for ASD: A neuropsychological evaluation or other comprehensive tool to identify impact & needs.
With general application: No
To receive services after enrolling: Yes
LD/ADHD/ASD documentation submitted to: Disability Services for Students
ASD Specific Program: NR
Special Ed. HS course work accepted: NR
Specific course requirements of all applicants: Yes
Separate application required for program services: Yes
Total # of students receiving LD/ADHD/ASD services: 120
Acceptance into program means acceptance into college: No

Admissions

Admissions criteria are the same for all applicants. Typically, students who are admitted to the university are in the top 30 percent of their class, have a B average in college-preparatory courses, and have taken 4 years of college-prep math, 3–4 years of a science lab, and 3–4 years of a foreign language and 3–4 years of social sciences; SAT average range is 1500–1800, ACT average 24, but there are no cutoffs (or equivalent ACT). There are no alternative options for admissions. DSS has no involvement in any admissions decision. However, there is a member of the admissions staff with a background in special education.

Additional Information

The Center for Academic Resources offers academic support to all UNH undergraduate students who are matriculated in 4-year degree programs. They support students in their development of the cognitive-skills and academic-strategies needed to succeed in college. For students with a demonstrated academic need who meet income or disability criteria (as specified in their federal TRIO SSS grant) free peer subject-area tutoring and other learning and enrichment services may be available.

General Support Services Information

Contact Information
Name of program or department: Disability Services for Students
Telephone: 603-862-0830
Fax: 603-862-4043
Website: http://www.unh.edu/disabilityservices

Accommodations or Services For Students With Learning Differences

Accommodations are decided upon an individual basis after a thorough review of appropriate, current documentation. The accommodations requests must be supported through the documentation provided and must be logically linked to the current impact of the condition on academic functioning.

Allowed in exams
Calculator: Yes
Dictionary: Yes
Computer: Yes
Spellchecker: Yes
Extended test time: Yes
Scribes: Yes
Proctors: Yes
Oral exams: Yes
Note-takers: Yes
Support services for students with LD: Yes
Support services for students with ADHD: Yes
Support services for students with ASD: Yes
Distraction-reduced environment: Yes
Tape recording in class: Yes
Electronic texts: Yes
Kurzweil reader: NR
Audio books: Yes
Other assistive technology: Not Applicable
Priority registration: Yes
Added costs of services: No
LD specialists: NR
ADHD coaching: No
ASD specialists: No
Professional tutors: No
Peer tutors: NR
Max. hours/wk. for services: NR
How professors are notified of student approved accommodations: By director

General Admissions Information

Office of Admissions: 603-862-1360

Entrance Requirements

Academic units required: 4 English, 3 math, 3 science, 2 science labs, 2 foreign language, 3 social studies.
Academic units recommended: 4 English, 4 math, 4 science, 3 science labs, 3 foreign language, 3 social studies, 1 visual/performing arts. High school diploma is required and GED is accepted. SAT or ACT required. If ACT, ACT with writing required. TOEFL required of all international applicants: minimum paper TOEFL 550 or minimum internet TOEFL 80.

Application deadline: 2/1
Notification: Rolling starting 1/15
Average GPA: 3.39
ACT Composite middle 50% range: 22-27
SAT Math middle 50% range: 500-610
SAT Critical Reading middle 50% range: 500-600
SAT Writing middle 50% range: 490-590
Graduate top 10% of class: 18
Graduated top 25% of class: 45
Graduated top 50% of class: 86

COLLEGE GRADUATION REQUIREMENTS

Course waivers allowed: No
Course substitutions allowed: Yes
In what course: May be substitution of courses for a foreign language requirement.

Additional Information

Environment: This public school was founded in 1866. It has a 2600-acre campus.

Student Body
Undergrad enrollment: 13,034
% Women: 54
% Men: 46
% Out-of-state: 53

Cost information
In-state Tuition: $17,624
Out-of-state Tuition: $31,424
Room & board: $10,938

Housing Information
University Housing: Yes
Percent living on campus: 56

Greek System
Fraternity: Yes
Sorority: Yes
Athletics: Division I

CALDWELL COLLEGE

9 Ryerson Avenue, Caldwell, NJ 07006-6195
Phone: 973-618-3500 • Fax: 973-618-3600
E-mail: admissions@caldwell.edu • Web: www.caldwell.edu
Support: CS • Institution: Private

PROGRAMS OR SERVICES FOR STUDENTS WITH LEARNING DIFFERENCES

The Office of Disability Services at Caldwell College is a dedicated office for students with documented disabilities that arranges for reasonable and appropriate accommodations for eligible students. The departments that comprise Academic Services are the cornerstone of Caldwell University's commitment to educational achievement. The primary mission is to attend to the holistic needs of Caldwell University students by integrating advisement, academic support and career counseling. Academic Services aspires to support and empower students from matriculation to graduation and beyond. The Academic Services departments are also committed to the ongoing improvement of the quality, accessibility and consistency of the programmatic offerings and academic support services rendered to all students, regardless of their level of preparedness. Guided by Caldwell's core values of respect, integrity, community and excellence, Academic Services supports and extends the University's mission to develop lifelong learners.

ADMISSION INFORMATION FOR STUDENTS WITH LEARNING DIFFERENCES

College entrance tests required: Yes
Interview required: No
Essay required: No
Additional Application Required for LD/ADHD/ASD: NR
What documentation required for LD: Psycho ed evaluation to include: relevant historical info, instructional interventions, related services, age diagnosed, objective data (aptitude, achievement, info processing), test scores (standard, percentile and grade equivalents) and describe functional limitations.
With general application: No
To receive services after enrolling: Yes
What documentation required for ADHD: Diagnosis based on DSM-V; history of behaviors impairing functioning in academic setting; diagnostic interview; history of symptoms; evidence of ongoing behaviors.
With general application: No
To receive services after enrolling: Yes
What documentation required for ASD: Psycho ed evaluation
With general application: NR
To receive services after enrolling: Yes
LD/ADHD/ASD documentation submitted to: Office of Disability Services
ASD Specific Program: NR
Special Ed. HS course work accepted: Yes
Specific course requirements of all applicants: Yes
Separate application required: No
Total # of students receiving LD/ADHD/ASD services: NR
Acceptance into program means acceptance into college: Students must be admitted to and enrolled in the university first and then request services.

ADMISSIONS

The average GPA is a 3.3 on a 4.0 scale, or a B average. Admissions looks for the completion of sixteen college prep courses, which should include: four years of English, two years of foreign language, two years of college prep mathematics, two years of science (one must be a lab science), one year of history, and other college prep courses. A student who has sixteen units but has not satisfied all the prerequisites may be admitted on the recommendation of the Committee on Admissions provided evidence is given of ability to pursue college work. ACT or SAT is required and the mid-50% range for SAT 900-1150 (Math and Critical Reading sections only). The equivalent in ACT terms would be 19-24. At least two written recommendations are required. Students should submit a graded essay/term paper written in the last year or submit a response to one of the provided questions. (If students complete the Common Application, the essay included on the Common Application will fulfill this requirement): Caldwell has partnered with ZeeMee, a free service that helps students bring their application to life. As part of a holistic review, Caldwell is committed to learning about the person behind the application. Students would simply copy and paste their ZeeMee digital portfolio link into the Caldwell University application.

ADDITIONAL INFORMATION

Individual and group tutoring in most academic subjects are available on a scheduled basis. Many drop-in sessions are also offered. Skill-specific workshops are presented regularly to help students develop and improve their study habits and writing techniques. The Writing Center staffed by professional and peer tutors, has regular hours for drop-in assistance. Students may be referred to the Academic Success Center by their professors for skill reinforcement, or they may arrange for their own tutoring by completing the form available in the Academic Success Center.

General Support Services Information

Contact Information
Name of program or department: Office of Disability Services/Learning Center
Telephone: 973-618-3645
Fax: 973-618-3488

Accommodations or Services for Students with Learning Differences

Accommodations are decided upon an individual basis after a thorough review of appropriate, current documentation. The accommodations requested must be supported through the documentation provided and must be logically linked to the current impact of the condition on academic functioning.

Allowed in exams
Calculator: Yes
Dictionary: Yes
Computer: Yes
Spellchecker: Yes
Extended test time: Yes
Scribes: Yes
Proctors: Yes
Oral exams: Yes
Note-takers: Yes

Services for students with LD: Yes
Services for students with ADHD: Yes
Services for students with ASD: Yes
Distraction-reduced environment: Yes
Tape recording in class: Yes
Audio books: NR
Electronic texts: Yes
Kurzweil Reader: Yes
Other assistive technology: Yes
Priority registration: No

Added costs for services: No
LD specialists: Yes
ADHD coaching: NR
ASD specialists: NR
Professional tutors: 5
Peer tutors: 30–40
Max. hours/wk. for services: Unlimited
How professors are notified of LD/ADHD: By both student and director

General Admissions Information

Office of Admissions: 973-618-3500

Entrance Requirements

Academic units required: 4 English, 2 mathematics, 2 science, (1 science labs), 2 foreign language, 1 history, 5 academic electives. High school diploma is required and GED is accepted. SAT or ACT required. TOEFL required of all international applicants: minimum paper TOEFL 500.

Application deadline: 4/1
Notification: NR
Average GPA: NR
ACT Composite middle 50% range: NR-NR

SAT Math middle 50% range: NR-NR
SAT Critical Reading middle 50% range: NR-NR
SAT Writing middle 50% range: NR-NR

Graduated top 10% of class: NR
Graduated top 25% of class: NR
Graduated top 50% of class: NR

COLLEGE GRADUATION REQUIREMENTS

Course waivers allowed: No
Course substitutions allowed: Yes
In what course: Students may receive substitutions in foreign language if documentation supports the need for it.

Additional Information

Environment: The campus is located 10 miles from Newark, New Jersey and 20 miles from New York City.

Student Body
Undergrad enrollment: 1,595
% Women: 70
% Men: 30
% Out-of-state: NR

Cost information
Tuition: $29,950
Room & board: NR
Housing Information
University Housing: Yes
Percent living on campus: 26

Greek System
Fraternity: No
Sorority: No
Athletics: Division II

Fairleigh Dickinson University—Florham Campus

285 Madison Avenue, Madison, NJ 07940
Phone: 800-338-8803 • Fax: 973-443-8088
E-mail: globaleducation@fdu.edu • Web: www.fdu.edu
Support: SP • Institution: Private

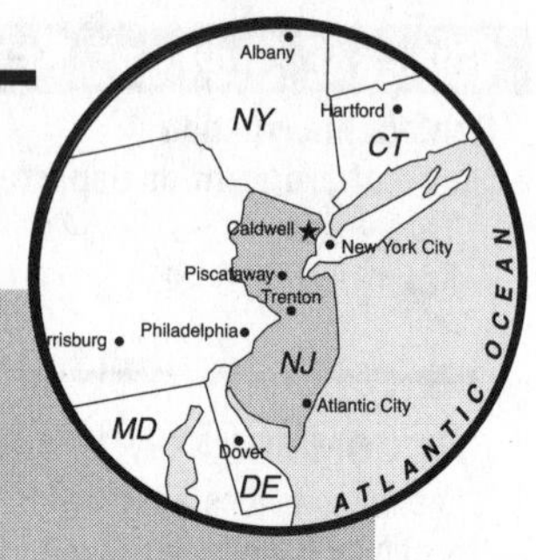

Programs or Services for Students with Learning Differences

The Regional Center for College Students with Learning Disabilities offers a structured plan of intensive advisement, academic support, and counseling services that is tailored to the unique needs of students with LD. The goal is to provide a framework within which college students identified with "Specific Learning Disabilities" will develop the confidence to succeed in their studies and the independence to do their best. Planning, learning strategies, professional tutors, counseling, and accommodations are the cornerstones of the Regional Center. Staffed by professionals with services at both the Metropolitan Campus and the Campus of Florham, the LD program and special services are free of charge. Assistance to students is intensive and the program is fully integrated into the coursework. Students are in touch with faculty on a regular basis. The program encourages involvement in the community, particularly service-type activities relevant to the students with LD. Performance data are routinely reviewed to identify students in need of more intensive help. Upon admission students are invited to attend a summer orientation session. During this time, students meet with center staff to develop an Individual Academic Plan in order to develop a class schedule with the right balance. For more information, visit www.fdu.edu/rcsld

Admission Information for Students with Learning Differences

College entrance test required: Yes
Interview required: No
Essay required: NR
Additional Application Required for LD/ADHD/ASD: NR
What documentation required for LD: Psycho-educational Evaluation: WAIS III, Woodcock- Johnson III, WIAT
With general application: No
To receive services after enrolling: Yes
What documentation required for ADHD: N/A to Regional Center Program
With general application: No
To receive services after enrolling: Yes
What documentation required for ASD: Psycho ed evaluation
With general application: No
To receive services after enrolling: Yes
LD/ADHD/ASD documentation submitted to: Support program/services
ASD Specific Program: NR
Special Ed. HS course work accepted: Yes
Specific course: Yes
Separate application required for program services: Yes
Total # of students receiving LD/ADHD/ASD services: 165
Acceptance into program means acceptance into college: NR

Admissions

Admissions decisions are made independently by FDU Admissions and the LD Program Admissions Directors. Students must be admitted to the university before applications can be reviewed by the Regional Center. Criteria include documentation of a primary diagnosis of a language based learning disability made by licensed professionals dated within 24 months of the application; evidence of adequate performance in mainstream college-prep high school courses; and evidence of motivation as reflected in recommendations. Students enrolled solely in special education high school classes are usually not admissible. Lower level mainstream classes are acceptable from high schools offering different levels in the same subjects. ACT/SAT are required but are secondary to the above criteria. Previous school achievement and positive recommendations are viewed as the best predictors for success. Students with a 2.5 GPA and 850 SAT can be accepted. General admissions require performance in the top 2/5 of class or "B" average. If applicants are below a 2.5 GPA they may be referred to the Petrocelli College Program which maintains a 2-year associates degree program on the Metropolitan Campus in Teaneck. Admission decisions are made after careful review.

Additional Information

Fairleigh Dickinson University maintains two campuses in New Jersey. The Metropolitan Campus for Professional and International Studies, situated in Bergen county, less than 10 miles from New York City. The College at Florham is located in suburban Morris County, New Jersey. Both campuses offer the services of the Regional Center. There is an additional opportunity for students desiring a two year degree via the Edwards William Program available through New College at the Metropolitan Campus.

General Support Services Information

Contact Information
Name of program or department: Office of Disability Support Services
Telephone: 973-443-8079
Fax: 201-692-2813

Accommodations or Services for Students with Learning Differences

Accommodations are decided upon an individual basis after a thorough review of appropriate, current documentation. The accommodations requests must be supported through the documentation provided and must be logically linked to the current impact of the condition on academic functioning.

Allowed in exams
Calculator: Yes
Dictionary: Yes
Computer: Yes
Spellchecker: Yes
Extended test time: Yes
Scribes: No
Proctors: Yes
Oral exams: Yes
Note-takers: No
Services for students with LD: Yes
Services for students with ADHD: No
Services for students with ASD: Yes
Distraction-reduced environment: Yes
Tape recording in class: Yes
Audio books: No
Electronic texts: NR
Kurzweil Reader: Yes
Other assistive technology: Yes
Priority registration: Yes
Added costs of services: No
LD specialists: Yes
ADHD coaching: NR
ASD specialists: NR
Professional tutors: Yes
Peer tutors: No
Max. hours/wk. for services: 4
How professors are notified of student approved accommodations: Both student and director

General Admissions Information

Office of Admissions: 800-338-8803

Entrance Requirements

Academic units required: 4 English, 3 math, 2 science, 2 science labs, 2 history, 3 academic electives. **Academic units recommended:** 4 English, 3 math, 3 science, 2 science labs, 2 foreign language, 2 history, 4 academic electives. High school diploma is required and GED is accepted. SAT or ACT required. If ACT, ACT with writing accepted. TOEFL required of all international applicants: minimum paper TOEFL 550 or minimum internet TOEFL 79.

Application deadline: NR
Notification: NR
Average GPA: 3.1
ACT Composite middle 50% range: NR-NR
SAT Math middle 50% range: 460-570
SAT Critical Reading middle 50% range: 450-560
SAT Writing middle 50% range: 460-560
Graduated top 10% of class: 14
Graduated top 25% of class: 36
Graduated top 50% of class: 75

COLLEGE GRADUATION REQUIREMENTS

Course waivers allowed: No
Course substitutions allowed: Yes
In what course: Mathematics and foreign language substitutions are available if appropriate to students with LD enrolled in the Center.

Additional Information

Environment: This private school was founded in 1942. It has a 178-acre campus.

Student Body
Undergrad enrollment: 2,396
% Women: 55
% Men: 45
% Out-of-state: 16
Cost information
Tuition: $36,386
Room & board: $12,294
Housing Information
University Housing: Yes
Percent living on campus: 62.6
Greek System
Fraternity: Yes
Sorority: Yes
Athletics: Division III

Fairleigh Dickinson University—Metropolitan Campus

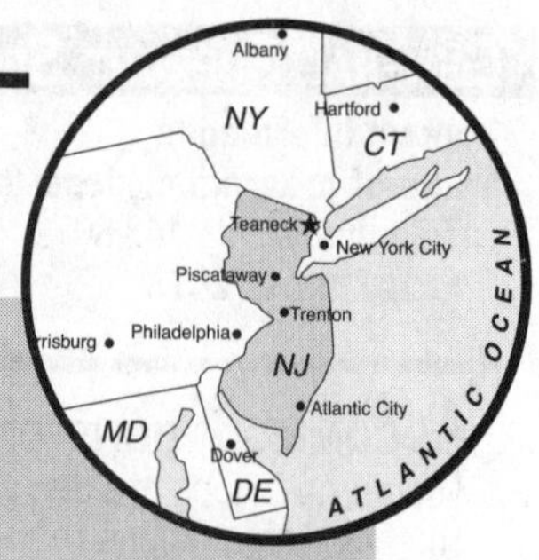

1000 River Road, Teaneck, NJ 07666-1966
Phone: 201-692-2087 • Fax: 201-692-7319
E-mail: globaleducation@fdu.edu • Web: www.fdu.edu
Support: SP • Institution: Private

Programs or Services for Students with Learning Differences

The Regional Center for College Students with LD offers a structured plan of intensive advisement, academic support, and counseling services tailored to the unique needs of students with language-based disabilities. The goal is to provide a framework within which college students identified with "Specific Learning Disabilities" will develop the confidence to succeed in their studies and the independence to do their best. Planning, learning strategies, professional tutors, counseling, and accommodations are the cornerstones of the Regional Center. Staffed by professionals at the Metropolitan Campus and the Campus of Florham, the LD program and special services are free. Assistance is intensive and the program fully integrated into the course work. Performance data is routinely reviewed to identify students in need of more intensive help. Upon admission students are invited to attend a summer orientation session.

Admission Information for Students with Learning Differences

College entrance tests required: Yes
Interview required: No
Essay required: NR
Additional Application Required for LD/ADHD/ASD: NR
What documentation required for LD: Psycho ed evaluation to include: relevant historical info, instructional interventions, related services, age diagnosed, objective data (aptitude, achievement, info processing), test scores (standard, percentile and grade equivalents) and describe functional limitations.
With general application: Yes if requested as part of Structured Program application
To receive services after enrolling: Yes
What documentation required for ADHD: Diagnosis based on DSM-V; history of behaviors impairing functioning in academic setting; diagnostic interview; history of symptoms; evidence of ongoing behaviors.
With general application: NR
To receive services after enrolling: Yes
What documentation required for ASD: Psycho ed evaluation
With general application: NR
To receive services after enrolling: Yes
LD/ADHD/ASD documentation submitted to: Support Program/Services
ASD Specific Program: NR
Special Ed. HS course work accepted: Yes
Specific course requirements for all applicants: Yes
Separate application required for program services: Yes
Total # of students receiving LD/ADHD/ASD services: 150
Acceptance into program means acceptance into college: Students must first be admitted to the University before a Regional Center application is reviewed for admission to the program.

Admissions

Admissions decisions are made independently by FDU Admissions and the LD Program Admissions Directors. Students must be admitted to the university before applications can be reviewed by the Regional Center. Criteria include documentation of a primary diagnosis of a language-based learning disability made by licensed professionals dated within 24 months of the application; evidence of adequate performance in mainstream college-prep high school courses; and evidence of motivation as reflected in recommendations. Students enrolled solely in special education high school classes are usually not admissible. Lower level mainstream classes are acceptable from high schools offering different levels in the same subjects. ACT/SAT required but are secondary to the above criteria. Previous school achievement and positive recommendations are viewed as the best predictors for success. Students with a 2.5 GPA and 850 SAT can be accepted. General admissions require performance in the top two-fifths of class or B average. If applicants have a GPA below a 2.5, they may be referred to the Petrocelli College Program, which maintains a two-year associate's degree program on the Metropolitan Campus in Teaneck.

Additional Information

Students with a language-based learning disability enrolled at both the Metropolitan and Florham campuses during their undergraduate career are provided comprehensive professional support free of charge. Students are provided with structured plans of intensive academic support and counseling services specific to the unique learning needs of each student. Freshman can receive up to four support sessions a week per semester, sophomores three supports a semester, juniors and seniors one or two supports per semester.

General Support Services Information

Contact Information
Name of program or department: Office of the Provost
E-Mail: mourton@fdu.edu
Telephone: 201-692-2460

Accommodations or Services for Students with Learning Differences

Accommodations are decided upon an individual basis after a thorough review of appropriate, current documentation. The accommodations requested must be supported through the documentation provided and must be logically linked to the current impact of the condition on academic functioning.

Allowed in exams
Calculator: Yes
Dictionary: No
Computer: Yes
Spellchecker: Yes
Extended test time: Yes
Scribes: No
Proctors: Yes
Oral exams: Yes
Note-takers: No
Services for students with LD: Yes
Services for students with ADHD: No
Services for students with ASD: Compass Program
Distraction-reduced environment: Yes
Tape recording in class: Yes
Audio books: NR
Electronic texts: No
Kurzweil Reader: Yes
Other assistive technology: Through the Regional Center, students have access to innovative assistive technologies. The university library has also begun to loan students Kindles and other portable reading devices.
Priority registration: N/A
Added costs for services: No
LD specialists: Yes
ADHD coaching: No
ASD specialists: No
Professional tutors: 10
Peer tutors: No
Max. hours/wk. for services: 8
How professors are notified of LD/ADHD: Letter from Regional Center and student

General Admissions Information

Office of Admissions: 201-692-2553

Entrance Requirements

Academic units required: 4 English, 3 math, 2 science, 2 science labs, 2 history, 3 academic electives, **Academic units recommended:** 4 English, 3 math, 3 science, 2 science labs, 2 foreign language, 2 history, 4 academic electives. High school diploma is required and GED is accepted. SAT or ACT required. If ACT, ACT with writing accepted. TOEFL required of all international applicants: minimum paper TOEFL 550 or minimum internet TOEFL 79.

Application deadline: NR
Notification: NR
Average GPA: 3.2
ACT Composite middle 50% range: NR-NR
SAT Math middle 50% range: 450-550
SAT Critical Reading middle 50% range: 440-530
SAT Writing middle 50% range: 430-540
Graduated top 10% of class: 18
Graduated top 25% of class: 45
Graduated top 50% of class: 83

COLLEGE GRADUATION REQUIREMENTS

Course waivers allowed: No
Course substitutions allowed: Yes
In what course: Math

Additional Information

Environment: This private school was founded in 1942. It has a 68-acre campus.

Student Body
Undergrad enrollment: 6,775
% Women: 60
% Men: 40
% Out-of-state: 14

Cost information
Tuition: $33,920
Room & board: $12,742

Housing Information
University Housing: Yes
Percent living on campus: 19.2

Greek System
Fraternity: Yes
Sorority: Yes
Athletics: Division I

Georgian Court University

900 Lakewood Avenue, Lakewood, NJ 08701-2697
Phone: 732-987-2700 • Fax: 732-987-2000
E-mail: admissions@georgian.edu • Web: www.georgian.edu
Support: SP • Institution: Private

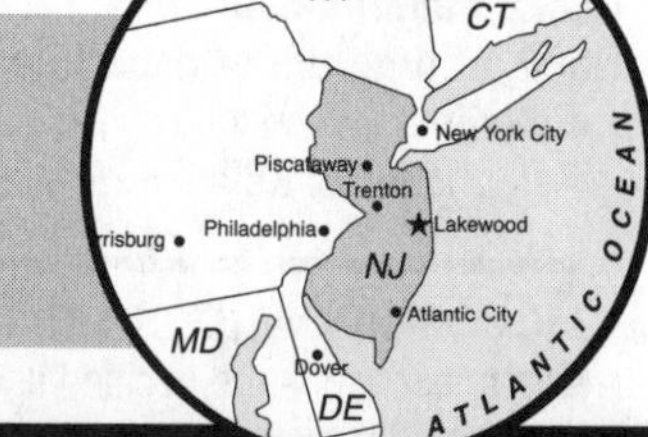

Programs or Services for Students with Learning Differences

The Learning Center (TLC) is an assistance program designed to provide an environment for students with mild to moderate learning disabilities who desire a college education. The program is not one of remediation, but it is an individualized support program to assist candidates in becoming successful college students. Emphasis is placed on developing self-help strategies and study techniques. To be eligible for the TLC program, all applicants must submit the following: documentation of a learning disability by a certified professional within a school system or state-certified agency; the documentation must be current, having been completed within the past 3 years and must include the identification and description of the learning disability, including the student's level of academic performance and the effect the disability has on the student's learning; a recent IEP; other evaluations or recommendations from professionals who have recently provided services to the student; and additional documentation on request. All applicants must have a personal interview.

Admission Information for Students with Learning Differences

College entrance tests required: Yes
Interview required: Yes
Essay required: No
Additional Application Required for LD/ADHD/ASD: NR
What documentation required for LD: Psycho ed evaluation to include: relevant historical info, instructional interventions, related services, age diagnosed, objective data (aptitude, achievement, info processing), test scores (standard, percentile and grade equivalents) and describe functional limitations.
With general application: Yes if requested as part of Structured Program application
To receive services after enrolling: Yes
What documentation required for ADHD: Diagnosis based on DSM-V; history of behaviors impairing functioning in academic setting; diagnostic interview; history of symptoms; evidence of ongoing behaviors.
With general application: Yes if requested as part of Structured Program application
To receive services after enrolling: Yes
What documentation required for ASD: Psycho ed evaluation
With general application: NR
To receive services after enrolling: Yes
LD/ADHD/ASD documentation submitted to: Both Admissions and the Learning Center
ASD Specific Program: NR
Special Ed. HS course work accepted: No
Specific course requirements of all applicants: Yes
Separate application required: No
Total # of students receiving LD/ADHD/ASD services: Varies each semester
Acceptance into program means acceptance into college: Students are simultaneously admitted into The Learning Center and Georgian Court College.

Admissions

Applicants must meet the following criteria: 16 academic units that include 4 years of English, 2 years of a foreign language, 2 years of math, 1 year of science lab, 1 year history, and electives. The class rank and transcript should give evidence of the ability to succeed in college. Students must submit SAT scores. Conditional admission may be offered to some applicants. The Associate Director of Admissions is the liaison between the admissions staff and the TLC.

Additional Information

College graduation requirements are not waived for TLC students. Reduced course load is recommended for students with learning disabilities, and program completion may take longer than 4 years. The program offers individuals one-on-one support with a professional staff member known as an Academic Development Specialist. Additionally, the program offers personalized tutoring/coaching program, guaranteed two hours per week of one-on-one sessions with Academic Development Specialists that include content tutoring, organizational, study, and testing taking skills.

General Support Services Information

Contact Information
Name of program or department: The Learning Center (TLC)
Telephone: 732-987-2650 or 732-987-2659
Fax: 732-987-2026

Accommodations or Services for Students with Learning Differences

Accommodations are decided upon an individual basis after a thorough review of appropriate, current documentation. The accommodations requested must be supported through the documentation provided and must be logically linked to the current impact of the condition on academic functioning.

Allowed in exams
Calculator: Yes
Dictionary: Yes
Computer: Yes
Spellchecker: Yes
Extended test time: Yes
Scribes: Yes
Proctors: Yes
Oral exams: Yes
Note-takers: Yes
Services for students with LD: Yes
Services for students with ADHD: Yes
Services for students with ASD: Yes
Distraction-reduced environment: Yes
Tape recording in class: Yes
Audio books: NR
Electronic texts: No
Kurzweil Reader: Yes
Other assistive technology: Yes
Priority registration: Yes
Added costs for services: Yes
LD specialists: Yes
ADHD coaching: NR
ASD specialists: NR
Professional tutors: 3
Peer tutors: No
Max. hours/wk. for services: Varies
How professors are notified of LD/ADHD: By both student and director

General Admissions Information

Office of Admissions: 732-987-2700

Entrance Requirements

Academic units required: 4 English, 2 math, 1 science, 1 science labs, 2 foreign language, 1 history, 6 academic electives. High school diploma is required and GED is accepted. SAT or ACT required. If ACT, ACT with writing accepted. TOEFL required of all international applicants: minimum paper TOEFL 550 or minimum internet TOEFL 79.

Application deadline: 8/1
Notification: NR
Average GPA: 3.25
ACT Composite middle 50% range: NR-NR
SAT Math middle 50% range: 420-540
SAT Critical Reading middle 50% range: 420-510
SAT Writing middle 50% range: 410-518
Graduated top 10% of class: 7
Graduated top 25% of class: 28
Graduated top 50% of class: 64

COLLEGE GRADUATION REQUIREMENTS

Course waivers allowed: No
Course substitutions allowed: Yes
In what course: Foreign language, if applicable

Additional Information

Environment: This private school, affiliated with the Roman Catholic Church, was founded in 1908. It has a 156-acre campus.

Student Body
Undergrad enrollment: 1,528
% Women: 74
% Men: 26
% Out-of-state: 5

Cost information
Tuition: $30,158
Room & board: $10,808

Housing Information
University Housing: Yes
Percent living on campus: 29

Greek System
Fraternity: No
Sorority: No
Athletics: Division II

KEAN UNIVERSITY

Office of Undergraduate Admissions, Union, NJ 07083-0411
Phone: 908-737-7100 • Fax: 908-737-7105
E-mail: admitme@kean.edu • Web: www.kean.edu
Support: CS • Institution: Public

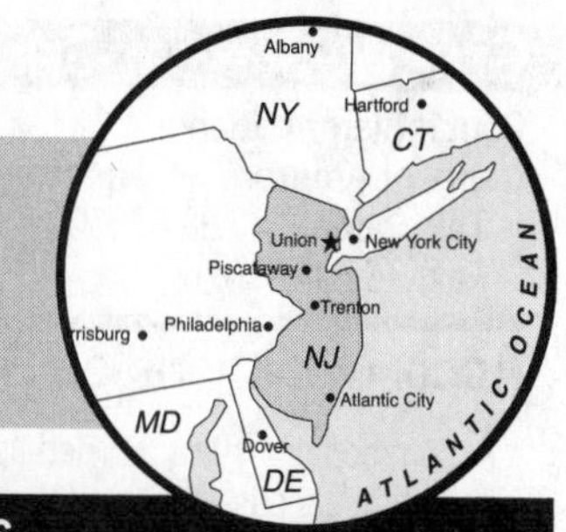

PROGRAMS OR SERVICES FOR STUDENTS WITH LEARNING DIFFERENCES

Kean University is committed to the full inclusion and equal opportunity for all persons with disabilities. Students who seek support services from the Office of Disability Services must be registered Kean University students with a current schedule. They are required to self-disclose their disability and submit current documentation to verify eligibility as defined under applicable law. To meet this requirement, documentation must be dated within the last five years, and address the present need for accommodations. This documentation will be reviewed on a case-by-case basis in conjunction with a personal intake interview. Academic accommodations are designed to provide equal access to course content while maintaining the academic standards that are required in all classes. The college may deny an accommodation, academic adjustment or request for assistive technology if determined to be unreasonable, or if the modification fundamentally alters an academic program.

ADMISSION INFORMATION FOR STUDENTS WITH LEARNING DIFFERENCES

College entrance test required: Yes
Interview required: Yes
Essay required: Not Applicable
Additional Application Required for LD/ADHD/ASD: Yes
What documentation required for LD: Educational and Psychological evaluations as well as Medical Verification
With general application: NR
To receive services after enrolling: Yes
What documentation required for ADHD: Educational and Psychological evaluations
With general application: NR
To receive services after enrolling: Yes
What documentation required for ASD: Educational and Psychological evaluations
With general application: NR
To receive services after enrolling: Yes
LD/ADHD/ASD documentation submitted to: Office of Disability Services
ASD Specific Program: Mentoring
Special Ed. HS course work accepted: NR
Specific course requirements of all applicants: NR
Separate application required for program services: FALSE
Total # of students receiving LD/ADHD/ASD services: NR
Acceptance into program means acceptance into college: NR

ADMISSIONS

There is no special admissions process for students with LD. All applicants must meet the same admission criteria, which include 4 years of English, 3 years of math, 2 years of social studies, 2 years of science, and 5 elective credits. Courses taken in special education may be considered. SAT/ACT results are required, and the average SAT range is 1000–1020 and the average ACT is 21. The minimum GPA is 2.8 and the average GPA is 3.0. Kean requires two recommendations and a personal essay. Although students are asked to write about their educational and career objectives, they can also share noteworthy accomplishments in their lives or discuss something or someone who helped them become the person they are today. The student must be highly motivated, able to do college work, be of at least average intelligence, have a documented learning disability, have areas of academic strength, and make a commitment to work responsibly and attend classes, tutoring, workshops, and counseling sessions. Students are encouraged to apply by early March.

ADDITIONAL INFORMATION

The Office of Disability Services provides services to students with disabilities including: Academic coaching and mentoring, testing and classroom accommodations, assistance in setting up tutoring appointments, training in assistive technology, equipment loaning program, adaptive testing center and study/computer area. The Center for Academic Success (CAS) is a cornerstone of Kean University's commitment to opportunity. The CAS is open to all students at Kean. It integrates all of the advisement, learning support and career counseling to provide full service to our students. This unique concept is implemented in a physical structure expressly designed for this very purpose. CAS and its programmatic offerings are designed to help Kean University realize its mission of educational access and excellence for its students. The primary goal of the center is to address the academic and informational needs of Kean University's students. It is regardless of their level of academic preparation. The center also has the goal of improving the quality, consistency and availability of academic support services to students. Through these efforts, CAS will seek to improve the retention and persistence to graduation rates for the university.

General Support Services Information

Contact Information
Name of program or department: Office of Disability Services
Telephone: 908-737-4910
Fax: 908-737-4865

Accommodations or Services For Students With Learning Differences

Accommodations are decided upon an individual basis after a thorough review of appropriate, current documentation. The accommodations requests must be supported through the documentation provided and must be logically linked to the current impact of the condition on academic functioning.

Allowed in exams
Calculator: Yes
Dictionary: Yes
Computer: Yes
Spellchecker: Yes
Extended test time: Yes
Scribes: Yes
Proctors: Yes
Oral exams: Yes
Note-takers: Yes
Support services for students with LD: Yes
Support services for students with ADHD: Yes
Support services for students with ASD: Yes
Distraction-reduced environment: Yes
Tape recording in class: Yes
Electronic texts: Yes
Kurzweil reader: NR
Audio books: Yes
Other assistive technology: Yes
Priority registration: Yes
Added costs of services: No
LD specialists: Yes
ADHD coaching: No
ASD specialists: Yes
Professional tutors: No
Peer tutors: Yes
Max. hours/wk. for services: NR
How professors are notified of student approved accommodations: By student

General Admissions Information

Office of Admissions: 908-737-7100

Entrance Requirements

Academic units required: 4 English, 3 math, 2 science, 2 science labs, 2 history, 5 academic electives.
Academic units recommended: 4 English, 3 math, 2 science, 2 science labs, 2 foreign language, 2 social studies, 2 history, 5 academic electives. High school diploma is required and GED is accepted. SAT or ACT required. If ACT, ACT with writing accepted. TOEFL required of all international applicants: minimum paper TOEFL 550 or minimum internet TOEFL 79.

Application deadline: 8/15
Notification: Rolling starting 11/1
Average GPA: 3.1
ACT Composite middle 50% range: 17-21
SAT Math middle 50% range: 430-520
SAT Critical Reading middle 50% range: 410-500
SAT Writing middle 50% range: NR-NR
Graduate top 10% of class: 11
Graduated top 25% of class: 28
Graduated top 50% of class: 66

COLLEGE GRADUATION REQUIREMENTS

Course waivers allowed: No
Course substitutions allowed: Yes
In what course: depending on documentation and major

Additional Information

Environment: This public school was founded in 1855. It has a 186-acre campus.

Student Body
Undergrad enrollment: 11,814
% Women: 60
% Men: 40
% Out-of-state: 2

Cost information
In-state Tuition: $5,790.25
Out-of-state Tuition: $9,091.25
Room & board:NR

Housing Information
University Housing: Yes
Percent living on campus: 15

Greek System
Fraternity: Yes
Sorority: Yes
Athletics: Division III

Monmouth University (NJ)

Admission, Monmouth University, West Long Branch, NJ 07764-1898
Phone: 732-571-3456 • Fax: 732-263-5166
E-mail: admission@monmouth.edu • Web: www.monmouth.edu
Support: CS • Institution: Private

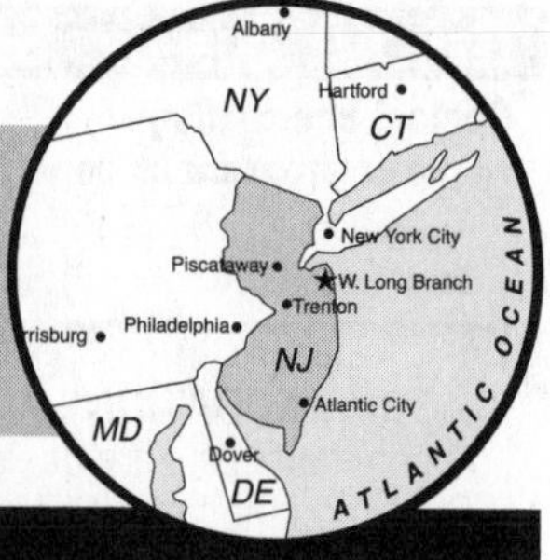

Programs or Services for Students with Learning Differences

Monmouth University recognizes the special needs of students with disabilities who are capable, with appropriate assistance, of excelling in a demanding university environment. Reasonable support services and a nurturing environment contribute to their success. Monmouth's commitment is to provide a learning process and atmosphere that allows students to pursue their educational goals, realize their full potential, contribute actively to their community and society, and determine the direction of their lives. Students are enrolled in regular courses and are not isolated from the rest of the student body in any manner. Students with documented disabilities may request reasonable accommodations and/or auxiliary aids. It is important that students disclose their disability and provide the required documentation to Department of Disability Services for Students. Much of their success has to do with individual recognition of their specific learning needs, and a willingness to self-advocate in a student-driven program.

Admission Information for Students with Learning Differences

College entrance test required: Yes
Interview required: N/A
Essay required: No
Additional Application Required for LD/ADHD/ASD: NR
What documentation required for LD: Copy of grade 12 IEP; and copies of most recent CST testing (psychoeducational evaluation, including WAIS-R and WJ3 results).
With general application: No
To receive services after enrolling: Yes
What documentation required for ADHD: Copy of high school IEP or 504 Plan; copy of educational and/or psychological test results; Monmouth University Disability Provider Form (if student is under the care of a treating physician and is prescribed medication).
With general application: No
To receive services after enrolling: Yes
What documentation required for ASD: Determined on a case-by-case basis.
With general application: No
To receive services after enrolling: Yes
LD/ADHD/ASD documentation submitted to: Support program/services
ASD Specific Program: NR
Special Ed. HS course work accepted: Yes
Specific course: Yes
Separate application required for program services: No
Total # of students receiving LD/ADHD/ASD services: NR
Acceptance into program means acceptance into college: NR

Admissions

There is no special admissions process for students with diagnosed disabilities. In addition to meeting the minimum GPA and SAT/ACT scores, academic courses required for general admission include: 4 years of English, 3 years of mathematics, 2 years social science, 2 years science and 5 additional academic electives. The average GPA is 3.38. The mid 50% ACT range is 22-26 and the mid 50% SAT range is Critical Reading 470-560 and Math 490-580.

Additional Information

Students with documented disabilities may request reasonable accommodations or auxiliary aids that will enable them to participate in and benefit from post secondary educational programs and activities. Monmouth University also offers an orientation to the Department of Disability Services for Students during the university's freshman orientation. Testing accommodations can include extended time, computer use of Microsoft Word, reader, private test setting, Dragon Naturally Speaking, and a calculator if appropriate. The Center for Student Success offers students academic and personal support designed to foster responsibility and enthusiasm for learning. Support services are focused on student academic and career goals and include: Academic Advising, service learning and community programs, tutoring and writing services.

General Support Services Information

Contact Information
Name of program or department: Department of Disability Services for Students
Telephone: 732-571-3460
Fax: 732-263-5126

Accommodations or Services for Students with Learning Differences

Accommodations are decided upon an individual basis after a thorough review of appropriate, current documentation. The accommodations requests must be supported through the documentation provided and must be logically linked to the current impact of the condition on academic functioning.

Allowed in exams
Calculator: Yes
Dictionary: Yes
Computer: Yes
Spellchecker: Yes
Extended test time: Yes
Scribes: Yes
Proctors: Yes
Oral exams: No
Note-takers: Yes
Services for students with LD: Yes
Services for students with ADHD: Yes
Services for students with ASD: Yes
Distraction-reduced environment: Yes
Tape recording in class: Yes
Audio books: Yes
Electronic texts: NR
Kurzweil Reader: Yes
Other assistive technology: Yes
Priority registration: No
Added costs of services: No
LD specialists: Yes
ADHD coaching: NR
ASD specialists: NR
Professional tutors: Yes
Peer tutors: Yes
Max. hours/wk. for services: Varies
How professors are notified of student approved accommodations: Student

General Admissions Information

Office of Admissions: 732-571-3456

Entrance Requirements

Academic units required: 4 English, 3 mathematics, 2 science, (1 science labs), 2 history, 5 academic electives. **Academic units recommended:** 2 foreign language, 2 social studies. High school diploma is required and GED is accepted. SAT or ACT required. If ACT, ACT with Writing component required. TOEFL required of all international applicants: minimum paper TOEFL 550 or minimum web TOEFL 79.

Application deadline: 3/1
Average GPA: 3.4
ACT Composite middle 50% range: 22-25
SAT Math middle 50% range: 490-590
SAT Critical Reading middle 50% range: 480-560
SAT Writing middle 50% range: 480-570
Graduated top 10% of class: 19
Graduated top 25% of class: 49
Graduated top 50% of class: 82

COLLEGE GRADUATION REQUIREMENTS

Course waivers allowed: No
Course substitutions allowed: No

Additional Information

Environment: The college is located on 125 acres in a suburb 60 miles south of New York City.

Student Body
Undergrad enrollment: 4,557
% % Women: 59
% % Men: 41
% Out-of-state: 12

Cost information
Tuition: $30,390
Room & board: $11,234
Housing Information
University housing: Yes
% Living on campus: 42

Greek System
Fraternity: Yes
Sorority: Yes
Athletics: Division I

Montclair State University

One Normal Avenue, Montclair, NJ 07043-1624
Phone: 973-655-4444 • Fax: 973-655-7700
E-mail: undergraduate.admissions@montclair.edu • Web: www.montclair.ed
Support: S • Institution: Public

Programs or Services for Students with Learning Differences

Montclair State University is committed to the full inclusion of students with disabilities in all curricular and co-curricular activities. The Disability Resource Center (DRC) will assist in receiving the accommodations and services necessary.

Admission Information for Students with Learning Differences

College entrance test required: Yes
Interview required: No
Essay required: Not Applicable
Additional Application Required for LD/ADHD/ASD: No
What documentation required for LD: Each student requesting accommodations through the Disability Resource Center is required to submit documentation to verify eligibility under Section 504 of the Rehabilitation Act of 1973 and the Americans with Disabilities Act Amendments Act (ADAAA).
With general application: No
To receive services after enrolling: No
What documentation required for ADHD: Each student requesting accommodations through the Disability Resource Center is required to submit documentation to verify eligibility under Section 504 of the Rehabilitation Act of 1973 and the Americans with Disabilities Act (ADA).
With general application: No
To receive services after enrolling: No
What documentation required for ASD: The term learning disabilities refers to a heterogeneous group of disorders characterized by significant difficulties in the acquisition and use of listening, speaking, reading, writing, reasoning, or mathematical abilities.
With general application: No
To receive services after enrolling: No
LD/ADHD/ASD documentation submitted to: Disability Resource Center
ASD Specific Program: NR
Special Ed. HS course work accepted: Yes
Specific course requirements of all applicants: NR
Separate application required for program services: False
Total # of students receiving LD/ADHD/ASD services: 300
Acceptance into program means acceptance into college: No

Admissions

All students with disabilities at the University met the university eligibility requirements and, once admitted are expected to meet all academic standards.

Additional Information

The DRC provides accommodations and services (Appropriate academic accommodations are determined on a case-by-case basis and must be supported by documentation). Academic Accomodations are note takers, readers, scribes, extended testing, textbooks on CD ,equipment loans and adaptive technology.

General Support Services Information

Contact Information
Name of program or department: Disability Resource Center
Telephone: 973-655-5431
Fax: NR
Website: http://www.montclair.edu/disability-resource-center/

Accommodations or Services for Students with Learning Differences

Accommodations are decided upon an individual basis after a thorough review of appropriate, current documentation. The accommodations requests must be supported through the documentation provided and must be logically linked to the current impact of the condition on academic functioning.

Allowed in exams
Calculator: Yes
Dictionary: Yes
Computer: Yes
Spellchecker: Yes
Extended test time: Yes
Scribes: Yes
Proctors: Yes
Oral exams: Yes
Note-takers: Yes
Support services for students with LD: Yes
Support services for students with ADHD: Yes
Support services for students with ASD: Yes
Distraction-reduced environment: Yes
Tape recording in class: Yes
Electronic texts: Yes
Kurzweil reader: NR
Audio books: Yes
Other assistive technology: Yes
Priority registration: Yes
Added costs of services: No
LD specialists: Yes
ADHD coaching: Yes
ASD specialists: No
Professional tutors: No
Peer tutors: NR
Max. hours/wk. for services: NR
How professors are notified of student approved accommodations: By student

General Admissions Information

Office of Admissions: 973-655-4444

Entrance Requirements

Academic units required: 4 English, 3 math, 2 science, 2 science labs, 2 foreign language, 2 social studies, 3 academic electives. High school diploma is required and GED is accepted. SAT or ACT recommended. TOEFL required of all international applicants: minimum paper TOEFL 550 or minimum internet TOEFL 80.

Application deadline: 3/1
Notification: Rolling starting 10/1
Average GPA: 3.24
ACT Composite middle 50% range: NR-NR
SAT Math middle 50% range: 440-550
SAT Critical Reading middle 50% range: 430-540
SAT Writing middle 50% range: 430-540
Graduate top 10% of class: 10
Graduated top 25% of class: 37
Graduated top 50% of class: 79

COLLEGE GRADUATION REQUIREMENTS

Course waivers allowed: No
Course substitutions allowed: Yes
In what course: Foreign Language, Physical Education, Public Speaking

Additional Information

Environment: This public school was founded in 1908. It has a 275-acre campus.

Student Body
Undergrad enrollment: 16,336
% Women: 62
% Men: 38
% Out-of-state: 3

Cost information
In-state tuition: $8,513
Out-of-state tuition: $17,060
Room & board: $13,884

Housing Information
University Housing: Yes
Percent living on campus: 31

Greek System
Fraternity: Yes
Sorority: Yes
Athletics: Division III

New Jersey City University

2039 Kennedy Boulevard, Jersey City, NJ 7305
Phone: 888-441-6528 • Fax: 201-200-2044
E-mail: admissions@njcu.edu • Web: www.njcu.edu
Support: SP • Institution: Public

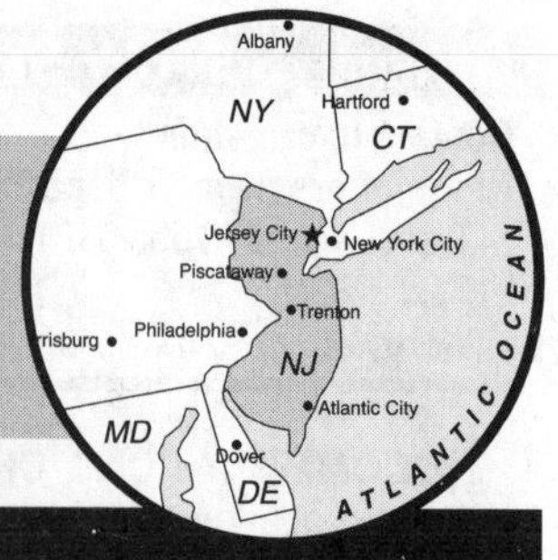

Programs or Services for Students with Learning Differences

Students with Disabilities are served by the Office of Specialized Services for Student with Disabilities at New Jersey City University. The Office of Specialized Services (OSS) provides NJCU students with disabilities equal access to college programs. The OSS serves as a resource for students with mobility, vision, hearing, learning, and other disabilities that are in need of campus accommodations. The OSS assists students, on an individual basis, in securing reasonable accommodations, including, but not limited to alternate testing arrangements, adaptive technology, and assistance in arranging other support services (e.g., sign language interpreters, books on tape, and note-taking support) supported by documentation. It is the student's responsibility to self-identify and request services. Students requesting academic adjustments are required to submit appropriate and recent documentation of their disability. Students wishing to obtain accommodations may do so by contacting the OSS Director. Reasonable accommodations are then determined after consultation between the student and the Director.

Admission Information for Students with Learning Differences

College entrance tests required: NR
Interview required: NR
Essay required: NR
Additional Application Required for LD/ADHD/ASD: NR
What documentation required for LD: Psycho ed evaluation to include: relevant historical info, instructional interventions, related services, age diagnosed, objective data (aptitude, achievement, info processing), test scores (standard, percentile and grade equivalents) and describe functional limitations.
With general application: NR
To receive services after enrolling: Yes
What documentation required for ADHD: Diagnosis based on DSM-V; history of behaviors impairing functioning in academic setting; diagnostic interview; history of symptoms; evidence of ongoing behaviors.
With general application: NR
To receive services after enrolling: Yes
What documentation required for ASD: Psycho ed evaluation
With general application: NR
To receive services after enrolling: Yes
LD/ADHD/ASD documentation submitted to: NR
ASD Specific Program: NR
Special Ed. HS course work accepted: NR
Specific course requirements of all applicants: NR
Separate application required: No
Total # of students receiving LD/ADHD/ASD services: NR
Acceptance into program means acceptance into college: Must be admitted and enrolled, and then request accommodations

Admissions

There is no separate application for students with disabilities. All applicants are expected to meet the same admission standards. Applicants must submit 2 letters of recommendations. Students may also write an essay to describe aspirations and motivations. ACT or SAT required. Courses required include: 4 English, 3 math, 4 science, 2 social studies, and 5 electives.

Additional Information

The Center for Student Success (CSS) offers access to peer and professional tutoring services and academic resources, enabling all NJCU students to attain the necessary skills, strategies, and behaviors necessary to improve their academic standing and to identify appropriate career objectives. The CSS provides: individual and small group peer tutoring in basic English and math; study halls in basic English and math; workshops on study skills, learning styles, information literacy, financial literacy, and success strategies; Access to computer-based learning skills materials and resources; referrals to on-campus academic and personal assistance programs; co-curricular transcript application; learning and study skills strategies; and exposure to leadership opportunities.

General Support Services Information

Contact Information
Name of program or department: Office of Specialized Services & Supportive Instruction (OSS/SI)
Telephone: 201-200-2091
Fax: 201-200-3083

Accommodations or Services for Students with Learning Differences

Accommodations are decided upon an individual basis after a thorough review of appropriate, current documentation. The accommodations requested must be supported through the documentation provided and must be logically linked to the current impact of the condition on academic functioning.

Allowed in exams
Calculator: Yes
Dictionary: Yes
Computer: Yes
Spellchecker: Yes
Extended test time: Yes
Scribes: Yes
Proctors: Yes
Oral exams: Yes
Note-takers: Yes
Services for students with LD: Yes
Services for students with ADHD: Yes
Services for students with ASD: Yes
Distraction-reduced environment: Yes
Tape recording in class: Yes
Audio books: NR
Electronic texts: Yes
Kurzweil Reader: No
Other assistive technology: Yes
Priority registration: NR
Added costs for services: No
LD specialists: Yes
ADHD coaching: Yes
ASD specialists: NR
Professional tutors: NR
Peer tutors: Yes
Max. hours/wk. for services: Unlimited
How professors are notified of LD/ADHD: By both student and director

General Admissions Information

Office of Admissions: 888-441-6528

Entrance Requirements

Academic units required: 4 English, 4 math, 4 science, 2 science labs, 4 social studies. **Academic units recommended:** 4 English, 4 math, 4 science, 3 science labs, 2 foreign language, 4 social studies. High school diploma is required and GED is accepted. SAT or ACT required. TOEFL required of all international applicants.

Application deadline: NR
Notification: NR
Average GPA: 2.92
ACT Avg Composite: 19 (15-22)
SAT Math Avg: 444 (370-600)
SAT Critical Reading Avg: 469 (390-610)
SAT Writing Avg: 419 (310-540)
Graduated top 10% of class: 9
Graduated top 25% of class: 29
Graduated top 50% of class: 61

COLLEGE GRADUATION REQUIREMENTS

Course waivers allowed: No
Course substitutions allowed: Yes
In what course: Each case is reviewed on an individual basis.

Additional Information

Environment: This public school was founded in 1927. It has a 17-acre campus.

Student Body
Undergrad enrollment: 6,317
% Women: 60
% Men: 40
% Out-of-state: 1

Cost information
In-state Tuition: $7,936
Out-of Tuition: $16,764
Room & board: $10,917

Housing Information
University Housing: Yes
Percent living on campus: 4

Greek System
Fraternity: Yes
Sorority: Yes
Athletics: Division III

Rider University

2083 Lawrenceville Road, Lawrenceville, NJ 08648-3099
Phone: 609-896-5042 • Fax: 609-895-6645
E-mail: admissions@rider.edu • Web: www.rider.edu
Support: CS • Institution: Private

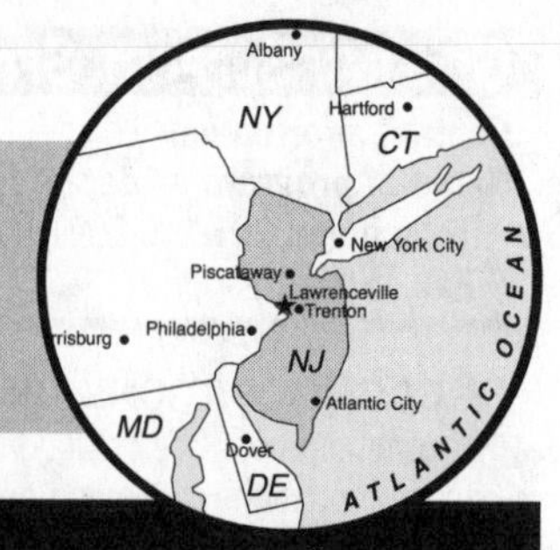

Programs or Services for Students with Learning Differences

Services for Students with Disabilities offer a range of services to help students with documented LD obtain appropriate accommodations. These services include screening and referral, informal assessment, and support services. The goal of the services is to assist students in becoming more independent and efficient learners. A learning disability specialist meets individually with students who have learning disabilities and/or attention deficit disorder. Students must initiate the request for this meeting and must supply documentation of the disability. These learning disability specialists conduct an intake interview and, based on the information resulting from this interview, refer students to appropriate support services. They also determine the appropriate academic adjustments.

Admission Information for Students with Learning Differences

College entrance test required: Yes
Interview required: No
Essay required: Not Applicable
Additional Application Required for LD/ADHD/ASD: No
What documentation required for LD: In most cases, an recent ADHD evaluation from a qualified assessor with appropriate adult-normed test scores is required.
With general application: Not Applicable
To receive services after enrolling: No
What documentation required for ADHD: Documentation from a qualified professional should include, at a minimum, a diagnosis, a statement of functional limitations with supporting recent evaluation data, and recommendations for accommodations.
With general application: Not Applicable
To receive services after enrolling: No
What documentation required for ASD: In most cases, a full psycho-educational evaluation, including cognitive and educational tests normed on the adult population, is required.
With general application: Not Applicable
To receive services after enrolling: No
LD/ADHD/ASD documentation submitted to: Services for Students with Disabilities
ASD Specific Program: NR
Special Ed. HS course work accepted: No
Specific course requirements of all applicants: Yes
Separate application required for program services: FALSE
Total # of students receiving LD/ADHD/ASD services: NR
Acceptance into program means acceptance into college: Not Applicable

Admissions

There is no special admissions process for students with learning disabilities. All students must submit the general university application. Admissions criteria are based on the following: high school academic record and GPA of 2.5 or better; SAT or ACT test results; and a college writing sample (essay). Courses required include 16 acceptable units from a college-prep curriculum: four years English, three years math, and the remaining in sciences, foreign language, social science, and humanities. The Rider Achievement Program is for academically admissible students who are just below the admissions criteria for the regularly admitted student. The Educational Opportunity Fund Program is the state-funded program for academically disadvantaged or economically disadvantaged students.

Additional Information

The Writing Lab provides individual and small group tutoring in writing, reading comprehension, and study strategies. The staff offers study strategy workshops and students have access to computers. The Mathematics Skill Lab provides a math course for students who do not meet the placement criteria for college level math. The course is taught via individual tutoring, structured workshops, and computer-assisted instruction. The MSL staff offers weekly tutorial sessions for Finite Math, helps students prepare for the Algebra & Trig Qualifying Exam, and provides tutoring for other courses. The Student Success Center provides a peer tutoring program for students needing extra help. Courses in College Reading and Introduction to Academic Reading are available.

General Support Services Information

Contact Information
Name of program or department: Services for Students with Disabilities
Telephone: (609) 895-5492
Fax: (609) 895-5507
Website: Rider.edu/SSD

Accommodations or Services For Students With Learning Differences

Accommodations are decided upon an individual basis after a thorough review of appropriate, current documentation. The accommodations requests must be supported through the documentation provided and must be logically linked to the current impact of the condition on academic functioning.

Allowed in exams
Calculator: Yes
Dictionary: Yes
Computer: Yes
Spellchecker: Yes
Extended test time: Yes
Scribes: Yes
Proctors: Yes
Oral exams: Yes
Note-takers: Not Applicable
Support services for students with LD: Yes
Support services for students with ADHD: Yes
Support services for students with ASD: Yes
Distraction-reduced environment: Yes
Tape recording in class: Yes
Electronic texts: Yes
Kurzweil reader: NR
Audio books: Yes
Other assistive technology: Yes
Priority registration: Yes
Added costs of services: No
LD specialists: Yes
ADHD coaching: Yes
ASD specialists: No
Professional tutors: Yes
Peer tutors: Yes
Max. hours/wk. for services: NR
How professors are notified of student approved accommodations: By student

General Admissions Information

Office of Admissions: 609-896-5042

Entrance Requirements

Academic units required: 4 English, 3 math. **Academic units recommended:** 4 math, 4 science, 2 science labs, 2 foreign language, 2 social studies, 2 history. High school diploma is required and GED is accepted. SAT or ACT required. If ACT, ACT with writing required. TOEFL required of all international applicants: minimum paper TOEFL 550 or minimum internet TOEFL 80.

Application deadline: NR
Notification: Rolling starting 12/15
Average GPA: 3.28
ACT Composite middle 50% range: 19-25
SAT Math middle 50% range: 460-560
SAT Critical Reading middle 50% range: 450-550
SAT Writing middle 50% range: 450-540
Graduate top 10% of class: 14
Graduated top 25% of class: 37
Graduated top 50% of class: 75

COLLEGE GRADUATION REQUIREMENTS

Course waivers allowed: No
Course substitutions allowed: Yes
In what course: With appropriate documentation foreign language and math courses may be substituted, except if they are essential to the student's major.

Additional Information

Environment: This private school was founded in 1865. It has a 280-acre campus.

Student Body
Undergrad enrollment: 4,128
% Women: 57
% Men: 43
% Out-of-state: 23

Cost information
Tuition: $37,650
Room & board: $13,770
Housing Information
University Housing: Yes
Percent living on campus: 55

Greek System
Fraternity: Yes
Sorority: Yes
Athletics: Division I

Seton Hall University

Office of Admission, Seton Hall, South Orange, NJ 07079
Phone: 800-THE-HALL • Fax: 973-275-2339
E-mail: thehall@shu.edu • Web: www.shu.edu
Support: CS • Institution: Private

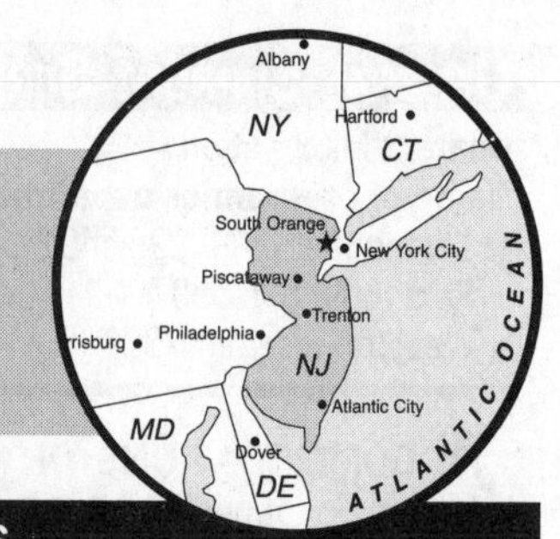

Programs or Services for Students with Learning Differences

The mission of Disability Support Services (DSS) is to provide students with disabilities equal access to all university programs and activities, while raising campus-wide awareness of issues impacting this student population. DSS works collaboratively with academic departments and student affairs offices to engage and support the intellectual and social development of students with disabilities. To this end, DSS employs policies and programming to promote academic excellence, the development of self-advocacy skills, and increased student leadership opportunities. Accommodations are provided based on submission of appropriate documentation, which is reviewed by DSS staff in compliance with university policy, Section 504 of the Rehabilitation Act, the Americans with Disabilities Act (ADA), and the New Jersey Law against Discrimination (NJLAD).

Admission Information for Students with Learning Differences

College entrance tests required: Yes
Interview required: No
Essay required: N/A
Additional Application Required for LD/ADHD/ASD: NR
What documentation required for LD: Psychoeducational evaluation. Please the DSS website for information on documentation criteria: https://www13.shu.edu/offices/disability-support-services/forms.cfm.
With general application: No
To receive services after enrolling: Yes
What documentation required for ADHD: Yes
With general application: NR
To receive services after enrolling: Yes
What documentation required for ASD: Psycho ed evaluation
With general application: NR
To receive services after enrolling: Yes
LD/ADHD/ASD documentation submitted to: Disability Support Services
ASD Specific Program: NR
Special Ed. HS course work accepted: No
Specific course requirements for all applicants: Yes
Separate application required for program services: No
Total # of students receiving LD/ADHD/ASD services: 200

Admissions

There is no special admission process for students with learning disabilities, and all applicants must meet the same admission criteria. Courses required include 4 years of English, 3 years of math, 1 year of science lab, 2 years of a foreign language, 2 years of social studies, and 4 electives. If students have been waived from a world language via their IEP, the requirement will be waived if it is not a core requirement of a particular program. The minimum SAT is 900. Students need to rank in the top 40 percent of their class, and a minimum 2.5 GPA is preferred.

Additional Information

In coordinating its activities with other departments of the university (such as Residence Life and Academic Services), Student Support Services works to assure that the university remains in compliance with all federal laws and regulations. The DSS office provides the following services to individuals with LD (with appropriate documentation): reduced course load, extended time to complete assignments, tape recorders, note-taking, taped texts, readers, extended time for in class assignments, assistive technology (calculator, word processor, etc.), extended time for testing, and a distraction-reduced environment. The recommendation from DSS is that students meed with their instructor at least one week before each scheduled exam to determine how exam accommodations will be implemented.

General Support Services Information

Contact Information
Name of program or department: Disability Support Services (DSS)
Telephone: 973-313-6003
Fax: 973-761-9185

Accommodations or Services for Students with Learning Differences

Accommodations are decided upon an individual basis after a thorough review of appropriate, current documentation. The accommodations requested must be supported through the documentation provided and must be logically linked to the current impact of the condition on academic functioning.

Allowed in exams
Calculator: Yes
Dictionary: Yes
Computer: Yes
Spellchecker: Yes
Extended test time: Yes
Scribes: Yes
Proctors: Yes
Oral exams: Yes
Note-takers: Yes
Services for students with LD: Yes
Services for students with ADHD: Yes
Services for students with ASD: Yes
Distraction-reduced environment: Yes
Tape recording in class: Yes
Audio books: NR
Electronic texts: Yes
Kurzweil Reader: Yes
Other assistive technology: Assistive Technology (hardware and software) is allocated based on each student's individual needs.
Priority registration: No
Added costs for services: No
LD specialists: Yes
ADHD coaching: NR
ASD specialists: Yes
Professional tutors: Yes
Peer tutors: Yes
Max. hours/wk. for services:
How professors are notified of LD/ADHD: Student

General Admissions Information

Office of Admissions: (800) THE HALL

Entrance Requirements

Academic units required: 4 English, 3 math, 1 science, 1 science labs, 2 foreign language, 2 social studies, 4 academic electives. SAT or ACT required. If ACT, ACT with writing accepted. TOEFL required of all international applicants: minimum paper TOEFL 550.

Application deadline: NR
Notification: Rolling starting 11/15
Average GPA: 3.47
ACT Composite middle 50% range: 22-27
SAT Math middle 50% range: 510-610
SAT Critical Reading middle 50% range: 490-590
SAT Writing middle 50% range: 490-600
Graduated top 10% of class: 37
Graduated top 25% of class: 61
Graduated top 50% of class: 86

COLLEGE GRADUATION REQUIREMENTS

Course waivers allowed: Yes
In what course: Course substitutions for mathematics and world languages are available as long as they are not core courses required for the student's major. These determinations are based on documented need.
Course substitutions allowed: Yes
In what course: Students may request course substitutions through the DSS office for mathematics and world languages. DSS's recommendation is then submitted to the dean of each school or college for review and approval.

Additional Information

Environment: This private school, affiliated with the Roman Catholic Church, was founded in 1856. It has a 58-acre campus.

Student Body
Undergrad enrollment: 5,497
% Women: 59
% Men: 41
% Out-of-state: 22
Cost information
Tuition: $35,940
Room & board: $11,522
Housing Information
University Housing: Yes
Percent living on campus: 41
Greek System
Fraternity: No
Sorority: No
Athletics: Division I

New Mexico Institute of Mining and Technology

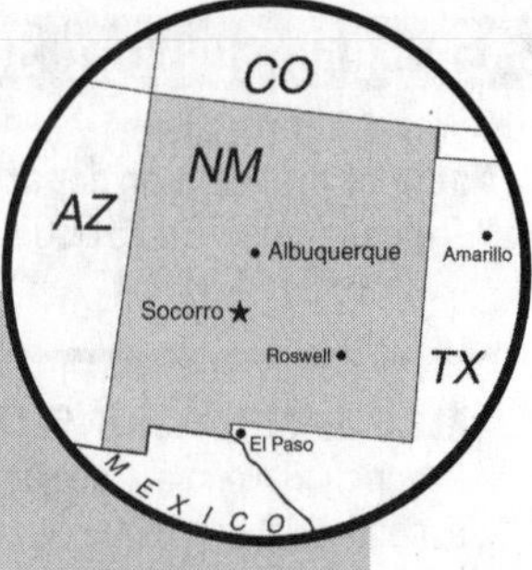

Campus Station, Socorro, NM 87801
Phone: 575-835-5424 • Fax: 575-835-5989
E-mail: admission@admin.nmt.edu • Web: www.nmt.edu
Support: S • Institution: Public

Programs or Services for Students with Learning Differences

New Mexico Tech does not have a specific program for students with LD. Services for students with disabilities are available in the Counseling and Student Health Center. Students must present recent documentation completed within the previous 3 years. The documentation should be sent to the Office for Counseling and Disability Services. New Mexico Tech sends a letter to all admitted students asking those with disabilities to contact the Office for Counseling and Disability Services. There is a special application required after admission and enrollment to receive services or accommodations. The counseling staff works with students with disabilities on an individual basis to accommodate their special needs. Students may also use the counseling service to reduce their stress, think through problems or difficulties, clarify options, and express and explore feelings.

Admission Information for Students with Learning Differences

College entrance tests required: Yes
Interview required: No
Essay required: No
Additional Application Required for LD/ADHD/ASD: NR
What documentation required for LD: Psycho ed evaluation to include: relevant historical info, instructional interventions, related services, age diagnosed, objective data (aptitude, achievement, info processing), test scores (standard, percentile and grade equivalents) and describe functional limitations.
With general application: No
To receive services after enrolling: Yes
What documentation required for ADHD: Diagnosis based on DSM-V; history of behaviors impairing functioning in academic setting; diagnostic interview; history of symptoms; evidence of ongoing behaviors.
With general application: No
To receive services after enrolling: Yes
What documentation required for ASD: Psycho ed evaluation
With general application: NR
To receive services after enrolling: Yes
LD/ADHD/ASD documentation submitted to: Office for Counseling and Disability Services
ASD Specific Program: NR
Special Ed. HS course work accepted: NR
Specific course requirements of all applicants: Yes
Separate application required: Yes
Total # of students receiving LD/ADHD/ASD services: 24
Acceptance into program means acceptance into college: Students must be admitted to and enrolled in the university first and then request services.

Admissions

There is no special admission process for students with LD. The minimum GPA is a 2.5. The college requires an ACT composite score of 21 or higher or an SAT score of 970 or higher. The college will accept the SAT, but prefers the ACT. The GED is accepted with a score of 50 or higher. High school course requirements include 4 years of English, 2 years of science (including biology, physics, chemistry, and earth science), 3 years of math, and 3 years of social science, of which one must be history. Students are encouraged to self-disclose their disability during the admission process.

Additional Information

Students will work with staff to determine appropriate accommodations or services. These services may include coordinating academic accommodations, extended time for tests, calculators in exams, skills classes in study strategies and time management, and tutorial services available for all students on campus.

General Support Services Information

Contact Information
Name of program or department: Office of Counseling and Disability Services
Telephone: 575-835-6619
Fax: 575-835-5959

Accommodations or Services for Students with Learning Differences

Accommodations are decided upon an individual basis after a thorough review of appropriate, current documentation. The accommodations requested must be supported through the documentation provided and must be logically linked to the current impact of the condition on academic functioning.

Allowed in exams
Calculator: Yes
Dictionary: No
Computer: Yes
Spellchecker: Yes
Extended test time: Yes
Scribes: Yes
Proctors: Yes
Oral exams: Yes
Note-takers: Yes
Services for students with LD: Yes
Services for students with ADHD: Yes
Services for students with ASD: Yes
Distraction-reduced environment: Yes
Tape recording in class: Yes
Audio books: NR
Electronic texts: Yes
Kurzweil Reader: No
Other assistive technology: Yes
Priority registration: Yes
Added costs for services: No
LD specialists: No
ADHD coaching: NR
ASD specialists: NR
Professional tutors: No
Peer tutors: 50
Max. hours/wk. for services: Unlimited
How professors are notified of LD/ADHD: By both student and director

General Admissions Information

Office of Admissions: 575-835-5424

Entrance Requirements

Academic units required: 4 English, 3 math, 2 science, 2 science labs, 2 social studies, 1 history, 3 academic electives. **Academic units recommended:** 4 English, 4 math, 4 science, 3 science labs, 2 foreign language, 3 social studies, 1 history. High school diploma is required and GED is accepted. SAT or ACT required. If ACT, ACT with writing accepted. TOEFL required of all international applicants: minimum paper TOEFL 540.

Application deadline: 8/1
Notification: Rolling starting 3/1
Average GPA: 2.90
ACT Avg Composite: 30
SAT Avg Math: 560
SAT Avg Critical Reading: 610
SAT Avg Writing: 550
Graduated top 10% of class: 36
Graduated top 25% of class: 64
Graduated top 50% of class: 86

COLLEGE GRADUATION REQUIREMENTS

Course waivers allowed: No
Course substitutions allowed: No

Additional Information

Environment: This public school was founded in 1889. It has a 320-acre campus.

Student Body
Undergrad enrollment: 1,633
% Women: 30
% Men: 70
% Out-of-state: 15.7

Cost information
In-state Tuition: $5,563
Out-of Tuition: $18,087
Room & board: $7,586

Housing Information
University Housing: Yes
Percent living on campus: 50

Greek System
Fraternity: No
Sorority: No
Athletics: Other

New Mexico State University

PO Box 30001, Las Cruces, NM 88003-8001
Phone: 575-646-3121 • Fax: 575-646-6330
E-mail: admissions@nmsu.edu • Web: www.nmsu.edu
Support: S • Institution: Public

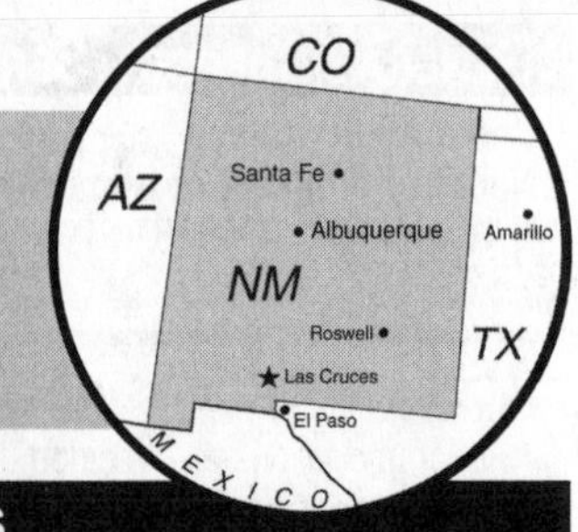

Programs or Services for Students with Learning Differences

Services for Students with Disabilities is a component of the Office of Student Development. The staff are committed to providing information and services that assist students with disabilities in personal and academic adjustment to the university community. Services for Students with Disabilities provides assistance with procuring auxiliary aids, coordinating services and resources, and discussing special needs and accommodations, and the staff serve as consultants regarding questions about various accommodations. They work with students to ensure that they have access to all of the programs and services that will affect their full participation in the campus community. Students are encouraged to contact Services for Students with Disabilities to discuss their needs and to register for the program. Students should complete the petition for Services for Students with Disabilities and return it with the appropriate documentation for evaluation and review. A review committee will determine their eligibility and the specific services and accommodations to be provided, and students will be notified by a coordinator. This process takes time, and students are encouraged to start the process as soon as possible.

Admission Information for Students with Learning Differences

College entrance tests required: Yes
Interview required: No
Essay required: No
Additional Application Required for LD/ADHD/ASD: NR
What documentation required for LD: Psycho ed evaluation to include: relevant historical info, instructional interventions, related services, age diagnosed, objective data (aptitude, achievement, info processing), test scores (standard, percentile and grade equivalents) and describe functional limitations.
With general application: No
To receive services after enrolling: Yes
What documentation required for ADHD: Diagnosis based on DSM-V; history of behaviors impairing functioning in academic setting; diagnostic interview; history of symptoms; evidence of ongoing behaviors.
With general application: No
To receive services after enrolling: Yes
What documentation required for ASD: Psycho ed evaluation
With general application: NR
To receive services after enrolling: Yes
LD/ADHD/ASD documentation submitted to: Services for Students with Disabilities
ASD Specific Program: NR
Special Ed. HS course work accepted: Yes
Specific course requirements of all applicants: Yes
Separate application required: No
Total # of students receiving LD/ADHD/ASD services: 90
Acceptance into program means acceptance into college: Students must be admitted to and enrolled in the university first and then request services.

Admissions

Admission criteria are the same for all students. Admission can be granted on a regular status or provisional status. Regular admission requires high school GPA of 2.5 and 21 ACT or 970 SAT. Course requirements include 4 years of English, 2 years of science, 3 years of math, and 3 years of social studies (1 must be history). Provisional status is possible for students who have a high school GPA of 2.1 and 18 ACT. Students admitted provisionally must take at least 6, but not more than 12, credits in a regular semester and at least 3, but not more than 6, credits in a summer session.

Additional Information

The Student Success Center offers students the skills they need to excel in college. Students work with learning facilitators to develop or maximize the skills needed for college success. Assistance is offered in time management, concentration, memory, test preparation, test-taking, listening/note-taking, textbook-reading techniques, math and science study skills, reasoning skills, writing, spelling, and grammar. Student Accessibility Services is a program of academic and personal support with the goal of improving the retention and graduation of undergraduate students with disabilities. A mentor is provided for all participants to help motivate them, and tutors help with study skills in specific subjects. Students may have tutors in two subjects and can meet weekly. Other services available are early registration, note-taking services, readers, and test accommodations including extended time, a quiet location, scribes, readers, or other assistance with exams. All services are free.

General Support Services Information

Contact Information
Name of program or department: Student Accessibility Services
Telephone: 505-646-6840
Fax: 505-646-5222

Accommodations or Services for Students with Learning Differences

Accommodations are decided upon an individual basis after a thorough review of appropriate, current documentation. The accommodations requested must be supported through the documentation provided and must be logically linked to the current impact of the condition on academic functioning.

Allowed in exams
Calculator: Yes
Dictionary: No
Computer: Yes
Spellchecker: Yes
Extended test time: Yes
Scribes: Yes
Proctors: Yes
Oral exams: Yes
Note-takers: Yes
Services for students with LD: Yes
Services for students with ADHD: Yes
Services for students with ASD: Yes
Distraction-reduced environment: Yes
Tape recording in class: Yes
Audio books: NR
Electronic texts: Yes
Kurzweil Reader: Yes
Other assistive technology: Yes
Priority registration: Yes
Added costs for services: No
LD specialists: No
ADHD coaching: NR
ASD specialists: NR
Professional tutors: No
Peer tutors: 50
Max. hours/wk. for services: Unlimited
How professors are notified of LD/ADHD: By both student and director

General Admissions Information

Office of Admissions: 575-646-3121

Entrance Requirements

Academic units required: 4 English, 4 math, 2 science, 2 science labs, 1 foreign language. High school diploma is required and GED is accepted. SAT or ACT required. If ACT, ACT with writing accepted. TOEFL required of all international applicants: minimum paper TOEFL 500.

Application deadline: NR
Notification: NR
Average GPA: 3.26
ACT Composite Avg: 22
SAT Math Avg: 475 (420-530)
SAT Critical Reading Avg: 530 (400-660)
SAT Writing Avg: 445 (320-570)
Graduated top 10% of class: 20
Graduated top 25% of class: 46
Graduated top 50% of class: 78

COLLEGE GRADUATION REQUIREMENTS

Course waivers allowed: Yes
In what course: Students need to negotiate with the college in which they are majoring.
Course substitutions allowed: Yes
In what course: Students need to negotiate with the college in which they are majoring.

Additional Information

Environment: This public school was founded in 1888. It has a 900-acre campus.

Student Body
Undergrad enrollment: 12,526
% Women: 53
% Men: 47
% Out-of-state: 34

Cost information
Room & board: NR
Housing Information
University Housing: Yes
Percent living on campus: 18

Greek System
Fraternity: Yes
Sorority: Yes
Athletics: Division I

Santa Fe U. of Art & Design

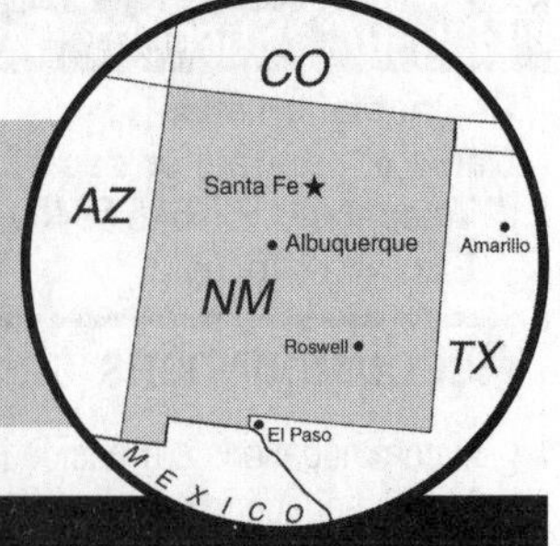

1600 St. Michaels Drive, Santa Fe, NM 87505-7634
Phone: 505-473-6937 • Fax: 505-473-6127
E-mail: admissions@santafeuniversity.edu • Web: www.santafeuniversity.edu
Support: S • Institution: Private

Programs or Services for Students with Learning Differences

Student Services houses support services programs designed to assist eligible students to graduate from Santa Fe University. There is no formal disabilities program at the university, but the students do have access to many services and accommodations. Students may receive services in basic skills instruction for reading, study strategies, writing, math, humanities, and science. Students work with the professional staff to set up a support program that meets their specific needs. The initial meeting is during registration. To be eligible for services, students with learning disabilities must provide a current psychoeducational evaluation that identifies their learning disability. Once this documentation is on file with the Academic Resource Center, students may meet with staff to identify the necessary accommodations and services needed to be successful in college.

Admission Information for Students with Learning Differences

College entrance tests required: Yes
Interview required: No
Essay required: No
Additional Application Required for LD/ADHD/ASD: NR
What documentation required for LD: Complete request at http://santafeuniversity.edu/public/default_site/files/Disability_Accommodations_Request_Form.pdf
With general application: No
To receive services after enrolling: Yes
What documentation required for ADHD: Diagnosis based on DSM-V; history of behaviors impairing functioning in academic setting; diagnostic interview; history of symptoms; evidence of ongoing behaviors.
With general application: No
To receive services after enrolling: Yes
What documentation required for ASD: Psycho ed evaluation
With general application: NR
To receive services after enrolling: Yes
LD/ADHD/ASD documentation submitted to: Academic Resource Center
ASD Specific Program: NR
Special Ed. HS course work accepted: Yes
Specific course requirements of all applicants: Yes
Separate application required: No
Total # of students receiving LD/ADHD/ASD services: NR
Acceptance into program means acceptance into college: Students are admitted to the college and to the Academic Resource Center after applying for services.

Admissions

There is no separate admission process for students with LD/ADHD. Students with LD/ADHD are required to meet the general admission criteria. This includes course requirements of 3 years of English, 2 years of math, 2 years of science, 2 years of social science, and a recommendation of 2 years of a foreign language. Each applicant is evaluated individually. All traditional first-time candidates for admission are required to go through an on-campus interview process. If students are unable to come to campus because of distance or time, the college will arrange a telephone interview. If admitted, students with a GPA inconsistent with their level of ability arrange for academic support from the Academic Resource Center. Copies of diagnostic examinations not more than 3 years old must document the student's learning disability or ADHD. The results of these tests are sent to the Academic Resource Center after the student is admitted.

Additional Information

Throughout the academic year, the Disabilities Service Office works to support the needs of students with disabilities by providing an initial interview, assessment of accommodation needs, and ongoing support. Services provided by the college could include, but are not limited to, the following: alternative testing, specialized tutoring, academic advisement and career planning, note-takers, interpreters for the hearing impaired, screen-reader software, other assistive technology, peer tutoring, resource information, and referrals. ARC offers students free tutoring in most subjects taught at Santa Fe University of Art & Design. Tutoring helps students more fully understand course material and develop academic strategies helpful in all courses. Individual tutoring is available from professional staff as well as peer tutors. Peer tutors are Santa Fe University students who have excellent academic records, have taken the courses they tutor, and have been trained to work with students with a wide range of needs and learning styles. Tutors also facilitate study groups for many courses offered at the university. These groups provide opportunities to discuss course content, compare notes with other students, and develop success strategies. Accommodations are provided on an individual basis.

General Support Services Information

Contact Information
Name of program or department: Disabilities Services
Telephone: 505-473-6570
Fax: 505-473-6286

Accommodations or Services for Students with Learning Differences

Accommodations are decided upon an individual basis after a thorough review of appropriate, current documentation. The accommodations requested must be supported through the documentation provided and must be logically linked to the current impact of the condition on academic functioning.

Allowed in exams
Calculator: Yes
Dictionary: Yes
Computer: Yes
Spellchecker: Yes
Extended test time: Yes
Scribes: Yes
Proctors: Yes
Oral exams: Yes
Note-takers: Yes
Services for students with LD: Yes
Services for students with ADHD: Yes
Services for students with ASD: Yes
Distraction-reduced environment: Yes
Tape recording in class: Yes
Audio books: NR
Electronic texts: Yes
Kurzweil Reader: Yes
Other assistive technology: Yes
Priority registration: No
Added costs for services: No
LD specialists: No
ADHD coaching: NR
ASD specialists: NR
Professional tutors: 2
Peer tutors: 5–15
Max. hours/wk. for services: 3
How professors are notified of LD/ADHD: By both student and director

General Admissions Information

Office of Admissions: 505-473-6937

Entrance Requirements

Academic units required: 4 English, 2 math, 2 science, 2 science labs, 2 social studies, **Academic units recommended:** 4 English, 2 math, 2 science, 2 science labs, 2 foreign language, 2 social studies, 4 academic electives. High school diploma is required and GED is accepted. SAT or ACT not used. If ACT, ACT with writing accepted. TOEFL required of all international applicants: minimum paper TOEFL 550 or minimum internet TOEFL 79.

Application deadline: NR
Notification: Rolling starting 9/12
Average GPA: NR
ACT Composite middle 50% range: NR-NR
SAT Math middle 50% range: NR-NR
SAT Critical Reading middle 50% range: NR-NR
SAT Writing middle 50% range: NR-NR
Graduated top 10% of class: NR
Graduated top 25% of class: NR
Graduated top 50% of class: NR

COLLEGE GRADUATION REQUIREMENTS

Course waivers allowed: Yes
In what course: This is done on an individual basis, depending on the experience of the individual student.
Course substitutions allowed: Yes
In what course: Again, it is done on a case-by-case basis, but substitution is common for all students here.

Additional Information

Environment: This private school was founded in 1874. It has a 100-acre campus.

Student Body
Undergrad enrollment: 950
% Women: 54
% Men: 46
% Out-of-state: 78

Cost information
Tuition: $28,836
Room & board: $8,984
Housing Information
University Housing: Yes
Percent living on campus: NR

Greek System
Fraternity: No
Sorority: No
Athletics: 0

Adelphi University

Levermore Hall 114, Garden City, NY 11530
Phone: 516-877-3050 • Fax: 516-877-3039
E-mail: admissions@adelphi.edu • Web: www.adelphi.edu
Support: SP • Institution: Private

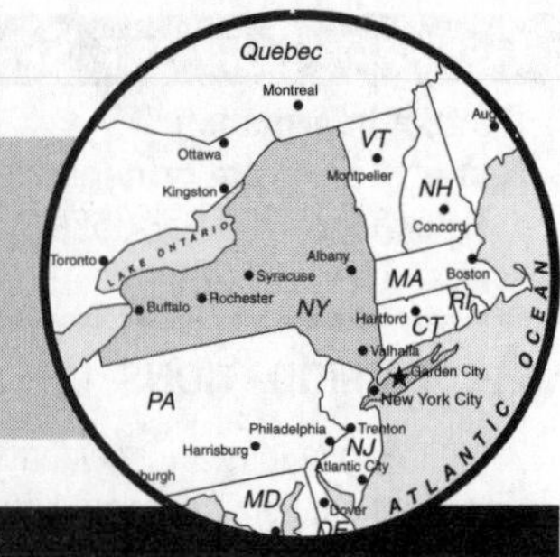

Programs or Services for Students with Learning Differences

The approach of the Learning Resource Program at provides an atmosphere where students with LD/ADHD can realize their potential. The program is specially designed for students unable to process oral and written materials in conventional ways, but who excel in other ways. Each student is provided with the support of an interdisciplinary team of experienced professionals in tutoring and counseling. More than 17 professionals provide all instruction, counseling, and assessments with advanced degrees in special education and social work. Students meet individually with an educator and a counselor who work as a team. There is a mandatory summer program prior to freshman year. Students attend tutoring sessions two times a week, participate in all the program's services, and sign an agreement acknowledging their academic commitment. The Bridges to Adelphi Program (additional fee) is based on social learning theory and cognitive behavioral principles as theoretical foundations.

Admission Information for Students with Learning Differences

College entrance tests required: Yes, by Admissions
Interview required: Yes
Essay required: Yes
Additional Application Required for LD/ADHD/ASD: NR
What documentation required for LD: WAIS, WJ, and specific LD diagnosis with Psycho ed evaluation
With general application: NR
To receive services after enrolling: Yes
What documentation required for ADHD: Comprehensive evaluation with written interpretive report or ADHD certification, WAIS and Achievement Testing
With general application: NR
To receive services after enrolling: Yes
What documentation required for ASD: BAP requires an interview and Psycho Ed
With general application: NR
To receive services after enrolling: Yes
LD/ADHD/ASD documentation submitted to: Learning Resource Program
ASD Specific Program: NR
Special Ed. HS course work accepted: No
Specific course requirements of all applicants: NR
Separate application required: Yes
Total # of students receiving LD/ADHD/ASD services: 125
Acceptance into program means acceptance into college: Yes

Admissions

TThe Learning Resource Program conducts a highly individualized assessment of each candidate's application and documentation. Candidates may or may not meet admission criteria to the University based on standardized test scores. Criteria for admission include: Primary diagnosis of specific LD or ADHD, average to superior intelligence (WAIS), social maturity, demonstrated motivation to participate in the Program and able to meet the intellectual challenges and responsibilities of university life. These qualities are assessed in interviews with the professional staff and through recommendations. Applicants will have succeeded in college prep courses and shown progress in their academic careers. Two letters of recommendation are required. A recent psycho Ed evaluation providing clear evidence of a specific LD and/or AD/HD and suggested reasonable accommodations must be included. Judgment of the professional staff will determine eligibility for the program.

Additional Information

In the Learning Resource Program students receive intensive academic tutoring and individual counseling. Course content and requirements are never compromised for students with LD but program procedures do help to ease the way in the classroom. BAP staff consists almost exclusively of Adelphi graduate students who are studying psychology, social work, education, or communication disorders. Each student is assigned at least two staff members to work with them a minimum of four times per week on academic issues. These meetings focus on executive functioning strategies to help the student remain aware of, and plan for, upcoming assignments, exams and meetings; and assignment completion, exam preparation, and research.

General Support Services Information

Contact Information
Name of program or department: Learning Disabilities Program
Telephone: 516-877-4710
Fax: 516-877-4711

Accommodations or Services for Students with Learning Differences

Accommodations are decided upon an individual basis after a thorough review of appropriate, current documentation. The accommodations requested must be supported through the documentation provided and must be logically linked to the current impact of the condition on academic functioning.

Allowed in exams
Calculator: Yes
Dictionary: Yes
Computer: Yes
Spellchecker: Yes
Extended test time: Yes
Scribes: Yes
Proctors: Yes
Oral exams: Yes
Note-takers: Yes
Services for students with LD: Yes
Services for students with ADHD: Yes
Services for students with ASD: Yes
Distraction-reduced environment: Yes
Tape recording in class: Yes
Audio books: NR
Electronic texts: Yes
Kurzweil Reader: Yes
Other assistive technology: Yes
Priority registration: Yes
Added costs for services: Yes
LD specialists: Yes
ADHD coaching: Yes
ASD specialists: Yes
Professional tutors: No
Peer tutors: No
Max. hours/wk. for services: 3–5
How professors are notified of LD/ADHD: By both student and program

General Admissions Information

Office of Admissions: 516-877-3050

Entrance Requirements

Academic units recommended: 4 English, 3 mathematics, 3 science, 2 foreign language, 4 Social Studies, History, English, Math, Science or Foreign Language. High school diploma is required and GED is accepted. SAT or ACT required for some. If ACT, ACT with Writing component required. TOEFL required of all international applicants: minimum paper TOEFL 550.

Application deadline: NR
Average GPA: 3.4
ACT Composite middle 50% range: 22-28
SAT Math middle 50% range: 520-620
SAT Critical Reading middle 50% range: 500-600
SAT Writing middle 50% range: 510-610
Graduated top 10% of class: 26
Graduated top 25% of class: 64
Graduated top 50% of class: 92

COLLEGE GRADUATION REQUIREMENTS

Course waivers allowed: No
Course substitutions allowed: No

Additional Information

Environment: The university is located on a 75-acre campus 20 miles from New York City.

Student Body
Undergrad enrollment: 5,000
% % Women: 69
% % Men: 31
% Out-of-state: 8

Cost information
Tuition: $29,300
Room & board: $12,330

Housing Information
University housing: Yes
% Living on campus: 23

Greek System
Fraternity: Yes
Sorority: Yes
Athletics: Division II

Barnard College

3009 Broadway New York, NY 10027
Phone: 212-854-2014 • Fax: 212-854-6220
E-mail: admissions@barnard.edu • Web: www.barnard.edu
Support: S • Institution: Private

Programs or Services for Students with Learning Differences

In 1978, Barnard established a program to provide services for students with disabilities which enhance their educational, professional and personal development. The Office of Disability Services (ODS) serves students with visual, mobility and hearing disabilities, and students with invisible disabilities such as chronic medical conditions, learning disabilities/ADD, psychological disabilities and substance use/recovery. The Office of Disability Services' mission is to provide support services to students, faculty and staff which encourage Barnard students with disabilities to become self-sufficient in managing their own accommodations.

Admission Information for Students with Learning Differences

College entrance test required: Yes
Interview required: Not Applicable
Essay required: Not Applicable
Additional Application Required for LD/ADHD/ASD: Not Applicable
What documentation required for LD: N/A
With general application: Not Applicable
To receive services after enrolling: Not Applicable
What documentation required for ADHD: N/A
With general application: Not Applicable
To receive services after enrolling: Not Applicable
What documentation required for ASD: N/A
With general application: Not Applicable
To receive services after enrolling: Not Applicable
LD/ADHD/ASD documentation submitted to: Office of Disability Services
ASD Specific Program: No
Special Ed. HS course work accepted: Yes
Specific course requirements of all applicants: Yes
Separate application required for program services: True
Total # of students receiving LD/ADHD/ASD services: NR
Acceptance into program means acceptance into college: Not Applicable

Admissions

Students are held to the same admissions criteria as students without any needs for accommodations.

Additional Information

To register with ODS, you will need to have an intake session with our Director or Accommodations Coordinator. Call the office at 212-854-4634 to set up an appointment time. Accommodations are not retroactive, so we can only set up accommodations for your classes or exams after you have your intake meeting with us so it's important to register with ODS early in the semester to use your accommodations for all your coursework. Intakes are not conducted past the second to last full week of classes. Students may register throughout the semester, however, no intake meetings are conducted during midterm exams, final exams, or the last two weeks of the semester unless a student has a brand new diagnosis that was just found out in the last two weeks of the semester. It's imperative that ODS has at least two weeks prior to final exams to get accommodations set up for students, so we'd be happy to meet with new students for accommodations for the following semester after final exams end. At your appointment, ODS staff will likely spend some time chatting with you in order to get to know you and your needs. ODS staff will explain ODS policies and procedures for accessing accommodations, complete an intake packet with you, and create an accommodation plan for you!

General Support Services Information

Contact Information
Name of program or department: Office of Disability Services
Telephone: 212-854-4634
Fax: 212-854-6275
Website: NR

Accommodations or Services for Students with Learning Differences

Accommodations are decided upon an individual basis after a thorough review of appropriate, current documentation. The accommodations requests must be supported through the documentation provided and must be logically linked to the current impact of the condition on academic functioning.

Allowed in exams
Calculator: Yes
Dictionary: Yes
Computer: Yes
Spellchecker: Yes
Extended test time: Yes
Scribes: Yes
Proctors: Yes
Oral exams: No
Note-takers: Yes
Support services for students with LD: Yes
Support services for students with ADHD: Yes
Support services for students with ASD: Yes
Distraction-reduced environment: Yes
Tape recording in class: Yes
Electronic texts: No
Kurzweil reader: NR
Audio books: Yes
Other assistive technology: No
Priority registration: No
Added costs of services: No
LD specialists: No
ADHD coaching: Yes
ASD specialists: Yes
Professional tutors: No
Peer tutors: Yes
Max. hours/wk. for services: NR
How professors are notified of student approved accommodations: By both student and director

General Admissions Information

Office of Admissions: 212-854-2014

Entrance Requirements

Academic units recommended: 4 English, 3 math, 3 science, 3 foreign language, 3 history, High school diploma or equivalent is not required. . If ACT, ACT with writing accepted. TOEFL required of all international applicants: minimum paper TOEFL 600 or minimum internet TOEFL 100.

Application deadline: 1/1
Notification:4/1
Average GPA: 3.9
ACT Composite middle 50% range: 29-32
SAT Math middle 50% range: 620-720
SAT Critical Reading middle 50% range: 640-730
SAT Writing middle 50% range: 650-740
Graduate top 10% of class: 81
Graduated top 25% of class: 94
Graduated top 50% of class: 99

COLLEGE GRADUATION REQUIREMENTS

Course waivers allowed: No
In what course: NR
Course substitutions allowed: No
In what course: NR

Additional Information

Environment: This private school was founded in 1889. It has a 4-acre campus.

Student Body
Undergrad enrollment: 2,556
% Women: 100
% Men: 00
% Out-of-state: 74

Cost information
Tuition: $48,614
Room & board: $9,230
Housing Information
University Housing: Yes
Percent living on campus: 91

Greek System
Fraternity: No
Sorority: Yes

Canisius College

2001 Main Street, Buffalo, NY 14208
Phone: 716-888-2200 • Fax: 716-888-3230
E-mail: admissions@canisius.edu • Web: http://www.canisius.edu
Support: CS • Institution: Private

Programs or Services for Students with Learning Differences

Students are encouraged to self identify as learning disabled or special needs. The College is committed to creating equal access for all students with disabilities. It is our goal to help meet the needs of individuals registered and documented through the office, whether the disability is permanent or temporary.

Admission Information for Students with Learning Differences

College entrance test required: Yes
Interview required: No
Essay required: Not Applicable
Additional Application Required for LD/ADHD/ASD: Not Applicable
What documentation required for LD: Written confirmation supplied by a Medical Provider
With general application: Not Applicable
To receive services after enrolling: Not Applicable
What documentation required for ADHD: Written confirmation Supplied by a Medical Provider
With general application: Not Applicable
To receive services after enrolling: Not Applicable
What documentation required for ASD: Written confirmation supplied by a Medical Provider
With general application: Not Applicable
To receive services after enrolling: Not Applicable
LD/ADHD/ASD documentation submitted to: Accessibility Support Services
ASD Specific Program: Reasonable Housing Accomondations
Special Ed. HS course work accepted: Not Applicable
Specific course requirements of all applicants: Yes
Separate application required for program services: False
Total # of students receiving LD/ADHD/ASD services: NR
Acceptance into program means acceptance into college: Not Applicable

Admissions

There is no special admissions criteria for students with learning disabilities. When reviewing the application for admission, the Admissions Committee looks for students with at least a solid B average in a college preparatory program of study. Rigor of curriculum, including the types of courses being taken in the senior year, is considered the most important factor in the admissions decision.

Additional Information

Students must self-identify with the GRIFF Center for Academic Engagement , complete the Accessibility Support intake form, and provide current documentation. The student then meets with a professional in AS to discuss the accommodations, and to become familiar with the procedures. Students can receive alternative texts, note takers, readers, talking calculators, and assistive listening devices . The Griff Center Proctor Site is a designated area for students that need testing accommodations due to a disability or to make up a missed exam. Test accommodations are determined on a case-by-case basis.

General Support Services Information

Contact Information
Name of program or department: Accessibility Support Services
Telephone: 716-888-2476
Fax: 706-888-3212
Website: NR

Accommodations or Services for Students with Learning Differences

Accommodations are decided upon an individual basis after a thorough review of appropriate, current documentation. The accommodations requests must be supported through the documentation provided and must be logically linked to the current impact of the condition on academic functioning.

Allowed in exams
Calculator: Yes
Dictionary: Yes
Computer: Yes
Spellchecker: Yes
Extended test time: Yes
Scribes: Yes
Proctors: Yes
Oral exams: Yes
Note-takers: Yes
Support services for students with LD: Yes
Support services for students with ADHD: Yes
Support services for students with ASD: Yes
Distraction-reduced environment: Yes
Tape recording in class: Yes
Electronic texts: Yes
Kurzweil reader: NR
Audio books: Yes
Other assistive technology: Yes
Priority registration: No
Added costs of services: No
LD specialists: Yes
ADHD coaching: Yes
ASD specialists: Not Applicable
Professional tutors: Yes
Peer tutors: No
Max. hours/wk. for services: 47
How professors are notified of student approved accommodations: By director

General Admissions Information

Office of Admissions: 716-888-2200

Entrance Requirements

Academic units required: 4 English, 3 math, 3 science, 2 science labs, 2 foreign language, 4 social studies, **Academic units recommended:** 4 English, 4 math, 4 science, 2 science labs, 4 foreign language, 4 social studies, 4 academic electives, High school diploma is required and GED is accepted. SAT or ACT required. If ACT, ACT with writing accepted. TOEFL required of all international applicants: minimum paper TOEFL 550 or minimum internet TOEFL 79.

Application deadline: 5/1
Notification: Rolling starting 12/15
Average GPA: 3.47
ACT Composite middle 50% range: 21-27
SAT Math middle 50% range: 480-600
SAT Critical Reading middle 50% range: 470-580
SAT Writing middle 50% range: NR-NR
Graduate top 10% of class: 18
Graduated top 25% of class: 50
Graduated top 50% of class: 88

COLLEGE GRADUATION REQUIREMENTS

Course waivers allowed: Yes
In what course: Based on applicable documentation mainly math and foreign languages.
Course substitutions allowed: Yes
In what course: primarily math and foreign languages.

Additional Information

Environment: This private school, affiliated with the Roman Catholic-Jesuit Church, was founded in 1870. It has a 32-acre campus.

Student Body
Undergrad enrollment: 2,671
% Women: 54
% Men: 46
% Out-of-state: 9.4

Cost information
Tuition: $33,282
Room & board: $12,766
Housing Information
University Housing: Yes
Percent living on campus: 45.9

Greek System
Fraternity: Yes
Sorority: Yes
Athletics: Division I

CUNY—Hunter College

695 Park Ave, Room N203, New York, NY 10065
Phone: 212-772-4490 • Fax: 212-650-3472
E-mail: admissions@hunter.cuny.edu • Web: www.hunter.cuny.edu
Support: CS • Institution: Public

Programs or Services for Students with Learning Differences

The Office of AccessABILITY's goal is to enhance the educational experience for students with disabilities at Hunter College. Our mission is to ensure a comprehensively accessible college experience for all students with disabilities. The program is also committed to promoting access and awareness as a resource to all members of the Hunter College community.

Admission Information for Students with Learning Differences

College entrance test required: Yes
Interview required: No
Essay required: Not Applicable
Additional Application Required for LD/ADHD/ASD: Yes
What documentation required for LD: The support and services provided by the Office of AccessABILITY are based upon current supporting medical, educational and/or psychological documentation. All documents are kept confidential and will only be used for support and accommodation purposes.
With general application: No
To receive services after enrolling: Yes
What documentation required for ADHD: The support and services provided by the Office of AccessABILITY are based upon current supporting medical, educational and/or psychological documentation. All documents are kept confidential and will only be used for support and accommodation purposes.
With general application: No
To receive services after enrolling: Yes
What documentation required for ASD: The support and services provided by the Office of AccessABILITY are based upon current supporting medical, educational and/or psychological documentation. All documents are kept confidential and will only be used for support and accommodation purposes.
With general application: No
To receive services after enrolling: Yes
LD/ADHD/ASD documentation submitted to: Office of AccessABILITY
ASD Specific Program: NR
Special Ed. HS course work accepted: Not Applicable
Specific course requirements of all applicants: Yes
Separate application required for program services: True
Total # of students receiving LD/ADHD/ASD services: 350
Acceptance into program means acceptance into college: No

Admissions

There is no special admissions process for students with learning disabilities. Students must self identify and submit related documentation based on disability to secure related accommodations and services.

Additional Information

Accommodations utilized by students with learning disabilities include reduced course load and priority registration, extended time to complete assignments, note taking, extended time for tests, separate area, scribe,taped texts and a reader, calculator for tests and more. There are also auxiliary services provided by the Office of Accessibility including priority registration, readers, tutoring referrals, special workshops and seminars LEADS Counseling.

General Support Services Information

Contact Information
Name of program or department: Office of AccessABILITY
Telephone: 212-650-3581
Fax: 212-650-3449
Website: http://www.hunter.cuny.edu/studentservices/access/admission

Accommodations or Services for Students with Learning Differences

Accommodations are decided upon an individual basis after a thorough review of appropriate, current documentation. The accommodations requests must be supported through the documentation provided and must be logically linked to the current impact of the condition on academic functioning.

Allowed in exams
Calculator: Yes
Dictionary: Yes
Computer: Yes
Spellchecker: Yes
Extended test time: Yes
Scribes: Yes
Proctors: Yes
Oral exams: Yes
Note-takers: Yes
Support services for students with LD: Yes
Support services for students with ADHD: Yes
Support services for students with ASD: Yes
Distraction-reduced environment: Yes
Tape recording in class: Yes
Electronic texts: Yes
Kurzweil reader: NR
Audio books: Yes
Other assistive technology: Yes
Priority registration: Yes
Added costs of services: No
LD specialists: Yes
ADHD coaching: Yes
ASD specialists: Yes
Professional tutors: No
Peer tutors: No
Max. hours/wk. for services: NR
How professors are notified of student approved accommodations: By both student and director

General Admissions Information

Office of Admissions: 212-772-4490

Entrance Requirements

Academic units required: 2 English, 2 math, 1 science, 1 science labs, **Academic units recommended:** 4 English, 3 math, 2 science, 2 foreign language, 4 social studies, 1 academic electives, 1 visual/performing arts. High school diploma is required and GED is accepted. SAT or ACT required. TOEFL required of all international applicants: minimum paper TOEFL 500.

Application deadline: 3/15
Notification: Rolling starting 1/15
Average GPA: NR
ACT Composite middle 50% range: NR-NR
SAT Math middle 50% range: 540-640
SAT Critical Reading middle 50% range: 520-620
SAT Writing middle 50% range: NR-NR
Graduate top 10% of class: NR
Graduated top 25% of class: NR
Graduated top 50% of class: NR

COLLEGE GRADUATION REQUIREMENTS

Course waivers allowed: Yes
In what course: with appropriate documentations: foreign language
Course substitutions allowed: Yes
In what course: foreign language

Additional Information

Environment: This public school was founded in 1870.

Student Body
Undergrad enrollment: 16,550
% Women: 64
% Men: 36
% Out-of-state: 3

Cost information
In-state tuition: $6,330
Out-of-state tuition: $16,800
Room & board: $8,655

Housing Information
University Housing: Yes
Percent living on campus: NR

Greek System
Fraternity: No
Sorority: NR
Athletics: Division III

Clarkson University

8 Clarkson Ave, Box 5605, Potsdam, NY 13699
Phone: 315-268-6480 • Fax: 315-268-7647
E-mail: admission@clarkson.edu • Web: www.clarkson.edu
Support: CS • Institution: Private

Programs or Services for Students with Learning Differences

In order to assure equal access for students with disabilities, Clarkson UniversityÃ‚â ™s Office of Accommodative Services provides reasonable accommodations to qualified students in compliance with Section 504 of the Rehabilitation Act of 1973, and Title III of the Americans with Disabilities Act (ADA) of 1990, as amended in 2008. The mission of the Office of Accommodative Services at Clarkson is to assure access to the University and its programs for students with disabilities. We determine, coordinate and provide reasonable accommodations, educate and advocate for an accessible and hospitable learning environment, and promote responsibility and self-advocacy on the part of the individuals we serve.

Admission Information for Students with Learning Differences

College entrance test required: Yes
Interview required: No
Essay required: Not Applicable
Additional Application Required for LD/ADHD/ASD: No
What documentation required for LD: Psych Ed evaluation
With general application: No
To receive services after enrolling: No
What documentation required for ADHD: Psych Ed evaluation
With general application: No
To receive services after enrolling: No
What documentation required for ASD: Psych Ed evaluation
With general application: No
To receive services after enrolling: No
LD/ADHD/ASD documentation submitted to: Office of Accommodative Services
ASD Specific Program: No
Special Ed. HS course work accepted: Not Applicable
Specific course requirements of all applicants: NR
Separate application required for program services: False
Total # of students receiving LD/ADHD/ASD services: 190
Acceptance into program means acceptance into college: No

Admissions

The admission process and criteria are the same for all students applying to Clarkson. Documentation should be submitted to the Office of Accommodative services after being admitted. Courses required include 4 years of English, 3-4 years of math, 1-4 years of science (chemistry and physics required for engineering majors). Interviews are helpful. Talented high school juniors can apply after 11th grade and enter early.

Additional Information

There are many resources available to support students with disabilities. Student Support Services offers academic support. Some services include weekly small group tutoring. The Writing Center offers one-to-one help with academic and personal projects, like essays, reports, labs and presentations. All students can seek out tutoring resources, each student must manage their own time and complete assignments independently. A student needs to study at least 2 to 3 hours outside of class for each hour of class.

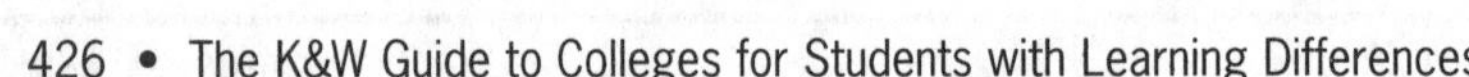

General Support Services Information

Contact Information
Name of program or department: Office of Accommodative Services
Telephone: 315-268-7643
Fax: 315-268-2400
Website: http://clarkson.edu/oas

Accommodations or Services for Students with Learning Differences

Accommodations are decided upon an individual basis after a thorough review of appropriate, current documentation. The accommodations requests must be supported through the documentation provided and must be logically linked to the current impact of the condition on academic functioning.

Allowed in exams
Calculator: Yes
Dictionary: Yes
Computer: Yes
Spellchecker: Yes
Extended test time: Yes
Scribes: Yes
Proctors: Yes
Oral exams: Yes
Note-takers: Yes
Support services for students with LD: Yes
Support services for students with ADHD: Yes
Support services for students with ASD: Yes
Distraction-reduced environment: Yes
Tape recording in class: Yes
Electronic texts: Yes
Kurzweil reader: NR
Audio books: Yes
Other assistive technology: Yes
Priority registration: Yes
Added costs of services: No
LD specialists: Yes
ADHD coaching: Yes
ASD specialists: No
Professional tutors: No
Peer tutors: NR
Max. hours/wk. for services: NR
How professors are notified of student approved accommodations: By both student and director

General Admissions Information

Office of Admissions: 315-268-6480

Entrance Requirements

Academic units required: 4 English, 3 math, 1 science, and 4 units from above areas or other academic areas. **Academic units recommended:** 4 math, 4 science, High school diploma is required and GED is accepted. SAT or ACT required. If ACT, ACT with writing accepted. TOEFL required of all international applicants: minimum paper TOEFL 550 or minimum internet TOEFL 80.

Application deadline: 1/15
Notification: Rolling starting 2/1
Average GPA: 3.7
ACT Composite middle 50% range: 24-30
SAT Math middle 50% range: 560-660
SAT Critical Reading middle 50% range: 520-630
SAT Writing middle 50% range: 490-600
Graduate top 10% of class: 36
Graduated top 25% of class: 72
Graduated top 50% of class: 95

COLLEGE GRADUATION REQUIREMENTS

Course waivers allowed: Yes
In what course: on a case-by-case basis
Course substitutions allowed: Yes
In what course: on a case by case basis

Additional Information

Environment: This private school was founded in 1896. It has a 640-acre campus.

Student Body
Undergrad enrollment: 3,257
% Women: 30
% Men: 70
% Out-of-state: 26
Cost information
Tuition: $46,132
Room & board: $14,556
Housing Information
University Housing: Yes
Percent living on campus: 84
Greek System
Fraternity: Yes
Sorority: Yes
Athletics: Division III

Colgate University

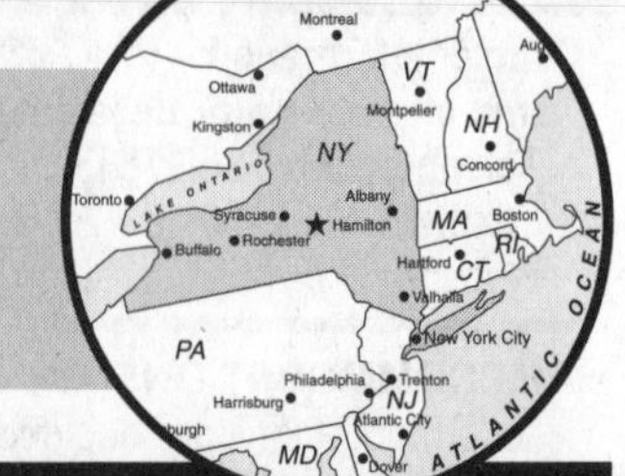

13 Oak Drive, Hamilton, NY 13346
Phone: 315-228-7401 • Fax: 315-228-7544
E-mail: admission@colgate.edu • Web: www.colgate.edu
Support: CS • Institution: Private

Programs or Services for Students with Learning Differences

Colgate provides for a small student body a liberal arts education that will expand individual potential and ability to participate effectively in society's affairs. There are many resources available for all students. Colgate's goal is to offer resources and services within the campus-wide support system that are responsive to the various talents, needs, and preferences of students with disabilities. For the university to understand and prepare for the accommodations that may be requested, students are asked to complete a confidential self-assessment questionnaire and provide appropriate documentation about their disability. The Director of Academic Support and Disability Services works with students and faculty to assure that the needs of students with disabilities are met, serves as clearinghouse for information about disabilities, provides training and individual consultation for all members of the Colgate community, and provides academic counseling and individualized instruction. Seeking help early and learning to be a self-advocate are essential to college success.

Admission Information for Students with Learning Differences

College entrance tests required: Yes
Interview required: No
Essay required: No
Additional Application Required for LD/ADHD/ASD: NR
What documentation required for LD: Psycho ed evaluation to include: relevant historical info, instructional interventions, related services, age diagnosed, objective data (aptitude, achievement, info processing), test scores (standard, percentile and grade equivalents) and describe functional limitations.
With general application: No
To receive services after enrolling: Yes
What documentation required for ADHD: Diagnosis based on DSM-V; history of behaviors impairing functioning in academic setting; diagnostic interview; history of symptoms; evidence of ongoing behaviors.
With general application: No
To receive services after enrolling: Yes
What documentation required for ASD: Psycho ed evaluation
With general application: NR
To receive services after enrolling: Yes
LD/ADHD/ASD documentation submitted to: Academic Support
ASD Specific Program: NR
Special Ed. HS course work accepted: No
Specific course requirements of all applicants: Yes
Separate application required: No
Total # of students receiving LD/ADHD/ASD services: NR
Acceptance into program means acceptance into college: Students must be admitted to and enrolled in the university first and then request services.

Admissions

There is no special admission process for students with learning disabilities. The Office of Admissions reviews the applications of all candidates for admission. The admissions staff looks for evidence of substantial achievement in a rigorous secondary school curriculum, one counselor recommendation, standardized testing, a personalized essay, and extracurricular involvement. Also valued are qualities such as curiosity, originality, thoughtfulness, and persistence. Admission is very competitive. Criteria include 16 courses in a college-preparatory program (20 recommended): 4 years of English, 3–4 years of math, 3–4 years of science, 3–4 years of social studies, and 3 years of a foreign language. The ACT average is 29 or the SAT Reasoning Test average is 1348. Three SAT Subject Tests of the applicant's choice are required if the applicant submits the SAT Reasoning Test. However, SAT Subject Tests are not required if the applicant submits the ACT.

Additional Information

Students are encouraged to seek help early; meet with professors at the beginning of each semester to discuss approaches and accommodations that will meet their needs; and seek assistance from the Director of Academic Support and Disability Services, administrative advisor, and faculty advisor. Modifications in the curriculum are made on an individual basis. Colgate provides services in support of academic work on an as-needed basis, such as assistance with note-takers, tape-recorded lectures, tutors, readers, and assistive technology. There is a Writing and Speaking Center and tutoring, and skills help is available in writing, reading, and study strategies. Services and accommodations are available for undergraduate and graduate students. Students must complete a Special Needs Identification Form and mail to: Lynn Waldman, Director of Academic Support and Disability Services, Center for Learning, Teaching, and Research, 101A Lathrop Hall, Colgate University, 13 Oak Drive, Hamilton, NY 13346.

General Support Services Information

Contact Information
Name of program or department: Academic Program Support and Disability Services
Telephone: 315-228-7375
Fax: 315-228-7831

Accommodations or Services for Students with Learning Differences

Accommodations are decided upon an individual basis after a thorough review of appropriate, current documentation. The accommodations requested must be supported through the documentation provided and must be logically linked to the current impact of the condition on academic functioning.

Allowed in exams
Calculator: Yes
Dictionary: Yes
Computer: Yes
Spellchecker: Yes
Extended test time: Yes
Scribes: Yes
Proctors: Yes
Oral exams: Yes
Note-takers: Yes
Services for students with LD: Yes
Services for students with ADHD: Yes
Services for students with ASD: Yes
Distraction-reduced environment: Yes
Tape recording in class: Yes
Audio books: NR
Electronic texts: Yes
Kurzweil Reader: Yes
Other assistive technology: Yes
Priority registration: Yes
Added costs for services: No
LD specialists: Yes
ADHD coaching: NR
ASD specialists: NR
Professional tutors: No
Peer tutors: Yes
Max. hours/wk. for services: Unlimited
How professors are notified of LD/ADHD: By student

General Admissions Information

Office of Admissions: 315-228-7401

Entrance Requirements

Academic units required: 4 English, 3 math, 3 science, 2 science labs, 3 foreign language, 3 social studies. **Academic units recommended:** 4 English, 4 math, 4 science, 4 science labs, 4 foreign language, 4 social studies. High school diploma is required and GED is accepted. SAT or ACT required. If ACT, ACT with writing accepted. TOEFL required of all international applicants.

Application deadline: 1/15
Notification: 4/1
Average GPA: 3.67
ACT Composite middle 50% range: 29-32
SAT Math middle 50% range: 650-750
SAT Critical Reading middle 50% range: 630-720
SAT Writing middle 50% range: NR-NR
Graduated top 10% of class: 72
Graduated top 25% of class: 92
Graduated top 50% of class: 98

COLLEGE GRADUATION REQUIREMENTS

Course waivers allowed: Yes
Course substitutions allowed: Yes
In what course: Foreign language—all requests are considered case-by-case.

Additional Information

Environment: This private school was founded in 1819. It has a 515-acre campus.

Student Body
Undergrad enrollment: 2,875
% Women: 54
% Men: 46
% Out-of-state: 73

Cost information
Tuition: $47,855
Room & board: $11,510

Housing Information
University Housing: Yes
Percent living on campus: NR

Greek System
Fraternity: Yes
Sorority: Yes
Athletics: Division I

Concordia College (NY)

171 White Plains Road, Bronxville, NY 10708
Phone: 914-337-9300 • Fax: 914-395-4636
E-mail: admission@concordia-ny.edu • Web: www.concordia-ny.edu
Support: CS • Institution: Private

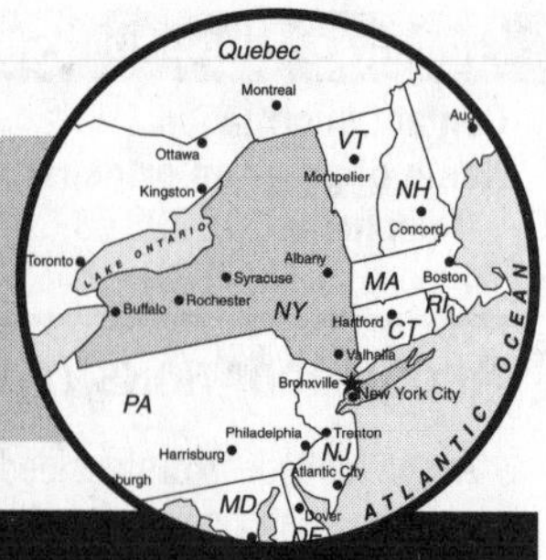

Programs or Services for Students with Learning Differences

Concordia Connection is a program for students with LD who have demonstrated the potential to earn a college degree. Their commitment is to provide an intimate, supportive, and caring environment where students with special learning needs can experience college as a successful and rewarding endeavor. This is a mainstream program. Students are fully integrated into the college. During the fall and spring semesters, students are registered for four or five classes. Additionally, students are registered for a one-credit independent study, which incorporates a weekly, 1-hour group session with the director and staff that focuses on the development of individualized learning strategies. Progress is monitored, and an assessment of learning potential and academic levels is provided. The program's director coordinates support services and works with the assigned freshman advisor to assure an optimal course plan each semester. A one summer orientation and academic seminar is required for all new Concordia Connection students.

Admission Information for Students with Learning Differences

College entrance tests required: Yes
Interview required: No
Essay required: Yes
Additional Application Required for LD/ADHD/ASD: NR
What documentation required for LD: Psycho ed evaluation to include: relevant historical info, instructional interventions, related services, age diagnosed, objective data (aptitude, achievement, info processing), test scores (standard, percentile and grade equivalents) and describe functional limitations.
With general application: No
To receive services after enrolling: Yes
What documentation required for ADHD: Diagnosis based on DSM-V; history of behaviors impairing functioning in academic setting; diagnostic interview; history of symptoms; evidence of ongoing behaviors.
With general application: No
To receive services after enrolling: Yes
What documentation required for ASD: Psycho ed evaluation
With general application: NR
To receive services after enrolling: Yes
LD/ADHD/ASD documentation submitted to: Admissions
ASD Specific Program: NR
Special Ed. HS course work accepted: No
Specific course requirements of all applicants: Yes
Separate application required: No
Total # of students receiving LD/ADHD/ASD services: 32–50
Acceptance into program means acceptance into college: Students must be admitted to and enrolled in the university first and then request services. Some are reviewed by the LD program, which provides a recommendation to the Admissions Office.

Admissions

Students wishing to apply should submit the following documents to the Admissions Office: a Concordia application and the student's current transcript; SAT/ACT scores; documentation of LD, which must minimally include a WAIS–IV profile with subtest scores that was completed within the past year and the student's most recent IEP; recommendations from an LD specialist and a guidance counselor; and an essay describing the nature of the LD, the effect on learning patterns, and the student's reason for pursuing college. Visits are encouraged. Applicants must be high school graduates, have a diagnosed LD, have college-prep courses, and be committed to being successful. General admissions criteria include a B average, ACT/SAT scores (used to assess strengths and weaknesses rather than for acceptance or denial), and college-preparatory courses in high school (foreign language is recommended but not required). Students with LD who self-disclose and provide documentation will be reviewed by the Admissions Office and the director of Concordia Connection.

Additional Information

The Concordia Connection provides services to all students. These include test-taking modifications, taped text books, computer access, and tutoring. Although there are no charges for students requesting peer tutoring, there is a $6,000 charge for program services. Skills courses for credit are offered in time management, organizational skills, and study skills. The 1-day summer orientation helps students get acquainted with support services, get exposure to academic expectations, review components and requirements of the freshman year, develop group cohesion, and explore individualized needs and strategies for seeking assistance.

General Support Services Information

Contact Information
Name of program or department: The Concordia Connection Program
Telephone: 914-337-9300, ext. 2361
Fax: 914-395-4500

Accommodations or Services for Students with Learning Differences

Accommodations are decided upon an individual basis after a thorough review of appropriate, current documentation. The accommodations requested must be supported through the documentation provided and must be logically linked to the current impact of the condition on academic functioning.

Allowed in exams
Calculator: Yes
Dictionary: Yes
Computer: Yes
Spellchecker: Yes
Extended test time: Yes
Scribes: Yes
Proctors: Yes
Oral exams: Yes
Note-takers: Yes
Services for students with LD: Yes
Services for students with ADHD: Yes
Services for students with ASD: Yes
Distraction-reduced environment: Yes
Tape recording in class: Yes
Audio books: NR
Electronic texts: No
Kurzweil Reader: No
Other assistive technology: No
Priority registration: Yes
Added costs for services: Yes
LD specialists: Yes
ADHD coaching: NR
ASD specialists: NR
Professional tutors: 3–6
Peer tutors: 10–20
Max. hours/wk. for services: 10
How professors are notified of LD/ADHD: By both student and director

General Admissions Information

Office of Admissions: 914-337-9300

Entrance Requirements

High school diploma is required and GED is accepted. SAT or ACT required. If ACT, ACT with writing recommended. TOEFL required of all international applicants: minimum paper TOEFL 550.

Application deadline: 3/15
Notification: Rolling starting 1/15
Average GPA: 2.7
ACT Composite middle 50% range: 16-20
SAT Math middle 50% range: 415-505
SAT Critical Reading middle 50% range: 420-500
SAT Writing middle 50% range: 415-480
Graduated top 10% of class: NR
Graduated top 25% of class: NR
Graduated top 50% of class: NR

COLLEGE GRADUATION REQUIREMENTS

Course waivers allowed: No
Course substitutions allowed: Yes
In what course: Substitution of American Sign Language for foreign language

Additional Information

Environment: This private school, affiliated with the Lutheran Church, was founded in 1881. It has a 33-acre campus.

Student Body
Undergrad enrollment: 887
% Women: 67
% Men: 33
% Out-of-state: 27

Cost information
Tuition: $27,740
Room & board: $10,265
Housing Information
University Housing: Yes
Percent living on campus: 68

Greek System
Fraternity: No
Sorority: No
Athletics: Division II

Cornell University

Undergraduate Admissions, 410 Thurston Avenue, Ithaca, NY 14850
Phone: 607-255-5241 • Fax: 607-255-0659
E-mail: admissions@cornell.edu • Web: www.cornell.edu
Support: S • Institution type: 4-year Private

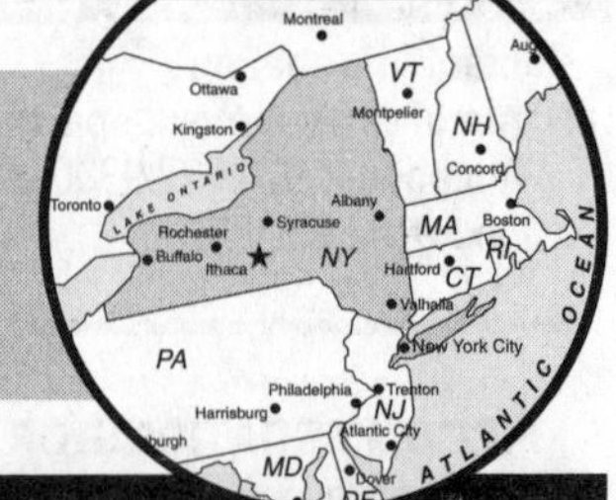

Programs or Services for Students with Learning Differences

Cornell University strives to be an accessible community where students with disabilities have an equitable opportunity to fully participate in all aspects of university life. Students with disabilities must submit requests for disability services to the Student Disability Services (SDS) office. The SDS staff is responsible for determining appropriate and effective federally mandated support services for eligible students. The university provides support services for a broad range of disabilities. There is not a specific program designed for students with learning disabilities. Once a student has been approved for disability services, many units across campus are responsible for fulfilling access needs. Students are directly involved in the process of arranging accommodations with instructors and for following established procedures for using disability services.

Admission Information for Students with Learning Differences

College entrance test required: NR
Interview required: No
Essay required: Not Applicable
Additional Application Required for LD/ADHD/ASD: NR
What documentation required for LD: Guidelines for documentation are available at http://sds.cornell.edu/Getting_Started/Doc_Guides/index.html
With general application: NR
To receive services after enrolling: Yes
What documentation required for ADHD: Guidelines for documentation are available at http://sds.cornell.edu/Getting_Started/Doc_Guides/index.html
With general application: NR
To receive services after enrolling: Yes
What documentation required for ASD: Guidelines for documentation are available at http://sds.cornell.edu/Getting_Started/Doc_Guides/index.html
With general application: NR
To receive services after enrolling: Yes
LD/ADHD/ASD documentation submitted to: Student Disability Services
ASD Specific Program: NR
Special Ed. HS course work accepted: NR
Specific course requirements of all applicants: Yes
Separate application required for program services: NR
Total # of students receiving LD/ADHD/ASD services: NR
Acceptance into program means acceptance into college: NR

Admissions

Cornell does not have a special admissions process for students with learning disabilities. All students applying to Cornell are expected to meet admissions criteria. General admission requirements include 16 units of English, math, science, social studies, and foreign language. Each of the seven undergraduate colleges has its own specific requirements. Admission is very competitive and most of the admitted students rank in the top 10 percent of the class, at least, and have taken AP and honors courses in high school. Disability documentation should not be sent along with the admissions application, but should be sent directly to Student Disability Services after acceptance to Cornell.

Additional Information

Students are encouraged to complete a disability self-identification form that is included on the New Students website. Once Student Disability Services has received current and complete documentation of a disability, the staff will work with students to determine effective and reasonable accommodations. Diagnostic testing, remedial courses, and tutors specifically selected to work with students with LD are not available at Cornell. The Learning Strategies Center provides general supportive services including classes and workshops in reading comprehension, organizational skills, note-taking, and exam preparation. The Learning Strategies Center is available to all students.

General Support Services Information

Contact Information
Name of program or department: Student Disability Services
Telephone: 607-254-4545
Fax: 607-255-1562
Website: http://sds.cornell.edu/index.html

Accommodations or Services for Students With Learning Differences

Accommodations are decided upon an individual basis after a thorough review of appropriate, current documentation. The accommodations requests must be supported through the documentation provided and must be logically linked to the current impact of the condition on academic functioning.

Allowed in exams
Calculator: Yes
Dictionary: Yes
Computer: Yes
Spellchecker: Yes
Extended test time: Yes
Scribes: Yes
Proctors: Yes
Oral exams: Yes
Note-takers: Yes
Support services for students with LD: Yes
Support services for students with ADHD: Yes
Support services for students with ASD: Yes
Distraction-reduced environment: Yes
Tape recording in class: Yes
Electronic texts: Yes
Kurzweil reader: NR
Audio books: Yes
Other assistive technology: Yes
Priority registration: No
Added costs of services: No
LD specialists: No
ADHD coaching: No
ASD specialists: No
Professional tutors: No
Peer tutors: Not Applicable
Max. hours/wk. for services: NR
How professors are notified of student approved accommodations: By student

General Admissions Information

Office of Admissions: 607-255-5241

Entrance Requirements

Academic units required: 4 English, 3 math, **Academic units recommended:** 3 science, 3 science labs, 3 foreign language, 3 social studies, 3 history. High school diploma or equivalent is not required. SAT or ACT required. If ACT, ACT with writing accepted. TOEFL required of all international applicants: minimum paper TOEFL 600 or minimum internet TOEFL 100.

Application deadline: 1/2
Notification: NR
Average GPA: NR
ACT Composite middle 50% range: 30-34
SAT Math middle 50% range: 680-780
SAT Critical Reading middle 50% range: 650-750
SAT Writing middle 50% range: NR-NR
Graduate top 10% of class: 89
Graduated top 25% of class: 97
Graduated top 50% of class: 100

COLLEGE GRADUATION REQUIREMENTS

Course waivers allowed: No
Course substitutions allowed: Not Applicable

Additional Information

Environment: This private school was founded in 1865. It has a 745-acre campus.

Student Body
Undergrad enrollment: 14,315
% Women: 52
% Men: 48
% Out-of-state: 65

Cost information
Tuition: $50,953
Room & board: $13,900
Housing Information
University Housing: Yes
Percent living on campus: 55

Greek System
Fraternity: Yes
Sorority: Yes
Athletics: Division I

Dowling College

Idle Hour Boulevard, Oakdale, NY 11769-1999
Phone: 800-369-5464 • Fax: 631-563-3827
E-mail: admissions@dowling.edu • Web: www.dowling.edu
Support: SP • Institution: Private

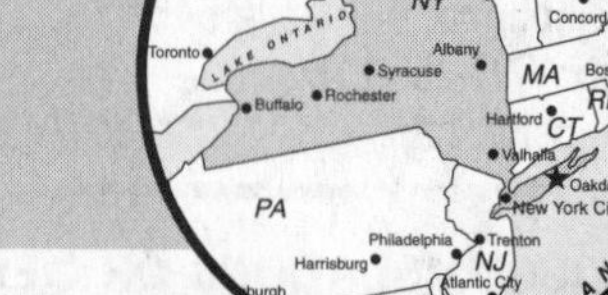

Programs or Services for Students with Learning Differences

Dowling College's Program for Potentially Gifted College Students (it is still a program devoted to students with learning disabilities; however, as one recent graduate noted, "We learn differently, we do not have a disability") is a small, individualized program that provides for cognitive development. The college is looking for students who are committed to life-long learning who have taken academically demanding courses in high school. They seek students who are eager and willing to persevere to achieve their goals. Additionally, students need to be interested and involved in community and extracurricular activities. There is a fee of approximately $2,000 per semester for services from the LD program. Students must submit a recent psychoevaluation and an IEP to be eligible to receive services or accommodations. Students are encouraged to make sure that their IEPs include all of the necessary accommodations. Students sign a contract promising to attend tutoring sessions and all of their classes. Services are available all four years; additionally, for those who have completed an undergraduate program at Dowling, a graduate program is now offered.

Admission Information for Students with Learning Differences

College entrance test required: No
Interview required: Yes
Essay required: Not Applicable
Additional Application Required for LD/ADHD/ASD: Yes
What documentation required for LD: IEP or documentation from a physician
With general application: Not Applicable
To receive services after enrolling: Yes
What documentation required for ADHD: IEP
With general application: Not Applicable
To receive services after enrolling: Yes
What documentation required for ASD: IEP, psychological
With general application: Not Applicable
To receive services after enrolling: Yes
LD/ADHD/ASD documentation submitted to: Peter Hausman Center
ASD Specific Program: NR
Special Ed. HS course work accepted: Yes
Specific course requirements of all applicants: Yes
Separate application required for program services: Yes
Total # of students receiving LD/ADHD/ASD services: NR
Acceptance into program means acceptance into college: Not Applicable

Admissions

Students must be admitted to Dowling College first and then may request an application to the Dowling College Academic Access Program . Applicants to Dowling College are encouraged to submit either the ACT or SAT. Students should have 16 academic courses in high school, including four years of English. Students must have an interview. Once a student with LD has been admitted to the college, s/he may submit an application to the LD program. Both student and parent are required to complete an application. Students must submit their most recent IEP and psychoeducational evaluation. An interview is required, and the director looksfor students with tenacity and motivation. Approximately 25 students are admitted to the program each year.

Additional Information

College Academic Access Program offers support services, and a liaison between professors and students, weekly writing workshops and early individualized class selection. In addition, students who have specific discipline needs will visit the student service center. The program will concentrate on developing individualized academic strategies for success; tutors are trained to provide academic support. This is a lab school at which students with learning disabilities receive tutoring at least twice a week in learning strategies. Students are eligible to receive all accommodations or services that are listed in their most recent IEP. For students who will not be serviced in the Dowling College Academic Access Program, there is the Hausman Center.

General Support Services Information

Contact Information
Name of program or department: Peter Hausman Center
Telephone: 631 244-3144
Fax: 631 244-1098
Website: NR

Accommodations or Services For Students With Learning Differences

Accommodations are decided upon an individual basis after a thorough review of appropriate, current documentation. The accommodations requests must be supported through the documentation provided and must be logically linked to the current impact of the condition on academic functioning.

Allowed in exams
Calculator: Yes
Dictionary: Yes
Computer: Yes
Spellchecker: Yes
Extended test time: Yes
Scribes: Yes
Proctors: Yes
Oral exams: Yes
Note-takers: Yes
Support services for students with LD: Yes
Support services for students with ADHD: Yes
Support services for students with ASD: Yes
Distraction-reduced environment: Yes
Tape recording in class: Yes
Electronic texts: No
Kurzweil reader: NR
Audio books: Yes
Other assistive technology: No
Priority registration: Yes
Added costs of services: Yes
LD specialists: Yes
ADHD coaching: Yes
ASD specialists: Not Applicable
Professional tutors: Yes
Peer tutors: Yes
Max. hours/wk. for services: NR
How professors are notified of student approved accommodations: By student

General Admissions Information

Office of Admissions: 800-369-5464

Entrance Requirements

Academic units recommended: 4 English, 3 math, 2 science, 3 social studies, and 4 units from above areas or other academic areas. High school diploma is required and GED is accepted. SAT or ACT not used.

Application deadline: NR
Notification: NR
Average GPA: 2.8
ACT Composite middle 50% range: NR-NR
SAT Math middle 50% range: 410-520
SAT Critical Reading middle 50% range: 410-520
SAT Writing middle 50% range: NR-NR
Graduate top 10% of class: 6
Graduated top 25% of class: 19
Graduated top 50% of class: 50

COLLEGE GRADUATION REQUIREMENTS

Course waivers allowed: Yes
In what course: Foreign language for students who are language deficient with FL exemption on IEP
Course substitutions allowed: No
In what course: NR

Additional Information

Environment: This private school was founded in 1959. It has a 157-acre campus.

Student Body
Undergrad enrollment: 1,700
% Women: 55
% Men: 45
% Out-of-state: 10

Cost information
Tuition: $29,100
Room & board: $11,120
Housing Information
University Housing: Yes
Percent living on campus: 17

Greek System
Fraternity: Yes
Sorority: Yes
Athletics: Division II

HOFSTRA UNIVERSITY

100 Hofstra University, Hempstead, NY 11549
Phone: 516-463-6700 • Fax: 516-463-5100
E-mail: admission@hofstra.edu • Web: www.hofstra.edu
Support: SP • Institution: Private

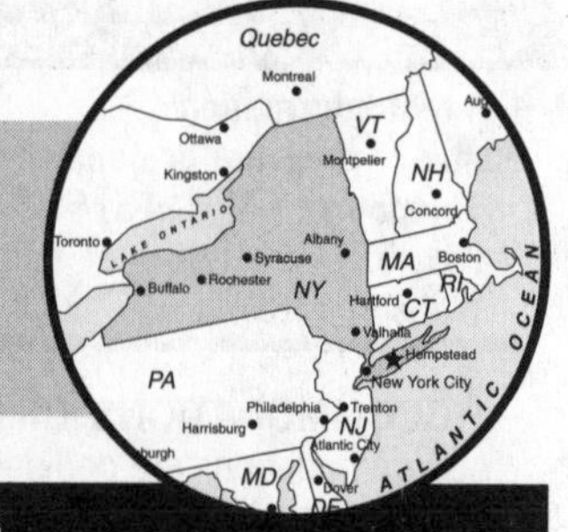

PROGRAMS OR SERVICES FOR STUDENTS WITH LEARNING DIFFERENCES

The Program for Academic Learning Skills (PALS) seeks candidates who have been diagnosed with LD and show above average intellectual ability and emotional stability. The program concentrates on identifying qualified applicants for entrance to the university and on enhancing the skills that will help students achieve academic success. Normally, candidates will be accepted into PALS for a period of one academic year. Students enrolled in the Academic Coaching program and their learning specialist will write up a set of mutually agreed upon goals for the term and will work toward meeting those specified goals. A summary of progress, the extent to which the student's goals were met, and ideas for future goals and objectives should the student re-enroll the following semester will be completed by the learning specialist at the end of each term. In addition to up to 90 minutes of individual sessions with a learning specialist per week, students enrolled in the Academic Coaching program are offered opportunities to attend study skills workshops and utilize online instructional assessments and tools designed to help them develop more efficient and effective college survival skills. To be eligible for the program, students must have a documented disability and must complete an application and interview process. The interview process will assist SSD staff in determining the student's knowledge of academic strengths and weaknesses, level of commitment to academic improvement, and desire to participate actively in Academic Coaching sessions. There is a fee for Academic Coach by semester.

ADMISSION INFORMATION FOR STUDENTS WITH LEARNING DIFFERENCES

College entrance test required: No
Interview required: Not Applicable
Essay required: Recommended
Additional Application Required for LD/ADHD/ASD: No
What documentation required for LD: Psychoeducational or neuropsychological exam.
With general application: Not Applicable
To receive services after enrolling: No
What documentation required for ADHD: Psychoeducational or neuropsychological exam.
With general application: Not Applicable
To receive services after enrolling: No
What documentation required for ASD: Psychoeducational or neuropsychological exam.
With general application: Not Applicable
To receive services after enrolling: No
LD/ADHD/ASD documentation submitted to: Student Access Services
ASD Specific Program: Academic Coaching
Special Ed. HS course work accepted: Yes
Specific course requirements of all applicants: NR
Separate application required for program services: False
Total # of students receiving LD/ADHD/ASD services: 198
Acceptance into program means acceptance into college: Not Applicable

ADMISSIONS

Students are admitted to PALS through Hofstra's Office of Admission and Student Access Services. Students complete the undergraduate admission application, and indicate on the application that they are interested in applying for PALS enrollment. In addition to the required admission materials, students submit comprehensive documentation of their specific disability. Documentation requirements can be found at hofstra.edu/PALS. Students enrolled in the Academic Coaching program and their learning specialist will write up a set of mutually agreed upon goals for the term and will work toward meeting those specified goals. A summary of progress, the extent to which the student's goals were met, and ideas for future goals and objectives should the student re-enroll the following semester will be completed by the learning specialist at the end of each term. In addition to up to 90 minutes of individual sessions with a learning specialist per week, students enrolled in the Academic Coaching program are offered opportunities to attend study skills workshops and utilize online instructional assessments and tools designed to help them develop more efficient and effective college survival skills.

ADDITIONAL INFORMATION

Enrollment in PALS is a two-semester (one-year) commitment. Students enrolled in PALS are billed a one-time, $12,500 charge during their first year at Hofstra. However, this one-time fee entitles the student to continue meeting with a learning specialist for the duration of his or her academic program at Hofstra.

General Support Services Information

Contact Information
Name of program or department: Student Access Services
Telephone: 516-463-4999
Fax: 516-463-7070
Website: www.hofstra.edu/SAS

Accommodations or Services For Students With Learning Differences

Accommodations are decided upon an individual basis after a thorough review of appropriate, current documentation. The accommodations requests must be supported through the documentation provided and must be logically linked to the current impact of the condition on academic functioning.

Allowed in exams
Calculator: Yes
Dictionary: Yes
Computer: Yes
Spellchecker: Yes
Extended test time: Yes
Scribes: Yes
Proctors: Yes
Oral exams: Yes
Note-takers: Yes
Support services for students with LD: Yes
Support services for students with ADHD: Yes
Support services for students with ASD: Yes
Distraction-reduced environment: Yes
Tape recording in class: No
Electronic texts: Yes
Kurzweil reader: NR
Audio books: Yes
Other assistive technology: Yes
Priority registration: No
Added costs of services: Yes
LD specialists: Yes
ADHD coaching: Yes
ASD specialists: Yes
Professional tutors: No
Peer tutors: NR
Max. hours/wk. for services: NR
How professors are notified of student approved accommodations: By student

General Admissions Information

Office of Admissions: 516-463-6700

Entrance Requirements

Academic units required: 4 English, 3 math, 3 science, 1 science labs, 2 foreign language, 3 social studies, **Academic units recommended:** 4 math, 4 science, 2 science labs, 3 foreign language, 4 social studies. High school diploma is required and GED is accepted. SAT or ACT considered if submitted. If ACT, ACT with writing recommended. TOEFL required of all international applicants: minimum paper TOEFL 550 or minimum internet TOEFL 80.

Application deadline: NR
Notification: NR
Average GPA: 3.62
ACT Composite middle 50% range: 24-29
SAT Math middle 50% range: 550-640
SAT Critical Reading middle 50% range: 540-620
SAT Writing middle 50% range: NR-NR
Graduate top 10% of class: 27
Graduated top 25% of class: 63
Graduated top 50% of class: 91

COLLEGE GRADUATION REQUIREMENTS

Course waivers allowed: Yes
In what course: Foreign Language Substitution.
Course substitutions allowed: NR

Additional Information

Environment: This private school was founded in 1935. It has a 240-acre campus.

Student Body
Undergrad enrollment: 6,824
% Women: 54
% Men: 46
% Out-of-state: 36

Cost information
Tuition: $39,400
Room & board: $13,950

Housing Information
University Housing: Yes
Percent living on campus: 47

Greek System
Fraternity: Yes
Sorority: Yes
Athletics: Division I

IONA COLLEGE

715 North Avenue, New Rochelle, NY 10801
Phone: 914-633-2502 • Fax: 914-633-2182
E-mail: admissions@iona.edu • Web: www.iona.edu
Support: SP • Institution: Private

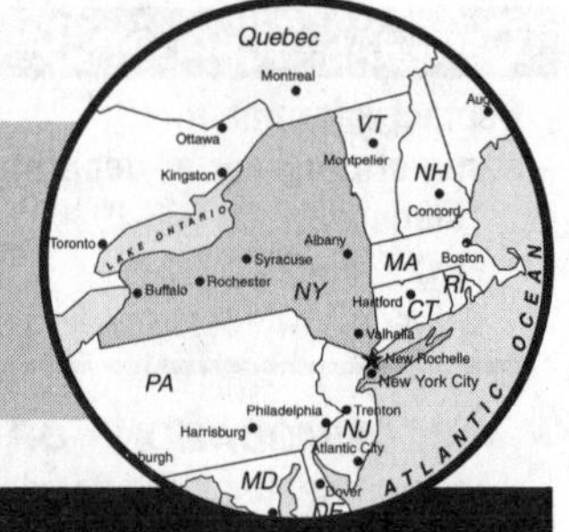

PROGRAMS OR SERVICES FOR STUDENTS WITH LEARNING DIFFERENCES

The College Assistance Program (CAP) offers comprehensive support and services for students with LD/ADHD. CAP is designed to encourage success by providing instruction tailored to individual strengths and needs. Students take standard full-time course requirements to ensure the level of quality education expected of all degree candidates. Professional tutors teach individually appropriate strategies that cross disciplines. CAP staff encourages students to become involved members of the college community. All CAP freshmen must participate in a 2-week summer orientation. During the orientation, the staff instructs and guides students in intensive writing instruction and study and organizational and time management skills; students are oriented to the college and services; individual learning styles are explored; opportunities are provided for the students to practice self-advocacy; several workshops are offered in areas that meet the student's specific needs; and individual fall classes are developed. Semester services include supplementary advisement, counseling, regularly scheduled weekly skill-based tutoring with an LD professional, study groups, skills workshops, and provision of appropriate documented accommodations.

ADMISSION INFORMATION FOR STUDENTS WITH LEARNING DIFFERENCES

College entrance test required: Yes
Interview required: Yes
Essay required: No
Additional Application Required for LD/ADHD/ASD: NR
What documentation required for LD: ADHD Verification Form
With general application: Psycho ed evaluation to include: relevant historical info, instructional interventions, related services, age diagnosed, objective data (aptitude, achievement, info processing), test scores (standard, percentile and grade equivalents) and describe functional limitations.
To receive services after enrolling: Yes
What documentation required for ADHD: Diagnosis based on DSM-V; history of behaviors impairing functioning in academic setting; diagnostic interview; history of symptoms; evidence of ongoing behaviors.
With general application: NR
To receive services after enrolling: Yes
What documentation required for ASD: 1.A Psychoeducational Report or Neuropsychological Report 2.A full scale IQ Report with scores and interpretation
With general application: NR
To receive services after enrolling: Yes
LD/ADHD/ASD documentation submitted to: College Assistance Program
ASD Specific Program: NR
Special Ed. HS course work accepted: No
Specific course requirements of all applicants: Yes
Separate application required for program services: Yes
Total # of students receiving LD/ADHD/ASD services: NR
Acceptance into program means acceptance into college: Students must be admitted to the college and to CAP simultaneously.

ADMISSIONS

All applicants must meet the same admission criteria, which include 4 years of English, 1 year of American history, 1 year of social studies, 2 years of a foreign language (waivers granted), 1 year of natural science, and 3 years of math. Students should send the following to the CAP office: a complete psychological evaluation conducted within the past 2 years that includes the WAIS or WAIS subtest scores, a comprehensive report, a copy of the most recent IEP, and two letters of recommendation (one from an LD instructor). A personal interview is required. CAP is designed for students with LD and ADHD who have been mainstreamed in their academic courses in high school. Students should be average or above average in intellectual ability, socially mature, emotionally stable, and motivated to work hard.

ADDITIONAL INFORMATION

CAP services include a freshman summer college transition program, supplementary academic advising and program planning based on each student's learning style, priority registration, 2 hours per week of scheduled skill-based individual tutoring with a professional learning specialist (additional tutoring sessions are possible), small group tutoring and workshops, testing accommodations, alternative testing procedures, special equipment, self-advocacy training, referrals to additional services on campus, and counseling services. The CAP director works with faculty to help them understand the problems faced by students with LD and explore creative ways to support the learning process. The Samuel Rudin Academic Resource Center (ARC) offers free services to all students who wish to improve their learning skills or who want academic support. ARC provides free reasonable services to all students with documented LD/ADHD.

General Support Services Information

Contact Information
Name of program or department: College Assistance Program (CAP)
Telephone: 914-633-2159
Fax: 914-633-2011

Accommodations or Services for Students with Learning Differences

Accommodations are decided upon an individual basis after a thorough review of appropriate, current documentation. The accommodations requested must be supported through the documentation provided and must be logically linked to the current impact of the condition on academic functioning.

Allowed in exams
Calculator: Yes
Dictionary: Yes
Computer: Yes
Spellchecker: Yes
Extended test time: Yes
Scribes: Yes
Proctors: Yes
Oral exams: No
Note-takers: Yes
Services for students with LD: Yes
Services for students with ADHD: Yes
Services for students with ASD: Yes
Distraction-reduced environment: Yes
Tape recording in class: Yes
Audio books: NR
Electronic texts: Yes
Kurzweil Reader: Yes
Other assistive technology: Yes
Priority registration: Yes
Added costs for services: Yes
LD specialists: Yes
ADHD coaching: NR
ASD specialists: NR
Professional tutors: 10–15
Peer tutors: No
Max. hours/wk. for services: Unlimited
How professors are notified of LD/ADHD: By student

General Admissions Information

Office of Admissions: 914-633-2502

Entrance Requirements

Academic units required: 4 English, 3 math, 3 science, 2 science labs, 2 foreign language, 2 social studies, 1 history, 1 academic electives, **Academic units recommended:** 4 math, 2 history, 3 academic electives. High school diploma is required and GED is accepted. SAT or ACT required. If ACT, ACT with writing accepted. TOEFL required of all international applicants: minimum paper TOEFL 550 or minimum internet TOEFL 80.

Application deadline: 2/15
Notification: Rolling starting 12/1
Average GPA: 2.96
ACT Composite middle 50% range: 20-25
SAT Math middle 50% range: 440-550
SAT Critical Reading middle 50% range: 450-550
SAT Writing middle 50% range: NR-NR
Graduate top 10% of class: 8
Graduated top 25% of class: 25
Graduated top 50% of class: 56

COLLEGE GRADUATION REQUIREMENTS

Course waivers allowed: NR
Course substitutions allowed: NR

Additional Information

Environment: This private school, affiliated with the Roman Catholic Church, was founded in 1940. It has a 35-acre campus.

Student Body
Undergrad enrollment: 3,271
% Women: 51
% Men: 49
% Out-of-state: 25

Cost information
Tuition: $34,384
Room & board: $14,400

Housing Information
University Housing: Yes
Percent living on campus: 41

Greek System
Fraternity: Yes
Sorority: Yes
Athletics: Division I

Le Moyne College

1419 Salt Springs Road, Syracuse, NY 13214-1301
Phone: 315-445-4300 • Fax: 315-445-4711
E-mail: admission@lemoyne.edu • Web: www.lemoyne.edu
Support: S • Institution: 4-year Private

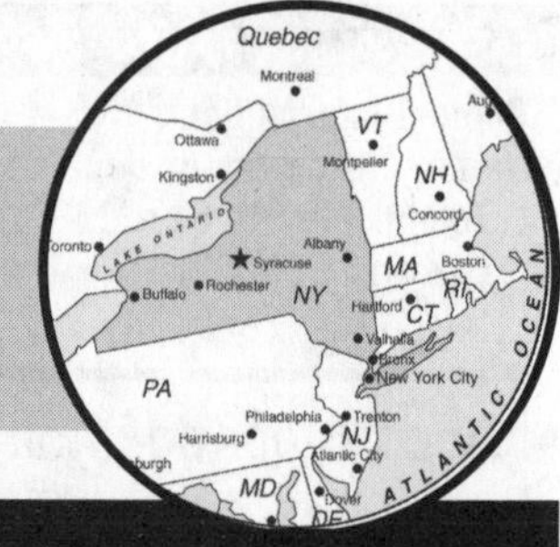

Programs or Services for Students with Learning Differences

Le Moyne College welcomes people with disabilities and, in compliance with Section 504 of the Rehabilitation Act of 1973, as amended, and the Americans with Disabilities Act of 1990, supports students' entitlements and does not discriminate on the basis of disability. Academic support services for students with disabilities are coordinated by the Director of Disability Support Services in the Academic Support Center. Students with Special Needs have access to the same support services provided to all students–individual sessions with professionals in the Academic Support Center (ASC) regarding study skills and learning strategies, ASC Workshops provided each fall semester, and individual and small-group tutoring in writing, mathematics, foreign languages, economics, and the natural sciences. In addition, students with disabilities receive individualized services through the ASC. Our goal is to create collaborative partnerships that put students in the driver's seat of their education to enhance their chances for academic success.

Admission Information for Students with Learning Differences

College entrance tests required: Yes
Interview required: No
Essay required: Yes
Additional Application Required for LD/ADHD/ASD: NR
What documentation required for LD: Psycho ed evaluation to include: relevant historical info, instructional interventions, related services, age diagnosed, objective data (aptitude, achievement, info processing), test scores (standard, percentile and grade equivalents) and describe functional limitations.
With general application: No
To receive services after enrolling: Yes
What documentation required for ADHD: Diagnosis based on DSM-V; history of behaviors impairing functioning in academic setting; diagnostic interview; history of symptoms; evidence of ongoing behaviors.
With general application: No
To receive services after enrolling: Yes
What documentation required for ASD: Psycho ed evaluation
With general application: NR
To receive services after enrolling: Yes
LD/ADHD/ASD documentation submitted to: Support Program/Services
ASD Specific Program: NR
Special Ed. HS course work accepted: No
Specific course requirements for all applicants: NR
Separate application required for program services: No
Total # of students receiving LD/ADHD/ASD services: NR
Acceptance into program means acceptance into college: NR

Admissions

Admissions to Le Moyne College is the same for all applicants. Besides a general college-prep program, it is recommended that all potential students visits the campus and interviews. For the student with learning disabilities there is an essay that is required and an interview that is recommended. The high school record is very important. Class rank, recommendations, standardized test scores, and the essay are used in the admissions process to assess the applicant. Foreign language requirement may be substituted dependent on the documentation presented by the applicant.

Additional Information

The office provides and arranges accommodations for students with special needs due to learning, emotional, and temporary or permanent diagnostic referrals, review of previously administered diagnostic tests, informal academic advising, presentation of self-advocacy skills for students, and liaison and advocacy measures with faculty and staff. If applicable you will also need to connect with appropriate adult services agencies. Students with documented disabilities may be eligible for one or more of the following services: note-takers, recorded texts, access to adaptive technologies, time extensions for exams and alternative testing sites.

General Support Services Information

Contact Information
Name of program or department: Disability Support Services
Telephone: 315-445-4118
Fax: 315-445-6014

Accommodations or Services for Students with Learning Differences

Accommodations are decided upon an individual basis after a thorough review of appropriate, current documentation. The accommodations requested must be supported through the documentation provided and must be logically linked to the current impact of the condition on academic functioning.

Allowed in exams
Calculator: Yes
Dictionary: Yes
Computer: Yes
Spellchecker: Yes
Extended test time: Yes
Scribes: N/A
Proctors: Yes
Oral exams: N/A
Note-takers: Yes
Services for students with LD: Yes
Services for students with ADHD: Yes
Services for students with ASD: Yes
Distraction-reduced environment: Yes
Tape recording in class: Yes
Audio books: NR
Electronic texts: Yes
Kurzweil Reader: Yes
Other assistive technology: Yes
Priority registration: Yes
Added costs for services: NR
LD specialists: No
ADHD coaching: NR
ASD specialists: NR
Professional tutors: Yes
Peer tutors: Yes
Max. hours/wk. for services: NR
How professors are notified of LD/ADHD: Student

General Admissions Information

Office of Admission: 315-445-4300

Entrance Requirements

Academic units required: 4 English, 3 mathematics, 3 science, 3 foreign language, 4 social studies. **Academic units recommended:** 4 mathematics, 4 science, (3 science labs). High school diploma is required and GED is accepted. SAT or ACT required; TOEFL required of all international applicants; minimum paper TOEFL 550, minimum computer TOEFL 213, minimum web-based TOEFL 79.

Application deadline: None
Average GPA: 3.37
ACT Composite middle 50% range: 21–26
SAT Math middle 50% range: 500–610
SAT Critical Reading middle 50% range: 480–590
SAT Writing middle 50% range: NR
Graduated top 10% of class: 22%
Graduated top 25% of class: 53%
Graduated top 50% of class: 88%

COLLEGE GRADUATION REQUIREMENTS

Course waivers allowed: N/A
Course substitutions allowed: Yes
In what course: Course substitutions are provided on a case-by-case basis. American Sign Language may be accepted by some majors.

Additional Information

Environment: The college is located on 161 acres in a city environment.

Student Body
Undergrad enrollment: 2,786
% Women: 60%
% Men: 40%
% Out-of-state: 6%

Cost Information
Tuition: $28,380
Room and board: $10,890

Housing Information
University housing: Yes
% Living on campus: 50%

Greek System
Fraternity: No
Sorority: No
Athletics: Division II

LONG ISLAND U.—POST

720 Northern Boulevard, Brookville, NY 11548
Phone: 516-299-2900 • Fax: 516-299-2137
E-mail: enroll@cwpost.liu.edu • Web: www.liu.edu
Support: SP • Institution type: 4-year Private

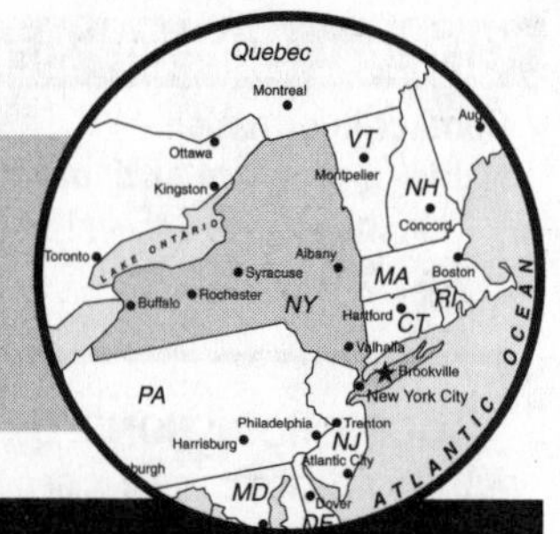

PROGRAMS OR SERVICES FOR STUDENTS WITH LEARNING DIFFERENCES

The Academic Resource Program (ARP), is housed in our Learning Support Center, is a comprehensive, structured, fee-for-service support program designed to meet the needs of students certified as having a LD and/or ADHD. Students are provided with one-on-one sessions with a trained learning assistant; an up-to-date computer lab with assistive technology; weekly meetings with an ARP administrator; and as needed, sessions with our social worker, time management counselor, and/or Bridges to Post counselor. The staff is committed to working with each individual student enrolled in the program to help students learn the strategies and skills needed to transition and succeed in college. The staff provides each student with the opportunity, structure, and support necessary to help him or her develop the academic, social, problem-solving, and strategic skills to achieve goals. This is accomplished through a structured program and an approach that is designed to assist the individual student. The key ingredient is, of course, the student and the student's desire to succeed and willingness to be actively involved in the program.

ADMISSION INFORMATION FOR STUDENTS WITH LEARNING DIFFERENCES

College entrance tests required: Yes
Interview required: Yes
Essay required: Yes
Additional Application Required for LD/ADHD/ASD: NR
What documentation required for LD: Psycho ed evaluation to include: relevant historical info, instructional interventions, related services, age diagnosed, objective data (aptitude, achievement, info processing), test scores (standard, percentile and grade equivalents) and describe functional limitations.
With general application: Yes if requested as part of Structured Program application
To receive services after enrolling: Yes
What documentation required for ADHD: Diagnosis based on DSM-V; history of behaviors impairing functioning in academic setting; diagnostic interview; history of symptoms; evidence of ongoing behaviors.
With general application: Yes if requested as part of Structured Program application
To receive services after enrolling: Yes
What documentation required for ASD: Psycho ed evaluation
With general application: NR
To receive services after enrolling: Yes
LD/ADHD/ASD documentation submitted to: Academic Resource Program
ASD Specific Program: NR
Special Ed. HS course work accepted: Yes
Specific course requirements of all applicants: NR
Separate application required: Yes
Total # of students receiving LD/ADHD/ASD services: 65–75
Acceptance into program means acceptance into college: Students must be admitted to the University first and then request an application for the program.

ADMISSIONS

Admission to the ARP is separate and distinct from admission to the university. Upon receipt of an acceptance letter from the Office of Admissions, prospective students should contact the Learning Support Center at 516-299-3057 to request an application for the Academic Resource Program. The student must submit the completed Academic Resource Program application, together with the required essay, and a Diagnostic Evaluation conducted within the past three years. Upon receipt of the completed application essay, and required psychological-educational evaluations, the staff will contact eligible candidates to schedule a personal interview, which is an integral part of the admission to ARP process.

ADDITIONAL INFORMATION

Learning assistants help freshmen make the transition from high school to college. They assist all Academic Resource Program students in time management, organizational skills, note-taking techniques, study skills, and other necessary learning strategies. Each student is responsible for his or her attendance and participation in these sessions. Freshmen and sophomores meet with a learning assistant for two hours per week. Students are welcome to schedule more hours if necessary. Juniors and seniors are given the opportunity to schedule and contract more flexible hours with the Academic Resource Program staff.

General Support Services Information

Contact Information

Name of program or department: Academic Resource Center

Telephone: 516-299-3057

Fax: 516-299-2126

Accommodations or Services for Students with Learning Differences

After a thorough review of the documentation and interview conducted with the student, ARP administrators decide upon the appropriate reasonable accommodations. All approved reasonable accommodations will be discussed with the student and will be listed on the student's Accommodations Form.

Allowed in exams
Calculator: Yes
Dictionary: Yes
Computer: Yes
Spellchecker: Yes
Extended test time: Yes
Scribes: Yes
Proctors: Yes
Oral exams: NR
Note-takers: Yes
Services for students with LD: Yes
Services for students with ADHD: Yes
Services for students with ASD: Yes
Distraction-reduced environment: Yes
Tape recording in class: Yes
Audio books: NR
Electronic texts: Yes
Kurzweil Reader: Yes
Other assistive technology: Yes
Priority registration: No
Added costs for services: Yes
LD specialists: Yes
ADHD coaching: NR
ASD specialists: NR
Professional tutors: 10–15
Peer tutors: 10
Max. hours/wk. for services: Unlimited
How professors are notified of LD/ADHD: By student with appropriate Accommodations Form

General Admissions Information

Office of Admission: 516-299-2900

Entrance Requirements

Academic units required: 4 English, 2 math, 2 science (2 science labs), 2 foreign language, 3 social studies, 1 academic elective. **Academic units recommended:** 4 English, 4 math, 4 science (4 science labs), 4 foreign language, 4 social studies. High school diploma is required, and GED is accepted. TOEFL required of all international applicants: minimum paper TOEFL 500.

Application deadline: None
Average GPA: 3.00
ACT Composite middle 50% range: NR
SAT Math middle 50% range: 440–550
SAT Critical Reading middle 50% range: 440–530
SAT Writing middle 50% range: NR
Graduated top 10% of class: 10%
Graduated top 25% of class: 26%
Graduated top 50% of class: 61%

COLLEGE GRADUATION REQUIREMENTS

Course waivers allowed: Yes

In what course: A specific computer course can be taken to satisfy the core math requirement. English 7 and 8 (anthology courses) can be taken instead of a foreign language. These are for core requirements only.

Course substitutions allowed: Yes

In what course: A specific computer course can be taken to satisfy the core math requirement. English 7 and 8 (anthology courses) can be taken instead of a foreign language. These are for core requirements only.

Additional Information

Environment: The college is located in Long Island, about 30 minutes from New York City.

Student Body
Undergrad enrollment: 4,925
% Women: 62%
% Men: 38%
% Out-of-state: 13%
Cost Information
Tuition: $30,046
Room & board: $11,840
Housing Information
University housing: Yes
% Living on campus: 37%
Greek System
Fraternity: Yes
Sorority: Yes
Athletics: Division II

Manhattanville College

2900 Purchase Street, Purchase, NY 10577
Phone: 914-323-5124 • Fax: 914-694-1732
E-mail: admissions@mville.edu • Web: www.mville.edu
Support: SP • Institution: Private

Programs or Services for Students with Learning Differences

The Higher Education Learning Program (H.E.L.P.) serves as a center of support for students with documented learning disabilities. It is designed to assist students to successfully meet the academic challenges of the college curriculum. H.E.L.P. offers a range of services that are individualized to meet the needs of each student. Professionals are trained and experienced working with this population to provide instruction. No separate application is required for the H.E.L.P. Center. Students must register with the ODS first before accessing the H.E.L.P. Center. The Academic Resource Center (ARC) offers academic support free of charge to all students. At the ARC students may receive support, individually and in groups and the emphasis is on learning and gaining independence. The ARC has professional mathematics instructors available every day. In addition there are peer tutors and Supplemental Instructors for many subjects. Students are encouraged to look for the SI leaders who may be assigned to their courses, and take advantage of this opportunity to enhance their academic success.

Admission Information for Students with Learning Differences

College entrance tests required: Yes
Interview required: No
Essay required: No
Additional Application Required for LD/ADHD/ASD: NR
What documentation required for LD: Current documentation of disability by a qualified professional is required.
With general application: NR
To receive services after enrolling: Yes
What documentation required for ADHD: Current documentation of disability by a qualified professional is required.
With general application: NR
To receive services after enrolling: Yes
LD/ADHD/ASD documentation submitted to: Director of Disability Services
ASD Specific Program: NR
Special Ed. HS course work accepted: NR
Specific course requirements of all applicants: Yes
Separate application required: No
Total # of students receiving LD/ADHD/ASD services: 150
Acceptance into program means acceptance into college: No

Admissions

All applicants must meet the general admission requirements. The criteria includes: 3.0 GPA and 4 years of English, 3 years of math, 2 years of science, 2 years of history and 5 academic electives. The college is test optional. Students are not required to submit standardized test scores with their applications for admission to the college, except international and home-schooled applicants. Teacher and counselor recommendation is required plus a personal essay. Interviews are encouraged. Some students may be admitted as Transitional students under the premise that they may need additional support in order to be successful in college. The overall goals and objectives of the program are to: provide to develop connections with other students and key staff from many resource centers; encourage the development of personal goals and plan for college and for life learning; and to enable students to recognize components of a successful college experience including health and wellness issues, time management, and study skills. Students admitted through the Transitional Acceptance Program fall under the oversight of the Center for Academic Success during their first semester. Students are required to attend a series of workshops through the Student Enrichment Program to ease their transition. Students must also successfully complete 12 credits with at least a 2.0 grade point average by the end of their first semester. Although 12 credits must be successfully completed by the end of the first semester, we recommend that students register for no fewer than 15 to 16 credits per semester. If these criteria are met, the student will no longer be considered a transitional student. If these criteria are not met, the student could be placed on academic probation or dismissed from the college.

Additional Information

The H.E.L.P. Center offers the following services: one-to one tutoring, study skills instruction, reading strategies, writing support, organizational skills, time management technique, All instruction is provided by certified teachers. Services are customized to match each student's learning style. During freshman year, students meet with their assigned tutor to work on time management skills, completion of all assignments, and to take responsibility for their own learning. Upperclassmen may meet with their tutors for either two or three hours per week, continuing to receive strategy-based instruction to address their specific needs. ARC provides instruction, enhancement, and ongoing support, and serves students at all levels. The Pathways And Connections (PAC) Program is a fee-based program for students with Autism Spectrum and related disorders.

General Support Services Information

Contact Information
Name of program or department: Office of Disability Services and HELP Center
Telephone: 914-323-7127 (Disability Services) or 914-323-5313 (HELP
Fax: 914-323-7218

Accommodations or Services for Students with Learning Differences

Accommodations are determined on an individual basis with thorough review of appropriate documentation and an intake interview. The accommodations requested must be supported by the documentation provided and linked to the current impact on academic functioning. The accommodations listed below are available to those for whom they are appropriate.

Allowed in exams
Calculator: Yes
Dictionary: No
Computer: Yes
Spellchecker: Yes (on computer)
Extended test time: Yes
Scribes: Yes
Proctors: Yes
Oral exams: Yes
Note-takers: Limited volunteers
Services for students with LD: Yes
Services for students with ADHD: Yes
Services for students with ASD: Yes
Distraction-reduced environment: Yes
Tape recording in class: Yes
Audio books: NR
Electronic texts: Yes
Kurzweil Reader: Yes
Other assistive technology: Yes
Priority registration: No
Added costs for services: HELP only
LD specialists: HELP only
ADHD coaching: NR
ASD specialists: NR
Professional tutors: 8–10 in HELP center
Peer tutors: Yes for all students
Max. hours/wk. for services: 3 for HELP
How professors are notified of LD/ADHD: Letter sent by ODS Director

General Admissions Information

Office of Admissions: 914-323-5464

Entrance Requirements

Academic units required: 4 English, 3 math, 2 science, 2 social studies, 5 academic electives. High school diploma is required and GED is accepted. SAT or ACT recommended. If ACT, ACT with writing recommended. TOEFL required of all international applicants: minimum paper TOEFL 550 or minimum internet TOEFL 80.

Application deadline: 3/1
Notification: NR
Average GPA: NR
ACT Composite middle 50% range: 21-26
SAT Math middle 50% range: 480-580
SAT Critical Reading middle 50% range: 490-580
SAT Writing middle 50% range: 480-590
Graduated top 10% of class: NR
Graduated top 25% of class: NR
Graduated top 50% of class: NR

COLLEGE GRADUATION REQUIREMENTS

Course waivers allowed: No
Course substitutions allowed: Yes by application

Additional Information

Environment: This private school was founded in 1841. It has a 100-acre campus.

Student Body
Undergrad enrollment: 1,798
% Women: 64
% Men: 36
% Out-of-state: 30
Cost information
Tuition: $34,870
Room & board: $14,520
Housing Information
University Housing: Yes
Percent living on campus: 64
Greek System
Fraternity: No
Sorority: No
Athletics: Division III

Marist College

3399 North Road, Poughkeepsie, NY 12601-1387
Phone: 845-575-3226 • Fax: 845-575-3215
E-mail: admission@marist.edu • Web: www.marist.edu/
Support: SP • Institution: Private

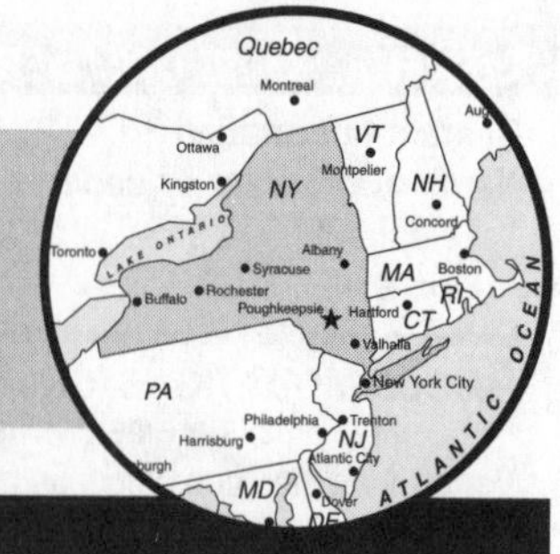

Programs or Services for Students with Learning Differences

Marist College believes that bright, motivated students with specific learning disabilities are more similar than they are different from other college students and can achieve a higher education. Marist offers a program of support for students with learning disabilities through the Learning Disabilities Program. Students receive a complement of academic services designed to meet individual needs. The program focuses on the development and use of strategies to promote independence and personal success. The philosophy of the program does not emphasize remediation but rather the development of compensatory strategies. Each student is enrolled in credit-bearing courses and completes the same degree requirements as all students. Program staff work closely with faculty and administration, and students are encouraged to discuss their learning disabilities with faculty. Participation in the program is available on a continual basis for as long as the LD specialist and the student agree is necessary.

Admission Information for Students with Learning Differences

College entrance test required: No
Interview required: Yes
Essay required: Required
Additional Application Required for LD/ADHD/ASD: NR
What documentation required for LD: Psych/Ed Eval & Medical Documentation
With general application: Yes
To receive services after enrolling: Yes
What documentation required for ADHD: For LD Program a Psych/Ed Evaluation is required for all applicants.
With general application: Yes
To receive services after enrolling: Yes
What documentation required for ASD: Psych / Ed Evaluation
With general application: Yes
To receive services after enrolling: Yes
LD/ADHD/ASD documentation submitted to: Office of Special Services
ASD Specific Program: NR
Special Ed. HS course work accepted: No
Specific course requirements of all applicants: Yes
Separate application required for program services: Yes
Total # of students receiving LD/ADHD/ASD services: 250
Acceptance into program means acceptance into college: Yes

Admissions

Students with LD must submit an application for admission and all required materials to the Office of Admissions. A supplementary application for the LD support program must also be completed and sent directly to the OSS. A copy of the transcript and recommendations is also required. Additionally, students must submit to the OSS the results of the WAIS–IV, including subtest scores; their calculated IQ and an accompanying narrative; achievement testing with current levels of functioning in reading, mathematics, and written language; an essay describing what the student thinks is important about them as a person; and a $25 fee. ACT/SAT scores are optional. Those most qualified and suited to the program will be invited to interview. Students accepted into the program should have an acceptance and understanding of their LD; know their academic strengths and weaknesses; have taken college-prep courses; provide recommendations that communicate strengths, motivation to succeed, and willingness to accept and access supports; and have sound study skills and work habits. Admission to the program is competitive, and students are encouraged to apply early.

Additional Information

Upon enrollment, students complete a comprehensive survey of their abilities and attitudes toward academics. This survey is combined with diagnostic evaluations and the comprehensive record of students' performance to develop an individual support service plan. Students meet an LD specialist two times a week and typically concentrate on writing skills, note-taking, organizational skills, study skills, and testing strategies. Accommodations may include accommodated testing procedures, note-takers, scribes, readers, alternative texts, and use of adaptive equipment/software. A program fee is charged only for the services of the learning specialist. Students in the program also have access to content tutors and a counselor who can address academic, career, and personal issues. Services and accommodations are available for undergraduate and graduate students.

General Support Services Information

Contact Information
Name of program or department: Office of Special Services
Telephone: 845-575-3274
Fax: 845.575.3011
Website: https://www.marist.edu/specialservices/

Accommodations or Services For Students With Learning Differences

Accommodations are decided upon an individual basis after a thorough review of appropriate, current documentation. The accommodations requests must be supported through the documentation provided and must be logically linked to the current impact of the condition on academic functioning.

Allowed in exams
Calculator: Yes
Dictionary: Not Applicable
Computer: Yes
Spellchecker: Not Applicable
Extended test time: Yes
Scribes: Yes
Proctors: Yes
Oral exams: Not Applicable
Note-takers: Yes
Support services for students with LD: Yes
Support services for students with ADHD: Yes
Support services for students with ASD: NR
Distraction-reduced environment: Yes
Tape recording in class: Yes
Electronic texts: Yes
Kurzweil reader: NR
Audio books: Yes
Other assistive technology: Yes
Priority registration: No
Added costs of services: Yes
LD specialists: Yes
ADHD coaching: No
ASD specialists: No
Professional tutors: No
Peer tutors: Yes
Max. hours/wk. for services: NR
How professors are notified of student approved accommodations: By student

General Admissions Information

Office of Admissions: 845-575-3226

Entrance Requirements

Academic units required: 4 English, 3 math, 3 science, 2 science labs, 2 foreign language, 2 social studies, 1 history, 2 academic electives. **Academic units recommended:** 4 math, 4 science, 3 science labs, 3 foreign language. High school diploma is required and GED is accepted. SAT or ACT considered if submitted. If ACT, ACT with writing accepted. TOEFL required of all international applicants: minimum paper TOEFL 550 or minimum internet TOEFL 80.

Application deadline: 2/1
Notification: 4/1
Average GPA: 3.3
ACT Composite middle 50% range: 23-28
SAT Math middle 50% range: 530-630
SAT Critical Reading middle 50% range: 520-620
SAT Writing middle 50% range: 520-630
Graduate top 10% of class: 26
Graduated top 25% of class: 61
Graduated top 50% of class: 87

COLLEGE GRADUATION REQUIREMENTS

Course waivers allowed: NR
Course substitutions allowed: No

Additional Information

Environment: This private school was founded in 1929. It has a 180-acre campus.

Student Body
Undergrad enrollment: 5,576
% Women: 59
% Men: 41
% Out-of-state: 47

Cost information
Tuition: $33,250
Room & board: $14,850

Housing Information
University Housing: Yes
Percent living on campus: 69

Greek System
Fraternity: Yes
Sorority: Yes

Athletics: Division I

MARYMOUNT MANHATTAN COLLEGE

221 East 71st Street, New York, NY 10021
Phone: 212-517-0430 • Fax: 212-517-0448
E-mail: admissions@mmm.edu • Web: www.mmm.edu
Support: SP • Institution: Private

PROGRAMS OR SERVICES FOR STUDENTS WITH LEARNING DIFFERENCES

Marymount Manhattan College's Program for Academic Access includes a full range of support services that center on academic and personal growth for students with learning disabilities. Students who have been admitted to the full-time program are required to demonstrate commitment to overcoming learning difficulties through regular attendance and tutoring. Academic advisement and counseling is provided to assist in developing a program plan suited to individual needs. The college is looking for highly motivated students with a commitment to compensate for their learning disabilities and to fully participate in the tutoring program. Once admitted into the program, students receive a program plan suited to their needs, based on a careful examination of the psycho-educational evaluations. Full time students sign a contract to regularly attend tutoring provided by professionals experienced within the field of LD. In addition to assisting students in the development of skills and strategies for their coursework, LD specialists coach participants in the attitudes and behavior necessary for college success. Professors assist learning specialists in carefully monitoring students' progress throughout the academic year and arranging for accommodations. Students must submit a current and complete Psycho ed evaluation that meets the documentation guidelines by giving clear and specific evidence of the disability and its limitations on academic functioning in the diagnosis summary statement. Students with ADD must have a licensed physician, psychiatrist or psychologist provide a complete and current (within the last 3 years) documentation of the disorder.

ADMISSION INFORMATION FOR STUDENTS WITH LEARNING DIFFERENCES

College entrance test required: Yes
Interview required: Yes
Essay required: Yes
Additional Application Required for LD/ADHD/ASD: NR
What documentation required for LD: Psychoeducational evaluation within the last 3 years.
With general application: No
To receive services after enrolling: Yes
What documentation required for ADHD: Signed letter from psychiatrist or psychologist with diagnostic code.
With general application: No
To receive services after enrolling: Yes
What documentation required for ASD: Psycho ed evaluation
With general application: No
To receive services after enrolling: Yes
LD/ADHD/ASD documentation submitted to: Support program/services
ASD Specific Program: NR
Special Ed. HS course work accepted: No
Specific course: Yes
Separate application required for program services: No
Total # of students receiving LD/ADHD/ASD services: 30
Acceptance into program means acceptance into college: NR

ADMISSIONS

Admission to Marymount Manhattan College's Program for Academic Access is based on a diagnosis of dyslexia, ADD, or other primary learning disability; intellectual potential within the average to superior range; and a serious commitment in attitude and work habits to meeting the program and college academic requirements. Prospective students are required to submit the following: high school transcript or GED. Students are expected to have college prep courses in high school but foreign language is not required for admission; ACT or SAT are required; results of a recent complete Psycho ed evaluation (within one year); letters of recommendation from teachers, tutors, or counselors; and have a personal interview. Students may be admitted to the college through the Program for Academic Access. Students interested in being considered for admission through the program must self disclose their LD/ADD in a personal statement with the application. There is no fixed deadline for the application, however there are a limited number of slots available. Completed files received by mid-January are at an advantage to be elligible for selection.

ADDITIONAL INFORMATION

There are three LD professionals associated with the program. Students have access to two hours of tutoring per week with a learning specialist, drop-in tutoring and monthly parent meetings. Skills classes are offered in study skills, reading, vocabulary development and workshops in overcoming procrastination and study reading and effectiveness. The following services are offered to students with appropriate documentation: the use of calculators, computer and spell checker in exams; extended time on tests; proctors; oral exams; distraction-free testing environment; tape recorder in class; books on tape; Kurzweil software, note-takers, separate and alternative forms of testing; and priority registration.

GENERAL SUPPORT SERVICES INFORMATION

Contact Information
Name of program or department: Disability Services
Telephone: 212-774-0724
Fax: 212-774-4875

ACCOMMODATIONS OR SERVICES FOR STUDENTS WITH LEARNING DIFFERENCES

Accommodations are decided upon an individual basis after a thorough review of appropriate, current documentation. The accommodations requests must be supported through the documentation provided and must be logically linked to the current impact of the condition on academic functioning.

Allowed in exams
Calculator: Yes
Dictionary: Yes
Computer: Yes
Spellchecker: Yes
Extended test time: Yes
Scribes: No
Proctors: Yes
Oral exams: Yes
Note-takers: Yes
Services for students with LD: Yes
Services for students with ADHD: Yes
Services for students with ASD: Yes
Distraction-reduced environment: Yes
Tape recording in class: Yes
Audio books from learning ally: Yes
Electronic texts: NR
Kurzweil Reader: No
Other assistive technology: Yes
Priority registration: Yes
Added costs of services: Yes
LD specialists: Yes
ADHD coaching: NR
ASD specialists: NR
Professional tutors: NR
Peer tutors: No
Max. hours/wk. for services: 2
How professors are notified of student approved accommodations: Student

GENERAL ADMISSIONS INFORMATION

Office of Admissions: 212-517-0430

ENTRANCE REQUIREMENTS

Academic units required: 4 English, 3 math, 3 science, 3 social studies, 4 academic electives. **Academic units recommended:** 2 science labs, 2 foreign language. High school diploma is required and GED is accepted. SAT or ACT required. If ACT, ACT with writing accepted. TOEFL required of all international applicants: minimum internet TOEFL 80.

Application deadline: NR
Notification: Rolling starting 9/1
Average GPA: 3.34
ACT Composite middle 50% range: 20-26
SAT Math middle 50% range: 440-550
SAT Critical Reading middle 50% range: 470-590
SAT Writing middle 50% range: 480-580
Graduated top 10% of class: NR
Graduated top 25% of class: NR
Graduated top 50% of class: NR

COLLEGE GRADUATION REQUIREMENTS

Course waivers allowed: No
Course substitutions allowed: No

ADDITIONAL INFORMATION

Environment: This private school was founded in 1936. It has a 1-acre campus.

Student Body
Undergrad enrollment: 1,928
% Women: 77
% Men: 23
% Out-of-state: 59
Cost information
Tuition: $27,360
Room & board: $15,500
Housing Information
University Housing: Yes
Percent living on campus: 38
Greek System
Fraternity: No
Sorority: No
Athletics: NR

NEW YORK UNIVERSITY

665 Broadway, New York, NY 10012
Phone: 212-998-4500 • Fax: 212-995-4902
E-mail: admissions@nyu.edu • Web: www.nyu.edu
Support: CS • Institution: Private

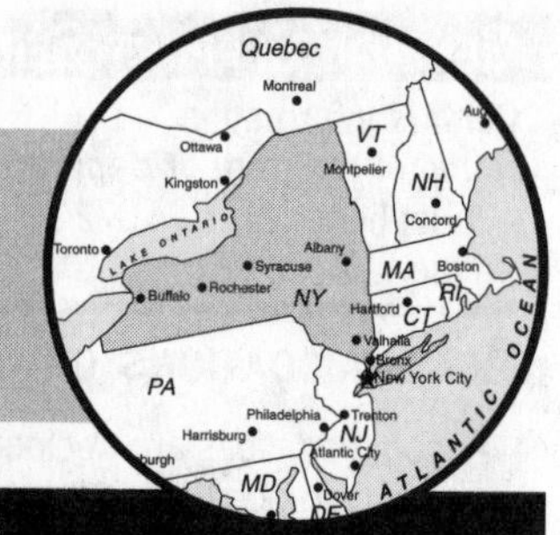

PROGRAMS OR SERVICES FOR STUDENTS WITH LEARNING DIFFERENCES

The Henry and Lucy Moses Center for Students with Disabilities (CSD) works with students with a documented disability or disabilities who register with the office to obtain appropriate accommodations and services. This process is designed to encourage independence, backed by a strong system of supports. Each student who is approved through CSD works with a staff specialist to develop an individualized and reasonable accommodation plan. Reasonable accommodations are adjustments to policy, practice, and programs that "level the playing field" for students with disabilities and provide equal access to NYU's programs and activities. Accommodation plans and other related services are based on each student's disability documentation and NYU program requirements and are therefore determined on a case-by-case basis.

ADMISSION INFORMATION FOR STUDENTS WITH LEARNING DIFFERENCES

College entrance tests required: No
Interview required: No
Essay required: Yes
Additional Application Required for LD/ADHD/ASD: NR
What documentation required for LD: Psycho ed evaluation to include: relevant historical info, instructional interventions, related services, age diagnosed, objective data (aptitude, achievement, info processing), test scores (standard, percentile and grade equivalents) and describe functional limitations.
With general application: No
To receive services after enrolling: Yes
What documentation required for ADHD: Diagnosis based on DSM-V; history of behaviors impairing functioning in academic setting; diagnostic interview; history of symptoms; evidence of ongoing behaviors.
With general application: No
To receive services after enrolling: Yes
What documentation required for ASD: Psycho ed evaluation
With general application: NR
To receive services after enrolling: Yes
LD/ADHD/ASD documentation submitted to: Moses Center for Students with Disabilities
ASD Specific Program: NR
Special Ed. HS course work accepted: Yes
Specific course requirements for all applicants: Yes
Separate application required for program services: No
Total # of students receiving LD/ADHD/ASD services: NR
Acceptance into program means acceptance into college: Separate application required after student has enrolled

ADMISSIONS

The NYU Admissions Committee reviews each application holistically, considering and carefully evaluating many significant factors, including the following: the Common Application and NYU Supplement, School Report (including a letter from a student's guidance counselor and a transcript), a combination of standardized test scores the student chooses to submit (e.g., SAT, ACT, SAT Subject Test, AP, IB, or other national examination scores), one Teacher Evaluation, audition or portfolio submissions for art and music applicants to the Steinhardt School of Culture, Education, and Human Development and all applicants to the Tisch School of the Arts. The committee also takes into account each applicant's unique talents, personal attributes, accomplishments, and goals.

ADDITIONAL INFORMATION

In addition to academic accommodations, CSD provides academic support services to registered students. Students may meet with a learning consultant on a restricted basis and may attend several academic strategy based workshops throughout the semester.

General Support Services Information

Contact Information
Name of program or department: Henry and Lucy Moses Center for Students with Disabilities
Telephone: 212-998-4980
Fax: 212-995-4114

Accommodations or Services for Students with Learning Differences

Accommodations are determined through a careful review of appropriate and current documentation. The accommodations requested must be supported by the documentation provided and must be linked to the current impact on academic functioning. Reasonable accommodations do not negate requirements for successful completion of a program, course, or services or adherence to acceptable standard or behavior. It is important to note that some accommodations are not appropriate in all courses.

Allowed in exams
Calculator: Yes
Dictionary: Yes
Computer: Yes
Spellchecker: Yes
Extended test time: Yes
Scribes: Yes
Proctors: Yes
Oral exams: No
Note-takers: Yes
Services for students with LD: Yes
Services for students with ADHD: Yes
Services for students with ASD: Yes
Distraction-reduced environment: Yes
Tape recording in class: Yes
Audio books: NR
Electronic texts: Yes
Kurzweil Reader: Yes
Other assistive technology: Yes
Priority registration: Yes
Added costs for services: No
LD specialists: Yes
ADHD coaching: NR
ASD specialists: NR
Professional tutors: Yes (NYU Writing Center)
Peer tutors: Yes (University Learning Center)
Max. hours/wk. for services: Students may schedule one session per week at the Writing Center; tutoring at the College Learning Center is determined by subject area and schedule.
How professors are notified of LD/ADHD: Student

General Admissions Information

Office of Admissions: 212-998-4500

Entrance Requirements

Academic units required: 4 English, 3 math, 3 science, 3 science labs, 3 foreign language, 3 social studies, 3 history. **Academic units recommended:** 4 English, 4 math, 4 science, 4 science labs, 4 foreign language, 4 social studies, 4 history. High school diploma is required and GED is accepted. If ACT, ACT with writing required. TOEFL required of all international applicants: minimum internet TOEFL 100.

Application deadline: 1/1
Notification: 4/1
Average GPA: 3.59
ACT Composite Avg: 29 (23-36)
SAT Math middle 50% range: 630-740
SAT Critical Reading middle 50% range: 610-710
SAT Writing middle 50% range: 620-720
Graduated top 10% of class: NR
Graduated top 25% of class: NR
Graduated top 50% of class: NR

COLLEGE GRADUATION REQUIREMENTS

Course waivers allowed: No
Course substitutions allowed: Yes
In what course: Determined by the student's Office of the Dean on a case-by-case basis.

Additional Information

Environment: The university has an urban campus in New York City.

Student Body
Undergrad enrollment: 24,985
% Women: 57
% Men: 43
% Out-of-state: 64

Cost information
Tuition: $43,746
Room & board: $16,782
Housing Information
University Housing: Yes
Percent living on campus: 44

Greek System
Fraternity: Yes
Sorority: Yes
Athletics: Division III

Rochester Inst. of Technology

60 Lomb Memorial Drive, Rochester, NY 14623-5604
Phone: 585-475-5502 • Fax: 585-475-7424
E-mail: admissions@rit.edu • Web: www.rit.edu
Support: SP • Institution: Private

Programs or Services for Students with Learning Differences

There is no separate academic program exclusively for students with disabilities; all students apply to a Rochester Institute of Technology degree program and major. Students with disabilities who require academic and/or residential accommodations should submit a request and relevant documentation to the RIT Disability Services Office. Currently about 700 students with disabilities are registered with the office, the majority of whom have learning disabilities and/or attention deficit disorders. The office also offers support with time management, organization, and study skills strategies to registered students upon request. Please see www.rit.edu/dso for information. RIT is home to the National Technical Institute for the Deaf; please see www.ntid.rit.edu for more information.

Admission Information for Students with Learning Differences

College entrance test required: Yes
Interview required: No
Essay required: No
Additional Application Required for LD/ADHD/ASD: NR
What documentation required for LD:
With general application: No
To receive services after enrolling: Yes
What documentation required for ADHD: Psycho ed evaluation
With general application: No
To receive services after enrolling: Yes
What documentation required for ASD: Psycho ed evaluation
With general application: No
To receive services after enrolling: Yes
LD/ADHD/ASD documentation submitted to: Support program/services
ASD Specific Program: NR
Special Ed. HS course work accepted: No
Specific course: No
Separate application required for program services: 3
Total # of students receiving LD/ADHD/ASD services: NR
Acceptance into program means acceptance into college: NR

Admissions

There is no special admissions process for students with learning disabilities. However, students with learning disabilities may include a supporting essay. Although an interview is not required, it is recommended. The required scores on the SAT or ACT will depend on the program the student is applying to within RIT. It is also helpful to identify compensatory strategies used in high school and what will be needed for success in college. The admission decision is made jointly by the program chairperson and Director of Admissions. Applicants are encouraged to indicate a second and third program choice. If RIT is unable to offer an admission to the first choice program, an applicant may be qualified for admission to one of the alternative choices. Factors considered in a general admission decision include, but are not limited to: overall GPA and rank in class, rigor of course work, grades in content courses, appropriateness of courses for academic major, competitiveness of high school, standardized test(s), recommendation from school counselor, recommendations from those familiar with the student's academic performance, and an essay.

Additional Information

The RIT Academic Support Center offers a range of learning supports to all students, including time management and organization support through the Structured Monitoring program, math and physics tutoring, study skills strategies, and weekly academic success workshops. Please see www.rit.edu/asc for more information. RIT offers a "Spectrum Support Program" for interested students with autism spectrum disorders (www.rit.edu/ssp) and TRiO Student Support Services for qualified students (www.rit.edu/trio).

General Support Services Information

Contact Information
Name of program or department: Disability Services
Telephone: 585-475-2023
Fax: 585-475-2215

Accommodations or Services for Students with Learning Differences

Accommodations are decided upon an individual basis after a thorough review of appropriate, current documentation. The accommodations requests must be supported through the documentation provided and must be logically linked to the current impact of the condition on academic functioning.

Allowed in exams
Calculator: Yes
Dictionary: Yes
Computer: Yes
Spellchecker: Yes
Extended test time: Yes
Scribes: Yes
Proctors: Yes
Oral exams: Yes
Note-takers: Yes
Services for students with LD: Yes
Services for students with ADHD: Yes
Services for students with ASD: Yes
Distraction-reduced environment: Yes
Tape recording in class: Yes
Audio books from learning ally: Yes
Electronic texts: NR
Kurzweil Reader: Yes
Other assistive technology: Yes
Priority registration: Yes
Added costs for services: NR
LD specialists: Yes
ADHD coaching: Yes
ASD specialists: Yes
Professional tutors: NR
Peer tutors: Yes
Max. hours/wk. for services: NR
How professors are notified of student approved accommodations: Director

General Admissions Information

Office of Admissions: 585-475-6631

Entrance Requirements

Academic units required: 4 English, 2 math, 2 science, 1 science labs, 4 social studies, 10 academic electives. **Academic units recommended:** 4 English, 3 math, 3 science, 2 science labs, 3 foreign language, 4 social studies, 5 academic electives. High school diploma is required and GED is accepted. SAT or ACT required. If ACT, ACT with writing accepted. TOEFL required of all international applicants: minimum paper TOEFL 550 or minimum internet TOEFL 79.

Application deadline: 2/1
Notification: Rolling starting 3/15
Average GPA: 3.6
ACT Composite middle 50% range: 26-31
SAT Math middle 50% range: 580-690
SAT Critical Reading middle 50% range: 550-660
SAT Writing middle 50% range: 520-630
Graduated top 10% of class: 34
Graduated top 25% of class: 69
Graduated top 50% of class: 96

COLLEGE GRADUATION REQUIREMENTS

Course waivers allowed: No
Course substitutions allowed: No
In what course: This is rarely requested but a discussion could be entertained.

Additional Information

Environment: This private school was founded in 1829. It has a 1300-acre campus.

Student Body
Undergrad enrollment: 13,543
% Women: 32
% Men: 68
% Out-of-state: 46

Cost information
Tuition: $36,596
Room & board: $11,918

Housing Information
University Housing: Yes
Percent living on campus: 55

Greek System
Fraternity: Yes
Sorority: Yes
Athletics: Division III

St. Bonaventure University

3261 West State Road, St. Bonaventure, NY 14778
Phone: 716-375-2434 • Fax: 716-375-4005
E-mail: admissions@sbu.edu • Web: www.sbu.edu
Support: S • Institution: Private

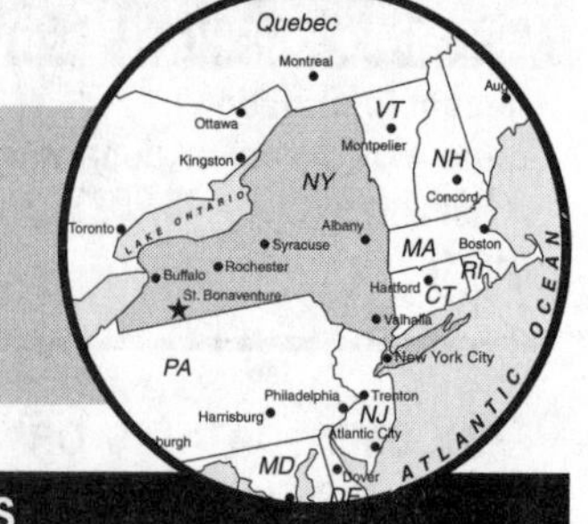

Programs or Services for Students with Learning Differences

St. Bonaventure does not operate a specialized LD program but does provide services to students with identified disabilities. In the spirit of the federal mandates, reasonable accommodations are made for otherwise qualified students with disabilities. St. Bonaventure's Teaching and Learning Center is an intrinsic element of the university's goal of academic excellence. The credo is to assist, not do. Once authentic, current documentation has been received, a careful review of the records will be conducted and an evaluation of appropriate accommodations will be made. Students who wait to identify themselves until after registration may find that some accommodations are not immediately available. Students with learning disabilities/ attention deficit hyperactivity disorder who wish to request accommodations must meet with the coordinator of Services for Students with Disabilities. It is the student's responsibility to deliver accommodation letters to professors after accommodations have been arranged. Accommodations are arranged each semester. Students are encouraged to discuss the disability with professors and arrange for specific accommodations for test-taking and other course requirements. Students must contact the coordinator of Services for Students with Disabilities to request a course substitution. The students need to accept responsibility for their own academic excellence, and assistance will be provided.

Admission Information for Students with Learning Differences

College entrance tests required: Yes
Interview required: No
Essay required: No
Additional Application Required for LD/ADHD/ASD: NR
What documentation required for LD: Psycho ed evaluation to include: relevant historical info, instructional interventions, related services, age diagnosed, objective data (aptitude, achievement, info processing), test scores (standard, percentile and grade equivalents) and describe functional limitations.
With general application: No
To receive services after enrolling: Yes
What documentation required for ADHD: Diagnosis based on DSM-V; history of behaviors impairing functioning in academic setting; diagnostic interview; history of symptoms; evidence of ongoing behaviors.
With general application: No
To receive services after enrolling: Yes
What documentation required for ASD: Psycho ed evaluation
With general application: NR
To receive services after enrolling: Yes
LD/ADHD/ASD documentation submitted to: Services for Students with Disabilities
ASD Specific Program: NR
Special Ed. HS course work accepted: Yes
Specific course requirements of all applicants: Yes
Separate application required: No
Total # of students receiving LD/ADHD/ASD services: 50–100
Acceptance into program means acceptance into college: Students must be admitted to and enrolled in the university first and then request services.

Admissions

Students with learning disabilities must meet regular admission standards and complete the same admissions process as all applicants. The mid 50 percent ACT score range is 23–24, and for SAT it is 1070–1110. The minimum GPA is a 3.0. Course requirements include 4 years of English, 4 years of social studies, 3 years of math, 3 years of science, and 2 years of a foreign language. Special education courses may be considered. It is recommended that students self-disclose their disability in a personal statement. Once students are accepted and have enrolled, they are encouraged to self-disclose their learning disability, if this has not already been done, and provide appropriate documentation to the Office of Services for Students with Disabilities. Documentation is reviewed and appropriate accommodations are arranged.

Additional Information

Students with LD may obtain assistance with assessing learning strengths and weaknesses and consult one-on-one or in groups to acquire a greater command of a subject, get help with a specific assignment, or discuss academic challenges. Services might include, but are not limited to: alternative testing arrangements, taped texts and classes, access to word processors/spellchecker, note-takers, tutors, peer mentors, time management and study skills training, and weekly individual appointments. Assistance can be offered in requesting books on tape. Tutoring services are available to all students and are not intended to be a substitute for independent study or preparation.

General Support Services Information

Contact Information
Name of program or department: Disability Support Services
Telephone: 716-375-2065
Fax: 716-375-2071
Website: www.sbu.edu/dss

Accommodations or Services For Students With Learning Differences

Accommodations are decided upon an individual basis after a thorough review of appropriate, current documentation. The accommodations requests must be supported through the documentation provided and must be logically linked to the current impact of the condition on academic functioning.

Allowed in exams
Calculator: Yes
Dictionary: Yes
Computer: Yes
Spellchecker: Yes
Extended test time: Yes
Scribes: Yes
Proctors: Yes
Oral exams: Yes
Note-takers: Yes
Support services for students with LD: Yes
Support services for students with ADHD: Yes
Support services for students with ASD: Yes
Distraction-reduced environment: Yes
Tape recording in class: Yes
Electronic texts: Yes
Kurzweil reader: NR
Audio books: Yes
Other assistive technology: No
Priority registration: No
Added costs of services: No
LD specialists: No
ADHD coaching: No
ASD specialists: No
Professional tutors: No
Peer tutors: Yes
Max. hours/wk. for services: NR
How professors are notified of student approved accommodations: By student

General Admissions Information

Office of Admissions: 716-375-2434

Entrance Requirements

Academic units recommended: 4 English, 3 math, 3 science, 3 science labs, 2 foreign language, 4 social studies. High school diploma is required and GED is accepted. SAT or ACT required. If ACT, ACT with writing accepted. TOEFL required of all international applicants: minimum paper TOEFL 550.

Application deadline: 7/1
Notification: Rolling starting 10/15
Average GPA: 3.4
ACT Composite middle 50% range: 21-27
SAT Math middle 50% range: 470-590
SAT Critical Reading middle 50% range: 460-580
SAT Writing middle 50% range: 445-550
Graduate top 10% of class: 19
Graduated top 25% of class: 47
Graduated top 50% of class: 74

COLLEGE GRADUATION REQUIREMENTS

Course waivers allowed: No
Course substitutions allowed: Yes
In what course: foreign language

Additional Information

Environment: This private school, affiliated with the Roman Catholic Church, was founded in 1858. It has a 500-acre campus.

Student Body
Undergrad enrollment: 1,687
% Women: 49
% Men: 51
% Out-of-state: 27
Cost information
Tuition: $30,424
Room & board: $11,128
Housing Information
University Housing: Yes
Percent living on campus: 75
Greek System
Fraternity: No
Sorority: No
Athletics: Division I

St. Lawrence University

Payson Hall, Canton, NY 13617
Phone: 315-229-5261 • Fax: 315-229-5818
E-mail: admissions@stlawu.edu • Web: www.stlawu.edu
Support: CS • Institution: Private

Programs or Services for Students with Learning Differences

The Office of Academic Services for Students with Special Needs provides services to members of the university who either have identified themselves or believe they may have some type of learning disability. The office has several purposes: to serve students who are learning-challenged by documented disabilities; help students get the academic help that they need; put students in touch with other people on campus who can help; advise and counsel students; and educate everyone on campus about special needs. The office works with students in developing IEPs for the purpose of receiving reasonable accommodations in their educational and residential life concerns. The service will also make referrals and advocate at several on-campus services, and if necessary, connect with state or regional support agencies. There is a Writing Center for help with writing assignments, peer tutors for general assistance with academic work, and a Counseling Center and Health Center. As appropriate to the disability, documentation should include a diagnostic statement identifying the disability, date of the current diagnostic evaluation, and the date of the original diagnosis; a description of the diagnostic criteria and/or diagnostic test used; a description of the current functional impact of the disability; treatments, medications, and assistive devices/services currently prescribed or in use; a description of the expected progression or stability of the impact of the disability over time; and the credentials of the diagnosing professionals. Recommendations from professionals with a history of working with the individual provide valuable information for the review process. They will be included in the evaluation of requests for accommodation and/or auxiliary aids.

Admission Information for Students with Learning Differences

College entrance test required: NR
Interview required: Not Applicable
Essay required: Not Applicable
Additional Application Required for LD/ADHD/ASD: NR
What documentation required for LD: Documentation requirements to received accommodations from the Disability and Accessibility Services Office are made on a case-by-case basis.
With general application: NR
To receive services after enrolling: Yes
What documentation required for ADHD: Documentation requirements to received accommodations from the Disability and Accessibility Services Office are made on a case-by-case basis.
With general application: NR
To receive services after enrolling: Yes
What documentation required for ASD: Documentation requirements to received accommodations from the Disability and Accessibility Services Office are made on a case-by-case basis.
With general application: NR
To receive services after enrolling: Yes
LD/ADHD/ASD documentation submitted to: Disability and Accessibility Services
ASD Specific Program: NR
Special Ed. HS course work accepted: Not Applicable
Specific course requirements of all applicants: NR
Separate application required for program services: FALSE
Total # of students receiving LD/ADHD/ASD services: 143
Acceptance into program means acceptance into college: NR

Admissions

There is no special admissions process for students with learning disabilities. All applicants must meet the same admission criteria, which include recommended courses of 4 years of English, 3 years of math, 3 years of science, 3 years of a foreign language, and 3 years of social studies, test optional for the SAT/ACT (middle 50 percent SAT 1750–1940). An interview is recommended and can be done off campus with an alumni representative. Counselor and 2 teacher recommendations.

Additional Information

Students need to be self-starters (to seek out the service early and follow through). As soon as possible, students should provide the official documents that describe the learning disability, the office helps develop the IEP—and notify the professors about the learning disability. Academic requirements required for graduation are waived. Services and accommodations are available for undergraduate and graduate students.

General Support Services Information

Contact Information
Name of program or department: Disability and Accessibility Services
Telephone: 315-229-5678
Fax: NR

Accommodations or Services For Students With Learning Differences

Accommodations are decided upon an individual basis after a thorough review of appropriate, current documentation. The accommodations requests must be supported through the documentation provided and must be logically linked to the current impact of the condition on academic functioning.

Allowed in exams
Calculator: Yes
Dictionary: Yes
Computer: Yes
Spellchecker: Yes
Extended test time: Yes
Scribes: Yes
Proctors: Yes
Oral exams: Yes
Note-takers: Yes
Support services for students with LD: Yes
Support services for students with ADHD: Yes
Support services for students with ASD: Yes
Distraction-reduced environment: Yes
Tape recording in class: Yes
Electronic texts: Yes
Kurzweil reader: NR
Audio books: Yes
Other assistive technology: Yes
Priority registration: No
Added costs of services: No
LD specialists: Yes
ADHD coaching: No
ASD specialists: Yes
Professional tutors: No
Peer tutors: Yes
Max. hours/wk. for services: 2
How professors are notified of student approved accommodations: By student

General Admissions Information

Office of Admissions: 315-229-5261

Entrance Requirements

Academic units recommended: 4 English, 4 math, 4 science, 4 foreign language, 2 social studies, 2 history. High school diploma is required and GED is accepted. SAT or ACT considered if submitted. If ACT, ACT with writing accepted. TOEFL required of all international applicants: minimum paper TOEFL 600 or minimum internet TOEFL 82.

Application deadline: 2/1
Notification: NR
Average GPA: 3.56
ACT Composite middle 50% range: 26-30
SAT Math middle 50% range: 550-660
SAT Critical Reading middle 50% range: 550-650
SAT Writing middle 50% range: 540-640
Graduate top 10% of class: 45
Graduated top 25% of class: 77
Graduated top 50% of class: 95

COLLEGE GRADUATION REQUIREMENTS

Course waivers allowed: No
Course substitutions allowed: No

Additional Information

Environment: This private school was founded in 1856. It has a 1000-acre campus.

Student Body
Undergrad enrollment: 2,435
% Women: 55
% Men: 45
% Out-of-state: 59.1

Cost information
Comprehensive fee: **$59,982**

Housing Information
University Housing: Yes
Percent living on campus: 98.8

Greek System
Fraternity: Yes
Sorority: Yes

Athletics: Division III

St. Thomas Aquinas College

125 Route 340, Sparkill, NY 10976
Phone: 845-398-4100 • Fax: 845-398-4372
E-mail: admissions@stac.edu • Web: www.stac.edu
Support: SP • Institution: Private

Programs or Services for Students with Learning Differences

The mission of Pathways is to facilitate the academic performance of bright college students with LD and ADHD so that they may demonstrate their knowledge and abilities. Pathways program services are comprehensive and specialized. Pathways has an emphasis on individualized services. We focus on the development of effective learning strategies and attitudes by critically evaluating and educating students about their specific needs and abilities. The aim is to break the pattern of helplessness often created in students with learning deficits, foster a spirit of active learning, to teach students to maximize strengths in order to compensate for weaknesses, and to inspire confidence in the students' own abilities. At the heart of the program are mentoring sessions. Students meet twice weekly with a professional mentor in one-to-one sessions tailored to meet specific needs. Mentors are not tutors, but guides who help students develop learning strategies, improve organizational and editing skills, understand course concepts, and negotiate academic life. Incoming freshmen must attend a four-day residential summer program.

Admission Information for Students with Learning Differences

College entrance test required: NR
Interview required: Yes
Essay required: Not Applicable
Additional Application Required for LD/ADHD/ASD: Not Applicable
What documentation required for LD: Same as LD documentation, plus documentation of ADHD by an appropriate professional
With general application: No
To receive services after enrolling: Not Applicable
What documentation required for ADHD: Psycho ed evaluation
With general application: No
To receive services after enrolling: Not Applicable
What documentation required for ASD: Within three years: Adult intelligence test (WAIS-IV); full educational evaluation; report describing impact of disability on student's current functioning.
With general application: No
To receive services after enrolling: Not Applicable
LD/ADHD/ASD documentation submitted to: Disability Services
ASD Specific Program: NR
Special Ed. HS course work accepted: NR
Specific course requirements of all applicants: NR
Separate application required for program services: Yes
Total # of students receiving LD/ADHD/ASD services: NR
Acceptance into program means acceptance into college: No

Admissions

Pathways has a separate application and admissions process from the college itself. Admission to Pathways is extremely competitive. Students must be accepted by the college before their Pathways application is evaluated; however, students should apply to the college and to Pathways at the same time. (SAT or ACT scores are required for regular college admission.) The following must be submitted to Pathways: a completed Pathways application; high school transcripts (college transcripts for transfers); a letter of recommendation from a teacher; most recent IEP if available; and a comprehensive diagnostic assessment including an adult intelligence test (WAIS-IV), measures of achievement, and the specific effects of the LD/ADHD on the student's current academic performance. Reports are required; scores on an IEP are insufficient documentation. Students must also have a personal interview with Pathways staff. Transfer applications are accepted.

Additional Information

Pathways has a director, associate director, and trained staff of mentors. Mentors are professionals with post-college education and experience in some aspect of teaching. The director and assistant director also provide mentoring. Students come to mentoring sessions having already attended classes and prepared initial course work. Pathways students are required to attend regularly scheduled sessions with their own mentor and are encouraged to drop-in for additional help as needed. Study groups in specific skills and content areas are offered dependent upon student need and staff expertise. Pathways students are also provided with academic counseling, course advisement, and priority registration. The required summer program for incoming Pathways freshmen is designed to learn the specific needs of each student, to begin preparing them for academic rigors of higher education, and to build a sense of trust and community within the group.

General Support Services Information

Contact Information
Name of program or department: Disability Services
Telephone: 845-398-4088
Fax: 845-398-4151
Website: http://www.stac.edu

Accommodations or Services For Students With Learning Differences

Accommodations are decided upon an individual basis after a thorough review of appropriate, current documentation. The accommodations requests must be supported through the documentation provided and must be logically linked to the current impact of the condition on academic functioning.

Allowed in exams
Calculator: Yes
Dictionary: Yes
Computer: Yes
Spellchecker: Yes
Extended test time: Yes
Scribes: Yes
Proctors: Yes
Oral exams: Not Applicable
Note-takers: Yes
Support services for students with LD: Yes
Support services for students with ADHD: Yes
Support services for students with ASD: Yes
Distraction-reduced environment: Yes
Tape recording in class: Yes
Electronic texts: Yes
Kurzweil reader: NR
Audio books: Yes
Other assistive technology: NR
Priority registration: Yes
Added costs of services: Yes
LD specialists: Yes
ADHD coaching: No
ASD specialists: Yes
Professional tutors: No
Peer tutors: No
Max. hours/wk. for services: NR
How professors are notified of student approved accommodations: By student

General Admissions Information

Office of Admissions: 845-398-4100

Entrance Requirements

Academic units required: 4 English, 3 math, 3 science, 2 science labs, 2 foreign language, 4 social studies. **Academic units recommended:** 4 math, 3 foreign language. High school diploma is required and GED is accepted. SAT or ACT required. If ACT, ACT with writing accepted. TOEFL required of all international applicants: minimum paper TOEFL 530.

Application deadline: NR
Notification: Rolling starting 11/1
Average GPA: 3.01
ACT Composite middle 50% range: 18-22
SAT Math middle 50% range: 420-530
SAT Critical Reading middle 50% range: 410-520
SAT Writing middle 50% range: 410-510
Graduate top 10% of class: NR
Graduated top 25% of class: NR
Graduated top 50% of class: NR

COLLEGE GRADUATION REQUIREMENTS

Course waivers allowed: No
In what course: NR
Course substitutions allowed: Yes
In what course: Foreign language; Speech; Math (only when math is not a requirement of the major)

Additional Information

Environment: This private school was founded in 1952. It has a 47-acre campus.

Student Body
Undergrad enrollment: 1,696
% Women: 56
% Men: 44
% Out-of-state: 13

Cost information
Tuition: $28,240
Room & board: $12,030
Housing Information
University Housing: Yes
Percent living on campus: 33.5

Greek System
Fraternity: NR
Sorority: NR
Athletics: Other

STATE UNIVERSITY OF NEW YORK AT BINGHAMTON

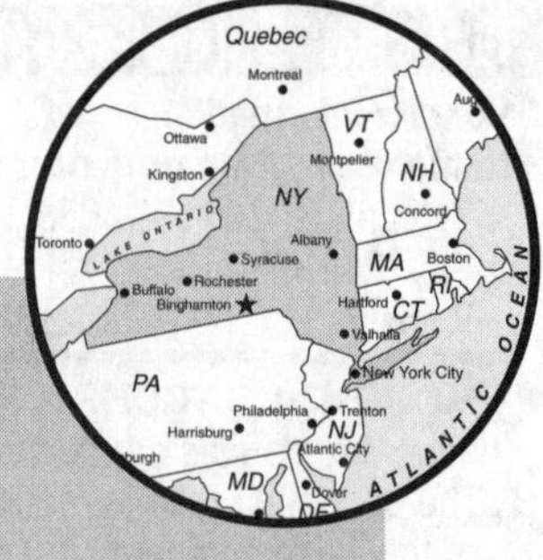

PO Box 6001, Binghamton, NY 13902-6001
Phone: 607-777-2171 • Fax: 607-777-4445
E-mail: admit@binghamton.edu • Web: www.binghamton.edu
Support: CS • Institution: Public

PROGRAMS OR SERVICES FOR STUDENTS WITH LEARNING DIFFERENCES

The Services for Students with Disabilities office provides assistance to students with physical or learning disabilities. They operate on the philosophy that the individuals they serve are students first and their disabilities are secondary. Support services assist students in taking advantage of the opportunities at Binghamton and in making their own contributions to the university community.

ADMISSION INFORMATION FOR STUDENTS WITH LEARNING DIFFERENCES

College entrance test required: Yes
Interview required: No
Essay required: Not Applicable
Additional Application Required for LD/ADHD/ASD: Yes
What documentation required for LD: No documentation is required for admission to Binghamton University, however guidelines for ADHD admission are available at the SSD websitehttp://binghamton.edu/ssd/new-students/disability-documentation-guidelines.html
With general application: No
To receive services after enrolling: Yes
What documentation required for ADHD: There are no requirements for documentation for ASD in order to be admitted to Binghamton University
With general application: No
To receive services after enrolling: Yes
What documentation required for ASD: No documentation / diagnostic testing is required for admission to Binghamton University, however guidelines for LD admission are available at the SSD website http://binghamton.edu/ssd/new-students/disability-documentation-guidelines.html
With general application: No
To receive services after enrolling: Yes
LD/ADHD/ASD documentation submitted to: Services for Students with Disabilities
ASD Specific Program: No
Special Ed. HS course work accepted: Not Applicable
Specific course requirements of all applicants: NR
Separate application required for program services: Yes
Total # of students receiving LD/ADHD/ASD services: NR
Acceptance into program means acceptance into college: No

ADMISSIONS

Binghamton University welcomes applications from all qualified individuals. While there are no special admissions procedures or academic programs expressly for students with disabilities, the Services for Students with Disabilities Office provides a wide range of support services to enrolled students. Diagnostic tests are not required for admissions, but students are encouraged to meet with the director of Services for Students with Disabilities and provide documentation to determine appropriate accommodations. Through nonmatriculated enrollment, students can take courses but are not enrolled in a degree program. If they do well, they may then apply for matriculation, using credits earned toward their degree. General admission criteria includes 4 years of English, 2.5 years of math, 2 years of social science, 2 years of science, and 2 years of 2 foreign languages or 3 years of 1 foreign language. The mid 50 percent score range on the SAT is 1100–1330.

ADDITIONAL INFORMATION

Students with LD/ADHD may use all campus-wide services, plus receive accommodations and services through SSD. Accommodations that are available for students with appropriate documentation include extended testing times; low-distraction environments for tests; scribes; proctors; use of calculators, dictionaries, computers, and spellchecker during exams; and assistive technology including voice recognition software, screen readers software, print enlargement, assistive listening devices, and variable speed tape recorders on loan. Tutorial services are provided for 4 hours per week to undergraduate students at no charge. However, SSD can arrange for more than 4 hours per week at the student's expense. The university's Center for Academic Excellence provides peer tutoring to any student at no cost. The university has offered courses in college study, coping skills, and applying study skills to career research. Availability of these courses each year is dependent on staffing. Students are provided memos of reasonable accommodation written by the SSD director or learning disabilities specialist to be given to their professors. Services and accommodations are available for undergraduate and graduate students.

General Support Services Information

Contact Information
Name of program or department: Services for Students with Disabilities
Telephone: 607-777-2686
Fax: 607-777-6893

Accommodations or Services For Students With Learning Differences

Accommodations are decided upon an individual basis after a thorough review of appropriate, current documentation. The accommodations requests must be supported through the documentation provided and must be logically linked to the current impact of the condition on academic functioning.

Allowed in exams
Calculator: Yes
Dictionary: No
Computer: Yes
Spellchecker: No
Extended test time: Yes
Scribes: Yes
Proctors: Yes
Oral exams: Not Applicable
Note-takers: Yes
Support services for students with LD: Yes
Support services for students with ADHD: Yes
Support services for students with ASD: Yes
Distraction-reduced environment: Yes
Tape recording in class: Yes
Electronic texts: Yes
Kurzweil reader: NR
Audio books: Yes
Other assistive technology: Yes
Priority registration: No
Added costs of services: Not Applicable
LD specialists: Yes
ADHD coaching: No
ASD specialists: Yes
Professional tutors: No
Peer tutors: Not Applicable
Max. hours/wk. for services: NR
How professors are notified of student approved accommodations: By student

General Admissions Information

Office of Admissions: 607-777-2171

Entrance Requirements

Academic units required: 4 English, 3 math, 2 science, 3 foreign language, 2 social studies. **Academic units recommended:** 4 math, 4 science, 4 social studies, 4 history. High school diploma is required and GED is accepted. SAT or ACT required. If ACT, ACT with writing required. TOEFL required of all international applicants: minimum paper TOEFL 560 or minimum internet TOEFL 83.

Application deadline: NR
Notification: NR
Average GPA: 3.7
ACT Composite middle 50% range: 27-31
SAT Math middle 50% range: 630-703
SAT Critical Reading middle 50% range: 600-680
SAT Writing middle 50% range: 580-670
Graduate top 10% of class: NR
Graduated top 25% of class: NR
Graduated top 50% of class: NR

COLLEGE GRADUATION REQUIREMENTS

Course waivers allowed: No
Course substitutions allowed: Yes
In what course: Foreign Language on a case by case basis

Additional Information

Environment: This public school was founded in 1946. It has a 930-acre campus.

Student Body
Undergrad enrollment: 13,491
% Women: 48
% Men: 52
% Out-of-state: 8

Cost information
In-state Tuition: $6,470
Out-of-state Tuition: $19,590
Room & board: $13,198

Housing Information
University Housing: Yes
Percent living on campus: 51

Greek System
Fraternity: Yes
Sorority: Yes
Athletics: Division I

STATE UNIVERSITY OF NEW YORK—DELHI

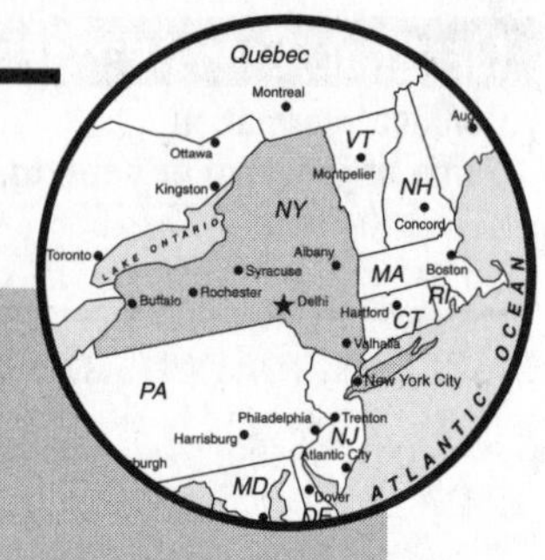

Bush Hall, Two Main Street, Delhi, NY 13753
Phone: 607-746-4550 • Fax: 607-746-4104
E-mail: enroll@Delhi.edu • Web: www.delhi.edu
Support: CS • Institution type: 2-year Public

PROGRAMS OR SERVICES FOR STUDENTS WITH LEARNING DIFFERENCES

SUNY—Delhi provides students with learning disabilities with academic support services and equipment, including tutors, exams in distraction-free environments, and enlarged-video-display computer terminals. The coordinator of services often confers with students regarding their unique learning, study, and time management needs.

ADMISSION INFORMATION FOR STUDENTS WITH LEARNING DIFFERENCES

College entrance tests required: No
Interview required: No
Essay required: No
Additional Application Required for LD/ADHD/ASD: NR
What documentation required for LD: Psycho ed evaluation to include: relevant historical info, instructional interventions, related services, age diagnosed, objective data (aptitude, achievement, info processing), test scores (standard, percentile and grade equivalents) and describe functional limitations.
With general application: No
To receive services after enrolling: Yes
What documentation required for ADHD: Diagnosis based on DSM-V; history of behaviors impairing functioning in academic setting; diagnostic interview; history of symptoms; evidence of ongoing behaviors.
With general application: No
To receive services after enrolling: Yes
What documentation required for ASD: Psycho ed evaluation
With general application: NR
To receive services after enrolling: Yes
LD/ADHD/ASD documentation submitted to: The Coordinator of Students with Disabilities
ASD Specific Program: NR
Special Ed. HS course work accepted: NR
Specific course requirements of all applicants: Yes
Separate application required: No
Total # of students receiving LD/ADHD/ASD services: NR
Acceptance into program means acceptance into college: Students must be admitted to and enrolled in the university first and then request services.

ADMISSIONS

The admission requirements are the same for all students. It is always helpful if students with learning disabilities present themselves as confident, independent, goal-oriented, and self-directed learners. The minimum GPA and course requirements depend on the major. Admissions counselors will refer students to the coordinator if the student provides information about a disability. To be eligible for services, students must disclose information about their learning disability/attention deficit hyperactivity disorder and meet with the coordinator of Services for Students with Disabilities.

ADDITIONAL INFORMATION

The Resnick Learning Center coordinates with the academic departments to offer a variety of resources, programs, and services to prepare students for the rigors of the college experience. The Center provides alternative testing services for students who need a distraction-free environment, a private room, use of a computer to read exams, scribes, oral exams or enlarged print. Services provided in the center include: Academic Advising/Academic Warning System; Career and Business Development; Tutoring-both on site and online; Math Center; Writing Center; International Student Services; English Language Learners (ELL); Access and Equity (formerly Disability Services); Educational Opportunity Program; Academic Exploration Program.

General Support Services Information

Contact Information
Name of program or department: The Resnick Learning Center
Telephone: 607-746-4593
Fax: 607-746-4368

Accommodations or Services for Students with Learning Differences

Accommodations are decided upon an individual basis after a thorough review of appropriate, current documentation. The accommodations requested must be supported through the documentation provided and must be logically linked to the current impact of the condition on academic functioning.

Allowed in exams
Calculator: Yes
Dictionary: Yes
Computer: Yes
Spellchecker: Yes
Extended test time: Yes
Scribes: Yes
Proctors: Yes
Oral exams: Yes
Note-takers: Yes
Services for students with LD: Yes
Services for students with ADHD: Yes
Services for students with ASD: Yes
Distraction-reduced environment: Yes
Tape recording in class: Yes
Audio books: NR
Electronic texts: No
Kurzweil Reader: Yes
Other assistive technology: Yes
Priority registration: No
Added costs for services: No
LD specialists: Yes
ADHD coaching: Yes
ASD specialists: NR
Professional tutors: Yes
Peer tutors: Yes
Max. hours/wk. for services: 2 per course
How professors are notified of LD/ADHD: By student

General Admissions Information

Office of Admission: 607-746-4550

Entrance Requirements

Academic units required: 4 English, 1 math, 1 science, 3 social studies, 1 history. **Academic units recommended:** 2 math, 2 science (1 science lab). High school diploma is required, and GED is accepted.

Application deadline: None
Average GPA: NR
ACT Composite middle 50% range: NR
SAT Math middle 50% range: NR
SAT Critical Reading middle 50% range: NR
SAT Writing middle 50% range: NR
Graduated top 10% of class: NR
Graduated top 25% of class: NR
Graduated top 50% of class: NR

COLLEGE GRADUATION REQUIREMENTS

Course waivers allowed: No
Course substitutions allowed: Yes
In what course: Math and foreign language

Additional Information

Environment: The university is on 1,100 acres in a small town setting in upstate New York.

Student Body
Undergrad enrollment: 2,751
% Women: 44%
% Men: 56%
% Out-of-state: 2%

Cost Information
In-state tuition: $5,270
Out-of-state tuition: $14,320
Room & board: $10,120

Housing Information
University housing: Yes
% Living on campus: 70%

Greek System
Fraternity: Yes
Sorority: Yes
Athletics: Division III

State University of New York—Farmingdale

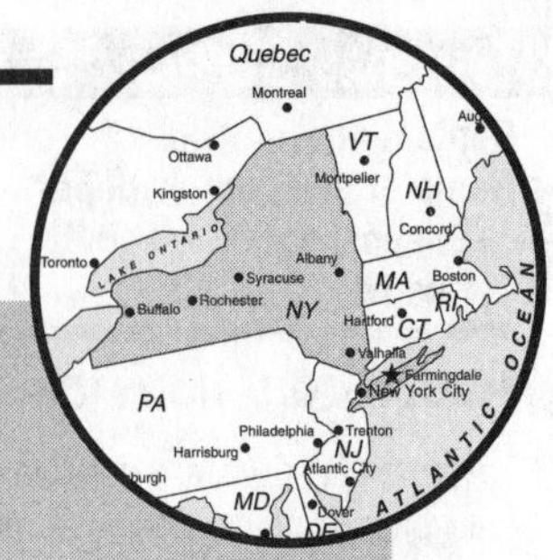

Admissions Office, 2350 Broadhollow Road, Farmingdale, NY 11735
Phone: 631-420-2200 • Fax: 631-420-2633
E-mail: admissions@farmingdale.edu • Web: www.farmingdale.edu
Support: CS • Institution type: 4-year Public

Programs or Services for Students with Learning Differences

There is no learning disabilities program at the college, but the Disability Services Center is dedicated to the principle that equal opportunity to realize one's full potential should be available to all students. In keeping with this philosophy, the staff offers services to students with disabilities in accordance with their needs. Students may be able to meet individually with a learning disability specialist or in group meetings. Services include academic remediation with emphasis on compensatory strategies, study skills strategies training, test accommodations, time management instruction, tutoring, and self-understanding of disability. The services offered strive to instill independence, self-confidence, and self-advocacy skills.

Admission Information for Students with Learning Differences

College entrance tests required: Yes
Interview required: Yes
Essay required: No
Additional Application Required for LD/ADHD/ASD: NR
What documentation required for LD: Psycho ed evaluation to include: relevant historical info, instructional interventions, related services, age diagnosed, objective data (aptitude, achievement, info processing), test scores (standard, percentile and grade equivalents) and describe functional limitations.
With general application: No
To receive services after enrolling: Yes
What documentation required for ADHD: Diagnosis based on DSM-V; history of behaviors impairing functioning in academic setting; diagnostic interview; history of symptoms; evidence of ongoing behaviors.
With general application: No
To receive services after enrolling: Yes
What documentation required for ASD: Psycho ed evaluation
With general application: NR
To receive services after enrolling: Yes
LD/ADHD/ASD documentation submitted to: Office of Support Services
ASD Specific Program: NR
Special Ed. HS course work accepted: Yes
Specific course requirements of all applicants: Yes
Separate application required: No
Total # of students receiving LD/ADHD/ASD services: 145–155
Acceptance into program means acceptance into college: Students must be admitted and enrolled in the university first (they can appeal a denial) and then request services.

Admissions

There is no special admissions procedure for applicants with learning disabilities. Students should self-identify on the application. Admission decisions are made by the Office of Admissions. Students are required to take the SAT/ACT. The university has rolling admissions. Almost all of the programs accept students throughout the year. The minimum GPA is 80 percent and SAT 1000 or ACT 21.

Additional Information

Students begin the process to receive support services by disclosing their disability to the Disability Services Center (DSC). Documentation providing diagnosis and how it impacts learning is required. Additional documentation may be required depending on specific disability. Services and accommodations available with appropriate documentation may include extended testing times; distraction-free environments; use of calculators, computers, and spellchecker; note-takers; scribes; proctors; assistive technology; tutors; and recording in classes.

General Support Services Information

Contact Information
Name of program or department: Disability Services Center
Telephone: 631-420-2411
Fax: 631-794-6173

Accommodations or Services for Students with Learning Differences

Accommodations are decided upon an individual basis after a thorough review of appropriate, current documentation. The accommodations requested must be supported through the documentation provided and must be logically linked to the current impact of the condition on academic functioning.

Allowed in exams
Calculator: Yes
Dictionary: No
Computer: Yes
Spellchecker: Yes
Extended test time: Yes
Scribes: Yes
Proctors: Yes
Oral exams: Yes
Note-takers: Yes
Services for students with LD: Yes
Services for students with ADHD: Yes
Services for students with ASD: Yes
Distraction-reduced environment: Yes
Tape recording in class: Yes
Audio books: NR
Electronic texts: Yes
Kurzweil Reader: Yes
Other assistive technology: Yes
Priority registration: No
Added costs for services: No
LD specialists: Yes
ADHD coaching: Yes
ASD specialists: NR
Professional tutors: No
Peer tutors: Yes
Max. hours/wk. for services: Unlimited
How professors are notified of LD/ADHD: By student

General Admissions Information

Office of Admission: 631-420-2200

Entrance Requirements

Academic units required: 4 English, 2 math, 1 science (1 science lab), 4 social studies. **Academic units recommended:** 4 English, 4 math, 3 science (3 science labs), 4 social studies. High school diploma is required, and GED is accepted. TOEFL required of all international applicants: minimum paper TOEFL 520, minimum computer TOEFL 190.

Application deadline: None
Average GPA: Rolling starting 11/1
ACT Composite middle 50% range: NR
SAT Math middle 50% range: 450–550
SAT Critical Reading middle 50% range: 430–530
SAT Writing middle 50% range: 420–500
Graduated top 10% of class: NR
Graduated top 25% of class: NR
Graduated top 50% of class: NR

COLLEGE GRADUATION REQUIREMENTS

Course substitutions allowed: Yes
In what course: Foreign language

Additional Information

Environment: Farmingdale is in the suburbs with easy access to New York City.

Student Body
Undergrad enrollment: 7,600
% Women: 42%
% Men: 58%
% Out-of-state: 1%

Cost Information
In-state tuition: $6,444
Out-of-state tuition: $14,320
Room & board: $11,618

Housing Information
University housing: Yes
% Living on campus: 10%

Greek System
Fraternity: No
Sorority: No
Athletics: Division III

State University of New York—Potsdam

44 Pierrepont Avenue, Potsdam, NY 13676
Phone: 315-267-2180 • Fax: 315-267-2163
E-mail: admissions@potsdam.edu • Web: www.potsdam.edu
Support: S • Institution: Public

Programs or Services for Students with Learning Differences

The State University of New York College—Potsdam is committed to the full inclusion of all individuals who can benefit from educational opportunities. Accommodative Services provides academic accommodations for all qualified students who have documented learning, emotional, and/or physical disabilities and a need for accommodations. The ultimate goal is to promote individuals' independence within the academic atmosphere of the university. Students are assisted in this process by the support services and programs available to all Potsdam students. Students must submit (written) documentation of the disability and the need for accommodations. After forwarding documentation, students are encouraged to make an appointment to meet with the coordinator to discuss accommodations. All accommodations are determined on an individual basis. Accommodative Services makes every effort to ensure access to academic accommodations.

Admission Information for Students with Learning Differences

College entrance tests required: Yes
Interview required: No
Essay required: No
Additional Application Required for LD/ADHD/ASD: NR
What documentation required for LD: Psycho ed evaluation to include: relevant historical info, instructional interventions, related services, age diagnosed, objective data (aptitude, achievement, info processing), test scores (standard, percentile and grade equivalents) and describe functional limitations.
With general application: No
To receive services after enrolling: Yes
What documentation required for ADHD: Diagnosis based on DSM-V; history of behaviors impairing functioning in academic setting; diagnostic interview; history of symptoms; evidence of ongoing behaviors.
With general application: No
LD/ADHD/ASD documentation submitted to: Support Services
ASD Specific Program: NR
Special Ed. HS course work accepted: No
Specific course requirements of all applicants: Yes
Separate application required: No
Total # of students receiving LD/ADHD/ASD services: 45–50
Acceptance into program means acceptance into college: Students must be admitted to and enrolled in the university first and then request services.

Admissions

Students with learning disabilities must meet the same admission criteria as all applicants to the university. General admissions requirements include an ACT of 20-plus or SAT of 960, 3.0 GPA, and 17 core courses including 3 years of math, 2 years of science, 4 years of social studies, 4 years of English, 3 years of a foreign language, and 1 year of fine or performing arts. There is no conditional or probational admission plan. Students are encouraged to self-disclose their disability and provide appropriate documentation to Accommodative Services.

Additional Information

Accommodations available through Accommodative Services include note-takers; test readers/books on tape; alternative testing such as extended time and/or distraction-reduced environment, exam readers/scribes, and use of word processor with spellchecker; and lending of some equipment. Additional services can include special registration and academic advising. Accommodative Services will assist students requesting non-academic auxiliary aids or services in locating the appropriate campus resources to address the request. The College Counseling Center provides psychological services. The early warning system asks each instructor to indicate at midpoint in each semester if a student is making unsatisfactory academic progress. Results of this inquiry are sent to the student and advisor. Student Support Services provides academic support, peer mentoring, and counseling. Tutoring is available for all students one-on-one or in small groups.

General Support Services Information

Contact Information

Name of program or department: Accommodative Services

Telephone: 315-267-3268

Fax: housese@potsdam.edu

Accommodations or Services For Students With Learning Differences

Accommodations are decided upon an individual basis after a thorough review of appropriate, current documentation. The accommodations requests must be supported through the documentation provided and must be logically linked to the current impact of the condition on academic functioning.

Allowed in exams
Calculator: Yes
Dictionary: Yes
Computer: Yes
Spellchecker: Yes
Extended test time: Yes
Scribes: Yes
Proctors: Yes
Oral exams: Yes
Note-takers: Yes
Support services for students with LD: Yes
Support services for students with ADHD: Yes
Support services for students with ASD: Yes
Distraction-reduced environment: Yes
Tape recording in class: Yes
Electronic texts: Yes
Kurzweil reader: NR
Audio books: Yes
Other assistive technology: Yes
Priority registration: Yes
Added costs of services: No
LD specialists: No
ADHD coaching: NR
ASD specialists: NR
Professional tutors: No
Peer tutors: Yes
Max. hours/wk. for services: NR
How professors are notified of student approved accommodations: By both student and director

General Admissions Information

Office of Admissions: 315-267-2180

Entrance Requirements

Academic units required: 4 English, 2 math, 2 science, 1 science labs, 4 social studies, 1 visual/performing arts. **Academic units recommended:** 4 English, 3 math, 3 science, 1 science labs, 3 foreign language, 4 social studies, 1 visual/performing arts. High school diploma is required and GED is accepted. SAT or ACT required for some. If ACT, ACT with writing accepted. TOEFL required of all international applicants: minimum paper TOEFL 550 or minimum internet TOEFL 79.

Application deadline: NR
Notification: Rolling starting 10/1
Average GPA: 87.03
ACT Composite middle 50% range: 22-28
SAT Math middle 50% range: 440-580
SAT Critical Reading middle 50% range: 437-570
SAT Writing middle 50% range: NR-NR
Graduate top 10% of class: 15
Graduated top 25% of class: 25
Graduated top 50% of class: 43

COLLEGE GRADUATION REQUIREMENTS

Course waivers allowed: No
Course substitutions allowed: Yes

Additional Information

Environment: This public school was founded in 1816. It has a 240-acre campus.

Student Body
Undergrad enrollment: 3,614
% Women: 57
% Men: 43
% Out-of-state: 3

Cost information
Room & board:NR

Housing Information
University Housing: Yes
Percent living on campus: 60

Greek System
Fraternity: Yes
Sorority: Yes
Athletics: Division III

State University of New York— Stony Brook University

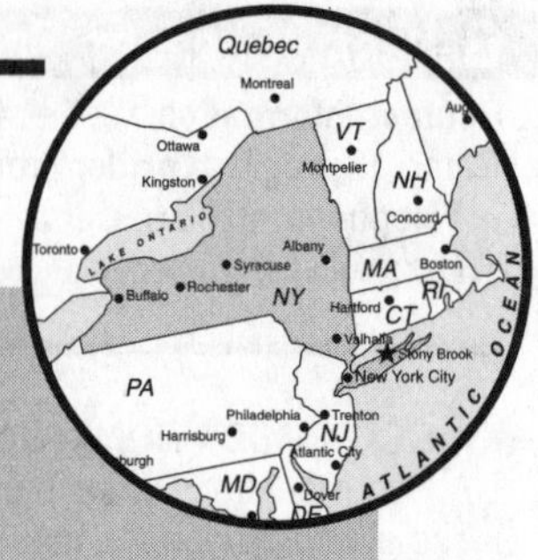

Office of Admissions, Stony Brook, NY 11794-1901
Phone: 631-632-6868 • Fax: 631-632-9898
E-mail: enroll@stonybrook.edu • Web: www.stonybrook.edu/
Support: CS • Institution: Public

Programs or Services for Students with Learning Differences

Disability Support Services (DSS) coordinates advocacy and support services for students with disabilities. These services assist integrating students' needs with the resources available at the university to eliminate physical or programmatic barriers and ensure an accessible academic environment. All information and documentation of student disabilities is confidential. Students are responsible for identifying and documenting their disabilities through the DSS office. Students receive assistance with special housing and transportation, recruitment of readers, interpreters, note-takers, test accommodations, and counseling. A learning disabilities specialist is available to refer students for diagnostic testing and educational programming, meet accommodation needs, and provide in-service training to the university community. A Supported Education Program offering individual counseling and group sessions is available for students with psychological disabilities. Students who anticipate requiring assistance should contact Disability Support Services as early as possible to allow time for implementing recommended services.

Admission Information for Students with Learning Differences

College entrance tests required: Yes
Interview required: No
Essay required: No
Additional Application Required for LD/ADHD/ASD: NR
What documentation required for LD: Psycho ed evaluation to include: relevant historical info, instructional interventions, related services, age diagnosed, objective data (aptitude, achievement, info processing), test scores (standard, percentile and grade equivalents) and describe functional limitations.
With general application: No
To receive services after enrolling: Yes
What documentation required for ADHD: Diagnosis based on DSM-V; history of behaviors impairing functioning in academic setting; diagnostic interview; history of symptoms; evidence of ongoing behaviors.
With general application: No
LD/ADHD/ASD documentation submitted to: DSS
ASD Specific Program: NR
Special Ed. HS course work accepted: No
Specific course requirements of all applicants: Yes
Separate application required: No
Total # of students receiving LD/ADHD/ASD services: 165
Acceptance into program means acceptance into college: Students must be admitted to and enrolled in the university first and then request services.

Admissions

Admission decisions are based on grades, GPA and/or class rank, and ACT/SAT. There is no separate or special admission because there are no developmental or remedial classes. However, each applicant who is identified as having a disability is given the special consideration of being reviewed by an admissions counselor and a DSS staff member jointly. All special circumstances are taken into consideration. Students are encouraged to self-disclose their disability in the application process. The director of Disabilities Services will review documentation from students with learning disabilities and provide a recommendation to the Office of Admissions.

Additional Information

Every semester the student should go to the DSS to meet with a counselor and fill out an accommodation request form to generate a letter to each professor that explains the accommodations. Types of services and accommodations available are pre-registration advisement, liaising with faculty and staff, taped texts, learning strategies and time management training, assistance in locating tutors, assistance in arranging for note-takers and readers, tutorial computer programs, proctoring and/or modified administration of exams, support groups, referrals to appropriate campus resources, peer advising, and aid in vocational decision making. Services and accommodations are available to undergraduate and graduate students. No skills classes are offered.

General Support Services Information

Contact Information
Name of program or department: Disabilities Support Services (DSS)
Telephone: 631-632-6748
Fax: 631-632-6747

Accommodations or Services for Students with Learning Differences

Accommodations are decided upon an individual basis after a thorough review of appropriate, current documentation. The accommodations requested must be supported through the documentation provided and must be logically linked to the current impact of the condition on academic functioning.

Allowed in exams
Calculator: NR
Dictionary: No
Computer: Yes
Spellchecker: Yes
Extended test time: Yes
Scribes: Yes
Proctors: Yes
Oral exams: No
Note-takers: Yes
Services for students with LD: Yes
Services for students with ADHD: Yes
Services for students with ASD: Yes
Distraction-reduced environment: Yes
Tape recording in class: Yes
Audio books: NR
Electronic texts: No
Kurzweil Reader: Yes
Other assistive technology: Yes
Priority registration: Yes
Added costs for services: No
LD specialists: Yes
ADHD coaching: NR
ASD specialists: NR
Professional tutors: No
Peer tutors: No
Max. hours/wk. for services: N/A
How professors are notified of LD/ADHD: By student

General Admissions Information

Office of Admissions: 631-632-6868

Entrance Requirements

Academic units required: 4 English, 3 math, 3 science, 2 foreign language, 4 social studies. **Academic units recommended:** 4 math, 4 science, 3 foreign language. High school diploma is required and GED is accepted. SAT or ACT required. If ACT, ACT with writing recommended. TOEFL required of all international applicants: minimum paper TOEFL 550 or minimum internet TOEFL 80.

Application deadline: NR
Notification: 4/1
Average GPA: 3.79
ACT Composite middle 50% range: 26-31
SAT Math middle 50% range: 600-720
SAT Critical Reading middle 50% range: 550-660
SAT Writing middle 50% range: 540-660
Graduated top 10% of class: 46
Graduated top 25% of class: 79
Graduated top 50% of class: 96

COLLEGE GRADUATION REQUIREMENTS

Course waivers allowed: No
Course substitutions allowed: Yes
In what course: Subsitutions possible for foreign language

Additional Information

Environment: This public school was founded in 1957. It has a 1450-acre campus.

Student Body
Undergrad enrollment: 16,831
% Women: 46
% Men: 54
% Out-of-state: 8

Cost information
In-state Tuition: $6,470
Out-of Tuition: $21,550
Room & board: $12,032

Housing Information
University Housing: Yes
Percent living on campus: 51

Greek System
Fraternity: Yes
Sorority: Yes
Athletics: Division I

State University of New York—University at Albany

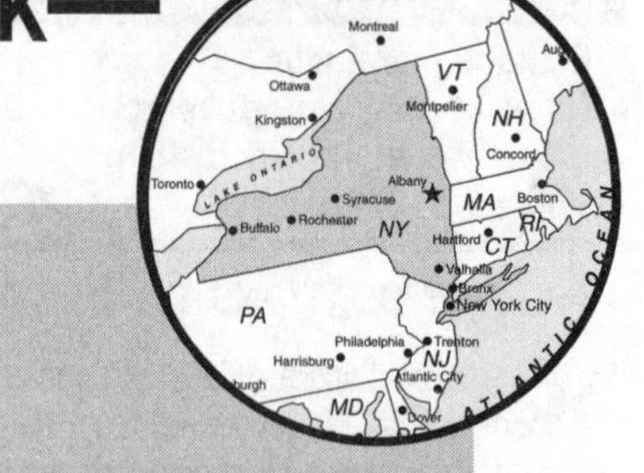

Office of Undergraduate Admissions, Albany, NY 12222
Phone: 518-442-5435 • Fax: 518-442-5383
E-mail: ugadmissions@albany.edu • Web: www.albany.edu
Support: CS • Institution: Public

Programs or Services for Students with Learning Differences

The University at Albany—State University of New York, in response to a growing population of successful students with learning disabilities and/or attention deficit disorder, created an Office of Learning Disabled Student Services. This office is now part of the newly created Disability Resource Center. The mission of the Didability Resource Center is to empower individual students, using appropriate supportive services, as well as acting as an expert resource for the university community. This includes assisting the student in developing the skills necessary to be a successful, independent learner, organizing class assignments, workload, social life and developing appropriate academic accommodations for classes as well as increasing campus awareness of the issues surrounding students with disabilities.

Admission Information for Students with Learning Differences

College entrance test required: Yes
Interview required: No
Essay required: No
Additional Application Required for LD/ADHD/ASD: NR
What documentation required for LD: Current psychological/educational evaluation (within the last 3 years). Documentation must state area of disability (state a diagnosis). Reasonable academic accommodations must be supported by documentation. Academic accommodations must not change the academic mission of the university nor may the accommodation decrease the academic standards of a course or plan of study. Foreign language is required for graduation. If the student had a foreign language exemption in high school, documentation must include what evaluation was used to support the exemption—NOT just a statement on the IEP that estudents disability adversely impact ability to learn a foreign language.
With general application: No
To receive services after enrolling: Yes
What documentation required for ADHD: Medical documenation is sufficient for individual appointments. Psychological-Educational evaluation (completed within the last 3 years) will need to be submitted to support any academic accommodations that the student may seek. Academic accommodations must not change the academic mission of the university nor may the accommodation decrease the academic standards of a course or plan of study.
With general application: No
To receive services after enrolling: Yes
What documentation required for ASD: Psycho ed evaluation
With general application: No
To receive services after enrolling: Yes
LD/ADHD/ASD documentation submitted to: Support program/services
ASD Specific Program: NR
Special Ed. HS course work accepted: Yes
Specific course: Yes
Separate application required for program services: 3

Admissions

There is no special application for applicants with learning disabilities and/or attention deficit disorder. For regular admissions, a student needs to have a High School average of 85% or higher, be in the top 1/3 of their class and obtain an acceptable standardized test score. The university does have a Talented Student Admissions program for those students that do not fit the standard profile. The minimum academic criteria for consideration has been set at an eleventh grade cumulative average of 80 and rank in the top 1/2 of the high school class at the end of 11th grade, as well as having an ACT/SAT scores deemed acceptable by the university.

Additional Information

Students visiting the University at Albany are encouraged to schedule an appointment to meet with the a staff member of the Disability Resource Center while they are on campus. The Disability Resource Center provides individual appointments to discuss academic concerns, develop study strategies, rehearse self advocacy scenarios and provide a "reality check" on the student's academic progress. The office receives and reviews documentation supplied by the student in regards to their disability. Appropriate academic accommodations are then developed based on the documentation supplied. The student and the director or assistant director discuss the academic accommodations that are developed and the mechanisms involved to receive the accommodation.

General Support Services Information

Contact Information
Name of program or department: Disability Resource Center
Telephone: 518-442-5490
Fax: 518 442 5400

Accommodations or Services for Students with Learning Differences

Accommodations are decided upon an individual basis after a thorough review of appropriate, current documentation. The accommodations requests must be supported through the documentation provided and must be logically linked to the current impact of the condition on academic functioning.

Allowed in exams
Calculator: Yes
Dictionary: Yes
Computer: Yes
Spellchecker: Yes
Extended test time: Yes
Scribes: Yes
Proctors: Yes
Oral exams: Yes
Note-takers: Yes
Services for students with LD: Yes
Services for students with ADHD: Yes
Services for students with ASD: Yes
Distraction-reduced environment: Yes
Tape recording in class: Yes
Kurzweil reader: Yes
Audio books from learning ally: Yes
Other assistive technology: Yes
Priority registration: Yes
Added costs of services: N/A
LD specialists: Yes
ADHD coaching: NR
ASD specialists: NR
Peer tutors: Yes
How professors are notified of student approved accommodations: Student

General Admissions Information

Office of Admissions: 518-442-5435

Entrance Requirements

Academic units required: 4 English, 2 math, 2 science, 2 science labs, 1 foreign language, 3 social studies, 2 history, 4 academic electives. **Academic units recommended:** 4 math, 3 science, 3 science labs, 3 foreign language. High school diploma is required and GED is accepted. SAT or ACT required. If ACT, ACT with writing required. TOEFL required of all international applicants: minimum paper TOEFL 550 or minimum internet TOEFL 79.

Application deadline: 3/1
Notification: NR
Average GPA: 3.5
ACT Composite middle 50% range: 22-26
SAT Math middle 50% range: 520-600
SAT Critical Reading middle 50% range: 490-580
SAT Writing middle 50% range: NR-NR
Graduated top 10% of class: 18
Graduated top 25% of class: 49
Graduated top 50% of class: 86

COLLEGE GRADUATION REQUIREMENTS

Course waivers allowed: No
Course substitutions allowed: Yes
In what course: Determined on a case-by-case basis with supporting documentation

Additional Information

Environment: This public school was founded in 1844. It has a 795-acre campus.

Student Body
Undergrad enrollment: 12,929
% Women: 48
% Men: 52
% Out-of-state: 6

Cost information
In-state Tuition: $6,470
Out-of Tuition: $19,590
Room & board: $12,426

Housing Information
University Housing: Yes
Percent living on campus: 58

Greek System
Fraternity: Yes
Sorority: Yes
Athletics: Division I

Syracuse University

100 Crouse-Hinds Hall, Syracuse, NY 13244-2130
Phone: 315-443-3611 • Fax: 315-443-4226
E-mail: orange@syr.edu • Web: www.syr.edu
Support: CS • Institution: Private

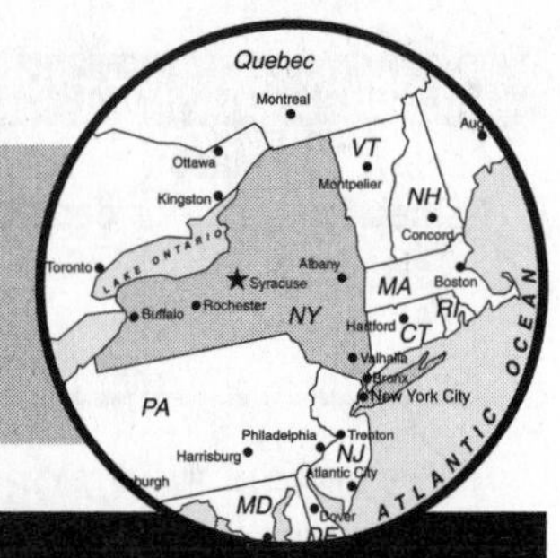

Programs or Services for Students with Learning Differences

The Office of Disability Services provides an integrated network of academic support, counseling, and advising services to meet the individual needs of students with diagnosed learning disabilities. Every student with learning disabilities who is accepted to the university is eligible for services and must provide diagnostic information from which appropriate academic accommodations are determined. Services are provided by a professional staff to assist students in developing a sense of independence as they learn to advocate for themselves and become involved in their college education.

Admission Information for Students with Learning Differences

College entrance tests required: Yes
Interview required: Yes
Essay required: Yes
Additional Application Required for LD/ADHD/ASD: NR
What documentation required for LD: Psycho ed evaluation to include: relevant historical info, instructional interventions, related services, age diagnosed, objective data (aptitude, achievement, info processing), test scores (standard, percentile and grade equivalents) and describe functional limitations.
With general application: No
To receive services after enrolling: Yes
What documentation required for ADHD: Diagnosis based on DSM-V; history of behaviors impairing functioning in academic setting; diagnostic interview; history of symptoms; evidence of ongoing behaviors.
With general application: No
LD/ADHD/ASD documentation submitted to: Office of Disability Services
ASD Specific Program: NR
Special Ed. HS course work accepted: No
Specific course requirements of all applicants: Yes
Separate application required: No
Total # of students receiving LD/ADHD/ASD services: 450
Acceptance into program means acceptance into college: Students must be admitted to and enrolled in the university first and then request services.

Admissions

All students must meet regular admission standards and submit the general application form. General admission criteria include 4 years of English, 3–4 years of math, 3–4 years of science, 3–4 years of social studies, and 2 years of a foreign language; an ACT of 25 or SAT of 1100-plus; and a B average (80 percent or a 3.0 GPA). However, consideration will be given to standardized testing scores in light of the disability. Students with learning disabilities may request substitutions for high school math or foreign language if documentation can substantiate a disability in any one of these areas. Students should include current testing and documentation. Students can write an accompanying letter describing their learning disability, their goals, and the services needed. Students' grades should show an upward trend. In the event that an applicant is denied admission to a specific course of study, an alternative offer may be suggested.

Additional Information

Students with identified learning disabilities are provided with an integrated network of academic and counseling services to meet their individual needs. Services include note-takers, proofreaders, readers for exams alternate format (electronic text) of textbooks, tutors, counseling, and advising. Accommodations include time extensions for exams, and alternative testing methods. The Office of Disability Services provides each student with an accommodation letter to be used when the students meet with instructors to verify their LD status. To take advantage of these support services, diagnosed students must submit recent documentation of their learning disability. Services are offered to undergraduate and graduate students.

General Support Services Information

Contact Information
Name of program or department: Office of Disability Services
Telephone: 315-443-4498
Fax: 315-443-1312
Website: disabilityservices.syr.edu

Accommodations or Services For Students With Learning Differences

Accommodations are decided upon an individual basis after a thorough review of appropriate, current documentation. The accommodations requests must be supported through the documentation provided and must be logically linked to the current impact of the condition on academic functioning.

Allowed in exams
Calculator: Yes
Dictionary: Yes
Computer: Yes
Spellchecker: Yes
Extended test time: Yes
Scribes: Yes
Proctors: Yes
Oral exams: Yes
Note-takers: Yes
Support services for students with LD: Yes
Support services for students with ADHD: Yes
Support services for students with ASD: Yes
Distraction-reduced environment: Yes
Tape recording in class: Yes
Electronic texts: Yes
Kurzweil reader: NR
Audio books: Yes
Other assistive technology: Yes
Priority registration: Yes
Added costs of services: No
LD specialists: Yes
ADHD coaching: No
ASD specialists: Yes
Professional tutors: Yes
Peer tutors: Yes
Max. hours/wk. for services: NR
How professors are notified of student approved accommodations: By student

General Admissions Information

Office of Admissions: 315-443-3611

Entrance Requirements

Academic units recommended: 4 English, 4 math, 4 science, 3 foreign language, 4 social studies, 4 history. High school diploma is required and GED is accepted. SAT or ACT required. If ACT, ACT with writing required. TOEFL required of all international applicants: minimum paper TOEFL 550 or minimum internet TOEFL 85.

Application deadline: 1/1
Notification: NR
Average GPA: 3.6
ACT Composite middle 50% range: 24-29
SAT Math middle 50% range: 560-660
SAT Critical Reading middle 50% range: 530-630
SAT Writing middle 50% range: 530-640
Graduate top 10% of class: 35
Graduated top 25% of class: 70
Graduated top 50% of class: 95

COLLEGE GRADUATION REQUIREMENTS

Course waivers allowed: Yes
In what course: Math and foreign language, reviewed on a case by case basis.
Course substitutions allowed: Yes
In what course: Math and foreign language

Additional Information

Environment: This private school was founded in 1870. It has a 200-acre campus.

Student Body
Undergrad enrollment: 15,196
% Women: 55
% Men: 45
% Out-of-state: 63

Cost information
Room & board:NR
Housing Information
University Housing: Yes
Percent living on campus: 75

Greek System
Fraternity: Yes
Sorority: Yes
Athletics: Division I

Utica College

1600 Burrstone Road, Utica, NY 13502-4892
Phone: 315-792-3006 • Fax: 315-792-3003
E-mail: admiss@utica.edu • Web: www.utica.edu
Support: CS • Institution: Private

Programs or Services for Students with Learning Differences

The Office of Learning Services provides academic support and advisement to students who identify themselves as disabled and who provide appropriate supporting documentation. Accommodations are determined on a case-by-case basis based on supportive documentation provided by the student. Students are responsible for initiating a request for accommodations; for providing documentation of a disability; and for contacting the Office of Learning Services as early as possible upon admission. The Office of Learning Services professional staff members determine eligibility for services based on documentation; consult with students about appropriate accommodations; assist students in self-monitoring the effectiveness of the accommodations; coordinate auxiliary services; provide information regarding rights and responsibilities of students; provide individualized educational advising; and serve as advocates for the student.

Admission Information for Students with Learning Differences

College entrance test required: No
Interview required: No
Essay required: Required
Additional Application Required for LD/ADHD/ASD: NR
What documentation required for LD: Psycho ed evaluation to include: relevant historical info, instructional interventions, related services, age diagnosed, objective data (aptitude, achievement, info processing), test scores (standard, percentile and grade equivalents) and describe functional limitations.
With general application: NR
To receive services after enrolling: Yes
What documentation required for ADHD: Diagnosis based on DSM-V; history of behaviors impairing functioning in academic setting; diagnostic interview; history of symptoms; evidence of ongoing behaviors.
With general application: NR
To receive services after enrolling: Yes
What documentation required for ASD: Psycho ed evaluation
With general application: NR
To receive services after enrolling: Yes
LD/ADHD/ASD documentation submitted to: Learning Services office
ASD Specific Program: NR
Special Ed. HS course work accepted: NR
Specific course requirements of all applicants: NR
Separate application required for program services: No
Total # of students receiving LD/ADHD/ASD services: 172
Acceptance into program means acceptance into college: Students must be admitted to and enrolled in the university prior to requesting services.

Admissions

Utica College requires standardized test scores (such as SAT and ACT) for specific programs. Students are evaluated on an individualized basis. Students should have four years of English, three years of social studies, three years of math, three years of science, and two years of foreign language. Students with disabilities are strongly encouraged to schedule an interview. Documentation of a disability should be sent to the Office of Learning Services. Students are not required to self-disclose the disability during the admission process.

Additional Information

The Office of Learning Services provides accommodations to students with disabilities based on appropriate and current documentation. Documentation would be a written evaluation completed by an appropriate professional which states the specific disability, what functional limitations the student has because of the disability, and which offers recommendations for academic accommodations. Services may include priority registration, specific skill remediation, learning and study strategy development, referrals for diagnostic evaluation, time management strategies, professional tutoring. Accommodations may include such items as: use of a tape recorder; time extensions for tests and/or alternative testing methods; note-takers; and separate location for tests. An accommodation letter is generated for each student stating what accommmodations are appropriate in each individual case. It is the responsibility of the students to meet with their instructors to discuss their disability and their accommodations.

General Support Services Information

Contact Information
Name of program or department: Learning Services office
Telephone: 315-792-3032
Website: http://www.utica.edu/student/development/learning/

Accommodations or Services For Students With Learning Differences

Accommodations are decided upon an individual basis after a thorough review of appropriate, current documentation. The accommodations requests must be supported through the documentation provided and must be logically linked to the current impact of the condition on academic functioning.

Allowed in exams
Calculator: Yes
Dictionary: Yes
Computer: Yes
Spellchecker: Yes
Extended test time: Yes
Scribes: Yes
Proctors: Yes
Oral exams: Yes
Note-takers: Yes
Support services for students with LD: Yes
Support services for students with ADHD: Yes
Support services for students with ASD: Yes
Distraction-reduced environment: Yes
Tape recording in class: Yes
Electronic texts: Yes
Kurzweil reader: NR
Audio books: Yes
Other assistive technology: Yes
Priority registration: Yes
Added costs of services: No
LD specialists: Yes
ADHD coaching: Not Applicable
ASD specialists: Yes
Professional tutors: No
Peer tutors: Not Applicable
Max. hours/wk. for services: NR
How professors are notified of student approved accommodations: By both student and director

General Admissions Information

Office of Admissions: 315-792-3006

Entrance Requirements

Academic units required: 4 English, 3 math, 3 science, 1 foreign language, 4 social studies, 1 visual/performing arts. High school diploma is required and GED is accepted. SAT or ACT required for some. If ACT, ACT with writing accepted. TOEFL required of all international applicants: minimum paper TOEFL 525.

Application deadline: NR
Notification: Rolling starting 9/1
Average GPA: 3.09
ACT Composite middle 50% range: 20-24
SAT Math middle 50% range: 440-560
SAT Critical Reading middle 50% range: 440-540
SAT Writing middle 50% range: 420-520
Graduate top 10% of class: 9
Graduated top 25% of class: 33
Graduated top 50% of class: 63

COLLEGE GRADUATION REQUIREMENTS

Course waivers allowed: Not Applicable
Course substitutions allowed: Yes

Additional Information

Environment: This private school was founded in 1946. It has a 128-acre campus.

Student Body
Undergrad enrollment: 3,084
% Women: 61
% Men: 39
% Out-of-state: 18

Cost information
Tuition: $19,446
Room & board: $10,434
Housing Information
University Housing: Yes
Percent living on campus: 35

Greek System
Fraternity: Yes
Sorority: Yes
Athletics: Division III

Appalachian State University

Office of Admissions, Boone, NC 28608-2004
Phone: 828-262-2120 • Fax: 828-262-3296
E-mail: admissions@appstate.edu • Web: www.appstate.edu
Support: CS • Institution: Public

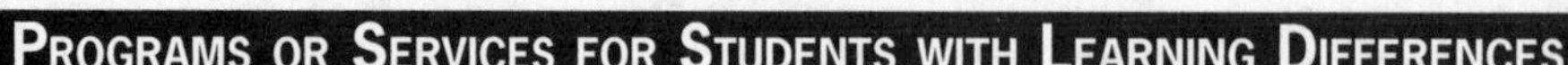

Programs or Services for Students with Learning Differences

The Office of Disability Services (ODS) and the Office of Equity, Diversity and Compliance strives to ensure that the dignity of students, employees and campus visitors is upheld when equal access to education and employment is guaranteed, respectful treatment is assured, and an appreciation of differences is fostered for all members of the university community. ODS works diligently to ensure that individuals with disabilities are provided equal access at ASU by broadening disability awareness, removing barriers and providing reasonable accommodations.

Admission Information for Students with Learning Differences

College entrance test required:
Interview required: No
Additional Application Required for LD/ADHD/ASD: NR
What documentation required for LD: Documentation must reflect the current impact and functional limitations of the impairment, be typed on office or practice letterhead, dated and signed by qualified professional. In-depth documentation can be found under documentation guidelines at ods.appstate.edu
With general application: No
To receive services after enrolling: Yes
What documentation required for ADHD: Documentation must reflect the current impact and functional limitations of the impairment, be typed on office or practice letterhead, dated and signed by qualified professional. In-depth documentation can be found under documentation guidelines at ods.appstate.edu
With general application: No
To receive services after enrolling: Yes
What documentation required for ASD: Documentation must reflect the current impact and functional limitations of the impairment, be typed on office or practice letterhead, dated and signed by qualified professional. In-depth documentation can be found under documentation guidelines at ods.appstate.edu
With general application: No
To receive services after enrolling: Yes
LD/ADHD/ASD documentation submitted to: Support program/services
ASD Specific Program: NR
Special Ed. HS course work accepted: Yes
Specific course: No
Separate application required for program services: Yes

Admissions

Individuals with disabilities must be accepted to the university through the established admission process required of all applicants. Admission is based solely on the university's requirements; neither the nature nor severity of a disability is considered in the admission process. Course requirements include 4 years English, 4 years math (Algebra I and II, geometry, and a higher level course), 3 years science (1 life science, 1 physical science and 1 lab course), 2 years social studies including US History, and 2 years foreign language . The average weighted GPA is 4.06. The average SAT (without writing) is 1158 and average ACT is 27. Appalachian does not conduct interviews with applicants as part of the application process. Interviews may be required in special circumstances and Appalachian will notify the applicant. Appalachian does not require letters of recommendations, resumes, essays or personal statements as part of the application for admission. However, Appalachian encourages applicants to submit a personal statement and/or resume. There is no predetermined topic, so this is a chance for the student to tell more about themselves (beyond grades and test scores). They will have access to enter supplemental information in their MyApp Portal once they have submitted their application for admission.

Additional Information

Tutoring is provided on a one-on-one basis for assistance with course content, as well as guidance in developing or improving learning skills. Tutors are trained in working with each student. Basic skills courses are available in memory skills, oral presentation, and note-taking strategies, reading textbooks, written language, math, time management techniques, and study strategies. Skills courses for no credit are offered in English and math. LD/ADHD coaching is available through the Office of Disability Services (ODS). Coaching is provided by ODS graduate assistants and consists of one-on-one meetings to minimize the frustrations of ADHD/LD and maximize your ability using feedback, guidance, and an ongoing partnership. Skills addressed include establishing and achieving semester goals, study and test strategies, time management and organizational planning, note-taking tips, and planning projects. Services and accommodations are available for undergraduates and graduates.

General Support Services Information

Contact Information
Name of program or department: Office of Disability Services
Telephone: 828-262-3056
Fax: 828-262-7904

Accommodations or Services For Students With Learning Differences

Accommodations are decided upon an individual basis after a thorough review of appropriate, current documentation. The accommodations requests must be supported through the documentation provided and must be logically linked to the current impact of the condition on academic functioning.

Allowed in exams
Calculator: Yes
Dictionary: Yes
Computer: Yes
Spellchecker: Yes
Extended test time: Yes
Scribes: Yes
Proctors: Yes
Oral exams: Yes
Note-takers: Yes
Support services for students with LD: Yes
Support services for students with ADHD: Yes
Support services for students with ASD: Yes
Distraction-reduced environment: Yes
Tape recording in class: Yes
Electronic texts: Yes
Kurzweil reader: NR
Audio books: Yes
Other assistive technology: Yes
Priority registration: Yes
Added costs of services: No
LD specialists: No
ADHD coaching: NR
ASD specialists: No
Professional tutors: No
Peer tutors: Not Applicable
Max. hours/wk. for services: NR
How professors are notified of student approved accommodations: By student

General Admissions Information

Office of Admissions: 828-262-2120

Entrance Requirements

Academic units required: 4 English, 4 math, 3 science, 1 science labs, 2 foreign language, 1 social studies, 1 history. High school diploma is required and GED is not accepted. SAT or ACT required. If ACT, ACT with writing accepted. TOEFL required of all international applicants: minimum paper TOEFL 525 or minimum internet TOEFL 75.

Application deadline: 3/15
Notification: Rolling starting 1/25
Average GPA: 4.14
ACT Composite middle 50% range: 23-28
SAT Math middle 50% range: 530-620
SAT Critical Reading middle 50% range: 530-620
SAT Writing middle 50% range: 500-600
Graduate top 10% of class: 21
Graduated top 25% of class: 61
Graduated top 50% of class: 92

COLLEGE GRADUATION REQUIREMENTS

Course waivers allowed: No
Course substitutions allowed: Yes

Additional Information

Environment: This public school was founded in 1899. It has a 1300-acre campus.

Student Body
Undergrad enrollment: 16,290
% Women: 54
% Men: 46
% Out-of-state: 8

Cost information
In-state Tuition: $3,961
Out-of-state Tuition: $17,786
Room & board: $7,845

Housing Information
University Housing: Yes
Percent living on campus: 34

Greek System
Fraternity: Yes
Sorority: Yes
Athletics: Division I

BREVARD COLLEGE

One Brevard College Drive, Brevard, NC 28712
Phone: 828-884-8300 • Fax: 828-884-3790
E-mail: admissions@brevard.edu
Support: CS • Institution: Private

PROGRAMS OR SERVICES FOR STUDENTS WITH LEARNING DIFFERENCES

Brevard College welcomes students who learn differently. Although the College does not offer a special program or curriculum for such students, the college has an excellent disabilities support service, as well as the Academic Enrichment Center, where any student can receive such services as counseling on academic matters, tutoring in a specific subject, advice on organizing work and/or managing time, assistance with reading skills, study skills, test taking skills, and arrange note-taking. The Director of the Office for Students with Special Needs and Disabilities reviews student documentation and identifies academic accommodations which are adjustments to course policies. The director works with students to determine what would be useful to use in a particular course, and what the student must do in order to obtain these accommodations. The director can also assist students with talking to their professors about the learning disability and accommodations.

ADMISSION INFORMATION FOR STUDENTS WITH LEARNING DIFFERENCES

College entrance tests required: No/Test Optional
Interview required: No
Essay required: N/A
Additional Application Required for LD/ADHD/ASD: NR
What documentation required for LD: Psycho ed evaluation to include: relevant historical info, instructional interventions, related services, age diagnosed, objective data (aptitude, achievement, info processing), test scores (standard, percentile and grade equivalents) and describe functional limitations.
With general application: No
To receive services after enrolling: Yes
What documentation required for ADHD: Diagnosis based on DSM-V; history of behaviors impairing functioning in academic setting; diagnostic interview; history of symptoms; evidence of ongoing behaviors.
With general application: No
LD/ADHD/ASD documentation submitted to: Office for Students with Special Needs & Disabilities
ASD Specific Program: NR
Special Ed. HS course work accepted: Yes
Specific course requirements for all applicants: NR
Separate application required for program services: No
Total # of students receiving LD/ADHD/ASD services: 45
Acceptance into program means acceptance into college: NR

ADMISSIONS

There is no special admission process for students with LD. Brevard asks for quite a bit of information from applicants and from those who know the applicants and their learning style. If applicants are aware of a learning disability, they are encouraged to provide the Office for Students with Special Needs & Disabilities with as much information as possible, for example, counseling testing and reports, recommendations, and assessments. Applicants must provide official transcripts, letters of recommendation from college counselor or dean, a teacher of English, and one other teacher or adult who has worked with the student and knows the student well. Brevard is Test-Optional and does not require students to submit the ACT or SAT. The average GPA is 3.07. Brevard looks for strong verbal ability as represented in an applicant's writing sample(s). This gives the college a chance to know what the student struggles with, what the student feels confident about, what the student wants to achieve by earning a degree. Conditional admission status is available for students who display some, but not all, of the indicators of success as a post-secondary liberal arts student.

ADDITIONAL INFORMATION

As the central academic resource and support center on campus, the Academic Enrichment Center is designed to enrich the academic life of all students by providing strong academic support services and enrichment programming. The AEC services are offered on the premise that all students who are successful in college are those who have learned to take charge of their own learning and to utilize available resources to attain their academic goals. Students can get support or develop skills by going to a career workshop, working on studying techniques, getting tutored by a fellow student, or meeting with professional staff for an individualized academic plan. Experiential Opportunities in the AEC include: one-on-one individualized attention from academic coordinators, student tutors, and even professors whenever students need it. The Writing or Math lab (staffed by both faculty and peer tutors) can provide help with a revision of a final paper or one-on-one help with algebra homework. There are also a variety of academic resource materials to prepare for graduate entrance exams, develop study strategies, and improve performance in current courses.

General Support Services Information

Contact Information
Name of program or department: Office for Students with Special Needs and Disabilities
Telephone: 828-884-8131
Fax: 828-884-8293

Accommodations or Services for Students with Learning Differences

Accommodations are decided upon an individual basis after a thorough review of appropriate, current documentation. The accommodations requests must be supported through the documentation provided and must be logically linked to the current impact of the condition on academic functioning.

Allowed in exams
Calculator: Yes
Dictionary: Yes
Computer: Yes
Spellchecker: Yes
Extended test time: Yes
Scribes: Yes
Proctors: Yes
Oral exams: Yes
Note-takers: Yes
Services for students with LD: Yes
Services for students with ADHD: Yes
Services for students with ASD: Yes
Distraction-reduced environment: Yes
Tape recording in class: Yes
Kurzweil reader: Yes
Audio books from learning ally: Yes
Other assistive technology: Yes
Priority registration: Yes
Added costs of services: No
LD specialists: Yes
ADHD coaching: NR
ASD specialists: NR
Peer tutors: Yes
How professors are notified of student approved accommodations: Student

General Admissions Information

Office of Admissions: 828-884-8300

Entrance Requirements

Academic units recommended: 4 English, 3 math, 3 science, 1 science labs, 2 foreign language, 4 social studies, 1 history, 4 academic electives. High school diploma is required and GED is accepted. SAT or ACT required for some. If ACT, ACT with writing accepted. TOEFL required of all international applicants: minimum paper TOEFL 537.

Application deadline: NR
Notification: Rolling starting 7/1
Average GPA: 3.07
ACT Composite middle 50% range: 17-22
SAT Math middle 50% range: 420-530
SAT Critical Reading middle 50% range: 420-520
SAT Writing middle 50% range: NR-NR
Graduated top 10% of class: 6
Graduated top 25% of class: 24
Graduated top 50% of class: 62

COLLEGE GRADUATION REQUIREMENTS

Course waivers allowed: No
Course substitutions allowed: Yes
In what course: Substitutions are done on a case-by-case basis. Foreign language is not required for graduation.

Additional Information

Environment: This private school, affiliated with the Methodist Church, was founded in 1853. It has a 120-acre campus.

Student Body
Undergrad enrollment: 705
% Women: 42
% Men: 58
% Out-of-state: 42

Cost information
Tuition: $27,550
Room & board: $9,650-$10,500

Housing Information
University Housing: Yes
Percent living on campus: 76

Greek System
Fraternity: No
Sorority: No
Athletics: Division II

Davidson College

PO Box 7156, Davidson, NC 28035-7156
Phone: 704-894-2230 • Fax: 704-894-2016
E-mail: admission@davidson.edu • Web: www.davidson.edu
Support: CS • Institution: Private

Programs or Services for Students with Learning Differences

Students enroll in Davidson with a proven record of academic achievement and the ability to utilize resources, persevere, and excel. The college provides services and accommodations to allow students an opportunity to continue to be successful. Special procedures have been developed for students handicapped by learning disabilities. Students who seek adapted instruction on the basis of a learning disability undergo an evaluation by college-designated learning specialists, usually at the student's expense. The results of the evaluation, made available to the college with the student's permission, may include recommendations for compensatory learning strategies to be used by the student and recommendations for services and accommodations to be provided by the college. Using these recommendations as a guide, the Student Learning Support Committee works with the student to develop a learning plan that enhances learning strengths and compensates for learning difficulties. If the learning plan recommends adjustment to academic requirements, the recommendation is considered by the Curriculum Requirements Committee and may result in the approval of the recommendation or the substitution of the academic requirement. All students seeking accommodations on the basis of an LD must provide recent documentation. The Dean of Students, with the student's permission, will notify professors of an individual student's need for adaptations. Accommodations are not universal in nature but are designed to meet the specific need of the individual to offset a specific disability.

Admission Information for Students with Learning Differences

College entrance tests required: Yes
Interview required: No
Essay required: No
Additional Application Required for LD/ADHD/ASD: NR
What documentation required for LD: Psycho ed evaluation to include: relevant historical info, instructional interventions, related services, age diagnosed, objective data (aptitude, achievement, info processing), test scores (standard, percentile and grade equivalents) and describe functional limitations.
With general application: No
To receive services after enrolling: Yes
What documentation required for ADHD: Diagnosis based on DSM-V; history of behaviors impairing functioning in academic setting; diagnostic interview; history of symptoms; evidence of ongoing behaviors.
With general application: No
LD/ADHD/ASD documentation submitted to: Dean of Student Services
ASD Specific Program: NR
Special Ed. HS course work accepted: No
Specific course requirements of all applicants: Yes
Separate application required: No
Total # of students receiving LD/ADHD/ASD services: 54
Acceptance into program means acceptance into college: Students must be admitted to and enrolled in the university first and then request services.

Admissions

There is no special admission process for students with LD, though the Admissions Office may seek comments from support staff knowledgeable about LD. Students are encouraged to self-disclose their ADHD. The admission process is very competitive, and the disclosure can help the Admissions Office more fairly evaluate the transcript. This disclosure could address any specific academic issues related to the LD, such as no foreign language in high school because of the specific LD or lower grades in math as a result of a math disability. The GPA is recalculated to reflect rigor with 97 percent of the accepted students having a recalculated GPA of 3.0. Students have completed at least 4 years of English, 3 years of math, 2 years of the same foreign language, 2 years of science, and 2 years of history/social studies. Courses taken in special education are not accepted. The mid 50 percent of students have an ACT between 28 and 31 or SAT between 1240 and 1420. Interviews are not required but are recommended.

Additional Information

Support services and accommodations available include, but are not limited to: referrals for appropriate diagnostic evaluation; individual coaching and instruction in compensatory strategies and study skills; consultation with faculty and staff; student support groups as requested; classroom accommodations such as extra test-taking time, taped texts, note-takers, use of tape recorders, use of computers with spellcheckers, and individual space for study or test-taking; reduced course loads; and course substitutions or waivers (rarely).

General Support Services Information

Contact Information
Name of program or department: Dean of Students Office
Telephone: 704-894-2225
Fax: 704-894-2849

Accommodations or Services for Students with Learning Differences

Accommodations are decided upon an individual basis after a thorough review of appropriate, current documentation. The accommodations requested must be supported through the documentation provided and must be logically linked to the current impact of the condition on academic functioning.

Allowed in exams
Calculator: Yes
Dictionary: Yes
Computer: Yes
Spellchecker: Yes
Extended test time: Yes
Scribes: Yes
Proctors: Yes
Oral exams: No
Note-takers: Yes
Services for students with LD: Yes
Services for students with ADHD: Yes
Services for students with ASD: Yes
Distraction-reduced environment: Yes
Tape recording in class: Yes
Audio books: NR
Electronic texts: No
Kurzweil Reader: No
Other assistive technology: No
Priority registration: No
Added costs for services: No
LD specialists: Yes
ADHD coaching: NR
ASD specialists: NR
Professional tutors: No
Peer tutors: 100
Max. hours/wk. for services: Unlimited
How professors are notified of LD/ADHD: By both student and director

General Admissions Information

Office of Admissions: 704-894-2230

Entrance Requirements
Academic units required: 4 English, 3 math, 2 science, 2 foreign language, and 2 units from above areas or other academic areas. **Academic units recommended:** 4 math, 4 science, 4 foreign language, and 4 units from above areas or other academic areas. High school diploma is required and GED is not accepted. SAT or ACT required. If ACT, ACT with writing recommended. TOEFL required of all international applicants: minimum paper TOEFL 600 or minimum internet TOEFL 100.

Application deadline: 1/2
Notification: 4/1
Average GPA: 4
ACT Composite middle 50% range: 29-32
SAT Math middle 50% range: 630-720
SAT Critical Reading middle 50% range: 630-720
SAT Writing middle 50% range: 610-720
Graduated top 10% of class: 55
Graduated top 25% of class: 91
Graduated top 50% of class: 91

COLLEGE GRADUATION REQUIREMENTS

Course waivers allowed: No
Course substitutions allowed: Yes
In what course: Substitutions in any appropriate course

Additional Information

Environment: This private school, affiliated with the Presbyterian Church, was founded in 1837. It has a 556-acre campus.

Student Body
Undergrad enrollment: 1,784
% Women: 50
% Men: 50
% Out-of-state: 75

Cost information
Tuition: $46,501
Room & board: $13,153
Housing Information
University Housing: Yes
Percent living on campus: 94

Greek System
Fraternity: Yes
Sorority: Yes
Athletics: Division I

Duke University

2138 Campus Drive, Durham, NC 27708-0586
Phone: 919-684-3214 • Fax: 919-668-1661
E-mail: undergrad-admissions@duke.edu • Web: www.duke.edu
Support: CS • Institution: Private

Programs or Services for Students with Learning Differences

Duke University does not provide a formal, highly structured program for students with LD. The university does provide, however, significant academic support services for students through the Academic Resource Center (ARC). Students who submit appropriate documentation of their learning disability to the ARC clinical director are eligible for assistance in obtaining reasonable academic adjustments and auxiliary aids. In addition, the ARC clinical director and instructors can provide individualized instruction in academic skills and learning strategies, academic support counseling, and referrals for other services. Students with learning disabilities voluntarily access and use the services of the ARC, just as they might access and use other campus resources. Student interactions with the ARC staff are confidential. The goals of the support services for students with learning disabilities are in keeping with the goals of all services provided through the ARC: to help students achieve their academic potential within the context of a competitive university setting, promote a disciplined approach to study, and foster active, independent learners.

Admission Information for Students with Learning Differences

College entrance tests required: Yes
Interview required: No
Essay required: No
Additional Application Required for LD/ADHD/ASD: NR
What documentation required for LD: Psycho ed evaluation to include: relevant historical info, instructional interventions, related services, age diagnosed, objective data (aptitude, achievement, info processing), test scores (standard, percentile and grade equivalents) and describe functional limitations.
With general application: No
To receive services after enrolling: Yes
What documentation required for ADHD: Diagnosis based on DSM-V; history of behaviors impairing functioning in academic setting; diagnostic interview; history of symptoms; evidence of ongoing behaviors.
With general application: No
LD/ADHD/ASD documentation submitted to: ARC
ASD Specific Program: NR
Special Ed. HS course work accepted: No
Specific course requirements of all applicants: NR
Separate application required: No
Total # of students receiving LD/ADHD/ASD services: 40–60
Acceptance into program means acceptance into college: Students must be admitted to and enrolled in the university first and then request services.

Admissions

There is no special admission process for students with LD. All applicants must meet the general Duke admission criteria. Most applicants are in the top 10% of their class and have completed a demanding curriculum including many AP and honors courses. The ACT with Writing or SAT Reasoning and 2 Subject tests are required. Duke considers the highest ACT composite score and highest sub scores on each section, regardless of test date, but will not recalculate the composite score. Students who take the ACT are not required to submit SAT or SAT Subject Tests. Duke uses the highest available SAT Critical Reading, Writing, and Math sub scores, plus the two highest subject test sub scores, regardless of the date those tests were taken. Students may elect "Score Choice" when releasing their SAT scores. Students must submit two teacher and one counselor recommendation. Applicants may also submit one optional personal recommendation from a coach, a director, a teacher from an elective course, a family member, or anyone else who knows the student well and will. This optional information will be considered in understanding the student as a person, but will not be formally evaluated as part of the application. Some students choose to disclose a disability in their application because it is an important element of their experiences or to share how they dealt with an obstacle. Duke considers this information in understanding a student's achievements and evaluates accomplishments within the context of opportunities or challenges presented to that student. Duke does not use information to deny admission to a student.

Additional Information

The Student Disability Access Office (SDAO) explores possible coverage and reasonable accommodations for qualified undergraduate, graduate and professional students who are disabled in compliance with Section 504 of the Federal Rehabilitation Act of 1973, the Americans with Disabilities Act (ADA) of 1990 and the ADA Amendments Act of 2008. SDAO provides and coordinate accommodations, support services and programs that enable students with disabilities to have equal access to all Duke University programs and activities.

GENERAL SUPPORT SERVICES INFORMATION

Contact Information
Name of program or department: Student Disability Access Office/Academic Resource Center (ARC)
Telephone: 919-684-5917
Fax: 919-684-5917

ACCOMMODATIONS OR SERVICES FOR STUDENTS WITH LEARNING DIFFERENCES

Accommodations are decided upon an individual basis after a thorough review of appropriate, current documentation. The accommodations requested must be supported through the documentation provided and must be logically linked to the current impact of the condition on academic functioning.

Allowed in exams
Calculator: No
Dictionary: Yes
Computer: Yes
Spellchecker: No
Extended test time: Yes
Scribes: Yes
Proctors: Yes
Oral exams: Yes
Note-takers: Yes
Services for students with LD: Yes
Services for students with ADHD: Yes
Services for students with ASD: Yes
Distraction-reduced environment: Yes
Tape recording in class: Yes
Audio books: NR
Electronic texts: Yes
Kurzweil Reader: No
Other assistive technology: Yes
Priority registration: No
Added costs for services: No
LD specialists: Yes
ADHD coaching: NR
ASD specialists: NR
Professional tutors: No
Peer tutors: 80
Max. hours/wk. for services: Unlimited
How professors are notified of LD/ADHD: By both student and director

GENERAL ADMISSIONS INFORMATION

Office of Admissions: 919-684-3214

ENTRANCE REQUIREMENTS

Academic units recommended: 4 English, 3 math, 3 science, 3 foreign language, 3 social studies. High school diploma is required and GED is not accepted. If ACT, ACT with writing required.

Application deadline: 1/2
Notification: 4/1
Average GPA: NR
ACT Composite middle 50% range: 31-34
SAT Math middle 50% range: 690-790
SAT Critical Reading middle 50% range: 670-760
SAT Writing middle 50% range: 680-780
Graduated top 10% of class: 90
Graduated top 25% of class: 8
Graduated top 50% of class: 2

COLLEGE GRADUATION REQUIREMENTS

Course waivers allowed: No
Course substitutions allowed: No

ADDITIONAL INFORMATION

Environment: This private school, affiliated with the Methodist Church, was founded in 1838. It has a 8500-acre campus.

Student Body
Undergrad enrollment: 6,646
% Women: 50
% Men: 50
% Out-of-state: 88
Cost information
Tuition: $45,800
Room & board: $13,290
Housing Information
University Housing: Yes
Percent living on campus: 82
Greek System
Fraternity: Yes
Sorority: Yes
Athletics: Division I

East Carolina University

Office of Undergraduate Admissions, Greenville, NC 27858-4353
Phone: 252-328-6640 • Fax: 252-328-6945
E-mail: admis@ecu.edu • Web: www.ecu.edu
Support: CS • Institution: Public

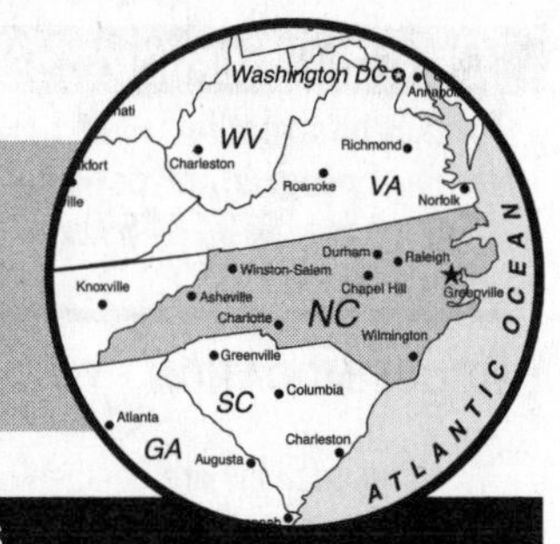

Programs or Services for Students with Learning Differences

STEPP Program: Supporting Transition and Education through Planning and Partnerships
The STEPP Program's mission is to provide students with learning disabilities with access and comprehensive support throughout the university experience. By partnering with these students, their families, and a variety of educational communities, the STEPP Program fosters a network of opportunities and resources to empower and support students from admission to graduation from East Carolina University. The STEPP Program offers comprehensive academic, social, and life-skills support to a select number of students with identified Specific Learning Disabilities who have shown the potential to succeed at ECU.

Admission Information for Students with Learning Differences

College entrance tests required: Yes
Interview required: No
Essay required: No
Additional Application Required for LD/ADHD/ASD: NR
What documentation required for LD: Psycho ed evaluation to include: relevant historical info, instructional interventions, related services, age diagnosed, objective data (aptitude, achievement, info processing), test scores (standard, percentile and grade equivalents) and describe functional limitations.
With general application: No
To receive services after enrolling: Yes
What documentation required for ADHD: Diagnosis based on DSM-V; history of behaviors impairing functioning in academic setting; diagnostic interview; history of symptoms; evidence of ongoing behaviors.
With general application: No
LD/ADHD/ASD documentation submitted to: Disability Support Services
ASD Specific Program: NR
Special Ed. HS course work accepted: Yes
Specific course requirements of all applicants: Yes
Separate application required: No
Total # of students receiving LD/ADHD/ASD services: 100–150
Acceptance into program means acceptance into college: Students must be admitted to and enrolled in the university first and then request services.

Admissions

A student with a disability applies for admission and is considered for admission in the same manner as any other applicant. Neither the nature nor the severity of one's disability is used as a criterion for admission. Students with learning disabilities are admitted solely on academic qualifications. Out-of-state students must present slightly higher GPAs and test scores, but the minimum is 2.0 depending on the SAT score. Test scores vary, but the minimum out-of-state ACT is 19 and in-state is 17, and the average ACT is 21. The minimum SAT out-of-state is 1000 and in-state is 900, and the average SAT is 1030. Students must have taken 4 years of English, 2 years of social science, and 3 years of science (1 year biology and 1 year physical science); 3 years of math and 2 years of a foreign language are recommended.

Additional Information

Once admitted to the university, students must self-identify and register with the Department for Disability Support Services. Students must show official verification of their disability. Students will be assigned to academic advisors from the department. Once students enter their major fields of study, the department will still be available to provide advising assistance but never to the exclusion of the individual's assigned academic advisor. Alternative testing accommodations may include extended time, a noise-free environment, reader-assisted test-taking, and other arrangements that satisfy the needs of the student. A maximum of double time can be allowed for students to complete a test or an exam. The university offers a modified language sequence for students enrolled in Spanish.

General Support Services Information

Contact Information
Name of program or department: Department for Disability Support Services
Telephone: 252-737-1016
Fax: 252-737-1025

Accommodations or Services for Students with Learning Differences

Accommodations are decided upon an individual basis after a thorough review of appropriate, current documentation. The accommodations requested must be supported through the documentation provided and must be logically linked to the current impact of the condition on academic functioning.

Allowed in exams
Calculator: Yes
Dictionary: Yes
Computer: Yes
Spellchecker: Yes
Extended test time: Yes
Scribes: Yes
Proctors: Yes
Oral exams: Yes
Note-takers: Yes
Services for students with LD: Yes
Services for students with ADHD: Yes
Services for students with ASD: Yes
Distraction-reduced environment: Yes
Tape recording in class: Yes
Audio books: NR
Electronic texts: Yes
Kurzweil Reader: Yes
Other assistive technology: Yes
Priority registration: Yes
Added costs for services: No
LD specialists: Yes
ADHD coaching: NR
ASD specialists: NR
Professional tutors: No
Peer tutors: 2
Max. hours/wk. for services: Unlimited
How professors are notified of LD/ADHD: By student

General Admissions Information

Office of Admissions: 252-328-6640

Entrance Requirements

Academic units required: 4 English, 4 math, 3 science, 1 science labs, 2 foreign language, 2 social studies, 1 history. **Academic units recommended:** 4 English, 4 math, 3 science, 1 science labs, 2 foreign language, 2 social studies, 1 history, 1 visual/performing arts. High school diploma is required and GED is accepted. SAT or ACT required. If ACT, ACT with writing accepted. TOEFL required of all international applicants: minimum paper TOEFL 500 or minimum internet TOEFL 80.

Application deadline: 3/15
Notification: Rolling starting 8/20
Average GPA: 3.76
ACT Composite middle 50% range: 20-24
SAT Math middle 50% range: 490-560
SAT Critical Reading middle 50% range: 470-550
SAT Writing middle 50% range: 450-540
Graduated top 10% of class: 16
Graduated top 25% of class: 44
Graduated top 50% of class: 80

COLLEGE GRADUATION REQUIREMENTS

Course waivers allowed: No
Course substitutions allowed: No

Additional Information

Environment: This public school was founded in 1907. It has a 1379-acre campus.

Student Body
Undergrad enrollment: 23,039
% Women: 58
% Men: 42
% Out-of-state: 12

Cost information
In-state Tuition: $4,157
Out-of Tuition: $19,731
Room & board: $9,319

Housing Information
University Housing: Yes
Percent living on campus: 26

Greek System
Fraternity: Yes
Sorority: Yes
Athletics: Division I

Elon University

100 Campus Drive, Elon, NC 27244-2010
Phone: 336-278-3566 • Fax: 336-278-7699
E-mail: admissions@elon.edu • Web: www.elon.edu
Support: S • Institution: Private

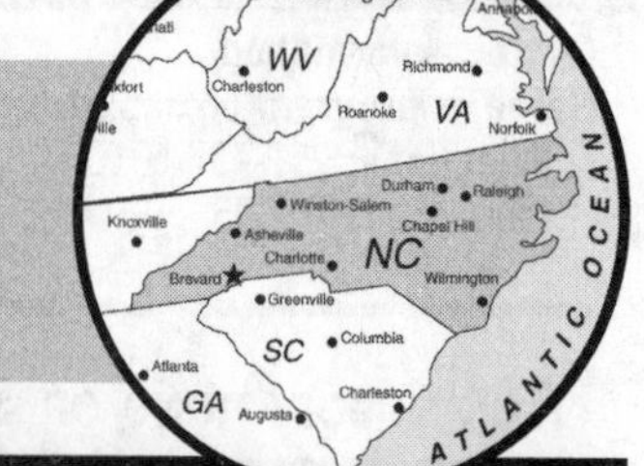

Programs or Services for Students with Learning Differences

Elon University is committed to the principle of equal opportunity. We assist students with disabilities in finding approaches and accommodations that provide them an opportunity to benefit from the many programs offered on campus. Faculty, staff, administrators, and students work together to find approaches and accommodations that enable students to benefit from the wide variety of programs and activities on campus.

Admission Information for Students with Learning Differences

College entrance tests required: Yes
Interview required: No
Essay required: No
Additional Application Required for LD/ADHD/ASD: NR
What documentation required for LD: Psycho ed evaluation to include: relevant historical info, instructional interventions, related services, age diagnosed, objective data (aptitude, achievement, info processing), test scores (standard, percentile and grade equivalents) and describe functional limitations.
With general application: No
To receive services after enrolling: Yes
What documentation required for ADHD: Diagnosis based on DSM-V; history of behaviors impairing functioning in academic setting; diagnostic interview; history of symptoms; evidence of ongoing behaviors.
With general application: No
LD/ADHD/ASD documentation submitted to: Disability Services
ASD Specific Program: NR
Special Ed. HS course work accepted: No
Specific course requirements of all applicants: Yes
Separate application required: No
Total # of students receiving LD/ADHD/ASD services: NR
Acceptance into program means acceptance into college: Students must be admitted and enrolled prior to requesting services.

Admissions

Students with disabilities must meet the same admissions criteria as other applicants. There is no special admission process. Most important factors in admissions are academic rigor, grades, ACT (with writing) or SAT and counselor recommendation, activities, involvement and essay. GPA is converted to 4.0 scale, and then Elon gives weight to honors, AP or IB courses. Courses required include 4 years English, 3 years math, 2 years foreign language, 3 years social studies, and 3 years science. Students may be admitted with one deficiency. Disclosing a disability is totally up to the applicant.

Additional Information

Students must provide current documentation to request accommodations. They are encouraged to be proactive and develop an ongoing conversation with their professors and service providers. Every student is assigned an advisor, a professor or an administrator who helps students get information regarding programs, tutors and special needs. All students have access to The Tutoring Center and Writing Center. Waivers for foreign language or math courses are never approved. However, students may request a foreign language substitution. Documentation is required that demonstrates the presence of deficits that make learning a foreign language extremely difficult, as well as, a history of poor grades in the subject. Students who have never taken such classes will be asked to enroll; performance will be evaluated before the end of the drop/add period and a decision will be made regarding the substitution.

General Support Services Information

Contact Information
Name of program or department: Disabilities Services
Telephone: 336-278-6500
Fax: 336-278-6514

Accommodations or Services for Students with Learning Differences

Accommodations are decided upon an individual basis after a thorough review of appropriate, current documentation. The accommodations requested must be supported through the documentation provided and must be logically linked to the current impact of the condition on academic functioning.

Allowed in exams
Calculator: Yes
Dictionary: Yes
Computer: Yes
Spellchecker: Yes
Extended test time: Yes
Scribes: Yes
Proctors: NR
Oral exams: No
Note-takers: Yes
Services for students with LD: Yes
Services for students with ADHD: Yes
Services for students with ASD: Yes
Distraction-reduced environment: Yes
Tape recording in class: Yes
Audio books: NR
Electronic texts: Yes
Kurzweil Reader: Yes
Other assistive technology: No
Priority registration: Yes
Added costs for services: No
LD specialists: No
ADHD coaching: NR
ASD specialists: NR
Professional tutors: No
Peer tutors: 100
Max. hours/wk. for services: Unlimited
How professors are notified of LD/ADHD: By both student and director

General Admissions Information

Office of Admissions: 336-278-3566

Entrance Requirements

Academic units required: 4 English, 3 math, 3 science, 1 science labs, 2 foreign language, 1 social studies, 2 history. **Academic units recommended:** 4 English, 4 math, 3 science, 1 science labs, 3 foreign language, 1 social studies, 2 history. High school diploma is required and GED is accepted. SAT or ACT required. If ACT, ACT with writing accepted. TOEFL required of all international applicants: minimum paper TOEFL 550 or minimum internet TOEFL 79.

Application deadline: 1/10
Notification: 3/20
Average GPA: 3.97
ACT Composite middle 50% range: 25-29
SAT Math middle 50% range: 560-650
SAT Critical Reading middle 50% range: 550-640
SAT Writing middle 50% range: 550-650
Graduated top 10% of class: 24
Graduated top 25% of class: 58
Graduated top 50% of class: 90

COLLEGE GRADUATION REQUIREMENTS

Course waivers allowed: No
Course substitutions allowed: Yes
In what course: Not generally, but on a case-by-case basis—rarely in foreign language and even more rarely in math, especially if the course is required in the student's major. Students will need sufficient documentation.

Additional Information

Environment: This private school, affiliated with the United Church of Christ Church, was founded in 1889. It has a 575-acre campus.

Student Body
Undergrad enrollment: 5,903
% Women: 59
% Men: 41
% Out-of-state: 72

Cost information
Tuition: $31,773
Room & board: $10,998

Housing Information
University Housing: Yes
Percent living on campus: 62

Greek System
Fraternity: Yes
Sorority: Yes
Athletics: Division I

Guilford College

5800 West Friendly Avenue, Greensboro, NC 27410
Phone: 336-316-2100 • Fax: 336-316-2954
E-mail: admission@guilford.edu • Web: www.guilford.edu/
Support: CS • Institution: Private

Programs or Services for Students with Learning Differences

The Learning Commons (LC) serves the learning needs of a diverse campus by providing professional and peer tutoring, workshops, advocacy, and realistic encouragement. The focus is on self-advocacy and the articulation of both strengths and weaknesses. Faculty tutors work one-on-one with students on time management, study skills, test-taking, reading, and writing. A large student tutoring service offers course-specific tutoring. The center sponsors workshops on subjects pertaining to academic success. Faculty allow the usual accommodations requested by students: extra time, permission to use a computer for in-class work, testing in a less distracting environment, tape-recording classes, and so on.

Admission Information for Students with Learning Differences

College entrance tests required: No
Interview required: No
Essay required: Yes
Additional Application Required for LD/ADHD/ASD: NR
What documentation required for LD: Psycho ed evaluation to include: relevant historical info, instructional interventions, related services, age diagnosed, objective data (aptitude, achievement, info processing), test scores (standard, percentile and grade equivalents) and describe functional limitations.
With general application: No
To receive services after enrolling: Yes
What documentation required for ADHD: Diagnosis based on DSM-V; history of behaviors impairing functioning in academic setting; diagnostic interview; history of symptoms; evidence of ongoing behaviors.
With general application: No
LD/ADHD/ASD documentation submitted to: Disability Resources
ASD Specific Program: NR
Special Ed. HS course work accepted: Yes
Specific course requirements of all applicants: NR
Separate application required: N/A
Total # of students receiving LD/ADHD/ASD services: NR
Acceptance into program means acceptance into college: Students must be admitted to and enrolled in the college first and then request services.

Admissions

Students with LD must meet the same criteria as other students. The general admission criteria include the mid 50 percent range for the ACT of 21–26 (or the SAT, 950–1210) and a 2.8–3.4 GPA. Typically, admitted students have 4 years of English, 3 years of math, 3–4 years natural science, 3 years of social studies, and 2 years of a foreign language. With appropriate documentation, students with LD can substitute some high school courses in areas that impact their ability to learn. The Disability Resources Committee reviews files to make certain that the college can provide appropriate support services.

Additional Information

Guilford is a writing-intensive place. The writing program is revision-driven and utilizes peer-editing and response groups. The LC offers individualized professional tutoring in writing as well as opportunities to work with trained student writing tutors. The LC offers other services, including professional tutors to work one-on-one with students on time management, study skills, test-taking, and reading, math. A large student tutoring service offers course-specific tutoring. The center also sponsors workshops and seminars on subjects pertaining to academic success. Students are encouraged to speak with professors early concerning particular needs. Guilford waives the foreign language requirement if students submit appropriate documentation and petition through Disability Resources.

General Support Services Information

Contact Information
Name of program or department: Disability Resources
Telephone: 336-316-2253
Fax: 336-316-2946

Accommodations or Services for Students with Learning Differences

Accommodations are decided upon an individual basis after a thorough review of appropriate, current documentation. The accommodations requested must be supported through the documentation provided and must be logically linked to the current impact of the condition on academic functioning.

Allowed in exams
Calculator: Yes
Dictionary: Yes
Computer: Yes
Spellchecker: Yes
Extended test time: Yes
Scribes: Yes
Proctors: No
Oral exams: Yes
Note-takers: Yes
Services for students with LD: Yes
Services for students with ADHD: Yes
Services for students with ASD: Yes
Distraction-reduced environment: Yes
Tape recording in class: Yes
Audio books: NR
Electronic texts: Yes
Kurzweil Reader: Yes
Other assistive technology: Yes
Priority registration: No
Added costs for services: No
LD specialists: Yes
ADHD coaching: NR
ASD specialists: NR
Professional tutors: 2
Peer tutors: 20–40
Max. hours/wk. for services: NR
How professors are notified of LD/ADHD: By student

General Admissions Information

Office of Admissions: 336-316-2100

Entrance Requirements

Academic units recommended: 4 English, 3 mathematics, 3 science, 2 foreign language, 3 social studies, 3 history. High school diploma is required and GED is accepted. SAT or ACT recommended. If ACT, ACT with Writing component accepted. TOEFL required of all international applicants: minimum paper TOEFL 550.

Application deadline: 2/15
Average GPA: 3.2
ACT Composite middle 50% range: 20-26
SAT Math middle 50% range: 480-580
SAT Critical Reading middle 50% range: 460-610
SAT Writing middle 50% range: 450-580
Graduated top 10% of class: 11
Graduated top 25% of class: 33
Graduated top 50% of class: 69

COLLEGE GRADUATION REQUIREMENTS

Course waivers allowed: Quantitative Literacy may be waived with approval from Disability Resources.
Course substitutions allowed: Yes
In what course: Foreign language

Additional Information

Environment: The college is located on a suburban campus in a culturally diverse city in Greensboro, North Carolina.

Student Body
Undergrad enrollment: 2,166
% Women: 55
% Men: 45
% Out-of-state: 45

Cost information
Tuition: $32,090
Room & board: $8,800

Housing Information
University housing: Yes
% Living on campus: 77

Greek System
Fraternity: No
Sorority: No
Athletics: Division III

LENOIR-RHYNE COLLEGE

Admissions Office, Hickory, NC 28603
Phone: 828-328-7300 • Fax: 828-328-7378
E-mail: admission@lrc.edu • Web: www.lrc.edu
Support: S • Institution: Private

PROGRAMS OR SERVICES FOR STUDENTS WITH LEARNING DIFFERENCES

The Lenoir-Rhyne College Disability Services Office strives to provide the highest quality service to each student with a disability through appropriate modification of college policies, practices and procedures. It is the mission of the office to ensure that every student with a disability has an equal chance to benefit from college programs. Furthermore, the office emphasizes personal independence and responsibility, on the part of the student, in the provision of services. The office will also serve as a campus and community resource for information about people with disabilities and the issues that affect them.

ADMISSION INFORMATION FOR STUDENTS WITH LEARNING DIFFERENCESES

College entrance test required: Yes
Interview required: No
Essay required: Yes
Additional Application Required for LD/ADHD/ASD: NR
What documentation required for LD: Full psychoeducational evaluation with IQ scores listed
With general application: No
To receive services after enrolling: Yes
What documentation required for ADHD: Full psychoeducational evaluation with IQ scores listed
With general application: No
To receive services after enrolling: Yes
With general application: No
To receive services after enrolling: Yes
LD/ADHD/ASD documentation submitted to: Support program/services
ASD Specific Program: NR
Special Ed. HS course work accepted: No
Specific course: Yes
Separate application required for program services: No

ADMISSIONS

There is no special admissions process for students with learning disabilities. All students are reviewed on an individual case-by-case basis. Basic admissions criteria include: 2.0 GPA, top 50% class rank, 850 SAT or 17 ACT, 4 years English, 3 years math, 1 year history, 2 years foreign language.

ADDITIONAL INFORMATION

Advising and Academic Services Center offers a variety of services to help students achieve academic success through Group Peer Tutoring, Advising and Assessment, and Academic Skills Counseling. With appropriate documentation students with LD/ADD may be appropriate for some of the following services/accommodations: the use of calculators, dictionary, computer or spellcheck in exams; extended time on tests; distraction-free environment; scribe; proctor; oral exams; note taker; tape recorder in class; books on tape; and substitution of the foreign language requirement. (Extensive documentation is required for foreign language substitution). Services to students with disabilities varies depending on the type and nature of the disability. There is also the Lohr Learning Commons that provides assistance with writing,public speaking, course-specific tutoring,math tutoring lab, and general learning strategies. And a separate Writing Center to assist students in improving writing ability.

General Support Services Information

Contact Information
Name of program or department: Disability Services Office
Telephone: 828.328.7296
Fax: 828.267.3441

Accommodations or Services For Students With Learning Differences

Accommodations are decided upon an individual basis after a thorough review of appropriate, current documentation. The accommodations requests must be supported through the documentation provided and must be logically linked to the current impact of the condition on academic functioning.

Allowed in exams
Calculator: Yes
Dictionary: Yes
Computer: Yes
Spellchecker: Yes
Extended test time: Yes
Scribes: Yes
Proctors: Yes
Oral exams: Yes
Note-takers: Yes
Support services for students with LD: Yes
Support services for students with ADHD: Yes
Support services for students with ASD: Yes
Distraction-reduced environment: Yes
Tape recording in class: Yes
Electronic texts: Yes
Kurzweil reader: NR
Audio books: Yes
Other assistive technology: Yes
Priority registration: No
Added costs of services: No
LD specialists: No
ADHD coaching: No
ASD specialists: Not Applicable
Professional tutors: No
Peer tutors: NR
Max. hours/wk. for services: NR
How professors are notified of student approved accommodations: By both student and director

General Admissions Information

Office of Admissions: 828.328.7300

Entrance Requirements

Academic units required: 4 English, 3 math, 1 science, 1 science labs, 2 foreign language, 1 history, **Academic units recommended:** 4 English, 4 math, 2 science, 1 science labs, 3 foreign language, 2 history. High school diploma is required and GED is accepted. SAT or ACT required. If ACT, ACT with writing required. TOEFL required of all international applicants: minimum paper TOEFL 500 or minimum internet TOEFL 79.

Application deadline: NR
Notification: NR
Average GPA: NR
ACT Composite middle 50% range: NR-NR
SAT Math middle 50% range: 440-550
SAT Critical Reading middle 50% range: 440-550
SAT Writing middle 50% range: 440-550
Graduate top 10% of class: NR
Graduated top 25% of class: NR
Graduated top 50% of class: NR

COLLEGE GRADUATION REQUIREMENTS

Course waivers allowed: No
Course substitutions allowed: Yes
In what course: Foreign Language if deemed appropriate

Additional Information

Environment: This private school, affiliated with the Lutheran Church, was founded in 1891. It has a 100-acre campus.

Student Body
Undergrad enrollment: 1,587
% Women: 58
% Men: 42
% Out-of-state: 18

Cost information
Tuition: $33,730
Room & board: $11,600

Housing Information
University Housing: Yes
Percent living on campus: 51

Greek System
Fraternity: Yes
Sorority: Yes
Athletics: Division II

NORTH CAROLINA STATE UNIVERSITY

Box 7103, Raleigh, NC 27695
Phone: 919-515-2434 • Fax: 919-515-5039
E-mail: undergrad_admissions@ncsu.edu • Web: www.ncsu.edu/
Support: CS • Institution: Public

PROGRAMS OR SERVICES FOR STUDENTS WITH LEARNING DIFFERENCES

Services for students with learning disabilities are handled by the LD coordinator through the Disability Services Office. The functions of the coordinator include identifying students with learning disabilities, helping to accommodate and interpret the needs of these students to the faculty, and providing services to students according to their individual needs. The purpose of the services is to ensure that students with documented learning disabilities receive appropriate accomodations to equalize their opportunities while studying at NCSU.

ADMISSION INFORMATION FOR STUDENTS WITH LEARNING DIFFERENCES

College entrance tests required: Yes
Interview required: No
Essay required: N/A
Additional Application Required for LD/ADHD/ASD: NR
What documentation required for LD: Psycho ed evaluation to include: relevant historical info, instructional interventions, related services, age diagnosed, objective data (aptitude, achievement, info processing), test scores (standard, percentile and grade equivalents) and describe functional limitations.
With general application: No
To receive services after enrolling: Yes
What documentation required for ADHD: Diagnosis based on DSM-V; history of behaviors impairing functioning in academic setting; diagnostic interview; history of symptoms; evidence of ongoing behaviors.
With general application: No
LD/ADHD/ASD documentation submitted to: Disability Support Services
ASD Specific Program: NR
Specific course requirements for all applicants: Yes
Separate application required for program services: Yes
Total # of students receiving LD/ADHD/ASD services: 260–300
Acceptance into program means acceptance into college: Separate application required after student has enrolled

ADMISSIONS

Admission to the university for students with learning disabilities is determined on the basis of academic qualifications, and they are considered in the same manner as any other applicant. There is no pre-admission question regarding a learning disability. A cover letter from applicants, stating that a learning disability exists, alerts the admission staff to consider that there may be unusual circumstances. Self-disclosure of the learning disability could explain the high school record, such as late diagnosis and onset of LD accommodations or difficulty in particular subjects. General admission criteria include a minimum ACT 24 or SAT 1100. Over 75 percent of the students have at least a 3.5 GPA; minimum course requirements include four years English, three years math (including algebra I, algebra II, and geometry), two years social studies (including U.S. History), three years science (including one life science, one physical science, and one laboratory science), and two years of the same foreign language.

ADDITIONAL INFORMATION

All enrolled students may receive services and accommodations through the coordinator of learning disabilities of the DSO if they present appropriate documentation. The documentation should include a written report with a statement specifying areas of learning disabilities. Services and accommodations available with appropriate documentation include extended testing times for exams; reduced distraction testing environments; use of calculators, dictionaries, computers, or spellcheckers during exams; proctors; scribes; note-takers; audio format; assistive technology; and priority registration. If new needs are identified, services are modified or developed to accommodate them.

General Support Services Information

Contact Information
Name of program or department: Disability Services Office
Telephone: 919-515-7653
Fax: 919-513-2840

Accommodations or Services For Students With Learning Differences

Accommodations are decided upon an individual basis after a thorough review of appropriate, current documentation. The accommodations requests must be supported through the documentation provided and must be logically linked to the current impact of the condition on academic functioning.

Allowed in exams
Calculator: Yes
Dictionary: Yes
Computer: Yes
Spellchecker: Yes
Extended test time: Yes
Scribes: Yes
Proctors: Yes
Oral exams: Yes
Note-takers: Yes
Support services for students with LD: Yes
Support services for students with ADHD: Yes
Support services for students with ASD: Yes
Distraction-reduced environment: Yes
Tape recording in class: Yes
Electronic texts: Yes
Kurzweil reader: NR
Audio books: Yes
Other assistive technology: Yes
Priority registration: Yes
Added costs of services: No
LD specialists: No
ADHD coaching: No
ASD specialists: No
Professional tutors: No
Peer tutors: NR
Max. hours/wk. for services: NR
How professors are notified of student approved accommodations: NR

General Admissions Information

Office of Admissions: 919-515-2434

Entrance Requirements

Academic units required: 4 English, 4 math, 3 science, 1 science labs, 2 foreign language, 1 social studies, 1 history, **Academic units recommended:** 4 English, 4 math, 3 science, 1 science labs, 2 foreign language, 1 social studies, 1 history. High school diploma is required and GED is not accepted. SAT or ACT required. If ACT, ACT with writing accepted. Minimum paper TOEFL 563 or minimum internet TOEFL 85.

Application deadline: 1/15
Notification: NR
Average GPA: 3.67
ACT Composite middle 50% range: 27-31
SAT Math middle 50% range: 590-680
SAT Critical Reading middle 50% range: 570-650
SAT Writing middle 50% range: 540-630
Graduate top 10% of class: 51
Graduated top 25% of class: 87
Graduated top 50% of class: 99

COLLEGE GRADUATION REQUIREMENTS

Course waivers allowed: No
Course substitutions allowed: NR

Additional Information

Environment: This public school was founded in 1887. It has a 2110-acre campus.

Student Body
Undergrad enrollment: 24,111
% Women: 45
% Men: 55
% Out-of-state: 10

Cost information
In-state Tuition: $6,407
Out-of-state Tuition: $23,926
Room & board: $10,635

Housing Information
University Housing: Yes
Percent living on campus: 32

Greek System
Fraternity: Yes
Sorority: Yes
Athletics: Division I

St. Andrews University

1700 Dogwood Mile, Laurinburg, NC 28352
Phone: 910-277-5555 • Fax: 910-277-5020
E-mail: admissions@sapc.edu • Web: sa.edu
Support: CS • Institution: Private

Programs or Services for Students with Learning Differences

St. Andrews University, a branch of Webber International University, acknowledges its responsibility, both legally and educationally, to serve students with learning disabilities by providing reasonable accommodations. These services do not guarantee success, but endeavor to assist students in pursuing a quality postsecondary education. The Office of Disability Services and The Center for Academic Success at St. Andrews offer a range of support services for students with disabilities. These services are meant to help students devise strategies for meeting college demands and to foster independence, responsibility, and self-advocacy. The Office of Disability Services responds to each request for services and helps students develop a viable plan for personal success. The Office of Disability Services at St. Andrews University is committed to ensuring that all student information remains confidential. Students may begin the process for requesting accommodations, by visiting this site: https://www.sa.edu/student-life/disability-accommodations.

Admission Information for Students with Learning Differences

College entrance tests required: Yes
Interview required: No
Essay required: SAT/ACT writing required
Additional Application Required for LD/ADHD/ASD: NR
What documentation required for LD: Psycho ed evaluation to include: relevant historical info, instructional interventions, related services, age diagnosed, objective data (aptitude, achievement, info processing), test scores (standard, percentile and grade equivalents) and describe functional limitations.
With general application: No
To receive services after enrolling: Yes
What documentation required for ADHD: Diagnosis based on DSM-V; history of behaviors impairing functioning in academic setting; diagnostic interview; history of symptoms; evidence of ongoing behaviors.
With general application: No
LD/ADHD/ASD documentation submitted to: Office of Disability Services
ASD Specific Program: NR
Special Ed. HS course work accepted: Only as accepted for regular college entrance
Specific course requirements of all applicants: Yes
Separate application required: Yes
Acceptance into program means acceptance into college: Students must be admitted to and enrolled in the university first and then request services.

Admissions

Each application is reviewed on an individual basis. Factors considered are an SAT minimum of 800 or ACT minimum of 17 and students' high school profiles and courses attempted, as well as a minimum GPA of 2.5; an essay and counselor and/or teacher recommendations are optional but strongly recommended. Courses recommended include 3 credits of college prep English, 3 credits of math including Algebra II and Geometry, 3 credits of science, 3 credits of social studies, and 1 years of a foreign language. Prospective students are strongly encouraged to visit the campus. Students with learning disabilities complete the regular admissions application. Students with a diagnosis of attention deficit hyperactivity disorder are required to show achievement and ability testing (adult version) that validates the DSM–IV diagnosis. All students must meet the same admissions criteria. For the Admissions Committee to make the most informed decision, students are encouraged to self-disclose the existence of a learning disability in their personal statement. Any other personal information indicating the student's ability to succeed in college should also be included with the application. All documentation of a specific learning disability should be sent separately with an application for services to the Office of Disability Services at St. Andrews. Application forms for disability services are on the college website.

Additional Information

All accommodations are based on the submitted current documentation. Each case is reviewed individually. Disability Services reserves the right to determine eligibility for services based on the quality of the submitted documentation. The services and accommodations include note-taking, extended time on tests, alternative test formats, separate locations for tests, books on tape through Recordings for the Blind and Dyslexic or from readers, and content tutoring through individual departments. Franklin Language Masters and audiotape equipment are available for loan. All computers in computer labs are equipped with spellchecker and there are two Kurzweil Readers in the Center for Academic Success.

General Support Services Information

Contact Information
Name of program or department: Office of Disability Services and Center for Academic Success
Telephone: 910-277-5667
Fax: 910-277-5746

Accommodations or Services for Students with Learning Differences

Accommodations are decided upon an individual basis after a thorough review of appropriate, current documentation. The accommodations requested must be supported through the documentation provided and must be logically linked to the current impact of the condition on academic functioning.

Allowed in exams
Calculator: Yes
Dictionary: Yes
Computer: Yes
Spellchecker: Yes
Extended test time: Yes
Scribes: Yes
Proctors: Yes
Oral exams: Yes
Note-takers: Yes
Services for students with LD: Yes
Services for students with ADHD: Yes
Services for students with ASD: Yes
Distraction-reduced environment: Yes
Tape recording in class: Yes
Audio books: NR
Electronic texts: Yes
Kurzweil Reader: Yes
Other assistive technology: Yes
Priority registration: No
Added costs for services: No
LD specialists: Yes
ADHD coaching: NR
ASD specialists: NR
Professional tutors: NR
Peer tutors: 5–15
Max. hours/wk. for services: As needed
How professors are notified of LD/ADHD: By student

General Admissions Information

Office of Admissions: 910-277-5555

Entrance Requirements

Academic units required: 3 English, 3 math, 3 science, 1 foreign language, 3 social studies. High school diploma is required and GED is accepted. If ACT, ACT with writing accepted. TOEFL required of all international applicants: minimum paper TOEFL 550.

Application deadline: NR
Notification: Rolling starting 8/1
Average GPA: 3.2
ACT Composite middle 50% range: NR-NR
SAT Math middle 50% range: 355-605
SAT Critical Reading middle 50% range: NR-NR
SAT Writing middle 50% range: 330-590
Graduated top 10% of class: 7
Graduated top 25% of class: 30
Graduated top 50% of class: 66

COLLEGE GRADUATION REQUIREMENTS

Course waivers allowed: No
Course substitutions allowed: Yes
In what course: Foreign language

Additional Information

Environment: This private school, affiliated with the Presbyterian Church, was founded in 1958. It has a 600-acre campus.

Student Body
Undergrad enrollment: 617
% Women: 54
% Men: 46
% Out-of-state: 59

Cost information
Tuition: $23,682
Room & board: NR

Housing Information
University Housing: Yes
Percent living on campus: 85

Greek System
Fraternity: NR
Sorority: NR
Athletics: Division II

U. of N. Carolina at Asheville

CPO #1320 Asheville, NC 28804-8502
Phone: 828-251-6481 • Fax: 828-251-6482
E-mail: admissions@unca.edu • Web: www.unca.edu
Support: S • Institution: Public

Programs or Services for Students with Learning Differences

The goal of the Office of Academic Accessibility is to provide students with disabilities equal access to university courses, programs, services, and activities in a self-reliant manner when possible. To register with the Office of Academic Accessibility, students complete several forms and provide appropriate documentation of their disability and functional limitations.

Admission Information for Students with Learning Differences

College entrance test required: Yes
Interview required: No
Essay required: Not Applicable
Additional Application Required for LD/ADHD/ASD: Yes
What documentation required for LD: Diagnostic statement identifying the disability including ICD or DSM classification. Description of the current functional impact to student's experiences. Assessment method(s) used and assessment score reports used in the determination of the diagnosis, when applicable.
With general application: Not Applicable
To receive services after enrolling: Yes
What documentation required for ADHD: Diagnostic statement identifying the disability including ICD or DSM classification. Description of the current functional impact to student's experiences. Assessment method(s) used and assessment score reports used in the determination of the diagnosis, when applicable.
With general application: Not Applicable
To receive services after enrolling: Yes
What documentation required for ASD: Diagnostic statement identifying the disability including ICD or DSM classification. Description of the current functional impact to student's experiences. Assessment method(s) used and assessment score reports used in the determination of the diagnosis, when applicable.
With general application: Not Applicable
To receive services after enrolling: Yes
LD/ADHD/ASD documentation submitted to: Office of Academic Accessibility
ASD Specific Program: No
Special Ed. HS course work accepted: Not Applicable
Specific course requirements of all applicants: Yes
Separate application required for program services: False
Total # of students receiving LD/ADHD/ASD services: NR
Acceptance into program means acceptance into college: Not Applicable

Admissions

Admissions criteria and procedures for the university are the same for students with and without disabilities.

Additional Information

Through Academic Accessibility, the university seeks to meet individual needs by coordinating and implementing programs,services and activities for students with disabilities. Prospective students interested in inquiring about the services we provide are welcome and encouraged to contact our staff by phone, at 828-250-3979, or e-mail, at academicaccess@unca.edu. Additional information is provided on our website, at oaa.unca.ed

General Support Services Information

Contact Information
Name of program or department: Office of Academic Accessibility
Telephone: 828-232-5050
Fax: 828-251-6592
Website: oaa.unca.edu

Accommodations or Services for Students with Learning Differences

Accommodations are decided upon an individual basis after a thorough review of appropriate, current documentation. The accommodations requests must be supported through the documentation provided and must be logically linked to the current impact of the condition on academic functioning.

Allowed in exams
Calculator: Yes
Dictionary: Yes
Computer: Yes
Spellchecker: Yes
Extended test time: Yes
Scribes: Yes
Proctors: Yes
Oral exams: Yes
Note-takers: Yes
Support services for students with LD: Yes
Support services for students with ADHD: Yes
Support services for students with ASD: Yes
Distraction-reduced environment: Yes
Tape recording in class: Yes
Electronic texts: Yes
Kurzweil reader: NR
Audio books: Yes
Other assistive technology: Yes
Priority registration: Yes
Added costs of services: No
LD specialists: No
ADHD coaching: Yes
ASD specialists: No
Professional tutors: Yes
Peer tutors: Yes
Max. hours/wk. for services: NR
How professors are notified of student approved accommodations: By student

General Admissions Information

Office of Admissions: 828-251-6481

Entrance Requirements

Academic units required: 4 English, 4 math, 3 science, 1 science labs, 2 foreign language, 1 social studies, 1 history. **Academic units recommended:** 4 academic electives, High school diploma is required and GED is not accepted. SAT or ACT required. If ACT, ACT with writing required. TOEFL required of all international applicants: minimum paper TOEFL 550 or minimum internet TOEFL 79.

Application deadline: 2/15
Notification: Rolling starting 12/15
Average GPA: 3.42
ACT Composite middle 50% range: 23-28
SAT Math middle 50% range: 520-610
SAT Critical Reading middle 50% range: 530-640
SAT Writing middle 50% range: 510-610
Graduate top 10% of class: 21
Graduated top 25% of class: 52
Graduated top 50% of class: 91

COLLEGE GRADUATION REQUIREMENTS

Course waivers allowed: Yes
In what course: Math, foreign language, and others on an individual basis.
Course substitutions allowed: Yes
In what course: Math, foreign language, and others on an individual basis.

Additional Information

Environment: This public school was founded in 1927. It has a 265-acre campus.

Student Body
Undergrad enrollment: 3,858
% Women: 56
% Men: 44
% Out-of-state: 11

Cost information
In-state tuition: $4,041
Out-of-state tuition: $20,436
Room & board: $8,746

Housing Information
University Housing: Yes
Percent living on campus: 39

Greek System
Fraternity: Yes
Sorority: Yes
Athletics: Division I

The University of North Carolina at Chapel Hill

Jackson Hall, Chapel Hill, NC 27599-2200
Phone: 919-966-3621 • Fax: 919-962-3045
E-mail: unchelp@admissions.unc.edu • Web: www.unc.edu
Support: CS • Institution: 4-Year Public

Programs or Services for Students with Learning Differences

The Academic Success Program, or ASP (www.unc.edu/asp), is one of the many programs within the Learning Center. We provide accommodations and services for undergraduate, professional and graduate students who have a documented learning disability and/or attention-deficit/hyperactivity disorder (AD/HD). The staff determines legally mandated accommodations and collaborates with the Department of Disability Services in providing them. The staff also provides a variety of services to eligible students, including learning strategy sessions and coaching.

Admission Information for Students with Learning Differences

College entrance tests required: Yes
Interview required: NR
Essay required: NR
Additional Application Required for LD/ADHD/ASD: NR
What documentation required for LD: Psycho ed evaluation to include: relevant historical info, instructional interventions, related services, age diagnosed, objective data (aptitude, achievement, info processing), test scores (standard, percentile and grade equivalents) and describe functional limitations.
With general application: No
To receive services after enrolling: Yes
What documentation required for ADHD: Diagnosis based on DSM-V; history of behaviors impairing functioning in academic setting; diagnostic interview; history of symptoms; evidence of ongoing behaviors.
With general application: No
What documentation required for ASD: Diagnosis based on DSM-V; history of behaviors impairing functioning in academic setting; diagnostic interview; history of symptoms; evidence of ongoing behaviors.
With General Application: No
To receive services after enrolling: Yes
LD/ADHD/ASD documentation submitted to: Admissions
ASD Specific Program: NR
Special Ed. HS course work accepted: Yes
Specific course requirements of all applicants: NR
Separate application required: No
Total # of students receiving LD/ADHD/ASD services: 450
Acceptance into program means acceptance into college: No, students must be admitted to and enrolled in the university first and then request services.

Admissions

All applicants must meet the same admission criteria. Teacher recommendation and counselor statement are required. Students must submit either the SAT or ACT with writing. There is one long and one short essay required. UNC does not use formulas or cutoffs for admission. They look for and celebrate diversity of interests, backgrounds, and aspirations. UNC focuses first on academics using courses, GPA tests, recommendations, and essays. Rigor of courses is very important. Beyond academics they look at leadership and service, and character.

Additional Information

Coaching is a creative partnership between students and their coach. Accommodations provided include note-takers, taped textbooks, tutors in math or foreign languages, extended time on tests, distraction-free test environments, readers during exams, scribes to write dictated test answers, and computers for writing test answers. Using the student's current course work, LDS can teach a range of strategies, including how to plan, draft, and edit papers; how to take lecture notes and reading notes; how to read critically and efficiently; how to manage time; and how to prepare for and take exams. Group experiences are available to students each semester based on their expressed interests. These can include support groups that promote understanding, acceptance, and pride; academic workshops that allow students to help one another learn specific skills; seminars that provide topical information from campus experts as well as other students; and panel discussions between students and university personnel.

Support Services Information

Contact Information
Name of program or department: Accessibility Resources & Service
Telephone: 919-962-8300
Fax: 919-962-4748
Website: http://learningcenter.unc.edu/ldadhd-services/

Accommodations or Services For Students With Learning Differences

Accommodations are decided upon an individual basis after a thorough review of appropriate, current documentation. The accommodations requests must be supported through the documentation provided and must be logically linked to the current impact of the condition on academic functioning.

Allowed in exams
Calculator: Yes
Dictionary: Yes
Computer: Yes
Spellchecker: Yes
Extended test time: Yes
Scribes: Yes
Proctors: Yes
Oral exams: Yes
Note-takers: Yes
Support services for students with LD: Yes
Support services for students with ADHD: Yes
Support services for students with ASD: Yes
Distraction-reduced environment: Yes
Tape recording in class: Yes
Electronic texts: Yes
Kurzweil reader: NR
Audio books: Yes
Other assistive technology: Yes
Priority registration: Yes
Added costs of services: No
LD specialists: Yes
ADHD coaching: Yes
ASD specialists: No
Professional tutors: No
Peer tutors: NR
Max. hours/wk. for services: NR
How professors are notified of student approved accommodations: By both student and director

General Admissions Information

Office of Admissions: 919-966-3621

Entrance Requirements

Academic units required: 4 English, 4 math, 3 science, 1 science labs, 2 foreign language, 1 social studies, 1 history, 1 academic electives. High school diploma is required and GED is not accepted. SAT or ACT required. If ACT, ACT with writing accepted. TOEFL required of all international applicants: minimum paper TOEFL 600 or minimum internet TOEFL 100.

Application deadline: 1/15
Notification: NR
Average GPA: 4.63
ACT Composite middle 50% range: 27-32
SAT Math middle 50% range: 610-700
SAT Critical Reading middle 50% range: 590-690
SAT Writing middle 50% range: 590-700
Graduate top 10% of class: 77
Graduated top 25% of class: 96
Graduated top 50% of class: 99

COLLEGE GRADUATION REQUIREMENTS

Course waivers allowed: No
Course substitutions allowed: Yes
In what course: Math and foreign language only; through a staff reviewed process students can apply to take an alternative course to fulfill the requirement.

Additional Information

Environment: This public school was founded in 1789. It has a 729-acre campus.

Student Body
Undergrad enrollment: 18,415
% Women: 58
% Men: 42
% Out-of-state: 17

Cost information
In-state Tuition: $6,648
Out-of-state Tuition: $31,730
Room & board: $10,902
Housing Information
University Housing: Yes
Percent living on campus: 52

Greek System
Fraternity: Yes
Sorority: Yes
Athletics: Division I

THE UNIVERSITY OF NORTH CAROLINA AT CHARLOTTE

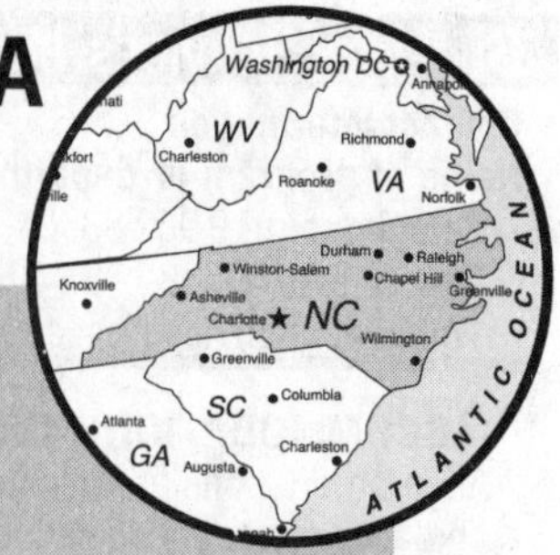

9201 University City Boulevard, Charlotte, NC 28223-0001
Phone: 704-687-5507 • Fax: 704-687-6483
E-mail: unccadm@uncc.edu • Web: www.uncc.edu/
Support: CS • Institution: Public

PROGRAMS OR SERVICES FOR STUDENTS WITH LEARNING DIFFERENCES

The mission of Disability Services reflects the university's commitment to diversity by ensuring access to educational opportunities for persons with disabilities. The professional staff in Disability Services assists students with disabilities, including learning disabilities, through an interactive process based on their individual needs.

ADMISSION INFORMATION FOR STUDENTS WITH LEARNING DIFFERENCES

College entrance test required: Yes
Interview required: No
Essay required: Not Applicable
Additional Application Required for LD/ADHD/ASD: No
What documentation required for LD: Psycho ed evaluation to include: relevant historical info, instructional interventions, related services, age diagnosed, objective data (aptitude, achievement, info processing), test scores (standard, percentile and grade equivalents) and describe functional limitations.
With general application: No
To receive services after enrolling: No
What documentation required for ADHD: Diagnosis based on DSM-V; history of behaviors impairing functioning in academic setting; diagnostic interview; history of symptoms; evidence of ongoing behaviors.
With general application: No
To receive services after enrolling: No
What documentation required for ASD: Psycho ed evaluation
With general application: No
To receive services after enrolling: No
LD/ADHD/ASD documentation submitted to: Office of Disability Services
ASD Specific Program: NR
Special Ed. HS course work accepted: NR
Specific course requirements of all applicants: Yes
Separate application required for program services: No
Total # of students receiving LD/ADHD/ASD services: 83
Acceptance into program means acceptance into college: No

ADMISSIONS

All applicants must meet the general admissions requirements and any special requirements for acceptance into a particular program of study. Students go through the regular application process. Courses required include 4 years English, 4 years math (1 beyond algebra II) 3 years science, 2 years foreign language, 2 years social studies (1 history recommended), and 2 years of electives. The university reserves the right to withhold the admission of any applicant who fails to meet any of the requirements for admission. Once students have been admitted and enrolled they may request the necessary services. The mid 50% of the admitted students have a GPA of ¾-4/0. SAT 1480-1730 and ACT 21-26.

ADDITIONAL INFORMATION

Services offered are based on the student's disability documentation, the functional impact of the disability upon the student and an interactive process between the student and the Disability Services counselor. UNC Charlotte has a Tutoring Center and a Writing Center available to all students. Academic Services at UNC Charlotte enriches the academic community by offering a broad range of initiatives promoting student success, ensuring access, and enhancing the educational experience of all students. Through transition programs, learning communities, support for student-athletes, academic advising, career services, experiential learning, university-wide honors programs, disability services, tutorial programs, and initiatives for underrepresented students, Academic Services cultivates life skills critical to successful graduation and global citizenship. Advocating for the needs of a diverse student population, Academic Services utilizes an integrated student-centered approach that reinforces rigorous academic expectations and encourages student engagement from the time of enrollment through graduation.

General Support Services Information

Contact Information
Name of program or department: Office of Disability Services
Telephone: 704-687-0040
Fax: 704-687-1395

Accommodations or Services For Students With Learning Differences

Accommodations are decided upon an individual basis after a thorough review of appropriate, current documentation. The accommodations requests must be supported through the documentation provided and must be logically linked to the current impact of the condition on academic functioning.

Allowed in exams
Calculator: Yes
Dictionary: No
Computer: Yes
Spellchecker: No
Extended test time: Yes
Scribes: No
Proctors: No
Oral exams: No
Note-takers: Yes
Support services for students with LD: NR
Support services for students with ADHD: NR
Support services for students with ASD: NR
Distraction-reduced environment: Yes
Tape recording in class: Yes
Electronic texts: No
Kurzweil reader: Yes
Audio books: No
Other assistive technology: Yes
Priority registration: No
Added costs of services: No
LD specialists: Yes
ADHD coaching: NR
ASD specialists: NR
Professional tutors: No
Peer tutors: Yes
Max. hours/wk. for services: NR
How professors are notified of student approved accommodations: By student

General Admissions Information

Office of Admissions: 704-687-5507

Entrance Requirements

Academic units required: 4 English, 4 math, 3 science, 1 science labs, 2 foreign language, 1 social studies, 1 history. **Academic units recommended:** 3 foreign language. High school diploma is required and GED is accepted. SAT or ACT required. If ACT, ACT with writing recommended. TOEFL required of all international applicants: minimum paper TOEFL 523 or minimum internet TOEFL 70.

Application deadline: 6/1
Notification: Rolling starting 11/1
Average GPA: 3.9
ACT Composite middle 50% range: 22-25
SAT Math middle 50% range: 510-600
SAT Critical Reading middle 50% range: 500-580
SAT Writing middle 50% range: 470-560
Graduate top 10% of class: 22
Graduated top 25% of class: 57
Graduated top 50% of class: 87

COLLEGE GRADUATION REQUIREMENTS

Course waivers allowed: NR
Course substitutions allowed: NR

Additional Information

Environment: This public school was founded in 1946. It has a 1,000-acre campus.

Student Body
Undergrad enrollment: 22,732
% Women: 48
% Men: 52
% Out-of-state: 5

Cost information
In-state Tuition: $3,628
Out-of-state Tuition: $16,799
Room & board: $10,220

Housing Information
University Housing: Yes
Percent living on campus: 23

Greek System
Fraternity: Yes
Sorority: Yes
Athletics: Division I

The University of North Carolina at Greensboro

1400 Spring Garden Street, Greensboro, NC 27402-6170
Phone: 336-334-5243 • Fax: 336-334-4180
E-mail: admissions@uncg.edu • Web: www.uncg.edu
Support: CS • Institution: Public

Programs or Services for Students with Learning Differences

The University of North Carolina—Greensboro is committed to equality of educational opportunities for qualified students with disabilities. The goal of Disabled Student Services is to provide a full range of academic accommodations. Students who need tests offered in a nontraditional format may request this service. Modifications may include extended test times, private rooms, readers, scribes, or the use of word processors for essay examinations. Documentation must verify the use of special accommodations. The Disability Services Office provides a handbook for students to use as a helpful guide in making their experience at UNCG a positive one.

Admission Information for Students with Learning Differences

College entrance tests required: Yes
Interview required: No
Essay required: No
Additional Application Required for LD/ADHD/ASD: NR
What documentation required for LD: Psycho ed evaluation to include: relevant historical info, instructional interventions, related services, age diagnosed, objective data (aptitude, achievement, info processing), test scores (standard, percentile and grade equivalents) and describe functional limitations.
With general application: No
To receive services after enrolling: Yes
What documentation required for ADHD: Diagnosis based on DSM-V; history of behaviors impairing functioning in academic setting; diagnostic interview; history of symptoms; evidence of ongoing behaviors.
With general application: No
LD/ADHD/ASD documentation submitted to: Disabled Student Services
ASD Specific Program: NR
Special Ed. HS course work accepted: NR
Specific course requirements of all applicants: Yes
Separate application required: No
Total # of students receiving LD/ADHD/ASD services: 200
Acceptance into program means acceptance into college: Students must be admitted to and enrolled in the university first and then request services.

Admissions

There is no special admissions process for students with learning disabilities. Admission is competitive and based on academic qualifications. Students with learning disabilities must submit the regular application and are considered for admission in the same manner as any other applicant. No pre-admission inquiry regarding the learning disability is made. It is highly recommended that the SAT or ACT be taken with accommodations (if eligible) if this gives a better estimate of the student's ability.

Additional Information

Trained staff members are available for counseling to assist students with academic and/or personal problems. Voluntary note-takers are solicited through DSS, and photocopying is available. Students will meet with their faculty advisor to discuss courses that need to be taken, and DSS will stamp the students' registration cards to verify that they are registered with DSS and warrant priority registration. Assistance in securing taped textbooks through Recording for the Blind is provided, and a file of available readers is available for instances when materials are not available through RFB. Students are provided with information regarding campus tutorials and labs. Individual tutors are provided when it seems necessary. Students can receive help with study skills and time management techniques.

General Support Services Information

Contact Information
Name of program or department: Disabled Student Services
Telephone: 336-334-5440
Fax: 336-334-4412

Accommodations or Services for Students with Learning Differences

Accommodations are decided upon an individual basis after a thorough review of appropriate, current documentation. The accommodations requested must be supported through the documentation provided and must be logically linked to the current impact of the condition on academic functioning.

Allowed in exams
Calculator: Yes
Dictionary: Yes
Computer: Yes
Spellchecker: Yes
Extended test time: Yes
Scribes: Yes
Proctors: Yes
Oral exams: Yes
Note-takers: Yes
Services for students with LD: Yes
Services for students with ADHD: Yes
Services for students with ASD: Yes
Distraction-reduced environment: Yes
Tape recording in class: Yes
Audio books: NR
Electronic texts: Yes
Kurzweil Reader: Yes
Other assistive technology: Yes
Priority registration: Yes
Added costs for services: No
LD specialists: Yes
ADHD coaching: NR
ASD specialists: NR
Professional tutors: No
Peer tutors: Yes
Max. hours/wk. for services: Depends on needs
How professors are notified of LD/ADHD: By both student and director

General Admissions Information

Office of Admissions: 336-334-5243

Entrance Requirements

Academic units required: 4 English, 4 math, 3 science, 1 science labs, 2 foreign language, 2 social studies. High school diploma is required and GED is not accepted. SAT or ACT required. If ACT, ACT with writing required. TOEFL required of all international applicants: minimum paper TOEFL 550 or minimum internet TOEFL 79.

Application deadline: 3/1
Notification: Rolling starting 9/15
Average GPA: 3.62
ACT Composite middle 50% range: 20-25
SAT Math middle 50% range: 470-550
SAT Critical Reading middle 50% range: 470-560
SAT Writing middle 50% range: 440-540
Graduate top 10% of class: 13
Graduated top 25% of class: 41
Graduated top 50% of class: 79

COLLEGE GRADUATION REQUIREMENTS

Course waivers allowed: NR
In what course: NR
Course substitutions allowed: NR
In what course: NR

Additional Information

Environment: This public school was founded in 1891. It has a 357-acre campus.

Student Body
Undergrad enrollment: 15,951
% Women: 66
% Men: 34
% Out-of-state: 5

Cost information
In-state Tuition: $4,129
Out-of-state Tuition: $18,991
Room & board: $7,774

Housing Information
University Housing: Yes
Percent living on campus: 34

Greek System
Fraternity: Yes
Sorority: Yes
Athletics: Division I

The University of North Carolina Wilmington

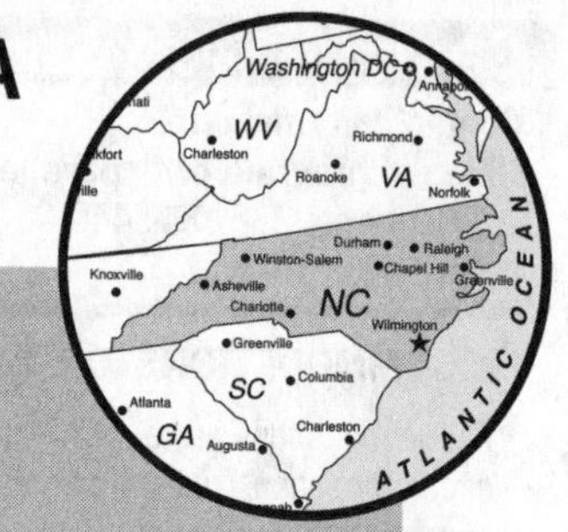

601 South College Road, Wilmington, NC 28403-5904
Phone: 910-962-3243 • Fax: 910-962-3038
E-mail: admissions@uncw.edu • Web: www.uncw.edu
Support: CS • Institution: Public

Programs or Services for Students with Learning Differences

The university's goal is to provide access to all of its academic programs, support services, and extracurricular activities and enrich students' academic and vocational experiences while in college. The coordinator of Disability Services (DS) meets with the student to appraise special needs, make referrals, and arrange for special accommodations. The university has devoted much time and energy to meeting the requirements of Section 504 and the ADA. This effort is exemplified by the accommodating services offered through DS for students with learning disabilities and by special cooperation of the faculty. As the number of students with learning disabilities attending UNCW increases, so does the university's commitment to making facilities and programs more accessible.

Admission Information for Students with Learning Differences

College entrance tests required: Yes
Interview required: No
Essay required: Yes
Additional Application Required for LD/ADHD/ASD: NR
What documentation required for LD: Psycho ed evaluation to include: relevant historical info, instructional interventions, related services, age diagnosed, objective data (aptitude, achievement, info processing), test scores (standard, percentile and grade equivalents) and describe functional limitations.
With general application: No
To receive services after enrolling: Yes
What documentation required for ADHD: Diagnosis based on DSM-V; history of behaviors impairing functioning in academic setting; diagnostic interview; history of symptoms; evidence of ongoing behaviors.
With general application: No
LD/ADHD/ASD documentation submitted to: Disability Services
ASD Specific Program: NR
Special Ed. HS course work accepted: No
Specific course requirements of all applicants: Yes
Separate application required: N/A
Total # of students receiving LD/ADHD/ASD services: 250
Acceptance into program means acceptance into college: Students must be admitted to and enrolled in the university first and then request services.

Admissions

Students with learning disabilities must meet the same entrance requirements as all other applicants. Course requirements include 4 years of English, 3 years of math, 3 years of science, 2 years of social studies, and 2 years of a foreign language. UNCW requires one recommendation from a guidance counselor or a core academic teacher. Most students admitted to UNCW have SAT test scores between 1160 and 1230 or, ACT scores between 26 and 28, and the average GPA is 3.68. The university prefers that students respond to the essay question posed by UNCW rather than sending an essay they have prepared for another institution.

Additional Information

Services are provided based on individual needs as assessed through recent diagnostic information and a personal interview. As new needs are identified, services may be modified or developed to accommodate them. Newly accepted students interested in services should complete and sign the disclosure form that is included with the letter of acceptance. This information should then be forwarded to the Disability Services. Current documentation must be sent to the Director of DS after acceptance to the university. Diagnostic testing must be conducted by a licensed professional, and an adequate report must include specific educational recommendations. There are no special classes or programs designed just for students with learning disabilities. Services and accommodations are offered to undergraduate and graduate students.

General Support Services Information

Contact Information
Name of program or department: Disability Services (DS)
Telephone: 910-962-7555
Fax: 910-962-7556

Accommodations or Services for Students with Learning Differences

Accommodations are decided upon an individual basis after a thorough review of appropriate, current documentation. The accommodations requested must be supported through the documentation provided and must be logically linked to the current impact of the condition on academic functioning.

Allowed in exams
Calculator: Yes
Dictionary: No
Computer: Yes
Spellchecker: Yes
Extended test time: Yes
Scribes: Yes
Proctors: Yes
Oral exams: Yes
Note-takers: Yes
Services for students with LD: Yes
Services for students with ADHD: Yes
Services for students with ASD: Yes
Distraction-reduced environment: Yes
Tape recording in class: Yes
Audio books: NR
Electronic texts: Yes
Kurzweil Reader: Yes
Other assistive technology: Yes
Priority registration: Yes
Added costs for services: No
LD specialists: Yes
ADHD coaching: NR
ASD specialists: NR
Professional tutors: No
Peer tutors: Yes
Max. hours/wk. for services: Depends on needs
How professors are notified of LD/ADHD: By student

General Admissions Information

Office of Admissions: 910-962-3243

Entrance Requirements

Academic units required: 4 English, 4 math, 3 science, 1 science labs, 2 foreign language, 1 social studies, 1 history. High school diploma is required and GED is accepted. SAT or ACT required. If ACT, ACT with writing required. TOEFL required of all international applicants: minimum internet TOEFL 71.

Application deadline: 2/1
Notification: 4/1
Average GPA: 4.1
ACT Composite middle 50% range: 23-27
SAT Math middle 50% range: 560-630
SAT Critical Reading middle 50% range: 560-630
SAT Writing middle 50% range: 520-620
Graduate top 10% of class: 24
Graduated top 25% of class: 62
Graduated top 50% of class: 95

COLLEGE GRADUATION REQUIREMENTS

Course waivers allowed: Not Applicable
Course substitutions allowed: Not Applicable

Additional Information

Environment: This public school was founded in 1947. It has a 656-acre campus.

Student Body
Undergrad enrollment: 13,218
% Women: 61
% Men: 39
% Out-of-state: 13.3

Cost information
In-state Tuition: $4,188
Out-of-state Tuition: $18,054
Room & board: $9,466

Housing Information
University Housing: Yes
Percent living on campus: 30.5

Greek System
Fraternity: Yes
Sorority: Yes
Athletics: Division I

Wake Forest University

PO Box 7305, Winston Salem, NC 27109
Phone: 336-758-5201 • Fax: 336-758-4324
E-mail: admissions@wfu.edu • Web: www.wfu.edu
Support: CS • Institution: Private

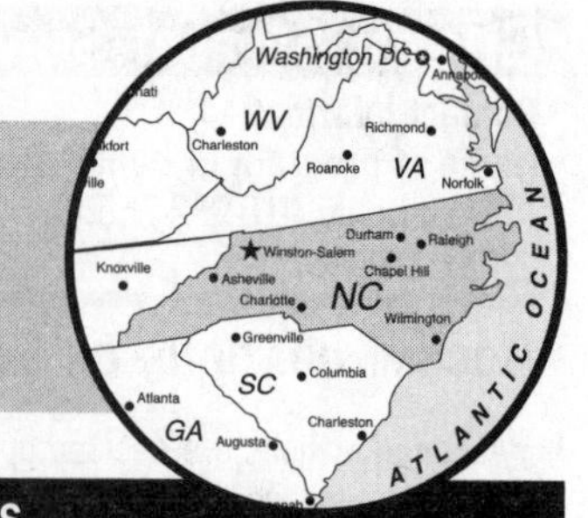

Programs or Services for Students with Learning Differences

The Learning Assistance Center (LAC) offers support for academic success. For students with documented disabilities, the program director will work with the student and members of the faculty to help implement any approved course accommodations. The students with learning disabilities have a series of conferences with staff members who specialize in academic skills and who help design an overall study plan to improve scholastic performance in those areas needing assistance. If special course accommodations are needed, the LAC staff will serve as an advocate for the students with members of the faculty.

Admission Information for Students with Learning Differences

College entrance tests required: No
Interview required: No
Essay required: Yes
Additional Application Required for LD/ADHD/ASD: NR
What documentation required for LD: Psycho ed evaluation to include: relevant historical info, instructional interventions, related services, age diagnosed, objective data (aptitude, achievement, info processing), test scores (standard, percentile and grade equivalents) and describe functional limitations.
With general application: No
To receive services after enrolling: Yes
What documentation required for ADHD: Diagnosis based on DSM-V; history of behaviors impairing functioning in academic setting; diagnostic interview; history of symptoms; evidence of ongoing behaviors.
With general application: No
To receive services after enrolling: Yes
What documentation required for ASD: Psycho ed evaluation
With general application: NR
To receive services after enrolling: Yes
LD/ADHD/ASD documentation submitted to: LAC
ASD Specific Program: NR
Special Ed. HS course work accepted: No
Specific course requirements of all applicants: Yes
Separate application required: No
Total # of students receiving LD/ADHD/ASD services: 221
Acceptance into program means acceptance into college: Students must be admitted to and enrolled in the university first and then request services.

Admissions

There are no special admissions procedures for students with learning disabilities. Students with LD submit the general Wake Forest University application and are expected to meet the same admission criteria as all applicants. Wake Forest does not accept the ACT. The mid 50 percent range for the SAT is 1240–1360. Course requirements include 4 years of English, 3 years of math, 1 year of science, 2 years of social studies, and 2 years of a foreign language. Students should self-disclose to the Learning Assistance Center after admission. Services are available to all enrolled students with documentation on file. Students are encouraged to provide a recent psychoeducational evaluation.

Additional Information

The Learning Assistance Program staff will assist students with learning disabilities to learn new approaches to studying and methods for improving reading comprehension, note-taking, time management, study organization, memory, motivation, and self-modification. The LAC offers peer tutoring services. In addition to one-on-one tutoring in many academic subjects, the LAC provides collaborative learning groups comprised of two to five students. The LAC also assists students who present special academic needs. Accommodations are determined based on appropriate documentation. All students with or without learning disabilities are eligible for group or individual tutoring in basic academic subjects. The tutors are advanced undergraduates or graduate students who have demonstrated mastery of specific subject areas and are supervised by the LAC staff for their tutoring activities. The LAC also offers all students individual academic counseling to help develop study, organization, and time management strategies that are important for successful college-level learning.

General Support Services Information

Contact Information
Name of program or department: Learning Assistance Center (LAC)
Telephone: 336-758-5929
Fax: 336-758-1991

Accommodations or Services for Students with Learning Differences

Accommodations are decided upon an individual basis after a thorough review of appropriate, current documentation. The accommodations requested must be supported through the documentation provided and must be logically linked to the current impact of the condition on academic functioning.

Allowed in exams
Calculator: No
Dictionary: Yes
Computer: Yes
Spellchecker: Yes
Extended test time: Yes
Scribes: No
Proctors: No
Oral exams: No
Note-takers: No
Services for students with LD: Yes
Services for students with ADHD: Yes
Services for students with ASD: Yes
Distraction-reduced environment: Yes
Tape recording in class: Yes
Audio books: NR
Electronic texts: No
Kurzweil Reader: No
Other assistive technology: No
Priority registration: No
Added costs for services: No
LD specialists: Yes
ADHD coaching: NR
ASD specialists: NR
Professional tutors: No
Peer tutors: 150
Max. hours/wk. for services: NR
How professors are notified of LD/ADHD: By both student and letter from Director

General Admissions Information

Office of Admissions: 336-758-5201

Entrance Requirements

Academic units required: 4 English, 3 math, 1 science, 2 foreign language, 2 social studies. **Academic units recommended:** 4 English, 4 math, 4 science, 4 foreign language, 4 social studies. High school diploma is required and GED is accepted. SAT or ACT considered if submitted. If ACT, ACT with writing required. TOEFL required of all international applicants: minimum paper TOEFL 600.

Application deadline: 1/1
Notification: NR
Average GPA: 3.66
ACT Composite middle 50% range: 28-32
SAT Math middle 50% range: 620-730
SAT Critical Reading middle 50% range: 590-690
SAT Writing middle 50% range: 610-710
Graduated top 10% of class: 77
Graduated top 25% of class: 93
Graduated top 50% of class: 99

COLLEGE GRADUATION REQUIREMENTS

Course waivers allowed: No
Course substitutions allowed: Yes
In what course: Foreign language only. If there is a documented language-based LD and a good faith effort has been made by the student to learn a foreign language without success, then two courses from an approved list of classics and humanities courses may be substituted.

Additional Information

Environment: This private school was founded in 1834. It has a 340-acre campus.

Student Body
Undergrad enrollment: 4,871
% Women: 53
% Men: 47
% Out-of-state: 79

.Cost information
Tuition: $47,120
Room & board: $12,996

Housing Information
University Housing: Yes
Percent living on campus: 77

Greek System
Fraternity: Yes
Sorority: Yes
Athletics: Division I

WESTERN CAROLINA UNIVERSITY

102 Camp Building, Cullowhee, NC 28723
Phone: 828-227-7317 • Fax: 828-227-7319
E-mail: admiss@email.wcu.edu • Web: www.wcu.edu
Support: CS • Institution: Public

PROGRAMS OR SERVICES FOR STUDENTS WITH LEARNING DIFFERENCES

The Office of Disability Services attempts to respond to the needs of students with learning disabilities by making services and assistive technologies available as needed.

ADMISSION INFORMATION FOR STUDENTS WITH LEARNING DIFFERENCES

College entrance tests required: Yes
Interview required: No
Essay required: No
Additional Application Required for LD/ADHD/ASD: Yes
What documentation required for LD: Psycho ed evaluation to include: relevant historical info, instructional interventions, related services, age diagnosed, objective data (aptitude, achievement, info processing), test scores (standard, percentile and grade equivalents) and describe functional limitations.
With general application: No
To receive services after enrolling: Yes
What documentation required for ADHD: Diagnosis based on DSM-V; history of behaviors impairing functioning in academic setting; diagnostic interview; history of symptoms; evidence of ongoing behaviors.
With general application: No
To receive services after enrolling: Yes
What documentation required for ASD: Psycho ed evaluation
With general application: NR
To receive services after enrolling: Yes
LD/ADHD/ASD documentation submitted to: Office of Disability Services (ODS)
ASD Specific Program: NR
Special Ed. HS course work accepted: No
Specific course requirements of all applicants: Yes
Separate application required: No
Total # of students receiving LD/ADHD/ASD services: 100–120
Acceptance into program means acceptance into college: Students must be admitted to and enrolled in the university first and then request services.

ADMISSIONS

Students with learning disabilities are admitted under the same standards as students who do not have learning disabilities. WCU does not have a strict minimum GPA, but the average GPA for enrolled students in fall of 2011 was a 3.54 and the course requirements include 4 years of English, 4 years of math, 3 years of science, 3 years of social studies, and 2 years of a foreign language. The non-standardized ACT/SAT is acceptable. Students not admissible through the regular admission process may be offered a probationary admission and must begin in the summer prior to freshman year. The admission decision is made by the Admissions Office.

ADDITIONAL INFORMATION

To qualify for services, students must be enrolled at the university and have updated medical documentation. The following are examples of services or accommodations are available for students with appropriate documentation: the use of calculators, dictionaries, computers, or spellcheckers during exams; extended time on tests; quiet environments; scribes; proctors; oral exams; note-takers; tape recorders in class; text in alternate format; and priority registration. All students have access to tutoring, writing and math centers, a Technology Assistance Center, and counseling and psychological services. Admitted students should maintain good class attendance, strive for good grades, cooperate with counselors and advisors, set realistic career goals, and meet with the Office of Disability Services to arrange accommodations. Services and accommodations are available for all enrolled students.

General Support Services Information

Contact Information
Name of program or department: Office of Disability Services (ODS)
Telephone: 828-227-3886
Fax: 828-227-7078
E-mail: disabilityservices@wcu.edu

Accommodations or Services for Students with Learning Differences

Accommodations are decided upon an individual basis after a thorough review of appropriate, current documentation. The accommodations requested must be supported through the documentation provided and must be logically linked to the current impact of the condition on academic functioning.

Allowed in exams
Calculator: Yes
Dictionary: Yes
Computer: Yes
Spellchecker: Yes
Extended test time: Yes
Scribes: Yes
Proctors: Yes
Oral exams: Yes
Note-takers: Yes
Services for students with LD: Yes
Services for students with ADHD: Yes
Services for students with ASD: Yes
Distraction-reduced environment: Yes
Tape recording in class: Yes
Audio books: NR
Electronic texts: Yes
Kurzweil Reader: Yes
Other assistive technology: Yes
Priority registration: Yes
Added costs for services: No
LD specialists: Yes
ADHD coaching: NR
ASD specialists: NR
Professional tutors: Varies
Peer tutors: 20–50
Max. hours/wk. for services: NR
How professors are notified of LD/ADHD: By student

General Admissions Information

Office of Admissions: 828-227-7317

Entrance Requirements

Academic units required: 4 English, 4 math, 3 science, 3 science labs, 2 foreign language, 2 social studies, 1 history, 4 academic electives. **Academic units recommended:** 4 English, 4 math, 3 science, 3 science labs, 2 foreign language, 2 social studies, 1 history, 8 academic electives. High school diploma is required and GED is accepted. SAT or ACT required. If ACT, ACT with writing required. TOEFL required of all international applicants: minimum paper TOEFL 550 or minimum internet TOEFL 79.

Application deadline: 3/1
Notification: Rolling starting 9/1
Average GPA: 3.2
ACT Composite Avg: 21
SAT Math Avg: 500 (340-720)
SAT Critical Reading Avg: 494 (370-720)
SAT Writing Avg: 462 (270-690)
Graduated top 10% of class: 13
Graduated top 25% of class: 39
Graduated top 50% of class: 79

COLLEGE GRADUATION REQUIREMENTS

Course waivers allowed: Yes
In what course: Individually considered
Course substitutions allowed: Yes
In what course: Individually considered

Additional Information

Environment: This public school was founded in 1889. It has a 682-acre campus.

Student Body
Undergrad enrollment: 8,787
% Women: 54
% Men: 46
% Out-of-state: 6.8

Cost information
In-state Tuition: $3,669
Out-of Tuition: $14,062
Room & board: $8,016

Housing Information
University Housing: Yes
Percent living on campus: 42.3

Greek System
Fraternity: Yes
Sorority: Yes
Athletics: Division I

Dakota College at Bottineau

105 Simrall Boulevard, Bottineau, ND 58318
Phone: 800-542-6866 • Fax: 701-288-5499
E-mail: ken.grosz@dakotacollege.edu • Web: www.misu-b.nodak.edu
Support: CS • Institution type: 2-year Public

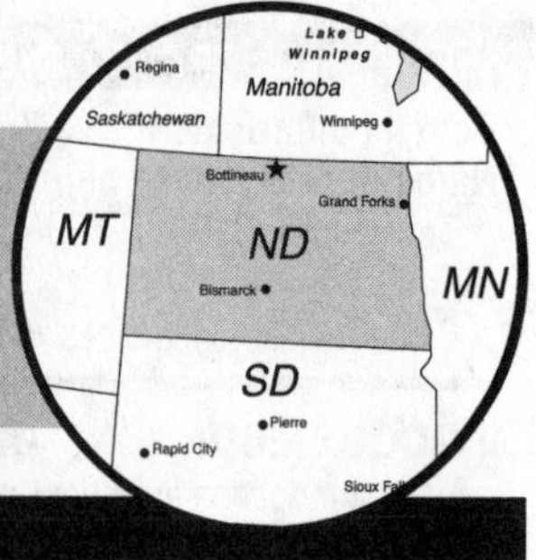

Programs or Services for Students with Learning Differences

The Learning Center provides a variety of academic support services to eligible students with LD. The Learning Center also provides individualized or small group instruction in English, algebra, biology, basic computer use, and other areas. Individuals are also provided with services that best meet their needs. In addition, study skills and reading improvement classes are offered for credit. An LD specialist/math instructor and an English/social studies instructor provide assistance in this program. Students planning to enroll at Dakota College at Bottineau should send documentation of their disability that is no more than 3 years old to the Learning Center. The documentation should include an intelligence assessment (preferably the WAIS–R), achievement testing (such as the Woodcock-Johnson psychoeducational battery), and education recommendations such as accommodations provided in high school and a recent IEP. Students should visit the Learning Center as soon as they arrive on campus. Students will be asked to complete an application, and the Learning Center instructor will review the students' class schedules and arrange for tutoring if deemed necessary.

Admission Information for Students with Learning Differences

College entrance tests required: Yes
Interview required: No
Essay required: No
Additional Application Required for LD/ADHD/ASD: NR
What documentation required for LD: Psycho ed evaluation to include: relevant historical info, instructional interventions, related services, age diagnosed, objective data (aptitude, achievement, info processing), test scores (standard, percentile and grade equivalents) and describe functional limitations.
With general application: No
To receive services after enrolling: Yes
What documentation required for ADHD: Diagnosis based on DSM-V; history of behaviors impairing functioning in academic setting; diagnostic interview; history of symptoms; evidence of ongoing behaviors.
With general application: No
To receive services after enrolling: Yes
What documentation required for ASD: Psycho ed evaluation
With general application: NR
To receive services after enrolling: Yes
LD/ADHD/ASD documentation submitted to: Learning Center
ASD Specific Program: NR
Special Ed. HS course work accepted: Yes
Specific course requirements of all applicants: NR
Separate application required: No
Total # of students receiving LD/ADHD/ASD services: 10–20
Acceptance into program means acceptance into college: Students must be admitted to and enrolled in the university first and then request services.

Admissions

Dakota College at Bottineau has an open admission policy. Applicants must present a high school diploma or equivalent such as a GED. Standardized tests are not required. Students are encouraged to self-disclose their disability during the application process so that the university may provide information about accessing support once enrolled. All students who enroll are asked to complete a questionnaire that asks them to identify academic support services that they feel they may need once on campus.

Additional Information

The Learning Center offers free tutoring and is open to all students. Sessions are adapted to fit a student's schedule. Individual tutoring is available. Students may receive accommodations that include class scheduling, though priority registration is not offered. Skills courses are offered in note-taking strategies, test-taking tips, and memory aids. There is a one-credit reading improvement course that helps improve reading comprehension. Additional accommodations based on appropriate documentation could include extended testing times, note-takers, distraction-free testing environments, tape recorders in class, and e-text versions of textbooks.

General Support Services Information

Contact Information
Name of program or department: Learning Center
Telephone: 701-228-5479
Fax: 701-228-5614

Accommodations or Services for Students with Learning Differences

Accommodations are decided upon an individual basis after a thorough review of appropriate, current documentation. The accommodations requested must be supported through the documentation provided and must be logically linked to the current impact of the condition on academic functioning.

Allowed in exams
Calculator: Yes
Dictionary: Yes
Computer: Yes
Spellchecker: Yes
Extended test time: Yes
Scribes: NR
Proctors: NR
Oral exams: Yes
Note-takers: Yes
Services for students with LD: Yes
Services for students with ADHD: Yes
Services for students with ASD: Yes
Distraction-reduced environment: Yes
Tape recording in class: Yes
Audio books: NR
Electronic texts: Yes
Kurzweil Reader: No
Other assistive technology: Yes
Priority registration: No
Added costs for services: No
LD specialists: Yes
ADHD coaching: NR
ASD specialists: NR
Professional tutors: 2
Peer tutors: 2–5
Max. hours/wk. for services: Varies
How professors are notified of LD/ADHD: By both student and director

General Admissions Information

Office of Admission: 800-542-6866

Entrance Requirements

High school diploma is required, and GED is accepted.

Application deadline: None
Average GPA: 3.1
ACT Composite middle 50% range: 19–24
SAT Math middle 50% range: N/A
SAT Critical Reading middle 50% range: N/A
SAT Writing middle 50% range: N/A
Graduated top 10% of class: NR
Graduated top 25% of class: NR
Graduated top 50% of class: NR

COLLEGE GRADUATION REQUIREMENTS

Course waivers allowed: No
Course substitutions allowed: No

Additional Information

Environment: The campus is located in a small town 80 miles from Minot, North Dakota.

Student Body
Undergrad enrollment: 812
% Women: 48%
% Men: 52%
% Out-of-state: 26%

Cost Information
In-state tuition: $3,856
Out-of-state tuition: $5,416
Room & board: $4,950

Housing Information
University housing: Yes
% Living on campus: N/A

Greek System
Fraternity: No
Sorority: No
Athletics: NAIA

North Dakota State University

PO Box 6050, Dept 5230, Fargo, ND 58108
Phone: 701-231-8643 • Fax: 701-231-8802
E-mail: ndsu.admission@ndsu.edu • Web: www.ndsu.edu
Support: S • Institution: Public

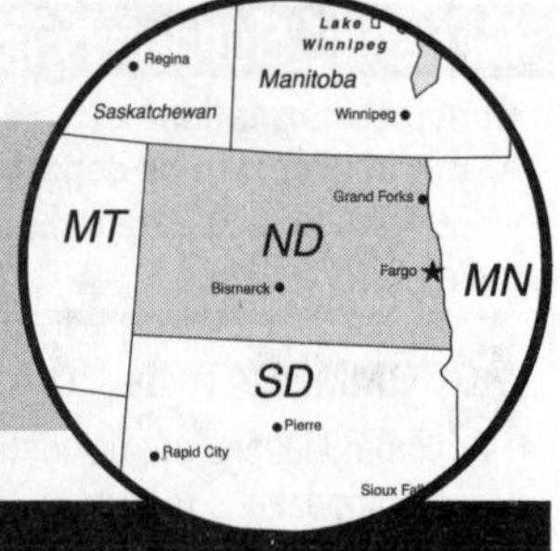

Programs or Services for Students with Learning Differences

The mission of NDSU Disability Services is to ensure equal access to educational opportunities for students with disabilities to fully participate in the university environment. Disability Services (DS) assists both students with disabilities, and faculty and staff working with students with disabilities. DS staff members can provide individual consultation regarding the possible presence of a disability, making referrals when appropriate; determine eligibility for accommodations and services, explain how to access services, provide assistance when arranging accommodations; consult with students, faculty and staff and partner with NDSU personnel to implement appropriate accommodations; and make referrals to other available support services. Disability Services staff members work to promote equal access to academic programs, promote self-awareness and advocacy skill development, educate campus community about disability-related issues and collaborate with various support services.

Admission Information for Students with Learning Differences

College entrance tests required: Yes
Interview required: N/A
Essay required: N/A
Additional Application Required for LD/ADHD/ASD: NR
What documentation required for LD: Psycho ed evaluation to include: relevant historical info, instructional interventions, related services, age diagnosed, objective data (aptitude, achievement, info processing), test scores (standard, percentile and grade equivalents) and describe functional limitations.
With general application: No
To receive services after enrolling: Yes
What documentation required for ADHD: Diagnosis based on DSM-V; history of behaviors impairing functioning in academic setting; diagnostic interview; history of symptoms; evidence of ongoing behaviors.
With general application: No
To receive services after enrolling: Yes
What documentation required for ASD: Psycho ed evaluation
With general application: NR
To receive services after enrolling: Yes
LD/ADHD/ASD documentation submitted to: Disability Services
ASD Specific Program: NR
Special Ed. HS course work accepted: N/A
Specific course requirements of all applicants: Yes
Separate application required: No
Total # of students receiving LD/ADHD/ASD services: NR
Acceptance into program means acceptance into college: Students must be admitted to and enrolled in the university first and then request services.

Admissions

Students with learning disabilities submit the general application form and are expected to meet the same admission standards as all other applicants. The ACT range is 20-22, and the minimum GPA is 2.5. Applicants are expected to have taken high school courses in math, including algebra; English; science labs; and social studies. Students with learning disabilities may include a self-disclosure or information explaining or documenting their disability.

Additional Information

Skills courses are offered. A technology lab/resource room is available for student use. Individual, career, and academic counseling along with support groups are available through the NDSU Counseling Center. TRIO-Student Support Services Program provides tutoring and small group instruction in study strategies, reading, computers, math, and science. The Academic Collegiate Experience (ACE) offers group tutoring. Individuals with learning disabilities or attention deficit hyperactive disorder may utilize these services. Students need to apply and qualify for TRIO-Student Support Services.

General Support Services Information

Contact Information
Name of program or department: Disability Services
Telephone: 701-231-8463
Fax: 701-231-5205

Accommodations or Services for Students with Learning Differences

Accommodations are decided on an individual, case-by-case basis after a thorough review of appropriate, current documentation and a student intake. The accommodations requested must be supported by the documentation provided and are based on the functional limitations of the disability.

Allowed in exams
Calculator: Yes
Dictionary: NR
Computer: NR
Spellchecker: NR
Extended test time: Yes
Scribes: Yes
Proctors: Yes
Oral exams: Yes
Note-takers: Yes
Services for students with LD: Yes
Services for students with ADHD: Yes
Services for students with ASD: Yes
Distraction-reduced environment: Yes
Tape recording in class: Yes
Audio books: NR
Electronic texts: Yes
Kurzweil Reader: Yes
Other assistive technology: Yes
Priority registration: Yes
Added costs for services: No
LD specialists: No
ADHD coaching: NR
ASD specialists: NR
Professional tutors: No
Peer tutors: 20–50
Max. hours/wk. for services: Unlimited
How professors are notified of LD/ADHD: By student

General Admissions Information

Office of Admissions: 701-231-8643

Entrance Requirements

Academic units required: 4 English, 3 math, 3 science, 3 science labs, 3 social studies. High school diploma is required and GED is accepted. SAT or ACT required. If ACT, ACT with writing accepted. TOEFL required of all international applicants: minimum paper TOEFL 525 or minimum internet TOEFL 71.

Application deadline: 8/1
Notification: Rolling starting 8/1
Average GPA: 3.43
ACT Composite middle 50% range: 21-26
SAT Math middle 50% range: 500-630
SAT Critical Reading middle 50% range: 480-630
SAT Writing middle 50% range: 460-520
Graduate top 10% of class: 15
Graduated top 25% of class: 41
Graduated top 50% of class: 71

COLLEGE GRADUATION REQUIREMENTS

Course waivers allowed: NR
Course substitutions allowed: NR

Additional Information

Environment: This public school was founded in 1890. It has a 258-acre campus.

Student Body
Undergrad enrollment: 12,037
% Women: 45
% Men: 55
% Out-of-state: 57

Cost information
Out-of-state Tuition: $16,381
Room & board: $6,910

Housing Information
University Housing: Yes
Percent living on campus: 36

Greek System
Fraternity: Yes
Sorority: Yes
Athletics: Division I

UNIVERSITY OF JAMESTOWN

6081 College Lane, Jamestown, ND 58405-0001
Phone: 701-252-3467 • Fax: 701-253-4318
E-mail: admissions@uj.edu • Web: www.uj.edu
Support: CS • Institution: Private

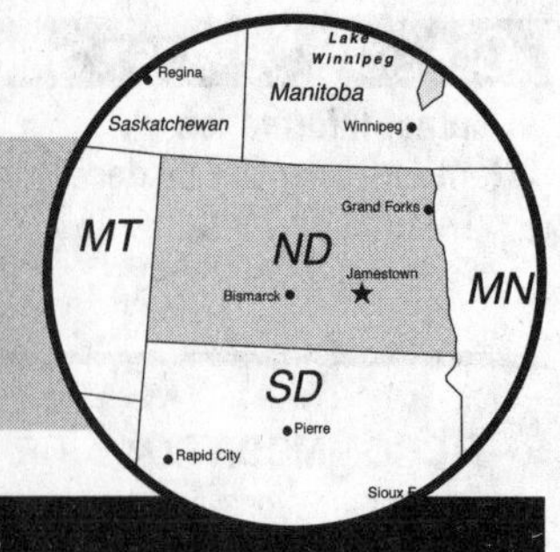

PROGRAMS OR SERVICES FOR STUDENTS WITH LEARNING DIFFERENCES

The Learning and Academic Advising Center mission statement is to create a purposeful,learner-centered environment that supports students' academic development. The Academic Advising program is designed to help students design an educational plan that is compatible with their goals.

ADMISSION INFORMATION FOR STUDENTS WITH LEARNING DIFFERENCES

College entrance test required: Yes
Interview required: No
Essay required: Not Applicable
Additional Application Required for LD/ADHD/ASD: NR
What documentation required for LD: Documentation that outlines diagnosis and functioning limitations of the disability
With general application: No
To receive services after enrolling: Yes
What documentation required for ADHD: Documentation that outlines diagnosis and functioning limitations of the disability
With general application: No
To receive services after enrolling: Yes
What documentation required for ASD: Documentation that outlines diagnosis and functioning limitations of the disability
With general application: No
To receive services after enrolling: Yes
LD/ADHD/ASD documentation submitted to: Learning and Academic Advising Center
ASD Specific Program: NR
Special Ed. HS course work accepted: Yes
Specific course requirements of all applicants: Yes
Separate application required for program services: True
Total # of students receiving LD/ADHD/ASD services: 37
Acceptance into program means acceptance into college: No

ADMISSIONS

The application gives the admissions counselors insight into the student. University of Jamestown undergraduate Admissions Criteria is a GPA of 2.5 and an minimum ACT of 19. Each applicant is reviewed on an individual basis.

ADDITIONAL INFORMATION

The student is encouraged to meet with the director of the Learning and Academic Advising Center when they arrive on campus to register with disability services, determine accommodations, and find out about available resource. The Center will help identify and coordinate reasonable accommodations for qualified students with disabilities. Each incoming first year student is assigned a faculty advisor. Tis faculty member will be available to answer any questions about academic programs. The Center also provides assistance with reading skills, study skills and time management. Their peer tutors are specially trained to assist students in most subject areas. It's free of charge.

GENERAL SUPPORT SERVICES INFORMATION

Contact Information
Name of program or department: Learning and Academic Advising Center
Telephone: 7012523467
Fax: 7012534318
Website: www.uj.edu

ACCOMMODATIONS OR SERVICES FOR STUDENTS WITH LEARNING DIFFERENCES

Accommodations are decided upon an individual basis after a thorough review of appropriate, current documentation. The accommodations requests must be supported through the documentation provided and must be logically linked to the current impact of the condition on academic functioning.

Allowed in exams
Calculator: Yes
Dictionary: Yes
Computer: Yes
Spellchecker: Yes
Extended test time: Yes
Scribes: Not Applicable
Proctors: Yes
Oral exams: Yes
Note-takers: Yes
Support services for students with LD: Yes
Support services for students with ADHD: Yes
Support services for students with ASD: Yes
Distraction-reduced environment: Yes
Tape recording in class: Yes
Electronic texts: Not Applicable
Kurzweil reader: NR
Audio books: No
Other assistive technology: Not Applicable
Priority registration: No
Added costs of services: No
LD specialists: Yes
ADHD coaching: No
ASD specialists: No
Professional tutors: No
Peer tutors: Yes
Max. hours/wk. for services: NR
How professors are notified of student approved accommodations: By both student and director

GENERAL ADMISSIONS INFORMATION

Office of Admissions: 701-252-3467

ENTRANCE REQUIREMENTS

Academic units recommended: 4 English, 3 math, 4 science, 2 foreign language, 3 social studies, High school diploma is required and GED is accepted. SAT or ACT required. If ACT, ACT with writing accepted. TOEFL required of all international applicants: minimum paper TOEFL 525 or minimum internet TOEFL 70.

Application deadline: NR
Notification: Rolling starting 8/1
Average GPA: 3.46
ACT Composite middle 50% range: 18-28
SAT Math middle 50% range: 385-581
SAT Critical Reading middle 50% range: 371-579
SAT Writing middle 50% range: NR-NR
Graduate top 10% of class: 20
Graduated top 25% of class: 41
Graduated top 50% of class: 49

COLLEGE GRADUATION REQUIREMENTS

Course waivers allowed: Yes
In what course: A petition process is in place for all students to petition a general education requirement.
Course substitutions allowed: Yes
In what course: A petition process is in place for all students to petition a general education requirement.

ADDITIONAL INFORMATION

Environment: This private school, affiliated with the Presbyterian Church, was founded in 1883. It has a 110-acre campus.

Student Body
Undergrad enrollment: 888
% Women: 52
% Men: 48
% Out-of-state: 53

Cost information
Tuition:$19,930
Room & board: $7,066

Housing Information
University Housing: Yes
Percent living on campus: 76

Greek System
Fraternity: No
Sorority: No
Athletics: NAIA

Bowling Green State University

110 McFall Center, Bowling Green, OH 43403-0085
Phone: 419-372-BGSU • Fax: 419-372-6955
E-mail: choosebgsu@bgsu.edu • Web: www.bgsu.edu
Support: S • Institution: Public

Programs or Services for Students with Learning Differences

The philosophy of the university is to level the playing field for students with LD and/or ADHD through the provision of appropriate accommodations and advocacy. The Office of Disability Services is evidence of BGSU's commitment to provide a support system that assists in conquering obstacles that persons with disabilities may encounter as they pursue their educational goals and activities. ODS provides services on an as-needed basis. The Study Skills Lab is open to all BGSU students, and the extent of participation is determined by the student. No grades are given in the lab, participation is voluntary, and the program is individualized. The lab is not a tutorial service, but students will be shown efficient techniques for studying, reading textbooks, taking notes, time management, and strategies for effective test-taking and test-preparation.

Admission Information for Students with Learning Differences

College entrance test required: Yes
Interview required: No
Essay required: Yes
Additional Application Required for LD/ADHD/ASD: NR
What documentation required for LD: Psychoeducational evaluation
With general application: No
To receive services after enrolling: Yes
What documentation required for ADHD: Neuropsychological Evaluation, Developmental History
With general application: No
To receive services after enrolling: Yes
What documentation required for ASD: Psycho ed evaluation
With general application: No
To receive services after enrolling: Yes
LD/ADHD/ASD documentation submitted to: Support program/services
ASD Specific Program: NR
Special Ed. HS course work accepted: No
Specific course: Yes
Separate application required for program services: No
Total # of students receiving LD/ADHD/ASD services: NR
Acceptance into program means acceptance into college: NR

Admissions

There is no special application or special admissions process. Core courses preferred include: 4 years English, 3 years math, 3 years science, 3 years social studies, 2 years foreign language, 1 year art. Students with LD may substitute foreign language with another core course. The minimum GPA is approximately 2.0. Students with LD submit the regular application and are encouraged to self-disclose their LD and arrange an interview with ODS to allow staff to discuss any documentation they may require and any concerns of the students. Additional information such as school or medical history that describes specific strengths and weaknesses is helpful in determining services necessary, once the student is admitted. Information documenting the LD should be sent to ODS. Students should submit the results of a psychoeducational evaluation or other testing and documentation that establishes the presence of a specific LD. Students should indicate accommodations that have worked successfully in high school. There is a Summer Freshman Program for freshmen applicants who do not meet the academic standards for fall admission.

Additional Information

General services include priority registration; advising by sharing information on instructor's teaching and testing styles; Writing Lab for effective strategies; Study Skills Center for effective study skills, test-taking strategies, time management, and textbook reading skills; Math Lab, a walk-in lab for understanding basic and advanced concepts; computerized technology; note-takers, readers, and scribes; letters to professors explaining the disability and modifications needed; advocacy; and books on tape. To be eligible for test accommodations, students are required to provide documentation that provides a clear indication/recommendation for the need requested. Staff work with the student to reach consensus on the type of accommodation. Test accommodations may include extended time, oral exams, take-home exams, open-book exams, readers, scribes, computers and spellcheck or grammar check, calculators, scratch paper, speller's dictionaries, question clarification, modification of test response format, and a quiet room.

General Support Services Information

Contact Information
Name of program or department: Office of Disability Services
Telephone: (419) 372-8495
Fax: (419) 372-8496

Accommodations or Services For Students With Learning Differences

Accommodations are decided upon an individual basis after a thorough review of appropriate, current documentation. The accommodations requests must be supported through the documentation provided and must be logically linked to the current impact of the condition on academic functioning.

Allowed in exams
Calculator: Yes
Dictionary: Yes
Computer: Yes
Spellchecker: Yes
Extended test time: Yes
Scribes: Yes
Proctors: Yes
Oral exams: Yes
Note-takers: Yes
Support services for students with LD: Yes
Support services for students with ADHD: Yes
Support services for students with ASD: Yes
Distraction-reduced environment: Yes
Tape recording in class: Yes
Electronic texts: Yes
Kurzweil reader: NR
Audio books: Yes
Other assistive technology: Yes
Priority registration: Yes
Added costs of services: No
LD specialists: No
ADHD coaching: NR
ASD specialists: No
Professional tutors: No
Peer tutors: NR
Max. hours/wk. for services: NR
How professors are notified of student approved accommodations: By student

General Admissions Information

Office of Admissions: 419-372-BGSU

Entrance Requirements

Academic units recommended: 4 English, 3 math, 3 science, 2 science labs, 2 foreign language, 3 social studies, 1 visual/performing arts. High school diploma is required and GED is accepted. SAT or ACT required. If ACT, ACT with writing accepted. TOEFL required of all international applicants: minimum paper TOEFL 530 or minimum internet TOEFL 71.

Application deadline: 7/15
Notification: Rolling starting 8/1
Average GPA: 3.3
ACT Composite middle 50% range: 20-25
SAT Math middle 50% range: 460-580
SAT Critical Reading middle 50% range: 460-580
SAT Writing middle 50% range: 420-550
Graduate top 10% of class: 12
Graduated top 25% of class: 36
Graduated top 50% of class: 71

COLLEGE GRADUATION REQUIREMENTS

Course waivers allowed: No
Course substitutions allowed: Yes

Additional Information

Environment: This public school was founded in 1910. It has a 1250-acre campus.

Student Body
Undergrad enrollment: 14,334
% Women: 57
% Men: 43
% Out-of-state: 12

Cost information
Out-of-state Tuition: $16,632
Room & board: $8,496

Housing Information
University Housing: Yes
Percent living on campus: 42

Greek System
Fraternity: Yes
Sorority: Yes
Athletics: Division I

Case Western Reserve University

Wolstein Hall, Cleveland, OH 44106-7055
Phone: 216-368-4450 • Fax: 216-368-5111
E-mail: admission@case.edu • Web: www.case.edu
Support: CS • Institution: Private

Programs or Services for Students with Learning Differences

Disability Services are provided through the broader Educational Support Services Department in Student Affairs. Disability Services assists qualified students with disabilities to fully participate in their chosen programs at CWRU. Disability Services provides academic support, special accommodations and personal advising around disability issues. Students must provide current and appropriate documentation from a qualified professional in order to be considered for services.

Admission Information for Students with Learning Differences

College entrance test required: Yes
Interview required: No
Essay required: Not Applicable
Additional Application Required for LD/ADHD/ASD: No
What documentation required for LD: We request a neuropsychological evaluation or narrative from a qualified professional with a history with the student.
With general application: Not Applicable
To receive services after enrolling: No
What documentation required for ADHD: We prefer a neuropsychological evaluation but will accept a narrative from any qualified specialist the student has worked with on an on-going basis.
With general application: Not Applicable
To receive services after enrolling: No
What documentation required for ASD: We request a neuropsychological evaluation from a qualified specialist.
With general application: Not Applicable
To receive services after enrolling: No
LD/ADHD/ASD documentation submitted to: Disability Resources
ASD Specific Program: Social Skills Group
Special Ed. HS course work accepted: Yes
Specific course requirements of all applicants: NR
Separate application required for program services: No
Total # of students receiving LD/ADHD/ASD services: NR
Acceptance into program means acceptance into college: Not Applicable

Admissions

Students with learning disabilities are encouraged to apply to CWRU. Admission is highly competitive, but all applicants are evaluated on an individual basis. General admission criteria include: 4 years English, 3 years math, 3 years social science, 1 year science, and 2–4 years foreign language. Students must also submit a writing sample and are encouraged to have an interview. Most admitted students rank in the top 20 percent of their class and have an SAT I of 1180–1380 or an ACT of 27–31.

Additional Information

Students at Case are not required to disclose disability information to anyone. However, in order to use services and appropriate accommodations, students should notify Disability Resources in Educational Services for Students, 470 Sears Building. The associate director of disability resources or any other Education Services for Students staff member that is aware of a student's disability will keep this information confidential. Students decide who needs to know about their disability. ESS is the only department that will determine eligibility. Disability Resources will work closely with students and design an individual plan for accommodations. Included in that plan are strategies for disclosure to professors as well as identifying specific accommodations that will be needed for each course. Accommodations and services are available for students with a variety of disabilities including learning disabilities. The legal definition states that any mental of physical impairment that substantially limits one or more major life activity is a disability. Students are "fitted" with the services and accommodations that will be most helpful for their particular needs. Case is able to offer the following: testing accommodations, adaptive equipment and assistive technology, scheduling assistance. alternate format for print materials, note-taking assistance, and interpreters. This list is not exhaustive and other accommodations may be appropriate.

General Support Services Information

Contact Information
Name of program or department: Disability Resources
Telephone: (216) 368-5230
Fax: (216) 368-8826
Website: NR

Accommodations or Services For Students With Learning Differences

Accommodations are decided upon an individual basis after a thorough review of appropriate, current documentation. The accommodations requests must be supported through the documentation provided and must be logically linked to the current impact of the condition on academic functioning.

Allowed in exams
Calculator: Yes
Dictionary: Not Applicable
Computer: Yes
Spellchecker: Not Applicable
Extended test time: Yes
Scribes: Yes
Proctors: Yes
Oral exams: Yes
Note-takers: Yes
Support services for students with LD: Yes
Support services for students with ADHD: Yes
Support services for students with ASD: Yes
Distraction-reduced environment: Yes
Tape recording in class: Yes
Electronic texts: Yes
Kurzweil reader: NR
Audio books: Yes
Other assistive technology: Yes
Priority registration: Yes
Added costs of services: No
LD specialists: Yes
ADHD coaching: Yes
ASD specialists: Yes
Professional tutors: No
Peer tutors: Yes
Max. hours/wk. for services: 5
How professors are notified of student approved accommodations: By both student and director

General Admissions Information

Office of Admissions: 216-368-4450

Entrance Requirements

Academic units required: 4 English, 3 math, 3 science, 2 science labs, 2 foreign language, 3 social studies. **Academic units recommended:** 4 math, 3 science labs, 3 foreign language, 4 social studies. High school diploma is required and GED is accepted. SAT or ACT required. If ACT, ACT with writing required. TOEFL required of all international applicants: minimum paper TOEFL 577 or minimum internet TOEFL 90.

Application deadline: 1/15
Notification: 3/20
Average GPA: NR
ACT Composite middle 50% range: 30-33
SAT Math middle 50% range: 680-770
SAT Critical Reading middle 50% range: 620-720
SAT Writing middle 50% range: 620-720
Graduate top 10% of class: 71
Graduated top 25% of class: 91
Graduated top 50% of class: 99

COLLEGE GRADUATION REQUIREMENTS

Course waivers allowed: No
Course substitutions allowed: Yes
In what course: Math

Additional Information

Environment: This private school was founded in 1826. It has a 155-acre campus.

Student Body
Undergrad enrollment: 5,121
% Women: 45
% Men: 55
% Out-of-state: 60

Cost information
Tuition: $44,156
Room & board: $13,850
Housing Information
University Housing: Yes
Percent living on campus: 80

Greek System
Fraternity: Yes
Sorority: Yes
Athletics: Division III

Cedarville University

251 N.Main Street Cedarville, OH 45314
Phone: 937-766-7700 • Fax: 937-766-7575
E-mail: admiss@cedarville.edu • Web: www.cedarville.edu

Support: S • Institution: Private

Programs or Services for Students with Learning Differences

The mission of Disability Services is to facilitate an environment where students with a diagnosed disability can have equal access to educational opportunities and campus life. Each student who applies to Disability Services is evaluated on an individual basis. The office will generate an official Letter of Accommodation that specifies the student's approved accommodations. There is also an Academic Peer Coaching service, mentors and resources to help with anxiety, time management, concentration and more.

Admission Information for Students with Learning Differences

College entrance test required: Yes
Interview required: No
Essay required: Not Applicable
Additional Application Required for LD/ADHD/ASD: No
What documentation required for LD: Documentation is recommended. There is a process.
With general application: Not Applicable
To receive services after enrolling: No
What documentation required for ADHD: Documentation is recommended. There is a process.
With general application: Not Applicable
To receive services after enrolling: No
What documentation required for ASD: Documentation is recommended. There is a process.
With general application: Not Applicable
To receive services after enrolling: No
LD/ADHD/ASD documentation submitted to: Disability Services at The Cove
ASD Specific Program: NR
Special Ed. HS course work accepted: Not Applicable
Specific course requirements of all applicants: Yes
Separate application required for program services: False
Total # of students receiving LD/ADHD/ASD services: 50
Acceptance into program means acceptance into college: Not Applicable

Admissions

3.0 GPA, 21 ACT, and file review; if below but close to criteria, students are placed into foundation courses.

Additional Information

Cedarville University Disability Services for students is a part of the Academic Enrichment Center-The Cove. The Cove provides academic resources and support to facilitate learning. There is one-on-one consultations, meeting with learning specialists, supplemental instruction and learning and study strategies. There is help with time management, reading and comprehension, dorm room organization and note-taking.

General Support Services Information

Contact Information
Name of program or department: Disability Services at The Cove
Telephone: 937-766-7437
Fax: 937-766-7419
Website: http://www.cedarville.edu/Offices/Academic-Enrichment/Disabilities.aspx

Accommodations or Services for Students with Learning Differences

Accommodations are decided upon an individual basis after a thorough review of appropriate, current documentation. The accommodations requests must be supported through the documentation provided and must be logically linked to the current impact of the condition on academic functioning.

Allowed in exams
Calculator: Yes
Dictionary: Yes
Computer: Yes
Spellchecker: Yes
Extended test time: Yes
Scribes: Yes
Proctors: Yes
Oral exams: Yes
Note-takers: Yes
Support services for students with LD: Yes
Support services for students with ADHD: Yes
Support services for students with ASD: Yes
Distraction-reduced environment: Yes
Tape recording in class: Yes
Electronic texts: Yes
Kurzweil reader: NR
Audio books: Yes
Other assistive technology: Yes
Priority registration: Yes
Added costs of services: No
LD specialists: Yes
ADHD coaching: Yes
ASD specialists: Yes
Professional tutors: No
Peer tutors: Yes
Max. hours/wk. for services: NR
How professors are notified of student approved accommodations: By both student and director

General Admissions Information

Office of Admissions: 937-766-7700

Entrance Requirements

Academic units recommended: 4 English, 2 science labs, 3 foreign language, 2 social studies, 2 history. High school diploma is required and GED is accepted. SAT or ACT required. If ACT, ACT with writing accepted. TOEFL required of all international applicants: minimum paper TOEFL 550 or minimum internet TOEFL 80.

Application deadline: 8/1
Notification: Rolling starting 9/1
Average GPA: 3.64
ACT Composite middle 50% range: 23-28
SAT Math middle 50% range: 520-640
SAT Critical Reading middle 50% range: 540-650
SAT Writing middle 50% range: 520-630
Graduate top 10% of class: 30
Graduated top 25% of class: 61
Graduated top 50% of class: 86

COLLEGE GRADUATION REQUIREMENTS

Course waivers allowed: Yes
In what course: math, foreign language; if appropriate - case by case basis
Course substitutions allowed: Yes
In what course: math, foreign language; if appropriate - case by case basis

Additional Information

Environment: This private school, affiliated with the Baptist Church, was founded in 1887. It has a 400-acre campus.

Student Body
Undergrad enrollment: 3,353
% Women: 52
% Men: 48
% Out-of-state: 61.3

Cost information
Tuition: $27,910
Room & board: $6,880

Housing Information
University Housing: Yes
Percent living on campus: 83.6

Greek System
Fraternity: No
Sorority: No
Athletics: Division II

Central Ohio Technical College

1179 University Drive, Newark, OH 43055-1767
Phone: 740-366-9222 • Fax: 740-364-9531
E-mail: thoudesh@cotc.edu • Web: www.cotc.edu
Support: CS • Institution type: 2-year Public

Programs or Services for Students with Learning Differences

Technical College and The Ohio State University at Newark ODS provides FREE programs and services designed to help students have full access to college life. All students are encouraged to contact the Office for Disability Services in the early stages of their college planning. Pre admission services include information about academic support services, specialized equipment, transition issues, admission requirements, and meetings with staff counselors.

Admission Information for Students with Learning Differences

College entrance test required: No
Interview required: N/A
Essay required: No
Additional Application Required for LD/ADHD/ASD: NR
What documentation required for LD: Psychological report, IEP, MFE/ETR, or other diagnostic assessments
With general application: No
To receive services after enrolling: Yes
What documentation required for ADHD: Psychological report, IEP, MFE/ETR, or other diagnostic assessments
With general application: No **To receive services after enrolling:** Yes
What documentation required for ASD: Psychological report, IEP, MFE/ETR, or other diagnostic assessments
With general application: No
To receive services after enrolling: Yes
LD/ADHD/ASD documentation submitted to: Support program/services
ASD Specific Program: NR
Special Ed. HS course work accepted: N/A
Specific course: No
Separate application required for program services: No
Total # of students receiving LD/ADHD/ASD services: NR
Acceptance into program means acceptance into college: NR

Admissions

Admission is open to all applicants with a high school diploma or the GED, except in health programs. There are no specific course requirements. ACT/SAT tests are not required. The application process is the same for all students. There is no requirement to provide disability-related information to the Admissions Office. Documentation of your disability should be sent directly to DS. Eligibility for services/accommodations from DS is a separate process from admissions. All prospective students are encouraged to contact DS in the early stages of their college planning. Preadmission services include information about academic support services, transition issues, admission requirements, and appropriate documentation and meetings with staff disability professionals.

Additional Information

A degree modification, or course requirement substitution is permitted if the modification does not constitute a fundamental change in the degree and is supported by the student's documentation of a disability. In order to substitute a required class, the student files an appeal petition, discusses the academic difficulties with ODS and requests assistance from ODS in the petition process. Students meet with the advisor for the degree, and discusses the disability related needs and potential modifications. Once a substitution is determined, the student completes the course information on the Petition to Substitute Required Course form. Lastly, the student returns to the ODS and requests that the appropriate staff member help complete the "Academic Reason(s) Justification for the Request" section of the form. If the request is reasonable, the staff member advocates for the student throughout the process. The Tutoring Center and the Assistive Technology Lab are for students with learning disabilities and ADHD. All students are automatically eligible for services. The tutoring program includes peer tutoring in almost any course, scheduled at the student's convenience for 2 hours each week per course. The Assistive Technology Lab has resources to improve reading, math, and language skills; word processing; and study aids for some courses and national tests. The Study Skills Workshop Series provides assistance in improving study skills and 50-minute workshops on time management, learning styles/memory, test preparation and taking, reading textbooks effectively, and note taking. Students also have access to proctors, individualized instruction designed to meet special needs, advocacy assistance, coaching, and assistance with accommodations.

General Support Services Information

Contact Information
Name of program or department: Office for Disability Services
Telephone: 740-366-9441
Fax: 740-364-9646

Accommodations or Services for Students with Learning Differences

Accommodations are decided upon an individual basis after a thorough review of appropriate, current documentation. The accommodations requests must be supported through the documentation provided and must be logically linked to the current impact of the condition on academic functioning.

Allowed in exams
Calculator: Yes
Dictionary: No
Computer: Yes
Spellchecker: No
Extended test time: Yes
Scribes: Yes
Proctors: Yes
Oral exams: Yes
Note-takers: Yes
Services for students with LD: Yes
Services for students with ADHD: Yes
Services for students with ASD: Yes
Distraction-reduced environment: Yes
Tape recording in class: Yes
Audio books from learning ally: Yes
Electronic texts: NR
Kurzweil Reader: Yes
Other assistive technology: Yes
Priority registration: No
Added costs of services: No
LD specialists: Yes
ADHD coaching: NR
ASD specialists: NR
Professional tutors: Yes
Peer tutors: Yes
Max. hours/wk. for services: NR
How professors are notified of student approved accommodations: Student

General Admissions Information

Office of Admission: 740-366-9222

Entrance Requirements

Open admissions. High school diploma or GED accepted. ACT score of 14 on the English section and 15 on the Math section. Some programs have additional requirements.

Application deadline: None
Average GPA: NR
ACT Composite middle 50% range: NR
SAT Math middle 50% range: NR
SAT Critical Reading middle 50% range: NR
SAT Writing middle 50% range: NR
Graduated top 10% of class: NR
Graduated top 25% of class: NR
Graduated top 50% of class: NR

COLLEGE GRADUATION REQUIREMENTS

Course waivers allowed: No
Course substitutions allowed: No

Additional Information

Environment: The campus is located in a small town with easy access to Columbus.

Student Body
Undergrad enrollment: 3,725
% Women: 71
% Men: 29
% Out-of-state: 1

Cost information
In-state Tuition: $4,200
Out-of-state Tuition: $6,960
Room & board: NR

Housing Information
University Housing: NR
Percent living on campus: 1

Greek System
Fraternity: No
Sorority: No
Athletics: NR

College of Mount St. Joseph

5701 Delhi Road, Cincinnati, OH 45233
Phone: 513-244-4531 • Fax: 513-244-4629
E-mail: admissions@mail.msj.edu • Web: www.msj.edu
Support: SP • Institution: Private

Programs or Services for Students with Learning Differences

Project EXCEL is a comprehensive academic support program for students with learning disabilities enrolled in the college. The program's goals are to assist students in the transition from a secondary program to a college curriculum and to promote the development of learning strategies and compensatory skills that will enable students to achieve success in a regular academic program. The structure of the program and supportive environment at the Mount give Project EXCEL its singular quality. Project EXCEL offers students individualized attention and a variety of support services to meet specific needs, including supervised tutoring by professional tutors; monitoring of student progress; instruction in learning strategies, time management, and coping skills; and academic advising with attention to the students' specific learning needs. Students admitted to the program must maintain a 2.25 overall GPA, and their progress is evaluated on an ongoing basis.

Admission Information for Students with Learning Differences

College entrance test required: Yes
Interview required: Yes
Essay required: Yes
Additional Application Required for LD/ADHD/ASD: NR
What documentation required for LD: Psychoeducational evaluation less than 3 years old
With general application: No
To receive services after enrolling: Yes
What documentation required for ADHD: Yes
With general application: No
To receive services after enrolling: Yes
What documentation required for ASD: Psycho ed evaluation
With general application: No
To receive services after enrolling: Yes
LD/ADHD/ASD documentation submitted to: Support program/services
ASD Specific Program: NR
Special Ed. HS course work accepted: Yes
Specific course: Yes
Separate application required for program services: Yes
Total # of students receiving LD/ADHD/ASD services: 75
Acceptance into program means acceptance into college: NR

Admissions

Admission to Project EXCEL is multi-stepped, including: an interview with the program director; completed general admission application; completed Project EXCEL forms (general information, applicant goal and self-assessment, and educational data completed by high school); psycho-educational evaluation; transcript; ACT minimum of 15 or SAT of 700–740; and a recommendation. The application is reviewed by the Project EXCEL Director and Project EXCEL Admission Committee. The diagnostic evaluation must indicate the presence of specific LD and provide reasonable evidence that the student can successfully meet college academic requirements. Academic performance problems that exist concomitantly with a diagnosed ADD/ADHD will be considered in the review of the student's diagnostic profile. Students can be admitted to the college through Project EXCEL. Students not meeting all EXCEL admission requirements may be admitted part-time or on a probationary basis. Apply early. Other students not meeting admission requirements can take up to 6 hours per semester to a maximum of 13 hours. At that point, if they have a 2.0+ GPA they are admitted to the college.

Additional Information

Project EXCEL students are assisted with course and major selection. Students are offered individualized attention and a variety of support services to meet specific needs, including supervised tutoring, monitoring of student progress, writing lab, note takers, accommodated testing, instruction in learning strategies, time management, and coping skills; liaison with faculty and academic advising with attention to specific learning needs. Students enroll in regular classes and must fulfill the same course requirements as all Mount students. The curriculum is closely supervised, and specialized instruction is offered in writing, reading, and study skills to fit the individual needs of the students. The program director serves as student advisor.

General Support Services Information

Contact Information
Name of program or department: Project EXCEL
Telephone: 513-244-4623
Fax: 513-244-4629

Accommodations or Services for Students with Learning Differences

Accommodations are decided upon an individual basis after a thorough review of appropriate, current documentation. The accommodations requests must be supported through the documentation provided and must be logically linked to the current impact of the condition on academic functioning.

Allowed in exams
Calculator: Yes
Dictionary: Yes
Computer: Yes
Spellchecker: Yes
Extended test time: Yes
Scribes: Yes
Proctors: Yes
Oral exams: Yes
Note-takers: Yes
Services for students with LD: Yes
Services for students with ADHD: Yes
Services for students with ASD: Yes
Distraction-reduced environment: Yes
Tape recording in class: Yes
Audio books from learning ally: Yes
Electronic texts: NR
Kurzweil Reader: Yes
Other assistive technology: No
Priority registration: No
Added costs of services: Yes
LD specialists: Yes
ADHD coaching: NR
ASD specialists: NR
Professional tutors: Yes
Peer tutors: NR
Max. hours/wk. for services: NR
How professors are notified of student approved accommodations: Both student and director

General Admissions Information

Office of Admissions: 513-244-4531

Entrance Requirements

Academic units required: 4 English, 3 mathematics, 3 science, (1 science labs), 2 foreign language, 1 social studies, 1 history, 1 visual/performing arts, 1 academic elective. **Academic units recommended:** 4 English, 4 mathematics, 4 science, (2 science labs), 2 foreign language, 2 social studies, 2 history, 1 visual/performing arts, 2 academic electives. High school diploma is required and GED is accepted. SAT or ACT required. If ACT, ACT with Writing component recommended. TOEFL required of all international applicants: minimum paper TOEFL 510 or minimum web TOEFL 64.

Application deadline: 8/15
Average GPA: 3.2
ACT Composite middle 50% range: 20-24
SAT Math middle 50% range: 430-540
SAT Critical Reading middle 50% range: 430-520
SAT Writing middle 50% range: NR
Graduated top 10% of class: 16
Graduated top 25% of class: 39
Graduated top 50% of class: 73

COLLEGE GRADUATION REQUIREMENTS

Course waivers allowed: No
Course substitutions allowed: No
In what course: Decisions made on a case-by-case basis

Additional Information

Environment: The Mount is a Catholic, coeducational, liberal arts college located approximately 15 miles from downtown Cincinnati.

Student Body
Undergrad enrollment: 1,690
% Women: 62
% Men: 38
% Out-of-state: 18

Cost information
Tuition: $24,200
Room & board: $7,860

Housing Information
University housing: Yes
% Living on campus: 23

Greek System
Fraternity: No
Sorority: No
Athletics: Division III

HOCKING COLLEGE

3301 Hocking Parkway, Nelsonville, OH 45764
Phone: 740-753-3591 • Fax: 740-753-1452
E-mail: admissions@hocking.edu • Web: www.hocking.edu
Support: CS • Institution type: 2-year Public

PROGRAMS OR SERVICES FOR STUDENTS WITH LEARNING DIFFERENCES

The Accessibility Resources Office services the various needs of individuals with disabilities and is committed to promoting their full participation in college life. Accessibility services are provided for students with permanent, chronic or temporary conditions. Hocking College will make reasonable modifications to its practices and will provide certain individualized services and accommodations as needed to assure nondiscrimination on the basis of disability. Students or applicants for admission are encouraged to meet with the Accessibility Resources Office specialists. Individualized Accommodations may include: testing accommodations, referral to The Learning Connection TRIO program and the Counseling Center advising and/or counseling with priority scheduling.

ADMISSION INFORMATION FOR STUDENTS WITH LEARNING DIFFERENCES

College entrance tests required: Yes
Interview required: No
Essay required: No
Additional Application Required for LD/ADHD/ASD: NR
What documentation required for LD: Psycho ed evaluation to include: relevant historical info, instructional interventions, related services, age diagnosed, objective data (aptitude, achievement, info processing), test scores (standard, percentile and grade equivalents) and describe functional limitations.
With general application: No
To receive services after enrolling: Yes
What documentation required for ADHD: Diagnosis based on DSM-V; history of behaviors impairing functioning in academic setting; diagnostic interview; history of symptoms; evidence of ongoing behaviors.
With general application: No
To receive services after enrolling: Yes
What documentation required for ASD: Psycho ed evaluation
With general application: NR
To receive services after enrolling: Yes
LD/ADHD/ASD documentation submitted to: ACODS
ASD Specific Program: NR
Special Ed. HS course work accepted: N/A
Specific course requirements of all applicants: No
Separate application required: Yes
Total # of students receiving LD/ADHD/ASD services: 171
Acceptance into program means acceptance into college: Students must be admitted to and enrolled in the university first and then request services.

ADMISSIONS

The college has open enrollment for any student with a high school diploma or equivalent. Students are not required to take any specific courses or have any specific test score on the ACT/SAT. Students requesting accommodations or services for learning disabilities must be admitted and enrolled, and then they may request services. Current documentation should be submitted.

ADDITIONAL INFORMATION

ACODS staff and the student work together to identify individual needs and then determine which of the support services and accommodations would enable the student to achieve academic potential. Strategies used to assist students with disabilities include assistance with instructional and supportive needs; aligning interests and abilities with instructors and program effectiveness; assuring individual program implementation consistent with the identified needs of the student; evaluating problematic situations regarding modes of presentation that affect student performance and potential for success; assisting on course assignments, troubleshooting learning problems, and assisting in solutions to situations that inhibit success; helping to obtain tutoring services; priority scheduling; liaising with community agencies; and serving as an advocate. For those who qualify, the Access Center staff can assist with advising, tutoring, and test-taking and also arrange for campus transportation and classroom access. In addition, the Access Center can link students with other college services and external service agencies. Eligibility is determined on the basis of the presence of a disability and a need for services and accommodations to support an equal educational opportunity. Documentation of the disability is required as well as the student's stated experience with services and accommodations that have been effective in the past. Quest for Success is a program designed especially for new students to help them prepare to start technical classes in the fall. Additional services include professional tutors in some mathematics and communications courses, Compu-Lenz to enlarge type on a computer screen and reduce glare, academic advising, and an educational coordinator to act as a liaison with college instructors and community agencies.

General Support Services Information

Contact Information
Name of program or department: Office of Disability Services (ACODS)
Telephone: 740-753-7107
Fax: 740-753-6082

Accommodations or Services for Students with Learning Differences

Accommodations are decided upon an individual basis after a thorough review of appropriate, current documentation. The accommodations requested must be supported through the documentation provided and must be logically linked to the current impact of the condition on academic functioning.

Allowed in exams
Calculator: Yes
Dictionary: No
Computer: Yes
Spellchecker: Yes
Extended test time: Yes
Scribes: Yes
Proctors: Yes
Oral exams: Yes
Note-takers: Yes
Services for students with LD: Yes
Services for students with ADHD: Yes
Services for students with ASD: Yes
Distraction-reduced environment: Yes
Tape recording in class: Yes
Audio books: NR
Electronic texts: Yes
Kurzweil Reader: Yes
Other assistive technology: Yes
Priority registration: No
Added costs for services: No
LD specialists: Yes
ADHD coaching: NR
ASD specialists: NR
Professional tutors: 3
Peer tutors: 25–40
Max. hours/wk. for services: Unlimited
How professors are notified of LD/ADHD: By student

General Admissions Information

Office of Admission: 740-753-7049

Entrance Requirements

Academic Units Recommended: 4 English, 3 math, 3 science, 4 social studies, 2 foreign language. Open admissions. High school diploma or GED accepted. Specific ACT or SAT scores are not required.

Application deadline: None
Average GPA: NR
ACT Composite middle 50% range: NR
SAT Math middle 50% range: NR
SAT Critical Reading middle 50% range: NR
SAT Writing middle 50% range: NR
Graduated top 10% of class: NR
Graduated top 25% of class: NR
Graduated top 50% of class: NR

COLLEGE GRADUATION REQUIREMENTS

Course waivers allowed: NR
Course substitutions allowed: Yes
In what course: Any with an appropriate substitution

Additional Information

Environment: The college is located on 150 acres in a rural area with easy access to Columbus.

Student Body
Undergrad enrollment: 4,235
% Women: 50%
% Men: 50%
% Out-of-state: 2%

Cost Information
In-state tuition: $3,669
Out-of-state tuition: $7,338
Room & board: $6,300

Housing Information
University housing: Yes
% Living on campus: 10%

Greek System
Fraternity: Yes
Sorority: Yes
Athletics: Intramural

Kent State University

161 Michael Schwartz Center, Kent, OH 44242-0001
Phone: 330-672-2444 • Fax: 330-672-2499
E-mail: kentadm@kent.edu • Web: www.kent.edu
Support: CS • Institution: Public

Programs or Services for Students with Learning Differences

The goals and philosophy of the Student Accessibility Services (SAS) program are to promote student independence and self-advocacy at the college level. The university believes that the ability to do college work is highly correlated with grades in high school. Students with learning disabilities who receive accommodations in high school and who are academically successful are most likely to be successful at KSU. Students should meet with an SAS staff member approximately 6 months before enrollment to discuss needs and accommodations.

Admission Information for Students with Learning Differences

College entrance test required: NR
Interview required: No
Essay required: Not Applicable
Additional Application Required for LD/ADHD/ASD: NR
What documentation required for LD: There are multiple ways for students to provide their documentation to SAS, which can include: a. A completed Disability Verification Form completed by a licensed professional and/or properly credentialed professional (e.g. medical doctor, psychiatrist, c
With general application: NR
To receive services after enrolling: Yes
What documentation required for ADHD: There are multiple ways for students to provide their documentation to SAS, which can include: a. A completed Disability Verification Form completed by a licensed professional and/or properly credentialed professional (e.g. medical doctor, psychiatrist, c
With general application: NR
To receive services after enrolling: Yes
What documentation required for ASD: There are multiple ways for students to provide their documentation to SAS, which can include: a. A completed Disability Verification Form completed by a licensed professional and/or properly credentialed professional (e.g. medical doctor, psychiatrist, c
With general application: NR
To receive services after enrolling: Yes
LD/ADHD/ASD documentation submitted to: Student Accessibility Services
ASD Specific Program: NR
Special Ed. HS course work accepted: NR
Specific course requirements of all applicants: Yes
Separate application required for program services: NR
Total # of students receiving LD/ADHD/ASD services: NR
Acceptance into program means acceptance into college: NR

Admissions

Students with LD must meet the same admission criteria as all other applicants. There is no special admissions procedure for students with LD. Documentation of the student's disability is required. In addition to having completed standard college preparatory courses, applicants should be able to type or use a computer and a calculator and have skills in performing addition, subtraction, multiplication, and division using natural numbers, integers, fractions, and decimals. Students should also have highly developed study skills based on their specific strengths. The students most likely to be admitted and succeed are those who have completed the recommended college preparatory curriculum in high school, who have achieved a cumulative high school grade point average of 2.6 or higher, and whose composite ACT score is 21 or better (combined SAT score of 980 in critical reading and math).

Additional Information

It is recommended that all documentation be submitted prior to enrolling, although students are welcome to register with the office at any time during the academic year. All students with documentation of a learning disability may utilize the academic and counseling services, such as academic advising; developmental education courses for freshmen students with deficits in reading, writing, and math; individual and small group tutoring; support groups; and individual and group study skills help through the Academic Success Center. The peer mentoring program, through the Academic Success Center, matches a student with a personal study coach—someone who can help them acquire the skills and motivation necessary for academic success. Supplemental Instruction (SI) is a national program that offers peer-facilitated group study sessions for students enrolled in large, high-risk liberal arts and science courses. (High-risk courses are courses that have a D, F, or withdrawal rate of at least 30 percent.) The basic difference between SI and other tutoring services offered at the Academic Success Center is that SI leaders actually attend classes along with the students they are tutoring. Each SI leader has already taken the course and earned an A or a B. The writing tutoring program is designed to help all students strengthen their writing skills and develop gradually as independent writers.

General Support Services Information

Contact Information
Name of program or department: Student Accessibility Services
Telephone: 330 672 3391
Fax: 330 672 3763
Website: www.kent.edu/sas

Accommodations or Services For Students With Learning Differences

Accommodations are decided upon an individual basis after a thorough review of appropriate, current documentation. The accommodations requests must be supported through the documentation provided and must be logically linked to the current impact of the condition on academic functioning.

Allowed in exams
Calculator: Yes
Dictionary: Yes
Computer: Yes
Spellchecker: Yes
Extended test time: Yes
Scribes: Yes
Proctors: Yes
Oral exams: Yes
Note-takers: Yes
Support services for students with LD: Yes
Support services for students with ADHD: Yes
Support services for students with ASD: Yes
Distraction-reduced environment: Yes
Tape recording in class: Yes
Electronic texts: Yes
Kurzweil reader: NR
Audio books: Yes
Other assistive technology: Yes
Priority registration: Yes
Added costs of services: No
LD specialists: Yes
ADHD coaching: NR
ASD specialists: NR
Professional tutors: No
Peer tutors: Yes
Max. hours/wk. for services: NR
How professors are notified of student approved accommodations: By student

General Admissions Information

Office of Admissions: 330-672-2444

Entrance Requirements

Academic units recommended: 4 English, 4 math, 3 science, 2 science labs, 2 foreign language, 3 social studies, 1 visual/performing arts. High school diploma is required and GED is accepted. SAT or ACT required. If ACT, ACT with writing accepted. TOEFL required of all international applicants: minimum paper TOEFL 525 or minimum internet TOEFL 71.

Application deadline: 5/1
Notification: Rolling starting 10/1
Average GPA: 3.36
ACT Composite middle 50% range: 21-25
SAT Math middle 50% range: 470-580
SAT Critical Reading middle 50% range: 480-580
SAT Writing middle 50% range: 460-560
Graduate top 10% of class: 14
Graduated top 25% of class: 39
Graduated top 50% of class: 77

COLLEGE GRADUATION REQUIREMENTS

Course waivers allowed: No
Course substitutions allowed: NR

Additional Information

Environment: This public school was founded in 1910. It has a 1200-acre campus.

Student Body
Undergrad enrollment: 23,607
% Women: 60
% Men: 40
% Out-of-state: 13
Cost information
Room & board:NR
Housing Information
University Housing: Yes
Percent living on campus: 28
Greek System
Fraternity: Yes
Sorority: Yes
Athletics: Division I

Miami University

301 S. Campus Avenue, Oxford, OH 45056
Phone: 513-529-2531 • Fax: 513-529-1550
E-mail: admission@miamioh.edu • Web: www.miamioh.edu/
Support: CS • Institution: Public

Programs or Services for Students with Learning Differences

The Student Disability Services staff coordinates university and community resources to meet the academic and personal needs of students with LD; assist faculty in understanding the characteristics and needs of these students; and provide services on an individual basis to students with appropriate documentation. Appropriate services and accommodations are determined through a flexible, interactive process that involves the student and the coordinator and are arranged through dialogue with faculty and staff responsible for implementing many of these services or accommodations. Decisions about services and accommodations for students with LD are made on the basis of the disability documentation and the functional limitations caused by the disability, as well as the current needs of the student. Students with ADHD must meet with the LD coordinator to initiate services after discussing disability-related needs and providing documentation of the disability and its impact on learning.

Admission Information for Students with Learning Differences

College entrance tests required: Yes
Interview required: No
Essay required: No
Additional Application Required for LD/ADHD/ASD: NR
What documentation required for LD: Psychoeducational evaluation
With general application: NR
To receive services after enrolling: Yes
What documentation required for ADHD: Psychoeducational evaluation
With general application: NR
To receive services after enrolling: Yes
LD/ADHD/ASD documentation submitted to: Admission Office
ASD Specific Program: NR
Special Ed. HS course work accepted: NR
Specific course requirements of all applicants: NR
Separate application required: No
Total # of students receiving LD/ADHD/ASD services: NR
Acceptance into program means acceptance into college: Students must be admitted to and enrolled in the university first and then request services.

Admissions

Students with LD are admitted to Miami through the regular admission process; therefore, it is important to ensure that the information in the application accurately reflects a student's academic ability and potential. Students with academic deficiencies may still be qualified for admission. Students may choose to self-disclose LD or ADHD on their application, either through a personal essay or the extenuating circumstances statement. Also, students may voluntarily choose to submit other information that may help the Admission Office to understand their unique learning strengths and needs.

Additional Information

Services for students with LD include priority registration; classroom accommodations such as test modifications, extended exam times, and so on; liaison with faculty; campus advocacy; counseling; and career awareness. In addition, students with LD can utilize services through the Rinella Learning Center, which works with students encountering academic difficulties. Its tutorial assistance program provides peer tutors. The Bernard B. Rinella Jr. Learning Center has special services designed to help students experiencing academic problems. In meeting with a learning specialist, students' existing learning strategies will be assessed, and new effective strategies will be introduced. Topics of time management, note-taking, test-taking, writing, and organization will be covered. New study strategies will be reinforced through individual conferences with a learning specialist, peer mentoring, and/or tutoring.

General Support Services Information

Contact Information
Name of program or department: Office of Disability Resources
Telephone: 513-529-1541
Fax: 513-529-8799

Accommodations or Services for Students with Learning Differences

Accommodations are decided upon an individual basis after a thorough review of appropriate, current documentation. The accommodations requested must be supported through the documentation provided and must be logically linked to the current impact of the condition on academic functioning.

Allowed in exams
Calculator: NR
Dictionary: NR
Computer: NR
Spellchecker: NR
Extended test time: Yes
Scribes: NR
Proctors: NR
Oral exams: NR
Note-takers: NR
Services for students with LD: Yes
Services for students with ADHD: Yes
Services for students with ASD: Yes
Distraction-reduced environment: Yes
Tape recording in class: Yes
Audio books: NR
Electronic texts: Yes
Kurzweil Reader: Yes
Other assistive technology: Yes
Priority registration: Yes
Added costs for services: No
LD specialists: Yes
ADHD coaching: NR
ASD specialists: NR
Professional tutors: No
Peer tutors: 100–220
Max. hours/wk. for services: NR
How professors are notified of LD/ADHD: By student

General Admissions Information

Office of Admissions: 513-529-2531

Entrance Requirements

Academic units recommended: 4 English, 4 math, 3 science, 2 foreign language, 2 social studies, 1 history, 1 visual/performing arts. High school diploma is required and GED is accepted. SAT or ACT required. If ACT, ACT with writing accepted. TOEFL required of all international applicants: minimum paper TOEFL 550 or minimum internet TOEFL 80.

Application deadline: 2/1
Notification: 3/15
Average GPA: 3.76
ACT Composite middle 50% range: 26-30
SAT Math middle 50% range: 590-690
SAT Critical Reading middle 50% range: 550-650
SAT Writing middle 50% range: 540-650
Graduated top 10% of class: 36
Graduated top 25% of class: 68
Graduated top 50% of class: 94

COLLEGE GRADUATION REQUIREMENTS

Course waivers allowed: No
Course substitutions allowed: Yes
In what course: Foreign language and math only if it is determined not to be an essential component of the curriculum and/or major.

Additional Information

Environment: This public school was founded in 1809. It has a 2000-acre campus.

Student Body
Undergrad enrollment: 16,387
% Women: 51
% Men: 49
% Out-of-state: 35

Cost information
In-state Tuition: $13,533
Out-of Tuition: $30,233
Room & board: $11,644

Housing Information
University Housing: Yes
Percent living on campus: 46

Greek System
Fraternity: Yes
Sorority: Yes
Athletics: Division I

Muskingum University

163 Stormont Street, New Concord, OH 43762
Phone: 740-826-8137 • Fax: 614-826-8100
E-mail: jzellers@muskingum.edu
Support: SP • Institution: Private

Programs or Services for Students with Learning Differences

The PLUS Program provides college students who have learning disorders with the opportunity to reach their academic potential. The program is built upon a proven model of Embedded Learning Strategies Instruction blended with a Learning Conversation approach. This model facilitates life-long learning, essential to success in college, work, and life pursuits. Through Learning Strategy Instruction, Learning Consultants assist students by providing systematic and explicit instruction in learning strategies that are embedded in course content. Learning strategy instruction areas include time and materials management, organization, test-taking, note-taking, reading, writing, memory and study skills, among others. Through Learning Conversations, Learning Consultants provide the context within which students may appreciate that they can succeed, recognize the factors that influence their success, develop a possibility perspective, improve self-confidence, and understand their unique learning profile and what it means for their learning. The success of students can be attributed in part to the highly qualified, professional adult Learning Consultants who engage students in academic support services. Students participating in the Full PLUS Program receive an average of one contact hour per week for each eligible course for an average total of 3-4 hours per week. Maintenance PLUS Program students receive one half hour of PLUS tutorial services per week for each eligible course. Both levels of service are provided with additional services, including a Primary Learning Consultant who acts as liaison to home, faculty, and others; guidance to promote favorable number of courses; optimal course selection and balanced course load; continuum of services to provide a range of individual support for short term needs.

Admission Information for Students with Learning Differences

College entrance tests required: Yes
Interview required: Yes
Essay required: Yes
Additional Application Required for LD/ADHD/ASD: NR
What documentation required for LD: Yes
With general application: NR
To receive services after enrolling: Yes
What documentation required for ADHD: Yes
With general application: NR
To receive services after enrolling: Yes
LD/ADHD/ASD documentation submitted to: PLUS Program
ASD Specific Program: NR
Special Ed. HS course work accepted: Yes
Specific course requirements of all applicants: Yes
Separate application required: No
Total # of students receiving LD/ADHD/ASD services: 130–160
Acceptance into program means acceptance into college: Joint admission to Muskingham University and PLUS Program

Admissions

The PLUS Program reflects the university's commitment to the ultimate success of its students. Course and graduate requirements are not compromised for PLUS students. Each applicant is evaluated by a committee for the potential to complete degree requirements and succeed in the campus residential environment. Students should have a university preparatory curriculum. Generally 4 years of English, Algebra I and II, and Geometry; at least 2 years of science with lab and social sciences are recommended for admissions. To apply to the PLUS Program, an applicant should complete all materials required for regular admission to the university. In addition, PLUS applicants should submit a recent comprehensive evaluation, which includes aptitude testing, achievement testing, and a diagnostic summary. Admission to the university and the PLUS Program are based upon application materials and a personal interview. Rolling admissions apply. Due to the great demand for the PLUS Program services, early application is strongly advised.

Additional Information

Muskingum University offers the First Step Transition Program, a two-week summer transition program to help bridge the gap between high school and university life.

General Support Services Information

Contact Information
Name of program or department: PLUS Program, Center for Advancement of Learning or Disability Education Office
Telephone: 740-826-8284 or 740-826-6132
Fax: 740-826-8285

Accommodations or Services for Students with Learning Differences

The Disability Education Office provides federally mandated accommodations to qualified students at no charge. Individuals seeking these services must self-identify and provide specific documentation to the DEO. Accommodations are provided at no charge and are coordinated with or without PLUS Program services.

Allowed in exams
Calculator: Yes
Dictionary: Yes
Computer: Yes
Spellchecker: Yes
Extended test time: Yes
Scribes: Yes
Proctors: Yes
Oral exams: Yes
Note-takers: Yes
Services for students with LD: Yes
Services for students with ADHD: Yes
Services for students with ASD: Yes
Distraction-reduced environment: Yes
Tape recording in class: Yes
Audio books: NR
Electronic texts: Yes
Kurzweil Reader: Yes
Other assistive technology: Yes
Priority registration: Yes
Added costs for services: Yes for PLUS Program
LD specialists: Yes
ADHD coaching: NR
ASD specialists: NR
Professional tutors: Yes
Peer tutors: No
Max. hours/wk. for services: 3–4
How professors are notified of LD/ADHD: NR

General Admissions Information

Office of Admissions: 740-826-8137

Entrance Requirements

Academic units required: 4 English, 2 math, 2 science, 1 science labs, 2 foreign language, 1 social studies, 2 history. **Academic units recommended:** 4 English, 3 math, 3 science, 2 science labs, 2 foreign language, 1 social studies, 2 history. High school diploma is required and GED is accepted. SAT or ACT required. If ACT, ACT with writing accepted. TOEFL required of all international applicants: minimum paper TOEFL 550 or minimum internet TOEFL 79.

Application deadline: 8/1
Notification: Rolling starting 10/1
Average GPA: 3.45
ACT Composite avg: 31 (26-36)
SAT Math avg: 603 (400-800)
SAT Critical Reading avg: 530 (330-800)
SAT Writing avg: 543 (380-800)
Graduated top 10% of class: 28
Graduated top 25% of class: 43
Graduated top 50% of class: 70

COLLEGE GRADUATION REQUIREMENTS

Course waivers allowed: No
Course substitutions allowed: No

Additional Information

Environment: This private school, affiliated with the Presbyterian Church, was founded in 1837. It has a 245-acre campus.

Student Body
Undergrad enrollment: 1,728
% Women: 55
% Men: 45
% Out-of-state: 8

Cost information
Tuition: $24,000
Room & board: $9,760

Housing Information
University Housing: Yes
Percent living on campus: 71

Greek System
Fraternity: Yes
Sorority: Yes
Athletics: Division III

NOTRE DAME COLLEGE

4545 College Road, South Euclid, OH 44121
Phone: 216-381-1680 • Fax: 216-373-5278
E-mail: admissions@ndc.edu • Web: www.notredamecollege.edu
Support: SP • Institution: Private

PROGRAMS OR SERVICES FOR STUDENTS WITH LEARNING DIFFERENCES

The Mission of the Academic Support Center (ASC) is to provide quality educational opportunities and support services above and beyond those required by law to individuals with documented learning disabilities, a group that is traditionally under-served in postsecondary education. The mission of the Academic Support Center parallels the mission of Notre Dame College, which is to educate a diverse population in the liberal arts for personal, professional, and global responsibility. The services provided by the ASC are structured and comprehensive, thus enabling a student with a documented learning disability to succeed in college. Prior to being admitted to the center, the student must meet the admission requirements of Notre Dame College. To participate in the ASC, the student must submit documentation of a learning disability. This documentation must include a psychoeducational evaluation that has been conducted within the past 3 years. Refer to web link on documentation.

ADMISSION INFORMATION FOR STUDENTS WITH LEARNING DIFFERENCES

College entrance test required: Yes
Interview required: No
Essay required: No
Additional Application Required for LD/ADHD/ASD: NR
What documentation required for LD: Psycho-educational evaluation conducted within the last three years and a current Individual Education Plan (IEP)
With general application: No
To receive services after enrolling: Yes
What documentation required for ADHD: Psycho-educational evaluation conducted within the last three years and a current Individual Education Plan (IEP)
With general application: No
To receive services after enrolling: Yes
What documentation required for ASD: Psycho ed evaluation
With general application: No
To receive services after enrolling: Yes
LD/ADHD/ASD documentation submitted to: Support program/services
ASD Specific Program: NR
Special Ed. HS course work accepted: No
Specific course: Yes
Separate application required for program services: No
Total # of students receiving LD/ADHD/ASD services: 130

ADMISSIONS

In fulfilling its mission, Notre Dame College seeks to attract students of diverse religious, racial, educational, and socioeconomic backgrounds and those of various ages and personal experiences. Notre Dame College admits students who demonstrate potential for success in rigorous academic work. The credentials of each applicant are individually evaluated with consideration to a combination of academic record, entrance examination performance, and evidence of potential for success in college studies. The following distribution of courses is considered to be standard academic preparation: 4 units of English, 3 units of math (including Algebra I, Geometry, and Algebra II), 3 units of science with laboratory experience, 3 units of social studies, 2 units of a foreign language, and 1 unit of fine arts.

ADDITIONAL INFORMATION

There are a number of support resources offered on the college campus. Some are direct support for students with a diagnosed disability and others are for all the students on campus. For example,the mission of the Student Success Resources is to provide direction and support for students as they connect to the campus. Students in the learning support program ASC) are given a Academic Support Center Student Guide when they start Notre Dame College. In the Guide is a listing of staff, tutors who have specific expertise, how to initiate services, scheduling of exams and initiating note-takes, and more.

General Support Services Information

Contact Information
Name of program or department: Academic Support Center for Students with Learning Differences
Telephone: 216-373-5185
Fax: 216-937-0357

Accommodations or Services for Students with Learning Differences

Accommodations are decided upon an individual basis after a thorough review of appropriate, current documentation. The accommodations requests must be supported through the documentation provided and must be logically linked to the current impact of the condition on academic functioning.

Allowed in exams
Calculator: Yes
Dictionary: Yes
Computer: Yes
Spellchecker: Yes
Extended test time: Yes
Scribes: Yes
Proctors: Yes
Oral exams: Yes
Note-takers: Yes
Services for students with LD: Yes
Services for students with ADHD: Yes
Services for students with ASD: Yes
Distraction-reduced environment: Yes
Tape recording in class: Yes
Audio books from learning ally: Yes
Electronic texts: NR
Kurzweil Reader: Yes
Other assistive technology: Yes
Priority registration: Yes
Added costs of services: Yes
LD specialists: Yes
ADHD coaching: NR
ASD specialists: NR
Professional tutors: Yes
Peer tutors: N/A
Max. hours/wk. for services: NR
How professors are notified of student approved accommodations: Student

General Admissions Information

Office of Admissions: 216-381-1680

Entrance Requirements

Academic units recommended: 4 English, 3 mathematics, 3 science, (3 science labs), 2 foreign language, 3 social studies, 0 history, 1 fine art. High school diploma is required and GED is accepted. SAT or ACT required. If ACT, ACT with Writing component accepted. TOEFL required of all international applicants: minimum paper TOEFL 550.

Application deadline: NR
Notification: Rolling starting 9/1
Average GPA: 3.0
ACT Composite middle 50% range: 17-21
SAT Math middle 50% range: 393-520
SAT Critical Reading middle 50% range: 440-528
SAT Writing middle 50% range: NR
Graduated top 10% of class: 4
Graduated top 25% of class: 22
Graduated top 50% of class: 62

COLLEGE GRADUATION REQUIREMENTS

Course waivers allowed: No
Course substitutions allowed: Yes
In what course: Logic may be substituted for math with proper documentation. NDC does not require a foreign language.

Additional Information

Environment: Notre Dame College is located in South Euclid, Ohio, a suburb under 30 minutes east of downtown Cleveland, Ohio. The college sits on a wooded 53-acre campus.

Student Body
Undergrad enrollment: 835
% Women: 63
% Men: 37
% Out-of-state: 3

Cost information
Tuition: $18,670
Room & board: $6,648

Housing Information
University housing: Yes
% Living on campus: 29

Greek System
Fraternity: No
Sorority: No
Athletics: NAIA

Oberlin College

101 North Professor Street, Oberlin, OH 44074
Phone: 440-775-8411 • Fax: 440-775-6905
E-mail: college.admissions@oberlin.edu • Web: www.oberlin.edu
Support: CS • Institution: Private

Programs or Services for Students with Learning Differences

Personnel from the Office of Services for Students with Disabilities (OSSD) provide services, as well as coordinate accommodations, to meet the needs of students who have disabilities. Their goal is to maximize the student's entire educational potential while helping him or her develop and maintain independence. The program philosophy is one that encourages self-advocacy. Students who are diagnosed by OSSD personnel as having LD, as well as those who can provide documentation of a current diagnosis of LD, are eligible for services. To verify a previously diagnosed LD, a student must provide a psychological assessment, educational test results, and a recent copy of an IEP that specifies placement in a learning disabilities program. These documents will be reviewed by personnel from OSSD to determine eligibility. Students requesting services are interviewed by a learning disability counselor before a service plan is developed or initiated.

Admission Information for Students with Learning Differences

College entrance tests required: Yes
Interview required: No
Essay required: No
Additional Application Required for LD/ADHD/ASD: NR
What documentation required for LD: Psycho ed evaluation to include: relevant historical info, instructional interventions, related services, age diagnosed, objective data (aptitude, achievement, info processing), test scores (standard, percentile and grade equivalents) and describe functional limitations.
With general application: No
To receive services after enrolling: Yes
What documentation required for ADHD: Diagnosis based on DSM-V; history of behaviors impairing functioning in academic setting; diagnostic interview; history of symptoms; evidence of ongoing behaviors.
With general application: No
To receive services after enrolling: Yes
What documentation required for ASD: Psycho ed evaluation
With general application: NR
To receive services after enrolling: Yes
LD/ADHD/ASD documentation submitted to: SSD
ASD Specific Program: NR
Special Ed. HS course work accepted: Yes
Specific course requirements of all applicants: Yes
Separate application required: No
Total # of students receiving LD/ADHD/ASD services: 200
Acceptance into program means acceptance into college: Students must be admitted to and enrolled in the university first and then request services.

Admissions

There is no special admissions procedure for students with LD. All applicants must meet the same admission requirements. Courses required include 4 years of English and math and at least 3 years of social science and science. The average GPA is typically a B average or better. ACT scores range between 25 and 30; SAT Reasoning test scores range between 1100 and 1320, and SAT Subject Test scores range between 560 and 680 on each Subject Test. Students who self-disclose and provide documentation may have their files read by OSSD personnel, who will provide a recommendation to the Office of Admissions. Students who can provide valid and recent documentation of a psychoeducational diagnosis of LD may receive services. The report must include the name, title, and credentials of the professional. All letters must be typed on letterhead, signed, and dated. It would be useful if the report contains the following components: diagnosis and a description of the methodology used; previous history and prognosis of the disability; description of the current functional limitations and explanation of how the diagnosis substantially limits a major life activity; the severity of the condition; an explanation of past services and accommodations; recommendations and rationale as to why the accommodations are requested.

Additional Information

A Learning Resource Center and an Adaptive Technology Center are available for all students. Skills classes are offered for college credit in reading, study skills, and writing. OSSD can arrange one or all of the following services for students with learning disabilities: quiet space for exams; extended examination times, up to twice the time typically allotted, based on diagnosis; oral exams; scribes; individual academic, personal, and vocational counseling; computer resources for additional academic skill development and assistance; alternate text; priority academic scheduling; peer tutoring; new student orientation assistance; and faculty/staff consultation. In addition, OSSD can provide information about other support services sponsored by the college.

General Support Services Information

Contact Information
Name of program or department: Disability Services
Telephone: 440-775-5588
Fax: 440-775-5589

Accommodations or Services for Students with Learning Differences

Accommodations are decided upon an individual basis after a thorough review of appropriate, current documentation. The accommodations requested must be supported through the documentation provided and must be logically linked to the current impact of the condition on academic functioning.

Allowed in exams
Calculator: Yes
Dictionary: Yes
Computer: Yes
Spellchecker: Yes
Extended test time: Yes
Scribes: Yes
Proctors: Yes
Oral exams: Yes
Note-takers: Yes
Services for students with LD: Yes
Services for students with ADHD: Yes
Services for students with ASD: Yes
Distraction-reduced environment: Yes
Tape recording in class: Yes
Audio books: NR
Electronic texts: Yes
Kurzweil Reader: Yes
Other assistive technology: Yes
Priority registration: Yes
Added costs for services: No
LD specialists: Yes
ADHD coaching: NR
ASD specialists: NR
Professional tutors: No
Peer tutors: 38
Max. hours/wk. for services: Unlimited
How professors are notified of LD/ADHD: By both student and director

General Admissions Information

Office of Admissions: 440-775-8411

Entrance Requirements

Academic units required: 4 English, 3 math, 3 science, 3 foreign language, 3 social studies. **Academic units recommended:** 4 math, 4 science. High school diploma is required and GED is accepted. SAT or ACT required. If ACT, ACT with writing recommended. TOEFL required of all international applicants: minimum paper TOEFL 600.

Application deadline: 1/15
Notification: 4/1
Average GPA: 3.58
ACT Composite middle 50% range: 28-32
SAT Math middle 50% range: 620-720
SAT Critical Reading middle 50% range: 640-730
SAT Writing middle 50% range: 640-730
Graduated top 10% of class: 61
Graduated top 25% of class: 91
Graduated top 50% of class: 100

COLLEGE GRADUATION REQUIREMENTS

Course waivers allowed: No
Course substitutions allowed: Yes
In what course: Case-by-case

Additional Information

Environment: This private school was founded in 1833. It has a 450-acre campus.

Student Body
Undergrad enrollment: 2,961
% Women: 55
% Men: 45
% Out-of-state: 92

Cost information
Tuition: $49,928
Room & board: $13,630

Housing Information
University Housing: Yes
Percent living on campus: 77

Greek System
Fraternity: No
Sorority: No
Athletics: Division III

The Ohio State University—Columbus

Student Academic Services Building, Columbus, OH 43210
Phone: 614-292-3980 • Fax: 614-292-4818
E-mail: askabuckeye@osu.edu • Web: www.osu.edu
Support: CS • Institution: Public

Programs or Services for Students with Learning Differences

The Office for Disability Services (ODS) at Ohio State University offers a variety of services for students with documented disabilities, including learning disabilities, hearing or visual impairments, attention deficit disorders, and psychiatric or medical disabilities. The mission of ODS is to provide and coordinate support services and programs that enable students with disabilities to maximize their educational potential. ODS serves as a resource to all members of the university community so that students with disabilities can freely and actively participate in all facets of university life.

Admission Information for Students with Learning Differences

College entrance tests required: Yes
Interview required: No
Essay required: N/A
Additional Application Required for LD/ADHD/ASD: NR
What documentation required for LD: Psycho ed evaluation to include: relevant historical info, instructional interventions, related services, age diagnosed, objective data (aptitude, achievement, info processing), test scores (standard, percentile and grade equivalents) and describe functional limitations.
With general application: No
To receive services after enrolling: Yes
What documentation required for ADHD: Diagnosis based on DSM-V; history of behaviors impairing functioning in academic setting; diagnostic interview; history of symptoms; evidence of ongoing behaviors.
With general application: No
With general application: NR
To receive services after enrolling: Yes
LD/ADHD/ASD documentation submitted to: Support Program/Services
ASD Specific Program: NR
Special Ed. HS course work accepted: No
Specific course requirements for all applicants: Yes
Separate application required for program services: No
Total # of students receiving LD/ADHD/ASD services: 278
Acceptance into program means acceptance into college: NR

Admissions

A variety of staff members provide different functions. Some of the functions include: assistive technology, counseling, testing accommodations and scribes/readers. All eligible students are assigned to a disability counselor who coordinates services and accommodations. The counselor collaborates on issues such as learning strategies, advocacy, and transition issues.

Admissions

Students with LD are admitted under the same criteria as regular applicants. However, consideration can be given to students with LD with support from ODS in instances where the student's rank, GPA, or lack of courses, such as foreign language, have affected performance in high school. Applicants interested in services should submit a general application for admission; complete the section under optional personal statement that gives students the opportunity to provide information if they feel that their high school performance was adversely affected by special circumstances; and submit documentation of the disability to ODS, including the latest IEP and the results of the last psychoeducational testing. In some cases, ODS will be asked to consider supporting an appeal of an admissions decision. ODS will review the application, look at course work and deficiencies, review services received in high school and determine if the student's needs can be met at OSU if the student is not normally admissible, look at when a diagnosis was made and at the IEP, and make a recommendation to the Admissions Office. Students exceeding the minimum curriculum in math, natural resources, or foreign language will be given additional consideration. Other factors considered include the competitiveness of the high school, accelerated courses taken, if the applicant is a first-generation college student, or the student's cultural, economic, racial, or geographic diversity; outstanding talents; extracurricular activities; significant work experiences; or leadership positions.

General Support Services Information

Contact Information
Name of program or department: Disability Services
Telephone: 614-292-3307
Fax: 614-292-4190

Accommodations or Services for Students with Learning Differences

Accommodations are decided upon an individual basis after a thorough review of appropriate, current documentation. The accommodations requested must be supported through the documentation provided and must be logically linked to the current impact of the condition on academic functioning.

Allowed in exams
Calculator: Yes
Dictionary: Yes
Computer: Yes
Spellchecker: Yes
Extended test time: Yes
Scribes: Yes
Proctors: Yes
Oral exams: No
Note-takers: Yes
Services for students with LD: Yes
Services for students with ADHD: Yes
Services for students with ASD: Yes
Distraction-reduced environment: Yes
Tape recording in class: Yes
Audio books: NR
Electronic texts: Yes
Kurzweil Reader: No
Other assistive technology: Open Book, Zoomtext, JAWS, Read and Write Gold, Kurweil, voice recognition software (Dragon, Smart Nav)
Priority registration: Yes
Added costs for services: No
LD specialists: Yes
ADHD coaching: NR
ASD specialists: NR
Professional tutors: No
Peer tutors: Yes
Max. hours/wk. for services: N/A
How professors are notified of LD/ADHD: Student

General Admissions Information

Office of Admissions: 614-292-3980

Entrance Requirements

Academic units required: 4 English, 3 math, 3 science, 3 science labs, 2 foreign language, 2 social studies, 1 academic electives, 1 visual/performing arts. **Academic units recommended:** 4 English, 4 math, 3 science, 3 science labs, 3 foreign language, 3 social studies, 1 academic electives, 1 visual/performing arts. High school diploma is required and GED is accepted. SAT or ACT required. If ACT, ACT with writing accepted. TOEFL required of all international applicants: minimum paper TOEFL 550 or minimum internet TOEFL 79.

Application deadline: 2/1
Notification: 3/31
Average GPA: NR
ACT Composite middle 50% range: 27-31
SAT Math middle 50% range: 610-720
SAT Critical Reading middle 50% range: 560-670
SAT Writing middle 50% range: 560-660
Graduated top 10% of class: 62
Graduated top 25% of class: 95
Graduated top 50% of class: 99

COLLEGE GRADUATION REQUIREMENTS

Course waivers allowed: Yes
Course substitutions allowed: Yes
In what course: On a case-by-case basis and with appropriate supporting disability documentation, some students can petition for a substitution of the foreign language if it is not essential for the major. Math substitutions are rare.

Additional Information

Environment: This public school was founded in 1870. It has a 3469-acre campus.

Student Body
Undergrad enrollment: 45,289
% Women: 48
% Men: 52
% Out-of-state: 17.4

Cost information
In-state Tuition: $10,037
Out-of-state Tuition: $27,365
Room & board: $11,666

Housing Information
University Housing: Yes
Percent living on campus: 25.7

Greek System
Fraternity: Yes
Sorority: Yes
Athletics: Division I

Ohio University

120 Chubb Hall, Athens, OH 45701
Phone: 740-593-4100 • Fax: 740-593-0560
E-mail: admissions@ohio.edu • Web: www.ohio.edu
Support: S • Institution: Public

Programs or Services for Students with Learning Differences

Student Accessibility Services facilitates requests for accommodations in accordance with the Americans with Disabilities Act and Section 504 of the Rehabilitation Act. Students wishing to request accommodations should complete an application for accommodation and submit supporting documentation to SAS, preferably before you begin your first semester. Each eligible student will be assigned an Accessibility Coordinator who will assist the student in transition to college through determination of reasonable accommodations, referral to pertinent resources to support student success, assist students in developing self-advocacy skills, and to serve as a central point of contact for navigating the college experience. Accessibility Coordinators are available and willing to meet upon a student's request; however progress is not formally monitored by the SAS. There is not a separate support program to which a student applies for admission; rather all admitted students with a disability may request accommodation through the Student Accessibility Services.

Admission Information for Students with Learning Differences

College entrance test required: Yes
Interview required: No
Essay required: Yes
Additional Application Required for LD/ADHD/ASD: NR
What documentation required for LD: Prefer a recent, full Psycho ed evaluation to include: relevant historical info, instructional interventions, related services, age diagnosed, objective data (aptitude, achievement, info processing), test scores (standard, percentile and grade equivalents) and describe functional limitations. Recommended to contact SAS and speak with an Accessibility Coordinator to discuss your specific situation.
With general application: No
To receive services after enrolling: Yes
What documentation required for ADHD: Yes
With general application: No
To receive services after enrolling: Yes
What documentation required for ASD: Psycho ed evaluation
With general application: No
To receive services after enrolling: Yes
LD/ADHD/ASD documentation submitted to: Student Accessibility Services
ASD Specific Program: NR
Special Ed. HS course work accepted: Yes
Specific course: No
Separate application required for program services: No
Total # of students receiving LD/ADHD/ASD services: 400
Acceptance into program means acceptance into college: NR

Admissions

Applicants with learning disabilities are expected to meet the same admission criteria as all other applicants. General admission requires the applicant to be in the top 30 percent with 21 ACT or 990 SAT, or top 50 percent with 23 ACT or 1060 SAT. The mid 50 percent range for ACT is 22-26 and SAT 1030-1200. Course requirements include 4 years English, 3 years science, and 2 years of foreign language. Students can be admitted with deficiencies. Applicants with learning disabilities who meet the criteria should send documentation to special services after admission. Those students not meeting the admission criteria are encouraged to self-disclose by writing a narrative explaining the impact of the disability condition on the student's academic career as well as sending relevant documentation. This disclosure and accompanying documentation will be reviewed by Admissions. Students, in general, must demonstrate the ability to perform in a mainstream academic setting where support is available when needed. Counselor recommendation is very helpful for students who do not meet the traditional criteria.

Additional Information

General services provided include advising referral and liaison, academic adjustments and classroom accommodations, priority scheduling, free tutoring through the Academic Advancement Center (4 hours per course per week), and tutoring in writing and reading skills. Skills classes are offered in learning strategies, college reading skills, reading, speed, and vocabulary. Services are available to undergraduate and graduate students.

General Support Services Information

Contact Information
Name of program or department: Student Accessibility Services
Telephone: 740-593-2620
Fax: 740-593-0790
Website: NR

Accommodations or Services For Students With Learning Differences

Accommodations are decided upon an individual basis after a thorough review of appropriate, current documentation. The accommodations requests must be supported through the documentation provided and must be logically linked to the current impact of the condition on academic functioning.

Allowed in exams
Calculator: Yes
Dictionary: Yes
Computer: Yes
Spellchecker: Yes
Extended test time: Yes
Scribes: Yes
Proctors: Yes
Oral exams: Not Applicable
Note-takers: Yes
Support services for students with LD: Yes
Support services for students with ADHD: Yes
Support services for students with ASD: Yes
Distraction-reduced environment: Yes
Tape recording in class: Yes
Electronic texts: Yes
Kurzweil reader: NR
Audio books: Yes
Other assistive technology: Yes
Priority registration: Yes
Added costs of services: No
LD specialists: No
ADHD coaching: No
ASD specialists: No
Professional tutors: No
Peer tutors: NR
Max. hours/wk. for services: NR
How professors are notified of student approved accommodations: By student

General Admissions Information

Office of Admissions: 740-593-4100

Entrance Requirements

Academic units required: 4 English, 4 math, 3 science, 2 foreign language, 3 social studies, 4 academic electives, and 1 units from above areas or other academic areas. **Academic units recommended:** 4 English, 4 math, 3 science, 2 foreign language, 3 social studies, 4 academic electives, 1 visual/performing arts. High school diploma is required and GED is accepted. SAT or ACT required. If ACT, ACT with writing recommended.

Application deadline: 2/1
Notification: Rolling starting 9/15
Average GPA: 3.46
ACT Composite middle 50% range: 22-26
SAT Math middle 50% range: 500-610
SAT Critical Reading middle 50% range: 490-600
SAT Writing middle 50% range: 470-590
Graduate top 10% of class: 16
Graduated top 25% of class: 43
Graduated top 50% of class: 81

COLLEGE GRADUATION REQUIREMENTS

Course waivers allowed: No
In what course: NR
Course substitutions allowed: Yes
In what course: NR

Additional Information

Environment: This public school was founded in 1804. It has a 1762-acre campus.

Student Body
Undergrad enrollment: 23,513
% Women: 59
% Men: 41
% Out-of-state: 15

Cost information
Out-of-state Tuition: $19,566
Room & board: $10,734

Housing Information
University Housing: Yes
Percent living on campus: 46

Greek System
Fraternity: Yes
Sorority: Yes
Athletics: Division I

UNIVERSITY OF CINCINNATI

PO Box 210091, Cincinnati, OH 45221-0091
Phone: 513-556-1100 • Fax: 513-556-1105
E-mail: admissions@uc.edu • Web: www.uc.edu
Support: CS • Institution: Public

PROGRAMS OR SERVICES FOR STUDENTS WITH LEARNING DIFFERENCES

The University of Cincinnati does not have a specific or separate learning disability program. However, students with learning disabilities who use academic accommodations and support services available through the Disability Services and other resources of the university find they can be successful in achieving their academic objectives. The goal of Disability Services is to provide the necessary accommodations to students in order for them to become successful and independent learners. Remedial/developmental courses are available along with campus-wide tutoring. To receive support services, students must submit documentation from a licensed professional to the Disability Services Office (DSO). DSO staff will work with students and faculty to accommodate special needs.

ADMISSION INFORMATION FOR STUDENTS WITH LEARNING DIFFERENCES

College entrance tests required: Yes
Interview required: N/A
Essay required: N/A
Additional Application Required for LD/ADHD/ASD: NR
What documentation required for LD: Psycho ed evaluation to include: relevant historical info, instructional interventions, related services, age diagnosed, objective data (aptitude, achievement, info processing), test scores (standard, percentile and grade equivalents) and describe functional limitations.
With general application: No
To receive services after enrolling: Yes
What documentation required for ADHD: Diagnosis based on DSM-V; history of behaviors impairing functioning in academic setting; diagnostic interview; history of symptoms; evidence of ongoing behaviors.
With general application: No
To receive services after enrolling: Yes
What documentation required for ASD: Psycho ed evaluation
With general application: NR
To receive services after enrolling: Yes
LD/ADHD/ASD documentation submitted to: Disability Services Office
ASD Specific Program: NR
Special Ed. HS course work accepted: Yes
Specific course requirements for all applicants: Yes
Separate application required for program services: N/A
Total # of students receiving LD/ADHD/ASD services: NR
Acceptance into program means acceptance into college: No

ADMISSIONS

There is no special admission procedure for students with learning disabilities. All students submit the university's general application form. Requests for substitutions/waivers of admission requirements should be made to the admissions office. The University of Cincinnati expects all baccalaureate students to have completed the following articulation requirements: four units of college-prep English, three units of college-prep math, two units of science, two units of social science, two units of a single foreign language, one unit of fine arts, two additional units of any of these. ACT/SAT scores are also required for baccalaureate programs. Branch campuses require a high school diploma or GED for admission. ACT/SAT scores are recommended but not required.

ADDITIONAL INFORMATION

Disabilities Services provides support services and accommodations including but not limited to: note-taking, tutors, readers, taped textbooks, testing accommodations, scribes, loan of equipment, and library disability services. Peer tutoring is available to all students at no cost. Students with appropriate documentation may request course substitutions in math or foreign language. Skill development classes are offered for all students in areas such as time management, organizational skills, and study skills. Developmental courses are also available on the branch campuses.

General Support Services Information

Contact Information
Name of program or department: Disability Services
Telephone: 513-556-6823
Fax: 513-556-1383
Website: http://www.uc.edu/aess/disability.html

Accommodations or Services For Students With Learning Differences

Accommodations are decided upon an individual basis after a thorough review of appropriate, current documentation. The accommodations requests must be supported through the documentation provided and must be logically linked to the current impact of the condition on academic functioning.

Allowed in exams
Calculator: Yes
Dictionary: Yes
Computer: Yes
Spellchecker: Yes
Extended test time: Yes
Scribes: Yes
Proctors: Yes
Oral exams: No
Note-takers: Yes
Support services for students with LD: Yes
Support services for students with ADHD: Yes
Support services for students with ASD: Yes
Distraction-reduced environment: Yes
Tape recording in class: Yes
Electronic texts: Yes
Kurzweil reader: NR
Audio books: Yes
Other assistive technology: Yes
Priority registration: Yes
Added costs of services: No
LD specialists: Yes
ADHD coaching: No
ASD specialists: No
Professional tutors: No
Peer tutors: NR
Max. hours/wk. for services: NR
How professors are notified of student approved accommodations: By both student and director

General Admissions Information

Office of Admissions: 513-556-1100

Entrance Requirements

Academic units required: 4 English, 4 math, 3 science, 3 social studies, and 3 units from above areas or other academic areas. **Academic units recommended:** 2 foreign language. High school diploma is required and GED is accepted. SAT or ACT required. If ACT, ACT with writing required. TOEFL required of all international applicants: minimum paper TOEFL 517 or minimum internet TOEFL 66.

Application deadline: 3/1
Notification: Rolling starting 10/1
Average GPA: 3.46
ACT Composite middle 50% range: 23-28
SAT Math middle 50% range: 530-660
SAT Critical Reading middle 50% range: 510-630
SAT Writing middle 50% range: 490-610
Graduate top 10% of class: 20
Graduated top 25% of class: 48
Graduated top 50% of class: 83

COLLEGE GRADUATION REQUIREMENTS

Course waivers allowed: No
Course substitutions allowed: Yes
In what course: We will offer course substitutions in foreign language and in rare occasions, if given Departmental approval, mathematics. Most importantly is to ensure that the substitution does not create a fundamental alteration of the program.

Additional Information

Environment: This public school was founded in 1819. It has a 392-acre campus.

Student Body
Undergrad enrollment: 24,407
% Women: 50
% Men: 50
% Out-of-state: 11

Cost information
In-state Tuition: $9,322
Out-of-state Tuition: $24,656
Room & board: $10,750

Housing Information
University Housing: Yes
Percent living on campus: 24

Greek System
Fraternity: Yes
Sorority: Yes
Athletics: Division I

University of Dayton

300 College Park, Dayton, OH 45469-1310
Phone: 937-229-4411 • Fax: 937-229-4729
E-mail: admission@udayton.edu • Web: www.udayton.edu
Support: CS • Institution: Private

Programs or Services for Students with Learning Differences

The University of Dayton is: one of the nation's ten largest Catholic universities and Ohio's largest private university, with undergraduate and graduate programs; a university founded in 1850 by the Society of Mary (Marianists), a Roman Catholic teaching order of priests and brothers; a residential learning community with more than 70 academic programs in arts and sciences, business administration, education and allied professions, engineering and law; a diverse community committed to educating the whole person and to linking learning and scholarship with leadership and service; a vibrant living-learning environment, where modern campus housing blurs the line between living and learning.

Admission Information for Students with Learning Differences

College entrance tests required: Yes
Interview required: No
Essay required: N/A
Additional Application Required for LD/ADHD/ASD: NR
What documentation required for LD: Psycho ed evaluation to include: relevant historical info, instructional interventions, related services, age diagnosed, objective data (aptitude, achievement, info processing), test scores (standard, percentile and grade equivalents) and describe functional limitations.
With general application: No
To receive services after enrolling: Yes
What documentation required for ADHD: Diagnosis based on DSM-V; history of behaviors impairing functioning in academic setting; diagnostic interview; history of symptoms; evidence of ongoing behaviors.
With general application: No
To receive services after enrolling: Yes
What documentation required for ASD: Psycho ed evaluation
With general application: NR
To receive services after enrolling: Yes
LD/ADHD/ASD documentation submitted to: Support Program/Services
ASD Specific Program: NR
Special Ed. HS course work accepted: N/A
Specific course requirements for all applicants: Yes
Separate application required for program services: No
Total # of students receiving LD/ADHD/ASD services: NR
Acceptance into program means acceptance into college: Students must be admitted and enrolled prior to requesting services.

Admissions

Applications for admission are reviewed for specific academic majors or, when applicable, for undeclared status in an academic division. Five factors are considered when we assess your preparation for a chosen field of study: your selection of courses in preparation for college, your grade record and pattern throughout high school, your class standing or ranking, results of either the SAT or ACT, and your character and record of leadership and service. Balanced consideration is given to all aspects of your college-preparation. While no minimum grade point average, class rank, or standardized test score is specified, these measures must provide evidence of your readiness for college studies in your chosen academic program.

Additional Information

Because the university recognizes that students have individually unique academic and personal strengths and weaknesses, the Office of Learning Resources (OLR) provides support services to students such as drop-in tutoring (peer-facilitated), with additional support models (Supplemental Instruction) linked to specific classes, and writing support across the curriculum. All OLR support services are provided free of charge. OLR services are most effective if the student takes advantage of them before he or she falls too far behind or receives too many low grades. Every individual student with a disability is guaranteed equal access to all educational programs and services at the University of Dayton. OLR serves qualified students with disabilities after they have been accepted to the University of Dayton and registered with OLR. Students with disabilities must submit appropriate, current documentation of their disability (see website for specific requirements) and participate in the interactive process. There is no obligation for any student to identify a disability; however, students who wish to receive reasonable accommodations must submit proper documentation, participate in an interactive assessment interview with the OLR Disabilities Staff, request in writing the need for specific services following established published guidelines and deadlines. The Ryan C. Harris Adaptive Learning Lab is specifically designed with assistive technology for students with various physical and cognitive disabilities. Staff members provide technical assistance and proctored testing.

General Support Services Information

Contact Information
Name of program or department: Office of Learning Resources
Telephone: 937-229-2066
Fax: 937-229-3270
Website: http://go.udayton.edu/disability

Accommodations or Services For Students With Learning Differences

Accommodations are decided upon an individual basis after a thorough review of appropriate, current documentation. The accommodations requests must be supported through the documentation provided and must be logically linked to the current impact of the condition on academic functioning.

Allowed in exams
Calculator: Yes
Dictionary: Yes
Computer: Yes
Spellchecker: Yes
Extended test time: Yes
Scribes: Yes
Proctors: Yes
Oral exams: No
Note-takers: Yes
Support services for students with LD: Yes
Support services for students with ADHD: Yes
Support services for students with ASD: Yes
Distraction-reduced environment: Yes
Tape recording in class: Yes
Electronic texts: Yes
Kurzweil reader: NR
Audio books: No
Other assistive technology: Yes
Priority registration: Yes
Added costs of services: No
LD specialists: Yes
ADHD coaching: Yes
ASD specialists: Yes
Professional tutors: No
Peer tutors: Yes
Max. hours/wk. for services: NR
How professors are notified of student approved accommodations: By student

General Admissions Information

Office of Admissions: 937-229-4411

Entrance Requirements

Academic units recommended: 4 English, 4 math, 4 science, 1 science labs, 2 foreign language, 4 social studies, 4 history, 4 computer science, 4 visual/performing arts. High school diploma is required and GED is accepted. SAT or ACT required. If ACT, ACT with writing accepted. TOEFL required of all international applicants: minimum paper TOEFL 523 or minimum internet TOEFL 70.

Application deadline: 3/1
Notification: 2/15
Average GPA: 3.62
ACT Composite middle 50% range: 24-29
SAT Math middle 50% range: 530-640
SAT Critical Reading middle 50% range: 510-610
SAT Writing middle 50% range: 510-610
Graduate top 10% of class: 24
Graduated top 25% of class: 54
Graduated top 50% of class: 87

COLLEGE GRADUATION REQUIREMENTS

Course waivers allowed: No
Course substitutions allowed: Yes
In what course: Courses specific to the disability that do not change the essential functions of the program.

Additional Information

Environment: This private school, affiliated with the Roman Catholic Church, was founded in 1850. It has a 259-acre campus.

Student Body
Undergrad enrollment: 8,529
% Women: 47
% Men: 53
% Out-of-state: 47

Cost information
Tuition: $39,090
Room & board: $12,190

Housing Information
University Housing: Yes
Percent living on campus: 71

Greek System
Fraternity: Yes
Sorority: Yes
Athletics: Division I

Ursuline College

2550 Lander Road, Pepper Pike, OH 44124-4398
Phone: 440-449-4203 • Fax: 440-684-6138
E-mail: admission@ursuline.edu • Web: www.ursuline.edu
Support: SP • Institution: Private

Programs or Services for Students with Learning Differences

Ursuline College is a small Catholic college committed to helping students with learning disabilities succeed in their courses and become independent learners. The Program for Students with Learning Disabilities (FOCUS) is a voluntary, comprehensive fee-paid program. The goals of the FOCUS program include providing a smooth transition to college life, helping students learn to apply the most appropriate learning strategies in college courses, and teaching self-advocacy skills. To be eligible for FOCUS admission, a student must present documentation of an LD, which consists of a WAIS-R, the Woodcock-Johnson, and any other standardized measures of achievement. The psychoeducational evaluation must clearly indicate that the student has a specific learning disability and should have been conducted within the last 3 years. Students must have average to above-average intellectual ability and an appropriate academic foundation to succeed in a 4-year liberal arts college.

Admission Information for Students with Learning Differences

College entrance test required: Yes
Interview required: No
Essay required: NR
Additional Application Required for LD/ADHD/ASD: Yes
What documentation required for LD: A diagnosis from a qualified professional which includes any testing information and assessment the evaluator deems necessary and appropriate.
With general application: No
To receive services after enrolling: Yes
What documentation required for ADHD: A speech diagnosis of an ASD based on current DSM criteria from a qualified professional.
With general application: No
To receive services after enrolling: Yes
What documentation required for ASD: A diagnosis from a qualified professional which includes actual test scores.
With general application: No
To receive services after enrolling: Yes
LD/ADHD/ASD documentation submitted to: U.R.S.A. Disabilities Services
ASD Specific Program: NR
Special Ed. HS course work accepted: No
Specific course requirements of all applicants: NR
Separate application required for program services: Yes
Total # of students receiving LD/ADHD/ASD services: 25
Acceptance into program means acceptance into college: No

Admissions

To participate in the FOCUS program, students must first meet with the LD specialist to discuss whether the program is suitable for them. Students must then meet the requirements for clear or conditional admission to the college by applying to the admissions office and completing all regular admission procedures. Students with learning disabilities usually meet the same requirements for admission to the college as all other students: 2.5 GPA and an ACT score of 17 or an SAT score of 850 for a "clear" admission, although consideration may be given. Courses recommended for admission include: 4 years English, 3 years social studies, 3 years math, 3 years science, 2 years foreign language. A student may receive a "conditional" admission if the GPA and ACT are lower. Students with conditional admission are limited to 12 credit hours per semester for the first year. The final admission decision is made by the Office of Admissions.

Additional Information

The FOCUS group is a program that features an orientation which provides a smooth transition to the college, acquaints students with mentors and other students including mentors, and introduces students to high-tech equipment and computers in the ARC; individual bi-weekly 1-hour sessions with LD specialist to work on developing time-management and organizational skills, design learning strategies for success in college, and learn note taking and test-taking skills; individual weekly 1-hour sessions with a writing specialist who provides assistance with writing assignments in specific courses and who helps with developing skills in writing effective sentences, paragraphs, and essays; weekly academic-skills support groups with LD specialist to learn coping skills, develop self-advocacy skills, and receive support for dealing with classroom issues; and academic advising for guidance on choosing appropriate courses and scheduling appropriate number of credits each semester. A liaison also exists between FOCUS and career counseling. Focus students have been members of our graduating classes for almost ten years and have been successful in the fields of nursing (largest private nursing school in Ohio), education, fashion, business, and special studies.

General Support Services Information

Contact Information
Name of program or department: U.R.S.A. Disabilities Services
Telephone: 440-646-8123
Fax: NR
Website: http://www.ursuline.edu/Student_Life/URSA/focus.html

Accommodations or Services For Students With Learning Differences

Accommodations are decided upon an individual basis after a thorough review of appropriate, current documentation. The accommodations requests must be supported through the documentation provided and must be logically linked to the current impact of the condition on academic functioning.

Allowed in exams
Calculator: Yes
Dictionary: Yes
Computer: Yes
Spellchecker: Yes
Extended test time: Yes
Scribes: Yes
Proctors: Yes
Oral exams: Yes
Note-takers: Yes
Support services for students with LD: Yes
Support services for students with ADHD: Yes
Support services for students with ASD: Yes
Distraction-reduced environment: Yes
Tape recording in class: Yes
Electronic texts: Yes
Kurzweil reader: NR
Audio books: Yes
Other assistive technology: Yes
Priority registration: Yes
Added costs of services: Yes
LD specialists: Yes
ADHD coaching: Yes
ASD specialists: Yes
Professional tutors: Yes
Peer tutors: Yes
Max. hours/wk. for services: NR
How professors are notified of student approved accommodations: By student

General Admissions Information

Office of Admissions: 440-449-4203

Entrance Requirements

Academic units recommended: 4 English, 3 math, 3 science, 2 science labs, 2 foreign language, 3 social studies, 1 visual/performing arts, and 1 units from above areas or other academic areas. High school diploma is required and GED is accepted. SAT or ACT required. If ACT, ACT with writing accepted. TOEFL required of all international applicants: minimum paper TOEFL 500 or minimum internet TOEFL 60.

Application deadline: 2/1
Notification: NR
Average GPA: 3.31
ACT Composite middle 50% range: 19-24
SAT Math middle 50% range: 440-535
SAT Critical Reading middle 50% range: 425-590
SAT Writing middle 50% range: 415-565
Graduate top 10% of class: 16
Graduated top 25% of class: 45
Graduated top 50% of class: 74

COLLEGE GRADUATION REQUIREMENTS

Course waivers allowed: No
Course substitutions allowed: Yes
In what course: This is evaluated according to the student's specific needs on a case by case basis

Additional Information

Environment: This private school, affiliated with the Roman Catholic Church, was founded in 1871. It has a 110-acre campus.

Student Body
Undergrad enrollment: 655
% Women: 93
% Men: 07
% Out-of-state: 7.6

Cost information
Tuition: $988 per credit
Room & board: $9,964-$12,920

Housing Information
University Housing: Yes
Percent living on campus: 25

Greek System
Fraternity: No
Sorority: No
Athletics: Division II

Wright State University

3640 Colonel Glenn Highway, Dayton, OH 45435
Phone: 937-775-5700 • Fax: 937-775-4410
E-mail: admissions@wright.edu • Web: www.wright.edu
Support: CS • Institution: Public

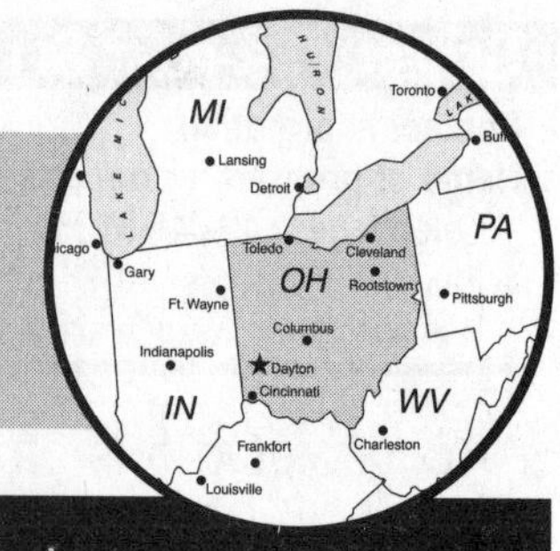

Programs or Services for Students with Learning Differences

Students with disabilities are encouraged to participate in all facets of university life according to their abilities and interests and to develop independence and responsibility to the fullest extent possible. The philosophy of the university is intended to stimulate students to pursue the career of study regardless of their learning disability. Through the Office of Disability Services, the university provides a comprehensive array of services on a campus with a long history of commitment to students with physical, visual, and/or learning disabilities. A pre-service interview is required of all prospective students to discuss service needs. Eligibility for services is determined after documentation is received and the student has an individual interview.

Admission Information for Students with Learning Differences

College entrance tests required: Yes
Interview required: Yes
Essay required: No
Additional Application Required for LD/ADHD/ASD: NR
What documentation required for LD: Psycho ed evaluation to include: relevant historical info, instructional interventions, related services, age diagnosed, objective data (aptitude, achievement, info processing), test scores (standard, percentile and grade equivalents) and describe functional limitations.
With general application: No
To receive services after enrolling: Yes
What documentation required for ADHD: Diagnosis based on DSM-V; history of behaviors impairing functioning in academic setting; diagnostic interview; history of symptoms; evidence of ongoing behaviors.
With general application: No
To receive services after enrolling: Yes
What documentation required for ASD: Psycho ed evaluation
With general application: NR
To receive services after enrolling: Yes
LD/ADHD/ASD documentation submitted to: Office of Disability Services
ASD Specific Program: NR
Special Ed. HS course work accepted: No
Specific course requirements of all applicants: Yes
Separate application required: Yes
Total # of students receiving LD/ADHD/ASD services: 175
Acceptance into program means acceptance into college: Students must be admitted to and enrolled in the university first and then request services.

Admissions

The university has an open admission policy for in-state students. ACT/SAT is used for placement, not admission. The mid 50 percent range for the ACT is 18–24, and for the SAT, it is 990–1140. Students with LD must meet the same criteria as all applicants and must be accepted to the university prior to requesting services. However, out-of-state students are encouraged to self-disclose their learning disability and submit documentation to the Office of Disability Services prior to applying to the university if they would like to discuss eligibility for admission and services available on campus and determine if Wright State is a good fit for them. It is recommended that students self-disclose the LD if GPA or test scores are low and the student feels that LD disclosure is important in explaining academic or testing information. The director of Disability Services encourages students and their families to visit and interview. Admissions will ask ODS to review documentation, transcripts, and so on, and meet with the student to determine readiness for college. Students with a college-prep curriculum in high school have been more successful at Wright State than those who took a general curriculum. The final decision rests with the Admissions Office.

Additional Information

Wright State Office of Disability Services offers testing accommodations, counseling, math learning center and tutoring services for all students. Develomental courses are offered in writing and math. Supplemental instruction helps students review course concepts, improve study habits, and be better prepared for exams and assignments. A trained supplemental instructor student leader works with a professor in consultation to provide group study sessions.

General Support Services Information

Contact Information
Name of program or department: Office of Disability Services
Telephone: 937-775-5680
Fax: 937-775-5699
Website: www.wright.edu/disability-services

Accommodations or Services for Students with Learning Differences

Accommodations are decided upon an individual basis after a thorough review of appropriate, current documentation. The accommodations requests must be supported through the documentation provided and must be logically linked to the current impact of the condition on academic functioning.

Allowed in exams
Calculator: Yes
Dictionary: Yes
Computer: Yes
Spellchecker: Yes
Extended test time: Yes
Scribes: Yes
Proctors: Yes
Oral exams: Yes
Note-takers: Yes
Support services for students with LD: Yes
Support services for students with ADHD: Yes
Support services for students with ASD: Yes
Distraction-reduced environment: Yes
Tape recording in class: Yes
Electronic texts: Yes
Kurzweil reader: NR
Audio books: Yes
Other assistive technology: Yes
Priority registration: No
Added costs of services: No
LD specialists: Yes
ADHD coaching: Yes
ASD specialists: Yes
Professional tutors: No
Peer tutors: Yes
Max. hours/wk. for services: 2
How professors are notified of student approved accommodations: By student

General Admissions Information

Office of Admissions: 937-775-5700

Entrance Requirements

Academic units required: 4 English, 3 math, 3 science, 3 science labs, 2 foreign language, 3 social studies, 1 visual/performing arts. High school diploma is required and GED is accepted. SAT or ACT required. If ACT, ACT with writing accepted. TOEFL required of all international applicants: minimum internet TOEFL 61.

Application deadline: NR
Notification: Rolling starting 9/9
Average GPA: 3.26
ACT Composite middle 50% range: 19-25
SAT Math middle 50% range: 450-590
SAT Critical Reading middle 50% range: 460-590
SAT Writing middle 50% range: 430-560
Graduate top 10% of class: 17
Graduated top 25% of class: 37
Graduated top 50% of class: 68

COLLEGE GRADUATION REQUIREMENTS

Course waivers allowed: Yes
In what course: Considered on a case by case basis, however waivers are traditionally not offered.
Course substitutions allowed: Yes
In what course: Any course will be considered

Additional Information

Environment: This public school was founded in 1964. It has a 557-acre campus.

Student Body
Undergrad enrollment: 12,722
% Women: 52
% Men: 48
% Out-of-state: 2

Cost information
In-state Tuition: $8,730
Out-of-state Tuition: $17,098
Room & board: $9,304

Housing Information
University Housing: Yes
Percent living on campus: 20

Greek System
Fraternity: Yes
Sorority: Yes
Athletics: Division I

XAVIER UNIVERSITY (OH)

3800 Victory Parkway, Cincinnati, OH 45207-5311
Phone: 513-745-3301 • Fax: 513-745-4319
E-mail: xuadmit@xavier.edu • Web: www.xavier.edu
Support: CS • Institution: Private

PROGRAMS OR SERVICES FOR STUDENTS WITH LEARNING DIFFERENCES

The Learning Assistance Center (LAC) provides support services to facilitate learning. The LAC has two main purposes: tutoring and disability services. Our tutoring services are available to all Xavier students and include subject specific tutoring, drop-in sessions, study skills assistance and Supplemental Instruction (SI). For students with documented disabilities, our disability services provides accommodations such as extended time on exams, reduced distraction testing environment, note taking assistance, and assistive technology. We provide these services in a positive and encouraging environment which promotes appreciation for diversity and Cura Personalis.

ADMISSION INFORMATION FOR STUDENTS WITH LEARNING DIFFERENCES

College entrance tests required: Yes
Interview required: No
Essay required: Yes
Additional Application Required for LD/ADHD/ASD: NR
What documentation required for LD: Psycho ed evaluation to include: relevant historical info, instructional interventions, related services, age diagnosed, objective data (aptitude, achievement, info processing), test scores (standard, percentile and grade equivalents) and describe functional limitations.
With general application: No
To receive services after enrolling: Yes
What documentation required for ADHD: Diagnosis based on DSM-V; history of behaviors impairing functioning in academic setting; diagnostic interview; history of symptoms; evidence of ongoing behaviors.
With general application: No
To receive services after enrolling: Yes
What documentation required for ASD: Psycho ed evaluation
With general application: NR
To receive services after enrolling: Yes**LD/ADHD/ASD documentation submitted to:** LAC
ASD Specific Program: NR
Special Ed. HS course work accepted: Yes
Specific course requirements of all applicants: Yes
Separate application required: No
Total # of students receiving LD/ADHD/ASD services: 265
Acceptance into program means acceptance into college: Students must be admitted to and enrolled in the university first and then request services.

ADMISSIONS

There is no special admissions process for students with disabilities. The middle 50 percent GPA is 3.20–3.88; the middle 50 percent class rank is 62–89 percent; the middle 50 percent ACT score is 23–28; and the middle 50 percent SAT score is 1060–1230.

ADDITIONAL INFORMATION

All students have access to the Math Lab, Writing Center, and Tutoring Center. Accommodations and services are available for undergraduates and graduates. Documentation required for a student with LD is a copy of the last IEP and results of the last psychoeducational test battery. Students with ADHD should submit a copy of a recent diagnostic report that states the DSM–IV diagnosis, symptoms, instruments and procedures used to make the diagnosis, and the dosage, type and frequency of your current medication. In addition to this documentation, students must fill out paperwork and sign a release form at the beginning of each semester. This enables the staff at the Learning Assistance Center to contact professors and arrange for accommodations.

General Support Services Information

Contact Information
Name of program or department: Disability Services, Learning Assistance Center
Telephone: 513-745-3280
Fax: 513-745-3387
Website: www.xavier.edu/learning-assistance-center/

Accommodations or Services for Students with Learning Differences

Accommodations are decided upon an individual basis after a thorough review of appropriate, current documentation. The accommodations requests must be supported through the documentation provided and must be logically linked to the current impact of the condition on academic functioning.

Allowed in exams
Calculator: Yes
Dictionary: Yes
Computer: Yes
Spellchecker: Yes
Extended test time: Yes
Scribes: Yes
Proctors: Yes
Oral exams: Yes
Note-takers: Yes
Support services for students with LD: NR
Support services for students with ADHD: NR
Support services for students with ASD: NR
Distraction-reduced environment: Yes
Tape recording in class: Yes
Electronic texts: Yes
Kurzweil reader: Yes
Audio books: Yes
Other assistive technology: Yes
Priority registration: Yes
Added costs of services: No
LD specialists: Yes
ADHD coaching: NR
ASD specialists: NR
Professional tutors: No
Peer tutors: NR
Max. hours/wk. for services: 1
How professors are notified of student approved accommodations: NR

General Admissions Information

Office of Admissions: 513-745-3301

Entrance Requirements

Academic units recommended: 4 English, 3 math, 3 science, 2 foreign language, 3 social studies, 5 academic electives, and 1 units from above areas or other academic areas. High school diploma is required and GED is accepted. SAT or ACT required. If ACT, ACT with writing accepted. TOEFL required of all international applicants: minimum paper TOEFL 550 or minimum internet TOEFL 79.

Application deadline: NR
Notification: Rolling starting 10/15
Average GPA: 3.59
ACT Composite middle 50% range: 22-27
SAT Math middle 50% range: 490-590
SAT Critical Reading middle 50% range: 490-590
SAT Writing middle 50% range: 480-590
Graduate top 10% of class: 23
Graduated top 25% of class: 53
Graduated top 50% of class: 84

COLLEGE GRADUATION REQUIREMENTS

Course waivers allowed: NR
Course substitutions allowed: NR
In what course: Foreign language

Additional Information

Environment: This private school, affiliated with the Roman Catholic-Jesuit Church, was founded in 1831. It has a 146-acre campus.

Student Body
Undergrad enrollment: 4,572
% Women: 54
% Men: 46
% Out-of-state: 52

Cost information
Tuition: $34,050
Room & board: $11,380
Housing Information
University Housing: Yes
Percent living on campus: 52

Greek System
Fraternity: No
Sorority: No
Athletics: Division I

Oklahoma State University

219 Student Union, Stillwater, OK 74078
Phone: 405-744-5358 • Fax: 405-744-7092
E-mail: admissions@okstate.edu • Web: www.okstate.edu
Support: S • Institution: Public

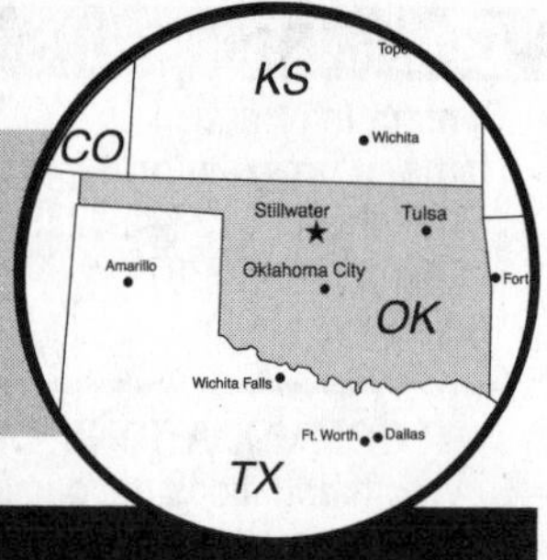

Programs or Services for Students with Learning Differences

Oklahoma State University does not have a formal learning disabilities program but uses a service-based model to assist the students in obtaining the necessary accommodations for specific learning disabilities. Students with learning disabilities may request priority enrollment and a campus orientation to assist in scheduling classes. Other services developed in coordination with the faculty work to minimize the students' difficulties in relation to course work. These services could include test accommodations, course substitutions, and independent study. The underlying philosophy of this program is to provide assistance to students to facilitate their academic progress. Student Disability Services (SDS) also acts as a resource for faculty and staff.

Admission Information for Students with Learning Differences

College entrance tests required: Yes
Interview required: No
Essay required: N/A
Additional Application Required for LD/ADHD/ASD: NR
What documentation required for LD: Psycho ed evaluation to include: relevant historical info, instructional interventions, related services, age diagnosed, objective data (aptitude, achievement, info processing), test scores (standard, percentile and grade equivalents) and describe functional limitations.
With general application: No
To receive services after enrolling: Yes
What documentation required for ADHD: Diagnosis based on DSM-V; history of behaviors impairing functioning in academic setting; diagnostic interview; history of symptoms; evidence of ongoing behaviors.
With general application: No
To receive services after enrolling: Yes
What documentation required for ASD: Psycho ed evaluation
With general application: NR
To receive services after enrolling: Yes**LD/ADHD/ASD documentation submitted to:** Support Program/Services
ASD Specific Program: NR
Special Ed. HS course work accepted: No
Specific course requirements for all applicants: Yes
Separate application required for program services: No
Total # of students receiving LD/ADHD/ASD services: 60–70
Acceptance into program means acceptance into college: Separate application required after student has enrolled

Admissions

There is no special admissions policy for students with LD. However, if ability to meet admission criteria was impacted by a disability (such as late identification, no accommodations, or high school courses waived), students should include a personal statement with their application and contact Disability Services. General admission requirements include minimum ACT 24 or SAT 1090 or a 3.0 GPA and rank in the top third of the class. Course requirements include four units English, three units math, two units lab science, three units history & citizenship skills (economics, geography, government, or non-western culture), and three units from previous areas and/or computer science and/or foreign language. Students with appropriate documentation may be allowed to substitute courses for math or foreign language. Students not meeting admission requirements may qualify for admission through: (1) Alternative Admission for students whose high school achievement is slightly below the standards and/or deficient in no more than one curricular unit (2) Summer Provision Program for students who meet all the curricular requiremetns and have a GPA of 2.5 or above, or ACT of 18 or above or SAT of 870 or above. These students may enter in the summer on probation and may be required to take placement tests prior to a final acceptance.

Additional Information

There is a math lab and a writing center for all students. All students with LD/ADHD requesting accommodations or services must provide appropriate and current documentation. All diagnostic testing and documentation should be sent to Student Disability Services. There are currently 100 students with learning disabilities and 40 with ADHD receiving services on campus. The university also operates the Oklahoma City Technical Institute, which offers two-year, career-oriented programs.

General Support Services Information

Contact Information
Name of program or department: Student Disability Services (SDS)
Telephone: 405-744-7116
Fax: 405-744-8380

Accommodations or Services for Students with Learning Differences

Accommodations are decided upon an individual basis after a thorough review of appropriate, current documentation. The accommodations requested must be supported through the documentation provided and must be logically linked to the current impact of the condition on academic functioning.

Allowed in exams
Calculator: Yes
Dictionary: Yes
Computer: Yes
Spellchecker: Yes
Extended test time: Yes
Scribes: Yes
Proctors: Yes
Oral exams: Yes
Note-takers: Yes
Services for students with LD: Yes
Services for students with ADHD: Yes
Services for students with ASD: Yes
Distraction-reduced environment: Yes
Tape recording in class: Yes
Audio books: NR
Electronic texts: Yes
Kurzweil Reader: Yes
Other assistive technology: WYNN software, Open Book, JAWS, MAGic, Dragon Naturally Speaking, CCTV, Braille printer
Priority registration: Yes
Added costs for services: No
LD specialists: No
ADHD coaching: NR
ASD specialists: NR
Professional tutors: NR
Peer tutors: No
Max. hours/wk. for services: Unlimited
How professors are notified of LD/ADHD: Both student and director

General Admissions Information

Office of Admissions: 405-744-5358

Entrance Requirements

Academic units required: 4 English, 3 math, 3 science, 3 science labs, 2 social studies, 1 history. High school diploma is required and GED is accepted. SAT or ACT required. If ACT, ACT with writing accepted. Minimum paper TOEFL 500 or minimum internet TOEFL 61.

Application deadline: NR
Notification: NR
Average GPA: 3.52
ACT Composite middle 50% range: 22-27
SAT Math middle 50% range: 500-620
SAT Critical Reading middle 50% range: 470-590
SAT Writing middle 50% range: NR-NR
Graduate top 10% of class: 27
Graduated top 25% of class: 56
Graduated top 50% of class: 85

COLLEGE GRADUATION REQUIREMENTS

Course waivers allowed: NR
Course substitutions allowed: NR

Additional Information

Environment: This public school was founded in 1890. It has a 840-acre campus.

Student Body
Undergrad enrollment: 21,046
% Women: 49
% Men: 51
% Out-of-state: 27
Cost information
In-state Tuition: $ 4,620
Out-of-state Tuition: $17,820
Room & board: $8,190
Housing Information
University Housing: Yes
Percent living on campus: 47
Greek System
Fraternity: Yes
Sorority: Yes
Athletics: Division I

THE UNIVERSITY OF TULSA

800 South Tucker Drive, Tulsa, OK 74104
Phone: 918-631-2307 • Fax: 918-631-5003
E-mail: admission@utulsa.edu • Web: www.utulsa.edu
Support: CS • Institution: Private

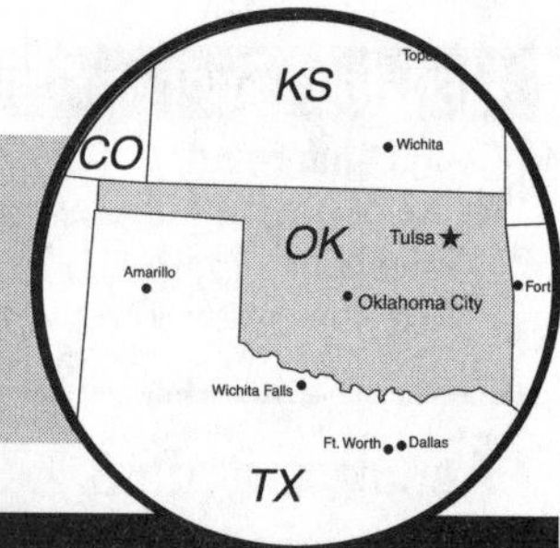

PROGRAMS OR SERVICES FOR STUDENTS WITH LEARNING DIFFERENCES

The Center for Student Academic Support offers a comprehensive range of academic support services and accommodations to students with disabilities. The goal is to provide services which will, in combination with the resources and talents of the student, maximize the students' independence for full participation in the curriculum and provide an opportunity to achieve career goals. The policy of the University of Tulsa, in keeping with the Americans with Disabilities Act, is to provide reasonable accommodations for students with disabilities, including students with learning disabilities. Students who have specific disabilities that might impact their full access and participation in university programs are urged to provide the relevant documentation and make an appointment with the director of the Center for Student Academic Support.

ADMISSION INFORMATION FOR STUDENTS WITH LEARNING DIFFERENCES

College entrance test required: Yes
Interview required: No
Essay required: Not Applicable
Additional Application Required for LD/ADHD/ASD: Yes
What documentation required for LD: Self-report application form and documentation from health care professional with diagnosis and description of functional limitations.
With general application: No
To receive services after enrolling: Yes
What documentation required for ADHD: Self-report application form and documentation from health care professional with diagnosis and description of functional limitations.
With general application: No
To receive services after enrolling: Yes
What documentation required for ASD: Self-report application form and documentation from health care professional with diagnosis and description of functional limitations.
With general application: No
To receive services after enrolling: Yes
LD/ADHD/ASD documentation submitted to: Center for Student Academic Support
ASD Specific Program: Social Opportunities Program
Special Ed. HS course work accepted: No
Specific course requirements of all applicants: NR
Separate application required for program services: Yes
Total # of students receiving LD/ADHD/ASD services: 59
Acceptance into program means acceptance into college: No

ADMISSIONS

All students must meet the general admissions requirements. Students with disabilities are not required to disclose information about the disability, but may voluntarily disclose or request information from CSAS. The university does not consider disabilities in the decision-making process, even if there is knowledge of the disability, without a request and disclosure by the applicant. Students may provide verification of the disability that should be submitted directly to CSAS. General admission requirements include: 4 years of English, 3 years of math, 4 years of science, and 2 years of foreign language. No course substitutions are allowed. The average ACT is above 21 and for the SAT is 1080–1140. Students applying to the nursing or athletic training programs must submit a special application. Conditional admission is available for freshmen and probational admission is an option for transfer students. The student with learning disabilities also needs to complete the application form and intake sheet. Also required is documentation presented from a doctor stating diagnostic material and diagnosis of the disorder.

ADDITIONAL INFORMATION

Accommodations students might qualify for depending upon their documentation and needs include: extended time on tests, priority registration, testing in self-contained environment, use of spelling aids on written exams, texts on tape, note-takers, preferential seating, tests given orally, and enlarged print tests. Concerns regarding requests for a referral for evaluation of a learning disability should be directed to the Coordinator of the Center for Student Academic Support. Students with LD must provide documentation that includes tests of intellect and of achievement administered by a professional. Students with documented ADHD must provide behavior checklist (one completed by a doctor), a test of intellect, a test of attention, and a clinical interview that includes a history of the ADHD.

General Support Services Information

Contact Information
Name of program or department: Center for Student Academic Support
Telephone: 918-631-2315
Fax: 918-631-3459
Website: www.utulsa.edu/CSAS

Accommodations or Services For Students With Learning Differences

Accommodations are decided upon an individual basis after a thorough review of appropriate, current documentation. The accommodations requests must be supported through the documentation provided and must be logically linked to the current impact of the condition on academic functioning.

Allowed in exams
Calculator: Yes
Dictionary: Yes
Computer: Yes
Spellchecker: Yes
Extended test time: Yes
Scribes: Yes
Proctors: Yes
Oral exams: Yes
Note-takers: Yes
Support services for students with LD: Yes
Support services for students with ADHD: Yes
Support services for students with ASD: Yes
Distraction-reduced environment: Yes
Tape recording in class: Yes
Electronic texts: Yes
Kurzweil reader: NR
Audio books: Yes
Other assistive technology: NR
Priority registration: Yes
Added costs of services: Yes
LD specialists: Yes
ADHD coaching: Yes
ASD specialists: No
Professional tutors: No
Peer tutors: Yes
Max. hours/wk. for services: NR
How professors are notified of student approved accommodations: By student

General Admissions Information

Office of Admissions: 918-631-2307

Entrance Requirements

Academic units recommended: 4 English, 4 math, 3 science, 3 science labs, 2 foreign language, 3 social studies, 1 computer science, 1 visual/performing arts. High school diploma is required and GED is accepted. SAT or ACT required. If ACT, ACT with writing accepted. TOEFL required of all international applicants: minimum paper TOEFL 550 or minimum internet TOEFL 80.

Application deadline: NR
Notification: Rolling starting 12/15
Average GPA: 3.9
ACT Composite middle 50% range: 26-32
SAT Math middle 50% range: 570-700
SAT Critical Reading middle 50% range: 560-700
SAT Writing middle 50% range: NR-NR
Graduate top 10% of class: 73
Graduated top 25% of class: 91
Graduated top 50% of class: 99

COLLEGE GRADUATION REQUIREMENTS

Course waivers allowed: Yes
In what course: Any applicable courses.
Course substitutions allowed: Yes
In what course: Any applicable courses.

Additional Information

Environment: This private school, affiliated with the Presbyterian Church, was founded in 1894. It has a 209-acre campus.

Student Body
Undergrad enrollment: 3,478
% Women: 42
% Men: 58
% Out-of-state: 43

Cost information
Tuition: $37,580
Room & board: $11,116

Housing Information
University Housing: Yes
Percent living on campus: 71

Greek System
Fraternity: Yes
Sorority: Yes
Athletics: Division I

Lewis & Clark College

0615 SW Palatine Hill Road Portland, OR 97219-7899
Phone: 503-768-7040 • Fax: 503-768-7055
E-mail: admissions@lclark.edu • Web: www.lclark.edu
Support: CS • Institution: Private

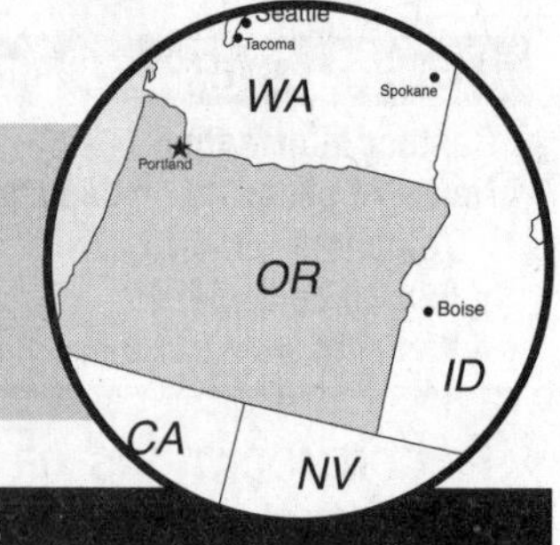

Programs or Services for Students with Learning Differences

To serve and support students with disabilities in the CAS, graduate school and law school. To help students appreciate their distinctive ways of learning and develop strategies for success based on their strengths and to develop strong self-advocacy skills. To help the LC community develop positive modes of interacting with students with disabilities.

Admission Information for Students with Learning Differences

College entrance test required: No
Interview required: Not Applicable
Essay required: Not Applicable
Additional Application Required for LD/ADHD/ASD: Not Applicable
What documentation required for LD: Psycho-educational assessment or verification of diagnosis with recommendation for accommodation.
With general application: Not Applicable
To receive services after enrolling: Not Applicable
What documentation required for ADHD: Verification of diagnosis with recommendation for accommodation.
With general application: Not Applicable
To receive services after enrolling: Not Applicable
What documentation required for ASD: Full battery of diagnostic psycho-educational assessments
With general application: Not Applicable
To receive services after enrolling: Not Applicable
LD/ADHD/ASD documentation submitted to: Student Support Services
ASD Specific Program: NR
Special Ed. HS course work accepted: Not Applicable
Specific course requirements of all applicants: Yes
Separate application required for program services: False
Total # of students receiving LD/ADHD/ASD services: NR
Acceptance into program means acceptance into college: Not Applicable

Admissions

When admitting new students, our admissions staff look for individuals from diverse backgrounds, with diverse talents and interests, students who will not only meet the rigorous academic challenges of a Lewis & Clark education, but will also take full advantage of the opportunities for individual achievement and growth offered here. Successful Lewis & Clark applicants will have completed a rigorous curriculum including at a minimum: 4 years of English 4 years of mathematics 3-4 years of history/social science 2-3 years of a foreign language 3 years of lab science 1 year of fine arts The best predictor of academic success at Lewis & Clark is a student's record in their core academic courses. Grades for such courses taken in years 11 and 12 are very important. We look not only at your performance in a challenging curriculum, but at the following criteria as well: SAT or ACT scores (unless applying through the Test-Optional Portfolio Path); Secondary School Report (first-year students only); Teacher Evaluation completed by a teacher who has taught you in an academic course (English, mathematics, science, foreign language, history, or social studies) in 10th-12th grade. Personal essay, leadership, community service and work experience, and extracurricular involvements.

Additional Information

In order to access accommodations, students need to meet with a representative from the Student Support Services Office and provide their documentation. The staff will work with a student on study skills, test-taking skills and curriculum planning. The following are available for all students: The Writing Center, Tutoring, Physics Help Center, Chemistry Help Center, and Counseling Services.

General Support Services Information

Contact Information
Name of program or department: Student Support Services
Telephone: 503-768-7192
Fax: 503-768-7197
Website: lclark.edu/offices/student_support_services/

Accommodations or Services for Students with Learning Differences

Accommodations are decided upon an individual basis after a thorough review of appropriate, current documentation. The accommodations requests must be supported through the documentation provided and must be logically linked to the current impact of the condition on academic functioning.

Allowed in exams
Calculator: Yes
Dictionary: Yes
Computer: Yes
Spellchecker: Yes
Extended test time: Yes
Scribes: Yes
Proctors: Yes
Oral exams: Yes
Note-takers: Yes
Support services for students with LD: Yes
Support services for students with ADHD: Yes
Support services for students with ASD: Yes
Distraction-reduced environment: Yes
Tape recording in class: Yes
Electronic texts: Yes
Kurzweil reader: NR
Audio books: Yes
Other assistive technology: Yes
Priority registration: No
Added costs of services: No
LD specialists: Yes
ADHD coaching: Yes
ASD specialists: No
Professional tutors: No
Peer tutors: Yes
Max. hours/wk. for services: 16
How professors are notified of student approved accommodations: By director

General Admissions Information

Office of Admissions: 503-768-7040

Entrance Requirements

Academic units recommended: 4 English, 4 math, 3 science, 2 science labs, 2 foreign language, 3 social studies, 1 visual/performing arts. High school diploma is required and GED is accepted. SAT or ACT required for some. If ACT, ACT with writing accepted. TOEFL required of all international applicants: minimum paper TOEFL 575 or minimum internet TOEFL 91.

Application deadline: 3/1
Notification: 4/1
Average GPA: 3.88
ACT Composite middle 50% range: 27-31
SAT Math middle 50% range: 590-670
SAT Critical Reading middle 50% range: 600-720
SAT Writing middle 50% range: 580-630
Graduate top 10% of class: 48
Graduated top 25% of class: 82
Graduated top 50% of class: 97

COLLEGE GRADUATION REQUIREMENTS

Course waivers allowed: No
Course substitutions allowed: Yes
In what course: Foreign Language

Additional Information

Environment: This private school was founded in 1867. It has a 137-acre campus.

Student Body
Undergrad enrollment: 2,209
% Women: 61
% Men: 39
% Out-of-state: 89

Cost information
Tuition: $44,744
Room & board: $11,218

Housing Information
University Housing: Yes
Percent living on campus: 70

Greek System
Fraternity: No
Sorority: No
Athletics: Division III

Oregon State University

104 Kerr Administration Building, Corvallis, OR 97331-2106
Phone: 541-737-4411 • Fax: 541-737-2482
E-mail: osuadmit@oregonstate.edu • Web: oregonstate.edu/
Support: S • Institution: Public

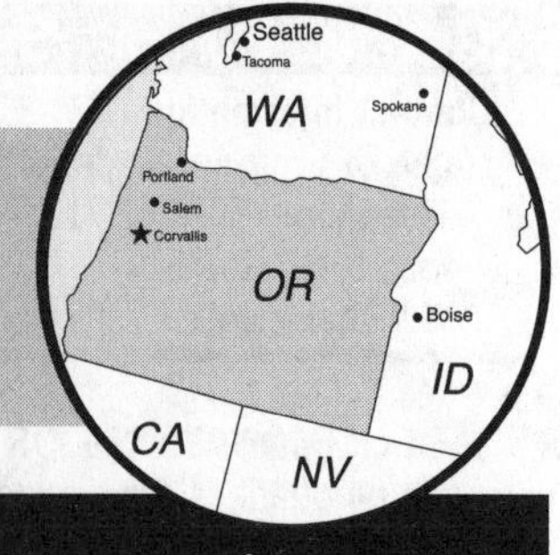

Programs or Services for Students with Learning Differences

OSU is committed to providing equal opportunity for higher education to academically qualified students without regard to disability. Disability Access Services (DAS) strives to be sensitive to the individual needs of students by offering a variety of services. Services rendered are dependent on the type of learning disability. Services are provided to ensure an equal opportunity to succeed but do not guarantee success. Self-advocacy and independence are promoted. DAS is available for all students who need extra services. The Educational Opportunities Program (EOP) offers students who are learning disabled, economically disadvantaged, or first-generation college-bound a variety of remedial courses for credit. EOP tries to provide tutoring for any undergraduate class if tutors are available. To be recognized as a person with a learning disability, students are required to submit documentation from a qualified educational evaluator. Preferred diagnostic testing would include at least one test in each of the following categories: cognitive, achievement, and processing. Other documentation specifying a learning disability without testing in the three categories mentioned must include an in-depth valid assessment of the disability by a qualified professional.

Admission Information for Students with Learning Differences

College entrance tests required: Yes
Interview required: No
Additional Application Required for LD/ADHD/ASD: NR
What documentation required for LD: Psycho ed evaluation to include: relevant historical info, instructional interventions, related services, age diagnosed, objective data (aptitude, achievement, info processing), test scores (standard, percentile and grade equivalents) and describe functional limitations.
With general application: No
To receive services after enrolling: Yes
What documentation required for ADHD: Diagnosis based on DSM-V; history of behaviors impairing functioning in academic setting; diagnostic interview; history of symptoms; evidence of ongoing behaviors.
With general application: No
To receive services after enrolling: Yes
What documentation required for ASD: Psycho ed evaluation
With general application: NR
To receive services after enrolling: Yes
LD/ADHD/ASD documentation submitted to: Support Program/Services
ASD Specific Program: NR
Special Ed. HS course work accepted: No
Specific course requirements for all applicants: Yes
Separate application required for program services: No
Total # of students receiving LD/ADHD/ASD services: 179
Acceptance into program means acceptance into college: Separate application required after student has enrolled

Admissions

All students must submit the general application for admission. If a student does not meet admissions requirements, admission will be denied. Enclosed with the notification, the student will receive information regarding petitioning for special admission. Students who want to petition their admission on the basis of a learning disability must submit all information required in the petition. Petitioning students must utilize the services of EOP. The director of DAS helps to make admission decisions and may recommend EOP for the student with LD. Regular admission requires a 3.0 GPA and special admit for students with 2.5. Students requesting services should self-identify; submit documentation of their LD, including educational history and diagnostic testing administered by professionals; and include information describing cognitive strengths and weaknesses, recommendations for accommodations or services, and any other additional information in the form of a family history. Students must also submit a handwritten 1–2 page statement outlining educational goals and explaining motivation to succeed at OSU. Students admitted through the EOP Program must start in the summer and attend a required DAS orientation in the beginning of fall. EOP admission decision is made jointly between Admissions and EOP.

Additional Information

Students with LD, whether admitted regularly or as special admits, are encouraged to apply for additional assistance from EOP, which can provide special counseling, tutoring, and intensive practice in study skills. Accommodations in instruction and related academic work may include alternative test methods such as extended testing time and use of resources such as calculators. Accommodations are negotiated with instructors, academic departments, and the college as appropriate. Personal counseling is available through the Counseling Center. The director acts as a liaison between students and faculty.

General Support Services Information

Contact Information
Name of program or department: Disability Access Services (DAS)
Telephone: 541-737-4098
Fax: 541-737-7354

Accommodations or Services for Students with Learning Differences

Accommodations are decided upon an individual basis after a thorough review of appropriate, current documentation. The accommodations requested must be supported through the documentation provided and must be logically linked to the current impact of the condition on academic functioning.

Allowed in exams
Calculator: Yes
Dictionary: No
Computer: Yes
Spellchecker: Yes
Extended test time: Yes
Scribes: Yes
Proctors: Yes
Oral exams: Yes
Note-takers: Yes
Services for students with LD: Yes
Services for students with ADHD: Yes
Services for students with ASD: Yes
Distraction-reduced environment: Yes
Tape recording in class: Yes
Audio books: NR
Electronic texts: Yes
Kurzweil Reader: Yes
Other assistive technology: Assistive Listening Devices
Priority registration: Yes
Added costs for services: No
LD specialists: No
ADHD coaching: NR
ASD specialists: NR
Professional tutors: NR
Peer tutors: Available at Academic Success Center
Max. hours/wk. for services: N/A
How professors are notified of LD/ADHD: Both student and director

General Admissions Information

Office of Admissions: 541-737-4411

Entrance Requirements

Academic units required: 4 English, 3 math, 3 science, 2 science labs, 2 foreign language, 3 social studies, **Academic units recommended:** 3 science labs. High school diploma is required and GED is accepted. SAT or ACT required. If ACT, ACT with writing required. TOEFL required of all international applicants: minimum paper TOEFL 550 or minimum internet TOEFL 80.

Application deadline: 9/1
Notification: Rolling starting 10/15
Average GPA: 3.58
ACT Composite middle 50% range: 21-28
SAT Math middle 50% range: 490-630
SAT Critical Reading middle 50% range: 480-610
SAT Writing middle 50% range: 470-590
Graduate top 10% of class: 24
Graduated top 25% of class: 54
Graduated top 50% of class: 89

COLLEGE GRADUATION REQUIREMENTS

Course waivers allowed: NR
Course substitutions allowed: NR
In what course: Math, foreign language. Courses may only be substituted to meet core requirements not major requirements.

Additional Information

Environment: This public school was founded in 1858. It has a 421-acre campus.

Student Body
Undergrad enrollment: 24,612
% Women: 46
% Men: 54
% Out-of-state: 29

Cost information
In-state Tuition: $8,535
Out-of-state Tuition: $27,195
Room & board: $11,691

Housing Information
University Housing: Yes
Percent living on campus: 17

Greek System
Fraternity: Yes
Sorority: Yes
Athletics: Division I

UNIVERSITY OF OREGON

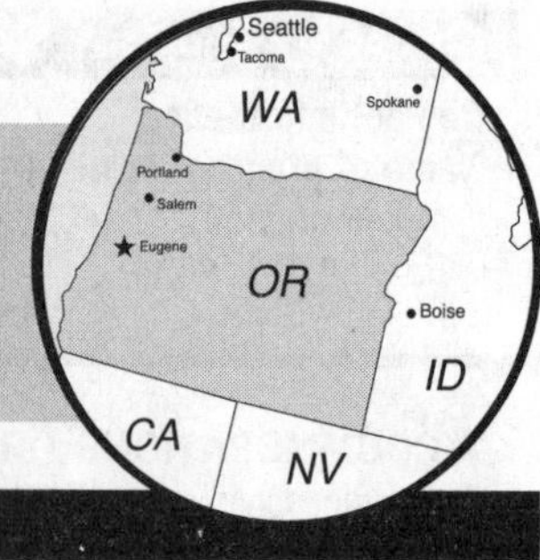

1217 University of Oregon, Eugene, OR 97403-1217
Phone: 541-346-3201 • Fax: 541-346-5815
E-mail: uoadmit@uoregon.edu • Web: www.uoregon.edu
Support: CS • Institution: Public

PROGRAMS OR SERVICES FOR STUDENTS WITH LEARNING DIFFERENCES

At the University of Oregon, the Accessible Education Center (AEC) promotes inclusive teaching strategies and coordinates services and support to students with currently documented learning disabilities and Attention Deficit Hyperactivity Disorder. During university orientation programs students discuss their needs, challenges, educational goals, and available services. Accommodations are determined on a case-by-case basis after admission and an individual appointment. A faculty notification letter outlining suggested accommodations is provided when requested, and is shared at the students' discretion. The university is actively engaged in universal design instructional strategies to minimize the need for individualized accommodations when possible. Successful students are motivated, hardworking, and able to articulate their strengths and challenges.

ADMISSION INFORMATION FOR STUDENTS WITH LEARNING DIFFERENCES

College entrance tests required: Yes
Interview required: No
Essay required: Yes
Additional Application Required for LD/ADHD/ASD: NR
What documentation required for LD: Psycho ed evaluation to include: relevant historical info, instructional interventions, related services, age diagnosed, objective data (aptitude, achievement, info processing), test scores (standard, percentile and grade equivalents) and describe functional limitations.
With general application: No
To receive services after enrolling: Yes
What documentation required for ADHD: Diagnosis based on DSM-V; history of behaviors impairing functioning in academic setting; diagnostic interview; history of symptoms; evidence of ongoing behaviors.
With general application: No
To receive services after enrolling: Yes
What documentation is required for ASD: Diagnosis based on DSM-V; history of behaviors impairing functioning in academic setting; diagnostic interview; history of symptoms; evidence of ongoing behaviors.
With general application: No
To receive services after enrolling: Yes
LD/ADHD/ASD documentation submitted to: Both Admissions and Accessible Education Center
ASD Specific Program: NR
Special Ed. HS course work accepted: Yes
Specific course requirements of all applicants: Yes
Separate application required: No
Total # of students receiving LD/ADHD/ASD services: 350
Acceptance into program means acceptance into college: Student must be admitted and enrolled in the university first and then request services.

ADMISSIONS

Students with learning disabilities must meet the same admission criteria as all other applicants. Courses recommended for admission include: 4 years of English, 3 years of math including Algebra II, 3 years of science, 2 years of a second language, and 3 years of social studies. The average SAT is 1117 and the average GPA is 3.59. Students not meeting the regular admission requirements who have extenuating circumstances due to a learning disability may request additional consideration of their application by a special committee. A completed application form, a graded writing sample, two letters of recommendation, and documentation of the disability with information about how it has influenced the student's ability to meet minimum admission requirements are required for special admission consideration based on disability.

ADDITIONAL INFORMATION

Students are encouraged to take an active role in registering for and utilizing services. Once admitted, students should meet with AEC to review documentation and discuss educational goals. Typical support includes modification of testing procedures, including additional testing time, dictation of responses, text to speech formats, and distraction reduced testing environments; permission to record lectures, access to instructor or classmate notes; Assistive Technology Program with alternate print formats; faculty liaison to assist in communicating needs to instructors and to help negotiate reasonable accommodations or inclusive design strategies in courses and programs. For graduation the university requires two terms of writing classes for all degrees. The BS degree requires one year of college math, and the BA degree requires two years of a second language (American Sign Language is accepted). Writing and math labs are available on campus.

General Support Services Information

Contact Information
Name of program or department: Accessible Education Center
Telephone: 541-346-1155
Fax: 541-346-6013

Accommodations or Services for Students with Learning Differences

Accommodations are determined an individual basis after a thorough review of appropriate, current documentation and an individual meeting with the student. The accommodations requested must be supported through the documentation provided and must be logically linked to the current impact of the condition on academic functioning.

Allowed in exams
Calculator: Yes
Dictionary: Yes
Computer: Yes
Spellchecker: Yes
Extended test time: Yes
Scribes: Yes
Proctors: Yes
Oral exams: Yes
Note-takers: Yes
Services for students with LD: Yes
Services for students with ADHD: Yes
Services for students with ASD: Yes
Distraction-reduced environment: Yes
Tape recording in class: Yes
Audio books: Yes
Electronic texts: Yes
Kurzweil Reader: Yes
Other assistive technology: Yes
Priority registration: Yes
Added costs for services: Yes
LD specialists: Yes
ADHD coaching: No
ASD specialists: No
Professional tutors: Yes
Peer tutors: Yes
Max. hours/wk. for services: NR
How professors are notified of LD/ADHD: By student and notification letter

General Admissions Information

Office of Admissions: 541-346-3201

Entrance Requirements

Academic units required: 4 English, 3 math, 3 science, 2 foreign language, 3 social studies. **Academic units recommended:** 1 science labs. High school diploma is required and GED is accepted. SAT or ACT required. If ACT, ACT with writing accepted. TOEFL required of all international applicants: minimum paper TOEFL 500 or minimum internet TOEFL 61.

Application deadline: 1/15
Notification: Rolling starting 4/1
Average GPA: 3.61
ACT Composite middle 50% range: 22-27
SAT Math middle 50% range: 500-610
SAT Critical Reading middle 50% range: 500-620
SAT Writing middle 50% range: 490-600
Graduated top 10% of class: 29
Graduated top 25% of class: 64
Graduated top 50% of class: 93

COLLEGE GRADUATION REQUIREMENTS

Course waivers allowed: No
Course substitutions allowed: Yes
In what course: In extreme cases with appropriate documentation.

Additional Information

Environment: This public school was founded in 1876. It has a 295-acre campus.

Student Body
Undergrad enrollment: 20,538
% Women: 53
% Men: 47
% Out-of-state: 41

Cost information
In-state Tuition: $8,505
Out-of Tuition: $30,240
Room & board: $11,785

Housing Information
University Housing: Yes
Percent living on campus: 20

Greek System
Fraternity: Yes
Sorority: Yes
Athletics: Division I

Western Oregon University

345 N Monmouth Avenue, Monmouth, OR 97361
Phone: 503-838-8211 • Fax: 503-838-8067
E-mail: wolfgram@wou.edu • Web: www.wou.edu
Support: S • Institution: Public

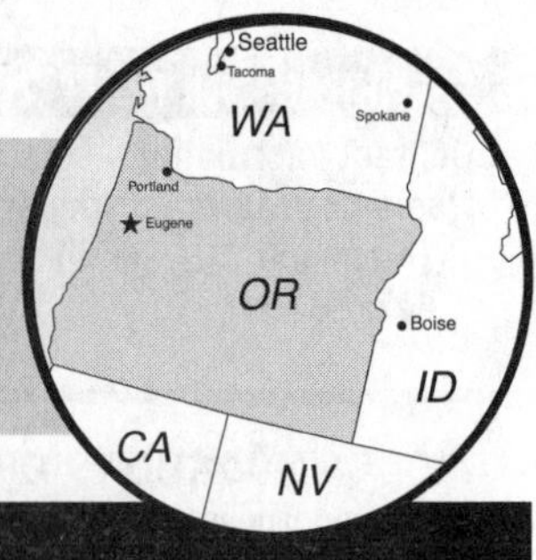

Programs or Services for Students with Learning Differences

The mission of the Office of Disability Services (ODS) is to remove barriers to learning for students with disabilities and to help ensure that these students access the tools and processes they need to create a successful experience at Western and beyond. These goals are realized by providing support services and information to help students develop skills such as self-advocacy, independence, identification and use of resources, appropriate use of problem-solving techniques, and accepting responsibility for one's actions. ODS strives to meet the individual needs of students with disabilities. The Student Enrichment Program (SEP) is designed to help students find success in college. The program's goals are to help SEP students develop writing, math, learning, and critical-thinking skills; maintain the necessary GPA to achieve individual goals; develop interpersonal communication skills; and achieve autonomy and maintain a sense of self-worth. Students who could benefit from SEP are those who enter the university without being completely prepared. SEP staff focuses on working with individual needs. Eligibility is based on federal guidelines determined by first-generation college-bound, financial need, or physical or learning disability; additionally, the student must have demonstrated academic need for the program.

Admission Information for Students with Learning Differences

College entrance tests required: No
Interview required: No
Essay required: No
Additional Application Required for LD/ADHD/ASD: NR
What documentation required for LD: Psycho ed evaluation to include: relevant historical info, instructional interventions, related services, age diagnosed, objective data (aptitude, achievement, info processing), test scores (standard, percentile and grade equivalents) and describe functional limitations.
With general application: No
To receive services after enrolling: Yes
What documentation required for ADHD: Diagnosis based on DSM-V; history of behaviors impairing functioning in academic setting; diagnostic interview; history of symptoms; evidence of ongoing behaviors.
With general application: No
To receive services after enrolling: Yes
What documentation required for ASD: Psycho ed evaluation
With general application: NR
To receive services after enrolling: Yes
LD/ADHD/ASD documentation submitted to: Office of Disability Services
ASD Specific Program: NR
Special Ed. HS course work accepted: No
Specific course requirements of all applicants: Yes
Separate application required: Yes
Total # of students receiving LD/ADHD/ASD services: 60–70
Acceptance into program means acceptance into college: Student must be admitted and enrolled in the university first and then request services.

Admissions

General admission requires a 2.75 GPA and ACT/SAT scores, which are used only as alternatives to the required GPA. Applicants with a 2.50–2.74 are admissible with 21 ACT or 1000 SAT. Course requirements include 4 years of English, 3 years of math, 3 years of science, 3 years of social science, and 2 years of the same foreign language ("C-" or better in courses). Alternatives to course requirements require either a score of 470 or above on three SAT Subject Tests. A limited number of students who do not meet the regular admission requirements, alternatives, or exceptions may be admitted through special action of an Admissions Committee. Submit a letter of petition stating why they don't meet the admission requirements and what they are doing to make up deficiencies, and three letters of recommendation from school and community members.

Additional Information

Skills classes are offered in academic survival strategies (no credit) and critical thinking (college credit). Other services include advocacy, computer stations, note-takers, readers and taping services, alternative testing, advisement, and assistance with registration. CEP offers counseling; basic math courses; advising; individualized instruction in reading, study skills, writing, and critical thinking; monitor programs; and workshops on study skills, research writing, math anxiety, rapid reading, note-taking, and time management. Services and accommodations are available for undergraduate and graduate students.

General Support Services Information

Contact Information
Name of program or department: Office of Disability Services
Telephone: 503-838-8250
Fax: 503-838-8721

Accommodations or Services for Students with Learning Differences

Accommodations are decided upon an individual basis after a thorough review of appropriate, current documentation. The accommodations requested must be supported through the documentation provided and must be logically linked to the current impact of the condition on academic functioning.

Allowed in exams
Calculator: Yes
Dictionary: Yes
Computer: Yes
Spellchecker: Yes
Extended test time: Yes
Scribes: Yes
Proctors: Yes
Oral exams: Yes
Note-takers: Yes
Services for students with LD: Yes
Services for students with ADHD: Yes
Services for students with ASD: Yes
Distraction-reduced environment: Yes
Tape recording in class: Yes
Audio books: NR
Electronic texts: No
Kurzweil Reader: No
Other assistive technology: Yes
Priority registration: Yes
Added costs for services: No
LD specialists: No
ADHD coaching: NR
ASD specialists: NR
Professional tutors: No
Peer tutors: Yes
Max. hours/wk. for services: N/A
How professors are notified of LD/ADHD: By both student and director

General Admissions Information

Office of Admissions: 503-838-8211

Entrance Requirements

Academic units required: 4 English, 3 math, 3 science, 1 science labs, 2 foreign language, 3 social studies, **Academic units recommended:** 4 English, 3 math, 3 science, 1 science labs, 2 foreign language, 3 social studies. High school diploma is required and GED is accepted. SAT or ACT not used. If ACT, ACT with writing required. TOEFL required of all international applicants: minimum paper TOEFL 500.

Application deadline: NR
Notification: Rolling starting 1/1
Average GPA: 3.24
ACT Composite middle 50% range: 22-17
SAT Math middle 50% range: 530-420
SAT Critical Reading middle 50% range: 540-420
SAT Writing middle 50% range: 510-410
Graduated top 10% of class: 11
Graduated top 25% of class: 35
Graduated top 50% of class: 71

COLLEGE GRADUATION REQUIREMENTS

Course waivers allowed: No
Course substitutions allowed: Yes
In what course: Decisions are made on a case-by-case basis.

Additional Information

Environment: This public school was founded in 1856. It has a 157-acre campus.

Student Body
Undergrad enrollment: 4,808
% Women: 60
% Men: 40
% Out-of-state: 18

Cost information
In-state Tuition: $8,723
Out-of Tuition: $22,257
Room & board: $9,416
Housing Information
University Housing: Yes
Percent living on campus: 26

Greek System
Fraternity: Yes
Sorority: Yes
Athletics: Division II

BUCKNELL UNIVERSITY

Office of Admissions, 1 Dent Drive Lewisburg, PA 17837
Phone: 570-577-3000 • Fax: 570-577-3538
E-mail: admissions@bucknell.edu • Web: www.bucknell.edu
Support: CS • Institution: Private

PROGRAMS OR SERVICES FOR STUDENTS WITH LEARNING DIFFERENCES

The Office of Accessibility Resources (formerly referred to as the Office of Disability Services) exists to ensure access, provide support, and help to navigate or remove barriers for students, faculty, staff, and visitors to our campus. Our office is committed to providing a strong support system for individuals with disabilities, and is committed to ensuring that no otherwise qualified individual with a disability will be denied participation in or the benefits of any of our programs on the basis of a disability.

ADMISSION INFORMATION FOR STUDENTS WITH LEARNING DIFFERENCES

College entrance test required: Yes
Interview required: No
Essay required: Not Applicable
Additional Application Required for LD/ADHD/ASD: Yes
What documentation required for LD: Educational Psychological evaluation
With general application: Not Applicable
To receive services after enrolling: Yes
What documentation required for ADHD: Psychological evaluation
With general application: Not Applicable
To receive services after enrolling: Yes
What documentation required for ASD: Educational Psychological evaluation
With general application: Not Applicable
To receive services after enrolling: Yes
LD/ADHD/ASD documentation submitted to: Office of Accessability Resources
ASD Specific Program: Office of Accessibility Resources
Special Ed. HS course work accepted: Yes
Specific course requirements of all applicants: Yes
Separate application required for program services: False
Total # of students receiving LD/ADHD/ASD services: 208
Acceptance into program means acceptance into college: Not Applicable

ADMISSIONS

Same for all students. Bucknell University uses the Common Application.

ADDITIONAL INFORMATION

The student contacts the Director of OARS for an intake interview. During this "meeting" that can happen in person or by phone. The Director, during this conversation, will identify the documentation the student needs to submit. It is then reviewed and the student is notified whether the accommodation request is approved.

The Office of Accessibility Resources (OAR) provides direct support services. The OAR arranges, facilitates,and/or coordinates necessary accommodations and academic adjustments to meet the individual needs of the student. Additionally, the Teaching & Learning Center offers study groups led by a trained peer facilitator and also a Tutoring Program.

General Support Services Information

Contact Information
Name of program or department: Office of Accessability Resources
Telephone: 570-577-1188
Fax: 570-577-1826
Website: http://www.bucknell.edu/Accessibility

Accommodations or Services for Students with Learning Differences

Accommodations are decided upon an individual basis after a thorough review of appropriate, current documentation. The accommodations requests must be supported through the documentation provided and must be logically linked to the current impact of the condition on academic functioning.

Allowed in exams
Calculator: Yes
Dictionary: Yes
Computer: Yes
Spellchecker: Yes
Extended test time: Yes
Scribes: Yes
Proctors: Yes
Oral exams: Yes
Note-takers: Yes
Support services for students with LD: NR
Support services for students with ADHD: Yes
Support services for students with ASD: Yes
Distraction-reduced environment: Yes
Tape recording in class: Yes
Electronic texts: Yes
Kurzweil reader: NR
Audio books: Yes
Other assistive technology: Yes
Priority registration: No
Added costs of services: No
LD specialists: Yes
ADHD coaching: Yes
ASD specialists: Yes
Professional tutors: Yes
Peer tutors: Yes
Max. hours/wk. for services: NR
How professors are notified of student approved accommodations: By both student and director

General Admissions Information

Office of Admissions: 570-577-3000

Entrance Requirements

Academic units required: 4 English, 3 math, 2 science, 2 foreign language, 2 social studies, 2 history, 1 academic electives. **Academic units recommended:** 4 English, 4 math, 2 science, 2 science labs, 4 foreign language, 2 social studies, 2 history, 1 academic electives, High school diploma is required and GED is accepted. SAT or ACT required. If ACT, ACT with writing accepted. TOEFL required of all international applicants: minimum paper TOEFL 600 or minimum internet TOEFL 100.

Application deadline: 1/15
Notification: 4/1
Average GPA: 3.54
ACT Composite middle 50% range: 28-32
SAT Math middle 50% range: 620-710
SAT Critical Reading middle 50% range: 590-680
SAT Writing middle 50% range: 590-690
Graduate top 10% of class: 65
Graduated top 25% of class: 91
Graduated top 50% of class: 99

COLLEGE GRADUATION REQUIREMENTS

Course waivers allowed: No
In what course: Foreign Language
Course substitutions allowed: Yes
In what course: Foreign Language

Additional Information

Environment: This private school was founded in 1846. It has a 446-acre campus.

Student Body
Undergrad enrollment: 3,569
% Women: 52
% Men: 48
% Out-of-state: 77

Cost information
Tuition: $49,878
Room & board: $12,216

Housing Information
University Housing: Yes
Percent living on campus: 91

Greek System
Fraternity: Yes
Sorority: Yes
Athletics: Division I

CHATHAM UNIVERSITY

Woodland Road Pittsburgh, PA 15232
Phone: 412-365-1825 • Fax: 412-365-1609
E-mail: admission@chatham.edu • Web: www.chatham.edu
Support: S • Institution: Private

PROGRAMS OR SERVICES FOR STUDENTS WITH LEARNING DIFFERENCES

The PACE Center offers a wide variety of academic support and access to services.
PACE coordinates services and determines accommodations on a case-by-case basis and they are implemented only after the student's needs are documented.Tutoring is available for the majority of courses offered. Peer tutors are recommended by faculty and trained by PACE staff to provide helpful assistance. Students may receive up to two hours of tutoring per week in each course. The tutoring is free. There is also Academic Coaching/skill building available.

ADMISSION INFORMATION FOR STUDENTS WITH LEARNING DIFFERENCES

College entrance test required: Yes
Interview required: No
Essay required: Not Applicable
Additional Application Required for LD/ADHD/ASD: No
What documentation required for LD: Documentation may consist of medical or educational records, and reports and assessments from health care providers, educational psychologists, teachers, or the educational system.
With general application: NR
To receive services after enrolling: No
What documentation required for ADHD: No specific documentation is required but documentation must be provided by a qualified professional that states the diagnosis, functional limitations and recommendations for accommodations, adaptive devices, and support services.
With general application: NR
To receive services after enrolling: No
What documentation required for ASD: Documentation may consist of medical or educational records, and reports and assessments from health care providers, educational psychologists, teachers, or the educational system.
With general application: NR
To receive services after enrolling: No
LD/ADHD/ASD documentation submitted to: PACE Center
ASD Specific Program: No
Special Ed. HS course work accepted: Yes
Specific course requirements of all applicants: Yes
Separate application required for program services: False
Total # of students receiving LD/ADHD/ASD services: NR
Acceptance into program means acceptance into college: NR

ADMISSIONS

Chatham University has a test-optional policy. If the student chooses not to submit scores they should send the following (in addition to the application): Resume, graded writing sample, and on campus interview.

ADDITIONAL INFORMATION

Accommodations are determined on a case-by-case basis and are implemented only after the student's needs are documented. Documentation of a disability can take a variety of forms. Students are encouraged to make an appointment with the Director to discuss any challenges the student may faces in regards to their educational program. Accommodations can include but are not limited to: alternate text formats, distraction free environment for testing, note-taker services, screen reading (Kruzweil) and self-advocacy development.

General Support Services Information

Contact Information
Name of program or department: PACE Center
Telephone: 412-365-1611
Fax: 412-365-1660
Website: http://chatham.edu/academics/support/index.cfm

Accommodations or Services for Students with Learning Differences

Accommodations are decided upon an individual basis after a thorough review of appropriate, current documentation. The accommodations requests must be supported through the documentation provided and must be logically linked to the current impact of the condition on academic functioning.

Allowed in exams
Calculator: Yes
Dictionary: Yes
Computer: No
Spellchecker: Yes
Extended test time: Yes
Scribes: Yes
Proctors: Yes
Oral exams: Yes
Note-takers: Yes
Support services for students with LD: Yes
Support services for students with ADHD: Yes
Support services for students with ASD: Yes
Distraction-reduced environment: Yes
Tape recording in class: Yes
Electronic texts: Yes
Kurzweil reader: NR
Audio books: Yes
Other assistive technology: Yes
Priority registration: No
Added costs of services: No
LD specialists: No
ADHD coaching: Yes
ASD specialists: No
Professional tutors: Yes
Peer tutors: Yes
Max. hours/wk. for services: NR
How professors are notified of student approved accommodations: By both student and director

General Admissions Information

Office of Admissions: 412-365-1825

Entrance Requirements

Academic units required: 4 English, 2 math, 2 science, and 3 units from above areas or other academic areas. **Academic units recommended:** 4 English, 3 math, 3 science, 2 foreign language, 3 social studies. High school diploma is required and GED is accepted. SAT or ACT considered if submitted. If ACT, ACT with writing accepted. TOEFL required of all international applicants: minimum paper TOEFL 500 or minimum internet TOEFL 60.

Application deadline: 8/1
Notification: Rolling starting 10/15
Average GPA: 3.57
ACT Composite middle 50% range: 21-26
SAT Math middle 50% range: 470-560
SAT Critical Reading middle 50% range: 485-585
SAT Writing middle 50% range: 460-580
Graduate top 10% of class: 23
Graduated top 25% of class: 53
Graduated top 50% of class: 87

COLLEGE GRADUATION REQUIREMENTS

Course waivers allowed: No
In what course: NR
Course substitutions allowed: Yes
In what course: Physical Education

Additional Information

Environment: This private school was founded in 1869. It has a 39388-acre campus.

Student Body
Undergrad enrollment: 1,034
% Women: 83
% Men: 17
% Out-of-state: 19

Cost information
Tuition:$34,195
Room & board: $11,042

Housing Information
University Housing: Yes
Percent living on campus: 52

Greek System
Fraternity: No
Sorority: No
Athletics: Division III

DREXEL UNIVERSITY

3141 Chestnut Street, Philadelphia, PA 19104
Phone: 215-895-2400 • Fax: 215-895-1285
E-mail: enroll@drexel.edu • Web: www.drexel.edu
Support: CS • Institution: Private

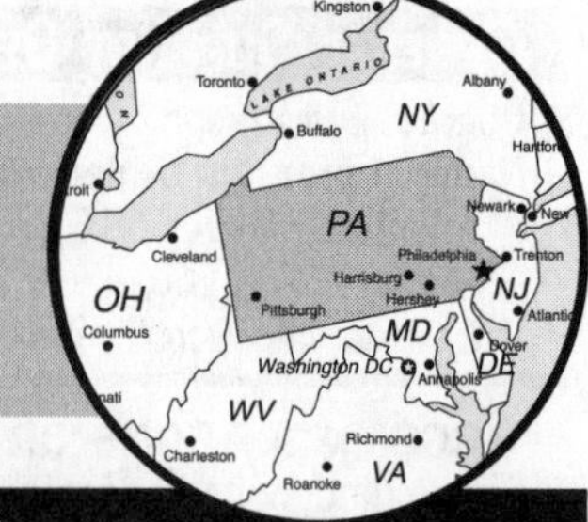

PROGRAMS OR SERVICES FOR STUDENTS WITH LEARNING DIFFERENCES

Drexel University does not have a specific learning disability program, but services are provided through the Office of Disability Resources (ODR). The professional staff works closely with the students who have special needs to ensure that they have the opportunity to participate fully in Drexel University's programs and activities. Drexel's ODR offers an individualized transition program for students with disabilities upon request. Students need to contact the ODR.

ADMISSION INFORMATION FOR STUDENTS WITH LEARNING DIFFERENCES

College entrance tests required: Yes
Nonstandardized tests accepted: Yes
Interview required: No
Essay required: No
Additional Application Required for LD/ADHD/ASD: NR
What documentation required for LD: Psycho ed evaluation to include: relevant historical info, instructional interventions, related services, age diagnosed, objective data (aptitude, achievement, info processing), test scores (standard, percentile and grade equivalents) and describe functional limitations.
With general application: No
To receive services after enrolling: Yes
What documentation required for ADHD: Diagnosis based on DSM-V; history of behaviors impairing functioning in academic setting; diagnostic interview; history of symptoms; evidence of ongoing behaviors.
With general application: No
To receive services after enrolling: Yes
What documentation required for ASD: Psycho ed evaluation
With general application: NR
To receive services after enrolling: Yes
LD/ADHD/ASD documentation submitted to: Office of Disability Resources (ODR)
ASD Specific Program: NR
Special Ed. HS course work accepted: No
Specific course requirements of all applicants: Yes
Separate application required for services: No
Total # receiving LD/ADHD services: 270
Acceptance into program means acceptance into college: Students must be admitted and enrolled at the university first, then they may request services.

ADMISSIONS

The regular admission requirements are the same for all students, and there is no special process for students with learning disabilities or any other type of disability. Students are encouraged to-self disclose and provide current documentation of their disabilities to the ODR. General admission criteria include recommended courses of 4 years of English, 3 years of math, 1 year of science, 1 year of social studies, 7 electives (chosen from English, math, science, social studies, foreign language, history, or mechanical drawing). The average SAT score is 1180, and the average GPA is 3.4; an interview is recommended. For additional information, contact the Admissions Office at Drexel University directly.

ADDITIONAL INFORMATION

Accommodations may be provided, if appropriate and reasonable, and may include extra time for exams, adaptive technologies, note-takers, priority scheduling, instruction modifications, reduced course loads, and course substitutions. All accommodation eligibility is determined on a case-by-case basis. Tutors are not an accommodation in college, but are available for all students at Drexel through the Learning Centers. Currently there are nearly 270 students with LD eligible for services and accommodations. The Drexel Autism Support Program (DASP) exists to provide a peer-mediated community of practice for current Drexel students that promotes academic excellence, self-advocacy, and social integration. DASP does not require its participants to provide documentation of a diagnosis or disability. Current Drexel students may apply by e-mailing dasp@drexel.edu with their interest in joining the program. A program administrator will follow up in scheduling the initial, in-person conversation.

General Support Services Information

Contact Information
Name of program or department: Office of Disability Resources
Phone: 215-895-1401
Fax: 215-895-1402

Accommodations or Services for Students with Learning Differences

Accommodations are decided upon an individual basis after a thorough review of appropriate, current documentation. The accommodations requested must be supported through the documentation provided and must be logically linked to the current impact of the condition on academic functioning.

Allowed in Exams
Calculator: Yes
Dictionary: Yes
Computer: Yes
Spellchecker: Yes
Extended test time: Yes
Scribes: Yes
Proctors: Yes
Oral exams: Yes
Note-takers: Yes
Services for students with LD: Yes
Services for students with ADHD: Yes
Services for students with ASD: Yes
Distraction-reduced environment: Yes
Tape recording in class: Yes
Audio books from learning ally: NR
Electronic texts: Yes
Kurzweil Reader: Yes
Other assistive technology: Yes
Priority registration: Yes
Added costs: No
LD Specialists: 1
ADHD coaching: NR
ASD specialists: NR
Professional tutors: Yes
Peer tutors: Yes
Max. hours/wk. for services: Varies
How professors are notified of LD/ADHD: By the student

General Admissions Information

Office of Admissions: 215-895-2400

Entrance Requirements

Academic units required: 3 math, 1 science, 1 science labs. **Academic units recommended:** 1 foreign language. High school diploma is required and GED is accepted. SAT or ACT required. If ACT, ACT with writing accepted. TOEFL required of all international applicants: minimum paper TOEFL 550.

Application deadline: 1/15
Notification: NR
Average GPA: 3.47
ACT Composite middle 50% range: 24-29
SAT Math middle 50% range: 560-670
SAT Critical Reading middle 50% range: 530-630
SAT Writing middle 50% range: 520-630
Graduated top 10% of class: 29
Graduated top 25% of class: 61
Graduated top 50% of class: 90

Additional Information

Environment: This private school was founded in 1891. It has a 40-acre campus.

Student Body
Undergrad enrollment: 16,896
% Women: 47
% Men: 53
% Out-of-state: 53
Cost information
Tuition: $44,646
Room & board: $14,367
Housing Information
University Housing: Yes
Percent living on campus: 26
Greek System
Fraternity: Yes
Sorority: Yes
Athletics: Division I

EAST STROUDSBURG U. OF PA

East Stroudsburg University, East Stroudsburg, PA 18301-2999
Phone: 570-422-3542 • Fax: 570-422-3933
E-mail: undergrads@po-box.esu.edu • Web: www4.esu.edu
Support: CS • Institution: Public

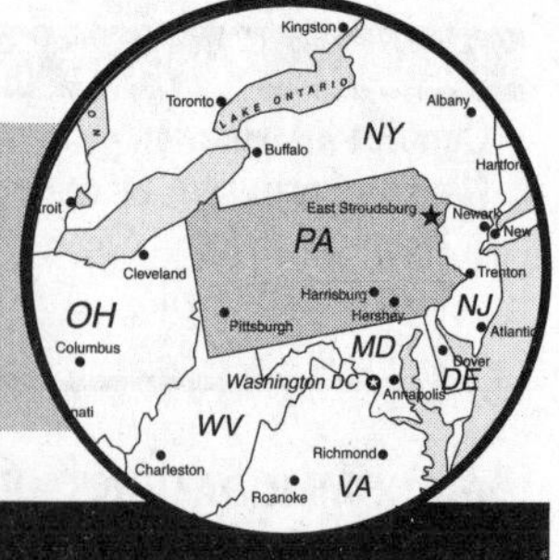

PROGRAMS OR SERVICES FOR STUDENTS WITH LEARNING DIFFERENCES

East Stroudsburg University of Pennsylvania is committed to providing equal educational access to otherwise qualified students with disabilities. Individuals with disabilities are guaranteed certain protections and rights of equal access to programs and services under section 504 of the Rehabilitation Act of 1973 and the Americans with Disability Act (ADA). Therefore, East Stroudsburg University of Pennsylvania recognizes the responsibility of the university community to provide equal educational access and full participation in any university program and activity. East Stroudsburg University of Pennsylvania believes that an individual's access to opportunities for achievement and personal fulfillment must be determined solely on the basis of the person's ability and interest. East Stroudsburg University of Pennsylvania and the Pennsylvania State System of Higher Education promotes a broad definition of diversity that appreciates disability as an integral part of the human experience.

ADMISSION INFORMATION FOR STUDENTS WITH LEARNING DIFFERENCES

College entrance tests required: Yes
Interview required: No
Essay required: Yes
Additional Application Required for LD/ADHD/ASD: NR
What documentation required for LD: Psychoeducational evaluation; reevaluation done within 3 years; must have been completed no earlier than 10th grade and functional limitation impact on learning.
With general application: NR
To receive services after enrolling: Yes
What documentation required for ADHD: Psychoeducational evaluation and/or medical evaluation that includes medical history, diagnostic assessment instruments, diagnosis, and functional limitations.
With general application: NR
To receive services after enrolling: Yes
LD/ADHD/ASD documentation submitted to: Disability Services
ASD Specific Program: NR
Special Ed. HS course work accepted: Yes
Specific course requirements of all applicants: Yes
Separate application required: No
Total # of students receiving LD/ADHD/ASD services: 190
Acceptance into program means acceptance into college: Student must be admitted and enrolled in the university first and then request services.

ADMISSIONS

Students with LD file the general application and are encouraged to complete the section titled "Disabilities Information" and forward documentation of their disability to the Office of Disability Services. For general admission, academic achievement is the primary factor considered in the selection process. ESU looks for a good match between what each applicant can contribute to the university and how the university can meet each applicant's expectations through a whole-person assessment. ESU is interested in student contributions to their school and community, activities and achievements, aspirations, and anything else that would help evaluate potential success at ESU. SAT or ACT are used as a common yardstick to help in the selection process. SAT Subject Tests are not required.

ADDITIONAL INFORMATION

Students with learning disabilities may work individually or in groups with the disabilities specialist. All students enrolled in the university have the opportunity to take skills classes in reading, composition, and math. Other services include workshops in time management and test-taking strategies that are offered to all students. The Learning Center provides individual and group tutoring by peer tutors free of charge to ESU students. Tutors are assigned on a first-come, first-served basis, and students must complete and submit a request form in order to receive tutoring. East Stroudsburg University is the home of the Alpha Chapter of Delta Alpha Pi International Honor Society, an international honor society for students with disabilities who have achieved academic success. Services and accommodations are available for undergraduate and graduate students.

General Support Services Information

Contact Information
Name of program or department: Office of Disability Services
Telephone: 570-422-3954
Fax: 717-422-3898

Accommodations or Services for Students with Learning Differences

Accommodations are decided upon an individual basis after a thorough review of appropriate, current documentation. The accommodations requests must be supported through the documentation provided and must be logically linked to the current impact of the condition on academic functioning.

Allowed in exams
Calculator: Yes
Dictionary: Yes
Computer: Yes
Spellchecker: Yes
Extended test time: Yes
Scribes: Yes
Proctors: No
Oral exams: No
Note-takers: Yes
Services for students with LD: Yes
Services for students with ADHD: Yes
Distraction-reduced environment: Yes
Tape recording in class: Yes
Audio books from learning ally: Yes
Electronic texts: NR
Kurzweil Reader: Yes
Other assistive technology: Yes
Priority registration: Yes
Added costs of services: No
LD specialists: Yes
ADHD coaching: NR
ASD specialists: NR
Professional tutors: Yes
Peer tutors: Yes
Max. hours/wk. for services: 2
How professors are notified of student approved accommodations: Student

General Admissions Information

Office of Admissions: 570-422-3542

Entrance Requirements

Academic units recommended: 4 English, 4 math, 3 science, 2 science labs, 2 foreign language, 3 social studies. High school diploma is required and GED is accepted. SAT or ACT required. TOEFL required of all international applicants: minimum paper TOEFL 560 or minimum internet TOEFL 83.

Application deadline: 4/1
Notification: Rolling starting 12/1
Average GPA: NR
ACT Composite middle 50% range: NR-NR
SAT Math middle 50% range: 460-550
SAT Critical Reading middle 50% range: 440-530
SAT Writing middle 50% range: 440-530
Graduated top 10% of class: 7
Graduated top 25% of class: 30
Graduated top 50% of class: 72

COLLEGE GRADUATION REQUIREMENTS

Course waivers allowed: No
Course substitutions allowed: No

Additional Information

Environment: This public school was founded in 1893. It has a 213-acre campus.

Student Body
Undergrad enrollment: 6,372
% Women: 55
% Men: 45
% Out-of-state: 25

Cost information
In-state Tuition: $5,804
Out-of-state Tuition: $14,510
Room & board: $6,658

Housing Information
University Housing: Yes
Percent living on campus: 42.25

Greek System
Fraternity: No
Sorority: No
Athletics: Division II

EDINBORO U. OF PENNSYLVANIA

219 Meadville Street, Edinboro, PA 16444
Phone: 814-732-2761 • Fax: 814-732-2420
E-mail: eup_admissions@edinboro.edu • Web: www.edinboro.edu/
Support: CS • Institution: Public

PROGRAMS OR SERVICES FOR STUDENTS WITH LEARNING DIFFERENCES

Edinboro is actively involved in providing services for students with learning disabilities. The Office for Students with Disabilities (OSD) provides services that are individually directed by the program staff according to expressed needs. There are different levels of services offered depending on the student's needs. Level 1 offers supervised study sessions with trained peer advisors up to 10 hours per week; writing specialist by appointment one to two hours weekly; required appointment every two weeks with professional staff to review progress; and all services in Basic Service. Level 2 includes peer advising up to three hours weekly and all services in Basic Service. Basic Service provides assistance in arranging academic accommodations, including alternate test arrangements; priority scheduling; consultation with staff; and an alternate format of textbooks. Level 1 and 2 are fee-for-service levels.

ADMISSION INFORMATION FOR STUDENTS WITH LEARNING DIFFERENCES

College entrance tests required: Yes
Interview required: No
Essay required: N/A
Additional Application Required for LD/ADHD/ASD: NR
What documentation required for LD: Psychological evaluation
With general application: No
To receive services: Yes
What documentation required for ADHD: Psychological evaluation
With general application: No
To receive services: Yes
What documentation required for ASD: Psychological evaluation
With general application: No
To receive services: Yes
LD/ADHD/ASD documentation submitted to: OSD
ASD Specific Program: NR
Special Ed. HS course work accepted: Yes
Specific course requirements for all applicants: NR
Separate application required for program services: No
Total # of students receiving LD/ADHD/ASD services: 270
Acceptance into program means acceptance into college: Students must be admitted and enrolled in the university first and then request services.

ADMISSIONS

Students with LD submit the general application form. Upon receipt of the application by the Admissions Office, it is suggested that students identify any special services that may be required and contact the OSD so that a personal interview may be scheduled. Occasionally, OSD staff are asked for remarks on certain files, but it is not part of the admission decision. Students must provide a multifactored educational assessment; grade-level scores in reading, vocabulary and comprehension, math, and spelling; an individual intelligence test administered by a psychologist, including a list of the tests given; and a list of recommended accommodations. Evaluations submitted must have been completed recently (recommend within 3 years) and should meet the guidelines as published College Board, www.collegeboard.org. Students are reviewed for academic promise, motivation, and positive attitude.

ADDITIONAL INFORMATION

Students with LD are paired with peer advisors who help them with study skills, organizational skills, and time management skills. Students are recommended for different levels of services based on their needs. Students are not required to select a particular level, but OSD strongly recommends that students enroll for Level 1 if they have less than a 2.5 GPA. Specific academic scheduling needs may be complex, but students working through the OSD are given priority in academic scheduling. Tutoring is available for all students through Academic Support Services.

General Support Services Information

Contact Information
Name of program or department: Office for Students with Disabilities (OSD)
Telephone: 814-732-2462
Fax: 814-732-2866

Accommodations or Services for Students with Learning Differences

Accommodations are decided upon an individual basis after a thorough review of appropriate, current documentation. The accommodations requested must be supported through the documentation provided and must be logically linked to the current impact of the condition on academic functioning. requested accommodations must not alter curriculum.

Allowed in exams
Calculator: Yes
Dictionary: Yes
Computer: Yes
Spellchecker: Yes
Extended test time: Yes
Scribes: Yes
Proctors: Yes
Oral exams: No
Note-takers: No
Distraction-reduced environment: Yes
Tape recording in class: Yes
Services for students with LD: Yes
Services for students with ADHD: Yes
Services for students with ASD: Yes
Audio books from learning ally: Yes
Electronic texts: Yes
Kurzweil Reader: Yes
Other assistive technology: We have an Assistive Tech Center on campus for evaluations and training of Assistive equipment.
Priority registration: Yes
Added costs for services: Yes
LD specialists: Yes
ADHD coaching: No
ASD specialists: No
Professional tutors: No
Peer tutors: 80–100
Max. hours/wk. for services: 8
How professors are notified of LD/ADHD: Student

General Admissions Information

Office of Admissions: 814-732-2761

Entrance Requirements
Academic units recommended: 4 English, 3 math, 3 science, 2 foreign language, 4 social studies, 1 computer science. High school diploma is required and GED is accepted. SAT or ACT required for some. If ACT, ACT with writing required. TOEFL required of all international applicants: minimum paper TOEFL 500 or minimum internet TOEFL 61.

Application deadline: NR
Notification: Rolling starting 9/15
Average GPA: 3.15
ACT Composite middle 50% range: 17-23
SAT Math middle 50% range: 410-520
SAT Critical Reading middle 50% range: 415-520
SAT Writing middle 50% range: NR-NR
Graduated top 10% of class: 5
Graduated top 25% of class: 20
Graduated top 50% of class: 51

COLLEGE GRADUATION REQUIREMENTS

Course waivers allowed: No
In what course: Case-by-case basis only for substitutions
Course substitutions allowed: No

Additional Information

Environment: This public school was founded in 1857. It has a 585-acre campus.

Student Body
Undergrad enrollment: 6,472
% Women: 56
% Men: 44
% Out-of-state: 11

Cost information
In-state Tuition: $5,554
Out-of-state Tuition: $8,332
Room & board: $7,130

Housing Information
University Housing: Yes
Percent living on campus: 29

Greek System
Fraternity: Yes
Sorority: Yes
Athletics: Division II

Gannon University

109 University Square, Erie, PA 16541
Phone: 814-871-7240 • Fax: 814-871-5803
E-mail: admissions@gannon.edu • Web: www.gannon.edu
Support: SP • Institution: Private

Programs or Services for Students with Learning Differences

Gannon's Program for Students with Learning Disabilities (PSLD) provides special support services for students who have been diagnosed with either LD or ADHD who are highly motivated for academic achievement. PSLD faculty are committed to excellence and strive to offer each student individually designed instruction. Students in the program may select any academic major offered by the university. Freshman-year support includes weekly individual sessions with instructor-tutors and a writing specialist. They also provide an advocacy seminar course that includes participation in small group counseling. Students should check the appropriate box on the admissions application if this service applies.

Admission Information for Students with Learning Differences

College entrance test required: Yes
Interview required: No
Essay required: Recommended
Additional Application Required for LD/ADHD/ASD: No
What documentation required for LD: Diagnosing physician report and recommendations
With general application: Not Applicable
To receive services after enrolling: No
What documentation required for ADHD: Diagnosing physician report and recommendations
With general application: Not Applicable
To receive services after enrolling: No
What documentation required for ASD: WAIS
With general application: Not Applicable
To receive services after enrolling: No
LD/ADHD/ASD documentation submitted to: Office of Disability Services
ASD Specific Program: No
Special Ed. HS course work accepted: No
Specific course requirements of all applicants: NR
Separate application required for program services: FALSE
Total # of students receiving LD/ADHD/ASD services: 50
Acceptance into program means acceptance into college: Not Applicable

Admissions

Admissions is based on several factors including academic courses, grades, rank in class, and counselor recommendation. ACT/SAT test required. The minimum GPA and test scores required very based on the academic program and the university will notify the applicants if they do not meet the minimum requirements. Personal statement/essay is optional but recommended as it assists the university in evaluating eligibility beyond test scores and academic record. Courses required include 16 units of which 4 must be in English. Students diagnosed with a learning disability and who are interested in the Hannon's PSLD Program will also need: personal letters of recommendation from teachers, counselor or school administrators, WAIS/WISC scores and sub scores (abbreviate WISC/WAIS scores are not accepted). The WAIS/WISC are not required if the primary diagnosis is ADHD. Records from any professional with whom the student has worked, such as psychologist, physician, reading specialist or math specialist. Students admitted conditionally must enter as undeclared majors until they can achieve a 2.0 GPA.

Additional Information

Specific features of the program include biweekly or more as needed, tutoring sessions with the program instructors and tutors to review course material, and focus on specific needs; weekly sessions with the writing specialist for reviewing, editing, and brainstorming. Additional services available are taping of classes, extended time on exams, scribes as prescribed. Basic services are free, and there is a $600 yearly fee for support services.

General Support Services Information

Contact Information
Name of program or department: Office of Disability Services
Telephone: 814-871-5522
Fax: 814-871-7422
Website: www.gannon.edu

Accommodations or Services For Students With Learning Differences

Accommodations are decided upon an individual basis after a thorough review of appropriate, current documentation. The accommodations requests must be supported through the documentation provided and must be logically linked to the current impact of the condition on academic functioning.

Allowed in exams
Calculator: No
Dictionary: No
Computer: Yes
Spellchecker: No
Extended test time: Yes
Scribes: Yes
Proctors: Yes
Oral exams: No
Note-takers: Yes
Support services for students with LD: Yes
Support services for students with ADHD: Yes
Support services for students with ASD: Yes
Distraction-reduced environment: Yes
Tape recording in class: Yes
Electronic texts: No
Kurzweil reader: NR
Audio books: Yes
Other assistive technology: Not Applicable
Priority registration: Yes
Added costs of services: Yes
LD specialists: Yes
ADHD coaching: Yes
ASD specialists: No
Professional tutors: Yes
Peer tutors: Yes
Max. hours/wk. for services: NR
How professors are notified of student approved accommodations: By both student and director

General Admissions Information

Office of Admissions: 814-871-7240

Entrance Requirements

Academic units required: 4 English, 2 social studies, 1 history, 3 academic electives. **Academic units recommended:** 4 English, 4 math, 4 science, 3 science labs, 2 foreign language, 2 social studies, 1 history, 3 academic electives, 1 computer science, 1 visual/performing arts. High school diploma is required and GED is accepted. SAT or ACT required. If ACT, ACT with writing accepted. TOEFL required of all international applicants: minimum paper TOEFL 550 or minimum internet TOEFL 79.

Application deadline: NR
Notification: NR
Average GPA: 3.53
ACT Composite middle 50% range: 20-25
SAT Math middle 50% range: 463-570
SAT Critical Reading middle 50% range: 460-560
SAT Writing middle 50% range: 433-550
Graduate top 10% of class: 24
Graduated top 25% of class: 50
Graduated top 50% of class: 81

COLLEGE GRADUATION REQUIREMENTS

Course waivers allowed: No
In what course: Foreign Language

Additional Information

Environment: This private school, affiliated with the Roman Catholic Church, was founded in 1925. It has a 13-acre campus.

Student Body
Undergrad enrollment: 3,115
% Women: 56
% Men: 44
% Out-of-state: 27.24

Cost information
Tuition: $29,300
Room & board: $4,800-$5,830

Housing Information
University Housing: Yes
Percent living on campus: 43.63

Greek System
Fraternity: Yes
Sorority: Yes
Athletics: Division II

Kutztown U. of Pennsylvania

Admissions Office, Kutztown, PA 19530-0730
Phone: 610-683-4060 • Fax: 610-683-1375
E-mail: admissions@kutztown.edu • Web: www.kutztown.edu
Support: CS • Institution: Public

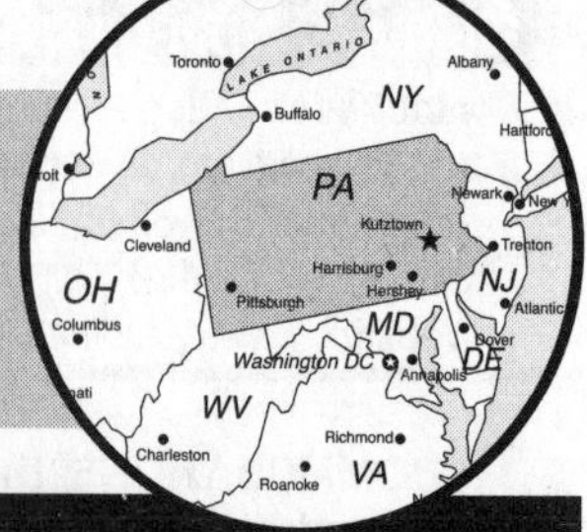

Programs or Services for Students with Learning Differences

The philosophy of the university is to provide equal opportunity to all individuals. Disability Services provides all necessary and reasonable accommodations while fostering independence in the students. The services provided are in accordance with the needs of the students and the academic integrity of the institution. The office acts as an information and referral resource, provides direct services, coordinates services provided by other departments/agencies, and serves as a liaison between students with disabilities and university personnel working with students. Since information regarding a student's disability is not obtained through the admission process, it is the student's responsibility upon acceptance to the university to identify himself/herself to the Disability Services Office. Students are encouraged to do this as early as possible upon admission. Students should inquire about accommodations to assess the university's capability of responding to special needs and provide the students with an opportunity to assess the services available at the university. The director of Disability Services works together with all university offices to help provide specific services as warranted by a diagnosis or clear need, as well as creative solutions to problems with which students with disabilities are confronted.

Admission Information for Students with Learning Differences

College entrance test required: Yes
Interview required: No
Essay required: No
Additional Application Required for LD/ADHD/ASD: NR
What documentation required for LD: Psycho-educational evaluation, including aptitude and achievement
With general application: No
To receive services after enrolling: Yes
What documentation required for ADHD: Criteria in line with the DSM-IV criteria for ADD/ADHD
With general application: No
To receive services after enrolling: Yes
What documentation required for ASD: Psycho ed evaluation
With general application: No
To receive services after enrolling: Yes
LD/ADHD/ASD documentation submitted to: Support program/services
ASD Specific Program: NR
Special Ed. HS course work accepted: No
Specific course: No
Separate application required for program services: No
Total # of students receiving LD/ADHD/ASD services: 350
Acceptance into program means acceptance into college: NR

Admissions

There is no special admissions process for students with learning disabilities. All applicants are expected to meet the same admission criteria. Course requirements include: 4 years English, 3 years math, 3 years social studies. Conditional Admission is available.

Additional Information

The director of Disability Services for ADA is the initial resource person and record keeper who validates the existence of a disability and the need for any specific accommodations. Academic assistance is provided through the Department of Academic Enrichment. Students with LD are eligible to receive services and accommodations prescribed in the psychoeducational evaluation, extended time on exams, use of a recorder, use of calculator, testing in a separate location, readers, spell check and grammar check on written assignments, scribes, alternative texts, tutorial assistance, early advisement and priority registration, computer assistive technology, and referrals. Tutors are available to all students, and arrangements are made at no cost to the student.

General Support Services Information

Contact Information
Name of program or department: Disability Services Office
Telephone: 610-683-4108
Fax: 610-683-1520
Website: http://www.kutztown.edu/DSO

Accommodations or Services for Students With Learning Differences

Accommodations are decided upon an individual basis after a thorough review of appropriate, current documentation. The accommodations requests must be supported through the documentation provided and must be logically linked to the current impact of the condition on academic functioning.

Allowed in exams
Calculator: Yes
Dictionary: Yes
Computer: Yes
Spellchecker: Yes
Extended test time: Yes
Scribes: Yes
Proctors: Yes
Oral exams: No
Note-takers: Yes
Support services for students with LD: Yes
Support services for students with ADHD: Yes
Support services for students with ASD: NR
Distraction-reduced environment: Yes
Tape recording in class: Yes
Electronic texts: Yes
Kurzweil reader: NR
Audio books: Yes
Other assistive technology: NR
Priority registration: Yes
Added costs of services: No
LD specialists: Yes
ADHD coaching: No
ASD specialists: No
Professional tutors: No
Peer tutors: Yes
Max. hours/wk. for services: 3
How professors are notified of student approved accommodations: By both student and director

General Admissions Information

Office of Admissions: 610-683-4060

Entrance Requirements

Academic units required: 4 English, 3 math, 3 science, 2 science labs, 3 social studies. High school diploma is required and GED is accepted. SAT or ACT required. If ACT, ACT with writing accepted. TOEFL required of all international applicants: minimum paper TOEFL 550 or minimum internet TOEFL 79.

Application deadline: NR
Notification: Rolling starting 10/1
Average GPA: 3.16
ACT Composite middle 50% range: 17-22
SAT Math middle 50% range: 430-520
SAT Critical Reading middle 50% range: 430-530
SAT Writing middle 50% range: 410-510
Graduate top 10% of class: 5
Graduated top 25% of class: 19
Graduated top 50% of class: 54

COLLEGE GRADUATION REQUIREMENTS

Course waivers allowed: No
In what course: NR
Course substitutions allowed: Yes
In what course: Only with strong diagnostic recommendation and departmental approval - foreign language and math

Additional Information

Environment: This public school was founded in 1866. It has a 325-acre campus.

Student Body
Undergrad enrollment: 8,293
% Women: 54
% Men: 46
% Out-of-state: 11.1

Cost information
In-state Tuition: $7,060
Out-of-state Tuition: $17,650
Room & board: $9,070

Housing Information
University Housing: Yes
Percent living on campus: 44.7

Greek System
Fraternity: Yes
Sorority: Yes
Athletics: Division II

Lehigh University

27 Memorial Drive West, Bethlehem, PA 18015
Phone: 610-758-3100 • Fax: 610-758-4361
E-mail: admissions@lehigh.edu • Web: www.lehigh.edu
Support: CS • Institution: Private

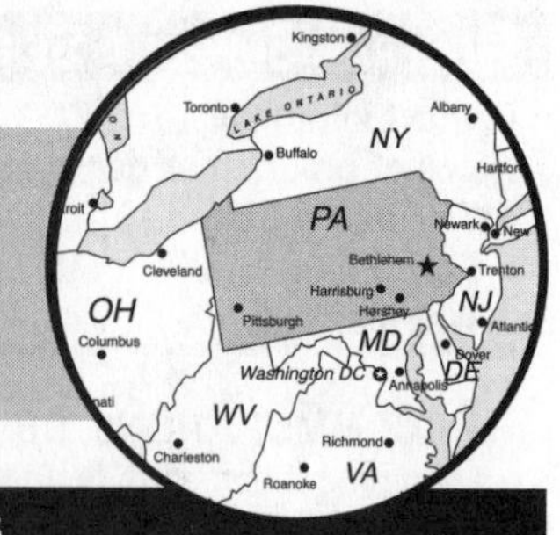

Programs or Services for Students with Learning Differences

Lehigh University is committed to ensuring reasonable accommodations to students who are substantially limited by a diagnosed disability. Students requesting academic accommodations are required to submit for review current documentation of their disability. If a student is not certain whether he or she has a learning disability, the Director of Academic Support Services can conduct a comprehensive intake interview and screening process. If a complete diagnostic evaluation seems appropriate, the student will be provided with referrals to community-based professionals who can perform a comprehensive evaluation at the student's expense. The ultimate goal is to ensure that students with disabilities have an opportunity to grow independently to their fullest potential at a competitive university. It is the responsibility of students with disabilities to identify themselves to the appropriate university contact person and provide the required documentation to receive accommodations. Given the specific nature of each person's disability, reasonable accommodations will be determined on an individual basis by the appropriate university contact person. Students who are eligible for accommodations must sign a professor notification and accommodation form at the beginning of each semester that students are requesting accommodations.

Admission Information for Students with Learning Differences

College entrance tests required: Yes
Interview required: No
Essay required: No
Additional Application Required for LD/ADHD/ASD: NR
What documentation required for LD: Psycho ed evaluation to include: relevant historical info, instructional interventions, related services, age diagnosed, objective data (aptitude, achievement, info processing), test scores (standard, percentile and grade equivalents) and describe functional limitations.
With general application: No
To receive services after enrolling: Yes
What documentation required for ADHD: Diagnosis based on DSM-V; history of behaviors impairing functioning in academic setting; diagnostic interview; history of symptoms; evidence of ongoing behaviors.
With general application: No
LD/ADHD/ASD documentation submitted to: Office of Academic Support Services
ASD Specific Program: NR
Special Ed. HS course work accepted: No
Specific course requirements of all applicants: Yes
Separate application required: No
Total # of students receiving LD/ADHD/ASD services: 95
Acceptance into program means acceptance into college: Students must be admitted and enrolled prior to requesting services.

Admissions

There is no special admission process for students with learning disabilities. All applicants must meet the same admission criteria. Applicants must submit either the SAT Reasoning Test or the ACT with the optional Writing section. An on-campus interview is recommended. Applicants' evaluations are based on many factors, including a challenging college-prep curriculum that included AP and honors courses.

Additional Information

The Peer Mentor Program assists first-year students with the transition from high school to a competitive university. The peer mentors are composed of upperclass students who have a diagnosed learning disability or attention deficit hyperactivity disorder. Each mentor has demonstrated leadership capability and has been academically successful at Lehigh University. First-year students are matched with a peer mentor by college and/or major. The rationale for matching students in this manner is because upperclass students of the same major and/or college have most likely taken the same courses and professors and have experienced the same challenges as the freshman with whom they have been matched. The first-year students who have participated in the Peer Mentor Program and who have worked with the Office of Academic Support Services have traditionally performed significantly better than students who have not participated in support services. Program participation is voluntary, and students may choose to withdraw from the program at any time. The Center for Writing and Math provides assistance with any writing assignments, including brainstorming, rough-draft preparations, and critiques of final draft and assistance in calculus and other math courses. The Center for Academic Success has peer tutors available in most freshman- and sophomore-level courses. Ten free hours of tutoring per course per semester are provided. The tutors provide assistance with study skills, note-taking skills, and time management techniques.

General Support Services Information

Contact Information
Name of program or department: Academic Support Services
Telephone: 610-758-4152
Fax: 610-758-5293
Website: http://studentaffairs.lehigh.edu/disabilities

Accommodations or Services for Students with Learning Differences

Accommodations are decided upon an individual basis after a thorough review of appropriate, current documentation. The accommodations requests must be supported through the documentation provided and must be logically linked to the current impact of the condition on academic functioning.

Allowed in exams
Calculator: No
Dictionary: No
Computer: Yes
Spellchecker: No
Extended test time: Yes
Scribes: Yes
Proctors: No
Oral exams: Yes
Note-takers: Yes
Support services for students with LD: Yes
Support services for students with ADHD: Yes
Support services for students with ASD: Yes
Distraction-reduced environment: Not Applicable
Tape recording in class: Yes
Electronic texts: Yes
Kurzweil reader: NR
Audio books: Yes
Other assistive technology: Yes
Priority registration: Yes
Added costs of services: No
LD specialists: Yes
ADHD coaching: NR
ASD specialists: No
Professional tutors: No
Peer tutors: Yes
Max. hours/wk. for services: NR
How professors are notified of student approved accommodations: By student

General Admissions Information

Office of Admissions: 610-758-3100

Entrance Requirements

Academic units required: 4 English, 3 math, 2 science, 2 science labs, 2 foreign language, 2 social studies, 3 academic electives. High school diploma or equivalent is not required. SAT or ACT required. If ACT, ACT with writing required. TOEFL required of all international applicants: minimum paper TOEFL 570 or minimum internet TOEFL 90.

Application deadline: 1/1
Notification: 4/1
Average GPA: NR
ACT Composite middle 50% range: 29-32
SAT Math middle 50% range: 640-740
SAT Critical Reading middle 50% range: 590-680
SAT Writing middle 50% range: NR-NR
Graduate top 10% of class: 60
Graduated top 25% of class: 89
Graduated top 50% of class: 98

COLLEGE GRADUATION REQUIREMENTS

Course waivers allowed: No
Course substitutions allowed: Not Applicable

Additional Information

Environment: This private school was founded in 1865. It has a 1600-acre campus.

Student Body
Undergrad enrollment: 5,075
% Women: 44
% Men: 56
% Out-of-state: 73

Cost information
Tuition: $45,860
Room & board: $12,280
Housing Information
University Housing: Yes
Percent living on campus: 67

Greek System
Fraternity: Yes
Sorority: Yes
Athletics: Division I

Mercyhurst University

Admissions, Erie, PA 16546
Phone: 814-824-2202 • Fax: 814-824-2071
E-mail: admissions@mercyhurst.edu • Web: admissions.mercyhurst.edu
Support: SP • Institution: Private

Programs or Services for Students with Learning Differences

The Learning Differences program at Mercyhurst College is designed to assist students who have been identified as having LD. The emphasis is on students' individual strengths, abilities and interests, as well as learning deficits. This program consists of a structured, individualized set of experiences designed to assist students with LD, ADHD and ASD to get maximum value from their educational potential and earn a college degree. Students selecting the structured program for students with learning differences pay an additional fee for this service and must submit a recent psychological evaluation that includes the WAIS or WISC scores (completed with the past 5 years); three letters of recommendation; SAT/ACT scores; and a written statement from a professional which documents the student's disability. Students choosing the structured program (Level II) have the option to attend summer sessions prior to entrance; classes may include guided practice while enrolled in actual college class, learning strategies, and use of assistive technology. The program lasts 3 weeks and costs approximately $1,600 (includes room, board and tuition). Students with learning differences who feel that they do not require a structured program may opt to receive support services through level I program at no additional charge. Our AIM program supports ASD students in all areas of the college experience, including campus life as well as class work. Students are evaluated in key domains that are essential to higher education and vocational success.

Admission Information for Students with Learning Differences

College entrance tests required: Yes
Interview required: Yes
Essay required: Yes
Additional Application Required for LD/ADHD/ASD: NR
What documentation required for LD: Psycho ed evaluation to include: relevant historical info, instructional interventions, related services, age diagnosed, objective data (aptitude, achievement, info processing), test scores (standard, percentile and grade equivalents) and describe functional limitations.
With general application: Yes if requested as part of Structured Program application
To receive services after enrolling: Yes
What documentation required for ADHD: Diagnosis based on DSM-V; history of behaviors impairing functioning in academic setting; diagnostic interview; history of symptoms; evidence of ongoing behaviors.
With general application: Yes if requested as part of Structured Program application
To receive services after enrolling: Yes
What documentation required for ASD: Psycho ed evaluation
LD/ADHD/ASD documentation submitted to: Admissions Office
ASD Specific Program: NR
Special Ed. HS course work accepted: No
Specific course requirements of all applicants: Yes
Separate application required: Yes
Total # of students receiving LD/ADHD/ASD services: 162
Acceptance into program means acceptance into college: Students must be admitted to and enrolled in the university first and then request services.

Admissions

To be eligible for any of the services at Mercyhurst, students with LD must adhere to the regular admission requirements and meet the regular admission criteria. Students who do not meet the regular admissions standards are referred to Mercyhurst—McAuley and/or Mercyhurst—North East for consideration into the two-year division. Some students may be admitted on probation pending the completion of developmental course work. The college reserves the right to reject any student not meeting admission standards. The admission decisions are made jointly by the director of Programs for Students with Learning Differences and the Office of Admission. Upon acceptance to the college, if the student wishes special services, she/he must identify herself/himself to the Admissions Office and, at that time, choose to receive services in one of two options available to students with documented learning differences. These programs are a structured program and a basic service program. Admission to Mercyhurst University does not guarantee admission to AIM, as applications to the university and to this highly selective support program are separate and distinct processes.

Additional Information

The Structured Program for Students with Learning Differences provides special services, advocacy, alternative testing, Assisstive Technology, community skills, drop-in services, Kurzweil 3000, electronic text book search, midterm progress reports, notetakers, peer tutoring, professional advising/priority registration, special three-week Summer Orientation Program prior to freshman year, optional study hall (required of all freshmen), and a support group.

General Support Services Information

Contact Information
Name of program or department: Learning Differences Program
Telephone: 814-824-3048
Fax: 814-824-2589

Accommodations or Services For Students With Learning Differences

Accommodations are decided upon an individual basis after a thorough review of appropriate, current documentation. The accommodations requests must be supported through the documentation provided and must be logically linked to the current impact of the condition on academic functioning.

Allowed in exams
Calculator: Yes
Dictionary: Yes
Computer: Yes
Spellchecker: Yes
Extended test time: Yes
Scribes: Yes
Proctors: Yes
Oral exams: Yes
Note-takers: Yes
Support services for students with LD: Yes
Support services for students with ADHD: Yes
Support services for students with ASD: Yes
Distraction-reduced environment: Yes
Tape recording in class: No
Electronic texts: Yes
Kurzweil reader: NR
Audio books: No
Other assistive technology: Yes
Priority registration: Yes
Added costs of services: Yes
LD specialists: Yes
ADHD coaching: Yes
ASD specialists: Yes
Professional tutors: No
Peer tutors: Yes
Max. hours/wk. for services: NR
How professors are notified of student approved accommodations: By both student and director

General Admissions Information

Office of Admissions: 814-824-2202

Entrance Requirements

Academic units required: 4 English, 3 math, 2 science, 1 science labs, 2 foreign language, 5 social studies,
Academic units recommended: 4 English, 3 math, 3 science, 2 science labs, 2 foreign language, 5 social studies. High school diploma is required and GED is accepted. SAT or ACT required. If ACT, ACT with writing accepted. TOEFL required of all international applicants: minimum paper TOEFL 550 or minimum internet TOEFL 79.

Application deadline: NR
Notification: Rolling starting 11/1
Average GPA: 3.37
ACT Composite middle 50% range: 21-26
SAT Math middle 50% range: 470-570
SAT Critical Reading middle 50% range: 470-580
SAT Writing middle 50% range: 460-560
Graduate top 10% of class: 21
Graduated top 25% of class: 29
Graduated top 50% of class: 87

COLLEGE GRADUATION REQUIREMENTS

Course waivers allowed: Yes
In what course: foreign languages, and only on an individual basis.
Course substitutions allowed: No

Additional Information

Environment: This private school, affiliated with the Roman Catholic Church, was founded in 1926. It has a 88-acre campus.

Student Body
Undergrad enrollment: 2,680
% Women: 56
% Men: 44
% Out-of-state: 48

Cost information
Tuition: $29,600
Room & board: $10,800

Housing Information
University Housing: Yes
Percent living on campus: 68

Greek System
Fraternity: No
Sorority: No
Athletics: Division II

Messiah College

One College Avenue, Mechanicsburg, PA 17055
Phone: 717-691-6000 • Fax: 717-691-2307
E-mail: admiss@messiah.edu • Web: www.messiah.edu
Support: S • Institution: Private

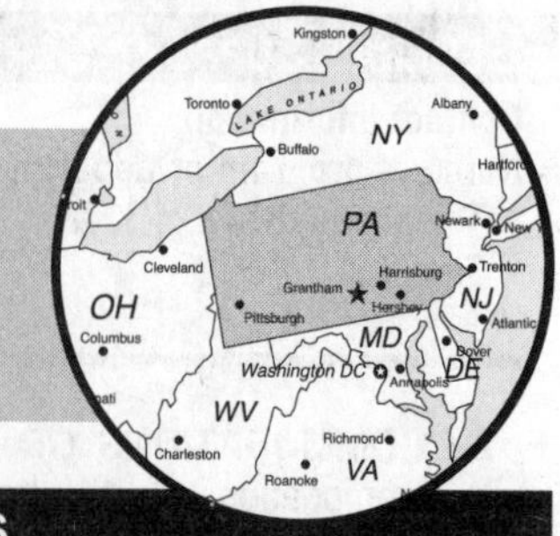

Programs or Services for Students with Learning Differences

Messiah College is a Christian college committed to providing reasonable accommodations to qualified students with disabilities. Students who feel they may qualify for services should meet with the Office of Disability Service's (ODS) staff. At that meeting, ODS staff will discuss the documentation process, services available, and their educational goals. Services and accommodations rendered will be based on the individualized needs of the students. Such services/accommodations are granted to create an equal opportunity for student success, but do not in any way waive class expectations. Therefore, classroom success is not guaranteed. To be recognized as a student with a disability, students are required to submit documentation from a qualified educational evaluator stating their diagnosis, how such a diagnosis creates a "substantial impairment" and in which life activities, and a list of accommodations that will be needed by the student in order to benefit from the program. Students who do not have documentation but who think they may have a disability may seek assistance from ODS by locating screening services. Any costs incurred for an evaluation are the responsibility of the student. ODS finds most students registered with the office to be motivated, hardworking, and interested and willing to meet their educational goals.

Admission Information for Students with Learning Differences

College entrance tests required: Yes
Interview required: No
Additional Application Required for LD/ADHD/ASD: NR
What documentation required for LD: Complete psychoeducational report from a qualified examiner, to include all test details; IEP/504 service plan suggested with few exceptions, report should be less than three years old.
With general application: NR
To receive services after enrolling: Yes
What documentation required for ADHD: Same as for LD
With general application: NR
To receive services after enrolling: Yes
LD/ADHD/ASD documentation submitted to: Office of Disability Services
ASD Specific Program: NR
Special Ed. HS course work accepted: Yes
Specific course requirements for all applicants: Yes
Separate application required for program services: No
Total # of students receiving LD/ADHD/ASD services: 25–30
Acceptance into program means acceptance into college: Student must be admitted to college first and may then request services.

Admissions

All applicants must meet the same admission criteria. There is an extensive application process including: letters of recommendation; ACT/SAT; high school transcript; essays, and a review by the Admissions officer/committee. Admission requirements include a high school transcript, SAT or ACT scores, and four English, two math, two natural sciences, two social studies, and six electives (prefer that two of these be in foreign language), and a Christian life recommendation. Messiah College makes all efforts to avoid any possible prejudice in the admission process. Students with disabilities are encouraged to self-disclose and request an interview with the ODS Director, but not to include documentation of the disability in the actual admissions packet.

Additional Information

Documentation should include a recent multi-disciplinary evaluation appropriate to the disability claimed. Neither an IEP nor a written 504 plan is sufficient to determine eligibility, but may be helpful when included along with a comprehensive evaluation report. Commonly provided accommodations by the Office of Disability Services include: extended time for test-taking; proctored exams in an alternate location; assistance with getting notes; disability coaching support; advocacy with instructors; alternate format textbooks;transition services; peer tutoring; referral source for other required services. Other accommodations are considered on an individual basis. Additionally, The Learning Center offers assistance with time management, motivation, goal setting, reading skills, note-taking, learning theory, and taking exams, in addition to providing a range of tutorial services through trained peer tutors. The Writing Center provides peer tutors for written projects. Other supports include math tutors and Supplemental Instruction, primarily in the sciences. Personal counseling is available through the Engle Health Center. The staff at ODS encourages and develops students self advocacy, but may act as a liaison between students and faculty when needed.

General Support Services Information

Contact Information
Name of program or department: Office of Disability Services
Telephone: 717-796-5382
Fax: 717-796-5217

Accommodations or Services For Students With Learning Differences

Accommodations are decided upon an individual basis after a thorough review of appropriate, current documentation. The accommodations requests must be supported through the documentation provided and must be logically linked to the current impact of the condition on academic functioning.

Allowed in exams
Calculator: Yes
Dictionary: Yes
Computer: Yes
Spellchecker: Yes
Extended test time: Yes
Scribes: Yes
Proctors: Yes
Oral exams: Yes
Note-takers: Yes
Support services for students with LD: Yes
Support services for students with ADHD: Yes
Support services for students with ASD: Yes
Distraction-reduced environment: Yes
Tape recording in class: Yes
Electronic texts: Yes
Kurzweil reader: NR
Audio books: Yes
Other assistive technology: Yes
Priority registration: Yes
Added costs of services: No
LD specialists: No
ADHD coaching: NR
ASD specialists: Yes
Professional tutors: No
Peer tutors: NR
Max. hours/wk. for services: NR
How professors are notified of student approved accommodations: By student

General Admissions Information

Office of Admissions: (717) 691-6000

Entrance Requirements

Academic units required: 4 English, 2 math, 2 science, 2 science labs, 2 foreign language, 2 social studies, 4 academic electives. **Academic units recommended:** 4 English, 3 math, 3 science, 3 science labs, 2 foreign language, 2 social studies, 2 history, 4 academic electives. High school diploma is required and GED is accepted. SAT or ACT required. If ACT, ACT with writing accepted. TOEFL required of all international applicants: minimum paper TOEFL 550 or minimum internet TOEFL 80.

Application deadline: NR
Notification: 9/15
Average GPA: 3.71
ACT Composite middle 50% range: 21-28
SAT Math middle 50% range: 510-630
SAT Critical Reading middle 50% range: 500-620
SAT Writing middle 50% range: 490-600
Graduate top 10% of class: 32
Graduated top 25% of class: 63
Graduated top 50% of class: 91

COLLEGE GRADUATION REQUIREMENTS

Course waivers allowed: No
Course substitutions allowed: Yes
In what course: If documentation is clear, students may be afforded a foreign language substitution.

Additional Information

Environment: This private school was founded in 1909. It has a 471-acre campus.

Student Body
Undergrad enrollment: 2,819
% Women: 61
% Men: 39
% Out-of-state: 37

Cost information
Tuition: $32,350
Room & board: $9,920

Housing Information
University Housing: Yes
Percent living on campus: 86

Greek System
Fraternity: NR
Sorority: NR
Athletics: Division III

Millersville U. of Pennsylvania

P.O. Box 1002, Millersville, PA 17551-0302
Phone: 717-871-4625 • Fax: 717-871-2147
E-mail: admissions@millersville.edu • Web: www.millersville.edu
Support: S • Institution: Public

Programs or Services for Students with Learning Differences

The Office of Learning Services promotes and encourages the unique learning styles of all Millersville University students through advocacy, assistive technology, collaboration, and direct services with the University community. Through excellence in service delivery, the Office of Learning Services fosters a climate that ensures student access and equity at Millersville University.

Admission Information for Students with Learning Differences

College entrance test required: Yes
Interview required: No
Essay required: Not Applicable
Additional Application Required for LD/ADHD/ASD: No
What documentation required for LD: Evaluation/ Re-evaluation report
With general application: Not Applicable
To receive services after enrolling: No
What documentation required for ADHD: Evaluation/ Re-evaluation report
With general application: Not Applicable
To receive services after enrolling: No
What documentation required for ASD: Evaluation/ Re-evaluation report
With general application: Not Applicable
To receive services after enrolling: No
LD/ADHD/ASD documentation submitted to: Office of Learning Services
ASD Specific Program: NR
Special Ed. HS course work accepted: Not Applicable
Specific course requirements of all applicants: NR
Separate application required for program services: False
Total # of students receiving LD/ADHD/ASD services: 354
Acceptance into program means acceptance into college: Not Applicable

Admissions

Typical first year students have achieved a solid B average in high school and earned an above average ACT or SAT. The University has their own application form online.

Additional Information

The Office of Learning Services coordinates academic accommodations and related services for students with learning and physical disabilities. Students must complete a Special Assistance Request Form. For a student with learning disabilities the first page and the page labeled Learning Disability are required together with a complete psycho-educational, psychological, neuropsychological, or evaluation report as the official documentation.

General Support Services Information

Contact Information
Name of program or department: Office of Learning Services
Telephone: 717-871-5554
Fax: 717-871-7943
Website: NR

Accommodations or Services for Students with Learning Differences

Accommodations are decided upon an individual basis after a thorough review of appropriate, current documentation. The accommodations requests must be supported through the documentation provided and must be logically linked to the current impact of the condition on academic functioning.

Allowed in exams
Calculator: Yes
Dictionary: Yes
Computer: Yes
Spellchecker: Yes
Extended test time: Yes
Scribes: Yes
Proctors: Yes
Oral exams: Yes
Note-takers: Yes
Support services for students with LD: Yes
Support services for students with ADHD: Yes
Support services for students with ASD: Yes
Distraction-reduced environment: Yes
Tape recording in class: Yes
Electronic texts: Yes
Kurzweil reader: NR
Audio books: Yes
Other assistive technology: Yes
Priority registration: Yes
Added costs of services: No
LD specialists: Yes
ADHD coaching: Yes
ASD specialists: No
Professional tutors: No
Peer tutors: Yes
Max. hours/wk. for services: NR
How professors are notified of student approved accommodations: By director

General Admissions Information

Office of Admissions: 717-871-4625

Entrance Requirements

Academic units required: 4 English, 3 math, 3 science, 2 science labs, 3 social studies, 2 history. **Academic units recommended:** 2 foreign language, 4 academic electives, High school diploma is required and GED is accepted. SAT or ACT required. If ACT, ACT with writing recommended. TOEFL required of all international applicants: minimum paper TOEFL 550 or minimum internet TOEFL 70.

Application deadline: NR
Notification: Rolling starting 9/15
Average GPA: NR
ACT Composite middle 50% range: 19-24
SAT Math middle 50% range: 450-550
SAT Critical Reading middle 50% range: 450-550
SAT Writing middle 50% range: 430-530
Graduate top 10% of class: 9
Graduated top 25% of class: 29
Graduated top 50% of class: 66

COLLEGE GRADUATION REQUIREMENTS

Course waivers allowed: Yes
In what course: Foreign language
Course substitutions allowed: Yes
In what course: Foreign language

Additional Information

Environment: This public school was founded in 1855. It has a 250-acre campus.

Student Body
Undergrad enrollment: 7,084
% Women: 56
% Men: 44
% Out-of-state: 5

Cost information
In-state tuition: $8,460
Out-of-state tuition: $17,650
Room & board: $12,188

Housing Information
University Housing: Yes
Percent living on campus: 33

Greek System
Fraternity: Yes
Sorority: Yes
Athletics: Division II

Misericordia University

301 Lake Street, Dallas, PA 18612
Phone: 570-674-6205 • Fax: 570-675-2441
E-mail: kdefeo@misercordia.edu • Web: www.misericordia.edu
Support: SP • Institution: Private

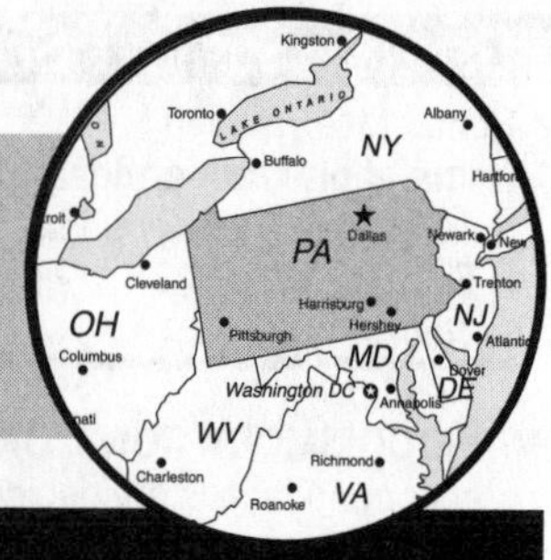

Programs or Services for Students with Learning Differences

In 1979, the Alternative Learners Project (ALP) was founded as the first of its kind in Pennsylvania to provide support to students with learning disabilities. With a dedicated Alternative Learning Manager, a professional staff of highly qualified full time coordinators and an abundance of cooperation and support from an exceptional faculty and administration, the ALP serves a population of approximately 40 students with disabilities per year. All students who participate in ALP are enrolled in regular college courses and are supported by an assortment of services delivered by a specially trained full time staff. Services include "Learning Strategies" which are designed to make students more efficient learners, and accommodations designed to work around students' disabilities whenever possible. Upon entry, each student develops a program of accommodation (POA), and participates in individual weekly meetings with a Program Coordinator. The ultimate goal of ALP is to help students with learning differences succeed independently in college.

Admission Information for Students with Learning Differences

College entrance tests required: Yes
Interview required: Yes
Essay required: Yes
Additional Application Required for LD/ADHD/ASD: NR
What documentation required for LD: Psycho ed evaluation to include: relevant historical info, instructional interventions, related services, age diagnosed, objective data (aptitude, achievement, info processing), test scores (standard, percentile and grade equivalents) and describe functional limitations.
With general application: Yes if requested as part of Structured Program application
To receive services after enrolling: Yes
What documentation required for ADHD: Diagnosis based on DSM-V; history of behaviors impairing functioning in academic setting; diagnostic interview; history of symptoms; evidence of ongoing behaviors.
With general application: Yes if requested as part of Structured Program application
To receive services after enrolling: Yes
What documentation required for ASD: Psycho ed evaluation
With general application: Yes if requested as part of Structured Program application
To receive services after enrolling: Yes
LD/ADHD/ASD documentation submitted to: ALP office
ASD Specific Program: NR
Special Ed. HS course work accepted: No
Specific course requirements of all applicants: Yes
Separate application required: Yes
Total # of students receiving LD/ADHD/ASD services: variable
Acceptance into program means acceptance into college: Applications are reviewed simultaneously by Admissions and ALP

Admissions

Misericordia University's experience with students with learning disabilities is that students who are highly motivated and socially mature have an excellent chance to be successful. Each applicant has to submit a standard application to the Admissions Office. In addition, students must send a written cover letter to the ALP Manager summarizing the disability, and indicate a desire to participate in the ALP. Additionally, a copy of the psycho-educational report should be submitted along with the high school transcript and three letters of recommendation (one should be written by a special education professional, if appropriate). Class rank is usually above the top 60 percent. Although ACT/SAT scores are required by the university for traditional admissions, they are not used in the ALP Admissions decision. Students and their parents will be invited to campus for an interview. Following the interview, the ALP Manager reviews all information and notifies the student directly regarding admission to the program.

Additional Information

The ALP students can participate in the BRIDGE Program. The BRIDGE program brings ALP students to campus one week prior to the start of freshman year and features a series of assessments and workshops designed to assist students in identifying both strengths and needs in their learning styles. They receive training in the use of the Learning Strategies Curriculum, designed to help students become more effective and efficient learners. The ALP staff works with students to establish their Program of Accommodations.

General Support Services Information

Contact Information
Name of program or department: Alternative Learners Project (ALP)
Telephone: 570-674-8126
Fax: 570-674-3026

Accommodations or Services for Students with Learning Differences

Accommodations are decided upon an individual basis after a thorough review of appropriate, current documentation. The accommodations requested must be supported through the documentation provided and must be logically linked to the current impact of the condition on academic functioning.

Allowed in exams
Calculator: Yes
Computer: Yes
Spellchecker: Yes
Extended test time: Yes
Scribes: Yes
Proctors: Yes
Oral exams: Yes
Note-takers: Yes
Services for students with LD: Yes
Services for students with ADHD: Yes
Services for students with ASD: Yes
Audio books: Yes
Distraction-reduced environment: Yes
Tape recording in class: Yes
Electronic texts: Yes
Kurzweil Reader: Yes
Other assistive technology: Yes
Priority registration: No
Added costs for services: Yes
LD specialists: Yes
ADHD coaching: No
ASD specialists: No
Professional tutors: N/A
Peer tutors: 100
Max. hours/wk. for services: 10
How professors are notified of LD/ADHD: By Program Coordinators

General Admissions Information

Office of Admissions: 570-674-6264

Entrance Requirements

Academic units required: 4 English, 4 math, 4 science, 4 social studies. High school diploma is required and GED is accepted. SAT or ACT required. If ACT, ACT with writing accepted. TOEFL required of all international applicants: minimum paper TOEFL 500.

Application deadline: NR
Notification: Rolling starting 9/1
Average GPA: 3.35
ACT Composite middle 50% range: 22-27
SAT Math middle 50% range: 490-570
SAT Critical Reading middle 50% range: 480-570
SAT Writing middle 50% range: NR-NR
Graduated top 10% of class: 24
Graduated top 25% of class: 56
Graduated top 50% of class: 84

COLLEGE GRADUATION REQUIREMENTS

Course waivers allowed: No
In what course: N/A
Course substitutions allowed: No
In what course: N/A

Additional Information

Environment: This private school, affiliated with the Roman Catholic Church, was founded in 1924. It has a 120-acre campus.

Student Body
Undergrad enrollment: 2,400
% Women: 68
% Men: 32
% Out-of-state: 25

Cost information
Tuition: $28,300
Room & board: $12,460

Housing Information
University Housing: Yes
Percent living on campus: 42

Greek System
Fraternity: No
Sorority: No
Athletics: Division III

NEUMANN UNIVERSITY

One Neumann Drive, Aston, PA 19014
Phone: 610-558-5616 • Fax: 610-361-2548
E-mail: neumann@neumann.edu • Web: www.neumann.edu
Support: S • Institution: Private

PROGRAMS OR SERVICES FOR STUDENTS WITH LEARNING DIFFERENCES

Neumann University, consistent with its Mission Statement, is committed to providing equal education opportunities to all qualified students with disabilities. In accordance with Section 504 of the Rehabilitation Act of 1973 and Title III of the Americans with Disabilities Act of 1990, Neumann University will provide appropriate and reasonable accommodations, which allow equal access to its educational programs.

ADMISSION INFORMATION FOR STUDENTS WITH LEARNING DIFFERENCES

College entrance test required: Yes
Interview required: No
Essay required: Not Applicable
Additional Application Required for LD/ADHD/ASD: Yes
What documentation required for LD: A letter from a physician, on official letterhead, signed by the physician, that details the diagnosis of ADHD, together with the patient's history of the condition, the prescribed treatment of the condition, and any side effects of the condition that may affect postsecondary study.
With general application: No
To receive services after enrolling: Yes
What documentation required for ADHD: An Evaluation Report (Psychological, Psychoeducational, Psychiatric, or Neuropsychological) that shows an appropriate diagnosis of ASD with the record of tests taken, the interpretation of those tests, and interviews that lead to the diagnosis.
With general application: No
To receive services after enrolling: Yes
What documentation required for ASD: Evaluation Reports (Psychological, and Educational or Psychoeducational) that demonstrates and appropriate diagnosis of LD with the record of tests taken and the interpretation of those tests and interviews that leads to the diagnosis of LD.
With general application: No
To receive services after enrolling: Yes
LD/ADHD/ASD documentation submitted to: ARC - Disabilities Services Office
ASD Specific Program: NR
Special Ed. HS course work accepted: Yes
Specific course requirements of all applicants: Yes
Separate application required for program services: True
Total # of students receiving LD/ADHD/ASD services: 105
Acceptance into program means acceptance into college: No

ADMISSIONS

Neumann University's undergraduate admissions have a rolling admissions policy.Interviews are not required, but strongly recommended.

ADDITIONAL INFORMATION

A student declares his/her disability to Neumann University by providing the Disabilities Services Coordinator of the John C. Ford Academic Resource Center (ARC) with current documentation of the disability by a recognized authority. The declaration remains confidential unless the student provides the Coordinator with written permission to release this information. Once the documentation of the disability is on record, Neumann University will provide reasonable accommodations to assist the student in fulfilling his/her academic pursuits. By law, the University is not responsible for making special accommodations for a student who has not declared and documented his/her disabilities. If a student wishes to appeal a decision regarding an academic matter, the student must follow the grievance procedure as stated in the Academic Information of the University catalog. Once the documentation of the disability has been filed, the student is also responsible for communicating his/her particular needs to the Disabilities Services Coordinator prior to the start of each semester. At this time, the student may fill out and sign a Disclosure and Notification Form, which gives ARC personnel permission to contact the appropriate faculty member(s) regarding the student's particular needs. Students are also invited and encouraged to discuss their needs with their teachers, the Director of Counseling, and the Director of Health Services

General Support Services Information

Contact Information
Name of program or department: ARC - Disabilities Services Office
Telephone: 610-361-5471
Fax: 610-358-4564
Website: http://www.neumann.edu/academics/arc/disabilities.asp

Accommodations or Services for Students with Learning Differences

Accommodations are decided upon an individual basis after a thorough review of appropriate, current documentation. The accommodations requests must be supported through the documentation provided and must be logically linked to the current impact of the condition on academic functioning.

Allowed in exams
Calculator: Yes
Dictionary: Yes
Computer: Yes
Spellchecker: Yes
Extended test time: Yes
Scribes: Yes
Proctors: Yes
Oral exams: Yes
Note-takers: Yes
Support services for students with LD: Yes
Support services for students with ADHD: Yes
Support services for students with ASD: Yes
Distraction-reduced environment: Yes
Tape recording in class: Yes
Electronic texts: Yes
Kurzweil reader: NR
Audio books: Yes
Other assistive technology: Yes
Priority registration: Yes
Added costs of services: No
LD specialists: No
ADHD coaching: Yes
ASD specialists: Yes
Professional tutors: No
Peer tutors: Yes
Max. hours/wk. for services: NR
How professors are notified of student approved accommodations: By both student and director

General Admissions Information

Office of Admissions: 610-558-5616

Entrance Requirements

Academic units required: 4 English, 2 math, 2 science, 2 foreign language, 2 social studies, 4 academic electives. **Academic units recommended:** 3 science, High school diploma is required and GED is accepted. SAT or ACT required. If ACT, ACT with writing accepted. TOEFL required of all international applicants: minimum paper TOEFL 550 or minimum internet TOEFL 70.

Application deadline: NR
Notification: Rolling starting 9/15
Average GPA: 3.04
ACT Composite middle 50% range: 17-21
SAT Math middle 50% range: 410-500
SAT Critical Reading middle 50% range: 410-490
SAT Writing middle 50% range: 390-480
Graduate top 10% of class: NR
Graduated top 25% of class: NR
Graduated top 50% of class: NR

COLLEGE GRADUATION REQUIREMENTS

Course waivers allowed: No
Course substitutions allowed: Yes
In what course: Students with certain documented disabilities, such as severe dyslexia, can, with the approval of the Vice President for Academic Affairs, substitute certain specific courses for those courses required for graduation.

Additional Information

Environment: This private school, affiliated with the Roman Catholic Church, was founded in 1965. It has a 55-acre campus.

Student Body
Undergrad enrollment: 2,403
% Women: 64
% Men: 36
% Out-of-state: 31

Cost information
Tuition: $25,792
Room & board: $11,754

Housing Information
University Housing: Yes
Percent living on campus: 32

Greek System
Fraternity: No
Sorority: No
Athletics: Division III

Penn. State U.—University Park

201 Shields Building, University Park, PA 16802
Phone: 814-865-5471 • Fax: 814-863-7590
E-mail: admissions@psu.edu • Web: www.psu.edu
Support: S • Institution: Public

Programs or Services for Students with Learning Differences

The goal of Penn State's academic support services for students with learning disabilities is to ensure that students receive appropriate accommodations so that they can function independently and meet the academic demands of a competitive university. Students with learning disabilities should be able to complete college-level courses with the help of support services and classroom accommodations. To receive any of the support services, students must submit documentation of their learning disability to the learning disability specialist in the Office for Disability Services (ODS). Documentation should be a psychoeducational report from a certified or licensed psychologist completed within the past 3 years. The report should include measures of intellectual functioning and measures of achievement that describe current levels of functioning in reading, mathematics, and written language. Students with ADHD should have the professional who diagnosed them complete the ADHD Verification Form and submit it to the Office for Disability Services.

Admission Information for Students with Learning Differences

College entrance test required: Yes
Interview required: Not Applicable
Essay required: Not Applicable
Additional Application Required for LD/ADHD/ASD: Not Applicable
What documentation required for LD: See: http://equity.psu.edu/ods/guidelines/ad-hd
With general application: Not Applicable
To receive services after enrolling: Not Applicable
What documentation required for ADHD: See: http://equity.psu.edu/ods/guidelines/asd
With general application: Not Applicable
To receive services after enrolling: Not Applicable
What documentation required for ASD: See: http://equity.psu.edu/ods/guidelines/learning-disorders
With general application: Not Applicable
To receive services after enrolling: Not Applicable
LD/ADHD/ASD documentation submitted to: Student Disability Resources
ASD Specific Program: NR
Special Ed. HS course work accepted: Not Applicable
Specific course requirements of all applicants: Yes
Separate application required for program services: Yes
Total # of students receiving LD/ADHD/ASD services: NR
Acceptance into program means acceptance into college: Not Applicable

Admissions

There is no special application process for students with learning disabilities or attention deficit hyperactivity disorder, and these students are considered for admission on the same basis as other applicants. The minimum 50 percent of admitted students have a GPA between 3.52 and 3.97 and an ACT score between 26 and 30 or an SAT score between 1750 and 1990. Course requirements include 4 years of English, 3 years of math, 3 years of science, 2 years of a foreign language, and 3 years of social studies. If the applicant's high school grades and test scores are low, students may submit a letter explaining why their ability to succeed in college is higher than indicated by their academic records. The Admissions Office will consider this information as it is voluntarily provided. The acceptable ACT or SAT score will depend on the high school grades and class rank of the student. Two-thirds of the evaluation is based on high school grades and one-third on test scores. Once admitted, students must submit documentation of their learning disability to receive support services. Students may seek admission as a provisional or nondegree student if they do not meet criteria required for admission as a degree candidate. Any student may enroll as a nondegree student.

Additional Information

Students with LD are encouraged to participate in the Buddy Program; incoming students are matched with a senior buddy who is a current student with a disability and is available to share experiences with a junior buddy. Other services include providing audiotaped textbooks, arranging course substitutions with academic departments (when essential requirements are not involved), providing test accommodations, and providing individual counseling. Assistance with note-taking is offered through the ODS. Services are offered in a mainstream setting. The Learning Assistance Center operates a Math Center, Tutoring Center, Writing Center, and Computer Learning Center. Students may receive academic help either individually or in small groups for a number of different courses. One-on-one academic assistance is available through the Office of Disability Services. Graduate clinicians provide individual assistance with study skills, time management, and compensatory learning strategies.

General Support Services Information

Contact Information
Name of program or department: Student Disability Resources
Telephone: 814-863-1807
Fax: 814-863-3217
Website: http://equity/psu.edu/ods/

Accommodations or Services For Students With Learning Differences

Accommodations are decided upon an individual basis after a thorough review of appropriate, current documentation. The accommodations requests must be supported through the documentation provided and must be logically linked to the current impact of the condition on academic functioning.

Allowed in exams
Calculator: Not Applicable
Dictionary: Yes
Computer: Yes
Spellchecker: Yes
Extended test time: Yes
Scribes: Yes
Proctors: Yes
Oral exams: Yes
Note-takers: Yes
Support services for students with LD: Yes
Support services for students with ADHD: Yes
Support services for students with ASD: Yes
Distraction-reduced environment: Yes
Tape recording in class: Yes
Electronic texts: Yes
Kurzweil reader: NR
Audio books: Yes
Other assistive technology: Yes
Priority registration: Yes
Added costs of services: Not Applicable
LD specialists: No
ADHD coaching: No
ASD specialists: Yes
Professional tutors: No
Peer tutors: Not Applicable
Max. hours/wk. for services: NR
How professors are notified of student approved accommodations: By student

General Admissions Information

Office of Admissions: 814-865-5471

Entrance Requirements

Academic units required: 4 English, 3 math, 3 science, 2 foreign language, 3 social studies. **Academic units recommended:** 3 foreign language. High school diploma is required and GED is accepted. SAT or ACT required. If ACT, ACT with writing accepted. TOEFL required of all international applicants: minimum paper TOEFL 550 or minimum internet TOEFL 80.

Application deadline: NR
Notification: Rolling starting 10/15
Average GPA: 3.6
ACT Composite middle 50% range: 25-29
SAT Math middle 50% range: 560-670
SAT Critical Reading middle 50% range: 530-630
SAT Writing middle 50% range: 540-640
Graduate top 10% of class: 41
Graduated top 25% of class: 82
Graduated top 50% of class: 98

COLLEGE GRADUATION REQUIREMENTS

Course waivers allowed: No
Course substitutions allowed: Yes
In what course: Foreign Language

Additional Information

Environment: This public school was founded in 1855. It has a 7,264-acre campus.

Student Body
Undergrad enrollment: 40,742
% Women: 46
% Men: 54
% Out-of-state: 31

Cost information
In-state Tuition: $16,572
Out-of-state Tuition: $30,404
Room & board: $10,920

Housing Information
University Housing: Yes
Percent living on campus: 34

Greek System
Fraternity: Yes
Sorority: Yes
Athletics: Division I

Seton Hill University

One Seton Hill Drive, Greensburg, PA 15601
Phone: 724-838-4255 • Fax: 724-830-1294
E-mail: admit@setonhill.edu • Web: www.setonhill.edu
Support: S • Institution: Private

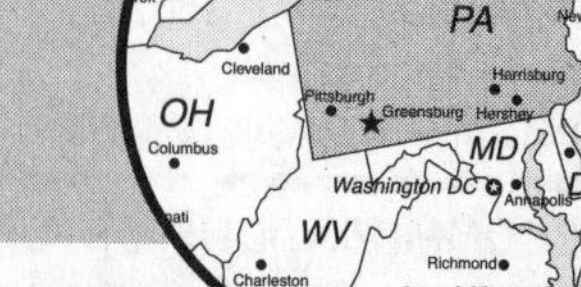

Programs or Services for Students with Learning Differences

Students who are eligible for, and are requesting, accommodations under the Americans with Disabilities ACT are required to register with the Coordinator of Disabled Student Services. Students work individually with the disability services coordinator to determine what learning or environmental supports are needed based on the documentation and recommendations for accommodations in the report. An individualized plan of accommodation will be developed with the student. It is the student's responsibility to implement the plan. The student should advise the coordinator of Disability Services if they experience any difficulties with their accommodation plan.

Admission Information for Students with Learning Differences

College entrance tests required: Yes
Interview required: No
Essay required: No
Additional Application Required for LD/ADHD/ASD: NR
What documentation required for LD: Psycho ed evaluation to include: relevant historical info, instructional interventions, related services, age diagnosed, objective data (aptitude, achievement, info processing), test scores (standard, percentile and grade equivalents) and describe functional limitations.
With general application: No
To receive services after enrolling: Yes
What documentation required for ADHD: Diagnosis based on DSM-V; history of behaviors impairing functioning in academic setting; diagnostic interview; history of symptoms; evidence of ongoing behaviors.
With general application: No
To receive services after enrolling: Yes
What documentation required for ASD: Psycho ed evaluation
With general application: NR
To receive services after enrolling: Yes
LD/ADHD/ASD documentation submitted to: Disability Services
ASD Specific Program: NR
Special Ed. HS course work accepted: NR
Specific course requirements of all applicants: Yes
Separate application required: No
Total # of students receiving LD/ADHD/ASD services: NR
Acceptance into program means acceptance into college: Students must be admitted to and enrolled in the university first and then request services.

Admissions

Students with documented learning disabilities may request course substitutions for deficiencies in entrance courses based on the LD. Pre admission interviews are not required but are recommended. The admissions office can also determine if an applicant might be appropriate to be admitted through the C.A.P.S Program. Within the C.A.P.S. Program there are two academic support programs, the pre-freshman year Opportunity Program and Student Support Services. The Admissions Office primarily determines acceptance into these two programs. Students who feel they would benefit from the C.A.P.S. Program services may also apply by submitting an application that can be obtained through the C.A.P.S. Program Office.

Additional Information

There is a summer program that targets English and study skills. These are required programs for students with weak transcripts or SAT/ACT scores who otherwise meet admissions standards. The Opportunity Program is a weeklong learning experience that prepares students for the University's demanding academic culture. It is designed to provide students with an academic experience that will ease their transition from high school to college. The program provides services that assist the students in maximizing and enhancing academic potential. Accommodations once in the college may include, but are not limited to, preferential seating, note-taking services, tape-recorded lectures, extended time for projects, extended time for quizzes and tests, testing in distraction-reduced environments, alternative testing formats, tutoring, counseling, course substitutions, use of assisted technologies (e.g., spellcheckers), computer-based programs, and scribe services. Students are responsible for notifying professors about their disability and requesting accommodations. Course substitution requests are reviewed and considered on an individual basis. Skills classes for college credit are offered in time management techniques, note-taking strategies, test-taking strategies, and text reading.

General Support Services Information

Contact Information
Name of program or department: Disability Services
Telephone: 724-838-4295
Fax: 724-830-4233

Accommodations or Services for Students with Learning Differences

Accommodations are decided upon an individual basis after a thorough review of appropriate, current documentation. The accommodations requested must be supported through the documentation provided and must be logically linked to the current impact of the condition on academic functioning.

Allowed in exams
Calculator: Yes
Dictionary: Yes
Computer: Yes
Spellchecker: Yes
Extended test time: Yes
Scribes: Yes
Proctors: Yes
Oral exams: Yes
Note-takers: Yes
Services for students with LD: Yes
Services for students with ADHD: Yes
Services for students with ASD: Yes
Distraction-reduced environment: Yes
Tape recording in class: Yes
Electronic texts: Yes
Audio books: NR
Kurzweil Reader: Yes
Other assistive technology: Yes
Priority registration: No
Added costs for services: No
LD specialists: No
ADHD coaching: NR
ASD specialists: NR
Professional tutors: No
Peer tutors: 60
Max. hours/wk. for services: Unlimited
How professors are notified of LD/ADHD: By student

General Admissions Information

Office of Admissions: 724-838-4255

Entrance Requirements

Academic units required: 4 English, 2 math, 1 science, 1 science labs, 2 social studies, 4 academic electives. **Academic units recommended:** 4 English, 2 math, 1 science, 1 science labs, 2 foreign language, 2 social studies, 4 academic electives. High school diploma is required and GED is accepted. SAT or ACT recommended. If ACT, ACT with writing recommended. TOEFL required of all international applicants: minimum paper TOEFL 550.

Application deadline: 8/15
Notification: Rolling starting 9/1
Average GPA: 3.62
ACT Composite middle 50% range: 20-27
SAT Math middle 50% range: 460-590
SAT Critical Reading middle 50% range: 470-580
SAT Writing middle 50% range: 450-570
Graduated top 10% of class: 18
Graduated top 25% of class: 52
Graduated top 50% of class: 78

COLLEGE GRADUATION REQUIREMENTS

Course waivers allowed: Yes
In what course: All appropriate waivers are reviewed and considered. Essential elements of a student's program cannot be waived.
Course substitutions allowed: Yes
In what course: All appropriate substitutions are reviewed and considered. Essential elements of a student's program cannot be substituted.

Additional Information

Environment: This private school, affiliated with the Roman Catholic Church, was founded in 1883. It has a 200-acre campus.

Student Body
Undergrad enrollment: 1,620
% Women: 65
% Men: 35
% Out-of-state: 26

Cost information
Tuition: $32,520
Room & board: $5,500-$6,805

Housing Information
University Housing: Yes
Percent living on campus: 56

Greek System
Fraternity: No
Sorority: No
Athletics: Division II

UNIVERSITY OF PITTSBURGH

4227 Fifth Avenue, Pittsburgh, PA 15260
Phone: 412-624-7488 • Fax: 412-648-8815
E-mail: oafa@pitt.edu • Web: www.pitt.edu
Support: CS • Institution: Public

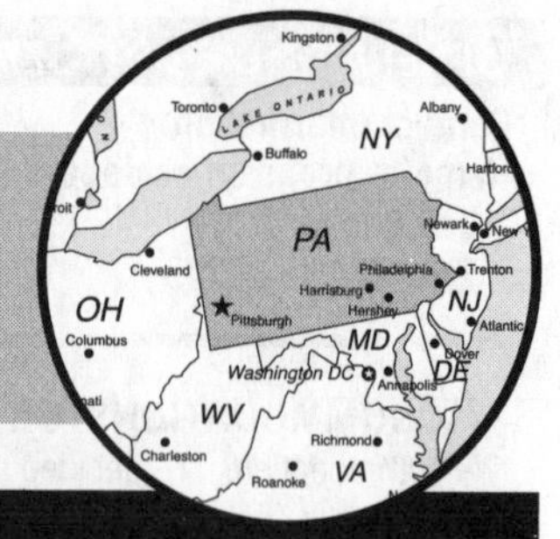

PROGRAMS OR SERVICES FOR STUDENTS WITH LEARNING DIFFERENCES

To access services, students must refer themselves to Disability Resource Services and submit documentation of their learning disability. Once eligibility is established, students meet regularly with a DRS disability specialist who will assist the student in accessing resources and developing an individualized, comprehensive educational plan. The objective of DRS is to work closely with students to empower them to plan and implement a successful academic experience.

ADMISSION INFORMATION FOR STUDENTS WITH LEARNING DIFFERENCES

College entrance tests required: Yes
Interview required: N/A
Essay required: N/A
Additional Application Required for LD/ADHD/ASD: NR
What documentation required for LD: Psycho ed evaluation to include: relevant historical info, instructional interventions, related services, age diagnosed, objective data (aptitude, achievement, info processing), test scores (standard, percentile and grade equivalents) and describe functional limitations.
With general application: No
To receive services after enrolling: Yes
What documentation required for ADHD: Diagnosis based on DSM-V; history of behaviors impairing functioning in academic setting; diagnostic interview; history of symptoms; evidence of ongoing behaviors.
With general application: No
To receive services after enrolling: Yes
What documentation required for ASD: Psycho ed evaluation
With general application: NR
To receive services after enrolling: Yes
LD/ADHD/ASD documentation submitted to: Support Program/Services
ASD Specific Program: NR
Special Ed. HS course work accepted: No
Specific course requirements for all applicants: Yes
Separate application required for program services: No
Total # of students receiving LD/ADHD/ASD services: 225
Acceptance into program means acceptance into college: Students must be admitted to and enrolled in the university first and then request services.

ADMISSIONS

Students with learning disabilities must meet the same admission criteria established for all applicants. It is important to have applications reviewed based on more than just the high school record and SAT/ACT scores. U Pitt recommends that students submit any supplemental information that they feel will help the committee get to know them better. The committee is looking for students who are well-rounded both in and out of the classroom. The Personal Essay is optional. However, applicants should definitely submit a personal essay if they want: scholarship consideration; consideration into the guaranteed admission to graduate/professional school; special consideration in the review process due to extenuating circumstances affecting a term or so of grades; and they would like the committee to review more than just the high school transcript and SAT/ACT scores. Likewise, while not required, letter(s) of recommendation from a person or people who knows the student well can help the admission office get to know the student better.

ADDITIONAL INFORMATION

DRS individually designs and recommends services to enhance the skills and personal development of the student. Services available may include: exam accommodations, use of calculators, computer or spell checker in exams, scribes, proctors, controlled environments, alternative format, instructional strategy assistance, and assistive technology. There are three disability specialists on staff.

General Support Services Information

Contact Information
Name of program or department: Disability Resources and Services
Telephone: 412-648-7890
Fax: 412-624-3346
Website: NR

Accommodations or Services For Students With Learning Differences

Accommodations are decided upon an individual basis after a thorough review of appropriate, current documentation. The accommodations requests must be supported through the documentation provided and must be logically linked to the current impact of the condition on academic functioning.

Allowed in exams
Calculator: No
Dictionary: Yes
Computer: Yes
Spellchecker: Yes
Extended test time: Yes
Scribes: Yes
Proctors: Yes
Oral exams: No
Note-takers: Yes
Support services for students with LD: Yes
Support services for students with ADHD: Yes
Support services for students with ASD: Yes
Distraction-reduced environment: Yes
Tape recording in class: Yes
Electronic texts: Yes
Kurzweil reader: NR
Audio books: Yes
Other assistive technology: Yes
Priority registration: No
Added costs of services: No
LD specialists: Yes
ADHD coaching: No
ASD specialists: Yes
Professional tutors: No
Peer tutors: NR
Max. hours/wk. for services: NR
How professors are notified of student approved accommodations: By both student and director

General Admissions Information

Office of Admissions: 412-624-7488

Entrance Requirements

Academic units required: 4 English, 3 math, 3 science, 3 science labs, 2 foreign language, 2 social studies, 3 academic electives. **Academic units recommended:** 4 English, 4 math, 4 science, 4 science labs, 3 foreign language, 3 social studies, 5 academic electives. High school diploma is required and GED is not accepted. SAT or ACT required. If ACT, ACT with writing required. TOEFL required of all international applicants: minimum paper TOEFL 600 or minimum internet TOEFL 100.

Application deadline: NR
Notification: Rolling starting 9/1
Average GPA: 4
ACT Composite middle 50% range: 26-31
SAT Math middle 50% range: 600-690
SAT Critical Reading middle 50% range: 580-660
SAT Writing middle 50% range: 570-670
Graduate top 10% of class: 50
Graduated top 25% of class: 83
Graduated top 50% of class: 99

COLLEGE GRADUATION REQUIREMENTS

Course waivers allowed: No
Course substitutions allowed: Yes
In what course: There is a process in place for students to request a course substitution if their disability supports the request.

Additional Information

Environment: This public school was founded in 1787. It has a 132-acre campus.

Student Body
Undergrad enrollment: 18,908
% Women: 51
% Men: 49
% Out-of-state: 26.7

Cost information
In-state Tuition: $17,292
Out-of-state Tuition: $28,058
Room & board: $10,900

Housing Information
University Housing: Yes
Percent living on campus: 44

Greek System
Fraternity: Yes
Sorority: Yes
Athletics: Division I

Widener University

One University Place, Chester, PA 19013
Phone: 610-499-4126 • Fax: 610-499-4676
E-mail: admissions.office@widener.edu • Web: www.widener.edu
Support: CS • Institution: Private

Programs or Services for Students with Learning Differences

Disabilities Services is a structured mainstream support service designed to assist students enrolled in one of Widener's standard academic programs. Students wishing to use Disabilities Services must submit documentation that describes the nature of the learning disability including relevant evaluations and assessments. Each student at Disabilities Services has the option of meeting once or twice a week with a learning specialist in our academic coaching program. Typically, academic coaching sessions focus on time management, study skills, social and emotional adjustment, and academic planning. Disabilities Services serves as a campus advocate for the needs of students with LD by making sure that accommodations are provided when appropriate. Participation in our services is included in the basic tuition charge. Thus, there is no extra fee.

Admission Information for Students with Learning Differences

College entrance tests required: Yes
Interview required: No
Essay required: Yes
Additional Application Required for LD/ADHD/ASD: NR
What documentation required for LD: Psycho ed evaluation to include: relevant historical info, instructional interventions, related services, age diagnosed, objective data (aptitude, achievement, info processing), test scores (standard, percentile and grade equivalents) and describe functional limitations.
With general application: No
To receive services after enrolling: Yes
What documentation required for ADHD: Diagnosis based on DSM-V; history of behaviors impairing functioning in academic setting; diagnostic interview; history of symptoms; evidence of ongoing behaviors.
With general application: No
To receive services after enrolling: Yes
What documentation required for ASD: Psycho ed evaluation
With general application: NR
To receive services after enrolling: Yes
LD/ADHD/ASD documentation submitted to: Enable
ASD Specific Program: NR
Special Ed. HS course work accepted: Yes
Specific course requirements of all applicants: NR
Separate application required: No
Total # of students receiving LD/ADHD/ASD services: 200
Acceptance into program means acceptance into college: Students must be admitted to and enrolled in the university first and then request services.

Admissions

Students with learning disabilities submit the general application form. Admission decisions are made by the Office of Admissions. Students should submit their application, an essay, and recommendations. ACT scores range between 17 and 27 and SAT scores range between 750 and 1300. There are no specific course requirements for admissions. High school GPA range is 2.0–4.0.

Additional Information

Disabilities Services is a personalized academic support and counseling service designed to help students with learning disabilities who meet university entrance requirements cope with the rigors of academic life. Students can sign up for academic coaching to meet with counselors who can help them understand and accept their disabilities; individualize learning strategies; teach self-advocacy; and link the students with the other Academic Support Services available at Widener. This office assures that professors understand which accommodations are needed. The Writing Center provides assistance with writing assignments and is staffed by professors. The Math Center offers individualized and group tutoring and is staffed by professors and experienced tutors. In addition, the Tutoring Office provides individual and group tutoring for the majority of undergraduate Widener courses.

General Support Services Information

Contact Information
Name of program or department: Disability Services
Telephone: 610-499-1266
Fax: 610-499-1192

Accommodations or Services for Students with Learning Differences

Accommodations are decided upon an individual basis after a thorough review of appropriate, current documentation. The accommodations requested must be supported through the documentation provided and must be logically linked to the current impact of the condition on academic functioning.

Allowed in exams
Calculator: Yes
Dictionary: Yes
Computer: Yes
Spellchecker: Yes
Extended test time: Yes
Scribes: Yes
Proctors: Yes
Oral exams: Yes
Note-takers: Yes
Services for students with LD: Yes
Services for students with ADHD: Yes
Services for students with ASD: Yes
Distraction-reduced environment: Yes
Tape recording in class: Yes
Audio books: NR
Electronic texts: Yes
Kurzweil Reader: Yes
Other assistive technology: Yes
Priority registration: Yes
Added costs for services: No
LD specialists: Yes
ADHD coaching: NR
ASD specialists: NR
Professional tutors: 1
Peer tutors: Yes
Max. hours/wk. for services: Unlimited
How professors are notified of LD/ADHD: By student

General Admissions Information

Office of Admissions: 610-499-4126

Entrance Requirements

Academic units required: 4 English, 3 math, 3 science, 2 foreign language, 3 social studies, 3 academic electives.
Academic units recommended: 4 English, 4 math, 4 science, 2 science labs, 2 foreign language, 4 social studies, 3 academic electives. High school diploma is required and GED is accepted. SAT or ACT required. TOEFL required of all international applicants: minimum paper TOEFL 500.

Application deadline: NR
Notification: Rolling starting 10/1
Average GPA: 3.45
ACT Composite middle 50% range: 21-25
SAT Math middle 50% range: 470-570
SAT Critical Reading middle 50% range: 460-550
SAT Writing middle 50% range: NR-NR
Graduated top 10% of class: 12
Graduated top 25% of class: 41
Graduated top 50% of class: 81

COLLEGE GRADUATION REQUIREMENTS

Course waivers allowed: No
Course substitutions allowed: No

Additional Information

Environment: This private school was founded in 1821. It has a 110-acre campus.

Student Body
Undergrad enrollment: 3,554
% Women: 56
% Men: 44
% Out-of-state: 40

Cost information
Tuition: $40,418
Room & board: $13,092

Housing Information
University Housing: Yes
Percent living on campus: 47

Greek System
Fraternity: Yes
Sorority: Yes
Athletics: Division III

Brown University

PO Box 1876, Providence, RI 02912
Phone: 401-863-2378 • Fax: 401-863-9300
E-mail: admission@brown.edu • Web: www.brown.edu
Support: CS • Institution: Private

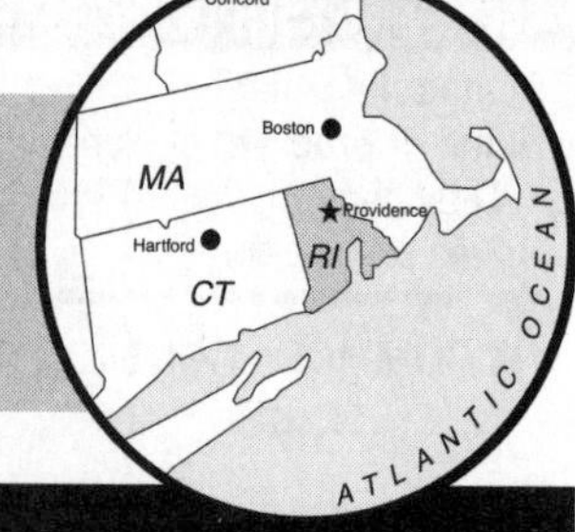

Programs or Services for Students with Learning Differences

Brown has a long history of providing accommodations and services to students with learning disabilities. There are no specific general education requirements which can be helpful to students for whom a particular area may be very challenging. Documentation guidelines are available on the SEAS website as well as information about services and accommodations: http://www.brown.edu/campus-life/support/accessibility-services/

Admission Information for Students with Learning Differences

College entrance test required: Yes
Interview required: N/A
Essay required: No
Additional Application Required for LD/ADHD/ASD: NR
What documentation required for LD: A current, complete psycho-educational evaluation is required and will hopefully have been done when the student could be evaluated using adult scales. Aptitude testing such as the WAIS III; achievement testing such as the Woodcock-Johnson IV; and information processing as appropriate are required. We require that the evaluation come from a qualified provider and that they use objective measures to make the diagnosis.
With general application: No
To receive services after enrolling: Yes
What documentation required for ADHD: We prefer to have the same documentation that we request for documenting a learning disability. We require that the evaluation come from a qualified provider and that they use objective measures to make the diagnosis.
With general application: No
To receive services after enrolling: Yes
What documentation required for ASD: The same documentation provided for LD/ADHD is often helpful, but sometimes documentation comes from a therapist.
With general application: No
To receive services after enrolling: Yes
LD/ADHD/ASD documentation submitted to: Support program/services
ASD Specific Program: NR
Special Ed. HS course work accepted: No
Specific course: Yes
Separate application required for program services: No
Total # of students receiving LD/ADHD/ASD services: NR
Acceptance into program means acceptance into college: NR

Admissions

Same as for all students; students can submit additional information about their disability (one page) if they believe it will be helpful to Admission in reviewing their application. Ninety-four percent of incoming freshmen rank in the top ten percent of their high school class. The 25 to 75 percent range of the ACT in 30-36 and 700-800 on each SAT section.

Additional Information

Brown University has as its primary aim the education of a highly qualified and diverse student body. Brown's commitment to students with disabilities is based on awareness of what students require for success and seeks to foster an environment in which that success may be achieved. Group tutoring is offered for introductory courses in science, math, economics, and statistics. Students are assigned to small groups that meet weekly to review important or difficult topics covered in class that week. Tutors have either taken the course or proven competency, and have been trained by the Academic Support Staff. Students can receive assistance with quick questions in introductory and intermediate biology, chemistry, and physics. Students with disabilities who believe they may need accommodations should self-identify by registering with SEAS. SEAS staff will conduct a review and analysis prior to making a recommendation regarding the provision of reasonable accommodations. Requests for accommodations are evaluated individually, based on documentation, and completion of the registration process.

General Support Services Information

Contact Information
Name of program or department: Student and Employee Accessibility Services (SEAS)
Telephone: 401-863-9588
Fax: 401-863-1444

Accommodations or Services For Students With Learning Differences

Accommodations are decided upon an individual basis after a thorough review of appropriate, current documentation. The accommodations requests must be supported through the documentation provided and must be logically linked to the current impact of the condition on academic functioning.

Allowed in exams
Calculator: Yes
Dictionary: Yes
Computer: Yes
Spellchecker: Yes
Extended test time: Yes
Scribes: Yes
Proctors: Yes
Oral exams: No
Note-takers: Yes
Support services for students with LD: NR
Support services for students with ADHD: Yes
Support services for students with ASD: Yes
Distraction-reduced environment: Yes
Tape recording in class: Yes
Electronic texts: Yes
Kurzweil reader: NR
Audio books: Yes
Other assistive technology: Yes
Priority registration: Not Applicable
Added costs of services: Not Applicable
LD specialists: Yes
ADHD coaching: Yes
ASD specialists: Not Applicable
Professional tutors: No
Peer tutors: Yes
Max. hours/wk. for services: 2
How professors are notified of student approved accommodations: By student

General Admissions Information

Office of Admissions: 401-863-2378

Entrance Requirements

Academic units required: 4 English, 3 math, 3 science, 2 science labs, 3 foreign language, 2 history, 1 academic electives. **Academic units recommended:** 4 English, 4 math, 4 science, 3 science labs, 4 foreign language, 1 social studies, 2 history, 1 academic electives, 1 computer science, 1 visual/performing arts. High school diploma is required and GED is not accepted. If ACT, ACT with writing recommended. Minimum paper TOEFL 600 or minimum internet TOEFL 100.

Application deadline: 1/1
Notification: NR
Average GPA: NR
ACT Composite middle 50% range: 31-34
SAT Math middle 50% range: 690-780
SAT Critical Reading middle 50% range: 680-780
SAT Writing middle 50% range: 690-780
Graduate top 10% of class: 91
Graduated top 25% of class: 100
Graduated top 50% of class: 100

COLLEGE GRADUATION REQUIREMENTS

Course waivers allowed: Not Applicable
Course substitutions allowed: Not Applicable

Additional Information

Environment: This private school was founded in 1764. It has a 146-acre campus.

Student Body
Undergrad enrollment: 6,652
% Women: 53
% Men: 47
% Out-of-state: 94

Cost information
Tuition: $50,224
Room & board: $13,200

Housing Information
University Housing: Yes
Percent living on campus: 76

Greek System
Fraternity: Yes
Sorority: Yes
Athletics: Division I

BRYANT UNIVERSITY

Office of Admission, 1150 Douglas Pike, Smithfield, RI 02917-1291
Phone: 401-232-6000 • Fax: 401-232-6731
E-mail: admission@bryant.edu • Web: www.bryant.edu
Support: CS • Institution: Private

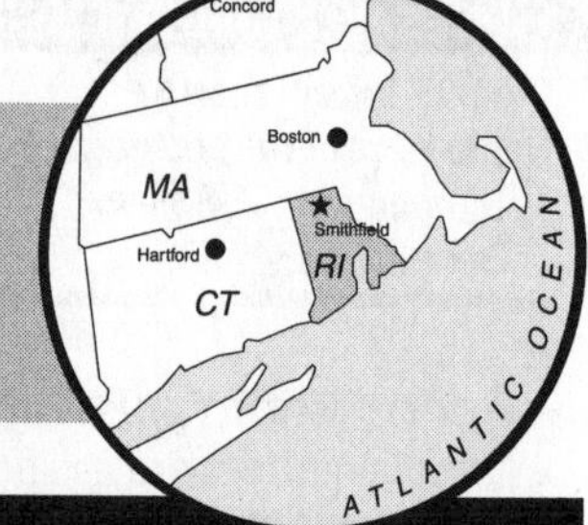

PROGRAMS OR SERVICES FOR STUDENTS WITH LEARNING DIFFERENCES

Bryant University offers services for students with learning disabilities. The Academic Center for Excellence (ACE) is dedicated to helping Bryant students achieve their goal of academic success. Basically, the center provides study skills training to help students become self-reliant, independent, and confident learners. This is achieved through an internationally accredited peer tutoring program and study skills instruction by professional staff. Group sessions as a mode of instruction are encouraged and the staff engages in a partnership with students to help them achieve their goals. The Learning Specialist provides support for students with LD. In keeping with the philosophy of empowering Bryant students to achieve their goals of academic success, they also will receive assistance in learning how to access the comprehensive academic support services offered by the Academic Success Programs.

ADMISSION INFORMATION FOR STUDENTS WITH LEARNING DIFFERENCES

College entrance tests required: No/Test Optional
Interview required: N/A
Essay required: N/A
Additional Application Required for LD/ADHD/ASD: NR
What documentation required for LD: Psycho ed evaluation to include: relevant historical info, instructional interventions, related services, age diagnosed, objective data (aptitude, achievement, info processing), test scores (standard, percentile and grade equivalents) and describe functional limitations.
With general application: No
To receive services after enrolling: Yes
What documentation required for ADHD: Diagnosis based on DSM-V; history of behaviors impairing functioning in academic setting; diagnostic interview; history of symptoms; evidence of ongoing behaviors.
With general application: No
To receive services after enrolling: Yes
What documentation required for ASD: Psycho ed evaluation
With general application: NR
To receive services after enrolling: Yes
LD/ADHD/ASD documentation submitted to: Support Program/Services
ASD Specific Program: NR
Special Ed. HS course work accepted: N/A
Specific course requirements for all applicants: Yes
Separate application required for program services: No
Total # of students receiving LD/ADHD/ASD services: NR
Acceptance into program means acceptance into college: NR

ADMISSIONS

Students are encouraged to self-disclose a learning challenge. All documentation should be sent to ACE. General admission criteria include an average GPA of 3.0. ACT/SAT are not required as Bryant is Test-Optional. A minimum of 16 units with the following courses is recommended: 4 years of English; 4 years of college prep math, including a year beyond Algebra II; 2 years of history or social science; 2 years of lab sciences; 2 years of foreign language. Interviews are not required but are encouraged.

ADDITIONAL INFORMATION

Students with documented learning differences need to submit documentation and request academic accommodations through Access Services in the Academic Center for Excellence. Comprehensive documentation completed within the past three years must address the current impact of disability on the academic performance. Students are encouraged to submit their documentation after their acceptance and decision to enroll at Bryant. At the start of each semester, students will need to meet with someone from the ACE staff to discuss academic needs and request reasonable accommodations. The Academic Success Programs provide access to learning specialists who provide individualized assistance and group workshops on college-level study skill development. Examples of some of the programs and services offered include: The Academic Center for Excellence, which is staffed by professional math specialists and peer tutors. The peer tutors are trained and certified by The College Reading and Learning Association and offer both one-on-one and group appointments for a variety of academic subjects. Learning Labs allow students to work with a specialist or peer tutor on math, economics, finance or accounting assignments. The Writing Center provides one-on-one services with professional writing specialists and student writing consultants, who are also CRLA trained and certified. The Writing Center staff work with students at all stages of the writing process, including brainstorming, outlining, thesis development, and draft editing. As a liaison among students, faculty, and administration, ACE encourages students with LD requiring special accommodations to schedule an appointment with a Learning Specialist as soon as they register for courses each semester.

General Support Services Information

Contact Information
Name of program or department: Academic Center for Excellence
Telephone: 401-232-6746
Fax: 401-232-6038

Accommodations or Services for Students with Learning Differences

Accommodations are decided upon an individual basis after a thorough review of appropriate, current documentation. The accommodations requested must be supported through the documentation provided and must be logically linked to the current impact of the condition on academic functioning.

Allowed in exams
Calculator: Yes
Dictionary: No
Computer: Yes
Spellchecker: Yes
Extended test time: Yes
Scribes: N/A
Proctors: N/A
Oral exams: N/A
Note-takers: N/A
Services for students with LD: Yes
Services for students with ADHD: Yes
Services for students with ASD: Yes
Distraction-reduced environment: Yes
Tape recording in class: Yes
Audio books: NR
Electronic texts: N/A
Kurzweil Reader: Yes
Other assistive technology: N/A
Priority registration: No
Added costs for services: No
LD specialists: Yes
ADHD coaching: NR
ASD specialists: NR
Professional tutors: 6
Peer tutors: 50
Max. hours/wk. for services: NR
How professors are notified of LD/ADHD: Both student and director

General Admissions Information

Office of Admissions: 401-232-6000

Entrance Requirements

Academic units required: 4 English, 4 math, 2 science, 2 science labs, 2 foreign language, 2 history. **Academic units recommended:** 4 English, 4 math, 3 science, 2 science labs, 2 foreign language, 3 history. High school diploma is required and GED is accepted. SAT or ACT considered if submitted. If ACT, ACT with writing accepted. TOEFL required of all international applicants: minimum paper TOEFL 550 or minimum internet TOEFL 80.

Application deadline: 2/1
Notification: 3/15
Average GPA: 3.36
ACT Composite middle 50% range: 23-28
SAT Math middle 50% range: 550-640
SAT Critical Reading middle 50% range: 515-600
SAT Writing middle 50% range: 500-590
Graduated top 10% of class: 20
Graduated top 25% of class: 52
Graduated top 50% of class: 87

COLLEGE GRADUATION REQUIREMENTS

Course waivers allowed: No
In what course: N/A
Course substitutions allowed: No
In what course: N/A

Additional Information

Environment: This private school was founded in 1863. It has a 420-acre campus.

Student Body
Undergrad enrollment: 3,320
% Women: 42
% Men: 58
% Out-of-state: 87

Cost information
Tuition: $39,241
Room & board: $14,553

Housing Information
University Housing: Yes
Percent living on campus: 82

Greek System
Fraternity: Yes
Sorority: Yes
Athletics: Division I

Providence College

Harkins 103, Providence, RI 02918
Phone: 401-865-2535 • Fax: 401-865-2826
E-mail: pcadmiss@providence.edu • Web: www.providence.edu
Support: CS • Institution: Private

Programs or Services for Students with Learning Differences

The director of the Office of Academic Services and the faculty of the college are very supportive and are diligent about providing comprehensive services. The goal of the college is to be available to assist students whenever help is requested. After admission, the assistant director for Disability Services meets with the learning disabled students during the summer, prior to entry, to help them begin planning for freshman year. Students are monitored for four years. The college makes every effort to provide "reasonable accommodations."

Admission Information for Students with Learning Differences

College entrance tests required: No
Interview required: N/A
Essay required: N/A
Additional Application Required for LD/ADHD/ASD: NR
What documentation required for LD: Psycho ed evaluation to include: relevant historical info, instructional interventions, related services, age diagnosed, objective data (aptitude, achievement, info processing), test scores (standard, percentile and grade equivalents) and describe functional limitations.
With general application: No
To receive services after enrolling: Yes
What documentation required for ADHD: Diagnosis based on DSM-V; history of behaviors impairing functioning in academic setting; diagnostic interview; history of symptoms; evidence of ongoing behaviors.
With general application: No
To receive services after enrolling: Yes
What documentation required for ASD: Psycho ed evaluation
With general application: NR
To receive services after enrolling: Yes
LD/ADHD/ASD documentation submitted to: Support Program/Services
ASD Specific Program: NR
Special Ed. HS course work accepted: N/A
Specific course requirements for all applicants: Yes
Separate application required for program services: No
Total # of students receiving LD/ADHD/ASD services: NR
Acceptance into program means acceptance into college: Separate application required after student has enrolled

Admissions

There is no special admissions process for students with learning disabilities. However, an interview is highly recommended, during which individualized course work is examined. General course requirements include four years English, three years math, three years foreign language, two years lab science, two years social studies, and two years electives. Students with learning disabilities who have lower test scores but a fairly good academic record may be accepted. The admission committee has the flexibility to overlook poor test scores for students with learning disabilities. Those who have higher test scores and reasonable grades in college-prep courses (C-plus/B) may also gain admission. Students should self-identify as learning disabled on their application.

Additional Information

The following services and accommodatations are available for students presenting appropriate documentation: the use of calculators, dictionaries and computers during exams; extended time on tests; distraction-free testing environment; scribes; proctors; oral exams; note-takers; tape recorders in class; assistive technology; and priority registration. Skills seminars (for no credit) are offered in study techniques and test-taking strategies. All students have access to the Tutorial Center and Writing Center. Services and accommodations are available for undergraduate and graduate students.

General Support Services Information

Contact Information
Name of program or department: Office of Academic Services—Office of Disability Support Services
Telephone: 401-865-1121
Fax: 401-865-1219

Accommodations or Services for Students with Learning Differences

Accommodations are decided upon an individual basis after a thorough review of appropriate, current documentation. The accommodations requested must be supported through the documentation provided and must be logically linked to the current impact of the condition on academic functioning.

Allowed in exams
Calculator: Yes
Dictionary: Yes
Computer: Yes
Spellchecker: Yes
Extended test time: Yes
Scribes: Yes
Proctors: Yes
Oral exams: Yes
Note-takers: Yes
Services for students with LD: Yes
Services for students with ADHD: Yes
Services for students with ASD: Yes
Distraction-reduced environment: Yes
Tape recording in class: Yes
Audio books: NR
Electronic texts: Yes
Kurzweil Reader: No
Other assistive technology: N/A
Priority registration: Yes
Added costs for services: No
LD specialists: Yes
ADHD coaching: NR
ASD specialists: NR
Professional tutors: No
Peer tutors: 45–50
Max. hours/wk. for services: Unlimited
How professors are notified of LD/ADHD/ASD: Student

General Admissions Information

Office of Admissions: 401-865-2535

Entrance Requirements

Academic units required: 4 English, 4 math, 3 science, 2 science labs, 3 foreign language, 2 social studies, 2 history. **Academic units recommended:** 4 English, 4 math, 4 science, 2 science labs, 4 foreign language, 2 social studies, 2 history. High school diploma is required and GED is not accepted. SAT or ACT considered if submitted. If ACT, ACT with writing required. TOEFL required of all international applicants: minimum internet TOEFL 90.

Application deadline: 1/15
Notification: 4/1
Average GPA: 3.41
ACT Composite middle 50% range: 23-28
SAT Math middle 50% range: 530-630
SAT Critical Reading middle 50% range: 520-620
SAT Writing middle 50% range: 520-630
Graduate top 10% of class: 9
Graduated top 25% of class: 69
Graduated top 50% of class: 94

COLLEGE GRADUATION REQUIREMENTS

Course waivers allowed: Yes
In what course: Depends on student's disability
Course substitutions allowed: Yes
In what course: Depends on student's disability

Additional Information

Environment: Providence College has a 105-acre campus located in a small city 50 miles south of Boston.

Student Body
Undergrad enrollment: 3,804
% Women: 57
% Men: 43
% Out-of-state: 88

Cost information
Tuition: $42,385
Room & board: $12,750

Housing Information
University housing: Yes
% Living on campus: 78

Greek System
Fraternity: No
Sorority: No
Athletics: Division I

Rhode Island College

Undergrad Admissions, 600 Mt. Pleasant Avenue, Providence, RI 02908
Phone: 401-456-2776 • Fax: 401-456-9525
E-mail: dsc@ric.edu • Web: www.ric.edu
Support: CS • Institution type: 4-year Public

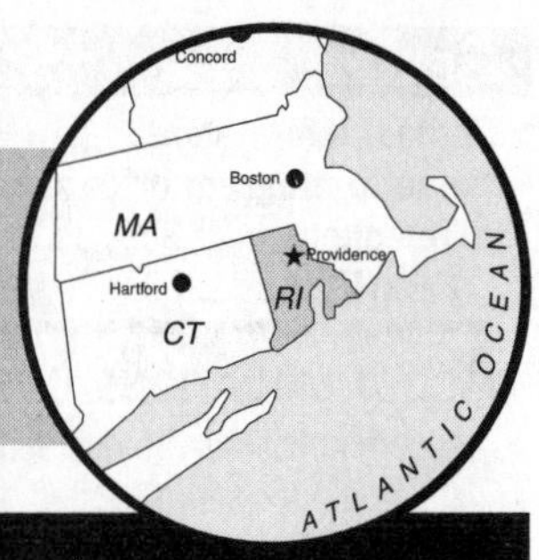

Programs or Services for Students with Learning Differences

Rhode Island College strives to create and promote an environment that is conducive to learning for all students. Necessary accommodations require that administration, faculty, and staff be consistent and use flexibility in making adaptations, and that the students be flexible in adapting to and using alternative modes of learning and instruction. Students with disabilities may self-identify at any point, but are encouraged to do so at admission. A registration card is sent to all new students. Filling out this card and returning it to the Office of Student Life starts the process. Faculty is responsible for stating at the beginning of each semester verbally or in writing that the instructor is available to meet individually with students who require accommodations. The college wants students to feel comfortable requesting assistance, and faculty and fellow students are encouraged to be friendly and supportive. The college feels that the presence of students with individual ways of learning and coping serves as a learning experience for the professor, student, and class.

Admission Information for Students with Learning Differences

College entrance tests required: Yes
Interview required: No
Essay required: No
Additional Application Required for LD/ADHD/ASD: NR
What documentation required for LD: Psycho ed evaluation to include: relevant historical info, instructional interventions, related services, age diagnosed, objective data (aptitude, achievement, info processing), test scores (standard, percentile and grade equivalents) and describe functional limitations.
With general application: No
To receive services after enrolling: Yes
What documentation required for ADHD: Diagnosis based on DSM-V; history of behaviors impairing functioning in academic setting; diagnostic interview; history of symptoms; evidence of ongoing behaviors.
With general application: No
To receive services after enrolling: Yes
What documentation required for ASD: Psycho ed evaluation
With general application: NR
To receive services after enrolling: Yes
LD/ADHD/ASD documentation submitted to: Both Admissions Office and Office of Student Life
ASD Specific Program: NR
Special Ed. HS course work accepted: No
Specific course requirements of all applicants: NR
Separate application required: Yes
Total # of students receiving LD/ADHD/ASD services: 177
Acceptance into program means acceptance into college: Students must be admitted to and enrolled in the university first and then request services.

Admissions

Admission requirements are the same for all applicants. Freshman requirements include 4 years of English, 2 years of a foreign language, 3 years of mathematics (Algebra I, Algebra II, and geometry), 2 years of social studies, 2 years of science (biology and chemistry or physics), 0.5 unit in the arts, and 4.5 additional college-preparatory units. Most accepted students rank in the upper 50 percent of their class. SAT or ACT scores required. Students with LD/ADHD should submit the general application for admission. If a student does not meet admission requirements and is considered as a conditional admit, this would be done regardless of having an LD or ADHD.

Additional Information

The Paul V. Sherlock Center on Disabilities, founded at Rhode Island College in 1993, is a University Center on Excellence in Developmental Disabilities Education, Research, & Service. Since 1963, University Centers on Excellence in Developmental Disabilities (UCEDDs) have worked towards a shared vision that individuals with disabilities participate fully in their communities. Independence, productivity, and community inclusion are key components of this vision.

GENERAL SUPPORT SERVICES INFORMATION

Contact Information
Name of program or department: Disability Services, Student Life Office
Telephone: 401-456-8061
Fax: 401-456-8702

ACCOMMODATIONS OR SERVICES FOR STUDENTS WITH LEARNING DIFFERENCES

Accommodations are decided upon an individual basis after a thorough review of appropriate, current documentation. The accommodations requested must be supported through the documentation provided and must be logically linked to the current impact of the condition on academic functioning.

Allowed in exams
Calculator: Yes
Dictionary: Yes
Computer: Yes
Spellchecker: Yes
Extended test time: Yes
Scribes: Yes
Proctors: No
Oral exams: Yes
Note-takers: Yes
Services for students with LD: Yes
Services for students with ADHD: Yes
Services for students with ASD: Yes
Distraction-reduced environment: Yes
Tape recording in class: Yes
Audio books: NR
Electronic texts: Yes
Kurzweil Reader: Yes
Other assistive technology: Larger screen monitors, network printers, adjustable computer tables, a clearview optiplex enlarger and various specialized software
Priority registration: Yes
Added costs for services: No
LD specialists: Yes
ADHD coaching: NR
ASD specialists: NR
Professional tutors: No
Peer tutors: Yes
Max. hours/wk. for services: Unlimited
How professors are notified of LD/ADHD/ASD: By both student and director

GENERAL ADMISSIONS INFORMATION

Office of Admissions: 401-456-8234

ENTRANCE REQUIREMENTS

Academic units required: 4 English, 3 math, 2 science, 2 science labs, 2 foreign language, 2 social studies, 5 academic electives. SAT or ACT required. If ACT, ACT with writing required. TOEFL required of all international applicants: minimum paper TOEFL 550 or minimum internet TOEFL 80.

Application deadline: 3/15
Notification: Rolling starting 12/15
Average GPA: NR
ACT Composite middle 50% range: 16-21
SAT Math middle 50% range: 400-510
SAT Critical Reading middle 50% range: 400-520
SAT Writing middle 50% range: 400-500
Graduated top 10% of class: 11
Graduated top 25% of class: 35
Graduated top 50% of class: 75

COLLEGE GRADUATION REQUIREMENTS

Course waivers allowed: Yes
In what course: English and others if not required by student's major
Course substitutions allowed: Yes
In what course: English and others if not required by student's major

ADDITIONAL INFORMATION

Environment: The campus is located a few miles from downtown Providence.

Student Body
Undergrad enrollment: 7,446
% Women: 68
% Men: 32
% Out-of-state: 14.4

Cost information
In-state Tuition: $7,118
Out-of Tuition: $18,779
Room & board: $10,394

Housing Information
University Housing: NR
Percent living on campus: 15.4

Greek System
Fraternity: Yes
Sorority: Yes
Athletics: Division III

UNIVERSITY OF RHODE ISLAND

Newman Hall Kingston, RI 2881
Phone: 401-874-7100 • Fax: 401-874-5523
E-mail: admission@uri.edu • Web: www.uri.edu
Support: CS • Institution: Public

PROGRAMS OR SERVICES FOR STUDENTS WITH LEARNING DIFFERENCES

Disability Services for Students will assist students in arranging accommodations, facilitate communication between students and professors, and help them to develop effective coping skills like time management, study skills, stress management, etc. Accommodations are provided case-by-case to meet the specific needs of individual students. Students are encouraged to have an on-going relationship with DSS and the professional staff is able to meet with students as often as desired. Students with LD/ADHD who want to access services or accommodations must provide DSS with current documentation and communicate what needs are requested. Students are also expected to keep up with their requested accommodations (pick up, deliver and return letters in timely manner) and be involved in the decision-making process when it comes to their needs. Students are encouraged to make accommodation requests as early as possible and/or prior to the beginning of each semester.

ADMISSION INFORMATION FOR STUDENTS WITH LEARNING DIFFERENCES

College entrance test required: Yes
Interview required: No
Essay required: NR
Additional Application Required for LD/ADHD/ASD: NR
What documentation required for LD: Full psychoeducational testing including aptitude, achievement and information processing
With general application: No
To receive services after enrolling: Yes
What documentation required for ADHD: Same as above or full diagnostic letter from Psychiatrist or Neurologist
With general application: No
To receive services after enrolling: Yes
What documentation required for ASD: Psycho ed evaluation
With general application: No
To receive services after enrolling: Yes
LD/ADHD/ASD documentation submitted to: Admissions
ASD Specific Program: NR
Special Ed. HS course work accepted: No
Specific course: Yes
Separate application required for program services: No
Total # of students receiving LD/ADHD/ASD services: 500
Acceptance into program means acceptance into college: NR

ADMISSIONS

All applicants are expected to meet the general admission criteria. There is not a special process for students with LD/ADHD. General admission requirements expect students to rank in the upper 50% of their high school class and complete college preparatory courses including English, math, social studies, science and foreign language. If there is current documentation of a language-based LD there is a waiver for the foreign language admissions requirement, but students must self-disclose during the admission process.

ADDITIONAL INFORMATION

Students need to provide the Disability Services for Students office with current documentation of their disability that includes: psycho-educational testing completed by a professional evaluator (see www.uri.edu/disability_services for more information). DSS will assist students in arranging for accommodations, help to facilitate communication between students and professors, work with students to develop effective coping strategies, assist students with identifying appropriate resources and provide referrals, and offer support for various issues, such as academic skill enhancement, and mentoring for 1st year students. Accommodations are based solely on documented disabilities and eligible students have access to services such as: priority registration, extended time on exams, permission to tape record lectures and access to a note taker. The university is one of 22 institutions nationwide to receive U.S. Dept of Education Grants that trains faculty and administrators to promote inclusion of students with disabilities.

General Support Services Information

Contact Information
Name of program or department: Disability Services for Students
Telephone: 401-874-2098
Fax: 401-874-5694
Website: NR

Accommodations or Services For Students With Learning Differences

Accommodations are decided upon an individual basis after a thorough review of appropriate, current documentation. The accommodations requests must be supported through the documentation provided and must be logically linked to the current impact of the condition on academic functioning.

Allowed in exams
Calculator: Yes
Dictionary: No
Computer: Yes
Spellchecker: No
Extended test time: Yes
Scribes: Yes
Proctors: Yes
Oral exams: No
Note-takers: Yes
Support services for students with LD: Yes
Support services for students with ADHD: Yes
Support services for students with ASD: Yes
Distraction-reduced environment: Yes
Tape recording in class: Yes
Electronic texts: Yes
Kurzweil reader: NR
Audio books: Yes
Other assistive technology: Yes
Priority registration: Yes
Added costs of services: No
LD specialists: Yes
ADHD coaching: Yes
ASD specialists: Yes
Professional tutors: No
Peer tutors: Not Applicable
Max. hours/wk. for services: NR
How professors are notified of student approved accommodations: By both student and director

General Admissions Information

Office of Admissions: 401-874-7100

Entrance Requirements

Academic units required: 4 English, 3 math, 2 science, 1 science labs, 2 foreign language, 2 social studies, 5 academic electives. High school diploma is required and GED is accepted. SAT or ACT required. If ACT, ACT with writing accepted. TOEFL required of all international applicants: minimum internet TOEFL 79.

Application deadline: 2/1
Notification: Rolling starting 1/31
Average GPA: 3.46
ACT Composite middle 50% range: 22-26
SAT Math middle 50% range: 510-600
SAT Critical Reading middle 50% range: 500-590
SAT Writing middle 50% range: 490-580
Graduate top 10% of class: 19
Graduated top 25% of class: 50
Graduated top 50% of class: 86

COLLEGE GRADUATION REQUIREMENTS

Course waivers allowed: No
Course substitutions allowed: Yes
In what course: foreign language

Additional Information

Environment: This public school was founded in 1892. It has a 1300-acre campus.

Student Body
Undergrad enrollment: 13,641
% Women: 54
% Men: 46
% Out-of-state: 44.6

Cost information
In-state Tuition: $11,128
Out-of-state Tuition: $27,118
Room & board: $11,700

Housing Information
University Housing: Yes
Percent living on campus: 44

Greek System
Fraternity: Yes
Sorority: Yes
Athletics: Division I

CLEMSON UNIVERSITY

105 Sikes Hall, Clemson, SC 29634-5124
Phone: 864-656-2287 • Fax: 864-656-2464
E-mail: cuadmissions@clemson.edu • Web: www.clemson.edu
Support: S • Institution: Public

PROGRAMS OR SERVICES FOR STUDENTS WITH LEARNING DIFFERENCES

Student Disability Services coordinates the provision of reasonable accommodations for students with disabilities. All reasonable accommodations are individualized, flexible, and confidential based on the nature of the disability and the academic environment. Students requesting accommodations must provide current documentation of the disability from a physician or licensed professional. High school IEP, 504 plan, and/or letter from a physician or other professional will not be sufficient to document some disabilities. While such documentation can be helpful in establishing the student's learning history, a recent (typically less than 3 years old) evaluation is still necessary to confirm current needs. Reasonable accommodations can be made in the instructional process to ensure full educational opportunities. The objective is to provide appropriate services to accommodate the student's learning differences, not to change scholastic requirements.

ADMISSION INFORMATION FOR STUDENTS WITH LEARNING DIFFERENCES

College entrance tests required: Yes
Interview required: No
Essay required: No
Additional Application Required for LD/ADHD/ASD: NR
What documentation required for LD: Psycho ed evaluation to include: relevant historical info, instructional interventions, related services, age diagnosed, objective data (aptitude, achievement, info processing), test scores (standard, percentile and grade equivalents) and describe functional limitations.
With general application: No
To receive services after enrolling: Yes
What documentation required for ADHD: Diagnosis based on DSM-V; history of behaviors impairing functioning in academic setting; diagnostic interview; history of symptoms; evidence of ongoing behaviors.
With general application: No
To receive services after enrolling: Yes
What documentation required for ASD: Psycho ed evaluation
With general application: NR
To receive services after enrolling: Yes
LD/ADHD/ASD documentation submitted to: Student Disability Services
ASD Specific Program: NR
Special Ed. HS course work accepted: Yes
Specific course requirements of all applicants: Yes
Separate application required: No
Total # of students receiving LD/ADHD/ASD services: 135, ADHD
Acceptance into program means acceptance into college: Students must be admitted to and enrolled in the university first and then request services.

ADMISSIONS

All students must satisfy the same admission criteria for the university. There is no separate application process for students with disabilities. General admission requirements include an ACT score of 22–27 or an SAT Reasoning score of 1080–1260, and course requirements include 4 years of English, 3 years of math, 3 years of science lab, 3 years of a foreign language, and 3 years of social studies. Students may request a waiver of the foreign language requirement by submitting a request to the exception committee. It is recommended that students self-disclose their learning disability if they need to explain the lack of a foreign language in their background or other information that will help admissions to understand their challenges.

ADDITIONAL INFORMATION

Appropriate accommodations are discussed with each student individually and confidentially. Some of the accommodations offered are assistive technology; note-takers, readers, and transcribers; course substitutions; exam modifications, including computers, extended time, private and quiet rooms, readers, and scribes; priority registration; and recorded lectures. All students have access to peer tutoring, supplemental instruction, a writing lab, and departmental tutoring. Assistive technology available includes screen readers, and scanners. Study skills instruction is available in topics such as time management techniques and test strategies. Peer mentoring is available. There are currently 135 students with learning disabilities and 345 students with ADHD receiving services.

General Support Services Information

Contact Information
Name of program or department: Student Disability Services
Telephone: 864-656-6848
Fax: 864-656-6849

Accommodations or Services for Students with Learning Differences

Accommodations are decided upon an individual basis after a thorough review of appropriate, current documentation. The accommodations requested must be supported through the documentation provided and must be logically linked to the current impact of the condition on academic functioning.

Allowed in exams
Calculator: Yes
Dictionary: Yes
Computer: Yes
Spellchecker: Yes
Extended test time: Yes
Scribes: Yes
Proctors: Yes
Oral exams: Yes
Note-takers: Yes
Services for students with LD: Yes
Services for students with ADHD: Yes
Services for students with ASD: Yes
Distraction-reduced environment: Yes
Tape recording in class: Yes
Audio books: NR
Electronic texts: Yes
Kurzweil Reader: Yes
Other assistive technology: Yes
Priority registration: Yes
Added costs for services: No
LD specialists: No
ADHD coaching: NR
ASD specialists: NR
Professional tutors: No
Peer tutors: Yes
Max. hours/wk. for services: Unlimited
How professors are notified of LD/ADHD: Student

General Admissions Information

Office of Admissions: 864-656-2287

Entrance Requirements

Academic units required: 4 English, 3 math, 3 science, 3 science labs, 2 foreign language, 1 social studies, 1 history, 2 academic electives, 1 computer science, 1 visual/performing arts, and 1 units from above areas or other academic areas. **Academic units recommended:** 4 math, 4 science labs, 3 foreign language. High school diploma is required and GED is accepted. SAT or ACT required. If ACT, ACT with writing required. TOEFL required of all international applicants: minimum paper TOEFL 550.

Application deadline: 5/1
Notification: Rolling starting 2/15
Average GPA: 4
ACT Composite middle 50% range: 27-31
SAT Math middle 50% range: 590-690
SAT Critical Reading middle 50% range: 560-660
SAT Writing middle 50% range: NR-NR
Graduate top 10% of class: 56
Graduated top 25% of class: 86
Graduated top 50% of class: 98

COLLEGE GRADUATION REQUIREMENTS

Course waivers allowed: NR
Course substitutions allowed: NR

Additional Information

Environment: This public school was founded in 1889.

Student Body
Undergrad enrollment: 18,016
% Women: 47
% Men: 53
% Out-of-state: 35

Cost information
In-state Tuition: $13,022
Out-of-state Tuition: $31,940
Room & board: $8,718

Housing Information
University Housing: Yes
Percent living on campus: 41

Greek System
Fraternity: Yes
Sorority: Yes
Athletics: Division I

College of Charleston

66 George Street, Charleston, SC 29424
Phone: 843-953-5670 • Fax: 843-953-6322
E-mail: admissions@cofc.edu • Web: http://cofc.edu
Support: CS • Institution: Public

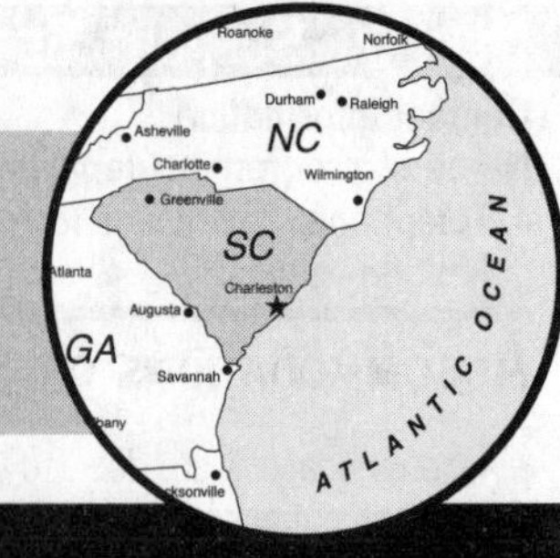

Programs or Services for Students with Learning Differences

The Center for Disability Services is dedicated to ensuring that all programs and services of the College are accessible; to providing reasonable and effective accommodations while promoting independence of the students; to offering educational opportunities to student, faculty and staff that enhances understanding of the various types of disabilities, promoting an environment respectful of all; and to serving as a resource center for faculty, staff, students, and the community.

Admission Information for Students with Learning Differences

College entrance test required: Yes
Interview required: No
Essay required: Not Applicable
Additional Application Required for LD/ADHD/ASD: Yes
What documentation required for LD: Psycho ed evaluation
With general application: No
To receive services after enrolling: Yes
What documentation required for ADHD: A current evaluation administered by an appropriately credentialed professional.
With general application: No
To receive services after enrolling: Yes
What documentation required for ASD: A current psychoeducational evaluation administered by an appropriately credentialed professional.
With general application: No
To receive services after enrolling: Yes
LD/ADHD/ASD documentation submitted to: Center for Disability Services
ASD Specific Program: No
Special Ed. HS course work accepted: NR
Specific course requirements of all applicants: Yes
Separate application required for program services: True
Total # of students receiving LD/ADHD/ASD services: 4620
Acceptance into program means acceptance into college: No

Admissions

When you apply, the College of Charleston admissions committee looks at many things in your application, including your academic preparation, GPA, rank in class, SAT/ACT scores, talents and leadership qualifications. We want you to do well here, so we will review your high school curriculum, GPA, rank and test scores first. Leadership, extra-curricular activities and other achievements are important, but are of secondary importance in our decision-making process. Here is the mid-range student profile (where the middle 50 percent of our accepted students fall) for our primary admission factors . If you take a test more than once, we only consider the highest score of each section across all of your exams.

Additional Information

Please see our website for details. Once the complete application packet is turned in, a SNAP administrator evaluates the completeness of the application and supporting documentation and makes a recommendation of SNAP approval or denial. A letter of approval or denial will be e-mailed to your College of Charleston email account approximately one week from receipt of your application packet. Included within this e-mail are the Student's Guide to SNAP Services and a set of forms to be completed by the student. Reasonable accommodations will be provided once the completed forms have been returned to SNAP. Students applying for alternative courses will receive an additional e-mail one to two weeks after the initial approval e-mail notifying them of their alternative status. If denied, you may appeal to the Director of the Center for Disability Services.

General Support Services Information

Contact Information
Name of program or department: Center for Disability Services
Telephone: 843-953-1431
Fax: 843-953-7731
Website: http://disabilityservices.cofc.edu

Accommodations or Services for Students with Learning Differences

Accommodations are decided upon an individual basis after a thorough review of appropriate, current documentation. The accommodations requests must be supported through the documentation provided and must be logically linked to the current impact of the condition on academic functioning.

Allowed in exams
Calculator: Yes
Dictionary: Yes
Computer: Yes
Spellchecker: Yes
Extended test time: Yes
Scribes: Yes
Proctors: Yes
Oral exams: Yes
Note-takers: Yes
Support services for students with LD: Yes
Support services for students with ADHD: Yes
Support services for students with ASD: Yes
Distraction-reduced environment: Yes
Tape recording in class: Yes
Electronic texts: Yes
Kurzweil reader: NR
Audio books: Yes
Other assistive technology: Yes
Priority registration: Yes
Added costs of services: No
LD specialists: Yes
ADHD coaching: Yes
ASD specialists: Not Applicable
Professional tutors: No
Peer tutors: Yes
Max. hours/wk. for services: 2
How professors are notified of student approved accommodations: By student

General Admissions Information

Office of Admissions: 843-953-5670

Entrance Requirements

Academic units required: 4 English, 4 math, 3 science, 3 science labs, 3 foreign language, 2 social studies, 1 history, 3 academic electives, 1 visual/performing arts, and 1 units from above areas or other academic areas. **Academic units recommended:** 4 English, 4 math, 2 history, 1 computer science, High school diploma is required and GED is accepted. SAT or ACT required. If ACT, ACT with writing accepted. TOEFL required of all international applicants: minimum paper TOEFL 570 or minimum internet TOEFL 80.

Application deadline: 4/1
Notification: NR
Average GPA: 3.9
ACT Composite middle 50% range: 23-28
SAT Math middle 50% range: 510-600
SAT Critical Reading middle 50% range: 520-610
SAT Writing middle 50% range: NR-NR
Graduate top 10% of class: 21
Graduated top 25% of class: 54
Graduated top 50% of class: 90

COLLEGE GRADUATION REQUIREMENTS

Course waivers allowed: No
Course substitutions allowed: Yes
In what course: Math/logic Foreign language

Additional Information

Environment: This public school was founded in 1770. It has a 52-acre campus.

Student Body
Undergrad enrollment: 10,468
% Women: 63
% Men: 37
% Out-of-state: 34.7

Cost information
In-state tuition: $10,900
Out-of-state tuition: $28,444
Room & board: $11,629

Housing Information
University Housing: Yes
Percent living on campus: 30.8

Greek System
Fraternity: Yes
Sorority: Yes
Athletics: Division I

Limestone College

1115 College Drive, Gaffney, SC 29340-3799
Phone: 864-488-4549 • Fax: 864-487-8706
E-mail: admiss@limestone.edu • Web: www.limestone.edu
Support: CS • Institution: Private

Programs or Services for Students with Learning Differences

In addition to free disability services offered by all institutions, the Program for Alternative Learning Styles (PALS) was developed to comprehensively service students with learning disabilities. Therefore, only students with documented learning disabilities are eligible to receive program services. For program purposes, LD refers to students with average to above average intelligence (above 90) who have a discrepancy between measured intelligence and achievement. PALS's biggest advantage is the follow-up system that is in place for the PALS students. Each student is very carefully monitored as to his or her progress in each course he or she takes. The students who are not successful are typically those students who do not take advantage of the system. Deliberate accountability helps students remain aware of their status and offers assistance to improve on negative reports. The tracking system is specifically designed to keep PALS personnel, the professors and the students informed about their progress toward a degree from Limestone College.

Admission Information for Students with Learning Differences

College entrance tests required: No
Interview required: Yes
Essay required: N/A
Additional Application Required for LD/ADHD/ASD: NR
What documentation required for LD: Psycho ed evaluation to include: relevant historical info, instructional interventions, related services, age diagnosed, objective data (aptitude, achievement, info processing), test scores (standard, percentile and grade equivalents) and describe functional limitations.
With general application: No
To receive services after enrolling: Yes
What documentation required for ADHD: Diagnosis based on DSM-V; history of behaviors impairing functioning in academic setting; diagnostic interview; history of symptoms; evidence of ongoing behaviors.
With general application: No
To receive services after enrolling: Yes
What documentation required for ASD: Psycho ed evaluation
With general application: NR
To receive services after enrolling: Yes
LD/ADHD/ASD documentation submitted to: Disability Services
ASD Specific Program: NR
Special Ed. HS course work accepted: Yes
Specific course requirements for all applicants: Yes
Separate application required for program services: No
Total # of students receiving LD/ADHD/ASD services: 150 (PALS and LD)
Acceptance into program means acceptance into college: Yes

Admissions

Students who self-disclose their LD and want the services of PALS must first be admitted to Limestone College either fully or conditionally. Students must submit a high school transcript with a diploma or GED certificate, SAT or ACT scores (though a minimum score is not required to seek admission via PALS), and the general college application. The minimum GPA is a 2.0. To receive services through PALS, students must submit their most recent psychological report (completed within the past 3 years) documenting an LD. In addition, only intelligence test scores from the Stanford Binet and/or Wechsler Scales will be acceptable. All available information is carefully reviewed prior to acceptance. Students may be admitted provisionally via PALS, if approved by the PALS Admissions Committee and enrolled in PALS. Students interested in PALS must arrange for an interview with the director of PALS to learn what will be expected of the student and what the program will and will not do for the student. After the interview is completed, students will be notified of their eligibility for PALS and be given the opportunity to sign a statement indicating their wish to participate or not to participate.

Additional Information

During the regular academic year, students will receive special instruction in the area of study skills. Students are required to participate in a minimum of ten hours per week of supervised study hall. PALS personnel are in constant communication with students concerning grades, tutors, professors, accommodations, time management, and study habits. Tutorial services are provided on an individual basis so that all students can reach their maximum potential. Skills classes are offered in math and reading. Other services include counseling, personal test proctors, time management skills, and screening for the best ways to make accommodations. PALS does not offer training in social skills. The cost of the program is $2500 per semester.

General Support Services Information

Contact Information

Name of program or department: Program for Alternative Learning Styles (PALS)

Telephone: 864-488-8377

Fax: 864-487-8706

Accommodations or Services for Students with Learning Differences

Accommodations are decided upon an individual basis after a thorough review of appropriate, current documentation and personal interview. The accommodations requested must be supported through the documentation provided and must be logically linked to the current impact of the condition on academic functioning. Accommodation may be include, but not limited to:

Allowed in exams
Calculator: Yes
Dictionary: Yes
Computer: Yes
Spellchecker: Yes
Extended test time: Yes
Scribes: Yes
Proctors: Yes
Oral exams: Yes
Note-takers: Yes
Services for students with LD: Yes
Services for students with ADHD: Yes
Services for students with ASD: Yes
Distraction-reduced environment: Yes
Tape recording in class: Yes
Audio books: NR
Electronic texts: Yes
Kurzweil Reader: NR
Other assistive technology: Yes
Priority registration: No
Added costs for services: Yes (comprehensive PALS services)
LD specialists: Yes
ADHD coaching: NR
ASD specialists: NR
Professional tutors: 4–8
Peer tutors: 18–24
Max. hours/wk. for services: Unlimited
How professors are notified of LD/ADHD: By PALS staff

General Admissions Information

Office of Admissions: 864-488-4549

Entrance Requirements

Academic units required: 4 English, 3 math, 2 science, 2 science labs, 3 social studies. High school diploma is required and GED is accepted. SAT or ACT required. If ACT, ACT with writing accepted. TOEFL required of all international applicants: minimum paper TOEFL 500 or minimum internet TOEFL 75.

Application deadline: 8/25
Notification: Rolling starting 6/1
Average GPA: 3.18
ACT Composite middle 50% range: 2-2.3
SAT Math middle 50% range: 480-560
SAT Critical Reading middle 50% range: 450-530
SAT Writing middle 50% range: NR-NR
Graduated top 10% of class: 3
Graduated top 25% of class: 19
Graduated top 50% of class: 51

COLLEGE GRADUATION REQUIREMENTS

Course waivers allowed: No

In what course: Foreign language is not required at Limestone!

Course substitutions allowed: No

Additional Information

Environment: This private school was founded in 1845. It has a 115-acre campus.

Student Body
Undergrad enrollment: 1,059
% Women: 38
% Men: 62
% Out-of-state: 41.51
Cost information
Tuition: $23,000
Room & board: $7,800
Housing Information
University Housing: Yes
Percent living on campus: 57.83
Greek System
Fraternity: Yes
Sorority: NR
Athletics: Division II

Southern Wesleyan University

Wesleyan Drive, Central, SC 29630-1020
Phone: 864-644-5550 • Fax: 864-644-5972
E-mail: admissions@swu.edu • Web: www.swu.edu
Support: S • Institution: Private

Programs or Services for Students with Learning Differences

Southern Wesleyan University offers services to students with disabilities by coordinating the efforts of faculty, staff, under the director of the Student Success Coordinator in the Student Success Center. This is free academic assistance that includes peer tutors, writing coaches, online tutoring and Supplemental instruction. Supplemental Instruction (SI) is an academic assistance program designed to increase retention, improve student grades and increase graduation rates. SI accomplishes these goals by helping students learn to solve problems, organize classroom materials, develop effective study strategies and meet personal and faculty expectations. Supplemental Instruction is intended to be a semester-long series of weekly group study sessions led by an SI leader. The SI leader is an undergraduate who has successfully completed the course with an "A" average. All SI leaders are recommended by faculty. The SI leader attends the weekly lecture, takes notes, meets with the course instructor regularly, and then holds three study sessions weekly to provide support to students currently enrolled in the course.

Admission Information for Students with Learning Differences

College entrance tests required: Yes
Interview required: No
Essay required: N/A
Additional Application Required for LD/ADHD/ASD: NR
What documentation required for LD: Psycho ed evaluation to include: relevant historical info, instructional interventions, related services, age diagnosed, objective data (aptitude, achievement, info processing), test scores (standard, percentile and grade equivalents) and describe functional limitations.
With general application: No
To receive services after enrolling: Yes
What documentation required for ADHD: Diagnosis based on DSM-V; history of behaviors impairing functioning in academic setting; diagnostic interview; history of symptoms; evidence of ongoing behaviors.
With general application: No
LD/ADHD/ASD documentation submitted to: Student Services Learning Coordinator
ASD Specific Program: NR
Specific course requirements for all applicants: Yes
Separate application required for program services: No
Total # of students receiving LD/ADHD/ASD services: 12
Acceptance into program means acceptance into college: Students are admitted directly into the university and to Services for Students with Disabilities with appropriate documentation.

Admissions

All applicants must meet the same admission criteria. Courses taken in high school should include at least: must have: 4 years of English, 2 years of science, 2 years of social studies, and 2 years of math. Applicants should have a GPA of 2.3 (or rank in upper half of your graduating class at time of acceptance) and a composite SAT score of 860 (based on the critical reading/verbal and math sections) or an ACT score of 18.

Additional Information

Documentation of a disability goes to the student Learning Services Coordinator. The student must request services each semester by discussing with the coordinator what accommodations are appropriate and needed in each course. The coordinator sends a letter to the professor of each course the student has identified for needed accommodation. The student also receives a copy and arranges the logistics and details with professors. We emphasize that students must initiate the request and the arrangements. We encourage the student to develop the highest degree of independence possible during their college years and become prepared to compete successfully in their chosen career. There is a liaison person between faculty and students. Professors are available to students after class. Modifications can be made in test-taking, which could include extended time and a quiet place to take exams. Additionally, students may receive assistance with note-taking. All services are offered in response to students' requests.

General Support Services Information

Contact Information
Name of program or department: Services to Students with Disabilities
Telephone: 864-644-5036
Fax: 864-644-5979

Accommodations or Services for Students with Learning Differences

Accommodations are decided upon an individual basis after a thorough review of appropriate, current documentation. The accommodations requested must be supported through the documentation provided and must be logically linked to the current impact of the condition on academic functioning.

Allowed in exams
Calculator: Yes
Dictionary: Yes
Computer: Yes
Spellchecker: Yes
Extended test time: Yes
Scribes: Yes
Proctors: Yes
Oral exams: Yes
Note-takers: Yes
Services for students with LD: Yes
Services for students with ADHD: Yes
Services for students with ASD: Yes
Distraction-reduced environment: Yes
Tape recording in class: Yes
Audio books: NR
Electronic texts: N/A
Kurzweil Reader: No
Other assistive technology: voice recognition program
Priority registration: No
Added costs for services: No
LD specialists: No
ADHD coaching: NR
ASD specialists: NR
Professional tutors: 1
Peer tutors: 5–8
Max. hours/wk. for services: NR
How professors are notified of LD/ADHD: Both student and coordinator

General Admissions Information

Office of Admissions: 864-644-5550

Entrance Requirements

Academic units recommended: 4 English, 2 math, 2 science, 2 social studies. High school diploma is required and GED is accepted. SAT or ACT required. If ACT, ACT with writing accepted. TOEFL required of all international applicants: minimum paper TOEFL 500.

Application deadline: 8/1
Notification: NR
Average GPA: 3.5
ACT Composite middle 50% range: 18-22
SAT Math middle 50% range: 445-550
SAT Critical Reading middle 50% range: 430-540
SAT Writing middle 50% range: 420-520
Graduated top 10% of class: 13
Graduated top 25% of class: 34
Graduated top 50% of class: 75

COLLEGE GRADUATION REQUIREMENTS

Course waivers allowed: NR
In what course: NR
Course substitutions allowed: No
In what course: No

Additional Information

Environment: This private school, affiliated with the Wesleyan Church, was founded in 1906. It has a 330-acre campus.

Student Body
Undergrad enrollment: 1,456
% Women: 60
% Men: 40
% Out-of-state: 28

Cost information
Tuition: $19,950
Room & board: $8,410

Housing Information
University Housing: Yes
Percent living on campus: 55

Greek System
Fraternity: No
Sorority: No
Athletics: NAIA

The University of South Carolina—Columbia

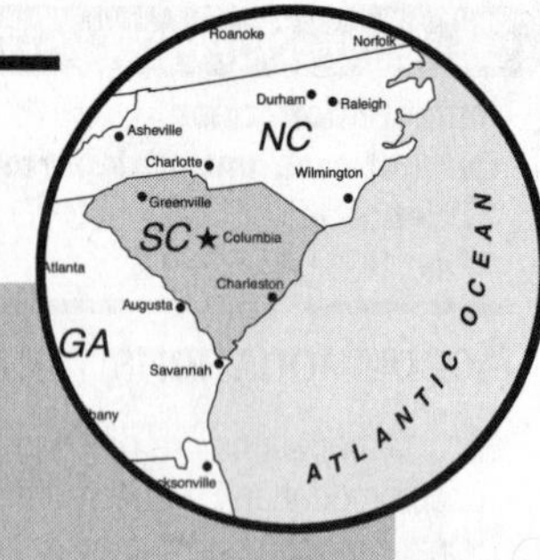

Office of Undergraduate Admissions, Columbia, SC 29208
Phone: 803-777-7700 • Fax: 803-777-0101
E-mail: admissions-ugrad@sc.edu • Web: www.sc.edu
Support: CS • Institution: Public

Programs or Services for Students with Learning Differences

The university's Office of Disability Services (ODS) provides educational support and assistance to students with LD who have the potential for success in a competitive university setting. The Office of Disability Services is specifically designed to empower them with the confidence to become self-advocates and to take an active role in their education. The university works with each student on an individualized basis to match needs with appropriate services. The services are tailored to provide educational support and assistance to students based on their specific needs. The Office of Disability Services recommends and coordinates support services with faculty, administrators, advisors, and deans. The nature and severity of LD may vary considerably. All requests are based on documented diagnostic information regarding each student's specific learning disability. The first step in accessing services from the Office of Disability Services is to self-disclose the disability and arrange an interview. During the interview, staff members will discuss the student's educational background and determine which services best fit his or her needs.

Admission Information for Students with Learning Differences

College entrance tests required: Yes
Interview required: Yes
Essay required: No
Additional Application Required for LD/ADHD/ASD: NR
What documentation required for LD: Psycho ed evaluation to include: relevant historical info, instructional interventions, related services, age diagnosed, objective data (aptitude, achievement, info processing), test scores (standard, percentile and grade equivalents) and describe functional limitations.
With general application: No
To receive services after enrolling: Yes
What documentation required for ADHD: Diagnosis based on DSM-V; history of behaviors impairing functioning in academic setting; diagnostic interview; history of symptoms; evidence of ongoing behaviors.
With general application: No
To receive services after enrolling: Yes
What documentation required for ASD: Psycho ed evaluation
With general application: NR
To receive services after enrolling: Yes
LD/ADHD/ASD documentation submitted to: ODS
ASD Specific Program: NR
Special Ed. HS course work accepted: No
Specific course requirements of all applicants: Yes
Separate application required: No
Total # of students receiving LD/ADHD/ASD services: 500
Acceptance into program means acceptance into college: Students must be admitted and enrolled in the university first (they can appeal a denial) and then request services.

Admissions

There is no special application or admission process for students with LD. Required scores on the SAT and ACT vary with class rank. Applicants must have a cumulative C-plus average on defined college-preparatory courses, including 4 years of English, 3 years of math, 3 years of science, 2 years of the same foreign language, 4 years of electives, and 1 year of physical education, as well as a 1200 SAT or 27 ACT. If they are denied admission or feel they do not meet the required standards, students may petition the Admissions Committee for an exception to the regular admissions requirements. Once admitted, students should contact the Educational Support Services Center to arrange an interview to determine which services are necessary to accommodate their needs.

Additional Information

Services are individually tailored to provide educational support and assistance. All requests are based on documented diagnostic information. The program is designed to provide educational support and assistance, including analysis of learning needs to determine appropriate interventions, consulting with the faculty about special academic needs, monitoring of progress by a staff member, study skills training, and tutorial referrals. Special program accommodations may include a reduced course load of 9–12 hours, waivers/substitutions for some courses, and expanded pass/fail options. Special classroom accommodations may include tape recorders, note-takers, and extended time on tests.

General Support Services Information

Contact Information
Name of program or department: Office of Student Disability Services
Telephone: 803-777-6142
Fax: 803-777-6741

Accommodations or Services for Students with Learning Differences

Accommodations are decided upon an individual basis after a thorough review of appropriate, current documentation. The accommodations requested must be supported through the documentation provided and must be logically linked to the current impact of the condition on academic functioning.

Allowed in exams
Calculator: Yes
Dictionary: Yes
Computer: Yes
Spellchecker: Yes
Extended test time: Yes
Scribes: Yes
Proctors: Yes
Oral exams: No
Note-takers: Yes
Services for students with LD: Yes
Services for students with ADHD: Yes
Services for students with ASD: Yes
Distraction-reduced environment: Yes
Tape recording in class: Yes
Audio books: NR
Electronic texts: Yes
Kurzweil Reader: Yes
Other assistive technology: Yes
Priority registration: Yes
Added costs for services: No
LD specialists: Yes
ADHD coaching: NR
ASD specialists: NR
Professional tutors: No
Peer tutors: No
Max. hours/wk. for services: 42.5
How professors are notified of LD/ADHD: By student

General Admissions Information

Office of Admissions: 803-777-7700

Entrance Requirements

Academic units required: 4 English, 4 math, 3 science, 3 science labs, 2 foreign language, 2 social studies, 1 history, 1 academic electives, 1 visual/performing arts, and 1 units from above areas or other academic areas. High school diploma is required and GED is accepted. SAT or ACT required. If ACT, ACT with writing required. TOEFL required of all international applicants: minimum paper TOEFL 550 or minimum internet TOEFL 77.

Application deadline: 12/1
Notification: 3/15
Average GPA: 4.15
ACT Composite middle 50% range: 24-29
SAT Math middle 50% range: 550-650
SAT Critical Reading middle 50% range: 540-630
SAT Writing middle 50% range: NR-NR
Graduated top 10% of class: 30
Graduated top 25% of class: 66
Graduated top 50% of class: 94

COLLEGE GRADUATION REQUIREMENTS

Course waivers allowed: Yes
In what course: Students with learning disabilities may petition their college for substitution of the required foreign language if the requirement is not an integral part of the degree program.
Course substitutions allowed: Yes
In what course: Students with learning disabilities may petition their college for substitution of the required foreign language if the requirement is not an intregal part of the degree program.

Additional Information

Environment: This public school was founded in 1801. It has a 384-acre campus.

Student Body
Undergrad enrollment: 24,180
% Women: 54
% Men: 46
% Out-of-state: 30

Cost information
In-state Tuition: $11,082
Out-of Tuition: $29,898
Room & board: $9,872

Housing Information
University Housing: Yes
Percent living on campus: 29

Greek System
Fraternity: Yes
Sorority: Yes
Athletics: Division I

Black Hills State University

1200 University Street, Unit 9078, Spearfish, SD 57799-9502
Phone: 605-642-6343 • Fax: 605-642-6254
E-mail: bhsuadmissions@bhsu.edu • Web: www.bhsu.edu
Support: S • Institution: Public

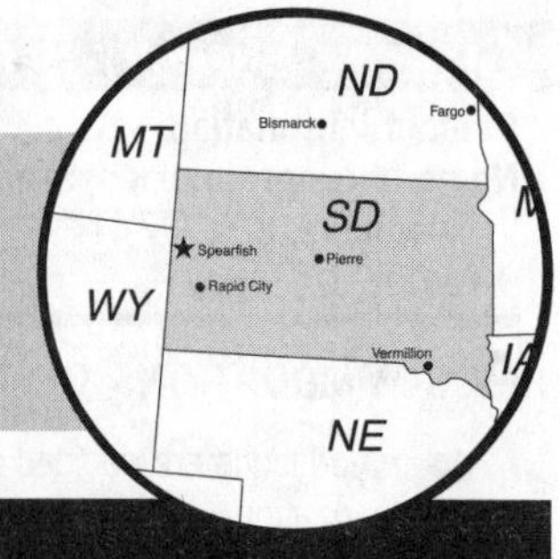

Programs or Services for Students with Learning Differences

BHSU has a full service Disability Services department as well as Student Support Services program that is a federal trio grant program that works with students with documented disabilities. The university offers tutoring centers in Math and Writing. Students with disabilities receive accommodation(s) based on documentation of their disability. Students requesting accommodation(s) are responsible for initiating services by providing the Disability Services Office with appropriate documentation. The documentation should be prepared by a professional (i.e. physician, psychologist, psychiatrist). It should include information about how the student's disability will affect his/her ability to equally access the educational opportunities, programs, and activities at Black Hills State University. It should also include recommendations for necessary accommodations.

Admission Information for Students with Learning Differences

College entrance tests required: Yes
Interview required: No
Essay required: No
Additional Application Required for LD/ADHD/ASD: NR
What documentation required for LD: Disability Documentation from a qualified professional.
With general application: No
To receive services after enrolling: Yes
What documentation required for ADHD: Disability Documentation from a qualified professional.
With general application: No
To receive services after enrolling: Yes
What documentation required for ASD: Disability Documentation from a qualified professional.
With general application: No
To receive services after enrolling: Yes
LD/ADHD/ASD documentation submitted to: Disability Services Liaison
ASD Specific Program: NR
Special Ed. HS course work accepted: No
Specific course requirements of all applicants: NR
Separate application required: Yes
Total # of students receiving LD/ADHD/ASD services: 65
Acceptance into program means acceptance into college: Students must be admitted to and enrolled in the university first and then request services.

Admissions

Students with LD must meet the same admission requirements as all applicants. Applicants must complete high school courses with a minimum grade point average (GPA) of 3.1. To become college-ready, it is recommended that high schools students complete at least five rigorous courses in key subject areas. Student athletes may also become ineligible to compete at the collegiate level if they waive the required coursework for all entering high school graduates.

Additional Information

Students accepted to BHSU need to submit their disability documentation to the Disability Services Liaison and then meet to discuss what accommodations that would be appropriate for the student. In addition to accommodation planning, the Disability Services Office provides direct services in the following areas: transition from secondary to post-secondary; academic planning and follow-up; advocacy; learning style assessment; study skill strategies; self-advocacy training; assistive technology instruction and access; and referrals and follow-up. To request a substitution for a course students should meet with disability services and provide a written request for the course requiring accommodation and the course requested as the accommodation. Students should provide a rationale including prior accommodations provided in the course (if any) and reasons why the student believes these were unsuccessful.

General Support Services Information

Contact Information
Name of program or department: Disability Services
Telephone: 605-642-6591
Fax: 605-642-6095

Accommodations or Services for Students with Learning Differences

Accommodations a provided based on a students Disability Documentation and set up on an individual basis. Some common accommodations are extended time on tests, tests in alternate setting, use of a calculator, note taking, assistive technology, and a variety of other accommodations that are based on the student's disability.

Allowed in exams
Calculator: Yes
Dictionary: Yes
Computer: Yes
Spellchecker: Yes
Extended test time: Yes
Scribes: Yes
Proctors: Yes
Oral exams: Yes
Note-takers: Yes
Services for students with LD: Yes
Services for students with ADHD: Yes
Services for students with ASD: Yes
Distraction-reduced environment: Yes
Tape recording in class: Yes
Audio books: NR
Electronic texts: Yes
Kurzweil Reader: Yes
Other assistive technology: Yes
Priority registration: No
Added costs for services: No
LD specialists: No
ADHD coaching: Yes
ASD specialists: NR
Professional tutors: 4
Peer tutors: 3–10
Max. hours/wk. for services: 40
How professors are notified of LD/ADHD: By both student and director

General Admissions Information

Office of Admissions: 605-642-6343

Entrance Requirements

Academic units required: 4 English, 3 mathematics, 3 science, (3 science labs), 3 social studies, 1 fine art. High school diploma is required and GED is accepted. If ACT, ACT with Writing component accepted. TOEFL required of all international applicants: minimum paper TOEFL 520.

Application deadline: NR
Average GPA: 3.1
ACT Composite middle 50% range: 18-23
SAT Math middle 50% range: NR
SAT Critical Reading middle 50% range: NR
SAT Writing middle 50% range: NR
Graduated top 10% of class: 6
Graduated top 25% of class: 24
Graduated top 50% of class: 60

COLLEGE GRADUATION REQUIREMENTS

Course waivers allowed: Yes
In what course: NR
Course substitutions allowed: Yes
In what courses: Depends on documentation

Additional Information

Environment: The university is located on 123 acres in a small town 45 miles northwest of Rapid City.

Student Body
Undergrad enrollment: 3,138
% Women: 63
% Men: 37
% Out-of-state: 21

Cost information
In-state tuition: $7,617
Out-of-state tuition: $10,097
Room & board: $6,330

Housing Information
University housing: Yes
% Living on campus: 46

Greek System
Fraternity: Yes
Sorority: Yes
Athletics: NAIA

South Dakota State University

SAD 200, Brookings, SD 57007-0649
Phone: 605-688-4121 • Fax: 605-688-6891
E-mail: sdsu.admissions@sdstate.edu • Web: www.sdstate.edu
Support: S • Institution: Public

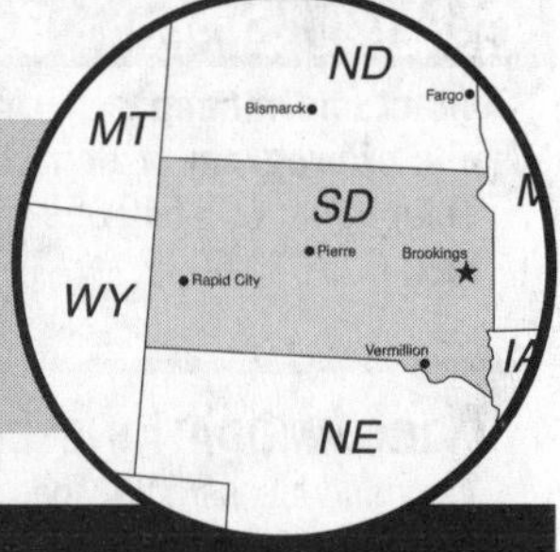

Programs or Services for Students with Learning Differences

South Dakota State University is committed to providing equal opportunities for higher education to academicallyqualified students with LDs. All students, including those with disabilities, have access to skill development courses inthe areas of general academic success skills, English composition, and mathematics. Free tutoring is available for allstudents in a wide variety of subject areas. They provide, through the Wintrode Tutoring Program , small group tutoring and walk-in review sessions in select courses, and it's from peers who have been through the same classes.

Admission Information for Students with Learning Differences

College entrance tests required: Yes
Interview required: No
Essay required: No
Additional Application Required for LD/ADHD/ASD: NR
What documentation required for LD: The Disability Services website is linked to the university's main page. On the DS site there are documentation forms that the student's medical/psychological professional is asked to complete.
With general application: NR
To receive services after enrolling: Yes
What documentation required for ADHD: The Disability Services website is linked to the university's main page. On the DS site there are documentation forms that the student's medical/psychological professional is asked to complete.
With general application: NR
To receive services after enrolling: Yes
LD/ADHD/ASD documentation submitted to: DS
Special Ed. HS course work accepted: NR
ASD Specific Program: NR
Specific course requirements of all applicants: Yes
Separate application required: Students mus be admitted to university first and then apply
Total # of students receiving LD/ADHD/ASD services: NR
Acceptance into program means acceptance into college: Students must be admitted to and enrolled in the university first and then request services.

Admissions

Students with learning disabilities must meet the same admission criteria as all applicants. For admission to SDS they look for one of the following academic achievements: 1) An ACT composite score of 18 or higher (SAT of 870 or higher) 2) a high school cumulative GPA of 2.6 or higher or 3) rank in the top 60 percent of the class. Students should also complete the following core courses with a "C" average or above: 4 years of English (or ACT English sub-score of 18) 3 years of advanced math—Algebra I and higher (or ACT math sub-score of 20), 3 years of laboratory science (or ACT science reasoning sub-score of 17), 3 years of social science (or ACT reading sub-score of 17), 1 year of fine arts (includes vocal, instrumental and studio arts), and basic computer skills (students should have basic keyboarding, word processing, spreadsheet and internet skills).

Additional Information

The Office of Disability Services provides assistance for students with a wide range of disabilities. The first step is to fillout the application for disability services. Along with this application, students need to send documentation of thedisability. After that, ODS will set up an appointment to discuss services provided that will enhance the students learningexperiences at SDSU. Some of the services include: alternative text formats, note taker, assistive technology, alternativeaccommodations for exams (testing in a distraction-free environment or providing readers for exams),extended time for testing, and referrals to other resources. Tutoring and Supplemental Instruction (SI) is offered to allSDSU students through the Wintrode Tutoring & SI Program. SI offers a series of weekly review sessions for students.

General Support Services Information

Contact Information
Name of program or department: Disability Services (DS)
Telephone: 605-688-4504
Fax: 605-688-4987

Accommodations or Services for Students with Learning Differences

Accommodations are decided upon an individual basis after a thorough review of appropriate, current documentation. The accommodations requested must be supported through the documentation provided and must be logically linked to the current impact of the condition on academic functioning.

Allowed in exams
Calculator: Yes
Dictionary: No
Computer: Yes
Spellchecker: Yes
Extended test time: Yes
Scribes: Yes
Proctors: Yes
Oral exams: Yes
Note-takers: Yes
Services for students with LD: Yes
Services for students with ADHD: Yes
Services for students with ASD: Yes
Distraction-reduced environment: Yes
Tape recording in class: Yes
Audio books: NR
Electronic texts: Yes
Kurzweil Reader: Yes
Other assistive technology: Yes
Priority registration: No
Added costs for services: No
LD specialists: No
ADHD coaching: NR
ASD specialists: NR
Professional tutors: Yes
Peer tutors: 25–32
Max. hours/wk. for services: Unlimited
How professors are notified of LD/ADHD: Through accommodation letters student presents to professors. Disability not discussed, only accommodations being requested.

General Admissions Information

Office of Admissions: 605-688-4121

Entrance Requirements

Academic units required: 4 English, 3 math, 3 science, 3 science labs, 3 social studies, 1 visual/performing arts. High school diploma is required and GED is accepted. SAT or ACT required. If ACT, ACT with writing accepted. TOEFL required of all international applicants: minimum paper TOEFL 500 or minimum internet TOEFL 61.

Application deadline: NR
Notification: NR
Average GPA: 3.37
ACT Composite middle 50% range: 20-26
SAT Math middle 50% range: 470-600
SAT Critical Reading middle 50% range: 430-560
SAT Writing middle 50% range: NR-NR
Graduate top 10% of class: 14
Graduated top 25% of class: 36
Graduated top 50% of class: 68

COLLEGE GRADUATION REQUIREMENTS

Course waivers allowed: No
Course substitutions allowed: No

Additional Information

Environment: The school is located on 220 acres in a rural area 50 miles north of Sioux Falls.

Student Body
Undergrad enrollment: 0
% Women: NR
% Men: NR
% Out-of-state: 37

Cost information
In-state tuition: $7,713
Out-of-state tuition: $9,795
Room & board: $6,548

Housing Information
University housing: Yes
% Living on campus: 42

Greek System
Fraternity: Yes
Sorority: Yes
Athletics: Division I

THE UNIVERSITY OF SOUTH DAKOTA

414 East Clark, Vermillion, SD 57069
Phone: 605-677-5434 • Fax: 605-677-6323
E-mail: admissions@usd.edu • Web: www.usd.edu
Support: CS • Institution: Public

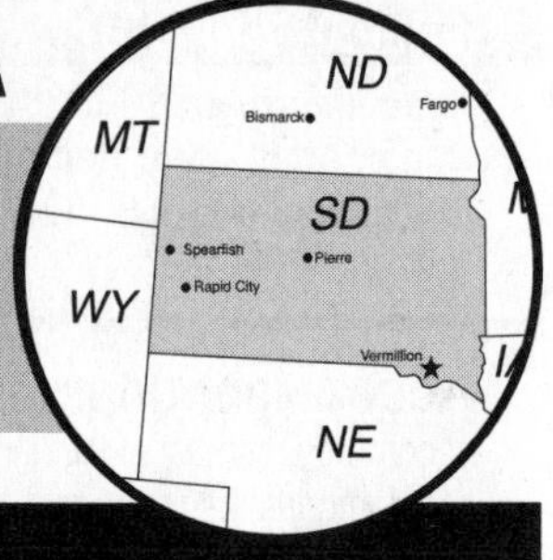

PROGRAMS OR SERVICES FOR STUDENTS WITH LEARNING DIFFERENCES

The University of South Dakota Disability Services (USDDS) operates on the premise that students at the university are full participants in the process of obtaining appropriate accommodations for their disabilities. Students are encouraged to make their own decisions and become self-advocates for appropriate accommodations or services. The three main goals are to: (1) help students become self-advocates; (2) provide better transition services into and out of college; and (3) to provide better instructional and support services. The university strives to ensure that all individuals with legally defined disabilities have access to the full range of the university's programs, services, and activities.

ADMISSION INFORMATION FOR STUDENTS WITH LEARNING DIFFERENCES

College entrance tests required: Yes
Interview required: N/A
Essay required: N/A
Additional Application Required for LD/ADHD/ASD: NR
What documentation required for LD: Psycho ed evaluation to include: relevant historical info, instructional interventions, related services, age diagnosed, objective data (aptitude, achievement, info processing), test scores (standard, percentile and grade equivalents) and describe functional limitations.
With general application: No
To receive services after enrolling: Yes
What documentation required for ADHD: Diagnosis based on DSM-V; history of behaviors impairing functioning in academic setting; diagnostic interview; history of symptoms; evidence of ongoing behaviors.
With general application: No
To receive services after enrolling: Yes
What documentation required for ASD: Psycho ed evaluation
With general application: NR
To receive services after enrolling: Yes
LD/ADHD/ASD documentation submitted to: Disability Services
ASD Specific Program: NR
Special Ed. HS course work accepted: Yes
Specific course requirements for all applicants: Yes
Separate application required for program services: Yes
Total # of students receiving LD/ADHD/ASD services: NR
Acceptance into program means acceptance into college: Separate registration required after student has enrolled

ADMISSIONS

For Freshmen Admission, students must have a minimum 2.6 GPA on a 4.0 scale in all high school courses, or be in the top 50 percent of their high school graduating class, or have a minimum 21 Composite Score on the ACT (minimum 990 SAT score), and complete the following courses with a cumulative grade point average of a C or higher (2.0 on a 4.0 scale): four years of English, three years of advanced math (algebra I or higher), three years of social science, three years of lab science, and one year of fine arts. Other requirements apply for Transfer Admission and Non-Traditional Admission. Non-Traditional Admission requirements apply for students who are age 24 or over and for those who did not graduate from high school. Please contact the Office of Admissions at 1-877-COYOTES [1-877-269-6837] for more information.

ADDITIONAL INFORMATION

Services are individualized for each student's learning needs. USDDS staff provides the following activities: planning, developing, delivering, and evaluating direct service programs; meeting individually with students ensuring that students receive reasonable and appropriate accommodations that match their needs; consulting with faculty; and providing academic, career, and personal counseling referrals. Classroom accommodations include test modification, note-taking assistance, readers, books on tape, specialized computer facilities, and tutors.

General Support Services Information

Contact Information
Name of program or department: Disability Services, Center for Disabilities, USDDS
Telephone: 605-677-6389
Fax: 605-677-3172

Accommodations or Services for Students with Learning Differences

Accommodations are decided upon an individual basis after a thorough review of appropriate, current documentation. The accommodations requested must be supported through the documentation provided and must be logically linked to the current impact of the condition on academic functioning.

Allowed in exams
Calculator: Yes
Dictionary: Yes
Computer: Yes
Spellchecker: Yes
Extended test time: Yes
Scribes: Yes
Proctors: Yes
Oral exams: Yes
Note-takers: Yes
Services for students with LD: Yes
Services for students with ADHD: Yes
Services for students with ASD: Yes
Distraction-reduced environment: Yes
Tape recording in class: Yes
Audio books: NR
Electronic texts: Yes
Kurzweil Reader: Yes
Other assistive technology: N/A
Priority registration: No
Added costs for services: No
LD specialists: Yes
ADHD coaching: NR
ASD specialists: NR
Professional tutors: NR
Peer tutors: Yes
Max. hours/wk. for services: Unlimited
How professors are notified of LD/ADHD: Student

General Admissions Information

Office of Admissions: 605-677-5434

Entrance Requirements

Academic units required: 4 English, 3 math, 3 science labs, 3 social studies. **Academic units recommended:** 4 math, 4 science, 2 foreign language, and 1 units from above areas or other academic areas. High school diploma is required and GED is accepted. SAT or ACT required. If ACT, ACT with writing accepted. TOEFL required of all international applicants: minimum paper TOEFL 550 or minimum internet TOEFL 81.

Application deadline: NR
Notification: Rolling starting 9/20
Average GPA: 3.37
ACT Composite middle 50% range: 20-25
SAT Math middle 50% range: 470-610
SAT Critical Reading middle 50% range: 400-440
SAT Writing middle 50% range: 410-510
Graduated top 10% of class: 15
Graduated top 25% of class: 37
Graduated top 50% of class: 72

COLLEGE GRADUATION REQUIREMENTS

Course waivers allowed: No
In what course: No courses will be waived for graduation based on disability.
Course substitutions allowed: No
In what course: No courses will be substituted for graduation based on disability.

Additional Information

Environment: This public school was founded in 1862. It has a 273-acre campus.

Student Body
Undergrad enrollment: 7,541
% Women: 63
% Men: 37
% Out-of-state: 33

Cost information
In-state Tuition: $4,164
Out-of-state Tuition:6246
Room & board: $7,089

Housing Information
University Housing: Yes
Percent living on campus: 33

Greek System
Fraternity: Yes
Sorority: Yes
Athletics: Division I

LEE UNIVERSITY

PO Box 3450, Cleveland, TN 37320-3450
Phone: 423-614-8500 • Fax: 423-614-8533
E-mail: admissions@leeuniversity.edu • Web: www.leeuniversity.edu
Support: CS • Institution: Private

PROGRAMS OR SERVICES FOR STUDENTS WITH LEARNING DIFFERENCES

Lee University provides an Academic Support Program for students. This service is free to students. It is the goal of the Lee University Academic Support Program to empower students to actualize all the academic potential that they can. The college offers a peer tutorial program that hires the best students on campus to share their time, experience, and insight in the course or courses that are most difficult for the students who need tutoring. In addition, the college provides direct assistance for any student to verify a learning disability. For these students, Lee University provides support teams, testing adjustments, classroom adjustments, tutoring, and personal monitoring. Students must initiate the request for special accommodations by applying at the Academic Support Program Office. Lee University is committed to the provision of reasonable accommodations for students with disabilities.

ADMISSION INFORMATION FOR STUDENTS WITH LEARNING DIFFERENCES

College entrance test required: Yes
Interview required: Not Applicable
Essay required: Not Applicable
Additional Application Required for LD/ADHD/ASD: Yes
What documentation required for LD: Full adult psychological evaluation completed within the last 3 years.
With general application: No
To receive services after enrolling: Yes
What documentation required for ADHD: Full adult psychological evaluation completed within the last 3 years.
With general application: No
To receive services after enrolling: Yes
What documentation required for ASD: Full adult psychological evaluation completed within the last 3 years.
With general application: No
To receive services after enrolling: Yes
LD/ADHD/ASD documentation submitted to: Academic Support Office
ASD Specific Program: No
ASD Specific Program: NR
Special Ed. HS course work accepted: No
Specific course requirements of all applicants: NR
Separate application required for program services: Yes
Total # of students receiving LD/ADHD/ASD services: 39
Acceptance into program means acceptance into college: No

ADMISSIONS

Each applicant is reviewed on a case-by-case basis. Each student must be able to perform successfully with limited support. The ACT minimum is 17; for the SAT it is 860. The minimum required GPA is 2.0. There are no specific course requirements. Students who do not meet the college policy for entrance are referred to a special committee for possible probational acceptance.

ADDITIONAL INFORMATION

The Academic Support Program is staffed by a director, office manager, and several student assistants. The program provides readers and books on tape. Benefits included in the program are tutoring sessions with friendly and comfortable surroundings; 2 hours of tutoring per week per subject; and tutoring in most subjects, including biology, psychology, English, mathematics, religion, science, sociology, history, and foreign language. Freshmen are channeled into a gateway class, which provides study skills and time management skills.

General Support Services Information

Contact Information
Name of program or department: Academic Support Office
Telephone: 423-614-8181
Website: leeuniversity.edu

Accommodations or Services For Students With Learning Differences

Accommodations are decided upon an individual basis after a thorough review of appropriate, current documentation. The accommodations requests must be supported through the documentation provided and must be logically linked to the current impact of the condition on academic functioning.

Allowed in exams
Calculator: Yes
Dictionary: Yes
Computer: Yes
Spellchecker: Yes
Extended test time: Yes
Scribes: Yes
Proctors: Yes
Oral exams: Yes
Note-takers: Yes
Support services for students with LD: Yes
Support services for students with ADHD: Yes
Support services for students with ASD: Yes
Distraction-reduced environment: Yes
Tape recording in class: Yes
Electronic texts: Yes
Kurzweil reader: NR
Audio books: Yes
Other assistive technology: Yes
Priority registration: Yes
Added costs of services: No
LD specialists: Yes
ADHD coaching: Yes
ASD specialists: No
Professional tutors: No
Peer tutors: Yes
Max. hours/wk. for services: 2
How professors are notified of student approved accommodations: By student

General Admissions Information

Office of Admissions: 423-614-8500

Entrance Requirements

Academic units required: 4 English, 3 math, 2 science, 1 foreign language, 2 social studies, 1 history. **Academic units recommended:** 4 English, 3 math, 2 science, 1 foreign language, 2 social studies, 1 history, 1 computer science. High school diploma is required and GED is accepted. SAT or ACT required. If ACT, ACT with writing accepted. TOEFL required of all international applicants: minimum paper TOEFL 450.

Application deadline: NR
Notification: Rolling starting 3/1
Average GPA: 3.56
ACT Composite middle 50% range: 21-27
SAT Math middle 50% range: 440-570
SAT Critical Reading middle 50% range: 460-610
SAT Writing middle 50% range: NR-NR
Graduate top 10% of class: 11
Graduated top 25% of class: 47
Graduated top 50% of class: 87

COLLEGE GRADUATION REQUIREMENTS

Course waivers allowed: No
Course substitutions allowed: No

Additional Information

Environment: This private school, affiliated with the Church of God Church, was founded in 1918. It has a 115-acre campus.

Student Body
Undergrad enrollment: 4,560
% Women: 59
% Men: 41
% Out-of-state: 56.58
Cost information
Tuition: $15,170
Room & board: $7,880
Housing Information
University Housing: Yes
Percent living on campus: 46.19
Greek System
Fraternity: Yes
Sorority: Yes
Athletics: Division II

MIDDLE TENNESSEE STATE U.

Cope Administration Building, 208, Murfreesboro, TN 37132
Phone: 615-898-2111 • Fax: 615-898-5478
E-mail: admissions@mtsu.edu • Web: www.mtsu.edu
Support: S • Institution: Public

PROGRAMS OR SERVICES FOR STUDENTS WITH LEARNING DIFFERENCES

The Disability & Access Center (DAC) provides accommodations that level the academic playing field for students with identified disabilities. The DAC supports students by providing accommodations on an individual basis that consider the student's strengths, course requirements and documentation. To register with the DAC, students schedule an appointment with the coordinator, complete the registration form, and provide the most current documentation of the disability.

ADMISSION INFORMATION FOR STUDENTS WITH LEARNING DIFFERENCES

College entrance tests required: Yes
Interview required: No
Essay required: N/A
Additional Application Required for LD/ADHD/ASD: NR
What documentation required for LD: Psycho ed evaluation to include: relevant historical info, instructional interventions, related services, age diagnosed, objective data (aptitude, achievement, info processing), test scores (standard, percentile and grade equivalents) and describe functional limitations.
With general application: No
To receive services after enrolling: Yes
What documentation required for ADHD: Diagnosis based on DSM-V; history of behaviors impairing functioning in academic setting; diagnostic interview; history of symptoms; evidence of ongoing behaviors.
With general application: No
To receive services after enrolling: Yes
What documentation required for ASD: Psycho ed evaluation
With general application: NR
To receive services after enrolling: Yes
LD/ADHD/ASD documentation submitted to: Support Program/Services
ASD Specific Program: NR
Special Ed. HS course work accepted: N/A
Specific course requirements for all applicants: Yes
Separate application required for program services: No
Total # of students receiving LD/ADHD/ASD services: 250–350
Acceptance into program means acceptance into college: Students must be admitted to and enrolled in the university first and then request services.

ADMISSIONS

There is no special admission process for students with LD. All students must meet the same general admission requirements. The minimum GPA is a 2.8 and/or ACT 20. Students should have four years of English, three years of math, two years of science, two years of social studies, two years of foreign language, and one year of visual/performing arts. Course substitutions are not allowed. The average ACT is 21 or 970 SAT. Students are encouraged to self-disclose a disability in a personal statement during the admission process, although this is not required.

ADDITIONAL INFORMATION

Students are encouraged to initiate contact with the DAC coordinator early in the semester to determine the necessary accommodations. Once enrolled in courses students schedule regular meetings with the coordinator in order to monitor progress and/or determine the need for adjustments to the accommodations. Services/resources provided include orientation to the DAC; orientation to the Adaptive Technology Center; assistance with the admission process; advising and strategic scheduling of classes; early registration of classes; tutorial services; test accommodations; note- takers, readers, scribes, books on tape; exploration of time management/note-taking strategies; career planning and employment strategies; and resume preparation. The Adaptive Technology Center provides training support for students, with disabilities in the use of adaptive/assistive technology application and devices. All disability documentation is confidential and is not released without the consent of the student.

General Support Services Information

Contact Information
Name of program or department: Disabled Student Services
Telephone: 615-898-2783
Fax: 615-898-4893

Accommodations or Services for Students with Learning Differences

Accommodations are decided upon an individual basis after a thorough review of appropriate, current documentation. The accommodations requested must be supported through the documentation provided and must be logically linked to the current impact of the condition on academic functioning.

Allowed in exams
Calculator: Yes
Dictionary: Yes
Computer: Yes
Spellchecker: Yes
Extended test time: Yes
Scribes: Yes
Proctors: Yes
Oral exams: Yes
Note-takers: Yes
Services for students with LD: Yes
Services for students with ADHD: Yes
Services for students with ASD: Yes
Distraction-reduced environment: Yes
Tape recording in class: Yes
Audio books: NR
Electronic texts: Yes
Kurzweil Reader: Yes
Other assistive technology: N/A
Priority registration: Yes
Added costs for services: No
LD specialists: No
ADHD coaching: NR
ASD specialists: NR
Professional tutors: No
Peer tutors: Yes
Max. hours/wk. for services: Unlimited
How professors are notified of LD/ADHD: Student

General Admissions Information

Office of Admissions: 615-898-2111

Entrance Requirements

Academic units required: 4 English, 4 math, 3 science, 1 science labs, 2 foreign language, 1 social studies, 1 history, 1 visual/performing arts. High school diploma is required and GED is accepted. SAT or ACT required. If ACT, ACT with writing accepted. TOEFL required of all international applicants: minimum paper TOEFL 500.

Application deadline: NR
Notification: NR
Average GPA: 3.41
ACT Composite middle 50% range: 19-25
SAT Math middle 50% range: 450-610
SAT Critical Reading middle 50% range: 480-630
SAT Writing middle 50% range: NR-NR
Graduated top 10% of class: NR
Graduated top 25% of class: NR
Graduated top 50% of class: NR

COLLEGE GRADUATION REQUIREMENTS

Course waivers allowed: N/A
In what course: On an individual basis
Course substitutions allowed: N/A
In what course: On an individual basis

Additional Information

Environment: The university is located 32 miles from Nashville.

Student Body
Undergrad enrollment: 20,140
% Women: 54
% Men: 46
% Out-of-state: 6

Cost information
In-state Tuition: $6,756
Out-of Tuition: $24,324
Room & board: $8,106

Housing Information
University Housing: Yes
Percent living on campus: 15

Greek System
Fraternity: Yes
Sorority: Yes
Athletics: NR

THE UNIVERSITY OF MEMPHIS

101 Wilder Tower, Memphis, TN 38152
Phone: 901-678-2111 • Fax: 901-678-3053
E-mail: recruitment@memphis.edu • Web: www.memphis.edu
Support: CS • Institution: Public

PROGRAMS OR SERVICES FOR STUDENTS WITH LEARNING DIFFERENCES

The university's LD/ADHD/ASD Program is designed to enhance academic strengths, provide support for areas of weakness, and build skills to help students with Learning, ADHD and Autism Spectrum Disorders compete in the college environment. The program encourages development of life-long learning skills as well as personal responsibility for academic success. Training in college survival skills and regular meetings with the staff are emphasized during the first year to aid in the transition to college. Specific services are tailored to individual needs, considering one's strengths, weaknesses, course requirements, and learning styles. Students are integrated into regular classes and are held to the same academic standards as other students; however, academic accommodations are available to assist them in meeting requirements. The LD/ADHD/ASD program places responsibility on students to initiate services and follow through with services once they are arranged. Most students who use the appropriate services are successful in their academic pursuits.

ADMISSION INFORMATION FOR STUDENTS WITH LEARNING DIFFERENCES

College entrance test required: Yes
Interview required: No
Essay required: No
Additional Application Required for LD/ADHD/ASD: NR
What documentation required for LD: A psycho-educational evaluation is requested for all students entering the LD/ADHD/ASD program. If uncertain, check with the LD/ADHD/ASD Coordinator to determine if documentation submitted is appropriate.
With general application: No
To receive services after enrolling: Yes
What documentation required for ADHD: A medical form, if the student is on medication, is required. For some students, a full psycho-educational evaluation may be requested. Check with the LD/ADHD/ASD Coordinator to determine if documentation submitted is appropriate.
With general application: No
To receive services after enrolling: Yes
What documentation required for ASD: A full psycho-educational evaluation is requested for all students entering the LD/ADHD/ASD program. If uncertain, check with the LD/ADHD/ASD Coordinator to determine if documentation submitted is appropriate.
With general application: No
To receive services after enrolling: Yes
LD/ADHD/ASD documentation submitted to: Support program/services
ASD Specific Program: NR
Special Ed. HS course work accepted: No
Specific course: Yes
Separate application required for program services: No

ADMISSIONS

The LD/ADHD/ASD services are open to any student admitted to the university who provides current, appropriate psycho-educational and other relevant medical information sufficient to establish the existence of a disability which causes substantial limitation.

ADDITIONAL INFORMATION

Some services are available to all students registered with DRS, however, academic services and accommodations are individually determined and are based on the student's current functional limitations outlined in the medical or professional documentation, the student's compensatory skills and the requirements of a particular course or program. The following general services are available to all students registered with DRS: Early registration, orientation to using disability services, assistance with strategic class scheduling to enhance academic success, semester plan for accommodations and services, memos to faculty about disability needs, advocacy relating to disability access issues, information and guidance on academic, social, career, and personal issues; orientation to and use of the Assistive Technology Lab, referral to other university departments and community agencies, liaison with state and federal rehabilitation agencies, and information about specific opportunities for students with disabilities.

General Support Services Information

Contact Information
Name of program or department: Disability Resources for Students
Telephone: 901-678-2880
Fax: 901-678-3070

Accommodations or Services for Students with Learning Differences

Accommodations are decided upon an individual basis after a thorough review of appropriate, current documentation. The accommodations requests must be supported through the documentation provided and must be logically linked to the current impact of the condition on academic functioning.

Allowed in exams
Calculator: Yes
Dictionary: Yes
Computer: Yes
Spellchecker: Yes
Extended test time: Yes
Scribes: Yes
Proctors: Yes
Oral exams: N/A
Note-takers: Yes
Services for students with LD: Yes
Services for students with ADHD: Yes
Services for students with ASD: Yes
Distraction-reduced environment: Yes
Tape recording in class: Yes
Audio books: Yes
Electronic texts: NR
Kurzweil reader: Yes
Other assistive technology: Yes
Priority registration: Yes
Added costs of services: No
LD specialists: Yes
ADHD coaching: NR
ASD specialists: NR
Professional tutors: Yes
Peer tutors: No
How professors are notified of student approved accommodations: Student

General Admissions Information

Office of Admissions: 901-678-2111

Entrance Requirements

Academic units required: 4 English, 3 math, 2 science, 1 science labs, 2 foreign language, 1 social studies, 1 history, 1 visual/performing arts. High school diploma is required and GED is accepted. SAT or ACT required. If ACT, ACT with writing accepted. TOEFL required of all international applicants: minimum paper TOEFL 550.

Application deadline: 7/1
Notification: NR
Average GPA: 3.33
ACT Composite middle 50% range: 20-25
SAT Math middle 50% range: 440-590
SAT Critical Reading middle 50% range: 440-570
SAT Writing middle 50% range: 410-560
Graduated top 10% of class: 1
Graduated top 25% of class: 42
Graduated top 50% of class: 79

COLLEGE GRADUATION REQUIREMENTS

Course waivers allowed: No
Course substitutions allowed: Yes
In what course: Course substitutions may be granted for foreign language requirements. Students with questions about specific course substitutions outside of foreign language should consult with their coordinator.

Additional Information

Environment: This public school was founded in 1912. It has a 1160-acre campus.

Student Body
Undergrad enrollment: 17,647
% Women: 61
% Men: 39
% Out-of-state: 10

Cost information
In-state Tuition: $400.50 per credit
Out-of-state Tuition: $888.50 per credit
Room & board: NR

Housing Information
University Housing: Yes
Percent living on campus: 14

Greek System
Fraternity: Yes
Sorority: Yes
Athletics: Division I

The U. of Tennessee at Chattanooga

615 McCallie Avenue, Chattanooga, TN 37403
Phone: 423-425-4662 • Fax: 423-425-4157
E-mail: utcmocs@utc.edu • Web: www.utc.edu
Support: CS • Institution: Public

Programs or Services for Students with Learning Differences

Disability Resource Center (DRC) at The University of Tennessee at Chattanooga is committed to ensuring that each individual has equal access to all educational opportunities and maximizes their potential regardless of the impact of their disability. OSD is also committed to supporting the ongoing development of an accessible university that embraces diversity. This mission is accomplished by: creating a physically, programmatically and attitudinally accessible environment where people are accepted and expected to participate fully regardless of their disability, and encouraging the development of an educational culture that embraces and celebrates people's differences.

Admission Information for Students with Learning Differences

College entrance tests required: No
Interview required: No
Essay required: No
Additional Application Required for LD/ADHD/ASD: NR
What documentation required for LD: Psycho ed evaluation to include: relevant historical info, instructional interventions, related services, age diagnosed, objective data (aptitude, achievement, info processing), test scores (standard, percentile and grade equivalents) and describe functional limitations.
With general application: No
To receive services after enrolling: Yes
What documentation required for ADHD: Diagnosis based on DSM-V; history of behaviors impairing functioning in academic setting; diagnostic interview; history of symptoms; evidence of ongoing behaviors.
With general application: No
To receive services after enrolling: Yes
What documentation required for ASD: Psycho ed evaluation
With general application: NR
To receive services after enrolling: Yes
LD/ADHD/ASD documentation submitted to: DRC
ASD Specific Program: NR
Special Ed. HS course work accepted: NR
Specific course requirements of all applicants: Yes
Separate application required: Yes
Total # of students receiving LD/ADHD/ASD services: 850
Acceptance into program means acceptance into college: Submit application to Admissions separate to DRC application.

Admissions

Students with disabilities submit a general application to the Admissions Office. Minimum admissions requirements are a 2.83 GPA (on a 4.0 scale) and an ACT composite score of 18(870 SAT) or 2.3 GPA and an ACT composite score of 21 (990 SAT); and 4 years of English, 3 years of math, 2 years of science lab, 1 year of American history, 1 year of European history, world history, or world geography, 2 years of a foreign language, and 1 year of fine arts. General applications are submitted online at http://www.utc.edu/Administration/Admissions/. Students may be admitted conditionally if they fall below these guidelines and have only 1 unit deficiency. If the course deficiency is due to impact of disability, an Appeals Committee will sometimes allow a probationary admittance if DRC works with prospective student to develop an accommodation plan. Students admitted on condition must earn at least a 2.0 GPA their first semester or suspension will result. The Dean of Admissions or Admission Committee may recommend conditions for acceptance. In order to receive accommodations in the classroom, students with disabilities need to submit application and documentation (listed above) to the Disability Resource Center. Application to the Disability Resource Center is a separate process and is not relevant to the admissions process.

Additional Information

DRC does not, as a matter of policy, seek on a student's behalf a waiver of any course work. Students admitted conditionally may be required to carry a reduced course load, take specific courses, have a specific advisor, and take specific programs of developmental study. Social skills development activities may involve video and role-playing situations in group form as well as during informal gatherings. There is a monthly publication, *The CAPsule*, for CAP students and parents. UTC offers developmental math and English courses for institutional credit. Services and accommodations are available for undergraduate and graduate students.

General Support Services Information

Contact Information
Name of program or department: College Access Program (CAP)
Telephone: 423-425-4006
Fax: 423-425-2288

Accommodations or Services for Students with Learning Differences

Accommodations are decided upon an individual basis after a thorough review of appropriate, current documentation. The accommodations requested must be supported through the documentation provided and must be logically linked to the current impact of the condition on academic functioning.

Allowed in exams
Calculator: Yes
Dictionary: NR
Computer: Yes
Spellchecker: Yes
Extended test time: Yes
Scribes: NR
Proctors: Yes
Oral exams: NR
Note-takers: Yes
Services for students with LD: Yes
Services for students with ADHD: Yes
Services for students with ASD: Yes
Distraction-reduced environment: Yes
Tape recording in class: Yes
Audio books: NR
Electronic texts: NR
Kurzweil Reader: Yes
Other assistive technology: Yes
Priority registration: Yes
Added costs for services: No
LD specialists: Yes
ADHD coaching: NR
ASD specialists: NR
Professional tutors: No
Peer tutors: No
Max. hours/wk. for services: NR
How professors are notified of LD/ADHD: By student

General Admissions Information

Office of Admissions: 423-425-4662

Entrance Requirements

Academic units required: 4 English, 3 mathematics, 2 science, (2 science labs), 2 foreign language, 1 social studies, 1 history, 1 visual/performing arts. High school diploma is required and GED is accepted. SAT or ACT required. If ACT, ACT with Writing component accepted. TOEFL required of all international applicants: minimum paper TOEFL 500 or minimum web TOEFL 61.

Application deadline: 5/1
Average GPA: 3.4
ACT Composite middle 50% range: 21-25
SAT Math middle 50% range: 470-590
SAT Critical Reading middle 50% range: 470-590
SAT Writing middle 50% range: NR
Graduated top 10% of class: NR
Graduated top 25% of class: 41%
Graduated top 50% of class: 81%

COLLEGE GRADUATION REQUIREMENTS

Course waivers allowed: No
Course substitutions allowed: Yes
In what course: NR

Additional Information

Environment: This public school was founded in 1886. It has a 120-acre campus.

Student Body
Undergrad enrollment: 10,084
% Women: 56
% Men: 44
% Out-of-state: 6

Cost information
In-state Tuition: $6,624
Out-of-state Tuition: $22,742
Room & board: $8,388

Housing Information
University Housing: Yes
Percent living on campus: 30

Greek System
Fraternity: Yes
Sorority: Yes
Athletics: Division I

The U. of Tennessee at Knoxville

320 Student Service Building, Knoxville, TN 37996-0230
Phone: 865-974-2184
E-mail: admissions@utk.edu • Web: www.utk.edu
Support: CS • Institution: Public

Programs or Services for Students with Learning Differences

The mission of the Office of Disability Services is to provide each student with a disability an equal opportunity to participate in the university's programs and activities. Students who are requesting support services are required to submit documentation to verify eligibility under the ADA of 1990. The documentation must include medical or psychological information from a certified professional. It is each student's responsibility to meet the essential qualifications and institutional standards; disclose the disability in a timely manner to ODS; provide appropriate documentation; inform ODS of accommodation needs; talk with professors about accommodations in the classroom, as needed; inform ODS of barriers to a successful education; maintain and return borrowed equipment; keep all appointments with ODS staff members or call to cancel or reschedule; be involved in their academic planning and course selection; and monitor their own progress toward graduation.

Admission Information for Students with Learning Differences

College entrance test required: Yes
Interview required: Not Applicable
Essay required: Not Applicable
Additional Application Required for LD/ADHD/ASD: Not Applicable
What documentation required for LD: Psycho ed evaluation
With general application: Not Applicable
To receive services after enrolling: Not Applicable
What documentation required for ADHD: Psycho ed evaluation
With general application: Not Applicable
To receive services after enrolling: Not Applicable
What documentation required for ASD: Psycho ed evaluation
With general application: Not Applicable
To receive services after enrolling: Not Applicable
LD/ADHD/ASD documentation submitted to: Office of Disability Services
ASD Specific Program: NR
Special Ed. HS course work accepted: Not Applicable
Specific course requirements of all applicants: NR
Separate application required for program services: Yes
Total # of students receiving LD/ADHD/ASD services: NR
Acceptance into program means acceptance into college: Not Applicable

Admissions

There is no special admission process for students with learning disabilities. The Office of Admissions makes every attempt to judge each application on its academic merits. Applicants believe that their academic record does not accurately reflect their situation, do not include documentation with admission materials. Applicants feel more information is needed to compete at an equal level with others seeking admission, they consider voluntarily self-identifying the disability and the circumstances to the Admissions Office. Qualified candidates with a disability will not be denied admissions solely on the basis of their disability. Applicants are required to have 4 English; 4 math; 3 natural science, including at least 1 biology, chemistry, or physics; 3 social studies; 2 foreign language; and 1 year of visual and performing arts.

Additional Information

The goals of ODS are to provide access to appropriate accommodations and support services; provide referrals and information for a variety of campus resources, including transportation and housing; encourage and assist students with disabilities to develop greater independence; increase faculty and staff understanding of the various needs of students with disabilities; and assist the university in interpreting legal mandates that address students with disabilities. Disability Services works with each student on a case-by-case basis to determine and implement appropriate accommodations based on documentation. Services could include note-takers, alternative testing arrangements such as extra time, books on tape, computers with speech input, separate testing rooms, tape recorders, and foreign language substitutions. Content tutors are available on campus through different departments.

General Support Services Information

Contact Information
Name of program or department: Office of Disability Services (ODS)
Telephone: 865-974-6087
Fax: 865-974-9552

Accommodations or Services for Students with Learning Differences

Accommodations are decided upon an individual basis after a thorough review of appropriate, current documentation. The accommodations requested must be supported through the documentation provided and must be logically linked to the current impact of the condition on academic functioning.

Allowed in exams
Calculator: Yes
Dictionary: Yes
Computer: Yes
Spellchecker: Yes
Extended test time: Yes
Scribes: Yes
Proctors: Yes
Oral exams: Yes
Note-takers: Yes
Services for students with LD: Yes
Services for students with ADHD: Yes
Services for students with ASD: Yes
Distraction-reduced environment: Yes
Tape recording in class: Yes
Audio books: NR
Electronic texts: Yes
Kurzweil Reader: Yes
Other assistive technology: Dragon Naturally Speaking, Kurzweil, Co-Writer, Write Out Loud, Brailler, Inspiration, Intellitools, Franklin Language Master, JAWS
Priority registration: Yes
Added costs for services: No
LD specialists: Yes
ADHD coaching: NR
ASD specialists: NR
Professional tutors: No
Peer tutors: Yes
Max. hours/wk. for services: N/A
How professors are notified of LD/ADHD: Both student and director

General Admissions Information

Office of Admissions: 865-974-2184

Entrance Requirements

Academic units required: 4 English, 4 math, 3 science, 3 science labs, 2 foreign language, 1 social studies, 1 history, 1 visual/performing arts. High school diploma is required and GED is accepted. SAT or ACT required. If ACT, ACT with writing accepted. TOEFL required of all international applicants: minimum paper TOEFL 523 or minimum internet TOEFL 70.

Application deadline: 12/1
Notification: Rolling starting 10/1
Average GPA: 3.89
ACT Composite middle 50% range: 24-30
SAT Math middle 50% range: 530-630
SAT Critical Reading middle 50% range: 520-630
SAT Writing middle 50% range: NR-NR
Graduate top 10% of class: 54
Graduated top 25% of class: 90
Graduated top 50% of class: 100

COLLEGE GRADUATION REQUIREMENTS

Course waivers allowed: No
Course substitutions allowed: Yes
In what course: Foreign languages and math, if appropriate

Additional Information

Environment: This public school was founded in 1794. It has a 520-acre campus.

Student Body
Undergrad enrollment: 21,863
% Women: 49
% Men: 51
% Out-of-state: 11

Cost information
In-state Tuition: $10,190
Out-of-state Tuition: $28,380
Room & board: $9,926

Housing Information
University Housing: Yes
Percent living on campus: 33

Greek System
Fraternity: Yes
Sorority: Yes
Athletics: Division I

The U. of Tennessee at Martin

200 Hall-Moody, Martin, TN 38238
Phone: 731-881-7020 • Fax: 731-881-7029
E-mail: admitme@utm.edu • Web: www.utm.edu
Support: CS • Institution: Public

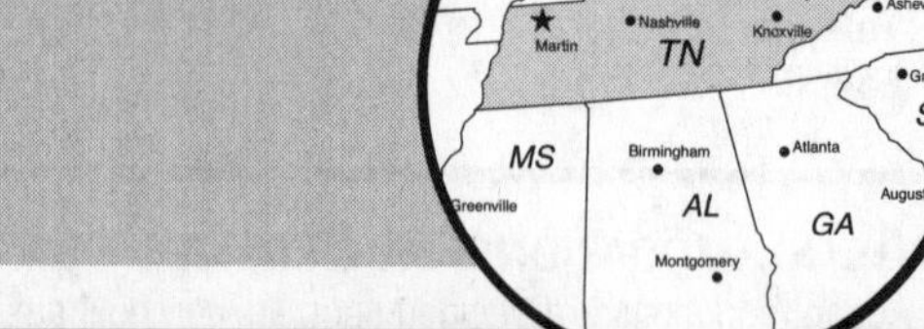

Programs or Services for Students with Learning Differences

The university believes students with learning disabilities can achieve success in college without academic compromise and can become productive, self-sufficient members of society. Students must self-identify with ODS by completing the "ODS Introductory Questionnaire" and sending this back to the Office with the appropriate documentation. ODS has a list of "reasonable accommodations" and are willing to work with the student to access what is needed. ODS is designed to complement and supplement existing university support services available for all students.

Admission Information for Students with Learning Differences

College entrance test required: Yes
Interview required: Not Applicable
Essay required: Not Applicable
Additional Application Required for LD/ADHD/ASD: Yes
What documentation required for LD: Psycho ed evaluation to include: relevant historical info, instructional interventions, related services, age diagnosed, objective data (aptitude, achievement, info processing), test scores (standard, percentile and grade equivalents) and describe functional limitations.
With general application: No
To receive services after enrolling: Yes
What documentation required for ADHD: Diagnosis based on DSM-V; history of behaviors impairing functioning in academic setting; diagnostic interview; history of symptoms; evidence of ongoing behaviors.
With general application: No
To receive services after enrolling: Yes
What documentation required for ASD: Psycho ed evaluation
With general application: No
To receive services after enrolling: Yes
LD/ADHD/ASD documentation submitted to: Disabilities Services Office
ASD Specific Program: NR
Special Ed. HS course work accepted: NR
Specific course requirements of all applicants: NR
Separate application required for program services: Yes
Total # of students receiving LD/ADHD/ASD services: 40
Acceptance into program means acceptance into college: No

Admissions

Basically, applicants must meet regular admission criteria. Qualified students with learning disabilities should apply to ODS once they have received an acceptance from the Office of Admissions.. Documentation should be sent to ODS. Applicants are selected on the basis of intellectual potential (average to superior), motivation, academic preparation, and willingness to work hard.

Additional Information

Students make an appointment with the ODS office and meet with an ODS advisor. The advisor will determine what reasonable accommodations and services will be needed and the procedures for receiving services. Students with appropriate documentation may be eligible to receive the following services: extended testing times; distraction-free testing environments; use of calculators, dictionaries, computers, and spellcheckers during exams; proctors; oral exams; note-takers; taper recorders in class; books on tape; and tutoring. Services and accommodations are provided to undergraduate and graduate students.

General Support Services Information

Contact Information
Name of program or department: Disabilities Services Office
Telephone: 731-881-7719
Fax: 731-881-1886
Website: www.utm.edu/departments/disabilities/

Accommodations or Services For Students With Learning Differences

Accommodations are decided upon an individual basis after a thorough review of appropriate, current documentation. The accommodations requests must be supported through the documentation provided and must be logically linked to the current impact of the condition on academic functioning.

Allowed in exams
Calculator: Yes
Dictionary: Yes
Computer: Yes
Spellchecker: Yes
Extended test time: Yes
Scribes: Yes
Proctors: Yes
Oral exams: Yes
Note-takers: Yes
Support services for students with LD: Yes
Support services for students with ADHD: Yes
Support services for students with ASD: Yes
Distraction-reduced environment: Yes
Tape recording in class: Yes
Electronic texts: Yes
Kurzweil reader: NR
Audio books: Yes
Other assistive technology: Yes
Priority registration: No
Added costs of services: No
LD specialists: No
ADHD coaching: No
ASD specialists: Yes
Professional tutors: No
Peer tutors: Yes
Max. hours/wk. for services: NR
How professors are notified of student approved accommodations: By both student and director

General Admissions Information

Office of Admissions: 731-881-7020

Entrance Requirements

Academic units required: 4 English, 4 math, 3 science, 1 science labs, 2 foreign language, 1 social studies, 1 history, 1 visual/performing arts. High school diploma is required and GED is accepted. SAT or ACT required. If ACT, ACT with writing accepted. TOEFL required of all international applicants: minimum paper TOEFL 500 or minimum internet TOEFL 61.

Application deadline: NR
Notification: Rolling starting 4/1
Average GPA: 3.48
ACT Composite middle 50% range: 20-25
SAT Math middle 50% range: NR-NR
SAT Critical Reading middle 50% range: NR-NR
SAT Writing middle 50% range: NR-NR
Graduate top 10% of class: 17
Graduated top 25% of class: 46
Graduated top 50% of class: 80

COLLEGE GRADUATION REQUIREMENTS

Course waivers allowed: No
Course substitutions allowed: Yes
In what course: This varies and is subject to faculty approval.

Additional Information

Environment: This public school was founded in 1900. It has a 930-acre campus.

Student Body
Undergrad enrollment: 6,435
% Women: 58
% Men: 42
% Out-of-state: 5

Cost information
In-state Tuition: $6,918
Out-of-state Tuition: $20,862
Room & board: $5,896

Housing Information
University Housing: Yes
Percent living on campus: 30

Greek System
Fraternity: Yes
Sorority: Yes
Athletics: Division I

ABILENE CHRISTIAN UNIVERSITY

ACU Box 29000, Abilene, TX 79699
Phone: 325-674-2650 • Fax: 325-674-2130
E-mail: info@admissions.acu.edu • Web: www.acu.edu
Support: CS • Institution: Private

GENERAL SUPPORT SERVICES INFORMATION

Alpha Scholars Program is a Student Support Service Program funded under Title IV legislation governing TRIO programs. The program strives to assist students in programs that move them toward independence in learning and living. The staff is specially trained instructors, peer tutors, counselors, and administrators who focus on the problems encountered by college students. Staff members help qualifying students find and apply solutions to their problems. Students qualify for services if they are a first-generation college student, economically disadvantaged, or a student with disabilities. Alpha means one-on-one help, and the instruction and tutoring are tailored to the student's unique needs. Students with learning disabilities may receive special accommodation services to assist them in achieving success in their university studies. Documentation of the disability is required to receive disability accommodations. Students must make an appointment to determine if they qualify to receive services.

ADMISSION INFORMATION FOR STUDENTS WITH LEARNING DIFFERENCES

College entrance test required: Yes
Interview required: No
Essay required: Not Applicable
Additional Application Required for LD/ADHD/ASD: Yes
What documentation required for LD: Psychoeducational assessment or response to documentation form from qualified professional
With general application: No
To receive services after enrolling: Yes
What documentation required for ADHD: documentation of previous services
With general application: No
To receive services after enrolling: Yes
What documentation required for ASD: Full psychoeducational assessment (with subscores)
With general application: No
To receive services after enrolling: Yes
LD/ADHD/ASD documentation submitted to: Alpha Scholars Program
ASD Specific Program: No
Special Ed. HS course work accepted: No
Specific course requirements of all applicants: NR
Separate application required for program services: Yes
Total # of students receiving LD/ADHD/ASD services: 163
Acceptance into program means acceptance into college: No

ADMISSIONS

All students must be admitted to the university and meet the same criteria for admission. There is no special admission process for students with learning disabilities. Regular admissions criteria include 20 ACT or 930-plus SAT; college-preparatory courses including 4 years of English, 3 years of math, 3 years of science, and 2 years of a foreign language; and no specific GPA. Some students not meeting the admission criteria may be admitted conditionally. Students admitted conditionally must take specified courses in a summer term and demonstrate motivation and ability. Freshman applicants need to take the SAT Reasoning Test or ACT with Writing component.

ADDITIONAL INFORMATION

Alpha Scholars Program provides opportunities for individual instruction in basic skills areas such as writing, math, or study skills; assessment of learning preferences, strengths, and weaknesses; instruction and tutoring designed to fit the student's particular learning preferences and strengths and academic needs; classroom help if needed such as readers, note-takers, alternative testing arrangements; personal, career, and academic counseling; and workshops on topics such as time management skills, resume writing, career placement, and study skills.

General Support Services Information

Contact Information
Name of program or department: Alpha Scholars Program
Telephone: 325-674-2667
Fax: 325-674-6847
Website: www.acu.edu/alpha

Accommodations or Services For Students With Learning Differences

Accommodations are decided upon an individual basis after a thorough review of appropriate, current documentation. The accommodations requests must be supported through the documentation provided and must be logically linked to the current impact of the condition on academic functioning.

Allowed in exams
Calculator: Yes
Dictionary: Yes
Computer: Yes
Spellchecker: Yes
Extended test time: Yes
Scribes: Yes
Proctors: Yes
Oral exams: No
Note-takers: Yes
Support services for students with LD: Yes
Support services for students with ADHD: Yes
Support services for students with ASD: Yes
Distraction-reduced environment: Yes
Tape recording in class: Yes
Electronic texts: Yes
Kurzweil reader: NR
Audio books: Yes
Other assistive technology: Yes
Priority registration: No
Added costs of services: NR
LD specialists: Yes
ADHD coaching: Yes
ASD specialists: No
Professional tutors: No
Peer tutors: Yes
Max. hours/wk. for services: 20
How professors are notified of student approved accommodations: By student

General Admissions Information

Office of Admissions: 325-674-2650

Entrance Requirements

Academic units recommended: 4 English, 3 math, 3 science, 2 science labs, 2 foreign language, 1 history, and 1 units from above areas or other academic areas. High school diploma is required and GED is accepted. SAT or ACT required. If ACT, ACT with writing recommended. TOEFL required of all international applicants: minimum paper TOEFL 525 or minimum internet TOEFL 80.

Application deadline: 2/15
Notification: 2/15
Average GPA: 3.58
ACT Composite middle 50% range: 22-27
SAT Math middle 50% range: 480-590
SAT Critical Reading middle 50% range: 470-580
SAT Writing middle 50% range: 450-570
Graduate top 10% of class: 22
Graduated top 25% of class: 58
Graduated top 50% of class: 87

COLLEGE GRADUATION REQUIREMENTS

Course waivers allowed: No
Course substitutions allowed: No

Additional Information

Environment: This private school, affiliated with the Church of Christ Church, was founded in 1906. It has a 208-acre campus.

Student Body
Undergrad enrollment: 3,760
% Women: 59
% Men: 41
% Out-of-state: 14

Cost information
Tuition: $30,780
Room & board: $9,310

Housing Information
University Housing: Yes
Percent living on campus: 48

Greek System
Fraternity: Yes
Sorority: Yes
Athletics: Division I

Lamar University

PO Box 10009, Beaumont, TX 77710
Phone: 409-880-8888 • Fax: 409-880-8463
E-mail: admissions@hal.lamar.edu • Web: www.lamar.edu
Support: S • Institution: Public

Programs or Services for Students with Learning Differences

The Disability Resource Center (DRC) assures qualified students access to Lamar University's academic activities, programs, resources, and services. Students with disabilities may qualify for accommodations, academic adjustments and/or assistive technology. Students are encouraged to contact the DRC to schedule an appointment with the Director or Communication Access Coordinator and complete an Accommodation Request Form and submit appropriate disability documentation that supports the accommodation requests. Individualized accommodation plans are developed for each student based on the needs identified.

Admission Information for Students with Learning Differences

College entrance tests required: Yes

Interview required: N/A
Additional Application Required for LD/ADHD/ASD: NR
What documentation required for LD: Psychoeducational evaluation administered after sixteenth birthday; should contain relevant developmental, psychological, social, and educational history; cognitive abilities as well as achievement information.
With general application: NR
To receive services after enrolling: Yes
What documentation required for ADHD: Psychoeducational evaluation administered after sixteenth birthday; should contain relevant developmental, psychological, social, and educational history; cognitive abilities as well as achievement information.
LD/ADHD/ASD documentation submitted to: Support Program/Services
ASD Specific Program: NR
Special Ed. HS course work accepted: No
Specific course requirements for all applicants: Yes
Separate application required for program services: Yes
Total # of students receiving LD/ADHD/ASD services: 45
Acceptance into program means acceptance into college: Separate application required after student has enrolled

Admissions

Applicants with learning disabilities and/or ADHD must meet the general admission requirements. Services will be offered to enrolled students who notify The Disability Resource Center. Students must be in top half of their class and complete 14 "solid" credits to be admitted unconditionally, including four years English, three years math (algebra I–II and geometry or higher), two years science (physical science, biology, chemistry, physics, or geology), two and a half years social science, and two and a half years electives (foreign language is recommended). A very limited number of applicants not meeting the prerequisites may be admitted on "individual approval." Those not in the top half must achieve a minimum composite score of 1000 SAT/21 ACT. Some students may be considered on an Individual Approval basis if they fail to meet Unconditional Admission. These students are subject to mandatory advisement; six-credit limit in summer and 14 in fall term, and must successfully complete nine hours with 2.0 GPA; students must meet these provisions or leave for one year.

Additional Information

The Disability Resource Center offers a variety of services designed to assure qualified students access to the university's academic activities, programs, resources, and services. Services or accommodations could include priority registration; alternative testing accommodations; copying of class notes; classroom accommodations; note-takers; readers and textbooks on tape. Professional staff assist students with questions, problem solving, adjustment, decision making, goal planning, and testing. Skills classes in study skills are offered, including developmental writing, reading, and math for credit. Students are referred to other offices and personnel in accord with the needs and intents of the individual. Services and accommodations are available for undergraduate and graduate students.

General Support Services Information

Contact Information
Name of program or department: The Disability Resource Center
Telephone: 409-880-8347
Fax: 409-880-2225

Accommodations or Services for Students with Learning Differences

Accommodations are decided upon an individual basis after a thorough review of appropriate, current documentation. The accommodations requested must be supported through the documentation provided and must be logically linked to the current impact of the condition on academic functioning.

Allowed in exams
Calculator: Yes
Dictionary: Yes
Computer: Yes
Spellchecker: Yes
Extended test time: Yes
Scribes: Yes
Proctors: Yes
Oral exams: Yes
Note-takers: Yes
Services for students with LD: Yes
Services for students with ADHD: Yes
Services for students with ASD: Yes
Distraction-reduced environment: Yes
Tape recording in class: Yes
Audio books: NR
Electronic texts: Yes
Kurzweil Reader: Yes
Other assistive technology: computer screen reader, screen enlarger; Braille
Priority registration: Yes
Added costs for services: No
LD specialists: No
ADHD coaching: NR
ASD specialists: NR
Professional tutors: No
Peer tutors: Yes
Max. hours/wk. for services: 15
How professors are notified of LD/ADHD: Student

General Admissions Information

Office of Admissions: 409-880-8888

Entrance Requirements

Academic units recommended: 4 English, 3 math, 2 science, 2 social studies, 2 academic electives. High school diploma is required and GED is accepted.High school diploma is required and GED is not accepted. SAT or ACT required. TOEFL required of all international applicants: minimum paper TOEFL 500.

Application deadline: 8/1
Notification: NR
Average GPA: NR
ACT Composite middle 50% range: NR-NR
SAT Math middle 50% range: NR-NR
SAT Critical Reading middle 50% range: NR-NR
SAT Writing middle 50% range: NR-NR
Graduated top 10% of class: 10
Graduated top 25% of class: 27
Graduated top 50% of class: 90

COLLEGE GRADUATION REQUIREMENTS

Course waivers allowed: No
Course substitutions allowed: Yes
In what course: Appropriateness of a core course substitution is determined by the Coordinating Board of the State of Texas; other subsitutions are determined by student's academic department.

Additional Information

Environment: This public school was founded in 1923. It has a 200-acre campus.

Student Body
Undergrad enrollment: 9,551
% Women: 55
% Men: 45
% Out-of-state: 1

Cost information
In-state Tuition: $4,850
Out-of-state Tuition: $10,700
Room & board: $3,935

Housing Information
University Housing: Yes
Percent living on campus: 11

Greek System
Fraternity: Yes
Sorority: Yes
Athletics: Division I

MIDWESTERN STATE UNIVERSITY

3410 Taft Boulevard, Wichita Falls, TX 76308-2099
Phone: 940-397-4334 • Fax: 940-397-4672
E-mail: admissions@mwsu.edu • Web: www.mwsu.edu
Support: S • Institution: Public

PROGRAMS OR SERVICES FOR STUDENTS WITH LEARNING DIFFERENCES

The Mission of Disability Support Services (DSS) is to provide students with disabilities equal access to all educational, social and recreational programs through the coordination of services and reasonable accommodations, consultation and advocacy. DSS strives to provide services that will encourage students to become as independent and self-reliant as possible.

ADMISSION INFORMATION FOR STUDENTS WITH LEARNING DIFFERENCES

College entrance tests required: Yes
Interview required: No
Essay required: No
Additional Application Required for LD/ADHD/ASD: NR
What documentation required for LD: Psycho ed evaluation to include: relevant historical info, instructional interventions, related services, age diagnosed, objective data (aptitude, achievement, info processing), test scores (standard, percentile and grade equivalents) and describe functional limitations.
With general application: No
To receive services after enrolling: Yes
What documentation required for ADHD: Diagnosis based on DSM-V; history of behaviors impairing functioning in academic setting; diagnostic interview; history of symptoms; evidence of ongoing behaviors.
With general application: No
To receive services after enrolling: Yes
What documentation required for ASD: Psycho ed evaluation
With general application: No
To receive services after enrolling: Yes
LD/ADHD/ASD documentation submitted to: Disability Support Services
ASD Specific Program: NR
Special Ed. HS course work accepted: Yes
Specific course requirements of all applicants: Yes
Separate application required: Yes
Total # of students receiving LD/ADHD/ASD services: 83
Acceptance into program means acceptance into college: Students must be admitted to and enrolled in the university first and then request services.

ADMISSIONS

Unconditional acceptance by the university is available to the student who graduates from an accredited high school with course work as follows: 4 years of English, 3 years of math, 2 years of science; a class rank within the top 60 percent; and an ACT of 20-plus or SAT score of 840-plus. Admission by review is an alternative admission with the same high school units as mentioned previously, but a high school rank 40–60 percent, an ACT score of 14–19, or an SAT score of 560–839. Students whose high school transcript does not reflect ranking must submit scores of 1110 on the SAT Reasoning Test or 24 composite on the ACT to be considered for unconditional admission. Students with disabilities must apply to MSU through the regular admissions process.

ADDITIONAL INFORMATION

To obtain services, students must be accepted for admission at MSU, complete an application form from Disability Support Services and supply verification of the disability. MSU offers courses for students for credit in study skills, time management, and adapting to college life. The MSU Counseling Center can also provide individual counseling for personal, academic and career concerns.

General Support Services Information

Contact Information
Name of program or department: Disability Support Services (DSS)
Telephone: 940-397-4140
Fax: 940-397-4180

Accommodations or Services for Students with Learning Differences

The DSS assists students in advocating and understanding their disability and communicating with instructors, provide accommodations for the classroom and testing, and train and provide technology to help students with learning differences.

Allowed in exams
Calculator: Yes
Dictionary: Yes
Computer: Yes
Spellchecker: Yes
Extended test time: Yes
Scribes: Yes
Proctors: Yes
Oral exams: Yes
Note-takers: Yes
Services for students with LD: Yes
Services for students with ADHD: Yes
Services for students with ASD: Yes
Distraction-reduced environment: Yes
Tape recording in class: Yes
Audio books: NR
Electronic texts: Yes
Kurzweil Reader: Yes
Audio books: Yes
Other assistive technology: Yes
Priority registration: Yes
Added costs for services: No
LD specialists: No
ADHD coaching: NR
ASD specialists: NR
Professional tutors: No
Peer tutors: Yes
Max. hours/wk. for services: Yes
How professors are notified of LD/ADHD: By student

General Admissions Information

Office of Admissions: 940-397-4334

Entrance Requirements

Academic units required: 4 English, 3 mathematics, 2 science, 6 academic electives. High school diploma is required and GED is accepted. SAT or ACT required. If ACT, ACT with Writing component required. TOEFL required of all international applicants: minimum paper TOEFL 550.

Application deadline: 8/7
Notification: Rolling starting 9/1
Average GPA: 3.4
ACT Composite middle 50% range: 18-23
SAT Math middle 50% range: 450-560
SAT Critical Reading middle 50% range: 440-550
SAT Writing middle 50% range: 440-540
Graduated top 10% of class: 12
Graduated top 25% of class: 37
Graduated top 50% of class: 73

COLLEGE GRADUATION REQUIREMENTS

Course waivers allowed: No
Course substitutions allowed: Yes
In what course: College algebra, foreign languages

Additional Information

Environment: The campus is located 135 miles northwest of Dallas.

Student Body
Undergrad enrollment: 5,358
% Women: 58
% Men: 42
% Out-of-state: 5

Cost information
In-state tuition: $7,254
Out-of-state tuition: $9,204
Room & board: $6,450
Housing Information
University housing: Yes
% Living on campus: 20

Greek System
Fraternity: Yes
Sorority: Yes
Athletics: Division II

Schreiner University

2100 Memorial Boulevard, Kerrville, TX 78028-5697
Phone: 830-792-7217 • Fax: (830) 792-7226
E-mail: http://www.schreiner.edu/admission/index
Web: www.schreiner.edu • Support: SP • Institution: Private

General Support Services Information

Students admitted to the Learning Support Services program must be highly motivated, have the intellectual potential for success in a rigorous academic program, and have the ability to meet the demands of college life. Extensive learning support is given to each student, and the ultimate goal is for students to be able to succeed without special help. The Learning Support Services (LSS) program is staffed by LD specialists and many tutors. Students with learning disabilities are enrolled in regular college courses and receive individual tutorial assistance in each subject. Students in the program are held to the same high standards and complete the same curriculum requirements as all other degree candidates. In addition to the LSS staff, the Schreiner University faculty is dedicated to helping students realize their full potential.

Admission Information for Students with Learning Differences

College entrance tests required: Yes
Interview required: Yes
Essay required: Yes
Additional Application Required for LD/ADHD/ASD: NR
What documentation required for LD: Psycho ed evaluation to include: relevant historical info, instructional interventions, related services, age diagnosed, objective data (aptitude, achievement, info processing), test scores (standard, percentile and grade equivalents) and describe functional limitations.
With general application: Yes if requested as part of Structured Program application
To receive services after enrolling: Yes
What documentation required for ADHD: Diagnosis based on DSM-V; history of behaviors impairing functioning in academic setting; diagnostic interview; history of symptoms; evidence of ongoing behaviors.
With general application: Yes if requested as part of Structured Program application
To receive services after enrolling: Yes
What documentation required for ASD: Psycho ed evaluation
With general application: NR
To receive services after enrolling: No
LD/ADHD/ASD documentation submitted to: Admissions and Learning Support Services
ASD Specific Program: NR
Special Ed. HS course work accepted: No
Specific course requirements of all applicants: Yes
Separate application required: No
Total # of students receiving LD/ADHD/ASD services: 65
Acceptance into program means acceptance into college: Students admitted into the Learning Support Services program are automatically admitted into the college.

Admissions

Proof of high school diploma and all significant materials relevant to the specific learning disability must be submitted. Applicants should be enrolled in regular, mainstream English courses in high school. We recommend that students take a college-preparatory curriculum. However, admission would not be denied to a qualified candidate if some course work was not included. The Woodcock-Johnson Achievement Battery is preferred, but other tests are accepted. An interview is required and is an important part of the admissions decision. Applicants are considered individually and selected on the basis of their intellectual ability, motivation, academic preparation, and potential for success. For a candidate to be considered for admission, the following are required: all secondary school transcripts (transfer students must also supply transcripts of all attempted college work); medical or psychological statement of specific learning disability or attention deficit hyperactivity disorder; written report of the results of the WAIS-IV, including all subtest scores and verbal, performance, and full-scale IQ scores taken within 12 months of application for admission; current individual achievement test results showing level of proficiency in reading comprehension, word identification, word attack, spelling, writing (written language), math calculation, and applied mathematics; and a completed application with application fee must be submitted to the Office of Admissions.

Additional Information

The Learning Support Services Program is tailored to meet the needs of each participating student. Each LSS staff member is committed to helping students develop the independent study skills and strategies that are necessary for academic success. Individualized services may include study skills development; regularly scheduled tutoring for all classes; testing accommodations, including readers, scribes, and extended time; use of recorded textbooks; arrangements made for note-takers in lecture classes; and a freshman seminar class that addresses issues of specific concern to college students with learning disabilities.

General Support Services Information

Contact Information
Name of program or department: Learning Support Services (LSS)
Telephone: 830-792-7257
Fax: 830-792-7294

Accommodations or Services for Students with Learning Differences

Accommodations are decided upon an individual basis after a thorough review of appropriate, current documentation. The accommodations requested must be supported through the documentation provided and must be logically linked to the current impact of the condition on academic functioning.

Allowed in exams
Calculator: No
Dictionary: No
Computer: Yes
Spellchecker: Yes
Extended test time: Yes
Scribes: Yes
Proctors: Yes
Oral exams: Yes
Note-takers: Yes
Services for students with LD: Yes
Services for students with ADHD: Yes
Services for students with ASD: No
Distraction-reduced environment: Yes
Tape recording in class: Yes
Audio books: NR
Electronic texts: Yes
Kurzweil Reader: Yes
Audio books: No
Other assistive technology: No
Priority registration: No
Added costs for services: Yes
LD specialists: Yes
ADHD coaching: Yes
ASD specialists: No
Professional tutors: 15
Peer tutors: No
Max. hours/wk. for services: Unlimited
How professors are notified of LD/ADHD: By both student and director

General Admissions Information

Office of Admissions: 830-792-7217

Entrance Requirements

Academic units recommended: 4 English, 3 math, 3 science, 2 science labs, 2 foreign language, 2 social studies, 2 history, 1 computer science, 1 visual/performing arts. High school diploma is required and GED is accepted. SAT or ACT required. If ACT, ACT with writing required. TOEFL required of all international applicants: minimum paper TOEFL 550 or minimum internet TOEFL 79.

Application deadline: 8/1
Notification: NR
Average GPA: 3.59
ACT Composite middle 50% range: 19-24
SAT Math middle 50% range: 450-550
SAT Critical Reading middle 50% range: 440-540
SAT Writing middle 50% range: 420-520
Graduate top 10% of class: 11
Graduated top 25% of class: 36
Graduated top 50% of class: 70

COLLEGE GRADUATION REQUIREMENTS

Course waivers allowed: NR
Course substitutions allowed: NR

Additional Information

Environment: This private school, affiliated with the Presbyterian Church, was founded in 1923. It has a 175-acre campus.

Student Body
Undergrad enrollment: 1,182
% Women: 58
% Men: 42
% Out-of-state: 3
Cost information
Tuition: $24,030
Room & board: $9,806
Housing Information
University Housing: Yes
Percent living on campus: 63
Greek System
Fraternity: Yes
Sorority: Yes
Athletics: Division III

SOUTHERN METHODIST UNIVERSITY

PO Box 750181 Dallas, TX 75275-0181
Phone: 214-768-2058 • Fax: 214-768-0103
E-mail: ugadmission@smu.edu • Web: www.smu.edu
Support: CS • Institution: Private

PROGRAMS OR SERVICES FOR STUDENTS WITH LEARNING DIFFERENCES

The goal of Disability Accommodations & Success Strategies (DASS) is to provide students with documented disabilities services or reasonable accommodations in order to reduce the effects that a disability may have on their performance in a traditional academic setting. DASS provides individual attention and support for students needing assistance with various aspects of their campus experience such as notifying professors, arranging accommodations, referrals, and accessibility.

ADMISSION INFORMATION FOR STUDENTS WITH LEARNING DIFFERENCES

College entrance test required: Yes
Interview required: No
Essay required: No
Additional Application Required for LD/ADHD/ASD: NR
What documentation required for LD: A full psychoeducational assessment conducted, preferably, in the last three years. Needs to use comprehensive measures of potential and achievement.
With general application: No
To receive services after enrolling: Yes
What documentation required for ADHD: Report from either a licensed psychologist or physician trained in diagnosing ADHD. Evaluation needs to be conducted, preferably, within three years of the time student seeks accommodations. Documentation guidelines are posted on website.
With general application: No
To receive services after enrolling: Yes
What documentation required for ASD: Documentation from a licensed professional, detailing the diagnosed condition, its impact on the student, and recommendations in an academic setting.
With general application: No
To receive services after enrolling: Yes
LD/ADHD/ASD documentation submitted to: Support program/services
ASD Specific Program: NR
Special Ed. HS course work accepted: Yes
Specific course: Yes
Separate application required for program services: No
Total # of students receiving LD/ADHD/ASD services: NR
Acceptance into program means acceptance into college: NR

ADMISSIONS

There is no special admission process to the university for students with LD. If their standardized tests were administered under non-standard conditions, this will not weigh unfavorably into the admission decision. In addition to GPA and SAT or ACT scores, the admission committee weighs many factors during the course of the application process, including classroom performance, rigor of high school curriculum, quality of essays and recommendations, extracurricular activities, talents, character and life experiences. Minimum high school course requirements include: 4 units of English, 3 units of math (algebra I,II, geometry), 3 units of social science, 3 units of science (of which 2 must be lab science) and 2 consecutive units of foreign language. Standardized Test Requirements include: Official SAT I or ACT scores (Please note SMU does not require the ACT writing test) and SAT II scores are recommended for some home-school students. if a student plans to major or minor in music, dance, or theater, an audition is a requirement for admission.

ADDITIONAL INFORMATION

All students have access to tutoring, writing centers, study skills workshops, and classes to improve reading rate, comprehension, and vocabulary. Skills classes are offered in time management, test strategies, notetaking strategies, organizational skills, concentration, memory, and test anxiety. There are two learning specialists available to work with students with learning differences free of charge. There are currently 380 students with learning disabilities and/or ADHD receiving services. DASS also offers academic coaching for students with diagnosed learning disabilities, a study and reading skills course called ORACLE and a student-run organization called Students for New Learning. DASS does also collaborate with Residence Life and student housing regarding special needs of the student.

General Support Services Information

Contact Information
Name of program or department: Disability Accommodations & Success Strategies
Telephone: 214-768-1470
Fax: 214-768-1255

Accommodations or Services For Students With Learning Differences

Accommodations are decided upon an individual basis after a thorough review of appropriate, current documentation. The accommodations requests must be supported through the documentation provided and must be logically linked to the current impact of the condition on academic functioning.

Allowed in exams
Calculator: Yes
Dictionary: Yes
Computer: Yes
Spellchecker: Yes
Extended test time: Yes
Scribes: Yes
Proctors: Yes
Oral exams: Yes
Note-takers: Yes
Support services for students with LD: Yes
Support services for students with ADHD: Yes
Support services for students with ASD: Yes
Distraction-reduced environment: Yes
Tape recording in class: Yes
Electronic texts: Yes
Kurzweil reader: NR
Audio books: Yes
Other assistive technology: Yes
Priority registration: Yes
Added costs of services: No
LD specialists: Yes
ADHD coaching: Yes
ASD specialists: No
Professional tutors: No
Peer tutors: Yes
Max. hours/wk. for services: NR
How professors are notified of student approved accommodations: By student

General Admissions Information

Office of Admissions: 214-768-2058

Entrance Requirements

Academic units required: 4 English, 3 math, 3 science, 2 science labs, 2 foreign language, 3 social studies. **Academic units recommended:** 4 English, 4 math, 3 science, 2 science labs, 3 foreign language, 3 history, 3 academic electives. High school diploma is required and GED is not accepted. SAT or ACT required. If ACT, ACT with writing accepted. TOEFL required of all international applicants: minimum paper TOEFL 550 or minimum internet TOEFL 80.

Application deadline: 1/15
Notification: 4/1
Average GPA: 3.64
ACT Composite middle 50% range: 28-32
SAT Math middle 50% range: 620-720
SAT Critical Reading middle 50% range: 600-690
SAT Writing middle 50% range: 600-690
Graduate top 10% of class: 44
Graduated top 25% of class: 75
Graduated top 50% of class: 93

COLLEGE GRADUATION REQUIREMENTS

Course waivers allowed: No
Course substitutions allowed: Yes
In what course: Foreign Language

Additional Information

Environment: This private school, affiliated with the Methodist Church, was founded in 1911. It has a 210-acre campus.

Student Body
Undergrad enrollment: 6,411
% Women: 50
% Men: 50
% Out-of-state: 54

Cost information
Tuition: $44,694
Room & board: $16,125

Housing Information
University Housing: Yes
Percent living on campus: 57

Greek System
Fraternity: NR
Sorority: NR
Athletics: Division I

TEXAS A&M U.—COLLEGE STATION

PO Box 30014, College Station, TX 77843-3014
Phone: 979-845-3741 • Fax: 979-847-8737
E-mail: admissions@tamu.edu • Web: www.tamu.edu
Support: S • Institution: Public

PROGRAMS OR SERVICES FOR STUDENTS WITH LEARNING DIFFERENCES

The Department of Disability Services exists to promote an academic experience for all students that is fully inclusive and accessible. The philosophy of Disability Services is to empower students with the skills needed to act as their own advocate and succeed in the mainstream of the university environment. Services include accommodations counseling, evaluation referral, disability-related information, adaptive technology services, sign language interpreting, and transcription services for academically related purposes.

ADMISSION INFORMATION FOR STUDENTS WITH LEARNING DIFFERENCES

College entrance test required: Yes
Interview required: Not Applicable
Essay required: Not Applicable
Additional Application Required for LD/ADHD/ASD: Not Applicable
What documentation required for LD: Psycho ed evaluation
With general application: Not Applicable
To receive services after enrolling: Not Applicable
What documentation required for ADHD: Psycho ed evaluation
With general application: Not Applicable
To receive services after enrolling: Not Applicable
What documentation required for ASD: Psycho ed evaluation
With general application: Not Applicable
To receive services after enrolling: Not Applicable
LD/ADHD/ASD documentation submitted to: Disability Services
ASD Specific Program: NR
Special Ed. HS course work accepted: Not Applicable
Specific course requirements of all applicants: NR
Separate application required for program services: Yes
Total # of students receiving LD/ADHD/ASD services: NR
Acceptance into program means acceptance into college: Not Applicable

ADMISSIONS

General application requirements require that students submit an essay, ACT (with optional essay) or new SAT scores, and have at least 4 years of English, 3.5 years of math (Algebra I and II, geometry, and 0.5 credit of advanced math), 3 years of science (2 must be in biology, chemistry, or physics), and recommend 2 years of the same foreign language. Students ranked in the top 10 percent of their class are automatically admissible if they have taken the required courses. Students not in the top 10 percent but ranked in the top 25 percent must have a 1300 on the SAT with a score of 600-plus in math and verbal or a 30 on the ACT and have the course requirements. Applicants with learning disabilities submit the general application form and are considered under the same guidelines as all applicants. Students may have their application reviewed by requesting special consideration based on their disability and by providing letters of recommendation from their high school counselor stating what accommodations are needed in college to be successful. Admissions will be affected by the student's record indicating success with provided accommodations along with any activities and leadership skills. Students not meeting academic criteria for automatic admission may be offered admission to a summer provisional program. These students must take 9–12 credits and receive a grade of C in each of the courses.

ADDITIONAL INFORMATION

Accommodations are provided on an individual basis as needs arise. Disability Services is a resource for information, including, but not limited to, tutoring services, study and time management skills training, community resources, disability awareness, and various university services. Skills classes in math, reading, and writing are offered to the entire student body though the Student Learning Center. Some of these classes may be taken for college credit. Services and accommodations are available for undergraduate and graduate students. Services include an adaptive technology laboratory equipped with state-of-the-art technology for students with disabilities, including text-to-speech scanning for personal use. The Academic Success Center has tutors available for support and Academic Coaches. They can be reached at 979-845-4900.

General Support Services Information

Contact Information
Name of program or department: Disability Services
Telephone: 979-845-1637
Fax: 979-458-1214 • **Website:** http://disability.tamu.edu

Accommodations or Services For Students With Learning Differences

Accommodations are decided upon an individual basis after a thorough review of appropriate, current documentation. The accommodations requests must be supported through the documentation provided and must be logically linked to the current impact of the condition on academic functioning.

Allowed in exams
Calculator: Yes
Dictionary: Yes
Computer: Yes
Spellchecker: Yes
Extended test time: Yes
Scribes: Yes
Proctors: Yes
Oral exams: Yes
Note-takers: Yes
Support services for students with LD: Yes
Support services for students with ADHD: Yes
Support services for students with ASD: Yes
Distraction-reduced environment: Yes
Tape recording in class: Yes
Electronic texts: Yes
Kurzweil reader: NR
Audio books: Yes
Other assistive technology: Yes
Priority registration: Yes
Added costs of services: No
LD specialists: NR
ADHD coaching: Yes
ASD specialists: Yes
Professional tutors: No
Peer tutors: Not Applicable
Max. hours/wk. for services: NR
How professors are notified of student approved accommodations: By student

General Admissions Information

Office of Admissions: (979) 845-1060

Entrance Requirements

Academic units required: 4 English, 3 math, 3 science, 1 science labs, 2 foreign language, 3 social studies, 5 academic electives, 1 visual/performing arts, and 1 units from above areas or other academic areas. **Academic units recommended:** 4 English, 4 math, 4 science, 2 science labs, 2 foreign language, 4 social studies, 7 academic electives, 1 visual/performing arts, and 1 units from above areas or other academic areas. High school diploma is required and GED is accepted. SAT or ACT required. If ACT, ACT with writing required. TOEFL required of all international applicants: minimum paper TOEFL 550 or minimum internet TOEFL 80.

Application deadline: 12/1
Notification: Rolling starting 12/15
Average GPA: NR
ACT Composite middle 50% range: 25-30
SAT Math middle 50% range: 550-670
SAT Critical Reading middle 50% range: 520-640
SAT Writing middle 50% range: 490-610
Graduate top 10% of class: 66
Graduated top 25% of class: 91
Graduated top 50% of class: 99

COLLEGE GRADUATION REQUIREMENTS

Course waivers allowed: No
Course substitutions allowed: Yes
In what course: Math, foreign language. Handled on a case-by-case depending on the nature of the disability and requirements fo the major.

Additional Information

Environment: This public school was founded in 1876. It has a 5200-acre campus.

Student Body
Undergrad enrollment: 48,960
% Women: 49
% Men: 51
% Out-of-state: 4

Cost information
In-state Tuition: $6,149
Out-of-state Tuition: $24,742
Room & board: $10,338

Housing Information
University Housing: Yes
Percent living on campus: 22.9

Greek System
Fraternity: Yes
Sorority: Yes
Athletics: Division I

TEXAS A&M U.—KINGSVILLE

MSC 105, Kingsville, TX 78363
Phone: 361-593-2315 • Fax: 361-593-2195
E-mail: ksossrx@tamuk.edu • Web: www.tamuk.edu
Support: S • Institution: Public

PROGRAMS OR SERVICES FOR STUDENTS WITH LEARNING DIFFERENCES

The university is committed to providing an environment in which every student is encouraged to reach the highest level of personal and educational achievement. Students with disabilities may have special concerns and even special needs. Services vary according to the nature of the disability and are provided by the Center for Life Services and Wellness. Counseling services offer educational, vocational, and personal consultations, as well as tutoring, testing, and academic advising. Students with LD have access to note-takers, readers, writers, and other assistance that the university can provide. All students entering college as freshmen (or transfers with less than 30 hours) have the university's commitment to improve student achievement, retention, depth, and quality of instruction and services.

ADMISSION INFORMATION FOR STUDENTS WITH LEARNING DIFFERENCES

College entrance tests required: Yes
Interview required: Yes
Essay required: No
Additional Application Required for LD/ADHD/ASD: NR
What documentation required for LD: Psycho ed evaluation to include: relevant historical info, instructional interventions, related services, age diagnosed, objective data (aptitude, achievement, info processing), test scores (standard, percentile and grade equivalents) and describe functional limitations.
With general application: No
To receive services after enrolling: Yes
What documentation required for ADHD: Diagnosis based on DSM-V; history of behaviors impairing functioning in academic setting; diagnostic interview; history of symptoms; evidence of ongoing behaviors.
With general application: No
To receive services after enrolling: Yes
What documentation required for ASD: Psycho ed evaluation
With general application: NR
To receive services after enrolling: Yes
LD/ADHD/ASD documentation submitted to: DRC
ASD Specific Program: NR
Special Ed. HS course work accepted: Yes
Specific course requirements of all applicants: Yes
Separate application required: No
Total # of students receiving LD/ADHD/ASD services: 190
Acceptance into program means acceptance into college: Students must be admitted to and enrolled in the university first and then request services.

ADMISSIONS

All applicants must meet the same general admission criteria. Admission is very similar to open door admissions, and thus, most applicants are admitted either conditionally or unconditionally or on probation. Average ACT scores are 16-plus; for the SAT, they are 610-plus. Students with LD are encouraged to self-disclose during the application process. There are two types of admission plans: conditional and unconditional. Unconditional admission is met by achieving 970-plus on the SAT. Conditional admission is achieved by scoring 810–960 on the SAT.

ADDITIONAL INFORMATION

Each freshman receives academic endorsement; developmental educational classes in writing, math, or reading (if necessary); access to tutoring or study groups; and academic rescue programs for students in academic jeopardy. Skills classes are offered for no credit in stress management and test anxiety. Letters are sent to faculty each semester, hand delivered by the student. DRC provides tutoring on a limited basis. Students are responsible for registering with the DRC office EACH SEMESTER. Testing accommodations are available, but students are responsible for scheduling the tests. Accommodations include extended testing times, private rooms, scribes, and readers. DRC will also proctor the exam and return the test to the instructor. DRC relies on a volunteer program for note-takers. Services and accommodations are available to undergraduate and graduate students.

General Support Services Information

Contact Information
Name of program or department: Disability Resource Center (DRC)
Telephone: 361-593-3024
Fax: 361-593-2006

Accommodations or Services for Students with Learning Differences

Accommodations are decided upon an individual basis after a thorough review of appropriate, current documentation. The accommodations requested must be supported through the documentation provided and must be logically linked to the current impact of the condition on academic functioning.

Allowed in exams
Calculator: Yes
Dictionary: Yes
Computer: Yes
Spellchecker: Yes
Extended test time: Yes
Scribes: Yes
Proctors: Yes
Oral exams: Yes
Note-takers: Yes
Services for students with LD: Yes
Services for students with ADHD: Yes
Services for students with ASD: Yes
Distraction-reduced environment: Yes
Tape recording in class: Yes
Audio books: NR
Electronic texts: Yes
Kurzweil Reader: No
Other assistive technology: Yes
Priority registration: Yes
Added costs for services: No
LD specialists: No
ADHD coaching: NR
ASD specialists: NR
Professional tutors: No
Peer tutors: Yes
Max. hours/wk. for services: NR
How professors are notified of LD/ADHD: By student

General Admissions Information

Office of Admissions: 361-593-2315

Entrance Requirements

Academic units recommended: 4 English, 3 mathematics, 3 science, 3 foreign language, 4 social studies, 3 history, 3 academic electives. SAT or ACT required for some.

Application deadline: None
Notification: Rolling starting 9/1
Average GPA: NR
ACT Composite middle 50% range: 16–21
SAT Math middle 50% range: 410–540
SAT Critical Reading middle 50% range: 410–520
SAT Writing middle 50% range: NR
Graduated top 10% of class: NR
Graduated top 25% of class: NR
Graduated top 50% of class: NR

COLLEGE GRADUATION REQUIREMENTS

Course waivers allowed: Yes
In what course: Case-by-case decision made by provost
Course substitutions allowed: Yes
In what course: Case-by-case decision made by provost

Additional Information

Environment: The 246-acre university campus is located 40 miles southwest of Corpus Christi.

Student Body
Undergrad enrollment: 5,087
% Women: 47
% Men: 53
% Out-of-state: 2

Cost information
In-state Tuition: $1,380
Out-of-state Tuition: $7,590
Room & board: $3,966

Housing Information
University Housing: Yes
Percent living on campus: 30

Greek System
Fraternity: Yes
Sorority: Yes
Athletics: NR

TEXAS STATE U.—SAN MARCOS

429 North Guadalupe Street, San Marcos, TX 78666
Phone: 512-245-2364 • Fax: 512-245-8044
E-mail: admissions@txstate.edu • Web: www.txstate.edu
Support: CS • Institution: Public

PROGRAMS OR SERVICES FOR STUDENTS WITH LEARNING DIFFERENCES

The mission of the Office of Disability Services (ODS) is to assist students with disabilities to independently achieve their educational goals and enhance their leadership development by ensuring equal access to all programs, activities, and services. This is accomplished through a decentralizing approach in providing education and awareness so that programs, activities, and services are conducted "in the most integrated setting appropriate." Students with learning disabilities are encouraged to self-identify and to submit documentation once admitted. By identifying and assessing student needs, ODS provides direct services and refers students to appropriate resources on and off campus. ODS also promotes awareness of the special needs and abilities of students with disabilities through educational events and outreach activities.

ADMISSION INFORMATION FOR STUDENTS WITH LEARNING DIFFERENCES

College entrance tests required: Yes
Interview required: No
Essay required: N/A
Additional Application Required for LD/ADHD/ASD: NR
What documentation required for LD: Psycho ed evaluation to include: relevant historical info, instructional interventions, related services, age diagnosed, objective data (aptitude, achievement, info processing), test scores (standard, percentile and grade equivalents) and describe functional limitations.
With general application: No
To receive services after enrolling: Yes
What documentation required for ADHD: Diagnosis based on DSM-V; history of behaviors impairing functioning in academic setting; diagnostic interview; history of symptoms; evidence of ongoing behaviors.
With general application: No
To receive services after enrolling: Yes
What documentation required for ASD: Psycho ed evaluation
With general application: NR
To receive services after enrolling: Yes
LD/ADHD/ASD documentation submitted to: Support Program/Services
ASD Specific Program: NR
Special Ed. HS course work accepted: NR
Specific course requirements for all applicants: Yes
Separate application required for program services: No
Total # of students receiving LD/ADHD/ASD services: 527
Acceptance into program means acceptance into college: No

ADMISSIONS

Students with LD must meet the same admission requirements as other applicants. A student whose educational and/or personal goals for success have been negatively impacted by a disability may address any challenges in the essay with their application for admission. This information may be considered during the application process. General admission requirements include: four years English, three years math, three years natural science, three years social science, one year computer science, and two years foreign language; freshman requirements are based on class rank and ACT/SAT scores; a second quarter class ranking would require an ACT score of 22 or SAT score of 1010. The ODS is available to review disability documentation for applicants for admission. This enables the ODS to inform the applicant as to whether or not they will qualify for accommodations at SWT based on the SWT disability guidelines, available from the ODS upon request. Freshmen applicants whose test scores do not meet the minimum requirements for their class rank are eligible for a PAS review if they rank in the top three-quarters of their class. Students in the fourth quarter are not eligible for this review. A limited number of students whose academic record demonstrates potential for academic success at SWT will be offered admission. Factors considered in the review process include specific class rank, size of the graduating class, quality and competitive level of high school courses taken and grades earned,and the applicant's individual verbal and math scores on ACT or SAT.

ADDITIONAL INFORMATION

Specialized support services are based on the individual student disability-based needs. Services available could include special groups registration, recorded textbooks, recording of textbooks not available on tape, arranging for special testing accommodations including extended time and reader services, assistance in accessing adaptive computer equipment, assistance in locating volunteer readers and note-takers, liaison and advocacy between students, faculty and staff, referral for tutoring, disability management counseling, and information and referral to on and off-campus resources.

General Support Services Information

Contact Information
Name of program or department: Office of Disability Services
Telephone: 512.245.3451
Fax: 512.245.3452 • **Website:** http://www.ods.txstate.edu/

Accommodations or Services For Students With Learning Differences

Accommodations are decided upon an individual basis after a thorough review of appropriate, current documentation. The accommodations requests must be supported through the documentation provided and must be logically linked to the current impact of the condition on academic functioning.

Allowed in exams
Calculator: Yes
Dictionary: Yes
Computer: Yes
Spellchecker: Yes
Extended test time: Yes
Scribes: Yes
Proctors: Yes
Oral exams: Yes
Note-takers: Yes
Support services for students with LD: Yes
Support services for students with ADHD: Yes
Support services for students with ASD: Yes
Distraction-reduced environment: Yes
Tape recording in class: Yes
Electronic texts: Yes
Kurzweil reader: NR
Audio books: Yes
Other assistive technology: Yes
Priority registration: Yes
Added costs of services: No
LD specialists: Yes
ADHD coaching: Yes
ASD specialists: Yes
Professional tutors: No
Peer tutors: NR
Max. hours/wk. for services: NR
How professors are notified of student approved accommodations: By both student and director

General Admissions Information

Office of Admissions: 512-245-2364

Entrance Requirements

Academic units required: 4 English, 4 math, 4 science, 2 science labs, 2 foreign language, 2 social studies, 2 history, 7 academic electives, 1 visual/performing arts, and 1 units from above areas or other academic areas.
Academic units recommended: 4 English, 4 math, 4 science, 2 science labs, 2 foreign language, 2 social studies, 2 history, 6 academic electives, 1 visual/performing arts, and 1 units from above areas or other academic areas. High school diploma is required and GED is accepted. SAT or ACT required. If ACT, ACT with writing required. TOEFL required of all international applicants: minimum paper TOEFL 550 or minimum internet TOEFL 78.

Application deadline: 5/1
Notification: By both student and director
Average GPA: NR
ACT Composite middle 50% range: 21-25
SAT Math middle 50% range: 470-560
SAT Critical Reading middle 50% range: 460-560
SAT Writing middle 50% range: 440-530
Graduate top 10% of class: 12
Graduated top 25% of class: 48
Graduated top 50% of class: 93

COLLEGE GRADUATION REQUIREMENTS

Course waivers allowed: No
Course substitutions allowed: Yes
In what course: Substitutions are primarily considered for Math and Foreign Language courses.

Additional Information

Environment: This public school was founded in 1899. It has a 455-acre campus.

Student Body
Undergrad enrollment: 33,480
% Women: 57
% Men: 43
% Out-of-state: 2

Cost information
In-state Tuition: $7,536
Out-of-state Tuition: $19,236
Room & board: $7,840
Housing Information
University Housing: Yes
Percent living on campus: 20

Greek System
Fraternity: Yes
Sorority: Yes
Athletics: Division I

TEXAS TECH UNIVERSITY

PO Box 45005, Lubbock, TX 79409-5005
Phone: 806-742-1480 • Fax: 806-742-0062
E-mail: admissions@ttu.edu • Web: www.ttu.edu
Support: CS • Institution: Public

PROGRAMS OR SERVICES FOR STUDENTS WITH LEARNING DIFFERENCES

It is the philosophy of Texas Tech University to serve each student on a case-by-case basis. All services rendered are supported by adequate documentation. We firmly believe that all students should be and will become effective self-advocates. Students with disabilities attending Texas Tech will find numerous programs designed to provide services and promote access to all phases of university activity. Such programming is coordinated through the Dean of Students's Office with the assistance of an advisory committee of both disabled and non-disabled students, faculty, and staff. Services to disabled students are offered through a decentralized network of university and nonuniversity resources. This means that many excellent services are available, but it is up to the student to initiate them. Each student is encouraged to act as his or her own advocate and take the major responsibility for securing services and accommodations. The Disabled Student Services team, Dean of Students's Office, faculty, and staff are supportive in this effort.

ADMISSION INFORMATION FOR STUDENTS WITH LEARNING DIFFERENCES

College entrance tests required: Yes
Interview required: No
Essay required: No
Additional Application Required for LD/ADHD/ASD: NR
What documentation required for LD: Psycho ed evaluation to include: relevant historical info, instructional interventions, related services, age diagnosed, objective data (aptitude, achievement, info processing), test scores (standard, percentile and grade equivalents) and describe functional limitations.
With general application: No
To receive services after enrolling: Yes
What documentation required for ADHD: Diagnosis based on DSM-V; history of behaviors impairing functioning in academic setting; diagnostic interview; history of symptoms; evidence of ongoing behaviors.
With general application: No
To receive services after enrolling: Yes
What documentation required for ASD: Psycho ed evaluation
With general application: NR
To receive services after enrolling: Yes
LD/ADHD/ASD documentation submitted to: PASS
ASD Specific Program: NR
Special Ed. HS course work accepted: Yes
Specific course requirements of all applicants: Yes
Separate application required: Yes
Total # of students receiving LD/ADHD/ASD services: 600
Acceptance into program means acceptance into college: Students must be admitted to and enrolled in the university first and then request services.

ADMISSIONS

There is no special admissions process for students with LD, and all applicants must meet the same criteria. All students must have 4 years of English, 3 years of math, 2.5 years of social studies, 2 years of science, and 3.5 years of electives. Any applicant who scores a 1200 on the SAT or a 29 on the ACT is automatically admitted regardless of class rank. Some students are admissible who do not meet the stated requirements, but they must have a 2.0 GPA for a provisional admission. After a student is admitted, Disabled Student Services requires documentation that provides a diagnosis and an indication of the severity of the disability and offers recommendations for accommodations for students to receive services.

ADDITIONAL INFORMATION

Support services through Disabled Student Services include academic support services, which can help students develop habits enabling them to get a good education. Students may receive academic support services in the PASS (Programs for Academic Support Services) Center, which is open to all students on campus. Services offered free of charge include tutor referral services (paid by student); study skills group; hour-long workshops that target a variety of subjects from overcoming math anxiety to preparing for finals; a self-help learning lab with videotapes; computer-assisted instruction; individual consultations assisting students with specific study problems; and setting study skills improvement goals. All students with LD are offered priority registration. Services and accommodations are available for undergraduate and graduate students.

General Support Services Information

Contact Information
Name of program or department: Student Disability Services
Telephone: 806-742-2405
Fax: 806-742-4837
Website: www.depts.ttu.edu/sds/

Accommodations or Services For Students With Learning Differences

Accommodations are decided upon an individual basis after a thorough review of appropriate, current documentation. The accommodations requests must be supported through the documentation provided and must be logically linked to the current impact of the condition on academic functioning.

Allowed in exams
Calculator: NR
Dictionary: NR
Computer: NR
Spellchecker: NR
Extended test time: Yes
Scribes: Yes
Proctors: NR
Oral exams: NR
Note-takers: Yes
Support services for students with LD: Yes
Support services for students with ADHD: Yes
Support services for students with ASD: Yes
Distraction-reduced environment: NR
Tape recording in class: Yes
Electronic texts: Yes
Kurzweil reader: NR
Audio books: NR
Other assistive technology: NR
Priority registration: Yes
Added costs of services: Yes
LD specialists: Yes
ADHD coaching: Yes
ASD specialists: Yes
Professional tutors: Yes
Peer tutors: Yes
Max. hours/wk. for services: 7
How professors are notified of student approved accommodations: By student

General Admissions Information

Office of Admissions: 806-742-1480

Entrance Requirements

Academic units required: 4 English, 3 math, 3 science, 3 science labs, 2 foreign language, 3 social studies, 5 academic electives, 1 visual/performing arts, and 1 units from above areas or other academic areas. **Academic units recommended:** 4 English, 4 math, 4 science, 4 science labs, 2 foreign language, 6 academic electives, 1 visual/performing arts, and 2 units from above areas or other academic areas. High school diploma is required and GED is accepted. SAT or ACT required. If ACT, ACT with writing accepted. TOEFL required of all international applicants: minimum paper TOEFL 550 or minimum internet TOEFL 79.

Application deadline: 8/1
Notification: Rolling starting 10/1
Average GPA: NR
ACT Composite middle 50% range: 23-27
SAT Math middle 50% range: 520-620
SAT Critical Reading middle 50% range: 510-600
SAT Writing middle 50% range: 470-570
Graduate top 10% of class: 20
Graduated top 25% of class: 55
Graduated top 50% of class: 86

COLLEGE GRADUATION REQUIREMENTS

Course waivers allowed: No
Course substitutions allowed: Yes
In what course: Math, Foreign Language, and Physical Education.

Additional Information

Environment: This public school was founded in 1923. It has a 1839-acre campus.

Student Body
Undergrad enrollment: 29,237
% Women: 45
% Men: 55
% Out-of-state: 6

Cost information
In-state Tuition: $7,984
Out-of-state Tuition: $15,224
Room & board: $9,760

Housing Information
University Housing: Yes
Percent living on campus: 25

Greek System
Fraternity: Yes
Sorority: Yes
Athletics: Division I

University of Houston

Office of Admissions, Houston, TX 77204-2023
Phone: 713-743-1010 • Fax: 713-743-7542
E-mail: admissions@uh.edu • Web: www.uh.edu
Support: CS • Institution: Public

Programs or Services for Students with Learning Differences

The Center for Students with DisABILITIES provides a wide variety of academic support services to students with all types of disabilities. Our goal is to help ensure that these otherwise qualified students are able to successfully compete with non-disabled students by receiving equal educational opportunities in college as mandated by law. Through advocacy efforts and a deliberate, ongoing, public education program, the staff strives to heighten the awareness of disability issues, educational rights, and abilities of persons who have disabilities.

Admission Information for Students with Learning Differences

College entrance tests required: Yes
Interview required: No
Additional Application Required for LD/ADHD/ASD: NR
What documentation required for LD: Psycho ed evaluation to include: relevant historical info, instructional interventions, related services, age diagnosed, objective data (aptitude, achievement, info processing), test scores (standard, percentile and grade equivalents) and describe functional limitations.
With general application: No
To receive services after enrolling: Yes
What documentation required for ADHD: Diagnosis based on DSM-V; history of behaviors impairing functioning in academic setting; diagnostic interview; history of symptoms; evidence of ongoing behaviors.
With general application: No
To receive services after enrolling: Yes
What documentation required for ASD: Psycho ed evaluation
With general application: NR
To receive services after enrolling: Yes
LD/ADHD/ASD documentation submitted to: Support Program/Services
ASD Specific Program: NR
Special Ed. HS course work accepted: Yes
Specific course requirements for all applicants: Yes
Separate application required for program services: No
Total # of students receiving LD/ADHD/ASD services: 226
Acceptance into program means acceptance into college: Students must be admitted to and enrolled in the university first and then request services.

Admissions

Admission is automatic for Texas residents in the top 15 percent of the class. Other applicants must meet one of the following criteria: Top 16-25 percent of the class have an SAT score of 1000 or higher or an ACT score of 21 or higher; Top 26-50 percent class rank with an 1100 SAT score or higher or an ACT score of 24 or higher. Applicants who do not meet these admissions criteria will be reviewed in light of the applicant's academic rigor, community service, extracurricular activities, and surmounting obstacles to pursue higher education. Letters of reference from high school teachers, counselors, supervisors and activity leaders along with personal statements are welcome additions to an applicant's file.

Additional Information

Students who come from an educationally and/or economically disadvantaged background may be eligible to participate in the UH 'Challenger Program' which is designed to provide intense support to students who face obstacles in their efforts to successfully complete college. Services to all students include: tutoring, counseling, financial aid advisement, and social enrichment. Remedial reading, writing, and study skills courses for three hours of non-college credit are offered. There are also remedial courses for credit in English and college algebra. Other services include assistance with petitions for course substitutions, peer support groups, free carbonized paper for note-taking, textbooks and class handouts put on tape by office staff or volunteer readers, and advocacy for student's legal rights to "reasonable and necessary accommodations" in their course work. Extended tutoring is available at the Learning Support Services and Math Lab.

General Support Services Information

Contact Information
Name of program or department: Center for Students with Disabilities
Telephone: 713-743-5400
Fax: 713-743-5396

Accommodations or Services for Students with Learning Differences

Accommodations are decided upon an individual basis after a thorough review of appropriate, current documentation. The accommodations requested must be supported through the documentation provided and must be logically linked to the current impact of the condition on academic functioning.

Allowed in exams
Calculator: Yes
Dictionary: Yes
Computer: Yes
Spellchecker: Yes
Extended test time: Yes
Scribes: Yes
Proctors: Yes
Oral exams: Yes
Note-takers: Yes
Services for students with LD: Yes
Services for students with ADHD: Yes
Services for students with ASD: Yes
Distraction-reduced environment: Yes
Tape recording in class: Yes
Audio books: NR
Electronic texts: Yes
Kurzweil Reader: Yes
Other assistive technology: JAWS, Zoomtext, headmouse, Handiword, FmLoop, CCTV, voice activated software, etc.
Priority registration: Yes
Added costs for services: No
LD specialists: Yes
ADHD coaching: NR
ASD specialists: NR
Professional tutors: No
Peer tutors: Yes
Max. hours/wk. for services: 4
How professors are notified of LD/ADHD: Student

General Admissions Information

Office of Admissions: 713-743-1010

Entrance Requirements

Academic units required: 4 English, 4 math, 4 science, 4 social studies. **Academic units recommended:** 2 science labs, 2 foreign language, 1 computer science, 1 visual/performing arts. High school diploma is required and GED is accepted. SAT or ACT required. If ACT, ACT with writing accepted. TOEFL required of all international applicants: minimum paper TOEFL 550 or minimum internet TOEFL 79.

Application deadline: 7/1
Notification: Rolling starting 9/15
Average GPA: NR
ACT Composite middle 50% range: 23-28
SAT Math middle 50% range: 540-640
SAT Critical Reading middle 50% range: 510-610
SAT Writing middle 50% range: NR-NR
Graduate top 10% of class: 30
Graduated top 25% of class: 64
Graduated top 50% of class: 89

COLLEGE GRADUATION REQUIREMENTS

Course waivers allowed: NR
Course substitutions allowed: NR
In what course: foreign language

Additional Information

Environment: This public school was founded in 1927. It has a 551-acre campus.

Student Body
Undergrad enrollment: 34,716
% Women: 49
% Men: 51
% Out-of-state: 2

Cost information
In-state Tuition: $9,756
Out-of-state Tuition: $24,456
Room & board: $9,849

Housing Information
University Housing: Yes
Percent living on campus: 19

Greek System
Fraternity: Yes
Sorority: Yes
Athletics: Division I

The University of Texas at Austin

PO Box 8058, Austin, TX 78713-8058
Phone: 512-475-7399 • Fax: 512-475-7478
E-mail: http://bealonghorn.utexas.edu/ask/contac • Web: www.utexas.edu
Support: CS • Institution: Public

Programs or Services for Students with Learning Differences

Services for Students with Disabilities (SSD) provides a program of support and advocacy for students with LD. Services offered include assistance with learning strategies, note-takers for lectures, scribe/readers, and extended time for in-class work. There is also a Tutoring and Learning Center whose free services include study skill assistance, subject-area tutoring, life management skills, exam reviews, peer mentoring, and distance tutoring.

Admission Information for Students with Learning Differences

College entrance tests required: Yes
Interview required: No
Essay required: No
Additional Application Required for LD/ADHD/ASD: NR
What documentation required for LD: Current diagnostic report, comprehensive and include aptitude and achievement testing, and specific evidence of a learning disability
With general application: NR
To receive services after enrolling: Yes
What documentation required for ADHD: Information regarding onset, longevity, and severity of the symptoms; impact of ADHD on educational setting; medication history and current recommendations regarding medication, the exact DSM–IV diagnosis, and information concerning co-morbidity should also be included in the evaluation.
LD/ADHD/ASD documentation submitted to: Services for Students with Disabilities (SSD)
ASD Specific Program: NR
Special Ed. HS course work accepted: Yes
Specific course requirements of all applicants: Yes
Separate application required: N/A
Total # of students receiving LD/ADHD/ASD services: 305
Acceptance into program means acceptance into college: Students must be admitted to and enrolled in the university first and then request services.

Admissions

There is no special admissions process for students with learning disabilities. General admission criteria requires students to have a high school diploma and ACT/SAT results, and they are not interested in class rank or GPA. Course requirements include 4 years of English, 3 years of math, 3 years of science, 4 years of social studies, 3 years of a foreign language, 0.5 year of health, 1 year of fine arts, 1.5 years of physical education, and 1 year of computer science. For students not otherwise eligible to enter due to grades or scores, a study skills class is required plus other courses from a course list.

Additional Information

To receive services, students must meet an SSD coordinator. Students need to provide current documentation from an appropriate licensed professional. Services offered to students, when appropriate, assistance with learning strategies, and priority registration. The Assistive Technology gives students access to various supports to help them with their studies and testing with screen readers and other technology. There is a support group for UT students with ASD. Classroom accommodations include note-takers, assistive technology, scribes, readers, and extended testing times. In the Tutoring and Learning Center, students can access study skills assistance, subject area tutoring, life management skills assistance, and a special needs room with state of the art technology. Currently there are 305 students with LD and 745 with ADHD receiving services. Students may request that instructors make course materials displayed on Power Point slides available for review.

General Support Services Information

Contact Information
Name of program or department: Services for Students with Disabilities
Telephone: 512-471-6259
Fax: 512-475-7730
Website: ddce.utexas.edu/disability

Accommodations or Services for Students with Learning Differences

Accommodations are decided upon an individual basis after a thorough review of appropriate, current documentation. The accommodations requests must be supported through the documentation provided and must be logically linked to the current impact of the condition on academic functioning.

Allowed in exams
Calculator: Yes
Dictionary: Yes
Computer: Yes
Spellchecker: Yes
Extended test time: Yes
Scribes: Yes
Proctors: Yes
Oral exams: Yes
Note-takers: Yes
Support services for students with LD: Yes
Support services for students with ADHD: Yes
Support services for students with ASD: Yes
Distraction-reduced environment: Yes
Tape recording in class: Yes
Electronic texts: Yes
Kurzweil reader: NR
Audio books: Yes
Other assistive technology: Yes
Priority registration: Yes
Added costs of services: NR
LD specialists: Yes
ADHD coaching: No
ASD specialists: NR
Professional tutors: No
Peer tutors: NR
Max. hours/wk. for services: NR
How professors are notified of student approved accommodations: By student

General Admissions Information

Office of Admissions: 512-475-7399

Entrance Requirements

Academic units required: 4 English, 4 math, 4 science, 2 foreign language, 4 social studies, 6 academic electives, and 2 units from above areas or other academic areas. High school diploma is required and GED is accepted. SAT or ACT required. If ACT, ACT with writing required. TOEFL required of all international applicants: minimum paper TOEFL 550 or minimum internet TOEFL 79.

Application deadline: 12/1
Notification: NR
Average GPA: NR
ACT Composite middle 50% range: 26-31
SAT Math middle 50% range: 600-710
SAT Critical Reading middle 50% range: 570-680
SAT Writing middle 50% range: 560-680
Graduate top 10% of class: 72
Graduated top 25% of class: 92
Graduated top 50% of class: 98

College Graduation Requirements

Course waivers allowed: No
Course substitutions allowed: Yes
In what course: foreign language (only if criteria is met and process is followed)

Additional Information

Environment: This public school was founded in 1883. It has a 350-acre campus.

Student Body
Undergrad enrollment: 39,619
% Women: 52
% Men: 48
% Out-of-state: 5.3

Cost information
In-state Tuition: $9,806
Out-of-state Tuition: $34,676
Room & board: $11,456

Housing Information
University Housing: Yes
Percent living on campus: 18.8

Greek System
Fraternity: Yes
Sorority: Yes
Athletics: Division I

University of Texas— Pan American

1201 West University Drive, Edinburg, TX 78539-2999
Phone: 956-665-2999 • Fax: 956-665-2687
E-mail: admissions@utpa.edu • Web: www.utpa.edu
Support: S • Institution: Public

Programs or Services for Students with Learning Differences*

Disability Services is a component of the Division of Student Affairs at the University of Texas—Pan American. It is designed and committed to providing support services to meet the educational, career, and personal needs of persons with disabilities attending or planning to attend the university. Students requesting accommodations must provide documentation from a professional who is qualified to diagnose and verify the particular disability; and the testing and documentation must be current. Disability Services will use the documentation to properly prepare an assistance plan for the student to use while enrolled at the university.

Admission Information for Students with Learning Differences

College entrance tests required: Yes
Interview required: No
Essay required: N/A
Additional Application Required for LD/ADHD/ASD: NR
What documentation required for LD: Psycho ed evaluation to include: relevant historical info, instructional interventions, related services, age diagnosed, objective data (aptitude, achievement, info processing), test scores (standard, percentile and grade equivalents) and describe functional limitations.
With general application: No
To receive services after enrolling: Yes
What documentation required for ADHD: Diagnosis based on DSM-V; history of behaviors impairing functioning in academic setting; diagnostic interview; history of symptoms; evidence of ongoing behaviors.
With general application: No
To receive services after enrolling: Yes
What documentation required for ASD: Psycho ed evaluation
With general application: No
To receive services after enrolling: Yes
LD/ADHD/ASD documentation submitted to: Support Program/Services
ASD Specific Program: NR
Special Ed. HS course work accepted: No
Specific course requirements for all applicants: NR
Separate application required for program services: Yes
Total # of students receiving LD/ADHD/ASD services: 66
Acceptance into program means acceptance into college: Separate application required after student has enrolled

Admissions

Students with learning disabilities must meet the same admission requirements as all other applicants. The admissions requirements for entering freshmen are: a) graduation in top ten percent of high school class; or b) ACT Composite scores 18 or SAT Critical Reading and Math Composite of 860; c) recommended or higher graduation plan or GED certificate.

Additional Information

Disability Services provides the following services: assessment for special needs; note-takers; readers and writers; advisement, counseling, and guidance; assistance with admissions, orientation, registration; referral services to other university units; interpreting services; liaison between students, faculty, staff, and others; resolution of problems/concerns; computer hardware and software; Kurzweil Reader; and Juliet Pro embosser. There are workshops for students who need help with Effective Note Taking and Studying; Time Management; Learning Styles, Test Anxiety & Strategies, and Stress Management. Services and accommodations are available for undergraduate and graduate students.

General Support Services Information

Contact Information
Name of program or department: Disability Services
Telephone: 956-665-7005
Fax: 956-665-2450

Accommodations or Services for Students with Learning Differences

Disability Services provides the following services: note-takers; scribes; registration; referral services to other university services; interpreting services; alternative formats; liaison between students, faculty, staff, and others; resolution of problems/concerns; computer hardware and software; and assistive technology lab. Services and accommodations are available for undergraduate and graduate students.

Allowed in exams
Calculator: Yes
Dictionary: Yes
Computer: Yes
Spellchecker: Yes
Extended test time: Yes
Scribes: Yes
Proctors: Yes
Oral exams: Yes
Note-takers: Yes
Services for students with LD: Yes
Services for students with ADHD: Yes
Services for students with ASD: Yes
Distraction-reduced environment: Yes
Tape recording in class: Yes
Audio books: Yes
Electronic texts: Yes
Kurzweil Reader: No
Other assistive technology: JAWS, pocket talker, Braille format, readers, large print, etc.
Priority registration: No
Added costs for services: No
LD specialists: No
ADHD coaching: No
ASD specialists: No
Professional tutors: No
Peer tutors: No
Max. hours/wk. for services: 40
How professors are notified of LD/ADHD: Student

General Admissions Information

Office of Admissions: (956) 665-2999

Entrance Requirements

Academic units required: 4 English, 4 math, 4 science, 2 foreign language, and 3 units from above areas or other academic areas. High school diploma is required and GED is accepted. SAT or ACT required. If ACT, ACT with writing accepted. TOEFL required of all international applicants: minimum paper TOEFL 500 or minimum internet TOEFL 63.

Application deadline: 7/31
Notification: NR
Average GPA: NR
ACT Composite middle 50% range: 18-22
SAT Math middle 50% range: 440-540
SAT Critical Reading middle 50% range: 420-520
SAT Writing middle 50% range: 410-510
Graduated top 10% of class: 22
Graduated top 25% of class: 53
Graduated top 50% of class: 83

COLLEGE GRADUATION REQUIREMENTS

Course waivers allowed: Yes
In what course: It depends on the degree plan. Requests can be made through the Program Advisors, Department Chairs, and the VP for Academic Affairs. An appeal process is required.
Course substitutions allowed: Yes
In what course: On a case-by-case basis

Additional Information

Environment: This public school was founded in 1927. It has a 330-acre campus.

Student Body
Undergrad enrollment: 18,200
% Women: 56
% Men: 44
% Out-of-state: 0.45

Cost information
In-state Tuition: $6,134
Out-of-state Tuition: $17,182
Room & board: $7,444

Housing Information
University Housing: Yes
Percent living on campus: 4.3

Greek System
Fraternity: NR
Sorority: NR
Athletics: Division I

Brigham Young University

A-153 ASB, Provo, UT 84602-1110
Phone: 801-422-2507 • Fax: 801-422-0005
E-mail: admissions@byu.edu • Web: www.byu.edu
Support: CS • Institution: Private

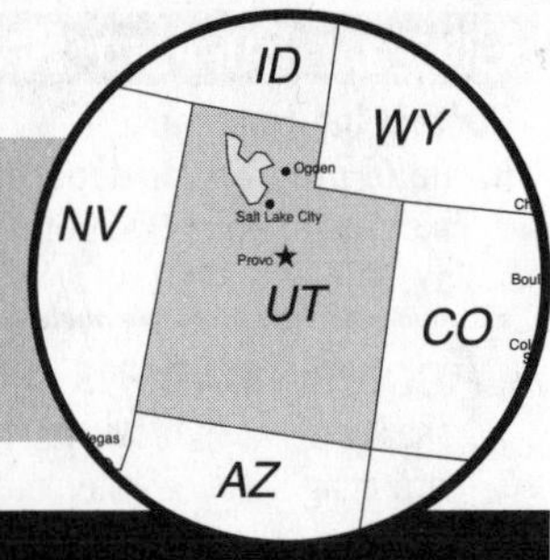

Programs or Services for Students with Learning Differences

The University Accessibility Center works to provide individualized programs to meet the specific needs of each student with a disability, assisting in developing strengths to meet the challenges, and making arrangements for accommodations and special services as required.

Admission Information for Students with Learning Differences

College entrance tests required: Yes
Interview required: N/A
Essay required: N/A
Additional Application Required for LD/ADHD/ASD: NR
What documentation required for LD: Psycho ed evaluation to include: relevant historical info, instructional interventions, related services, age diagnosed, objective data (aptitude, achievement, info processing), test scores (standard, percentile and grade equivalents) and describe functional limitations.
With general application: No
To receive services after enrolling: Yes
What documentation required for ADHD: Diagnosis based on DSM-V; history of behaviors impairing functioning in academic setting; diagnostic interview; history of symptoms; evidence of ongoing behaviors.
With general application: No
To receive services after enrolling: Yes
What documentation required for ASD: Psycho ed evaluation
With general application: NR
To receive services after enrolling: Yes
LD/ADHD/ASD documentation submitted to: Support Program/Services
ASD Specific Program: NR
Special Ed. HS course work accepted: N/A
Specific course requirements for all applicants: Yes
Separate application required for program services: Yes
Total # of students receiving LD/ADHD/ASD services: 110–130
Acceptance into program means acceptance into college: NR

Admissions

There is no special admission process for students with learning disabilities. Suggested courses include: four years English, three to four years math, two to three years science, two years history or government, two years foreign language, and two years of literature or writing. Evaluations are made on an individualized basis with a system weighted for college-prep courses and core classes.

Additional Information

Non-credit workshops and a study skill class are offered for all student and often recommended to students with learning concerns. The following topics are some examples: math anxiety, memory, overcoming procrastination, self-appreciation, stress management, test-taking, textbook comprehension, time management, and communication. Additional services include counseling support and advising. Services and accommodations are available for undergraduate and graduate students. There are academic learning services available through the Academic Learning Department. There is a Reading Center, Writing Center, Math Study Center, and a Study Skills Center. They are provided at no extra cost. There are several opportunities for obtaining tutors. An excellent volunteer program, also many of the general education classes offer labs where students can receive help free of charge.

General Support Services Information

Contact Information
Name of program or department: University Accessibility Center
Telephone: 801-422-2767
Fax: 801-422-0174

Accommodations or Services for Students with Learning Differences

Accommodations are decided upon an individual basis after a thorough review of appropriate, current documentation. The accommodations requested must be supported through the documentation provided and must be logically linked to the current impact of the condition on academic functioning.

Allowed in exams
Calculator: Yes
Dictionary: Yes
Computer: Yes
Spellchecker: Yes
Extended test time: Yes
Scribes: Yes
Proctors: Yes
Oral exams: Yes
Note-takers: Yes
Services for students with LD: Yes
Services for students with ADHD: Yes
Services for students with ASD: Yes
Distraction-reduced environment: Yes
Tape recording in class: Yes
Audio books: NR
Electronic texts: Yes
Kurzweil Reader: Yes
Other assistive technology: N/A
Priority registration: Yes
Added costs for services: No
LD specialists: Yes
ADHD coaching: NR
ASD specialists: NR
Professional tutors: 0
Peer tutors: 100
Max. hours/wk. for services:
How professors are notified of LD/ADHD: Both student and director

General Admissions Information

Office of Admissions: 801-422-2507

Entrance Requirements

Academic units recommended: 4 English, 4 math, 3 science, 2 foreign language, 2 history. High school diploma is required and GED is accepted. SAT or ACT required. If ACT, ACT with writing accepted. TOEFL required of all international applicants: minimum paper TOEFL 500.

Application deadline: 2/1
Notification: 2/28
Average GPA: 3.83
ACT Composite middle 50% range: 27-31
SAT Math middle 50% range: 580-680
SAT Critical Reading middle 50% range: 570-680
SAT Writing middle 50% range: 550-660
Graduated top 10% of class: 54
Graduated top 25% of class: 85
Graduated top 50% of class: 98

COLLEGE GRADUATION REQUIREMENTS

Course waivers allowed: No
In what course: NR
Course substitutions allowed: Yes
In what course: General education, foreign language, and/or math

Additional Information

Environment: This private school, affiliated with the Church of Jesus Christ of Latt Church, was founded in 1875. It has a 557-acre campus.

Student Body
Undergrad enrollment: 30,221
% Women: 48
% Men: 52
% Out-of-state: 66

Cost information
Tuition: $5,150
Room & board: $7,330

Housing Information
University Housing: Yes
Percent living on campus: 19

Greek System
Fraternity: No
Sorority: No
Athletics: Division I

Southern Utah University

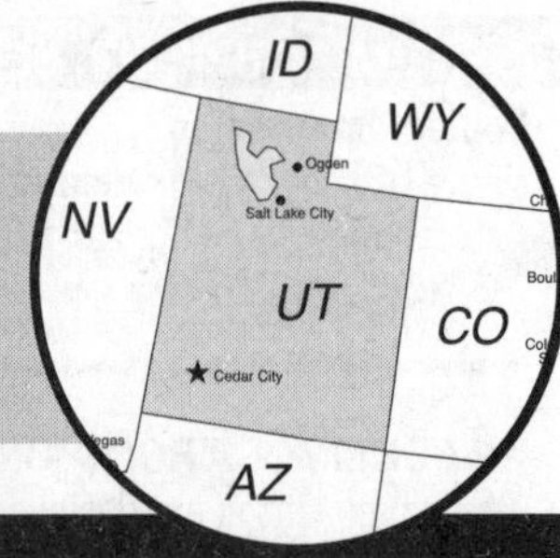

S. Utah University, 351 W University Boulevard, Cedar City, UT 84720
Phone: 435-586-7740 • Fax: 435-865-8223
E-mail: adminfo@suu.edu • Web: www.suu.edu

Support: S • Institution: Public

Programs or Services for Students with Learning Differences

The philosophy of the Office of Students with Disabilities is to promote self-sufficiency, achievement and support students with disabilities. OSD assists college students with developmental classes, skills courses, academic and tutorial support, and advisement. In particular, disabled students are encouraged and supported in advocating for themselves. The university provides a full variety of services and accommodations for all disabled students. The academic support coordinator assists students with enrollment in OSD and helps them identify academic areas where they feel a need to strengthen skills to assure college success.

Admission Information for Students with Learning Differences

College entrance tests required: Yes
Interview required: N/A
Essay required: N/A
Additional Application Required for LD/ADHD/ASD: NR
What documentation required for LD: Psycho ed evaluation to include: relevant historical info, instructional interventions, related services, age diagnosed, objective data (aptitude, achievement, info processing), test scores (standard, percentile and grade equivalents) and describe functional limitations.
With general application: No
To receive services after enrolling: Yes
What documentation required for ADHD: Diagnosis based on DSM-V; history of behaviors impairing functioning in academic setting; diagnostic interview; history of symptoms; evidence of ongoing behaviors.
With general application: No
To receive services after enrolling: Yes
What documentation required for ASD: Psycho ed evaluation
With general application: NR
To receive services after enrolling: Yes
LD/ADHD/ASD documentation submitted to: Support Program/Services
ASD Specific Program: NR
Special Ed. HS course work accepted: No
Specific course requirements for all applicants: Yes
Separate application required for program services: No
Total # of students receiving LD/ADHD/ASD services: 94
Acceptance into program means acceptance into college: Students must be admitted to and enrolled in the university first and then request services.

Admissions

Students with learning disabilities submit the general application form. Students must have at least a 2.0 GPA and show competency in English, math, science, and social studies. The university uses an admissions index derived from the combination of the high school GPA and results of either the ACT or SAT. If students are not admissible through the regular process, special consideration by a Committee Review can be gained through reference letters and a personal letter. The university is allowed to admit 5 percent in "flex" admission. These applications are reviewed by a committee consisting of the Director of Support Services and representatives from the Admissions Office. Students are encouraged to self-disclose their learning disability and submit documentation.

Additional Information

Students with disabilities are evaluated by the Office of Students with Disabilities to determine accommodations or services. The following accommodations or services may be available on a case-by-case basis for students with appropriate documentation: the use of calculators, dictionary, computer or spell checker in exams; extended testing time; scribes; proctors; oral exams; note-takers; distraction-free testing environments; tape recorders in class; books on tape; assistive technolgy; and priority registration. Tutoring is available in small groups or one-to-one, free of charge. Basic skills classes, for credit, are offered in English, reading, math, math anxiety, language, and study skills.

General Support Services Information

Contact Information
Name of program or department: Office of Students with Disabilities
Telephone: 435-865-8022
Fax: 435-865-8235

Accommodations or Services for Students with Learning Differences

Accommodations are decided upon an individual basis after a thorough review of appropriate, current documentation. The accommodations requested must be supported through the documentation provided and must be logically linked to the current impact of the condition on academic functioning.

Allowed in exams
Calculator: No
Dictionary: Yes
Computer: Yes
Spellchecker: Yes
Extended test time: Yes
Scribes: Yes
Proctors: Yes
Oral exams: Yes
Note-takers: Yes
Services for students with LD: Yes
Services for students with ADHD: Yes
Services for students with ASD: Yes
Distraction-reduced environment: Yes
Tape recording in class: Yes
Audio books: NR
Electronic texts: Yes
Kurzweil Reader: Yes
Other assistive technology: We evaluate our students with disabilities population and depending who we serve and the need, we will make accommodations.
Priority registration: Yes
Added costs for services: No
LD specialists: No
ADHD coaching: NR
ASD specialists: NR
Professional tutors: No
Peer tutors: No
Max. hours/wk. for services: N/A
How professors are notified of LD/ADHD: Both student and director, and by letter

General Admissions Information

Office of Admissions: 435-586-7740

Entrance Requirements

Academic units recommended: 4 English, 4 math, 3 science, 1 science labs, 2 foreign language, 3 social studies. High school diploma is required and GED is accepted. SAT or ACT required. If ACT, ACT with writing accepted. TOEFL required of all international applicants: minimum paper TOEFL 525 or minimum internet TOEFL 71.

Application deadline: 5/1
Notification: NR
Average GPA: 3.53
ACT Composite middle 50% range: 20-27
SAT Math middle 50% range: 450-570
SAT Critical Reading middle 50% range: 450-590
SAT Writing middle 50% range: 440-570
Graduate top 10% of class: 18
Graduated top 25% of class: 47
Graduated top 50% of class: 77

COLLEGE GRADUATION REQUIREMENTS

Course waivers allowed: NR
Course substitutions allowed: NR

Additional Information

Environment: This public school was founded in 1897. It has a 113-acre campus.

Student Body
Undergrad enrollment: 8,035
% Women: 57
% Men: 43
% Out-of-state: 21

Cost information
In-state Tuition: $495 per credit
Out-of-state Tuition: $1,501 per credit
Room & board: NR

Housing Information
University Housing: Yes
Percent living on campus: 10

Greek System
Fraternity: Yes
Sorority: Yes
Athletics: Division I

UNIVERSITY OF UTAH

201 South 1460 East, Salt Lake City, UT 84112
Phone: 801-581-7281 • Fax: 801-585-7864
E-mail: admissions@sa.utah.edu • Web: www.utah.edu
Support: CS • Institution: Public

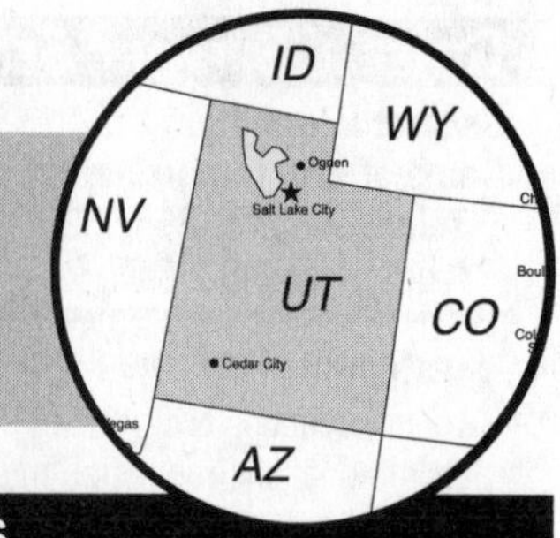

PROGRAMS OR SERVICES FOR STUDENTS WITH LEARNING DIFFERENCES

The Center for Disability Services at the University of Utah provides accommodations and support for students with disabilities who have current physical or psychological documentation that qualifies them for services. The goal is to provide assistance to encourage and enhance student's independence, maintain ongoing cooperative efforts to develop and maintain an accessible physical environment, and provide educational efforts to create a supportive psychological environment for students to achieve their educational objectives. A cooperative relationship is maintained with relevant campus departments to ensure the University of Utah complies with federal and state regulations regarding students with disabilities.

ADMISSION INFORMATION FOR STUDENTS WITH LEARNING DIFFERENCES

College entrance test required: Yes
Interview required: Not Applicable
Essay required: Not Applicable
Additional Application Required for LD/ADHD/ASD: Yes
What documentation required for LD: Psycho ed evaluation
With general application: No
To receive services after enrolling: Yes
What documentation required for ADHD: Psycho ed evaluation
With general application: No
To receive services after enrolling: Yes
What documentation required for ASD: Psycho ed evaluation
With general application: No
To receive services after enrolling: Yes
LD/ADHD/ASD documentation submitted to: Center for Disability Services
ASD Specific Program: NR
Special Ed. HS course work accepted: Not Applicable
Specific course requirements of all applicants: NR
Separate application required for program services: Yes
Total # of students receiving LD/ADHD/ASD services: 370
Acceptance into program means acceptance into college: No

ADMISSIONS

There is no special application process for students with learning disabilities. All applicants to the university must meet the general admission requirements. Students who do not meet the admission requirements as a direct result of their disability may be admitted on the condition that course deficiencies are filled prior to earning 30 semester hours at the university. Conditional admission is determined by the Center for Disability Services and the Admissions Office. Students must provide appropriate information regarding their disability and any services they received in high school due to their disability. Self-disclosure is recommended only if the student needs to inform the Admissions Office they are working with the Center for Disability Services to consider conditional admission. Otherwise disclosure is not recommended, but it is left to the student to make the decision.

ADDITIONAL INFORMATION

The University of Utah is committed to providing reasonable accommodations to students whose disabilities may limit their ability to function in the academic setting. To meet the needs of students and to make university activities, programs, and facilities accessible, the Center for Disability Services can provide the following services to students who provide documentation of a disability: assistance with admissions, registration, and graduation; orientation to the campus; referrals to campus and community services; guidelines for obtaining CDS services; general and academic advising related to disability; investigation of academic strengths and weaknesses; develop effective learning strategies; coordinate with academic and departmental advisors regarding program goals; coordinate reasonable accommodations of disability-related limitations with faculty and staff; liaison between student and faculty or staff; provide readers, scribes, note-takers, textbooks, and printed material recorded onto cassettes; and arrange for exam accommodations. The Center for Disability Services has the right to set procedures to determine whether the student qualifies for services and how the services will be implemented. Additionally, the center has the responsibility to adjust or substitute academic requirements that unfairly discriminate against the student with a disability and that are not essential to the integrity of a student's academic program. Students must provide appropriate documentation.

General Support Services Information

Contact Information
Name of program or department: Center for Disability Services
Telephone: 801-581-5020
Fax: 801-581-5487
Website: http://disability.utah.edu/

Accommodations or Services For Students With Learning Differences

Accommodations are decided upon an individual basis after a thorough review of appropriate, current documentation. The accommodations requests must be supported through the documentation provided and must be logically linked to the current impact of the condition on academic functioning.

Allowed in exams
Calculator: Yes
Dictionary: Yes
Computer: Yes
Spellchecker: Yes
Extended test time: Yes
Scribes: Yes
Proctors: Yes
Oral exams: Yes
Note-takers: Yes
Support services for students with LD: Yes
Support services for students with ADHD: Yes
Support services for students with ASD: Yes
Distraction-reduced environment: Yes
Tape recording in class: Yes
Electronic texts: Yes
Kurzweil reader: NR
Audio books: Yes
Other assistive technology: Yes
Priority registration: Yes
Added costs of services: No
LD specialists: Yes
ADHD coaching: NR
ASD specialists: No
Professional tutors: No
Peer tutors: NR
Max. hours/wk. for services: NR
How professors are notified of student approved accommodations: By student

General Admissions Information

Office of Admissions: 801-581-7281

Entrance Requirements

Academic units required: 4 English, 2 math, 3 science, 1 science labs, 2 foreign language, 1 history, 4 academic electives, **Academic units recommended:** 4 English, 4 math, 3 science, 2 science labs, 3 foreign language, 1 social studies, 2 history, 4 academic electives. High school diploma is required and GED is accepted. SAT or ACT required for some. If ACT, ACT with writing accepted. TOEFL required of all international applicants: minimum paper TOEFL 550 or minimum internet TOEFL 80.

Application deadline: 4/1
Notification: NR
Average GPA: 3.57
ACT Composite middle 50% range: 21-28
SAT Math middle 50% range: 510-660
SAT Critical Reading middle 50% range: 500-640
SAT Writing middle 50% range: 490-620
Graduate top 10% of class: 25
Graduated top 25% of class: 53
Graduated top 50% of class: 86

COLLEGE GRADUATION REQUIREMENTS

Course waivers allowed: No
Course substitutions allowed: Yes
In what course: Math Foreign Language

Additional Information

Environment: This public school was founded in 1850. It has a 1535-acre campus.

Student Body
Undergrad enrollment: 23,794
% Women: 44
% Men: 56
% Out-of-state: 20

Cost information
In-state Tuition: $7,130
Out-of-state Tuition: $24,955
Room & board: $9,000

Housing Information
University Housing: Yes
Percent living on campus: 13

Greek System
Fraternity: Yes
Sorority: Yes
Athletics: Division I

UTAH STATE UNIVERSITY

0160 Old Main Hill, Logan, UT 84322-0160
Phone: 435-797-1079 • Fax: 435-797-3708
E-mail: admit@usu.edu • Web: www.usu.edu
Support: CS • Institution: Public

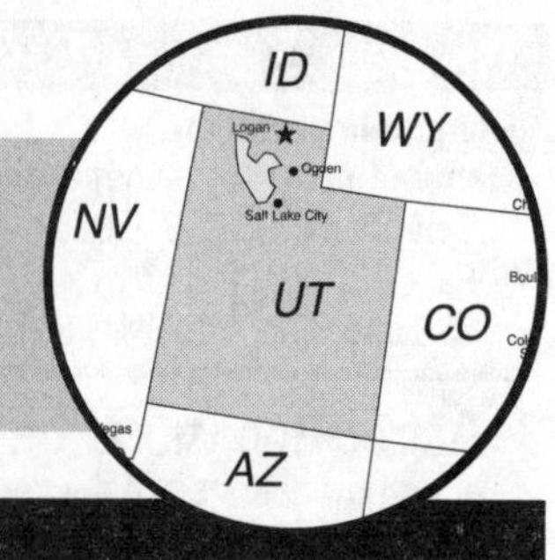

PROGRAMS OR SERVICES FOR STUDENTS WITH LEARNING DIFFERENCES

The mission of the Disability Resource Center (DRC) is to provide qualified persons with disabilities equal access to University programs, services, and activities. This is accomplished by the provision of reasonable and appropriate accommodations and fostering an environment which supports the understanding and acceptance of persons with disabilities throughout the university community. The DRC works to individually tailor services to student's specific needs so they can reach their full educational potential.

ADMISSION INFORMATION FOR STUDENTS WITH LEARNING DIFFERENCES

College entrance tests required: Yes
Interview required: No
Essay required: No
Additional Application Required for LD/ADHD/ASD: NR
What documentation required for LD: Psycho ed evaluation to include: relevant historical info, instructional interventions, related services, age diagnosed, objective data (aptitude, achievement, info processing), test scores (standard, percentile and grade equivalents) and describe functional limitations.
With general application: No
To receive services after enrolling: Yes
What documentation required for ADHD: Diagnosis based on DSM-V; history of behaviors impairing functioning in academic setting; diagnostic interview; history of symptoms; evidence of ongoing behaviors.
With general application: No
To receive services: Yes
What documentation required for ASD: Psychological evaluation preferred but letter from professional or copy of IEP/504 might suffice
With general application: No
To receive services after enrolling: Yes
LD/ADHD/ASD documentation submitted to: Disability Resource Center
ASD Specific Program: NR
Special Ed. HS course work accepted: Yes
Specific course requirements for all applicants: Yes
Separate application required for program services: Yes
Total # of students receiving LD/ADHD/ASD services: 712
Acceptance into program means acceptance into college: No, applications are completed independently of each other

ADMISSIONS

All students must submit the regular application and meet the established admissions requirements. A minimum 2.5 high school GPA, 17 ACT, and 90 admissions index are the minimum requirements for admission into a 4-year Bachelor Degree program. Applicants with a least a 2.0 high school GPA, 14 ACT, and 85 index score may be admitted into a 2-year Associate Degree program. In the 2-year degree program, the student can either earn an AS degree or an AA degree, or change to a 4-year bachelor degree after completing 24 credits with a minimum 2.5 GPA at USU. Please note that applicants must apply at least two months prior to the beginning of classes to be considered for admission into this associate degree program, and students cannot begin this associate degree program in summer.

ADDITIONAL INFORMATION

The Disability Resource Center provides the following services: registration assistance and priority registration, note takers, textbooks in alternative formats, accommodations for exams, including extended time and distraction reduced rooms with scribes/readers if appropriate. Basic skills courses are offered to all students by the Academic Resource Center (ARC) in time management, learning strategies, reading, math, and study strategies. Tutoring in math and supplemental instruction for some classes are also offered free of charge to all students by the ARC. The DRC has developed an assistive technology lab with computers and adaptive equipment to promote independence in conducting research and completing class assignments. If eligible, some DRC students may also access services provided by USU's Student Support Services program (TRIO). Workshops and individual services are also offered by the Health and Wellness Center and the Counseling and Psychological Services office.

General Support Services Information

Contact Information
Name of program or department: Disability Resource Center
Telephone: 435-797-2444
Fax: 435-797-0130

Accommodations or Services For Students With Learning Differences

Accommodations are decided upon an individual basis after a thorough review of appropriate, current documentation. The accommodations requests must be supported through the documentation provided and must be logically linked to the current impact of the condition on academic functioning.

Allowed in exams
Calculator: Yes
Dictionary: Yes
Computer: Yes
Spellchecker: Yes
Extended test time: Yes
Scribes: Yes
Proctors: Yes
Oral exams: Yes
Note-takers: Yes
Support services for students with LD: Yes
Support services for students with ADHD: Yes
Support services for students with ASD: Yes
Distraction-reduced environment: Yes
Tape recording in class: Yes
Electronic texts: Yes
Kurzweil reader: NR
Audio books: Yes
Other assistive technology: Yes
Priority registration: Yes
Added costs of services: No
LD specialists: Yes
ADHD coaching: No
ASD specialists: NR
Professional tutors: No
Peer tutors: NR
Max. hours/wk. for services: NR
How professors are notified of student approved accommodations: By both student and director

General Admissions Information

Office of Admissions: 435-797-1079

Entrance Requirements

Academic units required: 4 English, 3 math, 3 science, 1 science labs, 1 history, 4 academic electives, **Academic units recommended:** 2 foreign language. High school diploma is required and GED is accepted. SAT or ACT required. If ACT, ACT with writing accepted. TOEFL required of all international applicants: minimum internet TOEFL 71.

Application deadline: NR
Notification: NR
Average GPA: 3.51
ACT Composite middle 50% range: 20-27
SAT Math middle 50% range: 470-610
SAT Critical Reading middle 50% range: 480-600
SAT Writing middle 50% range: NR-NR
Graduate top 10% of class: 21
Graduated top 25% of class: 44
Graduated top 50% of class: 75

COLLEGE GRADUATION REQUIREMENTS

Course waivers allowed: Yes
In what course: Under certain circumstances
Course substitutions allowed: Yes
In what course: General Education math requirements may be substituted with other courses when a student can demonstrate that there is a substantial limitation that necessitates such an accommodation.

Additional Information

Environment: This public school was founded in 1888. It has a 400-acre campus.

Student Body
Undergrad enrollment: 25,259
% Women: 53
% Men: 47
% Out-of-state: 27

Cost information
In-state Tuition: $5,617
Out-of-state Tuition: $18,087
Room & board: $5,790

Housing Information
University Housing: Yes
Percent living on campus: NR

Greek System
Fraternity: Yes
Sorority: Yes
Athletics: Division I

CHAMPLAIN COLLEGE

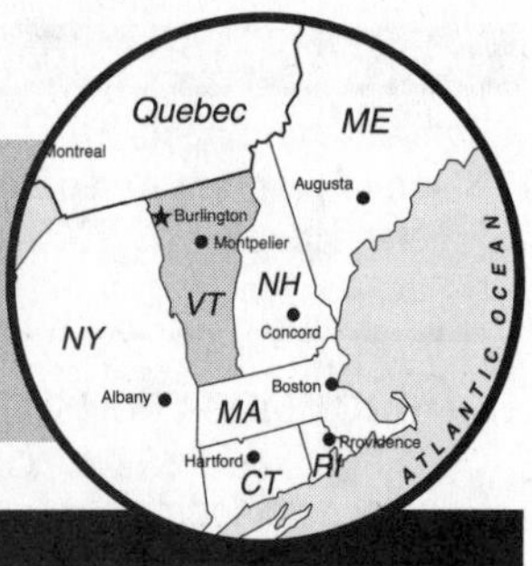

163 South Willard Street, Box 670, Burlington, VT 05402-0670
Phone: 802-860-2727 • Fax: 802-860-2767
E-mail: admission@champlain.edu • Web: www.champlain.edu/
Support: S • Institution: Private

PROGRAMS OR SERVICES FOR STUDENTS WITH LEARNING DIFFERENCES

Champlain College does not offer a special program for students with LD. Support services and academic accommodations are available when needed. Students with LD meet individually with a counselor at the start of the semester and are assisted in developing a plan of academic support. The counselor acts as liaison between the student and faculty. The college offers peer tutoring, writing assistance, accounting lab, math lab, and an oral communications lab. Mental health counseling is offered as is academic coaching. Students must provide documentation of the disability to the Office of Disability Services in the Counseling Department, which should include the most recent educational evaluation performed by a qualified individual, and a letter from any educational support service provider who has recently worked with the student would be most helpful. The letter should include information about the nature of the disability and the support services and/or program modifications provided.

ADMISSION INFORMATION FOR STUDENTS WITH LEARNING DIFFERENCES

College entrance tests required: Yes
Interview required: No
Essay required: Yes
Additional Application Required for LD/ADHD/ASD: NR
What documentation required for LD: Psycho ed evaluation to include: relevant historical info, instructional interventions, related services, age diagnosed, objective data (aptitude, achievement, info processing), test scores (standard, percentile and grade equivalents) and describe functional limitations.
With general application: No
To receive services after enrolling: Yes
What documentation required for ADHD: Diagnosis based on DSM-V; history of behaviors impairing functioning in academic setting; diagnostic interview; history of symptoms; evidence of ongoing behaviors.
With general application: No
To receive services after enrolling: Yes
What documentation required for ASD: Psycho ed evaluation
With general application: NR
To receive services after enrolling: Yes
LD/ADHD/ASD documentation submitted to: Counseling Department
ASD Specific Program: NR
Special Ed. HS course work accepted: Yes
Specific course requirements of all applicants: Yes
Separate application required: No
Total # of students receiving LD/ADHD/ASD services: 200
Acceptance into program means acceptance into college: Students must be admitted to and enrolled in the university first and then request services.

ADMISSIONS

There is no special admissions procedure for students with LD. The admissions process is fairly competitive. The most important part of the application is the high school transcript. Upward grade trend and challenging course work are looked on favorably. Recommendations and college essay are required. The average GPA is 3.15 and SAT 1144 with mid 50% 1030-1240 or ACT 26 with mid 50% 23-29. All admission decisions are based on an assessment of the academic foundation needed for success in the required courses at the bachelor's degree level. Strong writing skills are important for all applicants. Minimum recommended preparation includes successful completion of a college preparatory curriculum, including: 4 years of writing-and-reading-intensive English, 4 years of writing-and-reading-intensive history/social sciences, 3 years of college preparatory mathematics, at least through Algebra II. Many students take Pre-Calculus, Calculus or AP Calculus as juniors or seniors, and 3 years of lab science, plus 2 years of foreign language. Students are expected to take a full course load of challenging academic subjects senior year. Applicants are evaluated based on the demands of their secondary school curriculum, grades earned, rank in class, standardized test scores, writing ability, teacher and counselor recommendations, and academic growth. Strong writing skills are important for all applicants.

ADDITIONAL INFORMATION

Students with learning disabilities who self-disclose receive a special needs form after they have enrolled in college courses from the Counseling Department. The coordinator meets with each student during the first week of school. The first appointment includes a discussion about the student's disability and the academic accommodations that will be needed. Accommodations could include, but are not limited to, tutoring, extended time for tests, readers for tests, use of computers during exams, peer note-takers, tape recording lectures, and books on tape. With the student's permission, faculty members receive a letter discussing appropriate accommodations. The coordinators will continue to act as a liaison between students and faculty, consult with tutors, monitor students' academic progress, and consult with faculty as needed.

General Support Services Information

Contact Information
Name of program or department: Support Services for Students with Disabilities
Telephone: 802-865-6426
Fax: 802-860-2764

Accommodations or Services for Students with Learning Differences

Accommodations are decided upon an individual basis after a thorough review of appropriate, current documentation. The accommodations requested must be supported through the documentation provided and must be logically linked to the current impact of the condition on academic functioning.

Allowed in exams
Calculator: Yes
Dictionary: Yes
Computer: Yes
Spellchecker: Yes
Extended test time: Yes
Scribes: Yes
Proctors: Yes
Oral exams: Yes
Note-takers: Yes
Services for students with LD: Yes
Services for students with ADHD: Yes
Services for students with ASD: Yes
Distraction-reduced environment: Yes
Tape recording in class: Yes
Audio books: NR
Electronic texts: Yes
Kurzweil Reader: Yes
Other assistive technology: Yes
Priority registration: No
Added costs for services: No
LD specialists: No
ADHD coaching: NR
ASD specialists: NR
Professional tutors: Yes
Peer tutors: 30
Max. hours/wk. for services: N/A
How professors are notified of LD/ADHD: By student with a letter generated by the Disabilities Services Office

General Admissions Information

Office of Admissions: 802-860-2727

Entrance Requirements

Academic units required: 4 English, 3 math, 3 science, 3 science labs, 2 foreign language, 4 history, 4 academic electives, **Academic units recommended:** 4 math, 4 science, 4 foreign language. High school diploma is required and GED is accepted. SAT or ACT required. If ACT, ACT with writing accepted. TOEFL required of all international applicants: minimum internet TOEFL 79.

Application deadline: NR
Notification: NR
Average GPA: 3.2
ACT Composite middle 50% range: 23-29
SAT Math middle 50% range: 510-630
SAT Critical Reading middle 50% range: 520-630
SAT Writing middle 50% range: 490-600
Graduated top 10% of class: 10
Graduated top 25% of class: 34
Graduated top 50% of class: 77

COLLEGE GRADUATION REQUIREMENTS

Course waivers allowed: No
Course substitutions allowed: No

Additional Information

Environment: This private school was founded in 1878. It has a 19-acre campus.

Student Body
Undergrad enrollment: 3,400
% Women: 41
% Men: 59
% Out-of-state: 78

Cost information
Tuition: $37,436
Room & board: $14,050

Housing Information
University Housing: Yes
Percent living on campus: 64

Greek System
Fraternity: No
Sorority: No
Athletics: NR

GREEN MOUNTAIN COLLEGE

One Brennan Circle, Poultney, VT 05764-1199
Phone: 802-287-8000 • Fax: 802-287-8099
E-mail: admiss@greenmtn.edu • Web: www.greenmtn.edu
Support: CS • Institution: Private

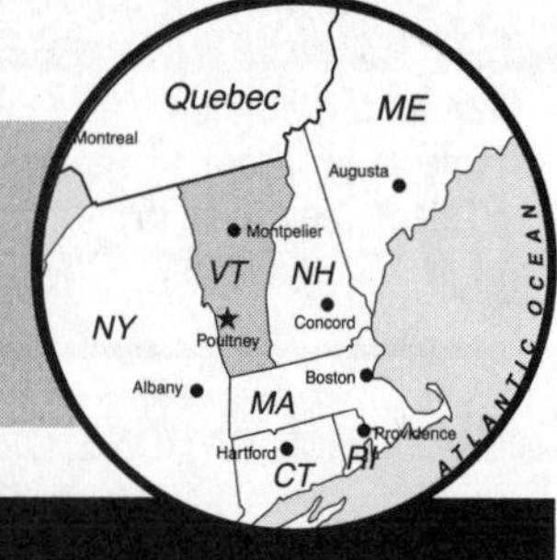

PROGRAMS OR SERVICES FOR STUDENTS WITH LEARNING DIFFERENCES

Green Mountain College provides accommodations for students with documented learning differences. The college believes that every student has the potential for academic success and strives to support students while teaching them independence and self-advocacy skills. The Calhoun Learning Center (CLC) functions as the primary source of information regarding academic issues relating to disabilities. Students seeking academic accommodations must self-identify and submit valid documentation of their learning needs. The CLC staff determines which students are eligible for academic accommodations and works with the student and staff to develop and implement an accommodation plan that will allow the student an opportunity to succeed at college. The CLC has six main functions: to provide academic support, primarily through one-on-one, small group, general content area tutoring; to serve as the campus Writing Center; to support courses specifically designed for underprepared students; to provide support for foreign students; to be the campus center for academic issues relating to disabilities; and to provide workshops and seminars and events with the goal of improving learning skills.

ADMISSION INFORMATION FOR STUDENTS WITH LEARNING DIFFERENCES

College entrance tests required: Yes
Interview required: No
Essay required: Yes
Additional Application Required for LD/ADHD/ASD: NR
What documentation required for LD: Psycho ed evaluation to include: relevant historical info, instructional interventions, related services, age diagnosed, objective data (aptitude, achievement, info processing), test scores (standard, percentile and grade equivalents) and describe functional limitations.
With general application: No
To receive services after enrolling: Yes
What documentation required for ADHD: Diagnosis based on DSM-V; history of behaviors impairing functioning in academic setting; diagnostic interview; history of symptoms; evidence of ongoing behaviors.
With general application: No
To receive services after enrolling: Yes
What documentation required for ASD: Psycho ed evaluation
With general application: NR
To receive services after enrolling: Yes
LD/ADHD/ASD documentation submitted to: Support Program/Services
ASD Specific Program: NR
Special Ed. HS course work accepted: Yes
Specific course requirements of all applicants: Yes
Separate application required: No
Total # of students receiving LD/ADHD/ASD services: 70
Acceptance into program means acceptance into college: Students must be admitted and enrolled at the college and then reviewed for LC services.

ADMISSIONS

There is no special admissions process for students with learning disabilities. Students face the same admission criteria, which include: ACT score of 19 or SAT score of 900; 2.0 GPA; 4 years of English, 2–3 years of history/social studies, 2 years of science (with lab), 3 years of math, and 2 years of a foreign language. All applications are carefully considered with the best interest of both the student and the college in mind.

ADDITIONAL INFORMATION

The Learning Center provides support services to all students which include: academic counseling for students on an individual basis and, when appropriate, making referrals to related college departments; offering and facilitating group sessions for students experiencing similar academic concerns; coordinating the delivery of services for students with disabilities that impact academic performance including responding to requests for reasonable and appropriate accommodations; conducting educational workshops designed to facilitate the mastery of study strategies and learning skills and to improve overall academic performance; coordinating the college tutorial program in consultation with individual academic departments; and collaborating with existing college components. The tutoring program uses a three-tiered approach: a drop-in clinic for immediate but temporary academic assistance; individually scheduled tutoring; or a more extensive schedule of one, two, or three tutoring sessions per week for tutorial help throughout a course. All new students take placement tests to assess their achievement in mathematics. Students underprepared in math are advised to take Intro to College Math and tutoring is available.

General Support Services Information

Contact Information
Name of program or department: The Calhoun Learning Center (CLC)
Telephone: 802-287-2180
Fax: 802-287-8288
Website: NR

Accommodations or Services For Students With Learning Differences

Accommodations are decided upon an individual basis after a thorough review of appropriate, current documentation. The accommodations requests must be supported through the documentation provided and must be logically linked to the current impact of the condition on academic functioning.

Allowed in exams
Calculator: Yes
Dictionary: Yes
Computer: Yes
Spellchecker: Yes
Extended test time: Yes
Scribes: Yes
Proctors: Yes
Oral exams: Yes
Note-takers: Yes
Support services for students with LD: Yes
Support services for students with ADHD: Yes
Support services for students with ASD: Yes
Distraction-reduced environment: Yes
Tape recording in class: Yes
Electronic texts: Yes
Kurzweil reader: NR
Audio books: Yes
Other assistive technology: Yes
Priority registration: Yes
Added costs of services: No
LD specialists: Yes
ADHD coaching: Yes
ASD specialists: No
Professional tutors: No
Peer tutors: Yes
Max. hours/wk. for services: NR
How professors are notified of student approved accommodations: By both student and director

General Admissions Information

Office of Admissions: 802-287-8000

Entrance Requirements

Academic units required: 4 English, 3 math, 3 science, 2 science labs, 1 foreign language, 3 social studies, 1 history, 5 academic electives, **Academic units recommended:** 4 math, 4 science, 2 foreign language, 2 history. High school diploma is required and GED is accepted. SAT or ACT required for some. If ACT, ACT with writing accepted. TOEFL required of all international applicants: minimum paper TOEFL 500 or minimum internet TOEFL 61.

Application deadline: NR
Notification: Rolling starting 9/1
Average GPA: NR
ACT Composite middle 50% range: 18-24
SAT Math middle 50% range: 460-530
SAT Critical Reading middle 50% range: 480-590
SAT Writing middle 50% range: 430-580
Graduate top 10% of class: NR
Graduated top 25% of class: NR
Graduated top 50% of class: NR

COLLEGE GRADUATION REQUIREMENTS

Course waivers allowed: No
Course substitutions allowed: Yes
In what course: math

Additional Information

Environment: This private school, affiliated with the Methodist Church, was founded in 1834. It has a 155-acre campus.

Student Body
Undergrad enrollment: 597
% Women: 51
% Men: 49
% Out-of-state: 85

Cost information
Tuition: $33,898
Room & board: $11,492

Housing Information
University Housing: Yes
Percent living on campus: 85

Greek System
Fraternity: No
Sorority: No
Athletics: Division III

Johnson State College

337 College Hill, Johnson, VT 05656-9408
Phone: 802-635-1219 • Fax: 802-635-1230
E-mail: jscadmissions@jsc.edu • Web: www.jsc.edu
Support: CS • Institution: Public

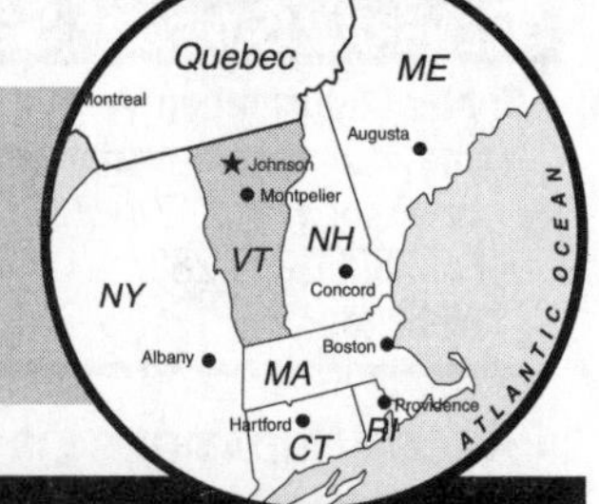

Programs or Services for Students with Learning Differences

Johnson State College provides services to students with disabilities through the Learning Specialist at the Academic Support Service Program. The fundamental purpose is to provide students with the appropriate services necessary to allow access to Johnson State College academic programs. Students with disabilities are integrated fully into the college community. In addition, students with disabilities may also be eligible for the TRiO program, which provides additional supports and services through the Learning Resource Center. The Learning Resource Center provides a friendly and supportive environment for any student who is academically struggling or underprepared to meet his or her educational goals. Services may include group and peer tutoring; professional tutoring in writing and math; and supplemental instruction in time management, study skills, organizational skills, and professional mentoring.

Admission Information for Students with Learning Differences

College entrance tests required: Yes
Interview required: No
Essay required: Yes
Additional Application Required for LD/ADHD/ASD: NR
What documentation required for LD: Follow AHEAD Guidelines—cognitive measurement WAIS–R and achievement tests within three years. Additional testing for specific LD is recommended (e.g. Denny Reading Test) although not required. Documentation must include diagnostic information, test scores and interpretation, and functional impact of disability on major life activities. Guidelines for documenting LD can be found at http://www.jsc.edu/Academics/Academic Support/StudentsWithDisabilities.aspx.
With general application: NR
To receive services after enrolling: Yes
What documentation required for ADHD: Follow ETS Guidelines for ADD documentation and forms to be completed by school personnel and diagnosing physician. Guidelines for documenting ADD can be found at http://www.jsc.edu/Academics/AcademicSupport/StudentsWithDisabilities.aspx.
LD/ADHD/ASD documentation submitted to: Support Program/Services
ASD Specific Program: NR
Special Ed. HS course work accepted: N/A
Specific course requirements for all applicants: Yes
Separate application required for program services: No
Total # of students receiving LD/ADHD/ASD services: 50+
Acceptance into program means acceptance into college: Students must be admitted to and enrolled in the university first and then request services.

Admissions

Students with disabilities who demonstrate the academic ability to be successful at the post-secondary level are eligible for acceptance. Applicants with a disability are encouraged to contact the Admissions Office so that accommodations can be made available, where appropriate, throughout the admission process. Course requirements include four years of English, three years of college preparatory mathematics, three years of social sciences, and two years of science (one course with a lab).

Additional Information

Academic Support Services provides tutoring, academic advising, personal counseling and mentoring, career exploration, college survival skills workshops, and assistance with establishing appropriate and reasonable accommodations. Students should be self-advocates and are responsible for notifying instructors to arrange for providing the approved accommodations.

General Support Services Information

Contact Information
Name of program or department: Academic Support Services
Telephone: 802-635-1259
Fax: 802-635-1454

Accommodations or Services for Students with Learning Differences

Accommodations are determined on an individual basis after a thorough review of appropriate, current documentation. Accommodations must be substantiated by the documentation and must be logically linked to the current impact of the specific diagnosis(es) on academic functioning.

Allowed in exams
Calculator: Yes
Dictionary: Yes
Computer: Yes
Spellchecker: Yes
Extended test time: Yes
Scribes: Yes
Proctors: Yes
Oral exams: No
Note-takers: Yes
Services for students with LD: Yes
Services for students with ADHD: Yes
Services for students with ASD: Yes
Distraction-reduced environment: Yes
Tape recording in class: Yes
Audio books: NR
Electronic texts: Yes
Kurzweil Reader: Yes
Other assistive technology: Kurzweil 3000, Inspiration Mapping Software, Dragon Naturally-Speaking Text Help, Read and Write Gold, digital recorders, Victor Vibe, Smart Pen
Priority registration: No
Added costs for services: No
LD specialists: Yes
ADHD coaching: NR
ASD specialists: NR
Professional tutors: 4–5
Peer tutors: 10–15
Max. hours/wk. for services: Unlimited
How professors are notified of LD/ADHD: Student

General Admissions Information

Office of Admissions: 802-635-1219

Entrance Requirements

Academic units required: 4 English, 2 math, 2 science, 1 science labs, 3 social studies, 2 history, **Academic units recommended:** 4 English, 3 math, 3 science, 2 science labs, 1 foreign language, 3 social studies, 3 history. High school diploma is required and GED is accepted. SAT or ACT required. If ACT, ACT with writing required. TOEFL required of all international applicants: minimum paper TOEFL 500 or minimum internet TOEFL 61.

Application deadline: NR
Notification: Rolling starting 12/1
Average GPA: NR
ACT Composite middle 50% range: 20-28
SAT Math middle 50% range: 430-550
SAT Critical Reading middle 50% range: 430-550
SAT Writing middle 50% range: NR-NR
Graduated top 10% of class: 34
Graduated top 25% of class: 66
Graduated top 50% of class: 68

COLLEGE GRADUATION REQUIREMENTS

Course substitutions allowed: Yes
In what course: Lower math may be substituted for one of the two math requirements if there is a math LD only.

Additional Information

Environment: This public school was founded in 1828. It has a 350-acre campus.

Student Body
Undergrad enrollment: 1,662
% Women: 62
% Men: 38
% Out-of-state: 28

Cost information
In-state Tuition: $8,568
Out-of Tuition: $19,008
Room & board: $8,446

Housing Information
University Housing: Yes
Percent living on campus: 38

Greek System
Fraternity: No
Sorority: No
Athletics: Division III

Landmark College

PO Box 820, Putney, VT 05346-0820
Phone: 802-387-6718 • Fax: 802-387-6868
E-mail: admissions@landmark.edu • Web: www.landmark.edu/
Support: SP • Institution: Private

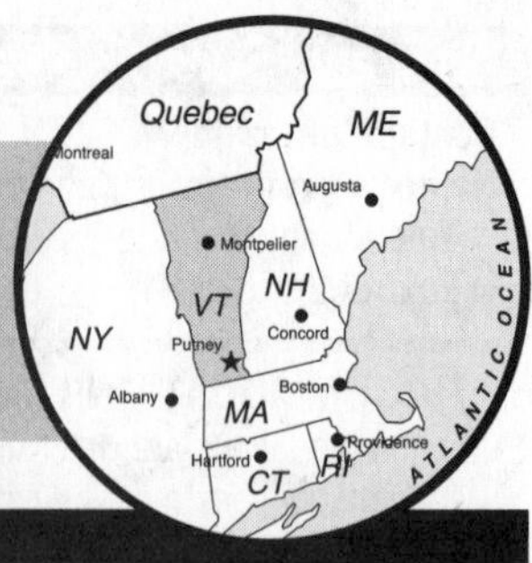

Programs or Services for Students with Learning Differences

Landmark College is the only accredited college in the country designed exclusively for students of average to superior intellectual potential with dyslexia, attention deficit hyperactivity disorder (AD/HD), or specific learning disabilities. Life-changing experiences are commonplace at Landmark College. Simply put, Landmark College knows how to serve students who learn differently better than any other place on earth. Landmark's beautiful campus offers all the resources students might expect at a high quality higher education institution, including a new athletic center, a student center, dining facility, cafe, residence halls, and academic resource center (library). The college has also invested substantially in technology, and offers a wireless network in all of its classrooms, along with LAN, telephone, and cable connections in all the residence rooms. Entering students are expected to bring a notebook computer, as these are used in nearly every class session. The college's programs extensively integrate assistive technologies, such as Dragon Naturally Speaking and Kurzweil text-to-speech software. What makes Landmark unique, though, is its faculty and staff. The college's 100+ full time faculty members are all highly experienced in serving students with learning disabilities and attention deficit disorders. Over 100 staff members provide an array of support services that are unusually comprehensive for a student population of less than 450 students.

Admission Information for Students with Learning Differences

College entrance test required: No
Interview required: NR
Essay required: Required
Additional Application Required for LD/ADHD/ASD: No
What documentation required for LD: Same documentation for all students.
With general application: NR
To receive services after enrolling: No
What documentation required for ADHD: Same documentation for all students.
With general application: NR
To receive services after enrolling: No
What documentation required for ASD: Refer to Landmark College's Website
With general application: NR
To receive services after enrolling: No
LD/ADHD/ASD documentation submitted to: NR
ASD Specific Program: Social Pragmatics
Special Ed. HS course work accepted: NR
Specific course requirements of all applicants: NR
Separate application required for program services: FALSE
Total # of students receiving LD/ADHD/ASD services: NR
Acceptance into program means acceptance into college: NR

Admissions

Applicants to Landmark College must have a diagnosis of dyslexia, attention deficit disorder, or other specific learning disability. The college offers rolling admissions, and enrolls academic semester students for fall and spring semesters. Enrolled students can earn up to 12 credits during the summer. A four-week skills development program is offered in the summer. A high school program, for students aged 16–18, is also offered in the summer. Diagnostic testing within the last three years is required, along with a diagnosis of a learning disability or AD/HD. One of the Wechsler Scales (WAIS-III or WISC-III) administered within three years of application is required. Scores, sub-test scores and their analysis are required to be submitted as well. Alternately, the Woodcock-Johnson Cognitive Assessment may be substituted if administered within three years of application.

Additional Information

The Landmark College Transition Program is a 2-week program for high school graduates and college students. A typical summer term includes pre-credit course work to develop skills and strategies to be successful in college credit work. Summer students work with professional faculty to: develop a writing process based on multi-modal writing techniques; to learn, integrate, and practice research-proven study skills; and to complete a communication or math course designed to integrate strategies and practice. Additionally there are small Group Individualized Instruction seminars, specific to strategy integration; Assistive technology training; and athletics and other activities. The Landmark Study Abroad Program has developed programs with students' diverse learning styles in mind. Faculty design and teach experiential courses in their specific disciplines that fulfill Landmark core requirements while helping students gain confidence and independence in new academic structures. Faculty accompany students abroad, providing them with the Landmark College academic experience in an international setting. Landmark also offers a 3-week summer session for high school students between the ages of 16 and 18 introducting students to the skills and strategies in reading and study skills -understanding and remembering readings; writing process—from pre-writing to final drafting—the Landmark way; and communication - self-advocacy, collaboration, and effective communication.

General Support Services Information

Contact Information
Name of program or department: Landmark College
Telephone: 802-387-4767
Fax: 802-387-6868

Accommodations or Services for Students with Learning Differences

Accommodations are decided upon an individual basis after a thorough review of appropriate, current documentation. The accommodations requests must be supported through the documentation provided and must be logically linked to the current impact of the condition on academic functioning.

Allowed in exams
Calculator: Yes
Dictionary: Yes
Computer: Yes
Spellchecker: Yes
Extended test time: Yes
Scribes: No
Proctors: No
Oral exams: Yes
Note-takers: No
Services for students with LD: Yes
Services for students with ADHD: Yes
Services for students with ASD: Yes
Distraction-reduced environment: Yes
Tape recording in class: Yes
Audio books: No
Electronic Texts: NR
Kurzweil reader: Yes
Other assistive technology: Yes
Priority registration: No
Added costs of services: No
LD specialists: Yes
ADHD coaching: NR
ASD specialists: NR
Professional tutors: Yes
Peer tutors: No
How professors are notified of student approved accommodations: N/A

General Admissions Information

Office of Admissions: 802-387-6718

Entrance Requirements
Academic units recommended: 4 English, 3 mathematics, 3 science, 1 foreign language, 3 social studies, 3 history, 1 visual/performing arts, 1 academic elective. High school diploma is required and GED is accepted. TOEFL required of all international applicants: minimum paper TOEFL 200.

Application deadline: None
Notification: Rolling starting 12/1
Average GPA: NR
ACT Composite middle 50% range: NR
SAT Math middle 50% range: NR
SAT Critical Reading middle 50% range: NR
SAT Writing middle 50% range: NR
Graduated top 10% of class: NR
Graduated top 25% of class: NR
Graduated top 50% of class: NR

COLLEGE GRADUATION REQUIREMENTS

Course waivers allowed: No
Course substitutions allowed: No

Additional Information

Environment: The college is located on 125 acres overlooking the Connecticut River Valley hills of Vermont and New Hampshire.

Student Body
Undergrad enrollment: 487
% Women: 32
% Men: 68
% Out-of-state: 95

Cost information
Tuition: $48,210
Room & board: $8,620

Housing Information
University housing: Yes
% Living on campus: 95

Greek System
Fraternity: No
Sorority: No
Athletics: No

Norwich University

Admissions Office, Northfield, VT 05663
Phone: 802-485-2001 • Fax: 802-485-2032
E-mail: nuadm@norwich.edu • Web: www.norwich.edu
Support: CS • Institution: Private

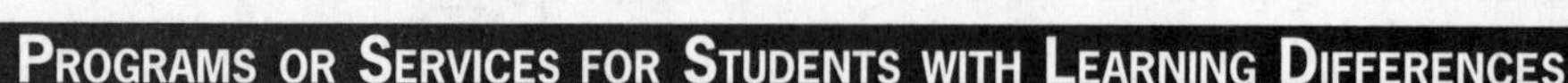

Programs or Services for Students with Learning Differences

Services for students with disabilities, available if you have a suspected or documented disability, are provided by the Coordinator of Specialized Student Services. The Coordinator of Specialized Student Services: helps you with the process of properly documenting your disability; orients you to your Educational Profile and Academic Accommodations; provides training and information about assistive technology; facilitates communication with faculty, staff, and family members, with your permission; provides academic coaching and counseling; and meets with you on an as-needed or regular basis.

Admission Information for Students with Learning Differences

College entrance tests required: Yes
Interview required: No
Essay required: No
Additional Application Required for LD/ADHD/ASD: NR
What documentation required for LD: Psycho ed evaluation to include: relevant historical info, instructional interventions, related services, age diagnosed, objective data (aptitude, achievement, info processing), test scores (standard, percentile and grade equivalents) and describe functional limitations.
With general application: No
To receive services after enrolling: Yes
What documentation required for ADHD: Diagnosis based on DSM-V; history of behaviors impairing functioning in academic setting; diagnostic interview; history of symptoms; evidence of ongoing behaviors.
With general application: No
To receive services after enrolling: Yes
What documentation required for ASD: Psycho ed evaluation
With general application: NR
To receive services after enrolling: Yes
LD/ADHD/ASD documentation submitted to: Academic Achievement Center
ASD Specific Program: NR
Special Ed. HS course work accepted: No
Specific course requirements of all applicants: Yes
Separate application required: No
Total # of students receiving LD/ADHD/ASD services: NR
Acceptance into program means acceptance into college: Students must be admitted to and enrolled in the university first and then request services.

Admissions

Students with learning disabilities submit a general application. Admission criteria include high school GPA of a C or better; an SAT score of 850 or equivalent ACT; participation in activities; and strong college recommendations from teachers, counselors, or coaches. There are no course waivers for admission. The university is flexible on ACT/SAT test scores. If grades and other indicators are problematic is recommended that students provide detailed information to give a better understanding the disability. A complete psychodiagnostic evaluation is required. A small number of students who do not meet the general admission requirements may be admitted if they show promise. An interview is highly recommended. There are limited provisional admission slots.

Additional Information

A telephone conversation or personal meeting with the LSC support personnel is encouraged prior to the start of college, so that work can begin immediately on preparing an individualized program. Students are responsible for meeting with each professor to discuss accommodations. Services begin with Freshman Placement Testing designed to assess each individual's level of readiness for college-level math. Other services include course advising with an assigned academic advisor and advocacy for academic petitions. Services and accommodations are available for undergraduate and graduate students.

General Support Services Information

Contact Information
Name of program or department: Academic Achievement Center (AAC)
Telephone: 802-485-2130
Fax: 802-485-2684

Accommodations or Services for Students with Learning Differences

Accommodations are decided upon an individual basis after a thorough review of appropriate, current documentation. The accommodations requested must be supported through the documentation provided and must be logically linked to the current impact of the condition on academic functioning.

Allowed in exams
Calculator: Yes
Dictionary: Yes
Computer: Yes
Spellchecker: Yes
Extended test time: Yes
Scribes: Yes
Proctors: Yes
Oral exams: Yes
Note-takers: No
Services for students with LD: Yes
Services for students with ADHD: Yes
Services for students with ASD: Yes
Distraction-reduced environment: Yes
Tape recording in class: Yes
Audio books: NR
Electronic texts: No
Kurzweil Reader: No
Other assistive technology: Yes
Priority registration: Limited
Added costs for services: No
LD specialists: Yes
ADHD coaching: NR
ASD specialists: NR
Professional tutors: 9
Peer tutors: 30
Max. hours/wk. for services: N/A
How professors are notified of LD/ADHD: By both student and director

General Admissions Information

Office of Admissions: 802-485-2001

Entrance Requirements

Academic units recommended: 4 English, 4 math, 4 science, 3 science labs, 2 foreign language, 3 social studies, 3 history. High school diploma is required and GED is accepted. SAT or ACT required. If ACT, ACT with writing accepted. TOEFL required of all international applicants: minimum paper TOEFL 500.

Application deadline: NR
Notification: Rolling starting 9/1
Average GPA: 3.12
ACT Composite middle 50% range: 21-26
SAT Math middle 50% range: 500-640
SAT Critical Reading middle 50% range: 480-580
SAT Writing middle 50% range: 460-620
Graduated top 10% of class: 11
Graduated top 25% of class: 37
Graduated top 50% of class: 74

COLLEGE GRADUATION REQUIREMENTS

Course waivers allowed: No
Course substitutions allowed: Yes
In what course: Foreign language, only with proof of inability to successfully function and after having gone through a lengthy petition process.

Additional Information

Environment: This private school was founded in 1819. It has a 1125-acre campus.

Student Body
Undergrad enrollment: 2,246
% Women: 26
% Men: 74
% Out-of-state: 84

Cost information
Tuition: $30,048
Room & board: $10,976

Housing Information
University Housing: Yes
Percent living on campus: 82

Greek System
Fraternity: No
Sorority: No
Athletics: Division III

UNIVERSITY OF VERMONT

University of Vermont Admissions, Burlington, VT 05401-3596
Phone: 802-656-3370 • Fax: 802-656-8611
E-mail: admissions@uvm.edu • Web: www.uvm.edu
Support: CS • Institution: Public

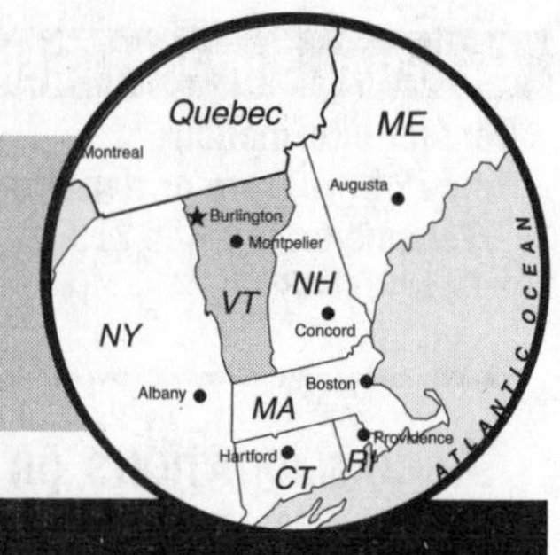

PROGRAMS OR SERVICES FOR STUDENTS WITH LEARNING DIFFERENCES

ACCESS provides Accommodations, Consultation, Collaboration, and Educational Support Services to students with documented disabilities. Among our extensive programs and services, ACCESS offers: exam accommodations, note taking, ebooks, meetings with Disability Specialists to receive advisement and advocacy around disability-related matters, as well as use of adaptive technology, unique opportunities for engagement and education related to identity development.

ADMISSION INFORMATION FOR STUDENTS WITH LEARNING DIFFERENCES

College entrance tests required: No
Interview required: No
Essay required: No
Additional Application Required for LD/ADHD/ASD: NR
What documentation required for LD: See www.uvm.edu/access/?Page=docguidelines/ld.html&SM=docguidelines/docsubmenu.html
With general application: No
To receive services after enrolling: Yes
What documentation required for ADHD: See www.uvm.edu/access/?Page=docguidelines/ld.html&SM=docguidelines/docsubmenu.html
With general application: No
To receive services after enrolling: Yes
Documentation for ASD: See www.uvm.edu/access/?Page=docguidelines/ld.html&SM=docguidelines/docsubmenu.html
With general application: No
To receive services after enrolling: Yes
LD/ADHD/ASD documentation submitted to: ACCESS
ASD Specific Program: NR
Special Ed. HS course work accepted: No
Specific course requirements of all applicants: Yes
Separate application required: No
Total # of students receiving LD/ADHD/ASD services: NR
Acceptance into program means acceptance into college: Students must be admitted to and enrolled in the university first and then request services.

ADMISSIONS

Students submit a common application to admissions. Documentation of a student's disability is sent directly to ACCESS. Students are encouraged to voluntarily provide documentation of their disability. ACCESS reviews documentation and may consult with Admissions if/when necessary as to how a student's disability has affected their academic record. Upon request, if time and resources allow, students may request a review of their documentation to assess for eligibility and/or entrance requirements if they feel their disability has impacted them in such a way that they are missing a requirement such as Foreign Language. Students with LD/ADHD should submit a current educational evaluation that includes a comprehensive measure of both cognitive and achievement functioning. Course requirements include 4 years English, 3 years Social Science, 3 years Math, 2 years Physical Sciences and 2 years Foreign Language. Self-disclosing in the application is a matter of personal choice. At UVM, disclosing a disability will absolutely not have a negative impact on a student's admissibility.

ADDITIONAL INFORMATION

UVM provides a multidisciplinary program for students with LD /ADHD emphasizing development of advocacy and reasonable and appropriate use of academic accommodations including: note-taking, reduced course load, extended test time, alternative test and media formats, technology use, audio format, readers/scribes, computer/spellchecker, tutoring, reading and writing skill development, academic advising and course selection, priority registration, learning strategies and study skills training, LD/ADHD support via peer and community leadership building opportunities, faculty consultation, trainings, diagnostic screenings/info sessions and evaluation referral.

General Support Services Information

Contact Information
Name of program or department: Academic Support Services
Telephone: 802-656-4075
Fax: 802-656-7957

Accommodations or Services for Students with Learning Differences

ACCESS provides Accommodations, Consultation, Collaboration, and Educational Support Services to students with documented disabilities. Among our extensive programs and services, ACCESS offers: exam accommodations, note taking, ebooks, meetings with Disability Specialists to receive advisement and advocacy around disability-related matters, as well as use of adaptive technology, unique opportunities for engagement and education related to identity development.

Allowed in exams
Calculator: Yes
Dictionary: No
Computer: Yes
Spellchecker: Yes
Extended test time: Yes
Scribes: Yes
Proctors: Yes
Oral exams: Yes
Note-takers: Yes
Services for students with LD: Yes
Services for students with ADHD: Yes
Services for students with ASD: Yes
Distraction-reduced environment: Yes
Tape recording in class: Yes
Audio books: No
Electronic texts: Yes
Kurzweil Reader: Yes
Other assistive technology: Yes
Priority registration: Yes
Added costs for services: No
LD specialists: Yes
ADHD coaching: No
ASD specialists: No
Professional tutors: No
Peer tutors: 150
Max. hours/wk. for services: 1–2
How professors are notified of LD/ADHD: By student

General Admissions Information

Office of Admissions: 802-656-3370

Entrance Requirements

Academic units required: 4 English, 3 math, 2 science, 1 science labs, 2 foreign language, 3 social studies. High school diploma is required and GED is accepted. SAT or ACT required. If ACT, ACT with writing accepted. TOEFL required of all international applicants: minimum paper TOEFL 550 or minimum internet TOEFL 79.

Application deadline: 1/15
Notification: 3/31
Average GPA: 3.53
ACT Composite middle 50% range: 25-30
SAT Math middle 50% range: 550-640
SAT Critical Reading middle 50% range: 550-650
SAT Writing middle 50% range: 540-650
Graduated top 10% of class: 32
Graduated top 25% of class: 74
Graduated top 50% of class: 96

COLLEGE GRADUATION REQUIREMENTS

Course waivers allowed: No
Course substitutions allowed: No

Additional Information

Environment: This public school was founded in 1791. It has a 460-acre campus.

Student Body
Undergrad enrollment: 10,973
% Women: 56
% Men: 44
% Out-of-state: 71

Cost information
In-state Tuition: $14,664
Out-of-state Tuition: $37,056
Room & board: $11,150

Housing Information
University Housing: Yes
Percent living on campus: 49

Greek System
Fraternity: Yes
Sorority: Yes
Athletics: Division I

The College of William & Mary

Office of Admissions, PO Box 8795, Williamsburg, VA 23187-8795
Phone: 757-221-4223 • Fax: 757-221-1242
E-mail: admission@wm.edu • Web: www.wm.edu
Support: S • Institution: Public

Programs or Services for Students with Learning Differences

Disability Services at the College of William and Mary are available to all students with disabilities. Reasonable accommodations upon request are evaluated on an individual and flexible basis. Program goals include fostering independence, encouraging self-determination, emphasizing accommodations over limitations, and creating an accessible environment to ensure that individuals are viewed on the basis of ability and not disability. Individual accommodations needs are considered on a case-by-case basis in consultation with the student. The staff works with students and faculty to implement reasonable supports. Students anticipating the need for academic support must provide pertinent documentation in a timely manner in order to facilitate the provision of the service. Additional documentation may be requested and accommodation requests can be denied if they do not seem to be substantially supported. Documentation for LD/ADHD must include a comprehensive report of psychoeducational or neuropsychological assessment. The documentation must demonstrate the impact of the disability on major life activities and support all the recommended accommodations.

Admission Information for Students with Learning Differences

College entrance tests required: Yes
Interview required: No
Essay required: N/A
Additional Application Required for LD/ADHD/ASD: NR
What documentation required for LD: Psycho ed evaluation to include: relevant historical info, instructional interventions, related services, age diagnosed, objective data (aptitude, achievement, info processing), test scores (standard, percentile and grade equivalents) and describe functional limitations.
With general application: No
To receive services after enrolling: Yes
What documentation required for ADHD: Diagnosis based on DSM-V; history of behaviors impairing functioning in academic setting; diagnostic interview; history of symptoms; evidence of ongoing behaviors.
With general application: No
To receive services after enrolling: Yes
What documentation required for ASD: Psycho ed evaluation
With general application: NR
To receive services after enrolling: Yes
LD/ADHD/ASD documentation submitted to: Support Program/Services
Special Ed. HS course work accepted: No
Specific course requirements for all applicants: Yes
Separate application required for program services: No
Total # of students receiving LD/ADHD/ASD services: 235
Acceptance into program means acceptance into college: NR

Admissions

Students go through a regular admissions process. Students must take either the SAT or ACT and three SAT Subject Tests are recommended. Results of non-standardized test administrations and documentation of disability may be submitted in support of any application, but are not essential for full consideration. Once admitted, students are fully mainstreamed and are expected to maintain the same academic standards as all other students.

Additional Information

The staff of Student Accessibility Services (SAS) seeks to create a barrier-free environment for students with disabilities by considering reasonable accommodations upon request. The staff works closely with all college departments to identify appropriate options for accommodating students with disabilities. Additionally, they offer services when students need special housing accommodations.

General Support Services Information

Contact Information
Name of program or department: Student Accessibility Services
Telephone: 757-221-2510
Fax: 757-221-2538

Accommodations or Services for Students with Learning Differences

Accommodations are decided upon an individual basis after a thorough review of appropriate, current documentation. The accommodations requested must be supported through the documentation provided and must be logically linked to the current impact of the condition on academic functioning.

Allowed in exams
Calculator: N/A
Dictionary: N/A
Computer: Yes
Spellchecker: N/A
Extended test time: Yes
Scribes: Yes
Proctors: N/A
Oral exams: No
Note-takers: Yes
Services for students with LD: Yes
Services for students with ADHD: Yes
Services for students with ASD: Yes
Distraction-reduced environment: Yes
Tape recording in class: Yes
Audio books: NR
Electronic texts: N/A
Kurzweil Reader: Yes
Other assistive technology: N/A
Priority registration: Yes
Added costs for services: No
LD specialists: No
ADHD coaching: NR
ASD specialists: NR
Professional tutors: NR
Peer tutors: NR
Max. hours/wk. for services: NR
How professors are notified of LD/ADHD: Director

General Admissions Information

Office of Admissions: 757-221-4223

Entrance Requirements

Academic units recommended: 4 English, 4 math, 4 science, 3 science labs, 4 foreign language, 4 social studies. High school diploma or equivalent is not required. SAT or ACT required. If ACT, ACT with writing accepted. TOEFL required of all international applicants: minimum paper TOEFL 600 or minimum internet TOEFL 100.

Application deadline: 1/1
Notification: 4/1
Average GPA: 4.19
ACT Composite middle 50% range: 28-32
SAT Math middle 50% range: 630-730
SAT Critical Reading middle 50% range: 630-730
SAT Writing middle 50% range: 620-720
Graduate top 10% of class: 81
Graduated top 25% of class: 96
Graduated top 50% of class: 100

COLLEGE GRADUATION REQUIREMENTS

Course waivers allowed: NR
In what course: Foreign language course substitution, NOT a waiver
Course substitutions allowed: NR
In what course: Documentation must exist that evidences impairment in specific area for consideration by the college's Committee on Degrees (which grants exception to school policy)

Additional Information

Environment: This public school was founded in 1693. It has a 1200-acre campus.

Student Body
Undergrad enrollment: 6,301
% Women: 56
% Men: 44
% Out-of-state: 30

Cost information
In-state Tuition: $15,674
Out-of-state Tuition: $36,158
Room & board: $11,382

Housing Information
University Housing: Yes
Percent living on campus: 74

Greek System
Fraternity: Yes
Sorority: Yes
Athletics: Division I

FERRUM COLLEGE

PO Box 1000, Ferrum, VA 24088
Phone: 540-365-4290 • Fax: 540-365-4366
E-mail: admissions@ferrum.edu • Web: www.ferrum.edu
Support: CS • Institution type: 4-year private

PROGRAMS OR SERVICES FOR STUDENTS WITH LEARNING DIFFERENCES

Ferrum College offers an array of services for students with documented disabilities, although the college does not offer a comprehensive program or monitoring services. Students motivated to accept the assistance and academic accommodations frequently find Ferrum's services to be excellent. Students can also consult with a disabilities specialist upon request about academics success strategies. While services are readily available, the student must assume the responsibility for requesting assistance and accepting offered options. Those students who are most successful are those who are highly motivated and those who are willing to implement self-advocacy skills.

ADMISSION INFORMATION FOR STUDENTS WITH LEARNING DIFFERENCES

College entrance test required: Yes
Interview required: No
Essay required: No
Additional Application Required for LD/ADHD/ASD: NR
What documentation required for LD: Current psycho-educational evaluation and statement of eligibility or other comparable documentation provided by a qualified professional.
With general application: No
To receive services after enrolling: Yes
What documentation required for ADHD: Current documentation with a statement of identification from a qualified professional.
With general application: No
To receive services after enrolling: Yes
What documentation required for ASD: Current documentation by a qualified professional that clearly explains the student's disability, strengths, needs, and relates needs to the tools used for evaluation.
With general application: No
To receive services after enrolling: Yes
LD/ADHD/ASD documentation submitted to: Support program/services
Special Ed. HS course work accepted: No
Specific course: Yes
Separate application required for program services: 3
Total # of students receiving LD/ADHD/ASD services: NR
Acceptance into program means acceptance into college: NR

ADMISSIONS

Students applying through the general admission criteria are encouraged to have an interview with the Office of Admissions. General admission criteria include: 4 years English, 3 years math 3 years science and 3 years social studies. The average GPA is 2.6. SAT/ACT required; and 50% have SAT between 400-499 (in each section) and 12-17 on the ACT.

ADDITIONAL INFORMATION

Ferrum offers several learning centers that are available for all students. Tutoring, study skills, and Gateway (a common first year experience course) helps students acclimate, and Ferrum Focus is a summer transitional course open to all entering freshmen. The tutoring center, writing center and a math center are academic support programs offered without additional fees. Through the ARC students can schedule tutoring with a peer tutor; arrange one-on-one tutoring; work with an academic counselor; attend peer led study groups; meet with professors during ARC office hours; and use a comfortable study area for individual or group study projects.

General Support Services Information

Contact Information
Name of program or department: Office of Academic Accessibility
Telephone: 540-365-4529
Fax: same as above

Accommodations or Services for Students with Learning Differences

Accommodations are decided upon an individual basis after a thorough review of appropriate, current documentation. The accommodations requests must be supported through the documentation provided and must be logically linked to the current impact of the condition on academic functioning.

Allowed in exams
Calculator: Yes
Dictionary: Yes
Computer: Yes
Spellchecker: Yes
Extended test time: Yes
Scribes: Yes
Proctors: Yes
Oral exams: Yes
Note-takers: Yes
Services for students with LD: Yes
Services for students with ADHD: Yes
Services for students with ASD: Yes
Distraction-reduced environment: Yes
Audio books: Yes
Tape recording in class: Yes
Kurzweil reader: Yes
Other assistive technology: Yes
Priority registration: No
Added costs of services: No
LD specialists: Yes
ADHD coaching: NR
ASD specialists: NR
Professional tutors: NR
Peer tutors: Yes
How professors are notified of student approved accommodations: Both student and director

General Admissions Information

Office of Admission: 540-365-4290

Entrance Requirements

Academic units recommended: 4 English, 3 math, 2 science (1 science lab), 2 foreign language, 3 social studies, 2 academic electives. High school diploma is required, and GED is accepted. TOEFL required of all international applicants: minimum paper TOEFL 550.

Application deadline: None
Notification: Rolling
Average GPA: 2.64
ACT Composite middle 50% range: 16–20
SAT Math middle 50% range: 390–490
SAT Critical Reading middle 50% range: 400–480
SAT Writing middle 50% range: NR
Graduated top 10% of class: 6%
Graduated top 25% of class: 19%
Graduated top 50% of class: 46%

COLLEGE GRADUATION REQUIREMENTS

Course substitutions allowed: Yes
In what course: Course substitution is discussed on a case-by-case basis and determined by the Academic Standards Committee.

Additional Information

Environment: The college is located in a rural area south of Roanoke.

Student Body
Undergrad enrollment: 1,484
% Women: 46%
% Men: 54%
% Out-of-state: 18%

Cost Information
Tuition: $26,375
Room & board: $8,530

Housing Information
University housing: Yes
% Living on campus: 80%

Greek System
Fraternity: No
Sorority: No
Athletics: Division III

HAMPTON UNIVERSITY

Office of Admissions, Hampton, VA 23668
Phone: 757-727-5328 • Fax: 757-727-5095
E-mail: admit@hamptonu.edu • Web: www.hamptonu.edu
Support: S • Institution: Private

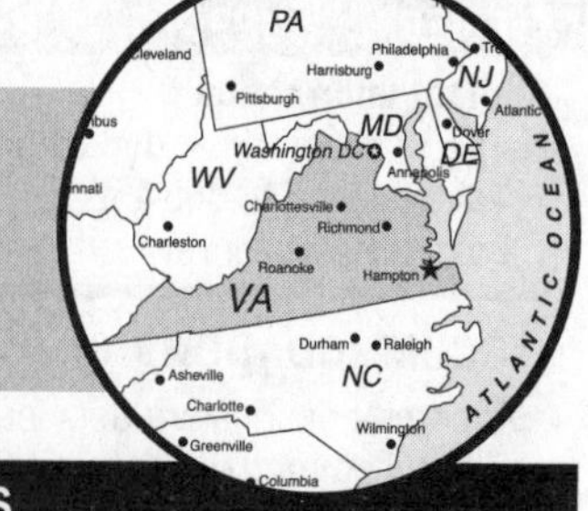

PROGRAMS OR SERVICES FOR STUDENTS WITH LEARNING DIFFERENCES

Hampton University is committed to assisting students with disabilities. They seek to help students achieve academic potential within the academically competitive curriculum by providing a variety of accommodations. Accommodations provided for students are in accordance to what is necessary and reasonable for the specific documented disability.

ADMISSION INFORMATION FOR STUDENTS WITH LEARNING DIFFERENCES

College entrance tests required: Yes
Interview required: No
Essay required: No
Additional Application Required for LD/ADHD/ASD: NR
What documentation required for LD: Psycho ed evaluation to include: relevant historical info, instructional interventions, related services, age diagnosed, objective data (aptitude, achievement, info processing), test scores (standard, percentile and grade equivalents) and describe functional limitations.
With general application: No
To receive services after enrolling: Yes
What documentation required for ADHD: Diagnosis based on DSM-V; history of behaviors impairing functioning in academic setting; diagnostic interview; history of symptoms; evidence of ongoing behaviors.
With general application: No
To receive services after enrolling: Yes
What documentation required for ASD: Psycho ed evaluation
With general application: NR
To receive services after enrolling: Yes
LD/ADHD/ASD documentation submitted to: Student Support Services
Special Ed. HS course work accepted: Yes
Specific course requirements of all applicants: Yes
Separate application required: No
Total # of students receiving LD/ADHD/ASD services: 30–40
Acceptance into program means acceptance into college: Students must be admitted to and enrolled in the university first and then request services.

ADMISSIONS

There is no special admission process for students with learning disabilities. Students are encouraged to send documentation directly to the Office of the Director of Compliance and Disability Services and not combine it with their application for admission to the university. Course requirements include: 4 English, 3 math, 2 foreign language, 2 science, 2 social science, and 6 electives.

ADDITIONAL INFORMATION

Accommodations in the classroom could include permission to record lectures, use of calculators, extended time for assignments and note sharing. Accommodations in an examination could include reduced-distraction environment, extended time, alternative test formats, readers/scribes, printed copies of oral instructions, and oral proctors. A student who would like to receive accommodations must contact the Office of the Director of Compliance and Disability Services and provide documentation of the disability that is not older than 3 years. The director is responsible for qualifying students with disabilities for reasonable academic accommodations within the university.

General Support Services Information

Contact Information
Name of program or department: Office of the Director of Compliance and Disability Services
Telephone: 757-727-5493
Fax: 757-727-4288

Accommodations or Services for Students with Learning Differences

Accommodations are available for students with supporting documentation. Documentation must be current no older than 3 years, and must clearly outline the disability, functional limitations and recommendations for accommodations in a competitive college environment.

Allowed in exams
Calculator: Yes
Dictionary: Yes
Computer: Yes
Spellchecker: Yes
Extended test time: Yes
Scribes: Yes
Proctors: Yes
Oral exams: Yes
Note-takers: Yes
Services for students with LD: Yes
Services for students with ADHD: Yes
Services for students with ASD: Yes
Distraction-reduced environment: Yes
Tape recording in class: Yes
Audio books: NR
Electronic texts: No
Kurzweil Reader: No
Other assistive technology: No
Priority registration: Yes
Added costs for services: No
LD specialists: No
ADHD coaching: NR
ASD specialists: NR
Professional tutors: No
Peer tutors: Yes
Max. hours/wk. for services: Unlimited
How professors are notified of LD/ADHD: By student

General Admissions Information

Office of Admissions: 757-727-5328

Entrance Requirements

Academic units required: 4 English, 3 math, 2 science, 2 science labs, 2 social studies, 6 academic electives, **Academic units recommended:** 2 foreign language. High school diploma is required and GED is accepted. SAT or ACT required for some. If ACT, ACT with writing accepted. TOEFL required of all international applicants: minimum paper TOEFL 525.

Application deadline: NR
Notification: NR
Average GPA: 3.22
ACT Composite middle 50% range: 19-24
SAT Math middle 50% range: 470-550
SAT Critical Reading middle 50% range: 470-540
SAT Writing middle 50% range: NR-NR
Graduate top 10% of class: 20
Graduated top 25% of class: 45
Graduated top 50% of class: 90

COLLEGE GRADUATION REQUIREMENTS

Course waivers allowed: NR
In what course: NR
Course substitutions allowed: NR
In what course: NR

Additional Information

Environment: This private school was founded in 1868. It has a 255-acre campus.

Student Body
Undergrad enrollment: 3,419
% Women: 66
% Men: 34
% Out-of-state: 73

Cost information
Tuition: $20,526
Room & board: $10,176

Housing Information
University Housing: Yes
Percent living on campus: 62

Greek System
Fraternity: Yes
Sorority: Yes
Athletics: Division I

JAMES MADISON UNIVERSITY

Sonner Hall, MSC 0101, Harrisonburg, VA 22807
Phone: 540-568-5681 • Fax: 540-568-3332
E-mail: admissions@jmu.edu • Web: www.jmu.edu
Support: CS • Institution: Public

PROGRAMS OR SERVICES FOR STUDENTS WITH LEARNING DIFFERENCES

The mission of the Office of Disability Services (ODS) is to assist the university in creating an accessible community where students with disabilities have an equal opportunity to fully participate in their educational experience at JMU. Disability Services provides, coordinates, and facilitates accommodations, support services, and programs that afford students with disabilities an equal opportunity to participate in life at JMU. The program assists students in the developmental process as they transition to higher education, independence, and effective self-advocacy and self-determination. ODS also serves as a resource for faculty and the JMU community as they strive to create inclusive opportunities for diverse needs. In order to fully evaluate requests for accommodations or auxiliary aids, JMU's Disability Services will need documentation of the disability that consists of a comprehensive evaluation by an appropriate professional that describes the current impact of the disability as it relates to the accommodation(s) requested. All requests for accommodations—including substitutions—are considered on a case-by-case basis. Students must register with Disability Services if they are planning to request reasonable accommodations. Current documentation is required to register for services.

ADMISSION INFORMATION FOR STUDENTS WITH LEARNING DIFFERENCES

College entrance tests required: Yes
Interview required: No
Additional Application Required for LD/ADHD/ASD: NR
What documentation required for LD: Psycho ed evaluation to include: relevant historical info, instructional interventions, related services, age diagnosed, objective data (aptitude, achievement, info processing), test scores (standard, percentile and grade equivalents) and describe functional limitations.
With general application: No
To receive services after enrolling: Yes
What documentation required for ADHD: Diagnosis based on DSM-V; history of behaviors impairing functioning in academic setting; diagnostic interview; history of symptoms; evidence of ongoing behaviors.
With general application: No
To receive services after enrolling: Yes
What documentation required for ASD: Psycho ed evaluation
With general application: NR
To receive services after enrolling: Yes
LD/ADHD/ASD documentation submitted to: Support Program/Services
Special Ed. HS course work accepted: Yes
Specific course requirements for all applicants: Yes
Separate application required for program services: No
Total # of students receiving LD/ADHD/ASD services: NR
Acceptance into program means acceptance into college: Separate application required after student has enrolled.

ADMISSIONS

During the admissions process, the admissions team at JMU is highly sensitive and knowledgeable concerning students with learning disabilities. Admission decisions are made without regard to disabilities and all prospective students are expected to present academic credentials that are competitive. After admission to JMU, the student should forward his or her documentation to ODS. Current recommendations for post-secondary accommodations are crucial for providing appropriate services in college. There are no specific courses required for admission into James Madison; however, students are expected to complete a solid college-prep curriculum. This would include four years of English, four years of mathematics (one year past algebra II), four years of social studies, three to five years of a foreign language and three years of laboratory sciences. The mid 50 percent range for the SAT is 1070–1230 and ACT is 24–28. Eighty-eight percent of the 2009–10 freshman class ranked in the top one-third of their high school class.

ADDITIONAL INFORMATION

The Office of Disability Services offers a number of services to students with disabilities including classroom accommodations such as extended time on tests, interpreters and other classroom accommodations for deaf and hard of hearing students, assistive technology labs; test proctoring; alternative texts and peer mentoring. Learning Strategies Instruction and Screening & Assessment services are available to all students, regardless of disability status. Additional on-campus services include: Learning Resource Centers (LRC). LRC consists of the following programs, tutoring and services available to all enrolled students: Communication Resource Center, Science & Math Learning Center, University Writing Center, Supplemental Instruction, Counseling and Student Development Center, and Career & Academic Planning.

General Support Services Information

Contact Information
Name of program or department: Office of Disability Services
Telephone: 540-568-6705
Fax: 540-568-7099
Website: www.jmu.edu/ods

Accommodations or Services For Students With Learning Differences

Accommodations are decided upon an individual basis after a thorough review of appropriate, current documentation. The accommodations requests must be supported through the documentation provided and must be logically linked to the current impact of the condition on academic functioning.

Allowed in exams
Calculator: Yes
Dictionary: Yes
Computer: Yes
Spellchecker: Yes
Extended test time: Yes
Scribes: Yes
Proctors: Yes
Oral exams: Yes
Note-takers: Yes
Support services for students with LD: Yes
Support services for students with ADHD: Yes
Support services for students with ASD: Yes
Distraction-reduced environment: Yes
Tape recording in class: No
Electronic texts: Yes
Kurzweil reader: NR
Audio books: Yes
Other assistive technology: Yes
Priority registration: Yes
Added costs of services: NR
LD specialists: Yes
ADHD coaching: Yes
ASD specialists: Yes
Professional tutors: No
Peer tutors: NR
Max. hours/wk. for services: NR
How professors are notified of student approved accommodations: By student

General Admissions Information

Office of Admissions: 540-568-5681

Entrance Requirements

Academic units required: 4 English, 4 math, 2 social studies, 2 history. High school diploma is required and GED is accepted. SAT or ACT required. If ACT, ACT with writing accepted. TOEFL required of all international applicants: minimum paper TOEFL 550.

Application deadline: 1/15
Notification: 4/1
Average GPA: NR
ACT Composite middle 50% range: 23-27
SAT Math middle 50% range: 520-610
SAT Critical Reading middle 50% range: 520-610
SAT Writing middle 50% range: NR-NR
Graduate top 10% of class: 23
Graduated top 25% of class: 41
Graduated top 50% of class: 97

COLLEGE GRADUATION REQUIREMENTS

Course waivers allowed: Yes
In what course: All accommodations for all students with disabilities are determined on a case by case basis relevant to the functional limitations experienced by the student and the concurrent need for mitigation by accommodation. Generally, Math requirements cannot be
Course substitutions allowed: NR

Additional Information

Environment: This public school was founded in 1908. It has a 712-acre campus.

Student Body
Undergrad enrollment: 19,396
% Women: 59
% Men: 41
% Out-of-state: 24

Cost information
In-state Tuition: $5,724
Out-of-state Tuition: $20,848
Room & board: $9,396

Housing Information
University Housing: Yes
Percent living on campus: 13

Greek System
Fraternity: Yes
Sorority: Yes
Athletics: Division I

Liberty University

1971 University Boulevard, Lynchburg, VA 24515
Phone: 434-582-2000 • Fax: 800-628-7977
E-mail: admissions@liberty.edu • Web: https://www.liberty.edu/
Support: CS • Institution: Private

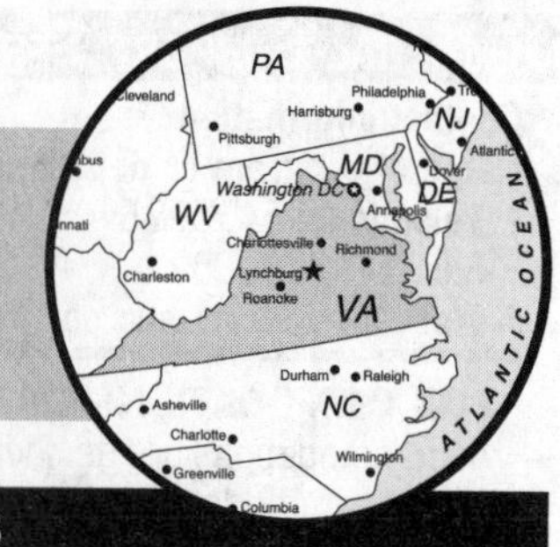

Programs or Services for Students with Learning Differences

The Office of Disability Academic Support, a component of the Center for Academic Support and Advising Services, was created to coordinate academic support services for Liberty University students who have documented disabilities. The Bruckner Learning Center helps all students plan, develop and maintain quality, university-wide academic support services.

Admission Information for Students with Learning Differences

College entrance test required: Yes
Interview required: No
Essay required: No
Additional Application Required for LD/ADHD/ASD: NR
What documentation required for LD: Their latest IEP and/or psychological testing profile or other written information that describes the learning disability.
With general application: No
To receive services after enrolling: Yes
What documentation required for ADHD: Diagnosis from a qualified professional.
With general application: No
To receive services after enrolling: Yes
What documentation required for ASD: Psycho ed evaluation
With general application: No
To receive services after enrolling: Yes
LD/ADHD/ASD documentation submitted to: Support program/services
Special Ed. HS course work accepted: Yes
Specific course: Yes
Separate application required for program services: No
Total # of students receiving LD/ADHD/ASD services: 300
Acceptance into program means acceptance into college: NR

Admissions

All applicants must submit an official transcript from an accredited high school and/or college, an official copy of a state high school equivalency diploma, or an official copy of the GED test results. The minimum acceptable unweighted GPA is 2.0. Applicants who fail to meet the minimum required GPA will be evaluated using other indicators of collegiate ability and may be admitted on Academic Warning. All applicants must submit ACT or SAT prior to admission. The minimum acceptable scores are SAT 800 or ACT 17.

Additional Information

If a student's entrance test scores indicate a deficiency in English or math, then the student will enroll in a basic composition class or fundamentals of math class. With the student's permission, instructors are provided with written communication providing information about the student's disability and suggestions of appropriate accommodations. Students with a specific learning disability can be assigned to a faculty advisor who has had training in LD. This person acts as a liaison between instructors and students regarding classroom accommodations. The Bruckner Learning Center provides individualized peer tutoring in most subjects on a weekly or drop-in basis. The Academic Opportunity Program (AOP) assists incoming freshmen in the adjustment of the rigors of college academically in their first semester. Students will be placed in groups of about 20 and have the same basic schedule. The AOP student schedule is created for the first semester to provide maximum success, allowing connections and study groups to be formed.

General Support Services Information

Contact Information
Name of program or department: Office of Disability Academic Support
Telephone: 434-582-2159
Fax: 434-582-2297

Accommodations or Services for Students with Learning Differences

Accommodations are decided upon an individual basis after a thorough review of appropriate, current documentation. The accommodations requests must be supported through the documentation provided and must be logically linked to the current impact of the condition on academic functioning.

Allowed in exams
Calculator: Yes
Dictionary: Yes
Computer: Yes
Spellchecker: Yes
Extended test time: Yes
Scribes: Yes
Proctors: Yes
Oral exams: Yes
Note-takers: Yes
Services for students with LD: Yes
Services for students with ADHD: Yes
Services for students with ASD: Yes
Distraction-reduced environment: Yes
Tape recording in class: Yes
Audio books: No
Kurzweil reader: Yes
Other assistive technology: Yes
Priority registration: Yes
Added costs of services: No
LD specialists: Yes
ADHD coaching: NR
ASD specialists: NR
Professional tutors: NR
Peer tutors: Yes
How professors are notified of student approved accommodations: Director

General Admissions Information

Office of Admissions: 434-582-2000

Entrance Requirements

Academic units recommended: 4 English, 3 math, 2 science, 2 science labs, 2 foreign language, 2 social studies, 4 academic electives. High school diploma is required and GED is accepted. SAT or ACT required. If ACT, ACT with writing accepted. TOEFL required of all international applicants: minimum paper TOEFL 500 or minimum internet TOEFL 60.

Application deadline: NR
Notification: NR
Average GPA: 3.48
ACT Composite middle 50% range: 20-27
SAT Math middle 50% range: 470-590
SAT Critical Reading middle 50% range: 480-600
SAT Writing middle 50% range: 460-580
Graduated top 10% of class: 23
Graduated top 25% of class: 47
Graduated top 50% of class: 78

COLLEGE GRADUATION REQUIREMENTS

Course waivers allowed: No
Course substitutions allowed: No

Additional Information

Environment: This private school, affiliated with the Baptist Church, was founded in 1971. It has a 4400-acre campus.

Student Body
Undergrad enrollment: 13,072
% Women: 52
% Men: 48
% Out-of-state: 59

Cost information
Tuition: $22,000
Room & board: $9,306

Housing Information
University Housing: Yes
Percent living on campus: 59

Greek System
Fraternity: No
Sorority: No
Athletics: Division I

OLD DOMINION UNIVERSITY

108 Rollins Hall, Norfolk, VA 23529-0050
Phone: 757-683-3685 • Fax: 757-683-3255
E-mail: admissions@odu.edu • Web: www.odu.edu
Support: CS • Institution: Public

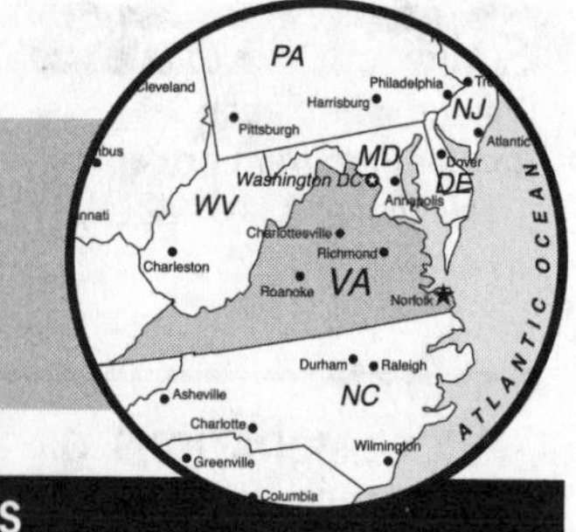

PROGRAMS OR SERVICES FOR STUDENTS WITH LEARNING DIFFERENCES

The Office of Educational Accessibility at Old Dominion University advocates for all students with disabilities in the pursuit of their educational objectives and enhances their overall university experiences by providing services and accommodations. The office helps to ensure equal access to all campus facilities and activities. It fosters acceptance by designing opportunities which highlight respect, awareness, and understanding for individuals with disabilities. It empowers students to become self-advocates in fulfilling their collegiate goals so they can find success at ODU and in their future endeavors.

ADMISSION INFORMATION FOR STUDENTS WITH LEARNING DIFFERENCES

College entrance test required: Yes
Interview required: No
Essay required: Not Applicable
Additional Application Required for LD/ADHD/ASD: No
What documentation required for LD: Please see the documentation guidelines listed on the office website: https:// www.odu.edu/educationalaccessibility.
With general application: NR
To receive services after enrolling: No
What documentation required for ADHD: Please see the documentation guidelines listed on the office website: https:// www.odu.edu/educationalaccessibility.
With general application: NR
To receive services after enrolling: No
What documentation required for ASD: Please see the documentation guidelines listed on the office website: https:// www.odu.edu/educationalaccessibility.
With general application: NR
To receive services after enrolling: No
LD/ADHD/ASD documentation submitted to: Office of Educational Accessibility
ASD Specific Program: No
Special Ed. HS course work accepted: NR
Specific course requirements of all applicants: Yes
Separate application required for program services: FALSE
Total # of students receiving LD/ADHD/ASD services: NR
Acceptance into program means acceptance into college: NR

ADMISSIONS

Admission to Old Dominion is based solely on the entrance requirements as described in the University Catalog. Disclosure of a disability during the admissions process is not required; neither the nature nor the severity of an individual's disability is used as criterion for admission. Recommended high school course work includes 4 years of English, 4 years of Mathematics, 3 years of Science, 3 years of Social Studies, and 3 years of Foreign Languages. For more information about the university and the admissions process, contact the Office of Admissions at (757) 683-3685.

ADDITIONAL INFORMATION

Accomodations are based upon the documentation that the student presents and the discussion that the student has with the office of Educational Accessibility professionals. The accommodations may have to be adjusted during the course of the academic career of the student at the University. Students are encouraged to seek out the Office each semester for any learning needs not being accommodated. Counseling and advising; study skills instruction; reading, writing, and math instruction; and tutorial assistance are available. Program staff design support services that focus on students' learning styles and special needs. There is a special section of Spanish for students with learning disabilities to meet the foreign language requirements, as well as developmental math, reading, spelling, and writing classes

General Support Services Information

Contact Information
Name of program or department: Office of Educational Accessibility
Telephone: 757-683-4655
Fax: 757-683-5356
Website: https://www.odu.edu/educationalaccessibility

Accommodations or Services for Students with Learning Differences

Accommodations are decided upon an individual basis after a thorough review of appropriate, current documentation. The accommodations requests must be supported through the documentation provided and must be logically linked to the current impact of the condition on academic functioning.

Allowed in exams
Calculator: Yes
Dictionary: Yes
Computer: Yes
Spellchecker: Yes
Extended test time: Yes
Scribes: Yes
Proctors: Yes
Oral exams: Yes
Note-takers: Yes
Support services for students with LD: Yes
Support services for students with ADHD: Yes
Support services for students with ASD: Yes
Distraction-reduced environment: Yes
Tape recording in class: Yes
Electronic texts: Yes
Kurzweil reader: NR
Audio books: Yes
Other assistive technology: Yes
Priority registration: Yes
Added costs of services: No
LD specialists: Yes
ADHD coaching: Yes
ASD specialists: Yes
Professional tutors: No
Peer tutors: Yes
Max. hours/wk. for services: NR
How professors are notified of student approved accommodations: By student

General Admissions Information

Office of Admissions: 757-683-3685

Entrance Requirements

Academic units required: 4 English, 3 math, 3 science, 3 foreign language, 3 social studies, **Academic units recommended:** 4 English, 4 math, 3 science, 3 foreign language, 3 social studies. High school diploma is required and GED is accepted. SAT or ACT required. If ACT, ACT with writing accepted. TOEFL required of all international applicants: minimum paper TOEFL 550 or minimum internet TOEFL 79.

Application deadline: 2/1
Notification: Rolling starting 10/15
Average GPA: 3.28
ACT Composite middle 50% range: 18-24
SAT Math middle 50% range: 460-570
SAT Critical Reading middle 50% range: 460-570
SAT Writing middle 50% range: NR-NR
Graduate top 10% of class: 8
Graduated top 25% of class: 32
Graduated top 50% of class: 71

COLLEGE GRADUATION REQUIREMENTS

Course waivers allowed: No
In what course: NR
Course substitutions allowed: Yes
In what course: Foreign language substitutions are available with sufficient documentation of a language processing disability.

Additional Information

Environment: This public school was founded in 1930. It has a 188-acre campus.

Student Body
Undergrad enrollment: 20,101
% Women: 54
% Men: 46
% Out-of-state: 7

Cost information
In-state Tuition: $9,480
Out-of-state Tuition: $26,220
Room & board: $10,404

Housing Information
University Housing: Yes
Percent living on campus: 23

Greek System
Fraternity: Yes
Sorority: Yes
Athletics: Division I

RADFORD UNIVERSITY

PO Box 6903, Radford, VA 24142
Phone: 540-831-5371 • Fax: 540-831-5038
E-mail: admissions@radford.edu • Web: www.radford.edu
Support: CS • Institution: Public

PROGRAMS OR SERVICES FOR STUDENTS WITH LEARNING DIFFERENCES

The Disability Resource Office (DRO) is committed to providing equal educational opportunities for individuals living with disabilities. The DRO serves and supports students, parents, and visitors seeking reasonable accommodations under the Americans with Disabilities Act. We are dedicated to the ongoing goal of access and inclusion for an individual to fully participate in the university experience.

ADMISSION INFORMATION FOR STUDENTS WITH LEARNING DIFFERENCES

College entrance test required: NR
Interview required: No
Essay required: Not Applicable
Additional Application Required for LD/ADHD/ASD: Yes
What documentation required for LD: Formal diagnosis functional limitations
With general application: Not Applicable
To receive services after enrolling: Yes
What documentation required for ADHD: Formal diagnosis functional limitations
With general application: Not Applicable
To receive services after enrolling: Yes
What documentation required for ASD: Formal diagnosis functional limitations
With general application: Not Applicable
To receive services after enrolling: Yes
LD/ADHD/ASD documentation submitted to: Disability Resource Office
ASD Specific Program: NR
Special Ed. HS course work accepted: Not Applicable
Specific course requirements of all applicants: NR
Separate application required for program services: True
Total # of students receiving LD/ADHD/ASD services:
Acceptance into program means acceptance into college: Not Applicable

ADMISSIONS

General admission standards and requirements

ADDITIONAL INFORMATION

The Learning Assistance and Resource Center helps student achieve academic success. In individual or group tutoring sessions, students acquire support from College Reading and Learning Association certified trained tutors. Writing tutors aid students with writing assignments for any discipline. Additionally,students can improve their learning skills through one-on-one consultations. With a learner-centered approach, the staff and tutors seek to meet each Radford University student's academic needs.

General Support Services Information

Contact Information
Name of program or department: Disability Resource Office
Telephone: 540-831-6350
Fax: 540-831-6525
Website: www.radford.edu/dro

Accommodations or Services for Students with Learning Differences

Accommodations are decided upon an individual basis after a thorough review of appropriate, current documentation. The accommodations requests must be supported through the documentation provided and must be logically linked to the current impact of the condition on academic functioning.

Allowed in exams
Calculator: Yes
Dictionary: Yes
Computer: Yes
Spellchecker: Yes
Extended test time: Yes
Scribes: Not Applicable
Proctors: Yes
Oral exams: Not Applicable
Note-takers: Yes
Support services for students with LD: Yes
Support services for students with ADHD: Yes
Support services for students with ASD: Yes
Distraction-reduced environment: Yes
Tape recording in class: Yes
Electronic texts: Yes
Kurzweil reader: NR
Audio books: Yes
Other assistive technology: Yes
Priority registration: Yes
Added costs of services: No
LD specialists: Yes
ADHD coaching: Yes
ASD specialists: Yes
Professional tutors: No
Peer tutors: Yes
Max. hours/wk. for services: NR
How professors are notified of student approved accommodations: By student

General Admissions Information

Office of Admissions: 540-831-5371

Entrance Requirements

Academic units recommended: 4 English, 4 math, 4 science, 4 science labs, 4 foreign language, 2 social studies, 2 history, High school diploma is required and GED is accepted. SAT or ACT recommended. If ACT, ACT with writing accepted. TOEFL required of all international applicants: minimum paper TOEFL 520 or minimum internet TOEFL 68.

Application deadline: NR
Notification: 4/1
Average GPA: 3.17
ACT Composite middle 50% range: 18-22
SAT Math middle 50% range: 440-520
SAT Critical Reading middle 50% range: 450-530
SAT Writing middle 50% range: 420-510
Graduate top 10% of class: 6
Graduated top 25% of class: 18
Graduated top 50% of class: 55

COLLEGE GRADUATION REQUIREMENTS

Course waivers allowed: Not Applicable
In what course: Determined on a case-by-case basis; generally no
Course substitutions allowed: Yes
In what course: Determined on a case-by-case basis

Additional Information

Environment: This public school was founded in 1910. It has a 191-acre campus.

Student Body
Undergrad enrollment: 8,880
% Women: 56
% Men: 44
% Out-of-state: 5

Cost information
In-state tuition: $6,788
Out-of-state tuition: $18,626
Room & board: $8,677

Housing Information
University Housing: Yes
Percent living on campus: 34

Greek System
Fraternity: Yes
Sorority: Yes
Athletics: Division I

ROANOKE COLLEGE

221 College Lane, Salem, VA 24153-3794
Phone: 540-375-2270 • Fax: 540-375-2267
E-mail: admissions@roanoke.edu • Web: www.roanoke.edu
Support: S • Institution: Private

PROGRAMS OR SERVICES FOR STUDENTS WITH LEARNING DIFFERENCES

Roanoke College is committed to providing equal access to educational opportunities for all students, in accordance with Section 504 of the Rehabilitation Act of 1973 and the Americans with Disabilities Act.

ADMISSION INFORMATION FOR STUDENTS WITH LEARNING DIFFERENCES

College entrance test required: Yes
Interview required: No
Essay required: Not Applicable
Additional Application Required for LD/ADHD/ASD: Yes
What documentation required for LD: All students disclosing ADD/ADHD will be required to show documentation of a psychological or medical evaluation with results that satisfy the diagnosis requirements set forth in the Diagnostic Statistical Manual (American Psychiatric Association). In other words, a declaration from a physician or counselor that a student has ADD/ADHD will need to be supported with documentation of the evaluations conducted resulting in diagnosis. See http://www.roanoke.edu/inside/a-z_index/center_for_learning_and_teaching/disability_support_services/registering_a_disability_and_requesting_accommodations
With general application: No
To receive services after enrolling: Yes
What documentation required for ADHD: Separate requirements are not specified for each disorder. The college policy can be found at: http://www.roanoke.edu/inside/a-z_index/center_for_learning_and_teaching/disability_support_services/registering_a_disability_and_requesting_accommodations
With general application: No
To receive services after enrolling: Yes
What documentation required for ASD: Separate requirements are not specified for each disorder. The college policy can be found at: http://www.roanoke.edu/inside/a-z_index/center_for_learning_and_teaching/disability_support_services/registering_a_disability_and_requesting_accommodations
With general application: No
To receive services after enrolling: Yes
LD/ADHD/ASD documentation submitted to: Disability Support Services
ASD Specific Program: No
Special Ed. HS course work accepted: NR
Specific course requirements of all applicants: Yes
Separate application required for program services: False
Total # of students receiving LD/ADHD/ASD services:
Acceptance into program means acceptance into college: No

ADMISSIONS

Admission to Roanoke College is based on individual qualifications. No separate standards are used for students with documented disabilities.

ADDITIONAL INFORMATION

All services are accessed through the Disability Support Services office and the Goode-Pasfield Center for Learning & Teaching. Any special considerations or accommodations requested by the student will not be allowed until testing results have been received and reviewed by the Coordinator of Disability Support Services. All requests are handled on a case by case basis. Students are encouraged to submit their documentation shortly after being admitted to the College.

General Support Services Information

Contact Information
Name of program or department: Disability Support Services
Telephone: 540-375-2247
Fax: 540-375-2485
Website: http://www.roanoke.edu/inside/a-z_index/center_for_learning_and_teaching/disability_support_services

Accommodations or Services for Students with Learning Differences

Accommodations are decided upon an individual basis after a thorough review of appropriate, current documentation. The accommodations requests must be supported through the documentation provided and must be logically linked to the current impact of the condition on academic functioning.

Allowed in exams
Calculator: Yes
Dictionary: Yes
Computer: Yes
Spellchecker: Yes
Extended test time: Yes
Scribes: No
Proctors: Yes
Oral exams: Yes
Note-takers: Yes
Support services for students with LD: Yes
Support services for students with ADHD: Yes
Support services for students with ASD: Yes
Distraction-reduced environment: Yes
Tape recording in class: Yes
Electronic texts: Yes
Kurzweil reader: NR
Audio books: No
Other assistive technology: No
Priority registration: No
Added costs of services: No
LD specialists: No
ADHD coaching: Yes
ASD specialists: No
Professional tutors: Yes
Peer tutors: Yes
Max. hours/wk. for services: 25
How professors are notified of student approved accommodations: By student

General Admissions Information

Office of Admissions: 540-375-2270

Entrance Requirements

Academic units required: 4 English, 3 math, 2 science, 2 science labs, 2 social studies, 5 academic electives, **Academic units recommended:** 4 foreign language, High school diploma is required and GED is accepted. SAT or ACT required. If ACT, ACT with writing accepted. TOEFL required of all international applicants: minimum internet TOEFL 80.

Application deadline: 3/15
Notification: Rolling starting 10/1
Average GPA: 3.5
ACT Composite middle 50% range: 21-27
SAT Math middle 50% range: 480-590
SAT Critical Reading middle 50% range: 490-610
SAT Writing middle 50% range: 480-598
Graduate top 10% of class: 15
Graduated top 25% of class: 45
Graduated top 50% of class: 78

COLLEGE GRADUATION REQUIREMENTS

Course waivers allowed: No
In what course: NR
Course substitutions allowed: No
In what course: NR

Additional Information

Environment: This private school, affiliated with the Lutheran Church, was founded in 1842. It has a 68-acre campus.

Student Body
Undergrad enrollment: 2,005
% Women: 59
% Men: 41
% Out-of-state: 47

Cost information
Tuition: $39,720
Room & board: $12,810
Housing Information
University Housing: Yes
Percent living on campus: 76

Greek System
Fraternity: Yes
Sorority: Yes
Athletics: Division III

University of Virginia

Office of Admission, Charlottesville, VA 22906
Phone: 434-982-3200 • Fax: 434-924-3587
E-mail: undergradadmission@virginia.edu • Web: www.virginia.edu
Support: CS • Institution: Public

Programs or Services for Students with Learning Differences

The University of Virginia is committed to providing equal access to educational and social opportunities for all disabled students. The Student Disability Access Center (SDAC) is housed within the university's Department of Student Health and serves as the coordinating agency for services to all students with disabilities. The SDAC assists students with disabilities to become independent self-advocates who are able to demonstrate their abilities both in the classroom and as members of the university community. The center provides a number of services, including review of documentation supporting the disability, determination of appropriate academic accommodations, and serving as a liaison with faculty and administrators. Information can be shared, with the student's permission, with university personnel who have an educational need to know. Once a learning disability is documented, the center assigns appropriate and reasonable accommodations and serves as a liaison with faculty and administrators. The center's primary purpose is to support the academic well-being of students with disabilities.

Admission Information for Students with Learning Differences

College entrance tests required: Yes
Interview required: No
Essay required: No
Additional Application Required for LD/ADHD/ASD: NR
What documentation required for LD: Psycho ed evaluation to include: relevant historical info, instructional interventions, related services, age diagnosed, objective data (aptitude, achievement, info processing), test scores (standard, percentile and grade equivalents) and describe functional limitations.
With general application: No
To receive services after enrolling: Yes
What documentation required for ADHD: Diagnosis based on DSM-V; history of behaviors impairing functioning in academic setting; diagnostic interview; history of symptoms; evidence of ongoing behaviors.
With general application: No
To receive services after enrolling: Yes
What documentation required for ASD: Psycho ed evaluation
With general application: NR
To receive services after enrolling: Yes
LD/ADHD/ASD documentation submitted to: LNEC
Special Ed. HS course work accepted: NR
Specific course requirements of all applicants: Yes
Separate application required: No
Total # of students receiving LD/ADHD/ASD services: NR
Acceptance into program means acceptance into college: Students must be admitted to and enrolled in the university first and then request services.

Admissions

The students with learning disabilities go through the same admissions procedure as all incoming applicants. After admission to the university, students must contact the SDAC to receive services. Students with learning disabilities admitted to the university have qualified for admission because of their abilities. No criteria for admission are waived because of a disability. All applicants to UVA have outstanding grades, a high rank in their high school class, excellent performance in advanced placement and honor courses, superior performance on ACT/SAT Reasoning and SAT Subject Tests, extracurricular success, special talents, and interests and goals. Letters of recommendation are required.

Additional Information

Following acceptance of an offer of admission to the university, students with an LD or ADHD are advised to contact the LNEC to identify their need for services. All students seeking accommodations while at the university must provide acceptable documentation of their disability, including, but not limited to, a neuropsychological or psychoeducational evaluation report, completed by a licensed clinical psychologist or clinical neuropsychologist, or other qualified provider that has been completed within 3 years of matriculation. Students are strongly encouraged to consult the Guidelines for Documentation of a Learning Disorder or ADHD available in the Information section of the SDAC website. Services and accommodations are available for undergraduate and graduate students.

General Support Services Information

Contact Information
Name of program or department: Student Disability Access Center (SDAC)
Telephone: 434-243-5181
Fax: 434-243-5188

Accommodations or Services for Students with Learning Differences

Accommodations are decided upon an individual basis after a thorough review of appropriate, current documentation. The accommodations requested must be supported through the documentation provided and must be logically linked to the current impact of the condition on academic functioning.

Allowed in exams
Calculator: Yes
Dictionary: Yes
Computer: Yes
Spellchecker: Yes
Extended test time: Yes
Scribes: Yes
Proctors: Yes
Oral exams: Yes
Note-takers: Yes
Services for students with LD: Yes
Services for students with ADHD: Yes
Services for students with ASD: Yes
Distraction-reduced environment: Yes
Tape recording in class: Yes
Audio books: NR
Electronic texts: Yes
Kurzweil Reader: Yes
Other assistive technology: Yes
Priority registration: NR
Added costs for services: No
LD specialists: Yes
ADHD coaching: NR
ASD specialists: NR
Professional tutors: No
Peer tutors: No
Max. hours/wk. for services: NR
How professors are notified of LD/ADHD: NR

General Admissions Information

Office of Admissions: 434-982-3200

Entrance Requirements

Academic units required: 4 English, 4 math, 2 science, 2 foreign language, 1 social studies, **Academic units recommended:** 5 math, 4 science, 5 foreign language, 4 social studies. High school diploma is required and GED is accepted. SAT or ACT required. If ACT, ACT with writing required. TOEFL required of all international applicants.

Application deadline: 1/1
Notification: 4/1
Average GPA: 4.234
ACT Composite middle 50% range: 29-33
SAT Math middle 50% range: 630-740
SAT Critical Reading middle 50% range: 620-720
SAT Writing middle 50% range: 620-720
Graduate top 10% of class: 89
Graduated top 25% of class: 97
Graduated top 50% of class: 99

COLLEGE GRADUATION REQUIREMENTS

Course waivers allowed: NR
Course substitutions allowed: NR
In what course: course substitution request. Additionally, students are required to demonstrate a "good faith effort" to fulfill the foreign language requirement before a course substitution would be considered.

Additional Information

Environment: This public school was founded in 1819. It has a 1167-acre campus.

Student Body
Undergrad enrollment: 16,736
% Women: 56
% Men: 44
% Out-of-state: 28

Cost information
In-state Tuition: $0
Out-of-state Tuition: $40,506
Room & board: $10,400

Housing Information
University Housing: Yes
Percent living on campus: 40

Greek System
Fraternity: Yes
Sorority: Yes
Athletics: Division I

EASTERN WASHINGTON UNIVERSITY

304 Sutton Hall, Cheney, WA 99004
Phone: 509-359-6692 • Fax: 509-359-6692
E-mail: admissions@ewu.edu • Web: www.ewu.edu
Support: S • Institution: Public

PROGRAMS OR SERVICES FOR STUDENTS WITH LEARNING DIFFERENCES

Although the university does not offer a specialized curriculum, personnel work with students to modify programs to meet individual needs. Disability Support Services (DSS) is dedicated to the coordination of appropriate and reasonable accommodations for students with disabilities. These accommodations are based on individual needs so that each student may receive an equal opportunity to learn to participate in campus life, to grow emotionally and socially, and to successfully complete a program of study that will enable him or her to be self-supporting and remain as independent as possible. This is facilitated through support services, information sharing, advisement, and referral when requested. Students who require services and support need to contact DSS so that the disability can be verified, specific needs determined, and timely accommodations made. In most cases, documentation by a professional service provider will be necessary. Information is kept strictly confidential. However, it is important to share information that will enable DSS staff to provide appropriate, reasonable, and timely services tailored to individual needs.

ADMISSION INFORMATION FOR STUDENTS WITH LEARNING DIFFERENCES

College entrance tests required: Yes
Interview required: No
Essay required: Yes
Additional Application Required for LD/ADHD/ASD: NR
What documentation required for LD: Psycho ed evaluation to include: relevant historical info, instructional interventions, related services, age diagnosed, objective data (aptitude, achievement, info processing), test scores (standard, percentile and grade equivalents) and describe functional limitations.
With general application: No
To receive services after enrolling: Yes
What documentation required for ADHD: Diagnosis based on DSM-V; history of behaviors impairing functioning in academic setting; diagnostic interview; history of symptoms; evidence of ongoing behaviors.
With general application: No
To receive services after enrolling: Yes
What documentation required for ASD: Psycho ed evaluation
With general application: NR
To receive services after enrolling: Yes
LD/ADHD/ASD documentation submitted to: Admissions Office and DSS
Special Ed. HS course work accepted: Yes
Specific course requirements of all applicants: Yes
Separate application required: No
Total # of students receiving LD/ADHD/ASD services: 200
Acceptance into program means acceptance into college: Students must be admitted to and enrolled in the university first and then request services.

ADMISSIONS

Individuals with disabilities are admitted via the standard admissions criteria that apply to all students. General admissibility is based on an index using GPA and test scores. The minimum GPA accepted is a 2.0. Required courses include 4 years of English, 3 years of math, 3 years of social science, 2 years of science (1 year of lab), 2 years of a foreign language (American Sign Language accepted), and 1 year of arts or academic electives. Special education courses are acceptable if they are courses that are regularly taught in the high school. However, all applicants must complete the required core courses. Students who do not meet the grade and test score admission scale may provide additional information to the Admission Office and request consideration through the special talent admissions process.

ADDITIONAL INFORMATION

Examples of services for students with specific learning disabilities include alternative format textbooks; equipment loans; alternative testing arrangements such as oral exams, extended time on tests, relocation of testing site; note-takers; tutorial assistance (available to all students); referral to a Learning Skills Center, Writers' Center, and/or Mathematics Lab; accessible computer stations; and a Kurzweil Reader. Examples of services for students with ADHD are consultation regarding reasonable and effective accommodations with classroom professors; alternative testing; alternative format textbooks; note-takers; taped lectures; equipment loans; referrals to a Learning Skills Center, a Math Lab, a Writers' Center, and counseling and psychological services; information on ADHD; and informal counseling. Skills classes for credit are offered in math, reading, time management, study skills, and writing skills. FOCUS is a structured first-year experience for selected, provisionally admitted students. The experience includes advising; academic instruction in math, English, and study strategies; and professional mentoring. Services and accommodations are offered to undergraduate and graduate students.

General Support Services Information

Contact Information
Name of program or department: Disability Support Services
Telephone: 509-359-6871
Fax: 509-359-7458

Accommodations or Services for Students with Learning Differences

Accommodations are decided upon an individual basis after a thorough review of appropriate, current documentation. The accommodations requested must be supported through the documentation provided and must be logically linked to the current impact of the condition on academic functioning.

Allowed in exams
Calculator: Yes
Dictionary: Yes
Computer: Yes
Spellchecker: Yes
Extended test time: Yes
Scribes: Yes
Proctors: Yes
Oral exams: Yes
Note-takers: Yes
Services for students with LD: Yes
Services for students with ADHD: Yes
Services for students with ASD: Yes
Distraction-reduced environment: Yes
Tape recording in class: Yes
Audio books: NR
Electronic texts: Yes
Kurzweil Reader: Yes
Other assistive technology: Yes
Priority registration: Yes
Added costs for services: No
LD specialists: No
ADHD coaching: NR
ASD specialists: NR
Professional tutors: 7
Peer tutors: 33
Max. hours/wk. for services: NR
How professors are notified of LD/ADHD: By both student and director

General Admissions Information

Office of Admissions: 509-359-6692

Entrance Requirements

Academic units required: 4 English, 3 math, 2 science, 2 science labs, 2 foreign language, 3 social studies, 1 visual/performing arts, and 1 units from above areas or other academic areas. High school diploma or equivalent is not required. SAT or ACT required. If ACT, ACT with writing accepted. TOEFL required of all international applicants: minimum paper TOEFL 525 or minimum internet TOEFL 71.

Application deadline: NR
Notification: Rolling starting 9/1
Average GPA: 3.21
ACT Composite middle 50% range: 18-23
SAT Math middle 50% range: 430-550
SAT Critical Reading middle 50% range: 420-540
SAT Writing middle 50% range: 410-520
Graduate top 10% of class: NR
Graduated top 25% of class: NR
Graduated top 50% of class: NR

COLLEGE GRADUATION REQUIREMENTS

Course waivers allowed: NR
In what course: NR
Course substitutions allowed: NR
In what course: NR

Additional Information

Environment: This public school was founded in 1882. It has a 335-acre campus.

Student Body
Undergrad enrollment: 11,300
% Women: 54
% Men: 46
% Out-of-state: 6

Cost information
Room & board:NR

Housing Information
University Housing: Yes
Percent living on campus: 19

Greek System
Fraternity: Yes
Sorority: Yes
Athletics: Division I

The Evergreen State College

2700 Evergreen Pkwy NW, Olympia, WA 98505
Phone: 360-867-6170 • Fax: 360-867-5114
E-mail: admissions@evergreen.edu • Web: www.evergreen.edu
Support: CS • Institution: Public

Programs or Services for Students with Learning Differences

For almost forty years, The Evergreen State College has consistently provided an integrated learning community for students. Instead of taking four or five separate, unrelated classes each quarter, students take one program that unifies these classes around a central theme, taught by two or three faculty members from different academic disciplines. Many programs continue for two or three consecutive quarters. This allows students to build specific skills to produce highly sophisticated work, even in introductory offerings. And, because learning is too important to be reduced to an arbitrary number or letter grade, students receive a narrative evaluation from the faculty. The student's accomplishments and achievements will be detailed to provide graduate schools and employers with a comprehensive overview of his or her undergraduate education.

Admission Information for Students with Learning Differences

College entrance tests required: Yes
Interview required: No
Additional Application Required for LD/ADHD/ASD: NR
What documentation required for LD: Psycho ed evaluation to include: relevant historical info, instructional interventions, related services, age diagnosed, objective data (aptitude, achievement, info processing), test scores (standard, percentile and grade equivalents) and describe functional limitations.
With general application: No
To receive services after enrolling: Yes
What documentation required for ADHD: Diagnosis based on DSM-V; history of behaviors impairing functioning in academic setting; diagnostic interview; history of symptoms; evidence of ongoing behaviors.
With general application: No
To receive services after enrolling: Yes
What documentation required for ASD: Psycho ed evaluation
With general application: NR
To receive services after enrolling: Yes
LD/ADHD/ASD documentation submitted to: Support Program/Services
Special Ed. HS course work accepted: No
Specific course requirements for all applicants: Yes
Separate application required for program services: No
Total # of students receiving LD/ADHD/ASD services: NR
Acceptance into program means acceptance into college: Separate application required after student has enrolled

Admissions

Students entering Evergreen directly from high school will be considered for admission on the following basis: Completion of college-preparatory course work in high school; Grade point average (GPA) and ACT or SAT test scores. A 2.8 cumulative GPA is recommended; a 2.0 cumulative GPA is required for admission consideration. The SAT writing test and subject tests are not required; Good standing in any college-level work attempted while in high school or after high school graduation. The quality of the college work will be taken into consideration as well. A personal statement is an important part of the application, too. This statement is desired from all applicants. However, Home School applicants must submit a personal statement. More information about the admission application process and the personal statement can be found on the web at admissions.evergreen.edu/application.

Additional Information

The Evergreen State College is committed to providing equal access, accommodations, and educational support for qualified students with disabilities. It is our goal to invite and celebrate diversity within our campus community. Our approach is designed to be holistic and to empower by promoting: self reliance, effective problem solving skills, enhanced academic and personal development, and equal access to college programs and activities for qualified students with disabilities.

General Support Services Information

Contact Information
Name of program or department: Access Services
Telephone: (360) 867-6364
Fax: NR
Website: http://www.evergreen.edu/access/

Accommodations or Services For Students With Learning Differences

Accommodations are decided upon an individual basis after a thorough review of appropriate, current documentation. The accommodations requests must be supported through the documentation provided and must be logically linked to the current impact of the condition on academic functioning.

Allowed in exams
Calculator: Yes
Dictionary: Yes
Computer: Yes
Spellchecker: Yes
Extended test time: Yes
Scribes: No
Proctors: No
Oral exams: No
Note-takers: Yes
Support services for students with LD: Yes
Support services for students with ADHD: Yes
Support services for students with ASD: Yes
Distraction-reduced environment: Yes
Tape recording in class: Yes
Electronic texts: Yes
Kurzweil reader: NR
Audio books: Yes
Other assistive technology: Yes
Priority registration: Yes
Added costs of services: No
LD specialists: Yes
ADHD coaching: Yes
ASD specialists: Yes
Professional tutors: No
Peer tutors: Not Applicable
Max. hours/wk. for services: NR
How professors are notified of student approved accommodations: By both student and director

General Admissions Information

Office of Admissions: 360-867-6170

Entrance Requirements

Academic units required: 4 English, 3 math, 2 science, 2 science labs, 2 foreign language, 3 social studies, 1 academic electives, and 1 units from above areas or other academic areas. High school diploma is required and GED is accepted. SAT or ACT required. If ACT, ACT with writing accepted. TOEFL required of all international applicants: minimum paper TOEFL 550 or minimum internet TOEFL 79.

Application deadline: NR
Notification: Rolling starting 11/1
Average GPA: 3.04
ACT Composite middle 50% range: 20-26
SAT Math middle 50% range: 450-560
SAT Critical Reading middle 50% range: 490-630
SAT Writing middle 50% range: 460-590
Graduate top 10% of class: 9
Graduated top 25% of class: 25
Graduated top 50% of class: 64

COLLEGE GRADUATION REQUIREMENTS

Course waivers allowed: Not Applicable
In what course: NR
Course substitutions allowed: Not Applicable
In what course: NR

Additional Information

Environment: This public school was founded in 1967. It has a 1000-acre campus.

Student Body
Undergrad enrollment: 3,872
% Women: 55
% Men: 45
% Out-of-state: 25

Cost information
Out-of-state Tuition: $21,927
Room & board: $9,492

Housing Information
University Housing: Yes
Percent living on campus: 23

Greek System
Fraternity: No
Sorority: No
Athletics: NAIA

Washington State University

PO Box 641067, Pullman, WA 99164-1067
Phone: 509-335-5586 • Fax: 509-335-4902
E-mail: admissions@wsu.edu • Web: www.wsu.edu
Support: S • Institution: Public

Programs or Services for Students with Learning Differences

The Access Center (AC) assists students who have a disability by providing academic accommodations. The program may also refer students to other service programs that may assist them in achieving their academic goals. AC will help students overcome potential obstacles so that they may be successful in their area of study. All academic adjustments are authorized on an individual basis. The program offers academic coaching. To be eligible for assistance, students must be currently enrolled at Washington State University. They also must submit documentation of their disability. For a learning disability, the student must submit a written report that includes test scores and evaluation. It is the student's responsibility to request accommodations if desired. It is important to remember that even though two individuals may have the same disability, they may not necessarily need the same academic adjustments. AC works with students and instructors to determine and implement appropriate academic adjustments. Many adjustments are simple, creative alternatives for traditional ways of learning.

Admission Information for Students with Learning Differences

College entrance tests required: Yes
Interview required: No
Essay required: No
Additional Application Required for LD/ADHD/ASD: NR
What documentation required for LD: Psycho ed evaluation to include: relevant historical info, instructional interventions, related services, age diagnosed, objective data (aptitude, achievement, info processing), test scores (standard, percentile and grade equivalents) and describe functional limitations.
With general application: No
To receive services after enrolling: Yes
What documentation required for ADHD: Diagnosis based on DSM-V; history of behaviors impairing functioning in academic setting; diagnostic interview; history of symptoms; evidence of ongoing behaviors.
With general application: No
To receive services after enrolling: Yes
What documentation required for ASD: Psycho ed evaluation
With general application: NR
To receive services after enrolling: Yes
LD/ADHD/ASD documentation submitted to: Access Center
Special Ed. HS course work accepted: Yes
Specific course requirements of all applicants: Yes
Separate application required: NR
Total # of students receiving LD/ADHD/ASD services: 125
Acceptance into program means acceptance into college: Students must be admitted and enrolled in the university first (they can appeal a denial) and then request services.

Admissions

All students must meet the general admission requirements. The university looks at the combination of scores on the ACT/SAT and the applicant's high school GPA. The standard admission criteria are based on an index score determined by 75 percent GPA and 25 percent SAT/ACT. Courses required include 4 years of English, 4 years of math, 2 years of science, 2 years of a foreign language, 3 years of social studies, 1 year of art. Only 15 percent of new admissions may be admitted under special admission. Documentation of the learning disability and diagnostic tests are required if requesting accommodations or services.

Additional Information

General assistance to students with learning disabilities includes pre-admission counseling; information about disabilities; referral to appropriate community resources; academic, personal, and career counseling; information about accommodations; information about the laws pertaining to individuals with disabilities; and self-advocacy. Typical academic adjustments for students with learning disabilities may include note-takers and/or audiotape class sessions; alternative testing arrangements; alternate print (mp3 files or text files); extended time for exams; essay exams taken on computer; and use of computers with voice output and spellcheckers. Services and accommodations are available for undergraduate and graduate students.

General Support Services Information

Contact Information
Name of program or department: Access Center (AC)
Telephone: 509-335-3417
Fax: 509-335-8511

Accommodations or Services for Students with Learning Differences

Accommodations are decided upon an individual basis after a thorough review of appropriate, current documentation. The accommodations requested must be supported through the documentation provided and must be logically linked to the current impact of the condition on academic functioning.

Allowed in exams
Calculator: Yes
Dictionary: Yes
Computer: Yes
Spellchecker: Yes
Extended test time: Yes
Scribes: Yes
Proctors: Yes
Oral exams: Yes
Note-takers: Yes
Services for students with LD: Yes
Services for students with ADHD: Yes
Services for students with ASD: Yes
Distraction-reduced environment: Yes
Tape recording in class: Yes
Audio books: Yes
Electronic texts: Yes
Kurzweil Reader: Yes
Other assistive technology: Yes
Priority registration: Yes
Added costs for services: No
LD specialists: No
ADHD coaching: NR
ASD specialists: NR
Professional tutors: No
Peer tutors: No
Max. hours/wk. for services: 5–10
How professors are notified of LD/ADHD: By student

General Admissions Information

Office of Admissions: 509-335-5586

Entrance Requirements

Academic units required: 4 English, 3 math, 2 science, 2 foreign language, 3 social studies, 1 visual/performing arts, and 1 units from above areas or other academic areas. **Academic units recommended:** 4 English, 4 math, 2 science, 2 foreign language, 3 social studies, 1 visual/performing arts, and 1 units from above areas or other academic areas. High school diploma is required and GED is accepted. SAT or ACT required. If ACT, ACT with writing accepted. TOEFL required of all international applicants: minimum paper TOEFL 550 or minimum internet TOEFL 79.

Application deadline: NR
Notification: Rolling starting 11/1
Average GPA: 3.32
ACT Composite middle 50% range: 20-26
SAT Math middle 50% range: 460-580
SAT Critical Reading middle 50% range: 450-570
SAT Writing middle 50% range: 440-550
Graduate top 10% of class: NR
Graduated top 25% of class: NR
Graduated top 50% of class: NR

COLLEGE GRADUATION REQUIREMENTS

Course waivers allowed: NR
Course substitutions allowed: NR

Additional Information

Environment: This public school was founded in 1890. It has a 1745-acre campus.

Student Body
Undergrad enrollment: 24,470
% Women: 52
% Men: 48
% Out-of-state: 10

Cost information
Room & board:NR

Housing Information
University Housing: Yes
Percent living on campus: 25

Greek System
Fraternity: Yes
Sorority: Yes
Athletics: Division I

Davis and Elkins College

100 Campus Drive, Elkins, WV 26241
Phone: 304-637-1230 • Fax: 304-637-1800
E-mail: admiss@davisandelkins.edu • Web: www.davisandelkins.edu
Support: SP • Institution: Private

Programs or Services for Students with Learning Differences

Davis and Elkins offers a comprehensive support program for college students with learning disabilities. The goals blend with the college's commitment to diversity and providing a personalized education. The program goes well beyond accommodations or services by providing individualized instruction to meet each student's needs. The goal of the LD program is to enable students diagnosed with LD/ADHD to function to the best of their ability. To meet this goal, each student meets at least weekly for a regularly scheduled session with one of the three experienced learning disabilities specialists. The main focus of these meetings is to develop learning strategies and academic skills. Students may request extra assistance and use the lab as a study area. There is a fee per year. Applicants must submit complete and current documentation of their disability.

Admission Information for Students with Learning Differences

College entrance tests required: Yes
Interview required: Yes
Essay required: Yes
Additional Application Required for LD/ADHD/ASD: NR
What documentation required for LD: Psycho ed evaluation to include: relevant historical info, instructional interventions, related services, age diagnosed, objective data (aptitude, achievement, info processing), test scores (standard, percentile and grade equivalents) and describe functional limitations.
With general application: Yes if requested as part of Structured Program application
To receive services after enrolling: Yes
What documentation required for ADHD: Diagnosis based on DSM-V; history of behaviors impairing functioning in academic setting; diagnostic interview; history of symptoms; evidence of ongoing behaviors.
With general application: Yes if requested as part of Structured Program application
To receive services after enrolling: Yes
What documentation required for ASD: Psycho ed evaluation
With general application: NR
To receive services after enrolling: Yes
LD/ADHD/ASD documentation submitted to: Supported Learning Program
Special Ed. HS course work accepted: No
Specific course requirements of all applicants: Yes
Separate application required: Yes
Total # of students receiving LD/ADHD/ASD services: 52
Acceptance into program means acceptance into college: Applications to the university and the LD program are separate. Must be accepted to the university before being accepted into the LD program.

Admissions

All applications are screened by the learning disabilities program director. Students must be admitted to Davis and Elkins College prior to being considered for the program. Students requesting admission to the program must meet admissions requirements; complete a separate application to the program; send current documentation completed within the past 2 years; provide recommendations for participation in the program by a counselor or a learning specialist; provide a copy of a recent IEP, if available; complete a handwritten essay requesting services and indicating why services are being requested; and have a personal interview with a member of the Supported Learning Program.

Additional Information

Services include individual sessions with certified LD specialists, individualized programs focusing on improved writing skills, test-taking techniques, note-taking and textbook usage, and time management strategies. Specialists help students develop a personalized program focusing on improving written work, identifying class expectations and preparing work to that level of expectation, test-taking skills, using textbooks and taking notes, and managing time effectively. Students also receive advising and registration assistance based on assessment information. Personnel in the LD program also assist the students with course selection and registration; orientation to college life; monitoring of classes throughout the year and interpreting feedback from professors; coordinating of tutoring, additional counseling, and career planning; and modifying instructional programs as needed.

General Support Services Information

Contact Information
Name of program or department: Supported Learning Program
Telephone: 304-637-1384
Fax: 304-637-1424

Accommodations or Services for Students with Learning Differences

Accommodations are decided upon an individual basis after a thorough review of appropriate, current documentation. The accommodations requested must be supported through the documentation provided and must be logically linked to the current impact of the condition on academic functioning.

Allowed in exams
Calculator: Yes
Dictionary: Yes
Computer: Yes
Spellchecker: Yes
Extended test time: Yes
Scribes: Yes
Proctors: Yes
Oral exams: Yes
Note-takers: Yes
Services for students with LD: Yes
Services for students with ADHD: Yes
Services for students with ASD: Yes
Distraction-reduced environment: Yes
Tape recording in class: Yes, under discretion of instructor
Audio books: NR
Electronic texts: Yes
Kurzweil Reader: Yes
Other assistive technology: Yes
Priority registration: N/A
Added costs for services: Yes
LD specialists: Yes
ADHD coaching: NR
ASD specialists: NR
Professional tutors: No
Peer tutors: 25–50
Max. hours/wk. for services: Mandatory one hour meeting per week, and 5 hours supervised study hall
How professors are notified of LD/ADHD: By both student and director

General Admissions Information

Office of Admissions: 304-637-1230

Entrance Requirements

Academic units required: 4 English, 1 mathematics, 3 science, (1 science labs), 1 foreign language, 3 social studies, 2 mathematics units must include algebra I or II and geometry **Academic units recommended:** 4 English, 1 mathematics, 3 science, (1 science labs), 1 foreign language, 3 social studies, 2 Mathematics units must include algebra I or II and geometry. High school diploma is required and GED is accepted. SAT or ACT required. If ACT, ACT with Writing component required. TOEFL required of all international applicants: minimum paper TOEFL 450.

Application deadline: NR
Notification: Rolling starting 9/30
Average GPA: 3.1
ACT Composite middle 50% range: 18-22
SAT Math middle 50% range: 420-510
SAT Critical Reading middle 50% range: 420-530
SAT Writing middle 50% range: NR
Graduated top 10% of class: 12
Graduated top 25% of class: 33
Graduated top 50% of class: 71

COLLEGE GRADUATION REQUIREMENTS

Course waivers allowed: Yes
In what course: Individual requests are reviewed by the dean.
Course substitutions allowed: Yes
In what course: Individual requests are reviewed by the dean.

Additional Information

Environment: The college is located in a community of 10,000 residents in the foothills of the Allegheny Mountain Range.

Student Body
Undergrad enrollment: 624
% Women: 63
% Men: 37
% Out-of-state: 23
Cost information
Tuition: $27,000
Room & board: NR
Housing Information
University housing: Yes
% Living on campus: 49
Greek System
Fraternity: Yes
Sorority: Yes
Athletics: Division II

MARSHALL UNIVERSITY

One John Marshall Drive, Huntington, WV 25755
Phone: 304-696-3160 • Fax: 304-696-3135
E-mail: admissions@marshall.edu • Web: www.marshall.edu
Support: SP • Institution: Public

PROGRAMS OR SERVICES FOR STUDENTS WITH LEARNING DIFFERENCES

Higher Education for Learning Problems (H.E.L.P.) is a comprehensive and structured tutoring support program for college students who have a diagnosed Specific Learning Disability and/or Attention-deficit Disorder. Both academic and remedial tutoring is available. The academic tutoring is done by graduate assistants so that we have the expertise in the subject matter. The remedial tutoring is done by Learning Disabilities Specialists. Through the academic component, students receive tutoring in the classes they are taking as well as receiving the needed accommodations in testing. The remedial component addresses skills areas such as reading, written expression, math, study skills, time management and organizational skills. H.E.L.P. encourages a feeling of camaraderie among the students enrolled in the program. Students attend class with all other students at Marshall University and they must meet the same standards as all other students. The H.E.L.P. Program boasts a high success rate with students.

ADMISSION INFORMATION FOR STUDENTS WITH LEARNING DIFFERENCES

College entrance test required: Yes
Interview required: Yes
Essay required: 5
Additional Application Required for LD/ADHD/ASD: NR
What documentation required for LD: A copy of the psychological and educational diagnoses. The psychological evaluation must be within the last three years. The educational evaluation must be within the last year.
With general application: No
To receive services after enrolling: Yes
What documentation required for ADHD: A copy of the psychological and educational diagnoses. The psychological evaluation must be within the last three years. The educational evaluation must be within the last year. There must be written documentation of the Attention-deficit Disorder.
With general application: No
To receive services after enrolling: Yes
What documentation required for ASD: N/A
With general application: No
To receive services after enrolling: Yes
LD/ADHD/ASD documentation submitted to: Support program/services
Special Ed. HS course work accepted: No
Specific course: Yes
Separate application required for program services: Yes
Total # of students receiving LD/ADHD/ASD services: 200
Acceptance into program means acceptance into college: NR

ADMISSIONS

Students must apply to both Marshall University and to the H.E.L.P. Program. Students applying to H.E.L.P. must have a diagnosed Specific Learning Disability and/or Attention-deficit Disorder. These students must submit: an application; updated psychological and educational evaluation; one-page, handwritten statement by the student (no assistance) regarding why college is desirable; and two recommendations stating why they feel the student should attend college. An interview with H.E.L.P. is required. It is best if students apply to H.E.L.P. at least six months in advance of the proposed entry date to college. There is a required 5-week summer HELP Program for incoming freshmen. Marshall University admission requires minimum GPA of 2.0, ACT 19, or SAT 910, plus 4 years English, 3 years social studies, 4 years math (including Algebra 1 and at least two higher units), and 3 years of laboratory science.

ADDITIONAL INFORMATION

The Summer Prep Learning Disabilities Program is offered through H.E.L.P. for our incoming freshmen. Students take one Marshall University class in the morning for credit, and receive one hour of tutoring daily for that class. In the afternoons, the students attend three hours of College Prep. Students are assigned to three, one hour sessions based on their areas of greatest need. The areas covered are basic reading skills, reading comprehension, written expression, study skills and math. The program is taught by Learning Disabilities Specialists. Students are taught in small groups, generally with five to six students per group. The cost for the Summer Prep Program is $1,000 for West Virginia residents, $1,400 for Metro area residents, and $2,200 for non-West Virginia residents. This does not include registration for classes students take through the university or housing. Students sign a release allowing H.E.L.P. to talk to professors and parents.

General Support Services Information

Contact Information
Name of program or department: NR
Telephone: NR
Website: www.marshall.edu/help

Accommodations or Services For Students With Learning Differences

Accommodations are decided upon an individual basis after a thorough review of appropriate, current documentation. The accommodations requests must be supported through the documentation provided and must be logically linked to the current impact of the condition on academic functioning.

Allowed in exams
Calculator: Yes
Dictionary: Yes
Computer: Yes
Spellchecker: Yes
Extended test time: Yes
Scribes: Yes
Proctors: Yes
Oral exams: Yes
Note-takers: No
Support services for students with LD: Yes
Support services for students with ADHD: Yes
Support services for students with ASD: Not Applicable
Distraction-reduced environment: Yes
Tape recording in class: Yes
Electronic texts: Yes
Kurzweil reader: NR
Audio books: Yes
Other assistive technology: Yes
Priority registration: Yes
Added costs of services: Yes
LD specialists: Yes
ADHD coaching: Yes
ASD specialists: No
Professional tutors: No
Peer tutors: No
Max. hours/wk. for services: NR
How professors are notified of student approved accommodations: By director

General Admissions Information

Office of Admissions: 304-696-3160

Entrance Requirements

Academic units required: 4 English, 4 math, 3 science, 3 science labs, 2 foreign language, 3 social studies, 1 visual/performing arts. High school diploma is required and GED is accepted. SAT or ACT required. If ACT, ACT with writing accepted. TOEFL required of all international applicants: minimum paper TOEFL 500.

Application deadline: NR
Notification: Rolling starting 9/1
Average GPA: 3.5
ACT Composite middle 50% range: 20-25
SAT Math middle 50% range: 430-480
SAT Critical Reading middle 50% range: 440-490
SAT Writing middle 50% range: NR-NR
Graduate top 10% of class: NR
Graduated top 25% of class: NR
Graduated top 50% of class: NR

COLLEGE GRADUATION REQUIREMENTS

Course waivers allowed: No
Course substitutions allowed: Yes
In what course: Math, Foreign Language

Additional Information

Environment: This public school was founded in 1837. It has a 70-acre campus.

Student Body
Undergrad enrollment: 9,518
% Women: 57
% Men: 43
% Out-of-state: 22

Cost information
In-state Tuition: $5,724
Out-of-state Tuition: $14,512
Room & board: $8,984

Housing Information
University Housing: Yes
Percent living on campus: NR

Greek System
Fraternity: NR
Sorority: NR
Athletics: Division I

West Virginia University

Admissions Office, Morgantown, WV 26506-6009
Phone: 304-293-2121 • Fax: 304-293-3080
E-mail: go2wvu@mail.wvu.edu • Web: www.wvu.edu
Support: S • Institution: Public

Programs or Services for Students with Learning Differences

The Office of Disability Services is available to all students on the campus of West Virginia University. Services are provided to qualified students with disabilities. It is the student's responsibility to provide appropriate documentation for the diagnosis prior to receiving accommodations based upon that disability. Each student's academic accommodations will be determined by the university on an individual basis. In order to meet the adult criteria of "disability" under federal laws individuals must provide documentation of how the significant impairment substantially limits their academic functioning. A "significant impairment" means below average functioning. An IEP or a 504 plan from the public school system is not documentation of a disability for the purposes of providing accommodations at the college level.

Admission Information for Students with Learning Differences

College entrance test required: Yes
Interview required: Yes
Essay required: Not Applicable
Additional Application Required for LD/ADHD/ASD: No
What documentation required for LD: Comprehensive evaluation report
With general application: No
To receive services after enrolling: No
What documentation required for ADHD: Comprehensive Psychoeducation evaluation report
With general application: No
To receive services after enrolling: No
What documentation required for ASD: Comprehensive Psychoeducation report
With general application: No
To receive services after enrolling: No
LD/ADHD/ASD documentation submitted to: NR
ASD Specific Program: NR
Special Ed. HS course work accepted: NR
Specific course requirements of all applicants: Yes
Separate application required for program services: Yes
Total # of students receiving LD/ADHD/ASD services: 500
Acceptance into program means acceptance into college: No

Admissions

There is no special admissions process for students with LD and ADHD. Students must meet admissions requirements. In-state students must have a 2.0 GPA and out-of-state students must have a 2.25 GPA and either a composite ACT of 20 or a combined SAT score of 950 to be considered for admission. Additionally, all applicants must have four years of English, three years of social studies, four years of math, three years of lab science, two years of same foreign language and one year of fine art. Students are not encouraged to self-disclose a disability in a personal statement during the application process. Appropriate services/accommodations will be determined after the student is admitted.

Additional Information

Requirements for the documentation of a LD include the following: a signed, dated comprehensive psychoeducational evaluation report indicating how the LD impacts academic performance and contributes to a "significant impairment" in academic functioning. The report should address Aptitude, Achievement, Processing, and should include the WAIS and full Woodcock-Johnson Battery. A description of the functional limitations, which impact against the educational effort, must be included in the diagnostic report. Additionally, a documented history of previous accommodations received should be included. Documentation of ADHD must be in the form of a signed and dated report, by either a psychiatrist, neuropsychologist or licensed psychologist trained in the differential diagnosis. Additional information is required. There are no LD specialists on staff; however, counselors are available to provide services to all students. Some accommodations that are available with appropriate documentation include: priority registration, extended testing time, note-takers, distraction-free environments, books on tape, and assistive technology.

General Support Services Information

Contact Information
Name of program or department: NR
Telephone: 304-293-6700
Fax: 304-293-3861

Accommodations or Services For Students With Learning Differences

Accommodations are decided upon an individual basis after a thorough review of appropriate, current documentation. The accommodations requests must be supported through the documentation provided and must be logically linked to the current impact of the condition on academic functioning.

Allowed in exams
Calculator: Yes
Dictionary: Yes
Computer: Yes
Spellchecker: Yes
Extended test time: Yes
Scribes: Yes
Proctors: Yes
Oral exams: Yes
Note-takers: Yes
Support services for students with LD: Yes
Support services for students with ADHD: Yes
Support services for students with ASD: Yes
Distraction-reduced environment: Yes
Tape recording in class: Yes
Electronic texts: Yes
Kurzweil reader: NR
Audio books: Yes
Other assistive technology: Yes
Priority registration: Yes
Added costs of services: Yes
LD specialists: No
ADHD coaching: NR
ASD specialists: No
Professional tutors: No
Peer tutors: Yes
Max. hours/wk. for services: NR
How professors are notified of student approved accommodations: Not Applicable

General Admissions Information

Office of Admissions: 304-293-2121

Entrance Requirements

Academic units required: 4 English, 4 math, 3 science, 3 science labs, 2 foreign language, 3 social studies, 1 visual/performing arts. High school diploma is required and GED is accepted. SAT or ACT required. If ACT, ACT with writing required. TOEFL required of all international applicants: minimum paper TOEFL 550 or minimum internet TOEFL 61.

Application deadline: 8/1
Notification: Rolling starting 9/15
Average GPA: 3.45
ACT Composite middle 50% range: 21-27
SAT Math middle 50% range: 470-580
SAT Critical Reading middle 50% range: 460-560
SAT Writing middle 50% range: NR-NR
Graduate top 10% of class: 20
Graduated top 25% of class: 46
Graduated top 50% of class: 77

COLLEGE GRADUATION REQUIREMENTS

Course waivers allowed: No
In what course: NR
Course substitutions allowed: NR
In what course: Foreign Language

Additional Information

Environment: This public school was founded in 1867.

Student Body
Undergrad enrollment: 22,498
% Women: 46
% Men: 54
% Out-of-state: 53

Cost information
In-state Tuition: $7,632
Out-of-state Tuition: $21,432
Room & board: $9,872

Housing Information
University Housing: Yes
Percent living on campus: 15

Greek System
Fraternity: Yes
Sorority: Yes
Athletics: Division I

West Virginia Wesleyan College

59 College Avenue, Buckhannon, WV 26201
Phone: 304-473-8510 • Fax: 304-473-8108
E-mail: admission@wvwc.edu • Web: www.wvwc.edu
Support: SP • Institution: Private

Programs or Services for Students with Learning Differences

West Virginia Wesleyan College's comprehensive program provides a solid foundational service delivered by master level professionals and two fee-based, optional programs assisting with the transition to college level academics. The Mentor Advantage Program provides an innovative, individualized support developed from research on the transition and persistence of post-secondary students with learning disabilities and from self-regulated learning theory. It is designed to create a bridge to academic regulation in the college environment. The program is composed of several elements: one-to-one professional organizational mentoring and academic strategic content tutoring, weekly small group discussion, and Day-time and Evening Check-In. Taken together, the Day-Time and Evening Check-In provide 12.5 hours, each weekday, of study time in a quiet environment with access to a professional mentor. Students may enroll in the program as a package or sign up for various components separately, depending on the student need. In addition, Wesleyan offers an individualized clinical learning program that focuses on the improvement of reading skills and language comprehension. Although the program is not an official site certified and endorsed by Lindamood-Bell ®, students work with instructors who have been trained in Lindamood-Bell ® Learning Techniques. Consistent application with this approach will improve skills required for accurate decoding, quick word recognition, and comprehension for the increased volume of information facing today's college student. Test scores and improved academic performance have validated a record of success with our students.

Admission Information for Students with Learning Differences

College entrance tests required: Yes
Interview required: No
Essay required: No
Additional Application Required for LD/ADHD/ASD: NR
What documentation required for LD: Psycho ed evaluation to include: relevant historical info, instructional interventions, related services, age diagnosed, objective data (aptitude, achievement, info processing), test scores (standard, percentile and grade equivalents) and describe functional limitations.
With general application: Yes if requested as part of Structured Program application
To receive services after enrolling: Yes
What documentation required for ADHD: Diagnosis based on DSM-V; history of behaviors impairing functioning in academic setting; diagnostic interview; history of symptoms; evidence of ongoing behaviors.
With general application: Yes if requested as part of Structured Program application
To receive services after enrolling: Yes
What documentation required for ASD: Psycho ed evaluation
With general application: NR
LD/ADHD/ASD documentation submitted to: Support Program/Services
Special Ed. HS course work accepted: Yes
Specific course requirements for all applicants: Yes
Separate application required for program services: No
Total # of students receiving LD/ADHD/ASD services: 40–45
Acceptance into program means acceptance into college: Students are admitted jointly into the college and SASS.

Admissions

The Director of the Learning Center reviews and decides the application outcome of students who disclose a disability. Applicants are encouraged to submit a psychoeducational evaluation if they believe it will help develop an accurate picture of student potential. General admission criteria include a GPA no lower than 2.0; four years English, three years math, two years science, two years social studies, one year history, and three years electives. No foreign language is required for admission. Submission of SAT or ACT testing is required.

Additional Information

West Virginia Wesleyan College provides excellent support programs to students with diagnosed learning disabilities, attention disorders, and other special needs. The heart of the program is the student relationship with the Comprehensive Advisor. Students work with their Comprehensive Advisor to cover the following areas: specialized academic advising; preferential preregistration for the first three semesters; implementation of accommodations to be used for college classes; development of academic, organizational, and self-monitoring strategies; discussion of priorities and motivational outlook; self-advocacy and social coaching, as needed; assistive technology lab with state-of-the-art software, opened during the day and evening; test taking Lab including readers, scribes, and word-processing, as needed; and note takers, as needed.

General Support Services Information

Contact Information
Name of program or department: Learning Center
Telephone: 304-473-8563
Fax: 304-473-8497

Accommodations or Services for Students with Learning Differences

Accommodations are decided upon an individual basis after a thorough review of appropriate, current documentation. The accommodations requests must be supported through the documentation provided and must be logically linked to the current impact of the condition on academic functioning.

Allowed in exams
Calculator: Yes
Dictionary: Yes
Computer: Yes
Spellchecker: Yes
Extended test time: Yes
Scribes: Yes
Proctors: Yes
Oral exams: Yes
Note-takers: Yes
Services for students with LD: Yes
Services for students with ADHD: Yes
Services for students with ASD: Yes
Distraction-reduced environment: Yes
Tape recording in class: Yes
Audio books: Yes
Electronic texts: NR
Kurzweil reader: Yes
Other assistive technology: Yes
Priority registration: Yes
Added costs of services: Yes
LD specialists: Yes
ADHD coaching: NR
ASD specialists: NR
Professional tutors: Yes
Peer tutors: Yes
Max. hours/wk. for services: 40
How professors are notified of student approved accommodations: Student

General Admissions Information

Office of Admissions: 304-473-8510

Entrance Requirements

Academic units required: 4 English, 3 math, 3 science, 1 science labs, 3 social studies, **Academic units recommended:** 2 foreign language. High school diploma is required and GED is accepted. SAT or ACT required. If ACT, ACT with writing accepted. TOEFL required of all international applicants: minimum paper TOEFL 500.

Application deadline: 8/15
Notification: Rolling starting 9/1
Average GPA: 3.48
ACT Composite middle 50% range: 20-25
SAT Math middle 50% range: 420-550
SAT Critical Reading middle 50% range: 420-540
SAT Writing middle 50% range: 500-530
Graduate top 10% of class: 25
Graduated top 25% of class: 53
Graduated top 50% of class: 82

COLLEGE GRADUATION REQUIREMENTS

Course waivers allowed: NR
In what course: There is no foreign language requirement. We have only one math requirement and a student can fill this with a college level Math for the Liberal Arts class.
Course substitutions allowed: NR
In what course: There is no foreign language requirement. We have only one math requirement and a student can fill this with a college level Math for the Liberal Arts class.

Additional Information

Environment: This private school, affiliated with the Methodist Church, was founded in 1890. It has a 120-acre campus.

Student Body
Undergrad enrollment: 1,389
% Women: 55
% Men: 45
% Out-of-state: 40
Cost information
Tuition: $28,574
Room & board: $8,248
Housing Information
University Housing: Yes
Percent living on campus: 80
Greek System
Fraternity: Yes
Sorority: Yes
Athletics: Division II

Alverno College

3400 South 43rd Street, Milwaukee, WI 53234-3922
Phone: 414-382-6101 • Fax: 414-382-6055
E-mail: admissions@alverno.edu • Web: www.alverno.edu
Support: S • Institution: Private

Programs or Services for Students with Learning Differences

Alverno College is a small liberal arts college for women with approximately 2,500 students. The Instructional Services Center (ISC) provides academic support to Alverno students, and assists Alverno applicants in meeting admissions requirements. ISC offers courses in reading, writing, critical thinking, math, and algebra in order to develop academic skills as required on the basis of new student assessment results. ISC also offers tutorial support, course-based study groups, and workshops to provide an opportunity for small groups of students to study together under the direction of a peer tutor or an ISC teacher. There is also a Student Accessibility Coordinator who assists the student with a disability to meet her academic potential through understanding of her learning needs, development of strategies and accommodations to maximize her strengths, and development of self-advocacy with faculty.

Admission Information for Students with Learning Differences

College entrance test required: Yes
Interview required: No
Essay required:
Additional Application Required for LD/ADHD/ASD: NR
What documentation required for LD: WAIS; WJ; WRAT-R: within 4-6 years
With general application: No
To receive services after enrolling: Yes
What documentation required for ADHD: Relevant historical information, description of current functional limitations pertaining to academic setting and recommendations for strategies and accommodations by qualified professional.
With general application: No
To receive services after enrolling: Yes
What documentation required for ASD: Psycho ed evaluation
With general application: No
To receive services after enrolling: Yes
LD/ADHD/ASD documentation submitted to: Support program/services
Special Ed. HS course work accepted: No
Specific course: Yes
Separate application required for program services: No
Total # of students receiving LD/ADHD/ASD services: 45
Acceptance into program means acceptance into college: NR

Admissions

Admission criteria are the same for all students coming directly from high school. General admission requirements include satisfactory scores on the SAT or ACT. Seventeen academic credits in college-prep courses with recommendations, including 4 years English, 2 years foreign language recommended, 3 years math, 3 years science, 3 years history or social studies; and rank in the top half of graduating class. There is a college transition program for students who do not meet the admissions criteria but have academic potential.

Additional Information

Classes are offered at a beginning level in reading and writing, math and algebra. Students may not substitute courses for math courses required to graduate, but intensive assistance is provided. Tutoring is provided through ISC. The college has a Math Resource Center and a Writing Resource Center available for all students. Individualized assistance is arranged based on student request or instructor/advisor referral. Peer tutoring provides assistance for students demonstrating a need for course content support. Study groups, primarily arranged to supplement difficult courses, are established at the request of the course instructor. Specially trained students, who have been recommended by faculty, provide the assistance in both of these situations. In other instances, instructors provide one-on-one support that extends beyond specific course content and assists the development of abilities such as critical thinking, analytical reading and writing, time management, and assessment preparation. Services and resources available to students include: Program orientation and needs assessment, individual registration, alternative testing, note-taking assistance, access to textbooks in alternative formats and classroom accommodations or modifications. The primary purpose of the Soref Center is to respond to individual questions and concerns to assist students in learning strategies and increasing their understanding of concepts and practices in math and science.

General Support Services Information

Contact Information
Name of program or department: Student Accessibility
Telephone: 414-382-6026
Fax: 414-382-6354

Accommodations or Services for Students with Learning Differences

Accommodations are decided upon an individual basis after a thorough review of appropriate, current documentation. The accommodations requests must be supported through the documentation provided and must be logically linked to the current impact of the condition on academic functioning.

Allowed in exams
Calculator: Yes
Dictionary: Yes
Computer: Yes
Spellchecker: Yes
Extended test time: Yes
Scribes: Yes
Proctors: Yes
Oral exams: Yes
Note-takers: Yes
Services for students with LD: Yes
Services for students with ADHD: Yes
Services for students with ASD: Yes
Distraction-reduced environment: Yes
Tape recording in class: Yes
Audio books: Yes
Electronic texts: NR
Kurzweil reader: Yes
Other assistive technology: Yes
Priority registration: No
Added costs of services: No
LD specialists: No
ADHD coaching: NR
ASD specialists: NR
Professional tutors: Yes
Peer tutors: Yes
Max. hours/wk. for services: 2
How professors are notified of student approved accommodations: Both student and director

General Admissions Information

Office of Admissions: 414-382-6101

Entrance Requirements

Academic units required: 4 English, 3 mathematics, 3 science, 3 social studies, 4 academic electives. **Academic units recommended:** 2 foreign language, 0 history. High school diploma is required and GED is accepted. SAT or ACT required. If ACT, ACT with Writing component accepted. TOEFL required of all international applicants: minimum paper TOEFL 520 or minimum web TOEFL 68.

Application deadline: NR
Notification: Rolling starting 9/1
Average GPA: 3.0
ACT Composite middle 50% range: 17-23
SAT Math middle 50% range: NR
SAT Critical Reading middle 50% range: NR
SAT Writing middle 50% range: NR
Graduated top 10% of class: NR
Graduated top 25% of class: NR
Graduated top 50% of class: NR

COLLEGE GRADUATION REQUIREMENTS

Course waivers allowed: No
Course substitutions allowed: No
In what course: Foreign language not required to graduate. Students must take a college Algebra class to graduate.

Additional Information

Environment: The campus is located in a suburban area on the southwest side of Milwaukee.

Student Body
Undergrad enrollment: 1,826
% Women: 100
% Men: 0
% Out-of-state: 4
Cost information
Tuition: $23,784
Room & board: NR
Housing Information
University housing: Yes
% Living on campus: 11
Greek System
Fraternity: No
Sorority: Yes
Athletics: Division III

Beloit College

700 College Street, Beloit, WI 53511
Phone: 608-363-2500 • Fax: 608-363-2075
E-mail: admiss@beloit.edu • Web: www.beloit.edu
Support: S • Institution: Private

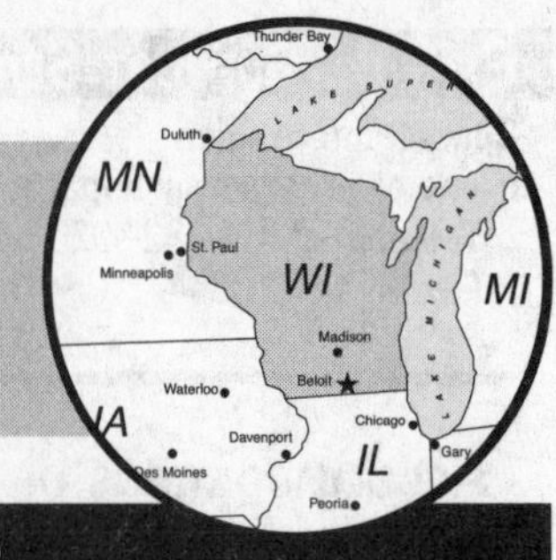

Programs or Services for Students with Learning Differences

The Learning Enrichment and Disability Services office provides academic enrichment opportunities (i.e. tutoring, one-on-one assistance) and support for all Beloit College students. For students with documented disabilities, we ensure that appropriate accommodations are implemented while educating the campus community regarding disability related laws, issues and concerns. In addition, we work with students with academic challenges and concerns (i.e. alert slips, academic probation) to assist them in implementing appropriate strategies to achieve personal and academic success. To accomplish these goals, we collaborate with faculty, staff and students and operate with a philosophy of student self-advocacy.

Admission Information for Students with Learning Differences

College entrance test required: No
Interview required: No
Essay required: Not Applicable
Additional Application Required for LD/ADHD/ASD: No
What documentation required for LD: Information from an appropriate professional which indicates the impact of the ADHD on this student.
With general application: No
To receive services after enrolling: No
What documentation required for ADHD: Psycho ed evaluation
With general application: No
To receive services after enrolling: No
What documentation required for ASD: Information from an appropriate professional which indicates the impact of the LD on this student.
With general application: No
To receive services after enrolling: No
LD/ADHD/ASD documentation submitted to: Joy de Leon
ASD Specific Program: NR
Special Ed. HS course work accepted: Yes
Specific course requirements of all applicants: NR
Separate application required for program services: False
Total # of students receiving LD/ADHD/ASD services: NR
Acceptance into program means acceptance into college: No

Admissions

There is no special admissions procedure for students with learning disabilities. Each student is reviewed individually, and the final decision is made by the Office of Admissions. The college is competitive in admissions, but there are no absolute GPA or test scores. A minimum of sixteen academic courses are required for admission. Courses recommended include 4 years of English, 4 years of math, 3 years of laboratory science, 2 years of a foreign language, and 3 years of social science or history.

Additional Information

Beloit College Learning Enrichment and Disability Services offers additional resources to all students in the areas of tutoring (most courses, including math and science), reading strategies, study strategies, time management, study groups, advising, mentoring, as well as assistance with computer usage and assistive technology. Improvement of writing and research skills as well as personal counseling, career guidance, and crisis intervention are also available at the college. Individual assistance and small group workshops are offered each semester.
Summer Bridge:
The Summer Bridge program at Beloit College is an educational pre-college orientation program designed to provide a smooth and successful transition to college. Students develop personal, academic, and social skills necessary for college success. Students learn Beloit College standards and expectations. Complete assessments that will help set and achieve goals. The program creates a network of faculty, staff, and peer connections in a supportive environment.

General Support Services Information

Contact Information
Name of program or department: Joy de Leon
Telephone: 6083632572
Fax: 608-363-7059
Website: https://www.beloit.edu/dss/

Accommodations or Services For Students With Learning Differences

Accommodations are decided upon an individual basis after a thorough review of appropriate, current documentation. The accommodations requests must be supported through the documentation provided and must be logically linked to the current impact of the condition on academic functioning.

Allowed in exams
Calculator: Not Applicable
Dictionary: No
Computer: No
Spellchecker: No
Extended test time: No
Scribes: No
Proctors: No
Oral exams: No
Note-takers: No
Support services for students with LD: Yes
Support services for students with ADHD: Yes
Support services for students with ASD: Yes
Distraction-reduced environment: No
Tape recording in class: No
Electronic texts: NR
Kurzweil reader: NR
Audio books: No
Other assistive technology: NR
Priority registration: Yes
Added costs of services: No
LD specialists: No
ADHD coaching: No
ASD specialists: No
Professional tutors: No
Peer tutors: Yes
Max. hours/wk. for services: NR
How professors are notified of student approved accommodations: By student

General Admissions Information

Office of Admissions: 608-363-2500

Entrance Requirements

Academic units recommended: 4 English, 3 math, 3 science, 3 science labs, 3 foreign language, 4 social studies. High school diploma is required and GED is accepted. SAT or ACT required for some. If ACT, ACT with writing accepted. Minimum paper TOEFL 550 or minimum internet TOEFL 80.

Application deadline: NR
Notification: Rolling starting 1/16
Average GPA: 3.35
ACT Composite middle 50% range: 24-30
SAT Math middle 50% range: 540-645
SAT Critical Reading middle 50% range: 540-695
SAT Writing middle 50% range: NR-NR
Graduate top 10% of class: 29
Graduated top 25% of class: 64
Graduated top 50% of class: 91

COLLEGE GRADUATION REQUIREMENTS

Course waivers allowed: Not Applicable
In what course: Student do not receive waivers, but substitutions are considered on an individual basis.
Course substitutions allowed: Yes
In what course: Substitutions are considered on an individual basis. They depend on the impact of the disability.

Additional Information

Environment: This private school was founded in 1846. It has a 75-acre campus.

Student Body
Undergrad enrollment: 1,358
% Women: 55
% Men: 45
% Out-of-state: 83
Cost information
Tuition: $44,590
Room & board: $7,890
Housing Information
University Housing: Yes
Percent living on campus: 87
Greek System
Fraternity: Yes
Sorority: Yes
Athletics: Division III

EDGEWOOD COLLEGE

1000 Edgewood College Drive, Madison, WI 53711-1997
Phone: 608-663-2294 • Fax: 608-663-2214
E-mail: admissions@edgewood.edu • Web: www.edgewood.edu
Support: CS • Institution: Private

PROGRAMS OR SERVICES FOR STUDENTS WITH LEARNING DIFFERENCES

Sponsored by the Sinsinawa Dominicans, Edgewood College is a community of learners that affirms both its Catholic heritage and its respect for other religious traditions. The liberal arts are the foundation of all our curricular offerings in the humanities, arts, sciences, and professional programs. Committed to excellence in teaching and learning, we seek to develop intellect, spirit, imagination, and heart. We welcome women and men who reflect the rich diversity of the world's cultures and perspectives. We foster open, caring, thoughtful engagement with one another and an enduring commitment to service, all in an educational community that seeks truth, compassion, justice and partnership.

ADMISSION INFORMATION FOR STUDENTS WITH LEARNING DIFFERENCES

College entrance tests required: Yes
Interview required: No
Essay required: No
Additional Application Required for LD/ADHD/ASD: NR
What documentation required for LD: Psycho ed evaluation to include: relevant historical info, instructional interventions, related services, age diagnosed, objective data (aptitude, achievement, info processing), test scores (standard, percentile and grade equivalents) and describe functional limitations.
With general application: No
To receive services after enrolling: Yes
What documentation required for ADHD: Diagnosis based on DSM-V; history of behaviors impairing functioning in academic setting; diagnostic interview; history of symptoms; evidence of ongoing behaviors.
With general application: No
To receive services after enrolling: Yes
What documentation required for ASD: Psycho ed evaluation
With general application: NR
To receive services after enrolling: Yes
LD/ADHD/ASD documentation submitted to: Support Program/Services
Special Ed. HS course work accepted: Yes
Specific course requirements for all applicants: No
Separate application required for program services: No (with the exception of the Cutting Edge Program—see below)
Total # of students receiving LD/ADHD/ASD services: NR
Acceptance into program means acceptance into college: NR

ADMISSIONS

Edgewood College offers rolling admission between September 1 and the following August 1 for fall enrollment. Campus tours and special visit days are available throughout the year. During the admission process you will be connected with an admissions counselor who will help you through the admission, financial aid, and housing processes. Generous financial aid is available to help make the exceptional Edgewood College education affordable.

ADDITIONAL INFORMATION

Edgewood College allows for foreign language course substitutions. There are also developmental writing and math courses. Other services include Summer Pre-orientation/Bridge Program, academic skills classes, individual academic coaching and learning support, Math/Science Tutoring Lab, Writing Center, content area tutoring, assistive technology training and career development services. Students are also able to participate in social skills and life skills classes offered through the Cutting Edge Program. Edgewood College was the first college in Wisconsin to offer inclusion in college for adult learners with intellectual and developmental disabilities. The Cutting-Edge program offers an alternative admissions process into the college along with a higher level of supports. The program strives to give the Cutting-Edge students, to the greatest degree possible, a college experience of academic, residential, and social inclusion. Through the use of peer mentors, the Cutting-Edge program provides students the opportunity to "fit in" to college by enrolling in undergraduate courses, residing in student housing, engaging in student life events, and pursuing service learning, internships and employment. Since its inception in 2007, the Cutting-Edge offers a non-degree program that includes a combination of pre-college level courses, life skills and social skills classes, general education courses—audited and modified—and internships. The Cutting-Edge students take regular college courses either for credit or audit. The Cutting-Edge program also provides career counseling and person-centered internship experiences that allow students to build their resumes and obtain gainful employment. During its development phase the college has found an increase in the admissions of "qualified" students with disabilities who have academically benefitted from the additional supports provided by the Cutting-Edge program. The Cutting-Edge program is developing occupational certificates for students who are unable to earn a bachelor's degree but who want to take courses for degree credit, and work towards terminal credentials.

General Support Services Information

Contact Information

Name of program or department: Accessibility Services for Students with Disabilities

Telephone: 608-663-8347

Fax: 608-663-2278

Accommodations or Services for Students with Learning Differences

Accommodations are decided upon an individual basis after a thorough review of appropriate, current documentation. The accommodations requested must be supported through the documentation provided and must be logically linked to the current impact of the condition on academic functioning.

Allowed in exams
Calculator: Yes
Dictionary: Yes
Computer: Yes
Spellchecker: Yes
Extended test time: Yes
Scribes: Yes
Proctors: Yes
Oral exams: Yes
Note-takers: Yes
Services for students with LD: Yes
Services for students with ADHD: Yes
Services for students with ASD: Yes
Distraction-reduced environment: Yes
Tape recording in class: Yes
Audio books: NR
Electronic texts: Yes
Kurzweil Reader: Yes
Priority registration: Yes
Added costs for services: No
LD specialists: Yes
ADHD coaching: NR
ASD specialists: NR
Professional tutors: No
Peer tutors: Yes
Max. hours/wk. for services: None
How professors are notified of LD/ADHD: Both student and director

General Admissions Information

Office of Admissions: 608-663-2294

Entrance Requirements

Academic units required: 4 English, 2 math, 2 science, 1 science labs, 2 foreign language, 2 social studies, 1 history, **Academic units recommended:** 4 English, 2 math, 2 science, 1 science labs, 2 foreign language, 2 social studies, 1 history. High school diploma is required and GED is accepted. SAT or ACT required. If ACT, ACT with writing accepted. TOEFL required of all international applicants: minimum paper TOEFL 525 or minimum internet TOEFL 71.

Application deadline: 8/15
Notification: Rolling starting 9/15
Average GPA: 3.37
ACT Composite middle 50% range: 20-25
SAT Math middle 50% range: 483-560
SAT Critical Reading middle 50% range: 448-598
SAT Writing middle 50% range: NR-NR
Graduate top 10% of class: 13
Graduated top 25% of class: 45
Graduated top 50% of class: 84

COLLEGE GRADUATION REQUIREMENTS

Course waivers allowed: NR

Course substitutions allowed: NR

Additional Information

Environment: This private school, affiliated with the Roman Catholic Church, was founded in 1927. It has a 55-acre campus.

Student Body
Undergrad enrollment: 1,813
% Women: 70
% Men: 30
% Out-of-state: 7.4
Cost information
Tuition: $26,550
Room & board: $9,400
Housing Information
University Housing: Yes
Percent living on campus: 29.6
Greek System
Fraternity: NR
Sorority: NR
Athletics: Division III

Marian University

45 South National Avenue, Fond du Lac, WI 54935
Phone: 920-923-7650 • Fax: 920-923-8755
E-mail: admissions@marianuniversity.edu • Web: www.marianuniversity.edu
Support: S • Institution: Private

Programs or Services for Students with Learning Differences

Marian University is committed to providing equal educational opportunities to students with learning disabilities and/or ADD/ADHD. The Coordinator for Disability Services and Academic Support is housed in the Center for Academic Support and Excellence, (CASE) Office. The Coordinator for Disability Services and Academic Support is dedicated to providing personal and academic support to students with disabilities from freshman year to graduation.

Admission Information for Students with Learning Differences

College entrance tests required: Yes
Interview required: No
Essay required: No
Additional Application Required for LD/ADHD/ASD: NR
What documentation required for LD: Psycho ed evaluation to include: relevant historical info, instructional interventions, related services, age diagnosed, objective data (aptitude, achievement, info processing), test scores (standard, percentile and grade equivalents) and describe functional limitations.
With general application: No
To receive services after enrolling: Yes
What documentation required for ADHD: Diagnosis based on DSM-V; history of behaviors impairing functioning in academic setting; diagnostic interview; history of symptoms; evidence of ongoing behaviors.
With general application: No
To receive services after enrolling: Yes
What documentation required for ASD: Psycho ed evaluation
With general application: NR
To receive services after enrolling: Yes
LD/ADHD/ASD documentation submitted to: Disability Services
Special Ed. HS course work accepted: NR
Specific course requirements of all applicants: Yes
Separate application required: No
Total # of students receiving LD/ADHD/ASD services: NR
Acceptance into program means acceptance into college: Students must be admitted to and enrolled in the university first and then request services.

Admissions

There is no special application or admissions procedure for students with learning disabilities. Admission criteria include a 2.0 GPA, a class rank within top 50 percent, and an ACT score of 18. All students, not just those with LD, are asked to meet two-thirds of these criteria. Students who do not meet two-thirds may be admitted on probation through a program called EXCEL. Students will be asked to submit 3 letters of recommendation supporting their ability to succeed in college-level course work. Students also may be asked to schedule a visit to Marian for a pre-admission interview during which their skills, attitudes, motivation, and self-understanding will be informally assessed. Students admitted provisionally may be admitted with limited credit status and may be required to take a freshman seminar course. Special education course work is accepted, but students are encouraged to be fully mainstreamed by senior year with minimal monitoring. Students who self-disclose their disability are given information on services available through the Center for Academic Support and Excellence (CASE) office.

Additional Information

Disability Services offers the following services and accommodations to students who disclose a disability and submit appropriate documentation: notetakers, audio books, audio players, scan and read software, distraction-free test environments, extended exam times, and test readers/scribes. The following support is also provided: organizational and study skills training, liaison with instructors/advisors, consultation, advocacy, referrals, and resource materials. The peer tutoring program helps students gain the confidence and skills necessary to successfully complete course work. Other services include information on community, state, and national resources, and course scheduling. Calculators are allowed in exams for students with a documented disability in math. Assistance is determined for each individual based on assessment. All students have access to the tutoring program, and the Learning and Writing Center. Services are available for undergraduate and graduate students. The EXCEL Program provides freshman with support as they transition to the college environment. The program offers smaller class sizes and encouragement and exposure to campus resources and services. To participate in the program, students must attend the EXCEL Summer Bridge Program and meet with an academic advisor bi-weekly. All first-year students are also assigned a Student Mentor to help them get acclimated.

General Support Services Information

Contact Information
Name of program or department: Disability Services
Telephone: 920-923-8951
Fax: 920-923-8135

Accommodations or Services for Students with Learning Differences

Accommodations are decided upon an individual basis after a thorough review of appropriate, current documentation. The accommodations requested must be supported through the documentation provided and must be logically linked to the current impact of the condition on academic functioning.

Allowed in exams
Calculator: Yes
Dictionary: No
Computer: Yes
Spellchecker: Yes
Extended test time: Yes
Scribes: Yes
Proctors: Yes
Oral exams: Yes
Note-takers: Yes
Services for students with LD: Yes
Services for students with ADHD: Yes
Services for students with ASD: Yes
Distraction-reduced environment: Yes
Tape recording in class: Yes
Audio books: NR
Electronic texts: Yes
Kurzweil Reader: Yes
Other assistive technology: Yes
Priority registration: Yes
Added costs for services: No
LD specialists: No
ADHD coaching: NR
ASD specialists: NR
Professional tutors: Yes
Peer tutors: Yes
Max. hours/wk. for services: Unlimited
How professors are notified of LD/ADHD: By Coordinator of Disability Services and Academic Support

General Admissions Information

Office of Admissions: 920-923-7650

Entrance Requirements
Academic units required: 4 English, 2 math, 1 science, 1 science labs, 1 history, **Academic units recommended:** 3 math, 2 science, 2 foreign language. High school diploma is required and GED is accepted. SAT or ACT required. If ACT, ACT with writing accepted. TOEFL required of all international applicants: minimum paper TOEFL 525.

Application deadline: NR
Notification: Rolling starting 9/15
Average GPA: 3.02
ACT Composite middle 50% range: 18-22
SAT Math middle 50% range: NR-NR
SAT Critical Reading middle 50% range: NR-NR
SAT Writing middle 50% range: NR-NR
Graduated top 10% of class: 9
Graduated top 25% of class: 30
Graduated top 50% of class: 66

COLLEGE GRADUATION REQUIREMENTS

Course waivers allowed: No
Course substitutions allowed: Yes
In what course: Foreign Language. Students must attempt the required course.

Additional Information

Environment: This private school, affiliated with the Roman Catholic Church, was founded in 1936. It has a 100-acre campus.

Student Body
Undergrad enrollment: 1,996
% Women: 75
% Men: 25
% Out-of-state: 7
Cost information
Tuition: $19,590
Room & board: $5,380
Housing Information
University Housing: Yes
Percent living on campus: 33
Greek System
Fraternity: Yes
Sorority: Yes
Athletics: Division III

Marquette University

PO Box 1881, Milwaukee, WI 53201-1881
Phone: 414-288-7302 • Fax: 414-288-3764
E-mail: admissions@Marquette.edu • Web: www.marquette.edu
Support: S • Institution: Private

Programs or Services for Students with Learning Differences

The Office of Disability Services (ODS) is the designated office at Marquette University to coordinate accommodations for all students with identified and documented disabilities. Accommodations are determined on a case-by-case basis, but the student must seek assistance prior to the need for accommodation. Relevant documentation from an appropriate licensed professional that gives a diagnosis of the disability and how it impacts on participation in courses, programs, jobs, activities and facilities at Marquette is required. The student and a staff member from ODS will discuss the student's disability and how it will impact on the requirements of the student's courses. Based upon this evaluation the ODS Coordinator provides a range of individualized accommodations.

Admission Information for Students with Learning Differences

College entrance test required: Yes
Interview required: No
Essay required: Not Applicable
Additional Application Required for LD/ADHD/ASD: Not Applicable
What documentation required for LD: Documentation completed by psychologist or psychiatrist that includes diagnosis, functional limitations, and accommodation suggestions.
With general application: Not Applicable
To receive services after enrolling: Not Applicable
What documentation required for ADHD: Documentation completed by psychologist or psychiatrist that includes diagnosis, functional limitations, and accommodation suggestions.
With general application: Not Applicable
To receive services after enrolling: Not Applicable
What documentation required for ASD: Psychoeducational Evaluation
With general application: Not Applicable
To receive services after enrolling: Not Applicable
LD/ADHD/ASD documentation submitted to: Office of Disability Services
ASD Specific Program: NR
Special Ed. HS course work accepted: Not Applicable
Specific course requirements of all applicants: NR
Separate application required for program services: False
Total # of students receiving LD/ADHD/ASD services: NR
Acceptance into program means acceptance into college: Not Applicable

Admissions

There is no special admissions process for students with LD and ADD. All applicants for admission must meet the same admission criteria. Marquette requires applicants to rank in the top 50 percent of their high school class (most rank in the top 25 percent) and have 4 years of English, 2-4 years of math and science, 2-3 years of social studies, and other additional subjects, although the foreign language requirement may be waived with appropriate documentation.

Additional Information

ODS provides a number of accommodations for students with LD and AD/HD including texts in alternate formats and alternative testing arrangements. If a student's disability requires a backup note taker, ODS assists students in locating or hiring note takers. Other methods of acquiring class material may include use of a tape recorder in class, and photocopying class notes or copies of lecture notes. Advance notice of assignments, alternative ways of completing an assignment, computer technology, taped textbooks and course or program modifications are also available. To assist students with reading-related disabilities, the Kurzweil Omni 3000 Education System is available. Students also have access to the campus Writing Center, tutors and general study skills assistance from the Office of Student Educational Services.

General Support Services Information

Contact Information
Name of program or department: Office of Disability Services
Telephone: 414-288-1645
Fax: 414-288-5799
Website: http://www.marquette.edu/disability-serv

Accommodations or Services For Students With Learning Differences

Accommodations are decided upon an individual basis after a thorough review of appropriate, current documentation. The accommodations requests must be supported through the documentation provided and must be logically linked to the current impact of the condition on academic functioning.

Allowed in exams
Calculator: Yes
Dictionary: Yes
Computer: Yes
Spellchecker: Yes
Extended test time: Yes
Scribes: Yes
Proctors: Yes
Oral exams: Yes
Note-takers: Yes
Support services for students with LD: Yes
Support services for students with ADHD: Yes
Support services for students with ASD: Yes
Distraction-reduced environment: Yes
Tape recording in class: Yes
Electronic texts: Yes
Kurzweil reader: NR
Audio books: Yes
Other assistive technology: Yes
Priority registration: Yes
Added costs of services: No
LD specialists: No
ADHD coaching: No
ASD specialists: No
Professional tutors: No
Peer tutors: Yes
Max. hours/wk. for services: 1
How professors are notified of student approved accommodations: By student

General Admissions Information

Office of Admissions: 414-288-7302

Entrance Requirements

Academic units required: 4 English, 2 science labs, **Academic units recommended:** 4 English, 3 science labs, 2 foreign language, 3 social studies, 2 history. High school diploma is required and GED is accepted. SAT or ACT required. If ACT, ACT with writing accepted. TOEFL required of all international applicants: minimum paper TOEFL 530 or minimum internet TOEFL 78.

Application deadline: 12/1
Notification: Rolling starting 1/31
Average GPA: NR
ACT Composite middle 50% range: 24-30
SAT Math middle 50% range: 540-660
SAT Critical Reading middle 50% range: 530-640
SAT Writing middle 50% range: 510-640
Graduate top 10% of class: 34
Graduated top 25% of class: 68
Graduated top 50% of class: 94

COLLEGE GRADUATION REQUIREMENTS

Course waivers allowed: No
Course substitutions allowed: Yes
In what course: Foreign language, math. Depends on the diagnosis.

Additional Information

Environment: This private school, affiliated with the Roman Catholic-Jesuit Church,, affiliated with the Jesuit Church, was founded in 1881. It has a 93-acre campus.

Student Body
Undergrad enrollment: 8,334
% Women: 53
% Men: 47
% Out-of-state: 67

Cost information
Tuition: $38,000
Room & board:NR
Housing Information
University Housing: Yes
Percent living on campus: 52

Greek System
Fraternity: Yes
Sorority: Yes
Athletics: Division I

Ripon College

PO Box 248, Ripon, WI 54971
Phone: 920-748-8337 • Fax: 920-748-8335
E-mail: adminfo@ripon.edu • Web: www.ripon.edu
Support: S • Institution: Private

Programs or Services for Students with Learning Differences

The Student Support Services (SSS) provides a wide variety of services on the campus, including academic and personal counseling, study skills information, and tutoring. Although the focus of the program is on first generation students, students of higher need, and students who are learning disabled, other students who feel they might qualify are encouraged to contact the SSS office. SSS is a voluntary program that has been in existence at Ripon College since 1974. For the many students who have used its services, SSS has provided a network of support for academic, financial, and personal concerns. A group of peer contacts serves SSS by meeting regularly with students to facilitate communication between SSS participants and the office staff. For students who qualify, SSS offers free tutoring in specific subject areas. (All-campus tutoring is also available.) The tutors are upperclass students who have been recommended by their professors and trained by the SSS staff. These tutors serve as a supplement to faculty assistance. The aim of the tutoring program is to help students develop independent learning skills and improve their course grades. Although federal guidelines require a restriction on who "qualifies," the door to SSS remains open to all eligible students.

Admission Information for Students with Learning Differences

College entrance tests required: Yes
Interview required: Yes
Essay required: No
Additional Application Required for LD/ADHD/ASD: NR
What documentation required for LD: Psycho ed evaluation to include: relevant historical info, instructional interventions, related services, age diagnosed, objective data (aptitude, achievement, info processing), test scores (standard, percentile and grade equivalents) and describe functional limitations.
With general application: No
To receive services after enrolling: Yes
What documentation required for ADHD: Diagnosis based on DSM-V; history of behaviors impairing functioning in academic setting; diagnostic interview; history of symptoms; evidence of ongoing behaviors.
With general application: No
To receive services after enrolling: Yes
What documentation required for ASD: Psycho ed evaluation
With general application: NR
To receive services after enrolling: Yes
LD/ADHD/ASD documentation submitted to: Support Program/Services
Special Ed. HS course work accepted: N/A
Specific course requirements for all applicants: Yes
Separate application required for program services: No
Total # of students receiving LD/ADHD/ASD services: 10
Acceptance into program means acceptance into college: Students must be admitted to and enrolled in the university first and then request services.

Admissions

Students with learning disabilities are screened by admissions and must meet the same admission criteria as all other applicants. There is no set GPA required; courses required include four years English, algebra and geometry, two years natural science, two years social studies, and seven additional units. Students with learning disabilities who self-disclose are referred to Student Support Services when making prospective visits to the campus in order to ascertain specific needs and abilities of the student.

Additional Information

SSS provides tutoring in subject areas; skills classes for no credit in time management, note-taking, test-taking strategies, reading college texts, writing papers, studying for and taking exams, and setting goals; and counseling/guidance. Student Support Services provides intensive study groups, LD support and internships. SSS provides students with peer contacts who provide students with one-on-one support and is useful in helping students adjust to college life, to provide a contact for the student to go to with problems or issues, organize group tutoring, and to help students open their minds and see hope in their future.

General Support Services Information

Contact Information
Name of program or department: Student Support Services
Telephone: 920-748-8107
Fax: 920-748-8382

Accommodations or Services for Students with Learning Differences

Accommodations are decided upon an individual basis after a thorough review of appropriate, current documentation. The accommodations requested must be supported through the documentation provided and must be logically linked to the current impact of the condition on academic functioning.

Allowed in exams
Calculator: Yes
Dictionary: No
Computer: Yes
Spellchecker: Yes
Extended test time: Yes
Scribes: Yes
Proctors: Yes
Oral exams: Yes
Note-takers: Yes
Services for students with LD: Yes
Services for students with ADHD: Yes
Services for students with ASD: Yes
Distraction-reduced environment: Yes
Tape recording in class: Yes
Audio books: NR
Electronic texts: Yes
Kurzweil Reader: Yes
Other assistive technology: Interactive computer technology speech recognition and Kurzweil Reading technology
Priority registration: No
Added costs for services: No
LD specialists: No
ADHD coaching: NR
ASD specialists: NR
Professional tutors: No
Peer tutors: 75
Max. hours/wk. for services: 3hrs/week/class
How professors are notified of LD/ADHD: Both student and director

General Admissions Information

Office of Admissions: 920-748-8337

Entrance Requirements

Academic units required: 4 English, 2 math, 2 science, 2 social studies, **Academic units recommended:** 4 math, 4 science, 2 foreign language, 4 social studies. High school diploma is required and GED is accepted. SAT or ACT required. If ACT, ACT with writing accepted. TOEFL required of all international applicants: minimum paper TOEFL 550 or minimum internet TOEFL 79.

Application deadline: NR
Notification: Rolling starting 9/15
Average GPA: 3.4
ACT Composite middle 50% range: 21-27
SAT Math middle 50% range: 500-620
SAT Critical Reading middle 50% range: 450-640
SAT Writing middle 50% range: NR-NR
Graduated top 10% of class: 21
Graduated top 25% of class: 51
Graduated top 50% of class: 80

COLLEGE GRADUATION REQUIREMENTS

Course waivers allowed: No
Course substitutions allowed: No

Additional Information

Environment: This private school was founded in 1851. It has a 250-acre campus.

Student Body
Undergrad enrollment: 794
% Women: 50
% Men: 50
% Out-of-state: 28

Cost information
Tuition: $36,214
Room & board: $8,177
Housing Information
University Housing: Yes
Percent living on campus: 89

Greek System
Fraternity: Yes
Sorority: Yes
Athletics: Division III

U. OF WISCONSIN—EAU CLAIRE

105 Garfield Avenue, Eau Claire, WI 54701
Phone: 715-836-5415 • Fax: 715-836-2409
E-mail: admissions@uwec.edu • Web: www.uwec.edu
Support: CS • Institution: Public

PROGRAMS OR SERVICES FOR STUDENTS WITH LEARNING DIFFERENCES

The University of Wisconsin—Eau Claire is committed to providing all students with an equal opportunity to fully participate in all aspects of the university community. Services for Students with Disabilities will work with students, faculty, staff, and community partners in a cooperative manner to review policies and procedures and to facilitate the provision of services and accommodations that will ensure that university facilities, programs, and activities are universally accessible.

ADMISSION INFORMATION FOR STUDENTS WITH LEARNING DIFFERENCES

College entrance tests required: Yes
Interview required: No
Essay required: N/A
Additional Application Required for LD/ADHD/ASD: NR
What documentation required for LD: Psycho ed evaluation to include: relevant historical info, instructional interventions, related services, age diagnosed, objective data (aptitude, achievement, info processing), test scores (standard, percentile and grade equivalents) and describe functional limitations.
With general application: No
To receive services after enrolling: Yes
What documentation required for ADHD: Diagnosis based on DSM-V; history of behaviors impairing functioning in academic setting; diagnostic interview; history of symptoms; evidence of ongoing behaviors.
With general application: No
To receive services after enrolling: Yes
What documentation required for ASD: Psycho ed evaluation
With general application: NR
To receive services after enrolling: Yes
LD/ADHD/ASD documentation submitted to: Support Program/Services
Special Ed. HS course work accepted: No
Specific course requirements for all applicants: Yes
Separate application required for program services: No
Total # of students receiving LD/ADHD/ASD services: NR
Acceptance into program means acceptance into college: Separate application required after student has enrolled

ADMISSIONS

Individuals with disabilities must complete the standard university application form. Applicants should carefully review the university's published admission criteria, including math and foreign language requirements. If an applicant with a disability wishes to request an exception to any admission requirements, s/he must: 1) include with the application a letter requesting the exception and explaining the rationale for the request, and 2) submit to the Services for Students with Disabilities Office appropriate documentation establishing both the existence of a disability and a resulting need for the exception being requested. Any information regarding a disability is treated as confidential information as defined by the Family and Educational Rights and Privacy Act (FERPA) at: http://www.ed.gov/offices/OII/fpco/ferpa/.

ADDITIONAL INFORMATION

Students must provide documentation prior to receiving appropriate accommodations. Some of the accommodations provided with appropriate documentation could include tutoring individually or in groups, readers, scribes, note-takers, taped textbooks, proofreaders, and exam accommodations, including extended time, readers, and separate testing rooms. The Academic Skills Center offers individualized tutoring in math preparation and background, composition, reading, and study skills. Many departments on campus provide tutors to help students with course content. Students take a form identifying appropriate accommodation requests completed by SSD staff to instructors. Students who are denied accommodations can appeal any denial by filing a complaint with the Affirmative Action Review Board. Services and accommodations are available to undergraduate and graduate students.

General Support Services Information

Contact Information
Name of program or department: Services for Students with Disabilities
Telephone: 715-836-5800
Fax: 715-831-2651
Website: www.uwec.edu/ssd

Accommodations or Services For Students With Learning Differences

Accommodations are decided upon an individual basis after a thorough review of appropriate, current documentation. The accommodations requests must be supported through the documentation provided and must be logically linked to the current impact of the condition on academic functioning.

Allowed in exams
Calculator: Yes
Dictionary: Yes
Computer: Yes
Spellchecker: Yes
Extended test time: Yes
Scribes: Yes
Proctors: Yes
Oral exams: Yes
Note-takers: Yes
Support services for students with LD: Yes
Support services for students with ADHD: Yes
Support services for students with ASD: Yes
Distraction-reduced environment: Yes
Tape recording in class: Yes
Electronic texts: Yes
Kurzweil reader: NR
Audio books: Yes
Other assistive technology: Yes
Priority registration: Yes
Added costs of services: No
LD specialists: Yes
ADHD coaching: Yes
ASD specialists: Yes
Professional tutors: No
Peer tutors: Yes
Max. hours/wk. for services: 4
How professors are notified of student approved accommodations: By student

General Admissions Information

Office of Admissions: 715-836-5415

Entrance Requirements

Academic units required: 4 English, 3 math, 3 science, 3 social studies, 4 academic electives. High school diploma is required and GED is accepted. SAT or ACT required. If ACT, ACT with writing accepted. TOEFL required of all international applicants: minimum paper TOEFL 550 or minimum internet TOEFL 79.

Application deadline: 8/25
Notification: Rolling starting 9/15
Average GPA: NR
ACT Composite middle 50% range: 22-26
SAT Math middle 50% range: 510-670
SAT Critical Reading middle 50% range: 500-640
SAT Writing middle 50% range: NR-NR
Graduate top 10% of class: 18
Graduated top 25% of class: 49
Graduated top 50% of class: 91

COLLEGE GRADUATION REQUIREMENTS

Course waivers allowed: No
In what course: NR
Course substitutions allowed: Yes
In what course: Physical Activity Courses and some general education courses

Additional Information

Environment: This public school was founded in 1916. It has a 333-acre campus.

Student Body
Undergrad enrollment: 9,894
% Women: 60
% Men: 40
% Out-of-state: 27

Cost information
In-state Tuition: $7,361
Out-of-state Tuition: $14,934
Room & board: $7,322

Housing Information
University Housing: Yes
Percent living on campus: 41

Greek System
Fraternity: NR
Sorority: NR
Athletics: Division III

U. OF WISCONSIN—MADISON

702 West Johnson Street, Suite 2104, Madison, WI 53715
Phone: 608-262-3961 • Fax: 608-262-7706
E-mail: onwisconsin@admissions.wisc.edu • Web: www.wisc.edu
Support: CS • Institution: Public

PROGRAMS OR SERVICES FOR STUDENTS WITH LEARNING DIFFERENCES

The McBurney Disability Resource Center provides students with disabilities equal access to the programs and activities of the University. Over 1,000 students with disabilities are currently registered with the McBurney Center. Students with disabilities who tend to do well have graduated from competitive high school or college programs and are reasonably independent, proactive in seeking assistance, and use accommodations similar to those offered here. For complete information about the McBurney Center, please visit our web site at www.mcburney.wisc.edu.

ADMISSION INFORMATION FOR STUDENTS WITH LEARNING DIFFERENCES

College entrance tests required: Yes
Interview required: No
Essay required: NR
Additional Application Required for LD/ADHD/ASD: NR
What documentation required for LD: Recent psychometric assessment with test analysis and interpretation
With general application: No
To receive services after enrolling: Yes
What documentation required for ADHD: Current comprehensive ADHD diagnostic evaluation report (within approximately the last three years)
With general application: No
To receive services after enrolling: Yes
What documentation required for ASD: Psycho ed evaluation
With general application: No
To receive services after enrolling: Yes
LD/ADHD/ASD documentation submitted to: Transition Services
Special Ed. HS course work accepted: No
Specific course requirements for all applicants: Yes
Separate application required for program services: Yes
Total # of students receiving LD/ADHD/ASD services: 675
Acceptance into program means acceptance into college: Separate application required after student has enrolled

ADMISSIONS

The admission review process is the same for all applicants. Factors in the review process may include self-disclosed disability information in the written statement, grades, rank, test scores, course requirements completed, and potential for success. Disclosure of disability will not have a negative effect on a student's admission application. If a student wishes to disclose a disability they may do so in the "additional statement" on the application. Suggested information to include is the date of diagnosis or the onset of the disability and the ramifications of the disability on course requirements, attendance, and academic performance. This information will be considered during the admission review by trained admission counselors. Any documentation about the disability should be submitted to the McBurney Disability Resource Center.

ADDITIONAL INFORMATION

The documentation must be completed by a professional qualified to diagnose an LD. The report must include results of a clinical interview and descriptions of the testing procedures; instruments used; test and subtest results reported in standard scores, as well as percentile rank and grade scores where useful; and interpretation and recommendations based on data gathered. It must be comprehensive and include test results where applicable in intelligence, reading, math, spelling, written language, language processing, and cognitive processing skills. Testing should carefully examine areas of concern/weakness, as well as areas of strengths; documentation should include a clear diagnostic statement based on the test results and personal history. Students may be eligible for advocacy/liaison with faculty and staff, alternative testing accommodations, curriculum modifications, disability management advising, learning skills training, liaison with vocational rehab, access to the McBurney Learning Resource Room, note-takers, peer support groups, priority registration, taped texts, and course materials.

General Support Services Information

Contact Information
Name of program or department: McBurney Disability Resource Center
Telephone: 608-263-2741
Fax: 608-265-2998

Accommodations or Services for Students with Learning Differences

Accommodations are decided upon an individual basis after a thorough review of appropriate, current documentation. The accommodations requested must be supported through the documentation provided and must be logically linked to the current impact of the condition on academic functioning.

Allowed in exams
Calculator: Yes
Dictionary: N/A
Computer: Yes
Spellchecker: Yes
Extended test time: Yes
Scribes: Yes
Proctors: No
Oral exams: Yes
Note-takers: Yes
Services for students with LD: Yes
Services for students with ADHD: Yes
Services for students with ASD: Yes
Distraction-reduced environment: Yes
Tape recording in class: NR
Audio books: Yes
Electronic texts: Yes
Kurzweil Reader: Yes
Other assistive technology: Yes
Priority registration: Yes
Added costs for services: No
LD specialists: Yes
ADHD coaching: NR
ASD specialists: Yes
Professional tutors: No
Peer tutors: Yes
Max. hours/wk. for services: .5
How professors are notified of LD/ADHD: Student

General Admissions Information

Office of Admissions: 608-262-3961

Entrance Requirements

Academic units required: 4 English, 4 math, 3 science, 3 foreign language, 3 social studies, 2 academic electives, **Academic units recommended:** 4 English, 4 math, 4 science, 4 foreign language, 4 social studies, 3 academic electives. High school diploma is required and GED is accepted. SAT or ACT required. If ACT, ACT with writing accepted. TOEFL required of all international applicants.

Application deadline: 2/1
Notification: Rolling starting 11/1
Average GPA: 3.85
ACT Composite middle 50% range: 27-31
SAT Math middle 50% range: 630-760
SAT Critical Reading middle 50% range: 560-660
SAT Writing middle 50% range: 600-690
Graduate top 10% of class: 54
Graduated top 25% of class: 91
Graduated top 50% of class: 100

COLLEGE GRADUATION REQUIREMENTS

Course waivers allowed: NR
Course substitutions allowed: NR

Additional Information

Environment: This public school was founded in 1848. It has a 933-acre campus.

Student Body
Undergrad enrollment: 31,662
% Women: 51
% Men: 49
% Out-of-state: 33

Cost information
In-state Tuition: $9,273
Out-of-state Tuition: $28,523
Room & board: $8,804

Housing Information
University Housing: Yes
Percent living on campus: 26

Greek System
Fraternity: Yes
Sorority: Yes
Athletics: Division I

U. of Wisconsin—Milwaukee

Department of Admissions and Recruitment, Milwaukee, WI 53211
Phone: 414-229-2222 • Fax: 414-229-6940
E-mail: uwmlook@uwm.edu • Web: www4.uwm.edu
Support: CS • Institution: Public

Programs or Services for Students with Learning Differences

The Accessibility Resource Center (ARC) offers a wide range of academic support services to students with learning disabilities, attention deficit hyperactivity disorders, Autism Spectrum Disorder and traumatic brain injuries. Our mission is to create an accessible university community for students with disabilities that fosters the development of each student's full potential. There is no waiting list or caps on participation. This program is well suited for students who are fairly independent and willing to seek the support services they need. Recommended academic accommodations are based on documentation of disability and disability related needs. The accommodations may include but are not limited to: note-taking assistance, exam accommodations, alternate format textbooks, priority registration. In addition to academic accommodations, staff is available to meet individually with students to work on study strategies, time management issues, and organization.

Admission Information for Students with Learning Differences

College entrance test required: Yes
Interview required: No
Essay required: No
Additional Application Required for LD/ADHD/ASD: NR
What documentation required for LD: Comprehensive and current psycho-educational or neuro-psychological assessment. Recommended testing instruments include the WAIS III and Wodcock-Johnson Tests of Achievement
With general application: No
To receive services after enrolling: Yes
What documentation required for ADHD: Preferred is a comprehensive and current psycho-educational or neuro-psychological assessment. Also accepted is completion of UWM's form of Certification of ADHD completed by a psychiatraist or psychologist. Form can be found on our website at www.sac.uwm.edu
With general application: No
To receive services after enrolling: Yes
What documentation required for ASD: Psycho ed evaluation
With general application: No
To receive services after enrolling: Yes
LD/ADHD/ASD documentation submitted to: Support program/services
Special Ed. HS course work accepted: Yes
Specific course: Yes
Separate application required for program services: Yes
Total # of students receiving LD/ADHD/ASD services: NR
Acceptance into program means acceptance into college: NR

Admissions

Admission into UWM is necessary for participation. Students apply directly to Enrollment Services or online. Online applications are encouraged. Apply online at apply.wisconsin.edu. The Accessibility Resource Center does not make admission decisions. Disability Documentation should be sent directly to the Accessibility Resource Center. Students need to apply online, and submit ACT scores, high school transcripts. Accommodations can be requested to take the placement tests by contacting the LD Program and submitting documentation of disability.

Additional Information

Students who meet eligibility criteria receive individual counseling and guidance. In addition, students may be eligible for academic accommodations based upon specific disability-related needs. These accommodations may include but are not limited to: Priority registration, note-taking assistance, exam accommodations, taped textbooks, and use of computer. To use the Computer & Assistive Technology Lab students must have an initial screening of the need for assistive technology. Specific, individualized recommendations for each student are evaluated. Eligible students will have portable, flexible access to technology. Assistive Technology is based on student need and there is training in the use of Assistive Technology.

General Support Services Information

Contact Information
Name of program or department: Accessibility Resource Center
Telephone: 414-229-6287
Fax: 414 229-2237

Accommodations or Services for Students with Learning Differences

Accommodations are decided upon an individual basis after a thorough review of appropriate, current documentation. The accommodations requests must be supported through the documentation provided and must be logically linked to the current impact of the condition on academic functioning.

Allowed in exams
Calculator: No
Dictionary: Yes
Computer: Yes
Spellchecker: Yes
Extended test time: Yes
Scribes: Yes
Proctors: Yes
Oral exams: Yes
Note-takers: Yes
Services for students with LD: Yes
Services for students with ADHD: Yes
Services for students with ASD: Yes
Distraction-reduced environment: Yes
Tape recording in class: Yes
Audio books: Yes
Electronic texts: NR
Kurzweil reader: Yes
Other assistive technology: Yes
Priority registration: Yes
Added costs of services: No
LD specialists: Yes
ADHD coaching: NR
ASD specialists: NR
Professional tutors: NR
Peer tutors: Yes
Max. hours/wk. for services: 3
How professors are notified of student approved accommodations: Student

General Admissions Information

Office of Admissions: 414-229-2222

Entrance Requirements

Academic units required: 4 English, 3 math, 3 science, 1 science labs, 3 social studies, 2 academic electives, and 2 units from above areas or other academic areas. **Academic units recommended:** 4 English, 4 math, 3 science, 1 science labs, 2 foreign language, 3 social studies, 2 academic electives, and 2 units from above areas or other academic areas. High school diploma is required and GED is accepted. SAT or ACT required for some. If ACT, ACT with writing accepted. TOEFL required of all international applicants: minimum paper TOEFL 520 or minimum internet TOEFL 68.

Application deadline: NR
Notification: Rolling starting 9/15
Average GPA: 3.05
ACT Composite middle 50% range: 19-24
SAT Math middle 50% range: NR-NR
SAT Critical Reading middle 50% range: NR-NR
SAT Writing middle 50% range: NR-NR
Graduated top 10% of class: 9
Graduated top 25% of class: 28
Graduated top 50% of class: 63

COLLEGE GRADUATION REQUIREMENTS

Course waivers allowed: No
Course substitutions allowed: Yes
In what course: On an individual basis determinations will be made for course substitutions generally in math and foreign language courses.

Additional Information

Environment: This public school was founded in 1956. It has a 93-acre campus.

Student Body
Undergrad enrollment: 23,004
% Women: 51
% Men: 49
% Out-of-state: 7

Cost information
In-state Tuition: $8,091
Out-of Tuition: $17,820
Room & board: $9,136

Housing Information
University Housing: Yes
Percent living on campus: 16

Greek System
Fraternity: NR
Sorority: NR
Athletics: Division I

UNIVERSITY OF WISCONSIN—OSHKOSH

Dempsey Hall 135, Oshkosh, WI 54901
Phone: 920-424-0202 • Fax: 920-424-1098
E-mail: oshadmuw@uwosh.edu • Web: www.uwosh.edu/home
Support: SP • Institution: Public

PROGRAMS OR SERVICES FOR STUDENTS WITH LEARNING DIFFERENCES

Project Success is a language remediation project that is based on mastering the entire sound structure of the English language. These students are academically able and determined to succeed, in spite of a pronounced problem in a number of areas. Help is offered in the following ways: direct remediation of deficiencies through the Orton-Gillingham Technique, one-on-one tutoring assistance, math and writing labs, guidance and counseling with scheduling course work and interpersonal relations, extended time, and by providing an atmosphere that is supportive. The goal is for students to become language independent in and across all of these major educational areas: math, spelling, reading, writing, comprehension, and study skills. As full-time university students, they will acquire language independence by mastering the entire phonetic structure of the American English language.

ADMISSION INFORMATION FOR STUDENTS WITH LEARNING DIFFERENCES

College entrance tests required: Yes
Interview required: No
Essay required: Yes
Additional Application Required for LD/ADHD/ASD: NR
What documentation required for LD: Psycho ed evaluation to include: relevant historical info, instructional interventions, related services, age diagnosed, objective data (aptitude, achievement, info processing), test scores (standard, percentile and grade equivalents) and describe functional limitations.
With general application: Yes if requested as part of Structured Program application
To receive services after enrolling: Yes
What documentation required for ADHD: Diagnosis based on DSM-V; history of behaviors impairing functioning in academic setting; diagnostic interview; history of symptoms; evidence of ongoing behaviors.
With general application: Yes if requested as part of Structured Program application
To receive services after enrolling: Yes
What documentation required for ASD: Psycho ed evaluation
LD/ADHD/ASD documentation submitted to: Admissions Office and Project Success
Special Ed. HS course work accepted: Yes
Specific course requirements of all applicants: Yes
Separate application required: Yes
Total # of students receiving LD/ADHD/ASD services: 350
Acceptance into program means acceptance into college: Students are accepted jointly to Project Success and the university; however, they must submit separate applications for the program and the university.

ADMISSIONS

Students may apply to Project Success in their junior year of high school. Applicants apply by writing a letter, in their own handwriting, indicating interest in the program and why they are interested. Applications are processed on a first-come, first-served basis. Those interested should apply at least 1 to 2 years prior to the student's desired entrance sememster. Students and parents will be invited to interview. The interview is used to assess family dynamics in terms of support for the student and reasons for wanting to attend college. The director is looking for motivation, stability, and the ability of the students to describe the disability. Acceptance into Project Success does not grant acceptance into the university. Admission to the university and acceptance into Project Success is a joint decision, but a separate process is required for each. General admissions procedures must be followed before acceptance into Project Success can be offered. ACT/SAT or GPA are not critical. Students who are admitted to UW—Oshkosh and Project Success not in full standing (all high school units completed, top 40 percent of graduating class, and ACT of 22-plus) must attend the Project Success summer program prior to freshman year.

ADDITIONAL INFORMATION

Incoming freshmen to Project Success must participate in an 6-week summer school program consisting of simultaneous multisensory instructional procedures (SMSIP). This program is used to teach study skills, reading, spelling, writing, and mathematical operations. The Project Success program offers the following remedial and support services for all students enrolled in its program: organizational tutors, mathematics courses/tutoring, remedial reading and spelling courses, English/written expression courses/tutoring, and content area tutoring. Additionally, students are eligible for extended time testing opportunities. Although Project Success does not offer taped texts, students are not prohibited from using them. Student requesting taped texts are referred to the UW—Oshkosh Disability Services office. Services and accommodations are available for undergraduate and graduate students.

General Support Services Information

Contact Information
Name of program or department: Project Success
Telephone: 920-424-3100
Fax: 920-424-0858

Accommodations or Services for Students with Learning Differences

Accommodations are decided upon an individual basis after a thorough review of appropriate, current documentation. The accommodations requested must be supported through the documentation provided and must be logically linked to the current impact of the condition on academic functioning.

Allowed in exams
Calculator: Yes
Dictionary: Yes
Computer: Yes
Spellchecker: No
Extended test time: Yes
Scribes: No
Proctors: Yes
Oral exams: No
Note-takers: Yes
Services for students with LD: Yes
Services for students with ADHD: Yes
Services for students with ASD: Yes
Distraction-reduced environment: Yes
Tape recording in class: Yes
Audio books: NR
Electronic texts: Yes
Kurzweil Reader: Yes
Other assistive technology: Yes
Priority registration: Yes
Added costs for services: No
LD specialists: Yes
ADHD coaching: NR
ASD specialists: NR
Professional tutors: No
Peer tutors: 80
Max. hours/wk. for services: NR
How professors are notified of LD/ADHD: By both student and director

General Admissions Information

Office of Admissions: 920-424-0202

Entrance Requirements

Academic units required: 4 English, 3 math, 3 science, 3 science labs, 3 social studies, 2 history, 4 academic electives, **Academic units recommended:** 4 math, 4 science, 4 science labs, 2 foreign language, 4 social studies, 1 history, 1 visual/performing arts. High school diploma is required and GED is accepted. SAT or ACT required. If ACT, ACT with writing accepted. TOEFL required of all international applicants: minimum paper TOEFL 525 or minimum internet TOEFL 70.

Application deadline: NR
Notification: Rolling starting 9/15
Average GPA: 3.3
ACT Composite middle 50% range: 20-24
SAT Math middle 50% range: NR-NR
SAT Critical Reading middle 50% range: NR-NR
SAT Writing middle 50% range: NR-NR
Graduated top 10% of class: 10
Graduated top 25% of class: 37
Graduated top 50% of class: 84

COLLEGE GRADUATION REQUIREMENTS

Course waivers allowed: Yes
In what course: UW—Oshkosh has special accommodations in place relating to the foreign language requirement.
Course substitutions allowed: Yes
In what course: Foreign language and several others in select areas

Additional Information

Environment: This public school was founded in 1871. It has a 192-acre campus.

Student Body
Undergrad enrollment: 12,322
% Women: 59
% Men: 41
% Out-of-state: 3

Cost information
In-state Tuition: $7,360
Out-of Tuition: $14,934
Room & board: $6,926
Housing Information
University Housing: Yes
Percent living on campus: 29

Greek System
Fraternity: Yes
Sorority: Yes
Athletics: Division III

U. of Wisconsin—Stevens Point

1108 Fremont Street, Stevens Point, WI 54481
Phone: 715-346-2441 • Fax: 715-346-3296
E-mail: admiss@uwsp.edu • Web: www.uwsp.edu
Support: S • Institution: Public

Programs or Services for Students with Learning Differences

The university does not have a formal program or a specialized curriculum for students with LD; rather, it provides all of the services appropriate to ensure equal access to all programs. Their philosophy is to provide what is mandated in order to enhance the student's academic success, and also to convey their concern for the student's total well-being. The director is a strong advocate for students. Students are encouraged to meet with the director prior to admissions for information about the services. A full range of accommodations are provided. The services provide a multisensory approach developing compensatory skills, not remediation, and utilize a developmental model for advising as well as psychosocial adjustment. Student success is contingent on many factors; some responsibilities belong to the student, others belong to the university, and others are shared by both. Students should make an appointment at the beginning of each semester; make their needs known; and be a self-advocate. Disability Services (DS) provides students with accommodations that are appropriate for the disability. Together, DS and the student can work toward effective accommodations and utilization of support services and establish a working relationship based on trust and communication.

Admission Information for Students with Learning Differences

College entrance test required: NR
Interview required: No
Essay required: Not Applicable
Additional Application Required for LD/ADHD/ASD: No
What documentation required for LD: Medical or psychological report identifying ADHD
With general application: NR
To receive services after enrolling: No
What documentation required for ADHD: Medical or psychological documentation completed by a professional qualified to document ASD.
With general application: NR
To receive services after enrolling: No
What documentation required for ASD: High school psychological report or other psychological report documenting a learning disorder
With general application: NR
To receive services after enrolling: No
LD/ADHD/ASD documentation submitted to: Disability and Assistive Technology Center
ASD Specific Program: NR
Special Ed. HS course work accepted: Not Applicable
Specific course requirements of all applicants: NR
Separate application required for program services: False
Total # of students receiving LD/ADHD/ASD services: NR
Acceptance into program means acceptance into college: NR

Admissions

There is no separate admission procedure for students with learning disabilities. However, students are encouraged to make a pre-admission inquiry and talk to the director of DS.

Additional Information

DS provides: accommodations that are appropriate to the disability, such as text-to-voice textbooks, note-takers, proctors and scribes, adaptive testing, assistive technology and advising, referral to tutoring and writing assistance, time management and study strategies training, notification to faculty/staff regarding necessary accommodations, referral for assessment for those not yet diagnosed, and a commitment to keeping scheduled appointments and a corresponding commitment to being timely. The Tutoring-Learning Center schedules one-on-one tutoring sessions and small-group tutoring; tutoring is free for students wanting help with reading or writing assignments. Tutoring in subject areas is done in groups and one-on-one in which there is a fee; however, for some students, the fee is covered by various support funding.

General Support Services Information

Contact Information
Name of program or department: Disability and Assistive Technology Center
Telephone: 715 346-3365
Fax: 715 346-4143
Website: www.uwsp.edu/special/disability/

Accommodations or Services For Students With Learning Differences

Accommodations are decided upon an individual basis after a thorough review of appropriate, current documentation. The accommodations requests must be supported through the documentation provided and must be logically linked to the current impact of the condition on academic functioning.

Allowed in exams
Calculator: Yes
Dictionary: Yes
Computer: Yes
Spellchecker: Yes
Extended test time: Yes
Scribes: Yes
Proctors: Yes
Oral exams: Not Applicable
Note-takers: Yes
Support services for students with LD: Yes
Support services for students with ADHD: Yes
Support services for students with ASD: Yes
Distraction-reduced environment: Yes
Tape recording in class: Yes
Electronic texts: Yes
Kurzweil reader: NR
Audio books: Yes
Other assistive technology: Yes
Priority registration: Yes
Added costs of services: No
LD specialists: No
ADHD coaching: No
ASD specialists: Yes
Professional tutors: No
Peer tutors: NR
Max. hours/wk. for services: NR
How professors are notified of student approved accommodations: By student

General Admissions Information

Office of Admissions: 715-346-2441

Entrance Requirements

Academic units required: 4 English, 3 math, 3 science, 3 social studies, 4 academic electives, **Academic units recommended:** 4 English, 4 math, 4 science, 4 social studies, 4 academic electives. High school diploma is required and GED is accepted. SAT or ACT required for some. If ACT, ACT with writing accepted. TOEFL required of all international applicants: minimum internet TOEFL 70.

Application deadline: NR
Notification: NR
Average GPA: 3.07
ACT Composite middle 50% range: 20-25
SAT Math middle 50% range: 410-523
SAT Critical Reading middle 50% range: 405-565
SAT Writing middle 50% range: 390-530
Graduate top 10% of class: 11
Graduated top 25% of class: 33
Graduated top 50% of class: 73

COLLEGE GRADUATION REQUIREMENTS

Course waivers allowed: No
Course substitutions allowed: Yes
In what course: Substitutions mostly granted for foreign language, speech and math.

Additional Information

Environment: This public school was founded in 1894. It has a 335-acre campus.

Student Body
Undergrad enrollment: 8,839
% Women: 52
% Men: 48
% Out-of-state: 11

Cost information
In-state Tuition: $7,674
Out-of-state Tuition: $15,940
Room & board: $3,414

Housing Information
University Housing: Yes
Percent living on campus: 39

Greek System
Fraternity: Yes
Sorority: Yes
Athletics: Division III

U. of Wisconsin—Whitewater

800 West Main Street, Whitewater, WI 53190-1791
Phone: 262-472-1440 • Fax: 262-472-1515
E-mail: uwwadmit@uww.edu • Web: www.uww.edu/
Support: CS • Institution: Public

Programs or Services for Students with Learning Differences

The University of Wisconsin—Whitewater Center for Students with Disabilities, Project ASSIST program offers support services for students with learning disabilities and ADD/ADHD. The Project ASSIST Summer Transition Program is a four-week program in which students enroll in a three credit study skills class, one credit New Student Seminar and non-credit Project ASSIST class. Areas addressed include learning strategies, comprehension concerns, written language skills, study habits, time management and self-advocacy skills. The philosophy of the program is that students with learning disabilities can learn strategies to become independent learners.

Admission Information for Students with Learning Differences

College entrance test required: Yes
Interview required: No
Essay required: 4
Additional Application Required for LD/ADHD/ASD: NR
What documentation required for LD: Diagnostic interview, assessment of aptitude (WAIS III), academic achievement (Woodcock-Johnson), information processing, specific diagnosis and test scores should be included in the summary report along with recommendations for accommodations. Response to Intervention, 504 Plans, and IEPs are helpful.
With general application: No
To receive services after enrolling: Yes
What documentation required for ADHD: History of early impairment, evidence of current impairment, diagnostic interview, any relevant testing, clearly stated specific diagnosis, rationale for specific accommodations
With general application: No
To receive services after enrolling: Yes
What documentation required for ASD: A specific diagnosis that conforms to DSM-IV criteria for Autism, Asperger's Syndrome, or Pervasive Developmental Disorder-Not Otherwise Specified. Documentation from psychologist, physician, psychiatrist or other appropriate professional. Response to Intervention, 504 Plans, and IEP documents can be helpful.
With general application: No
To receive services after enrolling: Yes
LD/ADHD/ASD documentation submitted to: Support program/services
Special Ed. HS course work accepted: Yes
Specific course: Yes
Separate application required for program services: Yes
Total # of students receiving LD/ADHD/ASD services: NR
Acceptance into program means acceptance into college: NR

Admissions

All applicants must meet the same criteria for admission. Students should apply to both the university and the Center for Students with Disabilities. General criteria include: Students apply to the university admissions and the Center for Students with Disabilities at the same time. Program staff review the documentation and application regarding eligibility for academic accommodations and Project ASSIST. Programs of Opportunity and Conditional admission to a limited number of students may be possible depending on review of documentation and reason for admission denial.

Additional Information

Tutoring services are provided in a one-to-one setting where students work with tutors on study, math and written language strategies in the context of specific course work. In addition, organizational tutoring is offered to assist students with time management and organization. Computer lab with assistive technology, small group support and academic advising available. Study areas available for student use with daytime and evening hours. In addition, drop-in tutoring is available each weekday and early evening. Access to copies of class notes to qualified students through Hawknotes system.

General Support Services Information

Contact Information
Name of program or department: Center for Students with Disabilities
Telephone: 262-472-4711
Fax: 262-472-4865

Accommodations or Services for Students with Learning Differences

Accommodations are decided upon an individual basis after a thorough review of appropriate, current documentation. The accommodations requests must be supported through the documentation provided and must be logically linked to the current impact of the condition on academic functioning.

Allowed in exams
Calculator: Yes
Dictionary: Yes
Computer: Yes
Spellchecker: Yes
Extended test time: Yes
Scribes: Yes
Proctors: Yes
Oral exams: Yes
Note-takers: Yes
Services for students with LD: Yes
Services for students with ADHD: Yes
Services for students with ASD: Yes
Distraction-reduced environment: Yes
Tape recording in class: Yes
Audio books: Yes
Electronic tetxts: NR
Kurzweil reader: Yes
Other assistive technology: Yes
Priority registration: Yes
Added costs of services: Yes
LD specialists: Yes
ADHD coaching: NR
ASD specialists: NR
Professional tutors: Yes
Peer tutors: Yes
Max. hours/wk. for services: NR
How professors are notified of student approved accommodations: Student

General Admissions Information

Office of Admissions: 262-472-1440

Entrance Requirements

Academic units required: 4 English, 3 math, 3 science, 1 science labs, 3 social studies, 4 academic electives, **Academic units recommended:** 4 math, 4 science, 2 foreign language, 4 social studies. High school diploma is required and GED is accepted. SAT or ACT recommended. If ACT, ACT with writing accepted. TOEFL required of all international applicants: minimum paper TOEFL 500.

Application deadline: NR
Notification: Rolling starting 9/15
Average GPA: NR
ACT Composite middle 50% range: 20-24
SAT Math middle 50% range: 480-600
SAT Critical Reading middle 50% range: NR-NR
SAT Writing middle 50% range: 470-610
Graduated top 10% of class: 9
Graduated top 25% of class: 32
Graduated top 50% of class: 77

COLLEGE GRADUATION REQUIREMENTS

Course waivers allowed: No
Course substitutions allowed: Yes
In what course: some math requirements, communications, foreign language

Additional Information

Environment: This public school was founded in 1868. It has a 385-acre campus.

Student Body
Undergrad enrollment: 9,231
% Women: 51
% Men: 49
% Out-of-state: 4

Cost information
In-state Tuition: $5,568
Out-of Tuition: $13,042
Room & board: $4,322

Housing Information
University Housing: Yes
Percent living on campus: 40

Greek System
Fraternity: NR
Sorority: NR
Athletics: Division III

Laramie County Community College

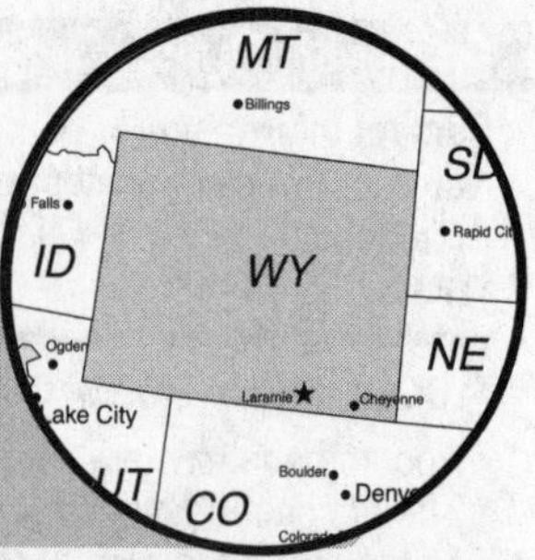

1400 East College Drive, Cheyenne, WY 82007 • Phone: 800-522-2993
E-mail: dss@lccc.wy.edu • Web: www.lccc.wy.edu
Support: CS • Institution type: 2-year Public

Programs or Services for Students with Learning Differences

Disability Support Services at Laramie County Community College provides comprehensive, confidential services for LCCC students with documented disabilities. Services and adaptive equipment are available to reduce mobility, sensory, and perceptual concerns. Services are provided free of charge to LCCC students. High school students are encouraged to contact DSS during their junior year to gather information.

Admission Information for Students with Learning Differences

College entrance tests required: No
Interview required: No
Essay required: No
Additional Application Required for LD/ADHD/ASD: NR
What documentation required for LD: Psycho ed evaluation to include: relevant historical info, instructional interventions, related services, age diagnosed, objective data (aptitude, achievement, info processing), test scores (standard, percentile and grade equivalents) and describe functional limitations.
With general application: No
To receive services after enrolling: Yes
What documentation required for ADHD: Diagnosis based on DSM-V; history of behaviors impairing functioning in academic setting; diagnostic interview; history of symptoms; evidence of ongoing behaviors.
With general application: No
To receive services after enrolling: Yes
What documentation required for ASD: Psycho ed evaluation
With general application: NR
To receive services after enrolling: Yes
LD/ADHD/ASD documentation submitted to: Disability Support Services Office
Special Ed. HS course work accepted: Yes
Specific course requirements of all applicants: NR
Separate application required: No
Total # of students receiving LD/ADHD/ASD services: 35
Acceptance into program means acceptance into college: Students must be admitted and enrolled prior to requesting services.

Admissions

Admission is open to all high school graduates or GED recipients. To register students for classes, LCCC needs to assess the student's skill level in three key areas (reading, English, and math). Admission to LCCC is not based on these scores. There are no specific course requirements.

Additional Information

Students requesting services will be required to provide a copy of current documentation. Laramie County Community College has adopted documentation guidelines as developed by the Consortium of Support Programs for Students with Disabilities, representing the postsecondary institutions of Colorado and Wyoming. Examples of services available include testing accommodations, readers/taped tests, scribes, extended time on exams, quiet rooms, use of calculators, special seating, textbooks on tape, tape recording of lectures, note-takers, assistive listening devices, assistive technology equipment, hardware and software programs, and priority registration. Appropriate accommodations are determined on a case-by-case basis between the DSS staff and the student.

General Support Services Information

Contact Information
Name of program or department: Disability Support Services
Telephone: 307-778-1359
Fax: 307-778-1262

Accommodations or Services for Students with Learning Differences

Accommodations are decided upon an individual basis after a thorough review of appropriate, current documentation. The accommodations requested must be supported through the documentation provided.

Allowed in exams
Calculator: Yes
Dictionary: Yes
Computer: Yes
Spellchecker: Yes
Extended test time: Yes
Scribes: Yes
Proctors: Yes
Oral exams: Yes
Note-takers: Yes
Services for students with LD: Yes
Services for students with ADHD: Yes
Services for students with ASD: Yes
Distraction-reduced environment: Yes
Tape recording in class: Yes
Audio books: NR
Electronic texts: Yes
Kurzweil Reader: Yes
Other assistive technology: Yes
Priority registration: Yes
Added costs for services: No
LD specialists: Yes
ADHD coaching: NR
ASD specialists: NR
Professional tutors: 5–15
Peer tutors: 10–20
Max. hours/wk. for services: Unlimited
How professors are notified of LD/ADHD: Accommodation letters

General Admissions Information

Office of Admission: 307-778-1117

Entrance Requirements

Open admissions but selective for some majors. Interview is required for equine training. ACT/SAT not required. High school diploma or GED accepted.

Application deadline: None
Notification: Rolling
Average GPA: NR
ACT Composite middle 50% range: NR
SAT Math middle 50% range: NR
SAT Critical Reading middle 50% range: NR
SAT Writing middle 50% range: NR
Graduated top 10% of class: NR
Graduated top 25% of class: NR
Graduated top 50% of class: NR

COLLEGE GRADUATION REQUIREMENTS

Course waivers allowed: No
Course substitutions allowed: Yes
In what course: Decided on a case-by-case basis depending on the documented disability and the student's course of study.

Additional Information

Environment: LCCC is 100 miles north of Denver, Colorado.

Student Body
Undergrad enrollment: 5,600
% Women: 58%
% Men: 42%
% Out-of-state: 10%

Cost Information
In-state tuition: $2,640
Out-of-state tuition: $5,952
Room & board: $6,742–$8,740

Housing Information
University housing: Yes
% Living on campus: 4%

Greek System
Fraternity: No
Sorority: No
Athletics: NJCAA

SHERIDAN COLLEGE

3059 Cofeen Avenue, Sheridan, WY 82801
Phone: 307-674-6446 • Fax: 307-674-3384
E-mail: admmissions@sheridan.edu • Web: www.sheridanc.edu
Support: S • Institution type: 2-year Public

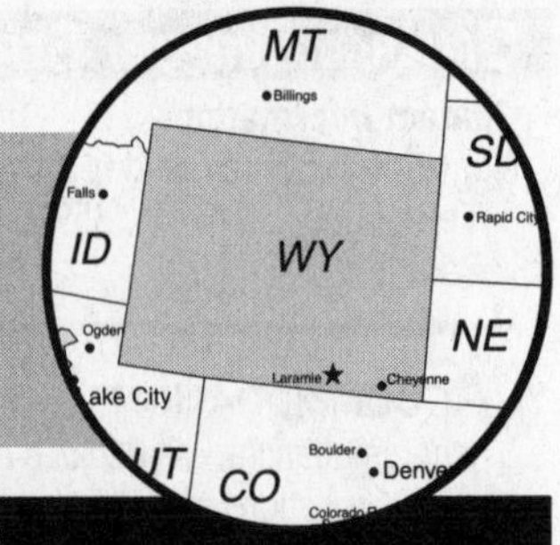

PROGRAMS OR SERVICES FOR STUDENTS WITH LEARNING DIFFERENCES

Sheridan College has limited services available for students with learning disabilities. Students who have been enrolled in special education classes in high school may find that the college does not have the extensive services necessary for them to be successful. Students need to be self-sufficient because the two advisor/counselors are able to allot only a small percentage of their time to work with students with disabilities. Students requesting accommodations must provide psychoeducational evaluations and have these sent to the Counseling/Testing Offices. The college reserves the right to evaluate if it can serve the needs of students.

ADMISSION INFORMATION FOR STUDENTS WITH LEARNING DIFFERENCES

College entrance tests required: No
Interview required: No
Essay required: No
Additional Application Required for LD/ADHD/ASD: NR
What documentation required for LD: Psycho ed evaluation to include: relevant historical info, instructional interventions, related services, age diagnosed, objective data (aptitude, achievement, info processing), test scores (standard, percentile and grade equivalents) and describe functional limitations.
With general application: No
To receive services after enrolling: Yes
What documentation required for ADHD: Diagnosis based on DSM-V; history of behaviors impairing functioning in academic setting; diagnostic interview; history of symptoms; evidence of ongoing behaviors.
With general application: No
To receive services after enrolling: Yes
What documentation required for ASD: Psycho ed evaluation
With general application: NR
To receive services after enrolling: Yes
LD/ADHD/ASD documentation submitted to: Admissions Office
Special Ed. HS course work accepted: N/A
Specific course requirements of all applicants: No
Separate application required: Yes
Total # of students receiving LD/ADHD/ASD services: 30
Acceptance into program means acceptance into college: Students must be admitted to and enrolled in the university first and then request services.

ADMISSIONS

There are no special admission procedures or criteria for students with learning disabilities. The college has open admissions, and any student with a high school diploma or GED is eligible to attend. All students are treated the same and must submit the general college application for admission. Any information on learning disabilities provided is voluntarily given by the student. Students with learning disabilities must submit psychoeducational evaluations. The admission decision is made by the director of the program.

ADDITIONAL INFORMATION

The college offers tutoring, quiet places to take tests, readers, extended testing times, recorders, note-takers, and the availability of a few Franklin Spellers. Remediation courses are offered in arithmetic skills, spelling, vocabulary, reading, writing, and algebra. Other aids for students with learning disabilities include test-taking strategies training, books on tape, tutoring one-on-one or in small groups in the Learning Center, and GED preparation and testing. Support services include career testing and evaluation, peer counseling, and personal and career development.

General Support Services Information

Contact Information
Name of program or department: Advising/Learning Center or Disabilities Service Coordinator & Tutor Program
Telephone: 307-674-6446 or 307-674-6646 ext: 2701
Fax: 307-674-3384

Accommodations or Services for Students with Learning Differences

Accommodations are decided upon an individual basis after a thorough review of appropriate, current documentation. The accommodations requested must be supported through the documentation provided and must be logically linked to the current impact of the condition on academic functioning.

Allowed in exams
Calculator: Yes
Dictionary: Yes
Computer: Yes
Spellchecker: Yes
Extended test time: Yes
Scribes: Yes
Proctors: Yes
Oral exams: Yes
Note-takers: Yes
Services for students with LD: Yes
Services for students with ADHD: Yes
Services for students with ASD: Yes
Distraction-reduced environment: Yes
Tape recording in class: Yes
Audio books: NR
Electronic texts: Yes
Kurzweil Reader: No
Other assistive technology: Yes
Priority registration: No
Added costs for services: No
LD specialists: No
ADHD coaching: NR
ASD specialists: NR
Professional tutors: No
Peer tutors: Yes
Max. hours/wk. for services: Unlimited
How professors are notified of LD/ADHD: By student

General Admissions Information

Office of Admission: 800-913-9139

Entrance Requirements

Open enrollment. Admissions does not require diploma or GED, but the financial aid office does to release federal aid.

Application deadline: 6/1
Notification: NR
Average GPA: NR
ACT Composite middle 50% range: NR
SAT Math middle 50% range: NR
SAT Critical Reading middle 50% range: NR
SAT Writing middle 50% range: NR
Graduated top 10% of class: NR
Graduated top 25% of class: NR
Graduated top 50% of class: NR

COLLEGE GRADUATION REQUIREMENTS

Course waivers allowed: Yes
In what course: Would have to be very particular circumstances
Course substitutions allowed: Yes
In what course: Would have to be very particular circumstances

Additional Information

Environment: The college is located on 64 acres in Sheridan.

Student Body
Undergrad enrollment: 3,500
% Women: 66%
% Men: 34%
% Out-of-state: 9%

Cost Information
In-state tuition: $2,578
Out-of-state tuition: $5,986
Room & board: $5,880

Housing Information
University housing: Yes
% Living on campus: 15%

Greek System
Fraternity: No
Sorority: No
Athletics: NJCAA

University of Wyoming

Dept 3435, Laramie, WY 82071
Phone: 307-766-5160 • Fax: 307-766-4042
E-mail: admissions@uwyo.edu • Web: www.uwyo.edu
Support: CS • Institution: Public

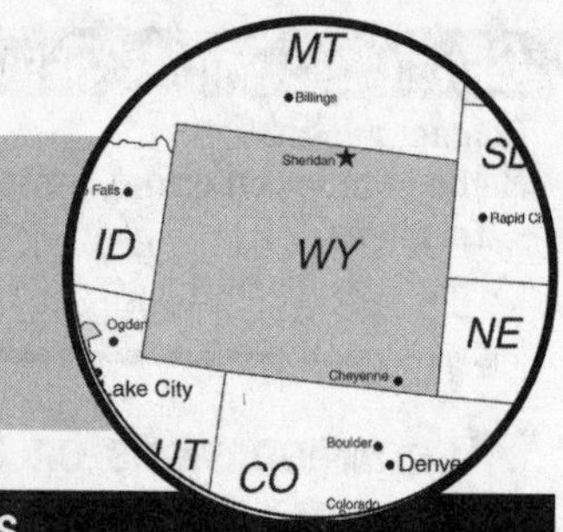

Programs or Services for Students with Learning Differences

University Disability Support Services (UDSS) offers academic support services to students with learning disabilities and physically handicapped students. Its goals are to promote the independence and self-sufficiency of students and encourage the provision of equal opportunities in education for students with disabilities. Any student enrolled at UW who has a documented disability is eligible for assistance. UDSS provides disability-related accommodations and services, technical assistance, consultations, and resource information. Recommended documentation includes a clear statement of the LD (documentation should be current, preferably having been completed within the past 3 years); a summary of assessment procedures and evaluation instruments used to make the diagnosis and a summary of the results, including standardized or percentile scores that support the diagnosis (LD testing must be comprehensive, including a measure of both aptitude and achievement in the areas of reading, mathematics, and written language); a statement of strengths and needs that will impact the student's ability to meet the demands of college; and suggestions of reasonable accommodations that may be appropriate. Accommodations are collaboratively determined by the student and the assigned disability support service coordinator.

Admission Information for Students with Learning Differences

College entrance test required: Yes
Interview required: No
Essay required: Not Applicable
Additional Application Required for LD/ADHD/ASD: NR
What documentation required for LD: None
With general application: NR
To receive services after enrolling: Yes
What documentation required for ADHD: None
With general application: NR
To receive services after enrolling: Yes
What documentation required for ASD: None
With general application: NR
To receive services after enrolling: Yes
LD/ADHD/ASD documentation submitted to: University Disability Support Services
ASD Specific Program: NR
Special Ed. HS course work accepted: NR
Specific course requirements of all applicants: NR
Separate application required for program services: Yes
Total # of students receiving LD/ADHD/ASD services: NR
Acceptance into program means acceptance into college: NR

Admissions

Students with learning disabilities must meet general admission requirements. If the students are borderline and have a documented learning disability, they are encouraged to self-identify to the director. Students who were diagnosed late in high school or began utilizing services late may be able to explain how this had an impact on academics. Students with learning disabilities who meet the general admission criteria request LD services after being admitted. Conditional admission is granted with a GPA of 2.5 or a GPA of 2.25 and an ACT score of 20 or an SAT score of 960. Students with learning disabilities not meeting admission criteria and not qualifying for assured or conditional admission may have their applications reviewed by the LD program director. The LD director will make a recommendation to the Office of Admissions.

Additional Information

Services include priority registration, readers, assistance with study skills, note-taking, test preparation, word processing orientation, equipment loan assistance, tutor referral, and advocacy for students via the University Accessibility Committee. Auditory systems are also used to provide access to print mediums for persons with LD. Synthesized speech reinforces visual cues. Grammar-checking software is available to proof documents and improve writing skills; writing skills may also be improved through the use of word prediction software. Dragon Dictate, a voice recognition program, may benefit those students who have learning disabilities that affect written expression. All students must take one course in math or quantitative reasoning to graduate.

General Support Services Information

Contact Information
Name of program or department: University Disability Support Services
Telephone: 307-766-6189
Fax: 307-766-4010

Accommodations or Services for Students With Learning Differences

Accommodations are decided upon an individual basis after a thorough review of appropriate, current documentation. The accommodations requests must be supported through the documentation provided and must be logically linked to the current impact of the condition on academic functioning.

Allowed in exams
Calculator: Yes
Dictionary: Yes
Computer: Yes
Spellchecker: Yes
Extended test time: Yes
Scribes: Yes
Proctors: Yes
Oral exams: No
Note-takers: Yes
Support services for students with LD: Yes
Support services for students with ADHD: Yes
Support services for students with ASD: Yes
Distraction-reduced environment: Yes
Tape recording in class: Yes
Electronic texts: Yes
Kurzweil reader: NR
Audio books: Yes
Other assistive technology: Yes
Priority registration: Yes
Added costs of services: Not Applicable
LD specialists: No
ADHD coaching: No
ASD specialists: No
Professional tutors: No
Peer tutors: No
Max. hours/wk. for services: NR
How professors are notified of student approved accommodations: By both student and director

General Admissions Information

Office of Admissions: 307-766-5160

Entrance Requirements

Academic units required: 4 English, 4 math, 4 science, 3 science labs, 2 foreign language, 3 social studies, 2 academic electives, and 2 units from above areas or other academic areas. **Academic units recommended:** 4 English, 4 math, 4 science, 3 science labs, 2 foreign language, 3 social studies, 2 academic electives, and 2 units from above areas or other academic areas. High school diploma is required and GED is accepted. SAT or ACT required. If ACT, ACT with writing accepted. TOEFL required of all international applicants: minimum paper TOEFL 540 or minimum internet TOEFL 76.

Application deadline: 8/10
Notification: NR
Average GPA: 3.48
ACT Composite middle 50% range: 22-27
SAT Math middle 50% range: 490-620
SAT Critical Reading middle 50% range: 480-615
SAT Writing middle 50% range: NR-NR
Graduate top 10% of class: 22
Graduated top 25% of class: 50
Graduated top 50% of class: 81

COLLEGE GRADUATION REQUIREMENTS

Course waivers allowed: No
Course substitutions allowed: No

Additional Information

Environment: This public school was founded in 1886. It has a 785-acre campus.

Student Body
Undergrad enrollment: 10,045
% Women: 52
% Men: 48
% Out-of-state: 32

Cost information
In-state Tuition: $ 3,570
Out-of-state Tuition: $14,310
Room & board: $10,037

Housing Information
University Housing: Yes
Percent living on campus: 24

Greek System
Fraternity: Yes
Sorority: Yes
Athletics: Division I

Quick Contact Reference List

ALABAMA

Alabama St. U.	Montgomery, AL 36101	University Counseling Center	334-229-4382
Auburn U.	Auburn, AL 36849-5149	Office of Accessibility	334-844-2096
Auburn U. at Montgomery	Montgomery, AL 36124-4023	Center for Disability Services	334-244-3754
Birmingham-Southern C.	Birmingham, AL 35254	Learning Disabilities Program	205-226-4727
Faulkner U.	Montgomery, AL 36109	Project Key	1-800-879-9816
Gadsden St. C.C.	Gadsden, AL 35999	Student Support Services Program	256-549-820
Huntingdon C.	Montgomery, AL 36106-2148	Disability Services	334-833-4577
Jacksonville St. U.	Jacksonville, AL 36265	Academic Center for Excellence	256-782-8380
Judson C.	Marion, AL 36756	LD Services	334-683-5112
Miles C.	Birmingham, AL 35208	Student Support Services	205-929- 1824
Samford U.	Birmingham, AL 35229	Disability Resources	205-726-4078
Spring Hill C.	Mobile, AL 36608	Coordinator of Academic Support	251-380-3466
Stillman C.	Tuscaloosa, AL 35403	Student Development Center	250-366-8894
Troy St. U.—Dothan	Dothan, AL 36304	Learning Disability Services	334-983-6556 ext. 221
Troy U.–Troy	Troy, AL 36082	Student Disability Services	800-551-9716
Tuskegee U.	Tuskegee, AL 36088	Tuskegee University Counseling Department	3347278244
U. of Alabama—Birmingham	Birmingham, AL 35294-1150	Office of Disability Services	205-348-4285
U. of Alabama—Huntsville	Huntsville, AL 35899	Disability Support Services	256-824-1997
The U. of Alabama–Tuscaloosa	Tuscaloosa, AL 35487-0132	Office of Disability Services	205-348-4285
U. of Montevallo	Montevallo, AL 35115	Services for Students w/ Disabilities	205-665-6250
U. of North Alabama	Florence, AL 35632	Disability Services	256-765-4214
U. of South Alabama	Mobile, AL 36688-0002	Special Student Services	251-460-7212
U. of West Alabama	Livingston, AL 35470	ADA Services	205-652-3653

ALASKA

U. of Alaska—Anchorage	Anchorage, AK 99508-8046	Disability Support Services	907-786- 4530
U. of Alaska—Fairbanks		Fairbanks, AK 99775-7480 Disability Services	907-474-5655
U. of Alaska—Southeast		Juneau, AK 99801-8681 Student Resource Center	907-796-6000

ARIZONA

Arizona St. U.	Tempe, AZ 85287-3202	Disability Resource Center	480-965-1234
Arizona St. U. West	Phoenix, AZ 85069-7100	Disability Resource Center	(480) 965-1234

Arizona St. U. Phoenix	Tempe, AZ 85287-0112	Disability Resource Center	(480)727-1368
Arizona St. U. Polytechnic	Tempe, AZ 85287-0112	Disability Resource Center	(480)727-1368
Arizona St. U. Tempe	Tempe, AZ 85287-0112	Disability Resource Center	(480)727-1368
Arizona St. U. aWest	Tempe, AZ 85287-0112	Disability Resource Center	(480)727-1368
Coconino C.C.	Flagstaff, AZ 86004	Disability Resources	928-226-4243
Embry Riddle Prescott NR	Prescott, AZ 86301	Disability Support Services	
Embry-Riddle Aero. U. AZ)	Prescott, AZ 86301-3720	Director Student Activities	928-777-6750
Gateway C.C.	Phoenix, AZ 85034	Special Services	602-286- 8250
Mesa C.C.	Mesa, AZ 85202	Disability Resources and Services	480-461-7447
Northern Arizona U.	Flagstaff, AZ 86011-4084	Disability Support Services	928-523-8773
Phoenix C.	Phoenix, AZ 85013	Disability Resource Center	602.285.7477
Pima C.C.	Tucson, AZ 85702	Disabled Student Resources	520-206-7286
Prescott C.	Prescott, AZ 86301	Learning Disability Program	928-350-1009
U. of Arizona	Tucson, AZ 85921	SALT	520-621-1427
U. of Phoenix	Phoenix, AZ 85040-1958	Disability Services Office	800-366-9699

ARKANSAS

Arkansas St. U.	State University, AR 72467	Disability Services	870-972-3964
Arkansas Tech U.	Russellville, AR 72801	Office of Disability Services	479-968-0302
Harding U.	Searcy, AR 72149	Student Support Services SSS)	501-279- 4019
Henderson St. U.	Arkadelphia, AR 71999-0001	Disability Services	870-230- 5453
Hendrix C.	Conway, AR 72032	Students with Disabilities	501-505- 2954
John Brown U.	Siloam Springs, AR 72761	Disability Services	479-524-7400
NW Arkansas C.C.	Bentonville, AR 72712	Learner Development Center	479-986-4076
Ouachita Baptist U.	Arkadelphia, AR 71998	Disability Services	870-245-5591
S. Arkansas U.	Magnolia, AR 71753-5000	Student Disability Special Services	870-235-4145
U. of Arkansas—Fayetteville	Fayetteville, AR 72701	Center for Educational Access	479-575-3104
U. of Arkansas—Little Rock	Little Rock, AR 72204	Disability Support Services	501-569-3143
U. of Arkansas—Pine Bluff	Pine Bluff, AR 71601-2799	Officeof Veterans & Disability Services	870-575-8089
U. of Central Arkansas	Conway, AR 72035	Disability Resource Center	501-450-3613
U. of the Ozarks		Clarksville, AR 72830 Student Success Center	479-979-1300
Williams Baptist C.	Walnut Ridge, AR 72476	Disability Services	870-759-4178

CALIFORNIA

Alliant Intl. U.	San Diego, CA 92131	Disability Services	415-955-2164
American Jewish University	Bel Air, CA 90077	Students with Disabilities	310-440-1586
Art Center C. of Design	Pasadena, CA 91103	Admissions	626-396-2373
Azusa Pacific U.	Azusa, CA 91702-7000	Learning Enrichment Center	(626) 815-3849
Bakersfield C.	Bakersfield, CA 93305	Support Services Program	661-395-4334
Biola U.	La Mirada, CA 90639	Learning Center	562-906-4542
Butte C.C.	Oroville, CA 95965	Services for Students with Disabilities	530-895-2455
C. of Redwoods	Crescent City, CA 95531	Disabled Student Spec.	707-464-2352
Cabrillo C.	Aptos, CA 95003	Learning Skills Program	831-479-6379
Calif. St. U.—San Bernardino	San Bernardino, CA 92407	Services to Students with Disabilities	909-537-5238
California Baptist U.	Riverside, CA 92504	Disability Services	951-343-4962
California C. of Arts	Oakland, CA 94618-1426	Learning Resource Center	510-594-3756
California Institute of Arts	Valencia CA 91355	Student Affairs Office	661-253-7874
California Institute of Tech.	Pasadena, CA 91125	Disability Services	626-395-6351
California Lutheran U.	Thousand Oaks, CA 91360	Center for Student Success	805-493-2360
California Polytechnic St. U.	San Luis Obispo, CA 93407	Disability Resource Center	805-756-1395
California St. Polytech U., Pomona	Pomona, CA 91768	Disability Resource Center	909-869-3333
California St. U.—Bakersfield	Bakersfield, CA 93311	Services for Students with Disabilities	661-654-3360
California St. U.—East Bay	Hayward, CA 94542	Learning Disabled Resources	510-885-3868
California St. U., Fullerton	Fullerton, CA 92834-6900	Disabled Student Services	657-278-3112
California St. U.—Long Beach	Long Beach, CA 90840	Disabled Student Services	562-985-5401
California St. U.—Monterey Bay	Seaside, CA 93955-8001	Student Disability Resources	831-582-3672
California St. U., Northridge	Northridge, CA 91330-8207	Disability Resources and Educational Services	818-677-2684
California St. U.—Sacramento	Sacramento, CA 95819	Services for Students With LD	916-278-6955
California St. U.—San Marcos	San Marcos, CA 92096-	Disabled Student Services	760-750-4905
California St. U., Stanislaus	Turlock, CA 95382	Disability Resource Services	NR
Cerritos C.C.	Norwalk, CA 90650	Disabled Students Programs & Svcs	562-860-2451 ext. 2335
Chapman U.	Orange, CA 92866	Center for Academic Success	714-516-4520
Charles R. Drew U. of Med	Los Angeles, CA 90059	Student Education Center	323-563-5886
Citrus C.C.	Glendora, CA 91741	Disabled Student Program	626-914-8675
City C. San Francisco	Orinda, CA 94563	Disabled Student Services	415-452-5481

Claremont McKenna C.	Claremont, CA 91711	Disability Support Services	909- 607-7377
College of the Siskiyous	Weed, CA 96094	Disabled Student Services	530-938-5297
Columbia C.C.	Sonora, CA 95370	Disabled Student Programs & Services	209-588-5134
Concordia U.	Irvine, CA 92612-3299	Disability Services	949-214-3039
Cuesta C.	San Luis Obispo, CA 93403	Academic Support	805-546-3148
De Anza C.	Sunnyvale, CA 94087	Disability Support Services	408-864-8753
Dominican U. of California	San Rafeal, CA 94901-2298	Tutoring and Disability Services	disabilityservices@dominican.edu
East Los Angeles C.	Monterey Pk, CA 90025	DSPS	323-265-8787
El Camino C.	Torrance, CA 90506	Special Resource Center	310-660-3295
Evergreen Valley C.	San Jose, CA 95135	Disabled Students Program	408-270-6447
Foothill C.	Los Altos, CA 94022	STEP	650-949-7017
Fresno Pacific U.	Fresno, CA 93702	Director of Academic Support Services	559-453-2247
Grossmont C.	Ramona, CA 92065	Disabled Students Programs & Services	619-644-7987
Harvey Mudd C.	Claremont, CA 91711	Dean of Students	909-621-8125
Holy Names U.	Oakland, CA 94619	Disability Support Services	510-436-1394
Humboldt St. U.	Arcata, CA 95521-8299	Student Disability Resource Center	707-826-4678
Humphreys C.	Stockton, CA 95207	Disability Services	209-478-0800
John F. Kennedy U.	Orinda, CA 94563	Student Disability Services	925-969-3362
Lake Tahoe C.C.	So. Lake Tahoe, CA 96150	Disability Resource Center	530-541-4660 ext. 249
Laney College	El Sobrante, CA 94803	Disability Resource Center	510-464-3428
Life Challenges & PCS	Los Angeles, CA 90039	LD Services	323-953-4000 ext. 2270
Life Pacific C.	San Dimas, CA 91773-3298		909-599-5433 ext. 363
Long Beach City C.	Long Beach, CA 90808	Disabled Student Program Services	562-938-4558
Loyola Marymount U.	Los Angeles, CA 90045	Disability Support Services	310-338-4216
Master's C.	Newhall, CA 91322	Disability Services	661-259- 2843
Menlo C.	Atherton, CA 94027	ASC	650-543-3845
Mills C.	Oakland, CA 94613	Student Access and Support Services (SASS)	5104303241
Mount St. Mary's C.	Los Angeles, CA 90049	Disability Services	310-954-4141
Notre Dame de Namur U.	Belmont, CA 94002-1908	PASS	650-508-3670
Occidental C.	Los Angeles, CA 90041-3314	Disability Services	(323) 259-2969
Orange Coast C.	Costa Mesa, CA 92628	Learning Center	714-432-5535
Oxnard C.	Oxnard, CA 93033	Educational Assistance Center	805-986-5830
Pacific Oaks C.	Pasadena, CA 31103	CARE Center	626-529-8262

Pacific Union C.	Angwin, CA 94508	Disability Support Services	707-965-7688
Pasadena City C.	Pasadena, CA 91106	Disabled Student Programs & Services	626-585- 7995
Patten U.	Oakland, CA94601	Admissions and Student Experience	510-261-8500 ext. 7809
Pepperdine U.	Malibu, CA 90263	NR	310-506-6500
Pitzer C.	Claremont, CA 91711	Academic Support Services	909-607-2821
Point Loma Nazarene U.	San Diego, CA 92106	Disability Resource Center	619-849-2273
Pomona C.	Claremont, CA 91711	Disability Services	909-607-2147
Reedley College	Reedley, CA 93654-2099	Disabled Students Programs & Services	559-638-0332
Saddleback C.	Carlsbad, CA 92008	Disabled Students Programs and Services	949-582-4885
San Diego City C.	San Diego, CA 92101	DSPS	619-388-3513
San Diego St. U.	San Diego, CA 92182-7455	Student Disability Services	619-564-6473
San Francisco Art Institute	San Francisco, CA 94133	Disabilities Services Coordinator	415-276-1060
San Francisco St. U.	San Francisco, CA 93132	Disability Programs and Resource Center	NR
San Jose St. U.	San Jose, CA 95192	Disability Resource Center	408-924-6000
Santa Barbara City C.	Santa Barbara, CA 93109	Disabled Student Services	805-965-0581
Santa Clara U.	Santa Clara, CA 95053	Disabilities Resources	408-554-4109
Santa Monica C.	Santa Monica, CA 90405	Disability Resources	310-434-4265
Santa Rosa Junior C.	Santa Rosa, CA 95401	Disability Resource Department	707-527-4278
Scripps C.	Claremont, CA 91711	Dean of Students Office	909-621-8277
Sierra C.	Rocklin, CA 95677	Learning Opportunities Center	916-660- 7230
Simpson U.	Redding, CA 96003-8606	Academic Success Center	530-226- 4783
Soka U. of America	Aliso Viejo, CA 92656-8081	Student Services	949-480-4139
Sonoma St. U.	Rohnert Park, CA 94928	Disabled Student Services	707-664-2677
St. Mary's C. of CA	Moraga, CA 94556	Student Disability Services	925-631-4358
Stanford U.	Stanford, CA 94305-6106	Office of Accessible Education	650-723-1066
Taft C.	Taft, CA 93268	Disabled Student Services	661-763-7748
U. of California, Irvine	Irvine, CA 92697-1075	Disability Services Center	9498247494
U. of California—Berkeley	Berkeley, CA 94720-4250	Disabled Students' Program	510-642-0518
U. of California—Davis	Davis, CA 95616	Learning Disability Center	530-752-3184
U. of California—Irvine	Irvine, CA 92717	Office of Disability Services	949-824-7494
U. of California—Los Angeles	Los Angeles, CA 90095	Office for Students with Disabilities	310-825-1501
U. of California—Riverside	Riverside, CA 92521	Services for Students w/ Disabilities	951-827-4538
U. of California–San Diego	La Jolla, CA 92093-0021	Office for Students with Disabilities	858.534.4382

U. of California—San Diego	La Jolla, CA 92093-0337	Office for Students with Disabilities	858-534-4382
U. of California–Santa Barbara	Santa Barbara, CA 93106-2014	The Disabled Students Program	805-893-2182
U. of California—Santa Barbara	Santa Barbara, CA 93106	Disabled Student Program	805-893-2668
U. of California–Santa Cruz	Santa Cruz, CA 95064	Disability Resource Center	(831) 459-2089
U. of La Verne	La Verne, CA 91750	Disabled Student Services	909-448-4441
U. of Redlands	Redlands, CA 92373-0999	Student Services	909-748-8108
U. of San Diego	San Diego, CA 92110-2492	Disability and Learning Differences Resource Center	NR
U. of San Francisco	San Francisco, CA 94117	Student Disability Services	4154222613
U. of Southern California	Los Angeles, CA 90089-0911	Disability Services and Programs	NR
U. of the Pacific	Stockton, CA 95211	Services for Students with Disabilities	209.946.3221
Vanguard U. of Southern CA	Costa Mesa, CA 92626	Student Disability Services	714-619-6478
Westmont C.	Santa Barbara, CA 93108	Disability Services	805-565-6186
Whittier C.	Whittier, CA 90608	Disability Services	562-907-4825
Woodbury U.	Burbank, CA 91510	Student Development	818-252-5254
COLORADO			
Colorado C.	Colorado Springs, CO 80903	Accessibility Resources	719-227-8294
Colorado Christian C.	Lakewood, CO 80226	Life Directions Center	303-963-3010
Colorado Mt. C.	Glenwood Springs, CO 81601	Disability Services	970-947-8256
Colorado School of Mines	Golden, CO 80401-1869	Student Disability Services	303-384-2595
Colorado St. U.	Fort Collins, CO 80523-1062	Resources for Disabled Students	(970) 491-6385
Colorado St. U.—Pueblo	Pueblo, CO 81001	Disabilities Resources Office	719-549- 2648
Fort Lewis C.	Durango, CO 81301	Name of Program/Services for Special Needs Students	970-247-7459
Mesa St. C.	Grand Junction, CO 81502-2647	Educational Access Services	970-248-1856
Metropolitan St. C. of Denver	Denver, CO 80217-3362	Access Center	303-556-8387
Northeastern Junior C.	Sterling, CO 80751	Disability and Transition Specialist	970-521-6727
Regis U.	Denver, CO 80221-1099	Disability Services	303-458-4941
U. of Colorado Boulder	Boulder, CO 80309-0552	Disability Services	303-492-8671
U. of Colorado—Boulder	Boulder, CO 80309-0107	Disability Services	303-492-8671
U. of Colorado—Col. Springs	Colorado Springs, CO 80933	Disability Services	719-255-3354
U. of Colorado—Denver	Denver, CO 80217	Disability Resources and Services	303-556-3450
U. of Denver	Denver, CO 80208	LEP	303-871-2372
U. of Northern Colorado	Greeley, CO 80639	Disability Support Services (DSS)	970-351-2289
Western St. C. of Colorado	Gunnison, CO 81231	Academic Resource Center	970-943-7056

CONNECTICUT

Albertus Magnus C.	New Haven, CT 06511	Academic Disability Services	203-773-8564
Central Connecticut St. U.	New Britain, CT 6050	Student Disability Services	860-832-1952
Eastern Connecticut St. U.	Willimantic, CT 06226	AccessAbility	860-465- 0189
Fairfield U.	Fairfield, CT 6824	Disability Support Services	203-254-4000 x: 2615
Housatonic C.	Bridgeport, CT 06608	Disability Support Services	203-332-5018
Mitchell C.	New London, CT 06320	Disability Student Services	860-701-5790
Post U.	Waterbury, CT 06723	Student Disability Services	203-596-4508
Quinnipiac C.	Hamden, CT 06518	Learning Services	203-582-5390
Quinnipiac U.	Hamden, CT 6518	The Learning Center	203-582-8628
Sacred Heart U.	Fairfield, CT 6825	NR	203-371-7823
Southern Connecticut St. U.	New Haven, CT 06515	Disability Resource Office	203-392-6828
Trinity C.	Hartford, CT 06106	Disability Services	860-297-4025
U of St. Joseph	West Hartford, CT 06117	Disability Services	860-231-5428
U. of Bridgeport	Bridgeport, CT 06604	Disability Services	203-576-4454
U. of Connecticut	W. Hartford, CT 06117	Center for Students with Disabilities	860-570-9204
U. of Hartford	West Hartford, CT 06117	Learning Plus	860.768.4312
U. of New Haven	West Haven, CT 06516	Campus Access Services	203-932-7332
Wesleyan U.	Middletown, CT 6459	Disability Resources	860-685-5581
Western Connecticut St. U.	Danbury, CT 06810	AccessAbility	203-837- 8225
Yale U.	New Haven, CT 06520	Resource Office for Disabilities	203-432-2324
Delaware St. U.	Dover, DE 19901	Student Accessibility Services	302-857-7304
Delaware Tech C.C.	Georgetown, DE 19947	Disability Services	302- 259-6045
U. of Delaware	Newark, DE 19716-6210	Disability Support Services	302-831-4643
Wesley C.	Dover, DE 19901-3875	Academic Support Services	302-736-2492

DISTRICT OF COLUMBIA

American U.	Washington, DC 20016-8001	Academic Support and Access Center	202-885-3360
Catholic U. of America, The	Washington, DC 20064-0001	Disability Support Services	202-319-5211
Corcoran C. of Art	Washington DC 20006-4804	Disability Services	202-639-1895
Gallaudet U.	Washington, DC 20002	Students with Disabilities	202-651-5256
George Washington U.	Washington, DC 20052	Disability Support Services	202-994-8250

Georgetown U.	Washington, DC 20057	Academic Support	202-687-8354
Howard U.	Washington, DC	Special Student Services	202-238-2420
The Catholic U. of America	Washington, DC 20064	Disability Support Services	202-319-5211
Trinity Washington University	Washington, DC 20017-1094	Disability Support Services	202-884-9358
U. of District of Columbia	Washington, DC 20008	Disability Resource Center	202-274-6417

FLORIDA

Baptist C. of Florida	Graceville, GL 32440	Disability Services	800-328-2660 ext 465
Barry U.	Miami Shores, FL 33161-6695	Office of Disability Services	305-899-3488
Beacon C.	Leesburg, FL 34748	Office of Admissions	855-220-5374
Broward C.	Ft. Lauderdale, FL 33301	Disability Services	954-201-7517
Clearwater Christian C.	Clearwater, FL 33759-4595	Disability Services	727-726-1153 ext 262
Eckerd C.	St. Petersburg, FL 33711	Disability Support Services	727-864-8248
Edison C.C.	Fort Meyers, FL 33906	Learning Assistance	937-778-8600
Edward Waters C.	Jacksonville, FL 32009	Disability Services	888-898-3191
Embry-Riddle Aeronaut. U. FL	Daytona Beach, FL 32114	Disability Services	386-226-7916
Flagler C.	St. Augustine, FL 32085-1027	Office of Services for Students with Disabilities	904 819-6460
Florida A&M U.	Tallahassee, FL 32307-3200	Center for Disability Access and Resources	(850) 599-3180
Florida Atlantic U.	Boca Raton, FL 33431	Office for Students with Disabilities	561-297-3880
Florida Gulf Coast U.	Fort Myers, FL 33965-6565	Adaptive Services	239-590-7930
Florida Institute of Tech.	Melborne, FL 32901-6975	Academic Support Services	321-674- 7110
Florida Institute of Tech	Melbourne, FL 32901-6975	Office of Disability Services	321-674-8050
Florida International U.	Miami, FL 33199	Disability Services	305-348-3532
Florida Memorial U.	Miami, FL 33054	CASR	305-626-3662
Florida Southern C.	Lakeland, FL 33801	Student Disability Services	863-680-4197
Florida St. U.	Tallahassee, FL 32306	Student Disability Resource Center	850-644-9566
Gulf Coast St. C.	Panama City, FL 32401	Disability Support Services	(850)769-1551
Hillsborough C.C.	Tampa, FL 33631-3127	Disabled Services	813-253-7757
Indian River St. C.	Fort Pierce, FL 34981	Disability Services	772-462-4699
Jacksonville U.	Jacksonville, FL 32211	Student Life	904-256-7067
Lynn U.	Boca Raton, FL 33431	Institute for Achievement & Learning	561-237-7013
Miami Int'l. U. of Art	Miami, FL 33132	Student Affairs	305.428.5900
New C. of Florida	Sarasota, FL 34243-2109	Student Disability Services	941-487-4637

Northwood U.—Florida Campus	West Palm Beach, FL 33409	Learning Center	561-478-5585
Nova Southeastern U.	Ft. Lauderdale, FL 33314	Student Disability Services	954-262-7185
Pensacola Jr. C.	Pensacola, FL 32504	Disability Support Services	850-484-1637
Ringling School of Art	Sarasota, FL 34234-5895	Academic Resource Center	941.359.7627
Rollins C.	Winter Park, FL 32789-4499	Disability Services	407-975-6463
Saint Thomas U.	Miami, FL 33054	Academic Enhancement	651-962-6315
Santa Fe C.C.	Gainsville, FL 32606	Disability Resource Center	352-395-4400
Seminole St. C.	Sanford, FL 32773	Disability Support Services	407-708-2505
Southeastern U.	Lakeland, FL 33801	Student Life	863-667-5157
St. Leo U.	Saint Leo, FL 33574-6665	Academic Student Support Services	352-588-8464
St. Petersburg Jr. C.	St. Petersburg, FL 33733	Disability Services	727-341-3398
Stetson U.	DeLand, FL 32723	Academic Success	386-822-7345
Tallahassee CC	Tallahassee, FL 32340	Disability Support Services	850-201-8430
Trinity Baptist C.	Jacksonville, FL 32221	Disability Services	800-786-2206
U. of Central Florida	Orlando, FL 32816-0111	Student Accessibility Services	407-823-2371
U. of Florida	Gainesville, FL 32611	Disability Resources Center	352-392-8565
U. of Miami	Coral Gables, FL 33124-4616	Office of Disability Services	305-284-2374
U. of North Florida	Jacksonville, FL 32224-2645	Disability Resource Center	904-620-2769
U. of South Florida	Tampa, FL 33620	Student Disability Services	813-974-4309
U. of South Florida - St. Petersburg	St. Petersburg, FL 33701-5016	Student Disability Services	727-873-4990
U. of Tampa	Tampa, FL 33606-1490	Student Disability Services	813-257-5757
U. of West Florida	Pensacola, FL 32514-5750	Dean of Students	850-474-2161
Warner U.	Lake Wales, FL 33859	Academic Skills Center	863-638- 7244

GEORGIA

Agnes Scott C.	Decatur, GA 30030-3770	Disability Services	404-471-6174
Andrew C.	Cuthbert, GA 31740	FOCUS	229-732-5908
Armstrong St. C.	Savannah, GA 31419	Disability Services	912-344-2572
Berry C.	Mount Berry, GA 30149-0159	NR	706-368-6960
Brenau U.	Gainesville, GA 30501	Learning Center	770-534-6134
Brewton-Parker C.	Mt. Vernon, GA 30445	Disability Support Services	912-583-3222
Clark Atlanta U.	Atlanta, GA 30314	Student Affairs	404-880- 8040
Clayton College & St. U.	Morrow, GA 30260	Disability Resource Center	678-466-5445

Columbus C.	Columbus, GA 31907	Disability Services	614-287-2570
Covenant C.	Lookout Mountain, GA 30750	Disability Services	706-419-1262
Darton C.	Albany, GA 31707	Disabled Student Services	229-317-6867
Emmanuel College	Franklin Springs, GA 30639	Counseling Services	706-245-2715
Emory U.	Atlanta, GA 30322	Disability Services	404-727-9877
Ft. Valley St. U.	Fort Valley, GA 31030-4313	Differently Abled Services	476-825-6744
Gainesville C.	Gainseville, GA 30503	Disability Services	678-717-3839
Georgia C. & St. U.	Milledgeville, GA 31061	Office of Disability Services	478-445-5931
Georgia Institute of Tech	Atlanta, GA 30332-0320	The Office of Disability Services	404-385-0733
Georgia Perimeter College	Clarkston, GA 30021	Ctr. for Disability Services	678-891-3385
Georgia Regents University	Augusta, GA 30904-2200	Testing & Disability Services	706-737-1469
Georgia Southern U.	Statesboro, GA 30460	Student Disability Resource Center	912-478-1566
Georgia St. U.	Atlanta, GA 30302-4009	Margaret A. Staton Office of Disabiltiy Services	404-413-1560
Kennesaw St. U.	Kennesaw, GA 30144-5591	Student Disability Support Services	470-578-2666
LaGrange C.	La Grange, GA 30240	Counseling Center	706-880-8313
Life U.	Marietta, GA 30060	Academic Assistance Center	770-794-3035 x.1720
Mercer U.	Macon, GA 31207-0003	Disability Services	478-301-2778
Mercer U.-Macon	Macon, GA 31207-0001	Access and Accommodations Office	478-301-2778
Morehouse C.	Atlanta, GA 30314	Counseling center	404-215-2636
North Georgia C. & St. U.	Dahlonega, GA 30597	Student Disability Resources	706-864-1819
Oglethorpe U.	Atlanta, GA 30319	Academic Success Center	404-504-1445
Paine C.	Augusta, GA 30901-3182	Disability Services	706-821-8345
Piedmont C.	Demorest, GA 30535	Academic Support Services	706-776-0101
Reinhardt U.	Waleska, GA 30183	Academic Support Office	770-720-5567
Savannah C. of Art and Design	Savannah, GA 31402-3146	SCAD Counseling and Student Support Services	912-525-6971
Shorter C.	Rome, GA 30165-4898	Academic Support Center	706-233-7323
South U.—Georgia	Savannah, GA 33411	Disability Services	912-201-8170
Southern Polytechnic St. U.	Marietta, GA 30060	Disability Services	678-915-7244
Spelman C.	Atlanta, GA 30314	Student Disability Services	404-270-5293
The Savannah C. of Art	Savannah, GA 31402-3146	Disability Services	912-525-6971
Truett-McConnell C.	Cleveland, GA 30528	Special Support Services	706-865-2134ext 172
U. of Georgia	Athens, GA 30602-1633	Disability Resource Center	706-542-8719

U. of North Georgia	Dahlonega, GA 30597	Student Disability Services	678-717-3855
U. of West Georgia	Carrollton, GA 30118	Accessibiity Services	678-839-6428
Valdosta St. U.	Valdosta, GA 31698	Access Office for Students with Disabilities	229-245-2498
HAWAII			
Brigham Young U.	Laie Oahu, HI 96762-1294	Services for Students with Special Needs	808-675-3518
Chaminade U. of Honolulu	Honolulu, HI 96816	Counseling Center	808-735-4845
Hawaii C.C.	Hilo, HI 96720	Ha'awi Kokua Program	808-934-2825
Hawaii Pacific U.	Honolulu, HI 96813	Disability Resources	808-566-2406
U. of Hawaii at Manoa	Honolulu, HI 96822	Kokua Program	NR
U. of Hawaii—Hilo	Hilo, HI 96720-4091	Disability Services	808-932-7623
IDAHO			
Albertson C. of Idaho	Caldwell, ID 83605	Disability Services	208-459-5683
Boise St. U.	Boise, ID 83725	Special Services	208-426-1583
C. of Idaho	Caldwell, ID 83605-4432	Learning Support and Disability Services	2084595141
Idaho St. U.	Pocatello, ID 83209-8270	ADA Disabilities Center	208- 282-3599
Lewis-Clark St. C.	Lewiston, ID 83501	Disability Services	208-792-2211
Northwest Nazarene U.	Nampa, ID 83686	Academic Support Center	208-467-8463
U. of Idaho	Moscow, ID 83844-4140	Disability Services Access	208-885-6307
ILLINOIS			
Augustana C.	Rock Island, IL 61201-2296	Dean of Students Office	309-794-7279
Aurora U.	Aurora, IL 60506	Disability Services	630-844-5267
Benedictine U.	Lisle, IL 60532-0900	Academic Resource Center	630-829-6512
Blackburn C.	Carlinville, IL 62626	Counseling Office/Learning Center	800-233-3550
Bradley U.	Peoria, IL 61625	Center for Learning Assistance	309-677-2845
C. of Du Page	Glen Ellyn, IL 60137	Special Student Services	630-942-2567
C. of Lake County	Grayslake, IL 60030	Disability Student Services	847-543-2055
Chicago St. U.	Chicago, IL 60628	Abilities Office	773-995-4401
Columbia C. (IL)	Chicago, IL 60605-1996	Services for Students with Disabilities	312-369-8296
DePaul University	Chicago, IL 60604	Center for Students with Disabilities	773-325-1677
Dominican U.	River Forest, IL 60305	Disability Support Services	708-524-6822
Eastern Illinois U.	Charleston, IL 61920	Student Disability Services	217-581-6583

Elgin C.C.	Elgin, IL 60123	Disability Services	847-214-7417
Elmhurst C.	Elmhurst, IL 60126	Disability Services	630-617-3753
Eureka C.	Eureka, IL 61530-1500	Learning Center	309-467-6520
Governors St. U.	University Park, IL 60466	Disability Services	708-235-3968
Greenville C.	Greenville, IL 62246-0159	Student Success	618-664-6611
Harper C.	Palatine, IL 60067	Center for Students with Disabilities	847-925-6266
Illinois C.	Jacksonville, IL 62650-2299	Templeton Counseling Center	217-245-3774
Illinois Institute of Tech	Chicago, IL 60616	Academic Resource Center	312-567-5744
Illinois St. U.	Normal, IL 61790-2200	Disability Concerns	309-438-5853
Illinois Wesleyan U.	Bloomington, IL 61702-2900	Disability Services	309-556-3231
Ivy Tech St. C.	Evansville, IL 47710	Special Needs	812-429-1386
John Wood C.C.	Quincy, IL 62301	Support Services Center	217-641-4343
Joliet Junior C.	Joliet, IL 60436	Project Achieve	815-280-2230
Kankakee C. C.	Kankakee, IL 60901	Disability Services	815-802-8632
Knox C.	Galesburg, IL 61401	Disability Support Services	309-341-7478
Lake Forest C.	Lake Forest, IL 60045	Dean's Office	847-735-5167
Lakeland C.	Mattoon, IL 61938	Special Needs Office	217-234-5372
Lewis U.	Romeoville, IL 60446	NR	NR
Lewis U.	Romeville, IL 60446-2200	Disability Resources	815-836-5284
Lincoln C.	Lincoln, IL 62656	Disability Services	217-732-3155
Loyola U. of Chicago	Chicago, IL 60611	Services for Students with Disabilities	773508-3700
MacMurray C.	Lebanon, IL 62254-1299	Disability Services	217-479-7176
McHenry C.C.	Crystal Lake, IL 60012	Special Needs	815-455-8676
McKendree C.	Lebanon, IL 62254-1299	Academic Support	618-537-6850
Millikin U.	Decatur, IL 62522-2084	Disability Services	217-424-3999
Monmouth C.	Monmouth, IL 61462	Teaching & Learning Center	309-457-2257
Moraine Valley C.C.	Palos Hills, IL 60465	Center for Disability Services	708-974-5711
Morton C.	Cicero, IL 60650	Academic Advising Center	708-656-8000
National-Louis U.	Evanston, IL 60201	Diversity, Access and Equity	312-261-3188
North Central C.	Naperville, IL 60566-7063	Student Disability Services	630-637-5264
North Park U.	Chicago, IL 60625-4895	OSESS	773-244-5737
Northern Illinois U.	DeKalb, IL 60115-2857	Disability Resource Center	815- 753-1303
Northwestern U.	Evanston, IL 60204	Services for Students with Disabilities	847-467-5530

Oakton Community C.	Des Plaines, IL 60116	ASSIST	847-635-1759
Olivet Nazarene U.	Bourbonnais, IL 60914	Learning Development Center	815-928-5669
Parkland C.	Champaign, IL 61821	Disability Services	217-353-2338
Quincy U.	Quincy, IL 62301	Academic Support Services	217-228-5288
Robert Morris C.	Chicago, IL 60605	Student Relations	312-935-2003
Rockford C.	Rockford, IL 61108-2393	Disability Support Services	815-226-4083
Roosevelt U.	Chicago, IL 60605	Academic Success Center	312-341-3810
Saint Francis Medical Center C. of Nursing	NR	Peoria, IL 61603	NR
Saint Xavier U.	Chicago, IL 60655	Learning Center	773-298-3308
Schl. of Art Inst. of Chicago	Chicago, IL 60603	Learning Center	312-499-4278
Shimer C.	Waukegan, IL 60079-0500	Dean of the College	312-235-3511
SIU-Carbondale	Carbondale, IL 62901-4710	Achieve Program	618-453-5738
SIU-Edwardsville	Edwardsville, IL 62026	Disability Support Services	618-650-3726
Southern Illinois U. Carbondale	Carbondale, IL 62901	Disability Support Services	(618) 453-5738
Southern Illinois U.-Edwardsville	Edwardsville, IL 62026-1047	Disability Support Services	618-650-3726
St. Anthony C. of Nursing	Rockford, IL 61108-2468	Student Affairs Office	815-395-5100
Trinity Christian C.	Palos Heights, IL 60463	OFFICE OF LEARNING SERVICES	708.239.4765
Trinity International C.	Deerfield, IL	Disability Services	847-317-8018
U. of Chicago	Chicago, IL 60637	Student Disability Services	773-702-7776
U. of Ill.—Urbana-Champaign	Urbana, IL 61801	Disability Resources	217-333-4603
U. of Illinois at Urbana-Champai	Urbana, IL 61801-3028	Disability Resources and Educational Services (DRES)	217-333-1970
U. of Illinois Springfield	Springfield, IL 62703-5407	Disability Services	217-206-6666
U. of Illinois—Chicago	Chicago, IL 60680	Disability Services	312-413-2183
U. of St. Francis	Joliet, IL 60435	Office of Disability Services	815-740-3204
Waubonsee C.C.	Sugar Grove, IL 60554	Access Ctr. for Students w/ Disabilities	630-466-7900 x2564
Western Illinois U.	Macomb, IL 61455-1390	Disability Resource Center	309-298-2512
Wheaton C.	Weaton, IL 60187	Disability Services	630-752-5941
Wheaton C. (IL)	Wheaton, IL 60187	Academic and Disability Services	630-752-5674

INDIANA

Anderson U.	Anderson, IN 46012	Disability Services	765-641-4223
Anderson U. (IN)	Anderson, IN 46012-3495	Disability Services for Students	765 6414223
Ball St. U.	Muncie, IN 47306	Office of Disabled Students	765-285-5293

Bethel C.	Mishawaka, IN 46545	Disability Resources and Services	651-638-6833
Butler U.	Indianapolis, IN 46208	Student Disability Services	317-940-9308
Calumet C. of St. Joseph	Whiting, IN 46394	Disability Services	877-700-9100
DePauw U.	Greencastle, IN 46135	Academic Services	765-658-6267
Earlham C.	Richmond, IN 47374	Academic Enrichment Center	765-983-1341
Franklin C.	Franklin, IN 46131-2623	Disability Services	3177388286
Goshen C.	Goshen, IN 46526-4794	Academic Resource & Writing Center	800-348-7422
Grace C. and Seminary	Winona Lake, IN 46590	Special Services Program	574-372-5100 ext. 6423
Hanover C.	Hanover, IN 47243	Disability Services	812-866-7215
Huntington C.	Huntington, IN 46750	Learning Center	260-359-4290
Indiana St. U.	Terre Haute, IN 47809	Disabled Student Services	812-237-2700
Indiana U. Bloomington	Bloomington, IN 47405-1106	Disability Services for Students	(812) 855-7578
Indiana U. East	Richmond, IN 47374-1289	Student Support Services	765-973-8257
Indiana U. Northwest	Gary, IN 46408-1197	Office of Affirmative Action and Employment Practices	(219) 980-6705
Indiana U. South Bend	South Bend, IN 46634-7111	Office of Disability Support Services	(574) 520-4460
Indiana U. Southeast	New Albany, IN 47150	Disability Services	(812) 941-2243
Indiana U.—Bloomington	Bloomington, IN 47405-7700	Disabled Student Services	812-855-7578
Indiana U.-Kokomo	Kokomo, IN 46904-9003	Career and Accessibility Center	765-455-9301
Indiana U.—Northwest	Gary, IN 46408	Student Support Services	219-980-6798
Indiana U.-Purdue U. Indianapolis	Indianapolis, IN 46202	Adaptive Educational Services	(317) 274-3241
Indiana U.—Purdue Univ.	Indianapolis, IN 46202-5143	Adaptive Educational Services	317-274-3241
Indiana Wesleyan U.	Marion, IN 46953-4999	Center for Student Success	765-677-2257
IPFW-Ft. Wayne	Ft. Wayne, IN 46805	Services for Students with Disabilities	260-481-6658
IVY Tech	Fort Wayne, IN 46805	Disability Services	260-481-2210
Manchester U.	N. Manchester, IN 46962	Success Center	260-982-5888
Marian U.	Indianapolis, IN 46222-1997	NR	NR
Purdue U.—Calumet	Hammond, IN 46323-2094	Disability Resources	219-989-2455
Purdue U.—North Central	Westville, IL 46391	Disability Services	219-785-5374
Purdue U.—West Lafayette	West Lafayette, IN 47907	Disability Resource Center	765-494-1247
Rose-Hulman Institute of Tech.	Terre Haute, IN 47803	Disability Services	812-877-8285
Saint Mary's C. (IN)	Notre Dame, IN 46556	Disability Resource Office	574-284-4262
St. Joseph's C.	Rensselaer, IN 47978	Office for Student Development	219-866-6404
St. Mary-of-the-Wood C.	St. Mary-of-the-Wood, IN 47876	Learning Resource Center	812-535-5271

Taylor U.	Upland, IN 46989-1001	Academic Enrichment Center	(765) 998 - 5391
Trine U.	Angola, IN 46703	Academic Support Services	2606654853
U. of Evansville	Evansville, IN 47722	Disability Services	812-479-2663
U. of Indianapolis	Indianapolis, IN 46227	Students with Disabilities	317-788-2140
U. of Notre Dame	Notre Dame, IN 46556	Disability Services	574-631-7141
U. of Saint Francis	Fort Wayne, IN 46808	Student Disability Services	260-399-8065
U. of Southern Indiana	Evansville, IN 47712	Disability Resources	812-464-1961
Valparaiso U.	Valparaiso, IN 46383	Disability Support Services	219-464-6496
Vincennes U.	Vincennes, IN 47591	STEP	812-888-4501
Wabash C.	Crawfordsville, IN 47933	Academic Support	765-361-6024

IOWA

Briar Cliff U.	Sioux City, IA 51104	Student Support Services	712-279-5230
Buena Vista U.	Storm Lake, IA 50588-1798	NR	NR
Central C.	Pella, IA 50219	Student Support Services	641-628-5247
Clarke C.	Dubuque, IA 52001	Learning Center	563-588-8107
Coe C.	Cedar Rapids, IA 52402	Academic Achievement Program	319-399-8547
Cornell C.	Mount Vernon, IA 52341	Academic Support and Advising	319-895- 4382
Des Moines Area C.C.	Ankney, IA 50021	Disability Services Office	515-964-6234
Dordt C.	Sioux Center, IA	Academic Skill Center	712-722-6487
Drake U.	Des Moines, IA 50311-4505	Student Disability Services	515-271-1835
Graceland U.	Lamoni, IA 50140	Student Support Services	641-784-5211
Grand View C.	Des Moines, IA 50316-1599	Academic Success	515-263-2971
Grinnell C.	Grinnell, IA 50112-1690	Disability Resources	6412693702
Hawkeye C.C.	Waterloo, IA 50704	Student Development	319-296-4014
Indian Hills C.C.	Ottumwa, IA 52501	Disability Services	641-683-5749
Iowa Central C.C.	Ft. Dodge, IA 50501	Special Populations	515-574-1045
Iowa St. U.	Ames, IA 50011-2011	Student Disability Resources	5152947220
Iowa Wesleyan C.	Mount Pleasant, IA 52641	Academic Resource Center	319-385-6334
Iowa Western C.C.	Council Bluffs, IA 51502	Program Director	712-325-3284
Loras C.	Dubuque, IA 52001	Learning Center	563-588-7134
Luther C.	Decorah, IA 52101-1045	Student Academic Support Services	563-387-1270
Morningside College	Sioux City, IA 51106-1751	Learning Center	712-274-5191
Mount Mercy U.	Cedar Rapids, IA 52402	Disability Services	319-363-8213 ext. 1204

Northwestern C. (IA)	Orange City, IA 51041	Disability Services	712-707-7454
Scott CC E. Iowa CC	Bettonderf, IA 52722	Services for Students with Disabilities	563-441-4027
Simpson C.	Indianola, IA 50125	Hawley Academic Resource Center	515-961-1524
Southeastern C.C.	W. Burlington, IA 52655	Disability Services	402-323-3412
St. Ambrose U.	Davenport, IA 52803-2898	Student Disability Services	563-333-6275
U. of Dubuque	Dubuque, IA 52001-5050	Academic Success Center	563-589-3757
U. of Iowa	Iowa City, IA 52242	Student Disability Services	319-335-1462
U. of Northern Iowa	Cedar Falls, IA 50614-0018	Student Disability Services	319-273-2677
Waldorf C.	Forest City, IA 50436	Learning Disability Program	641-584-8207
Wartburg C.	Waverly, IA 50677-0903	Pathways Center	319-352-8615
William Penn U.	Oskaloosa, IA 52577	Office of Academics Affairs	641-673-1010

KANSAS

Baker University	Baldwin City, KS 66006	Disability Resources	785-594-8352
Benedictine C.	Atchison, KS 66002	Disability Services Office	913-360-7968
Benedictine College	Atchison, KS 66002	Academic Assistance Center	913-360-7517
Bethany C.	Lindsborg, KS 67456-1897	McCann Learning Center	304-829-7402
Butler City C.C.	Eldorado, KS 67042	Disability Services	316-322-3166
Emporia St. U.	Emporia, KS 66801-5087	Disability Service	620-341-6637
Friends U.	Wichita, KS 67213	Student Retention	316-295-5237
Hutchinson C.C.	Hutchison, KS 67502	Disability Services	620-665-3554
Johnson County C.C.	Overland Park, KS 66210	Student Success Center	913-469-3521
Kansas City C.C.	Kansas City, KS 66112	Academic Resource Center	913-288-7664
Kansas St. U.	Manhattan, KS 66506	Student Access Center	785-532-6441
Manhattan Christian C.	Manhattan, KS 66502	Student Development	877-246-4622
McPherson C.	McPherson, KS 67460	Disability Services	620-242-0507
MidAmerica Nazarene U.	Olathe, KS 66062	Learning Resources Center	913-971-3582
Newman University	Wichita, KS 67213	Student Support Services	316-942-4291
Pittsburg St. U.	Pittsburg, KS 66762	Center for Student Accommodations	620-235-4309
Pratt C.C.	Pratt, KS 67124	Student Success	620-672-5641 ext. 215
U. of Kansas	Lawrence, KS 66045-7576	Academic Achievement and Access Center	784-864-4064
U. of St. Mary	Levenworth, KS 66048	Student Life	913-682-5151
Wichita St. U.	Wichita, KS 67260	Disability Services	316-978-3309

KENTUCKY

Bellarmine C.	Louisville, KY 40205	Disability Services Coordinator	502- 272-8480
Berea C.	Berea, KY 40404	Disability and Accessibility Services	859-985-3237
Bluegrass Comm. & Tech. College	Lexington, KY 40506-0235	Disability Support Services	859-246-6728
Brescia C.	Owensboro, KY 42301	Student Support Services	270-686-4259
Centre C.	Danville, KY 40422	Disability Services	859-238-5223
Cumberlands C.	Williamsburg, KY 40769	Academic Services	606-539-4214
Eastern Kentucky U.	Richmond, KY 40475	Project SUCCESS	859-622-2933
Georgetown C.	Georgetown, KY 40324	Counseling Center	502-863-7074
Kentucky Christian U.	Grayson, KY 41143	Special Student Services	606-474-3257
Kentucky St. U.	Frankfort, KY 40601	NR	NR
Kentucky Wesleyan C.	Owensboro, KY 42302	PLUS Center	270-852-3212
Lexington C.C.	Lexington, KY 40506-0235	Disability Support Services	859-246-6535
Lindsey Wilson C.	Columbia, KY 42728	Learning Disabilities	270-384-8080
Mid-Continent C.	Mayfield, KY 42066	A.C.E. Program	270-247-8521 ext. 354
Morehead St. U.	Morehead, KY 40351	Disability Services	606-783-5188
Murray St. U.	Murray, KY 42071	Office of Equal Opportunity	270-809-3155
Northern Kentucky U.	Highland Heights, KY 41099	Disability Programs and Services	589.572.5180
Southeast C.C.	Cumberland, KY 40823	Student Support Services	402-228-3468 ext. 1361
Thomas More C.	Crestview Hill, KY 41017	Student Support Services	859-344-3521
Transylvania U.	Lexington, KY 40508-1797	Disability Services	859-233-8502
U. of Kentucky	Lexington, KY 40506	Disability Resource Center	(859) 257-2754
U. of Louisville	Louisville, KY 40292	Disability Resource Center	502-852-6938
U. of Pikevile	Pikeville, KY 41501	Disability Student Services	(606) 218-5232
Western Kentucky U.	Bowling Green, KY 42101	Student Disability Services	270-745-5004

LOUISIANA

Louisiana C.	Pineville, LA 71359-0560	PATH Program	318-487-7629
Louisiana St. U.	Baton Rouge, LA 70803	Disability Services	225-578-5919
Loyola U. New Orleans	New Orleans, LA 70118-6195	Office of Disability Services	504-865-2990
McNeese St. U.	Lake Charles, LA 70609	Services for Students with Disabilities	337-475-5916
Nicholls St. U.	Thibodaux, LA 70310	Office of Disability Services	985-448-4429
Northwestern St. U. of Louisiana	Natchitoches, LA 71497	Academic and Career Engagement Center	318-357-6950

Our Lady of Holy Cross C.	New Orleans, LA 70131	Enrollment Services	504-398-2165
Southeastern Louisiana U.	Hammond, LA 70402	The Office of Disability Services	985-549-2247
Southern U. & A&M C.	Baton Rouge, LA 70813	Special Education	225-771-3950
Southern U. of New Orleans	New Orleans, LA 70126	Student Support Services	504-286-5106
Tulane U.	New Orleans, LA 70118	Goldman Office of Disability Services	504-862-8433
U. of Louisiana—Lafayette	Lafayette, LA 70504	Services for Students w/ Disabilities	337-482-5252
U. of Louisiana—Monroe	Monroe, LA 71209	Dean of the Faculty's Office	318-342-5431
U. of New Orleans	New Orleans, LA 70148	Student Affairs	504-280-6222

MAINE

Bates C.	Lewiston, ME 04240-9917	Dean's Office	207-786-6067
Bowdoin C.	Brunswick, ME 04011-8441	Dean's Office	207-725-3578
C. of Atlantic	Bar Harbor, ME 04609	Disability Services	207-288-5015
Colby C.	Waterville, ME 04901-8840	Dean's Office	207-859-4255
Eastern Maine Tech C.	Bangor, ME 04401	Academic Support Center	207-974-4658
Husson C.	Bangor, ME 04401	Dean of Students Office	207-992-1934
Husson U.	Bangor, ME 4401	OASIS	(207) 992-1934
Kennebec Valley Tech	Fairfield, ME 04937	Students With Disabilities	207-453-5019
Maine C. of Art	Portland, ME 04101	Student Affairs	207.699.5067
N. Maine Tech C.	Presque Isle, ME 04769	Student Affairs—TRIO	207-768-2747
Southern Maine C. C.	South Portland, ME 04106	Disability Services	207-741-5629
Thomas C.	Waterville, ME 04901	Center for Academic Support	207-859-1214
U. of Maine	Orono, ME 04469-5713	Disability Support Services	207-581-2319
U. of Maine at Farmington	Farmington, ME 4938	Learning Assistance Center Disabilities Services	207-778-7295
U. of Maine—Augusta	Bangor, ME 04401-4367	Cornerstone Program	207-621-3501
U. of Maine—Farmington	Farmington, ME 04938	Acad. Svcs. for Students w/ Disab.	207-778-7295
U. of Maine—Fort Kent	Fort Kent, ME 04743	Disability Services	207-834-7834
U. of Maine—Machias	Machias, ME 04654	Student Resources	207-255-1228
U. of Maine—Orono	Orono, ME 04469-5757	Onward Program/Disabilities	207-581-2325
U. of Maine-Presque Isle	Presque Isle, ME 4769	Student Support Services	207.9613
U. of New England	Biddeford, ME 04005-9599	Disability Services	207-221-4418
U. of Southern Maine	Portland, ME 04104	Support for Students with Disabilities	207-780-4706
Unity C.	Unity, ME 04988-0532	Learning Resource Center	207-948-3131 ext. 263

MARYLAND

Allegany C.	Cumberland, MD 21502	Student Success Center	301-784-5551
Anne Arundel C.C.	Arnold, MD 21012	Disabled Student Services	410-777-2306
Baltimore City C.C.	Baltimore, MD 21215	Disability Support Services Center	410-462-8589
C. of Norte Dame of Maryland	Baltimore, MD 21210	Disability Support Services	410-532-5379
C. of Southern MD—La Plata	La Plata, MD 20646	Academic Support Services	301-934-2251 ext. 7614
Capitol C.	Laurel, MD 20708	Dean of Student's Office	301-369-2800 ext. 3046
Carroll C.C.	Westminster, MD 21157	Student Support Services	410-386-8329
Catonsville C.C.	Catonsville, MD 21228	Special Student Population	443-840-4718
Cecil C.C.	North East, MD 20901	Academic Advising	410-287-6060 ext556
Columbia Union C.	Takoma Park, MD 20912	Center for Learning Resources	301-891-4184
Coppin St. U.	Baltimore, MD 21216-3698	Counseling Center	410-951-3510
Essex C.C.	Baltimore, MD 21237	Office of Special Services	443-840-1741
Frostburg St. U.	Frostburg, MD 21532	Disability Support Services	301-687-4738
Goucher C.	Baltimore, MD 21204-2794	NO program - disability support services	410-337-6178
Harford C.C.	Bel Air, MD 21015	Learning Support Services	443-412-2414
Hood C.	Fredrick, MD 21701	Disability Services	301-696-3550
Howard C.C.	Columbia, MD 21044	Learning Assistance Center	410-772-4822
John Hopkins U.	Baltimore, MD 21218	Institutional Equity	410-516-8075
Loyola C. MD	Baltimore, MD 21210	Center for Academic Services and Support	410-617-2663
McDaniel College	Westminster, MD 21157	Academic Skills Center	410-857-2504
Montgomery C.	Rockville, MD 20850	Disability Support Services	240-567-5058
Morgan St. U.	Baltimore, MD 2125	Counseling Center	443-885-3130
Mount St. Mary's U.	Emmitsburg, MD 21727	Learning Services	301-447-5006
Salisbury U.	Salisbury, MD 21801	Office of Student Disability Support Services	410-543-6070
Towson U.	Towson, MD 21252-0001	Disability Support Services	410-704-2638
U. of Baltimore	Baltimore, MD 21201	Disability Support Services	410-837-4775
U. of Maryland—C. Park	College Park, MD 20742-5235	Disability Support Services	301-314-7682
U. of Maryland—Eastern Shore	Princess Anne, MD 21853	Disabled Student Services	410-651-6461
U. of Maryland—U. College	Adelphi, MD 20783	Disability Services	301.314.7682
Washington C.	Chestertown, MD 21620	Disability Services	410-778-7883

MASSACHUSETTS

American International C.	Springfield, MA 01109-3184	Supportive Learning Services	413-205-3430
Amherst C.	Amherst, MA 1002	Accessibility Services	413-542-2337
Anna Maria C.	Paxton, MA 01612	Learning Center	508-849-3372
Art Institute of Boston—Lesley U.	Boston, MA 02215-2598	Center for Academic Achievement	617-582-4610
Assumption C.	Worcester, MA 01615	Disabled Students Services	508-767-7500
Babson C.	Babson Park, MA 2457	Disability Services	781-239-4508
Bay Path C.	Longmeadow, MA 01106	Office of Disability Services	413-565-1353
Bay Path U.	Longmeadow, MA 01106-2292	NR	413-565-1772
Becker C.	Worchester, MA 01609	Center for Academic Success	508-373-9704
Bentley C.	Waltham, MA 2452	Counseling & Student Development	781-891-2274
Bentley U.	Waltham, MA 2452	NR	781-891-2004
Berklee C. of Music	Boston, MA 02215	Advising Center	617-747-2310
Berkshire C.C.	Pittsfield, MA 01201	Services for Disabled Students	413-236-1605
Boston Architectural Center	Boston, MA 02115	Academic Services	617-585-0274
Boston C.	Chestnut Hill, MA 02467-3809	The Connors Family Learning Center	617-552-8093
Boston U.	Boston, MA 02215	Learning Disability Support Services	617-353-3658
Brandeis U.	Waltham, MA 02454-9110	Disabilities Services and Support	781.736.3470
Bridgewater St. C.	Bridgewater, MA 02325	Office for Students with Disabilities	508-531-1214
C. of the Holy Cross	Worcester, MA 01610-2395	Office of Disability Services	508-793-3693
Clark U.	Worcester, MA 01610-1477	Student Accessibility Services	508 798 4368
Curry C.	Milton, MA 02186	Program for Advancement of Learning	617-333-2385
Dean C.	Franklin, MA 02038	Disability Support Services	508-541-1764
Elms C.	Chicopee, MA 01013	Office of Students with Disabilities	413-265-2333
Emerson C.	Boston, MA 02116-1511	Disability Services Office	617-824-8592
Emmanuel C.	Boston, MA 2115	Disability Support Services	617-735-9923
Endicott C.	Beverly, MA 1915	Disability Services	978-998-7746
Fitchburg St. C.	Fitchburg, MA 01420-2697	Disability Services	978-665-3562
Framingham St. C.	Framingham, MA 01701	Academic Support	508-626-4906
Gordon C.	Wenham, MA 01984-1899	Academic Support Center	978.867.4746
Hampshire C.	Amherst, MA 01002	Center for Academic Support and Advising	413-559-5423
Harvard and Radcliffe C.s	Cambridge, MA 02318	Accessible Education Center	617-496-8707

Holyoke C.C.	Holyoke, MA 01040	College Disability Services	413-552-2417
Lasell C.	Newton, MA 02466	Academic Achivement Center	617-243-2306
Lesley C.	Cambridge, MA 02138	Disability Services	617-349-8194
Mass Bay C.C.	Wellesley Hills, MA 02181	Disability Services	781-239-2626
Mass. C. of Liberal Arts	North Adams, MA 01247	Learning Services Center	413-662-5309
Mass. C. of Pharmacy & Health	Boston, MA 02115-5896	Academic Support Services	617-732-2860
Mass. Institute of Tech	Cambridge, MA 02139	Disability Serivices	617-253-1674
Mass. Maritime Academy	Bussards Bay, MA 02532-1803	Disability Resource	508-830-5000 x2208
Massasoit C.C.	Brockton, MA 02402	Disability Services	508-588-9100 x1805
Merrimack C.	North Andover, MA 01845	Disability Services	978-837-5140
Montserrat C. of Art	Beverly, MA 01915	Academic Affairs	978-921-4242 ext. 1603
Mount Holyoke C.	South Hadley, MA 1075	AccessAbility Services	4135382634
Mt. Holyoke C.	South Hadley, MA 01075	Disability Services	413-538-2550
Mt. Ida C.	Newton, MA 01259	Learning Opportunities Program	617-928-4648
Mt. Wachusett C.C.	Gardner, MA 01440	Students with Disabilities	978-630-9178
N. Adams St. C.	N. Adams, MA 01247	Learning Center	413-662-5309
Nichols C.	Dudley, MA 01571	Advising Services	508-213-2212
North Shore C.C.	Danvers, MA 01923	SSC—Disabilities Services	978-762-4000 ext. 4501
Northeastern U.	Boston, MA 2115	Disability Resource Center	617.373.2676
Pine Manor C.	Chestnut Hill, MA 02167	Learning Resource Center	617-731-7181
Quinsigamond C.C.	Worcester, MA 01606	Disabilities Services	508-854-4471
Regis C.	Weston, MA 02493-1571	Disability Services	781-768-7384
Simmons C.	Boston, MA 02115	Academic Support	617-521-2473
Smith C.	Northampton, MA 01063	Office of Disability Services	413-585-2071
Springfield C.	Springfield, MA 01109	Student Support Service	413-748-3768
Springfield Tech C.C.	Springfield, MA 01105	Office of Disability Services	413-755-4551
Stonehill C.	Easton, MA 02357-5610	Accessibility Resources	508-565-1306
Suffolk U.	Boston, MA 2108	Office of Disability Services	6179946820
Tufts U.	Medford, MA 2155	Student Accessibility Services	617-627-4539
U. Mass.—Amherst	Amherst, MA 01003	Learning Disabilities Support Services	413-545-0892
U. Mass.—Boston	Boston, MA 02125-3393	Roth Center for Disability Services	617-287-7432
U. Mass.—Dartmouth	North Dartmouth, MA 02747	Disabled Student Services	508-999-8711
U. Mass.—Lowell	Lowell, MA 01854	Disability Services	978-934-4574

U. of Massachusetts Amherst	Amherst, MA 01003-9291	Disability Services	(413) 545-0982
Wellesley C.	Wellesley, MA 02481	POTC	781-283-2641
Wentworth Institute of Tech	Boston, MA 02115-5998	The Center for Wellness and Disability Services	(617) 989-4232
Western New England C.	Springfield, MA 01119	Student Disability Services	413-782-1257
Westfield St. U.	Westfield, MA 1086	Disabilities Services	413-572-8789
Wheaton C. (MA)	Norton, MA 2766	Disability Services	5082868215
Wheaton C. MA	Norton, MA 02766	Academic Support Services	508-286-3848
Wheelock C.	Boston, MA 2215	Disability Services	617 879 2030
Williams C.	Williamstown, MA 1267	NR	NR
Worcester Poly. Institute	Worcester, MA 01609	Student Disability Services	508-831-5235
Worcester Polytechnic Institute	Worcester, MA 1609	Office of Disability Services	508-831-4908
Worcester St. U.	Worcester, MA 01602-2597	Disability Services Office	508-929-8733
MICHIGAN			
Adrian C.	Adrian, MI 49221-2575	Academic Service Office	517-265-5161 ext. 4413
Albion C.	Albion, MI 49224	Learning Support Center	517-629-0825
Albion College	Albion, MI 49224	Disability Services	517-629-0825
Alma C.	Alma, MI 48801-1599	Center for Student Opportunity	(989) 463-7407
Andrews U.	Berrien Springs, MI 49104	Student Services	269-471-3227
Aquinas C.	Grand Rapids, MI 49506-1799	Academic Achievement Center	616-632-2166
C. of Creative Studies	Detroit, MI 48202	Student Success Services	313-664-7680
Calvin C.	Grand Rapids, MI 49546	Disability Services	616.526.6155
Central Michigan U.	Mount Pleasant, MI 48859	Academic Assistance	989-774-7506
Cornerstone U.	Grand Rapids, MI 49525	Learning Center	616-222-1596
Davenport U.	Grand Rapids, MI 49503	Disability Services	616-554-5687
Delta C.	Universal City, MI 48710	Learning Disabilities Services	989-686-9322
Eastern Michigan U.	Ypsilanti, MI 48197	Student Success	734-487-6694
Ferris St. U.	Big Rapids, MI 49307	Educational Counseling & Disabilities Services	231-591-3051
Finlandia U.	Hancock, MI 49930	Student Support Services	906-487-7346
Grand Rapids C.C.	Grand Rapids, MI 49503	Disability Support Services	616-234-4140
Grand Valley St. U.	Allendale, MI 49401	Disability Support Resources	616-331-2490
Hillsdale C.	Hillsdale, MI 49242	Health and Wellness	517-437-7341 ext. 2561
Hope C.	Holland, MI 49422-9000	NR	NR

Itaska C.C.	Grand Rapids, MI 55744	Support Services	218-322-2430
Kalamazoo C.	Kalamazoon, MI 49006	Dean of Students	269-337-7209
Kellogg C.C.	Battle Creek, MI 49017	Support Services	269-965-3931 ext. 2627
Kettering U.	Flint, MI 48504-6214	Wellness Center	810-762-9650
Kuyper C.	Grand Rapids, MI 49525	Academic Support	616-988-3688
Lansing C.C.	Lansing, MI 48901	Counseling Services	517-483-1904
Lawrence Tech. U.	Southfield, Mi 48075	Disability Services	248-204-4119
Lawrence Technological U.	Southfield, MI 48075-1058	Office of Disability Services	248.204.4100
Madonna U.	Livonia, MI 48150-1173	Educational Support Services	734-432-5641
Marygrove C.	Detroit, MI 48221	Support Services	313-927-1423
Michigan St. U.	East Lansing, MI 48824	Resource Center for Persons with Disabilities	517-884-1903
Michigan Tech.l U.	Houghton, MI 49931	Student Disability Services	906-487-2212
North Central Michigan C.	Petoskey, MI 49770	Educational Opportunity Program	231-348-6687
Northern Michigan U.	Marquette, MI 49855	Disability Services	906-227-1737
Northwood U.—Midland	Midland, MI 48640	Special Needs Services	989-837-4213
Oakland C.C.	Auburn Hills, MI 48309	ACCESS	248-232-4081
Oakland U.	Rochester, MI 48309	Disability Support Services	248-370-3266
Olivet C.	Olivet, MI 49076	Disability Services	269-749-7702
Rochester C.	Rochester Hills, MI 48307	Student Support Center	248-218-2014
Saginaw Valley St. U.	University Center, MI 48710	Disability Services	989-964-4168
Schoolcraft C.C.	Livonia, MI 48152	Learning Assistance Center	734-462-4436
Spring Arbor U.	Spring Arbor, MI	Disability Center	517-750-6479 x1479
SW Michigan C.	Dowagiac, MI 49047	Academic Support	269-782-1321
U. of Michigan–Ann Arbor	Ann Arbor, MI 48109-1316	Services for Students with Disabilities	734-763-3000
U. of Michigan—Ann Arbor	Ann Arbor, MI 48109	Services for Students with Disabilities	734-763-3000
U. of Michigan—Dearborn	Dearborn, MI48128-1491	Counseling & Support Services	313-593-5430
U. of Michigan-Flint	Flint, MI 48502	COUNSELING, ACCESSIBILITY, AND PSYCHOLOGICAL SERVICES (CAPS)	810-762-3456
Walsh C.	Troy, MI 48007-7006	Academic Advising	248-823-1386
Wayne St. U.	Detroit, MI 48202	Student Disability Services	(313) 577-1851
Western Michigan U.	Kalamazoo, MI 49008-5211	Disability Services for Students	269-387-2116

MINNESOTA

Augsburg C.	Minneapolis, MN 55454	CLASS Program	612-330-1218
Bemidji St. U.	Bemidji, MN 56601	Disability Services	NR
Bethel U.	Saint Paul, MN 55112	Disability Resources & Services	651-635-8759
Bimidji St. U.	Bimidji, MN 55601	Disability Services	218-755-3883
C. of Saint Benedict	Saint Joseph, MN 56374	Academic Advising	320-363-5687
C. of Saint Benedict/Saint John's U.	Collegeville, MN 56321-7155	Student Accessibility Services	320-363-5245
C. of St. Catherine, The	Saint Paul, MN 55105	O'Neill Learning Center	651-590-6563
C. of St. Scholastica, The	Duluth, MN 55811-4199	Academic Support Services	218-723-6552
Carleton C.	Northfield, MN 55057	Disability Services for Students	507-222-4080
Century College	White Bear Lk, MN 55110	Access Center	651-779-3354
Concordia C.—Moorhead	Moorhead, MN 56562	Disability Counseling	218-299-3514
Concordia C.—Saint Paul	Saint Paul, MN 55104-5494	Students with Disabilities	651-641-8272
Crown C.	St. Bonifacius, MN 55375	Disability Counseling	952-446-4216
Fond du Lac C.C.	Cloquet, MN 55720	Office of Students with Disabilities	218-879-0805
Gustavus Adolphus C.	St. Peter, MN 56082	Academic Advising: Dean of Students	507-933-7027
Hamline U.	Saint Paul, MN 55104	Disability Services	651-523-2521
Hibbing C.C.	Hibbing, MN 55746	Disability Services	218-262-6712
Inver Hills C.C.	Inver Grove Hgts, MN 55076	Disabled Student Services	651-450-3628
Lake Superior C.	Duluth, MN 55811	Disability Services	218-733-7650
Macalester C.	St. Paul, MN 55105	Robin Hart Ruthenbeck	651-696-6874
Mesabi C.C.	Virginia, MN 55792	Disability Services	218-749-0319
Minneapolis C.C.	Minneapolis, MN 55403	Office for Students with Disabilities	612-659-6733
Minnesota St. U.—Mankato	Mankato, MN 56002	Center for Academic Success	507-389-1791
Minnesota St. U.—Moorhead	Moorhead, MN 56563	Disability Services	218-477-2131
N. Hennepin C.C.	Brooklyn Pk, MN 55445	Disability Access Services	763-493-0556
Normandale C.C.	Bloomington, MN 55431	Office for Students with Disabilities	952-487-7035
North Central U.	Minneapolis, MN 55404	Disability Services	612-343-3510
Northwestern C.	St. Paul, MN 55113-1598	Disability Services	651-631-7446
Riverland C.C.	Austin, MN 55912	Student Success Center	507-433-0646
Rochester C.C.	Rochester, MN 55904	Disability Services	507-280-2968
Saint Cloud St. U.	Saint Cloud, MN 56301-4498	Student Disability Services	320-308-3117
Saint John's U.	Collegeville, MN 56321-7155	Academic Advising	320-363-5687

Saint Mary's U. of Minnesota	Winona, MN 55987-1399	Disability Support Services	507-457-1465
Southwest St. U.	Marshall, MN 56258	Learning Resources	507-537-7672
St. Olaf C.	Northfield, MN 55057-1098	Student Disability Service	507-786-3288
U. of Minnesota	Crookston, MN 56716	Office for Students w/ Disabilities	218-281-8587
U. of Minnesota—Duluth	Duluth, MN 55812-2496	Learning Disability Program	218-726-8727
U. of Minnesota, Morris	Morris, MN 56267	Disability Resource Center	320-589-6163
U. of Minnesota—Twin Cities	Minneapolis, MN 55455-0213	Disability Services	612-626-1333
U. of Minnesota–Twin Cities	Minneapolis, MN 55455-0213	Disability Resource Center	612-624-4120
U. of St. Thomas	St. Paul, MN 55105-1096	Enhancement Program	651-962-6315
Winona St. U.	Winona, MN 55987	Access Services for Students with Diabilities	507-457-5878
MISSISSIPPI			
Belhaven U.	Jackson, MS 39202	Office of Student Success	601.968.8865
Blue Mountain C.	Blue Mountain, MS 38610-0160		662-685-4771
Jackson St. U	Jackson, MS 39217	Disability Services	601-979-3704
Millsaps C.	Jackson, MS 39210-0001	Disability Services	601-974-1228
Mississippi C.	Clinton, MS 39058	Counseling & Testing Center	601-325-3354
Mississippi St. U.	Mississippi, MS 39762	Student Support Services	662-325-3335
Mississippi U. for Women	Columbus, MS 39701	Academic Support Services	662-241-7138
Rust C.	Holy Springs, MS 38635	Disability Services	662-252-8000 ext. 4909
U. of Mississippi	University, MS 38677	Services for Students with Disabilities	662-915-7128
U. of Southern Mississippi	Hattiesburg, MS 39406	Office of Disability Accmmodations	601-266-5024
William Carey C.	Hattiesburg, MS 39401-5499	Student Support Services	601-318-6208
MISSOURI			
Avila U.	Kansas City, MO 64145	Learning Center	816-501-3670
Barnes-Jewish C. of Nurs. & AH	St. Louis, MO 33132	Student Support Services	314-454-8686
Blue River C.C.	Blue Springs, MO 64015-7242	ACCESS Office	816-220-6651
C. of the Ozarks	Point Lookout, MO 65726	Academic Dean's Office	417-334-6411 ext. 2278
Calvary Bible C. and Theological Seminary	Kansas City, MO 64147	Academic Accommodations Office	8163220110 ext 1320
Central Missouri St. U.	Warrensburg, MO 64093	Office of Accessibility	660-543-4421
Columbia C.	Columbia, MO 65216	Student Support Center	573-875-7651
Culver-Stockton C.	Canton, MO 63435	Disability Services	(860) 917-1729
Drury C.	Springfield, MO 65802-9977	Assistive Student Services	417-873-6881

Evangel U.	Springfield, MO 65802	Academic Development Center	417-865-2811
Fontbonne C.	St. Louis, MO 63105	Academic Resource Center	314-719-3627
Hannibal-LaGrange C.	Hannibal, MO 63401	Academic Affairs	573-221-3675 ext. 253
Harris-Stowe St. C.	St. Louis, MO 63103	Disability Services	314-340-3648
Kansas City Art Institute	Kansas City, MO 64111-1762	Academic Resource Center	816-802-3485
Lincoln U.	Jefferson City, MO 65102-0029	Disability Services	573-681-5167
Lincoln U. (MO)	Jefferson City, MO 65101	Access & Ability Services	573-681-5162
Lindenwood U.	Saint Charles, MO 63301-1695	Student and Academic Support Services	636-949-4510
Longview Comm. C.	Lee Summit, MO 64081-2105	ACCESS Office	816-672-2252
Maple Woods C.C.	Kansas City, MO 64156	ACCESS Office	816-437-3192
Maryville U. of St. Louis	St. Louis, MO 63141-7299	Academic Success Center	314-529-9374
Mineral Area C.	Park Hills, MO 63601	Special Services	573-518-2152
Missouri Southern St. C.	Joplin, MO 64801-1595	Learning Center	417-659-3725
Missouri St. U.	Springfield, MO 65897	Learning Diagnostic Clinic	417-836-4192
Missouri Valley C.	Marshall, MO 65340	NR	660-831-4170
Missouri Western St. U.	Saint Joseph, MO 64507	Disability Services	816-271-4330
Northwest Missouri St. U.	Maryville, MO 64468	Student Support Services	660-562-1259
Park U.	Parkville, Mo 64152	Academic Support Services	816-584-6332
Penn Valley C.C.	Kansas City, MO 64110	Access Office	816-759-4152
Rockhurst U.	Kansas City, MO 64110	Office of Access Services	816-501-4689
Saint Louis U.	Saint Louis, MO 63103	Disability Services/Student Success Center	(314) 977-3484
Southeast Missouri St. U.	Cape Girardeau, MO 63701	Disability Services	573-651-5927
Southwest Baptist U.	Bolivar, MO 65613	University Success Center	417-328-1425
Southwest Missouri St. U.	Springfield, MO 65804	Learning Diagnostic Clinic	417-836-4787
St. Charles City C.C.	St. Peters, MO 63376	Disabled Student Services	636-922-8247
St. Louis C C.—Florissant Valley	St. Louis, MO 63135	ACCESS Office	314-513-4551
St. Louis C.C.—Forest Park	St. Louis, MO 63110	ACCESS Office	314-644-9039
St. Louis C.C.—Meramec	St. Louis, MO 63122	ACCESS Office	314-984-7673
Stephens C.	Columbia, MO 65215	Student Services	573-876-7212
Three River C.C.	Poplar Bluff, MO 63901	Student Support Services	573-840-9650
Truman St. U.	Kirksville, MO 63501	Disability Services	660-785-4478
U. of Missouri—Columbia	Columbia, MO 65203	Office of Disability Services	573-882-4696
U. of Missouri–Kansas City	Kansas City, mo 64114	Office of Services for Students with Disabilities	816-235-5696

U. of Missouri—Kansas City	Kansas City, MO 64110-2499	Services for Students with Disabilities	816-235-5696
U. of Missouri—Rolla	Rolla, MO 65409	Disability Support Services	573-341-6655
U. of Missouri—Saint Louis	Saint Louis, MO 63121	Disability Access Services	314-516-6554
Washington U.	Saint Louis, MO 63130-4899	Disability Resource Center	314-935-4153
Washington U. in St. Louis	St. Louis, MO 63130-4899	Disability Resources	314-935-5970
Webster U.	Saint Louis, MO 63119-3194	NR	(314)246-7700
Westminster C.	Fulton, MO 65251-1299	Learning Disabilities Program	573-592-5305
William Jewell C.	Liberty, MO 64068	Office of Disability Services	816-415-7556
William Woods U.	Fulton, MO 65251	Disability Services	573-592-1194
MONTANA			
Carroll C.	Helena, MT 59625-0002	Academic Resource Center	406-447-4504
Montana St. U.	Bozeman, MT 59717-2190	Disability, Re-Entry and Veteran Services	406-994-2824
Montana St. U—Northern	Harve, MT 59501	Assistant Dean of Students	406-265-4152
Montana Tech. College	Butte, MT 59701	Disability Services	406-496-4129
Rocky Mountain C.	Billings, MT 59102	Services for Academic Success	406-657-1128
The U. of Montana	Missoula, MT 59812	Disability Services for Students	406-243-2243
The U. of Montana—Western	Dillon, MT 59725	Disability Services	406-683-7900
U. of Great Falls	Great Falls, MT 59405	Center for Academic Excellence	406-791-5213
U. of Montana	Missoula, MT 59812	Disability Services for Students	406-243-2243
NEBRASKA			
Bellevue U.	Bellevue, NE 68005	Special Needs Services	402-557-7417
Concordia U., Nebraska	Seward, NE 68434-1556	NR	NR
Creighton U.	Omaha, NE 68178	Disability Support Services	402-280-2166
Dana C.	Blair, NE 68008	Academic Support Services	402-426-7343
Doane C.	Crete, NE 68333	Academic Support	402-826-8554
Grace U.	Omaha, NE 68108-3629	Dean of Women	402-449-2849
Hastings C.	Hastings, NE 68901-7621	Disability Services	402-461-7386
Metropolitan C.C.	Omaha, NE 68103	Special Needs Program	402-457-2580
Midland Lutheran C.	Fremont, NE 68025	Academic Support Center	402-941-6257
Nebraska Methodist C.	Omaha, NE 68114	Student Development Services	402-354-7214
U. of Nebraska—Kearney	Kearney, NE 68849	Academic Success	308-865-8988
U. of Nebraska–Lincoln	Lincoln, NE 68588-0417	Services for Students with Disabilities	402-472-3787

U. of Nebraska—Medical Center	Omaha, NE 68198-4265	Student Disability Services	402-559-5553
U. of Nebraska—Omaha	Omaha, NE 68182	Disability Services	402-554-2872
Union C.	Lincoln, NE 68506-4300	Teaching Learning Center	402-486-2506
Wayne St. C.	Wayne, NE 68787	STRIDE	402-375-7321
West Nebraska C.C.	Scottsbluff, NE 69361-1899	Counseling Center	800-348-4435
NEVADA			
Truckee Meadows C.C.	Reno, NV 89512	Disability Resource Center	775-673-7126
U. of Nevada—Las Vegas	Las Vegas, NV 89154	Disability Resource Center	702-895-0866
U. of Nevada—Reno	Reno, NV 89557	Disability Resource Center	775-784-6000
Western Nevada C.C.	Carson City, NV 89703	Disability Support Services	775-445-3275
NEW HAMPSHIRE			
Colby-Sawyer C.	New London, NH 03257	Disability Resources	603-526-3712
Dartmouth C.	Hanover, NH 03755	Student Disabilities Center	603-646-2014
Franklin Pierce U.	Rindge, NH 03461-0060	Academic Services	603-899-4044
Keene St. C.	Keene, NH 03435-2604	Office of Disability Services	603-358-2353
New England C.	Henniker, NH 03242	Academic Advising & Support Ctr.	603-428-2218
New Hampshire Tech	Concord, NH 03301	Support Services	603-271-7723
Plymouth St. U.	Plymouth, NH 3264	Support Services/Disability Services Office	603-535-2482
Rivier U.	Nashua, NH 03060	Special Needs Services	603-897-8479
Southern New Hampshire U.	Manchester, NH 03108	Disability Services	603-668-2211 x2386
St. Anselm C.	Manchester, NH 03102	Academic Advisment	603-641-7465
U. of New Hampshire	Durham, NH 3824	Disability Services for Students	603-862-0830
NEW JERSEY			
Bergen C.C.	Paramus, NJ 07652	Office of Special Services	201-612-5273
Bloomfield C.	Bloomfield, NJ 07003	Learning Needs	973-748-9000 x654
Brookdale C.C.	Lincroft, NJ 07738	Director of Disability Services	732-224-2730
C. of New Jersey, The	Ewing, NJ 06628-0718	Office for Students w/ Differing Abilities	609-771-2571
C. of St. Elizabeth	Morristown, NJ 07960-6989	Disability Services	973-290-4261
Caldwell College	Caldwell, NJ 07006-9165	Office of Disability Services	973-618-3645
Camden County C.	Blackwood, NJ 08012	PACS Program	856-227-7200 ext. 4430
Centenary C.	Hackettstown, NJ 07840	Disability Services	908-852-1400 ext. 2251
County C. of Morris	Randolph, NJ 07869	Horizons Program	973-328-5284

Drew U.	Madison, NJ 07940-1493	Office of Accessibility Resources	973 408-3962
Fairleigh Dickinson U.	Teaneck, NJ 07666	Reg. Ctr. for College Students with LD	201-692-2087
Fairleigh Dickinson U.—Florham			973-443-8734
Georgian Court U.	Lakewood, NJ 08701	The Learning Center	732-987-2650
Kean U.	Union, NJ 07083-0411	Office of Disability Services	908-737-4910
Middlesex C.C.	Edison, NJ 08818	Project Connections	732-906-2507
Monmouth U.	W. Long Branch, NJ 07764	Department of Disability Services for Students	732-571-3460
Montclair St. U.	Montclair, NJ 07043-1624	Disability Resource Center	973-655-5431
Mountclair St. U.	Montclair, NJ 07043	Disability Services	973-655-5431
New Jersery Institute of Tech.	Newark, NJ 070102-1982	Disability Services	973-596-3420
New Jersey City U.	Jersey City, NJ 07305	Project Mentor	201-200-2091
Ocean County C.	Toms River, NJ 08754	Disability Resource Center	732-255-0456
Princeton U.	Princeton, NJ 08544-0430	Disability Services	609-258-3061
Raritan Valley C.C.	Somerville, NJ 08876	Disability Services	908-526-1200 ext. 8418
Richard Stockton C. of NJ	Pomona, NJ 08240-0195	Learning Access Program	609-652-4988
Rider U.	Lawrenceville, NJ 08648-3099	Services for Students with Disabilities	(609) 895-5492
Rowan U.	Glassboro, NJ 08028	Academic Success Center	856-256-4234
Rutgers U.	Piscataway, NJ 08854-8097	Disability Services	973-353-5608
Salem C.C.	Carneys Point, NJ 08069	Center for Student Success	856-351-2700
Seton Hall U.	South Orange, NJ 07079	Disability Support Services	973-313-6003
St. Peter's C.	Jersey City, NJ 07306-5997	Special Needs Students	201-761-6032
Stevens Institute of Tech.	Hoboken, NJ 07030	Director of Counseling & Disability Services	201-216-5177
Sussex C.C.	Newton, NJ 07860	LD Program	973-300-2154
The C. of New Jersey	Ewing, NJ 08628-0718	Disability Support Services	609/771/3199
Thomas Edison St. C.	Trenton, NJ 08608-1176	Learners Services	609-984-1141 ext. 3415
Westminster Choir C. of Rider U.	Princeton, NJ 08540	Services for Students w/ Disabilities	609-896-5000 ext. 7365
William Paterson U. of NJ	Wayne, NJ 07470	Disability Services	973-720-2853

NEW MEXICO

C. of Santa Fe	Santa Fe, NM 84505	Center for Academic Excellence	505-473-6552
Eastern New Mexico U.	Portales, NM 88130	Services for Students with Disabilities	505-562-2280
N.M. Inst. of Mining & Tech.	Socorro, NM 87801	Services for Students with Disabilities	575.835.6619
New Mexico Highlands U.	Las Vegas, NM 87701	Disability & Testing Services	505-454-3252

New Mexico Junior C.	Hobbs, NM 88240	Special Needs Services	575-492-2574
New Mexico St. U.	Las Cruces, NM 88003	Services for Students with Disabilities	505-646-6840
U. of New Mexico	Albuquerque, NM 87131	Special Services Program	505-277-3506
U. of the Southwest	Hobbs, NM 88240	Office of Special Services	505-392-6564
Western New Mexico U.	Silver City, NM 88062	Special Needs Services	505-538-6498

NEW YORK

Adelphi U.	Garden City, NY 11530	Disability Support Services	5168773145
Bard C.	Annandale-on-Hudson, NY 12504	Disability Support Services	845-758-7532
Barnard C.	New York, NY 10027	Office of Disability Services	212-854-4634
C. of Mount Saint Vincent	Riverdale, NY 10471	NR	NR
C. of New Rochelle	New Rochelle, NY 10805-2339	Student Services	914-654-5364
C. of Performing Arts	New York, NY 10003	Student Disability Services	212.229.5626 x3135
C. of Saint Rose, The	Albany, NY 12203	Office of Students with Disabilities	518-337-2335
C. of St.n Island CUNY	Staten Island, NY 10314	Center for Student Accessibility	718-982-2510
Canisius C.	Buffalo, NY 14208	Accessibility Support Services	716-888-2476
Clarkson U.	Potsdam, NY 13699	Office of Accommodative Services	315-268-7643
Colgate U.	Hamilton, NY 13346	Academic Program Support	315-228-7375
Columbia U.	New York, NY10027	Disability Services	212-854-2388
Concordia C. NY)	Bronxville, NY 10708	The Concordia Connection	914-337-9300 ext. 2361
Cooper Union	New York, NY 10003	Dean of Students	212-353-4115
Cornell U.	Ithaca, NY 14850	Student Disability Services	607-254-4545
Corning C.C.	Corning, NY 14830	Counseling for Students with Disabilities	607-962-9262
Culinary Institute of America	Hyde Park, NY 12538	The Learning Strategies Center	845-451-1219
CUNY—Baruch C.	New York, NY 10010	Disability Services	646-312-4590
CUNY—Bronx C.C.	Bronx, NY 10453	Disability Services	718-289-5874
CUNY—Brooklyn C.	Brooklyn, NY 11210	Services for Students with Disabilities	718-951-5538
CUNY—C. of St.n Island	Staten Island, NY 10314	Disability Services	718- 982-2510
Hunter C., CUNY	New York, NY 10065	Office of AccessABILITY	212-650-3581
CUNY—John Jay C	New York, NY 10019	Services for Individuals with Disabilities	212-237-8185
CUNY—Kingsborough C.C.	Brooklyn, NY 11235	Special Services	718-368-5175
CUNY—LaGuardia C.C.	Long Island City, NY 11101	Office for Students with Disabilities	718-482-5278
CUNY—Lehman C.	Bronx, NY 10468	Disability Issues	718-960-8441

CUNY—Medgar Evers C.	Brooklyn, NY 11225	Differently Abled Student Services	718-270-5027
CUNY—New York City C. of Tech.	Brooklyn, NY 11201	Student Support Services	718-260-5143
CUNY—York C.	Jamaica, NY 11451	Disability Services	718-262-2073
D'Youville C.	Buffalo, NY 14201	Disability Services	716-829-7728
Daemen C.	Amherst, NY 14226	The Learning Center	716-839-8228
Dominican C.	Orangeburg, NY 10692-1210	Disability Services	845-848-4035
Dowling C.	Oakdale, NY 11769-1999	Peter Hausman Center	631 244-3144
Eastman School of Music	Rochester, NY 14627	Dean of Academic Affairs	585-274-1020
Elmira C.	Elmira, NY 14901	Education Services	607-735-1857
Eugene Lang C. of Liberal Arts	New York, NY 10003	Student Disability Services	201-229-5626x3135
Fashion Institue of Tech	New York, NY 10001-5992	Disability Support Services	212-217-4090
Five Towns C.	Dix Hills, NY 11746-5871	Academic Support Services	631-656-2129
Fordham U.	Bronx, NY 10458	The Office of Disability Services	718-817-0655
Hamilton C.	Clinton, NY 13323	Accessibility Services	(315) 859-4021
Hartwick C.	Oneonta, NY 13820-4020	AccessAbility Services	6074314467
Hilbert C.	Hamburg, NY 14075-1597	Academic Services	716-649-7900 ext. 257
Hobart and William Smith C.s	Geneva, NY 14456	Disability Services	315-781-3351
Hofstra U.	Hempstead, NY 11549	Student Access Services	516-463-4999
Houghton C.	Houghton, NY 14744	Student Academic Services	716-567-9262
Iona C.	New Rochelle, NY 10801	NR	NR
Ithaca C.	Ithaca, NY 14850-7002	Student Accessibility Services	607-274-1005
Keuka College	Keuka Park, NY 14478-0098	Academic Support Program	315-279-5636
Le Moyne C.	Syracuse, NY 13214-1301	Disability Support Services	315-445-4118
Long Island U.—Brooklyn	Brooklyn, NY 11021	Special Educational Services	718-488-1219
Long Island U.—C.W. Post	Brookville, NY 11548-1300	Academic Resource Center	516-299-3057
Manhattan C.	Riverdale, NY 10471	Learning Disabilites Program	718-862-7101
Manhattan School of Music	New York, NY 10027	Dean of Students	212-749-2802 ext. 4036
Manhattanville C.	Purchase, NY 10577	Higher Education Learning Program	914-323-3186
Marist	Poughkeepsie, NY 12601-1387	Office of Special Services	845-575-3274
Marymount Manhattan C.	New York, NY 10021	Disability Services	212-774-0724
Mercy C.	Dobbs Ferry, NY 10522	Support Services	914-674-7523
Molloy C.	Rockville Centre, NY 11570	DISABILITY SUPPORT SERVICES (DSS/STEEP)	516.323.3315
Mount Saint Mary C.	Newburgh, NY 12550	Disability Services	845-569-3638

New York U.	New York, NY 10011	Moses Center for Students with Disabilities	212-998-4980
Niagara U.	Niagara University, NY 14109	Office of Academic Support	716-286-8076
NY Institute of Tech	Old Westbury, NY 11568-8000	Office of Counseling & Wellness	516-686-7683
NYU Teaching & Learning Ctn.	New York, NY 10003	Para Educator for Young Adults	212-998-5185
Onondaga C.C.	Syracuse, NY 13215	Disability Services	315-498-2245
Parsons School of Design	New York, NY 10003	Student Disability Services	21.229.5626x3135
Paul Smith C.	Paul Smith's, NY 12970	Special Services	518-327-6358
Rensselaer Polytechnic Inst.	Troy, NY 12180	Disability Services	518-276-2746
Roberts Wesleyan C.	Rochester, NY 14624	Learning Center	585-594-6493
Rochester Inst. of Tech	Rochester, NY 14623	Learning Development Center	585-475-6988
Rockland C.C.	Suffern, NY 10901	Office of Disability Services	845-574-4541
Saint Bonaventure U.	St. Bonaventure, NY 14778	Services for Students with Disabilities	716-375-2065
Saint Francis C.	Brooklyn Heights, NY 11201	Student Health Services	718-489-5366
Saint John's U. NY)	Jamaica, NY 11439	Director of Student Services	718-990-6568
Saint Lawrence U.	Canton, NY 13617	Academic Svcs for Students with Special Needs	315-229-5104
Saint Thomas Aquinas C.	Sparkill, NY 10976	Pathways	845-398-4230
Sarah Lawrence C.	Bronxville, NY 10708-5999	Disability Services	914-395-2235
Schenectady C.C.	Schenectady, NY 12305	TRIO Student Support Services	518-381-1465
Siena C.	Loudonville, NY 12211	Services for Students with Disabilities	518-783-4239
St. Bonaventure U.	St. Bonaventure, NY 14778	Disability Support Services	716-375-2065
St. John's U.	Queens, NY 11439	Office of Disabilities Services	718-990-6384
St. Lawrence U.	Canton, NY 13617	Disability and Accessibility Services	315-229-5678
St. Thomas Aquinas C.	Sparkill, NY 10976	Disability Services	845-398-4088
St. University College at Buffalo	Buffalo, NY 14260	Office of Disability Services	716-645-2608
St. U. of New York at Binghamton (Binghamton U.)		Binghamton, NY 13902-6001 Services for Students with Disabilities	607-777-2686
SUNY—Alfred St. College	Alfred, NY 14802	Services for Students with Disabilities	607-587-4122
SUNY—Brockport	Brockport, NY 14420-2915	Office for Students with Disabilities	585-395-5409
SUNY—Broome C.C.	Binghamton, NY 134902	Learning Disabilities	607-778-5316
SUNY—The C. at Old Westbury	Old Westbury, NY 11568-0307	Office of Services for Students with Disabilities	516-628-5666
SUNY—C. of Tech	Cobelskill, NY 12043	Disability Support Services	518-255-5282
SUNY—Canton	Canton, NY 13617	Accommodative Services	315-386-7603
SUNY—Cayuga C.C.	Auburn, NY 13021	Office of Disability Services	315-255-1743 ext. 422
SUNY—Columbia Greene C.C.	Hudson, NY 12534	Dean of Students	518-828-4181 x3123

SUNY—Cortland	Cortland, NY 13045	Disabilities Services	607-753-2066
SUNY—Delhi	Delhi, NY 13753	Center for Academic Services	607-746-4593
SUNY—Farmingdale	Farmingdale, NY 11735	Support Svcs. for Stdnts. w/ Disabilities	631-420-2411
SUNY—Finger Lakes C.C.	Canandaigua, NY 14424	Services for Students w/Disablities	585-394-3500 ext. 1390
SUNY—Fredonia	Fredonia, NY 14063	Disabled Student Support	716-673-3270
St. U. of New York at Geneseo	Geneseo, NY 14454	Office of Disability Services	(585) 245-5112
SUNY—Hudson Valley C.C.	Troy, NY 12180	Disability Resource Center	518-266-8106
SUNY—Jamestown C.C.	Jamestown, NY 14702	Main Street Center	716-665-5220
SUNY—Jefferson C.C.	Watertown, NY 13601	Learning Skills Center	315-786-2335
SUNY—Mohawk Valley C.C.	Utica, NY 13501	Services for Students with Disabilities	315-792-5413
SUNY—Nassau C.C.	Garden City, NY 11530	Center for Students with Disabilities	516-572-7138
St. U. of New York at New Paltz	New Paltz, NY 12561	Disability Resource Center	845-257-3020
SUNY—Old Westbury	Old Westbury, NY 11568	Disability Services	516-876-3009
SUNY—Oneonta	Oneonta, NY 13820	Learning Support Services	607-436-2137
St. U. of New York–Oswego	Oswego, NY 13126-3599	Disability Support Services Office	(315) 312-3358
SUNY—Plattsburgh	Plattsburgh, NY 12901-2681	Student Support Services	518-564-2810
St. U. of New York - Potsdam	Potsdam, NY 13676	Accommodative Services	315-267-3268
SUNY—Purchase	Purchase, NY 10577	Special Services	914-251-6390
SUNY—Stony Brook U.	Stony Brook, NY 11794	Disabilities Support Services	631-632-6748
SUNY—University at Albany	Albany, NY 12222	Learning Disabilities Resource Program	518-442-5490
SUNY—University at Buffalo	Buffalo, NY 14222-1095	Disability Services	716-878-4500
Syracuse U.	Syracuse, NY 13244-2130	Office of Disability Services	315-443-4498
The C. at Brockport - SUNY	,	NR	(585) 395-5409
The C. of Saint Rose	Albany, NY 12203	Services for Students with Disabilities	518-485-3822
The City C. of New York of The City U. of New York	New York, NY 10031	The Accessability Center	212 650 7552
The Culinary Institute of America	Hyde Park, NY 12538	Learning Strategies Center	845-905-4631
Tompkins Cortland C.C.	Dryden, NY 13035	Baker Center for Learning	607-844-8222 ext. 4283
U. of Rochester	Rochester, NY 14627-0251	Disability Resources	585-275-9125
Union C.	Schenectady, NY 12308	DEean of Students	518-388-6061
Utica C.	Utica, NY 13502-4892	Learning Services office	315-792-3032
Vassar C.	Poughkeepsie, NY 12604	Office of Disability Services	845-437-7584
Vaughn C. of Aeronautics & Tech.	Flushing, NY 11369	Academic Support Services	718-429-6600
Vennessa Walker	Niagara University, NY 14109	Office of Disability Services	716.286.8541

Wagner C.	Staten Island, NY 10301	Academic Advisement Center	718-390-3278
Wells C.	Aurora, NY 13026	Academic Advising	315-364-3401
Westchester C.C.	Valhalla, NY 10595	Disabled Students	914-606-6552
Yeshiva U.	New York, NY 10033	Disability Services	917-326-4828
NORTH CAROLINA			
Appalachian St. U.	Boone, NC 28608-2004	Office of Disability Services	828-262-3056
Asheville-Buncombe Tech.	Asheville, NC 28801	Disability Support Services	828-398-7581
Barton C.	Wilson, NC 27893	Disability Services	252-399-6587
Belmont Abbey C.	Belmont, NC 28012	Academic Assistance	704-461-6776
Bennett C.	Greensboro, NC 27401	Center for Teaching, Learning, and Technology	336-517-1567
Brevard College	Brevard, NC 28712	Office for Stnts w/Special Needs & Disabilities	828-884-8131
Campbell U.	Buies Creek, NC 27506	Student Support Services	910-814-4364
Catawba C.	Salisbury, NC 28144	Academic Resource Center	704-637-4410
Central Piedmont C.C.	Charlotte, NC 28235	Services for Students with Disabilities	704-330-2722 x7279
Chowan College	Murfreesboro, NC 27855	Learning Center	252-398-6356
Davidson C.	Davidson, NC 28036	Dean of Students Office	704-894-2225
Duke U.	Durham, NC 27708	Student Disability Access Office	919-668-1267
East Carolina U.	Greenville, NC 27858	Disability Support Services	252-737-1016
Elizabeth City St. U.	Elizabeth City, NC 27909	Center for Special Needs Students	252-335-3527
Elon University	Elon, NC 27244	Disability Services	336-278-6500
Gardner-Webb U.	Boiling Springs, NC 28071	Disability Services	704-406-4271
Greensboro C.	Greensboro, NC 27401-1875	Disability Services	336-272-7102 ext. 591
Guilford C.	Greensboro, NC 27410	The Learning Commons	336-316-2451
Guilford Tech C.C.	Jamestown, NC 27282	Counseling Services	336-454-1126, ext. 50157
High Point U.	High Point, NC 27268	Disability Support	336-841-9061
Johnson C. Smith U.	Charlotte, NC 28216	Student Support Services	708-378-1116
Lees-McRae C.	Banner Elk, NC 28604	Disability Services	828-898-2561
Lenoir Rhyne U.	Hickory, NC 28603	Disability Services Office	828.328.7296
Livingstone C.	Salisbury, NC 28144	Empowering Scholars	704-216-6065
Mars Hill C.	Mars Hill, NC 28754	Special Education	828-689-1495
Meredith C.	Raleigh, NC 27607-5298	Disability Services	919-760-8427
Methodist C.	Fayetteville, NC 28311-1498	Disability Services	910-630-7402

Mt. Olive C.	Mount Olive, NC 28365	Teaching and Learning Center	919-658-2502 ext. 4013
Nash Community C.	Rocky Mount, NC 27804	Compensatory Education Dept.	252-451-8315
North Carolina School of the Arts	Winston-Salem, NC 27127-2189	Counseling Center	336-770-3288
North Carolina St. U.	Raleigh, NC 27695	Disability Services Office	919-515-7653
Richmond C.C.	Hamlet, NC 28345	Student Development	910-410-1867
Rockingham C.C.	Wentworth, NC 27375	Student Development	336- 342-4261 ext. 2243
Southwestern C.C.	Sylva, NC 28779	Student Support Services	800.447.4091, ext. 4420
St. Andrews U.	Laurinburg, NC 28352	Disability Services	910-277-5298
The U. of N. Carolina Chapel Hill	Chapel Hill, NC 27599-2200	Accessibility Resources & Service	919-962-8300
The U. of N. Carolina Greensboro	Greensboro, NC 27402-6170	Office of Accessibility Resources and Services	336-334-5440
U. of North Carolina at Asheville	Asheville, NC 28804-8502	Office of Academic Accessibility	828-232-5050
U. of North Carolina at Charlotte	Charlotte, NC 28223-0001	Office of Disability Services	704-687-0040
U. of North Carolina-Pembroke	Pembroke, NC 28372	Accessibility Resource Center	910-521-6695
U. of North Carolina–Wilmington	Wilmington, NC 28403-5904	NR	910-962-7555
UNC at Chapel Hill, The	Chapel Hill, NC 27599	Learning Disabilities Services	919-962-7227
Wake Forest U.	Winston-Salem, NC 27109	Learning Assistance Center	336-758-5929
Wake Tech C.C.	Raleigh, NC 27603	Disability Support Services	919-866-5668
Western Carolina U.	Cullowhee, NC 28723	Disability Services	828-227-2716
Western Piedmont C.C.	Morgantown, NC 28655	Disabled Student Services	828-448-3153
Wingate U.	Wingate, NC 28174	Disability Services	704-233-8269
Winston-Salem St. U.	Winston-Salem, NC 27110	Academic Resource Center	336-750-2138
NORTH DAKOTA			
Bismarck St. C.	Bismarck, ND 58506	Disability Support Services	701-224-5554
Dickinson St. U.	Dickinson, ND 58601-4896	Student Support Services	701-483-2999
Jamestown C.	Jamestown, ND 58405	Office of Admissions	701-252-5512
Maryville St. U.	Maryville, ND 58257	Academic Support Services	701-788-4675
Minot St. U.	Minot, ND 58707	Extended Learning Center	701-858-3822
North Dakota St. C.	Wahpeton, ND 58076-0002	Study Svcs. for Students w/ Disabilities	701-671-2623
North Dakota St. U.	Fargo, ND 58108	Disability Services	701-231-8463
U. of Jamestown	Jamestown, ND 58405-0001	Learning and Academic Advising Center	7012523467
U. of Mary	Bismarck, ND 58504	Learning Skill Services	701-355-8264
U. of North Dakota	Grand Forks, ND 58202	Disability Srvices for Students	701-777-3425

United Tribes Tech C.	Bismarck, ND 58504	Student Support Services	701-255-3285 x1471
Valley City St. U.	Valley City, ND 58072	Student Academic Services	701-845-7298
Williston St. C.	Williston, ND 58801	Enrollment Services	1-888-863-9455 ext 4222

OHIO

Antioch C.	Yellow Springs, OH 45387	Center for Academic Support Services	937-319-0093
Art Academy of Cincinnati	Cincinnati, OH 45202	Learning Assistance	513-562-6261
Ashland U.	Ashland, OH 44805	Disability Services	419-289-5953
Baldwin Wallace U.	Berea, OH 44017	Disability Services for Students	440-826-2147
Bluffton U.	Bluffton, OH 45817	Academic Development/Disability Services	4193583215
Bowling Green St. U.	Bowling Green, OH 43403-0085	Office of Disability Services	(419) 372-8495
C. of Mount Saint Joseph	Cincinnati, OH 45233-1630	Project Excel	513-244-4623
C. of Wooster	Wooster, OH 44691	Learning Center	330-263-2595
Capital U.	Columbus, OH 43209	Disability Concerns	614-236-6327
Case Western Reserve U.	Cleveland, OH 44106-7055	Disability Resources	(216) 368-5230
Cedarville U.	Cedarville, OH 45314	Disability Services at The Cove	937-766-7437
Central Ohio Tech C.	Newark, OH 43055	Office for Disability Services	740-366-9441
Clark St. C.C.	Springfield, OH 45505	Office of Student Services	937-328-6084
Cleveland Institute of Art	Cleveland, OH 44106	Office of Academic Services	216-421-7462
Cleveland Institute of Music	Cleveland, OH 44106	Office of Admissions	216-795-3107
Cleveland St. U.	Cleveland, OH 44115-2214	Office of Disability Services	216-687-2015
Columbus C. of Art and Design	Columbis, OH 43215	Disability Services	614-222-4004
Columbus St. C.C.	Columbus, OH 43216	Disability Services	614-227-2629
Cuyahoga C.C. Western	Parma, OH 44130	Access Office for Accommodation	216-987-5077
Denison U.	Granville, OH 43023	Office of Academic Support	740-587-6666
Franciscan U. of Seubenville	Stubenville, OH 43952-1763	Disability Services	740-284-5358
Franklin U.	Columbus, OH 43215-5399	Student Services	614-797-4700
Heidelburg C.	Tiffin, OH 44883	Learning Center	419-448-2301
Hiram C.	Hiram, OH 44234	Disability Services	330-569-5652
Hocking C.	Nelsonville, OH 45764	Office of Disability Services	740-753-3591
John Carroll U.	University Heights, OH 44118	Services for Students with Disabilities	216-397-4967
Kent St. U.- Kent Campus	Kent, OH 44242-0001	Student Accessibility Services	330 672 3391
Kenyon C.	Gambier, OH 43022-9623	Student Accessibility Support Services	7404275453

Lake Erie C.	Painesville, OH 44077-3389	Disability Coordination	4403757426
Lakeland C.C.	Kirtland, OH 44095	Services for Students with Disabilities	440-525-7245
Lorain County C.C.	Elyria, OH 44035	Office for Special Needs Services	440-366-4124
Lourdes C.	Sylvania, OH 43560	Disability Services	419-824-3834
Malone U.	Canton, OH 44709	Student Retention	330-471-8359
Marietta C.	Marietta, OH 45750	Counseling Center	740-376-4477
Miami U.	Oxford, OH 45056	Office of Disability Resources	513-529-1541
Miami U.—Hamilton	Hamilton, OH 45011	Special Services	513-785-3211
Mount St. Joseph U.	Cincinnati, OH 45233	Disability Services Office	513-244-4524
Mount Vernon Nazarene U.	Mount Vernon, OH 43050	Accessibility Services	740-392-6868
Mt. Union C.	Alliance, OH 44601	Disability Support Services	330-823-7372
Mt. Vernon Nazarene U.	Mount Vernon, OH 43050	Academic Support Services	740-392-6868
Muskingum C.	New Concord, OH 43762	PLUS Program	740-826-8280
North Central St. C.	Mansfield, OH 44901	Disability Services	419-755-4727
Notre Dame C. of Ohio	Cleveland, OH 44121	Disability Services	216-373-5185
Oberlin C.	Oberlin, OH 44074	Off. of Serv. for Students w/ Disab.	440-775-5588
Ohio Dominican C.	Coumbus, OH 42319	Academic Development	614-251-4233
Ohio Dominican U.	Coumbus, OH 42319-2099	Disability Servics	(614) 251-4233
Ohio Northern U.	Ada, OH 45810	Disability Resources	419-772-2534
Ohio St. U.	Marion, OH 43302	Learning Disabilities Services	614-292-3307
Ohio St. U.—Columbus	Columbus, OH 43210-1200	Office for Disability Services	614-292-3307
Ohio St. U.—Newark	Newark, OH 43055	Learning Assistance Services	740-366-9441
Ohio U.—Athens	Athens, OH 45701	Office for Institutional Equity	740-593-2620
Ohio Wesleyan U.	Delaware, OH 43015	Academic Advising	740-368-3105
Otterbein C.	Westerville, OH 43081	Academic Support Center	614-823-1618
Owens C.C.	Toledo, OH 43699	Disability Resource Services	419-661-7010
Raymond Walters C.	Cincinnati, OH 45236	Disability Services	513-729-8625
Shawnee St. U.	Portsmouth, OH 45662	Student Succes Center	740-351-3276
Sinclair C.C.	Dayton, OH 45402	Disability Services	937-512-5337
Terra St. C.C.	Fremont, OH 43420	Disability Services	419-559-2208
The Cleveland Institute of Art	Cleveland, OH 44106	Learning Support Services	2164217462
The Ohio St. U. at Mansfield	Mansfield, OH 44906	NR	NR
The Ohio St. U. at Marion	Marion, OH 43302	NR	NR

U. of Akron	Akron, OH 44325-2001	Services for Students with Disabilities	330-972-7928
U. of Cincinnati	Cincinnati, OH 45221-0091	Disability Services	513-556-6823
U. of Dayton	Dayton, OH 45469-1310	Office of Learning Resources	937-229-2066
U. of Findlay	Findlay, OH 45840	Supporting Skills System	419-422-8313
U. of Rio Grande	Rio Grande, OH 45774	Office of Accessibility	740-245-7439
U. of Toledo	Toledo, OH 43606-3390	Office of Accessibility	419-530-4981
Union Institute U.	Cincinnati, OH 45206	Disability Services	802-828-8740
Urbana U.	Urbana, OH 43078	Disability Services	937-484-1286
Ursuline C.	Pepper Pike, OH 44124-4398	U.R.S.A. Disabilities Services	440-646-8123
Walsh U.	North Canton, OH 44720-3396	Office of Accessibility Services	330-490-7529
Washington St. C.C.	Marietta, OH 45750	Student Development	740-374-8716
Whittenberg U.	Springfield, OH 45501	Academic Services	937-327-7924
Wilmington C.	Wilmington, OH 45177	Disability Services	937-382-6661
Wittenberg U.	Springfield, OH 45501	Disability Services	937-327-7958
Wright St. U.	Dayton, OH 45435	Office of Disability Services	937-775-5680
Xavier U.	Cincinnati, OH 45207-2612	Learning Assistance Center	513-745-3214
Xavier U. (OH)	Cincinnati, OH 45207-5311	Disability Services, Learning Assistance Center	513-745-3280
Youngstown St. U.	Youngstown, OH 44555	CSP Disability Services	330 941-1238

OKLAHOMA

Cameron U.	Lawton, OK 73505	Disability Services	580-581-2209
East Central U.	Ada, OK 74820	Disability Services	580-559-5677
Northeastern St. U.	Tahlequah, OK 74464	Student Affairs	918-456-5511 ext. 2120
Oklahoma Baptist U.	Shawnee, OK 74804	Student Services	405-878-2420
Oklahoma Christian U.	Oklahoma City, OK 73136-1100	Student Life	405-425-5907
Oklahoma City C.C.	Oklahoma City, OK 73159	Services to Students with Disabilities	405-682-7520
Oklahoma City U.	Oklahoma City, OK 73106	Campus Disability Services	4052085895
Oklahoma St. U.	Stillwater, OK 74078	Student Disability Services	NR
Oklahoma Wesleyan U.	Bartlesville, OK 74006	Disability Support Services	918.335.6200
Oral Roberts U.	Tulsa, OK 74171	Student Support Services	918-495-7018
Southeastern Oklahoma St. U.	Durant, OK 74701-0609	Student Support Services	580-745-2394
Southern Nazarene U.	Bethany, OK 73008	Student Support Services	405-491-6694
St. Gregory's U.	Shawnee, OK 74804	Disability Support Services	405-878-5310

Tulsa Junior C.	Tulsa, OK 74119	Disabled Student Resource Center	918-595-7115
U. of Central Oklahoma	Edmond, OK 73034	Disability Support Services	405-974-2516
U. of Oklahoma	Norman, OK 73019	Office of Disability Services	405-325-3852
The U. of Tulsa	Tulsa, OK 74104	Center for Student Academic Support	918-631-2315

OREGON

Blue Mountain C.C.	Pendelton, OR 97801	Services for Students with Disabilities	541-278-5934
Chemeketa C.C.	Salem, OR 97309	Office for Students with Disabilities	503-399-5192
Corban C.	Salem, OR 97301	Career and Academic Services	503-375-7012
Eastern Oregon U.	La Grande, OR 97850	Learning Center	541-962-3081
George Fox U.	Newberg, OR 97132	Disability Services	503-554-2314
Lane C.C.	Eugene, OR 97405	Disability Resources	541-463-3010
Lewis & Clark C.	Portland, OR 97219-7899	Student Support Services	503-768-7192
Linfield C.	McMinnville, OR 97128-6894	Learning Support Services	503-413-8219
Linn-Benton C.C.	Albany, OR 97321	Disability Services	541-917-4789
Marylhurst U.	Marylhurst, OR 97036-0261	Disability Services	503-636-8141 ext. 3344
Mt. Hood C.C.	Gresham, OR 97030	Disability Services	503-491-6923
Multnomah U.	Portland, OR 97220-5898	Academic Support Center	503-251-6501
Northwest Christian C.	Eugene, OR 97401	Career Development & Service Learning	541-684-7345
Oregon Institute of Tech	Klamath Falls, OR 97601	Diasability Services	541-885-1129
Oregon St. U.	Corvallis, OR 97331-2106	Disability Access Services	541-737-4098
Pacific U.	Forest Grove, OR 97116	Learning Support Services	503-352-2107
Portland St. U.	Portland, OR 97207	Disability Resource Center	503-725-4150
Rogue C.C.	Grants Pass, OR 97527	Disability Services	541-956-7337
Southern Oregon U.	Ashland, OR 97520-5032	Disability Resources	5415526213
U. of Oregon	Eugene, OR 97403-1217	Accessible Education Center	541-346-1155
U. of Portland	Portland, OR 97203-7147	Accessible Education Services	NR
Umpqua C.C.	Roseburg, OR 97470	Disability Services	541-440-7655
Warner Pacific C.	Portland, OR 97215	Career Services	503-517-1010
Western Oregon U.	Monmouth, OR 97361	Office of Disability Services	503-838-8250
Willamette U.	Salem, OR 97301	Disability Services	503-370-6471

PENNSYLVANIA

Albright C.	Reading, PA 19612	Learning Center - Academic Support	610-921-7662
Allegheny C.	Meadville, PA 16335	NR	NR
Alvernia U.	Reading, PA 19607-1799	Disabilities Services Office	610-568-1499
Arcadia U.	Glenside, PA 19038-3295	Learning Resource Network	215-572-4033
Bloomsburg U. of Pennsylvania	Bloomsburg, PA 17815	Accommodative Services	570-389-4491
Bryn Athyn C. of the New Church	Bryn Athyn, PA 19009	NR	267-502-2551
Bryn Mawr C.	Bryn Mawr, PA 19010-2859	Access Services	610-526-7351
Bucknell U.	Lewisburg, PA 17837	Office of Accessability Resources	570-577-1188
Bucks County C.C.	Newton, PA 18940	DisAbility Services	215-968-8182
C.C. of Allegheny County	Pittsburgh, PA 15212	Disability Services	412-237-4535
C.C. of Philadelphia	Philadelphia, PA 19130	Center on Disability	215-751-8050
Cabrini C.	Randor, PA 19087	Disability Resource Center	610-902-8572
California U. of Pennsylvania	California, PA 15419	Office for Students with Disabilities	724-938-5781
Carnegie Mellon U.	Pittsburgh, PA 15213	NR	412-268-1192
CCAC North	Pittsburgh, PA 15237	Disability Services	412-369-3649
Cedar Crest C.	Allentown, PA 18104	Disability and Accessibility Services	610-606-4673
Chatham U.	Pittsburgh, PA 15232	PACE Center	412-365-1611
Chestnut Hill C.	Philadelphia, PA 19118-2693	Disability Resource Center	215.753.3665
Cheyney U. of PA	Cheyney, PA 19319	Office of Social Equity	610-399-2430
Clarion U. of Pennsylvania	Clarion, PA 16214	Disability Support Services	814-393-2095
De Sales U.	Center Valley, PA 18034	Disability Services	610-282-1100, 1453
Delaware Valley C.	Doylestown, PA 18901	Learning Support Services	215-489-2490
DeSales U.	Center Valley, PA 18034	Academic Resource Center	610-282-1100 ext. 1455
Drexel U.	Philadelphia, PA 19104	Office of Disability Resources	215-895-1401
Duquesne U.	Pittsburgh, PA 15282	Special Services	412 396 6658
East Stroudsburg U. of PA	East Stroudsburg, PA 18301-2999	Office of Disability Services	570-422-3954
Eastern U.	St. Davids, PA 19087-3696	Cushing Center for Counseling	610-341-5837
Edinboro U. of Pennsylvania	Edinboro, PA 16444	Office for Students with Disabilities	814-732-2462
Elizabethtown C.	Elizabethtown, PA 17022-2298	Disability Services	717-361-1227
Franklin and Marshall C.	Lancaster, PA 17604-3003	Disability Services	7172913989
Gannon U.	Erie, PA 16541	Office of Disability Services	814-871-5522
Geneva C.	Beaver Falls, PA 15010	ACCESS Center	724-847-5566

Gettysburg C.	Gettysburg, PA 17325	Academic Advising	717-337-6579
Grove City College	Grove City, PA 16127	Services for Disabilities	724-458-2000
Gwynedd-Mercy U.	Gwyned Valley, PA 19437-0901	Disability Support Services	215-646-7300 ext. 427
Harcum Jr C.	Bryn Mawr, PA 19010	Disability Support Services	610-526-6036
Haverford C.	Haverford, PA 19041	Access and Disabilities Services	610-896-1324
Holy Family U.	Philadephia, PA 19114-2009	Office of Disability Services	267-341-3213
Immaculata U.	Immaculata, PA 19345-0702	Academic Success Services	610-647-4400 ext. 3900
Indiana U. of Penn	Indiana, PA 15705	Advising and Testing Center	724-357-4067
Juniata C.	Huntingdon, PA 16652	Academic Support	814-641-3152
King's C.	Wilkes-Baree, PA 18711	Academic Support	570-208-5841
King's C. (PA)	Wilkes-Barre, PA 18711	Academic Skills Center	570-208-5800
Kutztown U. of Pennsylvania	Kutztown, PA 19530-0730	Disability Services Office	610-683-4108
Lafayette C.	Easton, PA 18042	Academic Tutoring and Training Information Center (ATTIC)	610 330-5098
LaRoche C.	Pittsburgh, PA 15327	Disability Services	412-536-1177
LaSalle U.	Philadelphia, PA 19141-1199	Disability Services	215-951-1014
Lebanon Valley College	Annville, PA 17003-0501	Office of Disability Services	717-867-6028
Lehigh U.	Bethlehem, PA 18015	Academic Support Services	610-758-4152
Lock Haven U. of Pennsylvania	Lock Haven, PA 17745	Disability Services	570-484-2926
Luzerne County C.C.	Naanticoke, PA 18634	Office of Accessibility Services	570-740-0397
Lycoming C.	Williamsport, PA 17701	Office of Disability Support Services	570-321-4050
Mansfield U. of PA	Mansfield, PA 16933	Center of Services for Students with Disabilities	570-662-4691
Marywood U.	Scranton, PA 18509-1598	Disability Services	570-348-6211 ext. 2335
Mercyhurst U.	Erie, PA 16546	Learning Differences Program	814-824-3048
Messiah C.	Mechanicsburg, PA 17055	Office of Disability Services	717-796-5382
Millersville U. of Pennsylvania	Millersville, PA 17551-0302	Office of Learning Services	717-871-5554
Misericordia U.	Dallas, PA 18612	Alternative Learning Project	570-674-6205
Montgomery County C.C.	Blue Bell, PA 19422	Disability Service Center	215-641-6575
Moore C. of Art & Design	Philadelphia, PA 19103	Educational Support Services	215-965-4061
Moravian C.	Bethlehem, PA 18018	Disability Support Services	6108611401
Mount Aloysius C.	Cresson, PA 16630	Counseling & Disability Services	814-886-6336
Muhlenberg C.	Allentown, PA 18104-5596	Office of Disability Services	484-664-3825
Neumann C.	Aston, PA 19014-1298	Disability Services	610-361-5471
Neumann U.	Aston, PA 19014	ARC - Disabilities Services Office	610-361-5471

Northampton C.C.	Bethlehem, PA 18017	Disability Services	610-861-5342
Peirce C.	Philadelphia, PA 19102	Center for Academic Excellence	215-670-9251
Penn St. U.—Brandywine	Media, PA 19063-5596	Disability Services	610-892-1461
Penn St. U.—Erie, The Behrend C.	Erie, PA 16563	Disabilities & Learning Differences	814-898-7101
Penn St. U.—Lehigh Valley	Fogelsville, PA 18051-9999	Disability Services	610-285-5124
Penn St. U.—Mont Alto	Mont Alto, PA 17237-9703	Office of Disability Services	814-863-1807
Penn St. U.—Schuylkill	Schuylkill Haven, PA 17972-2208	Disability Services	570-385-6127
Penn St. U. Park	University Park, PA 16802	Student Disability Resources	814-863-1807
Pennsylvania C. of Tech	Williamsport, PA 17701	Disability Services	570-320-5225
Pennsylvania St. U.—U. Park	Univ. Park, PA 16802-3000	Office for Disability Services	814-863-1807
Philadelphia Biblical U.	Langhorne, PA 19047-2990	Disability Services	215-702-4270
Philadelphia U.	Philadelphia, PA 19144	Disability Service Office	215-951-6830
Point Park U.	Pittsburg, PA 15222	Academic Success	412-392-3870
Robert Morris U.	Moon Township, PA 15108	Center For Student Success	412-397-4342
Rosemont C.	Rosemont, PA 19010	Troy Chiddick	610 527-0200
Saint Francis U. PA)	Loretto, PA 15940	Student Success Services	814-472-3176
Saint Joseph's U. PA)	Philadelphia, PA 19131	Office of Student Educational Support Services	610-660-1081
Saint Vincent C. PA)	Latrobe, PA 15650-2690	Disability Support Services	724-805-2371
Seton Hill University	Greensburg, PA 15601	Disability Services	724-838-4295
Shippensburg U. of PA	Shippensburg, PA 17257-2299	Office of Disability Services	717-477-1364
Slippery Rock U. of PA	Slippery Rock, PA 16057	Office for Students with Disabilities	724-738-2203
Susquehanna U.	Selinsgrove, PA 17870	Office of Disability Services	570-372-4340
Swarthmore C.	Swarthmore, PA 19081	Student Disability Services	610-690-5014
Temple U.	Philadelphia, PA 19122-6096	Disability Resources and Services	215-204-1280
The U. of Scranton	Scranton, PA 18510	Center for Teaching & Learning Excellence (CTLE)	570-941-4038
Thiel C.	Greenville, PA 16125	Office of Disability Services	724-589-2125
Thomas Jefferson U., Col. of Health	Philadelphia, PA 19107	Student Life	215-503-8189
U. of Arts, The	Philadelphia, PA 19102	Educational Access Services	215-717-6616
U. of Pennsylvania	Philadelphia, PA 19104	Student Disability Services	215-573-9235
U. of Pittsburgh at Bradford	Bradford, PA 16701	Disability Resources and Services	814-362-7609
U. of Pittsburg-Greensburg	Greensburg, PA 15601	Disability Resources	724-836-7098
U. of Pittsburgh at Johnstown	Johnstown, PA 15904	Disability Services	814-269-7119
U. of Pittsburgh–Pittsburgh Campus	Pittsburgh, PA 15260	Disability Resources and Services	412-648-7890

U. of Scranton	Scranton, PA 18510-4699	Center for Teaching & Learning Excellence	570-941-4018
Ursinus C.	Collegeville, PA 19426	Center for Academic Support	610-409-3400
Villanova U.	Villanova, PA 19085	Disability Services	610-519-4095
Washington & Jefferson C.	Washington, PA 15301	NR	724-223-6008
West Chester U. of PA	West Chester, PA 19383	Office of Services for students with Disabilities	610-436-2564
Westminster C. (PA)	New Wilmington, PA 16172	Disability Resources Office	724-946-7192
Widener U.	Chester, PA 19013-5792	Disability Services	610-499-1266
Wilkes U.	Wilkes-Barre, PA 18766	Disability Support Services	(570) 408-4150
Wilson College	Chambersburg, PA 17201	Disability Services	717-264-4141 x3349
York C. of PA	York, PA 17405-7199	Disability Support Services	717-815-1785
PUERTO RICO			
Polytechnic U. of Puerto Rico	Hato Rey, PR 00919-2017	Counseling Office	787.622.8000 x.478
Pontifical Catholic U. of Puerto Rico	Ponce, PR 00717-0777	Disability Support Services	1.800.961.7696
U. of Puerto Rico—Humacao	Humacao, PR 00791-4300	SERPI	787-850-9383, ext. 9501 or 9589
U. of Puerto Rico—Mayaguez	Mayaguez, PR 00631-9000	Students with Disabilities	787-832-4040
RHODE ISLAND			
Brown U.	Providence, RI 2912	Student and Employee Accessibility Services	401-863-9588
Bryant U.	Smithfield, RI 02917	Disability Services	401-232-6746
C.C. of Rhode Island	Warwick, RI 02856	Disability Services for Students	401-825-2164
Johnson & Wales	Providence, RI 02903	Center for Academic Support	401-598-4689
Providence C.	Providence, RI 2918	Academic Support Services	NR
Rhode Island College	Providence, RI 02908	Disability Services Center	401-456-2776
Rhode Island School of Design	Providence, RI 2903	Disability Support Services	401-709-8469
Roger Williams U.	Bristol, RI 02809	Student Accessibility Services	401-254-3841
Salve Regina U.	Newport, RI 02840-4192	DIsability Services	(401) 341-2226
U. of Rhode Island	Kingston, RI 2881	Disability Services for Students	401-874-2098
SOUTH CAROLINA			
C. of Charleston	Charleston, SC 29424	Center for Disability Services	843-953-1431
The Citadel, The Military C. of South Carolina	Charleston, SC 29409	The Academic Support Center	843-953-1820
Clemson U.	Clemson, SC 29634-5124	Student Disability Services	8646566848
Coastal Carolina U.	Conway, SC 29528-6054	Accessibility and Disability Services	843-349-2503
Coker C.	Hartsville, SC 29550	Learning Support Services	843-383-8021

Columbia International U.	Columbia, SC 29203	Academic Success Services	803-807-5611
Converse C.	Spartanburg, SC 29302	Disability Services	864-577-2028
Erskine C.	Due West, SC 29639	Student Services	864-379-8701
Francis Marion U.	Florence, SC 295001	Counseling & Testing	843-661-1840
Furman U.	Greenville, SC 29613	Disability Services	864-294-2320
Lander U.	Greenwood, SC 29649-2099	Academic Success Center	864-388-8460
Limestone C.	Gaffney, SC 29340	Program for Alternative Learning Styles PALS)	864-488-8377
Newberry C.	Newberry, SC 29108	Academic, Disability, & International Services	803-321-5187
North Greenville C.	Tigerville, SC 29688	Learning Disability Liaison Office	800.468.6642
Presbyterian C.	Clinton, SC 29325	Office of Provost	800-476-7272 ext. 8234
Southern Wesleyan U.	Central, SC 29630-1020	Services to Students with Disabilities	864-644-5133
U. of South Carolina Aiken	Aiken, SC 29801	Disability Services	803-643-6815
USC—Columbia	Columbia, SC 29208	Office of Student Disability Services	803-777-6142
USC—Lancaster	Lancaster, SC 29721	Academic Success Center	803-313-7113
USC—Spartanburg	Spartanburg, SC 29303	Disability Services	864-503-5199
Winthrop U.	Rock Hill, SC 29733	Office of Disability Services	803-323-3290 x6174
Wofford C.	Spartanburg, SC 29303-3663	Health Services and Counseling	864-597-4371
York Tech C.	Clover, SC 29730	Disability Services—Special Resources Office	803-325-2894

SOUTH DAKOTA

Augustana U.	Sioux Falls, SD 57197	NR	605-274-4127
Black Hills St. U.	Spearfish, SD 57799	Student Assistant Center	605-642-6099
Dakota St. U.	Madison, SD 57042	Disability Services Office	605-256-5121
Dakota Wesleyan U.	Mitchell, SD 57301-4398	Disability Services	605-995-5121
Mount Marty C.	Yankton, SD 57078	Disability Services	605-668-1518
National American U.	Rapid City, SD 57709	Learner Services	605-721-5328
Northern St. U.	Aberdeen, SD 57401	Office of Disability Services	605-626-2371
South Dakota Scl of Mines & Tech.	Rapid City, SD 57701	Disability Services	605-394-1924
South Dakota St. U.	Brookings, SD 57007-0649	Disability Services	605-688-4504
U. of Sioux Falls	Sioux Falls, SD 57105	Learning Accessibility Services	605-331-6648
U. of South Dakota—Vermillion	Vermillion, SD 57069	Disability Services	605-677-6389

TENNESSEE

Austin Peay St. U.	Clarksville, TN 37044	Office of Disability Services	931-221-6230
Chattanooga St. Tech C.C.	Chattanooga, TN 37406	Disability Support Services	423-697-4404
Christian Brothers U.	Memphis, TN 38104	Student Disability Services	901-321-3536
Cleveland St. CC.	Clevland, TN 37320	Disabilities ACCESS Center	423-478-6217
Cumberland U.	Lebanon, TN 37087-3408	Disability Services	615-547-1397
East Tennessee St. U.	Johnson City, TN 37614	Disability Services (423) 439-5829	
Lee U.	Cleveland, TN 37320-3450	Academic Support Office	423-614-8181
Lipscomb U.	Nashville, TN 37204-3951	Disability Services	615-966-6301
Martin Methodist C.	Pulaski, TN 38472	Student Resources Center	931-363-9895
Maryville C.	Maryville, TN 37804-5907	Disability Services	865-981-8124
Middle Tennessee St. U.	Murfreesboro, TN 37132	Disabled Student Services	615-898-2783
Milligan C.	Milligan College, TN 37682	Disability Services	423-461-8981
Pellissippi St. C. C.	Knoxville, TN 37933	Disability Services	865-539-7091
Rhodes C.	Memphis, TN 38112	Office of Student Disability Services	901-843-3885
Southern Adventist U.	Collegeedale, TN 37315	Disability Support Services	423-236-2574
Tennessee St. U.	Nashville, TN 37209-1561	Disability Services	615-963-7400
Tennessee Tech U.	Cookeville, TN 38505	Disability Services	931-372-6119
Tennessee Wesleyan C.	Athens, TN 37371-0040	Academic Success Center	423-746-5275
Trevecca Nazarene U.	Nashville, TN 37210	Disability Services	615-248-1346
Tusculum C.	Greenville, Tn 37743	Disability Services	423-636-7300 ext. 5154
U. of Memphis	Memphis, TN 38152-6687	Disability Resources for Students	901-587-7195
U. of Memphis—Lambuth	Jackson, TN 38301	Student Academic Support	731-425-2500
U. of Tennessee-Chattanooga	Chattanooga, TN 37403	Disability Resource Center	423-425-4006
U. of Tennessee at Martin	Martin, TN 38238	Disabilities Services Office	731-881-7719
U. of Tennessee, Knoxville	Knoxville, TN 37996-0230	Office of Disability Services	865-974-6087
Union U.	Jackson, TN 38305	Office of Disability Services	731-661-6520
Vanderbilt U.	Nashville, TN 37203-1700	EAD Services	615-322-4705
Victory U.	Memphis, TN 38111-1375	Student Success Center	901-320-9753

TEXAS

Abilene Christian U.	Abilene, TX 79699	Alpha Scholars Program	325-674-2667
Amarillo C.	Amarillo, TX 79178	disAbility Services	806-345-5639

Angelo St. U.	San Angelo, TX 76909	Disability Services	325-942-2047
Austin C.C.	Cedar Park, TX 78613	Students Services	512-223-2126
Baylor U.	Waco, TX 76798	Access & Learning Accommodations	254-710-3605
Central Texas C.	Killeen, TX 76540	Disability Support	254-526-1863
Dallas Baptist U.	Dallas, TX 75211-9299	Disabled Student Services	214-333-5101
East Texas Baptist U.	Marshall, TX 75670	Academic Success & Graduate	903-923-2075
El Paso C.C.	El Paso, TX 79998	Center for Students with Disabilities	915-831-2426
Hardin-Simmons U.	Abilene, TX 79698	Office for Students with Disabilties	325-670-5842
Houston Baptist U.	Houston, TX 77074	Disability Services	2816493647
Howard Payne U.	Brownwood, TX 76801	The Collegium	325-649-8020
Jarvis Christian C.	Hawkins, TX 75765-1470	Academic Affairs	903-730-4890
Lamar St. College.—Orange	Orange, TX 77630	Disability Support Services	409-882-3370
Lamar U.	Beaumont, TX 77710	Disability Resource Center	409-880-8347
Laredo C.C.	Laredo, TX 78040	Special Service Center	956-721-5137
Le Tourneau U.	Longview, TX 75607-7001	Student Support Services	903-233-4460
Lee C.	Baytown, TX 77522	Services for Students with Disabilities	281-425-6384
Lubbock Christian U.	Lubbock, TX 79407	Disability Services	806-720-7156
McMurry U.	Abilene, TX 79697	Disability Services	325.793.4881
Midwestern St. U.	Wichita Falls, TX 76308-2099	Disability Services	940-397-4140
Northwood U. Texas Campus	Cedar Hill, TX 75104	Academic Office	972-293-5480
Our Lady of the Lake U.	San Antonio, TX 78207-4689	Student Success Center	210-431-4010
Prairie View A&M U.	Prairie View, TX 77446	Diagnostic Testing & Disability Services	936-261-3585
Rice U.	Houston, TX 77251-1892	Disability Support Services	713-348-5841
Saint Edward's U.	Austin, TX 78704	Academic Planning & Support Services	512-448-8557
Sam Houston St. U.	Huntsville, TX 77341	Service for Student with Disabilities	936-294-1828
Schreiner U.	Kerrville, TX 78028-5697	Learning Support Services	830-792-7258
Southern Methodist U.	Dallas, TX 75275-0181	Disability Accommodations & Success Strategies	214-768-1470
Southwestern U.	Georgetown, TX 78627-0770	Center for Academic Success & Records	512-863-1744
St. Edward's U.	Austin, TX 78704-6489	Student Disability Services	512-233-1659
St. Mary's U.	San Antonio, TX 78228-8503	Disability Support Services	210-436-6706
Stephen F. Austin St. U.	Nonacogdoches, TX 75962	Disability Services	936-468-3004
Texas A&M U.–C. Station	College Station, TX 77843-3014	Disability Services	979-845-1637
Texas A&M U.—C. Station	College Station, TX 77843	Disability Services	979-845-1637

Texas A&M U.—Corpus Christi	Corpus Christi, TX 78412-5503	Disability Services	361-825-5816
Texas A&M U.—Galveston	Galveston, TX 77553-1675	Counseling Center	409-740-4736
Texas A&M U.—Kingsville	Kingsville, TX 78363	Disability Resource Center	361-593-3024
Texas Christian U.	Fort Worth, TX 76129	Center for Academic Services-Disabilities Services	817-257-6567
Texas Lutheran U.	Seguin, TX 78156-5999	Disability Support Services	830-372-8009
Texas St. U.	San Marcos, TX 78666	Office of Disability Services	512.245.3451
Texas Tech U.	Lubbock, TX 79409-5005	Student Disability Services	806-742-2405
Texas Wesleyan U.	Fort Worth, TX 76105-1536	Disability Services	817-531-4468
Texas Woman's U.	Denton, TX 76204-5679	Disability Support Services	940-898-3835
Trinity U.	San Antonio, TX 78212-7200	Student Accessibility Services	210-999-7411
Tyler Jr. C.	Tyler, TX 75711	Support Services	903-510-2389
U of the Incarnate World	San Antonio, TX 78209-6397	Student Disability Services	210-829-3997
U. of Houston	Houston, TX 77204-2023	Center for Students with Disabilities	713-743-5400
U. of Houston—Downtown	Houston, TX 77002-1001	Office of Disability Services	713-226-5227
U. of Mary Hardin-Baylor	Belton, TX 76513	Disability Support Services	254-295-4696
U. of North Texas	Denton, TX 76203-5358	Office of Disability Accommodations	940-565-4323
U. of Texas—Arlington	Arlington, TX 76019-0111	Office for Students with Disabilities	817-272-3364
U. of Texas at Austin	Austin, TX 78713-8058	Services for Students with Disabilities	512-471-6259
U. of Texas at Dallas	Richardson, TX 75080-3021	Student AccessAbility	972-883-2098
U. of Texas—Pan American	Edinburg, TX 78539	Disability Services	956-665-7005
U. of Texas—Permian Basin	Odessa, TX 79762-0001	PASS Office	432-552-2630
U. of Texas at San Antonio	San Antonio, TX 78249-0617	Student Disability Services	NR
U. of Texas—Tyler	Tyler, TX 75799	Student Accessibility & Resources	903-566-7079
University of Texas—El Paso	El Paso, TX 79968	Disabled Student Services	915-747-5148
West Texas A&M U.	Canyon, TX 79016	Student Disability Services	806-651-2335
Wiley C.	Marshall, TX 75670	Academic Affairs	903-923-2474
UTAH			
Brigham Young U. UT)	Provo, UT 84602-1110	University Accessibility Center	801-422-2767
C. of Eastern Utah	Price, UT 84501	Disability Resource Center	435-613-5483
Snow C.	Ephraim, UT 84627	Academic Support Services	435-283-7321
Southern Utah U.	Cedar City, UT 84720	Disability Support Center	4358658022
U. of Utah	Salt Lake City, UT 84112	Center for Disability Services	801-581-5020

Utah St. U.	Logan, UT 84322-0160	Disability Resource Center	435-797-2444
Utah Valley St. College	Orem, UT 84058	Accessibility Services	801-863-8747
Weber St. U.	Ogden, UT 84408-1103	Student Services	801-626-6413
VERMONT			
Bennington C.	Bennington, VT 05701	Dean of Academic Services	802-442-5401
Burlington C.	Burlington, VT 05401	Student Support Services	802-862-9616 ext. 124
C. of St. Joseph	Rutland, VT 05701	Learning Center for Academic Support	802-773-5900 ext. 3239
Castleton St. C.	Castleton, VT 05735	Disability Services	802-468-1321
Champlain C.	Burlington, VT 05402-0670	Accommodation Services	802-651-5961
Green Mountain C.	Poultney, VT 05764-1199	NR	802-287-2180
Johnson St. C.	Johnson, VT 05656	Academic Support Services	802-635-1259
Landmark C.	Putney, VT 05346-0820	NR	NR
Lyndon St. C.	Lyndonville, VT 05851	Disability Services	802-626-6210
Marlboro C.	Marlboro, VT 05344	Disability Services	802-258-9335
Middlebury C.	Middlebury, VT 05753-6002	Student Accessibility Services	802-443-5936
New England Culinary School	Montpelier, VT 05602	Learning Services	802-225-3327
Norwich U.	Northfield, VT 05663	Academic Achievement Center	802-485-2130
Saint Michael's C.	Colchester, VT 05439	Academic Support Services	802-654-2818
Saint Michael's C.	Colchester, VT 5439	Office of Accessibility Services	802-654-2467
Southern Vermont C.	Bennington, VT 05201	Learning Differences Support Program	802-447-6360
U. of Vermont	Burlington, VT 05401	ACCESS	802-656-7753
Vermont Technical C.	Randolph Center, VT 05061	Services for Students with Disabilities	802-728-1278
VIRGINIA			
Averett U.	Danville, VA 24541	Disability Services	434 791-5754
Blue Ridge C.C.	Weyers Cave, VA 24486	Disability Services	540-453-2298
Bluefield C.	Bluefield, VA 24605	ACE Program	276-326-4606
Bridgewater C.	Bridgewater, VA 22812-1599	Academic Support Services	540-828-5370
C. of William & Mary, The	Williamsburg, VA 23187-8795	Disability Services	757-221-2510
C. of William and Mary	Williamsburg, VA 23187-8795	Student Accessibility Services	757-221-2509
Christopher Newport U.	Newport News, VA 23606	Dean of Students Office	757-594-7505

Eastern Mennonite U.	Harrisonburg, VA 22801	Disability Support Services	540-432-4233
Emory & Henry C.	Emory, VA 24327	Academic Support Services	276-944-6144
Ferrum C.	Ferrum, VA 24088	Accessibility Services	540-365-4262
George Mason U.	Fairfax, VA 22030-4444	Office of Disability Services	703-993-2474
Hampden-Sydney C.	Hampden-Sydney, VA 23943-0667	Office of Academic Success	434-223-6188
Hampton U.	Hampton, VA 23668	University Testing, Office of Compliance and Disability Services	757-727-5493
Hollins U.	Roanoke, VA 24020	Academic Affairs	540-362-6491
James Madison U.	Harrisonburg, VA 22807	Office of Disability Services	540-568-6705
Liberty U.	Lynchburg, VA 24502	Office of Disability Academic Support	434-582-2159
Longwood U.	Farmville, VA 23909	Office of Disability Resources	434-395-2391
Lynchburg C.	Lynchburg, VA 24501	Disability Services	434.544.8687
Mary Baldwin C.	Staunton, VA 24401	Learning Skills Center	540-887-7250
Marymount U.	Arlington, VA 22207	Student Access Services	703-526-6925
New River C.C.	Dublin, VA 24060	Center for Disability Services	540-674-3600 ext. 3619
Old Dominion U.	Norfolk, VA 23529-0050	Office of Educational Accessibility	757-683-4655
Patrick Henry C.C.	Martinsville, VA 24115	Student Support Services	276-656-0257
Radford U.	Radford, VA 24142	Disability Resource Office	540-831-6350
Randolph C.	Lynchburg, VA 24503-1555	Office of Disability Services	434-947-8132
Randolph-Macon C.	Ashland, VA 23005	Disability Support Services	804-752-7343
Regent U.	Virginia Beach, VA 23464	Disability Services	757-352-4894
Roanoke C.	Salem, VA 24153-3794	Disability Support Services	540-375-2247
Saint Paul's C.	Lawrenceville, VA 23868	Disability Services	651.846.1547
Shenandoah U.	Winchester, VA 22601-5195	Turning Point Program	540.665.4928
Sweet Briar C.	Sweet Briar, VA 24595	Academic Resource Center	434-381-6100 x6278
Thomas Nelson C.C.	Hampton, VA 23670	Disabled Student Services	757-825-2833
Tidewater C.C.	Portsmouth, VA 23703	Office of Educational Accessibility	757-822-2200
U. of Mary Washington	Fredericksburg, VA 22401	Office of Disability Resources	540-654-1266
U. of Richmond	Richmond, VA 23173	Disability Services	804-289-8119
U. of Virginia	Charlottesville, VA 22906	Student Disability Access Center	434-243-5180
U. of Virginia—College at Wise	Wise, VA 24293	Disability Support Services	276-328-0265
Virginia Commonwealth U.	Richmond, VA 23284	Disability Support Services	804-828-2144
Virginia Intermont College	Bristol, VA 24201-4298	Student Support Services	276-466-7906
Virginia Military Institute	Lexington, VA 24450-0304	Disability Services	540-464-7667

Virginia St. U.	Petersburg, VA 23806	Students with Disabilities Program	804-524-5061
Virginia Tech	Blacksburg, VA 24061	Services for Students with Disabilities	540-231-3788
Virginia Union U.	Richmond, VA 23220	Center for Student Success & Retention	804-342-3885
Virginia Wesleyan C.	Norfolk, VA 23502-5599	Learning Center	757-455-5704
Virginia Western Comm C.	Roanoke, VA 24038	Reach Student Support Services	540-857-7286
Washington and Lee U.	Lexington, VA 24450-0303	Student Academic Support	540-458-8746

WASHINGTON

Bates Tech C.	Tacoma, WA 98405	Disability Support Services	253-680-7010
Central Washington U.	Ellensburg, WA 98926-7463	Disability Services	509-963-2149
City U.	Bellevue, WA 98005	Student with Special Needs	1.800.426.5596 x5228
Cornish C. of the Arts	Seattle, WA 98121	Disability Support Services	206-726-5098
Eastern Washington U.	Cheney, WA 99004	Disability Support Services	509-359-4706
Everett C.C.	Everett, WA 98201	Center for Disability Services	425-388-9272
Evergreen St. C., The	Olympia, WA 98505	Access Services	360-867-6364
Gonzaga U.	Spokane, WA 99258	DREAM Office	509-313-4134
Heritage U.	Toppenish, WA 98948	Office of Student Affairs	509-865-8515
North Seattle C.C.	Seattle, WA 98103	Disability Services	206-934-36
Northwest U.	Kirkland, WA 98083	Academic Success Center	425-889-7823
Pacific Lutheran U.	Tacoma, WA 98447	Disability Support Services	253-535-7206
Pierce C.	Tacoma, WA 98446	Disability Support Services	253-964-6460
Saint Martin's U.	Lacey, WA 98503	Disability Support Services	360-438-4580
Seattle Pacific U.	Seattle, WA 98119-1997	Disability Support Services	(206) 281-2272
Seattle U.	Seattle, WA 98122	Student Academic Services	206-296-5710
Spokane Falls C.C.	Spokane, WA 99204	Disability Support Services	509-533-4166
Tacoma C.C.	Tacoma, WA 98465	Access Services	253-566-5328
The Evergreen St. C.	Olympia, WA 98505	Access Services	(360) 867-6364
U. of Puget Sound	Tacoma, WA 98416	Student Access & Accommodation	253-879-3395
U. of Washington	Seattle, WA 98195-5852	Disability Resources for Students	206-543-8924
U. of Washington-Bothell	Bothell, WA 98011	Disability Resources for Students	NR
Walla Walla C.	College Place, WA 99324-1198	Disability Services Office	509-527-6450
Washington St. U.	Pullman, WA 99164-1067	Access Center, Division of Student Affairs	509-335-3417
Western Washington U.	Bellingham, WA 98225	disAbility Resources	360-650-3083

Whatcom C.C.	Bellingham, WA 98226	Access & Disability Services	360-383-3043
Whitman C.	Walla Walla, WA 99362	Disabililty Support Services	(509) 527-5767
Whitworth C.	Spokane, WA 99251	Educational Support Services	509-777-4534
Yakima Valley C.C.	Yakima, WA 98907	Disability Services	509-574-4968
WEST VIRGINIA			
Bluefield St. C.	Bluefield, WB 24701	Student Support Services	304-327-4098
Concord U.	Athens, WV 24712	Office of Disability Services	304-384-6086
Davis & Elkins C.	Elkins, WV 26241	Supported Learning Program	304-637-1384
Fairmount St. U.	Fairmont, WV 26554	Disability Services	304-367-4686
Glenville St. C.	Glenville, WV 26351	Academic Support Center	304-462-6152
Marshall U.	Huntington, WV 25755	NR	NR
Mountain St. U.	Beckley, WV 25802	Student Affairs	304-929-1402
Ohio Valley U.	Vienna, WV 26105-8000	Academic Support	304-865-6127
Shepherd U.	Shepherdstown, WV 25443-5000	Disability Support Serv ice	3048765122
U. of Charleston	Charleston, WV 25304	Academic Success Center	304-357-4776
West Liberty St. C.	West Liberty, WV 26074-0295	Learning & Student Development Center	304-336-8216
West Virginia St. C.	Institute, WV 25112-1000	Disability Services	304-766-3168
West Virginia Tech	Montgomery, WV 25136	Student Support Services	304-442-3498
West Virginia U.	Morgantown, WV 26506-6009	NR	304-293-6700
West Virginia Wesleyan C.	Buckhannon, WV 26201	The Learning Center	304.473.8563
Wheeling Jesuit U.	Wheeling, WV 26003	Disability Services	304-243-4484
WISCONSIN			
Alverno C.	Milwaukee, WI 53234-3922	Student Accessibility	414-382-6026
Bellin C. of Nursing	Green Bay, WI 54305	Academic Affairs	920-433-6699
Beloit C.	Beloit, WI 53511	Joy de Leon	6083632572
Cardinal Stritch U.	Milwaukee, WI 53217-3985	Academic Support	414-410-4166
Carroll U. WI)	Waukesha, WI 53186	Disability Services	262-524-7335
Carthage C.	Kenosha, WI 53140	Office of Student Life	262-551-5802
Concordia U. WI)	Mequon, WI 53097	Learning Resource Center	262-243-4535
Edgewood C.	Madison, WI 53711-1997	Jumpstart College and Student Accessibility and Disabilities Services	6086638347
Gateway Technical C.	Kenosha, WI 53144	Special Needs	262-564-2300
Lawrence U.	Appleton, WI 54911-5699	Student Academic Success	920-832-6530

Marian University	Fond du Lac, WI 54935	Student Academic Services	920-923-8951
Marquette U.	Milwaukee, WI 53201-1881	Office of Disability Services	414-288-1645
Milwaukee Inst. of Art & Des.	Milwaukee, WI 53202	Disability Services	414-847-3347
Milwaukee School of Engineering	Milwaukee, WI 53202-3109	Student Accessibility Services	414-277-7281
Mount Mary C.	Milwaukee, WI 53222	Accessibility Services	414-443-3645
Mount Mary U.	Milwaukee, WI 53222-4597	Accessibility Services	414-930-3368
Northland C.	Ashland, WI 54806	Disability Services	715-682-1369
Ripon C.	Ripon, WI 54971	Student Support Services	920-748-8107
Saint Norbert C.	De Pere, WI 54115	Academic Support Services	920-403-1321
Silver Lake C.	Manitowoc, WI 54220	Disability Services	920-686-6115
St. Norbert C.	De Pere, WI 54115-2099	Academic Support Services	920-403-3874
U of Wisc.—Baraboo/Sauk County	Baraboo, WI 53913	Accessibility Services	608-355-5230
U. of Wisconsin-Eau Claire	Eau Claire, WI 54701	Services for Students with Disabilities	715-836-5800
U. of Wisconsin-Green Bay	Green Bay, WI 53411-7001	Disability Services Office	(920)465-2849
U. of Wisconsin—Green Bay	Green Bay, WI 53411-7001	Disability Services	920-465-2841
U. of Wisconsin—LaCrosse	LaCrosse, WI 54601-3742	Disability Resource Services	608-785-6900
U. of Wisconsin-Madison	Madison, WI 53715Ã‚â “1007	McBurney Disability Resource Center	608-263-2741
U. of Wisconsin—Madison	Madison, WI 53706	McBurney Disability Resource Center	608-263-2741
U. of Wisconsin—Milwaukee	Milwaukee, WI 53201	Learning Disabilities Program	414-229-4564
U. of Wisconsin—Oshkosh	Oshkosh, WI 54901-8662	Project Success	920-424-1033
U. of Wisconsin—Parkside	Kenosha, WI 53141	Learning Disabilities Support Services	262-595-2610
U. of Wisconsin—Platteville	Platteville, WI 53818	Services for Student with Disabilities	608-342-1818
U. of Wisconsin-River Falls	River Falls, WI 54022	Ability Services	715-425-0740
U. of Wisconsin-Stevens Point	Stevens Point, WI 54481	Disability and Assistive Technology Center	715 346-3365
U. of Wisconsin—Stout	Menomonie, WI 54751	Disabilities Services	715-232-2995
U. of Wisconsin—Superior	Superior, WI 54880	Disability Support Services	715-394-8087
U. of Wisconsin—Whitewater	Whitewater, WI 53190	Center for Students with Disabilities	262-472-1630
Viterbo U.	La Crosse, WI 54601	Academic Resource Center	608-796-3194
Western Tech. C.	La Crosse, WI 54602	Disability Services	608-785-9875
Wisconsin Indianhead Tech.	Shell Lake, WI 54871	Accommodation Support Services	715-468-2815 ext. 5350
Wisconsin Lutheran C.	Milwaukee, WI 53226	Disability Support Services	414-443-8797

WYOMING			
Central Wyoming C	Riverton, WY	Student Support Services	307-855-2228
Laramie County C.C.	Cheyenne, WY 82007	Disability Support Services	307-778-1266
U. of Wyoming	Laramie, WY 82071	University Disability Support Services	307-766-6189
CANADA—ALBERTA			
Grant MacEwan University	Edmonton, AB T51 2P2	Services for Students with Disabilities	780-497-5886
Lethbridge C.	Lethbridge, AB T1K 1L6	Accessibility Services	403-320-3202 ext. 5400
N. Alberta Inst. Tech.	Edmonton AB T5G 2R1	Services for Students with Disabilities	780-378-6133
S. Alberta Inst. Tech.	Calgary AB T2M OL4	Accessibility Services	403-774-5093
U. of Alberta	Edmonton AB T6G 2E8	Specialized Support & Disability Services	780-492-3381
U. of Calgary	Calgary AB T2N 1N4	Student Accessibility Services	403-220-8237
CANADA—BRITISH COLUMBIA			
C. of New Caledonia	Pr. George BC V2N 1P8	Disability Support Services	250-561-5838
Camosun C.	Victoria BC V8P 4X8	Disability Resource Center	250-370-3325
Capilano U.	N. Vancouver BC V71 3H5	Disability Services	604-983-7526
Kwantlen College	Surrey V3T BC 5H8	Services for Stud. With Disabilities	604-599-2003
Langara C.	Vancover BC V5Y 2Z6	Disability Services	604-323-5509
Okanagan C.	Kelowna BC V1Y 4X8	Disability Services	250-762-5445
Simon Fraser U.	Burnaaby BC V5A 1S6	Centre for Students with Disabilities	778-782-3312
U. of British Columbia	Vancouver BC V6T 1Z1	Access & Diversity	604-822-5844
U. of N. British Colum.	Prince Grge BC V2L 5P2	Disability Services	250-960-6355
U. of Victoria	Victoria BC V8W 3P2	Resource Center for Students with Disabilities	250-472-4947
CANADA—MANITOBA			
U. of Manitoba	Winnipeg MB R3T 2N2	Student Accessibility Services	204-474-7423
U. of Winnipeg	Winnipeg MB R3B 2E9	Accessibility Services & Resources Center	204-786-9971
CANADA—NEW BRUNSWICK			
Mt. Allison U.	Sackville NB EOA 3C0	Meighen Center for Learning Assistance	506-364-2527
U. of New Brunswick	Fredericton NB E3B 6E3	Student Accessibility Center	506-648-5680
CANADA—NEWFOUNDLAND			
Mem. U. Newfoundland	St. John's NF A1G 5S7	Blundon Centre for Students with Disabilities	709-864-2156

CANADa—NOVA SCOTIA

Dalhousie U.	Halifax NS B3H 4J2	Hill Accessibility Center	902-494-2836
NSCAD U.	Halifax NS B3J 3J6	Disability Services	902-494-8313
St. Mary's U.	Halifax NS B3H 3C3	Atlantic Center	902-420-5449

CANADA—ONTARIO

Algoma U. C.	S. Ste. Marie ON P6A 2G4	Academic Support Services	705-949-2301 ext. 4221
Cambrian C.	Sudbury ON P3A 3V8	Disability Services	705-566-8101 ext. 7420
Canadore C.	N. Bay ON P1B 8K9	Student Success Services	705-474-7600 ext. 5213
Carleton U.	Ottawa ON K1S 5B6	P. Menton Cntr for Stnts w/ Disabilities	613-520-6608
Centennial C.	Scarborough ON M1K 5E9	Disability Services	416-289-5000 ext. 2254
Durham C.	Oshawa ON L1H 7L7	Center for Students with Disabilities	905-721-3123
Fanshawe C.	London ON N5V 1W2	Accessibility Services	519-452-4282
George Brown C.	Toronto ON M5T 2T9	Accessibility Services	416-415-5000 ext. 2966
Humber College	Toronto ON M9W 5L7	Disability Services	416-675-5090
Lakehead U.	Thunder Bay ON P7B 5E1	Student Accessibility Services	807-343-8047
Loyalist College	Belleville ON K8N 5B9	AccessAbility Services	613-969-1913 ext. 2256
Mohawk College	Hamilton ON L8N 3T2	Accessible Learning Services	905-575-2211
Nippissing U.	N. Bay ON P1B 8L7	Student Accessibility Services	705-474-3450 ext. 4362
Ontario C. of Art	Toronto ON M5T 1W1	Center for Students with Disabilities	416-977-6000 ext. 339
Queen's U.	Kingston ON K7L 3N6	Disability Services	613-533-6000 ext. 74206
Seneca College	N. York ON M2J 2X5	Services for Students	416-491-5050 ext. 3150
Sheridan C.	Oakville ON L6H 2L1	Accessible Learning Services	905-815-4045
St. Clair C.	Windsor ON N9A 6S4	Disability Services	519-972-2727 ext. 4226
St. Lawrence C.	Brockville ON K6V 5X3	Accessibility	613-544-5400 ext. 1593
Trent U.	Peterborough ON K9J 7B8	Accessibility Services	705-748-1281
U. of W. Ontario	London ON N6A 3K7	Services for Students with Disabilities (SDC)	519-661-2147
U. of Waterloo	Waterloo ON N2L 3G1	AccessAbility Services	519-888-4567 ext. 35231
U. of Windsor	Windsor, ON N9B3P4	Student Disability Services	519-253-3000 x3461
York U.	N. York ON M3J 1P3	Learning Disability Services	416-736-5297
Western U.	London, ON N6A 3K7	Services for Students with Disabilities	519-661-2147

CANADA—PRINCE EDWARD ISLAND			
Holland College	Charlottetown PE C1A 4Z1	Student Academic Services	902-566-9619
CANADA—QUEBEC			
Concordia U.	Montreal PQ H4B 1R6	(ACSD) Access Center for Students with Disabilities	514-848-2424 ext. 3525
Dawson C.	Montreal PQ H3Z 1A4	Student AccessAbility Center	514-931-8731 ext. 1211
John Abbott C.	St. An. Belvue. PQ H9X 3L9	Student Access Center	514-457-6610
McGill U.	Montreal PQ H3A 1X1	Office of Student with Disabilities	514-398-6009
CANADA—SASKATCHEWAN			
SIAST-Kelsey	Saskatoon SK S7K 6B1	Learning Services	306-659-4048
U. of Saskatchewan	Saskatoon SK S7N 0W0	Disability Student Services	306-966-7273
CANADA—YUKON			
Yukon C.	Yukon YT Y1A 5K4	Learning Assistance Center	867-668-8785
IRELAND			
Maynooth U.	Maynooth, Co Kildare	Maynooth Access Programme	+ 353 1 708 6025
UNITED KINGDOM			
American International U —Richmond	Rich.-upon Thames TW10 6JP, Eng.	Students with Disabilities	617-450-5617

Alphabetical List of Colleges by Level of Support Services

SP: STRUCTURED PROGRAMS

College/University	State	Support
Adelphi University	New York	SP
American International College	Massachusetts	SP
American University	District of Columbia	SP
Anderson University (IN)	Indiana	SP
Augsburg College	Minnesota	SP
Barry University	Florida	SP
Beacon College	Florida	SP
Brenau University	Georgia	SP
Curry College	Massachusetts	SP
Davis and Elkins College	West Virginia	SP
Dean College	Massachusetts	SP
Dowling College	New York	SP
Fairleigh Dickinson University, Florham Campus	New Jersey	SP
Fairleigh Dickinson University, Metropolitan Campus	New Jersey	SP
Finlandia University	Michigan	SP
Florida A&M University	Florida	SP
Gannon University	Pennsylvania	SP
Georgian Court University	New Jersey	SP
Hofstra University	New York	SP
Iona College	New York	SP
Landmark College	Vermont	SP
Long Island University—Post	New York	SP
Loras College	Iowa	SP
Louisiana College	Louisiana	SP
Lynn University	Florida	SP
Manhattanville College	New York	SP
Marist College	New York	SP
Marshall University	West Virginia	SP
Marymount Manhattan College	New York	SP
Mercyhurst University	Pennsylvania	SP
Misericordia University	Pennsylvania	SP
Missouri State University	Missouri	SP
Mitchell College	Connecticut	SP
Mount Ida College	Massachusetts	SP
Mount St. Joseph University	Ohio	SP
Muskingum College	Ohio	SP
National-Louis University	Illinois	SP
New Jersey City University	New Jersey	SP
Northeastern University	Massachusetts	SP
Notre Dame College	Ohio	SP
Reinhardt College	Georgia	SP
Rochester Institute of Technology	New York	SP
Schreiner University	Texas	SP

Southern Illinois University—Carbondale	Illinois	SP
St. Thomas Aquinas College	New York	SP
University of Arizona	Arizona	SP
University of Denver	Colorado	SP
University of Indianapolis	Indiana	SP
University of the Ozarks	Arkansas	SP
University of Wisconsin—Oshkosh	Wisconsin	SP
Ursuline College	Ohio	SP
Vincennes University	Indiana	SP
Waldorf College	Iowa	SP
West Virginia Wesleyan College	West Virginia	SP
Westminster College	Missouri	SP

CS: COORDINATED SERVICES

College/University	State	Support
Abilene Christian University	Texas	CS
Adrian College	Michigan	CS
Appalachian State University	North Carolina	CS
Arizona State University	Arizona	CS
Boston College	Massachusetts	CS
Boston University	Massachusetts	CS
Brevard College	North Carolina	CS
Brigham Young University	Utah	CS
Brown University	Rhode Island	CS
Bryant University	Rhode Island	CS
Bucknell University	Pennsylvania	CS
Cal Polytechnic State University, San Luis Obispo	California	CS
Caldwell College	New Jersey	CS
California State Polytechnic University, Pomona	California	CS
California State University, Fullerton	California	CS
California State University, Long Beach	California	CS
California State University, Northridge	California	CS
California State University, San Bernardino	California	CS
Calvin College	Michigan	CS
Canisius College	New York	CS
Case Western Reserve University	Ohio	CS
The Catholic University of America	District of Columbia	CS
Central Ohio Technical College	Ohio	CS
Clark University	Massachusetts	CS
Clarkson University	New York	CS
Colby-Sawyer College	New Hampshire	CS
Colgate University	New York	CS
College of Charleston	South Carolina	CS
College of the Siskiyous	California	CS
Concordia College (NY)	New York	CS

CUNY—Hunter College	New York	CS
Dakota College at Bottineau	North Dakota	CS
Davidson College	North Carolina	CS
DePaul University	Illinois	CS
Drexel University	Pennsylvania	CS
Duke University	North Carolina	CS
East Carolina University	North Carolina	CS
East Stroudsburg Univ. of Pennsylvania	Pennsylvania	CS
Eastern Kentucky University	Kentucky	CS
Edgewood College	Wisconsin	CS
Edinboro University of Pennsylvania	Pennsylvania	CS
Emerson College	Massachusetts	CS
Emory University	Georgia	CS
Evangel University	Missouri	CS
The Evergreen State College	Washington	CS
Fairfield University	Connecticut	CS
Ferris State University	Michigan	CS
Ferrum College	Virginia	CS
Florida Atlantic University	Florida	CS
Florida State University	Florida	CS
The George Washington University	District of Columbia	CS
Georgia Southern University	Georgia	CS
Georgia State University	Georgia	CS
Grand View University	Iowa	CS
Green Mountain College	Vermont	CS
Guilford College	North Carolina	CS
Hocking College	Ohio	CS
Illinois State University	Illinois	CS
Indiana University—Bloomington	Indiana	CS
Iowa State University	Iowa	CS
Jacksonville State University	Alabama	CS
James Madison University	Virginia	CS
Johnson State College	Vermont	CS
Kansas State University	Kansas	CS
Kean University	New Jersey	CS
Kent State University	Ohio	CS
Kutztown University of Pennsylvania	Pennsylvania	CS
Laramie County Community College	Wyoming	CS
Lee University	Tennessee	CS
Lehigh University	Pennsylvania	CS
Lewis & Clark College	Oregon	CS
Liberty University	Virginia	CS
Limestone College	South Carolina	CS
Lincoln College	Illinois	CS
Loyola University of Chicago	Illinois	CS

Manchester College	Indiana	CS
McDaniel College	Maryland	CS
Menlo College	California	CS
Miami University	Ohio	CS
Michigan State University	Michigan	CS
Michigan Technological University	Michigan	CS
Monmouth University	New Jersey	CS
Montana Tech of the University of Montana	Montana	CS
Montclair State University	New Jersey	CS
New England College	New Hampshire	CS
New York University	New York	CS
North Carolina State University	North Carolina	CS
Northern Illinois University	Illinois	CS
Northwestern University	Illinois	CS
Norwich University	Vermont	CS
Oberlin College	Ohio	CS
Ohio State University—Columbus	Ohio	CS
Old Dominion University	Virginia	CS
Pine Manor College	Massachusetts	CS
Pittsburg State University	Kansas	CS
Providence College	Rhode Island	CS
Radford University	Virginia	CS
Reedley College	California	CS
Regis University	Colorado	CS
Rhode Island College	Rhode Island	CS
Rider University	New Jersey	CS
Rocky Mountain College	Montana	CS
Roosevelt University	Illinois	CS
Saint Andrews Presbyterian College	North Carolina	CS
San Diego State University	California	CS
San Francisco State University	California	CS
San Jose State University	California	CS
Santa Clara University	California	CS
Santa Monica College	California	CS
Santa Rosa Junior College	California	CS
Seton Hall University	New Jersey	CS
Sierra College	California	CS
Southern Connecticut State University	Connecticut	CS
Southern Illinois University—Edwardsville	Illinois	CS
Southern Methodist University	Texas	CS
Springfield College	Massachusetts	CS
St. Ambrose University	Iowa	CS
St. Catherine University	Minnesota	CS
St. Lawrence University	New York	CS
Stanford University	California	CS

State University of New York at Binghamton	New York	CS
State University of New York—Delhi	New York	CS
State University of New York—Farmingdale	New York	CS
State University of New York—University at Albany	New York	CS
Stetson University	Florida	CS
Stony Brook University	New York	CS
Syracuse University	New York	CS
Texas State University	Texas	CS
Texas Tech University	Texas	CS
Towson University	Maryland	CS
University of California—Berkeley	California	CS
University of California—Los Angeles	California	CS
University of California—San Diego	California	CS
University of California—Santa Barbara	California	CS
University of Central Florida	Florida	CS
University of Cincinnati	Ohio	CS
University of Colorado—Boulder	Colorado	CS
University of Colorado—Colorado Springs	Colorado	CS
University of Connecticut	Connecticut	CS
University of Dayton	Ohio	CS
University of Delaware	Delaware	CS
University of Florida	Florida	CS
University of Georgia	Georgia	CS
University of Hartford	Connecticut	CS
University of Houston	Texas	CS
University of Illinois at Urbana—Champaign	Illinois	CS
University of Iowa	Iowa	CS
University of Jamestown	North Dakota	CS
University of Kansas	Kansas	CS
University of Kentucky	Kentucky	CS
University of Maryland—College Park	Maryland	CS
University of Massachusetts Amherst	Massachusetts	CS
The University of Memphis	Tennessee	CS
University of Michigan—Ann Arbor	Michigan	CS
University of Montana	Montana	CS
University of Missouri—Columbia	Missouri	CS
University of Nevada—Las Vegas	Nevada	CS
University of New Hampshire	New Hampshire	CS
The University of North Carolina at Chapel Hill	North Carolina	CS
The University of North Carolina at Greensboro	North Carolina	CS
The University of North Carolina at Charlotte	North Carolina	CS
The University of North Carolina at Wilmington	North Carolina	CS
University of Notre Dame	Indiana	CS
University of Oregon	Oregon	CS
University of Pittsburgh—Pittsburgh Campus	Pennsylvania	CS

University of Rhode Island	Rhode Island	CS
University of San Francisco	California	CS
The University of Saint Francis (IN)	Indiana	CS
University of South Carolina—Columbia	South Carolina	CS
The University of South Dakota	South Dakota	CS
University of Southern California	California	CS
The University of Tennessee at Knoxville	Tennessee	CS
The University of Tennessee at Martin	Tennessee	CS
The University of Tennessee at Chattanooga	Tennessee	CS
The University of Texas at Austin	Texas	CS
University of Tulsa	Oklahoma	CS
University of Utah	Utah	CS
University of Vermont	Vermont	CS
University of Virginia	Virginia	CS
University of Wisconsin—Eau Claire	Wisconsin	CS
University of Wisconsin—Madison	Wisconsin	CS
University of Wisconsin—Milwaukee	Wisconsin	CS
University of Wisconsin—Whitewater	Wisconsin	CS
University of Wyoming	Wyoming	CS
Utah State University	Utah	CS
Utica College	New York	CS
Wake Forest University	North Carolina	CS
Washington University in St. Louis	Missouri	CS
Western Carolina University	North Carolina	CS
Western Connecticut State University	Connecticut	CS
Western Illinois University	Illinois	CS
Western Kentucky University	Kentucky	CS
Wheelock College	Massachusetts	CS
Widener University	Pennsylvania	CS
Wright State University	Ohio	CS
Xavier University (OH)	Ohio	CS

S: SERVICES

College/University	State	Support
Alverno College	Wisconsin	S
Arkansas State University	Arkansas	S
Auburn University Montgomery	Alabama	S
Barnard College	New York	S
Beloit College	Wisconsin	S
Black Hills State University	South Dakota	S
Bluegrass Community and Technical College	Kentucky	S
Bowling Green State University	Ohio	S
Cedarville University	Ohio	S
Champlain College	Vermont	S
Chatham University	Pennsylvania	S

Clemson University	South Carolina	S
The College of William & Mary	Virginia	S
Colorado State University—Pueblo	Colorado	S
Cornell University	New York	S
Drake University	Iowa	S
Eastern Illinois University	Illinois	S
Eastern Washington University	Washington	S
Elon University	North Carolina	S
Fitchburg State University	Massachusetts	S
Frostburg State University	Maryland	S
Grand Valley State University	Michigan	S
Grinnell College	Iowa	S
Hampton University	Virginia	S
Indian Hills Community College	Iowa	S
Lamar University	Texas	S
Le Moyne College	New York	S
Lenoir-Rhyne University	North Carolina	S
Louisiana State University—Baton Rouge	Louisiana	S
Loyola Marymount University	California	S
Marian University	Wisconsin	S
Marquette University	Wisconsin	S
Messiah College	Pennsylvania	S
Middle Tennessee State University	Tennessee	S
Midwestern State University	Texas	S
Millersville University of Pennsylvania	Pennsylvania	S
Minnesota State University, Moorhead	Minnesota	S
Montana State University—Billings	Montana	S
Morningside College	Iowa	S
Neumann University	Pennsylvania	S
New Mexico Institute of Mining & Tech.	New Mexico	S
New Mexico State University	New Mexico	S
Nicholls State University	Louisiana	S
North Dakota State University	North Dakota	S
Northern Arizona University	Arizona	S
Northern Michigan University	Michigan	S
Occidental College	California	S
Ohio University—Athens	Ohio	S
Oklahoma State University	Oklahoma	S
Oregon State University	Oregon	S
Pennsylvania State University—University Park	Pennsylvania	S
Ripon College	Wisconsin	S
Rivier College	New Hampshire	S
Roanoke College	Virginia	S
Salisbury University	Maryland	S
Santa Fe University of Art and Design	New Mexico	S
Seton Hill University	Pennsylvania	S

Sheridan College	Wyoming	S
Shimer College	Illinois	S
Smith College	Massachusetts	S
Sonoma State University	California	S
South Dakota State University	South Dakota	S
Southern Maine Community College	Maine	S
Southern Utah University	Utah	S
Southern Wesleyan University	South Carolina	S
St. Bonaventure University	New York	S
St. Olaf College	Minnesota	S
State University of New York—Potsdam	New York	S
Texas A&M University—College Station	Texas	S
Texas A&M University—Kingsville	Texas	S
Thomas More College	Kentucky	S
Tulane University	Louisiana	S
The University of Alabama in Huntsville	Alabama	S
The University of Alabama at Tuscaloosa	Alabama	S
University of Alaska—Anchorage	Alaska	S
University of Alaska—Fairbanks	Alaska	S
University of Arkansas—Fayetteville	Arkansas	S
University of Illinois at Springfield	Illinois	S
University of Minnesota, Morris	Minnesota	S
University of Missouri—Kansas City	Missouri	S
University of Montana—Western	Montana	S
University of Nebraska—Lincoln	Nebraska	S
University of New England	Maine	S
University of New Haven	Connecticut	S
University of New Orleans	Louisiana	S
The University of North Carolina at Asheville	North Carolina	S
University of Northern Colorado	Colorado	S
University of Northern Iowa	Iowa	S
University of Southern Indiana	Indiana	S
University of St. Francis	Illinois	S
University of the Pacific	California	S
The University of Texas—Pan American	Texas	S
University of Wisconsin—Stevens Point	Wisconsin	S
Washington State University	Washington	S
Wayne State College	Nebraska	S
West Virginia University	West Virginia	S
Western Oregon University	Oregon	S
Western State College of Colorado	Colorado	S
Wheaton College (IL)	Illinois	S
Wheaton College (MA)	Massachusetts	S
Whittier College	California	S
Winona State University	Minnesota	S

Programs Listed by Aspergers Foundation International

FOUR-YEAR COLLEGES

Arizona: Arizona State University; University of Arizona

Arkansas: Harding University

California: California State Polytechnic University, San Luis Obispo; California State University, San Bernardino; San Francisco State University; Santa Clara University; University of San Francisco

Connecticut: Trinity College

Florida: University of Central Florida; Florida Atlantic University

Georgia: Brenau University; Georgia State University; Reinhardt College

Illinois: University of Illinois at Urbana Champaign; Southern Illinois University-Carbondale; Southern Illinois University-Edwardsville

Indiana: Anderson University

Iowa: Iowa State University; Loras College; St. Ambrose University; University of Iowa

Massachusetts: Boston College

Michigan: Finlandia University; University of Michigan

Minnesota: Augsburg College

Missouri: Westminster College

Montana: Montana State University-Billings; Montana State University-Bozeman

Nebraska: Union College

New York: Bryant-Stratton College; Iona College; New York University; Rochester Institute of Technology; St. Bonaventure University; St. Lawrence University; State University of New York-Delhi

North Carolina: Appalachian State University; Brevard College

Ohio: Wright State University

Pennsylvania: College Misericordia; Dickinson College; East Stroudsburg University; Mercyhurst College, Penn State Mont Alto

Rhode Island: Johnson and Wales University

South Carolina: Limestone College

Tennessee: Middle Tennessee State University; University of Tennessee at Knoxville

Texas: Abilene Christian University; Southern Methodist University; University of Houston

Vermont: New England Culinary Institute; Norwich University

Virginia: Old Dominion University

West Virginia: West Virginia Wesleyan College

Wisconsin: University of Wisconsin-Oshkosh

TWO-YEAR COLLEGES

Arizona: Phoenix College; Pima Community College

California: Allan Hancock College; Contra Costa Community College; Glendale Community College; Mesa College; Saddleback College

Colorado: Front Range Community College: Pikes Peak Community College

Connecticut: Middlesex Community College

Florida: Hillsborough Community College; Okaloosa-Walton College

Hawaii: Hawaii Community College

Illinois: Harper College; Lewis and Clark Community College

Indiana: Ivy Tech Community College

Iowa: Des Moines Area Community College; Muscatine Community College

Massachusetts: Mount Wachusett Community College

Michigan: Kellogg Community College; Schoolcraft College; Southwestern Michigan College

ADDENDUM: INDEPENDENT LIVING OPTIONS

The following programs are options for students who may have LD/ADHD or other disabilities, but who want to continue to pursue independent living skills and education beyond high school.

School	Program Overview	Contact Information
Anchor to Windward, Inc.	Structured living experience Marblehead, MA 01945 781-990-3056 http://anchortowindward.org/	74 Atlantic Ave.
Bancroft NeuroHealth	Various therapeutic services for children and adults with autism, and other neurological impairments. Haddonfield, NJ 08033-0018 Ph: 856-524-7322 http://www.bancroftnj.org/	Bancroft Admissions Office Haddonfield Campus 425 Kings Highway East P.O. Box 20
Berkshire Hills Music Academy	Post-secondary school providing young adults with learning and developmental disabilities to live in a college setting while developing musical potential. www.berkshirehills.org Kristen Tillona: ktillona@berkshirehills.org	Two-year certificate program. Berkshire Hills Music Academy 48 Woodbridge Street South Hadley, MA 01075 Ph: 413-540-9720
Berkshire Center	College Internship Program and the Aspire Program—both are independent living experiences. Aspire for those with Asperger's and Non-verbal learning differences. (Also Brevard) Michael Gunther: admissions@cipworldwide.org	Admissions Director 40 Main St. Suite 3 Lee, MA 01238 Ph: (877) Know-CIP http://www.berkshirecenter.org/academicsupport.html
Casa de Amma	Young adults who function independently but require assistance and structure in daily living. Life-long residential community. contact.html	Casa de Amma 27231 Calle Arroyo San Juan Capistrano, CA 92675 Ph: (949) 496-9001 http://www.casadeamma.org/

Center for Adaptive Learning	18+ with a neurological disability, supportive living program. Concord, CA 94519 Ph: (925) 827-3863 info@c4al.org www.centerforadaptivelearning.org	Center for Adaptive Learning 3227 Clayton Road
Chapel Haven	Residential program teaching independent living to young adults. Ext 113 or 148 admission@chapelhaven.org www.chapelhaven.org	1040 Whalley Avenue New Haven, CT 06515 Ph: (203) 397-1714
Chapel Haven West	Residential program teaching independent living to young adults. Tucson, Arizona 85719 877-824-9378 admission@chapelhaven.org http://www.chapelhaven.org/west/	1701 N. Park Ave Tucson, AZ 85719 University of Arizona
College Excel	Support programs for young adults 18-27 years of age who are ready to begin or continue in college. Program provides college-accredited courses, skill development classes, tutoring, life skills education, and life coaching. Bend, OR 97702 http://www.collegeexcel.com/	1458 NW Century Dr Suite 201 Bend, OR 97701 541-388-3043 info@collegeexcel.com Mailing Address: 70 SW Century Dr Box 199
College Internship Programs	Post-secondary academic, internship and independent living experiences for age 18-25 with Asperger's and non-verbal learning differences. Students participate in the College Internship Programs and can also attend classes at local colleges or community colleges. Ph: (413) 243-2576 X34 http://cipworldwide.org/cip-berkshire/berkshire-overview/	CIP Bloomington Center 425 N. College Ave Bloomington, Indiana 47404 ph: 812-323-0600 X 22 http://www.cipbloomington.org CIP Berkshire 40 Main St. Suite 3 Lee, MA 01238

	CIP Brevard 3692 N. Wickham Road Melbourne, FL 32935 Ph: 321-259-1900 X11 sbrown@cipbrevard.org http://www.brevard.org CIP Berkeley Center 2070 Allston Way Suite 101 Berkeley, CA 94704 Ph: 510-704-4476 mpaul@cipberkeley.org www.cipberkeley.org CIP Amherst 4511 Harlem Rd Amherst, NY 14226 Ph: 716-839-2620 jcovert@cipamherst.org www.cipamherst.org CIP Long Beach 4510 E. Pacific Highway Long Beach, CA 90804 Ph: 716-839-2620 http://cipworldwide.org/cip-long-beach/long-beach-overview/ CIP National Admissions Office Maggi Sanderson 199 South St Pittsfield, MA 01201 admission@cipworldwide.org http://cipworldwide.org/contact/	
College Living Experience	College program for students with autism spectrum disorders, Asperger's nonverbal learning disorder, ADD/ADHD and other learning disabilities http://experiencecle.com/admissions/	National Admissions 401 North Washington St Suite 420 Rockville, MD 20850 800-486-5058

CLE Fort Lauderdale
6555 Nova Drive Suite 100
Fort Lauderdale, FL 33317
Ph: (800) 486 – 5058
Terri Shermett
http://www.experiencecle.com/locations/ft_lauderdale.aspx

CLE Austin TX
11801Stonehollow Dr.
Suite 100
Austin, TZX 78758
Ph: 800-486-5058
Bronwyn Towart
http://www.cleinc.net/locations/austin.aspx

CLE Denver CO
1391 Speer Blvd.
Suite 400
Denver. CO 80204
Ph: 800-486-5058
Sharon Heller
http://www.cleinc.net/locations/denver.aspx

CLE Monterey CA
787 Munras Ave. Suite 201
Montery, CA 93940
Ph: 800-486-5058
Audre Nelson
http://www.cleinc.net/locations/monterey.aspx

CLE Washington DC
401 North Washington St. Suite 420
Rockville Maryland 20850
Ric Kienzie
http://www.cleinc.net/locations/washington_dc.aspx

	CLE Costa Mesa, CA 2183 Fairview Road Suite 101 Costa Mesa, CA 92627 Ph: 800-486-5058 Jennifer Griffith http://experiencecle.com/ locations-2/costa- mesa-california/_Mesa.aspx 7150 Columbia Gateway, Suite J Columbia, MD 2104 7150 Columbia Gateway, Suite J Columbia, MD 21046 Toll-free: 800-486-5058	
Elmhurst Life Skills Academy ELSA	Program assists students with special needs in completing college and transitioning into independent adults. Locations in Florida, Colorado and Texas. Elmhurst Life Skills Academy	190 Prospect Avenue Elmhurst, Illinois 60126 Ph: (630) 617-3500 http://public.elmhurst.edu/elsa
Evaluation & Development Center	Center provides services to anyone 16+ who is vocationally handicapped to attain greater productivity and self-sufficiency. http://ehs.siu.edu/rehab/ service-programs/ evaluation-development/index.php edcinfo@siu.edu	Evaluation & Development Center 500 C. Lewis Lane Carbondale, Il 62901 Ph: (618) 453-2331
Gersh College Experience at Daemen College	Post-secondary, undergraduate program for students with neurobiological disorders, e.g. Asperger's ADHD, OCD, Tourette's Syndrome, Anxiety or Depression, Autism Spectrum and Nonverbal Learning disorders.	21 Sweet Hollow Rd Huntington, NY 11743 855-337-2438 http://gershexperience.com/ offerings/academic-support/
The Horizons School	Young adults with learning disabilities to live self-sufficient lives. Non-degree program focused on life and social skills and career development.	The Horizons School 2018 15th Ave. South Birmingham, AL 35205 Ph: (800)-822- 6242 www.horizonsschool.org

Independence Center	Young adults 18-30 transitional residential program. Los Angeles, CA 90034 Ph: (310) 202-7102 www.independencecenter.com	Independence Center 3640 S. Sepulveda Blvd., Ste. 102
Lesley University	Threshold Program is a comprehensive two-year non-degree campus-based program for highly motivated young adults with diverse learning disabilities and other special needs. http://www.lesley.edu/	Threshold Program Lesley University 29 Everett Street Cambridge, MA 02138 617-349-8181 threshld@lesley.edu
Life Development Institute	High school and post-secondary programs teaching independence. Glendale, AZ 85308 866-736-7811 info@life-development-inst.org http://lifedevelopmentinstitute.org/	Life Development Institute 18001 N. 79th Ave., E-71
LIFE Skills, Inc.	Young adults 18+ with developmental disabilities, brain injury or mental illness. Services to enhance higher levels of independence. http://www.swcrcinc.org/who.php	LIFE Skills, Inc. 44 Morris Street Webster, MA 01570 Ph: 508-943-0700 life-skills@life-skillsinc.org
Maplebrook School	11-21 residential and day school consisting of vocational and college programs. Ph: (845) 373-9511 www.maplebrookschool.org	Maplebrook School 5142 Route 22 Amenia, NY 12501
Minnesota Life College	Apartment living instructional program for young adults whose learning disabilities pose serious challenges to their independence. Must be 18+ and have completed K-12 education. Vocational skills and workforce readiness.	Minnesota Life College 7501 Logan Ave. South Suite 2A Richfield, MN 55423 Ph: (612) 869-4008 www.minnesotalifecollege.com
New York Institute of Technology Vocational Independence Program	18+ with significant learning disabilities and have received special education services during high school years. 3 year certificate program for vocational major or degree program. Ernest Vanbergeijk: evanberg@nyit.edu http://www.nyit.edu/vip/	VIP Program NY Institute of Technology Central Islip Campus 300 Carleton Avenue Central Islip, NY 11722 Ph: (631) 348-3117

OPTIONS at Brehm	Young adults with complex learning disabilities. Certificate. 2 year and 4 year degree programs. http://www.experienceoptions.org/	OPTIONS at Brehm 101 S Lewis Ln Carbondale, IL 62901 618-549-9752
PACE Program at National Louis University	18-30 years with cognitive and provides integrated services to empower students to become independent adults within the community. Ph: 224-233-2670 http://www.nl.edu/pace/	PACE National Louis University 5202 Old Orchard Road Suite 300 Skokie, Il 60077
Pathway at UCLA	Two year certificate program for students with developmental disabilities providing a blend of educational, social and vocational experiences. Ph: 310- 825-9971 https://www.uclaextension.edu/pathway/Pages/default.aspx	Pathway UCLA Extension 10995 Le Conte Avenue Suite 639 Los Angeles, CA 90024
Riverview School	Ages 12-20 in secondary program, 19-23 in post-secondary program (GROW). Co-ed residential school for students with complex language, learning and cognitive disabilities.	Riverview School Admissions Office 551 Route 6A East Cape Cod, MA 02537 Ph: (508) 888-0489 www.riverviewschool.org
University of Iowa R.E.A.C.H Realizing Educational and Career Hopes	A 2-year certificate for students with multiple learning and cognitive disabilities ask.education@uiowa.edu http://www.education.uiowa.edu/services/reach/home	N297 Lindquist Center Iowa City, IA 52242 319-335-5359
Vista Vocational & Life Center **Skills Center**	Three-year post-secondary training program for 18+ with neurological disabilities. Ph: (800) 399-8080 www.vistavocational.org	Vista Vocational & Life Skills 1358 Old Clinton Road Westbrook, CT 06498

Wellspring Foundation	Intensive residential treatment for various populations including girls 13-18 and adults. Highly structured programs designed to treat a wide range of emotional and behavioral problems including affective, personality, and attachment, eating and traumatic stress disorders.	The Wellspring Foundation, Inc. 21 Arch Bridge Road P.O. Box 370 Bethlehem, CT 06751 Ph: (203) 266-8002 www.wellspring.org

RECOMMENDED WEBSITES

Independent Educational Consultants Association
www.IECAonline.com

LDA of America
www.ldanatl.org

Council for Exceptional Children
www.cec.sped.org

Council for Learning Disabilities
www.cldinternational.org

INDEX

Notes

Notes

Notes

Notes

Notes

Notes

Notes

Notes

Notes

Notes

Notes

About the Authors

Marybeth Kravets, M.A., retired in 2010 as the College Counselor at Deerfield High School, a public high school, in Deerfield, Illinois after 31 years. She is now the Chief Education Officer/VP College Partnerships for Chicago Scholars, Chicago Illinois. Marybeth also has a private practice and provides educational and college consulting to high schools including Wolcott School, colleges, families and other professionals. She received her BA in education from the University of Michigan in Ann Arbor, and her MA in Counseling from Wayne State University in Detroit, Michigan. She is a Past President of the National Association for College Admission Counseling (NACAC) and also served as the President of the Illinois Association for College Admission Counseling. Marybeth Kravets is a recipient of the Harvard University Club of Chicago Community Service Award for her lifelong dedication to serving students who are economically challenged or challenged with learning differences. She has been a guest on the NBC'S Today Show several times and has appeared on many other radio and television programs. For additional information or to contact Marybeth Kravets for consultation email or call:

Marybeth Kravets
847-212-3687- Cell
847-236-1985- voicemail/fax
Marybeth@kravets.net

Imy F. Wax, MS, LCPC, CEP is a psychotherapist and educational consultant. Imy is a member of several professional and parental organizations. She has presented at both professional and parental conferences on such topics as "The Emotional Expectations of Parenting a Child with Learning Disabilities," and has written numerous articles in professional and parental journals. Imy conducts workshops for parents on raising children with learning disabilities and/or attention deficit/hyperactivity disorder, as well as, for school districts all over the United States, on the college process. She has been invited a number of times to speak at conferences and at schools in countries in Asia and South America. She has appeared as a guest on the NBC's *Today Show*, as well as, other television and radio shows. She is married to Howard Wax and has four children, two with learning disabilities and one who also has attention deficit/hyperactivity disorder. Her daughter was the inspiration for this book. For additional information or to contact Imy Wax for consultation or for presentations, email or call:

Imy Wax
847-945-0913
imy@imywax.com